EVERYMAN'S LIBRARY

EVERYMAN,
I WILL GO WITH THEE,
AND BE THY GUIDE,
IN THY MOST NEED
TO GO BY THY SIDE

THE DIARY OF
JOHN
EVELYN

EDITED BY E.S. DE BEER

SELECTED AND INTRODUCED
BY ROY STRONG

EVERYMAN'S LIBRARY

291

First included in Everyman's Library, 1907
New edition 2006
This edition selected from *The Diary of John Evelyn*, edited by
E. S. de Beer, Oxford University Press, 1959, by kind permission
of Oxford University Press.
Introduction © Roy Strong, 2006
Editorial matter © Everyman's Library, 2006
Typography by Peter B. Willberg

ISBN 1-85715-291-3

A CIP catalogue record for this book is available from the
British Library

Published by Everyman's Library,
Northburgh House, 10 Northburgh Street,
London EC1V 0AT

Distributed by Random House (UK) Ltd.,
20 Vauxhall Bridge Road, London SW1V 2SA

Printed and bound in Germany by GGP Media GmbH, Pössneck

GENERAL CONTENTS

———

INTRODUCTION

John Evelyn, Gentleman

John Evelyn was born on 31 October 1620 at Wotton in Surrey, on his father's estate which lay in well-wooded and watered gently hilly country between Guildford and Dorking. He was the second son and fourth child of Richard Evelyn and his heiress wife, Eleanor Stansfield. Evelyn records his father as follows: 'his countenance was cleare, & fresh colour'd, his eyes extraordinary quick & piercing, an ample fore head, in summ, a very well composed visage and manly aspect'. His mother he records equally: 'a proper personage ... inclyn'd to a religious Melancholy, or pious sadnesse; of a rare memory, and most exemplary life'. Even though Evelyn was not to come into Wotton until he was nearly eighty, his affection for the place shines out of the Diary pages. From his parents he inherited a high intelligence, powers of mental retention and observation, an introspective piety as well as an unswerving allegiance to the monarchy.

The Evelyns came from Shropshire and, ultimately, Normandy. They owed their financial well-being to Evelyn's grandfather, George, who had been given the monopoly in the manufacture of gunpowder in the aftermath of the Armada in 1588. That was to be retained by the family until the Civil War. Such good fortune meant that George was able to provide for all twenty-four children he had by two wives. John Evelyn's father, Richard, was the youngest son by the second wife and his portion was Wotton, an estate of some seven hundred acres which brought in an annual income of £4,000.

At the age of four Evelyn was sent to live with his grandfather near Lewes where he was to spend the next thirteen years. Quite early on he received instruction from a Frenchman and, after that, in 1630, was sent to the free school at Southover where he remained until he was seventeen. All three Evelyn brothers were admitted to the Middle Temple, also going up to Oxford, George, the eldest, to Trinity College,

John to Balliol, where he matriculated in May 1637, and was joined in 1640 by his younger brother, Richard. They left Oxford, as was customary, without taking a degree. During his childhood, Evelyn returned to Wotton only three times, once in 1632, following the marriage of his eldest sister, two years later, after her death in childbirth, and in 1635 on the occasion of his mother's death when he was fifteen. Only in retrospect did he regret that he did not go to Eton as was planned but which at the time he resisted.

Like his father before him, Richard Evelyn was able to provide for each of his family and so, contrary to the usual fate of younger sons, John was not forced to pursue a profession. In 1640 he inherited from his father some lands near Lewes and the sum of £4,000, which provided income enough to obviate the need for a profession. Evelyn, however, came of age during a period of increasing political turbulence. His career as an aspiring country gentleman began in the normal manner with attendance at court, but he was watching all the time how 'the political wheel was turning', deciding to 'absent [himself] from this ill face of things at home'. In 1641 he departed for the Netherlands, where he joined, very briefly, a company of English volunteers fighting with the Dutch army in the war against Spain.

The Low Countries were to form his first in-depth experience of foreign travel but on his return things had drifted from bad to worse. War broke out and he arrived too late to join the Royalist forces at the battle of Brentford. Parliament was quickly to assert its control over Surrey 'which had left both me and my Brothers [at Wotton] expos'd to ruine'. The Evelyn family, like so many others, wanted to keep out of the fray and so to avoid being caught up in the tide of events Evelyn obtained a licence from the king at Oxford in October 1643 to travel abroad, 'to observe things mechanically curious and usefull as well as the mysteries of government'. He was not to return to England until 1647 and, even though his account of these years was written in retrospect, no other document captures so vividly the English response to continental civilization.

Evelyn did not travel alone but with another Balliol man, James Thicknesse, and, once in Italy, they were to be joined by a third Oxford man, Thomas Henshaw. The first stop was Paris and Charles II's resident, Sir Richard Browne, whose embassy became a gathering place for Royalist exiles and whose chapel kept the Anglican liturgy alive. Here Evelyn was to perfect his French. In 1644 the party travelled south and, embarking at Cannes, landed at Genoa. Their progress through Italy ran Pisa, Livorno, Florence, Siena, Rome and Naples, an itinerary largely reversed on the return, this time Rome, Siena, Lucca, Florence, Bologna, Ferrara, Venice, Padua (where he stopped for a period to study medicine) and back via Verona, Milan, and over the Alps (with an horrendous crossing via the Simplon Pass) to Geneva, where he was laid low by smallpox. The winter of 1646 to 1647 was passed in Paris where he learned Spanish and Dutch and married the thirteen-year-old daughter of the ambassador. He did not cohabit with her until two years later.

By the time Evelyn returned to England the Civil War was all but over, the Royalist cause finished. The execution of Charles I was but a preface for the horrors which followed, the formal abolition of the monarchy and of the Church of England. For a period Evelyn joined the Royalist exiles in Paris but he and his wife returned to England in the aftermath of Charles II's defeat at the battle of Worcester. Like so many others he decided to come to terms with the status quo, determining 'to endeavor a settled life ... there being now so little appearance of any change for the better, all being intirely in the rebells hands'.

Evelyn took up residence at Sayes Court, an estate in Deptford formerly belonging to his father-in-law Sir Richard Browne, which had been seized by Parliament and sold. Evelyn had to buy it back and it was there in 1652 that he set out like so many other Royalists to create a private world, one in which the banned Anglican services were held in secret. There too he began to lay out the famous garden inspired by all that he had seen in both France and Italy. In this way both Evelyn and his wife sat out the 1650s, putting the eighteen-roomed, half-timbered old manor house in order and starting a family. The experience of these tumultuous years, it has been argued, made Evelyn wary of public life. It can equally be argued, from the minor offices he held after 1660, that his talents in this direction were limited. Of politics and administration he was to write: 'I acknowledge the burthen insupportable.' What he really yearned for was to be some kind of adviser to Charles II on cultural and scientific matters. That he never achieved and, although frequently in the orbit of both king and court, he was never to attain a major appointment. His books he constantly presented to Charles II, who probably found Evelyn a bit of a pious bore.

None the less the 1660s saw Evelyn at his apogee, serving on a whole range of committees dealing with matters as varied as the Royal Mint, the manufacture of saltpetre and the replanning of London in the aftermath of the Great Fire. His most onerous job was as a Commissioner for the Sick and Wounded during the Second and Third Dutch Wars. This brought him a modest salary of only £300. In 1671 membership of the new Council for Foreign Plantations (i.e. colonies) brought a better figure, £500. During this period he cast Sayes Court as a villa with the Thames as the Brenta and there he received the old queen mother, Henrietta Maria, and the Lord Chancellor, Clarendon, before his fall. He was clearly at his happiest as a founding member of the Royal Society, a setting in which his many talents could flourish.

In 1670 Evelyn was fifty, old in seventeenth-century terms, but he was to live another thirty-five years. Most of these were spent preoccupied with family affairs and the perpetuation of the dynasty. His energies were expended on his not very talented heir, John, and his grandson, Jack. Both needed jobs and the way to them was through Evelyn's friendship with Sidney Godolphin, later Lord Godolphin, first as a Commissioner of the Treasury and later as Lord Treasurer. But for Evelyn these were decades clouded by the fear of a Catholic coup and the events leading up to the Revolution in 1688 which were watched and recorded with emotion. And, although he was to come into his beloved Wotton on the demise of his brother in 1699, they had spent the previous year in 'tedious altercations' as to the terms of this inheritance. In the end Evelyn was forced to sell land both to pay off debts and pay portions to various claimants. He was also landed with a battle royal with the executrix who stripped the place bare.

Evelyn had already moved his family and possessions to Wotton in 1694. Sayes Court he let, once disastrously to the Russian tsar, Peter the Great, who wrecked the place. Afflicted with kidney disorders and the gravel, Evelyn became progressively more and more obsessed with guilt and remorse. But he achieved his objective and secured the future of the dynasty. Early in 1704 his grandson Jack was appointed Receiver-General of the Stamp Duties and the following year was married to Lord Godolphin's niece. Evelyn died at his house in Dover Street on 27 February 1706. His wife, Mary, was to outlive him by just three years.

Family and Friends

To understand the Diary Evelyn needs to be placed not only within the context of his own immediate family, but also his friends. His wife, Mary Evelyn, although married when only thirteen years of age, was an educated woman brought up in a Paris which saw the emergence of the *précieuses* and of the salon hostess. She, of course, spoke French and read both that language and Italian. She was also a stylish letter-writer in her own right and, in addition, studied drawing and mathematics. The marriage was a good one, Evelyn once writing to her: 'you are myselfe & I trust you with all'. None the less one feels that he selected her at an early age with the idea that he could form her, and indeed the first thing he was to present her with on marriage was a treatise on the role of a wife. In this context he was actually unconsciously repressive. This was an alliance of affection and respect, the norm for the seventeenth-century upper classes, and certainly not one fired by either romance or passion. The latter were to come to him in the form of Margaret Godolphin during what might, in modern parlance, be described as a mid-life crisis, one which he coped with by self-repression.

Margaret Blagge, as she began her life, was the daughter of a Royalist colonel from Suffolk and maid of honour to the Duchess of York and later to Catherine of Braganza, Charles II's queen. She was an extraordinarily attractive woman and Evelyn met her first by chance on 28 June 1669. Although a member of the licentious Restoration court, Margaret was a woman of deep piety and she and Evelyn, then aged fifty-two, formed a pact of spiritual friendship in 1672. In the Diary she is depicted as a star and it is difficult not to believe that he was not in some way in love with her, although this was sublimated into a role for him as her mentor in the pursuit of the spiritual life. In order to understand such a relationship we have to avoid projecting back onto it either the fruits of Freudian psychology or the biographical stripping away of the mask we associate with the Bloomsburys. The seventeenth century accepted such friendships outside marriage. A man, for instance, could address another man as 'dearest amico' or 'charissime' without any overtones of homosexuality. In Evelyn's case Margaret came at the end of a series of 'vertuous friendships' he had had with other women. The spirit of such a relationship lay partly in France in Catholic Devout Humanism and partly in the court of Charles I over which Henrietta Maria reigned as a Neoplatonic love goddess. In spite of their relationship Margaret eschewed a life of chastity and married, in 1675, Sidney Godolphin without telling anyone, not even Evelyn. She was to die three years later in childbirth, leaving both husband and spiritual mentor grief-stricken. Godolphin was to succeed his wife in a 'holy friend-ship' with Evelyn: 'And now you see I have putt you just in the place of her I have lost.' Evelyn was to write a *Life of Mrs Godolphin* which he eventually sent to her husband in 1702 but it was never acknowledged. It was not to be published until 1847.

The Evelyns had eight children, four of whom died in childhood or infancy. The loss of Richard, the precocious heir who died at five, followed by his brother George, devastated Evelyn: 'upon the sudaine I grieve so severe and stoical, as it had even twisted my countenance and given me a perug of Grey-haires ...' The almost debonaire young man caught by Nanteuil in his engraving gives way to the lined face we see in the portrait by Kneller. A similar outpouring attended the death of his favourite and talented daughter Mary in 1685, at the age of nineteen: 'O how desolate hast Thou left us, Sweete, obliging, happy Creature!' That blow was followed not long after by the elopement of her sister Elizabeth who was to die only months later of smallpox. A third daughter, Susanna, 'religious, discreete, Ingenious', was to make a successful match with William Draper, heir to a fortune. The solitary male heir, John, of whom his father expected too much, was to predecease him.

Outside of the family Evelyn knew more or less anyone of consequence at both the court of Charles II and James II. Sir Christopher Wren, the architect, and Samuel Pepys were clearly good friends. And others seem to fall within this inner circle: Thomas Browne, the author of *Religio Medici*, Dr John Beale, the Herefordshire pomologist, Robert Boyle, the natural philosopher, Abraham Cowley, the poet, and the diarist's father-in-law, Sir Richard Browne. All were reflections of Evelyn's intellectual interests as the quintessential gentleman virtuoso.

Author and Virtuoso

Evelyn was a hugely industrious man. Indeed his papers, now in the British Library, remain still to be fully explored. The range of his interests was polymathic: pedagogy, education, botany, garden history, medicine, anatomy, mathematics, physics, natural history, mechanics, grammar, law, philology, philosophy, poetry (he was a bad poet), painting, coins and medals, and theology. He was a workaholic, forever putting pen to paper on a whole range of subjects although, it has to be admitted, what he produced tended to be in character pendantic and worthy.

Evelyn's range of interests captures a particular moment in the history of thought, in his case one which still retains elements of the late Renaissance hermetic encyclopaedic tradition and, at the same time, moves forward to embrace the new realms of post-Baconian experimental science. Evelyn was a representative of a new upper-class ideal which added to the existing sphere of a gentleman's activities the role of dilettante or virtuoso in the arts and sciences, that is, to be a person who was interested in, and probably took part in, experiments and inventions, was able to identify classical imagery and delighted in assembling a cabinet of rarities or judging a work of art. All this was a manifestation of a new educational programme for the upper classes embodying a dramatic change in attitude to studies and learning as attributes. Such was the virtuoso, but that concept was allied to a second, the Horatian ideal of the quiet country life devoted to rural meditation. These were the notions which saw so many Royalist gentry, Evelyn included, through the dark years of the 1650s. And out of this partly was to come the nexus of ideas which led to the Royal Society.

The backward elements in Evelyn's make-up include his unswerving belief in the divinity of monarchy and also his lingering faith in natural signs and portents (which Pepys had shed). Evelyn refers, for example, to the famous comet of 1618, held to portend the outbreak of the Thirty Years' War, reflecting that its effects, in 1624, were 'still working in the prodigious revolutions now beginning in Europ'. *Vis-à-vis* the sighting of another comet in 1680 he writes, 'I pray God avert his Judgements', and, fourteen years later, describing a group living out the Second Coming in Buckinghamshire, he recalls a prophecy of the German divine Alstedius that the millennium 'should indeede begin the very year 1694'.

Evelyn was also a Platonist. The Neoplatonic love etiquette was still very much alive at the court of Charles I and it provided, as we have seen, part of the thought-context for his relationship with Margaret Godolphin. But Platonism suffuses the rest of his intellectual make-up. When advising after the Fire on the replanning of London, practicalities are swept away in favour of the ground-plan of a utopian city. The garden at Sayes Court was equally seen by him as a terrestial reflection of the Garden of Eden.

Virtuosi assembled cabinets of rarities, artefacts which reflected the exploration and appreciation of the twin worlds of God's creation both in nature and in art. Evelyn had his cabinet room over the porch at Sayes Court but he provides a vivid picture less of his own than of that formed by Sir Thomas Browne in Norwich, 'whose whole house & Garden being a Paradise & Cabinet of rarities, & that of the best collection, especialy Medails, books, Plants, natural things, did exceedingly refresh me . . .'

Note that such a collection included what was in the garden. Evelyn was interested in gardening and garden design even before he travelled. In the 1650s he laid out an Italianate garden for his brother at Wotton and later designed a garden for Henry Howard at Albury. Others consulted him about gardens and the Deptford garden was central to his thought, Sayes Court being billed as 'my poor villa'. Unlike, however, the Italian villa, which was in general for leisure, *otium*, and not business, *negotio*, Sayes Court embraced both aspects of human life, the *vita activa* as well as *contemplativa*, for besides having a garden inspired by those Evelyn had seen in France and Italy, it was also used as a laboratory. Evelyn's delight in the *furor hortensis* never vanished and he was planting an elm walk at Wotton even in his eighty-first year.

Throughout his life Evelyn worked on a massive book on gardens and gardening, the *Elysium Britannicum*. It was to remain unpublished until 2001, although he was to cannabalize it for some of his other publications like his *Kalendarium Hortense* (1664) and *Acetaria* (1699), a discourse on salads. Amongst his published works the most influential was his *Sylva, Or a Discourse of Forest-Trees, and the Propagation of Timber*. That appeared, dedicated to Charles II, in 1664 and was to go through several editions until well into the following century. The general thrust of the book was the importance of planting up the land around the country house with trees, a future source of wood for shipbuilding and hence the power of the Navy. But its publication set the trend for landowners to go in a direction which would lead to the landscape garden.

Other works include the earliest plea to curb urban air pollution, *Fumifugium* (1661), *Sculptura* (1662), on engraving and, in particular, the mezzotint, and *Numismata* (1697), a history of medals with the earliest account of the slender contribution of England. Evelyn was also acutely aware of the value of translations, a view fully in accord with Bacon's intellectual strategy, and he translated a series of works from the French on libraries, painting, archictecture and gardening. But even this does not cover fully his astonishing output, for unpublished works linger amongst his papers including an 830-page history of religion.

The Agonized Anglican

In an era in which Britain can be described as a country in a post-Christian state, it is perhaps difficult for a modern reader to come to terms with the centrality of faith in Evelyn's life. It provides the key to him. In that way he is a far truer reflection of the ethos of the era than Pepys. On the continent the Thirty Years' War had been a conflict between Counter-Reformation Catholicism and Protestantism. In England, uniquely, the Civil War was one between two interpretations of the Protestant tradition, the direct consequence of the ambiguities of the 1559 settlement. Evelyn belonged firmly to the Anglican tradition as it was defined by Richard Hooker at the turn of the sixteenth century, a spiritual world which found poetic expression in the work of George Herbert. This was an Anglicanism rooted in the *Book of Common Prayer* with a firm belief in order and decency in public worship.

The Civil War was to intensify Evelyn's loyalty to the Church of England, Cromwell's suppression of it being 'the mournfullest day that in my life I have seene'. Services using the *Book of Common Prayer* were held covertly and in March 1655 the eminent divine, Dr Jeremy Taylor, became his 'Ghostly Father'. All of this intensified a sense of piety and also the weight of sin, one which continued to grow rather than diminish as Evelyn got older. He relentlessly recorded every sermon he went to and also the times when he had received communion, which was about monthly. His birthday increasingly prompted introspective self-examination of a kind which in 1680, on the occasion of his sixtieth birthday, lasted a week: 'I began a more solemn survey of my whole Life, in order to the making, and confirming my peace with God ... And, oh, how difficult, & uncertaine, yet most necessarie worke.'

Evelyn feared above all a Catholic coup and watched aghast as a Catholic Chapel Royal opened in Whitehall Palace for James II and his queen. So alarmed was he at the drift of events that, as a Commissioner of the Privy Seal (1685–7) he refused to license a publisher to print what he categorized as popish books. After the Revolution of 1688 it was the moral state of the nation which appalled him. But religion also had its positive side for from first to last it provided a framework for life and action, tempered and controlled his emotions and thoughts and enabled him to come to terms with both tragedy and grief. These he accepted stoically as the will of God. Obedience to the tenets of the Christian faith inevitably made him draw back from the shop-soiled world of the Restoration court. He viewed with increasing disgust the corruption in public life and records his revulsion from scenes like those witnessed when the court was at Newmarket in 1671: 'feasting & revelling, more resembling a luxurious & abandon'd rout, than a Christian Court'.

Perceptions of an Age

All diarists have their limitations. Evelyn's Diary reflects a myriad of impulses. One is certainly dynastic, a desire to record family history and his own place within it. That is caught in the resounding opening sentence: 'I was born at about 20 minuts past two in the morning, [on Tuesday] being the xxxi, and last of October Anno 1620 ...' That quality of being a family chronicle runs through the text from start to finish.

Another was his desire to record things seen, both those natural and man-made. There is from time to time a strong response also to landscape caught, for instance, in his first glimpse of the south of France in 1644: 'a Country sweetely declining to the South & Mediterranean Coasts, full of Vine-yards, & Olive-yards, Orange trees, Myrtils, Pomegranads & like sweete Plantations'. Similarly architecture is a preoccupa-tion, stimulated by his continental travels. In 1671 he praises Euston as 'a very noble pile' and Althorpe five years later is similarly eulogized as 'a noble uniforme pile ... a la moderne'. And along with buildings went gardens, a perennial source of fascination.

The foreign travel entries, particularly those covering Italy, remain perhaps the most vivid record from the Stuart age of one man's response to the riches of Italian Renaissance and baroque culture. Much of Evelyn's life was devoted to introducing what he had seen to his own country. Less well known but equally interesting is the tour of England he made with his wife in 1654. Together they travelled as far south-west as Salisbury, north as York and east as Cambridge. In this we get glimpses of the devastation wreaked by the war. Lord Craven's house at Caversham he records as 'now in ruines' and Worcester cathedral as being 'extreamely ruin'd'. But always one is left wanting more.

That sums up the Diary's shortcoming, Evelyn's inability on the whole to be discursive. An entry like that for 5 January 1674 immediately excites: 'I saw an *Italian Opera* in musique, the first that had ben in *England* of this kind.' But he fails to go on and describe it which he was perfectly capable of doing and we feel short-changed. When he does go on we are given something memorable as when the king summoned him to his Closet to hold the candle while the famous miniaturist Samuel Cooper drew him. Or one recalls his account of his discovery of Grinling Gibbons or his description of the court at Lord Arlington's house at Euston in 1671 – a visit which saw the advent of a new mistress for the king, Louise de Kéroualle: 'It was universaly reported that the faire Lady— was bedded one of these nights, and the stocking flung, after the manner of a married Bride: I acknowledge she was for the most part in her undresse all day, and that there was fondnesse, & toying, with that young wanton ...' In this Evelyn reveals that beneath the austere surface sometimes a Pepys could lurk.

He could, when he chose, provide a pen-portrait as perceptive as any. When they occur it is usually on someone's demise. His depiction of Charles II remains unforgettable with its stunning opening line: 'A prince of many Virtues, & many greate Imperfections ...' Equally of the king's bastard, Monmouth: 'an excellent souldier, & dauncer, a favorite of the people, of an Easy nature, debauched by lust, seduc'd by crafty knaves ...' Women too could catch his eye. Lady Petty he neatly encapsulates as 'an extraordinary witt, as well as beauty, & a prudent Woman'. But again one is left wanting more.

INTRODUCTION

So what does this all add up to? This is some eighty turbulent years of English history as seen through the eyes of a member of the Anglican landowning Royalist oligarchy which returned to power in 1660. It is the record of a man who saw his ideals, ones ideals enshrined in an imaginary pre-1642 world, betrayed by a corrupt and dissipated court. Worse, he nearly saw the country turn Catholic, to him the ultimate betrayal. But the post-Baconian urge to observe, even things as gruesome as torture and amputations, and set them down never quite deserted him. If the Diary lacks humour and a sense of *joie de vivre*, perhaps the man did not in reality. Let his friend Samuel Pepys have the last word. In September 1665 they were both at the same dinner, one 'that in all my life I never met with so merry a two hours as our company that night was'. And who should the leading spirit be but John Evelyn who 'did make us all die almost from laughing'. And there let him rest.

Roy Strong

THE NATURE OF
THE DIARY

What is John Evelyn's Diary? The question is a pertinent one
for anyone about to rummage through what at times may
seem little more than a dispiriting list of one man's movements
laced with an obsession for attending sermons and recording
every biblical text upon which they were based. At the outset
the reader needs to grasp that you cannot read Evelyn's Diary
in the same way that you can that of his great contemporary,
Samuel Pepys. The latter indeed, forms something of a stum-
bling block, for it is so readable, so vivid, so gloriously frank
and indiscreet, so overflowing with *joie de vivre*, that poor
Evelyn, in comparison, may seem at first glance small beer.
But then it must be borne in mind that Pepys wrote in code
which was not deciphered until the Victorian period, so he
could give free rein to his indiscretions secure in the knowledge
no one could read them. Evelyn, on the other hand, wrote so
that his Diary could be picked up and read by anyone, albeit
it was composed with the eyes of descendants in mind. That
is a huge divide. To that must be added the sharply constrast-
ing nature of these two men, the one ebullient, outgoing,
lecherous, the other pious, repressed and reserved. Both provide penetrating insights into one of the most turbulent centu-
ries in the island's history. And on that score Evelyn wins for
whereas Pepys covers barely a decade, 1660 to 1669, Evelyn's
Diary runs over eighty years from 1620 to 1706.

In that way Evelyn provides us with a panorama of one
man's life, his family and his friends, running from the reign
of James I to that of Queen Anne, a journey in time through
the Personal Rule of Charles I, the Civil War, the Republic,
the Protectorate, the Restoration, the Revolution of 1688 and
beyond. This is a record by a highly educated man on the
periphery of the great ones and the great events of the age. So
inevitably it is crammed with entries which are of the utmost
fascination. But it is also crammed with an unending litany of

the humdrum, more so to twenty-first century eyes because we are living in what some have designated as a post-Christian era. That presents any editor with a dilemma. Does he jettison what many readers will today find of little interest, or not? I believe that to do so would result in a distortion of Evelyn the man. So I have, therefore, opted for a middle way, keeping most of the text but hoping that the reader will have the good sense to run his eye quickly through such passages. What will help him and has not been done before is to divide the text into thematic sections, thus providing a clear chronology as an anchor and, equally, facilitating dipping without resort to the index.

What Evelyn presents us with is a personal chronicle of a long, busy, useful and, it would seem, entirely blameless life in all its external manifestations. He records journeys, visits, things seen, encounters, crises, rites of passage and curiosities. But the reader will look in vain for the inner workings of his mind, apart from periodic glimpses of spiritual angst and the articulation of grief. Although, for instance, Evelyn was a prolific author and translator, at no point does he reveal why he embarked on this or that book or translation. Equally we get very little insight into his domestic life and, although he is able occasionally, particularly when he travels, to exhibit powers of description, his Diary lacks the visual perception one would expect from a man so interested in the arts. Also, as in the case of so many diarists, the urge to write ebbed and flowed.

The Diary survives in two forms. The first manuscript is entitled *De Vita Propria*, a text of seventy-six pages written late in life in 1697 and covering the years 1620 to 1644. The second manuscript is his *Kalendarium* covering a far longer period. Even in the case of the latter the section up to 1645 was written retrospectively in 1660 and a second covering 1649 to 1684 was written between 1680 and 1684. After 1684 all the entries are contemporary. But from what did Evelyn compile his retrospective entries? The answer to that is that they began as annotations to printed Almanacks starting in 1637. These he had bound and interleaved with blank sheets enabling him to write where he wanted and at different times discursive entries. All of this material was used to compile the definitive text by E. S. de Beer which was published in six volumes from 1955 onwards and upon which the present edition is based.

Two points, however, need to be made in respect of these retrospective compilations. The first concerns what in essence was a nascent version of the Grand Tour. Although that remains a fundamental text and one of the most fascinating passages in the Diary, it was compiled making ample use of contemporary guide books. That part of the Diary needs to be read with caution. The second is the treatment of the pre-Civil War period. Evelyn was only twenty-two when the war broke out. One thing is clear, the execution of the king traumatized him. Evelyn was a firm believer in the sanctity of monarchy. As a consequence of this he bestowed a golden haze on the pre-Civil War era, one not so different in mood from that accorded by John Aubrey in his *Brief Lives*. In 'the days of our fathers,' Evelyn writes, 'simple plain men as they were who courted and chose their wives for their modesty', people were pious, industrious and serious with a keen sense of duty and morality both in public and in private life. That indulgence for ennobling the reign of Charles I also affected his treatment of events. When it came to Oliver Cromwell's funeral, for example, he records it as 'the joyfullest funeral that ever I saw, for there were none that Cried, but dogs ...', leaving one wondering whether that was a true or a prejudiced account. And that idealization of the Caroline age was to be made all the more acute by the louche world of the Restoration court. So we emerge with a sharp sense that Evelyn was out of tune with the times, someone who, by his early twenties, was already living beyond his period and was to feel this ever more acutely as he grew older.

Roy Strong

NOTE ON THE TEXT

The text of this edition is that of the Oxford Standard Authors edition of *The Diary of John Evelyn*, edited by E. S. de Beer, 1959, from his six-volume edition for the Oxford English Texts (Clarendon Press, 1955).

In his 1959 edition De Beer uses the text of the principal manuscript of the Diary, the *Kalendarium*. Extracts from Evelyn's later recension of the Diary (*De Vita Propria*) he gives as footnotes, their source being indicated by the letter 'V'. They are limited to the more important passages that contain substantive additions to the *Kalendarium*.

Three kinds of brackets occur in the text: round brackets for Evelyn's parentheses; square brackets for Evelyn's marginal notes, and for words and sentences interlined by him after the text had been written: and pointed brackets for editorial interference, supplying letters and words omitted by Evelyn or replacing his very wild spellings by more recognizable ones.

SELECT BIBLIOGRAPHY

———

JOHN BOWLE, *John Evelyn and his World. A Biography*, Routledge & Kegan Paul, London, Boston and Henley, 1981.

JOHN EVELYN, *Elysium Britannicum, or The Royal Gardens*, ed. John E. Ingram, University of Pennsylvania Press, 2000.

FRANCIS HARRIS, *Transformations of Love: The Friendship of John Evelyn and Margaret Godolphin*, Oxford University Press, 2002.

W. G. HISCOCK, *John Evelyn and his Family Circle*, Routledge & Kegan Paul, London, 1955.

GEOFFREY KEYNES, *John Evelyn: A Study in Bibliophily with a Bibliography of His Writings*, The Grolier Club, New York, 1937.

SIR ROY STRONG, historian, writer and broadcaster, was Director of the National Portrait Gallery from 1967 to 1973 and of the Victoria and Albert Museum from 1974 to 1987. His books include *The Cult of Elizabeth*, *Gloriana*, *Henry, Prince of Wales*, *Painting the Past*, *The Story of Britain*, *Feast: A History of Grand Eating* and *The Laskett*.

CHRONOLOGY

DATE	AUTHOR'S LIFE	LITERARY CONTEXT
1620	Birth of John Evelyn on 31 October, fourth child of Richard Evelyn and Eleanor Stansfield, at his father's country estate of Wotton in Surrey.	Bacon: *Novum Organum*. Quarles: *A Feast for Worms*. First (anonymous) English translation of the *Decameron*.
1621		Burton: *The Anatomy of Melancholy*. Fletcher: *The Wilde-Goose Chase* (1st perf.). Donne writes most of his *Holy Sonnets* and many *Divine Poems* (to 1631).
1622	Birth of Richard, the youngest of the Evelyn siblings.	Middleton and Rowley: *The Changeling* (first perf.). Drayton: *The Poly-Olbion*.
1623		Shakespeare First Folio. Drummond of Hawthornden: *A Cypresse Grove*.
1624		Herbert of Cherbury: *De Veritate*. Henry Wotton: *Elements of Architecture*.
1625	John sent to live with his mother's father and stepmother at Cliffe, near Lewes in Sussex.	Third, expanded edition of Bacon's *Essays*.
1627	Death of his grandfather, John Stansfield.	Bacon: *New Atlantis*. Thomas May's translation of Lucan's *Pharsalia*.
1628		Earle: *Microcosmographie* (a collection of character sketches). Harvey publishes his theories on the circulation of the blood: *De Motu Cordis et Sanguinis*.

HISTORICAL EVENTS

Thirty Years' War in Europe (since 1618). Battle of the White Mountain: Bohemian Protestants defeated. Spanish troops invade the Palatinate: James I incenses public opinion by failing to intervene on behalf of his son-in-law, the Elector. Massacre of Protestants in the Valtalline. Pilgrim Fathers set sail in the *Mayflower* and found the first New England colony. Economic slump in England: James I blamed for his interference in the wool trade and use of monopolies. Bacon and Mompesson impeached by Commons. Death of Philip III and accession of Philip IV of Spain: ascendancy of Olivarez begins. Edinburgh University founded. Oxford Physic Garden (earliest in Britain) founded.

Spread of Arminianism within Church of England. James I's *Direction to Preachers* aims to suppress contentious (Calvinist) preaching; arouses fears of crypto-Catholicism, exacerbated by Arminian adherence to High Church ritual and emphasis on the authority of bishops, and the declining importance of the sermon. Inigo Jones's Banqueting Hall completed. Invention of slide-rule by William Oughtred.
Abortive expedition of Prince Charles and Buckingham to Spain to win hand of Infanta. Statute of Monopolies forbids royal granting of monopoly rights; allows 14-year exclusive rights for new inventions, the beginning of the patent laws.
Cardinal Richelieu comes to power in France. Frans Hals: 'The Laughing Cavalier'; Poussin: 'Echo and Narcissus'; Rubens: 'Massacre of the Innocents'; Bernini's sculpture of 'Apollo and Daphnis'.
Outbreak of plague in England. Death of James I; accession of Charles I. Marriage of Charles and Henrietta Maria. Buckingham's naval raid on Cadiz, an expensive fiasco. 1625–30: Wallenstein, new general-in-chief of Imperial forces, defeats Protestant armies under Mansfeld, and, with Tilly, overwhelms Denmark.
England and France at war (to 1630). Failure of Buckingham's naval expedition to relieve Huguenots besieged at La Rochelle. Charles I raises money by forced loans: Case of the Five Knights who unsuccessfully test the legality of confinement for those who refuse to comply. Charles buys great art collection of the Gonzaga dukes of Mantua. Inigo Jones completes Queen's Chapel at St James's Palace. Kepler compiles *Rudolphine Tables* for calculating astronomical positions.
Laud is made Bishop of London; Arminianism and support of the prerogative become inextricably linked in the minds of Presbyterians. New Parliament passes Petition of Right, masterminded by Sir Edward Coke and John Eliot, in protest against arbitrary taxation and church reform. King counters with declaration to promote religious conformity. Assassination of Buckingham.

xxvii

DATE	AUTHOR'S LIFE	LITERARY CONTEXT
1629		Andrewes: *Ninety-Six Sermons*. Milton: *On the Morning of Christ's Nativity*.
1630	At school in Southover, Lewes. Now living in Southover, following the remarriage of his step-grandmother.	Alsted: *Encyclopaedia*. 1630s: Lord Falkland's Great Tew home becomes centre for liberal thinkers out of sympathy with recent denominational controversy (Jonson, Carew, Waller, Earle, Chillingworth, Hyde, etc.).
1631		*Chloridia*, last court masque of Ben Jonson and Inigo Jones (1st 1605). Chapman: *Caesar and Pompey*. Death of Donne.
1632	John pays his first visit to Wotton, following the wedding of his eldest sister, Elizabeth. Declines his father's proposal that he should be sent to Eton, preferring to remain with his 'too indulgent grandmother'.	Milton: 'On Shakespeare'. Prynne: *Histrio-Mastix* (a Puritan attack on stage plays).
1633	Richard Evelyn is made Sheriff of Surrey and Sussex – the highest office in the county, tenable for one year.	Birth of Pepys. Death of George Herbert. Poems of Donne and Herbert (*The Temple*) published. Milton: *L'Allegro* and *Il Penseroso*. Cowley: *Poetical Blossomes*. Ford: *'Tis Pity She's a Whore* (printed). D'Avenant: *The Wits* (1st perf.). Phineas Fletcher: *The Purple Island*.
1634	Death of Elizabeth Darcy, the Evelyns' eldest daughter. John returns to Wotton for the funeral.	Milton: *A Masque* [*Comus*] (music by Henry Lawes). *Coelum Britannicum* (masque by Carew and Inigo Jones). Shirley: *The Triumph of Peace* (a masque with music by William Lawes).

CHRONOLOGY

HISTORICAL EVENTS

Opposition led by Eliot and Holles insists upon delaying the dissolution of Parliament to pass three further resolutions attacking Court policy. Ringleaders imprisoned. Charles rules for 11 years without Parliament. Great 'Puritan migration' to New England begins. Massachusetts charter granted. Rubens presents 'Peace and War' to Charles I. Vermuyden contracted to drain Great Fens (to 1652).
Birth of Charles, Prince of Wales, later Charles II. Charles I builds up royal art collection with many Italian masterpieces (1630s).

Magdeberg savagely sacked by Imperial troops under Tilly. Gustavus Adolphus of Sweden embarks on brief but brilliant military career, overthrowing Tilly at Breitenfeld. Henry Lawes becomes a court composer: his many songs include settings of Carew, Waller, Herrick, Suckling, Lovelace and Milton.
Royal proclamation banishes gentry and nobility to their country estates. Increasing isolation of the court; the queen's Catholic influence becoming stronger. Laud, effectively chief minister, enforces policy via hated prerogative courts of the Star Chamber and High Commission. Swedes victorious at Lech (death of Tilly) and at Lützen; death of Gustavus Adolphus at Lützen. Thomas Wentworth (later Earl of Strafford) Lord Deputy in Ireland. Van Dyck becomes court painter.

Laud becomes Archbishop of Canterbury. Birth of James, Duke of York, later James II. Wentworth's policy of 'Thorough' in Ireland brings in revenue for the Crown but also antagonizes Presbyterian settlers and their supporters in England. In France the Abbé de St Cyran appointed director of Port-Royal which becoms a centre for Jansenism. Port-Royal circle includes Angélique and Antoine Arnauld, Pascal and Quesnel. Condemnation of Galileo by Inquisition for upholding the Copernican system.

King follows a mercantilist, interventionist economic policy, winning the support of merchants and financiers. Cycle of good harvests during the 1630s contributes to enhanced prosperity. First writs for ship money on coastal counties, for naval defence. Laud's religious policy further antagonizes Puritans: conventicles are suppressed and King James's Declaration of Sports revised and read in churches, implying condemnation of the Puritan sabbath. Puritan William Prynne is pilloried and has his ears

DATE	AUTHOR'S LIFE	LITERARY CONTEXT
1634 *cont.*		
1635	John summoned to Wotton during his mother's final illness. After her death he returns to Lewes, accompanied, at her wish, by his younger brother Richard.	Milton: *Lycidas*. Selden: *Mare Clausum*. Shirley: *The Lady of Pleasure*. Quarles: *Emblems*. Caldéron: *La vida es sueño*. Death of Lope de Vega.
1637	John and Richard are admitted to the Middle Temple (Feb); John enters Balliol College, Oxford (May) as a Fellow-Commoner. He remains at Oxford three years, leaving without graduating (as was common practice among the gentry), and without over-exerting himself in his studies. Takes music lessons – the beginning of a lifelong interest in music – and is 'admitted into the dauncing, and Vaulting schole'. Begins making diary notes in printed almanacks.	Death of Ben Jonson. Chillingworth: *The Religion of the Protestants a Safe Way to Salvation*. Corneille: *Le Cid*. Descartes: *Discours de la méthode*.
1638		Cowley: *Loves Riddle*; *Naufragium Joculaire*. Suckling: *Aglaura*. John Wilkins: *The Discovery of a World in the Moon*.
1639		D'Avenant: *The Spanish Lovers*. Shirley/Newcastle: *The Country Captain*.
1640	John obtains part of a chamber in the Middle Temple and begins to spend some time in London, while refusing to study law (April). Death of his father, Richard Evelyn (Dec). By the terms of his father's will, John Evelyn inherits some land in Lewes and £4000 in money – enough for him to live on comfortably without the need of a profession.	Jonson: *Underwood*; translation of Horace's *Ars Poetica*; prose works – *The English Grammar*, and *Timbers, or Discoveries*. First volume of Donne's Sermons, prefaced by Walton's *Life of Donne*. Carew: *Poems*. Suckling: *Ballad upon a Wedding*. Killigrew: *The Parson's Wedding*. *Wit's Recreations* (collection of epigrams and epitaphs).

CHRONOLOGY

amputated after trial by Court of Star Chamber for libelling the queen in
Histrio-Mastix. Maryland founded by Catholics. Assassination of Wallenstein.
Van Dyck's equestrian portrait of Charles I.
Ship money extended to inland counties – an efficient tax but deeply
unpopular. Rubens' Banqueting House ceiling depicting apotheosis of
James I. War between France and Spain. Richelieu founds *L'Académie
française*.

Puritan pamphleteers Prynne, Bastwick, Burton and Lilburne are mutilated,
branded and imprisoned for seditious libel. Laud attempts to impose Book
of Common Prayer on the Presbyterian Kirk, leading to riots in St Giles'
Cathedral. Van Dyck paints triple portrait of Charles I to help Bernini
execute a bust.

Rex v. Hampden case confirms legality of ship money: John Hampden fined
for refusing to pay. Growing fear that ship money might be used to finance a
standing army. General Assembly of Church of Scotland assumes leadership of
national revolt, organizing Solemn League and Covenant against episcopacy.
Charles I mobilizes army. Monteverdi: *Madrigals of Love and War*.
First Bishops' War. English army repelled by Scots under Leslie. Treaty of
Berwick. General Assembly sweeps away episcopacy in Scotland. Strafford
recalled from Ireland; advises the king to call a new Parliament to vote the
necessary supply to continue the war.
Short Parliament (April-May) refuses to vote supply until grievances are
settled; dissolved when Opposition (led by Pym) found to be negotiating
with Scots. Scots defeat English at Newburn and take Newcastle (Aug).
Treaty of Ripon imposes subsidy of £25,000 on Charles I, thereby shackling
him to the Long Parliament (meets 3 Nov and not dissolved until March
1660). Even many moderates in Parliament are now hostile to the king,
though initially bent on reform, not revolution. However, Pym's 'keynote'
speech (7 Nov) demonstrates that a core of members are convinced of a
conspiracy to introduce despotism and papacy into the country – a fear
fuelled by the apocalyptic preaching of Puritan divines. Root and Branch
petition (11 Dec), signed by 15,000 Londoners, calls for abolition of
episcopacy. Laud imprisoned.

DATE	AUTHOR'S LIFE	LITERARY CONTEXT
1640 *cont.*		John Wilkins: *A Discourse Concerning a New Planet.* Corneille: *Horace.* Janssen: *Augustinus.*
1641	The diarist comes to the notice of Lord Arundel, a great patron of the arts, whose estate lies close to Wotton. Witnesses the execution of the Earl of Strafford (7 May). Departs for Holland (July) where he very briefly enrols as a volunteer in Peter Apsley's company at the siege of Genep before continuing on a tour of the Low Countries.	Milton's first three anti-episcopal pamphlets. Denham: *The Sophy.* Wither: *Heleluiah.* Brome: *The Joviall Crew.* First publication of *Diurnal Occurrences in Parliament.* Hartlib: *A Description of the Famous Kingdom of Macaria.* Descartes: *Meditationes de prima philosophia.* Corneille: *Cinna.*
1642	Spends time in London, Wotton (inherited by his older brother George) and Lewes. Makes an attempt to join the Royalist army but arrives at the battle of Brentford (12 November) too late to take part. Returns to Wotton for fear that the property would be seized and confiscated by Parliamentary forces.	Denham: *Cooper's Hill.* Death of Cavalier poets Cartwright and Godolphin. Lovelace: 'To Althea'. Fuller: *The Holy State and the Profane State.* Henry More: *Psychodia Platonica.*
1643	Moves from place to place to avoid taking Parliament's oath of loyalty. Obtains the king's leave to travel abroad and departs in November for Paris.	Thomas Browne: *Religio Medici.* Digby: *Observations* (on the above); *Of Bodies*; *Of the Immortality of Man's Soul.* Cowley: *The Puritan and the Papist.* Prynne: *The Sovereign Power of Parliament.* Corneille: *Polyeucte.* Caldéron: *El alcalde de Zalamea.*
1644	Mainly in Paris. Summer in Tours. Sets out for Italy in the autumn via Lyons and Marseilles. Travels by sea from Cannes to Genoa. Visits Pisa, Florence, and Siena, arriving in Rome on 4 November.	Milton: *On Education*; *Areopagitica.* Cleveland: *The Rebel Scot.* Overton: *Man's Mortality.* Descartes: *Principia philosophiae.* Arnauld: *Apologie pour Jansénius.*

HISTORICAL EVENTS

Riots in London (Jan). Triennial Act (Feb). Impeachment of Strafford, whose execution (May) Charles is obliged to sanction. Protestation (3 May) of Commons to country. Marriage of Princess Mary to William, son of Frederick Henry, Prince of Orange and Dutch Stadtholder. Henrietta Maria found to be soliciting aid from Louis XIII. Abolition of prerogative courts. Root and Branch Bill. Pym's Ten Propositions (24 June). Charles leaves for Scotland (Aug). Rebellion of Irish Catholics in Ulster (Oct) which Parliament cannot trust Charles with an army to suppress. Commons pass Grand Remonstrance (22 Nov) by a majority of only 159 to 148, the radical restructuring of the Church being repellant to moderate Anglicans led by Falkland, Hyde and Culpepper. Charles returns to London and is welcomed by the city (1 Dec). Riots against bishops; 12 bishops sent to the Tower. Monteverdi: *The Return of Ulysses*.

In an unprecedented move, Charles enters the Commons to arrest the Five Members – Pym, Hampden, Holles, Haslerig, Strode – but they have already fled. Militia Bill passed and bill excluding bishops from House of Lords. Parliament's Nineteen Propositions to the king are so harsh that he appears moderate in comparison. Edward Hyde (later Earl of Clarendon) becomes Charles's chief adviser; begins to build up a Royalist party. Parliament mobilizes army under Earl of Essex. King raises standard at Nottingham (21 Aug). Royalists win battle of Edgehill (Oct) but fail to take London. Parliament closes all theatres (to 1660). Pascal designs machine for adding and subtracting. Discovery of Tasmania and New Zealand. Rembrandt: 'Night Watch'. Monteverdi: *The Coronation of Poppaea*.

King rejects 'Propositions of Oxford'. Royalist victories at Roundaway Down, Bristol and Adwalton Moor. Prince Rupert takes Bristol. King unsuccessfully besieges Gloucester. Royalist defeats at Newbury and Winceby. Pym gains support of Scots by accepting the Covenant in England: Westminster Assembly of Divines set up to enforce it. Death of Pym leaves the more conservative Parliamentarians leaderless. Death of Louis XIII and regency of Anne of Austria: Mazarin becomes chief minister in France. Condé defeats Spanish at Rocroi; Condé and Turenne win a series of victories in this last phase of the Thirty Years' War, ensuring French supremacy. Invention of the barometer by Torricelli.

Sir Henry Vane the younger, an Independent with Republican leanings, rising to prominence in the Commons, closely allied with Oliver Cromwell, rising star of the Army. Scots invade England, joining with Parliamentary army to defeat Royalists at Marston Moor (first defeat of Prince Rupert's cavalry by Cromwell's Ironsides). Montrose forms Royalist army in Scotland and wins the first of his victories against the Covenanters. Second battle of Newbury (inconclusive). Book of Common Prayer replaced by the Directory of Public Worship. Parliament orders a strict observance of Sundays and

DATE	AUTHOR'S LIFE	LITERARY CONTEXT
1644 *cont.*		
1645	Extensive sight-seeing in Rome. Evelyn's interests include works of art from antiquity and the Renaissance, historical monuments, gardens and natural scenery, and natural history collections. Visits Naples and volcanic areas nearby. Leaves Rome in May, travelling via Florence and Bologna to Venice. Spends the next ten months in Venice and in Padua, where he studies anatomy and physiology.	Marvell: *Flecknoe, an English Priest at Rome.* Waller: *Poems.* Fuller: *Good Thoughts in Bad Times.* Herbert of Cherbury: *De Causis Errorum.*
1646	Leaves Venice and Padua in May. Visits Milan, and crosses the Simplon Pass to Geneva. Arrives in Paris in July. Becomes friendly with the English Resident, Sir Richard Browne and his family.	Vaughan: *Poems.* Milton: *Poems.* Suckling: *Fragmenta Aurea*; *The Goblins*; *Brennoralt.* Crashaw: *Steps to the Temple*; *The Delights of the Muses.* Browne: *Pseudodoxia Epidemica (Vulgar Errors).* Clarendon begins his *History of the Rebellion.*
1647	Evelyn marries Mary Browne, Sir Richard Browne's daughter and heiress (June). He is 26, she 12 or 13. Leaving her in the care of her parents, he returns to England to settle his affairs (Oct). Visits Charles I, now a prisoner at Hampton Court, with information from the Royalists in Paris. Begins a cypher correspondence with his father-in-law on the political situation in England.	Cowley: *The Mistress.* Cleveland: *Poems.* Jeremy Taylor: *The Liberty of Prophesying* (an Anglican argument for religious toleration).
1648		Herrick: *Hesperides*; *Noble Numbers.* Lovelace: *Lucasta*; *Epodes, Odes, Sonnets, Songs etc.* John Wilkins: *Mathematical Magick* (on mechanical geometry).

HISTORICAL EVENTS

forbids the celebration of Christmas. Ejection of Royalist or 'unsuitable' clergy from their livings begins (over a third by the end of the Interregnum). Execution of Laud (Jan). Cromwell and Independents obtain Self-Denying Ordinance (April): MPs no longer allowed to hold military command. New Model Army formed under Sir Thomas Fairfax: Cromwell is second-in-command but does not resign his seat. Charles rejects Uxbridge peace proposals. New Model Army wins decisive victories at Naseby (June) and Langport (July). Rupert surrenders Bristol. Montrose defeated at Philiphaugh (Sept). Matthew Hopkins' crusade against witches in the eastern counties results in over 200 executions.

King surrenders to Scots at Newark (May). Oxford capitulates (June). Intensifying of Presbyterian–Independent conflict. Propositions put to Charles in June still stipulate acceptance of the Covenant. Independents open separate negotiations with king. Levellers argue for the abolition of monarchy and the sovereignty of the people in *Remonstrance of Many Thousand Citizens*. Puritan soldiers sack and burn manor house and church at Little Gidding in Huntingdonshire, where in 1625 Nicholas Ferrar had set up an Anglican community of prayer. Episcopacy formally abolished.

Parliament pays Scots £40,000 to hand over Charles I (Feb). Cromwell dispatches Cornet Joyce to sieze the king, who is taken into Army custody. Cromwell, Ireton and others debate constitutional issues with Army 'agitators' at Putney. Cromwell, negotiating directly with king, produces the Heads of Proposals, less extreme than Parliament's Newcastle Propositions. Charles flees from Hampton Court to Carisbrooke Castle (Nov). Signs Engagement with Scots (Dec), accepting their support in subduing England in return for a three-year trial of Presbyterian church government. Lely paints 'The Children of Charles I'. Ordinances banning bear baiting and folk dancing.

Second Civil War. Cromwell defeats Scots at Preston (Aug). Army presses for trial of king, referred to in Ireton's Remonstrance as 'that man of blood'. Parliament continues to negotiate with him. In Pride's Purge Army forcibly reduces membership of Parliament to 150, known as 'The Rump'. The Rump and the Army become centres of power in the country. Fronde of the parlement begins in France (May). Peace of Westphalia ends the Thirty Years' War. France, Saxony and Bavaria chief territorial gainers; Habsburg power is contained. France and Spain fight on until 1659.

JOHN EVELYN

DATE	AUTHOR'S LIFE	LITERARY CONTEXT
1649	Returns to Paris in July, rejoining the community of Royalist exiles who come together regularly at Sir Richard Browne's Anglican chapel. Evelyn's first published work, *Of Liberty and Servitude*, a translation of a treatise by F. de la Mothe le Vayer.	Winstanley: *The True Levellers' Standard Advanced.* Lilburne/Overton: *England's New Chains Discovered.* Lilburne: *Agreement of the People.* Descartes: *Traité des passions de l'âme.* Madeleine de Scudéry: *Artamène, ou le Grand Cyrus* (10 vols to 1653).
1650		Hobbes: *Treatise of Human Nature*; *De Corpore Politico.* Marvell: *An Horatian Ode on Cromwell's Return from Ireland*; *Tom May's Death.* Henry Vaughan: *Silex scintillans.* Thomas Vaughan: *Magia adamica.* Taylor: *The Rule and Exercises of Holy Living.* John Playford: *The English Dancing Master.* Anne Bradstreet: *The Tenth Muse Lately Sprung up in America.*
1651	Death of Evelyn's elder sister, Jane Glanville.	Hobbes: *Leviathan.* Harvey: *De Generatione* (study of development of embryo). Donne: *Essays in Divinity.* Henry Vaughan: *Olor Iscanus* ('The Swan of Usk'). Henry Wotton: *Reliquiae Wottonianae.* D'Avenant: *Gondibert.* Cartwright: *Comedies, Tragedies, with other poems.* Taylor: *The Rule and Exercises of Holy Dying.* Corneille: *Andromède.*
1652	Returns to England where he manages to obtain possession of Sayes Court, a house in Deptford belonging to his father-in-law and sequestered by the Parliamentarians. Richard, his first son, is born in August.	Winstanley: *Law of Freedom.* Crashaw: *Carmen Deo Nostro.* Henry Vaughan: *The Mount of Olives, or Solitary Devotions.* English translation by Lovelace and others of La Calprenède's *Cléopâtre* (12 vols, to 1659).

HISTORICAL EVENTS

Trial and execution of Charles I (Jan). Publication of the anonymous
bestseller *Eikon Basilike* presenting him as a martyr. Monarchy and the House
of Lords abolished (Feb). All office holders subjected to an oath of loyalty 'to
the Commonwealth of England'. Economic depression. Winstanley and the
Diggers occupy common land on St George's Hill, Surrey (April),
denouncing all property as a Norman invention. Proliferation of disaffected
sectaries – Anabaptists, Ranters, Familists, Adamites, Brownists, Fifth
Monarchists, etc. Levellers are crushed as a political force and Lilburne
spends most of the 1650s in prison. Catholic Royalist uprising in Ireland:
Cromwell's troop capture and sack Drogheda (Sept). Charles II proclaimed
in Scotland. Princes' Fronde in France, with Condé opposing Mazarin.
Execution of Montrose. Cromwell defeats Scots at Dunbar. Ordinance
repealing penalties for non-attendance at church provided one attended
an alternative public place of worship, favours Independents, but also
Catholics. Society of Friends (Quakers) founded by George Foxe. Death
of William II of Orange; posthumous birth of Wiliiam III. John de Witt
(elected Grand Pensionary 1653) effectively becomes chief minister of a new
Dutch Republic (the United Provinces). Guericke invents air pump and
experiments with vacuums. Velasquez paints 'Pope Innocent X'. Carissimi:
Jephtha – one of the ealiest oratorios.

Charles II invades England from Scotland; defeated by Cromwell at
Worcester. Leaves Scotland open to annexation; negotiations for union
completed by 1654. English naval superiority over Dutch and French
confirmed. First English Navigation Acts to break hold of Dutch carrying
trade between Europe and America. Milton, commissioned by Council to
reply to Salmasius' indictment of the regicide government (*Defensio Regia*),
issues *Pro Populo Anglicano Defensio*. Cape Colony founded by Dutch. Lely's
portrait of Oliver Cromwell. Claude Lorraine: 'The Rest on the Flight into
Egypt'. Cavalli: *La Calisto*.

End of war in Ireland. Settlement of demobilized English troops on lands
of former Catholic rebels. Commercial rivalry provokes First Dutch War
(to 1654). Blake's victory off the Kentish Knock; his defeat off Dungeness.
Foreign policy financed by sale of Crown and Church lands, plus higher
taxation. Parliament passes Act of Pardon and Oblivion to reconcile
Royalists. Independent MPs pressing for disestablishment: Army radicals for
law reform and dissolution of the Rump. First coffee house in London in
Cornhill. Condé occupies Paris.

DATE	AUTHOR'S LIFE	LITERARY CONTEXT
1652 *cont.*	Gardening, studying and literary pursuits occupy Evelyn during the Commonwealth years. He continues Anglican worship, where necessary in private, and manages to avoid taking any oath of loyalty to the republican government.	Benlowes: *Theophila, or Love's Sacrifice*. Letters of Dorothy Osborne to William Temple (to 1654).
1653	Birth of second son, John Stansfield Evelyn, who dies the following year.	Marvell: *The Character of Holland*; *The Bermudas*. Taylor: *Eniautos* (sermons for the Christian year). Walton: *The Compleat Angler*.
1654	Embarks on a tour of England with his wife, taking in Salisbury, York and Cambridge. While in Oxford, Evelyn meets the scientist Sir John Wilkins and the architect Christopher Wren. He remains on friendly terms with the latter throughout his life.	Marvell: *The First Anniversary of the Government under His Highness the Lord Protector*. Orrery: *Parthenissa* (to 1665). Flecknoe's *Ariadne*, probably the first English opera. Playford: *A Breif Introduction to the Skill of Musick*. At Oxford, Bible translated into Irish, Welsh, Turkish and Malay (to 1658).
1655	Birth of a third son, also named John – Evelyn's only son to survive to adulthood. The Anglican divine Jeremy Taylor becomes Evelyn's 'ghostly father'.	Hobbes: *De Corpore*. Fuller: *Church History*. Dugdale: *Montasticon Anglicanum* (to 1673). Thomas Stanley: *A History of Philosophy* (to 1662). Taylor: *The Golden Grove* (a manual of daily prayers). Mme de Sévigné begins to write her *Letters*.
1656	Evelyn publishes a verse translation of Lucretius's *De Rerum Natura*, showing the relationship between Lucretius's views and the the findings of modern science. Meets leading scientist Robert Boyle, forming another lifelong friendship.	Harrington: *The Commonwealth of Oceana* (opposing Hobbes's *Leviathan*). Tradescant: *Museum Tradescantianum*. Cowley: *Poems*. D'Avenant: *The Siege of Rhodes* (opera). Pascal: *Les Provinciales* (to 1657).

Naval victories against Dutch. The Rump forcibly dissolved by Cromwell. Republicans such as Vane and Haslerig thus removed from positions of influence. The 'Barebones' Parliament consists of 140 members chosen from lists provided by separatist Puritan congregations. Its programme of radical reforms proves controversial and Cromwell allows it to surrender its power back to him. In December he becomes Protector under Lambert's 'Instrument of Government'. Cromwell is obliged to fall back on support from the Army, now purged of radicals.
Cromwell's first Parliament (to 1655). Staunch republicans criticize his ambitions. Disaffection of Quakers – who never forgive Cromwell for not abolishing tithes – and other radical sects. New Parliament is more Presbyterian and intolerant in religious matters; Triers and Ejectors instituted to review ecclesiastical appointments and restrict uncontrolled preaching. Expedition of Penn and Venables to Hispaniola (part of Cromwell's grand 'Western Design' to secure settlements in West Indies). Brazil revolts against Dutch. End of Frondes in France: Mazarin's authority confirmed.

Cromwell, living in Whitehall, assumes many of the external trappings of royalty. Country divided into districts, each policed by a major-general (to 1657). Secretary Thurloe given complete control of all printed material. Jews (expelled by Edward I) are encouraged to return to England. Jamaica seized. Trade boom. John Wallis's *Arithmetica Infinitorum* contains the germs of differential calculus. Poussin: 'Et in Arcadia Ego'; Rembrandt: 'Woman Bathing'.

Alliance of England and France against Spain; Spain blockaded throughout winter. Cromwell's foreign policy based on considerations of trade. Second Protectorate Parliament summoned. Bernini completes piazza of St Peter's, Rome. Huygens invents pendulum clock. Boyle and Hooke conduct experiments on air pump and combustion at Oxford. Velasquez: 'Las Meninas'.

DATE	AUTHOR'S LIFE	LITERARY CONTEXT
1657	Birth of a fourth son, George Evelyn, who dies in 1658.	Richard Baxter: *Call to the Unconverted.* Henry King: *Poems.*
1658	Evelyn is devastated by the death of his five-year-old son, Richard. Translates *The Golden Book of St John Chrysostom, Concerning the Education of Children.* Also publishes *The French Gardiner.*	Marvell: *A Poem upon the Death of His Late Highness the Lord Protector.* Dryden: *Heroique Stanzas* (on the death of Cromwell). D'Avenant: *The Cruelty of the Spaniards in Peru* (opera). Browne: *Hydriotaphia* (or *Urn Burial*); *The Garden of Cyrus.* Edward Phillips: *The New World of English Words* (Evelyn was a contributor to later editions.) Hobbes: *De Homine.*
1659	Publishes *A Character of England*, a satirical piece. Finishes the synopsis of *Elysium Britannicum*, an encyclopedic work on horticulture which occupies him occasionally for the rest of his life. Circulates a pamphlet, 'An Apology for the Royal Party' (November).	Harrington: *The Art of Law-giving; Aphorisms Political.* Sprat: *The Plague of Athens.* Stillingfleet: *Irenicum* (suggested a compromise with the Presbyterians). Shirley: *The Contention of Ajax and Ulysses.* Molière: *Les précieuses ridicules.* Boileau: *Satire I.*
1660	Evelyn vainly attempts to persuade a former schoolfellow, Colonel Herbert Morley, Lieutenant of the Tower of London, to forestall General Monck by declaring for the king (Jan). Following the Restoration, he is presented to Charles II (4 June) and attends the court frequently thereafter. Attached to Charles II as a man, he becomes over the years increasingly disapproving of his morals and his policies. Evelyn is one of the founder members of what was to become in 1662 the Royal Society, formed for 'the promoting of experimental	Pepys begins his *Diary* (to 1669). Milton: *The Readie and Easie Way to Establish a Free Commonwealth* and *Brief Notes Upon a Late Sermon* for which he is arrested and imprisoned. Bunyan arrested for preaching without a licence and spends next 12 years in Bedford gaol. Dryden: *Astraea Redux.* Cowley: *Ode, upon the Blessed Restoration.* Taylor: *Ductor Dubitantium* ('a general instrument of moral theology'); *The Worthy Communicant.*

HISTORICAL EVENTS

Cromwell rejects offer of crown, but accepts the Humble Petition and Advice which enhances his power. Invested as Lord Protector. Blake destroys Spanish treasure fleet at Santa Cruz. England becoming confirmed as a maritime power and gaining increasing prestige in Europe where Cromwell has a network of ambassadors in place.
Battle of the Dunes results in the acquisition of Dunkirk (sold to Louis XIV after the Restoration). Death of Cromwell (3 Sept). Protectorate passes to his son, Richard. Tea is introduced to England, from China via Holland.
Velasquez: 'The Rokeby Venus'; Rembrandt: 'Self-Portrait with a Stick'.

Richard Cromwell summons Third Protectorate Parliament but Army grandees force its dissolution (April). Old Rump of 1653 recalled (May); Richard made to resign. Lambert puts down Royalist rising (Aug). Republicans in Parliament suspicious of Lambert's intentions: Lambert forcibly dissolves Parliament (Sept), ruling through a Committee of Safety. General Monck, commanding the army of occupation in Scotland, declares in support of Parliament and Lambert marches north against him (Nov), reaching Newcastle; Monck plays for time, as Lambert's troops are fast deserting. John Rushworth's first great collection of state papers (for years 1618–29). Treaty of the Pyrenees between France and Spain.
Monck's army marches south (Jan), Lambert's army offering no opposition, and reaches London 3 February. Monck's declared aim is to establish a free and full Parliament; members of the Long Parliament expelled by Pride are allowed to return and Parliament votes for its own dissolution. Charles II issues Declaration of Breda (4 April), promising amnesty, liberty of conscience, settlement of land claims and army back-pay. The Convention Parliament, including a restored House of Lords, meets (25 April). On Monck's recommendation, it votes for Restoration. Charles returns from exile in Europe, reaching London 29 May. Act of Indemnity and Oblivion grants free pardon to all except those who participated in the trial and execution of Charles I. Of the 59 regicides, ten are executed (three more in 1662); others flee or are imprisoned. Edward Hyde (made Earl of Clarendon 1661) appointed Lord Chancellor. Secret marriage of James, Duke of York, to Clarendon's daughter, Anne Hyde. Marriage of Louis XIV and Maria Teresa of Spain. Death of Mary Stuart, Princess of Orange. Founding of The Royal Society (charter granted 1662) for 'the Improving of Natural Knowledge'. Founders and early members include Boyle, Hooke, Petty, Ray, Wilkins and Wren. Literary members besides Evelyn include Ashmole, Aubrey, Cowley, Dryden and Waller. Theatres re-open.

JOHN EVELYN

DATE	AUTHOR'S LIFE	LITERARY CONTEXT
1660 *cont.*	philosophy'. He remains actively involved with the Society for many years, frequently serving on its council. Compiles the first part of his *Kalendarium* (diary to 1645).	Falkland: *Discourses of Infallibility* and *A Reply*.
1661	Writes *A Panegyric to Charles the Second* for the king's coronation. Publishes *Fumifugium*, a short book proposing ways of ridding London of air pollution, *Tyrannus Or the Mode: in a Discourse of Sumptuary Lawes* and *Instructions Concerning Erecting of a Library* (translated from the French of Gabriel Naudé).	Robert Boyle: *The Sceptical Chymist*. Digby: *Discourse concerning the Vegetation of Plants*. Glanvill: *The Vanity of Dogmatizing*. Dryden: *To His Sacred Majesty*. Molière: *L'Ecole des maris*. La Calprenède: *Pharamond*. Scarron: *Nouvelles tragicomiques*.
1662	Appointed to a commission for the improvement of London streets. Publishes *Sculptura: or the History, and Art of Chalcography and Engraving in Copper*.	Fuller: *The History of the Worthies of England*. Stillingfleet: *Origines Sacrae*. Butler: *Hudibras* (part 1). Dryden: *To My Lord Chancellor*. Molière: *Ecole des femmes*. Mme de La Fayette: *La Princesse de Montpensier*. La Rochefoucauld: *Mémoires*. Bossuet: *Sermons*.
1663	Appointed to a commission for examining the work of the Royal Mint. Engages Edward Phillips, Milton's nephew, as a tutor for his son John (to 1665).	Shakespeare Third Folio. Robert Howard: *The Committee*. John Wilson: *The Cheats*. Cowley: *Verses on Several Occasions*. Herbert of Cherbury: *De religione Gentilium*. Thomas Stanley's edition of Aeschylus.
1664	Birth and death in infancy of a fifth son, another Richard. Publication of *Sylva, or a Discourse of Forest-Trees*, together with *Pomona* (a treatise on fruit-growing for cider) and *Kalendarium Hortense*, a garden almanack. Also publishes *A Parallel of the Ancient Architecture with the Modern*, a translation of Roland Fréart de Chambray,	Cotton: *Scarronides, or Virgile Travestie*. Killigrew's collected plays published. Etherege: *The Comical Revenge, or Love in a Tub*. Howard: *The Indian Queen*. Flecknoe: *Love's Kingdom*. Lucy Hutchinson begins her Memoirs of the life of Colonel Hutchinson.

HISTORICAL EVENTS

Execution of Earl of Argyll. On anniversary of Charles I's execution, bodies
of Cromwell, Ireton and Bradshaw are exhumed from Westminster Abbey
and reburied at Tyburn. Convention Parliament fails to secure
accommodation for its predominantly Presbyterian views. Fifth Monarchist
revolt. New 'Cavalier' Parliament with militant Anglican majority orders
burning of the Solemn League and Covenant and repeals 1642 statute
excluding bishops from the House of Lords. Militia Act places armed forces
under command of king. Corporation Act: local government officers to take
an oath of non-resistance, abjure the Covenant and take Anglican
communion. Death of Mazarin. Louis XIV assumes full powers in France;
Colbert put in control of finance and ecomomy.

Charles II marries the Portuguese Catholic princess, Catherine of Braganza.
In defiance of the king's promise of religious toleration, Parliament passes
Act of Uniformity: clergy are obliged to accept Book of Common Prayer
and 39 Articles in their entirety. Nearly 2000 Presbyterians give up their
livings. Licensing Act drastically reduces number of printing presses. Boyle's
Law. *Observations upon the Bills of Mortality* (Graunt/Petty) spreads interest in
scientific attempts to estimate the size of the population from the number of
registered deaths.

Attempt to impeach Clarendon. Staple Act confirms 1651 Navigation Acts,
closing off colonial trade to foreign shipping. Charles II encourages
colonialism by charters to Royal Africa Company, Carolina and Rhode
Island. Drury Lane Theatre opens. First Turnpike Act. Palladio's *First Book
of Architecture*.

English capture New Amsterdam from Dutch and rename it New York after
James, Duke of York. Triennial Act made compulsory. Conventicle Act to
suppress Dissenting congregations; sporadically enforced but religious
nonconformity too widespread to be stamped out. Wren builds the
Sheldonian Theatre at Oxford (to 1669). In France work starts on Versailles
under Le Vaux and Le Nôtre. Hals: 'Men ... and Women Governors of the
Haarlem Almshouse'.

DATE	AUTHOR'S LIFE	LITERARY CONTEXT
1664 *cont.*	the first of two translations from the French of anti-Jesuitical works. In anticipation of war with Holland, Evelyn is appointed one of four commissioners for sick and wounded seamen. He is given charge of Kent and Sussex.	Stillingfleet: *A Rational Account of the Grounds of the Protestant Religion.* Molière: *Tartuffe.*
1665	Sends his family to Wotton during the plague. Birth of a daughter, Mary. Evelyn remains at Deptford, but is often obliged to go through London. His work with the sick and wounded brings him in contact with Samuel Pepys, a government clerk in the naval service. This is the beginning of a lifelong friendship. Like his father before him, and not for the first time, Evelyn refuses the honour of a knighthood for his services.	Marvell: *The Character of Holland.* Bunyan: *The Holy City, or the New Jerusalem.* Dryden: *The Indian Emperor* (stars Nell Gwyn). Orrery: *Mustapha.* Boyle: *Occasional Reflections.* La Rochefoucauld: *Maximes.* La Fontaine: *Contes et nouvelles en vers.*
1666	Appointed to a commission for regulating the production of saltpetre (there had been a shortage of gunpowder). Asked to report on proposals for the repair of St Paul's cathedral: Evelyn urges the further consideration of Wren's plans. A week later, during the Great Fire, Evelyn is at first a spectator but becomes actively involved in checking the spread of the flames. Draws up project (as does Wren) for the rebuilding of the destroyed area, but general replanning of this kind proves impossible to implement. *The English Vineyard Vindicated.*	Marvell: *The Second* and *Third Advice to a Painter.* Waller: *Instructions to a Painter.* Bunyan: *Grace Abounding to the Chief of Sinners.* Tillotson: *The Rule of Faith.* A. Brome, *et al*, trans., *The Poems of Horace.* Boyle: *The Origin of Forms and Qualities.* Parliament censures the work of Hobbes. Molière: *Le Misanthrope*; *Le Médicin malgré lui.* Leibniz: *De Arte Combinatoria.*
1667	Persuades his friend Henry Howard, grandson of the Earl of Arundel, to present his late grandfather's library to the Royal Society, and the Arundel Marbles to the University of Oxford. Designs Howard's garden at Albury. Continues to visit his friend Edward Hyde,	Milton: *Paradise Lost.* Dryden: *Annus mirabilis*; *The State of Innocence and the Fall of Man.* Marvell: *The Last Instructions to a Painter.* Dryden/D'Avenant: *The Tempest.* Dryden/Newcastle: *Sir Martin Mar-all.*

HISTORICAL EVENTS

Outbreak of bubonic plague kills 70,000 Londoners and paralyses port for three months. Five Mile Act further restricts activities of Dissenting ministers. Second Dutch War (to 1667). English victory at Lowestoft and defeat at Bergen. Death of Philip IV of Spain. The Royal Society's *Philosophical Transactions* becomes the first scientific journal. Newton's theory of fluxions. Robert Hooke: *Micrographia*. Hooke's studies of microscopic fossils lead him to become one of the first proponents of a theory of evolution.

French join Dutch in war against England. Inconclusive Four Days' Battle at sea (1–4 June). Albemarle (fomerly G. Monck) victorious off Orfordness (25 July). Great Fire of London (2–6 Sept). *London Gazette* founded as organ of Government. Scottish Covenanters defeated at battle of Pentland Hills. Wenceslaus Hollar, draughtsman to the king since 1660, makes the last of his famous engravings of London pre-fire. Newton invents differential calculus. Spirit level invented. Vermeer: 'Allegory on the Art of Painting'.

Dutch raiding force sails up the Medway, sinks three ships and tows away the English flagship, the *Royal Charles*. Treaty of Breda ends war. Unpopularity of Court party leads king to dismiss Clarendon (Aug). Threatened with impeachment by the Commons, he flees to France (Nov). He is replaced by the no less unpopular 'Cabal' (formed from the initials of their names: Clifford, Arlington, Buckingham, Ashley Cooper and Lauderdale). Reform of Treasury; Exchequer certificates circulate as embryonic paper currency. Lauderdale begins to impose autocratic rule on Scotland. Newton's optical discoveries begin.

DATE	AUTHOR'S LIFE	LITERARY CONTEXT
1667 *cont.*	Earl of Clarendon after his fall from power. Birth of daughter, Elizabeth. *Public Employment and an Active Life Prefer'd to Solitude.* Alarmed by the Dutch fleet reaching Chatham, sends all his valuables away from Sayes Court.	Duchess of Newcastle: *Life* of her husband. Orrery: *The Black Prince.* More: *Enchiridion Ethicum.* Flecknoe: *Les Damoiselles a La Mode.* Birth of Swift. Death of Cowley, whose *Works* are published the following year, prefaced with a *Life* by Thomas Sprat. Sprat's *History of the Royal Society.* Racine: *Andromaque.*
1668	*An Idea of the Perfection of Painting* (translated from R. Fréart de Chambray).	Dryden: *Of Dramatick Poesy.* Traherne: *Centuries of Meditations.* Denham: *Poems and Translations.* Etherege: *She Would if She Could.* Shadwell: *The Sullen Lovers.* Glanvill: *Plus Ultra* (mentions Evelyn). Wilkins: *Essay Towards a Real Character, and a Philosophical Language.* Boileau: *Satires VIII–IX.*
1669	Birth of last child, Susanna. Evelyn cultivating Clarendon's successors and opponents, Sir Thomas Clifford and Lord Arlington, both of whom become personal friends. Hopes to use his political contacts to secure permanent ownership of Sayes Court (the lease of which had reverted to the king in 1660) and obtain reimbursement for his father-in-law for expenses incurred as ambassador in Paris during the exile. Evelyn created a doctor of civil law at Oxford. First meeting with Margaret Blagge (b. 1652), at that time maid of honour to the Duchess of York. Publishes *The History of the Three Late Famous Impostors.*	Dryden: *Tyrannic Love.* William Penn: *No Cross, No Crown.* Burnet: *Modest and Free Conference between a Conformist and a Nonconformist.* Molière: *L'Avare.* Racine: *Britannicus.*

CHRONOLOGY

Triple Alliance of England, Holland and Sweden to protect the Netherlands against France organized by Temple and Arlington. Louis XIV accepts a general peace: Treaty of Aix-la-Chapelle (May). Claude Lorraine: 'Landscape with the Angel Appearing to Hagar'. Dryden becomes Poet Laureate.

The Duke of York acknowledges his conversion to Roman Catholicism; Charles insists his two daughters are brought up as Anglicans. Sir William Coventry dismissed from Government and becomes focus of the first regular Opposition or 'Country' Party – convinced of corruption in high places, suspicious of Charles's foreign policy and beginning to suspect his loyalty to Protestantism. Death of Henrietta Maria. Christopher Wren becomes Surveyor-General of the King's Works. Newton made professor of mathematics at Cambridge.

DATE	AUTHOR'S LIFE	LITERARY CONTEXT
1670	In the third edition of *Sylva*, Evelyn is able to claim in his dedication to the king that it had been 'the *sole* Occasion of furnishing your almost exhausted *Dominions*, with more (I dare say) than *two Millions of Timber-Trees* ...' Evelyn had proposed in 1669 that an account of the Dutch war, refuting Dutch claims, should be published; the king now asks him to be the author. Death of Evelyn's younger brother Richard.	Dryden: *The Conquest of Granada.* Aphra Behn: *The Forced Marriage.* Birth of Congreve. Walton: *Life of George Herbert.* John Ray: *A Collection of English Proverbs.* Pascal: *Pensées.* Racine: *Bérénice.* Molière: *Le Bourgeois gentilhomme.* Spinoza: *Tractatus Theologico-politicus.*
1671	Through Clifford's and Arlington's influence Evelyn appointed to the Council for Foreign Plantations, an advisory body for the supervision of English colonies, with a salary of £500 a year. Discovers the young wood-carver Grinling Gibbons in Deptford and introduces him to Christopher Wren and Charles II who afterwards employ him. Visits Arlington at Euston Hall in Suffolk; accompanies Henry Howard to his palace at Norwich, also taking the opportunity to call on Sir Thomas Browne, with whom he had long corresponded.	Milton: *Paradise Regained*; *Samson Agonistes.* Traherne: *Thanksgivings.* Buckingham: *The Rehearsal.* Tillotson: *Sermons* (first of 14 volumes). Bossuet: *Exposition de la doctrine de l'Eglise catholique.*
1672	Evelyn's history of the Dutch war is still unfinished on the outbreak of the Third Dutch War, when his duties as a commissioner for the sick and wounded take over. Disapproves of Charles's Declaration of Indulgence but is not against some level of toleration: 'I think, there might be some relaxations without the least prejudice to the present Establishment, discreetely limited.' Attracted by her beauty, wit and piety,	Marvell: *The Rehearsal Transposed.* Dryden: *Marriage a-la-Mode*; *The Assignation*; *Of Heroik Plays.* Wycherley: *Love in a Wood.* Bunyan: *A Confession of my Faith and a Reason of my Practice.* Temple: *Observations upon the ... Netherlands.* Nehemiah Grew: *An Idea of a Philosophical History of Plants.* Birth of Addison and Steele. Molière: *Les Femmes savantes.* Racine: *Bajazet.*

HISTORICAL EVENTS

Rumours that the king is considering divorce, his wife having failed to produce an heir. Treaty of Dover: Charles to receive subsidies from Louis XIV; England and France to collaborate on a war against Holland. By a secret clause Charles undertakes to declare his Catholicism at a suitable moment, at which further financial and military help to be made available. Second Conventicle Act renews persecution of Protestant Dissenters. Death of Charles's favourite sister, Henriette, Duchess of Orléans. Wren rebuilding 52 London churches destroyed in the Great Fire, a project that occupies him for the rest of his life. Work on St Paul's begins in 1675 and is completed in 1710. Hudson's Bay Trading Company established. Vermeer: 'The Love Letter'. Murillo: 'Beggar Boys Throwing Dice'.

Colonel Blood attempts to steal the Crown Jewels and is pardoned. Grinling Gibbons, sculptor in wood, is launched in his career, working over the years in St Paul's Cathedral and other Wren churches, and in a number of royal palaces and aristocratic mansions.

Charles II's Declaration of Indulgence suspends penal laws against Protestant Nonconformists and Catholics alike. Viewed by many as part of a pro-French, Roman Catholic conspiracy. Third Dutch War. Louis invades Holland (June); halted by William of Orange who is elected Stadtholder after popular uprising overthrows republic and De Witt is murdered. Indecisive battle of Southwold Bay; Earl of Sandwich killed in action. Ashley Cooper made Earl of Shaftesbury and Lord Chancellor. The Stop of the Exchequer: repayment of Government debts suspended with the promise of an extra 6% interest to creditors as compensation – a radical step to finance the war. Pepys appointed Secretary to the Admiralty. The two Willem van de Velde, maritime painters, enter royal service.

DATE	AUTHOR'S LIFE	LITERARY CONTEXT
1672 *cont.*	Evelyn forms compact of friendship with Margaret Blagge (16 Oct), taking charge of her affairs and meeting weekly for prayer and discussion. Evelyn appointed Secretary of the Royal Society (to 1673).	
1673	Evelyn saddened by the resignation of Clifford – who felt unable on religious grounds to take the new Test – his conversion to Catholicism and subsequent death. Although acquainted with Danby from their days of exile in Paris, Evelyn has little hope of political favour: 'a man of excellent natural parts, but nothing generous or gratefull'.	Wycherley: *The Gentleman Dancing-Master*. Shadwell: *Epsom Wells*. Behn: *The Dutch Lover*. Ravenscroft: *The Careless Lovers*. Settle: *The Empress of Morocco*. D'Avenant: *Works*. Temple: *Essay on the Origin and Nature of Government*. Racine: *Mithradate*. Molière: *Le Malade imaginaire*.
1674	On Charles's request for an attack on the Dutch Evelyn supplies him with the Preface to his uncompleted history: it is published as *Navigation and Commerce*, but not until peace has been made and copies have to be withdrawn. Council of Trade and Foreign Plantations (as it had become) dissolved by Danby as too expensive.	Death of Milton, Herrick and Traherne. Shadwell: *The Enchanted Island* (opera). Rochester banished from court for his *Satyr on Charles II*. Hobbes' translation of Homer's *Odyssey*. Nathaniel Lee: *Nero*. Anthony à Wood: *Historia et Antiquitates Universitatis Oxoniensis*. Racine: *Iphigénie*. Boileau: *L'Art poétique*.
1675	Visits Oxford and Northampton. Secret marriage of Margaret Blagge and Sidney Godolphin.	Dryden: *Aureng-Zebe*. Wycherley: *The Country Wife*. Shadwell: *Psyche* (opera). Otway: *Alcibiades*. Lee: *Sophonisba, or Hannibal's Overthrow*. Rochester: *A Satyr Against Mankind*. Crowne: *Calisto* (a masque). Phillips: *Theatrum Poetarum*. Shaftesbury: *A Letter from a Person of Quality to his Friend in the Country*. Traherne: *Christian Ethics*.

Parliament makes supply dependent upon withdrawal of Declaration of Indulgence; Charles is obliged to concede. Parliamentary opinion, encouraged by Dutch propaganda and bribery, swinging towards William of Orange. Test Act: office holders must deny transubstantiation and prove they have recently taken Anglican communion. Clifford and the Duke of York resign, confirming the public's worst fears. Death of Clifford. Sir Thomas Osborne appointed Lord High Treasurer. Outrage at James's impending marriage to the Catholic Mary of Modena; Shaftesbury dismissed for his opposition. Chelsea Physic Garden founded by Society of Apothecaries. First public concerts held in London. Lully's *Tragédies-lyriques*. Huygens' *Horlogium Oscillatorum* contains earliest attempt to apply dynamics to bodies of finite size.

Parliament puts pressure on the king to end war with Dutch (Treaty of Westminster). Fall of Buckingham and Arlington. Osborne, created Earl of Danby, emerging as new chief minister. Anti-French and a strong supporter of the Anglican establishment, he is well placed to form a reliable majority for the Court party. Liberal bribery ensures Parliament's amenability to any requests for supply. However, not wishing to be too reliant on Parliament, Charles continues to apply to Louis for subsidies. The two branches of his policy are incompatible. Danby introduces good financial management. Shaftesbury, espousing cause of popular Protestantism, leads Opposition party in the Lords, supported by Buckingham and Halifax. Death of Clarendon. Organist and composer John Blow becomes Master of the the Children of the Chapel Royal. Leibniz designs a machine for multiplying and dividing.

A great deal of money changing hands in the 13th session of the Cavalier Parliament: Danby bribing MPs to support the Court (and offering them a Royal Proclamation for enforcing laws against Nonconformists to soften them up); the Dutch and Spanish bribing them to press for war with France; the French bribing them *not* to enter such a war. Supply granted for naval expenses only. For the first time Charles is solvent. A dispute between the two Houses over jurisdiction provokes a long prorogation. Royal Greenwich Observatory founded by Charles II in building designed by Christopher Wren. John Flamsteed appointed first Astronomer Royal.

DATE	AUTHOR'S LIFE	LITERARY CONTEXT
1676	Margaret and Godolphin announce their marriage and set up house. Evelyn publishes *A Philosophical Discourse of Earth*, a paper he had read at the Royal Society (better know by its later title of *Terra*).	Etherege: *The Man of Mode*. Wycherley: *The Plain-Dealer*. Otway: *Don Carlos*. Behn: *The Town-Fop*. Thomas Sydenham: *Observationes Medicae* (becomes a standard medical textbook for two centuries).
1677	Stays three weeks with Arlington at Euston (September).	Crowne: *The Destruction of Jerusalem*. Lee: *The Rival Queens*. Sedley: *Antony and Cleopatra*. Behn: *The Rover*. Durfey: *A Fond Husband*. Tate: *Poems*. Marvell: *An Account of the Growth of Popery and Arbitrary Government*. Robert Plot: *The Natural History of Oxford-shire*. Spinoza: *Ethics*. Racine: *Phèdre*.
1678	Death of Margaret Godolphin after the birth of her first child, Francis. Deeply affected himself, Evelyn is called upon to make the funeral arrangements by her grief-stricken husband. He continues his friendship with Sidney Godolphin, who entrusts Evelyn with his son's financial affairs and education. Evelyn, like most of his contemporaries, at first believes in the Popish Plot.	Bunyan: *The Pilgrim's Progress*. Cudworth: *The True Intellectual System of the Universe*. Dryden: *All For Love*. Henry and Thomas Vaughan: *Thalia Rediviva*. L'Estrange's popular digest of Seneca's *Morals*. Rymer: *The Tragedies of the Last Age Considered*. Mme de La Fayette: *La Princesse de Cleves*.
1679		Burnet: *The History of the Reformation* (part 1). Cowley: *The Civil War* (book 1). Hobbes: *Behemoth*.

CHRONOLOGY

The king makes another secret treaty with Louis XIV and becomes his pensioner. This enables him to rule without Parliament, which suits Louis as Parliament is generally inclined to press for war against him. Shaftesbury's Green Ribbon Club active during prorogation. Bacon's rebellion in Virginia. Artist Godfrey Kneller arrives in England and attaches himself to the court. Presence of microbes first detected by Van Leeuwenhoek (Holland).

Negotiations begin between French and Dutch. Louis continues to pay Charles to remain neutral. Danby recommends Parliament be summoned as he feels he will be able to obtain supply; Louis bribes the Opposition to oppose Danby's anti-French policies, ensuring a stalemate. Both Shaftesbury and Buckingham in receipt of such bribes – Louis in return promising not to interfere with their liberties or their religion. Buckingham, Shaftesbury, Salisbury and Wharton committed to Tower for refusing to admit the legality of Parliament's meeting after a 15-month prorogation. Supply voted for ships. Danby's Act for securing the Protestant Religion fails to pass. Louis scores more military successes against the Dutch. Commons renew their request that England support the Dutch against France. In atmosphere of increasing suspicion of Roman Catholic conspiracy, Sacheverell demands that the king make public his alliances. Amidst rowdy scenes, Parliament is adjourned. Anglo-Dutch treaty (Dec) appears to detach England from France. Marriage of Mary, daughter of the Duke of York, and William III, Prince of Orange, her cousin: a triumph for Danby in his efforts to forge a Protestant foreign policy.

Following the Dutch treaty, the Commons, after some prevarication, vote Charles supply (Feb), but he continues to follow his double foreign policy and signs another secret treaty with Louis XIV (May). France and Holland make peace at Nijmegen (July). The army Charles had raised is no longer needed and conjecture as to the use to which it might be put proves explosive. Titus Oates and Israel Tonge first give evidence on oath to Sir Edmund Berry Godfrey (18 Sept) of a Popish plot. Mysterious death of Sir Edmund (Oct). Five Roman Catholic lords sent to the Tower. Execution of Edward Coleman, the Duke of York's secretary. Discovery of incriminating letter from Danby to Montagu (English ambassador in France), endorsed by Charles and referring to French subsidies. Commons become convinced that the Court had been intriguing with the French to introduce Catholicism and arbitrary government. Move to impeach Danby: Lords refuse to commit him, and to prevent an interminable duel between the two houses, the king prorogues Parliament (Dec).

Cavalier Parliament finally dissolved (Jan). Ensuing general election the first to be fought on party lines: the Tories (opposed to excluding the Catholic Duke of York from the succession) being defeated by the Whigs, led by Shaftesbury, who support Exclusion. Parliament refuses to accept validity of Charles's pardon; Danby is committed to the Tower, where he remains for five years. First Exclusion Bill passed in the Commons. Charles II

DATE	AUTHOR'S LIFE	LITERARY CONTEXT
1679 *cont.*		
1680	Evelyn visits Cassiobury in Hertfordshire, the seat of the Earl of Essex. Marriage of John Evelyn, Jun. to Martha Spencer, daughter and co-heir of a London merchant. Compiles second part of the *Kalendarium* (1649–84). Attends trial of Lord Stafford for involvement in the Popish Plot, during which 'from this moment forward I had quite lost my opinion of Mr. Oates'.	Filmer's *Patriarcha, or the Natural Power of Kings* (written 1638 in defence of Divine Right). Temple: *Miscellanies* (also 1692 and 1701). 1680s: Bishop Burnet begins his memoirs, published in 1724 and 1734 as *The History of My Own Time*. Death of Rochester.
1681		Crowne: *Thyestes*. Dryden: *The Spanish Fryar; Absalom and Achitopel; His Majesty's Declaration Defended*. Ravenscroft: *The London Cuckolds*. Shadwell: *The Lancashire Witches*. Oldham: *Satyrs upon the Jesuits*. Henry Nevill: *Plato Redivivus*.
1682	Declines presidency of the Royal Society (and again in 1690 and 1693). Birth of first surviving grandson, John (Jack). Evelyn's *Life of Mrs Godolphin* probably composed between 1682 and 1684.	Dryden: *Religio Laici*. Otway: *Venice Preserved*. Nehemiah Grew: *The Anatomy of Plants*. William Petty: *Quantulumcumque, or a Tract concerning Money*. Death of Sir Thomas Browne.

prorogues, then dissolves Parliament. Habeas Corpus Amendment Act
upholds rights of political prisoners. Further executions in connection with
the Popish Plot. In October, another general election returns a Parliament
in favour of Exclusion, prorogued before it meets. Frenzy of pope-burnings,
riots, pamphleteering, informing, forging and denouncing during the recess
(to Oct 1680), in London and elsewhere. Charles creates a new ministry of
courtiers, known as The Chits: Sunderland, Secretary of State, and two
young Commissioners of the Treasury – Sidney Godolphin and Laurence
Hyde. Murder of Archbishop Sharp in Scotland by supporters of the
Covenant. Covenanter rising put down by the Duke of Monmouth.
Court forms an alliance with Spain (June), to give Charles's foreign policy
an anti-French complexion. New House of Commons passes second
Exclusion Bill (Nov), rejected by the Lords after Halifax and Shaftesbury
argue the issue for seven hours. Impeachment of Stafford, one of the five
Roman Catholic lords imprisoned in the Tower, resulting in his execution.
House of Lords considers placing limitations on a future Catholic king as a
compromise to Exclusion. Duke of Monmouth working hard to build up
popular support for his claim (he is the illegitimate son of Charles II): in the
meantime many leading public figures also in consultation with another
possible claimant, William of Orange (nephew to the king and the Duke of
York, and married to the latter's eldest daughter).

The Commons refuse to grant further supply until the Exclusion Bill passes
(Jan). The king prorogues, then dissolves Parliament. Louis secretly renews
subsidy to Charles II (March), both to maintain English neutrality and still
more to ensure a Catholic succession. New Parliament meets in Oxford
(March) in which Whigs fail to regain their majority. Prospect of civil war
causes the Opposition to draw back. Choice to be made between a regency
(which Charles claims to support) and Exclusion. Charles vehemently rejects
a proposal by Shaftesbury that the Duke of Monmouth should be named his
successor. Third Exclusion Bill read: Charles now in a position to dissolve
Parliament indefinitely, which he duly does. Wars of the Reunions: Louis
annexes Strasburg and invades Luxemburg. William of Orange seeks
English support against Louis. Charles's 'neutrality' now subjected to
constant strain. Louis raises siege of Luxemburg when Charles threatens to
recall Parliament. King riding on a tide of popularity as the Popish Plot
burns itself out: panders to this support by enforcing laws against Dissenters.
Moves against the Whigs. Shaftesbury imprisoned in the Tower for high
treason (released on bail 1682).
King revolutionizes structure of local government in order to assure himself
of loyal (Tory) justices, mayors, sheriffs, etc. Cities prevailed upon to
surrender their charters. Press brought under Court control. Charles II
founds the Royal Hospital, Chelsea, for old soldiers; Wren's new building is
finished in 1694. Elias Ashmole presents his collection of curiosities,
bequeathed to him by Tradescant, to Oxford University, thus founding the
Ashmolean Museum.

DATE	AUTHOR'S LIFE	LITERARY CONTEXT
1683	Growing friendship with Thomas Tenison, one of the most prominent Latitudinarians. Death of Sir Richard Browne. Blaming Shaftesbury for the Rye House Plot, Evelyn deplores the treatment of 'these unhappy lords', Essex (a friend) and Russell. Increasing disappointment in Charles II: regretting his subservience to Louis XIV and disapproving of his policy towards the City of London (Sir Robert Clayton, the Lord Mayor, is another friend).	Tenison: *A Discourse Concerning a Guide in Matters of Faith.* Oldham: *Poems and Translations.* Thomas Sydenham's treatise on gout, considered his masterpiece. Digby: *Chymical Secrets, and Rare Experiments in Physick and Philosophy.*
1684	Begins to update his *Kalendarium* on a regular basis until the end of his life.	Boyle: *Memoirs for the Natural History of Humane Blood.*
1685	A tragic year for Evelyn and his wife. Their daughter Mary – Evelyn's favourite – dies in March, aged 19. Her younger sister Elizabeth elopes in July; a month later, she too dies. Death of Charles II (Feb). Death of Arlington (July). Both died as Catholics and Evelyn is particularly grieved to learn from Pepys of Charles's deathbed conversion. A firm supporter of legitimacy and the monarchical principle, he disapproves of the Monmouth Rebellion and remains loyal to James II in spite of his Catholicism, even going so far as to request his brother George not to stand for Surrey against the Court candidate in the election. During the absence of the second Earl of Clarendon in Ireland, Evelyn acts as one of three Commissioners of the Privy Seal.	Crowne: *Sir Courtly Nice.* Dryden: *Threnodia Augustalis* (on the death of Charles II). Stillingfleet: *Origines Britannicae.*

CHRONOLOGY

Death of Shaftesbury (Jan). Supposed Rye House ('Protestant') plot to murder the king and the Duke of York is made the occasion to exact revenge on distinguished Whig leaders who were almost certainly innocent. Essex commits suicide in the Tower, Russell and Sidney are executed after trials which convict on the most dubious evidence. London forced to surrender its charter; under new constitution, all posts become subject to royal approval. Princess Anne, second daughter of the Duke of York, marries the Protestant Prince George of Denmark. War breaks out between Louis and the Spanish Netherlands. Habsburg–Ottoman War (to 1699). Turkish army reaches the gates of Vienna before it is repulsed. Newton demonstrates his theory of gravitation at meetings of the Royal Society (to 1684).

'Great Frost'. Frost Fair held on frozen Thames throughout January. Charles now in a strong enough position to secure the release from the Tower of Danby and of the three surviving Catholic lords. Persecution of Nonconformists intensifies: 1300 Quakers known to have been imprisoned during the winter of 1683–4. In England local government still able to gain some protection for the subject, but no such protection exists in Scotland, where military law is imposed (Dec). No longer worried about Charles's recalling Parliament, Louis seizes Luxemburg and imposes on the Spanish a 20-year 'truce' (Truce of Ratisbon). Hooke invents optical telegraph.

Death of Charles II (6 Feb). Coronation of James II and Mary of Modena with Anglican rites in Westminster Abbey (April). Titus Oates whipped through the streets of London (May). He is imprisoned for life for perjury (but freed after the 1688 Revolution). Monmouth lands at Lyme Regis to lead Protestant rising (June); defeated at Sedgemoor by Royalist army commanded by John Churchill – later Duke of Marlborough – (6 July). Monmouth executed (15 July). Judge Jeffreys conducts Bloody Assize in the West Country against alleged supporters of Monmouth (Sept). Jeffreys becomes Lord Chancellor. Louis's persecution of French Protestants culminates in the Revocation of the Edict of Nantes in France (Oct). Many Huguenot refugees flee to England. John Rose appointed first English Royal Gardener.

JOHN EVELYN

DATE	AUTHOR'S LIFE	LITERARY CONTEXT
1686	Evelyn twice refuses to apply the seal to licences for the sale of Roman Catholic literature. Fraternizes with Huguenot exiles, notably the Marquis of Ruvigny.	William Wake: *An Exposition of the Doctrine of the Church of England* ... (reply to Bossuet's *Exposition*, 1671). Plot: *The Natural History of Stafford-shire.* John Ray: *Historia Plantarum* (to 1704).
1687	Clarendon returns and Evelyn is relieved of his duties. However, the king replaces Clarendon with a Catholic Lord Privy Seal. After years of lobbying, Evelyn finally receives from the Crown £6000 in part-payment of debts owed to his late father-in-law.	Newton: *Principia Mathematica.* Halifax: *Letter to a Dissenter.* Dryden: *The Hind and the Panther.* Matthew Prior: *The Hind and the Panther Transversed* ... (satire on Dryden's poem). Behn: *The Lucky Chance.*
1688	Evelyn becoming increasingly disaffected with James's attempts to establish a Roman Catholic ascendancy. He approves of William of Orange's intervention. When James asks the bishops to produce a prayer against such an invasion, Evelyn requests Archbishop Sancroft to change the wording (inserting 'reformed' and 'protestant' before 'Church of England') so the Prince's adherents can use it conscientiously. His son joins William's army.	Halifax: *The Character of a Trimmer*; *Anatomy of an Equivalent.* Tenison: *Popery Not Founded on Scripture.* Dryden dismissed as Poet Laureate and succeeded in 1689 by Whig dramatist Thomas Shadwell. Behn: *Oroonoko*; *The Fair Jilt.* La Bruyère: *Les Caractères.*
1689	While favouring a regency, Evelyn accepts its impracticality and recognizes William and Mary as king and queen. Jacobite friends sometimes try to win him over but on the whole Evelyn approves of the new regime – its Protestantism, its religious tolerance and liberalism, its respect for the law and the individual, and not least the moral conduct of the court. Sir Godfrey Knetler paints Evelyn's portrait.	Behn: *The Lucky Mistake.* Dryden: *Don Sebastian.* Locke: three *Letters* on Toleration (to 1692). Birth of Richardson. Racine: *Esther.*

HISTORICAL EVENTS

James proceeds to alienate the Anglican Tory class on which his principal support is based. He tries in vain to bully them to repeal the Test Act. In Godden v. Hales he wins legal sanction for employing Catholic officers in the army. In August he forms a military camp on Hounslow Heath to overawe the city of London. In Ireland he builds up a strong, entirely Catholic army. He establishes a new Court of Ecclesiastical Commission and creates four Catholic peers Privy Councillors. In continuing Charles's attack on borough charters he also allies himself with the radical Dissenters, the Tories' bitterest enemies.

Catholic army commander, the Earl of Tyrconnel, becomes Lord Deputy in Ireland. James issues Declaration of Indulgence, suspending penal laws against Catholics and Dissenters. State visit of papal nuncio. James attacks the privileges of the Anglican universities.

Order in Council requiring revised Declaration of Indulgence to be read in all Anglican churches on two successive Sundays meets with protests from Archbishop Sancroft and six other bishops, who are then imprisoned in the Tower. They are tried for seditious libel but acquitted. Birth of James Edward ('the Old Pretender), a Catholic male heir for James II. William of Orange receives secret letter from six Whig and Tory peers and an Anglican cleric, inviting him to 'defend the liberties of England'. He arrives at Torbay in November, and is joined by John Churchill, Lieutenant-General of James's army. James and family flee to France, while William is welcomed in London. In December, surviving members of Charles II's parliaments are convened; they ask the prince to take over provisional government immediately. Austrians capture Belgrade.

William summons a Convention Parliament which meets in February. William and Mary accepted as joint sovereigns but a Bill of Rights is drawn up stating the limitations of their power (much to William's displeasure). A Mutiny Act makes the maintenance of a standing army legal for one year only. Toleration granted to Protestant Dissenters. James invades Ireland with French support, in an attempt to regain his throne. Siege of Londonderry. Scottish Jacobite army defeats Covenanter army at Killiecrankie but rising repressed at Dunkeld. Presbyterianism re-established as state religion in Scotland. In England Archbishop Sancroft, eight bishops and some 400 clergy refuse to take an Oath of Allegiance to William, considering their oath to James still valid; these 'Non-Jurors' are deprived of their livings. War of the League of Augsburg (to 1697): European coalition against France led by William. Peter the Great becomes Tsar of Russia. Purcell's opera, *Dido and Aeneas*, first performed at a girls' boarding school in Chelsea.

DATE	AUTHOR'S LIFE	LITERARY CONTEXT
1690	*Mundus Muliebris: or, the Ladies Dressing-Room Unlock'd*, in part by Evelyn's daughter Mary.	Dryden: *Amphitryon*. Locke: *An Essay Concerning Human Understanding*; two *Treatises of Government*. Browne: *A Letter to a Friend* (posthumous pub.). Petty: *Political Arithmetic*.
1691	Death of his nephew, another John Evelyn, leaves him the next male heir to Wotton.	Rochester: *Poems*. Richard Bentley: *Letter to Mill*. Ray: *Wisdom of God manifested in the Works of Creation*. Racine: *Athalie*.
1692	His brother formally bequeaths him the Wotton estate. Death of Robert Boyle. As one of his trustees, Evelyn is involved in the setting up of the Boyle Lectures.	Bentley delivers the first Boyle Lecture, printed in 1693 as *The Folly and Unreasonableness of Atheism*. L'Estrange's translation of Aesop's *Fables*. Dryden: *Cleomenes*. Temple: *Memoirs*.
1693	Evelyn's only surving daughter, Susanna, marries William Draper. Evelyn publishes *The Compleat Gard'ner*, a translation from the French of J. de la Quintinye.	Dryden: *A Discourse Concerning the Original and Progress of Satire*. Locke: *Some Thoughts Concerning Education*. Aubrey deposits manuscript of his *Lives* at the Ashmolean Museum. Congreve: *The Old Bachelor*.
1694	At his brother's wish, Evelyn and his wife move to Wotton. The Drapers occupy Sayes Court, which is afterwards let. His friend Dr Tenison becomes Archbishop of Canterbury.	Congreve: *The Double Dealer*. William Wotton: *Reflections Upon Ancient and Modern Learning*.
1695	Evelyn made Treasurer of Greenwich Hospital for old sailors. He and Sir Christopher Wren lay the first stone of the new building the following year.	Congreve: *Love for Love*. Locke: *The Reasonableness of Christianity*. John Woodward: *An Essay Toward a Natural History of the Earth*.

HISTORICAL EVENTS

William goes to Ireland and defeats Jacobite army at the Battle of the Boyne. Protestant ascendancy established in Ireland. Anglo-Dutch fleet defeated off Beachy Head. Whigs, as secret supporters of William for many years, increasingly resent his mistrust of their party and dependence on the Tories. However, he soon comes to mistrust the Tories – many of them are still in touch with James II. Parliamentary animosity against Halifax, one of William's most trusted ministers, forces him to resign. Turks recapture Belgrade.

William offers pardon to rebellious Highlanders who swear allegiance by the end of the year. Campaigns in Holland and presides over Allied Congress. Fall of Mons to Louis XIV. William and Mary's popularity waning in England, but Carmarthen's (the former Earl of Danby) skilful management (bribery) of the House ensures the king is voted the supply he requires. Death of French General, Louvois. Turks defeated by imperial forces at Slankamen.

MacDonald clan, who had not sworn allegiance in time, massacred at Glencoe. French fleet shattered by Anglo-Dutch fleet in battle of La Hogue, but land army is defeated at Steenkerk. Princess Anne withdraws from court after quarrelling with her sister, Queen Mary, who resents her close friendship with Sarah, Lady Marlborough. Mary sends Marlborough to the Tower for alleged treason, though he is released after a month. Ill-feeling between the parties running high in winter 1692–3, dominated by conflict in Parliament between Russell (Whig) and Nottingham (Tory). Purcell: *The Fairy Queen*; *Ode on St Cecilia's Day*.

On the advice of Sunderland, and overcoming his prejudices, William courts the Whig leaders and makes Whig appointments: Sir John Somers as Lord Keeper, Sir John Trenchard as a Secretary of State. The Whigs are the only party fully to support William's foreign policy. The strategy pays off and William's army estimates are passed with a huge majority (Dec). Resignation of Nottingham. French military victory at Neerwinden. Couperin becomes court organist at Versailles.

Earl of Shrewsbury, another leading Whig, induced to join the cabinet. A Whig 'Junta' consisting of Shrewsbury, Somers, Trenchard, Russell, Montagu and Wharton now hold the reins of power. Godolphin and Carmarthen are the only remaining Tories. William withdraws his opposition to the Whigs' Triennial Act, ensuring frequent Parliaments. Bank of England founded. Kneller paints his series of Hampton Court 'Beauties' (to 1695). Purcell: *Come ye sons of art*, ode for Queen Mary's birthday. Queen Mary dies from smallpox (Dec).

The Licensing Act expires and is not renewed: relative freedom of the press established. Resignation of Carmarthen. William serves with army in the Netherlands: captures Namur (Sept). Bank of Scotland created. General election returns overwhelmingly Whig House of Commons (Nov). Purcell: *Thou knowest, Lord, the secrets of our hearts* (anthem for Queen Mary's funeral).

DATE	AUTHOR'S LIFE	LITERARY CONTEXT
1696	Evelyn's son returns from Ireland, where he was one of the Commissioners of the Revenue, in very ill health.	Vanbrugh: *The Relapse.* Aubrey: *Miscellanies.* Prior: 'The Secretary'. John Toland: *Christianity not Mysterious* (seminal work of Deism). Sloane's *Catalogus Plantarum* (classifying all the plants he had discovered in Jamaica).
1697	Writes *De Vita Propria*, a biography of his early life. Publishes *Numismata*, a history of medals.	Vanbrugh: *The Provoked Wife.* Phalaris controversy (to 1699): Bentley proves the *Epistles of Phalaris* to be spurious. Swift writes satire based on this: *The Battle of the Books*, pub. 1704. Defoe: *An Essay upon Projects.* William Dampier: *A New Voyage Round the World.*
1698	Sayes Court is sub-let to Peter the Great, who causes considerable damage to house and garden, for which Evelyn receives compensation from the Treasury. Dispute with his brother George and other claimants on the estate about Evelyn's inheriting Wotton free of entail: he removes to Berkeley Street, London (July) pending its resolution.	Crowne: *Caligula.* Algernon Sidney: *Discourses Concerning Government.*
1699	Death of Evelyn's son, John (March). Legal dispute ended, not before George had presented a bill in the Commons and John petitioned against it in the Lords. Evelyn offers to pay £6500 into George's estate on his demise in order to inherit Wotton unentailed (June). Takes over from his son the lease of a house in Dover Street (July). Death of George Evelyn (Oct). *Acetaria: A Discourse of Sallets.*	Farquhar: *The Constant Couple.* Death of Racine.

CHRONOLOGY

HISTORICAL EVENTS

Parliament told of plot to murder William at Turnham Green. Commons propose an Oath of Association to defend the king and the Protestant succession. Jacobite invasion scare. Withdrawal of Secretary of State Shrewsbury from office. Godolphin resigns from the Treasury.
Window tax introduced. Friction at court between William's two favourites, Keppel and Portland. Death of Purcell.

Whig government with Somers as Lord Chancellor (April). Treaty of Ryswick: Louis obliged to return territories conquered in the Low Countries since the Peace of Nijmegen, and recognizes William as king of England. In November, Robert Harley leads Commons Opposition in seeking reduction in the size of the army. Eugene of Savoy defeats Turks at battle of Zenta.

Whitehall Palace destroyed by fire, only the Banqueting Hall remaining. Tsar Peter visits England, studying shipbuilding. The Great Powers waiting to divide up the Habsburg empire when Charles II of Spain should die. First Partition Treaty between England, France and the United Provinces makes the Electoral Prince of Bavaria the triumphant candidate; neither Habsburg nor Bourbon would thus become over-powerful – but it is not accepted by the Emperor. Marlborough reinstated in the army and Privy Council. General election in summer returns a xenophobic Tory majority. Anti-war, anti-army and anti-Dutch, they propose cutting down the army to 7000 men, all of whom should be Englishmen (William's experienced army contained many Dutchmen and some French Huguenots). William considers abdication. Thomas Savery's steam engine.
Death of the Electoral Prince of Bavaria (Jan) makes the prospect of war more likely and the need of an army more pressing. William obliged to sign Disbanding Bill, and even loses famous Dutch Blue Guards. Second Partition Treaty negotiated. Spain, the Spanish Netherlands and Spanish territory in America to go to Archduke Charles, second son of Emperor Leopold. It is signed in January 1700, but not by the Emperor (who resents the increase of French influence in Italy by the same treaty) or by Spain. At home a weak Tory ministry (Jersey, Lonsdale, Bridgewater) is unable to handle the more aggressively Tory Commons. Eddystone Rock, first high-seas lighthouse, completed. Peace of Karlowitz between Ottoman Empire and Austria.

JOHN EVELYN

DATE	AUTHOR'S LIFE	LITERARY CONTEXT
1700	Moves back to Wotton as its new owner.	Congreve: *The Way of the World*. Dryden: *Fables Ancient and Modern*.
1701	Evelyn had been dissatisfied with the conduct of divine service at Wotton; the death of the rector enables him to present to the living Ralph Bohun, former tutor to his son.	Swift: *A Discourse of the Contents and Dissensions between the nobles and the commons in Athens and Rome* (against the Irish land policy of William and his Dutch favourites). Defoe: *The True-born Englishman*, satirizing xenophobic prejudice. Sackville and Sedley: *Poems*.
1702		Defoe: *The Shortest Way with Dissenters*. Clarendon: *History of the Rebellion*. Farquhar: *The Twin Rivals*.
1703	Resigns the treasurership of Greenwich Hospital. Death of Pepys.	Steele: *The Lying Lover*.
1704	Evelyn's grandson Jack (eldest son of John) appointed Receiver-General of the Stamp Duties.	Swift: *A Tale of a Tub*. Newton: *Opticks*.
1705	Jack marries Anne Boscawen, a niece of Lord Godolphin.	Vanbrugh: *The Confederacy*. Steele: *The Tender Husband*. Addison: *The Campaign*.

CHRONOLOGY

Resentment of William's Dutch favourites lies behind a Commons vote that royal grants of land in Ireland should be taken back and put in the hands of trustees. When they further vote that all foreigners except Prince George be removed from the king's councils (April), William prorogues Parliament. Dismisses Somers in the hope of appeasing the Tories. Death of William's eleven-year-old nephew and heir. Death of Charles II of Spain, who, ignoring the Partition Treaty, leaves the whole of his inheritance to Philip of Anjou, second son of Louis XIV's heir: Louis repudiates the Treaty and accepts the will.

At first, in the interests of maintaining peace, England and Holland recognize the Bourbon succession in Spain. General election returns a small Tory majority. Portland and Whig ministers of the Junto impeached in Commons for concluding the Partition Treaty without reference to Parliament (later acquitted by Lords). But alarm spreads when French troops enter the Spanish Netherlands and the Whigs support William's own desire for war. Kentish freeholders petition Parliament to grant the king the necessary funds. Marlborough made Commander-in-Chief of English forces in Holland. Grand Alliance signed at The Hague between Britain, Holland and the Habsburg Emperor against Louis XIV's attempts to unify France and Spain. General election in December shows swing towards the Whigs: the Grand Alliance is accepted and supply voted. Act of Settlement fixes the succession (failing heirs to Mary's sister, Anne) on the House of Hanover, descendants of James I's daughter, Elizabeth, and the Elector Palatine. It also transfers the right to dismiss judges from the king to Parliament. James II dies at St Germain: Louis XIV recognizes his son as James III. Jethro Tull invents the seed drill.

Death of William after a fall from his horse (March). Anne becomes Queen. War declared (May) – War of the Spanish Succession (to 1713). Godolphin made Lord Treasurer, serving as chief minister until 1710. General election gives Tories a majority of 113 MPs (June). Marlborough's first victories in the autumn. Sir George Rooke destroys or captures Spanish treasure fleet in Vigo Bay. Completion of main buildings at Castle Howard, Yorkshire, Vanbrugh's first foray into architecture, collaborating with Hawksmoor.

Marlborough advances down the Rhine, ejecting the French from Cologne and Bonn. Portugal joins the Grand Alliance against Louis XIV. 'Beau' Nash becomes master of ceremonies at Bath and arbiter of fashion there for the next 50 years. Peter the Great founds the city of St Petersburg.

Two prominent Tories join Godolphin's government – Henry St John and Robert Harley. Marlborough reaches the Danube. He and Prince Eugene victorious at Blenheim. Gibraltar bombarded and captured by Admiral Rooke who then wins naval victory at Velez Malaga against Franco-Spanish fleet. Blenheim victory parade in London. Anne appoints commissioners to negotiate political union with Scotland (ends in Act of Union, 1707). Earl of Peterborough leads Anglo-Dutch expedition to capture Barcelona. Halley publishes his research on the orbit of comets. Foundation stone laid of Vanbrugh's Blenheim Palace at Woodstock, Oxfordshire.

JOHN EVELYN

DATE	AUTHOR'S LIFE	LITERARY CONTEXT
1706	Death of John Evelyn on 27 February, aged 85, at his Dover Street house. Of his children, only Susanna, the youngest, survives him. Wotton is inherited by his grandson, Jack, who becomes Sir John Evelyn in 1713.	Farquhar: *The Recruiting Officer*.
1818	The earliest edition of the Diary published.	

CHRONOLOGY

HISTORICAL EVENTS

Peterborough's army advances through Spain. Marlborough's victory at
Ramillies, expelling French from modern Belgium. Anglo-Portuguese army
under the Earl of Galway, enters Madrid in June (retaken by French in
August). Anne reluctantly makes leading Whig, Charles Spencer, 3rd Earl
of Sunderland, a Secretary of State.

CONTENTS

THE DIARY OF JOHN EVELYN

KALENDARIUM
My Journal &c:

PARENTAGE AND EARLY LIFE
(1620–1641)

I WAS BORNE about 20 minuts past two in the morning, [on Tuesday] being the xxxi, and last of October Anno 1620, after my Father had been married about 7 yeares, and that my Mother had borne him 3 Children viz. Two Daughters and one sonn, about the 33d Yeare of his age, and the 23d of my Mothers.

My Father, named Richard, was of a sanguine complexion, mix'd with a dash of Choler; his haire inclining to light, which (though exceeding thick) became hoary by that time he had attain'd to 30 years of age; it was somewhat curled towards the extremes; his beard, (which he ware a little picked, as the mode was,) of a brownish colour and so continu'd to the last, save that it was somewhat mingled with grey haires about his cheekes; which with his countenance was cleare, & fresh colour'd, his eyes extraordinary quick & piercing, an ample fore head, in summ, a very well composed visage and manly aspect: For the rest, he was but low of stature, but very strong: He was for his life so exact and temperat, that I have heard he had never in all his life been surpriz'd by excesse, being ascetic and sparing: His Wisdome was greate, and judgment most acute; of solid discourse, affable, humble and in nothing affected; of a thriving, neate, silent and methodical genius; discreetely severe, yet liberall upon all just occasions both to his Children, strangers, and servants; a lover of hospitality; and in briefe, of a singular & Christian moderation in all his actions; not illiterate, nor obscure; as having continu'd Justice of Peace, and of the Quorum; and served his Country in the Charge of high-Sheriff; being (as I take it) the last dignified with that office for Sussex and Surrey together the same Yeare, before their separation: He was yet a studious decliner of Honors and Titles; being already in that esteeme with his Country, that they could have

added little to him, besids their burthen: In fine, a person of that
rare conversation, that upon frequent recollection, and calling to
memory some Passages of his life, and discourse, I could never
charge him with the least passion, or inadvertancy: [His estate
esteem'd to be about £4000 per an: well wodded & full of
Timber:]*

My Mother's name was Elianor, sole daughter, & heyresse of
John Standsfield Esquire of an antient, and honorable Family
(though now extinct) in Shropshire; and Elianor Comber, of a
good and well knowne house in Sussex. [She was borne 17. Nov:
1598 in Cliff Sussex, neere Lewes.] She was of proper personage,

---

*Expanded in V, and followed by an additional notice: His Estate estem'd to be
nere £4000 per Annum: wooded to the value of £30000 in six Contiguous
Mannors, 3 Advousons; the whole lying in the two Countys aboue named;
wonderfully prosperous in all his Undertakings, the more remarkable, as without the accession of any lucrative Office, he pass'd his whole time in the Country, & in good husbandry, and tho' Master of an ample Royalty, no lover of field
Sports, which he freely indulg'd to the gentlemen his Neighbours:

    And here I must not omit to speake somthing in briefe of my Gr: father
George Evelyn, the parent of 24 Children, *vzt* 16 Sonns & 8 Daughters, of
which 22 were of *Rosa* his first Wife, and two onely of Joanna his sec⟨ond,⟩
mother of my Father, Richard, & Katherin, married to Thom: Staughton of
Staughton in Com: Sur: who left no male Issue living: The rest of my Unkles &
Aunts, surviving, had considerable Estates left and settl'd upon them, whereof
one was John of God-stone, Sole Master of the Powder-Works, of which my
Gr: Father had a pattent, deriv'd I think from My Greate Gr-Fa: who first is
sayd to be the first who brought that Invention into England out of Flander,
from whence & from Genōa we bought powder at excessive rates: And this
Manufacture continued in the above-nam'd Family 'till the Civil Wars & late
Rebellion; when it was taken from it, & since made a Droug by Severall:
[undertakers:]

    My Grandfather having thus disposd of his Sonns, the Eldest at Long Dit-
ton, a second at Everly in   & afterward at West-Deane neere Salisbury in Wilts, now fall'n to a Daughter, the Mother of the present Evelyn,
Earle of Kingston & son of William Perpoint: The Rest had Estates & portions, as many as lived, which would be too tedious to particulariz, whose
numerous Branches and Offspring I referr to our Pedegreè, where will be found
those Earles of Kent & Kingston to have ben raised from Decay by the Daughters of our Famely; besides severall others of the Nobility:

    My Gr: Father George making (after some yeares that he had resided at Long-
Ditton, (where he had a greate Estate) purch⟨a⟩s'd a greater of   *Owen*,
together with Six Mannors &c (already mentioned) in the same County of
Surrey, whether he removed; and continued all his life after, & at his Death
bequeathed it to his youngest son Richard my Father.

well timber'd, of a browne complexion; her eyes and haire of a lovely black; of constitution more inclyn'd to a religious Melancholy, or pious sadnesse; of a rare memory, and most exemplary life: for Oeconomiq prudence esteem'd one of the most conspicuous in her Country, which render'd her losse universaly deplor'd, both by those who knew, and such as onely heard of her. Thus much in briefe touching my Parents: nor was it reasonable I should speake lesse of them, to whom I owe so much. [oblig'd.]

The Place of my birth was Wotton, in the Parish of Wotton or Black-Heath in the County of Surrey, the then Mansion house of my Father, left him [as above] by my Grandfather, and now [afterwards] my Eldest Brothers. [In the red-Chamber having 2 windows directly towards the N and South respecting the Gardens.] It is situated in the most Sothern part of the Shire, and though in a Vally; yet realy upon a very greate rising, being on part of one of the most eminent hills in England for the prodigious prospect to be seen from its summit, though by few observed. [Lyth-hill, where one may discerne 12 or 13 shires, with part of the sea, in a serene day.] The house is large and antient, suitable to those hospitable times,* and so sweetely environ'd with those delicious streames and venerable Woods, as in the judgment of strangers, as well as Englishmen, it may be compared to one of the most tempting and pleasant seates in the Nation [for a great person & a wanton purse to render it Conspicuous:] for it has risings, meadows, Woods & Water in aboundance; not destitute of the most noble and advantagious accommodations; being but [within little more than] 20 miles from Lond: and yet so securely placed, as if it were an hundred: from Darking 3 miles, [6 from Gilford 12 from Kingston] which serves it aboundantly with provisions as well of Land as Sea: I will say nothing of the ayre because the præeminence is universaly given to Surrey; the soile being dry and sandy; but I should speake much of the Gardens, Fountaines and Groves that adorne it were they not as generaly knowne to be [amongst] the most natural & [most] magnificent that England afforded [til

---

* Expanded in V: The Building after the antient fashion of our Ancestors, (tho' nothing of modish as now the manner is) is not onely very Capacious, but exceedingly Commodious, & almost intirely of Brick:

this later & universal luxury of the whole nation since abounding in such expenses], and which indeede gave one of the first
examples to that elegancy since so much in vogue and followd,
for the managing of their Waters and other elegancies of that
nature: Let me add the contiguity of 5 or 6 Mannors, the
Patronage of the Livings about it; and (what Themistocles pronounc'd for none of the least advantages) the good Neighborhod,
all which conspire here to render it an honorable and handsom
royalty,* fit for the present Possessor my worthy Brother, and
noble Lady, whose constant Liberality give them title both to
the place, and the affections of all that know them: Thus with the
Poet:

> Nescio qua Natale solum dulcedine cunctos
> Ducit, et immemores ⟨non⟩ sinit esse sui.

I had given me the name of my Grandfather, my Mothers
Father, who together with a sister of Sir Tho: Evelyns of Long
Ditton, and Mr. Comber, a neere relation of my mothers, were
my susceptors. [I had given me two handsom pieces of very curiously wrought, & gilt plate.] The sollemnity yet (upon what
accident I know not, unlesse some indisposition in me) was perform'd in the Dining rome by Parson Higham the present
incumbent of the Parish, according to the forme prescribed by
the then glorious CHURCH of ENGLAND.

    1621. I was now (in reguard of my Mothers weaknesse, or
rather costome of persons of quality) put to Nurse to one Peter, a
neighbours wife, and tennant; of a good comely, brown, & whol-
some-complexion, and in a most sweete place towards the hills,
flanked with wood, and refreshed with streames, the affection
to which kind of solitude, I succked in with my very milke.
It appeares by a note of my Fathers that I succked till 17: Jan:
1622, or at least I came not home before.

    1623. The very first thing that I can call to memory, and from
which time forward, I began to observe, was, this yeare my
Youngest Brother, being in his Nurses armes, who being then
two Yeares and 9 dayes younger then my selfe, was the last child
of my deare Parents: [My Bro: Richard was borne at 10 at Night:
9: Nov: Saturday: 1622.]

* In V: with a Royalty about it of neere 7000 Akers.

1624. I was not initiated into any rudiments till neere 4 yeares of age; and then one Frier taught us at the Church-porch of Wotton; and I do perfectly remember the greate talke and stirr about il Conde Gundamar, now Ambassador from Spaine; for neere about this time was the match of our Prince with the Infanta propos'd, and the Effects of that Comet 1618 still working in the prodigious revolutions now beginning in Europ, especialy in Germany, whose sad commotions sprung from the Bohemians defection from the Emperor Mathias, upon which quarell the Sweds brake in, giving umbrage to the rest of the Princes, and the whole Christian world, cause to deplore it [as never since Injoying any perfect tranquility.]

1625. I was this yeare (being the first of the reigne of King Charles) sent by my Father to Lewes in Sussex, to be with my Grandfather, with whom I pass'd my Child-hood: This was that yeare in which the Pestilence was so Epidemical, that there dy'd in Lond. 5000 a Weeke; & I well remember the strict Watches, and examinations upon the Ways as we pass'd: and I was shortly after so dangerously sick of a Feavor, that (as I have heard), the Physitians despair'd of me.

1626. My Picture was drawne in Oyle by one Chanterell, no ill Painter.

1627. My Grandfather Standsfield dyed this Yeare on the 5. of Feb: and I remember perfectly the solemnity at his funerall; he was buried in the Parish [Church] of All-Soules, where my Grandmother (his second Wife) erected him a pious Monument.

About this time was the Consecration of the Church of South Malling neere Lewes; [Consecrated by Bp: Field Bp: of Oxon: One Mr. Coxhall preached on . . . . who was afterward minister:] the building whereof was chiefely procur'd by my Grandfather, to which he left a rent Charge of £20 per annum: which likewise I pay'd, til I sold the Impropriation, and that onely because it was so: I lay'd one of the first stones at the building of that Church: [I have often wish'd, I had kept it: til I had ben able to restore it all to the Church:]

It was not till the yeare 1628 that I was put to learne my Latine Rudiments, and to Write, of one Citolin, a Frenchman in Lewes.

1629. I very well remember that generall Muster, prævious to the Ile of Rès expedition; and that I was one day awaken'd in the

Morning with the newes of the Duke of Buckinghams being slaine by that wretch Felton, after our disgrace before La Rochelle.

And I now tooke so extraordinary a fansy to drawing, and designing, that I could never after weane my inclinations from it, to the expense of much precious tyme which might have been more advantagiously employd: [1630] For I was now put to schoole to one Mr. Potts in the Cliff; from whom on the 7th of Jan: (being the day after Epiphany) I went to the Free-schole at Southover neere the Towne, of which one Agnes Morley had been the Foundresse, and now Edw: Snatt the Master, under whom I remain'd till I was sent to the University. [This yeare my Grandmother (with whom I sojourn'd) being married to one Mr. Newton a learned and most religious Gent: We went from the Cliff, to dwell at his house in Southover.] I do most perfectly remember the jubilie which was universaly express'd for the happy birth of the Prince of Wales 29: May: now CHARLES THE 2D, our most gracious Sovraigne.

1631. There happen'd now an extraordinary dirth in Engl: corne bearing an excessive price: and in imitation of what I had seene my Father do, I began to observe matters more punctualy, which I did use to set downe in a blanke Almanac.

The Lord of Castelhavens arraignement for many shamefull exorbitances was now all the talke; and the birth of the Princesse Mary, afterward Princess of Orange.

1632. October 21 my Eldest sister was married to Edw: Darcy Esquire: who little deserved so excellent a person, a woman of so rare vertue: I was not present at the Nuptials; but I was soone after sent for into Surrey, and my Father would very willingly have weaned me from my fondnesse of my too indulgent Grand-mother, intending to have sent me to Eaton; but being neither so provident for my owne benefit, unreasonably terrified with the report of the severe discipline there; I was sent back againe to Lewes, which perversenesse of mine, I have since a thousand times deplor'd.

This was the first time, that ever my Parents had seene all their Children together in prosperity.

Whiles I was now trifling at home I saw London, where I lay one night onely, the next day dined at Bedington much delighted with the Gardens & curiosities there, as they then appear'd to me: Thenc we return'd to the Lady Darcys at Sutton, thence to Wotton, and the 16 of Aug: following 1633 back to Lewes.

1633. Nov: 3: this yeare was my Father made sherif the last (as I thinke) who served in that honorable office for Surry & Sussex befor they were disjoyned: he had 116 Servants in Liverys, every one liveryd in greene sattin doublets; divers Gentlemen and persons of quality besides waited on him in the same garbe & habit, which at that time (when 30 or 40 was the usual retinue of the High-Sherif) was esteem'd a greate matter; nor was this out of the least vanity, that my Father exceeded (who was one of the greatest decliners of it in the World) but because he could not refuse the Civility of his friends and relations who voluntarily came themselves, or sent in their Servants: But my Father was afterwards most unjustly & spitefully molested by that jeering Judge Richardson, for repreeving the execution of a Woman, to gratifie my L: of Lindsey then Admiral; but out of this he emerged with as much honor as trouble.

1634. The King made this Yeare his progresse into Scotland, and Duke James was borne.

Decemb: 15. my deare Sister Darcy departed this life, being ariv'd to her 20th yeare of age, in vertue advanc'd beyond her yeares, or the merit of her Husband the worst of men. It was believed that the indisposition caused by her prety infant, which was borne the 2d of June before, contributed much to her destruction; as infallibly both their deaths did to my Mothers, who not long survived her.

The 24 of December I was therefore sent for home the second tyme to celebrate the obsequies of my Sister, who was interr'd in a very honorable manner, in our Dormitory, joyning to the Parish-Church, where now her Monument stands.

1635. On Jan: 7th following I returned to Lewes:[1]

But my deare Mother, being now dangerously sick, I was the 3d of Sept: following sent for to Wotton; whom I found so far spent, that all human assistance failing, she in a most heavenly

1 Followed by a deleted entry: *July the 16, my Father being (as I understood) extreamely displeased at my Writing so ill a Character, I put my selfe to the Writing Schoole for a Moneth or two, till I had redressed that in some measure:*

manner departed this Life upon the 29 of the same moneth, about 8 in the Evening of Michaelmas-day. It was a malignant feavor which tooke her away, about the 37th of her age, and 22d of her marriage, to our irreparable losse, and the universal regret of all that knew her. Certaine it is, that the visible cause of her indisposition proceeded from griefe, upon the losse of her daughter, and the Infants that follow'd it; and it is as certaine, that when she perceived the perill, whereto its excesse had engaged her, she strove to compose her selfe, and allay it; but it was too late, and she was forc'd to succumb; Therefore summoning all her Children then living (I shall never forget it) she express'd her selfe in a manner so heavenly, with instructions so pious, and Christian, as made us strangely sensible of the extraordinary losse then imminent; after which, embracing every one of us in particular, she gave to each a Ring with her Blessing, and dismiss'd us. Then taking my Father by the hand, she recommended us to his care; and because she was extreamely zealous for the education of my Younger Bro: she requested my Father, that he might be sent with me to Lewes; and so having importun'd him that what he design'd to bestow on her Funeral, he would rather dispose among the poore (for that she feared, God had not a little punish'd her, for the pomp, and expense of my Sisters) she labourd to compose herselfe for the blessed change which She now expected. There was not a Servant in the house, whom she did not expressly send for, advise, and infinitely affect with her counsell; and thus she continu'd to employ her intervalls, either instructing her relations, or preparing of her selfe: for though her Physitians (who were Dr. Meverell, Dr. Clement, & Dr. Rand) had given over all hopes of her recovery, and Sir Sanders Duncomb tried his celebrated & famous powder upon her;* yet she was many days impairing, and endur'd the sharpest conflicts of her sicknesse with admirable patience, and a most christian resignation; reteining both her intellectuals, and ardent affections for her dissolution to the very article of her departure; which hapned, as I sayd, on the 29 of

---

* V adds: This knight is say'd to have first brought the use of *Sedanns* from *Naples* into *England*, but I remember few persons of Reputation would make use of them a good while after, it being held a conveyance for voluptuous persons & Women of pleasure to their leu'd Rendivozes incognito.

September after she had fallen into a Crisis by a profound sweate (the onely change through all her sicknesse) after which lay⟨i⟩ng her hand upon every one of her Children, and ⟨having⟩ taken solemn leave of my Father; with elevated heart, & eyes, she quietly expired, and resign'd her Soule to God.

Thus ended that prudent, and pious Woman in the flowre [almost] of her age, to the unconsolable affliction of her husband, irreparable losse of her Children, and universal regret of all that knew her: She was interrd as neere as might be, to her Daughter Darcy, the 3d of October, at night; but with no meane Ceremony.

It was the 3d of the ensuing November after my Bro: Geo: was gon back to Oxford, 'ere I return'd to Lewes, where I made way (according to instructions received of my Father) for my Bro: Rich: who was sent the 12th after.

This Yeare 1636, being extremely dry, the Pestilence much increased in Lond, and divers parts of England.

The 13th of Feb: I was especialy admitted (and as I remember my other Bro:) into the Middle-Temple Lond: though absent, and as yet at Schoole.*

There were now large contributions to the distressed Palatinate.

The 31 of October came my Father himselfe to see us, and return'd the 5t of November following.

The 10th of December he sent a Servant to bring us necessaries &c, and the Plague beginning now to cease

The 3d. of Apr: 1637 I was sent for from Schoole; where till about the last Yeare I had been extremely remisse in my studies; so as I went to the Universitie, rather out of shame of abiding longer at Schoole, than for any fitnesse, as by sad experience

---

* Expanded in V: 1636 Feb: 13 we were all three especially admitted tho' absent into the Midle Temple, as was then the Course of Education of young gentlemen after their studys in the Universitys, to acquaint them with the Municiple Laws of their owne Country; but whether he design'd any of us his younger sonn⟨s⟩ to that profession I know not, leaving them both very Competent Fortu⟨n⟩es: But so it was, that that Society new building a part of that ⟨Inn⟩ of Court, my Father bought us Chambers, with three Assig⟨n⟩ements, just over that of the afterwards famous Lawyer Sir Jo Maynard, but which we afterwards parted with to the learned Tho Henshaw Esquire my Fellow Traveller in Italy &c:

I found, which put me to relearne all that I had neglected, or but perfunctorily gaind.*

It was Apr: 5. that I return'd to Wotton (upon what occasion I do not well remember) and the 9th of May after, that I ariv'd at Oxford, where I was admitted Fellow-Communer of Balliol Colledge upon the 10th in the Chapell there, taking an Oath to be conformable to the Statutes, and Orders of that Society.

On the 29 of May I was MATRICULATED in the Vestry at St. Maries; UBI SUBSCRIPSI ARTICULIS FIDEI, ET RELIGIONIS, ET JURAMENTUM SUSCEPI DE AGNOSCENDA SUPREMA REGIÆ MAJESTATIS POTESTATE, ET DE OBSERVANDIS STATUTIS, PRIV-ILEGIIS, ET CONSUETUDINIBUS UNIVERSITATIS. Dr. R: Baily head of St. Johns, being then Vice-Chancelor. [afterwards Bishop.]

It appeares by a letter of my Fathers, that he was upon treaty with one Mr. Bathurst of Trinity Coll: (afterwards Doctor [& Præsident])† who should have been my Tutor; but least my Brothers Tutor Dr. Hobbs, (more zelous in his life, then indus-trious with his Pupils,) should receive it as an affront; and espe-cialy for that Fellow-Communers in Balliol were no more exemptd from Exercise than the meanest Scholars there; my Father sent me thither to one Mr. Geo: Bradshaw (*nomen invi-sum*) yet the sonn of an excellent Father, beneficed in our Coun-try of Surrey. I ever thought my Tutor had parts enough; but as his ambition [& I fear vices] made him very much suspected of the Colledg; so his grudg to the Governor of it Dr. Lawrence [Margaret Professor] (whom he afterwards supplanted) tooke up so much of his tyme, that he seldom, or never had any

---

* Re-written in V: 1637 Aprill the 3d I was sent from Schole to the University, rather out of shame of abiding longer *sub ferula*, than, for that fitnesse to have ben expected from one had well employed his time, which was indeede exceed-ingly interrupted by being so often sent for into the Country, & other Acci-dents not a little imputable to the ill method of my Scholemaster: and my owne negligence, inclined as I was ⟨to⟩ trifles, drawing & painting & other imperti-nencys:

† Expanded in V: since, & at present the most antient Doctor in the Univer-sity, a person of admirable Parts and Learning president of that Colledge; to which he has built a very fine Chapell, & a monument for himselfe:

opportunity to discharge his duty to his Scholars; which, I perceiving, associated my selfe with one Jam: Thicknesse (then a
Young man of the foundation, afterwards fellow of the house)
by whose learned and friendly Conversation I received a great
advantage.

At my first arival Dr. Parkhurst was Master, after his discease
Dr. Lawrence, a Chaplaine of his Majesties and Margaret Professor succeeded, an accute and Learned Person; nor do I so
much reproch his severity, considering that the extraordinary
remissenesse of discipline had (til his coming) much detracted
from the reputation of that Colledg.

There came in my tyme to the Coll: one Nathaniel Conopios
out of Greece, from [Cyrill] the Patriarch of Constantinople,
who returning many yeares after, was made (as I understood)
Bishop of Smyrna. [He was the first I ever saw drink Coffè,
which custome came not into England til 30 years after.]* After
I was somewhat settled there in my formalities, (for then was
the University exceedingly regular under the exact discipline
of William Lawd, Archbish: of Canterbury then Chancelor)

* Expanded in V: There came in my Time to the College one *Nathaniel*
Conopios out of Greece sent into England by the famous Patriarch *Cyrill*,
(whom the Jesuits murdred) this Priest learned in the Greeke had a pension
from Arch-Bishop Dr. *Laude* then Chancellor of the University, to whose
extraordnary care & vigilancy, she owes soly to that brave Prelate & Martyr,
the Discipline 'til then wonderfully neglected: *Conopios* after returning to
Constantinople upon the troubles in England, & violating all that was sacred:
was made Bishop of *Smyrna* and then (I think,) Patriarch of *Alexandria*, and
was the first that I ever saw drink *Caffè*, not heard of then in England, nor til
many yeares after made a common entertainement all over the nation, as since
that the Chineze *Thea*; Sack & Tabacco being til these came in, the Universal
liquor & Drougs, which maintained such a number of Taverns [& coffe
houses] as remaine to this day, & might well be spared: The *Demeans* of the
Crowne, after the Rebellion resum'd, was formerly sufficient to support almost
the whole Government, but being viciously squander'd by a successor who was
govern'd by wicked favorits, reduc'd him to such streites, that Smoke, & exotic
Drinks, were the greatest branches of the Revenue, so as had the people
become as temperat, as Christianity obliges, the Government would have sunk
in all appearance, now kept up, by Luxury, unknow⟨n⟩ to our Ancestors, who
relyed on the providence & blessing of God, on their honest and industrious
Course of life.

I added as benefactor to the Library of the Coll: these Bookes following:*

> Ex dono Johannis Evelyni hujus Coll:
>   Socio-Commensalis, Filij Richardi
>   Evelyni, è Com: Surriæ, Armigeri
> Zanchij Opera Voll: j. 2. 3m.
> Granado in Tho: Aquinatem Vol: j. 2. 3m.
> Novarini Electa Sacra, &
> Cresolij Anthologia Sacra. Authors (it seemes) desired by the
>   students of Divinity there.

Upon the 2d of July, being the first of the Moneth, I first received the B: Sacrament of the Lords Supper in the Colledg Chapell, one Mr. Cooper, a fellow of the house preching; and at this tyme was the Church of England in her greatest splendor, all things decent, and becoming the peace, and the Persons that govern'd.

The most of the following Weeke I spent in visiting the Colledges, and several rarities of the University, which do very much affect young comers; but I do not find any memoranda's of what I saw.

18 July, I accompanyd my Eldest Bro (who then quitted Oxford) into the Country; and the 9 of Aug: went to visite my friends at Lewes, whenc I returned the 12th ⟨to⟩ Wotton. 17 Sept: I received the B: Sacrament at Wotton-Church, and Octob: 23 went back to Oxon.

5: Nov: I received againe the holy Comm: in our Coll: Chapell: one Prouse, a Fellow (but a mad one) preaching.

December 9, I offerd at my first exercise in the Hall, and answerd myne Opponent: and upon the 11th following declaymed in the Chapell before the Master, Fellows & Scholars according to the Custome: The 15th after, I first of all Oppos'd in the Hall.

---

* Expanded in V: At my Admission into the Coll: every Gent: was used to give a Piece of Plate or Tankard, with their Escuchion and Inscription of the *Donor*: Mine was in Books to the value of the *plate*, which was all Coin'd into mony to inable the King to maintaine his Forces, & Court, which was quartered about Oxon: The P⟨l⟩ate was Gon but my Books remaine in the Library, which is absolutly the best of any Colledge perhaps in Europe:

The Christmas ensuing, being at a Comedy, which the Gent: of Excester-Coll: presented to the University, and standing (for the better advantage of seeing) upon a table in the Hall, which was neere to another in the darke; being constrain'd by the extraordinary presse to quit my station, in leaping downe to save my selfe I dash'd my right leg with such violence against the sharp edge of the other board, as gave me an hurt which held me in cure till almost Easter, and confined me to my study.

1638. The 22d of Jan, I would needes be admitted into the dauncing, and Vaulting Schole; of which late activity one Stokes (the Master) did afterwards set forth a pretty booke, which was publish'd with many witty Elogies before it.

Feb: 4th. one Mr. Wariner preachd in our Chapell after which followd the B: Sacrament and so also Mar: 25: when Mr. Wentworth preached, a kindsman of the Earle of Straffords.

Apr: 13th my Father order'd that I should begin to manage myne owne Expenses; which ('til then) my Tutor had don, at which I was much satisfied.

July 1: I received the B: Sacr: one Evet, preaching.

The 9th following, I went home to visite my friends and the 26t, with my Bro: and Sister to Lewes, where we aboad till the 31, and thence, to one Mr. Michaels of Haughton neere Arundel (where we were very well treated) and the 2d of Aug: to Portsmouth; and thence having surveyd the fortifications (a greate rarity in that blessed Halcyon tyme in England) my bro: Rich. and I passed into the Ile of Wight, to the house of my Lady Richards, in a place call'd Yaverland; but we returned to our Company the next morning, whom we over-tooke at Chichester, where having viewed the Citty, and faire Cathedrall, we lodg'd that night, and the day following return'd home.

9 Aug: I receiv'd the B: Sacrament in our Parish-Church.

About the beginning of September I was so afflicted with a quartan Ague, that I could by no meanes get rid of it untill the December following: This was that fatal Yeare, wherein the rebellious Scots oppos'd the King, upon pretence of the intro-duction of some new Ceremonies, and the Booke of Comm: Prayer; and madly began our Confusions, and their owne destruction too, as it proved in event.

⟨1639.⟩ I came back to Oxon (after my tedious indisposition, and to the infinite losse of my tyme) on the 14 of Jan: 1639, and now I began to looke upon the rudiments of Musick, in which I afterwards ariv'd to some formal knowledge, though to small perfection of hand because I was so frequently diverted, with inclinations to newer trifles.

14 ⟨April⟩, being Pascha Dr. Lawrence our Master preaching in the Chap: I received the B: S:

May 20, accompany'd with one Mr. Jo: Crafford (who afterwards, being my fellow-traveller in Italy, there chang'd his Religion) I tooke a journey of pleasure to see our Summerset-shire Bathes, Bristoll, Cirencester, Malmesbury, Abington, and divers other townes of lesser note; cursorily view'd, and return'd the 25t.

July 9, my Father sent for me home, and the 11th I receiv'd the B: Sa: at Wotton.

16. Sept: I went to Lewes, returning not till the 26t: so it was the 8th of Octob. e're I went back to Oxon.

December 14 according to injunctions from the heads of Colledges, I went (amongst the rest) to the Confirmation in St. Maryes; where after Sermon, the Bishop of Oxon: lay'd his hands upon us, with the usual forme of benediction prescrib'd: But this receiv'd (I feare) for the more part, out of curiosity, rather then with that due preparation and advise which had been requisite, could not be so effectual, as otherwise that admirable, and usefull institution might have been; and as I have since deplor'd it.

1640. Jan: 21, came my Bro: Richard from Schole, to be my Chamber-fellow at the University: he was admitted the next day, and Matriculated the 31th.

Feb: 16 was a Comm: againe in our Coll: and upon March the 25. my Father happning to be sick, sent both for me and my Bro: to come to him.

Apr: 11th, I went to Lond, to see the solemnity of his Majesties riding through the Citty in State to the Short Parliament, which began the 13 following; a very glorious and magnificent sight, the King circl'd with his royal diademe, and the affections of his People. But

The day after I return'd to Wotton againe, where I stay'd (my Fathers indisposition suffering greate intervalls) till Apr: 27th when I was sent to London to be first resident at the

Middle-Temple: so as my being at the University, in reguard of these avocations, was of very small benefit to me.

Upon May the 5t following, was the Parliament unhapily dissolved: and the 20th I return'd with my Bro: Geor: to Wotton, who was upon 28 of the same Moneth married at Albury, to Mrs. Caldwell (an heyresse of an antient Licestershire family) where part of the nuptials were celebrated.

June 10th, I repaired with my Bro: to the Tearme, to goe into our new Lodgings (that were formerly in Essex-Court) being a very handsome appartment just over against the Hall-Court; but 4 payre of stayres high; which gave us the advantage of the fairer prospect; but did not much contribute to the love of that impolish'd study; to which (I suppose) my Father had design'd me, when he payd £145 to purchasse our present lives, and assignements afterwards.

London, and especialy the Court, were at this period in frequent disorders, and greate insolencies committed by the abus'd and too happy Citty: in particular the Bish: of Canterburys Palace at Lambeth was assaulted by a rude rabble from Southwark; my Lord Chamberlayne imprison'd, and many Scandalous Libells, & invectives scatter'd about the streetes to the reproch of Government, and the fermentation of our since distractions; so that upon the 25. of June I was sent for to Wotton; and the 27th after, my Fathers indisposition augmenting, by advice of the Physitians, he repaired to the Bathe.

The 31. I went againe to Lond: to visite one Mr. Duncomb, a Relation of my Brothers Lady, who lay mortaly sick there, and the next day return'd: But on the 7th after, my Bro: Geo: and I, understanding the perill my Father was in upon a suddaine attaque of his infirmity; rod post from Guildford towards him, and found him indeede extraordinary weake. Yet, so, as that continuing his course, he held out till the 8th of September, when I returned ⟨with⟩ him home in his Litter; being, as we conceiv'd, something repair'd in his health.

Octob: 15. I went to the Temple, it being Michaelmas Tearme: and Oct: 30, I saw his Majestie (comming from his Northern expedition) ride in pomp, and a kind of Ovation, with all the markes of an happy Peace restor'd to the affections of his People; being conducted through Lond, with a most splendid Cavalcade; and on November following, the *third* (a day never to be mention'd without a curse) to that long, ungratefull, foolish and fatal Parliament, the beginning of all our sorrows for twenty yeares after, and the period of the most happy Monarch in the World—quis talia fando—.

But my Father being by this time enter'd into a Dropsy, which was an indisposition, the most unsuspected, being a person so exemplaryly temperate, and of admirable regiment; hastened me back to Wotton December 12. where the 24th following, being Thursday, between 12 and one at noone, departed this life, that excellent man, and indulgent parent; reteining his senses, and his piety to the last; which he most tenderly express'd in blessing us, whom he now left in the World, and the worst of tymes, whilst he was taken from the evill to come.

It was a sad, and lugubr(i)ous beginning of the Yeare, when on the 2d of Jan: 1640/1, we at night follow'd the mourning hearse to the Church at Wotton; where (after a Sermon, and funebral Oration, by the Minister) my Father was interr'd neere his formerly erected Monument, and mingled with the ashes of our Mother, his deare Wife.

But thus we were bereft of both our Parents in a period when we most of all stood in neede of their Counsell and assistance; especially my selfe of a raw, vaine, uncertaine and very unwary inclination; but so it pleased God, to make tryall of my Conduct, in a conjuncture of the greatest and most prodigious hazards, that ever the Youth of England saw; and if I did not amidst all this, impeach my Liberty, nor my Vertue, with the rest who made ship-wrack of both; it was more the infinite goodnesse, and mercy of God, then the least providence or discretion of myne owne, who now thought of nothing, but the pursute of Vanity, and the confus'd imaginations of Young men.

Upon the 27 of Jan: I went with my Bro: to London about finding my Fathers Office,[1] in which something that was then left me, was concern'd; there I aboad till the 17th of March when I returnd to Wotton.

Apr: 1: I went with my Bro: Rich: to Lewes to settle matters with some Tennants of mine there, and came back againe the 9th but upon the 15, I repaired to Lond: to heare, and see the famous Tryall of the Earle of Strafford, Lord Deputy of Ireland; who on

1 Probably an inquest on his property.

the 22d of March before had been summoned before both houses of Parliament, and now appear'd in Westminster-Hall, which was prepar'd with Scaffolds for the Lords and Commons, who together with the King, Queene, Prince, and flowre of the Noblesse were Spectators, and auditors of the greatest malice, and the greatest innocency that ever met before so illustrious an Assembly. It was Tho: Earle of Arundell & Surrey Earle Martial of England who was made high Stuard upon this occasion, and the Sequell is too well known.

On the 27th came over out of Holland the young Prince of Orange, with a splendid equipage, to make love to his Majesties eldest daughter, the now Princesse-Royall, and that evening were celebrated the pompous funeralls of the Duke of Richmond, who was carried in Effigie in a⟨n⟩ [open] Charriot through Lond: in greate solemnity.

29, I kissed the Prince of Wales his hand, in the Lobby behind the house of Lords, and return'd to Wotton on the 30th, where I receiv'd the B: Sacr: the next Sonday.

May: 7th I went againe to Lond: with my Bro: and on the 12th following beheld on Tower-hill, the fatal Stroake, which sever'd the wisest head in England from the Shoulders of the Earle of Strafford, whose crime coming under the cognizance of no human-Law, a new one was made, not to be a precedent, but his destruction, to such exorbitancy were things arived.

TRAVELS IN THE NETHERLANDS
(1641)

THE 23D I receiv'd the B: Sac: and the next day returned to Wotton, and went to Lond againe June 28 with my sister Jane: The day after I sate to one Vanderborcht for my Picture in Oyle,* which I presented her, being her request upon my resolutions to absent my selfe from this ill face of things at home, which gave

---

* Expanded and added to in V: I sate to one Vanderborgh for my Picture in Oyle, at Arundel house, whose servant that Excellent painter was, brought out of Germany, when that earle returned from *Vienna*, (whither he was sent Am⟨b⟩assador Extraordinary with greate pomp & charge; tho' without any

umbrage to wiser then my selfe, that the Medaill was turning, and our calamities but yet in their infancy: so upon July the 15, having procur'd a passe at the Costome-house where I repeated my oath of Allegeance, I went the 16th from Lond: to Gravesend, accompany'd with one Mr. Caryll, and our Servants, where we arived by 6 that Evening, with a purpose to take the first opportunity of a passage for Holland; but the Wind as yet not favourable, we had tyme to view the Blockhouse of that Towne, which answer'd to another over against it at Tilberry (famous for the Rendezvous of Queene Eliz: in the yeare 88:) which we found stor'd with 20 piece of Cannon, and other ammunition proportionable: The 19th we rod to Rochester, and having seene the Cathedrall, we went to Chatham to see the Sovraigne, a mo⟨n⟩strous Vessel so call'd, being for burthen, defense and ornament the richest that ever spread cloth before the Wind; and especially for this remarkable, that her building cost his Majestie the affections of his Subjects, who quarreld with him for a trifle (as it was manag'd by some of his seacret Enemys, who made this an occasion) refusing to contribute either to their

---

Effect, thro' the artifice of the Jesuited Spanyard, who govern⟨ed⟩ all in that Conjuncture:) with Vanderburgh the Painter he brought over Winceslaus *Hollar*, the *Sculptor*, who Ingrav'd not onely this unhapy Deputys Triall in Westminster Hall, but his Decapitation, as he did severall other Historicall things then relating to the Accidents hapning during the Rebellion in England, with greate Skill, besides many Cittys, Towne⟨s⟩, Landscaps not onely of this Nation, but of forraine parts, & divers portraits of famous person⟨s⟩ then in being, & things designed from the best pieces of the rare Paintings & Masters of which the Earle of Arundel was possessor, purchased by and Collected in his Travells, with incredible Expense; so as tho' *Hollars* were but *Etched* in Aq: Fortis I accou⟨n⟩t the Collection to be the most authentiq, and usefull, extant, who have spent their time & paines in publishing Pagan Storys, fancys & fables curiously indeed Ingraved but altogether Uselesse: Holler was the son of a gent: neere Prage in Bohemia, and my very good friend, perverted at last by the Jesuits at Antwerp to chang his Religion, a very honest simple well meaning man, who at last came over againe into England where he died: We have the whole History of the Kings ⟨Reign⟩, from his Triall in Westminster Hall & before to the Restauration of Char: IId represented in severall Sculptures, with that also of A. Bish Laude, by this indefatigable Artist, besides innumerable Sculps in the Works of Dugdal, ⟨Ashmole⟩ & other Historicall & usefull Works: I am the more particular upon this, for the fruite of that Collection, which I wish I had intire.

owne safty, or his glory.* We return'd againe this evening and
⟨on⟩ the 21, nine in the morning, embarqued in a Dutch Fregat
bound for Flushing, convoyd and accompanied by five other
stoute Vessells, whereoff one was a Man of Warr, whose assistance we might have needed, if the two Saile which we discover'd to make towards us about midnight (and with whom we all
prepar'd for an encounter) had proved to be the enemy which we
apprehended; but finding them Norrway-Marchands onely, as
we approch'd, we at 4 in the morning discry'd the coast of Flanders, and by noone, with a fresh Gale (which made it the most
pleasant passage could be wished) we landed safely at Flushing
in Zeland.

And now me thought the Seane was infinitely chang'd, to see
so prety and neate a towne in the frontier: Here we first went to
view the Pr: of Oranges house and garden, the Wales whereof
are washed with Neptune continualy; after that the State-house,
which are generaly in all the Low countries magnificently built;
but being desirous to over-take the League which was then
before Genep, 'ere the summer should be too far expir'd, we
went this Evening to Midelbrogh, another sweete towne in this
Iland of Walcheria; and by night to Der-Veere, from whence
upon the 23d we embarqued for Dort: I may not forget that
being insufferably tormented with the stitch in my side, caus'd
through the impetuous motion of the Wagon, which running very swiftly upon the pav'd Cause-ways, give a wonderfull
concussion to such as are unacquainted with that manner of

---

* Expanded in V: we made a short excursion to *Chatham* (neere Rochester), to
see the *R. Sovraine* now lately built there, a glorious Vessel, of burden, Defence
and rich Ornament, doubtlesse one of the most admirable naval Fabriks, that
ever spread Cloth before the wind: She carried 1000 Brass: Cannon, & was
1200 Tunn, a rare sayler, the Work of the famous Naupegus Phynies Pet, Inventor of the Fregat fashion of Building to this day practiz'd: But what is to be
deplored, as to this Vessel, is, that it cost his Majestie the Affections of his Subjects, perverted by the Malcontent greate-ones, who tooke occasion to quarrell,
for his having raised a very slight Tax for the building of this & Equipping the
rest of the Navy, without an Act of Parliament; tho' by the suffrage of the Major
part of Judges, the king might legaly do, in times of imminent danger, of which
his Majestie was best apprais'd. But this not satisfie⟨in⟩g a jealous party, it was
condemn'd as unprecedential, & not justifiable as to the R. Prerogative, &
accordingly the Judges removed out of their places, fin'd & imprison'd:

travelling; the Fore-man perceiving me ready to drop from my seate, immediately cur'd and easd me of my payne, by unbout-toning my doublet, and applying an handfull of [could] couch-grasse to my side.

We passe from Der-Veere over many Townes, houses and ruines of demolish'd suburbs &c which have formerly ben swal-low'd up by the sea; at what time no lesse then eight of those Ilands had ben irrecoverably lost, which put me in mind of the deluge, and that description of the Poet.

—————culmen tamen altior hujus
Unda tegit, pressæque latent sub gurgite turres.

Met: j.

By reason of an adverse wind, we were this night constrain'd to Lodg in our Vessel; but on the next day we landed at Dort, the onely virgin, and first towne of Holland.

This Citty is commodiously situated on the river of . . . . . . by which it is furnish'd ⟨with⟩ all German Commodities, and especialy Rhenish-Wines and Timber: It hath almost at the extreamity a very spacious, and venerable Church; a stately Senat-house wherein was holden that famous Synod against the Arminians 1618; and in that hall hangeth a Picture of the Pas-sion, an exceeding rare, and much esteemed piece.

It was in this Towne that I first observed the Storkes building on their Chimnies, and frequently feeding in the Streetes, with-out that any dares to molest them.

Being desirous to hasten towards the Army, I tooke Wagon this afternoone to Roterdam, whither we were hurried in lesse than an houre, though it be ten-miles distant; so furiously do these Fore-men drive. I went first to visite the greate Church; the Doole, and the Burse, the publique statue of the learned Erasmus, which of brasse and a goodly piece; as we pass'd, they shew'd us his house; or rather the meane Cottage wherein he was borne, over which there are extant this distic in capital letters.

Ædibus his ortus, mundum decoravit Erasmus,
Artibus ingenuis, Religione, Fide.

The 26, I pass'd by a strait, and most commodious River through Delft, to the Hague; in which journey, I observ'd divers

Leprous poore Creatures dwelling, and permitted to ask the charity of passengers, which is convey'd them in a floating box that they cast out; they live in solitary huts on the brink of the Water; & I was told, contract their dissease from their too much eating of fish.

Ariv'd at the Hague, I went first to the Queene of Bohemias Court, where I had the honor to kisse her Majesties hand; and severall of the Princesses, her daughters: Prince Mauris was also there, newly come out of Germany: and my Lord Finch, not long before fled out of England from the fury of the Parliament.* It was a fasting-day with the Queene, for the unfortunat death of her husband, and therefore the Presence had been hung with black-Velvet, ever since his disscease; after some discourse with her Majestie we went to our Lodging, and spent the next day in contemplating that most divertissant, and noble Village.

The 28, I went, by the like passage to Leyden, and by the 29th to Utricht, being 30 English miles distant (as they reckon by houres). It was now Kermas, or a Faire in this Towne; the streetes swarming with Boores and rudenesse; so that early the next morning (having visited the antient Bishops Court, and the two very famous Churches) I satisfied my curiosity till my returne, and better leasure: The 30th we came to Rynen, where the Queene of Bohemia hath a neate, & well built Palace,

---

* Expanded in V: Arived at the *Hague*. We first went to the Q. of *Bohemias* mourning Court, where we had the honour to kisse her Majesties hand; severall of her Daughters & Princes standing about her, & since disposed of to severall German Princes, Electors, &c in Marriage: among these was the Princesse Elizabeth, celebrated by the famous *Des Cartes* for her profound Learning, afterwards a Protestant Abbesse in Germ(any), as her Sister *Louise*, was of a Popish, at Ponthoise in France, so rarely accomplisht in the art of Painting, that by a peculiar talent she would draw the Pourtraicture of any she saw by memory onely: I have of this Princesses hand the Picture of the Vicountesse Mourdaunt, which she sent my Wife in Oyle, and a long ingenious & facetious letter, all in *Rebus's*, & *Hieroglypics*, drawn with a pen very Curiously, expressing (without words) what pass'd at the Hague, directed to the old Earle of Norwich, from whom it came to my hands: Here were likewise Prince *Maurice*, nuly come out of Germany; he was Bro: to the Valiant *Pr: Rupert*: and in the time of the Rebellion, sailing for the *West Indys* in the Fleete under his Bro: was cast away in a Hurican: *Refugeès* from England, where the Greate Officers of State were (after this Buisinesse of Ship-mony (as they cald that Imposition) Imprisoned or Displact; One was Sir J. Finch, L. Keeper, escaping the fury of the Parliament, which design'd his head for the Block.

or Country house, built after the Italian manner, as I remember; and so crossing the Rhyne, upon which this Villa is situated, lodged that night in a Country-mans house.

The 31, I passed by Nimegen, built upon the rising brinke of the same River, having a strong Castle at one end of the Towne, which doth greatly improve the prospect: I went to see the Church, and the Fort of Naseburg, built by Pri: Maurice when he wonn this Citty, which in the time of Charles the 5t was an Imperial seate: The place is in Gelderland.

Two days after, being Aug: 2d, we ariv'd at the Leasure, where was then the whole Army encamped about Genep, a very strong Castle situated on the river Wahale, and Commanding all Cuke-Land; but being taken now foure ⟨or⟩ 5 days before, we had onely a sight of the demolitions, and upon the next Sunday was the thankesgiving-Sermonds, perform'd in Coll: Gorings Regiment (eldest sonne of the since Earle of Norwich) by Mr. Goffe, his Chaplaine (now turn'd Roman, and Fa: Confessor to the Q: Mother) his text being taken out of 107: Psal: v. 9th, and the evening spent in shooting of the Canon, and other expressions of Military Triumphs.

Now (according to the complement) I was receiv'd a Voluntéere in the Company of Cap: Apsley, of whose Cap: Lieutennant, Honywood (Apsley being absent) I received many civilities.

Aug: 3 at night we rod about the lines of Circumvallation, the Generall being then in the field: The next day I was accommodated with a very spatious, and commodious Tent for my Lodging, as before I was with an horse, which I had at command, and an Hutt, which during the excessive heates, was a very greate conveniency; for the sun peircing the Canvass of the Tent, it was during the day unsufferable, and at night, not seldome infested by the mists and foggs, which ascended from the river.

Upon the 6t as the turne came about, I watched on a horneworke, neere our quarters; and traild a pike; being the next morning reliev'd by a company of French: This was our continual duty, till the Castle was refortified, and all danger of quitting that station secur'd.

The 7th I went to see a Convent of Franciscan Friers, not far from our Tents, where we found them at their devotions; and both their Chapell, & Refectory full of the goods of such poore

people as at the approch of the Army, had fled with them thither
for Sanctuary. On the day following I went to view all the
trenches, aproches, and Mines &c of the besiegers; and in particular I tooke speciall notice of the Wheele-bridg, which
Engine his Excellency, had made, to run over the moate, when
they storm'd the Castle; as it is since described (with all the
other particulars of his seige) by the Author of that incomparable Worke, Hollandia illustrata: the incredible thicknesse of
the Walls, and ramparts of Earth, which a mine had broaken,
and crumbl'd all to ashes, did much astonish me.

Upon the 8, I din'd in the horse quarters, with Sir Robert
Stone, and his Lady; Sir William Stradling and divers Cavaliers;
where there was very good cheere, but hot service for a young
drinker as I then was: so that being pretty well satisfied with the
confusion of Armies, & seiges (if such, that of the United-
Provinces may be call'd, where their quarters, and encampments
are so admirably regular, and orders so exactly observed, as few
Cittys, the best disciplin'd, do in the World exceede it, for all
Conveniences) I tooke my leave of the League, and Camerades;
and on the 12 of Aug. embarked upon the Wahal (where the
Prince had made a huge bridge of boates), in the company of
three grave divines, who entertaynd us a greate part of our passage with a long dispute concerning the lawfulnesse of Church
Musick: Here we sailed by the Towne of Teile, where we landed
some of our fraight, and about five a clock we touch'd at a pretty
Towne nam'd Bommel, that had divers English in Garnison; it
stands upon Contribution Land, which subjects the environs to
the Spanish incursions: We saild also by an exceeding strong
fort, call'd Lovestine (the appellative of a well knowne party in
Holland) [famous for the Escape of the learned Grotius by a
Stratagem of his Lady convey⟨ing him⟩ out instead of a Trunk of
Books] and soone after by another Towne Worcom, but we
landed at the opposite Gorcom that night; a very strong &
considerable frontiere.

13 We arived late at Roterdam, where was at that time their
annual Mart or Faire, so furnish'd with pictures (especially
Landscips, and Drolleries, as they call those clownish representations) as I was amaz'd: some of these I bought and sent into
England. The reason of this store of pictures, and their cheape-
nesse proceede from their want of Land, to employ their Stock;

so as 'tis an ordinary thing to find, a common Farmor lay out two, or 3000 pounds in this Commodity, their houses are full of them, and they vend them at their Kermas'es to very greate gaines.*

Here I first saw an Eliphant, who was so extreamely well disciplin'd and obedient, that I did never wonder at any thing more: It was a beast of a mo⟨n⟩strous size, yet as flexible and nimble in the joynts (contrary to the vulgar tradition) as could be imagin'd from so prodigious a bulke, & strange fabrick; but I most of all admired at the dexterity, and strength of his proboscis, on which he was able to support two, or three men, and by which he tooke, and reached what ever was offer'd him; his teeth were but short being a femal, and not old, as they told us. I was also shew'd a Pelican, or rather (as I conjectur'd) the Onocratulus of Pliny, having a large bill, tip'd with red, and pointing downewards a little reflected; but what is most prodigious, the under part, annex't to a gullet, so wide, and apt to extend; and would easily have swallowd, a little child: The plumage was white, wall-eyd, the legge red and flatt footed; but in nothing resembling the picture, and description of the fabulous Pelican; which when I told the testy old-man who shew'd it; he was very wroth. There was also a Cock with 4 leggs; but what was most strange, with two rumps or vents, one whereof was at his breast; by which he likewise voyded dongue, as they assur'd us: There was with this fowle an hen having two large Spurrs growing out at her sides, and penetrating through the feathers of her wings.

Upon Aug. 17 I passed againe through Delft, visited the Church, where was the monument of Prince William of Nassau, a peace of rare art; There lyeth likewise intombed with him, his sonn & successor Grave Maurice.

The Senat-house of this Citty, hath a very stately Portico, supported with very choyce Pillars of black-marble; being, as I remember of one entire stone: and within, there hangs up a certaine weight⟨y⟩ vessell of Wood (not much unlike to a butter-Churne) which the adventurous Woman that hath two husbands

---

* In V: so as 'tis an ordinary thing to find a Common Farmer to lay out 500 or 600 pounds & more in this Commodity, & that keepe Painters at work in their house: and some not ill don, & generaly vended at these Faire⟨s⟩, whence so many Dutch paintings are carryed all Europ over:

at one time is to weare for a time about the Towne, her head
comming out at the hole, & the rest hanging on her shoulders,
as a pennance for incontinency:

From hence we went the next day to see Risewick, a stately
country house of the Prince of Oranges; but for nothing more
remarkable then the delicious walkes planted with Lime-trees,
and the moderne paintings within. We return'd this evening to
the Hague, and the next day went to visite the Hoff, or Princes-
Court, with the adjoyning Gardens, which were full of ornament, close-Walkes, Statues, Marbles, Grotts, Fountaines, and
artificiall Musique &c. There is to this Palas a very stately Hall,
not much inferior to ours of Westminster, hung round with
Colours, and other Trophys taken from the Spanyard; & the
sides below are furnish'd with shopps. I return'd the next day to
Delft, and thence to Rotterdam, whenc againe to the Hague
Aug: 20: (as my buisinesse requird, which was to bring some
Company on their way) and that Evening ariv'd at Leyden
where immediatly I mounted a Wagon, which that night (as late
as it was) brought us to Harlaem and almost to the end of my
Last Journey; for I tooke such a Cold, as was like to kill me:
About 7 in the Morning, I came to Amsterdam, where being
provided of a Lodging, I procur'd to be brought to a Synagogue
of the Jewes (it being then Saturday) whose Ceremonies, Ornaments, Lamps, Law, and Scholes afforded matter for my wonder
and enquiry: The Women were secluded from the men, being
seated above in certaine Galleries by themselves, and having
their heads mabbl'd with linnen, after a fantasticall & somewhat
extraordinary fashion: From hence I went to a place (without
the Towne) calld Over-kirk, where they had a spacious field
assign'd them for their dead, which was full of Sepulchers, and
Hebrew Inscriptions, some of them very stately, of cost: In one
of these Monuments, looking through a narrow crevise, where
the stones were disjoynted, I perceived divers bookes to lye,
about a Corps (for it seemes ⟨they use⟩ when any learned Rabby
dies, to bury some of his Bookes with him, as I afterwards
learn'd): of these, by the helpe of a stick that I had in my hand,
I raked out divers leaves, which were all writen in Hebrew Characters but much impair'd with age, & lying. As we return'd we
stepp'd in to see the Spin-house of Amsterdam, which is a kind
of Bride-well, where incorrigible and Lewd Women are kept in

Discipline and Labour; but in truth all is so sweete and neate, as there seemes nothing lesse agreable then the persons and the place. Here we were shew'd an Hospital erected for poore Travelors and Pilgrimes (as they told us) by Queene Eliz: of England, and another maintaind by the Citty. The State, or Senat-house of this vast Towne is (if the designe be perfected) one of the most costly, and magnificent pieces of Architecture in Europ; especialy for the materialls, & the Carvings, which exceedes all description. In the Doole, there is paynted on a very large table Maria de Medices her statue to the breast, supported by fower royal Diademes, the Worke of one Vandall, who hath set his name thereon. 1. Sept: 1638.

Upon Soneday, I went to heare an English Sermon, at the Presbyterian congregation; where they had chalked up the Psalmes upon a slate, which were that day to be sung; so placed, as all the congregation might see it, without the bidding of a Cleark: There was after sermon a Christning celebrated according to their fansy, which was homely enough. I was told, that after such an age no Minister was permitted to preach but had his maintenance continu'd during life.

I now expressly chang'd my Lodging, out of a desire to converse amongst the Sectaries that swarm'd in this Citty, to which gaine made every new-fangle acceptable. It was at a Brownists house, where we had an extraordinary good Table; There was in pension with us my L: [Keeper] Finch, and one Sir Jo: Fotherbee; here I also found an English Carmelite, that was travelling through Germanie towards Rome with another Irish Gentleman. I went to see the Weesehouse, which is a foundation like our Charter-house in designe, for the education of decay'd Persons, Orphans, and poore Children, where they are taught severall occupations; and, as I learn'd, the Wenches are so well brought up to housewifry, that men of good worth (who seeke that chiefely in a Woman) frequently take their Wifes from this Seminary. Hence we were carried to see the Rasp-house, where the lusty Knaves are compelld to labour, and it is a very hard labour, the rasping of Brasill, & Log-wood for the Diers, appointed them by their Task-masters. Thence to the Dull-house, a place for mad persons & fooles, like our Bethleem: But none did I so much admire as an Hospitall for their lame and decrepid souldiers, it being for state, order & accommodations one of the worthiest things that I thinke the world can shew of that nature: Indeede it is most remarkable, what provisions are here made and maintain'd for publique and charitable purposes, and to protect the poore from misery, and the Country from beggers.

It was on a Sunday morning about 11, that I purposely went to the Bourse (after the sermons were ended) to see their Dog-market, which lasts till two after-noone. I do not looke on the structure of this Exchange to be comparable to that of Sir Tho: Gresshams in our Citty of Lond: yet in one respect it exceeds, that ships of considerable burthen ride at the very key contiguous to it; and realy it is by extraordinary industry, that as well this Citty, as almost generaly the Townes of Holland, are so accommodated with Grafts,[1] Cutts, Sluces, Moles & Rivers, that nothing is more frequent then to see a whole Navy of Marchands & others environ'd with streetes & houses, every particular mans Barke, or Vessell at anker before his very doore, and yet the Streetes so exactly straite, even, & uniforme that nothing can be more pleasing, especialy, being so frequently planted and shaded with the beautifull lime trees, which are set in rowes before every mans house, affording a very ravishing prospect.

The next day we were entertain'd at a kind of Tavern, calld the Briloft, appertaining to a rich Anabaptist, where in the upper romes of the house were divers pretty Water workes rising 108 foote from the ground, which seem'd very rare, till the Engine was discovered: here were many quaint devices, fountaines, artificiall musique, noyses of beasts & chirping of birds &c: but what I most admir'd then, was a lamp of brasse, projecting eight soccketts from the middle stemm, like to those we use in Churches, which having counterfeit lights or Tapers in them, had streames of Water issuing, as out of their Wieekes or Snuffs: the whole branch hanging all this while loose upon a ⟨s⟩talk in the middst of a beame, and without any other perceptible commerce with any pipe; so that unlesse it were by compression of the ayre with a syringe, I could not comprehend how it should be don. There was likewise shew'd as a rarity, a Chime of Purselan dishes, which fitted to clock-worke, rung many changes, and tunes without breaking.

1 Properly ditches or moats; here canals with quays (Dutch *gracht*).

At another place of this Citty, we saw divers other Water-workes; but nothing more surpriz'd me than that stately, and indeede incomparable quarter of the Towne, calld the Keisers-Graft, or Emperors Streete, which appeares to be a Citty in a Wood, through the goodly ranges of the stately & umbragious Lime-trees, exactly planted before each-mans doore, and just at the margent of that goodly Aquæ-duct, or river, so curiously wharfed with Clincar'd, (a kind of White sun-bak'd brick) & of which material the spacious streetes on either side are paved. This part of Amesterdam is built, and gained upon the maine Sea, supported by Piles at an immense Charge, but with ever-lasting foundations. Prodigious it is to consider those multi-tudes, and innumerable Assemblys of Shipps, & Vessels which continualy ride before this Citty, which is certainely the most busie concourse of mortall men, now upon the face of the whole Earth & the most addicted to commerce: Nor must I forget the Ports[1] & Issues of the Towne, which are very noble Pieces of Architecture, some of them modern; and so are their Churches (though more Gotick) where in their Turrets or Steeples, (which are adorn'd after a particular manner for cost, & invention) the Chimes of Bells are so rarely manag'd, and artificialy rung, that being curious to know whither the motion were from any extraordinary Engine, I went up into that of St. Nicholas (as I take it) where I found one who play'd all sorts of Compositions from the tablature before him, as if he had fingerd an Organ; for so were the hammers fastned with wyers, to severall keyes, put into a frame 20 foote below the Bells, upon which (by help of a Wooden instrument not much unlike a Weavers Shuttle that guarded his hand) he struck on the keys, and playd to admira-tion; all this while, through the clattering of the Wyers, dinn of the too neerely sounding bells, & noise that his wooden-gloves ⟨made⟩, the confusion was so greate, that it was impossible for the Musitian to heare any thing himselfe, or any that stoode neere him; Yet to those, who were at a distance, and especialy in the streetes, the harmony, and the time were most exact & agre-able. The South-Church is richly paved with Blak, and White-marble: The West is a new fabric: Generaly, there are in all the Churches in Holland Organs, Lamps, Monuments &c:

1 Gates.

carefully preserved from the fury, and impiety of popular reformers, whose zeale has foolishly transported them in other places rather to act like madmen, then religious.

Upon St. Bartholomews-day I went to Hundius's shop to buy some Mapps, greately pleasd with the designes of that inde-fatigable Person: Mr. Bleaw, the setter-forth of the Atlas's & other Workes of that kind is worthy seeing: At another shop I furnish'd my selfe with some shells, & Indian Curiosities; and so towards the end of August quitted the Towne, returning back againe to Harlem by that straite River which runs betweene them; and in earnest it is a most stupendious prospect, to looke back upon Amsterdam at the end of this River cutt 10 miles in length as straite as a line without the least flexure, and of compe-tent breadth to saile by one another: By the way it is not to be omitted, we were shew'd a Cottage where they told us dwelt a Woman, who had then been married to her 25th Husband; and being now a Widdow, was prohibited to marry for the future; yet it could not be proved, that she had ever made any of her hus-bands away, though the suspicion had brought her divers times to trouble.

Harlem is a very delicat Towne, and hath one of the fairest Churches of the Gotique designe, I had ever seene: There hang in the Steeple (which is very high) two Silver-bells, which they report were brought from Damiate in Egypt, by an Earle of Holland, in memory of whose successe, they are rung out every Evening. In the Nave or body of the Church, hang the goodliest branches of brasse for tapers that ever I had seene, esteemed of greate value for the curiosity of the Workmanship: also a very faire payre of Organs, which I could not find they made any use of in Divine-Service or so much as to assist them in their singing of Psalmes (as I suppos'd) but onely for shew, and to recreate the people before and after their Devotions, whilst the Burgomasters were walking and conferring about their affaires:

There likewise hangs up, neere the West-Window (as I remember) two modells of Shipps, compleately equipp'd, in memory of that invention of Saws under their keeles, with which they cutt the Chayne before the port of Damiate. Having visited this Church, the Fishmarket, and made some enquiry about the Printing-house, the Invention whereof is sayd to have been in this towne, I return'd to Leyden, that renowned University of

Batavia: Here, the better to take view of the Citty, I was carried
up to the Castle or Pyrgus, built on a very steepe mount artificialy cast up, as 'tis reported, by Hengist the Saxon at his returne
out of England; as a place to retyre to when by any unexpected
accident, the Inhabitants should be threatned with suddaine
inundations. There is nothing observable in it besides a very
profound Well, in which they say a very monstrous fish was
found, and drawne forth when being beseiged, those of this
Castle were almost famished, the throwing of which over the
wales amongst the assaylants, caus'd them to raise the seige.
The Churches are many, and very faire. In one of them lyes
interr'd that Prodigy of Learning, the noble & illustrious
Joseph Scaliger, without any extraordinary inscription, as having himselfe left so many Monuments of his Worth behind
him, more lasting then Marble, besides his Library to this
University.

The 28, I went to see their Colledg, and Schooles, which are
nothing extraordinary; and was Matriculated by the then Mag-
nificus Proffessor who first in Latine demanded of me where my
Lod⟨g⟩ing in the Towne was; my Name, Age, birth; & to what
faculty I addicted my selfe; then recording my Answers in a
Booke, he administred an Oath to me, that I should observe the
Statutes, & Orders of the University, whiles I stay'd, and then
deliver'd me a tickett, by virtue whereof I was made Excise-free;
for all which worthy Priveleges, and the paines of Writing, he
accepted of a Rixdollar. Here was the famous Dan: Heinsius,
whom I so long'd to see; as well as the E⟨l⟩zivirian Printing
house & shop, renown'd for the politenesse of the Character, &
Editions of what he has publish'd through Europ. I went also to
visite their Garden of Simples, which was indeede well stor'd
with exotic Plants, if the Catalogue presented to me by the
Gardiner be a faithfull register. But amongst all the rarities of
this place I was much pleasd with a sight of their Anatomy
Schole, Theater & Repository adjoyning, which is very well furnish'd with Naturall curiosities; especially with all sorts of Skeletons, from the Whale & Eliphant, to the Fly, and the Spider,
which last is a very delicat piece of Art, as well as Nature, how
the bones (if so I may name them) of so tender an Insect, could
possibly be separated from the mucilaginous parts of that
minute animal. Here is the Sceletus of a Man on Horse-back, of

a Tigar, and sundry other creatures: The Skinns of Men & Women tentur'd[1] on frames & tann'd: Two faire and entire Mummies, Fishes, Serpents, Shells, divers Urnes; The figure of Isis cut in wood of a greate Proportion & Antiquity; a large Crocodile; The head of the Rynoceros; The Leomarinus, Torpedo, many Indian Weapons, Curiosities out of China, & of the Eastern Countries; so as it were altogether ⟨impossible⟩ to remember all, or take particular notice of them; though I could not forget that knife which they here shew'd us, newly taken out of a Drunken Dutch-mans gutts, by an incision in his side, after the sottish fellow had swallow'd it, when tempting to make himselfe vomit, by tickling his throat with the handle of it, he let it slip out of his fingers into his stomac, and had it taken out againe by the operation of that dextrous Chyrurgeon, whose Picture is together with his Patients preserv'd in this excellent Collection, and both the Persons living at my being in Holland.

There is somewhat without the Towne a faire Maill, curiously planted: Returning to my Lodging I was shew'd the happy Monke, whom they report to have been the first inventor of Typography, his statue being cut in stone, and set over the doore; but this is much controverted, by others who strive the glory of it besides John Guttenberg.[2]

I was the next day brought acquainted with a Burgundian-Jew who had married an Apostate Kentish-Woman: I asked him divers questions, and, amongst the rest, remember he told me that the World should never end: That our Soules transmigrated; & that even those of the most holy persons did Pennance in the bodys of bruits after death; & so he interpreted the banishment & salvage life of Nebucadnezar. That all the Jewes should rise againe and be lead to Jerusalem: That the Romans onely were the occasion of our Saviours death, whom he affirm'd (as the Turkes do) to be a greate Prophet but not the Messias: He shewed me severall bookes of their devotion, which he had translated into English for the instruction of his Wife; and told me that when their Messias came all the Ships, Barkes, & Vessells of Holland should by the powers of certaine strange Whirle-winds, be loosed from their Ankers and transported in a

1 Tentered, stretched.
2 This passage is misplaced: it refers to Haarlem.

moment to all the desolat ports & havens throug⟨h⟩out the world, where ever the dispersion was, to convey their Breathren & Tribes to the Holy Citty; with other such like stuff, and so I tooke my leave of the lying-Jew, whom I found to be a merry dronken fellow; but would by no meanes handle any mony (for something which I purchas'd of him) it being Saturday; but bid me leave it in the Window of his house: meaning to receive it on Sonday following.

Sep: 1. I went hence to Delft, thence to Roterdam the next morning, and two days after back to the Hague againe to bespeake a Suite of Armor which I causd to be made to fit me, with the harnasse of an Horse man.

I [now] rod out of Towne to see the Monument of the Woman, reported to have borne as many Children as are dayes in the Yeare: The Basins wherein they were baptis'd, together with a large Inscription of the mat⟨t⟩er of fact is affixed to the Tomb, & inchased in a Compartment of Carved Worke, in the Church of Lysdune, a desolate plase.

As I return'd we diverted to one of the Princes Palaces call'd the Hoff van Hounslers dyck, which is in truth a very magnificent Cloyster'd and quadrangular building: The Gallery is prettily paynted with severall huntings; and at one end thereof, a Gordian Knot, with severall rusticall Instruments so artificially represented, as would deceive an accurate Eye to discerne it from true Relievo. There is in this house a faire Staire-Case well contrived, having in the Domo, or Ceiling the rape of Ganymede painted, and other pendent figures, the Worke of F: Couenberg, of whose hand I bought an excellent drollery, which I afterwards parted with to my Bro: Geo: Evelyn of Wotton, where now it hangs: To this Palace joynes a faire Garden and Parke, curiously planted with Limes.

Being furnish'd at the Hague with some things which I wanted, I returned September 8th towards Roterdam through Delfts-haven, and Seedam, where was at that time Coll: Gorings Winter-quarters: This Towne has heretofore been very much talk'd of for Witches.

September 10th I tooke Wagon for Dort, to be present at the Reception of Queene-Mother Maria de Medices Dowager of France, Widdow of Henry the Greate, and Mother to the French King Lewes xiiith, and Queene of England, whence she newly ariv'd toss'd to and fro by the various fortune of ⟨her⟩ life; From this Citty she design'd for Collin,[1] conducted by the Earle of Arundell, and the Here van Brederod: I saw at this enterview the Princesse of Orange, and the Lady her daughter, afterward married to the house of Brandenbourg: There was little remarkable in this reception befitting the greatenesse of her Person, but an universal discontent, which accompany'd that unlucky Woman whereever she went. The next day I return'd to Roterdam to dispatch a servant of mine with some things into England.

Sep: 12th, I went towards the *Busse* [Bosleduke] passing by the Schone of the Grave, a most invincible fort, neere to which is another calld Jack a tra, not far from Ingle: We arrived at Bosleduc on Sep: 16. at the time when the new Citadell was advancing with innumerable hands, and incomparable inventions for the draining of the Waters out of the Fenns & Moraces about it, being by Bucketts, Mills, Cochleas, Pumps and the like. Here were now 16 companies, and 9 tropes of Horse: They were also cutting of a new River to passe from the towne to a Castle not far from it, and here we split our skiff terribly, falling fowle upon another through negligence of the Master, who was faine to run on ground to our no little hazard: At our arrival a Souldier conveyed us to the Governor, where our names were taken, and our Persons examin'd very strictly.

17th I was permitted to walke the round, and view the Workes; and obtained Licence to visite a pretty Convent of Religious Women of the Order of St. Clara, permitted (it seemes) to enjoy their Monastery & maintenance undisturb'd by articles & capitulations at the Surrender of the Towne, now 12 yeares since; Where we had a Collation & very Civil entertaynement. They had a very neate Chapell, in which the heart of the Duke of Cleve, their Founder lies inhum'd under a plate of Brasse: Within the Cloyster is a Garden, and in the middle of it an over-growne Lime-tree, out of whose stem, neere the roote, issue 5 upright & exceeding tall suckers or boles, the like whereof for evenesse & height I had not observd.

The Chiefe Church of this City is curiously carved within, & without; furnish'd with a paire of Organs, & a magnificent Font,

1 Cologne.

or Baptistery all of Copper. The 18, I went to see that most impregnable Fort & Towne of Hysdune, where I was exceedingly oblig'd to one Coll: Crombe, the Lieutenant-Governor, who would needes make me accept the honor of being Cap: of the Watch, & to give the Word this night. The Fortification is very irregular; but esteem'd one of the most considerable for strength, & situation, not onely of the Neither-Lands, but of the World.

On the 18 we departed towards Gorcum, in which passage we discover'd a Party lurking on the shore neere Bomel; but they were to⟨o⟩ weake to atacque us, being in a Mart-Ship, and well provided to receive them: Here, Sir Kenelme Digby travelling towards Colin met us. The next morning we ariv'd at Dort, passing by the Decoys where they catch innumerable quantities of Fowle.

On the 22d I went to Roterdam againe to receive a Passe, which I expected from the Cardinal Infanta, then Governor for the K: of Spaine his Bro: in Flanders, being desirous to see that Country in my returne for England whither I was now shaping my Course: And within two days after, having obtain'd another from his Highnesse the Pr: of Orange, upon the 24th of September I departed through Dort, attempting to sayle by the Keele, an obscure harbor so call'd, which the winds not permitting, we were constrayn'd to lye that night at Anker: 25th the next morning we made another Essay, but were againe repuls'd as far as Dort: The 26t, we put to sea afresh from the Keele; but a suddaine storme rising, with the Wind, and the Women (passengers) out-cries, we were forc'd to retyre into Harbor, where there lay threescore Vessells expecting fairer Weather. But we, impatient of the tyme, and inhospitablenesse of the Place set out againe the next morning early having the tyde propitious, though a most contrary and impetuous wind, passing so tirrible & overgrowne a Sea, as put us all in very greate jeopardy of our Lives; for we had much ado to keepe our selves above water, the billows breaking so desperately upon our Vessell, 'til it pleased God about noone to drive us in at a Towne calld William-Stat, a Place garnison'd by the English, where the Governor hath a faire house; the Workes, and especialy the Counterscarp is worthy of note, curiously hedg'd with a quick,[1] and planted with a stately

1 Quickset.

row of Limes on the Ramparts. The Church is of a round structure with a Cupola: Here I encounter'd two Polish noble-men,
who were travelling out of Germany, and had beene in Italy, very
accomplish'd persons.

It was now the 28 of Sept: when failing of an appointement,
I was constrain'd to returne againe to Dort, for a Bill of
Exchange; but it was the 1 of Octob: 'ere I could get back, when
at the Keele I numberd 141 Vessells, who durst not yet adventure
this fowle Passage: but we animated by the Master of a stout
Barke, after a small encounter of Weather ariv'd by 4 that
Evening at Stenebergen; In which passage we sailed over a Sea
call'd the Plaet, which is an exceeding dangerous Water by reason of two contrary tydes which meete very impetuously: Here,
because of the many Shelfes we were forc'd to tyde it along the
Channell in sight of two prety Townes call'd Oude Towne, &
Sommers Dyke: but 'ere we could gaine the Place the ebb was so
far spent, that we were compell'd to foote it at least a league
in a most pelting shower of raine. This is an exceeding impregnable fort.

Octob: 2. with a Gent: of the Rhyne-graves, I went in a Cart
(for it was no better, nor other accommodation could we procure) of two Wheeles & one horse to Bergen-op-Zome; by the
way meeting divers partys of his Highnesse Army, now retiring
towards their Winter-Quarters; the Convoy-Skiffs riding by
thousands, alongst the harbour. Having viewed the Workes
(which are wonderfull strong) and the Fort, built heretofore by
our Country-men the English, adjacent to the Towne; the
Church & Market-place, we spent the night with severall Commanders & Souldiers ⟨then⟩ in the Towne. The next morning
imbarked (for I had refus'd a Convoy of Horse which was
offered me) and came early to Lillo, landing short of the Fort, by
reason the tyde was against us, which constrain'd us to Land one
the beach, where we marched halfe-leg-deepe in mudd, ere we
could gaine the Dyke, which for being 5 or 6 miles distant from
Lillo we were forced to walke on foote very wett, and discompos'd: Then entering a Boate we pass'd the Ferry, and came into
the Castle; being first examin'd by the Sentinel, and conducted
to the Governor, who demanded my Passe, to which he set his
hand, and asked 2 Rixdollars for a fee, which me thought
appeared very unhandsome in a Souldier of his quality; I told

him, that I had already purchas'd my Passe to the Commissaries
at Roterdam, at which, in a great fury snatching the Paper out
of my hand, he flung it scornefully under a table, and bad me
try whether I could get to Antwerp without his permission: But
when I drew out the mony, he return'd it as scurvily againe; bidding me pay 14 dutch shill: to the Cantore or Searcher for my
contempt, which I was also glad to do with a greate deale of
Caution & danger, conceiling my Spanish-passe, it being a
matter of Imprisonment; for that the States were therein
treated by the names of Rebells; Besides all these exactions,
I g⟨a⟩ve the Commissary 6 shill: more, to the Souldiers something, and 'ere perfectly cleare of this Severe Frontiere 31 stivers
to the Man-of-Warr who lay blocking up the River, twixt Lillo,
and the opposit Sconce call'd Lifkinshoeek; Two such
Fortresses, as for their circuit are hardly to be paralleld in all
Europ besides. Thus on 4 of Octob: being (as I remember) Sonday, we passed the Forts of Santa Cruce; St. Philippo, Callò,
and St. Maria all appertaining to the Spaynard: Out of
St. Maria's came some Dons a'board us; and now I made use
onely of my other Passe, to which one of them put his hand,
receiving 6 guilders as a gratuity; These after they had sufficiently searched our Vessel, left us very courteously: Then we
pass'd by another Man-of-Warr to which we Lower'd o⟨u⟩r
top-saile, and so after many importunate accidents of this
nature twixt these two jealous States, we at last ariv'd safe at
Antwerp about 11 in the morning.

Here so soone as I had provided me of a Lodging (which are
in this Citty very handsome & convenient) I lost little tyme; but
with the conduct of one Mr. Lewkner, spent the afternone (being
a little refresh'd) in seeing divers Churches, Coledges, Monasteries &c: I exceedingly admir'd that sumptuous and most magnificent Church of the Jesuites, being a very glorious fabrique
without; & within wholy incrusted with marble inlayd & polish'd into divers representations of histories, Landskips, Flowers
&c. Upon the high Altar is plac'd the Statue of the B: Vergin &
our Saviour in White-marble, which has a bosse in the girdle
consisting of a very faire and rich Saphyre, with divers other
stones of price. There hang up in this Church divers Votive
tables & Reliques, containing the Pictures or Emblemes of severall dissasters, & recoveries. The Quire is a most glorious piece;

and the Pulpet supported with fowre Angels, adorn'd with other
carvings & rare Pictures wrought by the hand of Rubens now
newly deceased: I went hence unto the Vrou-kirke or Notre
Dame d'Anvers, which is the Cathedrall of this Citty: It is a very
venerable fabrique, built after the Gotick manner, and especialy
the Tower, which is in truth of an excessive height: This
I ascended, that I might the better take a view of the Country
about it, which happning on a day when the sunn shone exceedingly hot, and darted the rayes without any interruption,
afforded so bright a reflection to us who were above, and had a
full prospect of both the Land & Water about it, that I was
much confirm'd in my opinion of the Moones being of some
such substance as this earthly Globe consists of; perceiving all
the subjacent Country (at so smale an horizontal distance) to
repercusse such a light as I could hardly looke against; save
where the River, and other large Water within our View appeard
of a more darke & uniforme Colour, resembling those spotts in
the Moone, attributed to the seas there &c according to our new
Philosophy & the Phænomenas by optical Glasses: I number'd in this Church 30 priveleg'd Altars, whereof that of
St. Sebastians was rarely paynted.

Next we went to see Jerusalem Church, affirm'd to have been
founded by one, who upon divers greate Wagers, went to & fro
betweene that Citty & Antwerp on foote; by which he procur'd
greate Summs of mony which he bestow'd in this pious structure.[1] Hence to St. Marys Chapell, where I had some Conference with two English Jesuites, Confessors to Coll: Gage his
Regiment: These Fathers, conducted us to the Cloyster of Reli-
gious-Women where we heard a Dutch sermon at a Quarantia,
or Exposure of the Sacrament as they tearme it.

The Senat-house of this City is a very spacious and magnificent building.

Octob: 5. I visited the Jesuites-Scholes (which for the fame of
their method & institution, I had greately desir'd to see): they
were divided into 4 Classes with a several Inscription over each
of them; as, Ad majorem Dei gloriam the 1. Over the 2d was
Princips diligentiæ; the 3d Imperator Byzantiorum; over the 4th

---

1 This passage is misplaced: it (and, probably, the rest of the paragraph)
belongs to Bruges.

& Upmost Imperator Romanorum; under these, the Scholars &
Pupils had their Places or formes, with titles & priority according to their proficiency: Their dormitorys & Lodgings above,
were exceeding neate; Prisons they have for the offenders, &
lesse diligent; a Court to recreate themselves in, wherein is an
Aviary of Birds; besides Eagles, Foxes, Monke(y)s &c to divert
the Boys withall at their times of remission. To the house joyn'd
a Music, & Mathematical Scholes where they were also initiated
into those Studys; & lastly a pretty Chapell. I pass'd hence to the
greate Streete which is built after a more Italian mode, in
the middle whereof is erected a glorious Crucifix of White &
black-marble greater then the life. This is a very faire and noble
Streete; cleane, & sweete to admiration.

The Oesters-house, belonging to the East-India Company is
a most beautifull Palace, adorn'd with more then 300 Windows:
From hence walking into the Gun-garden I was suffer'd to see as
much of the Citadell as is easily permitted to strangers: It is
doubtlesse the most matchlesse piece of modern Fortification in
the World; for all contrivances of force, and resistance; incomparably accommodated with Logiaments for the Souldiers, &
magazines of Warr: The Graffs, ramparts, & Platformes are stupendious. Returning hence by the Shop of Plantine, I bought
some bookes for the namesake onely of that famous Printer: But
there was nothing about this Citty, which more ravished me
then those delicious shades and walkes of stately Trees, which
render the incomparably fortified Workes of the Towne one of
the Sweetest places in Europ; nor did I ever observe a more
quiet, cleane, elegantly built, and civil place then this magnificent and famous Citty of Antwerp, which caused me to spend
the next day in farther contemplation of it, & reviewing what
I had seene before; some few Palaces, Churches, Convents &
Ports &c 'til Evening, when I was invited to Signor Duerts, a
Portuguese by nation, an exceeding rich Merchant, whose
Palace I found to be furnish'd like a Princes; and here his three
Daughters, entertain'd us with rare Musique, both Vocal, &
Instrumental, which was finish'd with an handsome Collation:
And so I tooke leave of the Ladys, and of sweete Antwerp as late
as it was, embarquing my selfe for Bruxelles upon the Scheld, in
a Vessel which deliver'd us to a second boate (in another River)
drawn or taw'd by horses. In this passage we frequently chang'd

our Barge by reason of the Bridges thwarting our Course so frequently: Here I observed many numerous Familys to inhabite
their Vessells & floating dwellings, which were so built &
divided by Cabines, as few houses on land enjoy'd better accommodation; stor'd with all sorts of Utensiles; neate, Chambers, a
pretty Parlour, and kept so sweete and polite, as nothing could
be more refreshing: The rivers on which they are drawne, being
very cleare, & still waters & passe through a most pleasant
Country on both the bankes: We had in our Boate a very good
Ordnary, and excellent Company: The Cutt is as straite as a line
can possibly lay it for the space of 20 English-miles; and what
I much admir'd was, neere the mid-way, another artificial River,
which intersects this at right-angles; but upon an eminence of
Ground, which is therefore caryed in a Channel or Aqæduct of
stone so far abouve the other, as that the Waters neither mingle,
nor hinder one anothers passage. We came to a Towne call'd
Villefrow where is a very faire Castle, and here all the Passengers
went on shore to Wash at a certaine fountaine issuing out of a
Pillar, and so came abord againe. On the Margent of this long
tract, are aboundance of Shrines, and Images defended from the
injuries of the Weather, by the Niches of stone wherein they are
placed. Thus at 9 in the Morning, being Octob: 7th we ariv'd
at Bruxelles, where after I had a little dispatch'd some addresses;
I went first to visite the State-house neere the Market-Place;
being for the carving in free-stone a most laborious, &
⟨strangely⟩ finish'd Piece; well worth the observing.

The flesh-shambles is also built of stone: I was infinitely
pleas'd with certaine small Engines, and divices by which a silly
Girle or Boy was able to draw-up, or let-downe huge Bridges,
which in divers parts of the Citty crossed the Channell, for the
benefit of Passengers. The Wales of this Towne are very intyre,
and full of Towers at competent distances. The Cathedrall is
built upon a very high, & exceeding steepe ascent, to which we
mounted by faire stepps of stone: Hence I walked to a Convent
of English Nunns, with whom I sate discoursing most part of
this afternoone.

Octob: 8: (being the Morning I came away) I went to see the
Princes Court, which is an antient confus'd building, large &
irregular, not much unlike the Hofft, at the Hague; for there is
here likewise a very large Hall, where they vend all sorts of

Wares: Through this we passed by the Chapell which is indeede rarely ⟨arch'd⟩ and in the middle of it (at present) the Hearse or Catapalco of the late Arch-dutchesse, the wise & pious Clara Eugenia: Out of this, we were by a Spanyard conducted to the Lodgings, tapissryd with incomparable Aras; and adorn'd with many excellent pieces of Rubens; old, and young Breugle, Titian, Steen-wick; with stories of most of the late actions in the Netherlands. The Library I would very faine have seene; but by an accident, we could not at this tyme; Yet peeping through the key-hole, I perceived that the Bookes were placed in Presses, which were onely cancell'd[1] with gilt-wyre. There is a faire Terrace which respects the Vine-yard, in which upon Pedestalls are fix'd the Statues of all the Spanish Kings of the house of Austria; the opposite Wales paynted by Rubens, being an history of the late tumults in Belgia; in the last piece, the Arch-Dutchesse shutts a greate payre of Gates upon Mars, who is made comming forth out of Hel, arm'd, & in a menacing posture; which, with that other of the Infantas taking leave of Don Phelip the IVth is a most incomparable table. From this wee walked into the Parke, which for being intirely within the Walles of the Citty is particularly remarkable; nor lesse divertissant, then if in the most solitary recesses; So naturally it is furnish'd with whatever may render it agreable, melancholy & Country-like: for here is a stately Heronry; divers springs of Water & artificial Cascads, Rocks, Grotts, one whereoff being compos'd of the Extravagant[2] rootes of trees, and so cunningly built & hung together with Wyres, lookes very Extravagantly: There are in this Parke both Fallow & Red-deare. From hence we were led into the Manage, and out of that into a most sweete and delicious Garden, where was another Grott, of more neate & costly materials, full of noble Statues, and entertaining us with artificial musique: But it was the hedge of Water, which in forme of Lattice-Worke the Fontaniere caused to ascend out of the earth by degrees exceedingly pleased & surprizd me; for thus with a pervious Wall, or rather Palisad-hedge of Water, was the whole Parterr environd: There is likewise a faire Aviary; and in the Court next it are kept divers sorts of Animals, rare & exotic

1 Enclosed with lattice-work.
2 Straggling.

fowle; as Eagles, Cranes, Storkes, Bustars, Pheasants of Severall kinds, & a Duck having 4 Wings &c: In another division of the same Close, Connys of an almost perfect yellow Colour: There was no Court now in the Palace, the Infanta Cardinal, who was the Governor of Flanders being dead but newly, & every body in deepe Mourning, which made us quitt the Towne sooner than happly we should else have don.

It was now neere eleaven, when I repaird to his Majesties Agent Sir Henry De Vic, who very courteously receivd me and accommodated me with a Coach & six-horses, which carried me from Bruxelles to Gant, where it was to meete my Lord of Arundel, Earle Martial of England, who had requested me when I was at Antwerp to send it for him, if I went not thither my selfe.

Thus taking leave of Bruxelles, and a sad Court, yet full of Gallant Persons (for in this small Cittye the acquaintance being universal, Ladys & Gentlemen I perceiv'd had greate diversions and frequent meetings) I hasted towards Gant: Upon the Way, I met with divers little Wagons, pretily con-triv'd and full of pedling Merchandises, which were drawne by Mastive-Dogs, harnass'd compleately like so many Coach-horses; in some 4, in others six, according to the Charge they drew; as in the Towne of Bruxelles it selfe I had observed: In Antwerp I saw (as I remember) 4 dogs draw 5 lusty Chil-dren in a Charriot to my greate astonishment; the Master commands them whither he pleases, crying his Wares about the streetes.

I baited by the Way to refresh our horses at a pretty Towne call'd Ouse, and by 6 that Evening ariv'd at Ghendt.

Ghendt is an extravagant Citty of so vast a Circumference, that it is reported to be no lesse then 7 Leagues in compasse; but there is not an halfe part of it now built; much of it remain-ing in feilds and desolate pastures, even within the Wales, which has marvailous strong Gates towards the West, and two faire Churches, in one of which I heard a Sermon. Here I beheld the Palace wherein John of Gaunt, and Charles the Vt were borne, whose statue stands erected in the Market-place upon an high Pillar, with his sword drawn, to which (as I was told) the Magistrates and Burgers were wont to repaire upon a cer-taine day every yeare, with roaps about their necks, in toaken of submission & pennance for an old Rebellion of theirs: but now the Weede is changed into a blew ribbon. Here is planted the Basilisco, or monstrous gun so much talked of. ⟨The⟩ Ley and Scheld meeting in this vast Citty divide it into 26 Ilands which are united togethere by many bridges somewhat resembling Venice.

This night I supp'd with the Abbot of Andoyne, a pleasant and courteous Priest:

Octob: 8: I passed by Boate to Bruges, taking in a Convoy of 14 Musqueteeres by the way at a Redout, because the other side of the River being contribution land, was subject to the inrodes & depredations of the borduring States. This River was cut by the famous Marq: Spinola, and is, in my judgment, a wonderfull piece of Labour, and worthy publique worke, being in some places forced through the maine rock to an incredible depth for 30 miles: At the end of each mile is built a small Redout which communicats a line to the next; and so the whole way, from whence we received many volyes of shot in complement to my Lord Marshall who was in our Vessell a passenger with us: Thus about 5 that Evening we were met by the Magistrates of Bruges, who came out to convoy my Lord to his Lodging at whose cost he was entertayn'd that night. The morning after we went to see the State-house and adjoyning Aquæduct; the Church and Market-place, where I remember we saw Cheezes, & Butter [pild up] like heapes of Mortar: Also the Fortifications and grafts, which are incredibly strong & large:

The 9th we ariv'd at Ostend, by a straite & artificial River: Here with leave of the Captaine of the Watch, I was caryed to survey the river and harbour which fortifies one side thereof: The East & South are mud & earth Wales, one of the strongest places in my life I had seene: I then went to the Church of St. Peters, and the Cloyster of the Franciscans; & tooke more than ordinary notice of all for the memorable seige it endur'd not long before, of 3 yeares, 3 moneths, 3 Weekes & 3 dayes.

Octob: 10, I went by Wagon (accompany'd with a jovial Commissary) to Dynkirk, the journey was made all on the sea sands: On our arivall we first viewed the Court of Guards, The Workes, Towne-house and new Church (which is indeede very beautifull within) and another wherein they shew'd us an excellent piece of our B: Saviours bearing the Crosse. The Harbour in two Channells coming up to the Towne was choaked with a multitude of Prizes.* From hence I the next day marched 3 English miles towards the Packet-boate being a pretty Fregat of 6 Gunns, which embarked us for England about 3 in the afternoone: At our going off the Schrnken fort (against which our Pinnac ankerd) saluted my L: Martial with 13 greate gunns, which we answerd with 3. and so (not having the Wind favourable) after a little motion, ankerd that night before Calis: About midnight we weigh'd, and at 4 in the morning being not far from Dover, we could not yet make the Peere till 4 that afternoone, the wind proving contrary and driving us Westward; but at the last we got on shore, being the afternoone of Octob: 12th.

From Dover I that night rood Post to Canterbery, where I visited the Cathedrall, now in greatest splendor, those famous Windoes being intire, since demolish'd by the Phanatiques: The next morning by Sitinbourn, I came to Rochester; and thence to Graves-End, where a Light-horse-man (as they call it) taking us in, we spent our tide as far as Greene-Wich, whence after we had a little refresh'd at the Colledge (for by reason of the Contagion then in Lond: we baulked the Inns) we came to London, landing at Arundel Stayers, where I tooke leave of his Lordship, and retyr'd to my Lodgings in the Middle Temple, being about two in the morning the 14th of October.

---

* Expanded in V: The Harbour consists of two channels coming-up to the Towne, & was exceedingly full of Vessels, & aboundance of Prizes, which the Pikcarrons of this den of Thieves, take from the *Hollanders*, not without reciprocall Losses; so as one sees the streets full of Mariners & Souldiers, wanting legs & armes, the fruite of these adventurous people; The Port was at this time very inconvenient for any save those *Corsaire* Vessels, apt after stormes to be obstructed: But as the Towne is since exceedingly Inlarged; so the Fortifications, & Harbour has at the Cost of a million starling and more ben made one of the strongest Fortifications in *Europ*, & the *Peeres* far extended into the Sea, to ke⟨e⟩p it cleare of the rolling sands, rendered it at present capable to receive Men of War of greate burden: This greate Worke was begun & finished at the prodigious Expense of the French King, who bought it of our Charles the IId, by a greate oversight, as Polititians thinke: for tho in time of Peace, it be in no such importance, yet as it exceedingly strengthens all that Galic Coast; so in time of wars it proves a Cruel thorn in our sides; whilst the Harbour of *Dover* were it repaired, there might have ben a Sound between the two sides of that straite, made capable of shuting up that passage upon any occasion: But whether yet this was practicable, many doubted:

OCTOB: 16 I went to see my Bro: at Wotton, being the 31 of this Moneth (unfortunate for the Irish rebellion which brake out the 23) one & twenty Yeares of age.

No: 7: I received the B: Sac, at the Church of Wotton; and in the afternoone went to give my L: Martial a Visite at Albury:

Nov: 8 I went to Lewes to see my friends in Sussex, accompany'd with my two Brothers. The 13th I return'd, and the 23d to Lond: where on the 25t following I saw his Majestie ride through the Citty, after his comming out of Scotland and a peace proclaym'd, with greate acclamations and joy of the giddy people.

Decemb: 15, I was elected one of the Comptrollers of the Middle-Temple-Revellers, as the fashion of the Young Students & Gentlemen was; the Christmas being kept this Yeare with greate Solemnity; but being desirous to passe it in the Country, I got leave to resigne my Staffe of Office, and went with my Bro: Richard to Wotton. [Statues & heads set up in Temple hall:]

⟨1642⟩ Jan: 10th I gave a Visite to my Co: Hatton of Ditton and went the next to London, [13 Christend Mr. Smiths Sonn at Fan-Church for my Bro: George] returning the next day, but not to Wotton till the 18th.

29, I went againe to Lond, where I stayd till 5 March following, studying a little; but dauncing and fooling more:

[6: Feb: I received the B: S: at the Midle Temp: Church Dr. Littleton preaching: as also on Quadragessim Sunday:]

The 23d Mar: I tooke a journey with my Brothers to Northampton faire to buy some saddle horses, & returnd the 28 by St. Albans, where we visited the Church, and the ruines of old Verulame, where the L: Chancelor Bacons contemplative monument is the sole ornament worth remembring.

Apr: 13: I went from Wotton to Godstone [to visite Sir J. Evelyn] returning within two dayes: The 19 to Lond, where I remayn'd till May: 2d, & thence on the 5 to Lond. againe, tempted to adventure some monyes upon the Irish reduction; but there remaining some Scrupules, it did not succeede: so on the 23 I returnd to Wotton, till the 7th of June when I went

againe to Lond: whence on the 23d to Lewes in Sussex, returning the 25t.

July 6, I visited my Bro: at Wotton, from whence with both
my Bro: & sister we went Aug: 2 a journey of pleasure to Lewes,
where we left my sister for the rest of the Summer, returning on
the 5.

22 I went to Lond, & came back to Wotton 24th.

30th to Ditton: Sep: 2, to Wotton: Octob: 3d to Chichester,
and thence the next day to see the Seige of Portsmouth; for now
was that blody difference betweene the King and Parliament
broaken out, which ended in the fatal Tragedy so many yeares
after: It was on the day of its being render'd to Sir William
Waler, which ⟨gave⟩ me opportunity of taking my leave of Coll:
Goring the Governor now embarquing for France:

On the 6t I went from Portsmouth to ⟨Southampton⟩, lay at
Winchester, where I visited the Castle, Schole, Church & K:
Arthyrs round table; but especialy the Church and its Saxon
Kings Monuments, which I esteemed a worthy antiquity: On
the 7th I return'd to Wotton by Farne-ham & Guildford.

Octob: 3d was fought that signal Battaile at Edgehill:

31 I was 22 yeares of age.

No: 12: was the Battaile of Braineford[1] surprisingly fought, &
to the greate consternation of the Citty, had his Majestie (as
'twas beelievd he would) pursu'd his advantage: I came in with
my horse and Armes just at the retreate; but was not permitted
to stay longer then the 15th by reason of the Armys marching to
Glocester, which had left both me and my Brothers expos'd
to ruine, without any advantage to his Majestie.*

1 Brentford.
* Expanded, with errors, in V: I came with my Horse & Armes, & with some
mony presented to his Majestie by my Bro: was assigned to ride Volunteere,
amongst the Gent: in Pr: *Ruperts* Troop, who was general of the Horse: But the
King marching to *Glocester*, by which the Gentlemen whose Estates were in
Surry & Sussex lay in the immediate power of the Rebells, & would certainly
have ben seized as delinquents; nothing of my appearing in Armes, being
known, I was advis'd, to obtaine of his Majestie, leave to Travell; since my
Estate in the County, would have maintained more against his Majestie, than
I could, for him: So as having a Passe procur'd me by sir Ed: Nicholas, then Secretary of state, & a friend of our Family, (whence he had his rise in greate measure) under his Majesties hand, I began to resolve on my Returne & preparation
to passe into France:

Decemb: 7: I went from Wotton to Lond, to see the so much celebrated line of Communication, & on the 10th return'd: [no body knowing of my having ben in his Majesties Army:]

⟨1643⟩ Jan: 17 I went to Lewes, & return'd the 21:

[26 receivd the B: Sac:]

Feb: 7: to Lond: againe, returning the 11th.

March 3d To: Lond: from thence on the 10th to Hartingford-berry to Visite my Cousen Keightly:

The 11th I went to see my L: of Salisburys Palace at Hatfeild; where the most considerable rarity besides the house, (inferior to few for its Architecture then in England) was the Garden & Vineyard rarely well water'd and planted: They also shewd us the Picture of Secretary Cicil in Mosaique-worke very well don by some Italian hand.

I must not forget what amaz'd us exceedingly on the night before; viz, a shining clowd in the ayre, in shape resembling a sword, the poynt reaching to the North; it was as bright as the Moone, the rest of the skie being very serene; it began about 11 at night, and vanish'd not 'til about one, seene by all the South of England.

On the 13, I returnd to Lond, & on the 15 went to Wotton:

Apr: 2d I receiv'd the B: S:

The 10th I went to Ditton: 11th to Lond: 12 to Hartingford-bery againe: 15 to Hatfeild, and neere the Towne of Hartford went to se⟨e⟩ Sir J: Harris his house new built: 19 I return'd to Lond; calling in by the Way to see his Majesties House and Gardens at Theobalds, (since demolish'd by the Rebells) thence on the 21 to Wotton.

May 2d I went to Lond; where I saw the furious & zelous people demolish that stately Crosse in Cheapeside: The 4th I return'd with no little regrett for the Confusion that threaten'd us:

On the 15, to Lond: againe returning the 17th and resolving to possesse my selfe in some quiet if it might be, in a tyme of so greate jealosy, I built (by my Brothers permission,) a study, made a fish-pond, Iland and some other solitudes & retire-ments at Wotton, which gave the first occasion of improving them to those Water-Workes and Gardens, which afterwards succeded them, and became the most famous of England at that tyme.*

July 2: I received the B: Sac: On the 11th I went with my Bro: to Godstone to see Sir Jo: Evelyn:

The 12th I return'd, and sent my Black-[manage-]horse and furniture with a friend to his Majestie then at Oxford.

23 July, The Covenant being pressed, I absented my selfe; but finding it impossible to evade the doing of very unhandsome things; and which had been a greate Cause of my perpetuall motions hitherto betweene Lond: and Wotton: October the 2d, I obtayn'd a Lycense of his Majestie dated at Oxford, & sign'd by the King, to travell againe, so as on November 6, lying by the way at Sir Ralph Whitfeilds at Bletchinglee, (whither both my Brothers had conducted me) I arived at Lond: on the 7th and two dayes after tooke boate at the Tower-Wharfe, which carryd me as far as Sittinburne, though not without danger, I being onely in a payre of Oares expos'd to an hidious storme; but it pleas'd God, that we got in before the perill was considerable: From thence by Post I went to Dover accompany'd with one Mr. Thicknesse a very deare friend of mine:

TRAVELS IN FRANCE
(1643–1644)

ON THE 11TH having a reasonable good Passage, though the Weather were snowy & untoward enough, we came before Calais;

* Expanded in V: It was now, that yet *Balancing* whether I should go immediatly abroad, or stay a while to see what *Issue* this difference between the K. & Parliament would produce, that I made (by my Bro: permission) the stews & receptacles for Fish, and built a little study over a Cascade, to passe my Malencholy houres shaded there with Trees, & silent Enough: This trifle, however despicable, was the Occasion of my Bro: vast Expence, when some yeares after, he Inlarged the Gardens, built the Portico, & Cutt the Mount into the present shap(e) it now is of, with the fountaines in the Parterr, which were amenitys not frequent in the best Noble mens Gardens in England: This being finished whilst I was abroad, was conducted by a Relation of ours, *Georg(e) Evelyn* who had ben in *Italy*, but was mistaken in the Architecture of the Portico, which tho' making a magnificent shew, has greate faults in the *Colonade*, both as to the Order, which should have ben [Doric] *Corinthian* & the Ornaments, the rest is very tollerable:

where as we went on shore, mistaking the tyde, our shallop struck with no little danger on the sands; but at length we gott off.

Calais is an extraordinary well fortified Place consider'd in the old Castle, & new Citadell reguarding the Sea: The Haven consists of a long banke of Sand lying opposite to it: The Market-place and Church are very remarkeable things, besides those reliques of our once dominion there, so as I remember there was engraven in stone upon the front of an antient dwelling which was shew'd us, these words God save the King, in English, together with the name of the Architect and date: The Walls of the Towne are likewise very substantial, but the situation towards the Land not Pleasant in the least, by reason of the Marishes and low-grounds about it. The next day (being the 12th) after diner we tooke horse with the Messagere, hoping to have that night ariv'd at Bollogne; but there fell so greate a Snow, accompanied with hayle, raine & suddaine darknesse, as we had much a doe to retrive the next Village; and in this passage being to goe crosse a Vally where a Causeway and a Bridge was built over a small river, the raine that had fallen making it now an impetuous streame for neere a quarter of a mile, my horse slipping his ⟨footing⟩ had almost been the occasion of my perishing: This night we none of us went to bed, for the Souldiers in those parts leaving little in the Villages, we had enough to do to get ourselves dry by morning, between the fire and the fresh straw:

The next day early we ariv'd at Bollogne, where we were willing to recover some rest, though to the losse of a day:

Boullogne is a double towne, one part of it situate on an high rock or downes; the other call'd the Lower Towne is yet with a greate declivity towards the Sea; both of them defended by a strong Castle which stands on a notable Eminence: Under the Towne runs the River de Liane, which is yet but an inconsiderable brooke: This place is yet both a County, & a Bishoprick, but for nothing more remarkable to us, then the Seige of Hen: 8., when he made use of those letherne greate Gunns, which I have since beheld in the Tower of Lond: with this motto on them, Non Marte Opus est, cui non defficit Mercurius, if at least the history be true, which my L: Herbert doubts:

The next morning, through some danger of Partys surprizing us, we came to Monstreuil; It is built on the Summit of a most conspicuous hill, environd with faire & ample Meadows; but all the Suburbs had been from time to time ruin'd, and now lately burnt by the Spanish inroads. This Towne is exceedingly fortified with two very profound ditches, yet without Water; The walls about the Bastions, and Citadell are a noble piece of Masonry: The Church is more glorious without then within: The Market-place large, but the Inhabitans miserably poore.

From Montreuil we came the next day to Abbeville (having passd all this way in continual expectation of the Volunteeres as they call them) a Towne that affords a most gracious aspect towards the hill from whence we descended; nor indeede dos it deceive the Eye, for it is handsomly built, and has many pleasant & usefull streames passing through it, the maine river being the Somme which dos after wards discharge it selfe into the Sea at St. Valery almost in view of the Towne. The Principal Church is a very handsome piece of Gotique Architecture, and the Ports and Ramparts swee⟨t⟩ly built and planted for defence & ornament: In the morning they brought us choyce of Gunns & Pistolls to sell at reasonable rates, and neately made, being here a merchandize of greate account; so as the Towne abounds in Gun-Smiths.

Henc we advanc'd to Beavais, another Towne of good noate, and the first Vineyards we came at: The next day to Beaumont, & the morrow to Paris, having taken our repast at St. Denys within t⟨w⟩o Leagues of that greate Citty.

St. Denys is a towne considerable onely for its stately Cathedrall, and Dormitory of the French Kings who lye there inhum'd, as ours at Westminster: Not omitting the Treasury esteemed one of the richest in Europ.

The Church was built by K: Dagobert, but since much enlarged; being now no lesse then 390 foote long & 100 in bredth: 80 in height without comprehending the cover; it has also a very high shaft of stone, and the gates are of brasse:

Here whiles the Monke conducted us, we were shew'd the antient, and moderne Sepulchers of their Kings beginning from the founder to Lewes his son, with Charles Martel, Pepin ⟨his⟩ son, & father of Charlemagne, these lye in the Quire, & without more then as many more; amongst the rest Bertrand du Gues⟨c⟩lin Constable of France; in the Chapell of Charles V. all his posterity, and neere him that magnificent Sepulchre of Francis the first, with his Children, Warrs, Victories & Triumphs engraven in Marble: In the Nave of the Church lyes

the Catap⟨h⟩alc or hearse of Lewes XII. Hen: 2d; a noble tomb
of Fr: 2, and Charles IX.

We lay at Paris at the Ville de Venize, where after I had
something refresh'd, & put my selfe in equipage, I went to visite
Sir Rich: Browne, his Majesties Resident with the French King:

On the 5 of December, came the Earle of Norwich, Extraordinary Ambassador, whom in a Coach & six horses I went to
meete, at the Palais of Monsieur de Bassompieres, at Chaliot,
where I had the honor to see that gallant Person his Gardens,
Tarraces and rare Prospect: My L: was waited on by the Master
of the Ceremonies, and a very greate Cavalcade of men of
Quality to the Palais Cardinal. Where on the 23d he had Audience of the Fr: King and the Q: Regent his Mother, in the
Golden Chamber of Presence; from thenc I conducted him to
his Lodging in the rüe St. Denys & so tooke my Leave.

December 24 I went with some company to see some
remarkable places about the Citty; as the Isle, and how 'tis
encompassed by the Seine and Oyse rivers: The City is divided
into thre⟨e⟩ Parts, whereof the Towne is greatest: The City lyes
betwixt it and the University in forme of an Iland; Over the river
Seine is built a stately bridg (call'd Pont Neuf,) by Hen 3d 1578,
finished by Hen: 4th his Successor: It consists of 12 Arches, in
the middst of which ends the poynt of an Iland handsomely
built about with artificers houses. The Bridg above is very commodiously divided into one large Passage for Coaches, and two
for footemen 3 or 4 foote higher, and of convenient breadth for
8, or 10 to goe on brest; all of hewn free-stone the best I thinke
in Europ & growing in the very streetes, though more plentifully at Mont-Martyre within a mile of it. On the Middle of this
stately bridge upon one side stands that famous statue of Henry
le grand on horse-back exceeding the natural proportion by
much, and on the 4 faces of a stately Pedestal (which is all compos'd of various sorts of Polish'd-Marble and rich mouldings) is
engraven in brasse Inscriptions of his Victories, & most signal
actions: The statue and horse is of Copper, being the Worke of
the greate John di Bolognia, & sent from Florence by Ferdinando the first, and Cosimo the second, Unkle & Cousin to
Mary di Medices wife of Henry, whose statue it represents: The
Place where it is erected is enclos'd with a very strong and beautifull grate of Yron; about which there are allways Montebancs

shewing their feates to the idle passengers. From hence is a rare
Prospect towards the Louver, & Suburbs of St. Germaines, the
⟨Isle⟩ du Palais and Notre Dame. At foote of this Bridge is a
water-house, at the front whereof a greate height is the Story of
our B: Saviour and the Woman of Samaria powring Water out
of a bucket; above a very rare dyal of severall motions with a
chime &c: The Water is conveyd with huge Wheeles, pumps &
other Engines from the river beneath: But the confluence of the
People, multitude of Coaches and severall accidents passing
every moment over this Bridge is the greater miracle, and to a
new Spectator, a most prodigious, yet agreable diversion: Other
bridges there are as that of Notre dame, the Pont au Change &c
fairly built with houses of stone which are layd over this river;
onely the Pont St. Anne landing the Suburbe of St. Germaines
at the Thuilleries is built of Wood, having likewise a Water-
house in the middst of it, & a statue of Neptune (as the other)
casting Water out of a Whales mouth of lead; but much
inferiour to the Samaritans.

The University lyes South-West on an higher grownd, contiguous to, but the lesser part of, Paris: The⟨y⟩ reckon no lesse
than 65 Colleges, but they in nothing approch ours at Oxford
for state and order: Within the University dwell the Booke-
sellers: Onely the Scholes (of which more hereafter) are very
regular:

The Suburbs are those of St. Denys, Honoré, St. Marcel,
Jaques, St. Michel, St. Victoire, and St. Germaines which last is
the largest and where the nobility and Persons of best quality are
seated: And truely Paris, comprehending the Suburbs is certainely for the material the houses are built with, and many
noble and magnificent piles, one of the most gallant Cittys in
the World, and best built: large in Circuit, of a round forme,
infinitly populous; but situat in a botome environd with gentle
declivities, which renders some places very durty, and makes it
smell as if sulphure were mingled with the mudd: Yet is it pav'd
with a kind of freestone of neere a foote square which renders it
more easy to walke on then our pibbles of London:

On Christmas-Eve I went to see the Cathedrall Nostre
Dame; it was built by Philip August, but begun by K: Robert
son of Hugh Capet: It consists of a Gotique fabrique, sustaynd
with 120 pillars which make two allys in the Church round

about the Quire, without comprehending the Chapells, long 174 paces, large[1] 60: high 100: The Quire is enclosd with stone worke, graven with the Sacred History, and containes 45 Chapells cancelld with yron: At the front of the chiefe entrance are statues in relievo of the Kings 28 in number from Chi⟨l⟩debert unto Philip the founder, and above them two high towers square built, and another of a smaller size bearing a spire in the middle where the body of the Church formes a Crosse: The greate Towres ascend by 389 steps, having 12 Gallerys from one to the other: They greately reverence the Crucifix over the Skreene of the Quire with an Image of the B: Virgin cut out of a piece; some moderne Paintings there are good hanging on the Pillars; but the most Conspicuous statue is the huge Colosse of St. Christopher, with eleven other figures of men, houses, prospects & rocks about this gygantique piece, being of one stone, and more remarkable for its bulke than any other perfection. This is the prime church of France for dignity, having Archdeacons, Vicaries, Cannons, Priests and Chaplaines good store, to the number of 127. It is also the Palace of the Archbishop: The young king being now there with a greate and martial Guard, who enter'd the Nave of the Church with their drumms & Fifes, at their ceasing was entertaind with the Church musique, and so I left him.

Jan: 4 I passd with one Mr. Jo: Wall an Irish gent, who had been a Frier in Spaine, and after Reader in St. Isodor's Chayre at Rome; but now, I know not how, getting away, pretended himselfe a souldier of fortune, and absolute Cavaliere, having as he told us been Cap: of horse in Germany: It is certaine he was an excellent disputant, and so strangly given to it, that nothing could passe him, and he would needes perswade me to goe along with him this morning to the Jesuites Colledge to be witnesse of his polemical talent: We found the Fathers in their Church at the rüe St. Anthoine, there one of them shewd us the body of that nob⟨l⟩e fabrique which indeed for its Cupola, pavings, incrustations of marble; the Pulpit, Altars (especialy the highAltar) Organ, Lavatorium &c but, above all the richly carvd, and incomparable front, I esteeme for one of the most perfect pieces of Architecture in Europ, emulating even some of the

1 Broad: a gallicism.

greatest now at Rome it selfe: But this not being what our Frier sought, he lead us into the adjoyning Convent where having shewed us the Library they began a very hot dispute upon some poynts of divinity, which our Cavalier contested onely to shew his excessive pride, and to that indiscreete height, as the Jesuits would hardly bring us to our Coach, being put beside all patience:

The next day we went into the University, and enter'd into the College of Navarre, which is a well-built spacious Quad-rangle, having a very noble Library; Thenc to the Sorbonne, an antient fabrique built by one Robert de Sorbonne whose name it retaynes; but the restauration which the late Cardinal de Rich-lieu has made to it of most excellent moderne building, together with the sumptuous Church of admirable Architecture is far superior to the rest: The Cupola, Portico and whole designe of the Church is very magnificent: We enter'd into some of the Scholes, and in that of Divinity we found a grave Doctor in his chaire with a multitude of Auditors, who all are Writers after his dictats, this they call a Course: After we had sate a little, up starts our Cavalier and ru⟨d⟩ely enough begins to dispute with the Doctor, at which (and especialy to see a fellow clad in the Spanish habit which is in Paris the greatest bugbare imaginable) both the Scholars & Doctor fell into such a fit of laughter, as no body could be heard speake for a while; but silence being obtaind, he began to speake Latine, and make his Apology in so good a style, that their derision was turn'd to admiration, & beginning to argue, he so baffled the Professor that with univer-sal applause they all rose up and did him very great honors, waiting on us to the very streete and Coach, & testif⟨y⟩ing a greate deale of satisfaction.

On the 6t, I alterd my Lod⟨g⟩ing to the rüe de Seine. The 18 I tooke a Master of the French Tongue.

Feb: 2d I heard the newes of my Nephew Georges birth; which was on Jan: 15: English style 1645.

Feb: 3d I put my selfe in mourning for the French Kings death Lewes xiii; and having occasion to go to the Exchange, was curious to see the buildings about it, which as to the late addition is very noble, but the Gallerys where they sell their petty Merchandize nothing so stately as ours at London; no more then the place where they walke below, being onely a low

Vault: The Palais (as they call it above) was built in the time of
Philip the faire, noble and spacious; and the greate Hall annex'd
to it bravely arch'd with stone, having a range of Pillars in the
middle, round which, and at the sides, are shops of all kinds;
especialy bookesellers; the other side is full of pewes for the
Clearkes of the Advocates, which (as ours at Westminster)
swarme here: At one of the Ends stands an Alter were daily
Masse is sayd, within are severall Chambers, Courts, Treasures
&c above that most rich and glorious Sale de L'Audiens; the
Chamber of St. Lewes, and other Superior Courts where the
Parliament sits richly guilt on Embossed carvings & fretts guilt
with gold & exceedingly beautified: Within the Place where
they utter their wares is another narroer Gallery full of shopps
and Toys &c which lookes downe into the Prison-Yard:
Descending by a large payre of stayres we passed by St.
Chapelle, which is a Church built by St. Lewes 1242 after the
Gotique manner; what is most observable, is, that it stands upon
another church which is under it, sustained by pillars at the sides
which seeme to be very weake, which makes it appeare somewhat extraordinary in the Artist: This Chapell is wonderfull
famous for its Reliques which they pretend to be the almost
intyre Crowne of Thornes, the Achat Patine, rarely sculptur'd,
judg⟨e⟩d one of the Largest & best in Europ: There was now a
very beautifull spire to be cover'd with gold erecting: Below in
the Court (which is very spacious, as capable to hold many
Coaches, & inviron'd with shopps of all sorts, especialy
Engravers, Gold-smiths, Watch-makers &c) is a fayre Fountaine and Portico: Returning home we passd by the Isle du
Palais which consists of a triangular building of brick, whereof
one side reguards the river inhabited with Gold-smiths; within
the Court are privat dwellings: The Front lookes on the greate
Bridge possessd by Montebankes, Operators and Puppet Play-
ers: On the other Part, the Vale de Misere, where is an every-
days Market of all sorts of Provision, especialy Bread, even to
admiration the quantity consider'd; hearbs, Flowers, Orange-
trees, choyce shrubbs; besides Powltry & the like, and here is a
shop cal'd Noahs-Arke, where are to be had for mony all the
Curiosities naturall or artificial imaginable, Indian or Europan, for
luxury or Use, as Cabinets, Shells, Ivorys, Purselan, Dried fishes,
rare Insects, Birds, Pictures, & a thousand exotic extravagances:

Passing hence we view'd the Port Dauphine, which is an Arch of excellent Workmanship, the streete, bearing the same name, ample, & straite.

On the 4th I went to see the Marais de Temple, where is a noble Church and Palace, heretofore dedicated to the Knights of that order; but now converted to a Piazza not much onlike ours of Covent Garden; but far larger, & not so pleasant; though built about with divers considerable Palaces: From hence we went to St. Genevefe a Church of greate devotion, and another of their Amazons, sayd to have deliver'd the Citty on a tyme from the English: for which she is esteem'd the Tutelary saint of Paris: The Church stands upon a steepe eminence of ground, & has an exceeding high spire; It is governd by Canons Reguler:

We next drove to the Palace Royal, where Henry the fourth has built a faire quadrangle of stately Palaces arched underneath; in the middle of a Spacious Area, stands on a noble Pedistal the Brasen Statue of Lewes 13th which though made in imitation of that in the Roman Capitol; is nothing so much esteemd as that on the Pont Noeufe:

We went to visite some Hospitals, that of the Quinz-Vingts in rue St. Honorè is realy a noble foundation; but above all the Hostel Dieu for men & Women neere Nostre Dame, to a Princly, pious and prodigious expense: That of the Charite neere my Lodging is another, built by Q: Mary di Medices, where I have taken greate satisfaction to see how decently and Christianly the sick People are tended, yea even to delicacy; being sometymes (as I have seene them) served by ⟨noble⟩ Persons men and Women: The⟨y⟩ have also Gardens, Walkes, Fountaines: Here are divers People Cutt for the stone with greate successe yearely in May:

The two Chasteletts (suppos'd to have been built by Julius Cæsar) are the Places of Judicature in Criminal Causes under the Lieutenant Civil and Præsidial, to which is a strong Prison; the Courts are magnificent & spacious.

The 8th I tooke Coach and went to see the famous Garden Royale,* which is an Enclosure wall'd in, consisting of all sorts of

* V adds: (for all Publique Works & things beare the Title of Royal, & whatever a *flower* de *Lyce* is painted ⟨on⟩ tho' but upon a signe post: as the Boote Royal, the heart, the Hat all is Royal &c).

varietys of grounds, for the planting & culture of Medical simples. It is certainely for all advantages very well chosen, having within it both hills, meadows, growne Wood, & Upland, both artificial and naturall; nor is the furniture inferiour, being very richly stord with exotic plants: has a fayre fountaine in the middle of the Parterre, a very nob⟨l⟩e house, Chapel, Laboratory, Orangerie & other accommodations for the Præsident, who is allwayes one of the Kings chiefe Physitians:

We pass'd from hence quite to the other side of the Towne, and at some distance from it, to the Bois de Vincennes, going by the Bastille which is the Fortresse Tower and Magazine of this great Citty: It is vastly spacious within, and there the grand Master of the Artillery has his house, with faire Gardens & Walkes:

The Bois de Vincennes has in it a square, and noble ⟨Castle⟩, with a magnificent apartiment fit for a royal Court, not forgetting the Chapell: It is the chiefe Prison for persons of Quality: about it is a Parke wall'd in, and full of Deere, and there is in one part of it a grove of goodly Pine trees:

I went the next day to consider the Louvre more atentively, with all its severall Courts and Pavilions. One of the Quadrangles begon by Hen: 4: and finish'd by the two last Lewes's his son, & Grandchild, is a superb, but mix'd Structure: the Cornices, mouldings and Compartiments, together with the insertions of severall colour'd marbles being of infinite expense. Hence through the Long Gallery which is ⸺ foote, pav'd with white & black marble, richly fretted & paynted a fresca by Monsieur Per⸺ and others: but the front reguarding the River, though of exceeding rare worke for the Carving, yet wants of that magnificence which a playner & truer designe would have contributed to it: In the Court aux Thuilleries is a princely fabrique, especialy that incomparable winding stayres of stone, which hanging without support at the pozzo in the middle, together with the Cupola, I take to be as bold & noble a piece of Architecture as any in Europ of the kind: To this is a Corps de Logis worthy of so greate a Prince: Under these buildings through a Garden which has an ample fountaine, was the Kings Printing-house & that famous Letter so much esteem'd; & here I bought divers of the Clasique Authors, Poets & others: Hence we returnd through another Gallery, larger then the other, but nothing so long, where hung the Pictures of all the Kings & Queenes and prime nobility of France; descending henc we were let into a lower very large roome call'd the Sale des Antiques, which is a Vaulted Cimelia[1] destin'd onely to set statues in, amongst which stands that so celebrated Diana of the Ephesians said to be the same which utterd Oracles in that renowned Temple: besides those Collosean Figures of marble   Not forgetting the huge Globe which is hung up in Chaynes: The pavings, inlayings & incrustations of this Hall are very rich and glorious. In another more privat Garden towards the Queenes apartiment is a noble Walke or Cloyster under Arches, whose tarrac is pav'd with stones of a greate breadth; this, and the pleasant Aviary, Fountaine and stately Cypresses has prospect towards the river; where is to be seene a prodigious number of Barges & boates of incredible length, full of hay, Corne, Wood, Wine & other Commodities which this Vast Citty consumes.

Under the Long Gallery we have describ'd dwell Gold-Smiths, Paynters, Statuaries, Architects, who being the most famous for their art in Christendom are here stipendiated by the King: Into that of Monsieur Saracins we enterd, who was then moulding for an Image of a Madona, to be cast in gold, of a very greate bignesse, to be sent by the Q: Regent to Lauretto as an offering for the birth of the Dauphine, now the young King: I this day finish'd with a Walke in the greate Garden of the Thuilleres, which is rarely contriv'd for Privacy, shade, company, by Groves, Plantations of tall trees, especialy that in the middle being of Elmes, the other of Mulberys; & that Labyrinth of Cypresse; not omitting the noble hedges of Pome-granads, the fountaines, Piscianas, Aviary, but above all the artificial Echo, redoubling the words so distinctly, and as it is never without some faire Nymph singing to its gratefull returnes: standing at one of the focus's, which is under a tree or little Cabinet of hedges, the Voyce seemes to descend from the Clowds; and at another, as if it were under grownd: This being at the botome of the Garden, we were let into another, which being kept with all imaginable accuratenesse, in reguard of the Orangery, precious Shrubbs, & rare fruites, seem'd a Paradise: From a Tarrac in this Place we might see so many Coaches (as late in the yeare as it

1 *Cimelium*, a treasure, plural *cimelia; cimeliarchium*, a treasury.

was) going towards the Course (which is a place neere adjoyning of neere an English mile long, & planted with 4 rows of Trees, making a large Circle in the middle) that one would Conceive were impossible to be maintained in the whole Citty: This Corso is wall'd about neere breast-high with squar'd freestone, has a very stately Arch at the Entry, with noble Sculpture & statues about it, built by Mary di Medices; and here it is that the Gallants, & the Ladys of the Court take the ayre & divert themselves, as with us in Hide-Parke, the middle Circle being Capable to containe an hundred Coaches to turne commodiously, & the larger of the Plantations for 5 or 6 Coaches a breast:

Returning againe through the Thuilleries, at a certaine building on one side of the Wall, we went to see divers Wild beast(s) kept for the King's pleasure, as a Beare, a Wolfe, a Wild-boare, a Leopard &c:

Feb: 27 accompanyd with some English Gent: we tooke horse to see St. Germains en Lay, which is a stately Country-house of the Kings, some 5 leagues from Paris: By the way we alighted at St. Cloes, where upon an Eminence neere the River, the Arch-Bishop of Paris, has a Garden (for the house is not very considerable) so rarely waterd, & furnish'd with fountaines, statues, & groves: as I had never seene an(y)thing exceeding it: The Walkes are very faire; above all that fountaine of the Laocoon in a very ample square poole or Piscina, casting waters neere 40 foote in height, and having about it a multitude of Statues and basines, is a most glorious & surprizing object: Those three at descent of the hill, and dispos'd in a round walke are very remarkable; but nothing is more esteem'd than the Cascada falling from the greate stepps into the lowest & longest Walke from the Mons Parnassus, which consists of a Grotto or shell house erected on the summit of the hill; & herein are divers water-workes, and unlucky contrivances to wet the Spectators: This is coverd with a fayre Cupola, the Walls paynted with the Muses, statues placed thick about it, whereof some antique and good: In the upper Walkes are two Perspectives very pretty ones, seeming to enlarge the allys; and in this Garden there are a world of other incomparable diversions: The Palace (as I sayd) is not extraordinary: the out walles onely painted a fresca; in the Court is a Volary, and the statues of Char: the 9th and Hen: 3: 4th & Lewes the 13th on horsback, being Mezzo-relievo'd in

Plaster: I must not forgett, that in the Garden neere the house is a small Chapell, and under shelter, the figure of Cleopatra taken from the Belveders original, with divers others: From the Tarrac above, is a Tempest well paynted, & thence an excellent Prospect towards Paris, the meadows, & river.

At an Inn in this Village, neere the bridge is an host, who treates all the greate Persons in Princely lod⟨g⟩ings, for furniture & Plate; but they pay well for it, as I hav don: Indeede the entertainement is very splendid, and not unreasonable, considering the excellent manner of dressing their meate, and the service; here are many debauches & excessive revellings as being out of all noyse & observance.

From hence about a leage farther, we went to the Cardin a Richlieus Villa at Ruell; the House is but small, but fairely built in forme of a Castle, moated about; The Offices are towards the Way side, and over against it are large Vineyards walled in: But though the House be not of the greatest, the Gardens about it are so magnificent, as I much doubt whither Italy have any exceeding it for all varietyes of Pleasure: That which is neerest the Pavillion is a Parterre, having in the middst divers noble brasse statues perpetualy spouting Water into an ample Bassin, with other figures of the same metall: But that which is most admirable is the vast enclosure and variety of ground in the larger Garden, as containing Vineyards, Corne fields, Meadows, Groves, whereoff one is of Perennial Greenes; and Walkes of vast lengthes, so accurately kept & cultivated that nothing can be more agreable and tempting: In one of these Walkes within a square of tall trees, or rather a Grove, is a basilisc of copper, which as it is managed by the Fontaniere, casts Water neere 60 foote in height, and will of it selfe ⟨moove⟩ round so swiftly, that it is almost impossible to escape wetting: This leads to the Citroniere where there is a very noble conserve of all those rarities, and at the end of it the Arco of Constantine painted in Oyle on a Wall, as big as is the real one at Rome, so don to the life, that a man very well skilld in Painting may mistake it for stone, & sculpture; and indeede it is so rarely perform'd that it is almost impossible to believe it Paynting, but to be a Worke of solid stone: The skie, and hills which seeme to be betweene the Arches, are so naturall, that swallows & other birds, thinking to fly through, have dash'd themselves to pieces against the Walls:

I was infinitely taken with this agreable cheate: At the farther part of this Walke is that plentifull, though artificial Cascad of Water, which rolles downe a very steepe declivity, and over the marble degrees, & basins, with an astonishing noyse and fury, Each basin hath a jetto in it & flowing like sheetes of transparent glasse; especialy that which rises over the greate shell of lead, from whenc it glides silently downe a Channell, through the middle of a most spacious gravell Walke, that terminates in a Grotto, resembling the Yawning mouth of hell: Here are also fountaines that cast Water of an exceeding height; and Piscinas very large, in which two of them have Ilands for fowle, of which here is store, one of these Ilands has a receptacle for them built of natural Rock with extravagant stones neere 50 foote high, growne over with Mosse, Ivy &c, & shaded at a competent distance with tall trees: In this rupellary nidary do the fowle breede & lay Eggs: Hence we were brought to a large & very rare Grotto of shell-worke, ar⟨t⟩ificialy stuck on in the shapes of Satyres & other wild fansys: In the middle stands a table of Marble, on which a fountaine playes in divers formes of glasses, cupps, crosses, fanns, crownes &c. Then the Fountaniere represented a showre of raine from the topp, which was mett with the slender pissers from beneth; at the going out, two extravagant Musqueteeres shot us with a streame of water comming out very fiercely from their musket barrilles. Before this Grotto is a long poole into which run divers spouts of Water from leaden Escholop bassins: The viewing of this Paradise made us bring night to St. Germains.

The first building of this Palace is of Charles the 5 calld the Sage; but Francis the first (that true Virtuoso) made it compleate, speaking in the style of the magnificence then in fashion, which was with to⟨o⟩ greate a mixture of the Gotic; as may be seen in what there is of his in the old Castle, an irregular piece, as built on the old foundation, having a moate about it: It has yet some spacious & handsome romes of state in it, & a chapell neately paynted: The New Castle is at some distance divided from this by a Court; of a lower but more modern designe, built by Hen: 4th: to this belongs six incomparable Tarraces built of brick & stone descending in Cascads towards the river, & cut out of the naturall hill, having under them goodly Gallerys vaulted, whereof 4 have subterranean Grotts & rocks, where is represented severall objects in manner of sceanes, & other motions by the force of Water, to be shown by the light of torches onely: Especialy that of Orpheus, with his musique, & the Animals which daunce after his harp: In the 2d is the King and Dolphin; in the 3d the Neptune sounding with his trumpet, his charriot drawne by sea-horses: In the 4th the story of Perseus & Andromeda; not to insist on the mills, the solitude of Eremits, men a fishing, birds chirping & the many other devices: There is also a dry Grott, to ⟨refresh⟩ in; all of them rendring an incomparable prospect towards the River, & the goodly Country about it, especialy the Forrest: At the bottom is a Parterr; the Uppmost Tarrac is neere halfe a myle in length, with double declivities arched and balusterd with stone, of vast & royal cost: In the Pavilion of the new Castle are many faire romes well paynted, & leads into a very noble Garden and Parke, where there is a pall-maill, in the midst of which, at one of the sides, a Cappell Cupol'd with stone, though little, yet of an handsome order of Architecture: Out of the Parke you goe into the Forrest, which being very large is stor'd with Deare, Wild-boares, Wolves & other wild game: The Tennis Court, & Cavalerizzo for the menag'd horses are also observable.

We returnd to Paris by Madrid, another Villa of the Kings built by Francis the first, and cald by that name, to absolve him of his Oath, that he would not go from Madrid, in which he was Prisoner in Spayne, but from whence he made his Escape. This house is also built in a Park walled in: We next call'd in at the de bonnes ⟨hommes⟩, which being rare situated has a faire Chapel & Library.

March: 1: I went to see the Count de Lion Courts Palac in the rüe de Siene, which is well built, towards his study & bed-Chamber joynes a little Garden, which though very narrow, is yet by the addition of an excellently painted Perspective strangly enlarg'd to appearance; to this there is another part, supported by Arches, in which there runns a Streame of water, which rising in the Aviary out of a statue, seemes to flow for some miles, by being artificially continud in the painting, where it sinkes downe at the Wall, & then this I never saw a more agreable deceipt: At the end of this Garden is a little Theater which is made to change with divers pretty seanes, & the stage so ordered, that with figures of men & Women paynted on light boards, & cut out, a person who stands under neath makes to act as if they were speaking by guiding them, & reciting words in diferent tones, as the Parts require: We were lead hence into a pretty round Cabinet, where was a neate invention for reflecting of lights by lining divers sconces with thin shining plates of gilded Copper:

The next mor⟨n⟩ing being reccommended to one Monsieur de Hausse, President du Parliament, and once Ambassador at Venice for the French King, we were very civily receiv'd, & shew'd his Library: amongst his Payntings a rare Venus & Adonis of Veronezes; a St. Anthony after the first manner of Correggio; A Madona of Palma rare.

March the 6, being Sonday I went to Charenton 2 leagues from Paris, to heare & see the manner of the French-Protestant Churches service: The place of meeting they call the Temple, being a very faire & spacious roome built of Free-stone, and very decently adorn'd within with payntings of the Tables of the Law, the Lords Prayer & Creede: The Pulpit stands at the upper end in the middle, having a Parque or Enclosure of seates about it, where the Elders, & persons of greatest quality & strangers sit: The rest of the Congregation on formes & low stooles, but none in Pewes, as in our Churches, to their greate disgrace and nothing so orderly as here, where the stoles & other comber are removd when the Assembly rises: I was greately pleasd with their harmonious singing the Psalmes, which they all learen perfectly well from the tablature, which, I heard, their children are as duely taught, as their Catechisme:* In this passage we went by that famous bridge over the Marne where that renown'd Eccho returnes the Voice 9 or 10 times being provoked with a good singer:

The Next day, being Mar: 7th I set forwards with some Company, towards Fontaine Bleau, which is a sumptuous Palace of

---

* V adds: The Communion Table Stands (as I remember neer one of the side Walls or some distance from it: & the Preacher after a short prayer in the Pulpet, (having before finish'd their Forme of Devotion bellow) puts on his Hat, which I thought to be very fit, in reguard he represents the Doctor who Teaches: but I did not so well like the men & Congregation that are to be looked on as Scholars & Auditors to be so Covered: & it were not amisse that oure ministers imitated the French in our Pulpits, & Taught in their Graduat Capps.

the Kings (like ours of Hampton-Court) about 14 leagues from
the Citty: by the Way we passe through a Forest so prodigiously
encompassd with hidious rocks of a Certaine whiteish hard
stone, congested one upon another in Mountainous heights,
that the like I believe is no where to be found more horrid &
solitary: It abounds with Staggs, Wolves, Boares & sometimes
more salvage bea(s)ts, there being not long after, a Lynx or
Ownce killd amongst them who had devowrd some passengers:
Upon the Summite of one of these gloomy Precipices, intermingled with Trees & Shrubbs & monstrous protuberances of
the huge stones which hang over & menace ruine, is built an
Hermitage: passing these solitudes, not without howrly expectation of Rogues who frequently lurke about these denns & do
mischiefe (& for whom we were all well appoynted with our
Carabines) we arived that Evening at the Village, where we lay
at the Horne, going the next morning early to the Palace: The
Fabrique of this house is nothing so stately & uniforme, as
Hampton Court: but Fra: the 1st began much to beautifie it;
most of all Hen: 4th, and not a little the last King: It abounds
with very faire Halls, Chambers & Gallerys: In the longest
which is 360 foote long & 18 broad is paynted with the Victoryes
of that greate Prince Grand-father to the present: That of Francis the i: cal'd the grand Galery, has all the Kings Palaces
paynted on it: Above these in 60 pieces of incomparable Worke
the history of Ulysses out of Homer don by Primaticcio in
Fresca in the tyme of Hen: 3d and esteemed amongst the most
renown'd in Europ for the designe: The Cabinet is full of incomparable Pictures, especialy a Woman of Raphael: In the Hall of
the Guards is a piece of Tapissry painted on the wall very naturally, representing the Victoryes of Charles the 7th against our
Countrymen. In the Sale des Festines, is a rare Chimny-piece,
and Hen: 4th on horse-back of White-marble esteemed worth
18000 Crownes: Clementia and Pax nobly don: Upon Columns
of Jasper 2 Lyons of Brasse: The new stayres, and an halfe Circular Court is of modern & good Architecture, & so is a Chapell
built by Lewes XIIIth all of Jasper and severall incrustations of
Marble through the inside: Having seene the romes we went to
the Volary which has a Cupola in the middle of it; also greate
trees & bushes, it being full of birds who dranke at two fountaines: There is also a faire Tennis-Court, & noble stables; but

the Beauty of all are the Gardens: In the Court of the Fountaines stand divers Antiquities, & statues, a Mercury especialy:
In the Queenes Garden is the figure of a Diana making a fountayne with a world of other brasse statues: The Greate Garden
being 180 thoises long and 154 wide has in the Center the Fountayne of Tyber in a Colossean figure of brasse, with the Wolfe
over Romulus & Rhemus: also at each corner of the Garden
rises a fountaine. In the Garden of the Piscina is an Hercules of
White-marble; next is that of Pines, and without that a Canale
of an English mile in length, at the end of which rises three jettos in the forme of a flowre de lys of an exceeding height; at the
margent are incomparable Walkes planted with trees: Here the
Carps come familiarly to hand: Hence they brought us to a
Spring which they report being first discover'd by a dog, gave
occasion of beautif⟨y⟩ing this place both with the Palace and
Gardens; The White & horrid rocks at some distance in the
Forest yeald one of the most august & stupendious prospects
imaginable. The Parke about it is very large, & the Towne full of
noble-mens houses.

    Next morning we were invited by a Paynter who was keeper
of the Pictures & rarities to see his owne collection: we were lead
through a Gallery of old Rossos worke, at end of which is
another Cabinet were 3 Madonas of Raphael, 2 of Andr: de
Serto: In the Academy where the Paynter himselfe wrought was
a St. Michael of Raphael very rare: St. Jo: Baptist of Leonardo,
& a Womans head: a Queene of Sicily [& St. Margarit] of
Raphael, 2 more Madonas whereof one very large of the same
hand; some more Pictures of del Sartos: a St. Jerome of Perino
del Vagas: The Rape of Proserpine very good, with a greate
quantity of drawings.

    Returning part of our way to Paris that day, we visited an
house cal'd Maison Rouge incomparable for its Prospect, Grott,
& Fountaines one whereoff rises 50 foote from the ground, &
resembles the noise of a tempest, battailia of gunns & other
meteors at its issue: Thenc we went to Essone an house belonging to Monsieur Essling, who is a greate Vertuoso, there are
many good payntings in it; but nothing so observable as his
Gardens & Fountaines & Pooles of Fish, especialy that in a triangular forme, the water cast out into the ⟨channel⟩ by a multitude of heads about it: There is also a noble Cascado, and Prety

Bathes with all accommodations: Under a marble table is a
fountaine of Serpents twisting about a Globe: We alighted next
at Corbeil, a towne famous for the Seige of Hen: 4th, an old
place & high built: Here we slept, & so returnd the next morning to Paris.

On the 18 with one Sir Jo: Cotton a Cambridg-shire Knight
I went a journey into Normandy: The 1 day we passed by Gail-
lon which is the Archbishops of Roüens Palac, the Gardens are
highly commended, but we went not in, intending to reach Pon-
toise by dinner: The Towne is built in a very gallant place, has a
noble Bridge over the Oise, and is bravely refreshd with Fountaines. This is the first Towne in Normandy and the farthest ter-
roire that the Vineyards extend on this side the Country, which
is fuller of Playnes, Wood & Enclosures, with some downes
towards the sea very like England. We lay this night at a small
Vilage calld Magny; The next day descending an extraordinary
steepe hill we din'd at Fleury; and after riding 5 leagues downe
St. Catherine to Rouen, which affords a goodly Prospect to the
ruines of that Chapell & mountaine. This Country dos so
abound with Wolves, that a sheepheard whom I met told us, one
of his Companions was strangled by one but the day before, &
that in the middst of his flock: The feilds are most of them
planted with Peares, & Apples & other Cider fruites: It is also
plentifully furnish'd with quarries of stone & slat, & hath Yron
in aboundance.

I lay at the White Crosse in Rouen which is a very large
Citty, situat on the Seine, having two smaller rivers besides calld
the Aubelt and Lobes: There stand yet the ruines of a magnificent bridge of stone now supplyd by one of boates onely,
to which there come up Vessells of considerable burthen:
The other side of the Water consists of Meadow; and there
have the reformed a Church: The Cathedrall of the Citty is
Nost⟨r⟩e Dame, built as they acknowledge by the English, and
inded some English words graven in Gotic Characters upon the
Front seeme to confirm it. The Towers & whole Church is full
of Carving: It has 3 steeples with a Pyramid; in one of these
I saw the famous bell so much talk'd off, being 13 foote in height,
32 large, the diameter 11, & we⟨igh⟩ing 40000 pounds: In the
Chapel d'Amboise, built by a Cardinal of that name, lyes his
body, with severall faire monuments: The Quire has behind it a

greate Dragon paynted on the Wall, which they affirme to have don much harme to the Inhabitans till vanquish'd by St Romain their Archbishop, for which there is an annual Procession. It was now neere Easter, and many Images were exposd, with scenes & stories representing the Passion made up of little Puppets, to which there was great resort & devotion with offerings. There is before the Church a faire Palace. St. Owen is another goodly Church and Abby with very fine Gardens belonging to it: Here the King hath Lodgings when he makes his progresse through these parts.

The structure where the Court of Parliament is kep⟨t⟩ is very magnificent, containing very faire halles & chambers, especialy La Chambre d'orée. The Towne house is also well built; and so are some gentlemens houses; but the most part of the rest are of Timber like our Merchants of London in the wodden part of the Citty.

Upon Easter moneday we went from Rouen, din'd at Totes, a solitary inn betweene that & Diepe where we ariv'd March 21: This Towne is situated betwene two Mountaines not unpleasantly; is washed on the north by our English Seas: The Port is commodious, but the entrance difficult: It has one very ample & faire streete, in which a pretty Church: In the afternoone I walked up the hill to view the Fort Pollet which consists of a strong Earth-Worke and commands the Haven, as on the other side dos the Castle which is also well fortified with the Citadel before it; nor is the towne it selfe a little strong: This place exceedingly abounds in workemen that make and sell curiosities of Ivory and Tortoise shells, in which they turne, and make many rare toyes; & indeed whatever the East Indys afford of Cabinets, Purcelan, natural & exotic rarities are here to be had with aboundant choyce:

The 23d we passd all along by the Coast, a very rocky & rugged way, which forc'd ⟨us⟩ many times to alight till we came to Haver de Grace, where we lay that night: The next morning we were admitted to see the Citadell which is both very strong and regular, and in reguard of its situation altogether impregnable: It is also excellently stor'd with Artillery and ammunition of all sorts, the works furnish'd with faire brasse Canon; the allogiaments of the Garnison very uniforme, a spacious place for drawing up the souldiers, a pretty Chapell, and faire house

for the Governor. The Duke of Richlieu being now in the Fort
we went to salute him who received us very civilly, and commanded that we should be shew'd what ever we desired to see:
That which I tooke more especiall notice of was this motto upon
the Canon, out of the Prince of Latine Poets—Ratio Ultima
Regum: The Citadel was built by the late Card: de Richlieu,
unkle of the present duke, and may be esteemed one of the
strongest in France: The haven is very capacious: When we had
don here we embarqued our selves & horses to passe over to the
other side, being about 4 or 5 leagues to a Towne calld Homfleur,
where dissembogues the Seine into the sea: The place seemes to
be a poore fisher-towne, observable for nothing so much as the
odd, yet usefull habites which the good-Women weare, of beares
& others skinns, as of ruggs &c at Diepe and all along those
maritime Coasts: The 25, being the day after we ariv'd at Caen, a
very noble and beautifull Towne situat on the river Orne which
passes quite through it, joynd onely by a bridg consisting of one
intire arch: We lay at the Angel, where we were very well usd,
the place being aboundantly furnish'd with Provisions at a
cheape rate. The most considerable object is the greate Abby
and Church, large & rich; built after the Gotish manner, with
two spires [& a middle blunter one:] at the West end, & all of
stone: The Quire round & large.

Leaving this Monastry, we went to the Castle, which is very
strong and fayre; and so is the Towne-house built on the fore-
mention'd bridg which unites the two townes: Here are Scholes,
and an University for the Jurists: All the whole Towne is handsomly built of that excellent stone, so well knowne by that name
even in England:* Here I was lead to a very pretty Garden
belonging (as I remember) to a Churchman, which being
planted with hedges of Alaternus, had a skreene of an exceeding height at Entrance, acurately cutt in topiary worke with
well understood Architecture, consisting of Pillars, Nices,[1]
Freezes & other ornaments with greate curiosity; some of
the Colomns curiously wreathed, others in spirall forme, all
according to art.

---

* V adds: of which almost all the Churches were built 'til the *Isle* of Purbeck
[Portland] was brought into use and found far better:
1 Niches.

From Caen we went on the 28th towards Paris; the first night lying at Evreux, a Bishops seate, being an antient towne with a faire Cathedral; so the next day we ariv'd safe at Paris.

April 1st I went more exactly to see the roomes of that incomparable Palace of Luxemburge in the Fauxbourgs St. Germains, built by Mary de Medices and I thinke one of the most noble, entire and finish'd Pile⟨s⟩ that is standing in any Citty of the World, taking it with the Garden and all its accomplishments: The Gallery is of the Painting ⟨of⟩ P: Rubens, being the history of the Foundresses life, rarely designe⟨d⟩ and greate, at the end of it is the Duke of Orleans's Library, rarely furnish'd with excellent bookes, all bound in Mar⟨o⟩quin & guilded: the Valans of the shelves being of greene Velvet, freing'd with gold; in the Cabinet joyning to it, are onely the smaler Volumes, with 6 Cabinets of Medails; and an incomparable ⟨collection⟩ of shells and Achates, whereof some are prodigiously rich & glorious; this Duke being very learn'd in Medails, and Plants, nothing of that kind escapes him. There are other spacious, noble & princly furnish'd roomes which looke towards the Gardens, which are nothing inferior to the rest: The Court below is formd into a Squar by a Corridor, having over the chiefe Entrance a stately Cupola cover'd with stone, the rest is cloysterd & arch'd on Pillasters of rustique-worke; The Tarace ascending before the Front, pav'd with white & black marble is balustred about with white marble exquisitely polish'd: Onely the hall below is lowe, and the stayre-case somewhat of an heavy designe; but the faciata respecting the Parter, which is also arched & vaulted with stone, is of admirable beauty, & full of Sculpture: The Gardens containe neere an English mile in Compasse, enclos'd with a stately wall, & in good ayre, which renders it certainly one of the sweetest places imaginable; The Parterr is indeede of box; but so rarely designd, and accurately kept cut; that the ⟨e⟩mbrodery makes a stupendious effect, to the Lodgings which front it; 'tis divided into 4 Squares, & as many circular knots; having in the Center a noble Basin of Marble neere 30 foot diameter (as I remember) in which a Triton of brasse holds a Dolphin that casts a girandola of water neere 30 foote high which plays perpetualy, & the water is excellent, being convey'd from Arceuil, whence it is derived by an Aquæduct of stone built after the old Roman magnificence. About this ample Parter, the

spacious Walkes & all included, runs a bordure of free-stone
adorn'd with Pedistalls for Potts & Statues; and part of it
neere the Stepps of the Terrace, with a raile & baluster of pure
white marble: The Walkes are exactly faire, long & variously
descending, & so justly planted with limes, Elmes & other
Trees, that nothing can be more delicious & surprizing, especially that of the hornebeame hedge, which being high & stately,
butts full upon the fountaine: Towards the farther end is an
excavation intended for a Vast Piscina, but never finish'd; &
neere it is an enclosure for a Garden of simples, rarely entertaind, & here the Duke keepes Tortoises in greate number who
use the pole of Water at one side of the Garden: here is also a
Conservatory for Snow: At the upper part (towards the Palace)
is a grove of tall Elmes cutt into a Starr, every ray being a Walke
whose center is a large fountaine: The rest of the Ground is
made into severall enclosures (all hedge Worke or rowes of
Trees) of whole fields, meadowes, boscages, some of them containing divers ackers: Next the streete side, & more contiguous
to the house are knotts in trayle or grasse Worke, where likewise
runs a fountaine; Towards the Grotto, & Stables, inclos'd within
a Wall is a Garden of choyce flowers, in which the Duke spends
many thousand pistoles: In summ, nothing is wanting to render
this Palace, & Gardens perfectly beautyfull & magnificent; nor
is it one of the least diversions, to behold the infinite numbers of
Persons of quality, & Citizens, & strangers who frequent it, and
to whom all accesse is freely permitted: so as you shall meete
some walkes & retirements full of Gallants & Ladys, in others
melancholy Fryers, in others studious Scholars, in others jolly
Citizens; some sitting & lying on the Grasse, others, running, &
jumpi(n)g, some playing at bowles, & ball, others dancing
& singing; and all this without the least disturbance, by reason
of the amplitude of the place; & what is most admirable, you see
no Gardners or people at Worke in it, and yet all kept in such
exquisite order, as if they did nothing else but worke; It is so
early in the mornings that all is dispatch'd, and don without the
least confusion: I have been the larger in the description of this
Paradise, for the extraordinary delight I have taken in those
sweete retirements. The Cabinet, and Chapell, neerer the Garden Front has some choyce Pictures in it: All the houses neere
this are also very noble Palaces: especialy Petite Luxemburge:

The ascent of the Streete is both for breadth, & situation and building incomparable.

I went the next to view Paris from the top of St. Jaques-Steeple, (esteem'd the highest in the Towne): from whenc I had a full view of the whole Citty & suburbs, both which I do not judge to be so large as London; though the dissimilitude of their severall formes & situations, this round, London, long; render it very difficult to determine; but there is no comparison between the buildings, Palaces & materials; This being intirely of Stone, and infinitely sumptuous; though I esteeme our Piazzas to exceede theirs.*

Henc I tooke a turne in St. Inocents Church-yard where the story of the devouring quality of the ground (consuming Bodys in 24 houres), the Vast Charnells of Bones, Tombs, Piramids and sepultures tooke up much of my time, together with the Hiero-glypical Characters of Nicolas Flamens Philosophical Worke, who had both founded this Church, & divers other charitable workes, as himselfe testifies in his booke: Here I observd that divers clearks got their livelyhod by inditing letters for poore mayds & other ignorant people, who come to them for advise, and write for them into the Country, both to their Sweete-hearts, Parents & friends, every large grave stone a little Ele-vated serving them for Table:

There is joyning also to this Church A Common fountaine with good relievo upon it:

The next Morning I was had by a friend to Monsieur Morines Garden; a person who from an ordinary Gardner, is ariv'd to be one of the most skillfull & Curious Persons of France for his rare collection of Shells, Flowers & Insects: His Garden is of an exact Oval figure planted with Cypresse, cutt flat & set as even as a Wall could have form'd it: The Tulips,

---

* V adds: As since the dismal Conflagration, dos all our publique buildings, Theaters, Churches, Especialy st. *Paules* (next to st. Peters at Rome) now in greate forewardnesse, all the Churches in Christendome, besides, the Exchanges, Halls of the severall Companys; Hospitals & other publique struc-tures, which are of Portland Stone, (little inferior to Marble) tho' indeed not so thick of Palaces: All which with the Bridge, rivage, & addition of Beautifull Suburbs, puts it out of Controversy, that London almost by halfe exceedes *Paris* for amplitude, Prospect & Commerce, not onely *Paris*, but any of the Cittys in *Europe*.

Anemonies, Ranunculus's, Crocus's &c being of the most exquisite; were held for the rarest in the World, which constantly
drew all the Virtuosi of that kind to his house during the season;
even Persons of the most illustrious quality: He lived in a kind of
Hermitage at one side of his Garden where his Collection of
Purselan, of Currall, whereof one is carved into a large Crucifix,
is greately esteemed: besids his bookes of Prints, those of
Alberts, Van Leydens, Calot, &c. But the very greatest curiosity
which I esteemd, for being very ingenious and particular, was his
collection of all the Sorts of Insects, especialy of Buter flys, of
which he had so great Variety; that the like I had never seene:
These he spreads, & so medicates, that no corruption invading
them he keepes in drawers, so plac'd that they present you with a
most surprizing & delightfull tapissry: besides he shewd me the
remarkes he had made of their propagation, which he promisd
to publish: some of these, as also of his best flowers, he had
caus'd to be painted in miniature by rare hands, & some in oyle:*

The 6t, I sent my sister, my owne Picture, in Water Colours,
which she requested of me: & went to see divers of the fairest
Palaces of the Towne; as that of Vendosme; very large & stately:
That of Longueville, Guyse, Conde, Chevereuse, Nevers,
esteemed one of the best in Paris towards the River.

The Palas Cardinal bequeath'd by Richlieu to the King (on
condition to be cald by his name) & where during my aboad the
King resided because of the building of the Louvre, I often went

---

* V adds: Two pleasant Storys are not to be forgotten. which concerne his
Flowers, the first of two or 3 *Tulip bulbs* reckoned to be valued at 100 pistoles;
which he having wrap'd up in a paper, & left upon the Table in his house, a
Stranger comming in, with his friend to Visite the old man, & finding no body
in the roome, taking the rootes to be but a kind of Onion, Eate them up; one
may imagine what rage *Morine* was in, at the losse: Another who was a *Florist*,
being very importunat, to have some seeds of a speciall *Anemonie* for a price
they Could not agree on; came one day, as desiring onely to walke in the Garden, having a very long Cloake on (as the Priests & churchme⟨n⟩ usualy ware)
pass'd thro' the Beds of those Flowers then in seede, when observing his time,
he so drew the bottome of his Cloake as if spread by the aire, that the ⟨glew⟩, to
which the seedes do allways stick; that in 2 or 3 turnes aboundance of it stuck
to his Cloake; & so taking leave of our F⟨l⟩orist, when he came to his
house, brushing & picking off the ⟨glew⟩ & seeds, adhering to them; almost
quite rob'd Mr. Morine of that which he asked so much for, which I note for a
very ingenious Theft:

to; it is a very noble house, though somewhat low; The Gallerys, paintings there of the most illustrious Persons of both Sexes, the Queenes Bathes, Presence (in which the rich carved and gilded roofe) Theater, & large Garden, in which is an ample Fountaine, Grove, & Maille; are worthy of remarke:

Here I also frequently went to see them ride & exercise the Greate-horse; especialy at the Academy of Monsieur du Plessis, & de Veaus; which are particular Scholes of that Art frequented by the Nobility; & where besides the riding of the Greate horse Young-Gentlemen are taught to Fence, daunce, play on Musique & some skill in Fortification & the Mathematics: and truely the designe is admirable & very worthy; some of them being at the Charge of keeping neere an hundred brave horse, all of them manag'd to the great saddle.*

On the 12th I tooke Coach to see a generall Muster of all the Gens d'Armes about the Citty, before their Majesties and all the Grandees in the Bois de Boulogna neere Paris: They were reputed to be neere 20000 souldiers; besides spectators, who certainely much exceeded them in number: And here they performed all their motions, and being drawne up horse & foote into severall figures, represented a battell and fell to fighting in jeast, but did it so artificialy, as they had been reall Enemys, & in Earnest:

---

* V adds: & on solemn Occasions there is running at the Ring, & other Cavalier Exercises for prises of Value, which the Ladys Spectators propose to Crowne the Victor, & this is perform'd with extraordinary Pompe & no small charge in all sort of Gallantry: Of these Academys are many in *Paris*, & hardly any Towne of Note in France but has one or two, dedicated to these Souldierly diversions; some having so many Scholars, as that they keepe neere 100 horses, train'd up for their exercise, which indeede render the French Noblemen & Gent: so far superior in Horsemanship to other Nations: But this sort of Education, was, I think, first deriv'd from *Naples*, where are the best Horses: There is scarse a Prince in Europ, but what have ben scholars in the French Academys, & which by Consequence has leven'd them all, with the mode as well as Language of France, & disposed them to an undervaluing of their owne Countrys, with infinite prejudice to the rest of Europ; The *French*, naturaly active, insinuating & bold having with their trifles & new modes allmost debaucht all the sobriety of former times, Continualy aspiring to inlarge their Tyranny, by all the arts of dissimulation; & tretchery: Tho' it cannot be deneyed; that there are many worthy persons of probity, & greate Learning among them, who are weary of the intollerable yoake under which they Groone:

The Summer now drawing neere, and determining to spend the rest of it in some more remote Towne upon the river of Loyer; On the 19 of Aprill I tooke leave of Paris, and by the way of the Messenger agreed for my Passage to Orleans:

The Way from Paris to this City (as indeede most of the roades of France) is paved with a small square free-stone; so that the Country does not much molest the Travelor with dirt and ill way as ours in England dos; onely 'tis somewhat hard to the poore horses feete which causes them to ride more temperately, seldome going out of the trot, or *grand pas*, as they call it:

We passed by divers Wall'd Townes or Villages as the manner is frequently to secure them: Amongst others of note Chartres[1] & Estampes where we lay the first night: This has a faire Church: The next day we had excellent Way; but had like to come short home; for no sooner were we entred two or three leagues into the Forest of Orleans (which extends it selfe for many miles) after dinner; but the Company behind us, were set on by Rogues who shooting from the hedges and frequent Covert, slew fowre upon the spot, the rest flying: Amongst the slayne was a Captaine of Swisses of the Regiment of Picardy, a person much lamented: This disaster made such an Alarme in Orleans at our arival; that the Prevost-Martial with his assistants going in pursuite, brought in two whom they had shot, and exposed them in the greate Market-place, to see if any would take cognizance of them. I have greate Cause to give God thankes for this Escape; this happend on

Apr: 20 when comming to Orleans, and lying at the White-Crosse (where I found Mr. John Nicholas, eldest sonne to Mr. Secretary) there kitten'd a Cat on my bed, which left on it a Young one having 6 Eares, eight leggs, two bodys from the navil downe-wards, & two tayles: which strange Monster, I found dead; but warme by me in the Morning when I awaked. The 21 I went about to view the Citty, which is very well built of stone, upon the side of the Loyre; about the middle of the river is a very prety Iland full of Walkes, & faire Trees with some houses; this is contiguous to the Towne by a stately bridge of stone, reaching to the opposite suburbs, built likewise upon the edge of an hill from whenc is a beautifull prospect: At one of

1 Evelyn's error for Chastres, now Arpajon.

the extreames of the bridge are strong toures; and about the middle neere one side, the statue of the Virgin Mary, or Pieta, with a Christo Morto in her lap, as big as the life; At one side of the Crosse kneeles Charles the viith arm'd, and at the other Jane d'Arc the famous Pucele arm'd also like a Cavalier with boots & spurrs, her hayre dischevel'd as the Virago who deliver'd the Towne from our Countrymen, what time they beseig'd it: The valiant Creature being afterward burnt at Rouen for a Witch. The figures are all cast in Copper with a Pedistall full of Inscriptions, as well as a faire Columne joyning to it, which is all adornd with flowre de lyces & a Crucifix, with two saints, proceding as it were from two branches out of its Capital:

To this is made an annual procession, with a Masse sung before it on the 12 of May, with infinite Ceremony & Concourse of people:

The Wine of this Place is so grosse & strong that the Kings Cup-bearers are (as I was assurd) sworne never to give the King any of it: But it is else a very noble liquor, & much of it transported into other Countrys:

The Language for being here spoken in greate purity, as well for divers other Priveleges, & the University, makes the Towne to be much frequented by strangers, especialy Germans; which causes the English to make no long sojourne here; but such as can drinke & debauch:

The Citty stands in the County of Beaulse, was once styld a Kingdome, afterwards a Dutchy, as at present, & belongs to the 2d sonne of France: Many Councils have been celebrated here, and some Kings Crown'd. The University is very antient: divided now by the students into that of 4 Nations French, High-dutch, Normans and Picardins who have each their respective protectors, severall Officers, Treasurers, Consuls, Seal'es &c. There are in it two reasonable faire Libraries publique: whenc one may borrow a booke to on⟨e⟩s Chamber, giving but a note under hand, which is a costome extraordinary, & a confidence that has cost many Liberarys deare. The first Church I went to visite was that of St. Croix: It has been a stately fabric but now much ruind by the late Civil Warrs: They report the towre of it, to have beene the highest in France: There is the beginning of a faire reparation: about this Cathedrall is a very Spacious Cymeterie.

The Towne hous is also very nobly built, with an high towre to it: The Streetes, Market-place (some whereof are deliciously planted with Limes) are both ample & very straite; so exquisitely paved with a kind of pibble, that I have not seene a neater Towne in France: In fine, this Citty was by Francis the first esteemed the most agreable in his vast dominions:

On the 28, taking Boate on the Loir, I went towards Blois; the passage & River, being both very divertissant: Thus we went by Mehun, and Baugency where we din'd: Thence to a little Towne call'd St. Dieu where we repos'd that night. Thence quitting our Barke we hired horses to carry us to Blois by the Way of Chambourg, a famous house of the Kings built in the middle of a solitary Parke by Fran: I: the Enclosure is a Wall, and full of deere: That which made me desirous of seeing this Palace was the extravagance of the designe, especialy the Stayre-Case mention'd by the Architect Palladio: The⟨y⟩ report 1800 worke-men were employ'd in this fabrique together during the space of twelve yeares, which makes me wonder it was not finish'd, it being no greater than divers Gentlemens houses in England; both for rome and circuit. The Carvings are indeede very rich & full: The Stayre Case is devis'd with 4 Entries, or ascents, which thwart one another so, that though 4 severall persons meete, yet they never come in sight, but by the small loope holes, till they land: It consists of 274 stepps as I remember, & is indeede a worke very extraordinary; but of far greater expense, than use or beauty: The Chimnys of the house appeare like so many Towres: About the whole is a large deepe moate; The Country about it full of Corne & Wine, with many faire noblemens houses.

Being ariv'd at Blois this Evening, on the 30th of April which was the morrow I went to view the Towne, which is both very hilly, uneven and rag⟨g⟩ed.

The situation is on the side of the Loire, having suburbs joynd by a stately bridg of stone, upon which is a Pyramid with an Inscription I could not read as I passed:

The Castle has at the Entery Lewes the 12 on horseback in stone as big as the life, under a Gotic State.

Under this a very wide payre of Gates nailed full of Wolves heads & Wild Boares: Behind the Castle the Present Duke Gastion had begun a faire building, through which we walked into a large Garden, esteemed for its furniture one of the rarest

in Europ, especialy for simples and exotic plants, in which he
takes extraordinary delight: On the right hand is a longe Gallery
full of antient Statues & Inscriptions both of Marble and
Brasse: The length of it being 300 paces, divides the Garden into
higher & lower ground: having a very nob⟨l⟩e fountaine: There
is likewise the Portraiteure of an Hart taken in the forest by
Lewes the 12th which has 24 Antlers on its head. Henc we went
to the Collegiat Church of St. Saviours, where we saw many
Sepulchers of the Earles of Blois.

On Sunday, being May-day, we walked up into the Pall-mall,
which is very long and so nobly shaded with tall trees (being in
the middst of a greate Wood) as, unlesse that of Tours, I had
not seene a statlier: from hence we proceeded, with a friend of
mine through the adjoyning Forest to see if we could meete any
Wolves, which are here in such numbers, that they often come
and take the Children out of the very Streetes; for all which, will
not the Duke (who is Sovraigne here) permitt them to be
destroy'd: Thus we walked 5 or 6 miles out right, but met with
none. Yet a Gentleman, who was resting himselfe under a tree,
with his horse grazing by him; told us that halfe an houre before
two Wolves had set upon his horse, and had in probability
devour'd him but for a dog which lay by him that frighted them:
At a little Village at the end of this Wood we eate excellent
Creame; and visited a Castle which was there builded on a very
steepe Cliff: so we return'd:

Bloys is a towne where the Language is exactly spoken, the
Inhabitans very courteous, the [ayre] so good that it is for that
cause the ordinary nursery of the Kings Children; & the People
so ingenious, that for Goldsmiths Worke, & Watches no place
in France affords the like: The Pastures about the river are very
rich and pleasant.

Tuesday the 2d of May, we tooke boate againe, passing by
Charmont, a prow'd Castle on the left hand; before it a sweete
Iland, deliciously shaded with tall trees: A little distance from
hence, at Ambois, we went on shore; this is a very agreable Village, built of stone, and cover'd with blew Slate (as all the
Townes generaly are upon the Loyre) but the Castle was that
which chiefly invited us, the thicknesse of whose towres from
the River to the top being admirable: We enterd by the draw-
bridg, which has an invention to let one fall unhappily if not

præmonished: It is full of halls, & spacious Chambers, and one
Stayre Case large enough and sufficiently commodious to
receive a Coach and land it on the very towre, as they told us it
had been don: There is some artillery in it, but that which is
most prodigious & observable is in that antient Chapell a staggs
head, or branches hung up in chaynes, consisting of 20 brow
antlers, the beame bigger than a mans middle, and of an incredible length: Indeede it is monstrous, and I cannot conceive how
it should be artificial: they shew also the ribbs and Vertebras of
the same beast; which might haply be made counterfeit of
Whalebone. Leaving the Castle, we pass'd Mont Louis, a Village having never an house above-ground; but such onely as are
hewn out of the maine rocks of excellent free-stone; here &
there the funnell of a Chimny appearing through the Surface
amongst the Vineyards which are over them; and in this manner
they inhabite the Caves, as it were sea-Cliffs, one side of the
river for many miles together: And now we come within sight of
Tours whither we were designd for the rest of the tyme I resolv'd
to spend in France, the sejourne being so absolutely agreeable:

Tours is situat on the easy side of an hill on the river of Loyre,
having a faire bridg of stone cald St. Edme: the Streetes very
long, straite, spacious, well built, & exceeding cleane: The Suburbs very greate and pleasant, joynd to the Citty by another
bridg: On the 5, we were carry'd about the Towne to see severall
places; especialy St. Martins both Church and Monastry, which
is a vast piece of Gotic building, having 4 Square toures, faire
Organs, a stately Altar, where they shew strangers the bones &
ashes of St. Martine, with other reliques. From hence we walk'd
to the Mall, which is without comparison the noblest for length,
& shade the best in Europ, having 7 rowes of the talest & goodliest Elmes I had ever beheld, the innermost of which do so
embrace each other, & at such a prodigious height, as nothing
can be more solemn & majestical: Here we play'd a party or two,
and then walked about the Towne Walles, which are built of
square stone fill'd with Earth, & having a moate; no Citty in
France exceeding it in beauty or delight.

On the 6t we went to St. Gratian, reported to have bene built
by our Country-men: The dyal and Clock-worke is much
esteem'd: The Church has two handsom towres & spires of
stone, & the whole fabric is very noble & venerable; To this

joynes the Palace of the Arch-bishop, consisting both of old, and new building: with many faire romes in it, & a faire Garden to it: Here I grew acquainted with one Monsieur Mercy, a very good Musitian: The Archbish: also treated me very Courteously: Hence we went to Visite divers other Churches, Chapells & Monasteries for the greatest part neately built, & full of pretty Payntings, especialy the Covent of the Capucins which has a prospect over the whole Citty, & many faire Walkes in Cascade:

On the 8th, I went to see their Manifactures in silke (for in this Towne they drive a very considerable trade with Silk-Wormes) their pressing & wateri⟨n⟩g the Grograns & Chambletts: with weights of an extraordinary poyse put into a rolling Engine.

Here I tooke a Master of the Language, and studyed the tongue very dilligently; recreating my selfe sometimes at the Maill, & sometymes about the Towne.

The house just over against the place I lay at had been formerly a Palace of the Kings, ha⟨v⟩ing the outside totaly coverd with innumerable flore de lyes, emboss'd out of the stone: here Mary de Medices had her Court when she was compelld to retyre from Paris by the Persecution of the greate Cardinal.

It was on the 21 I receiv'd the newes of the sicknesse and death of my Sister in Law, Wife to my Bro: Geo: Evelyn.

On the 25 was the Fest Dieu, and a goodly Procession of all the Religious Orders, the whole streetes hung with their best Tappissrys, and most precious moveables expos'd, silkes, Damasks, Velvets, Plate & Pictures in aboundance, the Streets strew'd with flowres, and full of pageantry, banners & bravery:

On the June the 6t I went forth to visite that goodly & venerable Abby of Marmoustier, by water; it being one of the greatest, & principall in the Kingdome: To it is a very ample Church of Stone; with a very high Pyramid: Here amongst other reliques the Monkes shew'd us the holy Ampoule, the same with that which sacres their Kings at Rhemes, this being that which anoynted Hen: 4th. Hence ascending many stepps we went into the Abbots Palac, where we were shew'd a monstrous vast Tunn (as big as that at Heidelberg) which they report St. Martine (as I remember) did fill with one cluster of Grapes growing there.

The next day we walked about 2 miles from the Citty to an extraordinary agreable solitude Calld Du Plessis, The house belongs to the King, & has many pretty Gardens, the fullest of Nightingalls that ever I saw: In the Chapell lyes buryed the famous Poet Ronsard: Returning, we stepp'd into a Covent of Franciscans calld St. Cosme, where the Cloyster is painted with the miracles of their St. Francis à Paula, whose ashes lye in their Chapell. The Tomb has 4 small Pyramids of Marble at each Corner:

On the 9 June: I was invited abroad to a Vineyard, which was so artificialy planted, and supported with arched poles, that stooping downe one might see from end to end a very greate length, under the Vines, the bunches hanging downe in aboundance:

On the 20th we tooke hors & rid to see certaine natural Caves, calld Goutiere, neere Colombieres, where there is a Spring within the bowells of the Earth very deepe, so excessive cold, that the dropps, meeting with some lapidescent matter, converts them into an hard stone, which hangs about it like Isicles; having many others in the forme of Comfitures & suggar plumms as wee call them: Neere this we went under the ground, almost two furlongs, being lighted with candles, to view the source & spring which serves the whole Citty, by a passage cutt through the maine rock of Free-stone.

On the 28, I went out of Towne to see the Palace & Gardens of Chevareux, which is a sweete place:

The 30th I walked out on the Vinyards as fare as Roche Corbé, to the ruines of an old & very strong ⟨Castle⟩ sayd to have ben built by the English: The height is excessive, & the precipice on a dreadfull Cliff, from whence the Country & River yeald a most incomparable Prospect.

27 July I heard excellent Musique at the Jesuites, who have here a Schole and Convent; but a meane Chapell: We had now store of those admirable Melons so much celebrated in France for the best, of the whole Kingdome. But I was about this tyme so exceedingly tormented with my gumms, by a new tooth which was growing, that I was faine to be lanced two or three times to give it passage, & aswage the paine:

Aug: 1: My Valet de Chambre, One Garro, a Spaynard, borne in Biscay, for some misdemeanors, I was forc'd to discharge; he demanded of me (besides his Wages) no lesse then 100 Crownes to cary him to his Country, which I refusing to pay, as no part of

our agreement; he had the impudence to arest me, and serve me
with a Processe: so the next day I was call'd on to appeare in full
Court, where both our Advocats pleaded before the Lieutennant Civile: But it was so unreasonable a pretence, that the
Judge had not patience to heare it out, but immediately acquitting me, was so civil, as after he had extreamely reproch'd the
Advocate who tooke part with my servant, he rose from the
Bench, and making a courteous excuse to me, that being a
stranger I should be so barbarously usd, conducted me through
the Court to the very streete dore: This Varlet afterwards threat-
en'd to Pistol me.

The next day I waited on the Lieutennant to returne him
thankes for his greate humanity:

On the 18 came the Queene of England to Towers newly
ariv'd in France, and taking this Citty in her way to Paris; she
was very nobly receiv'd both by people and Cleargy, who went to
meete her with all the Train'd bands: After the Harangue, the
Archbish: entertaind her Majestie at his owne Palac, Where
I did my duty to her: The 20th, she set forwards towards Paris.

Sep: 8: came two of my Kindsmen from Paris to Towers,
where I settled them in their Pension and exercises.

On the 14 we tooke post for Richlieu, passing by l'Isle
Bouchart, a Village in the way.

The 15 We ariv'd at the towne, and went to se⟨e⟩ the Cardinals Palace neere it: The Towne is built in a low marshy-ground,
having a small river cutt by hand, very even & straite, capable of
bringing up a small Vessell: It consists of one onely considerable
streete; the houses on both sides (as indeede they are throughout
the Towne) built most exactly uniforme, after a modern handsome designe: I⟨t⟩ has a large goodly Market-house and Place,
opposite to which the Church built all of free-stone, having two
pyramids of stone which stand hollow from the Towers: The
church is well built, & of a well orderd Architecture, within
handsomly pav'd & adorn'd: To this Towne belongs an Academy,
where besides the exercise of the Horse, Armes, Dauncing &c
All the Siences are read in the Vulgar French; Professors stipendiated by the greate Cardinal, who by this, the Cheape living
there, & divers Priveledges, not onely designd the improvement
of the vulgar Language, but to draw People & strangers to the
Towne: But sin⟨c⟩e the Cardinals death, it is thinly inhabited, it

standing so much out of the way, & in a place not well situated either for health or pleasure: It being onely the Name of the Place, and an old house there standing, & belonging to his Ancestors, which allurd him to build: This pretty Towne is also handsomly wall'd about, & moated, with a kind of slight fortification, two fayre-Gates & draw-bridges: Before the Gate towards the Palace is a most spacious Circle where the faire is annualy kept.

About a flite-shot off the towne on the left hand is the Cardinals house, being a most princely pile, though upon an old designe, not altogether gotique, but mix'd: it has a cleare moate environing it. The roomes are stately, most richly furnishd, with Tissue, Damasque, Aras, Velvet: Pictures, Statues, Vases, & all sorts of Antiquities; especialy the Cæsars, all of Oriental Alabaster: The long Gallery is paynted with the famous Acts of the Founder; the roofe with the life of Julius Cæsar; at the end of it, is a Cupola or singing theater, supported with very stately pillars of black marble: The Court is very ample; and the Chapell, antiently belonging to his family: The Gardens without are very large & the Parterrs of incomparable imbrodry, set with frequent statues both brasse, & Marble: The Groves, Meadows & severall excellent Walkes are a real Paradise: So on the 16th we returnd to Towers; from whence after 19 Weekes sejourne we went towards the more Southern parts of France minding now to shape my Course so as I might Winter in Italy:

September 16th with my friend Mr. Thicknesse, and our guide, we went the first day 7 leagues to a Castle cal'd Chenonceaux built by Cath: di Medices, and now belonging to the Duke of Vendosme; it stands on a bridg: In the Gallery amongst divers other excellent statues, is that of Scipio Africanus of Oriental Alabaster: 21 We pass'd by Ville-Franche, where we din'd, & so by Muneton, lying at Viaron, au Mouton which was 20 leagues: The next day by Mung, to Bourge 4 leagues, where we spent the day: This towne is the Capital of Berry, an University, and much frequented by the Dutch, situated on the river Eure: It stands high; strong & well placed for defence: It is inviron'd with Meadows, and excellent Vines, which makes living very cheape: In the Suburbs of St. Privé there is a fountayne of sharp Waters, which they report wholesome against the Stone: They shew'd us also a vast tree, which they say stands just in the

Center of France: The French tongue is purely spoken in this place: We went to see St. Stephens Church which is the Cathedrall, well built à la Gotic, full of sepulchres withoutside; with the representation of the final Judgement over one of the Ports: Here they shew the Chapel of Claud de la Chastre, a famous Souldier who had serv'd six kings of France in their Warrs. Then we went to St. Chapell, built much like at Paris, full of reliqu⟨e⟩s; and the bones of one Briat a Gyant of 15 Cubits-high: This was built by Jo: Duke of Berry; and there is shew'd the Coronet of the Dukedome. The grosse Tour is a Pharos for defence of the towne; nor did I ever see a stronger, in thicknesse 18 foote fortified with graft & workes: There is still a garnison in it, and a strange engine wherewith to fling great stones: and the yron Cage where Lewes duke of Orleans was kept by Charles the 8th. Neere to the Towne-house stands the Colledge of Jesuites, where was heretofore an Amphitheatre: here I was courteously entertayn'd by a Jesuite who had us into the Garden, where wee fell amaine into disputation: The house of Jaques Coeur is worth seeing. Bourges is an Archbishopric, & Primate of Aquitaine. Having sufficiently visited this Towne, I tooke my leave of Mr. Nicholas, & some other English there, & proceeded on my journey 23d by Douleroy, Pont du Charge, and lay that evening at Coulaivre: 13 Leagues. The 24 by Franchede, St. Menau: thenc to Moulins where we din'd: This is the chiefe towne of the Bourbonois, on the river Allier very navigable: The Streetes are faire, The Castle has a noble Prospect, having been the seate of the Dukes: Here is a pretty Parke and Garden: After dinner came manny who offer'd knives & Cisars to sell, it being a Towne famous for those trifles: This Dutchy of Bourbon is ordinarily assignd to the dowry of the Queenes of France:

Hence we tooke horse for Varenne, an obscure Village where we lay that night; The next day we deviated some what out of the way to see the towne of Bourbon l'Archambaut, from whose antient & ragged Castle is deriv'd the name of the present Royal Family of France. The Castle stands on a flinty rock, over looking the Towne: In the middst of whose streetes are some Bathes of medicinal Waters, some of them excessive hott, but nothing so neately wald, & adornd as ours in Sommersetshire; & indeede they are chiefly usd to drinke off, our Queene being then lodg'd there for that cause: After dinner I went to see the

St. Chapel, a prime place of devotion, where is kept one of the
Thornes of our Saviors Crowne, & a piece of the real Crosse;
excellent paintings in glasse, some few statues of stone & Wood,
which they shew for curiosities: Hence we Went forward to
Palisse a Vilage that lodg'd us that night.

On the 26t we ariv'd at Rouanne, where we quitted our
Guide, and tooke Post for Lions:

Roan seemd to me one of the pleasantest & agreeable places
for a retyr'd Person imaginable; for besides the situation, which
is on the Loire, there are excellent provisions, cheape & aboundant: It being late e're we left this Towne, we rod no farther than
Tarrara that night (passing St. Saforin) a little desolate Village,
standing in a Vally neere a very pleasant streame encompass'd
with fresh meadows, & Vineyards: The Hills, which we rod over
before we descended, and after on Lions side, are so high &
mountainous, that fir & pine grow frequently on them; and the
ayre mithought was much alterd, as well as houses, built flatter,
& more after the Easterne manner: Before I went to bed, I tooke
a Landskip of this pleasant Terrace: But there followd so greate
a Tempest of thunder & lightning, as I never in my life had then
observ'd the like.

The 27th we rod post by Pont-Charu to Lions which being
but 6 leagues we soone accomplish'd, having made 85 leagues
from Toures in 7 dayes:

Here at Lions at the Lion d'or, rüe de Flandre I encounter'd
divers of mine acquaintance who comming from Paris, were
design'd for Italy: We lost no time in se⟨e⟩ing the Citty, because
of being ready to accompany these Gentlemen in their journey:
Lions is incomparably situated upon a Confluence of Rivers
Saone & Rhodanus, which washes the Walls of the Citty in a
very rapid streame: Each of these has its bridg; that over the
Rhone consists of 28 Arches. But what appeares most extrava-
gant, & very stately are the two high Cliffs, cal'd St. Just &
St. Sebastian, upon one of which stands a strong fort, guarisond:
We visited the Cathedrall St. Jean, and there one of the fairest
Clockes for art & buisy invention that ever I had seene: The fab-
rique of the Church is Gotic; as is likewise that of St. Estienne,
& St. Croix joyning to it: On the top of one of the Towres of
St. Jeans (for it has 4) we beheld the Whole Citty, & Country
with a prospect reaching even to the very Alpes themselves

many leagues distant. The Archbishops Palace is fairely built: The Church of St. Niser is the greatest: That of the Jacobins well built: Here are divers other fine Churches, and very noble buildings, which we had not time to visite, onely that of the Charite, or greate Hospital for the poore infirme people, which entertaining about 1500 Soules, with Schoole, Granary, Gardens & all conveniencies is of a wonderfull expense, and worthy the seeing. The place of the Belle Court is very spacious, especialy observable for the view it affords, so various & agreable, of hills, rocks, Vineyards, gardens, Precipices, & other extravagant & incomparable advantages[1] abounding in this Citty, and presenting themselves together: The Pall-mall is set with faire trees: In fine this stately, cleane & noble Citty (built all of stone) abounds in Persons of Quality, & rich Merchands: Those of Florence obtaining greate Priveleges above the rest. In the Towne-house they shew two tables d'airain on which is engraven Claudius's Speech pronounc'd to the Senat concerning the franchising of the Towne with the Roman Priveleges; there are also divers other Antiquities to be seene.

Sept: 30 we bargain'd with a Waterman to transport us as far as Avignon upon the River; so we embarqued from Lions, and got the first night to Vienne in Dauphine: This is an Archbishoprick and the Province gives title to the Heyre aparent of France; here we lay, and supp'd; having (amongst other dainties) a dish of Truffles, which is a certaine earth-nut, found out by an hogg, train'd up to it, & for which those Creatures, are sold at a greate price: It is in truth an incomparable meate: We were shewd the ruines of an Amphitheatre, reasonable entire, and many handsome Palaces: especialy that of Pontius Pilat, which we saw, not far from the Towne at the foote of a solitary Mountaine, neere the River, having 4 pinacles: Here 'tis reported he pass'd his exile, and precipitated himselfe into the Lake not far from it: The house is modernly built, & seemes to be the seate of some Gentleman; being in a very pleasent place though somewhat melancholy.

The Cathedral of Vienne is St. Maurice, & there are many other pretty buildings worth the seeing, but nothing more then

1 Rising grounds, vantage-grounds.

the Mills where the⟨y⟩ hammer & polish the Sword-blades, which is a greate Curiosity:

Henc the next Morning we Swam (for the river runns so exceedingly rapid, that we were onely steerd) to a small Vilage call'd Tain, where we dynd; Over against this is another Towne nam'd Tournon where is an exceeding strong Castle under a very high precipice; To the Castle joynes the Jesuits Coledge who have a fayre Library: The Prospect was so tempting, that I could not forbeare to designe it with my Crayon.

After we had eaten we came to Valence, a Capital Citty, carr⟨y⟩ing the title of a Dutchy; But the Bishop is now sole Lord Temporal of it, & the Country about it: The Towne having an University famous for the Civil Law is much frequented: but the Churches are none of the fairest, having been greately defac'd in the time of the Warrs: Yet are the Streets full of pretty fountaines: The Citadell strong, & Garnisond: Here we pass'd that night, and the next morning by Pont St. Esprit, which is 2412 yards in length & consists of 22 Arches; in the Pillars or piles of the Arches are Windoes (as it were) to receive the Water when it is high and full; here we went on shore, it being very dangerous to passe the bridg with a boate:

Hence leaving our barque, we tooke horse (se⟨e⟩ing but at some distance the Towne & Principality of Orange) and lodging one night on the Way ariv'd by noone at Avignon: This Citty has belong'd to the Popes ever since Clem: the 6ts tyme, being Anno 1352, alienated by Jeane Queene of Naples & Sicily. Entring the Gates of this towne the Souldiers at the Guard tooke our Pistols & Carbines from us, and examin'd us very strictly; after that having obtain'd the Governors leave, & Vice-Legat to tarry for 3 dayes, we were civily conducted to our lodging.

The City is plac'd on the Rhodanus, and divided from the newer part, or Towne (which is situate on the other side of the River) by a very faire bridge of stone, which has been broken, at one of whose extreames is a very high rock on which a strong Castle well furnish'd with Artillery. The Walls of the Citty (being all square huge free stone) are absolutely the most neate and best in repaire that in my life I ever saw: It is full of well built Palaces: Those of the Vice Legats & Archbish: being the

most magnificent: Many sumptuous Churches, especialy that of
St. Magdalene & St. Martial, wherein the Card: d'Amboise is
the most observable: That of the Celestines where Clement the
8th lies buried, the Altar whereof is exceeding rich; but for nothing I more admir'd it than the Tomb of Madona Laura Petrarchs
celebrated Mistris.

We were in the Arsenale, Popes Palace, and in the Synagogue
of the Jewes, who are in this towne distinguish'd by their red
hats:

Vaucluse so much renound for the solitude of the learned
Petrarch, we beheld from the Castle; but could not goe to visite
it, for want of time; being now taking Mules, & a guide for Marcelles:

Sep: 30 we lay at Loumas, the next morning came to Aix;
having pass'd that most dangerous & extreamely rapid river of
Durance: In this tract all the Heathes or Commons are cover'd
with Rosemary, Lavander, Lentiscs & the like sweete shrubbs
for many miles together, which to me was then a very pleasant
sight:

Aix is the chiefe Citty of Province, being a Parliament &
Presidial towne, with other royal Courts & Metrapolitan jurisdiction: It is well built, the houses exceeding high, & Streetes
ample: The Cathedrall St. Sauveurs is a noble pile, adornd with
innumerable figures (especialy that of St. Michael). The Baptis-
tarie, the Palace, the Court, built in a most specious Piazza are
very faire: The Duke of Guizes house is worth the seeing, being
furnish'd with many Antiquities in, and about it. The Jesuites
have also here a royal Colledge, and the City is an University.
From hence Octob: 7 we had a most delicious journey to
Marselles throug⟨h⟩ a Country, sweetely declining to the South
& Mediterranean Coasts, full of Vine-yards, & Olive-yards,
Orange trees, Myrtils, Pomegranads & the like sweete Plantations, to which belong innumerable pleasantly situated Villas, to
the number of above 15 hundred; built all of Free-stone, and
most of them in prospect shewing as if they were so many
heapes of snow dropp'd out of the clowds amongst those perennial greenes: It was almost at the shutting in of the Gates that
we got in at

Marcelles: This Towne stands on the Sea-Coast upon a
sweete rising; tis well wall'd, & has an excellent Port for Ships, &

Gallys, securd by an huge Chayne of Yron which draw crosse
the harbour at pleasure; & there is a well fortified tower: besides
this, there are also three other Forts or small Castles, especialy
that cald the If built on a rock: Ratonneau, & that of St. John
strongly garnison'd. But the Castle commanding the Citty, is
that of Nostre dame de la Guard: In the Chapel hang up divers
Crocodiles Skinns: We went then to Visite the Gallys being
about 25 in number. The Captaine of the Gally royal gave us
most courteous entertainement in his Cabine, the Slaves in the
interim playing both on loud & soft musique very rarely: Then
he shew'd us how he commanded their motions with a nod, &
his Wistle, making them row out; which was to me the newest
spectacle I could imagine, beholding so many hundreds of mis-
erab⟨l⟩y naked Persons, having their heads shaven cloose, &
onely red high bonnets, a payre of Course canvas drawers, their
whole backs, & leggs starke naked, doubly chayned about
their middle, & leggs, in Cupples, & made fast to their seates:
and all Commanded in a trise, by an Imperious & cruell sea-
man: One Turke amongst them he much favourd, who waited
on him in his Cabine, but naked as he was, & in a Chayne lock'd
about his leg; but not coupled.

    Then this Gally, I never saw any thing more richly carv'd &
Guilded (the Sovraigne excepted) and most of the rest were
exceeding beautiful: Here, after we had bestow'd something
amongst the Slaves, the Cap: sent a band of them to give us
musique at dinner where we lodged. I was amaz'd to contemplate how these miserable Catyfs lye in their Gally, considering
how they were crowded together; Yet was there hardly one but
had some occupation or other: by which as leasure, in Calmes,
& other times, permitts, they get some little monye; in so much
as some have after many Yeares of cruel Servitude been able to
purchase their liberty: Their rising forwards, & falling back at
their Oare, is a miserable spactacle, and the noyse of their
Chaines with the roaring of the beaten Waters has something
of strange & fearfull in it, to one unaccostom'd. They are ruld,
& chastiz'd with a bulls-pizle dry'd upon their backs, & soles of
their feete upon the least dissorder, & without the least humanity: Yet for all this they are Cherefull, & full of vile knavery: We
went after dinner to see the church of St. Victoire, where that
Saints head is reserv'd in a shrine of silver which weighs 600

lbs: Thence to Nostre Dame, exceedingly well built: This is the Cathedrall: Then the Duke of Guizes Palace; The Palais of Justice; the Maison du Roy. But there is nothing more strange than the infinite numbers of slaves, working in the Streets, & carying burthens with their confus'd noises, & gingling of their huge Chaynes: The Chiefe negoce of the Town is silkes & drougs out of Africa, Syria and Egypt: Also Barbara-horses which come hither in great numbers: The Towne is governd by 4 Captaines, & has 3 Consuls, and one Assessor: Three Judges royal; The Marchants have also a Judge for ordinary causes: Here we bought Umbrellos against the heate, and consulted of our jorney to Canes by Land, for feare of the Pickaron Turkes who make prize of many small Vessells about these parts, finding never a Gally bound for Genöa whither we were design'd: so on Octob: 9 we tooke our Mules, passing the first night very late in sight of St. Baume, & the solitary Grott, where the⟨y⟩ affirme Mary Magdalen did her pennance: the next day we lay at Perigeux; which is a Citty built on an old foundation, witnesse the ruines of a most stately Amphitheater, which I went out to designe, being about a flight-shoote from the towne: They call it now the Rolsies: There is also a very strong towre neere the Towne calld the Visone: But the towne and Citty are built at some distance from each other: It is a Bishoprick, & has a Cathedral, with divers noble-mens houses all in sight of that sea: The place formerly cald (and well knowne by Antiquaries) Forum Julij:

Oct: 10, as we proceeded on our way we passd by the ruines of a stately Aquæ-duct; the soile about the Country being rocky; yet full of Pines, & rare simples:

On the 11th we lay at Canes, which is a small port on the Mediterranean; here we agree'd with a Sea-man to transport us to Genöa, so having procurd a bill of Health (without which there is no admission at any Towne in Italy) we embarq'd on the 12 of Octob: touching at the Ilands of St. Margaret, & St. Honore, lately retaken from the Spanyards with so much bravery by Prince Harcourt: here, having payd some small duty, we bought divers trifles offerd us by the Souldiers but without going on Land: Thenc we Coasted within 2 leagues of Antibo which is the utmost towne of France: Thence by Nice a Citty in Savoy, built all of brick, which gives it a very pleasant aspect towards the sea, having a Castle built very high that commands it: Thus we also sail'd by Morgus now cald Monaco (having passd Villa Franca, heretofore Portus Herculis); where ariving after the Gates were Shut we were forc'd to abide in our Barque all night, which was put into the haven, the wind comming contrary; In the morning we were hastned away having no time permitted us (by our avaritious Master with whom we had made a bargaine) to goe up to see this strong and considerable Place: it now belongs to a Prince of the family of the Grimaldi of Genoa, who has put both it & himselfe under protection of the French: The situation (for that I could contemplat at pleasure) is on such a promontory of solid stone & rock, as I never beheld the like: The towne-Walls very fayre: Within it we were told was an ample Court, and a Palace furnish'd with the most princly & rich moveables imaginable, also collection of Statues, Pictures, & especially of Massie plate to an infinite value: Next we saild by Menton, and Vintimiglia, being the first Citty of the Republique of Genöa; supp'd at Onela where we ankerd and lay on shore, The next morning we coasted in view of the Ile of Corsica, then passd St. Remes, all whose rivage is incomparably furnish'd with Ever-greens Orange, Citron, & even Date-trees: Port Mauritio, Where we also lay; The next morning by Drano, Araisso famous for the best Corrall fishing, which here growes in aboundance upon the rocks, deepe, & continualy coverd with the Sea: By Albenga, & Finale a very faire & strong Towne belonging to the K: of Spayne, for which reason a Monsieur in our Vessell was extreamely afraide, as likewise the Patron of our Barke (for that they frequently catch a French Prize, as they creepe by these shores, to go into Italy) who ply'd both sayles & Oares to get under protection of a Genoeze-Gally that passd not farr before us, and in whose company we sayld a Lee as far as the Cape of Savona: a Towne built at the rise of the Apennines; for all this Coast (except a little at St. Remes) is an high and steepe mountainous ground, consisting all of rock-marble, without any grasse, tree, or rivage, most terrible to looke on: A strange object it is to consider how some poore cotages stand fast on the declivities of these precipices, & what steps they ascend to them; but they consist of all sorts of most precious marbles:

Here on the 15, forsaking our Gally we encounterd a little foule Weather, which made us creepe Terra, Terra as they call it; and so a Vessell that encounter'd us advis'd us to do: But our Patron, striving to double the point of Savona, making out into the Wind, put us all into an incredible hazard; for blowing very hard from Land 'twixt those horrid gapps of the Mountaines, it set so violently, as rais'd on the sudaine a⟨n⟩ over growne Sea, so as we could not then by any meanes recover the Weather shore for many houres, inso much that what with the Water already enterd, & the confusion of fearfull Passengers (of which one was an Irish Bishop & his Bro: a Priest, confessing some as at the Article of Death) we were almost uterly abandon'd to despaire; Our Pilot himselfe giving us for gon: But so it pleas'd God on the suddaine (and as now we were almost sinking downe right, wearied with pumping, & laving out the Water) to appease the Wind, that with much adoe & greate perill we recover'd the Shore, which we now kept within lesse then halfe a league, in view & sent of those pleasant Villas, & fragrant Orchards which are situated on this Coast, full of Princly retirements for the Sumptuousnesse of their buildings & noblenesse of the planta- tions; especialy those at St. Pietro d'Arena, from whence (the wind spiring as now it did) might perfectly be smelt the peculiar joys of Italy, in the natural perfumes of Orange, Citron, & Jass- mine flowres, for divers leagues to seaward. (So on)

TRAVELS IN ITALY I: GENOA TO VITERBO (1644)

OCTO: 16 WE got to Anker under the Pharos or Watch-towre erected on an high rock, at the mouth of the Mole of Genoa; the weather being yet so fowle, that for two houres at least we dast not stand in to the haven: Towards the evening adventur'd and came on shore by the Prattique-house, where after strict exami- nation of the Syndics, we were had to the Ducal Palace, and there our names beeing taken, we were conducted to our Inne, which was at one Zacharias an Englishmans, where we were almost amazd at the consideration of the danger we had escaped, never thinking to have seene that evening alive: I shall never forget a story of our host Zacharye, who upon the relation of our perill, quitted us with another of his owne, being ship-wrack'd as he affir(m)'d solemnly, in the middle of a greate sea some where in the West-Indies: That he swam no lesse then 22 leagues to another Iland, with a tinder-box wraped up in his hayre, which was not so much as wett all that way: That picking up the Carpenters tooles with other provisions in a Chest, he & the Carpenter, that accompany'd him (good swimmer(s) it seemes both) floated the Chest before them, and ariving at last in a place full of Wood, they built another Vessell, and so escaped; the rest being all cast away: After this story we no more talk'd of our danger, for Zachary put us quite downe, though we were all Travellors.

Octob: 17, accompany'd with a most courteous Marchand, who had long liv'd in the Towne, calld Mr. Tomson, we went to vieue the rarities: The Citty is built in the hollow, or boosome of a Mountaine, whose ascent is very steepe, high & rocky; so as from the Lanterne, & Mole, to the hill it represents the Shape of a Theater; the Streetes & buildings so ranged one above the other; as our seates are in Playhouses: but by reason of their incomparable materials, beauty & structure: never was any artificial sceane more beautifull to the eye of the beholder; nor is any place certainly in the World, so full for the bignesse of well designed & stately Palaces; as may easily be concluded by that rare booke in a large folio, which the greate Virtuoso & Painter Paule Rubens has publish'd, that containes but one onely Street & 2 or 3 Churches.

The first Palace of note that we went to Visite was that of Hieronymo del Negros, to which we pass'd by boate crosse the harbour; here I could not but observe the suddaine & devlish passion of a sea-man who plying us, was intercepted by another fellow, that interposd his boate before him, & tooke us in; for the teares gushing out of his eyes, he put his finger in his mouth & almost bit it off by the joynt, shewing it to his antagonist, as an assurance to him of some bloudy revenge, if ever he came neere that part of the harbour any more: And indeede this beautifull Citty is more stayn'd with such horrid acts of revenge & murthers, than any one place in Europ, or haply the World besides where there is a political government; which renders it very unsafe to strangers: This makes it a gally matter to carry a knife about one whose poynt is not broken off.

This Palas of Negros is richly furnish'd with the rarest Pictures, & other collections & moveables: but nothing which more delighted me then the terrac, or hilly Garden, where there stands a grove of stately trees, furnish'd with artificial Sheepe, Shepheards, & Wild beasts, so naturaly cut in a grey-stone, fountaines, rocks, & Piscina's, that casting your eyes one way, you would imagine your selfe in a Wildernesse & silent Country, side-ways in the heart of a greate Citty, & backwarde in the middst of the Sea; and that which is most admirable, all this within one Aker of ground, and I thinke the most stupendious & delightfull in the whole World: In this house I first tooke notice of those red plaster flores, which are made so hard, and kept so polite, that for some time, one would take them for whole pieces of Porphyrie: I have frequently wonderd, we never practis'd it in England for Cabinets, & romes of state, for it appeare⟨s⟩ to me beyond any invention whatev⟨e⟩r of that kind; but by their carefull covering them with Canvas, & fine mattresses, where there is much passage, I suppose them not so lasting in their glory, & happly they are often repaird.

There are in this Citty innumerable other Palaces of particular Curiositys, for the Marchands being prodigiously rich, have like our neighbours the Hollanders, little or no extent of ground to employ their Estates in; & therefore, as they on Pictures & hangings; so these on Marble houses, & rich furniture. One of the greatest remarke for Circuit, is that of the Prince d'Orias, which reaches from the very Sea, to the Summit of the Mountaines: The House without is most magnificently built, nor lesse gloriously furnish'd, having whole tables, & beadsteads of massy silver, besides many of them set with Achates, Onyxes, Cornelians, Lazulis, Pearle, Turquizes, & other precious stones: The Pictures & Statues innumerable: To this Palace there belongs three Gardens, the first whereoff is beautified with a tarrac supported by pillars of Marble: There is also a fountaine of Eagles, and one of Neptune with other Sea-Gods, all of the purest white marble that ever myne eyes beheld: These stand in a most ample basine of the same stone; and at the side of this Garden is such an Aviary as Sir Fra: Bacon describes in his Sermones fidelium or Essays, where in grow trees of more then 2 foote diameter, besides, Cypresse, Myrtils, Lentiscs & other rare shrubs, which serve to nestle & pearch all sorts of birds, who have ayre, & place enough under their wyrie Canopy, supported with huge Iron Worke very stupendious to consider, both as to the fabrick, & the Charge. The other two Gardens are full of Orange-trees, Citrons & Pomegranads, Fountaines, Grotts & Statues; amongst which one of Jupiter of a Colossal magnitude, under which is the Sepulchre of a beloved dog, for which one of this family received of the King of Spaine 500 crownes a yeare during the life of that faithfull animal. The Conserve of Water here is a most admirable piece for art, and so is likewise that incomparable grotto over against it.

We went hence to the Palace of the Dukes, where is also the Court of Justice; Thence to the Marchants Walke rarely covered: Neere the Ducal Palace we saw the publique Armory, which was almost all new, and one of the neatest kept & order'd that I had ever seene, for the quantity, being sufficient for 30000 men: Here we were shew'd many rare inventions & engines of Warr peculiar to that Armory, as in whose state gunns were first put in use: The Guarnison of the Towne consists chiefly of Germans & Corsicans:

We went the next day to see the famous Strada Nova, which is the same I formerly mentioned to have ben designd[1] by the famous Rubens: It is for statlinesse of the buildings, paving & evenesse of the Streete, certainly far superior to any in Europ for the number of houses: That of Don Carlo d'Orias is a most magnificent & prowd structure: Here in the Gardens of the house of the old Marquis Spinola I saw such huge Citrons hanging on the trees, applyd like our Abricotts to the Walles, that one would have believd incredible should have been supported by so weake branches: This whole Streete is built of polish'd Marbles &c:

Having thus spent the tyme in seeing the Palaces we went next to see the Churches which are nothing lesse splendid then the Palaces; That of St. Francis being totaly built of Parian marble: St. Laurenzo in the navil (as it were of the City) of white and black polish'd stone, the inside wholy incrusted with marble, and other precious materials; where, on the Altar of St. John stand those 4 sumptuous Columns of Porphyrie; here we were shew'd that prodigious Emrald so greately esteem'd by the Friers; being it may be one of the largest in the world.

---

1 In the older sense, drawn.

But it is the Church of Santo Ambrosio belonging to the Jesuites which when finish'd will exceede all the rest; and that of the Anunciada founded at the Charges of one family, a piece in the present & future designe never to be out done for cost & art, though a kingdome should joyne in the expense & intention.

From the Churches we walked to the Mole, a worke of solid huge Stones Stretching it selfe for neere 600 paces into the maine Sea; this secures the Harbour, which was heretofore of no safty: doubtlesse of all the wonders of Italy, for the art, & nature of the designe nothing dos parallel this: hence we passd over to the Pharos or Lanterne, which is a towre of incredible height; here we tooke horses, & made the circuite of the Citty, as far as the new Walles (built of a prodigious height & herculean indus- try; witnesse those vast pieces of whole mountaynes, which they have hew'n away, & blowne up of gunpowder to render steepe & inaccessible) would suffer us: These Wales, are besides their height of a wonderfull extent beyond the utmost building of the City, not much lesse then 20 English miles; Upon one of these promontories we could easily discerne the Iland of Corsica which is many leagues off at Sea; & from the same precipice east-ward we saw a Vale having a most violent torrent running through a most desolate & barren Country, & then turning your eyes more northward those pleasant & delicious Villas of St. Pietro d'Arena which presents another Genoa to you, the ravishing retirements of the Genoezi nobility: thence with much paine we descended towards the Arsenale, where all the Gallys lie in excellent order.

They are much affected to the Spanish mode & stately garbe in this Citty, where (by reason of the narownesse of their Streetes) they passe onely in their Sedans & Litters, & not in Coaches.

Octob: 19, we agreed with a Filuca and embarqud towards Ligorne; but the sea being this day very high (but not very dan- gerous, in reguard the billows did not breake) we resolv'd for feare of a storme to put in at Porta Venere, which we made, betweene two such narrow & horrid rocks, as the waves dashing with extraordinary velocity against them, put us in no small per- ill; but we were soone deliverd into as greate a Calme, & a most ample harbor, being the Golpho di Specia; whence we could see Plinies Delphini Promontorium, now cald Cap fino: Here stood that famous City of Luna, whenc the port, was namd Lunaris, being about 2 leagues over, more resembling a lake, than an haven; yet bravely defended both with Castles, and excessive high mountaines: Here at Lerici (a towne where we landed) being Sonday was a greate procession carr⟨y⟩ing about the Streetes together with the Sacrament, in solemne devotion: After dinner we tooke post-horses that caryd us bravely through whole groves of Olive-trees; the way somwhat rugged & hilly, at first; but afterwards pleasant: thus we pass'd through the townes of Sarazana, Massa & the vast Marble quaries of Carrara where we lodg'd in an obscure Inn at a place cald Viregio: The next day by morning we ariv'd at Pisa, where I met with my old friend Mr. Tho: Henshaw, who was then newly come out of Spaine, & from whose Company I never parted till more then a yeare after:

Pisa, for the famous mention thereof in History, whiles it con-tended with Rome, Florence, Sardinia, Sicily, & even Carthage herselfe, is as much worthy the seeing as any city in Italy:

The Palace & Church of St. Stephano (where the order of Knighthod cald by that name was instituted) drew first our curiosity, the outside theroff being altogether of polish'd marble; It is within full of tables relating to their Order, over which hang divers banners & pendents, with severall other Trophes taken by them from the Turkes, against whom they are particularly oblig'd to fight; being, though a religious Order; yet permitted to marry: At the front of the Palace stands a fountaine, & the Statue of the greate duke Cosimo.

The Campanile or Settezonio, built by one John Oenipont a German, consists of severall orders of pillars; 30 in a row, designd to be much higher: It stands alone, on the right side of the Domo or Cathedrall, strangely remarkable for this, that the beholder would expect every moment when it should fall; being built exceedingly declining by a rare adresse of the imortal Architect: and realy I take it to be one of the most singular pieces of workmanship in the World; how it is supported from immediately falling would puzzle a good Geometrician.

The Domo standing neere it is a superbe structure beautified with 6 Colomns of greate antiquity; & the gates are of brasse of admirable workmanship: Here is the Cemitere cald Campo Santo, made of divers Gally ladings of earth, brought formerly from Jerusalem, which being of a Carcofagus nature consumes dead bodys in the space of fourty houres. Tis clo⟨i⟩stred about

with marble Arches, & here lyes buried the learned Philip
Decius who taught in this University.

At one side of this Church stands an ample & well wrought
Marble Vessell, that heretofore containd the Tribute of the City
payd yearely to Cæsar: it is plac'd as I remember on a Pillar of
Opite stone with divers other antique Urnes: Neere to this & in
the same feild is the Baptisterie of San Giovanni built of pure
white marble, and coverd with so artificial a Cupola, that the voice
or word utter'd under it seemes to breake out of a Clowd: The
Font & Pulpit supported with 4 lyons is of inestimable value for
the preciousnesse of the materials: The Place where all these
buildings stand they call the Area: Hence we went to see the
Colledge to which joynes a Gallery so furnish'd with natural rarities, stones, minerals, shells, dryd Animals, Scelletos &c, as is
hardly to be seene the like in Italy: to this the Physique-Garden
lyes, where is a noble Palme tree from which I gatherd a long
branch: It has also very fine Waterworkes in it. The River Arno it
is which runs quite through the middle of this stately Citye,
whenc that Streete is nam'd Longarno, so ample that even the
Greate Dukes Gallys (built in the Arsenale here) are easily conveyd to Livorno; but what is most worth observeing is that
incomparable sole Arch which stretches from banke to banke, the
like of which (serving for a bridge) is no where in Europe; That
which renders it so famous is the extreame flatnesse of it. The
Duke has also in this Towne a Stately Palace, before which Ferdinando the 3ds statue is plac'd: over against it, is the Exchange all
built of Marble. Since this Citty came to be under the Dukes of
Tuscany ⟨it⟩ is extreamely de-populated & thinn of Inhabitants;
though there be hardly in Italy, any which exceedes it for stately
Edifices: Yet the situation is very low & flat; which accommodates
it with Spacious Gardens & even feilds within the Wales of it.

Octob: 21 we tooke Coach to Livorno (where I furnish'd my
selfe with a bill of Exchange) through the Greate Dukes new
Parke, full of huge Corke-trees, the under wood all Myrtils:
amongst which were many Buffolos feeding which is ⟨a⟩ monstrous kind of wild Ox, short-nosd, and with hornes revers'd;
those who worke with them, command them as our Beare-
Wards do the Beares, with a ring through the nose & a Coard:
Much of this Parke, as well as a greate part of the Country about
it, is very fenny and of very ill ayre.

Ligorne is the prime port belonging to all the Dukes Territories; heretofore a very obscure towne, but since Ferdinando at present has so strongly fortified it (after the moderne way) draind the marches, by cutting that Channell thence to Pisa, navigable for 16 miles, & raised a Mole, emulating that of Genoa to secure the shipping, it is becom a Port of incredible receipt; Strengthend with divers fanales & Skonces: It has also a Place for the Gallys where they lye very safe:* Just before the sea is an ample Piazza for the Market, where are erected those incomparable Statues, with the fowre slaves of Copper much exceeding the life for proportion; & in the judgment of most Artists one of the best pieces of modern Worke that was ever don.

Here is in Ligorne, & especialy this Piazzo, such a concourse of Slaves, consisting of Turkes, Mores and other Nations, as the number & confusion is prodigious; some buying, others selling; some drinking, others playing, some working, others sleeping, fighting, singing, weeping & a thousand other postures & Passions; yet all of them naked, & miserably Chayn'd, with a Canvas onely to hide their shame: Here was now a Tent erected, where any idle fellow, weary of that trifle, might stake his liberty against a few Crownes; which if lost (at Dice or other hazard) he was immediately chaynd, & lead away to the Gallys, where he was to serve a tearme of Yeares, but whence they seldome returnd; and many sottish persons would in a drunken bravado trye their fortune. The houses of this neate Towne are very uniforme, and excellently paynted a fresca on the out wales, being the representation of many of their Victories against the Turkes: The houses though low (in reguard of the Earth-quakes which frequently happen here to their greate terror, as did one during my being in Italy) are very well built; and the Piazz⟨a⟩, with the Church, whose 4 Columns at the Portico are of black marble Polish'd, is very fayre & commodious; and gave the first hint to the building both of the Church & Piazza in Covent-Garden with us, though very imperfectly pursu'd.

* V adds: It is said that this Port with all its Accommodations, was design'd & carried ⟨on⟩, by Duke *Dudly*, who pretended to be *Duke* of *Northumberland*, but claiming Title by a *Spurious* branch, & not legitimate, was entertain'd at Florence, & made one of the Dukes *Councill*: His knowledge in Maritime Affaires &c appeares to be very greate, by the 3 greate *Volumes* publish⟨ed⟩ in the *Italian* tonge, intitl'd *Arcano del Mare*:

From Livorno Octo: 22 I tooke Coach againe to Empoly, where we lay, & the next day ariv'd at Florence, being reccommended to the house of one Sig: Baritiere in the Piazza dal Spirito Santo, where I was exceedingly well treated:

Florenc is situated at the foote of the Apennines, the west part full of stately Groves, & pleasant Meadows, beautified with more then a thousand houses & country Palaces of note, appertaining to Gentlemen of the Towne:

The river Arno, which glids in a broad, but very shallow channell, runs through this Citty, dividing it as 'twere in the middle, and over this passe fowre most sumptuous bridges: of Stone: On that which was neerest our quarter stands in white marble the 4 seasons; on another, are the Goldsmits shops; at the head of the former stands a Columne of Opite upon which a Statue of Justice with her balances & Sword cut all out of Porphyrie, and for this the most remarkable, that 'twas the first which (after many yeares that art was utterly lost), had ben carv'd out of that hard material & brought to perfection; which they say was don by hardning the tooles in the juice of certayne herbs: This Statue was erected in that corner, for that there Cosimo was first saluted with the newes of Siennas being taken. Neere this is the famous Palazzo di Strozzi consisting of a rustique manner, a Princly piece of Architecture if any in the World be. Hence we went to the Palace of Pitie built by that family, but of late infinitely beautified by Cosimo, with huge Square stones, [with a terrace at each side rustic uncut balustradoed, with a fountain that ends in a Cascade seene from the greate gate and so a vista to the Gardens] of the Dorique, Ionic & Corinthian Order, in which nothing is more admirable than the vacant Stayre-case, Marbles, Statues, Urnes, Pictures, Court, Grotto & Water-workes: In the Quadrangle [where is a huge jetto of Water in a Volto of 4 faces, & noble statues at each Square, especially the *Diana* of Porphyrie above the grotto:] I remember we were shew'd a monstrous greate Load-stone: The Garden is full of all Variety, hills, dales, rocks, Groves, aviaries, Vivaries, fountaines, [Especialy on⟨e⟩ of 5 Jettos, the middle basin being one of the longest stones that ever I saw:] & what ever may render such a Paradise deligh⟨t⟩full; & to this the Duke has added an ample Laboratorie, over against which a fort standing on a hill, where they told us his highnesse Treasure is kept [I saw in this Garden a rose grafted on an Orange Tree: much topiarie work & Columns in Architecture about the hedges]: In this Palace it is the Duke ordinarily resides, living with his Swisse Guards after the frugal Italian way, and even Selling what he can spare of his Wines, at the Cellar under his very house: [& which was odd, wicker bottles dangling over the very chiefe Entrance into the Palace; serving for a Vintners bush.]

Next we went to see the Church of Santo Spirito where the Altar & Reliquary is most rich, & full of precious stones, especialy 4 pillars of a kind of Serpentine, & some of blew: Hence to another of the Dukes Palaces cal'd Palazzo Vecchio, before which is the statue of David, & Hercules killing of Cacus, the worke of Baccio Bandinelli, the other of Michael Angelo. The quadrangle about this is of the Corinthian order, & in the hall many rare marbles; as those of Leo the tenth, and Clement the viith, both Popes of the Medicean family: also the Acts of Cosimo in rare Painting. In the Chapell is conserv'd, (as they would make us believe) the Original Gospel of St. John, writen with his owne hand; together with the so famous Florentine Pandects; here are likewise divers precious stones; & neere it another pendent towre (like that at Pisa) always threatning ruine: Hence we goe to the Publique Court of Justice, under which is a stately Arcade for men to walke in; & over that the shops of divers rare Artists, who continualy worke for the Greate Duke; and above this that so renowned *Ceimeliarcha* or Repository where in are divers hundreds of admirable Antiquities, Statues of Marble & Mettal, Vasas of Porphyrie &c but amongst the statues none so famous as the S⟨c⟩ipio, the boare &c: the Idol of Apollo brought from the Delphic Temple, & two Triumphant Columnes: Over these hang the Pictures to the life of the famous Persons & Illustrious men, whither excelling in Arts or Armes to the number of 300, taken out of the Musæum of Paulus Jovius; Then they lead us into a large Square roome, in the middle whereoff stood a Cabinet of an octangular forme so adornd and furnish'd with Christals, Achat, Sculptures &c as certainely exceedes any description: Upon it is a globe of Ivory rarely carv'd, Hercules his Labours in Massy Silver, & many incomparable Pictures in small: Likewise another which had about it 8 oriental Columns of Alabaster, on each whereof was plac'd an head of a Cæsar, cover'd with a Canopy so richly beset with precious Stones, that they resembled a firmament of Starrs: This Cabinet was valued at 2 hundred thousand crownes: Within was our Saviours Passion, & 12 Apostles of incomparable Amber. In another with Calcidon Pillars was a Series of Golden Medaills. [In this Cabinet is call'd the *Tribuna*, in which is a pearle as big as an haizel nut: The Cabinet is of Ebonie, Lazuli & Jasper: Over the doore a round of *M: Angelo*, on the Cabinet Leo the tenth with other paintings of Raphaels, *del Sartos, Perugino*, & *Corregio* viz. a *St. John*, a *Virgin*, a *boy*, two Apostles & 2 heads of *Durer*, rar(e)ly carved. Here is also another rich Ebony Cabinet Cupola'd with a tortois shell & containing a Collection of gold Medails esteemd worth 50000 crounes, a wreathed Pillar of Oriental Alabaster, divers Paintings of *da Vinci, Pontorno, del Sarto*, an Ecce homo of Titian, a *boy* of *Bronzini* &c:

They also shew us a branch of Corall fix'd on the rock which they affirme dos still grow.]

In another roome is kept the Tabernacle appointed for the Chapel of St. Laurence, about which are placed divers small statues of Saints of precious materials, a piece of that Art & Cost, as having been these 40 yeares in perfecting, is certainly one of the most curious & rare things in the World.

Here were divers incomparable tables of Pietra Commessa, which is a marble ground inlayd with severall sorts of marbles & stones of divers colours, in the shapes of flowers, trees, beasts, birds & Landskips like the natural: In one is represented the Towne of Ligorne, by the same hand who inlayes the Altar of St. Laurence, Domenico Benotti of whom I purchas'd 19 pieces of the same worke for a Cabinet. In a Presse neere these they shew'd us an Yron-naile, one halfe whereof being converted into gold by one Thurnheuser a German Chymist, is look'd on as a greate rarity [but it plainly appears to have ben but sother'd:] There is a curious Watch, a monstrous Turcois as big as an Egge, on which is engraven an Emperors head: From hence we went into the Armory, where is conserved many antique habits, as that of the Chineze Kings, the Sword of *Charlemain*: an Italian lock for their wanton Wives or jealous Husbands: Hanibals headpiece; & a [huge] Load-stone [of a yard long] of that Vertue as it beares up 86 pounds weight very well: [in a chaine of 17 links, such as the slaves are tied to.] In the Presse of another roome they shew'd us such rare tourneries in Ivory, as are not to be describ'd for their curiosity: likewise a faire Pillar of Oriental Alabaster, and 12 vast, & compleate Services of Silver plate, & one of Gold, all of them of ⟨incomparable⟩ workmanship; besides a rich embrodred Saddle [of pearls] sent by the Emp: to this Duke [& here is that embrodred chaire set with precious stones, that he sits in when on St. *Johns* day he receives the Tribute of the Citties:]

On the 25, we went to see the Portico where the famous Statues of Judith & Olofernes stand; also that of the Medusa, all of Copper; but what is most admirable the rape of a Sabine [of Jo. de *Bolognia*] with another man under foote, the confusion & twining of whose members, consisting of one entire White marble, is most stupendious; this stands directly against the greate Piazza, where to adorne one fountaine are erected 4 marble statues, & 8 of brasse representing Neptune & his family of Sea Gods &c of a Colossean magnitude with 4 Sea horses in parian marble [of *Lamardati*,] & in the midst of a monstrous basin, a worke I thinke hardly to be paralleld in the World. [Here is also that famous Statue of David of M: Angelo, of Hercules & Cacus of *Baccio Bandinelli*, the *Persius* in Coper of *Benvenetos* & the *Judith* of Donatelli, which stand publiqly before the old Palace: The *Centaure* of *Bologna* huge Collossean figures:] Neere this stands Cosimo di Medici on horse-back in brasse on a Pedistal of Marble [& 4 Copper Bassrelievi of Jo. *Bolognia*] with divers Inscriptions: [But the *Ferdinando* on horsback is of *Pietro Tacca*:] Then we beheld with admiration the brazen boare which serves for another publique Fountaine.

After dinner we went to Visite divers Churches, And, in reguard the Duke & Court were there at devotions, first to the Annunciata; being a place of extraordinary repute for Sanctity; for here is a shrine that dos great Miracles, as they pretend, by innumerable Votive Tables & other trinkets, which almost quite cover the Wales of the whole Church: This is the Image of Gabriel who saluted the B: Virgin, and which the Artist having finish'd so well, as in despaire of performing so well on the Virgins face, they report was miraculously don for him whilst he slept. Others say 'twas long since painted by St. Luke himselfe: Who ever it was, infinite is the devotion of all Sexes to it, the Altar set off with 4 Colomns of Oriental Alabaster, and lightnd by 30 huge silver lamps (especialy two of them) and innumerable other Pictures drawne by rare Masters; as the Story of our Saviours Passion in brasse tables inserted in Marble the worke of Jo: de Bologna, & Baccio Bandinelli &c:

To this Church joynes a Convent, whose Cloister is painted in fresca very rarely: There is also neere it, an Hospital for 1000 persons, with Nurse Children & severall other charitable accommodations.

From this place we went to see the Dukes Cavalerizzo, where the Prince has a stable of incomparable Horses of all Countries, Arabs, Turks, Barbs, Gennets, English &c: which are continualy exercisd in the menage. Nere this is the Place where are kept several Wild-beasts, as Wolves, Catts, Bares, Tygers, & Lions: I tooke greate pleasure to see what an incredible height one of the Lyons would leape, for which I caused to be hung downe a joynt of mutton: They are loose in a deepe, Walld-Court, & therefore to be seene with much more delight than at the Tower of Lond, in their grates.[1]

[st. *Crosse* is the chiefe Cathedrall & its Altar-Piece is painted with the Miracles of S. Francis and rare sculpture, & so is the Sepulchre of the famous *Mich: Angelo*, wrought & design'd by his owne hand, being Painter, Sculptor, Architect, Poet: Here is also buried *Galileo*: To this joyns a large Covent of Franciscans, and the House where in Pope Urban VIII was born, but no considerable fabrick save for the painted out-side: st. Michaels Church, the Altar of the B. Virgin curiously Carved, in w⟨h⟩ite Marble, within full of statues.

St. Mary Florida, built by Arnulpho Lupo, with a vast Cupola of octogon forme—154 yards high, besids the Pinacle 36 yards higher: a globe of Gilt Copper: diameter 20. foote. The Pillars marble, and one of that bignesse as contains a pair of stayers which leads into the Borle: The whole structure of this Church is built of white, black Polished marbles even the very out-side, with a Gallery round it of stone, so as consider'd alltogether, tis reputed one of the nobl⟨e⟩st building⟨s⟩ in Europe: The Volto of the Domo is painted by Vasari & Zuchari: The Altar is of Bandinella, adorn'd with the statues of the Apostles. *Dantes* the Poet lys here interred, *Marsilius Ficinus* & Ph:

---

1 A missing leaf of K (or perhaps two leaves) is here supplied from V.

Brunelesius: who built the Cupala: By this church stands a Toure of the same Material, neere 400 f. high: so artific(i)aly that a man standing in a place call'd Canta della Pagl⟨i⟩a may *Uno intuito* see every square of the sides, all rarely beautified with Carving: In the same *Arëa* is the *Baptistary* or Church of st. *John*, 8 square of White & Bl: marble without, & incrusted within: The floore of divers Coloured stones, & the Cupola of rare Mosaick after the Greeke manner. In the Midst is the *Font* of one intire Alabaster exquisitly sculptur'd: but what transcends all description (& by many look'd-on as one of the worlds Wonders) are 3 paire of Brasen Gates, cast with the storys of the Bible: The Paving is Mosaick & so the Roofe & Domo: & in the Church the 12 Apostle marble before the Enterance: 2 Imperfect Columns of Porphyrie, ⟨brought⟩ from Pisa.

On the 17th ⟨27th⟩ I purchased the Pietra Comm⟨e⟩ssa Pieces for my Cabinet; bespoke 4. rare small statues of stucci made onely by that rare Artist *Vincetio Brocchi*: Collecting some Prints & drawings I went to see the renowned Church, Chapell & Library of St. *Laurences* in which the *Medicean* Family are buried, with Banners over them: The Church is wholy of White-marble in which a statue of the B.V. of *Parian* stone, with the Sepulcre of *Paulus Jovius* & the figures of *Cosmos* & *Damianus* Tutelares of the Medicean Family: Above is the Bibl⟨i⟩otheca, onely of Manuscripts, most in the Gr: & Oriental, & divers Latine Languages & ⟨they⟩ shewed us The Comedys of *Terrence*, interlined they say by his owne hand: Hence we were conducted to the third heaven if any be on Earth, the famous *Mausoleum* or Chapel where the *Dukes* are Inhum'd, it having now ben an hundred yeares building & not yet quite finished, for which a Million of Crowns of Gold is design'd: The Model is Octagonal, a figure much affected here, Every Square over-layed with various Colour'd Marble, Achati, Serpentine, Porphyrie, Lazuli, Amethists, Cornelians &c: perfect Jewels in their kind & in Each quarter the Armes of the Chiefe Towns of the Duke-dom, inlayed in their proper Blazoning, over them are Nices of black Touch for the statues of the Dukes; and (twixt the Escuchions & *Nices*) 8. huge Chests or Urnes of antique Forme of the most precious Marbles of various Coulors, the Ducal Cor'net & Scepter on a Cushion: The whole is cover'd with a *Domo* of rich Lapis Lazuli full of vaines of gold exceeding rich

& stellified with mother of Pearle: And when the new Altar is finish'd, it will doublesse be one of the most magnificent pieces of Art in the World: We concluded this day with st. Maria Novella & Monastery, which has in the Court 2 Pyramids of Marble upon Tortoises of Copper: In this church lies peter Martyr, the Pillars on which he was decapitated standing in the Towre. Here is also buried *Salernius Remigius* & others; and in the Splendid Chapell Jo. *Boccatius*, & Joseph Patriark of Constantinople: Neere this is st. Marks church & Library, belonging to the *Jacobites*, but infinite is the beauty & cost of the Chapel, designed by the famous J. de Bologne: In the Church lies *Angelus Politianus* and the Pious *Earle* of *Mirandula*: 2 famous s⟨c⟩holars: Thus having run thro the most memorable buildings & Curiositys of this noble Citty: we went to see the Manufactors of Silke, Damask, Velvet &c, which they report brings a yearly Revenu of two Millions of Gold; the streetes are most of the⟨m⟩ spacious, strait, & pav'd with flat broad Coarse Marble: which makes them very Cleane & faire; the Houses unive⟨r⟩saly well built of stone exceeding high, and of good Order; But the Inhabitans very thinn in them.

29 We tooke Horse for *Sienna*, alighting at *Poggio Imperiale* a house of Pleasure of the Duke, little distant from Florence, but having little time to Consider it, we refer'd it for our coming back from Rome:

We lay this night at st. *Cassiano*, & I think next day at Barbarini, a small Town, whence P. *Urbans* family: Then at *Poggio Bunci* famous for Snuff *Tabacco*, which the *Italians* of both sexes take excessivly, we dined, & that night arived at Sienna: (Note, that Snuff was not taken in England at this time nor some yeares after:)—this famous Citty stands on several rocky Hills, which makes it uneven, has an old ruin'd Wall about it, overgrown with *Caper* shrubbs: but the Air is incomparable, whence divers passe the heates of Summer there; Provisions cheape, the Inhabitans Courteous, & the Italian purely spoken. The Citty at a little distance presents the Traveller with an incomparable Prospect, occasion'd by the]¹ many playne brick Towers, which (whilst it was a Free state) were erected for defence; the tallest where off is call'd the Mangio, standing at the foote of the

1 K now resumes.

Piazza, which we went first to see the next day after our arival:
At the entrance of this Tower is a Chapel (open towards the
Piazza) of marble well adornd with Sculpture: On the other side
is the Signioria or Court of Justice, this is very well built, a la
Moderna, of brick; and indeede the Brick of Sienna is so rarely
made, that it lookes almost as well as Porphyrie it selfe, having
a kind of naturall politure. There is in this Senate-hous a very
faire hall, where they sometimes recreate the People with
publique Shews and Operas, as they call them. Towards the left
hand stand the statues of Romulus & Rhemus with the Wolfe,
all of brasse, plac'd on a Columne of Ophite stone, which they
report was brought from the renowned Ephesian Temple; and
these Ensignes, being it seemes the Armes of the Towne, are set
up in divers of the Streetes, publique Wayes both within & far
without the City:

The Piazza compasses the faciata of the Court and Chapel,
and being made with descending steps, much resembles the figure of an Escalop-shell, with the white ranges of Paving inter-
mix'd with the incomparable brick we described, & with which
generally the towne is well paved, which renders it marvailously
cleane: About this Market place (for so it is) are many faire
Palaces, though not built with excesse of elegance; Onely there
stands an Arch (the Worke of Baltazar di Sienna) built with
wonderfull diligence, no man being able to conceive how it is
supported; yet has it some imperceptable contignations which
do not betray themselves easily to the Eye.

On the edge of the Piazza is a goodly Fountaine beautified
with Statues, the water issuing out of the wolves mouth, being
the Worke of Jacopo Quercei, a famous Artist: There are likewise divers other publique Fountaines in the City of good
designe. After this we walk'd to the Sapienza, which is the University or Coledge rather, where the high Germans enjoy many
particular priveleges, who addict themselves to the Civil Law:
And indeede this Place has produc'd divers excellent Scholars;
besides those three Popes Alex: 3, Pius the 2d & the 3d of that
name, the learned Æneas Silvius, both of that antient house of
the Piccolomini.

The Chiefe streete is calld Strada Romana. Pius the 2d has
built a most stately Palace of Square stone, with that incomparable Portico joyning neere to it.

This Towne is commanded by a Castle, which hath to it 4 bastions, and a Garison of Souldiers, neere which a list to ride horses in, much frequented in summer by the Gallants.

Not far hence is the Church and Convent of the Dominicans, where in the Chapel of St. Catharine of Sienna, they shew her head, the rest of her body being translated to Rome: Then we went up to the Domo or Cathedral, which is both without and within of large square stones of black & white marble polish'd, of inexpressable beauty; as likewise is the front, being much adorn'd with Sculpture and rare statues: In the middle is a stately Cupola bearing two other Columns of sundry streaked Colour'd marble; about the body of the church on a Cornic within are inserted the heads of all the Popes; the Pulpit infinitely beautified with marble figures, a piece of exquisite worke; but what exceedes all description is the Pavement, where (besides the various Emblemes & other figures in the nave of the Cathedral) the Quire is wrought with the History of the Bible, so artificialy express'd in the natural Colours of marble, that few painters are able to exceede it with the Pensil: Here stands a Christo rarely cut in marble, and on the high Altar, a large brasen Vessell of admirable invention & Art. The Organs are exceeding sweete & well tun'd. On the lef⟨t⟩ side of the Altar is the Library where in are Painted the Acts of Æneas Sylvius & others by Raphael: and here they shew'd us an Arme of st. Jo: the Baptist, wherewith they say he baptis'd o⟨u⟩r B: Saviour in Jordan; given by the King of Peloponesus to one of the Popes, as an inscription testifies: also St. Peters Sword wherewith he smote of Malchus's Eare. Just against the Cathedral we went into the Hospital where they entertaine & refresh such Pilgrimes as goe to Rome, 3 or 4 dayes gratis: In the Chapell belonging to it lye⟨s⟩ the body of St. Susorius their founder as yet uncorrupted though dead many hundreds of yeares; they also shew one of the Nailes that pierced our Saviour; and st. Jo: Chrisostomes Comment on the Gospel writen by his owne hand: below the hill stands the poole cal'd Fonte Brande, where fish are nourish'd for Pleasure more then foode.

St. Francis Church is a large pile, neere which (yet a little without the Citty) growes a tree which they report in their Legend grew from the Saints Staff, which going to sleepe he fix'd in the ground, and found it miraculously a huge growne-tree at his waking; they affirme that the wood of it in decoctions cures sundry diseases.

Nov: 2d We went from Sienna, desirous to be present at the Cavalcad of the new Pope Innocentio decimo, who had not as yet made the grand Procession to st. Jo: de Laterano: We set out by Porto Romano, the Country all about the towne being rare for hunting and Game; so as Wild-Boare and Venison is frequently sold in the shops in many of the Townes about it: And first we pass'd neere Mont Oliveto, where the monastrie of that Order is pleasantly situated, and worth the seeing: Passing over a bridg (which by the Inscription shews it to have been built by Prince Matthias) we went through Buon-Convento famous for the Death of the Emperor Hen: 7th who was here poyson'd in the holy Eucharist: Thence we came to Torniero where we din'd. This Village lyes in a sweete Vally in view of Mount Alcini famous for the rare Muscatello; twas heretofore Mons Ilicinus. After 3 miles more we goe by St. Querico, and lay at a Privat Osteria neere it, where, after we were provided of Lodging, in came Cardinal Donghi a Genoeze by birth, now come from Rome; He was so civil as to entertaine us with greate respect, hearing we were English, for that he told us he had been once in our Country; amongst other discourse, he related how a Dove was seene to sit upon the Chayre in the Conclave, at the Election of Pope Innocent, which he magnified as a greate good Omen, with several other particulars which we enquir'd of him, till our Suppers parted us: I remember he came in great state, with his owne Bed-stead, & all the furniture; yet would by no meanes suffer us to resigne the room we had taken up in the Lodging, before his arival.

We rod next morning by Monte Pientio, or as vulgarly Monte Mantumiato, which is of an excessive height, ever & anon peeping above any Clowds with its snowy head; till we had climed to the Inn at Radicofany, built by Ferdinando the Greate Duke for the necessary refreshment of travellers in so inhospitable a place: as we ascended, we enter'd a very thick, soled and darke body of Clowds, which look'd like rocks at a little distance, which dured us for neere a mile going up; they were dry misty Vapours hanging undissolved for a vast thicknesse, & altogether both obscuring the Sunn & Earth, so as we seemed to be rather in the Sea than the Clowdes, till we having pierc'd quite through, came into a most serene heaven, as if we had been above all human Conversation, the Mountaine appearing more like a greate Iland, than joynd to any other hills; for we could perceive nothing but a Sea of thick Clowds rowling under our feete like huge Waves, ever now & then suffering the top of some other mountaine to peepe through, which we could discover many miles off, and betweene some breaches of the Clowds, Landskips and Villages of the subjacent Country: This was I must acknowledge one of the most pleasant, new & altogether surprizing objects that in my life I had ever beheld: On the summit of this horrid rock (for so it is) is built a very strong Fort Garnisond and somewhat beneath it, a small Towne, whose Provisions are drawne up with ropes & Engines, the Precipice being otherwise inaccessible. At one End of the Towne lye heapes of Rocks so strangely congested, & broaken, which have been broaken off from the ragged Mountaine, as would affright one with their horror and menacing postures. Just opposite to the Inn gusshed out a plentifull & most usefull fountaine which falls into a great trough of stone, bearing the Duke of Tuscany's Armes. Here we din'd, and I with my black-lead pen tooke the Prospect: it being also one of the utmost confines of the Etrurian State towards the St. Peters Patrimony, since the gift of Matilda to Greg: the VIIth, as is pretended: Here we passe a bridge of stone built by Pope Greg: XIIIth and thence immediately to Aquapendente, a Towne situated on a very raged rock, downe which precipitates an intire river of Water, which gives it the denomination with a most horrid roaring noise. We lay at the Post-house wher I could not choose ⟨but⟩ to observe the Capriccio of the Masters Motto under it

> L'Insegna della Posta, è posta a Posta
> In questa posta, fin che habbia à sua posta
> Ogn' un Cavallo a Vetturi in Posta.

Before 'twas darke we went to see the Monastery of the Franciscans, famous for 6. learned Popes, & sundry other greate Scholars, especialy the renown'd Physitian and Anatomist Fabritius de Aquapendente, who was bred & borne here.

On the 4th of November being next morning after a little riding we descend towards the Lake of Bolsena, which from hence (being above 20 miles in circuit) yeilds a most incomparable Prospect: neere the middle of it are 2. small Ilands, in one of which is a Convent of melancholy Capucines, & where those of the Farnezian family are interr'd: Pliny, calls it Tarquiniensis Lacus, and talkes of divers floting Ilands about it, but they appeard not to us, The Lake is invironed with mountaines; at one of whose sides we pass'd towards the Towne Bolsena, antiently Vulsinium, very famous in antiquity, as testifie divers rare sculptures in the Court of st. Christianas Church, the Urne, & Altar & Jasper Columns. After 7 miles riding (passing through a certaine Wood heretofore sacred to Juno) we came to Mount Fiascone, the head of Falisci, a famous people in old tyme, & heretofore Falernum, as renown'd for the excellent Wine, as now for the story of the Dutch Bishop, who lyes buried in Favionos Church with this Epitaph:

Propter Est, Est dominus meus mortuus est:

because he had drunke too much of the Wine; for it seemes he had commanded his Servant, to ride before, and (enquiring where the best liquor was,) to write Est upon the Vessells.

From Monte Fiascone we travell a plain and pleasant Champion to Viterbo, which presents it selfe with much state a farr off, in reguard of her many lofty pinacles and Towres; neither dos it deceive the expectation; for it is so exceedingly beautified with publique fountaines, especialy that at very entrance of the Port (being all of brasse, & adornd with many rare figures) as salutes the Passenger with a most agreable object, & refreshing waters. There are divers Popes buried in this Citty.

Neere the Towne is a sulphurous fountaine which continualy boiles; but having visited some other of the Antiquities & din'd, we tooke horse by the new way of Capranica, and so passing neere Mount Ciminus and the Lake we began to enter the Playnes of Rome, at which sight I confesse my thoughts were strangely elevated; but as soone allayed by such a dismal showre of raine which fell on us just as we were contemplating that prowd Mistriss of the World, and descending by the Vatican (for at that Port we enterd) so as before we got into the Citty, I was wett to the skin.

I CAME TO ROME on the 4th of November 1644 about 5 at night, and being greately perplex't for a convenient lodging, wandred up and downe on horse back, till one conducted us to one Monsieur Petits, a French mans, who entertaind strangers, being the very utmost house on the left hand as one ascends Monte Trinità, formerly Mons Pincius, neere the Piazza Spagnola. Here I alighted, delivered my horse to the Veturino, and having bargain'd with mine host for 20 crownes a moneth, I causd a good fire to be made in my Chamber, and so went to bed being very wet.

The very next morning (for resolv'd I was to spend no moment idly here) I got acquaintance with several persons that had long lived in Rome; being especialy reccommended to Father John a Benedictine Monke, and Superior of his Order for the English Colledg of Doway; a Person (to say truth) of singular learning, Religion and humanity; also to Mr. Patric Cary, an Abbot, and brother to our Learned Lord Falkland, a pretty witty young priest; but one that afterwards came over to our church: Dr. Bacon, and Gibbs, Physitians who had dependance of Cardinal Caponi, the latter an incomparable Poet; with Father Cortnèe the Chiefe of the Jesuites in the English Coledge, My Lord of Somerset: Bro: to the Marquis of Worcester, and some others: from whom I receiv'd instructions, how to behave our selves in Towne, what directions, Masters, and bookes to take in search and view of the Antiquities, Churches, Collections &c: and accordingly, the next day, being November 6t, I began to be very pragmatical.

And in the first place (as our Sights-man, for so they name certaine Persons in Rome, who get their living onely by leading strangers about to see the Citty) we first went to see the Palace of Farnezi, which is a most magnificent square structure, built by Michael Angelo of the 3 Orders of Columns, after the antient manner, & in a time when Architecture was but newly recovered from the Gotic barbarity: The Court, being square is tarrass'd, having two payre of staires which leade into the upper roomes; which conducted us to that famous Gallery painted by Caraccio, and then which nothing is certainly more rare of that Art in the whole world, so deepe, & well studied are all the figures, that it would require more judgment than, I confesse, I had, to deter-

mine whether they were flat, or emboss'd: Thence we pass'd into
another painted in Chiaro e Scuro, representing the fabulous
History of Hercules, then we went out on a Tarrace where was a
pretty garden even on the leads, for it is built in a place of the
Citty, that has no extent of grow⟨n⟩d backwards: The greate
Sale is wrought by Salviati, and Zuccharo; furnish'd with
statues, one of which being modern is the figure of a Farnese, in
a triumphant posture of white marble, worthy of Admiration.

Here we were shew'd the Musæum of Fulvius Ursinos,
replete with innumerable collections: But the Major Domo,
being absent we could not at this time see all that we had a desire
to, wherefore descending into the Court, we with greate astonishment began to contemplate those two incomparable statues of
the Hercules and Flora; so much celebrated by Pliny, and
indeede all Antiquity as two of the most rare pieces of Sculpture
in the World: There likewise stands an other moder⟨n⟩ statue of
Hercules, and two Gladiators, not to be despis'd for their worke;
from hence we were conducted into a 2d Court, where in a house,
or temporary shelter of boards onely we were shewd that most
stupendous, and never sufficiently to be admired, Toro of
Amphion, and Dirces, represented in 5 figures, much exceeding
the life in magnitude; all of purest white marble, being the contending worke of those famous Statuaries Apollonius and Tau-
risco, which they hew'd in the time of Augustus as now it
remaines unblemished, out of one entire stone; and certainely, it
is to be valued beyond all the marbles of the World, both for its
antiquity and workmanship: There are likewise divers other
heads, and busts, which I could not take so particular notice of.
At the enterance of this stately Palace, there stand two rare, &
vast Fountaines of Garnito stone, brough⟨t⟩ into this Piazza out
of Titus's Bathes; here, in summer the Gentlemen of Rome take
the fresco in their Coaches, and ⟨on⟩ foote: At the sides of this
Court we visited the Palace of Signor Pichini, who has a good
Collection of Antiquities, especialy that of the Adonis of Parrian
Marble which once my L: of Arundel would have purchas'd, if a
greate price would have been taken for it.

On the 7th we went into Campo Vacino by the ruines of the
Templum Pacis, built by Titus Vespatianus, and thought to
be the biggest & most ample as well as richly furnish'd of all
the Roman Dedicated places; It is now an heape, rather then a

Temple; yet dos the roofe, & Volto, continue firme, shewing it to
have formerly been of incomparable workmanship: This goodly
structure was (none knows how) consumed with fire, the very
night (by all computation) that our B: Saviour was borne.

From hence we passed by the place, rather then any signs,
of the Lake or Vorago into which Curtius is sayd to have precipitated himselfe for the love of his Country.

Neere this stand some Columns of white marble of exquisite
worke, supposd to be part of the Temple of Jupiter Tonans, built
by Augustus; the worke of the Capitals (being Corinthian) and
Architrave is excellent, & full of sacrificing utensiles. There are
also 3 other of Jupiter Stator.

The Oratories or Churches of st. Cosmo, and Damiano
opposite to these, heretofore the Temples of Romulus, a pretty
odd fabrique, with a Tribunal or Tholus within, wrought all of
Mosaic; the Gates before it are of brasse, & the whole adorne-
ment much obligd to Pope Urban the 8th. In this sacred place
lyes the bodys of those Two Martyrs, and in the Chapell at the
right hand, a rare Painting of Cavaliero Baglione.

Next this we entered st. Laurenzo in Miranda: The Inscription cut in the Marble or Architrave of its antient Portico (supported by a rang of most stately Columns) shew it to have been
the Temple of Faustina; It is now made a faire Church, with an
Hospital, which joynes to it.

On the same side we saw st. Adriano, heretofore sacred to
Saturne; before this was once placed a Miliary Column, as suppos'd to be set in the Center of all the Citty; and from whence
they Usd to compute the distance of all the Citties & places of
note, under the dominion of those Universal Monarchs: To this
Church are likewise brasen-gates, and a noble frontspeece: just
opposite, they shew'd us the heapes & ruines of Ciceros Palace:
Hence we went towards Mons Capitolinus, at foote of which
stands Septimius Severus's Arch, full, and entire, save where the
Pedistal & some of the lower members are chockd-up with
ruines & earth: This Arch is exceedingly inrich'd with Sculpture,
and Trophies, with a large Inscription: In the terrestrial & naval
battailes here graven is seen the Roman Aries; & this was the
first Triumphant Arch set up in Rome.

The Capitol, to which we climed, by a very broad ascent of
degrees, is built about a square Court, at right hand of which,

going up from Campo Vacino gusshes a plentifull streame from the statue of Tybur in Porphyrie, very antique, and another representing Rome; but above all is admirable the figure of Marforius, casting ⟨water⟩ into a most ample Concha. The front of this Court is crown'd with an incomparable fabrique, containing the Courts of Justice, and where the Criminal Notary sitts, and others: In one of the Halls, they shew the statues of Greg: the 13th and Paule the 3d with several others: To this joynes an handsome Towre, the whole faciata adorn'd with noble Statues both on the out side, & battlements, ascended by a double payre of staires and a stately posario. In the center of the Court stands that incomparable Horse bearing the Emp: Marcus Aurelius of Corinthian mettal, as big as the life, placed on a Pedistal of marble, with an inscription, and esteemed one of the noblest pieces of worke now extant in the world, antique, & very rare. There is also a vast head of a Coloseän magnitude fixed in the Wall of white marble: At the stayres descending (on either hand) are set two horses of white marble, govern'd by two naked slaves, taken to be Castor, & Pollux, brought from Pompeys Theatre: On the Balustrade, the Trophies of Marius against the Cimbrians, very antient, & instructive; & at the foote of the stepps, towards the left hand, that ⟨Colomna⟩ Miliaria, with the globe of brasse on it, being the same we mention'd to have formerly ben set in Campo Vacino.

On the same hand is the Palace of the Signiori Conservatori, or 3 Consuls, now the Civil Governors of the Citty, containing the fraternities or Halls & Guilds (as wee name them) of sundry Companys, and other Offices of State: Under the Portico within, are the two statues of Augustus Caesar, a Bacchus, and the so renown'd Colonna Rostrata of Duillius with the excellent Bassi Relievi. In a smaller Court, the statue of Constantine on a Fountaine, A Minervas head of brasse, and that of Commodus to which belongs an hand, the thumb whereoff is at the least an ell long, and yet proportionable; but the rest of the Collosse is lost. In a Corner of this Court stands the statue of an horse & lyon fighting, as big as the life, in White marble exceedingly valu'd: Likewise the rape of the Sabines, Two cumbent figures of Alex: and Mammea: Two monstrous feete of a certaine Colosse of Apollo: The Sepulchre of Agrippina, and the standard or antique measure of the Roman foote: Ascending by the stepps of the other coine, are inserted fowre basse-relievos, viz. the

triumph & Sacrifice of M: Aurelius, which last, for the antiquity
and rarenesse of worke, I caused my Painter Carlo Neapolitano,[1]
to copy out: Two statues of the Muses, and one of Adrian the
Emp: Above stands the figure of Marius, and by the wall Mar-
sias bound to a tree, all of them incomparable & antique: Above
in the Lobby is inserted into the Walls those antient Laws of
Brasse, call'd the Twelve Tables; a faire Madona of Pietro Perug-
gino, painted on the Wall; neere which the Archives full of
antient records: In the greate Hall are divers excellent Paintings
of Cavaliero Gioseppe d'Arpino, statue in brasse of Sixtus V.
and Leo X of marble: In another hall there are many modern
statues of their late Consuls and Governers, set about with
incomparable heads very antique; the rest are painted by the
hands of excellent Masters representing the Actions of M:
Scevola, Horatius Cocles &c: In the roome where the Conservatori now feast upon solemn dayes, 'tis tapissred with crimson
damasque embrodred with gold, having a state or baldaquino of
Crimson Velvet, very rich; the freeze above rarely painted: Here
is Romulus, & Rhemus sucking the Wolfe of brasse to the life,
with the shepheard Faustulus by them: Also that boy, plucking
the thorne out of his foote (so much admir'd by Artists) of
brasse, very antique, with some other holy statues & heads of
Saints. In a Gallery neere adjoyning are the names of the antient
Consuls, Prætors, & Fasti Romani &c so celebrated by the
Learned: Also the figure of an old Woman, and two other representing Poverty, with some more in fragments. In another Large
roome furnish'd with velvet is the statue of Adonis very rare, and
divers antique heads: In the next chamber an old statue of
Cicero, and another Consul, also an Hercules of brasse, two
womens heads of incomparable worke, six other statues, and
over the Chimny, a very rare basse-relievo, & other figures.

In a little Lobby before the Chapell, the statue of Hanibal the
Carthaginian, & a Bachus very antique: Two bustos, a Pan, &
Mercury with other old heads. All these noble & indeede incomparable statues &c, belong to the Citty, and cannot be disposed of
to any privat Persons, or remov'd hence, but are preserv'd for the
honor of the Place; though very greate summes have been offerd
for them by divers greate Princes, lovers of Art, & Antiquity.

1 Carlo Maratti.

We now left the Capitol, certainly one of the most renowned places in the World; even as now built by the designe of the famous M: Angelo. Returning home by Ara Cœli, we mounted to it by more then 100 marble stepps, not in devotion, as some I observd to do on their bare knees; but to see those two famous statues of Constantine in White marble plac'd there out of his Bathes: In this Church is a Madona reported to be painted by st. Luke, also a Culumn, on which we saw the print of a foote, which they affirme to have been the Angels, seene on the Castle of st. Angelo:

Here the feast of our B: Saviours Nativity being yearely celebrated, with divers pageants, they began to make the preparation; But thus having view⟨ed⟩ the Palace, & fountaine at the other side of the stayres, we returned weary to our Lodgings.

On the Tuesday, being the 7th, we went againe ⟨towards⟩ the Capitol towards the Tarpeian rock, where it has a goodly prospect towards the Tybur; thence descending by the Tullianum, where they told us st. Peter was imprison'd [St. Pietro da Vincoli], they shew'd us a Chapell, in which a rocky side of it, beares the impression of his face. [The painting of the *Ascension* is of *Raphael*.] In the nave of the Church gusshes a fountaine, which they say was caus'd by the Apostles prayer, when, having converted some of his fellow Captives, he wanted water to make them Christians: Then we walked about the Mount Palatinus, which with the Aventine we viewed very atentively, and from thence the once famous Circus Maximus, capable of holding 40000 spectators; It is now wholy converted into Gardens, and an heape of ougly ruines: Then we pass'd by the Forum Boarium, where they have a tradition Hercules slew Cacus; some ruines of his Temple remaining. Here they also shew'd us the Temple of Janus quadrifrontis, having 4 ports or arches importing the 4 Seasons, and at each side six niches for the annual monethes; it still remaines a very substantial & pretty intire antiquity. Neere to this is the Arcus Argentariorum. Bending now towards the River Tyber, we step'd into the Theater of Marcellus, capable once of 80000 persons, built by the greate Augustus, & dedicated to his Nephew, a piece for Architecture (as much as remaines) inferior to none; but now wholy converted into the house of the Savelli, one of the old Roman families.

They were now generaly buisie in erecting temporary Triumphs & Arches, with statues, and flatering Inscriptions, against his Holinesse's grand Procession to st. Jo: de Lateran, amongst which the Jewes also began one in testimony of gratitude for their protection under the Papal state: We walked hence to see the Palazzo Barberini, design'd by the now Pop⟨e⟩s Architect Cavaliere Bernini, & which I take to be as superbe, and princely an object, as any moderne building in Europ for the quantity: There is to it a double Portico, at the end of which, we ascended by two paire of Oval Stayres all of stone, & voide in the well; one of these landed us into a stately Hall, the Volto whereoff was newly painted a fresca by that rare hand of Pietro Berettieri, il Cortone: To this is annexed a Gallery compleately furnish'd ⟨with⟩ whatsoever Art can call rare & singular, & a Library full of worthy Collections, Medails, Marbles, and Manuscripts; but above all, for its unknowne material, and antiquity an Ægyptian Osyris: In one of the roomes neere this hangs the Sposaliccio of St. Sebastiano, the original of Hanibal Caraccio, of which I procured a Copy, little inferior to the prototype; a table in my judgment Superior to anything I had seene in Rome. Descending into the Court we spied a Vast Gulio, or Obelisque, broaken, having divers hieroglyphics cut on it:

November 8: We gave a visite to the Jesuites Church, the front whereoff, esteem'd as noble a piece of Architecture as any in Europe, the designe of Jacomo della Porta, & the famous Vignola: In this Church lyes the body of their renown'd Ignatius Liola, an arme of Xaverius their other Apostle: and at the right end of the high Altar their Champion Card: Bellarmine: Here Father Kercherus (Mathematical Professor, and of the Oriental Tongues) shew'd us many singular courtesies, leading us into their Colledge, and car⟨ry⟩ing us into their ⟨Refectory⟩, Dispensatory, Laboratory, Gardens; & finaly (through an hall hung round with the pictures of such of their Order as had been executed for their pragmatical & buisy adventures) into his owne study, where he with Dutch patience shew'd us his perpetual motions, Catoptrics, Magnetical experiments, Modells, and a thousand other crotchets & devises, most of them since published, either by himselfe, or his industrious Scholar Schotti. Returning home, we had time to view the Palazzo de Medici, which was an house of the Duke of Florence neere our Lodging upon the brow of Mons Pincius: having an incomparable Prospect towards the Campo Marzo. This is a very magnificent strong building, having a substruction very remarkable, and a Portico supported with Columns towards the Gardens with two huge Lions of marble at the end of the Balustrads: The whole out side of this facciata is ⟨incrusted⟩ with antique & rare Basse-relievis & statues: Descending into the Garden is a noble fountaine govern'd by a Mercury of brasse, and a little distance on the Left hand, a Lodge full of incomparable Statues, amongst which the Sabines, antique & singularly rare: In the Arcado neere this stand 24 statues of infinite price; and hard by a Mount planted with Cypresses, representing a fortresse, with a goodly fountaine in the middle: Here is also a row balustr'd with white marble, on which are erected divers statues and heads, covered over with the natural shrubbs, Ivys & other perennial Greenes, as in nices: At a little distance Those fam'd statues of the Niobe & her family, in all 15 as big as the life, of which we have ample mention in Pliny, being certainely to be esteemed amongst the best pieces of worke in the world, for the passions they expresse, & all other perfections of that stupendious art. There is likewise in this Garden a faire Obelisque full of Hieroglypics: At our going out, I tooke notice of the fountaine before the front, which cast water neere 50 foote in height, receiving it into a most ample basin of marble: Here they usualy rod the greate-horse every morning, which gave me much diversion from the Tarrace of my owne Chamber, where I could see all their motions. This Evening I was invited to heare rare musique at the Chiesa Nova, a building of incomparable ordinance; the black marble Pillars within lead us to that most precious Oratory of Philipus Nerius their founder: They being of the Oratory, secular Priests, & under no Vowe: There are in it divers good Pictures; as the Assumption, of Girolamo Mutiano; The Crucifix, the Visitation of Eliz: the Presentation of the B: Virgin, Christo Sepolto of Guido Rheno; Caravaggio, Arpino and others. This faire Church consists of 14 Altars; and as many Chapells; there is buried in it (besides their Saint) Cæsar Baronius the greate Annalist. Through this we went into the Sacristia, where the tapers being lighted, one of the Order, preach'd, after him stepp'd up, a Child, of about 8, or 9 years old, who pronounc'd an Oration, with so much grace as I never was better pleased in my life, then to heare Italian so well spoken, &

so intelligently: This course it seemes, they frequently use them to, to bring their scholars to an habit of speaking distinctly, & forming their action & assurance which none so much want, as ours in England. This being finish'd began their motettos, which (in a lofty Cupola richly painted) were sung by Eunuchs, and other rare Voices, accompanied with Theorbas, Harpsicors, & Viols; so as we were even ravish'd with the entertainement of that Evening. This roome is painted by Cortona, & has in it two figures in the Niches:

Before this Church passes one of the most stately streetes of Rome.

The 12th, I walked up to Dioclesians Bathes, whose ruines testifie the vastnesse of its original foundation and magnificence, as well as what M: Angelo tooke from the ornaments about it (by which 'tis sayd he restored the then almost lost art of Architecture) the excelency of the structure. This monstrous Pile was built by the Sweate of the Primitive Christians then under one of the 10 famous Persecutions.

Made out of one of these ruinous Cupolas onely, of incomparable worke, is the Church cald st. Bernardo: which is built in the just forme of an Urne with a Cover. Opposite to this is the Fontana delle Therme, otherwise cal'd Fons Felix, which has a ⟨basse-relievo⟩ in it of white-marble, representing Moses striking the rock which is adorn'd with Camels, Men, Women, Children drinking, as big as the life; a worke for the designe & vastnesse truely magnificent: the Water being conveyed no lesse then 22 Miles in an Aquæduct by Sixtus quintus, ex Agro Columnæ by the way of Præneste, as the Inscription testifies. Thus it gushes forth into 3 ample Lavors, raild about with stone, before which are plac'd two Lions of a strange black stone very rare & antique: Neere to this are the store-houses for the Cittys Corne; and right over against it the Church of st. Susanna, where were the Gardens of Salust. The faciata of this Church is extraordinary noble, the Soffito within guilded & full of Pictures; especialy famous is that of Susanna by Baldasser di Bologna. Also the Tribunal of the high Altar of exquisite worke, from whose incomparable stepps of marble you descend under grownd the repository of divers saints. The Picture over this Altar is the worke of Jacomo siciliano. And the foundation Bernardine Nunns.

From this, we bent towards Dioclesians Bathes againe, never satisfied with contemplating that moles, in which, after an hundred & fifty ⟨Thousand⟩ Christians were destined to burthens, building 14 yeares; he murthered them all; so as there had neede be a Monastery of Carthusians in memory of the cruelty: It is called Santa Maria degli Angeli, the Architecture M: Angelos, & the Cloister incompassing, walls in an ample Garden:

Hence we walked to Mont Alto's Villa, which enters by a stately Gate of stone: Tis built on the Viminalis, & is no other then a spacious Parke full of Fountaines, especialy that which salutes us at the front; stews for fish at the left hand: The Cypresse-Walkes are so beset with Statues, Inscriptions, Relievos, and other antient Marbles, as nothing can be more solemn & stately: But that which much surpriz'd me, were the monstrous Citron-Trees: In the Palace joining to it, are innumerable Collections of value: Returning, we step'd into st. Agneses Church where there is a Tribunal of antique Mosaique: and on the Altar a most rich Ciborio of Brasse, with a Statue of st. Agnese of Alabaster oriental. Hence to santa Constanza which has a noble Cupola: In this Church they shewd us a stone-ship borne upon a Columne, heretofore sacred to Baccus, as the relievo intimates, by the drunken Emblemes & instruments wrought upon it: The Altar is of rich Porphyrie as I remember. At our looking back, we had the intire view of the Via Pia, which downe to the two horses, before the Monte Cavallo before mention'd, I thinke to be one of the most glorious sights for state & magnificence that any City in the Earth can shew a Traveller: Thus we return'd by Porta Pia, and the Via Salaria, neere Campo Scelerato in whose glomy Caves the wanton Vestals were heretofore immur'd alive: Thenc into Via Felix, a straite & noble streete, but exceeding precipicious, till we came to the 4 Fountaines of Lepidus: These are built at the abbutments of 4 stately Wayes, making an exact Crosse of right angles, and the fountaines are as many Cumbent figures of Marble under very large niches of stone, the water powring into huge Basins: Here we enter'd the Church of st. Carlo, a singular fabrique for neatenesse as built all of a new white stone, & of an excellent oval designe: It has under it also another Church of a structure nothing lesse admirable: The Columns in the Superiour Church are worth the notice.

Next we came to santa Maria Maggiore, built upon the Esquiline Mountaine, which gives it a most conspicuous face to the streete at a great distance. The designe is mixt, partly antique, partly moderne: Here they affirme that B: Virgine appearing, shewed where it should be built, 300 yeares since: The first Pavement is rare & antique, & so is the Portico built by PP: Eugenius The 2d: The Ciborio is the worke of Paris Romano, and the Tribunal of Mosaic. We were shewed in the Church a Concha of Porphyrie wherein they say Patricius the founder lyes: This is one of the most famous of the 7 Roman Churches; and absolutely (in my opinion at least) after st. Peters the most magnificent; very greate are the stations, & Indulgences: but above all for incomparable glory & materials, are the two Chapels of Sixtus V: and Paulus Quintus. That of Sixtus was designed by Dom: Fontana, in which are two rare greate statues, some good Pieces of Painting: and here they pretended to shew us some of the holy Innocents bodyes slaine by the cruelty of Herod; as also that renown'd Tabernacle of metall gilt, sustained by 4 Angels, holding as many tapers, which is placed on the Altar: In this Chapel is likewise the statue of Sixtus in Copper, with basse-relievos of most of his famous acts in parrian marble. But that of P: Paulus, which we next enter'd, opposite to this, is beyond all imagination glorious, & therefore not to be describ'd; for tis so incircl'd with Achates & other most precious materials, as even altogether dazles & confounds the beholders: the Bassi relievos are for the most part of pure snowy marble intermixed with figures of molten brasse double guilt on Lapis Lazuli: The Altar a most stupendous piece; but most incomparable is the Cupola painted by Cavaliero Gioseppe, Rheni, and the present Baglioni, full of exquisite Sculptures: a most Sumptuos Sacristia, and the Piece over the Altar esteemed of the hand of st. Luke if you will believe it. Paule the 5t, hath here likewise built two other Altars, under the one lye the bones of the Apostle Matthias; In another Oratory is the statue of this Pope, and the head of the Congo Ambassador who dy'd, and was converted at Rome: In a 3d, design'd by M: Angelo lyes the body of Platina, and the Cardinal of Toledo; besides Honorius the 3d: Nicephorus the 4th: st. Hieroms Ashes and many others:

On the 14th we pass'd againe through the stately Capitol, & Campo Vacino towards the Amphitheater of Vespasianus, but

were first stayed to looke ⟨at⟩ Titus's Triumphal Arch, erected by
the people of Rome in honor of his victory at Jerusalem; on the
left hand whereof he is represented drawne in a Charriot with 4
horses a breast: On the right hand, or side of the Arch within, is
sculptur'd in figures, or basse relievo, as big as the life, (and in
one intire white marble) the Arke of the Covenant upon which
stands the seaven-branch'd Candlestick, describ'd in Leviticus,
as also the two Tables of the Law, all borne upon mens shoulders, by the barrs, as they are describ'd in some of st. Hieroms
bibles: Before this goes many crown'd & laureated figures & 12
Roman fasces, with other sacred Vessells; This I must confesse
did much confirme the Idea I before had, and therefore for the
light it gave to the holy history, I caused my Paynter Carlo to
copy it most exactly out: The rest of the worke of the Arch is of
the noblest, best understod Composita; and the Inscription is
this in capital Letters.

S. P. Q. R.
D: Tito. D. Vespasiani. F. ⟨VESPASIANO⟩ Augusto.

Before we left this Arch, we step'd into santa Maria Nova, where
they told us Simon Magus fell out of the ayre, at st. Peters
prayer, and burst himselfe to pieces upon a flint: And neere it a
rare monument of Marble, erected by the People of Rome in
memory of the Popes returne from Avignon. Being now pass'd
the ruines of Meta-Sudante, which stood before the Colosseum
(so cal'd, because there once stood here the statue of Comodus)
and was provided to refresh the Gladiators: we enter into the
mighty ruines of the Vespatian Amphitheatre, built by that
excellent Prince Titus; it is 830 Roman palmes in length (i) 130
paces, 90 in breadth at the Area: with Caves for the wild beasts
which us'd to be baited by men instead of doggs: The whole oval
Peripheria 2888 $\frac{4}{7}$ palmes; and capable to containe 87000 Spectators with ease and all imaginable accommodation; The 3 rowes
of Circles are yet entire, the first was for the Senators, & the
S⟨e⟩cond & middle for the Nobility, the 3d for the people:
At the dedication of this place were 5000 wild beasts slayn in
3 monethes during which the feast lasted to the expense of
10 milions of Gold: The Moles is all built of Tiburtine stone, a
vast height, by 30000 Jewes Captives, with the 5 order⟨s⟩ of

Architecture: It is without of a perfect Circle, and was once adorned thick with statues, remaining intire till of late that some of the stones were caried away to repaire the Citty wales, & build the Farnezian Palace: That which still appeares most admirable is the contrivance of the Porticos, vaults & staires, with the excessive altitude which certainely well deserves this distic of the ingenious Poet

> Omnis Cæsario cedat labor Amphitheatro
> Unum pro cunctis fama loquatur Opus.

Neere it is a small Chapell cal'd santa Maria della Pieta nel Col-iseo, which is erected on the steps, or stages very lofty, at one of its sides or ranges within, and where there lives onely a melan-cho⟨l⟩y Heremite: I ascended to the very top of it, and that with wonderfull admiration. From this we walked towards the Arch of Constantinus magnus, which is close by the Meta Sudante, a kind of Fountaine at which the Gladiators were us'd to refresh themselves, at the beginning of the famous Via Appia upon one side of Mont Celio: This Arch is perfectly intire, erected by the People in memory of his Triumph and Victory over Maxentius whom he vanquish'd at the Pons Milvius; now Ponte Mole; The Sculpture consists much of Trophes, and such like Ornaments.

Hence we went up to St. Gregorio in Monte Celio, where are many priviledg'd Altars, & there they shewed us an arme of that Saint, & other reliques: Before this Church stands a very noble Portico.

The 15 was wett, & I stirr'd not out. 16, I went to Visite Father John, Provincial of the Benedictines &c: The 17 I walked to Villa Burghesi, which is an house and ample Garden on Mons Pincius, yet somewhat without the Citty-Wales; circumscrib'd by another wall full of small turrets and banqueting houses, which makes it appeare at a distance like a little Towne, within it tis an Elysium of delight; having in the center of it a very noble Palace (but the enterance of the Garden, presents us with a very glorious fabrick, or rather dore-Case adorned with divers excellent marble statues): This Garden abounded with all sorts of the most delicious fruit, and Exotique simples: Fountaines of sundry inventions, Groves, & small Rivulets of Water: There is also adjoyning to it a Vivar-ium for Estriges, Peacoks, Swanns, Cranes, &c: and divers strange

Beasts, Deare & hares: The Grotto is very rare, and represents
among other devices artificial raines, & sundry shapes of Vessells,
Flowers &c: which is effected by ⟨changing⟩ the heads of the
Fountaines: The Groves are of Cypresse and Lawrell, Pine, Myr-
til, Olive &c: The 4 Sphinxes are very Antique and worthy observation: To this is a Volary full of curious birds: The House is built
of a Square fabric, with turrets, from which the Prospect towards
Rome, & the invironing hills is incomparable, cover'd as they were
with Snow (as commonly they continue even a greate part of
summer) which afforded a sweete refreshing: About the house
there is a stately Balustre of white Marble, with frequent jettos of
Water & adorned with statues standing on a multitude of Bases,
rendering a most gracefull ascent: The Wales of the house, are
covered with antique incrustations of history; as that of Curtius's
precipitation, the representation of Europa's ravishment, & that
of Leda &c: The Cornices above them consist of frutages & Festoons; betwixt which are Niches furnishd with statues, which
order is observed to the very roofe: In the Lodge at the Entry are
divers good statues of Consuls &c, with two Pieces of Field
Artillery upon Carriages (a mode much practiz'd in Italy before
the Greate-mens houses) which they looke on as a piece of state,
more then defence: In the first Hall within are the 12: Rom:
Emperors of most excellent marble, twixt them stand Porph⟨y⟩ry
Columns, & other precious stones of vast height & magnitude,
with Urnes of Oriental Alabaster; Tables of Pietra-Commessa:
And here is that renown'd Diana which Pompey worship'd ⟨of⟩
Easter-marble: The most incomparable Seneca of touch, bleeding
in a huge Vasa of Porphyrie ressembling the dropps of his blood:
The so famous Gladiator, Hermaphrodite, upon a quilt of stone;
from whence that small one of Ivory which I brought out of Italy
with me was admirably Copied by that signal Artist Hans
Fiammengo, esteemed one of the best statuaries in the World:
The new Piece of Daphny, and David, of Cavaliero Bernini,
observable for the incomparable Candor of the stone, & art of the
statuary plainely stupendious: We were also shewed a world of
rare Pictures of infinite Value, & of the best Masters; huge Tables
of Porphyrie, and two exquisitely wrought Vasas of the same; In
another chamber divers sorts of Instruments of Musique,
amongst other toyes, as that of the Satyre which so artificialy
express'd an human Voice, with the motion of eyes & head; that

would easily affright one who were not prepared for that most extravagant vision: They shew'd us also a Chayre, which Catches fast any who but sitts downe in it, so, as not to be able to stirr out of it, by certain springs conceiled in the Armes and back theroff, which at sitting downe surprizes a man on the suddaine, locking him in armes & thighs after a true tretcherous Italian guize: The Perspective is also considerable, compos'd by the position of look-ing-glasses, which renders a strange multiplication of things, resembling divers most richly furnish'd-roomes: Here stands a rare Clock of German-worke, in a word, ⟨nothing⟩ but magnifi-cent is to be seene in this Paradise.

The next day I went to the Vaticane, where in the morning I saw the Ceremony of Pamfilio the Popes Nephew's receiving a Cardinals hatt; which was indeede the first time I had ever beheld his Holinesse in Pontificalibus: The Ceremony was (after the Cardinals & Princes were met in the Consistory) in the Popes Chapell, where he was at the Altar invested with most pompous rites: Thence I pass'd through divers Galleries, Halls, & other Places filld with the rarest paintings; but had not time now to consider them.

On the 19 I went to visite St. Pietro, that most stupendious & incomparable Bascilicam, far surpassing any now extant in the World, & perhapps (Solomons Temple excepted) any that was ever built:

The largenesse of the Piazza before the Portico is worth observing, because it affords you a noble prospect of the Church; crowded up, for the most part in other places, where greate Churches are erected: In this is a fountaine out of which gushes a river, rather than a streame, which ascending a good height, breakes upon a round embosse of Marble into millions of pearles, which fall into the subjacent bason: making an horrible noise: I esteeme this, one of the goodliest fountains that ever I saw.

The Church was first began by st. Anacletus, when rather a Chapel, upon a foundation (as they give out) of the Greate Con-stantines, who in honor of the Apostles 'tis sayd, carried 12 baskets-full of sand to the Worke: After him Julius secundus tooke it in hand, unto which all his since successors, have more or less contributed. The Frontispiece is suppos'd to be the largest, and best studied piece of Architecture in the World: To this we went up by 4 stepps of marble: The first entrance is supported with huge Pillasters: The Volto within is certainely the richest in the Earth, overlayd with gold: next I considered the 5 large Anti-Ports, twixt which are Columns of enormous altitude & compass, with as many Gates of brasse, the worke & sculpture of Pollaiuolo the Florentine full of cast figures & histories in a deepe Relievo. Over this runns a tarrac of like amplitude & ornament, where the Pope upon sollemne times bestows his benedictions of the Vulgar. On each side of this Portico are two Campaniles or Towers, whereoff there was but one perfected, of admirable art, & aspect. Lastly on the top of all runns a Balustrade which edges it quite round, and upon this at equal distances, Christ & the 12 Disciples of gigantine bignesse & stature; yet below shewing no greater then the life.

Entring the Church, admirable is the bredth of the Volto or roofe, which is all carv'd with foliage & roses, overlayd with gold in nature of a deepe bass-relievo, a l'antique: The Nave or body of this Moles ⟨is⟩ in forme of a Crosse, such as the Crucifixes reppresent, whereof the foote part is the longest; and at the internodium of the Transum-part, arises the Cupola, which being all builded of stone, & of that prodigious height, is more in Compasse than that of the Pantheon (which was the largest amongst the old Romans, & is yet intire) or any else knowne in the whole World: The inside or Concave part, is covered with most exquisite mosaique representing the Celestial Hierarchie, by Cavaliero Giuseppe d'Arpino, full of starrs of gold: The Convex or out side expos'd to the aire is covered with lead, with huge ribbs of metall doubly guilt (as are also the ten other lesser Cupolas, for no fewer adorne this glorious structure) which gives a greate & admirable beauty & Splendor in all parts of the Citty: On the very Summit of this is fix'd a brasen Globe or Mundo gilt likewise over, & capable of receiving 35 Persons at once: This I entered, & engrav'd my name in, amongst other Travellors: Lastly the Crosse: The accesse to it is betweene the Leaden Covering and the stone or Convex Arch-Worke; a most miraculous, & truely stupendious piece of Art.

On the battlements of the Church (which is also all overlayd with Lead & marble) you would imagine your selfe in a Towne, so many Cupolas, Pinacles, Towers, Juttings; & not a few houses inhabited by men who dwell there, & have enough to do to looke after the vast reparations which continualy employs them.

Having seene this, we descended againe into the body of the Church, which is full of Collaterall Chapells & large Oratories, most of them exceeding that of ordinary Churches; but the Principal are fowre, incrusted with most precious marbles, & precious stones of various Colours, & adorn'd with an infinity of Statues, Pictures, stately Altars, & Reliques innumerable, & not indeede to be reckoned: onely the Altar-piece of st. Michael being of Mosaique I could not passe without particular note; because certainely one of the best of that kind in the Earth. The Chapel of Gregory the 13, where he is buried is most splendid:

Under the Cupola, and in the Center of the Church stands the high-Altar, consecrated first by Clement the 8th, adorn'd by Paulus V: and lately cover'd by Pope Urban the 8 with that stupendious Canopy of Corinthian brasse, which heretofore was brought from the Pantheon: It consists of 4 Wreath'd Columns partly channeld & incircl'd with vines, upon which hang little Puti, Birds, & Bees (the Armes of the Barberini) sustaining a Baldachino of the same Mettal: The 4 Columns weigh an hundred & ten thousand pounds, all over gilted with rich gold; and indeede with the Pedistalls, Crowne, & statues about it, a thing of that Art, vastnesse & magnificence beyond all that ever mans industry has produced of this kind & worthy the Celebration, as it is the Worke of Cavaliero Bernini A Florentine Sculptor, Architect, Painter & Poet: who a little before my Comming to the Citty, gave a Publique Opera (for so they call those Shews of that kind) where in he painted the seanes, cut the Statues, invented the Engines, composed the Musique, writ the Comedy & built the Theater all himselfe.

Opposite to either of these Pillars, under those Nices which with their Columne support the weighty Cupola before described, are placed 4 exquisite statues of Parian Marble, to which are 4 Altars: viz, that of Santa Veronica made by Fra: Mochi, over which is the Reliquary where they shew'd us the miraculous Sudarium indued with the Picture of our Saviours face.

The 4th hath over the Altar, and opposite to that of st. VERONICA the statue of st. Andrew, the worke of one Fiamingo, admirable for the rarenesse of it above all the other; & above is preservd the head of that Apostle richly inchas'd: It is

reported this excellent Sculptor dy'd mad, to see his statue plac'd
in a dissadvantageous light, by Bernino the chiefe Architect,
who found himselfe out don by this Artist: And indeede the vast
number of Reliques shew'd and kept in this Church, are without
number, as are also the precious Vessells of Gold, Silver, and
gemms, with the Vests & other incomparable services to be
seene in the Sacristy which were shewed us. Under the high-
Altar there is an ample & stately Grott inlayd with Pietra-
Commessa, wherein halfe of the bodys of St. Peter and St. Paule
are reserv'd, before which hang divers huge lamps of the richest
plate that continualy burne. About this, and contiguous to the
Altar runns a balustrad in forme of a Theatre of black-marble:
Towards the left, as you goe out of the Church by the Portico, a
little be neath the high Altar, sits an old brasse statue of st. Peter,
under the Soles of whose feete many devout persons rub their
heads, and touch their Chapletts: This was formerly cast from a
statue of Jupiter Capitolinus: In another place stands a Columne
(grated about with Yron) whereon they report our B: S: was
often wont to leane as he preached in the Temple; as likewise
⟨in⟩ the work of the Reliquary under the Cupola there are 8
wreathed Columns which were brought from the Temple of
Solomon. In another chapell they shew'd us the Chayre of st.
Peter, or (as they name it) the Apostolical Throne: But, amongst
all the Chapells one most glorious, having for Altar-piece a
Madona bearing a Cristo mortuo in White marble, on her
knees, the worke of Mich: Angelo: At the very upmost end of
the Cathedral are divers stately Monuments, especialy that of
Urban the VIIIth, amongst all which there is one observable for
two naked incumbent figures of an old, & a young woman, upon
which last, there now lyes a covering, or apern of brasse, to cover
those parts, which it seemes occasioned a [pigmalian] Spanyard
to be found in a la⟨s⟩civious posture, so rarely to the life was this
warme figure don: Round about the Cupola, and in many other
places of the Church are Confession-seates for all Languages as
Hebrew, Gr: Lat: Span: Ital: Fr: Engl: Irish, Welch, Sclavonic,
Dutch &c, as 'tis writen upon their frezes in Golden Capitals,
and there are still at Confessions some of all nations: Towards
the ⟨lower⟩ end of the Church, and on the side of a vast pillar
sustaining a weighty roofe is the depositum and statue of the
Countesse Matilda, a rare & incomparable piece, with basse

relievos about it of white marble the worke of Bernini, as also those of Sixtus the 4th, and Paulus III &c: Amongst the exquisite pieces in this sumptuous fabrique that of the Ship, St. Peter held up from sinking by our Saviour, and the emblems about it is the Mosaique of the famous Giotto who restor'd and made it perfect, after it had by the barbarians been defaced: nor is the pavement under the Cupola to be passed over without observation; which with the rest of the body and wales of the whole Church are all inlayd with the richest of piettra Commessa in the most splendid & glorious colours of polished marbles, Achats, Serpentine, Porphyrie, Calcedoine &c: wholy incrusted to the very roofe: Comming out by the Portico we entred, we were shew'd the Porto Santo never opned but at the yeare of Jubilie.

This glorious Foundation hath belonging to it 30 Canonics, 36 Beneficiates, 28 Clearkes benefic'd with innumerable Chaplaines &c, a Cardinal being always Arch-priest, as now was Franc: Barberini who also styl'd himselfe Protector of the English to whom he was indeede very courteous. Thus I came weary home, and full of admiration at what we had seene for that day:

November 20 I went to visite that antient See, and Cathedral of St. John de Laterana, and the holy places thereabout: This is a church of extraordinary devotion, though for outward forme not comparable to st. Peters, being of Gotique Ordonance: Before we went into the Cathedral the Baptisterie or Fonte of st. Jo: Baptist presented it selfe, it being formerly part of the Greate Constantines Palace, & as sayd his chamber, where by st. Silvester he was made a Christian; it is of an Octagonal shape, having before the entrance 8 faire Pillars of rich Porphyrie, the nobles⟨t⟩ doub⟨t⟩less in the world, consisting of one intire piece, their Capitells of divers orders, underpropping divers lesser Columnes of white-marble that support a noble Cupola, the moulding whereof is incomparably wrought. In the Chapell which they affirme to have been the lod⟨g⟩ing chamber of this Emperor all Women are prohibited to enter, for the malice of Herodias who caus'd him to loose his head: Here are deposited divers sacred Reliques of st. James, Mary Magdalen, st. Mathew &c and two goodly pictures: Another Chapel or Oratory neere it, is cald st. Jo: the Evangelist well adorn'd with Marbles and Tables, especialy those of Cavalier Gioseppe, and of Tempesta in fresca.

We went hence into another cald St. Venantius, in which is a Tribunal all of Mosaique in figures of Popes: here is likewise an Altar of the Madona much visited and divers Sclavonish Saints, companions of Pope John the 4th. The Portico of the Church is built with divers materials brought from P: Pilats house in Jerusalem; and here is that famous Porphyrie Chaire where the new created Pope ut Sexus sui periculum fieret, must sit bare, as tis affirm'd confidently. The next sight which drew us was a wonderfull concourse of people at their devotions before a place called Scala Sancta to which is built a most noble frontspiece: Being enter'd the Portico we saw those large stayers of marble, in number 28, which are never ascended but upon the knees, some lip-devotion us'd upon every step, upon which you may perceive divers red speccks of blood (under a grate) which they affirme to have been drops of our B: Saviours what time he was so barbarously missus'd by Herods souldiers; for these stayres are reported to be transferred hither from his palace in Jerusalem: At the top of these stayres is a chapell whereat they enter (but we could not be permitted) by Gates of Marble, being the same our Saviour passed when he went out of Herods-house, This they name the Sanctum Sanctorum, and over it we read this Epigraphe Non est in toto Sanctior orbe locus. Here, through a grate, we saw that picture of Christ, paynted, as they say, by the hand of st. Luke to the life, and so we descended againe, where the first thinge we took notice of (as indeed most worthy admiration) was the Obelisc before St. J: Laterano: It formerly lay in the Circo Maximo, & was erected here by Sixtus V: 1587 containing 112 foote in height without base, or pedistal: large it is at the foote 9½ one way, & 8 the other: This Pillar or Pyramid rather was brought first from Thebes at the utmost confines of Ægypt to Alexandria, from thence to Constantinople, thence to Rome, & is sayd by Ammianus Marcellinus to have been dedicated to Ramises K: of Ægypt: it was tran(s)ferred to this City by Constantius, the sonne of Const: Magnus: & is full of rare hieroglypics, serpents, men, owles, falcons, Oxen, Instruments &c, containing, as they affirme (and as Father Kercher

the Jesuite will shortly tell us in a booke hee is ready to publish)
all the recondite & abstruse learning of that people: It is
reported that the Vessell, Gally or floate, that brought this to
Rome so many hundred Leagues must needs have been of an
infinite bignesse & strange fabrique: The stone is one, & intire,
and was erected by the famous Dom: Fontana for that magnificent Pope Sixtus V: as the rest were, 'tis now crack'd in many
places, but solidly joyned:

Leaving this miraculous monument (before which is a stately
publique fountaine, with a statue of St. John in the middle of it)
we visited his Holynesse's Palace, being a little upon the left
hand: The designe of Fontana Pope Sixtus's Architect: This I
take to be one of ⟨the⟩ best Palaces of Rome; but not sta⟨y⟩ing
here, we enterd into the Church of St. Jo: de Laterana, which is
properly the Cathedral of the Roman See, as I learn'd by these
Verses engraven upon the Architrave of the Portico.

> Dogmate Papali datur, et simul Imperiali
> Quod sim cunctarum mater caput Ecclesiarum:
> Hinc Salvatoris cælestia regna datoris
> Nomine sanxerunt, cum cuncta peracta fuerunt;
> Sic Vos ex toto conversi supplice Voto
> Nostra quod hæc ædes; tibi Christe sit inclyta sedes.

'Tis cal'd Lateran from a noble famely dwelling it seemes here-
about on Mons Celius: The Church is built of Gotic ordonance,
& hath a stately Tribunal, the paintings are of Pietro Pisano: 'tis
the first Church that ever was consecrated with the Ceremonies
now introduc'd, and where Altars of stone supplied those of
wood heretofore in use & made like large Chests for the better
removing in times of persecution: Such an Altar is still the greate
one here preserved as a monument, because they hold st. Peter
celebrated Masse on it at Rome, for which cause none but the
Pope may now presume to make that use of it: The Pavement of
the Church is of all sorts of precious Marbles, and so are the very
walles of it to a great height, over which 'tis painted a fresca with
the life, and Acts of Constantine the Greate by most excellent
Masters: The Organs are rare, supported with 4 Columns: The
Suffitto is all richly gilded & full of Pictures. Opposite to the
Porte is an Altar of exquisite Architecture, with a Tabernacle on
it all of precious stones, the worke of one Targoni, on this is a

Cena of Plate, the invention of one Curtius Vanni of exceeding
value; the Tables hanging over it are of Gioseppe d'Arpino;
About this are 4 incomparable Columns formerly transported by
the Emp: Titus out of Asia, they are of brasse double gilt, about
12 foote in height, and the Walls betweene them are incrusted
with marble & set with statues in Niches, the Vacuum reported
to be fill'd with holy earth, which they say st. Helena sent
from Jerusalem to her sonn Constantine who set these pillars
where they now stand: At one side of this is an Oratory full of
rare Paintings & monuments, especially those of the greate
Connestable Colonna, out of this we came into the Sacristia full
also of good pictures of Albert & others: At the end of the
Church is a flat stone erected & supported by 4 pillars which they
affirme to have beene the exact height of our B: Saviours stature
when he conversed here on Earth, which, they say, never fitted
any mortal man that ever tryed it, but he was either taller, or
shorter. Two Columns likewise which rent at his Passion of the
Vaile of the Temple: The stone on which they threw Lotts for his
seamelesse Vesture, and the Pillar on which the Cock crow'd
after Peters abnegation and to omitt noe fine thing, the just
length of the Virgin Marys foote, as her shoo-maker, it seems,
affirmed. Here is indeede a most sumptuous Crosse besett with
preccious stones, & containing some of the very wood of the holy
Crosse it selfe: The heads of st. Peter, and St. Paule are conserv'd
here under St. Salvators Altar. In this Church were the two
famous Oecumenical Councils celebrated by P: Simmachus &
Martinus I. Stephanus &c: It is indeede furnish'd with the most
magnificent Monuments, especialy that of st. Helens being all of
Porphyrie: that of Card: Farneze, Martine the first of Coper: The
Pictures of Mary Magdalen, Martine the V: Laurent: Valla &c
are of Gaetano: Those of the Nuntiata: design'd by M: Angelo,
the greate Crucifix of Sermoneta. Under the chiefe Portico is the
Porta Sancta, opned but at the Jubilie: In a Chapel at one end of
the Porch is a statue of Hen: the 4th of France in brasse, it stands
in a darke hole, and so has don many yeares, for what reason I
could not learne; perhaps they did not believe him a th⟨o⟩rough
Proselyte. Other precious Reliqu⟨e⟩s are shew'd here, as the Calix
or Cup in which St. Jo: dranke the Poyson, the chayne that ty'd
him being led to Rome, & his Coate, which being once put on
3 dead men rais'd them to life, as they report; a robe of the B:

Virgins which she gave to Christ, and the towell with which he dried the Disciples feete; the reede, sponge, some of the blood & water of his precious side: some of the Virgins haire, the Table on which the Passover was celebrated, the rods of Aron & Moses, and many such bagatells:

Leaving this Venerable Church (for in truth it has a certaine majesty in it) we pass'd through a faire and large Hospital of good Architecture, and some Inscriptions put up by the Barberini the late Popes Nephew, Then by st. Silvia where there is a noble statue of S: Gregory P: began by M: Angelo, a st. Andrea, & here we were shewed the Bath of santa Cicilia: In the Church are divers rare paintings, especialy that story on the Wall of Guido Rheni: Thence we went to st. Giovanni e Paula where the Friers are reported to be greate Chymists, the quire, roofe & paintings in the Tribuna are excellent things: hence descending Mont Celius we come against the Vestigia's of the Palazzo Maggiore heretofore the Golden House of Nero; now nothing but an heape of vast & confused Ruines, to shew what time, and the vicissitude of human things doe change from the most glorious & magnificent, to the most deformed, and confused:

We next went into st. Sebastians Church, which has an handsome front: Then we passed by the place where Romulus & Rhemus were taken up by Faustulus: The Forum Romanum, and so by the edge of the Mons Palatinus, where we were shew'd the Ruines of Pompeys-house, the Church of st. Anacletus, and so into the Circus Maximus, heretofore capable of containing an hundred & sixty-thousand Spectators, now all but one entire heape of rubbish, part of it converted into a Garden of Potherbs. We concluded this evening with hearing the rare Voices and musique at the Chiesa nova.

On the 21 I was carried to a great Virtuoso one Cavalliero Pozzo, who shew'd us a rare Collection of all kind of Antiquities, a choice Library, over which are the Effigies of most of our late men of polite literature: That which was most new to me was his rare collection of the Antique Bassirelievos about Rome, which this curious man had caus'd to be design'd in divers folios: he shew'd us also many fine Medails, and amongst other curiousitys a pretty folding ladder, to be put in a small compasse, one of wood, another of cord: a number of choyce designes &

drawings. [He also shew'd us that stone *Pliny* calls *Enhydrus* [of the bignesse of a wallnut: it had plainly in it to the quantity of halfe a sponefull of Water, of a yellow pibble colour] & another in a ring without foile, paler than Amethyst, which yet he affirm'd to be the true *Carbuncle* & harder than the diamond: [twas set in a ring without foile or any thing at the bottome, so as t'was transparant of a greenish yellow, more lustrous than a Diamond.] He had very pretty things painted on Crimson Velvet, designed in black & shaded, hightned with white, I suppose in oyle, & set in frames:] [Cavaliero Pozzos Carbuncle

was of this shape & bignesse of a yellowish red, & far more sparkling than a diamond, though set transparantly without foile:] Hence we went on foote to the Suburra, and Erarium Saturni, where yet remaine some Ruines and an Inscription: Hence to st. Pietro in Vincoli one of the 7 Churches on the Esquiline, an old & much frequented place of greate devotion for the Reliques there: especialy the bodys of the Seaven Maccabean Breathren, these lye under the Altar: On the Wall is a st. Sebastian of Mosaic after the Græke manner; but what I chiefly reguarded was that noble Sepulchre of Pope Julius the Second the worke of M: Angelo, with that never sufficiently to be admired statue of Moses in White marble, those also of Vita Contemplativa & Activa are by the same incomparable hand: Behind these we walked a turne amongst the Bathes of Titus admiring the strange & prodigious receptacles of water, which the Vulgar call the Setti Sali, places of wonderfull amplitude & receipt, but now all in heapes: To this Church belongs a Monastery in the court of whose Cloisters grow two tall and very stately Palme-trees.

The 23d of this Moneth of November was the sollemne, and greatest ceremony of all the state Ecclesiastical, viz, the Cavalcado or Procession of his Sanctity Pope Inn⟨o⟩centius X to st. Jo: de Laterano which standing on the stepps of Ara Celi neere the Capitoll, I saw passe in this manner.

First went a guard of Swizzers to make way, and divers of the Avantguard of horse Car⟨ry⟩ing Lances: next follow'd those who caried the robes of the Cardinals, all two & two: then the Cardinals Mace-bearers, The Caudatari on Mules, The Masters of their horse: The Popes Barber, Taylor, Baker, Gardner & other

domesticall officers all on horse back in rich liveries: The
Squires belonging to the Guard. Then were lead by 5 men in
very rich liverys 5 noble Neapolitan Horses white as Snow,
coverd to the ground with trappings gloriously embrodered,
which is a Service payd by the King of Spaine for the Kingdomes of Naples & Sicily pretended fœdatorys to the Pope: 3
Mules of exquisite beauty & price trapped in Crimson Velvet,
next followd 3 rich Litters with Mules, the litters were empty:
After these the Master of the horse alone, with his Squires: 5
Trumpeters: The ⟨C⟩amerieri estra muros: The Fiscale & Con-
sistorial Advocates: Cappellani, Camerieri di honore, Cubiculari
& Chamberlaines cald Secreti, then followed 4 other Camerieri
with 4 Capps of the dignity Pontifical, which were Cardinals
hatts carried on staffs: 4 Trumpets, after them a number of
Noble Romans & Gentlemen of quality very rich, & follow'd by
innumerable Staffieri & Pages: The Secretaries of the Cancellaria, Abbreviatori-Acoliti in their long robes & on Mules:
Auditori di Rota, The Deane of the Roti, and Master of the
Sacred Palace, on Mules, with grave, but rich foote Clothes, &
in flat Episcopal hatts: Then went more of the Roman & other
nobility Courtiers with divers pages in most rich liveries on
horseback; After them 14 drums belonging to the Capitol: Then
the Marshals with their Staves, The 2 Sindics: The Conservators
of the Citty in robs of Crimson damasc; next them the knight
Confalonier & Prior of the P. R: in velvet tocqus: Six of his holynesse's Mace-bearers: Then the Captaine or Governor of the
Castle of St. Angelo upon a brave prancer: Next the Governor of
the Citty, on both sides of these 2 long rankes of Swizzers. The
Masters of the Ceremonies, The Crosse bearer on horse, with
two Priests on each hand a foote, Pages footemen & guards in
aboundance. Then next the Pope himselfe carried in a Litter, or
rather open chaire of Crimson Velvet richly embrodred, &
borne by two stately Mules; as he went holding up his two fingers, & blessing the people & multitudes upon their knees,
looking out of their windoes & houses with lowd viva's & acclamations of felicity to their new Prince: This was follow'd by the
Master of his chamber, Cuppbearer, Secretary, Physitian. Then
came the Cardinal Bishops, next the Cardinal Priests, Card:
Deacons, Patriarchs, Archbishops, and Bishops all in their several & distinct habits; some in red, others in greene flat hatts

with tossles, all on gallant Mules richly trapp'd with Velvet, &
lead by their servants in greate state & multitudes: After these
the Apostolical Protonotari, Auditor & Tresurer, Referendaries.
Lastly the Trumpets of the reareguard, 2 Pages of Armes in Hel-
mets with might⟨y⟩ feathers & Car⟨ry⟩ing Launces, 2 Captaines,
Then the Pontifical ⟨Standard⟩ of the Church, The two Alfieri,
or Cornets of the Popes light horse who all followed in Armor
& car⟨ry⟩ing launces, which with innumerable rich Coaches, litters & people made up the Proceeding; but what they did at st.
Jo: di Laterano I could not see by reason of the intollerable
Crowd; so as I spent most of the day in admiring of the two Triumphal Arches, which had been purposely erected a few days
before, and til now covered; the one by the Duke of Parma in the
foro Romano; the other by the Jewes in the Capitol with flatering Inscriptions, but of rare and excellent Architecture, decor'd
with statues, and aboundance of ornaments proper for the
Occasion, since they were but temporary, & made up of boards,
cloath &c painted & fram'd on the suddaine, but as to outward
appearance solid and very stately. The night ended with fireworkes; that which I saw was that which was built before the
Spa⟨n⟩ish Ambassadors house in the Piazza del Trinita, &
another of the French: The first appeard to be a mighty rock,
bearing the Popes Armes, a Dragon, and divers figures, which
being set on fire by one who flung a Roquett at it, tooke fire
immediately, yet preserving the figure both of the rock & statues
a very long time, insomuch as 'twas deemed ten thousand
reports of squibbs & crackers spent themselves in order: That
before the French Ambass: Palace (which, I also saw) was a
Diana drawne in a Chariot by her doggs, with aboundance of
other figures as big as the life which plaied with fire in the same
manner; in the meane time were all the windows or the whole
Citty set with innumerable Tapers, which put into lanterns of
sconces of severall colour'd oyl'd papers, that the win'd may not
annoy them, render a most glorious shew, in my conceite, nothing prettier; & besides these, there were at least 20 other glorious fire workes of vast charge & rare art for their invention
before divers Ambassadors, Princes & Cardinals Palaces, especialy that on the Castle of st. Angelo, being a Pyramid of lights
of an excessive height fastned to the ropes and cables which support the standard-pole; Thus were the streetes this night as light

as day, full of Bonfires, Canon roaring, Musique pla⟨y⟩ing, fountaines running Wine in all excesse of joy and Triumph.

On the 28 I went to se⟨e⟩ the Garden and house of the Aldobrandini, but now Cardinal Burghezes: This Palace is for Architecture and magnificence, pompe & state, having to it 4 fronts, &
a noble Piazza before it, one of the most considerable about the
Citty: Within the Court under Arches supported with Columns
of Marble are divers incomparable Statues; ascending the stayres
a rare figure of Diana of white-marble [or a woman in her
smock]: The st. Sebastian, & Hermaphrodite are of stupendious
art: For paintings, our Saviours head by Carragio, sundry pieces
of Raphael; whereof some in little: some of Bassano [Veroneze];
The Leda, and two admirable Venus's are of Titians Pensill [the
Chamber of Nudities]; so is the Psyche & Cupid, the head of
st. John borne by Herodias: Two heads of Albert Durer very
exquisite: We were shew'd here a glorious Cabinet, and Tables of
Florence-worke in stone: In the Garden are a world of fine fountaines, the wales all coverd with Citron trees which being rarely
spread invest the stone worke intirely; and towards the streete at
a back gate the port is so handsomly cloath'd with Ivy, as much
pleas'd me: About this Palace are divers noble & antique Bassi-
relievi; two especialy are placed on the ground, representing
Armor, & other military furniture of the Romans; beside these
stand about the Garden an infinity of rare statues, Altars, and
Urnes; above all for antiquity and curiosity (as being the onely
rarity of that nature now knowne to remaine in the World) is that
piece of old Roman Paynting, representing the Roman Sponsalia
or celebration of their Marriage, judged to be 1400 yeares old; yet
are the Colours very lively, and the designe very intire (tho found
deepe in the ground); for this morcell of paintings sake onely 'tis
sayd Burghesi purchas'd the house, because being on a wall in a
kind of banqueting-house in the Garden it Could not be
removed, but passe with the inheritance.

29: I a second time visited the Medicean Palace being neere
my Lodging, the more exactly to have a view of the noble Collections that adorne it; especialy the Bassrelievi & antique
frezes, inserted about the stone-worke of the house: The Saturne of mettal standing in the Portico is a rare piece; so is the
Jupiter & Apollo in the Hall, and now we were lead above
into those romes we could not see before; full of incomparable

Statues & Antiquities, above all, & happly preferrable to any in
the World are the two Wrestlers, for the inextricable mixture
with each others armes & leggs plainely stupendious; In the
great Chamber is the naked *Gladiator* whetting a knife; but the
Venus is without parallel, being the master piece of   whose
name you see graven under it in old Greeke characters, certainely nothing in Sculpture ever aproched this miracle of art.
[To this add *Marcius, Ganymede*, the two wrestlers, a little *Apollo*
playing on a pipe; some *Relievi* incrusted on the palace walles &
an Antique *Vasa* of Marble neere 6 foote high: I saw in one of
the Chambers, a Conceited *Chayre*, which folded into so many
varieties as to turne into a *bed*, a *bolster*, a *Table*, a *Couch*.] The
Cabinets & Tables of Pietra Commessa, I passe over, being the
proper invention of the Florentines; Of Pictures, I observed, the
Magdalen, st. Peter weeping, excellent paintings; & so refreshing myselfe with another walke about the Gardens, where
I tooke special notice of those two huge Vasas or Bathes of
stone, I went farther up the hill, to the Popes Palace at Monte
Cavallo, where I now saw the Garden more exactly, and found it
to be one of the most magnificent & Pleasant in Rome: I am
told the Gardner is annualy alow'd 2000 scudi for the keeping it: Here I observ'd the glorious hedges of myrtle above a
mans height; others of Laurell, Oranges, nay of Ivy, & Juniper:
The Close walkes and Rustic Grotto, and ⟨another⟩ admirable
Crypta whereof the Lavor or Basin is of one vast intire Porphyrie, the fairest that ever I beheld, antique: Below this falls a
plentifull Cascad of Water; the stepps of the Grott being all of
rich Mosaique, as is also the roofe: Here are hydraulic Organs; a
Fish-pond in an ample Bath: From hence we went to tast some
rare Greco, and so home.

  After this to the 6 of December I kept within for the most
part, being pretty weary of my continual walkings; so I entertain'd one Signor Alessandro who shew'd me upon the Theorba:

  The next excursion was over the river Tiber which I cross'd in a
Ferry-boate to see the Palazzo de Ghisi standing in Transtevere,
and fairely built, but famous onely for the painting a fresca on the
Volto of the Portic towards the Garden, the story is the Amours of
Cupid & Psyche, by the hand of the celebrated Raphael d'Urbin:
Here you shall always se⟨e⟩ Paynters designing, and Cop⟨y⟩ing

after it, it being esteem'd one of the rarest pieces of that Art in the world, & certainly with greate reason; not to omit that other incomparable fable of Galateo (as I remember) so carefully preserved in the Cuppord, at one of the ends of this walke to protect it from the aire, because it is a most stupendious lively painting: Here are likewise excellent things of Baldassarre & others: [Here at st. Crysogonos, the pillars at the high Altar, seeming of oriental Alabaster, the Friers assurd us they were of Congeal'd water found in an old Aquæduct.] Thenc we went to the noble house of the Duke of Bracciano fairely built with a stately court & fountaine: Next we walked to st. Marys Church, here was that Taberna Meritoria where the old Roman souldiers receiv'd their Triumphal Garland which they ever after wore: They report that in this holy place, there did rise a fountaine of Oyle for one whole day in the 3d yeare of Augustus, not long before our B: Saviours birth: The high-Altar is very faire, adorn'd with Columns of Porphyrie, here is also some Mosaic Worke about the Quire, & the Assumption an esteem'd peice: 'Tis sayd that this Church was the first that was dedicated to the Virgin at Rome. In the opposite Piazza is a very sumptuous Fountaine:

On Christmas-Eve at night I went not to bed, by reason that I was desirous to see the many extraordinary Ceremonyes perform'd then in their Churches, as mid-night Masses, & Sermons; so as I did nothing all this night but go from Church to Church in admiration at the multitude of sceanes, & pageantry which the Friers had with all industry & craft set out to catch the devout women & superstitious sort of people with, who never part from them without droping some mony in a vessell set on purpose: But especialy observable was the pupetry in the Church of the Minerva, representing the nativity &c: thenc I went & heard a Sermon at the Apollinare by which time it was morning.

On Christmas day his holynesse sa⟨y⟩ing Masse, the Artillery at st. Angelo went off: and all this day was exposd the Cradle of our Lord:

27. A great Supper is given the poore at the Hosp: of s: Jo: Laterano.

29 We were invited by the English Jesuites to dinner being their greate feast of Tho: of Canturbury: We din'd in their common Refectory, and afterward saw an Italian Comedy Acted by their Alumni before the Cardinals.

⟨1645⟩ Jan: We saw passe the new Officers of the People of Rome, especialy for their noble habit most conspicuous were the 3 Consuls, now call'd Conservators, who now take their places in the Capitol, having been sworne the day before betwene the hands of the Pope: We ended the day with the rare Musique at the Chiesa Nova.

6: Was the Ceremony of our Saviou⟨r⟩s Baptisme in st. Athanasius, and at Ara Celi a greate procession del Bambino as they call it, where was all the Magistrates & a wonderfull concurse of people:

7 A Sermon was preach'd to the Jewes at Ponte Sisto, who are constrain'd to sit, till the houre is don; but it is with so much malice in their countenances, spitting, humming, coughing & motion, that it is almost impossible they should heare a word, nor are there any converted except it be very rarely:

14 St. Peter & s: Paules heads are expos'd at st. J: Laterano:

15 The Zitelle or young Wenches which are to have portions given them by the Pope, being poore, and to marry them, walked in Procession to s: Peter, where the⟨y⟩ were shew'd the Veronica.

I went to the Ghetto, where the Jewes dwell, as in a suburbs by themselves; being invited by a Jew of my acquaintance to see a Circumcision: here I passed by the Piazza Judea (where their Serraglio begins) for being environd with wales, they are lock'd up every night: in this place remaines yet part of a stately fabric; which my Jew told me had been a Palace of theirs, for the Ambassador of ther Nation in former times, when their Country was Subject to the Romans. There was a large Inscription on it, that I could not stay to reade.

Being lead through the Synagogue into a privat house, I found a world of people in a Chamber: by & by came an old man who prepar'd & layd in order divers Instruments brought by a little child of about 7 years old in a box, These the man layd in a silver bason: The knife was much like a short Razor to shut into the haft: Then they burnt some Insense in a Censor, which perfum'd the rome all the while the ceremony was doing: In the basin was also a little cap made of white paper like a Capuchinshood, not bigger then my finger, also a paper of a red astringent powder, I suppose of bole: a small Instrument of Silver cleft in the midst, at one end to take up the prepuce withall, clowtes of fine linnen wrap'd up &c: These all in order the Women from out of another Chamber brought the Infant swadl'd, and deliver'd it to the Rabbie, who caried, and presented it before an Altar or Cuppord dress'd up, on which lay the 5 bookes of Moses, and the Commandments a little unrowled: Before this with profound reverence, and mumbling a few Words he waved the Child to & froo a while; then he delivered it to another Rabbie, who sate all this time upon a Table, he taking it in his hands put it betweene his thighs, whilest the other Jew unbound the blankets that were about it to come at the flesh: at this action all the company fell a singing of an hebrew hymn, and in as barbarous a tone, waving themselves to & fro, a ceremony they observe in all their devotions: The Infant now strip'd from the belly downewards, the Jew tooke the yard of the child and Chaf'd it within his fingers till it became a little stiff, then with the silver Instrument before describ'd (which was held to him in the basin) he tooke up as much of the Præputium as he could ⟨possibly⟩ gather, and so with the Razor, did rather Saw, then cutt it off; at which the miserable babe cry'd extreamely, whiles the rest continu'd their odd tone, rather like howling then singing: then the Rabby lifting the belly of the child to his face, & taking the yard all blody into his mouth he suck'd it a pretty while, having before taken a little V⟨i⟩negar, all which together with the blood he spit out into a glasse of red-wine of the Colour of french wine: This don he stripp'd downe the remainder of the fore-skin as farr and neere to the belly as he could, so as it appeared to be all raw, then he strew'd the read powder on it to stanch the bleeding and coverd it with the paper-hood, & upon all a Clowte, and so swath'd up the Child as before: All this while the⟨y⟩ continue their Psalme: Then two of the Women, and two men, viz, he who held the Child, and the Rabbin who Circumcis'd it (the rest I suppose were the Wittnesses) dranke some of the Wine mingl'd with the Vinegar, blood & spittle: so ended the slovenly ceremony, and the Rabbin cryes out to me in the Italian tongue perceiving me to be a stranger: Ecco Signior mio, Un Miracolo di dio; because the child had immediately left crying: The Jewes do all in Rome we⟨a⟩re yellow hatts, and live onely upon brokage & Usury, very poore and despicable beyond what they are in other territories of Princes where they are permitted.

18. I went to see the Popes Palace [the Vaticane] where he for the most part continualy keeps his Court: It was first built by P: Simachus, and since augmented to a vast pile of building by the

Successors: That part of it added by Sixtus Vtus is most magnificent; this lead us into divers tarraces arched sub dio, painted
with the historys of the Bible by Raphel, which are so esteemed,
that Workmen come from all parts of Europe to make their
studys from these designes; and certainely the whole World dos
not shew so much art; the foliage & Grotesque is admirable
about some of the Compartiments: In another ro⟨o⟩m are represented at large Mapps & plotts of most Countries in the World
in very vast tables, with briefe descriptions: The Stayres which
ascend out of s: Peters Portico into the first hall, are rarely contriv'd for ease, These leade into Sala di Gregorio XIII, the walls
wherof are halfe to the ⟨roof⟩ incrusted with most precious
marbles of various colours, & Workes; so is also the pavement
opere vermiculato; but what exceeds description is the Volto or
rooff itselfe, which is so exquisitely painted, that 'tis almost
impossible for the skillfullest eye to discerne whither it be the
worke of the Pensil upon a flatt, or of a toole, cutt in a deepe
Levati of stone: The Rota dentata in this admirable perspective
at the left hand as one goes out, the stella &c are things of art
incomparable: Certainely this is one of the most Superb & royall
Appartiments in the world, much too beautifull for a guard of
gigantique Swizzers who do nothing but drinke, and play at
Cards in it: [Going up these stayres there is painted st. Peter
walking on the sea towards our Saviour, with this inscription: ὁ
ζῆλος οὐ φέρει αναβολὴν.][1] Out of this I went into another
hall just before the chapell, calld the Sala del Conclave, full of
admirable paintings, amongst other the Assasination of Colignij
the greate French Admiral, murther'd by the D: of Guise in the
Parisian Massacre at the nuptials of Hen: 4th with Q: Margarite: Under this is written Coligni et Sociorum Cædes, on the
other side Rex Coligni necem probat.

  Now we came into the Popes Chapell, so much celebrated
for the Judgement painted by M: Angelo Buonaroti, the contemplation of which incomparable Worke tooke up much of
our tyme & wonder: It is a painting in fresca, upon a dead Wall
at the upper end of the Chapell just over the high Altar of a vast
designe and miraculous fantsy, considering the multitude of

1 'Zeal does not suffer delay.'

Nakeds, & variety of posture: The roofe is also full of rare worke: Hence we went into the Sacristia, where we were shew'd all the most precious Vestments, Copes &c, & furnitures of the Chapell, One Priestly Cope with the whole suite had been formerly sent from one of our English Henrys, & is shewn for a greate rarity, as indeede it is: We saw divers of the Popes Pantofles that are Kissed on his foote, having rich jewells embrodred on the instup: they are covered with crimson Velvet: Also his Tyara or Triple Crown, divers Miters, Crosiers, Crosses &c all bestudded with precious stones, gold and Pearle to an infinite value: A very large Crosse carved (as they affirme) out of the holy Wood it selfe: a world of Utensils, of Chrystal, Gold, Achat, Amber and other costly materials for the Altar: [The Sala *Clementinas* Suffito is painted by *Cherubin Alberti*, with an ample Landskep of *Paul Brills*.] Then we went into those Chambers painted with the historys of burning Rome quenched by the procession of a Crucifix: The victory of Constantine over Maxentius: St. Peters delivery out of Prison, all of them by the hand of the famous Julio Romano, and are therefore cal'd amongst the Virtuosi, the Paynters Academy, because you shall never come into them, but you find some young man or other designing from them, a civility which in Italy they do not refuse them where any rare pieces of the old and best Masters are extant; and which is occasion of breeding up many excellent men in that Profession: From hence we were conducted into a New Gallery, whose sides had painted on them most of the famous Places in Italy Townes & Territories, rarely don; and upon the Roofe the chiefe Acts of the Ro: Church since St. Peters pretended See there; It is doubtlesse one of the most magnificent Galleries this, in Europ: Out of this we came into the Consistory, which is a very noble roome, the Volto painted in Grotesque as I remember: The Upper end of it has a Throne, elevated, and a baldachino or Canopy of state for his holynesse, over it: From hence through a very extraordinary long Gallery (longer I thinke, then the French Kings at the Louvre) but onely of bare wales, we were brought into the Vaticane Library: This passage was now full of poore People, to each of whom the Pope (in his passage to st. Peters) gave a Mezzo grosse; I believe they were in number neer 1500, or 2000 Persons:

This Library is doubtlesse the most nobly built, furnish'd, and beautified in the World, ample, stately, light & cherefull, looking into a most pleasant Garden: The Walls & roofe are painted; not with Antiqu⟨e⟩s, & Grotesc's (like our Bodlean at Oxford) but Emblemes, Figurs, Diagramms, and the like learned inventions found out by the Wit, & Industry of famous Men, of which there are now whole Volumes extant: There were likewise the Effigies of the most Illustrious men of Letters & Fathers of the Church, with divers noble statues in white marble at the entrance, viz. Hippolitus and Aristides: The Generall Councils, are likewise painted upon the side Walls: [The largest roome was built by Sixtus Quintus 100 paces long, at the end is the Gallery of printed books: then the Gallery of the D: of Urbans Librarie amongst which are MSS: of incomparable Miniature, & divers China, Mexican, Samaritan, Abyssin & other Oriental books:] As to the ranging of the bookes, they are all shut up in Presses of Wainscot, & not expos'd on shelves to the naked ayre; nor are the most precious mix'd amongst the more ordinary, which are shew'd to the curious onely; Such as are those two Virgils written in Parchment, of more then a thousand yeares old; the like a Terence: The Acts of the Apostles in Golden Capital Letters: Petrarchs Epigramms written with his owne hand: Also an Hebrew Parchment made up in the antient manner from whence they were first cal'd Volumina, with the Cornua, but what we English do much enquire after, the Booke which our Hen: 8, writ against Luther: In another wing of the Edifice [200 paces long] were all the bookes taken from Heide⟨l⟩berg, of which the learned Greuter had been keeper & divers other greate Scholars: These Walls [& volto] are painted with the Machines invented by Domenico Fontana, for the erection of the Obelisque: and the true designe of Mahomets Sepulchre at Meca: Out of this we went to see the Conclave, where (at the Sede Vacante,) the Cardinals are shut up, till they are agreed upon a new Election, the whole manner whereof was describ'd to us: Hence into the Popes Armory; it is under the Library, and over the dore this Inscription Urbanus VIII Litteris Arma, Arma litteris. I hardly believe any Prince in Europ is able to shew a more compleately furnish'd Library of Mars, for the quality, and quantity; which is 40000 compleate for ho⟨r⟩se & foote, and most neately kept.

Out of this we pass'd againe, by the Long Gallery and at the lower end of it, downe a very large payr of stayres, round, without any Stepps or degrees as usualy, but descending with an evenesse so ample & easy, that an horse-litter or Coach may with ease be drawne up: The sides of the Vacuity are set with Columns: Those at Amboise on the Loyer in France, are something of this invention, but nothing so spruce: by these we descended into the Vatican Gardens, cald Belvedere, where entring first into a kind of Court, we were shew'd those incomparable statues (so fam'd by Pliny & Others) of Laocoan with his three sonns embrac'd by an huge serpent, all of one entire parrian stone, very white & perfect, somewhat bigger then the life, & the Worke of those three celebrated Sculptors Agesandrus, Polidorus, and Artimadorus Rhodians, as it was found amongst the ruines of Titus's Baths, and placed here: Plynie says this Statue is to be esteem'd before all pictures & statues in the World, and I am altogether of his opinion, for in my life I never beheld anything of Art approch it: Here is also Those two famous Images of Nylus with the children playing about him, and that of Tyber. Romulus & Rhemus about the Wolfe, that incomparable figure of the dying Cleopatra; The Venus and Cupid, rare pieces; The Mercury, Cybel, Hercules, Apollo, Antinous; most of which, are for defence against the Weather shut up in their Neeches with dores of Wainscot: We were likewise shew'd those Reliques of the Hadrian Moles; viz. the Pine, a vast piece of Mettall which stood on the summit of that Mausoleum; also a Peacock of Coper, supposed to have been part of Scipios Monument.

In the Garden without this (which containes a very Vast circuit of ground) are many stately Fountaines, especialy two, casting water into Antique lavors brought from Titus's Bathes: some faire Grotts & Water-works, with that noble Cascade where the ship daunces with divers other pleasant inventions, Walkes, Terraces, Meanders, Fruite-trees, and a most goodly Prospect over the greatest part of the Citty: One Fountaine under the Gate I must not omitt, consisting of three jettos of Water gushing out of the mouthes or proboscis of Bees (the Armes of the Late Pope) because of the Inscription

Quid miraris Apem, quæ mel de floribus haurit?
Si tibi mellitam guttúre fundit aquam:

Thus weary, & sated with fine sights we came to our Lodging this night.

On the 23d, We went without the Walls of the Citty to visite st. Paules; to which place 'tis sayd, the Apostle bore his owne head after Nero had caus'd it to be cut off: The Church was founded by the Greate Constantine; the maine roofe is supported with no lesse then 100 vast columns of marble, and the Mosaique worke of the greate Arch is wrought with a very antient story Anno 440, as that likewise of the Faciata. The Gates are brasse, made at Constantinople 1070, as you may reade by those Greeke Verses engraven on them. The Church is neere 500 foote long, and 258 in breadth, has 5 huge Iles joyn'd to it, upon the bases of one of whose Columns this old title Fl: Eugenius Asellus CC. Præf Urbis V.S.I. reparavit. Here they shew'd us that Miraculous Crucifix which they say spake to St. Brigit, and just before the Ciborio stand two excellent Statues. Here are buried part of st. Paule, & st. Peters bodys: The Pavement is richly interwoven with most precious oriental marbles, about the high-Altar where are likewise 4 excellent payntings, whereof one by the hand of a Woman cald Lavinia, a Bolognian Lady, which is the Lapidation of S. Stephen. The Tabernacle on this Altar is of incomparable Architecture; and the Pictures in the Chapel del Sacramento are of Lanfranchi: Divers other Reliques there be also in this Venerable Church, as a part of st. Anna, the head of the Woman of Samaria: The Chayne which bound st. Paule & the Eculeus us'd in tormenting the Primitive Christians: The Church stands in the Via Ost⟨i⟩ensis, about a mile from the Walls of the Citty, separated from any buildings neere it but the Tria Fontana to which (leaving our Coach) we walked, going over the mountaine or little rising upon which story says, an hundred seaventy & 4 thousand Christians had been Martyr'd by Maximianus, Dioclesian and other blody Tyrants: On this stands st. Vincents & Anastatius, likewise the Church of st. Maria Scala del Cielo, in whose Tribuna is a very faire Mosaique Worke. The Church of the Tre-Fontane (as they are cald) is perfectly well built although but small (where as that of st. Paules is but Gotique) having a noble Cupola in the middle: In this they shew the Pillar to which s: Paule was bound when his head was cut off, & from whence it made three prodigious leaps where there immediately brake out the 3 remaining fountaines which

gives denomination to this Church; The Waters are reported to
be Medicinable, and indeede seeme a little sharp: That most
excellent Picture of Peters Crucifixion is of Guido's: Over each
of the Fountains is erected an Altar, and a chayned ladle, for the
better tasting of the waters.

Hence we went to Dr. Gibb's a [famous poet &] Country-
man of Ours who had some intendency in Christ Hospital:
which he shewed us: The Infirmitory where the sick lay was all
rarely paved with variously colourd Marbles, and the Walls hung
with noble Pieces: The beds are very faire: In the middle is a
stately Cupola, under which an Altar decked with divers marble
statues, all in sight of the sick, who may both see, & heare Masse
as they lye in their beds: The Organs are very fine, & frequently
play'd on to recreate the people in paine: To this joyns an Apartiment destind to the Orphans, & there is a Schoole: The Children weare blew like ours in Lond: at an Hospital of the same
appellation: Here are 40 Nurses who give suck to such Children
as are accidentaly found expos'd & abandon'd: In another quarter are Children of bigger Groth 450 in number, who are taught
letters, In another 500 Girles under the tuition of divers Religious Matrons, in a Monastry as it were by it selfe: I was assurd
there were at least 2000 more maintain'd in other places: I think
one Appartiment had in it neere 1000 beds: These are in a very
long rome having an inner ⟨passage⟩ for those who attend, with
as much curiosity, sweetenesse and Conveniency as can be imagin'd, the Italians being generaly exquisitely neate: Under this
Portico the sick may walke out and take the ayre; Opposite to
this are other Chambers for such as are sick of maladies of a
more rare & difficult cure, & they have romes apart: At the end
of the long Corridore is one of the fairest & well stord Apothe-
carys shops that ever I saw, neere which chambers for Persons of
better quality who are yet necessitous: What ever the poore
bring is at their comming in delivered to a Tresurer, who makes
the Inventory, and is accoumptable to them, or their heyres if
they dye: To this building joynes the Palace of the Commenda-
tor, who with his Officers attending the sick make up 90 Persons, besides a Convent & an ample Church for the Friers and
Priest who daily attend: The Church is extreamely neate, and
the Sagrestia very rich: Indeede 'tis altogether one of the most
pious and worthy Foundations that ever I saw, nor is the benefit

small which divers Young Physitians & Chirurgions reape by
the experience they learne here amongst the sick, to whom those
students have universal accesse: The Hospital is built on the
antient Via Triumphalis. From this we ascended a very steepe
hill neere the Port st. Pancratio to that stately Fountaine cal'd
Acqua Paula, being the Aquæduct which Augustus had heretofore brought to Rome, now reedified by Paulus V: a rare piece of
Architecture, and serves the City after a journey of 35 miles, here
powering it selfe into divers ample Lavors, out of the mouthes of
Swanns, and Dragons, the armes of this Pope, which for that 'tis
situated on a very high mount, makes a most glorious show to
the Citty, especialy when the Sun darts on the waters as it
gusheth out:

We went next to St. Pietro Montorio, heretofore the M.
Janiculas, on which place the tradition goes St. Peter the
Apostle was crucified with his head revers'd; and upon that
very spot stands a round oratory of incomparable designe by
Bramante, the sumit whereoff is incircled with a Crown of
Columns. The Church adjoyning to it is exquisitly painted by
the inimitable hand of Raphel d'Urbin and amongst the rest of
the figures his own Effigie to the life: which peice is esteemd
one of the rarest in the World: Here had that ingenious Epe-
gramatist Martial his delicious ⟨Gardens⟩ & N. Pomphilus a
fair fountaine.

January 26. We were invited to see Cavaliero Gualdis Collection, a knight of eminent Learning, curiosity, and Civility to
Strangers: In his Study he shew'd us an antiq and I think, the
onely Tripos of Apollo extant, with its Bason on it, a ⟨Sistrum⟩,
the Sacrificing knife, the ⟨Acerra⟩ for Insence, divers old Lamps,
the Prefericolus, out of which they pourd the Wine that wash'd
the Victime. Divers antiq Rings, worne by the Romans, which
were first of Iron, then brass, after of Gold: Some excellant
Achats and Cornelians especialy that ⟨with⟩ Herculus's head,
perfectly to the life of the Farnezian statue; and another of Julius
Cæsar: Antinoüs: The two excellant Venus's. Divers Ægyptian
Idols; as the Canopus & Isis: a Book Engraven on the Bark of a
Tree, with the incisory Stylus, sharp at one extream, Triangular
at the other & flat with an edge to scrape out. The Roman Stater
and Ballance, Raffling Bones to cast dyes in use amongst the
Romans, Tessaras &c also (as he believed) the true Remora

which he had described in a print, with the history of that
⟨Fish's⟩ retentive property: It was about the bigness of an Hering
and not much unlike it in length or Shape, onely the upper Jaw
was sharp'd like a Pike, ⟨the nether⟩ seem'd as if wanting, & supplied with a Sucker like a Leach: He shewed us also the knee
Bone of a Gyant 23 Inchees in compass all Anotamist⟨s⟩ concluding it to have been of a Man, twas found at Trepone in
Sicilea. Divers Roman Locks and antiq keys, the forted horn
or ⟨trompet⟩ which of old the Romans Sounded at their Sacrifices and Wars: Some Hieroglypical stones, many natural
Curiosit⟨i⟩es, antient Armour, & not a few rare Pictures:

TRAVELS IN ITALY III: NAPLES
AND ROME AGAIN
(1645)

JANUARY 27. Having agreed with the ⟨Procachio⟩ for Lusty
Mules, ⟨accompanied⟩ with Sir John Manwood (formerly Governor of Dover Castle, an old Souldier, that had Maried the
famous Sir Jo: Ogles Daughter Mrs. Eutresia) Mr. Thomas
Henshaw ⟨and⟩ Mr. Borgh a Dutch Gentleman, that speaking
perfect English pass'd unsuspected in our Company (the
⟨Spaniards⟩ at that time having Wars with Holland) two Corti-
zans in Mans Apparell, who rid astride, booted, Sworded and
Spurd, & whereof one was marvelous pretty, and the Milaneze
Squire Signor Jo: Baptist their Gallant, our Servants & some
others, we set out from the Latine Port towards Naples: The
firs⟨t⟩ part of our way was well pav'd & full of Antiquities especially antient Sepulchers, Inscriptions and ruines; for it was
⟨their⟩ manner to bury much by famous high-roads, where they
also placed their Statues, thereby inciting the minds of Men to
gallant actions by the memory of their examples: In the right
hand we saw the ⟨Aquæduct⟩ of Ancq Martius, and those of
Claudius, and the new ones of Sixtus Vth, being a stately peice
of Arch work for near 20 Miles: Then we enter the Via Appia
'till we came near Frascati which we left on the other hand, riding by the Wood & Lake celebrated for the fiction of Heleon
and Diana, thence to Veletri, a Towne heretofore of the Volsci

where is a publique and faire statue of P: Urban the 8 in brasse, and a stately Fountaine in the streete, here we lay, and drank excellent Wine.

28 We dind at Sermoneta, descending all this morning downe a stony mountaine, unpleasant, yet full of Olive-trees; & anon passe a Towre built on a rock, kept by a small Watch or Guard against the Banditi, who are very rife in these parts, daily robbing and killing the Passengers, as my Lord Banbury and his Company found to their cost, a little before: To this Guard we gave some mony, and so were suffer'd to passe, which was still on the Appian to the Tres Tabernæ (whither the Breathren came from Rome to meete S. Paule Acts: 28:) The ruines wherof are yet very faire, resembling the remainder of some considerable Edifice, as may be judged by the vast stones, & fairenesse of the arched-worke. The Country invironing this passage is hilly but rich; at the right hand stretches an ample playne being the Pompt(i)ni Campi: We reposd this night at Piperno in the Post-house without the Towne; and here I was extreamely troubld with a sore hand which I brought from Rome with me by a mischance, which now began to fester, upon my base unlucky stiffne⟨c⟩ked trotting carrion Mule, & which are in the world the most wretched beasts.

In this Towne was the Poet Virgills Camilla borne:

The day following we were faine to hire a strong ⟨Convoy⟩ of about 30 Firelocks to guard us through the Cork-Woods (much infested with the Banditi) as far as Nova fossa, where was the Appij Forum, and now stands a reveren'd Church with a greate Monastry, the Place where Tho: Aquinas both studied, & lyes buried: Here we therefore all alighted, and were most curteously received by the Monks, who shew'd us many Reliqus of their learned Saint; and at the high-Altar the print forsooth of the mules hoofe, which he caused to kneele before the host: The Church is old, built after the Gotique manner, but the place is very agreeabley melancholy: After this pursuing the same noble Way (which before we left a little) the Appian, which we found in this journey to stretch from Capua to Rome it selfe, & afterwards as far as Brundusium: Built it was, by that famous Consul, 25 foote broad, every 12 foote something ascending for the ease, & firmer footing of horse and man: both the sides are also a little raisd, for those who travell on foote; the whole paved with a kind of beach stone, and (as I sayd) ever and anon adorn'd with some old ruine, sepulcher or fractur'd Statue: In one of these Monuments in Paulo ⟨terzos⟩ tyme Pancirollus tells us was found the body of a Young Lady swimming in a kind of Bath of precious oyle or liquor, fresh, & entire as she had been living, neither her face discolour'd, or her haire dissorderd: at her feete burnt a lamp which suddainely expir'd at the opening of the Vault, having flam'd as was computed by the conjecture that it was Tulliola the daughter of Cicero whose body was thus found now 1500 yeares, and as the Inscription testified.

We dined this day at Terr⟨a⟩cina heretofore the famous Anxur, which stands upon a very eminent Promontory, the Cercean by name:

Coming down againe I went towards the Sea-side to contemplate that stupendious strange Rock & promontory, Cleft by hand I suppose for the better passage: Within this is the Cercæan Cave. I went into it a good way, it makes a dreadfull noyes, by reason of the roaring, & impetuous Waves continualy assalting the beach, & that in an unusual horrid maner.

At the top, and an excessive height stands an old & very greate Castle:

We ariv'd this night at Fundi, a most dangerous passage for robbing; and so we pass'd by Galbas Villa; The Via Appia is here a noble prospect, having before consider'd how it was carried through vast mountaines of rocks for many miles, a most stupendious labour: here it is infinitely pleasant, beset with sepulchres and Antiquities, full of sweete shrubbs about the invironing hedges. At Fundi (here was Amiclas lost by silence) we had Oranges & Citrons for nothing, the trees growing in every corner infinitely charged with fruite, in all the poore peoples Orchyards:

29 We descried mount Cæcubus, famous for the generous Vine it heretofore produc'd; & so rid onward the Appian-Way beset with Myrtils, Lentiscus, bayes, Pomegranads, & whole Groves of orange-trees, and most delicious shrubbs, till we came to Formiana, where they shew'd us Ciceros Tomb standing in an Olive-grove, now a rudes of huge stones without any forme or beauty; for here that incomparable Orator was Murther'd: I shall never forget how exceedingly I was delighted with the

Sweetnesse of this passage, the Sepulchers mixed amongst the verdures of all Sorts; besides being now come within sight of that noble Citty Cajeta which gives a surprizing Prospect along the Tyrhen Sea, in manner of a Theater; & here we beheld that strangly cleft Rock, an hideous & frightfull spectacle; which they have a tradition hapn'd upon the Passion of our B: Saviour: But the hast of our Procaccio suffer'd us not to dwell so long on these objects, and the many antiquities of this Towne as we desired:

At Formia we saw Ciceros Grott, dining at Mola, & passing Senuessa, Garigliano (where once the Citty Minterna) & beheld the ruines of that vast Amphitheatre and Aquæduct yet standing; The River Liris which bounded the old Latium, Falernus, or Mons Massicus, celebrated for its wine, now nam'd Garo, and this night we lodg'd at a little Village call'd ⟨S.⟩ Agatha in the Falernian Feilds neere to Aurunca and Sessa. The next day, having passed Vulturnus, we come by the Torre di Francolesse where the valiant Hanibal in danger of Fabius Maximus escaped by debauching his Enemyes: And so we at last enter'd the most pleasant Plaines of Campania, now call'd Terra di Lavoro: In very truth I thinke the most fertile spot, that ever the Sunn shone upon: Here we saw the slender ruines of the once mighty Capüa contending at once both with Rome and Carthage for Splendor & Empire; now nothing but an heape of rubbish, with some goodly Vestigias of its pristine magnificence, discover'd in the remaining pieces of Temples, Arches, Theaters, Columns, Ports, Vaults, Collossas &c confounded together by the barbarous Goths & Longobards: There is yet a new Citty, neerer to the road by two miles, fairely raysd out of these heapes. The Passage from this Towne towards Naples (which is about 10, or 12 English post miles) is as straight as a line could lay it, & of a huge breadth, swarming with travellers more then ever I remember any of our greatest, & most frequented roads neere London: But what is extreamely divertissant, is the incomparable fertility of the feilds and grounds about it, which are planted about with fruit-trees, whose boles are serpented with excellent Vines, and they so exuberant, that 'tis commonly reported one Vine will loade 5 mules with its Grapes: but what much adds to the pleasure of these rusticities, is that the Vines climbing to the summit of the trees reach in festoons & fruitages from one tree to another, planted at exact distances, which shewing like a greene Chayne about a field, is pleasanter than any painting can describe it: Here likewise growes Rice, Canes for Suggar, Olives, Pomegranads, Mulberrys, Cittrons, Oranges, Figgs and infinite sorts of rare fruits: About the middle of the Way is the Towne Aversa, whither came 3 or 4 Coaches to meete our Lady travellers, of whom we now tooke leave, having ben very merry by the way with them, and the Capitano, who was their Gallant:

31 About noone We enterd the Citty of Naples, allighting at the 3 Kings, a Place of treatement to excesse, as we found by our very plentifull fare all the tyme we were in Naples, where provisions are miraculously cheape, & we seldome sat downe to fewer than 18 or 20 dishes of the most exquisite meate & fruites, enjoying the Creature:

The morrow after our arival in the afternoone We hired a Coach to carry us about the Towne, & first we went to Visite the Castle of St. Elmo, built on an excessive high rock, whence we had an intire prospect of the whole Citty, which lyes in shape of a Theatre upon the Sea brinke, with all the circumjacent Ilands, as far as Capra, famous for the debauch'd recesses of Tiberius.

This fort is the bridle of the Whole Citty, and was well stor'd, & Garrisond with natural[1] Spanyards: the strangenesse, of the precipice, & rarenesse of the Prospect in view of so many magnificent & stately Palaces, Churches & Monasteries, ⟨with⟩ the Arsenale, Mole, & distant Mount Vesuvius, all in full command of the Eye, is certainly one of the richest Landskips in the World: Hence we descended to another strong Castle, cald il Castello Nuovo, which protects the Shore, but they would by no intreaty permitt us to go in; the outward defence seemes to consist but in 4 tours very high, & an exceeding deepe graft, with thick Walls: Opposite to this is the Toure of St. Vincent, which is also very Strong: Then we went to the Vice-Roy's Palace, which is realy one of the noblest that I had seene in all Italy, partly old, & part of a newer Work, but we did not stay long here: Towards the Evening we tooke the ayre upon the

---

1 Native-born.

Mole, which is a streete upon the rampart or banke raysed in the sea for security of their Gallys in Port, built as that of Genoä: here I observ'd an incomparable rich Fountaine built in the middst of the Piazza, & adornd with divers rare statues of Copper representing the Sirens & deities of ⟨Parthenope⟩, spouting large streames of Water into an ample Concha, all of cast mettall & infinite Cost: this stands at the entrance of the Mole, where wee mett many of the Nobility, both on horse-back, & in their Coaches to take the fresco from the sea, as the manner is, it being in the most advantagious quarter for good ayre, delight & prospect: Here we saw divers goodly horses who handsomly become their riders, the Neapolitan Gentlemen: This Mole is about 500 paces in length, & pav'd with a square hewn stone.

From the Mole we ascend to a Church, a very greate antiquity formerly sacred to Castor & Pollux, as the Greeke let-ters carv'd in the Architrave testify, & the busts[1] of their two statues, converted now into a stately Oratory by the Theatines: Hence we went to the Cathedrall which is a most magnificent pile: and unlesse St. Peters in Rome certainly Naples exceeds all Cittys in the World for stately Churches & Monasteries: We were told that this day the Blood of St. Genuarius, & his head should be expos'd, and so we found it; but obtain'd not to see the miracle of the boiling of this blod, as was told us: The Next we went to see was St. Peters, richly adornd; the Chapel especialy, where the Apostle sayd Masse, as is testified on the Walle: After dinner we went to St. Dominic, where they shew'd us the Crucifix that is reported to have sayd these Words to St. Thomas: Bene de me scripsisti, Thoma. Hence to the Padri Olivetani famous for the monument of the learned Alexand: ab Alexandro.

We went the next day to visite the Church of Santa Maria Magiore, where we spent much tyme in surve⟨y⟩ing the Chapell of Izo: Joh: Pontanus, & in it the severall & excellent Sentences, & Epitaphs on himselfe, Wife, Children & Friends; full of rare witt, and worthy of recording, as already we find them in severall

---

1 Italian *busto*, 'a bulk or trunk without a head': so Torriano, 1659.

writers: In the same Chapell is shewed an arme of Titus Livius with this Epigraph.

Titi Livij ⟨brachium⟩, quod Anton Panormita à Patavinis impetravit. Jo:
Jovianus Pontanus multos post annos hoc in loco ponendum curavit.

From hence climbing a steepe hill we came to the Monastery of the Carthusians and Church, where (after we had turn'd about & considerd the goodly Prospect towards the Sea, and Citty; the one full of Gallys, and ships, the Other of stately Palaces, Churches, Monasteries, Castles, Gardens, delicious fields & meadows, Mount Vesuvius smoaking; the Promontory of Minerva, & Misenum; Capra, Prochyta, Ischia, Pausilipe, Puteoli and the rest, doubtlesse one of the most divertisant & considerable Vistas in the World) we went into the Church; which is most elegantly built; the very pavements of the common Cloyster being all layd with variously polish'd & rich marbles, richly figurd: here they shew'd a Massie Crosse of silver, much celebrated for the Workmanship & carving, & sayd to have ben 14 yeares in perfecting: The Quire also of this Church is of rare arte.

But above all to be admir'd is the yet unfinished Jesuites Church; a Piece, certainely if accomplish'd, not to me match'd in Europe: Hence we pass'd by the Palazza Caraffi full of antient & very noble statues; also the Palace of the Ursini.

The next day little, but visite some friends that were English merchants resident for their negotiation; Onely this morning at the Vice-roys Cavalerizzo, I saw the noblest horses that I had ever beheld, one of his sonns riding the Menage with that addresse & dexterity, as I had never seene any thing approch it.

Feb: 4th We were invited to the Collection of exotic rarities in the Museum of Ferdinando Imperati a Neapolitan Nobleman, and one of the most observable Palaces in the Citty: The repository full of incomparable rarities; amongst the Natural Herbals most remarkable was the Byssus Marina, & Pinna Marina: Male & femal Camelion; an Onacratulus & an extraordinary greate Crocodile: a Salamander; some of the Orcades Anates, held here for a strange rarity: The Male & female Manucodiata, the Male having an hollow on the back in which 'tis reported ⟨the female⟩ both layes, & hatches her Egg: The Mandragoras also of both Sexes: Papyrs made of severall reedes,

& some of silke, tables of the rinds of Trees writen with Japonique characters; and another of the branches of Palme: many Indian fruites: a Chrystal that had a pretty quantity of uncongeal'd Water within its cavity; a petrified fishers net: divers sorts of Tarantulas, being a kind of monstrous spiders, with lark-like clawes & somewhat bigger:

The [7] being Saturday we went 4 miles out of Towne on Mules to see that famous Vulcano or burning mountaine of Vesuvius; here we passe a faire Fountaine cal'd Labulla, which continualy boyles, supposed to proceede from Vesuvius; & thence over a river and bridg. Being now approching the [hill] as we were able with our Mules, we alighted, crawling up the rest of the proclivity, with extraordinary difficulty, now with our feete & hands, not without many untoward slipps, which did much bruise us on the various colourd Cinders with which the whole Mountaine is cover'd, some like pitch, others full of perfect brimstone, other metalique interspers'd with innumerable Pumices (of all which I made a collection) we at the last gain'd the summit, which I take to be one of the highest terraces in Europ (for 'tis of an excessive altitude) turning our faces towards Naples, it presents us one of the goodliest prospects in the World; & truely, I do not thinke there is a greater & more noble; all the Baiæ, Cuma, Elysian fields, Capra, Ischia, Prochita, Misenum, Puteoli, that goodly & gentile Citty, with a vast portion of the Tyrrhan Sea offering themselves to your view at once, & at so sweete & agreable a distance, as nothing can be more greate & delightfull. The mountaine consists of a double top; the one pointed very sharp, and commonly appearing above any clowds; the other blunt; here as we approch'd we met many large and gaping clefts & c⟨h⟩asm's, out of which issu'd such sulphurous blasts & Smoake, that we durst not stand long neere them: having gaind the very brim of the top, I layd my selfe on my belly to looke over & into that most frightfull & terrible Vorago, a stupendious pit (if any there be in the whole Earth) of neere three miles in Circuit, and halfe a mile in depth, by a perpendicular hollow cliffe, like that from the highest part of Dover-Castle, with now & then a craggy prominency jetting out: The area at the bottom is plaine, like a curiously even'd floore, which seemes to be made by the winds circling the ashes by its eddy blasts: in the middle & center, is a ⟨rising⟩, or hill

shaped like a greate browne loafe, appearing to consist of a sulphurous matter, continualy vomiting a foggy exhalation, &
ejecting huge stones with an impetuous noise & roaring, like
the report of many musquets discharging: This horrid
Barathrum engaged our contemplation for some whole houres
both for the strangnesse of the spectacle, and for the mention
which the old histories make of it, as one of the most stupendious
curiosities in nature, & which made the learned & inquisitive
Pliny adventure his life, to detect the causes, & to loose it in too
desperat an approch: It is likewise famous for the Stratagemm
of the rebell Spartacus, who did so much mischiefe to the state,
by his lurking & protection amongst these horid Caverns, when
it was more accessible, & lesse dangerous than now it is: But,
especialy, notorious it is, for the last conflagration, when in
Ann: 1630 it burst out beyond what it had ever don since the
memory of any history, spewing out huge stones, & fiery
pumices in such quantity, as not onely invoron'd the whole
mountaine, but totaly buried, & overwhelm'd divers Townes,
people & inhabitants, scattering the ashes more then an hundred miles distance, & utterly devasting all those goodly Vineyards, where formerly grew the most incomparable Greco;
when bursting through the bowels of the Earth it absorb'd the
very Sea and with its whirling Waters drew in divers Gallys &
other Vessells to their destruction; as is faithfully recorded:
Some there are who maintaine it the very Mouth of hell it selfe,
others of Purgatory, certainely it must be acknowledged one of
the most horrid spectacles in the World: We descen'd with infinite more ease, than we climbd up; namely through a deepe
Vallie of pure ashes (at the late erruption a flowing river of
mealted, & burning brimestone) and so we came at last to our
Mules, which with our Veturino, attended us neere the foote of
the Mountaine.

On Sunday, we with our Guide goe to visite the so much celebrated Baiæ, and natural rarities of the Places adjacent: Here
we enter the Mountaine Pausilipo, at the left hand of which they
shewd us the Poet Virgils Sepulchre, erected on a very steepe
rock, in forme of a Small rotunda, or cupulated Columne; but
almost over growne with bushes, & wild bay-trees: at this
entrance is this Inscription

Stanisi Cencovius
1589
Qui cineres? Tumuli hæc Vestigia, conditur olim,
⟨Ille⟩ hoc, qui cecinit Pascua, Rura, Duces.
Can. ⟨Rec⟩ MDLIII⟨I⟩.

After we were advanc'd into this noble, and altogether wonder-full Crypta, consisting of a passage, spacious enough for 2 Coaches to go on breast, cut through a rocky mountaine (as reported, by the antient Cimmerii) for neere three quarters of a mile; others say by L: Cocceius, who employd no lesse then an hundred thousand men at worke on it for 15 dayes, we came to the mid-way, where there is an orifice, or Well, boar'd quite through the whole diameter of this vast Mountaine, which admitts the light into a pretty Chapel, hewn out of the natural rock, wherein hang divers lamps perpetualy burning: The Way is pav'd under foote; but it dus not hinder the dust, which rises so excessively in this much frequented passage, that we were forc'd at mid day, to make use of a Torch; & so at length, with no small astonishment we were deliverd from the bowels of the earth into one of the most delicious, and incomparable Plaines in the World: the Orangs, the lemmons, Pomegranads, & other fruites blushing yet upon the perpetualy greene trees, for the Summer is here eternal; caus'd by the naturall & adventitious heate of the earth, so warmed through the Subterranean fires, as our guide alighting, and cutting up a turfe with his knife, & delivering it to me, I was hardly able to hold it in my hands: This Mountaine is exceedingly fruitefull in Vines, & there is nothing so rare & exotic, which will not grow in these invirons: Now we came to a lake of about two miles in circumference, inviron'd with hills: The Water of it, is fresh & swete on the surface, and salt at botome, some mineral-salt conjectur'd to be the cause; and 'tis reported of that profunditude in the middle, as that it has no botome soundable: The People call it Lago di Agnano, from the multitude of Serpents, which involv'd together about the Spring fall downe from the cliffy hills into it: & besides these it has no fish, neither will any live in it: The first thing we did here, was, the old experiment on a Dog, which we lead from that so mortal Cave commonly nam'd Grotto del Cane or Charons Cave: It is not above three, or four paces deepe, and about the height of a man, nor is it very broad: In this Cave whatever has life presently expires; of this we made tryal with two Doggs: which we bound with a Cord to a short pole to guide him the more directly into the farther part of the Den, where he was no soner enter'd, but without the least noyse or so much as strugling, except that he panted for breath, lolling out his tongue, his eyes being fixt, we drew him out dead, to all appearance; but then immediately plunging him into the adjoyning lake, within lesse space then halfe an houre, he recoverd againe, and swimming to shore ran away from us: Another Dog, on whom we try'd the former experiment of the Cave, without the application of the Water, we left starke dead upon the shore: It seemes this has also ben try'd on men, as well as beasts, as on that poore Creature which Peter of Toledo caus'd to go in; likewise on some Turkish Slaves, two Souldiers: & other foolehardy persons, who all perished, & could never be recover'd againe by the Water of the Lake, as are doggs, for which many learned reasons have ben offer'd; as Simon Majolus in his booke of the Canicular dayes: Colloq: 15. and certainely the most likely is, the effect of those hot & dry vapours which ascend out of the Earth, and then ⟨are⟩ condens'd by the ambient cold, as appeares by their converting into chrystaline drops on the top, whilst at the bottome 'tis so excessively hott, as extinguishing a torch held neere it, which lifted a little distance did sudaynely conceive flame againe:

Neere to this cave are the natural stoves of St. Germain, which are of the nature of Sudatories, in certaine Chambers partition'd with stone for the sick to sweate in. The vapours here are exceeding hot, and of admirable successe, especialy against the Goute, & other cold distempers of the nerves. Hence we climbd up an hill; the very high way in divers places even smoaking with heate like a fournace: The Mountaines were by the Greekes called Leucoÿ ei, and the fields Phlægrean; Hercules here vanquishd the Gyants assisted with lightning: Now we come to the Court of Vulcan, consisting of a Vally neere a quarter of a mile in breadth, the margent inviron'd with steepe cliffs, out of whose sides, & foote, belch forth fire & smoke in aboundance, making a noyse like a tempest of Water, and sometimes discharging in lowd reports like so many guns shot off: It is wonderfull the heate of this place, the earth it selfe being almost unsufferable; and which the subterraneal-fires have made so hollow by having wasted the matter for many

Yeares, that it sounds like a drumm to those who walke upon it: &
the water struggling thus with those fires, bubbls up, & sproutes
up aloft in the ayre: The mouthes of these spiracles are bestrew'd
with variously colour'd Cinders, which arise with the Vapor, as do
many colour'd stones according to the quality of the combustible
matter; insomuch as tis no little adventure to approch them, however daily frequented both by Sick & Well, who receiving the
fumes have been recover'd of diseases esteem'd incurable: Here we
found a world of sulphure made, which they refine in certaine
houses neere the Place, casting it into Canes: to a very greate val-
lue: Neere this we were shew'd an hill of Alume where is one of
the best mineries in the World, that yealds a considerable revenue;
also, some flowres of Brasse is found here: But, I could not but
smile, at those who perswade themselves, that here are the gates of
Purgatory; for which, it may be, they have erected a Covent,
nam'd St. Januarius, very neere it; reporting to have often heard
Schreeches & horrible lamentations ⟨proceed⟩ from these Caverns & Vulcano's, with divers other legends of birds, that are never
seene save on Sundayes, & which cast themselves into the lake at
night, appearing no more all the Weeke after:

Now we went to see the ruines of a very stately Temple or
Theater of 172 foote in length, & about 80 in breadth, throwne
downe by an Earth-quake not long since; it was consecrate to
Vulcan & under the ground are many strange meanders which
makes it be nam'd the Labyrinth: this place is so haunted with
Batts, that their perpetual fluttering about endangerd the putting out of our linkes:

Hence we passed those Sulphury-hills againe, which continualy boile & smoake, till we came to Puzzolo, formerly the
famous Puteoli, the landing-Place of St. Paule, when he came
into Italy, after the cruel tempest, describ'd in the Acts of the
Apostles: here we made a good dinner, and bought divers
Medailes & other curiosities, Antiquities &c of the Country
people, who daily find such things amongst the very old ruines
of those places: This Towne was formerly a Græke Colonie,
built by the Samians, a reasonable commodious Port, & full of
observable Antiquities: Here we saw the ruines of Neptunes
Temple, to whom this place was sacred: & neere it the stately
Palace & Gardens of Peter de Toledo formerly mention'd. After
dinner we visited that admirably built Temple of Augustus,

seeming to have ben hewn out of an intire rock, though indeede consisting of several square stones. 'Tis now converted to a Church in which they shewd us huge bones, which they affirme to have ben of some Gyant: Hence we went to se⟨e⟩ the ruines of the old Haven, so compact with that bituminous sand in which the materials are layd, as the like is hardly to be found; though all this has not ben sufficient to protect it from the fatal concussions of several Earthquakes (frequent here) which has almost demolish'd it: 13 vast piles of marble onely remaining, a stupendious worke in the bosome of Neptune; To this joynes the Bridg of Caligula; by which (having now embarqu'd our selves) we sail'd to the pleasant Baiæ almost 4 miles in length: all which way, that prowd Emperor would passe in Triumph: Here we row'd along towards a certaine Villa of the Orator Ciceros, where we were shew'd the ruines of his Academy, & at the foote of a Rock his Bathes, the Waters reciprocating their tides with the neighbouring sea: The Water is reported to be specificall for the Eyes & bowells: Hard at hand rises the Mount Gaurus, being, as I conceiv'd nothing save an heape of Pumices (which here floate in aboundance upon the sea) exhausted of all inflammable matter by the fire, which renders the⟨m⟩ light and porous, so as the beds of Niter which lyes deepe under them, having taken fire dos easily eject them: They dig much for fansied Treasures, sayd to be conceild about this place: From hence we Coasted neere the ruines of Portus Julius, where we might see divers stately Palaces that had ben swallow'd up by the sea after the Earthquakes: coming to shore we passe by the Lucrine Lake, so famous heretofore for its delicious Oysters; but now producing few, or none, as being divided from the sea, by a banke of incredible labour, the suppos'd worke of Hercules: Tis now halfe chock'd up with rubbish, & by part of the new Mountaine, which rose partly out of it, & partly out of the sea, and that in the Space of one onely Night & a day, to neere the altitude of a mile: this happned on the 29th September 1538, after many terrible Earthquakes, which ruined divers places thereabout: when at Midnight the sea retiring neere 200 paces, and yawning on the sudaine, it continued to vomite forth both flames, & firy stones in such quantity as produced by their fall this whole Mountaine; by a most firfull & tirrible prodigy; making the inhabitants of Puzzoli to leave their habitations, supposing the end of the World had ben come. From the left part of this, we walked to the Lacus Avernus, of a round forme & totaly inviron'd with mountaines: This Lake was fain'd by the Poetes for the Gates of Hel, by which Æneas Æn: 6, made his bold descent, & where they sacrificed to Pluto, & the Manes: Eustatius affirmes that our B: Saviour ascended from those Infernal regions in this very place: The Waters indeede are of a remarkable black colour; but I tasted of them without danger: Hence, they faigne that the River Styx has its sourse: At one side there off stands the handsome ruines of a Certaine Temple sacred to Apollo, or rather Pluto; but 'tis controverted, Opposite to this (having now lighted our Torches) we enter a vast Cave, in which having gon about two hundred paces, we passe a narrow Entry, which lead us into a roome of about 10 paces long, pro-portionable broad & high: The side-Wales and roofe retaine still the golden Mosaique, though now exceedingly decay'd by time: Here is a short Cell, or rather Niche cut out of the solid rock, somewhat resembling a Couch; in which they report the Sybilla lay, and utterd her Oracles; though by most, suppos'd to have been a Bath onely; This subterranean Grott, leads quite through to Cuma, but is in some places obstructed by the Earth which has sunk in; so as we were constrain'd back againe, & to creepe on our very bellys before we came to the light:

'Tis reported Nero had once resolved to cut a chanell for two greate Gallys that should have extended to Ostia, an hundred & fifty miles distant; and truely the attempt we here beheld with some amazement: The People call it now Licola:

From hence we ascended to that most antient Citty of Italy, the renowned Cuma, built by the Grecians: It stands on a very eminent Promontory, but is now an heape of ruines onely: A little below stands the Arco Felice, heretofore part of Apollos Temple, with the foundations of divers goodly buildings amongst whose heapes are frequently found divers statues & other Antiquities by such as dig for them: Neere this is the Lake Acherutia, & Acherron: Returning towards the shore we came to the Bagnie de Tritoli, and Diana, which are onely long narrow passages cutt through the maine rock, where the vapours ascend so hot, that entring with the body erect you will even faint away with excessive sweate; but stooping lower as suddaine a cold surprizes: These sudatories are much in request for many

Infirmityes, especially the venereal disease, & Fluxes; but it renders Women very unchast as 'tis reported: And now we enter'd
the haven of the Baiæ where once stood that famous Towne so
call'd from the Companion of Ulysses here buried; certainely
not without greate reason celebrated for one of the most delicious places that the Sunn shines on in the World, according to
that of *Hor*:

Nullus in Orbe locus Baijs prælucet ⟨amœnis⟩

though as to the stately fabrics there now remaine little save the
ruines, whereof the most intire is that of Dianas Temple, &
another of the Godesse Venus: This place being heretofore infinitely addicted to Lust and wantonesse. Here were those famous
pooles of Lampreys that would come to hand when call'd by
name as Martial tells us: Upon the sumite of the rock stands a
very strong Castle garison'd to protect the shore from Turkish
Pyrats: 'Twas once the retyring place of Julius Caesar: Passing by
the shore againe we entered Bauli observable from the monstrous Murthers of Nero committed on his Mother Agrippina,
her Sepulchre yet shew'd us in the rock which we enter'd, being
cover'd with sundry heads & figures of beasts: We saw there the
rootes of a tree turn'd into stone & are continualy dropping.

Thus having well viewed the foundations of the old Cimeria,
the Palaces of Marius, Pompey, Nero, Hortensius's & other Villas & Antiquities we proceeded towards the promontory of
Misenus renoun'd for the Sepulchre of Æneas's Trumpeter:
'Twas once a greate Citty, now hardly a ruine, say'd to have ben
built from this to the Promontory of Minerva which is 50 miles
distant, now discontinu'd & demolish'd by the frequent Earthquakes: Here was Cajus Marius's Villa where Tiberius Cæsar
died; and here runs the Traconaria or Aquæduct thought to be
dug by Nero, a stupendious passage, heretofore nobly arched
with marble as the ruines testifie: Hence we walked to those
receptacles of water cal'd Piscina mirabilis, being a vault of 500 f:
long and 22 in breadth, the roofe prop'd up with 4 rankes of
Square pillars 12 in a row, the walls are brick, plaster'd over with
such a composition as for strength & politure resembles white
marble: 'Tis conceivd it was built as a Conservatory for fresh
water by Nero, as were also the Centi Camerelli into which we
were next led: All these Crypta being now almost sunke into the

Earth, shew yet their former amplitude & magnificence:
Returning towards the Baiæ we againe passe the Elysian Fields
so celebrated by the Poets, nor unworthily for their situation &
verdure, being full of Myrtils & sweete shrubs, and having a
most incomparable prospect towards the tyrrhen sea: Upon the
Verge of these remaine the ruines of the Mercato di Sabato, formerly a Circus, over the Arches stand divers Urnes full of
Roman Ashes:

Feb: 8. We went to see the Arsenal, which was well furnish'd
with Gallies, and other Vessells: The Citty infinitely crowded
with Inhabitans, Gentlemen & Merchants. The Government is
held of the Pope by an annual tribute of 40000 ducats and a
White-Genet; but the Spanyard trusts more to the power of
those his natural Subjects there: Apulia and Calabria yeilding
him neere 4 milions of crownes yearely to maintaine it: The
Country is divided into 13 Provinces: 20 Archbishops: 107 Bish:
The Estates of the Nobility in default of the masculine line
reverting to the King: Besides the Vice-Roy, there is also
(amongst the chiefe Magistrates) an high Conestable, Admiral,
Chiefe-Justice, Great Chamb(e)rlaine, and Chancelor, with a
Secretary who being prodigiously avaritious do wonderfully
inrich themselves out of the miserable peoples labour, Silke,
Manna, Sugar, Oyle, Wine, Rice, Sulphur, Alome; for with all
these riches, is this delicious Country blest; the Manna falling at
certaine seasons upon the adjoyning hills, in forme of a thick
deuw: The very winter here is a summer, ever fruitefull, & continualy pregnant, so as in midst of February we had Melons,
Cheries, Abricots and many other sorts of fruite: The building
of the Citty is for the quantity the most magnificent of Europe,
the streetes exceeding large, well paved, having many Vaults, and
conveyances under them for the sullage which renders them
very sweete and cleane even in the midst of winter: To it
belongeth more then 3000 churches and monasteries, and those
the best built & adornd in Italy: they greately affect the Spanish
gravity in their habite, delight in good horses; the streetes are
full of Gallants, in their Coaches, on horseback, & sedans, from
hence brought first into England by Sir Sanders Duncomb: The
Women are generally well featur'd, but excessively libidinous;
the Country people so jovial and addicted to Musick, that the
very husbandmen almost universaly play on the guitarr, singing

and composing songs in prayse of their Sweete-hearts, & will go
to the field commonly with their fiddle; they are merry, Witty
and genial; all which I much attribute to the excellent quality of
the ayre: The French they have a deadly hatred to, so as some
of our Company were flouted at for wearing red Cloakes, as
then the mode was. Thus after two dayes respite, and feasting
our senses with fine sights & good cheere, I left this Ode, in
our Hosts Albus (wherein (as of many) it was his costome to
desire his Guests to write their Names and Impresse) as the Non
ultra of my Travells; sufficiently sated with rolling up and
downe, and resolving with my selfe to be no longer an Indi-
viduum vagum, if ever I got home againe; since from the report
of divers experienc'd and curious persons, I had ben assur'd there
was little more to be seene in the rest of the [civil] World, after
Italy, France, Flanders & the Low-Country, but plaine and
prodigious Barbarisme.

ODE.

Happy the man who lives content
With his owne Home, & Continent:
Those chiding streames his banks do curb
Esteemes the Ocean to his Orb;
Round which when he a Walke dos take,
Thinks t'have perform'd as much as Drake:
For other tongues he takes no thought
Then what his Nurse or Mother taught:
He's not disturb'd with the rude Cries
Of the Procaccio's Up & Rise;
But being of his Faire possess'd
From Travelling sets up his rest:
In her soft armes no sooner hurl'd
But he enjoyes another World,[1]

.   .   .   .
.   .   .   .
.   .   .   .
.   .   .   .

Scornes Us who Travell Lands & Seas,
Thinkes there's no Countries like to his:

1 There follow four lines deleted by Evelyn.

If then at Home, such Joyes be had,
Oh, how un-wise are We, how mad!

Neapoli 1644

Thus about the 7th of Feb: we return'd to Rome by the same way we came, not daring to adventure by Sea (as some of our Company consulted) for feare of the Turkish Pyrates hovering upon that Coast; nor made we any stay, save at Albano to view the celebrated place and Sepulchre of the famous Duelists who decided the antient quarell betweene their imperious Neighbours with the losse of their lives; and to tast of the Wine no lesse famous: These two Brothers the Horacij and Cur(i)acij lye buried neere the high way, under two antient Pyramids of stone, some what decay'd and overgrowne with rubbish:

15. Mr. Henshaw, and I tooke a walk by the Tyber, visited the Isola Tybertina (now St. Bartholomews) formerly cut in the shape of a ship, and wharfed with Marble, in which a lofty Obelisque represented the Mast: Here are the ruines of Æsculapius's Temple, converted now to a stately Hospital, & a pretty Convent: In the Church of St. Barthol: is the body of that Apostle: Opposite to it is the Convent & Church of St. Jo: Colavita, where I saw nothing remarkable save an old broken Altar with this Inscription.

Simoni Sanco Deo Fideo Sacrum, Sex Pompejus. S.P.F.
Colmussianus quinquenalis decur: bidentalis dono dedit:

Here was the Temple of *Fortuna Virilis*, and hence we walked to a Cupola, now a church, formerly dedicated to the Sunn: opposite to it Santa *Maria Schola Græca*, where formerly that Tongue was taught, & now said to be the 2d Church dedicated to the B: Virgin in all Rome, bearing also the Title of a Cardinalat: Behind this stands the Greate Altar of Hercules much demolish'd.

Neere this (being at the foote of *Mons Aventine*) are the Popes salt-houses, ascending the hill we came to *St. Sabina* an antient fabric, formerly sacred to Diana, there in a Chapell is an admirable Picture, the work of Livia Fontana, set about with columns of Alabaster, & in the middle of the Church is a stone they report cast by the Devil at St. Dominic, whilst he was at Masse: Hence we travelld towards an Heape of Rubbish called the Marmorata, on the bank of Tyber, a place or Magazine of stones & neere which formerly stood a Triumphal Arch, in honor of Horatius vanquishing the Tuscans: The ruines of the Bridg yet appeare: & now were we got to Mons *Testæceus* an heape of Potshards almost 200 foote high, thought to have ben amassed & thrown there by the Subjects of the Common-Wealth bringing their Tribute in Earthen Vessels, others (more probably) that it was formerly a quarter of the Towne where Potters lived: at the summet Rome affords a noble Prospect, & before it a spacious Greene cal'd the *Hippodrom* where heretofore Olympics were Celebrated, & the people Musterd as in our London Artillerie-ground: walking hence to the Citty old Wall, We with much admiration view the Pyramid or Tomb of C. Cestius, of White Marble, & is one of Romes most antient intire, Monuments.

At the left hand is the Port of *St. Paule*, once *Tergemina* out of which the three *Horatij* pass'd to encounter the *Cur(i)atij* of *Albano*: Hence bending homewards by *St. Saba* by *Antoninus* Bathes (which we enter'd), is the Marble Sepulchre of *Vespasian*: The thicknesse of the Walls, & stately ruines shew the enormous magnificence of these *Thermæ*: Hence we went by a corner of the *Circus Maximus*, viewing the place where stood the *Septizonium* demolish'd by *Sixtus* V. for feare of its falling: so passing by *M. Cœlius* we beheld the devotions of *St. Maria in Navicula* having a glorious front to the streete; so nam'd from a ship carv'd out in white Marble, & standing on a piedestal before it: supposd the Vowe of one escaping ship-wrack. Next this joynes Horti Mathæi, which of all the places about the Citty I onely omitted visiting, being as I was told yet inferior to no Garden in Rome, for statues, antient Monuments, Aviaries, Fountaines, Groves, & especialy a noble Obelisque: & maintain'd in beauty at the Expense of 6000 Crownes yearely: Which if not expended to keepe up its beauty, forfaits the Possession of a greater Revenue to another Family, as is reported, so curious are they of their Villas & places of Pleasure, even to excesse: Returning Weary to our Lodging, the next day we go to see the once famous *Circus Caracalla*, in the midst of which there now lay prostrate one of the most stately & antient Obelisks, (full of Ægyptian Hieroglyphi⟨c⟩s) that is now in the World, twas it seemes broken in 4 pieces when o'rethrowne by the Barbarians, & would have ben purchas'd &

transported into England by the magnificent *Thomas Earle* of *Arundel*, could it have ben well removed to the Sea: This is since set together, & plac'd on the stupendious Artificial Rock, made by *Innocentius Decimus* & serving for a Fountaine in Piazza Navona, the worke of Cavaliere Bernini, the Popes Architect. Neere this is the Sepulchre of Metellus of Massy stone, & pretty entire, now cal'd Capo di Bove. Hence to a small *Oratorie* nam'd *Domine quo vadis*; where the tradition is, our B: Saviour met St. Peter as he fled, & turn'd him back againe.

St. Sebastians was the next, a meane structure (the *faciata* except⟨e⟩d) but venerable Church, especialy for the Reliques & Grotts, in which lie the Ashes of many Holy men: Here is also kept the Pontifical chaire sprinkl⟨e⟩d with the Blood of *Pope Stephanus*, to which greate devotion is paied, also a Well full of Martyrs bones, & the Sepulchre of *St. Sebastian*, with one of the Arrows, the Vestigia of *Christ* when he met St. Peter at *Quo Vadis*: These are kept by the Fulgentine Monks who have here their Monasterie, & who led us down into a Grotto, which they affirm'd went divers furlongs under ground, the sides or Walls as we passed, fill'd with dead bones & bodies, laied as it were on shelfes, whereof some of them were shut up, with broad stones, & now & then a Crosse or Palme cut in them: here were also at the end of some of these subterranean passages square roomes, with Altars in them, pretending to have formerly ben the receptacles of Primitive Devots in the times of Persecution, nor seemes it improbable, thus we left those Catacombs.

The 17, I was invited (after dinner) to the Academie of the *Humorists*, kept in a spacious Hall, belonging to Signor Mancini, where the Witts of the Towne meete on certaine daies, to recite poems, & prevaricate on severall Subjects &c: The first that Speakes is cal'd the Lord, & stands in an eminent place, & then the rest of the virtuosi recite in order: by these ingenious Exercises the learn'd discourses, is the purity of the Italian Tongue daily improv'd: This roome is hung round, with enumerable devises or Emblemes all relating to something of *humidum* with Motos under them: Several other Academies there are of this nature, bearing the like fantastical titles: It is in this Accademie of the Humorists where they have the Picture of *Guarini* the famous Author of *Pastor fido*, once of this Society:

Over against this lives *Hippolito Vitelesco* the greate Statue
Colector, and he has a vast store of them & of the most esteem'd
in Rome to an incredible value [and his action, or rather passion
of kissing & embracing them is as pleasant as a Comedy:] but the
best part of the day we spent in hearing the Academic exercises.
Next morning we walked to st. Nicholas's in Carcere, it has a
faire front, & within part of the Bodys of *st. Mark & Marcellino*,
on the Tribuna is a painting of *Gentileschi*, & the Altar of *Caval:
Baglioni*, with some other rare paintings: coming round from
hence we passed by Circus flaminius, now totaly in ruines, formerly exceeding large: In the Afternoon we visited the *English
Jesuites* (being well acquainted with P: Stafford the Superior)
who courteously receev'd us: Their Church & College they call
st. Thomasso de gli Inglesi, & is a Seminarie, & shew in their
Church among other trifles the Relique of Beckett, their reputed
Martyr: Of Paintings there is one of *Durante*, & many representing the suffering of severall of their Society executed in England,
especially F: *Champion*: Next we went to see the Hospital of the
Pelerini, della S. Trinità, where I had seene the feete of many Pil-
grims wash'd by Princes, Cardinals & noble Romans, and serv'd
at Table, As the Ladys & Noble Women did to other poor Creatures in another roome; 'twas told us no lesse than foure hundred
fourty foure thousand had ben thus treated in the Jubilie of *1600*
and of Women 25500 as appears by the Register [which bring
store of money].

Returning homeward I saw the Palace of *Spada* belonging to
that Cardinal: it has a most magnificent hall painted by *Daniel
Volterra & Giulio Piacentino*, who made the fret in the little
Court: But the rare Perspectives are of Bolognesi: neere this is
the *Mont Pietà* instituted as a banc for the poore, who if the
summ be not greate, may have mony upon pawns &c: To this
joynes *st. Martino* to which belongs a *Schola*, or Corporation that
do many works of Charity: Hence we came through Campo di
Fiori or herb Market, in the midst of which is a fountaine casting Water out of a Dolphin in Coper, & in this Piazza, is common Execution don. I went this afternoone to visite my Lord
John Somerset, brother to the Marques of Worcester, who had
his Appartment in *Palazzo della Cancellaria* belonging to Card:
Francesco Barberini, as Vice-Chancelor of the Church of
Rome, & Protector of the English: The building is of the

famous Architect Bramanti, & is built of incrusted Marble with
4 ranks of noble lights, the principal Enterance of Fontanas
designe, and all of Marble, the Portico within sustaind with
massie Columns: In the second ⟨Peristyle⟩ above the Chambers
are rarely painted by Salviati & Vasari: & so ample is this Palace,
that 6 Princes with their families have ben receivd in it at a time
without incommoding each other:

Feb: the 20th: I went (as was my usual ⟨Costome⟩) & spent
an Afternoone in *Piazza Navona*, as well to see what Antiquities
I could purchase among the people, who hold Mercat there for
Medaills, Pictures, & such Curiosities, as to heare the Monte-
banks prate, & debite their Medicines. This was formerly the
Circus Agonalis dedicated to sports & Passtimes, and is now the
greatest Market of the Citty, having three most noble Fountaines, & the Stately Palaces of the Pamfilii, *st. Giacomo de Spag-
noli* belonging to that Nation, to which two Convents, for Friers
& Nunns all Spanish: In this Church was now erected a most
stately *Cataphalco* or *Chapelle Ardente* for the Death of the
Queene of Spaine: The Church all hung with black, & heare
I heard a Spanish sermon or funebral Oration, spent the rest of
the time in viewing the statues, divises, and Impreses hung
about the Walls, the Church, & Pyramid stuck with thousands
of lights & tapers, which made a glorious shew: The Statue of
st. James here is of *Sansovino*, & there are also some good Pictures [of *Carrachio*], the faciata too is faire: So returning home
I pass'd by the stumps of old Pasquin, at the Corner of a streete
call'd strada pontificia: Here they still past up their drolling
Lampons, & scurrilous Papers: This had formerly ben one of
the best statues for workmanship & Art, in all the Citty as the
remaining *bust* dos still shew. The 21, in the morning I tooke a
Walk up the Hill towards the Capuchins, where was then Card:
Onufrio (brother to the late P. *Urban* the VIIIth) of the same
order: Here's a prety church built by the Card: full of rare Pictures, & there lies the body of *s. Felix* that dos (they say) still do
Miracles: The Piece at the great Altar is of Lanfranc, 'tis a Lofty
Edifice, with a beautiful avenue of Trees, and in good aire: After
dinner passing along the *strada del* ⟨*Corso*⟩, I considerd the
Colonna d'Antonino passing under *Arco Portugallo* which is but a
relique, heretofore erected in honor of Domitian, cal'd now *Portugallo* from a Cardinal living neere it, a little farther on the right

hand stands the Column, in a small *Piazza*, heretofore set up in honor of *M: Aurelius Ant:* comprehending in a *basserelievo* of white marble his hostil acts against the *Parthians, Armenians, Germans* &c but is now somewhat decay'd, & bearing on the summit the Image of s. *Paule* of Gilded Coper: 'tis said to be CLXI foote high, & is ascended by 207 steps receiving light by 56 apertures, without defacing the sculpture: & here it is, that there is wrought that famous Miracle said to be caused by the Christian souldiers, of which *Baronius* Anno 176. A little distance off are the reliques of the Emperors Palace, the heads of whose Pillars shew them to have bin *Corinthian*. Turning a little down we came to another *Piazza* in which stands a sumptuous Vasa of Porphyrie, & a faire Fountaine, but the grace of this Merket, & indeede the admiration of the whole World, is the *Pantheon*, now call'd *S. Maria della Rotunda*: formerly sacred to all the Gods, & still remaining the most intire Antiquitie of the Citty, built by *Marcus Agrippa* as testifies the Architrave of the Portico, sustain'd by 13 Pilars of *Theban* Marble 6 foote thick, & 53 in height of one intire stone: In this Porch is an old Inscription: Entring the Church we admire the fabric, which is wholy cover'd with one Cupola, seemingly suspended in the aire, & receiving light by a hole in the middle onely: The structure is neere as high as broad, viz, 144 ⟨feet⟩ not counting the thicknesse of the Walls, which is 22 more to the top, all of white Marble, & til *Urban* the VIII converted the metall into Ordinance, to warr against the *Duke* of *Parma*, & part of it to make the high Altar in s. *Peters*, all over cover'd with *Corinthian* brasse, ascending by 40 degrees within the roof or Convex of the Cupola, rich carved with *octagons*, in the stone: There be *Niches* in the walls, in which stood heretofore the statues of *Jupiter* & the other Gods & Godesses, for here was that *Venus*, which had hung in her Eares the other *Union* that *Cleopatra* was about to dissolve & drink up, as she had don its fellow: There are severall of these *Niches* one above the other for the Celestial, Terrestrial & Subterranean Deities; but the place is now converted into a Church dedicated to the *B: Virgin* & all the Saints: The Pavement is incomparable and the vast folding-Gates of *Corinthian* brasse, in a word, 'tis of all the *Roman* Antiquities the most worthy notice: There lies interr'd in this Temple the famous *Raph: Urbine, Perin* del *Vaga, F. Zuccharo* & other painters: Returning home we passe by

Cardinal *Cajetans* Palace a noble piece of Architecture of Vin-
cenzo Ammannati, & is the grace of the whole Corso:

The 25t invited by a Frier *Dominican* whom we usualy heard
preach to a number of *Jewes*, to be Godfather to a Converted
Turk & a *Jew*, The Ceremonie was perform'd in the Church of S:
Maria sopra la Minerva neere the *Capitol*, They were clad in
White, then exorcis'd at their entering the church with aboundance of Ceremonies, when lead into the Quire, they were baptizd by a Bishop *in Pontificalibus*: The *Turk* lived afterwards in
Rome, sold hot-waters, & would bring us presents when he met
us, kneeling, & kissing the hemms of our Cloaks: But the Jew
was believ'd to be a Counterfeit: This Church situate on a spacious rising, was formerly consecrated to the Godesse Minerva:
'tis well built, & richly adorn'd, the body of s. *Catharine di Sienna*
is buried here, & the paintings of the Chapell of *Marcello
Venusti*, the *Madona* over the Altar of *Gio: da Fiesole* cal'd the
Angelic painter, & was of the order of these Monks: There are
many Charities dealt publiqly here, especialy at the procession
on the *Annuntiation* when I saw his holinesse with all the Cardinals, prelati &c *in pontificalibus*: Dowries being given to 300
poore Wenches, that were all clad in White: The *Pope* had his
Tiara on his head, & was carried on mens shoulders in an open
Chaire of armes, blessing the people as he passd along: The
statue of *Christ* at the Columna is esteem'd one of *M: Angelos*
Master-pieces: Here is interr'd Card: *Bembo*, & innumerable are
the paintings of the best Artists. The *Organ* is also accounted
one of the sweetest of *Rome*: We return'd by s: *Marco* a stately
Church, the pavement especialy, and that piece of P: *Perugino* of
the two Martyrs; adjoyning to this is a noble Palace built by the
famous *Bramanti*.

26t: Ascending a little up the hill we came to the *Forum Tra-
janum* where his *Culumna* stands yet intire, wrough⟨t⟩ with
admirable *Bass-relievo* & comprehending the *Dacian* War, the
figure⟨s⟩ at the upper part appearing of the same proportion
with those below: 'Tis ascended by 192 steps, inlightned with 44
apertures or windows, artificialy dispos'd; in height from the
piedestal 140 foote: It had once the Ashes of *Trajan* & statue in
place where now stands st. *Peters* of gilt brasse, erected by Pope
Sixtus quintus: The Sculpture of this stupendious pillar is
thought the work of *Apollodorus*; but what is very observable is

the descent to the *plinth* of the *Piedestal*, shewing how this Antient Cittie lies buried in her ruines now, this Monument being at first set up upon a rising ground:

After dinner we went to take the aire in *Card: Bentivoglios* delicious Gardens, now but newly deceas'd, he has a faire Palace built by several good Masters on part of the Ruines of *Constantines Thermæ*, well adorn'd with Columns and paintings, especialy of *Guido Rheni*.

On 27th in the Morning, Mr. Henshaw and myselfe walked to the Trophies of *Marius* erected in honor of his victorie over the Cymbrians, but these now taken out of their *Niches*, are plac'd on the balusters of the Capitol, so as their antient station is now but an informe[1] ruine: keeping on our way we came to st. *Crosse* in *Jerusalem*, built by Constantine, over the demolitions of the Temple of *Venus* & Cupid which he threw down, & 'twas here they report he reposited the wood of the true Crosse found by his Mother *Helena*, in honour whereof this Church was built, & memory of his victory over *Maxentius* when that holy signe appeard to him: The Edifice without is *Gotic*, but very glorious within, especialy the roofe, & one Tribune well painted: Here is a chapel dedicated to *st. Helena*, the floore whereof is of Earth brought from *Jerusalem*, the walls of faire Mosaic, in which they suffer no Women to enter save once a yeare: Under the high Altar of the Church is buried St. Anastasius in *Lydian* marble, Benedict of the VIIth and they shew a world of Reliques, expos'd at our request, with a Phial of our *B: Saviours* blood, two thornes of the Crowne, three Chips of the real Crosse, one of the Nailes, wanting a point, st. Thomas's doubting finger, and a fragment of the Title, being part of a thin board, some of *Judas's* pieces of silver, and innumerable more, if one had faith to believe it. To this venerable Church joynes a Monasterie, the Gardens taking up the space of an antient Amphitheater: Hence we pass'd beyond the walles out at the port of st. *Laurence* to that Saints Church & where his Ashes are enshrin'd: This was also built by the same Greate *Constantine*, famous for the Coronation of *Pietro Altisiodorensis* Emp: of *Constantinople* by *Honorius* the 2d. 'Tis sayd the Corps of *st. Stephen* the *proto-martyr* was deposited here by that of s. *Sebastian*, which it had no sooner

1 Shapeless.

touch⟨ed⟩ but *Sebastians* gave it place of its own accord. The Church has no lesse than 7 privileg'd Altars, & excellent Pictures; About the Walls is painted this Martyrs sufferings, & when they built them, the bones of divers saints, since translated to other churches: The front is *Gottic*. Returning we espied a small ruine of an Aquæduct, built by *Q. Martius* the *Prætor*, & so through that incomparable straite streete leading to Santa *Maria Major* return'd to our Lodging sufficiently tired. We were taken up the next morning in seing the impertinences of the Carnoval when all the world are as mad at Rome, as at other places, but the most remarkable were the 3 Races of the Barbarie horses, that run in the strada del *Corso* without riders, onely having spurrs so placed on their backs, & hanging downe by their sides, as with their motion to stimulate them; Then of Mares: Then of Asses, of Bufalos, of Naked Men [—old men, young, & boys:] and aboundance of idle & ridiculous Passetime: One thing yet is remarkable, their acting Comedies upon a Stage placed on a Cart, or *plaustrum* where the Scene or tiring place is made of bowghs, in a Pastoral & rural manner, this they drive from streete to streete with a yoake or two of Oxen, after the antient guise; The streetes swarming with whores, buffoones & all manner of rabble. 1 of March at the Greeke Church we saw the Eastern Ceremonies perform'd by a Bishop &c in that Tongue, & here the unfortunate Duke & Dutchesse of *Bullion* receiv'd their ashes, it being the first of Lent, there being now as much trudging up and downe of devotos: as the day before of prophan people; both now turn'd Saints alike to all appearance.

On Palme sonday was a greate procession, after a papal Masse, & on the 11th of Aprill, was exposd at *st. Peters st. Veronicas* Volto Santo, & next day the Speare, with a world of ceremonie: on Holy Thursday the *Pope* said Masse, & afterward carried processionaly the Host about the Chapell with an infinitie of Tapers; this finish'd his holinesse was carried in his open Chaire on Mens shoulders to the place where reading the Bull in *Cæna domini* he both Curses & blesses all in a breath, then the gunns againe went off: hence he went to the Ducal hall of the *Vatican* where he wash'd the feete of 12 poore-men, with all that ceremonie almost as tis don at Whitehall, they have Clothes, a dinner, & almes, which he gives with his owne hands, & serves at their Table: They have also gold & silver Medails, but their garments are of white wollan, long robes as we paint the Apostles: The same Ceremonies are don by the Conservators & other Officers of state at st. Jo: *de Lateran*: & now the Table on which they say our B: L. celebrated his last Supper is set out, & the heads of the Apostles; Every famous Church buisy in dressing up their pageantries, to represent the holy Sepulchre, of which we went to visite divers:

Good friday we went againe to s. *Peters*, where the Volto, Launce, & Crosse were all three exposd & worship'd together: All the confession Seates fill'd with devout people, & the Night a procession of severall people that most lamentably whipped themselves till all the blood staind their clothes, for some had shirts, others upon the beare back, with vizors & masks on their faces, at every 3 or 4 stepps, dashing the knotted & ravelld whip-cord over their shoulders as hard as they could lay it on, whilst some of the religious Orders & fraternities sung in a dismal tone, the lights, & Crosses going before, which shewd very horrible, & indeede a heathnish pomp: The next day was much ceremonie at s. Jo: de Laterano, so as this whole weeke we spent in running from Church to Church, all the towne in buisy devotion, greate silence, and unimaginable Superstition: Easterday was awakn'd with the Guns againe from *st. Angelo*, we went to s. *Peters*, where the pope himselfe celebrated Masse, shew'd the Reliques formerly nam'd, & gave a publique benediction, & so we went to dinner:

Monday, we went to heare Music in the *Chiesa Nova*, and though there were aboundance of Ceremonies at the other greate Churches, & greate exposure of Reliques, yet being wearied with sights, of this nature, & the season of the Yeare (Summer at *Rome* being very dangerous, by reason of the heates,) minding us of returning Northwards, we spent the rest of the time in visiting such places as we had not yet sufficiently seene: onely I do not forget the Pops benediction of the *Confalone* or Standard, & giving the hallowed palmes; & on Mayday, the greate Procession of the Universitie, & the *Mulatiers* at st. *Antonies*, & their seting up a foolish May-pole in the Capitol, very ridiculous:

We therefore now tooke Coach a little out of Towne, to visite the famous *Roma Subterranea*, being much like those of st. *Sebastians*: here in a Corn field, guided by two torches we crep't on our bellies into a little hole about 20 paces, which deliver'd us into a

large entrie that lead us into severall streetes or allies, a good
depth in the bowells of the Earth, a strange & fearefull passages
for divers miles, as *Bossius* has describ'd & measur'd them in his
book: we ever & anon came into pretty square roomes, that
seem'd to be Chapells, with Altars, & some adorn'd with antient
painting, very ordinary: That which renders the passages dreadfull is, the *Skeletons* & bodies, that are placd on the sides, in
degrees one above the other like shelves, whereof some are shut
up with a Course flat Stone, & *Pro Christo* or ✠ & Palmes
ingraven on them, which are suppos'd to have ben Martyrs: Here
in all liklyhood were the meetings of the Primitive *Christians*
during the Persecutions, as *Plinius Secundus* describes them: As I
was prying about, I found a glasse phiole as was conjecturd filld
with dried blood, as also two *lacrymatories*: Many of the bodyes,
or rather bones, (for there appeard nothing else) lay so intire, as if
placed so by the art of the Chirugion, which being but touch'd
fell all to dust: Thus after two or 3 miles wandring in this subterranean Meander we return'd to our Coach almost blind when we
came into the day light againe, & even choked with smoake: A
French bishop & his retinue adventuring it seemes too farr in
these denns, their lights going out, were never heard of more.

We were entertain'd at Night with an English play, at the
Jesuites where before we had dined, & the next at the *Prince Gal-
icanos*, who himselfe compos'd the Musique to a magnificent
Opera, where were *Cardinal Pamphilio* the Popes Nephew, the
Governors of Rome, the Cardinals, Ambassadors, Ladies & a
world of Nobilitie & strangers: after a Just & Turnament of severall young Gentlemen upon a formal Defy, which was perform'd in the Morning, to which we were invited, the prizes
distributed by the Ladies after the Knight Errantry way: The
Launces & swords running at tilt at the Barrieres with a greate
deele of clatter, but without any bloud shed, which gave much
diversion to the Spectators, & was very new to us Travellers:

The 5 we tooke Coach and went 15 miles out of the Cittie to
Frascati formerly *Tusculanum*, a villa of Card: *Aldobrandini*; built
for a Country house but for its elegance, situation & accommodation of plentifull water, Groves, Ascents & prospect, surpassing in my opinion the most delicious places that my eyes ever
beheld: Just behind the Palace (which is of excellent Architecture) and is in the center of the Inclosure, rises an high hill or

mountaine all over clad with tall wood, and so form'd by nature,
as if it had ben cut out by Art, from the summit whereof falls a
horrid Cascade seeming rather a greate River than a streame,
precipitating into a large Theater of Water representing a⟨n⟩
exact & perfect Raine-bow when the sun shines out: Under this
is made an artific⟨i⟩all Grott, where in are curious rocks,
hydraulic Organs & all sorts of singing birds moving, & chirping by force of the water, with severall other pageants and surprizing inventions: In the center of one of these roomes rises a
coper ball that continualy daunces about 3 foote above the pavement, by virtue of a Wind conveyed seacretly to a hole beneath
it, with many other devices to wett the unwary spectators, so as
one can hardly ⟨step⟩ without wetting to the skin: In one of
these Theatres of Water, is an *Atlas* spouting up the streame to
an incredible height, & another monster which makes a terrible
roaring with an horn; but above all the representation of a
storme is most naturall, with such fury of raine, wind and Thunder as one would imagine ones selfe in some extreame Tempest:
To this is a Garden of incomparable walkes & shady groves,
aboundance of rare Fruit, Orangs, Lemons, &c: and the goodly
prospect of Rome above all description, so as I do not wonder
that *Cicero* & others have celebrated this place with such
encomiums. The Palace is indeede built more like a Cabinet,
than any-thing compos'd of stone & morter, it has in the middle
an Hall furnish⟨ed⟩ with excellent Marbles, & rare Pictures,
especialy those of Cavalier *Gioseppe d'Arpino*, & the movables
are princely & rich, In a word this was the last piece of Architecture finishd by *Giacomo de la Porta*, who built it for *Pietro* Card:
Aldobrandini in the time of *Clement* the 8th.

On the 6t. we rested ourselves, & next day in Coach tooke our
last fare-well of visiting the Circumjacent places, & that was
Tivoli, or the old *Tyburtine*: After about 6 miles from *Rome* we
passe the Teverone, a bridge built ⟨by⟩ the Mother of *Severus*,
Mammea, and so by divers antient Sepulchres, amongst others,
that of *Valerius Volusi*, neere it the stinking sulphurous River over
the *Ponte Lucano* where we found an heape or Turret full of
Inscriptions, now call'd *Plautius* his Tomb. Ariv'd at *Tivoli* we
went first to see the Palace *d'Estè* erected on a plaine, but where
was formerly an hill: The Palace is very ample & stately: In the
Garden at the right hand are plac'd 16 vast Conchas of marble

jetting out Waters: in the midst of these stands a *Janus* quadrifrons that cast forth 4 girandolas, calld from the resemblance the *fontana di Speccho*; neere this a Place for Tilting: before the Ascent of the Palace is that incomparable fountain of *Leda*, & not far from that 4 sweete & delicious Gardens; descending thence two pyramids of Water, & in a Grove of trees neere it, the Fountaines of *Tethys*, *Esculapius*, *Arethusa*, *Pandora*, *Pomona* & *Flora*, then the pransing *Pegasus*, *Bacchus*, The Grott of *Venus*, The two Colosses of *Melicerta & Sybilla Tibertina*, all of exquisite Marble, Coper & other suitable adornments, The *Cupids* especialy are most rare, pouring out Water, & the Urnes on which are plac'd the 10 Nymphs: The Grotts are richly pav'd with *pietra Commessa*, Shells, Corall &c: Towards *Roma Triumphans*, leades a long & spacious Walk, full of Fountaines, under which is historiz'd the who⟨le⟩ *Ovidian* Metamorphosis in *mezzo Relievo* rarely sculptur'd, at the end of this, next the wall the Cittie of *Rome*, as it was in its beauty, all built of small models, representing that Citie with its Amphitheatres, Naumachia, Thermæ, Temples, Arches, Aquæducts, streetes & other magnificences, with a little streame runing through it for the River Tybur, gushing out of the Urne next the statue of that River: In another Garden a noble Aviarie, the birds artificial, & singing, til the presence of an Owle appeares, on which the⟨y⟩ suddainly chang their notes, to the admiration of the Spectators: Neere this is the Fountaine of Dragons belching large streames of water, with horrid noises: In another Grotto calld the *Grotta di Natura* is an hydraulic Organ, below this divers stews and fish-ponds, in one of which is the Statue of *Neptune* in his Chariot, on a seahorse, in another a *Triton*, & lastly a Garden of simples. There are besides in the Palace many rare statues, & Pictures, Bedsteds richly inlaied, & sundry other precious moveables: The whole said to have Cost the best part of a Milion. Having feasted our Curiositie with these artificial Miracles, & din'd, we went to see the so famous natural Precipice, & Cascade or Catadupe of the River *Anien* from the Mountaines of *Tivoli* which rushes down with that fury, that what with the mist it perpetualy casts up by breaking the waters against rocks, & what with the sun darting, forming a natural *Iris*, the prodigious depth of the Vorago is enough to astonish one that lookes on it. Upon the summite of this Rock stands yet the ruines, & some pillars & Cornishes of the Temple

of *Sibylla Tyburtina* or *Albumea*, a round fabric, as yet discovering
some of its pristine beauty: He⟨re⟩ was a greate deale of Gunpouder drying in the sun, & a little beneath Mills, belonging to
the *Pope*. And now we returne to Rome, whither we had 15 miles:
by the way we were shew'd (at some distance) the Citty *Preneste*,
The *Hadrian* Villa, now onely an heape of ruines, & so came late
to our Lodging, setting up our rest from visiting any more
Curiosities, but what happn'd to come in our way as my Companion Mr. Henshaw & I went to take the aire; onely I may not
omitt that diverting ourselves one afternoone in the *Piazza
Navona*, a *Montebank* there to allure Curious Strangers, taking of
a Ring from his finger, which seemd set with a dull darke stone a
little swelling out, like what we call (though untruely) a Toad-
stone, wetting his finger a little in his mouth, & but touching it,
it conceiv'd a luculent flame, as bright & big as a small wax-
candle, this blowing out, he repeated severall times, & I have
much regreted, that I did not think of purchasing the receipt of
making that composition, at what price soever, for though there
is a processe in *Jo: Baptista Porta*, & others how to do it, yet on
severall triales, they do none of them succeede.

May: 18 But being now disappointed of Monies long
expected, intending to see *Lauretto*, I was forc'd to returne by the
same way I came, desiring if possible to be at *Venice* by the
Ascension, & therefore diverted to take *Legorne* in the ⟨way⟩, as
well to furnish me with Credit by a Merchant there, as to take
order for the ⟨transporting⟩ such Collections as I had made at
Rome; when on my Way, turning about to behold this once & yet
glorious Citty, upon an Eminence of Ground I did not without
some regret give it my last farewell—

When my fix'd thoughts enjoyd their blest repose
Where liberall Nature her delights bestows,
Whilst they kept house at home, and knew no more
Than what might be survey'd from my owne dore;
When they were free, yet had no more extent
Than what is circumscrib'd in selfe-Content;
When in my owne Spheare mov'd, acquainted growne
With a blest temper, to excesse unknown:
When all my Cares (to better things inclyn'd)
A few square Ackers, & an hill confin'd;

An humble Cottage, & a silver Brooke,
A Shady Grove, a Choice Friend, & a Book:
Glad of my Chaster Nymph, Unknown to Courts,
Acquainted onely with the Country Sports:
Injoy'd the Seasons, and with chosen Flowres
Made Chaplets to bedeck the shady bowers,
Knit Love-knots in her haire, a thousand toyes,
(For Innocents embrace no other joyes)
Then liv'd I to my selfe, & slept secure
Within the Walls that did my Cares immure;
'Til on a Day (by chance) I spied a Book
In which a Neighbouring Shepheard us'd to looke:
He found it in a Cave, all foule & torne;
The first was wanting, and with Canker worne;
The Cover broidred with a slimie lace
Which a moist Snaile had wrought upon the place:
That which the Learned Worme had left I read,
Of vent'rous Knights, & Lands which flourished;
Of Armes & Arts, and many a bloudy field,
Citties renoun'd; Things that beliefe excell'd:
But still the chiefest seane of all was lay'd
Where the two Boys (exposd to be betray'd)
Found Wolves than Men more kind, & for a Tomb
Receivd a Nurse, they after call'd it *ROME*:
That Name she still retaines, & I suppos'd
It was with Walls, like our Shire-Towne inclosd:
Temples, Fanes, Statues, Amphitheaters
I fancied strange prodigious Creatures:
Triumphant Arches, Aquæ-ducts & more
Than e're I heard of, or had thought before:
Nor [farther was] I yet Concern'd, nothing did move
My fix't Desires: For I was then in Love:
Ah happy Swaine! hadst thou remain'd so still,
Content with little, Innocent of Ill:
Nor wanted ought; But ah the sad events
Of *Pan*, & other Shepherds discontents   The Civil
Exil'd me thence: Mark then with what an heart   Warrs
I left those Joyes, so *ROME*! from thee I part.
From thy proud Structures, *Temples* thee adorne,   Temples:
And stupend *Marbles* from far Countries born: Marbles:

Gulios so high, as if on top they bore
The Sunn to whom they sacred were before: Obeliscs:
Those *Obeliscs* so fam'd in Histories   Statues:
Discovering yet their lock'd-up Mysteries: Hercules in
The very Marbles live, here *Hercules*   *Farnezes*
Not so renoun'd of old, as at *Farneze*:   Palas
Transparant laune, her snowy thighs betraies,   Flora in
Whilst *Flora* with her bloomy Chaplet plaies: *Farnezes* Palas
The Youth *Adonis* a fierce Bore persues,   Adonis:
And in his reaking gore, hard tuscks imbrues: *Medicis*
It is a truth, nor can it be deny'd,   ⟨*Palas*⟩
This is the selfe-same *Niob* petrified: Niobe:
There strive the *Sabines*, by the Romans took,   Sabines:
And whilst they'r ravish'd, ravish those who look:
Had *Venus* here her Statue but espi'd,   Venus
She sure had call'd her Sister, or else dy'd   *Medicis*.
With Envy; and (could Godesse Mortal prove)
This had remaind her ⟨heyre⟩ [this] Queene of Love:
That *Steede* which so the *Capitol* dos grace,   Marc:
Wants nought save motion, yet dos without it pace: Aurelius in
For he's so full of Mettal, one would sweare   the *Capitol*
'Twere an inchanted *Horse* erected there:
Th' inveloup'd *Laocoon*, a Serpent twines   Laöcon in
And threids his Children, whilst the Father Pines   *Belvedere*:
Thro' anguish, and believe't, I did mistake   Vaticane
Myselfe, and fled, it is so like a Snake: Cleopatra
A dreadfull Asp, th' *Egy⟨p⟩tian* Queene dos kill,
Dead in the Storie, but here living still: The *Bull*
The furious *Bull*, calv'd from a rock, like this   at Farneze
There never was a *Metamorphosis*:   Palace:
The *Gladiator* who still seemes to fight,   Gladiator:
And the hard-soft, bed-rid *Hermaphrodite*:   Herma-
Chast *Daphne's* limbs into the Laurel shoote,   phrodite:
Whilst her swift feete the amorous Center roote;   Daphne in
How the rude bark invades her virgin Snow,   Villa *Bur-*
And dos to that well timber'd body grow!   *ghesi*
Here bleeding *Seneca* in's Bagnia lies,   Seneca:
And to's Spectators [dos] still Philosophise: Castor &
Castor & *Pollux*, bold *Bucephalus*,   Pollux
Old *Nile*, & the belov'd *Antinöus*:   Bucephalus

The reverend *Vatican*, & lofty Wall   in *Monte*
Of the Imperious & proud *Capitol*:   *Quirino*
Or in one Miracle to name them all,
First of *Apostles* fam'd Cathedrall.   Nilus ⎫ in
A thousand Wonders extant, more than these   Anti- ⎬ Vati
Tempt Travellers from the Antipodes: nous ⎭ cano
Such living *Pictures* from rare hands appeare,   Vatican.
As if mens shadows, reäl Bodys were: Capitolium
Like *Villa's*, *Fountaines*, & luxurious Fields   St. Peters
No Earths *Elizium* but thine *Rome*, yeilds!   Pictures.
Nor is the Eye alone thus entertain'd,   Villas:
But what may to the Intellect be gain'd,   Fountains:
Flourishes here: Source of Antiquitie,   Library
Apollo's ⟨Seate⟩, the *Muses* Monarchie: Vatican
Glory of Citties, for thy *Ruines* are   Ruines.
More glorious than be other *Citties* far:
With speaking stones, & breathing *Statues* set,
Justly art term'd the *Worlds sole Cabinet*:   Inscriptions.
Of all the *Vniverse* none dares Contend
With thee ô *ROME*, nor will thy Praises End:

TRAVELS IN ITALY IV: FLORENCE AGAIN, BOLOGNA, VENICE AND PADUA
(1645–1646)

MAY THE 18TH having taken leave of our Friends at *Rome*
I tooke Coach in Companie of two Courteous *Italian* Gentlemen, having sojourn'd in that Citty now about 7 moneths,
Autumn, Winter & Spring: In the Afternoone we ariv'd at an
house or rather Castle, of the duke of *Parmas* call'd *Capraruola*,
situate on the brow of an hill that over-looks a little Town, or
rather indeede a naturall & stupendious rock, witnesse those
vast Caves serving now for Celarige, where we were entertain'd
with most generous Wine of severall sorts, being just under the
foundation: The Palace was built by the famous Architect
Vignola at the cost of Card: *Alex: Farneze* in forme of an
Octagone, the Court in the middle being exactly round, after a
very extravagant manner, so as rather to resemble a Fort or
Castle. The Chambers yet within are all of them square, which

makes the Walls exceeding thick, & in particular one of these romes so artificialy contriv'd, that from the 2 opposite angles, one may overheare the least whisper: They say any perfect square dos it: Most of the Paintings are of *Succari*: It has a most stately entrie, on which spouts an artificial fountain within the porch: The Hall, Chapell, and infinite number of Lodging Chambers are remarkable, but most of all the Pictures, and witty inventions of *Hannibal Caraccio*, & the *Christo Morto* incomparable: Behind are the Gardens full of Statues and noble Fountaines, especialy that of the Shepherds:

Hence after dinner we tooke horse & lay that night at *Montrosso* 20 Miles from *Rome*: next day din'd at *Viterbo*, & lay at *St. Laurenzo*: Next day at *Radicofani*, & slept at *Turnera*: The 21 the afternoone having dind at *Sienna* where we could not passe admiring at the Greate Church built intirely both within and without with white & blak marble in polish'd square stones by *Macarino*, it shewing so beautifull after a shoure has fall'n. The floore within is of various colour'd Marbles representing the storie of both Testaments admirably wrought: Here lies Pius the 2d. The Bibliothec is painted by P: *Perugino* and *Raphael*, The life of *Æneas Sylvius* is in fresco, in the middle are the 3 graces of Marble Antique very curious: The front of this building though *Gotic* is yet very fine: Amongst other things they shew *S. Catherines* disciplining Cell, the doore whereof is halfe cut out into chipps by the Pilgrimes & devotees, being of deale wood. Setting out hence for *Pisa* we went againe to see the *Domo* in which *Henry* the seaventh Emp: lies buried, poysond by a Monk in the Eucharist: The bending Toure was built by *Busqueto Delichio*, a *Grecian* Architect, & may be looked on as a stupendious piece of art. In the Gallery of Curiosities is a faire Mummy, the taile of a Sea-horse, Corall growing in a Mans Skull, a Chariot Automatum, two pieces of rock Christall in one of which is a drop of Water, in the other 3 or 4 small wormes: Two Embalm'd Children, divers Petrifications &c: The Garden of Simples is well furnish'd, & has in it the mortiferous Yew or *Taxus* of the antients which the Superintendent Dr. Bellueccio affirmes his workmen cannot indure to clip above the space of halfe an houre at a time without retiring, for the paine of the head which surprizes them:

We went hence for *Ligorne* by Coach, where I tooke up 90 Crounes for the rest of my journey with letters of Credit for *Venice*, after I had sufficiently complaind of my defeate of Correspondence at *Rome*: The next day I came to Lucca, which is a small but pretty Territorie & State of itselfe: The Citty is neate, & well fortified, with noble & pleasant walkes of Trees on the Workes where the Gentry & Ladies use to take the aire: Tis situate on an ample plaine by the river *Serchio*, yet the Country about it is hilly: The Senat-house is magnificent: The Church of St. *Michael* a noble piece, so is also St. *Fredian*, more remarkable to us for the Corps of St. Richard an English King, who in his pilgrimage towards *Rome* died here. Next this we visited *St. Crosses*, a most incomparable structure all of Marble both without as well as within, & so adornd as may vie with many of the fairest even in *Rome* it selfe, witnesse the huge Crosse valued worth 15000 pounds, above all venerable for that Sacret *Volto*, which (as tradition gos) was miraculously put on the Image of *Christ*, & made by *Nicodemus*, whilst the Artist finishing the rest of the body, was meditating what face to set on it: The Inhabitans are exceedingly Civill to strangers above all places in *Italy*, & the⟨y⟩ speake the purest *Italian*, tis also cheape living, which causes Travellers to set up their rest here more than in *Florence* though a more celebrated Citty: Besides the Ladys here are very Conversable, and the Religious Women not at all reserv'd, of these we bought gloves & embroidred stomachers generaly worn by Gentlemen in these Countries. The Circuit of this State is but two easy days journey, & lies mixed with the Duke of *Tuscanies* but having Spaine for Protector (though the least bigotted of all *Roman* Catholicks) & being one of the best fortified Citties in Italy, it remaines in peace: This whole Country abounds in Excellent Olives &c:

Going hence for *Florence* & dining at Pistoia where (besides one Church) there was little observable, onely in the high way wee traversd a Rivulet of Salt-Water, being many miles from the Sea: The Country is extreamely pleasant, full of Gardens, & the roads as straite as a line for the best part of that whole day, & the hedges planted with trees at equal distances, very irriguous with cleare & plentifull streames: Rising early the next morning, we alighted att *Poggio Imperiale* being a Palace of the Greate Dukes, not far from the Citty, having omitted it in my former passage to *Rome*: The house is ascended to by a stately Gallery as it were of talle & overgrown *Cypresse* trees for neere halfe a mile, at the Enterance of these ranges are plac'd 2 Statues of *Tyber* & *Arno* of Marble. Those also of *Virgil*, Ovid, *Petrarch* & *Dantes*: The building is sumptuous, and curiously furnish'd within with Cabinets of *Pietro Comesso*, Tables, Pavements &c, which is a magnificence or work, particularly affected at Florence; The larger Pictures are of *Adam* & *Eve* by *Albert Durer* incomparable, as is that piece of Carving in wood by the same hand standing in a Cupboard: Here is don the whole *Austrian* line, the Dukes Mother sister to the Emperor & foundresse of this Palace, than which there is none in all Italy, that I have seene more magnificently adorn'd or Meubl'd.

We could not forbeare in this Passage to revisite the same & other Curiosities which we had both seene & omitted at our first being at *Florence*. We went therefore to see that famous Piece of *Andrea del Sarta* in the Annu⟨n⟩ciata: The storie is that this Painter in a time of dirth borrow'd a sack of Corne of the Religious of that Convent, & being demanded to repay it, wrought it out in this Picture, which represents *Joseph* sitting on a Sack of Corn & reading to the *B: Virgin*, a piece infinitly valued: There fell downe in the Cloister an old mans face painted in the wall in fresco, greately esteemd, & brake all into crumbs: The *Duke* sent his best Painters to make another instead of it, but none of them would presume to touch a pencil, where *Andrea* had wrought, like another *Apelles*; but one of them was so industrious & patient, that picking up the fragments he laied & fastned them so artificialy together, as the injury it had received was hardly discernable: *Del Sarta* lies buried in the same place: Here is also that piece of *Bartolomeo* who having spent his utmost skill in the face of the *Angel Gabriel*, & being troubl'd that he could not excede it in the Virgin Mother of God, he began the body, & to finish the Clothes & so left it, minding in the morning to work on the face; But when he came, no sooner had he drawn away the Cloth that was hung before it, to preserve it from the dust, when behold an admirable & ravishing face was found ready painted, at which Miracle all the Citty came in to Worship, tis now kept in the Chapell of the

Salutation, a place so inrich'd by the Devotas, as none save *Lau-retto* in *Italy* is said to exceede it: This picture they pretend was don by an *Angel*; tis always cover'd with 3 shutters, one of which is of massive silver: Mithinks tis very brown, the forehead & cheekes whiter, as if it had ben scraped with some thing: The⟨y⟩ report that those who have the honour of seeing it, never loose their sight as long as they live: happy then Wee: There is belonging to this Church a world of Plate, some whole statues of it & lamps innumerable, besides the Costly Vowes hung up, some of Gold, a Cabinet of precious Stones:

Visiting the Dukes Repository againe, we told at least 40 ranks of Porphyry & other statues, & 28 whole figures, many rare Paintings & Relievos: 2 Square Columns with Trophies: In one of the Galleries 24 figures, & 50 antique heads, a Bacchus of *M. Angelo* & one of *Bandinelli*, a head of *Bernini*, & a most lovely *Cupid* of Parian Marble, at the farther end two admirable Women sitting, & a Man fighting with a Centaure, & innumerable other nakeds: 3 figures in little of *Andrea*: an huge Candlestick of Amber, a woman of *Georgion*, a Table of Titians painting, & another representing God the Father sitting in the aire on the 4 Evangelists Animals, with divers smaler pieces of *Raphael*. A piece of pure Virgin Gold as big as an Egg: In the 3 Chamber of rarities is the 4 Square Cabinet valud at 80000 Crounes shewing every front with variety of curious work, one of birds & flowers of *Pietra Commessa*, the 2d a Descent from the Crosse of *M: Angelo*, on the 3d, our B: Savior & Apostles of Amber, on the 4th a Crucifix of the same, Twixt[1] the Pictures 2 naked Venus's of Titian, Adame & Eve of Durer, & severall other pieces of *Pordonon* & *del Frate*: Neere this, is a Globe of 6 foote diameter. In the Armorie, we saw an intire Elke, a Crocodile, & amongst the harnesse severall Targets, & horse armes antique, as that of *Charles* the V, two beset with Turcoises & other precious stones, an horses taile of an incredible length. Then passing the old Palace, which has an huge Hall for Feasts & Comedies, with a roofe rarely painted, & the side Walles of 6 very large Pictures representing batailes, the worke of *Gio: Vassari*: Here is a Magazine full of Plate, an harnesse of *Emralds*, the furniture of an Altar 4 foote high & six in length of Massy

1 'Entre les tableaux' in Evelyn's source—i.e. among.

Gold: In the middle is plac'd the statue of *Cosimo* II, the bass-relievos of precious stones: his breeches cover'd with diamonds; the Mouldings of this statue & other ornaments festoones &c. are garnish'd with jewells & huge pearles, dedicated to *St. Charles*, with this Inscription in Rubies. *Cosimus Secundus Dei gratia Magnus Dux Etruriæ, ex Voto*. There is also a King on horsebak of massy Gold 2 foote high, & an infinity of other suchlike rarities.

Looking on the Justice in Copper, set up on a Column by Cosmo 1555 after the Victorie over Sienna, we were told that when the Duke asking a Gentleman how he liked the piece; he answerd, that he liked it very well, but that it stood too high for poore men to come at it:

Prince *Leopold* has in this Citty a very excellent collection of Paintings especialy a St. *Catharine* of P: *Veroneze*, & a Venus of Marble vaild from the Navil to the feete, esteem'd to be of that greeke Workman who made the Venus at Medicis Palace in *Rome*, altogether as good, & better preserved, an inestimable statue, not long since found about *Boulognia*. Signor *Gaddi* is a letter'd person and has divers rarities statues, & Pictvres of the best Masters, & one bust of Marble as much esteem'd as the most antique in *Italy*. Many curious Manuscripts: his best paintings are a Virgin of *del Sarto* mention'd by *Vasari*, a *St. John* of *Raphael* & an *Ecce homo* of *Titian*.

They shew'd us the famous Academie de la Crusca which is a Hall hung about with Imprises & divices painted, all of them relating to Corne seifted from the brann, the seates are made like bread baskets, & other rustic Instruments usd about wheate, & the Cushions like sacks, of Satin:

Taking our last farewell of *St. Laurence*, and more particular notice of that piece of the R⟨e⟩surrection, it consists of an infinite number of Nudities, the work of *Pontarno*: On the left hand is the Martyrdom of St. *Laurence* of Bronzini rarely painted indeed: Here in a Chapell is the Tomb of *Pietro di Medices* & his bro: *Johns* of Coper, and rarely design'd, standing on 2 lions feete, which end in foliage, the work of M: Angelo, over against this Sepulchers of all the Ducal family: The altar has a statue of the Virgin Mary giving suck: & 2 Apostles: *Paulius Jovius* has the honor to be buried in the Cloister: Behind the quire is the superb Chapell of Ferdinand I, consisting of 8 faces, 4 plaine 4 hollowd a littl; in the 6 are to be the sepulchres & niches of Paragon, for the statue of the Prince now living: tis all of Coper gilt, and above a large table of Porphyrie for the Dukes Inscription in letters of Jasper: the whole Chapell, Walls, Pav⟨em⟩ent, roofe are nothing but precious stones, united with the Mouldings, which is also of gilded Coper, & so are the bases & Capitels of the Columns: The Custos or Tabernacle with the whole Altar is inlaied with Cornelius's, Lazuli, Serpentine, Achats, Onyxes: &c, on the other side are 6 huge Columns of rock Chrystal, 8 figures of precious stones of severall Colours inlayed in natural figures, not inferior to the best paintings, among which much Pearle, Diamond, Amethists, Topazes, indeede sumptuous & sparkling beyond description: The Windos without side are of White Marble: The Bibliotheca is the Architecture of *Raphael*, before the port is a square Vestibule of excellent Art, of all the orders without Confusion, & the Ascent to the Library from it incomparable: We numberd 88 shelves all MSS & bound in red, Chaind, in all about 3500 Volumes as they tell us:

The Arsenal has sufficient to arme 70000 men, accurately preserv'd & kept; with divers lusty pieces of Ordinance, whereof one for a ball of 300 pounds weight & another for 160 which weighs 72500 pounds:

The celebrated Masters at my being at Florence were for Pietro Commesso, a kind of Mosaique or inlaying of various Coloured Marbles & other more precious stones, were Domenico *Benotti*, & *Mazzotti*, The best Statuarie *Vincentio Brocchi* & Painter Piero *Berettini* called *Cortona*; The former statuarie makes those small statues in Plaster & Pastboard which so resemble Coper, that till one handles them they cannot be distinguishd, he has so rare an art of bronzing them: of this Artist I bought 4.

This Duke has a certaine daily tribute for every Curtezan or common Whore allow'd to practize that infamous trade in his Dominions & so has his holinesse the Pope, but not so much in value:

Taking now leave of our two jolly Companions Signor Giovanni & his Fellow, we tooke horses for *Bologna*, & by the way alighted at a Villa of the *Grand Dukes* call'd *Pratoline*, The House is a Square of 4 Pavilions, with a faire platform about it, balustr'd with stone, 'tis situate in a large meadow like an

amphitheater, ascending, having at the bottom a huge rock, with
Water running in a small Chanell like a Cascade, on the other
side the Gardens, the whole place seemes Consecrated to pleasure, & retirement in Summer: The Inside of the Palace may well
compare with any in Italy for furniture of Tapissry, beds &c: The
Gardens delicious & full of fountaines: In the Grove sits Pan
feeding his flock, the Water making a melodius sound through
his pipe, & an Hercules whose Club yeilds a Showre of Water,
which falling into a huge *Concha* has a Naked Woman riding on
the backs of Dolphins: In another Grotto is *Vulcan* & his family,
the walls richly composd of Coralls, Shells, Coper & Marble
figures; with the huntings of Severall beasts, moving by the force
of Water: Here having ben well wash'd for our Curiosity, we
went down a large Walk, at the sides whereof gushes out of
imperceptible pipes, couched under neath, slender pissings of
water, that interchangeably fall into each others Chanells, making a lofty & perfect arch, so as a man on horseback may ride
under it and not be wet with one drop, nay so high, as one may
walk with a speare in ones hand under each spout, this Canopi
or arch of Water, was mi thought one of the surprizings⟨t⟩ magnificences I had ever seene, & exceedingly fresh during the heate
of summer, at the End of this very long Walk stands a Woman
in white marble in posture of a Laundresse wringing Water out
of a piece of linnen very naturaly, into a vast Lavor, the work &
invention of the famous *Michael Angelo Buonaroti*: Hence we
ascended *Monte Parnasso*, where the Muses plaid to us on
Hydraulic Organs; neere this a greate Aviarie: The Sourse of all
these Waters are from the Rock in the Garden, on which the
statue of a Gyant representing the *Appennines* at the foote of
which stands this *Villa*: Last of all we came to the Labyrinth in
which a huge Colosse of *Jupiter*, that throws out a streame over
the Garden; This Moles is 50 foote in height, having in his body
a pretty Square chamber, his Eyes and mouth serving for the
Windos & dore: Having view'd these rarities we tooke horse &
supped that night at *il Ponte*, passing a dreadfull ridge of the
Appennines, in many places cap'd with Snow, which covers them
the whole summer long: We thence descend into a luxurious &
rich plaine; the next day passing through *Scarperia*, mounting
the hills againe, where the passage is so strait, & precipitious
towards the right hand, as with much care & danger we climbed

them, lodging ⟨at⟩ *Fiorenzuolo*, which is a Fort built among the Cliffs & rocks, & defending the Confines of the Greate Dukes Territories: The next day we passe by the *Pietra Mala* a burning Mountaine: at the summet of this prodigious Masse of hills, we had an unpleasant way to *Pianura*, where we slept that night, & were entertaind with excellent Wine: hence to *Scargalasino* & to bed to *Loiano*, this plaine begins about six Miles from *Bologna*.

This Towne belongs to the Pope, & is a famous University, situate in one of the fattest spots of Europe, for all sorts of Provisions: tis built like a ship, whereof the *Torre d'Asinello* may go for the Main-Mast: the Citty is of no greate strength, a trifling Wall about it, & is in Circuit neere five miles, & 2 in length: This *Torre d'Asinello* ascended by 447 stepps of a foote rise, seemes exceeding high, as being also but very narrow, & is the more conspicuous by another Tower cal'd *Garisenda* so artificialy built of brick (which increases the Wonder) as one would think it were allways ready to fall, tis not now so high as the other, but they say was formerly: but was so far taken down, for feare it should realy fall & do mischief: Next we went to see an Imperfect Church cald St. *Petronius*, shewing the intent of the founder had he gon on: from this our guid led us to the Schooles, which are indeede very magnificent: Then to St. Dominics, where that Saints body lies richly inshrind: The Stalls or seates of this good⟨l⟩y Chur⟨c⟩h has the historie of the Bible inlaied with severall woods, very curiously don, the work of one Fr: Damiano d'Bergomo, & a Frier of that Order: Amongst other Reliques they pretend to shew the two bookes of Esdras, writen with his own hand: Here lies buried Ja: Andreas & divers other learn'd persons: To the Church joynes the Convent, in the quadrangle where-of the⟨y⟩ shew'd us old Cypresses that they affirme were planted by their Saint: hence they led us to *St. Dominics* chamber, & gave us a tast of incomparable Wine: Then we went to the Palace of the *Legat*, a faire brick building (as are most of the houses & buildings of the Citty) full of excellent carving and mouldings, so as nothing in stone seemes to be better finish'd or Ornamentall, witnesse those incomparable Columns to be seene in many of their Churches, Convents & publique buildings, for the whole Towne is so cloysterd, that one may passe from house to house through the Streetes without being exposd either to raine or Sun:

Before the stately Hall of this Palace stands the Statue of
Paule the 4th and divers others, also the Monument of the
Coronation of Charles the 5t. The Piazza before it is absolutely
the most stately in all Italy, St. Marks at *Venice* onely excepted;
In the center of it is a Fountain of *Neptune*, a noble figure cast in
Coper: I here saw a Persian walking about in a very rich vest of
cloth of tissue, & severall other ornaments according to the
fashion of their Country, which did exceedingly please me, he
was a young handsom person of the most stately mîne I had ever
observd: faine I would have seene the Library of St. Saviours
famous for the quantity of rare Manuscripts, but could not, so
we went to St. *Francis's* a glorious pile & exceedingly adorn'd
within: After dinner I enquird out a Priest, and Dr. *Montalbano*,
to whom I brought recommendations from Rome: This was he
who invented or found out the famous composition of the *Lapis
illuminabil⟨i⟩s* or *Phosphorus*, which he shew'd me, their property
(for he shewd me severall) being to retaine the light of the sun
for some competent time, by a kind of imbibition, by a particular
way of Calcination: some of these presented a blew colour like
the flame of brimestone, others like coales of culinary fire: The
rest of the Afternoone was taken up in *St. Michall in bosco*, built
on a steepe hill, on the Edge of the Citty: & is for its fabric,
Celars, pleasant shade, & groves, Cellars, dormitory & prospect
one of the most delicious retirements that in my whole life I ever
saw: Art & nature contending whither shall exceede, so as 'till
now I never envied the life of a Frier, who here live so sweetely
as nothing can be more desird: The whole Towne, & Country to
a vast extent is under command of their eye, almost as far as
Venice itselfe and the sea: There are in this Convent many rare
Paintings of *Guido Rheni*, above all the little Cloister of 8 faces
painted by *Carrachio* in *fresco*: But the Carvings in Wood of the
Sacristie is stupendious; here is admirable inlay'd work about the
Chapell that even emulates the best of paintings the Work is
don so delicately & tender: The paintings of *St. Saviour* are of
Carrachio & *Leonardo*, & excelent things of *Raphael* which we
could not see: but in the Church of *St. John* there is an incomparable piece of St. *Cicilia* don by *Raphael*: As to other Paintings
there is in the Church of St. *Gregorio* an excelent picture of a
Bishop giving the habit of *St. Bernard* to a Souldier arm'd with
severall other figures in the piece, the work of *Guerchino*:

Indeede this Citty is full of rare Pieces, especialy of *Guido*, *Domenico*, and a Virgin nam'd *Isabell Sirani* now living, who has painted many excellent Pieces, & imitates *Guido* so well, that many skillfull Artists have ben deceiv'd: At the Mendicanti are the Miracles of St. *Eloy* by *Rheni* after the manner of *Caravagio*, but better: & here they shew'd us that famous piece of Hanibal *Carrach*, *Christs* calling St. *Mathew*: The Marques *Magniani* has the whole freeze of his Hall painted in fresco by the same hand:

   Many of the Religious men here nourish those Lap-dogs had so in delicijs by the Ladies, which they sell, they are a pigmie sort of Spaniels, whose noses they breake whe⟨n⟩ puppies, which in my opinion deformes them: At the end of the turning in one of the Wings of the Dormitorie of *St. Michael* I found a paper pasted neere the Window, containing the dimensions of most of the famous churches in Italy, compar'd with their Toures, & the length of this gallerie, a copy whereof I tooke.

	Braccia	Piedi di Bolognia	Cana di Roma
St. Pietro di Roma longo...	284	473	84
Cuppola del muro Alta....	210	350	60
Torre d'Asinello Alto....	208⁴/₅	348	59 ⟨palmi⟩: 6
Dormitorio de St. Mich: a Bologni ⟨Longo⟩....	254	423	72¹/₂

From hence being brought to a kingdome or subterranean territorie of Cellars, the Courteous Friars made us tast of variety of incomparable Wine & so we departed to our Inn:

   This Citty is famous also for *Salsicci*, & sell a World of Parmegiano Cheeze, with Botargo, Caviare &c: which makes some of their shops perfume the streetes with no agreable smell: here we furnish'd ourselves with Wash-balls, the best being made here, and a considerable commodity: This place has likewise ben famous for *Lutes*, made by the old Masters *Mollen*, *Hans Frey*, *Nic: Sconvelt*, which were of extraordinary price, & were most of them German Workmen. I observd the drawing Cattel about this Country (which is very rich & fertile, especially of Pasturage) are cover'd with *housses* of linnen freing'd at the bottome, that dangle about them, & preserve them from the flyes: which in summer are very troublesome to them.

From this pleasant Citty we went now towards *Ferrara*, carrying with us a *Bulletino* or Bill or Certificat of Sanità (costomarie in all these jealous parts of *Italy*, especialy the state of *Venice*) & so put our selves in a boate that was tawd with horses, & often interrupted by the sluces (inventions there to raise the Water for the use of mills, & to fill the artific(i)al chanells) at every of which we stayed till passage was made: Here we went by the Castle *Bentivoglio*, & about night arriv'd at an ougly Inn calld *Mal Albergo* agreable to its name, whence after we had supp'd, we Embarkd, & passe that night through the Fenns, where we were so pester'd with those flying *Glow-wormes* cald *Luccioli*, that one who had never heard of them, would thinke the Country full of sparks of fire, in so much as beating some of them downe & applying them to a book, I could reade in the darke, by the light they afforded; quitting now our Boate, we took Coach, & by morning, got to *Ferrara*, where before we were admitted entrance, our Gunns & Armes were taken from us, of Costome, the lock being taken of before, as we were advis'd: The Citty is situated in a low marshy Country, & therefore well fortified, perhaps by few excelld for the workes: The houses & streetes have nothing of beauty, excepting the Palace, & Church of st. Benedict, where the famous *Ariosto* lies buried: & some good Statues there are: The *Palazzo Del Diamante*, *Citadel*, Church of st. *Dominico*: The Market place, which is indeede very spacious, having in its center the Figure of *Nicholao Olaö* (once Duke of Ferrara) in Coper, on horse back: Tis in a word a durty Towne, & though the Streetes be large, they remaine illpav'd: Yet it is an University, & now belongs to the Pope: One thing I must not forget, that though there be not many fine houses in the Citty, yet the Inn where we lodg'd was a very noble Palace bear(in)g an *Angel* for its signe: We parted from hence about 3 in the after noone, & went some of our way on the Chanell, & then Imbark'd upon the *Po*, or *Padus*, by the Poets call'd *Eridanus*, where they faine *Phaeton* to have falln, after his rash attempt, & *Io:* metamorphosd into a Cow: There was in our Company, among others, a *Polonian* Bishop, who was exceedingly civill to me in this passage, & afterwards did me many kindnesses at *Venice*. We supp'd this night at a place call'd *Corbua*, neere the ruines of the antient Citty *Adria*, which gives name to the *Gulph* or *Sea*: After 3 miles we Imbarkd in a stout Vessell (having made

30 on the Po) & thro⟨ugh⟩ an artificial Chanell very strait, entred the *Adice*, which carried us by break of day into the Adriatic, & so sailing prosperously by *Chioza* (a Town upon an Iland in this sea) & *Palestina*, another; we came over against *Malamocco* (the chiefe port, & ankerage where our English Merchant men lie, that trade to Venice) where we arived about 7 at night, after we had stayed at the least two houres for our Permission to land, our Bill of Sanità being deliver'd according to costome: so soone as we came on shore we were conducted to the Dogana, where our Portmanteaus were visited, & so got to our lodging, which was at honest *Signor Paulo Rhodomants* at the *Aquila Nera* neere the Rialto, & one of the best quarters of the Towne. This journey from *Rome* to *Venice*, cost me 7: *Pistoles* & 13 *Julios*.

June. The next morning finding my-selfe extreamly weary, & beaten with my Journey, I went to one of their *Bagnias*, which are made, & treate after the Eastern manner, washing one with hot & cold water, with oyles, rubbing with a kind of Strigil, which a naked youth puts on his hand like a glove of seales Skin, or what ever it be, fetching off a world of dirt, & stretching out on⟨e⟩s limbs, then claps ⟨on⟩ a depilatorie made of a drug or earth they call *Resina*, that comes out of Turky, which takes off all the haire of the body, as resin dos a piggs. I think there is orpiment & lime in it, for if it lie on to long it burns the flesh: The curiosity of this Bath, did so open my pores that it cost me one of the greatest Colds & rheumes that ever I had in my whole life, by reason of my comming out without that caution necessary of keeping my selfe Warme for some time after: For I immediately began to visite the famous Places of the Citty And Travellers, do nothing else but run up & downe to see sights, that come into *Italy*: And this Citty, for being one of the most miraculously plac'd of any in the whole World, built on so many hundred Ilands, in the very sea, and at good distance from the Continent, deser⟨v⟩'d our admiration: It has neither fresh, nor any other but salt Water, save what is reserved in Cistrens, of the raine, & such as is daily brought them from *Terra firma* in boates: Yet it wa⟨nt⟩s nor fresh water, nor aboundance of all sorts of excellent Provisions, very cheape. 'Tis reported that when the *Hunns* overran all *Italy*, some meane fishermen & others left the Maine land, & fled to these despicable & muddy Ilands for Shelter, where in processe of time, & by Industry, it is growne to

the greatnesse of one of the most considerable states in the
World, consider'd as a *Republique* & having now subsisted
longer, than any of the foure antient Monarchies, & flourishing
in greate State, welth & glory by their Conquests of greate
Territories in Italy, Dacia, Greece, Candy, Rhodes, Slavonia, &
at present challenging the Empire of all the Adriatique Sea,
which they yearly espouse, by casting a gold ring into it, with
greate pomp & ceremony upon Ascention day: the desire of
seing this, being one of the reasons, that hastned us from *Rome*:
First the *Dodge* or Duke (having heard Masse) in his robes of
State (which are very particular & after the Eastern) together
with the Senat in their gownes, Imbarkd in their gloriously
painted, carved & gilded *Bucentoro*, invirond & follow'd by
innumerable Gallys, Gundolas, & boates filled with Spectators,
some dressed in Masqu⟨e⟩rade, Trumpets, musique, & Canons,
filling the whole aire with din: Thus having rowed out about a
league into the Gulph, the Duke at the prow casts into the Sea
a Gold ring, & Cup, at which a loud acclamation is Echod by
the greate Guns of the Arsenale, and at the *Liddo*: & so we
returnd: Two days after taking a *Gundola* which are their Water
Coaches, (for land ones many old men in this Citty never saw
any, or rarely a horse) we rowed up & downe the Channells,
which are as our Streetes; These *Vessells* are built very long &
narrow, having necks and tailes of steele, somewhat spreading at
the beake like a fishes taile, & kept so exceedingly polish'd as
giues a wonderfull lustre: some are adornd with carving, others
lined with Velvet, commonly black, with Curtains & tassals, &
the seates like Couches to lie stretch'd on, while he who rowes,
stands on the very edge of the boate, upright, and with one Oare
(bending forward as if they would precipitate into the Sea) rows,
& turnes, with incredible dexterity, thus passing from Channell
to Channell, & landing his fare or patron, at what house he
pleases: The beakes of these vessells are not unlike the Roman
antient Rostrums: The first thing I went to see of publique
building was the *Rialto*, celebrated for passing over the *grand
Canale* with one onely Arch, so large as to admitt a Gally to row
thro⟨ugh⟩ it, built of good Marble, & having on it, besides many
pretty shops, three stately & ample passages for people, without
any incumbrance, the 2 outmost nobly balustr'd with the same
stone, a piece of Architecture to be admir'd. It was Evening &

the Canale (which is their Hide-park, where the Noblesse go to take the aire) was full of Ladys & Gent; & there are many times very da⟨n⟩gerous stops by reason of the multitude of Gu⟨n⟩dalos, ready to sink one another, & indeede they affect to leane them so ⟨on⟩ one side, that one who is not accostom'd to it, would be afraid of over setting: Here they were singing, playing on harpsicords, & other musick & serenading their Mistriss's: In another place, racing, & other *passe tempi* on the Water, it being now exceeding hot: I went next day to their Exchange, a place like ours, frequented by Merchants, but nothing so magnificent; from thence my Guide had me to the *Fondigo di Todeschi* which is their magazine, & here the Merchants (as in a Coledge) having their lodging and diet many of them, especially Germons; the outside of this stately fabric is painted by *Geo: Castel Franco*, & *Titian* himselfe: hence I pass'd through the *Merceria*, which I take to be the most delicious streete in the World for the sweetenesse of it, being all the way on both sides, continualy tapissry'd as it were, with Cloth of Gold, rich Damasks & other silks, which the shops expose & hang before their houses from the first floore, & with that variety, that for neere halfe the yeare, which I spent chiefly in this citty, I hardly remember to have seene the same piece twice exposd, to this add the perfumers & Apothecaries shops, and the innumerable cages of Nightingals, which they keepe, that entertaines you with their melody from shop to shop, so as shutting your Eyes, you would imagine your selfe in the Country, when indeede you are in the middle of the Sea: besides there being neither rattling of Coaches nor trampling of horses, tis almost as silent as the field: This streete, pav'd with brick, and exceedingly cleane, brought us through an arch into famous *Piazzo* St. *Marco*, over this Porch, stands that admirable Clock, celebrated next to that of *Strasburg*, for its many movements, amongst which, about 12 & 6, which is their houre of *Ave Maria*, when all the towne are on their knees, comes forth the 3 Kings led by a Starr, & passing by the Imoge of Christ in his Mothers armes, do their reverence, & enter into the Clock by another doore: at the top of this turret another Automat strikes the quarters; & this I mention for a storie affirmd to me by an honest merchant, That walking on⟨e⟩ day in the Piazza he saw the fellow who kept the Clock, struck with this hammer so forcably, as he was stooping his head neere the bell to mend something amisse, at the instant of striking, that being stunn'd, he reel'd over the battlements, & brake his neck. The buildings about this *Piazza* are all Arched, on Pillars, within pav'd with white & black polish'd Marble, even to the Shops, the rest of the fabric as stately as any in Europ, being not onely marble, but the architecture of the famous *Sansovini*, who lies buried in *St. Jacomo* at the End of the *Piazzo*: The battlements of this noble range of building is raild with stone, & thick set with excellent statues, which add a wonderfull ornament; yet is one of the sides, much more Roman like than the other, I meane that which reguards the Sea, & where the church is placd: The other range is plainly Gotic, & so we entred into St. Marks Church, before which stand two brasse piedestals exquisitely cast, & figur'd, which beare as many tall masts, painted red, on which upon greate festivals, they hang flags & streamers: This famous Church is also Gotic, yet for the preciousnesse of the Materials, being of severall rich marbles, aboundanc of Porphyrie, serpentine &c: far exceeding any of *Rome*, St. *Peters* hardly excepted; & first I much admired the splendid historie of our B: Saviour, composd all of *Mosaic* over the faciata, below which, & over the chiefe Gate, are 4 horses cast in Coper, as big as the life, the same that formerly were transported from *Rome* by *Constantine* to *Byzantium*, & thence by the *Venetians* hither: Being come into the Church, you see nothing, & tread on nothing but is precious, The floore all inlayed with Achats, Lazulis, Calcedons, Jaspers, Porphyrie and other rich marbles, in admirable sort for the work, the walls sumptuously incrusted, & presenting to the Imagination the Shapes of Men, birds, trees, houses, flowers & a thousand varieties: The roofe is of incomparable Mosaic also: but what most admire is the new work of the Emblematic Tree at the other issue of the Church. In the midst of this rich Volto, rises 5 *Cupolas*, the middle very large, and sustayn'd by 36 marble Columns, 8 of which are of precious Marbles: Under these Cupola is the high Altar, on which stands a Reliquarie of severall sorts of Jewels engraven with figures after the *Greeke* manner, & set together with plates of pure Gold: The Altar is cover'd with a Canopy of *Ophit*, on which is Sculptur'd the storie of the Bible, & so on the Pillars (which are of Parian Marble) that support it. Behind these are 4 other Columns of transparant, & true Oriental *Alabaster*, which was brought hither out of the ruines of Salomons Temple, as they report. There are besides many Chapells, & notable Moniments of Illustrious Persons, Dukes, Cardinals &c as *Zeno*, *Jo: Soranzi* &c: & there is a vast *Baptisterie* of Coper, among other venerable Reliques a stone on which they say our B: Lord stood preaching to those of *Tyre* & *Sidon*, & neere the doore, an Image of Christ, much ador'd, as esteeming it very sacred, for that a rude fellow striking it, they say, there gush'd out a torrent of blood: In one of the Corners, lies the Body of St. *Isidore* brought hither 500 years since from the Iland *Chios*; a little farther they shew the picture of St. *Dominic* & *Francis*, affirm'd to have ben made by the *Abbot Joachim*, many yeares before any of them were born: Going out of the Church they shew'd us the stone where Alexand: 3d trod on the neck of the Emp: *Fred: Barbarossa*, pronouncing that of the Psalme *Super basiliscum* &c.

The dores of the Church are of massie Coper; The Pillars employd in this building are neere 500, most of them Porphyrie & Serpentine, & brought chiefly from *Athens* & other parts of Greece, formerly in their power: The 8 Porphyrie Columns at the front, that sustaine the horses are of immense bignesse & value: At the Corner of the Church are inserted into the maine Wall, 4 figures as big as the naturall cut in Porphyrie, whom they say are the Images of 4 Brothers who poysne'd one the other, by which meanes there Escheated to the Republique that vast Treasurey of Reliques, belonging to the Church: At the other Entrance, which looks towards the Sea, stands in a small Chapell that statue of our *Lady*, made (as they affirme) of the same stone or rock, out of which *Moses* brought Water to the Murmuring *Israelites* at *Horeb*, or *Meriba*: But when all is said, as to this Church, tis in my opinion much too dark, & dismal, & of heavy work: The fabric, as is much of Venice, both for bu(i)ldings & other fashions & circumstances much after the Greekes, their next neighbours:

The next day, by favour of the *French Ambassador* (who went to see the Reliquarie, call'd here the *Tresoro de San Marco*, & which very few even of Travellors are addmitted to see) I had admittance: The rarities I most observ'd (which is a large Chamber full of Presses) were the 12 breast plates or pieces of pure Golden Armour studied with precious stones, & as many Crownes of Gold, which they told us were dedicated to St. *Mark*,

by as many noble *Venetians* who had recovered their Wives taken
at Sea by the *Saracen*; Many curious Vasas of Achat, & the Cap
or Cornet of the Dukes of Venice, one of which had an extreame
rich & glorious Rubie set on it, esteemed at 200 thousand
Crownes; There were shew'd two Unicorns hornes, a world of
Vasas & Dishes of Achat set thick with precious Stones, & vast
pearles: Also divers heads of Saints, inchas'd in Gold: In another
part of this Treasurie we were shewed by a Priest (who first
vested himselfe in his sacerdotals, with the Stola about his neck)
the *Evangelium* of *St. Mark* the *Venetians* Patron or Tutelarie,
affirmed to be written by his owne hand, & whose Body (transported many yeares since from Alexandria) they shew buried in
this Church: Also a small Ampulla or glasse of our B: Saviou⟨r⟩s
blood, as they fancy: A greate morcell of the real Crosse, one of
the nailes, a Thorne, a fragment of the Column to which our
Lord was bound, when Scourged: The Labbarum or Ensigne
[Standard] of victorious *Constantine*, a piece of St. *Lukes* arme, a
rib of St. *Stephen*, a finger of Mary Magdalene & a world of
Reliques I could not remember. [The *Religioni de li Servi*, have
rare paintings of *P. Veroneze* especialy the *Magdalen*.]

From hence a French Gent: & myselfe got one to conduct us
to the Courts of Justice, the Senate house, & Ducal Palace:

The first Court, neere the Church, is almost quite built of several colourd & sorts of Marble, like chequer work, on the out
side, this is sustain'd with vast Pillars, not very Shapefull, but for
their Capitels observable, & that of 33 there are none like one
another. Under the fabrick ⟨is⟩ the Cloyster where merchants
meete morning and Evening, as also the grave Senators &
Gentlmen, to confer of State affaires, in their Gownes and Caps,
like so many Philosophers, & 'tis a very noble & solemn spectacle:
Hence we pass'd to another quadrangle in which stood two
Columns square of white Marble carved, which the⟨y⟩ affirm'd
had ben erected to hang one of their *dukes* on, who design'd to
make himselfe Sovraigne; Afterwards going through a stately
Arch, they shewd us divers Statues standing in *Niches* of greate
value, among which the so celebrated *Eve*, esteem'd worth its
weight in Gold, & is plac'd just opposite to the staires, where are
two *Colossus's* of *Mars* & *Neptune* the worke of *Sansovinus*, & so
we went up into a Coridore built with several Tribunals &
Courts of Justice, & by a rarely contriv'd staire-Case were landed

in the *Senate hall*, which appeare⟨s⟩ to be one of the most noble &
capacious roome⟨s⟩ of *Europ* being 76 paces long, 32 in breadth:
At the upper end are the Tribunals of the *Doge, Council of Ten*, &
assistants; In the body of the hall, lower ranks of seates, capable
of containing 1500 Senators, for they consist of no fewer, upon
grand debates: Here are those gallant Paintings of the final
Judgement, just over the Dukes Throne, the work of *Tintoret*, &
esteem'd amongst the best pieces in *Europe*: On the roof are the
famous Acts of the Repub⟨l⟩ick, painted by severall excellent
Masters, especialy *Bassano*; & next them the Effigies of the Severall Dukes with their *Elogies*. Then we turn'd into a greate
Court, painted with the battail of Lepanto, an incomparable
piece: Thence into the Chamber of the Council of *Ten*, all of
them painted by the most celebrated Masters: From hence, by
the special favour of an *Illustrissimo* we were carried to see the
private Armorie of the Palace, and so to the same Court we first
Enter'd, nobly built of polish'd white Marble, part of which being
the *Dukes* Court pro Tempore, there are two Wells, adornd with
incomparable Worke in Coper: This lead us to the sea-side,
where those two Columns stand of *Ophite* stone, in the intire
piece, & a greate height, one bearing the Statue of St. *Marks*
Lion, the other St. *Theodorus*: These Pillars were brought from
Greece, & set up by Nic: *Baraterius* the Architect; betweene which
publique Executions are don: Here having fed our Eyes with the
noble prospe⟨c⟩t of the Iland St. George, the Gallies, Gudolas, &
other Vessells, passing to & froo, we tooke a walke under the
Cloyster of the opposite side of this goodly *Piazza*, being a most
magnificent building, the designe of *Sansovino*: Here we went
into the *Zecca* or *Mint*, at whose entrance stand two prodigious
Gyants or *Hercules* of white marble: So we saw them Melt, beate,
& coyne *silver, Gold, Coper*; Then went up into the Procuratorie,
& a Library of excellent MSS & books that belongs to it, & the
publique: After this we Climb'd-up the Toure of St. *Marco*,
which we might as well have don on Horsebak, as tis said one of
the French-kings did; there being no stayres or steps, but
returnes that take up an intire Square upon the arches, broad
enough for a Coach: [namely 40 foote.] This steeple stands by it
selfe without any Church neere it, & is rather a Watch Toure in
the Corner of the great Piazza, 230 foote in height; They say the
foundation of it is exceeding deepe, on the top is an Angel that

turns with the Wind, & has a prospect down the Adriatic as far
as Istria & the Dalmatian side, with the surprizing sight of this
Mira⟨c⟩ulous Cittie which lies in the boosome of the sea in the
shape of a Lute, the numberlesse Ilands tack'd together by no
fewer than 450 bridges. At the foote of this Toure is a publique
Tribunal of incomparable Worke in white marble polish'd,
adornd with several brasse Statues, & figures of stone in *Mezzo
relievo*, the worke of some rare artist:

Twas now *Ascention* Weeke, & the greate Mart or faire of the
whole yeare now kept, every body at liberty, & jollie; the Noble-
men stalking with their Ladys on *Choppines* about 10 foote high
from the ground. These are high heeld shoos particularly
affected by these proude dames, or as some say, invented to
keepe them at home, it being so difficult to walke with them,
whence one being asked how he liked the *Venetian* Dames,
replyd, they were *Mezzo Carne, Mezzo Legno*; & he would have
none of them: The truth is their Garb is very odd, as seeming
allwayes in Masquerade, their other habite also totaly different
from all Nations: The⟨y⟩ weare very long crisped haire of severall
strakes and Colours, which they artificially make so, by washing
their heads in pisse, & dischevelling them on the brims of a
broade hat that has no head, but an hole to put out their head
by, drie them in the Sunn, as one may see them above, out of
their windos: In their tire they set silk flowers & sparkling
stones, their peticoates comming from their very armepetts, so
high as that their very breasts flub over the tying place; so as they
are neare three quarters & an halfe Aporn: Their Sleeves are
made exceeding wide, under which their smock sleeves as wide
& commo⟨n⟩ly tucked up to the shoulder, & shewing their
naked arme, through false Sleeves of Tiffany girt with a bracelet
or two: besides this they go very bare of their breasts & back,
with knots of poynts richly tagg'd, about their shoulders & other
places, of their body, which the⟨y⟩ usualy cover with a kind of
yellow Vaile of Lawn very transparant. Thus attir'd they set their
hands on the heads of two Matron-like servants or old women
to support them, who are mumbling their beades: Tis very
ridiculous to see how these Ladys crawle in & out of their *Gundolas* by reason of their Choppines, & what dwarfes they appeare
when taken down from their Wooden scafolds: Of these I saw
neere 30 together stalking, halfe as high more, as the rest of the

World; for Curtezans or the Citizens may not weare Chopines, but cover their bodies & faces with a vaile of a certaine glistring Taffata or Lustrèe, out of which they now & then dart a glaunce of their Eye, the whole face being otherwise intirely hid with it: Nor may the Common *Misses* or Whores, take this habite, but go about beare fac'd: To the corners of these Virgin Vailes hang broad but flat tassels of curious Point de Venize: The Married Women go in black Vailes: In the same Colour, but of fine Cloth, do all the Nobility weare, lind with taffata in Summer, with furre of the bellys of Squirills in the Winter, which all put on at a certaine day, girt with a girdle emboss'd with silver: The Vest, not much different from what our Batchelors of Art weare in Oxford, & an hood of Cloth made like a sack, cast over their left shoulder, & a round cloth black Cap, frieng'd with wooll: which is not so comely: They also weare their Collar open, to shew the diamond button of the Stock of their Shirt: But never have I seene pearle for oriency & bignesse comparable to what the Ladys weare, most noble families being very rich in jewells, especialy Pearle, which allways is left to the son or brother who is destin'd to Marry, which the eldest seldome do: The *Dodges* vest is of Crimson Velvet, the Procurator's &c. of Damasc very stately: Nor was I lesse surpriz'd with the strange variety of the severall Nations which we every day met with in the Streetes & Piazza of Jewes, Turks, Armenians, Persians, Moores, Greekes, Sclavonians, some with their Targets & boucklers, & all in their native fashions, negotiating in this famous *Emporium*, which is allways crouded with strangers. This night, having with my Lord Bruce taken our places before, we went to the Opera, which are Comedies [& other plays] represented in Recitative Music by the most excellent Musitians vocal & Instrumental, together with variety of Seeanes painted & contrived with no lesse art of Perspective, and Machines, for flying in the aire, & other wonderfull motions. So taken together it is doubtlesse one of the most magnificent & expensfull diversions the Wit of Men can invent: The historie was *Hercules* in Lydia, the Seanes chang'd 13 times, The famous Voices *Anna Rencia* a Roman, & reputed the best treble of Women; but there was an *Eunuch*, that in my opinion surpass'd her, and a *Genoveze* that sung an incomparable Base: This held us by the Eyes and Eares til two in the Morning when we went to the *Chetto* de San: Felice, to see the Noblemen & their Ladies at *Basset*, a Game at Cards which much use, but play not in publique & with all that have inclination to it, in Masquerad, without speaking so much as one word, & so come in, play, loose, or gaine, & go away as they please: This time of Licence is not all the yeare long, but onely in Carnoval, & this Ascention Weeke, neither are their Theaters open for that other Magnificenc, or for ordinary Comedians, save on these solemnities; they being a frugal & wise people and exact observer of all sumptuarie Laws.

There being at the time a ship bound for the Holy Land, I had now resolved to imbarke myselfe, intending to see Jerusalem, & others parts of Syria, Egypt, & Turky: but after I was provided of all necessaries, laied in Snow to coole our drink, bought some Sheepe, Poultry, Bisquit, Spirits & a little Cabinet of Drouggs &c. in case of sicknesse; our Vessell (whereof Cap: Powell was Master) happnd to be press'd for the service of the State, to Carry Provisions to *Candia*, which was now nuly attacqu'd by the Turkes; which altogether frustrated my designe, to my greate sorrow, it being but two or 3 daies before we hoped to set saile.

On the   of June we went to Padöa to the faire of their *St. Anthony*, in company of divers Passengers, the first *Terra firma* we landed at was *Fusina*, being onley an Inn, where we changed our Barge, & were then drawne up with horses through the River *Brenta*, a strait Chanell, as even as a line for 20 miles, the Country on both sides deliciously planted with Country Villas & gentlemens retirements, Gardens planted with Oranges, Figs, & other fruit, belonging to the *Venetians*. At one of these *Villas* we went on shore to see a pretty contrivd Palace: Observable in this passage was their buying their Water of those who farme the sluces, for this artificial river is in some places so shallow, that reserves of water are kept with sluces, which they open & shut with a most ingenious invention or Engine, so as to be governd even by a child: Thus they keep up the water, or dismisse it, till the next channell be either filled by the stop, or abated to the level of the other; for which every boate pays a certaine dutie: Thus we stayd neere halfe an houre, & more at 3 severall interruptions, so as it was evening ere we got to *Padoa*: Which is a very antient Cittie, if the tradition of *Antenors* being the founder be not a fiction: But thus speakes the Inscription over a stately Gate.

Hanc antiquissimam urbem literarum omnium asylum, cujus agrum fertilitatis lumen natura esse voluit, Antenor condidit, Anno ante Christum natum. M.C.XVIII. senatus autem Venetus his belli (propugnaculis) ornavit. The Towne stands on *Padus*, whence its name, & is generaly built like Bolonia, on Arches, & on Brick, so as one m⟨a⟩y walke all about it dry, & in the shade, which is very convenient in these hot Countries, & I think I was never in my whole life sensible of so burning a heate, as was this season, especialy the next day, which was that of the faire, which was fill'd with *Noble Venetians*, by reason of a greate & solemn Procession to their famous Cathedrall: Here passing by St. Lorenzo I met this Inscription

> C. Inclytus Antenor patriam Vox Nisa quietem
> Transtulit huc Henetum Dardanidumque fuga(s),
> Expulit Euganeos, Patavinam condidit urbem,
> Quem tegit hic humili marmore cæsa domus.

Under the Tomb, was a Cobler at his work: Being now come to St. Antonies (the streete most of the way, strait, well built, & outsides excellently painted in *fresco*) we surveied the spacious ⟨Piazza⟩, in which is erected a noble Statue of Coper on horse back, in memorie of one *Catta Malata*, a renouned Captaine: The Church *a la Greca*, consists of five handsome *Cupolas* leaded: At the left hand within is the Tomb of St. *Antonio*, and his Altar, about which a *Mezzo relievo* of the Miracles ascribd to their Saint, exquisitely wrought in white Marble by the 3 famous Sculptors *Tullius Lombardus, Jacobus Sansovinus,* & *Hieron Compagno*: a little higher is the Quire, walld parapet fashion with sundry coloured stone, in which are inserted divers tables of cast coper, of the historie of the Bible in halfe *relievo*, the work of *Andrëo Reccij.* The Altar within is of the same metall, which with the Candlestick & Bases, in my opinion, is as magnificent as any in *Italy*: The Wainscot also of the Quire is rarely inlayed & Carv'd: Here are the sepulchres of many famous persons, as of *Rudolpho Fulgosi* &c: & among the rest one that for an exploit at sea, has a Gally exquisitly carved on it: The Procession bore the banners, together with all the Treasure of the Cloyster, which was a very glorious sight: Henc walking over the *Prato della Valle* I went to see the Convent of *St. Justinas*, than which I never beheld a more magnificent: The Church is an incomparable

piece of Architecture, of *Andrea Paladios*, richly pav'd, with a
stately Cupola that Covers the high Altar, which inshrines the
ashes of that Saint: It is of *Pietra Commessa*, consisting of flowers
very natural: The Quire is also inlayd with the holy historie of
severall sorts of wood, with exceeding industry: at the far end, is
that rare Painting of St. *Justinas* Martyrdom, by *P: Veronese*, and
a stone, upon which they told us divers Primitive Christians had
be⟨en⟩ decapitated: & in another place (to which leads a small
cloister well painted) a dry well or pit, coverd with a brasse work
grate, where in are the bones of divers Martyrs. They shew here
likewise the Bones of *St. Luke* in an old alabaster Coffin, and
Three of the holy Innocents, the bodys of *St. Maximus* & *Pros-
docimus*: The Dormitory above is exceeding commodius &
stately; but what most pleas'd me were the old Cloyster, so well
painted with the legendarie Saints, mingled with many antient
Inscriptions, & pieces of *Urnes* dug up it seemes, at the foundation of the Church: Thus having spent the day in rambling,
I returnd the next to *Venice*: Our next sally was the *Arsenal*
thought to be one of the best furnish'd in the World: We entrd
by a strong port, allways guarded, & ascending a spacious
Gallery, saw armes of back, breast & head, for many Thousands,
in another were Saddles, & over them divers Ensignes taken
from the Turks: Another hall is for the meeting of the Senat:
passing a Graft, are the Smiths forges, where they are continualy
at work on Ankers & Iron work: Neere it a Well of fresh Water
which they impute to two Rinoceros's hornes which they say lie
in it, & will preserve it from ever being empoison'd: Then we
came to where the Carpenters were building, their Magazines of
Oares, Masts, &c for an hundred Gallys & ships, which have all
their aparell, & furniture neere them: Then the *fundarie*, where
they cast *Ordinance*: The forge is 450 paces long, & one of them
has 13 furnaces: There is one Canon weighing 16573 pounds cast
whilst *Henry* the 3d dined, & put into a Gally, built, rigg'd & fitted for launching within that time: They have also armes for 12
Galeasses, which are Vessells to row of almost 150 foote long,
and 30 large: not counting prow or poup, & contain 28 banks
each 7. men, & so carry 1300 Men: with 3 masts: In another a
Magazin for 50 Gallys, & place for some hundreds more: Here
stands the Bucentaur, with a most ample deck, & so contriv'd,
that the Slaves are not seene, having on the *Poup* a Thron for the

Dodge to sit, when he gos in tryumph to espouse the *Adriatic*:
here is also a gallery of 200 yards long for Cables, and over that a
Magazine of hemp: Over against these their Saltpeter houses &
a large row of Cells or houses to thrust their Gallys in, out of all
Weather: Over the Gate, as we go out, is a roome full of greate
& small Guns, some of which discharge 6 times at once: Then
there is a Court full of Cannon bullets, Chaines, Grapples,
Granados, &c: & over that Armes for 800000 men, & by themselves, armes for 400, taken from some that were in a plot
against the State; together with weapons of offence & defence
for 62 ships, 32 piece of Ordinance on Carriages taken from the
Turks, & one prodigious Mortar-piece: In a word, tis not to be
reckon'd up, what this large place containes of this sort: There
were now 23 Gallys, & 4 *Gally Grossi* here of 100 *Oares* of a side:
The whole Arsenal is walld about, & may be in Compasse about
3 miles, with 12 Toures for the Watch, besides that the sea invirons it: The Workmen who are ordinarily 500 march out of it in
militarie order, and every evening receive their pay thro⟨ugh⟩ a
small hole in the gate, where the Governor lives.

The next day I saw a wretch executed who had murther'd his
Master, for which he had his head chop'd off by an Axe that slid
down a frame of timber, betweene the two tall Columns in
St. Marcs Piazzo at the sea brink; the Executioner striking on
the Axe with a bettle, & so the head fell of the block:

Henc by *Gudola* we went to se⟨e⟩ *Grimanis* Palace, the portico whereoff is excellent work: Indeede the whole World cannot certainly shew a Citty of more stately buildings, considering
the extent of it, all of Square Stone, & as chargeable in their
foundations, as superstructure, as being all built upon Piles, at an
immense cost: We return'd home by the Church of St. *Johanne*
& *Paulo* before which is in Coper, the Statue of *Bartolomeo
Coleone* on horseback, double gilt, on a stately pedestal, the work
of *Andr: Verrochij* a *Florentine*: This is a very fine Church, & has
in it many rare Altar Pieces of the best Masters, especialy that
on the left hand of the two Friers slaine, which is of *Titian*.

The day after being Sonday, I went over to *St. Georgio* to the
Ceremonie of the Schismatic *Greekes*, who are permitted to have
their Church, though they are at defiance with *Rome*: They
allow of no Carved Images, but many painted, especialy the
storie of their Patron, & his dragon: Their rites differ not much

from the Latines, save that of communicating in both species, and distribution of the holy bread: We afterward fell into dispute with a *Candiot* concerning the procession of the *H: Ghost*: The Church is a noble fabric:

The Church of St. *Zacharia* is of Greeke building, by Leo the 4th Emp: and has buried the bones of the Prophet, with divers other saints: Neere this we visited *St. Lukes* famous for the Tomb of *Peter Aretine*.

Tuesday we continued to see severall other Churches, as *St. Maria* newly incrusted with Marble without, & adorn'd with Porphyrie, Ophit & Spartan stone: neere the Altar & under the Organ are Sculptures that are said to be of the famous Artist Praxitiles: To that of St: Paulo, I went purposely to see the Tomb of *Titian*: then to St. *John Evangelist*, where among other Heros, lies Andr: Balduarius the inventor of Oares applied to greate Vessells for fight: Also we saw *St. Rock* the roofe whereof is with the Schola or hall of that rich Confraternity admirably painted by *Tintoret*, especialy the *Crucifix* in the *Sacristia*: The Church of St. *Sebastiano* & Carmelites Monastrie:

Next day taking our Gudalo at St. Marks, I passd to the Iland of *St. Georgio Maggior*, where is a Convent of Benedictines, and a Church incomparably built, by *Andrea Palladio* the greate Architect: The Pavement, Cupola, Coire, Pictures, infinitely rich & sumptuous: The Cloyster ⟨h⟩as a fine Garden to it, which is a rare thing at Venice, though this be in an Iland a little distant from the Cittie, & has an Olive Orchard all invirond by the Sea: The new Cloyster now building, has a noble stayrecase to it, pav'd with white & black marble: From hence we visite S: *Spirito* & St. *Laurence* faire Churches in severall Ilands; but most remarkable that of the *Padri Olivetani* in *St. Helens* Iland, for the rare Paintings, & Carvings, with inlayd work &c:

We went next morning againe to *Padoä*, where next day we visited the Market, which is plentifully furnish'd, & exceedingly cheape, here we saw the greate Hall: built in a spacious *Piazza*, & one of the most ⟨magnificent⟩ in *Europe*: its ascent is by steps a good height, & of a reddish marble polish'd much us'd in these parts, & happly found not far off: 'tis almost 200 paces long, and 40 in bredth, all coverd with lead, without any sustaint of Columns: at the farther end stands the *bust* of *Titus Livius* the famous Historian. Neere ⟨which is⟩ the monument of *Speron*

Speronij, on the Ceiling is painted the *Cælestial Zodiaque*, & other Astronomical figures; without gos a *Corridor* in manner of a *Balcone* of the same Stone, and at entrie of the 3 gates, the head of some famous person, as *Albert Eremitano, Jul: Paullo*, Lawyers & *Peter Aponius*. In the *Piazza* is the *Podestas* & *Capitano Grandes* Palace, well built, but above all the *Monte Pietà*, the front whereof is of most excellent Architecture: There are of these in most of the Citties in Italy, where there's a continual banque of mony, to assist the poorer sort, upon any paune, & at reasonable Interest: together with Magazins for such goods ⟨as⟩ are reposited, til redeemed &c: We return'd home by the house where *Livy* was borne, full of Inscriptions, & pretty faire: hence to the *Scholes* of this flourishing & antient University, especialy for the studie of *Physic* & *Anatomie*: They are fairly built in quadrangle, with Cloysters beneath, & above with Columns: Over the greate gate, are the Armes of the *Venetian* State; & under the Lion of St. *Marc*

> *Sic ingredere ut teipso quotidie doctior, sic egredere ut indies*
> *Patriæ, Christianæque Reipublicæ utilior evadas: Ita demum*
> *Gymnasium à se feliciter ornatum existimabit.* ⟨CIꓛ .IꓛC.⟩

About the Court Walls, are carv'd in stone & painted the blazons of the Consuls of all the Nations, that from time to time have had that charge & honor in the Universitie: Which at my begin there was my worthy friend Dr. *Rogers*, who here tooke that Degree. It is above that the Scholes for the Lectures of the severall Siences are; but none of them comparable, or so much frequented as the Theater for Anatomies, which is excellently contriv'd both for the discector & spectators: I was this day invited to dinner, & in the afternoone being July 30th, received my *Matricula*, being resolved to spend some moneths here at study, especialy Physic & Anatomie, of both which here were now the most famous Professors then in *Europe*.

Next morning I went to see the Garden of Simples, rarely furnished with plants, and gave order to the Gardner to make me a Collection of them for an *hortus hyemalis*, by permission of the Cavalier Dr. Vestlingius their Præfect, & Botanic Professor, as well as *Anatomic*:

Next morning the *Earle* of *Arundel* (now in this Citty) and famous Collector of Paintings & Antiquities, invited me to go with him to see the Garden of *Mantua*, where as one enters stands a huge Colosse of Hercules. From hence to a place where was a roome cover'd with a noble Cupola built purposly for Musique, the fillings up, or *Core* 'twixt the Walls were of urnes & earthen potts for the better sounding, it was also well painted.

After dinner we walked to the Palace of *Foscari all' Arena*, there re⟨m⟩aining yet some appearances of an antient theater, though serving now for a Court onely before the house. There were kept in it two *Eagles*, a Crane, a Mauritanian Sheepe, a stag, and sundry foule as in a Vivarie: Three days after I returnd to *Venice*, and pass'd over to *Muran* famous for the best Glasses of the World, where having viewed their furnaces & seene them work, I made a Collection of divers Curiosities & Glasses which I sent for England by long sea: Tis the white flints which they have from *Pavia* which the⟨y⟩ pound & sieft exceedingly small, & mix with Ashes made of a Sea-Weede they bring out of *Syria*, & a white sand, that causes this manufacture to excell: The Towne is a *Podestaria* by it selfe, at some miles distant on the Sea from *Venice*, & like it, built upon severall small Ilands. In this place are excellent *Oysters*, small, & well tasted, like our *Colchester*, & they were the first, as I remember, that in my life I ever could eate; for I had naturaly an aversion to them. At our returne to *Venice* we met severall *Gudolas* full of *Venetian* Ladys, who come thus far in fine weather to take the aire, with Musique & other refreshments: Besides that *Muran* is it selfe a very nobly built towne, & has divers noblemens Palaces in it, and handsome Gardens: In coming back we saw the Ilands of St. *Christopher* & St. *Michael*, the last of which has a Church most incomparably inrich'd & incrusted with Marble & other architectonic Ornaments, which the Monkes very Courteously shew'd us: twas built & founded by *Margaret Æmiliana* of *Verona* who had ben a ⟨famous⟩ *Courtezan*, or rather sinner, purchasing a greate estate for the use of her body, & by this hoping to commute for her soule: Then rowed by the Iles of St. *Nicholas*, whose church with the Monuments of the *Justinian* family entertaind us a while, & so got home.

The next morning Cap: Powell (Master of the Vessell which had ben stop'd by the State, to go to Candy, & in which I was to Embark towards Turky) invited me on board, lying about 10 miles from *Venice*, where we had a good dinner, of English

pouderd beefe, & other good meate, with store of Wine, &
greate Gunns, as the manner is: After dinner the Captaine presented me with a stone he lately brought from *Gran⟨d⟩ Cairo*,
which he tooke from the Mumy-pitts, full of *Hieroglypics*, which
I designd on paper, with the true dimensions & sent in a letter to
Mr. ⟨Henshaw⟩, to communicate to Father Kircher, who was
then setting forth his greate work *Obeliscus Pamphilius*, where it
is described, though without mentioning my Name at all: The
stone was afterward brought for me into England, landed at
Wapping, where before I could heare of it, it was broken into
severall fragments, & utterly defaced to my no small affliction:
The Boate-swaine of the ship also gave me an hand & foote of
rare ⟨Mummy⟩, the nailes wheroff had ben overlaid with thin
plates of Gold, & the whole body perfect, when he brought it
out of *Egypt*, but the avarice of the Sailers & Ships Crue, brake
it in pieces & divided the body among them, which was greate
pitty: he presente⟨d⟩ me also with 2 Egyptian Idols, & some
loaves of the Bread which the *Coptics* use in the H: Sacrament,
with other curiosities:

August: 8 I had newes from *Padoä* of my Election to be *Syn-
dicus Artistarum*, which caused me (after two days idling in a
Country Villa, with the Consul of *Venice*) to hasten thither, that
I might dissingage my selfe of that honour, because it was not
onely Chargeable, but would have hindred my progresse; so as
the⟨y⟩ chose a Dutch Gentleman in my place, which did not
well please my Countrymen, who had not labourd a little to do
me the greatest honour, a stranger is Capable of in that Universitie: Being freed of this impediment, & taken leave of Dr. *Jani-
cius* a *Polonian*, & who was going Physitian in the *Venetian
Gallys* for *Candy*, I went againe to *Venice*, & made Collection of
severall Books, & some other tags: Three days after, I return'd to
Padoa, where I studied hard 'till the arivall of Mr. *Henshaw*,
Bramstone & some other English Gent: whom I had left at
Rome, & who made me go back with them to *Venice*, where I
spent some time in shewing them what I had seene there:

The 26 September my deare friend, & 'til now Constant fellow
Traveller Mr. *Thicknesse*, being oblig'd to returne into England
upon his particular Concerne, & who had served his Majestie in
the Warrs; I accompanied him part of his way, & 28, returnd to
Venice: On *Michaelmas* day I went with my *Lord Mowbray* (eldest

son to the *Earle* of *Arundell*, & a most worthy Person) to see the Collection of a Noble *Venetian* Signor *Rugini*: he has a stately Palace, richly furnish'd, with statues, heads of the *Roman Empp*, which are all plac'd in an ample roome: In the next was a Cabinet of *Medals* both *Latine* & *Greeke*, with divers curious shells, & two faire *Pearles* in 2 of them: but above all, he abounded in things petrified, Walnuts, Eggs, in which the *Yealk* rattl'd, a Peare, a piece of beefe, with the bones in it; an whole hedg-hog, a plaice on a Wooden Trencher turnd into Stone, & very perfect: Charcoale, a morsel of *Cork*, yet retaining its levitie, Sponges, Gutts, & a piece of Taffity: Part rolld up, with innumerable more; In another Cabinet, sustain by 12 pillars of oriental *Achat*, & raild about with Chrystal, he shew'd us severall noble Intaglias, of *Achat*, especialy a *Tiberius's* head, & a Woman in a Bath with her dog: Some rare *Cornelians*, *Onixes*, *Chrystals* &c in one of which was a drop of Water not Congeal'd but plainly moving up & down as it was ⟨shaken⟩: but above all was a *Diamond* which had growing in it a very faire *Rubie*; Then he shew'd us divers pieces of *Amber* wherein were several *Insects* in-tomb'd, in particular one cut like an heart, that contain'd ⟨in⟩ it a *Salamander*, without the least defect; & many curious pieces of Mosaic: The fabrique of this Cabinet was very ingenious thick set with *Achats*, *Turcoies*, & other precious stones, in the midst of which a *dog* in stone scratching his Eare, very rarely cut, & Antique, & comparable to the greatest Curiositie I had ever seene of that kind, for the accuratenesse of the work: The next chamber had a Bedstead all inlayd with *Achats*, *Chrystals*, *Cornelians*, *Lazuli* &c, esteemed worth 16000 Crounes: but for the most part the Bedsteds in *Italy* are all of forged Iron gilded, since tis impossible to keepe the wooden ones from the *Chimices*:

From hence I return'd to *Padoa*, when that Towne was so infested with Souldiers, that many houses were broken open in the night, some Murders committed; The *Nunns* next our lodging disturb'd, so as we were forc'd to be upon our guard, with *Pistols*, & other fire armes to defend our doores: And indeede the students themselves take a barbarous liberty in the Evenings, when they go to their strumpets, to stop all that go by the house, where any of their Companions in folly, are with them: This costome they call *Chi va li*; so as the streetes are very dangerous, when the Evenings grow dark; nor is it easy to reforme an intollerable usage, where there are so many strangers, of severall Nations: Using to drink my Wine coold with Snow & Ice, as the manner here is, I was so afflicted with an *Angina* & soare Throat, that it had almost cost me my life; for after all the remedies Cavalier *Vestlingius* (chiefe Professor here) could apply, old Salvatico (that famous Physitian) being call'd, made ⟨me⟩ be cupp'd & scarified in the back in 4 places, which began to give me breath, & consequently life, for I was in uttmost danger; but God being mercifull to me, I was after a fortnights being indis-posd abroad againe, when changing my Lodging, I went over against *Pozzo Pinto*, where I bought for Winter provision 3000 weight of excellent grapes, & pressed my owne Wine, which proved incomparable Liquor: This was on the 10 of *October*: Soone after came to Visite me from *Venice* Mr. Henry Howard, grand child to the *Earle of Arundel*: Mr. *Bramstone*, son to Judge Bramston Lord Chiefe Justice: & Mr. *Henshaw*, with whom I went againe to another part of the Citty to Lodge neere St. *Catharins* over against the Monasterie of Nunns, where we hired the whole house, and lived very nobly: Here I learned on the *Theorba* of Signor *Dominico Bassano*, who had a daughter, mar-ried to a *Doctor* of *Laws*, that played, and sung to 9 severall Instruments, with that skill, & addresse, as few Masters in Italy exceeded her, she likewise Composd divers excellent pieces: I had never seene any play on the Naples Viol before: She pre-sented me afterwards with 2 *Recitativas* of hers, both Words & Musique: & it ended in ⟨a⟩ Collation. The 31 of Octob: being my Birth-day, the *Nunns* of St. *Catherines* sent me flowers of silk-work: We were very studious all this Winter till Christmas, when on Twelfe day we invited all the English & Scotts in Towne (the Earle of Arundel excepted) to a Feast, which sunk our excellent Wine considerably:

1646. In January Signor *Molino* was chosen *Dodge*, but the extreame snow that fell, & the cold hindred my going to see the solemnity, so as I stirrd not from *Padoa* til *Shrovetide*, when all the world repaire to *Venice* to see the folly & madnesse of the *Carnevall*; The Women, Men & persons of all Conditions dis-guising themselves in antique dresses, & extravagant Musique & a thousand gambols, & traversing the streetes from house to house, all places being then accessible, & free to enter: There is abroad nothing but flinging of Eggs fill'd with sweete Waters,

& sometimes not over sweete; they also have a barbarous costome of hunting bulls about the Streetes & Piazzas, which is
very dangerous, the passages being generally so narrow in that
Citty: Likewise do the youth of the severall Wards & parrishes
contend in other Masteries or pastimes, so as tis altogether
impossible to recount the universal madnesse of this place during this time of licence: Now are the greate banks set up for those
who will play at Basset, the Comedians have also liberty & the
Operas to Exercise: Witty pasquils are likewise thrown about, &
the Mountebanks have their stages in every Corner: The diversion which chiefly tooke me up, was three noble *Operas* which
I saw, where was incomparable Voices, & Musique: The most
celebrated of which was the famous *Anna Rencha*, whom we
invited to a *Fishdinner*, after 4 daies in Lent, that they had given
over at the Theater; when accompanied with an *Eunuch* (whom
she brought with her) she entertaind us with rare Musique, both
of them singing to an Harpsichord: It growing late a Gentleman
of *Venice* came for her, to shew her the *Gallys* now ready to set
sayle for *Candia*: This Entertainement produc'd a second, which
was given us by the English Consul of the Merchants, inviting
us to his house, where he had the *Genòeze*, the most celebrated
base in *Italy*, who was of the late *Opera*: this divers⟨i⟩on held us
so late at night, that conveying a Gentlewoman (that supped
with us) to her *Gundola* at the usual place of landing; we were
shot at by two *Carbines* from out another *Gundola*, in which was
a *Noble Venetian* & his *Curtezana*, unwilling it seemes to be disturb'd, which made us run in, and fetch other weapons, not
knowing what the matter was, 'till we were informed of the
danger we might incurr, by pursuing it farther.

Three daies after this, I tooke my leave of *Venice*, and went to
Padoa to be present at the famous *Anatomie* Lecture, which is
here celebrated with extraordinary apparatus, & lasting almost
the whole Moneth, during which I saw three, a Woman, a
Child, & a Man dissected, with all the manual operations of the
Chirurgion upon the humane body: The one performed by Cav-
aliere *Vestlingius*, & *Dr. Jo. Athelsteinus Leoncenas*, of whom
I purchased those rare Tables of *Veines* & *Nerves*, & causd him to
prepare a third of the *Lungs*, *liver*, & *Nervi sexti par*: with the
Gastric vaines, which I transported into England, the first of

that kind had ben ever seene in our Country, & for ought I know, in the World, though afterwards there were others: [Given after to the R: Society:] When the Anatomie Lectures (which was in the Mornings) were ended, I went to see cures don in the *Hospitals*, and certainly, as there are the greatest helps, & skillfullest Physitians, so there are the most miserable & deplorable objects, to exercise upon, both of Men & Women; Whores, & Virgins, Old & Young; nor is there any I should think, so prevalent document, or lecture against the vice reigning in this licentious Country, than to be Spectator of the miserie, which these poore Creatures undergo, by Trepanning, Launcing, Salivating, Sweating, &c: They are indeede very carefully attended, and with extraordinary Charity: but I do not approve of their so freely admitting young Gentlemen Travellers to see their operations upon some of the femal Sex, who even in the midst of their tortures, are not very modest, & when they begin to be well, plainely lew'd: *March*: 20 I return'd to *Venice* where I tooke leave of my Friends: The 22d was invited to excellent *English* potted Venison, at Mr. *Hobbsons* a worthy Merchant: The 23d, I toke my leave ⟨of⟩ the *Patriarcke*, & the Prince of *Wertenburg*, & *Monsieur Grotius* (sonn to the learned Hugo,) now going a Commander to *Candia*, & in the afternoone receiv'd my Bills of Exchange of 300 *ducati* for my Journey of *Vandervoort* my Merchant, who shewed me his rare Collection of Italian Books, esteem'd very curious & of good value: The next day I was conducted to the *Ghetta* where the *Jewes* dwell (as in a Tribe & Ward) together, where I was present at a Mariage: The Bride was clad in White, sitting in a lofty chaire, & coverd also with a white vaile; Then t⟨w⟩o old *Rabbies* joynd them together, one of them holding a glasse of Wine in his hand, which in the midst of the ceremony, pretending to deliver to the Woman, he let fall, the breaking wherof, was to signifie the frailty of our nature, & that we must expect dissasters & crosses amidst all enjoyments: This don, we had a fine banquet, & were brought into the Bride chamber, where the bed was dress'd up with flowers, & the Counterpan, strewed in workes: At this ceremony we saw divers very beautifull *Portuguez*-Jewesses, with whom we had some conversation, & so went to dinner at our Lodging.

TRAVELS IN ITALY V: VICENZA AND MILAN
(1646)

THE NEXT DAY, I tooke leave of my Comrades at *Padoa*, & receiving some directions from *Cavallero Salvatico* how to govern my selfe, being of late incommoded with a salt defluction from my head (for which I had a little before ben let blood) I prepard for my Journey towards *Milan*: It was *Easter* Monday, that I was invited to Breakfast at the Earle of *Arundels*; I tooke my leave of him in his bed, where I left that greate & excellent Man in teares upon some private discourse of the crosses had befaln his Illustrious family: particularly the undutifullnesse of his *Grandson Philips* turning *Dominican* Frier [Since *Cardinal of Norfolke*], the unkindnesse of his *Countesse*, now in *Holland*; The miserie of his Countrie, now embroild in a Civil War &c: after which he causd his Gentleman to give me directions all written with his owne hand, what curiosities I should enquire after in my Journey, & so injoyning me to write sometimes to him, I departed: There staying for me below Mr. *Henry Howard* [now duke of Norfolk], Mr. *J: Digby*, son of Sir *Kenh⟨e⟩lme Digby* & other Gent: Who conducted me to the Coach that stood ready at the doore.

In company then with Mr. *Waller*, one Cap: *Wray* (son to Sir *Christopher*, whose *Father* had ben in armes against his Majestie & therefore by no meanes wellcome to us) with another gent: one Mr. *Abdy*, a modest & learned man, we got that night to *Vincenza*, passing by the *Euganian* hills, celebrated for the Prospects, and furniture of rare simples, which are found growing about them: The Wayes were something deepe, but the whole Country flat & even as a bowling greene; the common fields lying square, & orderly planted with fruite-trees, which the *Vines* run upon & embrace for ⟨many⟩ miles, with delicious streames creeping along the ranges.

Vincenza is a *Citty* in the Marquisate of *Treviso* yet appertaining to the *Venetians*, full of Gentlemen, & splendid Palaces, to which the famous *Palladio* borne here, has exceedingly contributed, as having ben the Architect: Most conspicuous is the Hall of Justice, it has to it a Toure of incomparable work: The lower Pillars are of the first order, those in the three upper Corridors *dorique*, under them shops in a spacious *Piazza*: The hall was built in imitation of that at *Padoä*, but of a nobler designe *a la moderna*: The next morning we visited the *Theater*, as being of that kind the most perfect now standing in all the World, & built by the forenam'd Artist, in exact imitation of the Antient Roman, & comprehensive of 5000 spectators: The Sceane which is all of stone represents an Imperial Citty, of Corinthian order, & decor'd with statues: over the *Scenario* is the Inscription

Virtuti ac Genio
Olympior: Academia
Theatrum hoc à Fundamentis erexit
Palladio Architect: 1584.

[The *Sceane* declines 11 foote, the *suffitto* painted with Clowdes.] To this there joynes a spacious hall for sollemn days to *Ballot in*, & a second for the *Academics*. In the *Piazza* is also the Podestà or Governors house, the faciata being of the Corinthian order, very noble. The Piazza it selfe so large, as to be capable of *Justs* & *Turnaments*, the Nobilitie of this Citty, being exceedingly addicted to this Knight Errantry, & other martial diversions: There is also in this place two Pillars erected, in imitation of those at St. *Marks* in *Venice*, bearing one of them a Winged *Lion*, the other the statue of St. *Jo: Baptist*: In a Word, this sweete Towne, has more well built Palaces than any of its dimensions in all *Italy*, besides a number begun, & not yet finished (but of stately designe) by reason of the domestic dissentions twixt them, & those of *Bres(c)ia* fomented by the Sage *Venetians*, least combining, they might think of recovering their antient liberty: for which reason likewise are permitted those dissorders & insolences comitted at *Padua* among the youth of these two *Territories*: Moreover it is no dishonor in this Country, to be some generations in finishing their Palaces, that without exhausting themselves by making a vast expense at once they may at last Erect a sumptuous pile: Count *Oleines* Palace is neere perfected of this nature, & of admirable Architecture. Count *Ulmarini* more famous for his Gardens, being without the Walls, especialy his *Cedrario* or Conserve of *Oranges*, Eleaven-score of my Paces long, set in exquisite order & ranges, & making a Canopie all the Way by their intermixing branches, for above 200 of my single paces, & which being full of fruite & blossomes, was one of the most delicious sights, that in my life I had seene. There was in the middle of this Garden, a Cupola made of Wyre, & supported by slender pillars of brick, so closely coverd with Ivy, both without & within, that nothing save greene was to

be perceived, that made an admirable effect, & was very extraordinarie, twixt the arches dangled festoones of the same: Here is
likewise a most inextricable Labyrinth. I had in this Towne a
Recommendation ⟨to⟩ a very civil & ingenious Apothecarie, cald
Angelico, who had a pretty Collection of Paintings: I would now
very faine have visited a Palace call'd the *Rotunda*, which was a
Mile out of Towne, belonging to Count *Martio Capra*, but one of
our Companions hasting to be gon, and little minding anything
save drinking & folly, causd us to take coach sooner than we
should: A little from the towne we passd the *Campo Martio*, set
out in imitation of antient *Rome*, wherein the Noblesse exercise
their horses, and the Ladys make the *Corso*, it is entred by a
stately Arch Triumphal the invention of *Palladio*. About mid
way (being now for *Verona*) we din'd at *Ostaria Nova*, & came
late to our resting place, which was the *Cavaletto*, just over the
Monument of the *Scaligeri*, formerly Princes of *Verona*, which is
adornd with many devices of Ladders, in stone, aluding to the
name: We were early next morning about the Citty, which is
built on the gentle declivity, & bottome of an hill, invirond with
some considerabl⟨e⟩ Mountaines, and downes of fine grasse, like
some places of the South of *England*, & on the other side with a
rich plaine & champion, where *Cajus Marius* gave that fatal
over-throw to the *Cimbrians*. The Citty is divided in the midst
by the *River Athesis* over which passe divers stately bridges, & on
its brinks many goodly Palaces, whereof one is rarely painted
with *Chiaro oscura* without side, as are divers in this drie Climate
of *Italy*: But the first thing that engag'd our curiosity & wonder
too, was the *Amphitheater*, which is the most intire now extant in
the World of Antient remaines: The Inhabitants call it the
Arena, having two *Porticos* one within the other, & is 34 rod long,
22 in bredth with 42 ranks of stone benches or seates, which
reach to the top: The vastnesse of the marble stones is stupendious: *L.V. ⟨Flaminius⟩, Consul Anno Urb: Con: LIII*. This I
esteeme one of the noblest Antiquities in Europ, worth the seeing, because it is so vast, & so intire, as having escaped the ruines
of other publique buildings for above 1400 Yeares: Other *Arches*
there are, as that of the Victorie of *Marius*: Temples, *Aquæducts*
&c, shewing still considerable reliques in severall places of the
Towne, & how magnificent it has formerly ben: It has besides 3
strong Castles, & large & noble Wall, & indeede, the whole
Citty bravely built, especialy the *Senate house*, where we saw

those celebrated statues of *Cornelius Nepos*, *Emilius Marcus*,
Plinie, *Vitruvius*, all of them honouring *Verona* with their birth,
as of later date, *Julius Cæsar Scaliger* that prodigie of Learning: In
the Evening we saw *Count Giusti's* Villa, wher are Walkes cutt
out of the maine rock, from whence we had the pleasant
Prospect of *Mantua*, & Parma, though at greate distance: At
Entrance of this Garden grows the goodliest *Cypresse* I fancy in
Europ, Cut in Pyramid, tis a prodigious tree both for breadth, &
height, intirely coverd, & thick to the base: A Civilian one Dr.
Cortone, shewd us (amongst other rarities) a St. *Dorothia* of
Raphaels incomparably painted: I would have seene the rare
drawings (especialy of *Parmensis*) belonging to Dr. *Marcello*,
another Advocate, but he was absent: Certainly this Citty
deserv'd all those Elogies, Scaliger has honour'd it with, for in
my opinion, tis situated in one of the most delightfullst places
that ever I came in, so sweetly mixed with risings, & Vallies, so
Elegantly planted with Trees, on which *Bacchus* seemes riding as
it were in Triumph every *Autumn*, for the Vines reach from tree
to tree; & here of all places I have travelld in *Italy*, would I fix
preferrable to any other, so as well has that learnd Man give⟨n⟩ it
the name of the very Eye of the World:

> *Ocelle Mundi, sidus Itali cæli,*
> *Flos urbium, flos ⟨corculumque amænarum⟩,*
> *Quot sunt, Eruntve, quot fuere, Verona.*

We trav⟨e⟩ll'd next morning over the downes, where Marius
fought, & fancied our selves about *Winchester* & the Countrie
towards *Dorsetshire*: We dind at an Inn call'd *Cavalli Caschieri*
neere *Peschiera* a very strong fort of the *Venetian Republique*, &
neere the *Lago* di *Garda*, which dissembogues into that of *Mantua* neere 40 miles in length, & for being so highly celebrated
by my *Lord Arundel* to me, as the most pleasant spot of *Italy*,
I observ'd it with the more diligence, alighting out of the Coach,
& going up to a grove of Cypresses growing about a *Gentlemans*
Country house, from whence indeede it presents a most surprizing Prospect: The hills & gentle risings about it, produces
Oranges, *Citrons*, *Olives*, *Figs* & other tempting fruits, & the
Waters abounding in excellent Fish, especialy *Trouts*: In the
middle of this Lake stands *Sermonea* on an Iland: Here *Cap:
Wray* bought a pretty Nag of the Master of our Inn where we
dined, for *8 Pistoles*, which yet his Wife our hostesse was so

unwilling to part with, that she did nothing but kisse, & weepe
& hang about the horses neck, till the *Captaine* rid away: so we
came this Evening to *Bres⟨c⟩ia*, which next morning (according
to our Costome) we traverst in search of Antiquities & new
sights: & here I purchasd my fine Carabine of [old] *Lazarino
Cominazzo* which cost me 9 pistols, this Citty being famous for
these fire Armes, & that workeman, with *Jo: Bap: Franco* the
best esteem'd; This Citty consists most in Arts, that make
Armes, every shop abounding in *Gunns*, Swords, Armorers &c,
most of which Workmen, come hither out of *Germanie*, of
which this is a Staple. The Citty stands in an incomparable fertil plaine, yet the Castle is built on an hill: The streetes abound
in faire Fountaines: The *Torre della Pallada* is of a noble Tuscan
order: & the Senate-house hardly inferior to any I ever saw:
Now also was repairing the *Domo* or *Cathedrall*, in it they shew
strangers a blew Crosse which they affirme fell downe from the
Clouds, at the very time it appeard to the Greate Constantine.
The Piazza is but indifferent: some of the houses arch'd as at
Padua: Willingly we would from hence visite *Parma*, *Piacenza*,
Mantua &c: but the Banditi & other dangerous Parties being
now abroad, who committed many Enormities, made us con-
ten⟨te⟩d with a Pisga⟨h⟩ sight of them. We dind next day at
Ursa Vecchio, & after dinner passe by an exceeding strong Fort
of the *Venetians* cald *Ursa Nova*, & is Frontier. Then by the
River Oglio, & so by *Sonano*, where we enter first into the *Spanish* Dominions, & that night arriv'd at *Crema*, which belongs to
Venice & very well defended: The *Podesta's* Palace is finely built,
& so is the Domo, & Tower to it: with an ample *Piazza*: Early
next ⟨day⟩, after 4 miles riding we enter'd into the State of
Milan, & pasd by *Lodi*, a Greate Citty, famous for *Cheeze*, &
even bearing up to the best *Parmeggiano*: We din'd at *Marig-
nano* ten-miles behether *Milan*, where we met halfe a dozen
suspicious *Cavalieres*, who yet did us no harme; & then passing
as through a continual Garden, we went on with exceeding
pleasure; for it is certainely the Paradise of all *Lumbardy*, the
high-ways being as even & straite, as a line could be laied, the
Fields to a vast extent, planted with fruit about the inclosures,
& Vines to every Tree at equal distances, and water'd with frequent Streames; There was likewise much Corne, & Olives in
aboundance.

Here, at approch of the Citty, some of our Company (in dread of the Inquisition, severer here than in any place of all Spaine) thought of throwing away some Protestant (by them call'd Heretical) books & papers: It was about 3 in the Afternoone that we came thither, where the Officers search'd us th⟨o⟩roughly for prohibited goods, but finding we were onely Gentlemen Travellers dismissd us for a small reward: so we went quietly to our Inn the *3 Kings*, where for that day we refreshed ourselves, as we had neede.

The morning come, we deliver'd our letters of recommendation to the learned and Courteous *Ferrarius* a Doctor of the *Ambrosian* College, who conducted us to all the remarkable Places of the Towne. The first of which was the famous *Cathedral* which we enter'd by a Portico so little inferior to that of *Rome* that when finish'd it will be hard to say which is the fairest; The materials being all of white & black Marble, with Columns of an incredible height, which are of Granito [Egyptian]: The outside of the Church is so full of Sculpture, that one may number 4000 statues all of white Marble, amongst which that one of St. Bartholemew is esteemed an excellent Masterpiece. The Church is very spacious [almost as long as S. Peters in Rome not so large]; about the Quire is a most incomparable Sculpture in snow white marble, containing the Sacred Storie, nor know I where it is exceeded: About the body of the Church are the Miracles of St. Char: *Borromeo*, & in the vault beneath his body, before the high Altar, grated & inchas'd in one of the vastest Chrystals in *Europe*; to this also belongs a rich Treasure. The Domo or Cupola is all of Marble both within & without, & even cover'd with ⟨huge⟩ planks of Marble, unfortunate in nothing save the *Gotick* designe: The Windows of the Church are most beautifully painted: The Organs, of which there are two, very faire, & excellent. The whole fabrique is erected in the midst of a faire Piazza, & in the very navill of the Citty. Hence we went to the Palace of the Archbishop, which is a quadrangle, famous for being the Architecture of *Theobaldi* who design'd much for *Phil:* 2d in the *Escurial*, & has built much in *Milan*: Hence I went into the Gouvernors Palace, who was then the *Condestable* of *Castile*: tempted by the glorious Tapissries & Pictures, I adventurd so far alone, that peeping into a Chamber where the greate Man was under the barbers hands, he sent one of his *Negros* (a slave) to know what I was, I made the best excuse I could & that I was onely admiring the Pictures, which he returning, & telling his Lord, I heard the Governor reply, It was some Spie, upon which I retir'd with all the Speede I could, pass'd the Guard of *Swisse*, got into the streete, and in a moment to my Company, who were gon to the *Jesuites* Church, which is in truth a noble Structure, the front especialy, after the moderne: After dinner we were conducted to St. *Celso*, a Church of rare Architecture, built by *Bramante*, & the Carvings of the *faciata* of marble of *Hannibal Fontana*, whom they esteeme at Milan equal with the best of the antients: In a roome joyning to the Church, is a *Madona* of Marble (like a Colosse) of the same Sculpturs work, which they will not expose to the aire: There are two *Sacristias*, in one a rare Virgin of Leonardo da Vinci, in the other, an other by *Raphael d'Urbino*, a piece which all the world admires: The *Sacristan* shew'd us here a world of rich Plate, Jewells, & Embrodred Copes which are kept in presses.

Next we went to see the greate Hospital, a quadrangular Cloyster, of a vast compasse: in earnest a royal fabric, & has to it of annual endowment 50 thousand crowns of Gold: There is in the middle of it a Crosse building for the sick, & just under it, an Altar so plac'd as to be seene in all places of the Infermarie: There are divers Colledges built in this quarter richly provided for, by the same *Borromeo* & his Nephew the last Card: *Fredrico*, some not yet finishd, but of excellent designe: Passing along we saw St. *Eustorgio*, wherein they told us there lay formerly the bodys of the 3 *Magi*, since translated to *Colin* in Germany: they yet reserve the Tomb, which is a Square Stone, on which is a Star ingraven, & under it:

Sepulchrum trium Magorum.

Here is also (as affirmed) some of the mony or golden Treasure, which they offerd our B: Saviour:—Passing by St. *Laurenzo* we espied 16 Columns of Marble, & the ruines of a building, which had ben a Temple dedicated to *Hercules*. So we concluded this days wandring at the Monasterie of Madona della Gratia, & in the Refectorie admir'd that celebrated *Cena domini* of L⟨e⟩onard: *da Vinci*, which takes up the intire Wall at the end, & is the same the greate *Virtuoso Francis* the first of *France* was so inamoured of, that he consulted to remove the whole Wall, by binding about with ribs of yron & timber, to convey it into France, being in deede one of the rarest paintings that ever *Leonardo* did, who was long in the service of that prince, & so deare to him, as the King coming to visite him in his old age & sicknesse he expired in his armes: But this incomparable piece is now exceedingly impaird:

Early next morning came the Learned *Dr. Ferarius* to visite us, & tooke us up in his Coach to go see the *Ambrosian Librarie*, where Card: Fred: *Borhomeo* has ⟨expended⟩ so vast a summ in building, & furnishing it with Curiosities, especialy paintings & drawings of inestimable value among Painters: It were a Schole fit to make the ablest Artist: Ther are many rare things of *Hans Breugill* viz. the 4 Elements, & in this roome stands the glorious Inscription of *Cavaliero Galeazzo Arconati*, to value his gift to the Librarie of severall drawings of *Da Vinci*: but these we could not see, the keeper of them being out of Towne, who allways carryed the keys with him: But my *Lord Martial* (who had seene them) told me, all but one booke are small, & that an huge folio contain'd 400 leaves, full of Scratches of Indiane &c: but whereas the Inscription pretends that our *King Charles* had offerd 1000 pounds for them; the truth is, & as my Lord him-selfe told me, 'twas his *Lordship* that treated with *Galeazzo* for himselfe, in the name, & by permission of the King, & that the *Duke of Feria* who was then Governour should make the bar-gain; but my Lord having seene them since, did not thinke them so much worth.

In the greate roome, where is a goodly Librarie, on the right hand of the doore, is a small wainscot closset, furnish⟨ed⟩ with rare *Manuscripts*: Two original letters of the *Grand Signor* were shew'd us, sent to two *Popes*, one of which was (as I remember) to Alex: 6. *Borgia*, & the other mentioning the head of the Launce, which pierc'd our B: Saviours side, sent as a present to the *Pope*. I would faine have gotten a copy of them, but could not, however they are I heare, translated into *Italian*, & therein a most honorable mention of Christ: from hence we revisited *St. Ambrose* Church; the high *Altar* is supported by 4 Porphyrie Columns, & under it lies the precious remaines of that holy Man; neere it they shewd us a pit or well, (an obscure place it is) where they say, St. Ambrose baptizd St. Augustine, & recited the *Te-deum*. They shew'd us likewise a fragment of the brasen

serpent which *Moses* made in the Wildernesse, if you will
believe it, it stands on a pillar in the Church, the place is also
famous for some Councils that have here ben held, & for the
Coronation of divers Italian Kings & Emperors: receiving the
Iron Crown from the Archbishop of this See: One more curiosity they shew, which is the Hist: of *Josephus* written on the bark
of trees:

The high Altar is infinitely rich: & to say the truth *Milan* is
one of the princliest Citties in *Europe*, it has no suburbs, but is
circld with a stately Wall for 10 miles, in the Center of a Country that seemes to flow with milk & hony: The aire is excellent,
the fields fruitfull to admiration, & consequently the Merkat
abounding with all sorts of provisions: The Citty has neere 100
Churches: 71 Monasteries: 40000 Inhabitans; It is of a Circular
figure fortified with bastions: full of sumptuous Palaces, & rare
Artists, especialy for Works in Chrystal, which is here cheape, as
being found among the *Alpes*: They are curious in Straw-worke
among the Nunns, even to admiration: It has a good river: but a
Citadell of some small distance from the Citty, & Commanding
it, that for its strength, Workes, & Munition of all kinds, the
whole world shewes none like it, tis garnisond onely with
Spaniards, & was built by *Galeatius* the second, consisting of
4 bastions, & those Works at the Angles & fronts: The Graft is
invested with brick, to an incredible depth, it has two strong
toures as one enters, & within is another fort, & spacious lodgings for the Souldiers, & to draw up in, in a word, no accommodation for streng⟨t⟩h wanting, & all exactly uniforme: They have
here also all sorts of Work & trades men:[1] an incomparable
Magazine of Armes, & Provisions: The fosse is of Spring Water,
& that grinds corne & the Ramparts vaulted underneth: At my
being now at *Milan* Don Juan Vasquez Coronada was Governor
of this Citadell.

But of all the curiosities of *Milan*, there is nothing more
worthy seeing, than the Collection of Signor *Septalla* a Canon
of St. *Ambros*, who is famous over Christendome for his learning & virtues: He shew'd us an *Indian* Wood, that had the perfect sent of Civet: & a Flint containing a good quantity of
Water within it, it is rather a pibble, cleare as Achat, so as you

1 Artificers or craftsmen.

may plainely discerne the Water: & has divers Chrystals that have Water moving in them, & some of them plants & leaves, in another hogs bristles: Much Amber full of Insects, & divers things of Woven *Amiantos*: In a Word *Milan* is a sweete place, & though the streetes are somewhat narrow, they abound in rich Coaches, are full of Noblesse, who every night frequent the *Course*.

Passing towards our Lodging, & Walking a turne in the Portico before the *Dome* a *Cavaliero* who pass'd by, hearing some of our Companie speaking English, looked a good while earnestly on us, and by & by sending his servant towards us, desir'd that we would honour him the next day at Dinner; This we looked on as an odd kind of Invitation, he not speaking at all to us himselfe: We returnd his Civilitie, with thanks, not fully resolv'd what to do, or what might be the meaning of it, in this jealous place: But on inquirie, 'twas told us he was a *Scots* Colonel, that had an honorable Command in the Citty, so we agreed to go: This Afternoone we were wholy taken up in seeing an *Opera*, represented by some *Neapolitans*, & performed all in excellent Musick, & rare Sceanes: in which there acted a celebrated Beauty:

Next morning we went to the *Colonels*, who had sent his servant againe to conduct us to his house; which in truth we found a noble Palace, richly furnish'd. There were also other Guest⟨s⟩, all Souldiers, and one of them a Scotch man, but not one of all their names could we learn: At dinner he excusd his rudenesse, that he had not himselfe spoken to us, telling us it was his costome, when he heard of any English Travlors (who but rarely would be knowne to passe through that Citty, for feare of the Inquisition) to invite them to his house, where they might be free: And indeede we had a most sumptuous dinner, with plenty of Excellent provision, & the wine so tempting, that after some healths had gon about, & we rissen from Table, the Colonel leade us into his hall, where there hung up divers Colours, Saddle, bridles, pistols & other Armes, being Trophies which he had with his owne hands taken from the Enemy; & amongst them would needes bestow a paire of *Pistols* on Cap: *Wray*, one of our fellow Travelors, & a good drinking Gent: & on me, a Turkish bridle woven with silk & very Curiously embossd, with other silk Trappings, to which hung an halfe moone finely wrought, which he had taken from a Basshaw that he had slaine: With this glorious spoile, I rid the rest of my Journey as far as Paris & brought it afterwards into England. Then he shew'd us a stable of brave horses, with his *Menage* & *Cavalerizzo*. Some of the horses he causd to be brought forth, which he mounted, and perform'd all the motions of an Excellent horse-man: When this was don, & he alighted, contrary to the advice of his Groome & Pages, (who it seemes knew the nature of the beast, & that their Master was a little spirited with Wine) needes he would have out a fiery horse, that had not yet ben Menag'd, & was very ungovernable; but was else a very beautifull Creature: This he mounting, the horse getting the raines, in a full carriere, ⟨rose⟩ so de⟨s⟩perately, as he fell quite back, crushing the Colonell so forceably against the Wall of the Manege, that though he sat on him like a *Centaure*, yet recovering the Jade on all foure againe, he desir'd to be taken down, & so led in, where he cast himselfe upon a Pallet, where with infinite lamentation, after some time, we tooke our leaves of him, being now speechlesse; and the next morning coming to visite him, we found before the doore, the Canopie, which they usualy carry over the Host, and some with lighted tapers, which made us suspect he was in very sad condition, & so indeede we found him, an Irish frier standing by his bed side, as Confessing him, or at least disguising a Confession & other Ceremonies, usd *in extremis*; for we afterwards learn'd, that the Gent: was a Protestant, and had this Frier his confident; which doubtlesse was a dangerous thing at *Milan*, had it ben but suspected: At our enterance he sighed grievously and held up his hands, but was not able to speake: After vomiting some bloud, he kindly tooke us all by the hand, & made signes, that he should see us no more, which made us take our leave of him with extreame reluctancy, & affliction for the Accident: This sad disaster made us Consult that very Evening about our departure from this Towne as soone as we could, not knowing how we might be enquird after, or engag'd, The Inquisition heare being so cruelly formidable, & inevitable on the least suspicion: The very next morning therefore discharging our Lodgings we agreed for a Coach to Carry us to the foote of the *Alpes*, not a little concernd for the death of the Colonell, which we now heard of, & that had so courteously entertain'd us:

OVER THE ALPS TO SWITZERLAND
(1646)

THE FIRST DAY then we got as far as *Castellanza*, by which runs a spacious river into *Lago Maggiore*: Here at dinner were two or three *Jesuites* who were very pragmatical & inquisitive, whom we declind conversation with as decently as we could: so we pursu'd our journey through a most fruitfull plaine, but the weather wet & uncomfortable: At night we lay at *Sesto* & next morning (leaving our Coach) Imbarked in a boate to waft us over the *Lago* (being one of the largest in Europe) & whence we could perfectly see the touring *Alps*, & amongst them *Il gran San Bernardo* esteemed the highest mountaine in Europe, appearing some miles above the Clouds: Through this vast Water passes the River *Ticinus* which discharges itselfe into the *Pò*, by which meanes *Helvetia* transports her Merchandizes into *Italy*, which we now begin to leave behind us: Having now sail'd about 2 leagues we were hal'd on shore at *Arona*, a strong Towne belonging to the Dutchy of *Milan*, where being examind by the Governor, & paying a small duty, we were dismiss'd: Opposite to this Fort is *Angiera*, another small Towne; the passage very pleasant, with the horrid prospect of the *Alps*, coverd with Pine trees, & Firrs & above them Snow: The next we pass'd was the pretty Iland, *Isabella*, that ⟨lies⟩ about the middle of the Lake, & has a faire house built on a Mount, indeede the whole Iland is a Mount, ascended by severall *Terraces* & walks all set about with Oranges & Citron trees, the reflection from the Water rendring the place very warme, at least during the Summer & Autumn: The next we saw was *Isola*, & left on our right hand the Ile of St Jovanni, & so sailing by another small Towne (built also upon an Iland) we ariv'd at night to *Marguzzo* an obscure village at the end of the Lake, & very foote of the Alpes, which now rise as it were suddainly, after some hundred of miles of the most even Country in the World, & where there is hardly a stone to be found, as if nature had here swept up the rubbish of the Earth in the Alpes, to forme & cleare the Plaines of *Lumbardy*, which hitherto we had pass'd since our coming from *Venice*:

In this wretched place, I lay on a bed stuff'd with leaves, which made such a Crackling, & did so prick my skin through the tick, that I could not sleepe: The next morning I was furnish'd with an Asse (for we could not get horses) but without stirrops, but we had ropes tied with a loope to put our feete in, that supplied other trappings, & thus with my gallant steede, bridld with my Turkish present, we pass'd thro a reasonable pleasant, but very narrow Vally, 'til we came to *Duomo*, where we rested, & having shew'd the *Spanish* passe, we brought from the Ambassador; The Governor would presse another on us: though onely that his Secretary might get a Croune: Here we exchang'd our *Asses* for *Mules* sure footed on the hills & precipices, as accustom'd to passe them, & with a Guide, which now we hired, we were brought that night, through very steepe, craggy, & dangerous passages, to a Village cal'd *Vedra*, being the last of the King of *Spaines* Dominion in the Dutchy of *Milan*, a very infamous wretched lodging:

Next morning we mount againe through strange, horrid & firefull Craggs & tracts abounding in Pine trees, & onely inhabited with Beares, Wolves, & *Wild Goates*, nor could we any where see above a pistol shoote before us, the horizon being terminated with rocks, & mountaines, whose tops cover'd with Snow, seem'd to touch the Skies, & in many places pierced the Clowdes. Some of these vast mountaines were but one intire stone, 'twixt whose clefts now & then precipitated greate Cataracts of Mealted Snow, and other Waters, which made a tirrible roaring, Echoing from the rocks & Cavities, & these Waters in some places, breaking in the fall, wett us as if we had pas'd through a mist, so as we could neither see, nor heare one another, but trusting to our honest Mules, jog on our Way: The narrow bridges in some places, made onely by felling huge Firtrees & laying them athwart from mountaine to mountaine, over Cataracts of stupendious depth, are very dangerous, & so are the passages & edges made by cutting away the maine rock: others in steps, & in some places we passe betweene mountaines that have ben broken & falln upon one another, which is very tirrible, & one had neede of a sure foote, & steady head to climb some of these precipices, harbours for the Beares, & Woulv⟨e⟩s, who sometimes have assaulted Travellers: In these straits we frequently alighted, freezing in the Snow, & anon frying by the reverberation of the Sun against the Cliffs as we descend lower, where we meete now & then a few miserable Cottages, built so upon the declining of the rocks, as one would expect their sliding down: Amongst these inhabite a goodly sort of People having monstrous Gullets or Wenns of flesse growing to their throats, some of which I have seene as big as an hundred pound bag of silver hanking under their Chinns; among the Women especialy, & that so ponderous, as that to Ease them, they many of them were ⟨a⟩ linnen cloth, bound about their head & coming under the chin to support it, but *quis tumidum guttur miratur in Alpibus?* Their drinking so much snow water is thought to be the Cause of it, the men using more wine, are not so *strumous* as the Women: but the very truth is, they are a race of people, & many greate Water-drinkers here have not those prodigious tumors: It runs as we say in the bloud, & is a vice in the race, & renders them so ougly, shrivel'd & deform'd, by its drawing the skin of the face downe, that nothing can be more fritefull; to which add a strange puffing habit, furrs, & barbarous Language, being a mixture of corrupt high *German*, *French*, & Italian: The people are of gigantic Stature, extreamely fierce & rude, yet very honest & trustie: This night, through unaccessible heights, we came in prospect of *Mons Sempronius*, now Mount *Sampion*, which has on its summit a few hutts, & a Chapell: Approching this, Captaine Wrays Water Spaniel, (a huge filthy Curr, that had follow'd him out of England), hunted an heard of Goates downe the rocks, into a river made by the dissolutions of the Snow: Ariv'd at our cold harbour (though the house had in every roome a Stove), supping with Cheeze & Milke & wretched wine to bed we go in Cupbords, & so high from the floore, that we climb'd them by a Ladder, & as we lay on feathers, so are Coverd with them, that is, betweene two tickes stuff'd with feathers, & all little enough to keepe one warme: The Ceilings of the roomes are strangely low for those tall people. The house was now in September, halfe cover'd with Snow, nor is there ever a tree or bush growing in many miles: from this unhospitable place then we hasted away early next morning, but as we were getting on our Mules, comes a huge young fellow, demanding mony for a Goate, Cap: Wrays Dog (he affirm'd) had kild the other day: expostulating the matter, & impatient of staying in the Cold, we set spurrs & endeavor'd to ride away, when a multitude of People, being by this time gotten together about us (it being Sonday morning & attending for the Priest to say Masse) stop our Mules, beate us off our saddles & imediately disarming us of our Carbines, drew us into one of the roomes of our Lodging, & set a guard upon us. Thus we continu'd Prisoners til Masse was ended, & then came there

halfe a Score grimm Swisse, & taking upon them to be Magistrates, sate downe on the Table, and condemn'd us to pay the
fellow a pistol for his Goate, & ten more for attempting to ride
away: Threatning that if we did not do it speedily they would
send us to another Prison, & keep us to a day of publique Justice, where, as they perhaps would have exaggerated[1] the Crime,
for they pretended we span'd our Carabines & would have shot
some of them (as indeede the Captaine, was about to do) we
might have had our heads cut off, for amongst these barbarous
people, a very small misdemeanor dos often meete that animad-
version: This we were afterwards told; & though the proceeding
appeerd highly unjust, upon Consultation among ourselves, we
thought it safer to rid our selves out of their hands, & the
trouble we were brought in, than to expostulate it among such
brutes, & therefore we patiently lay'd downe the mony, & with
fierce Countenances had our Mules, & armes deliverd us, and
glad to scape as we did: This was cold entertainement, but our
journey after was colder, the rest of the Way having (tis sai'd)
ben cover'd with Snow since the Creation; for that never man
remember'd it to be without; & because by the frequent Snow-
ing, the tracks are continualy fill'd up, we passe by severall tall
Masts, set up, to guide Those who travell, so as for many miles
they stand in ken of one another, like to our Beacons: In some
places of divided Mountaines, the Snow quite fills up the Cleft,
whilst the bottome being thaw'd, leaves it as it were a frozen
Arch of Snow, & that so hard, as to beare the greatest weight,
for as it snows often so it perpetualy freezes, & of this I was so
sensible, as it flaw'd the very skin of my face: Beginning now to
descend a little, Cap: Wrays horse, that was our Sumpter, (&
carried all our bagage) plunging thro a bank of loose Snow, slid
downe a firefull precipice, more than thrice the height of St
Paules, which so incens'd the Cholerique Cavalier his Master,
that he was sending a brace of bullets into the poore beast, least
the Swisse, that was our Guide, should recover him & run away
with his burden: but just as his hand was lifting up his Carbine,
We gave such a Shout, & pelted the horse so with Snow balls, as
with all his might plunging thro the Snow, he fell from another
steepe place into another bottome neere a path we were to

1 Emphasized, made much of; not in the modern depreciatory sense.

passe: It was yet a good while 'ere we got to him, but at last we recovered the place, & easing him of his Charge, hal'd him out of the Snow, where he had ben certainely frozen in, if we had not prevented it before night: It was (as we judg'd) almost two miles that he had slid & fall'n, & yet without any other harme, than the benumming of his limbs for the present, which with lusty rubbing & chafing he began to move, & after a little walking perform'd his journey well enough: All this Way (affrited with the dissaster of the Captaines horse) we trudg'd on foote, driving our Mules before us: & sometimes we fell, & sometimes slid thro this ocean of featherd raine, which after October is impassible: Towards night we came into a larger way, thro vast woods of Pines which cloth the middle parts of these rocks: here they were burning some to make *Pitch* & *Rosin*, piling the knotty branches, as we do to make Char-Coale, & reserving that which mealts from them, which harden into Pitch &c: & here we passd severall Cascads of dissolv'd Snow, that had made Channels of formidable depth in the Crevices of the Mountaines, & with such a firfull roaring, as for 7 long miles we could plainely heare it: It is from these Sourses, that the swift & famous *Rhodanus*, & the *Rhyne* which passe thro all France, & Germanie, derive their originals.

Late at night then we got to a Towne call'd *Briga* which is build at the foote of the *Alpes* in the *Valtoline*: Every doore almost had nailed on the outside, & next the Streete, a Beares, Wolfes or foxes-head & divers of them all Three, which was a Salvage kind of sight: but as the Alps are full of these beasts, the People often kill them:

The next morning we return'd our Guide, & tooke fresh Mules & another to conduct us to the Lake of *Geneva*, passing through as pleasant a Country, as that which before we had traveld, was melancholy & troublesome, & a strange & suddaine change it seem'd, for the reverberation of the Sunbeames darting from the Mountaines & rocks, that like a Wall range it on both sides, not above 2 flight shots in bredth for some hundreds of miles; renders the passage excessively hot: through such extreames we continud our Journey, whilst that goodly river the *Rhone* glided by us in a narrow & quiet chanell, almost in the middle of this Canton, & fertilizing the Country for Grasse & Corne which growes here in aboundance, for the Snow which waters it from the hills, brings downe with it a fertil liquor that dos wonderfully impregnat.

We ariv'd this night at a very pretty Towne, & Citty, for *Sion* (that is its name) is a Bishops seate, & the head of *Valesia*, & has a Castle: The Bishop who resides in it, has both Civile & Ecclesiastical Jurisdiction, & here our Host, (as the costome of these Cantons is) was one of the chiefest of the Towne, & having heretofore ben a Colonell in France us'd us exstreame Civily; being so displeas'd at the barbarous usage we received at Mount *Sampion*, as he would needes give us a letter, to the Governour of the Country, who resided at *St. Maurice* (which was in our Way to Geneva) to revenge the affront: This was a true old blade, & had ben a very curious *Virtuoso*, as we found by an handsome collection of *Books*, *Medails*, *Pictures*, *Shells* & other Antiquities; amongst other things he shew'd us two heads & hornes of the true *Capricorne*, which he told us, were frequently kill'd among the Mountaines: One branch of them was as much as I could well lift, & neere as high as my head, not much unlike the greater sort of Goates, save that they bent forewards, by help whereof they climb up, & hang on inaccessible rocks, from whence they now & then shoote them, & spake prodigious things of their leaping from crag to crag, & of their sure footing, notwithstanding their being cloven footed, unapt on⟨e⟩ would think to take hold, & walke so steadily on those tirrible ridges as they do: On⟨e⟩ of these *beames*, the Coll: would have bestowed on me, but the want of a Convenience to carry it along with me, caus'd me to refuse his courtesie: He told me that in the Castle there were some *Roman* & *Christian* Antiquities; & some Inscriptions he had in his owne Garden; but our time being short I could not perswad my Companions to stay & visite the places he would have had us seene, nor the offer he made to shew us the hunting of the Beare, Wolfe, & other wild beasts; inviting us to his Country house, where he told us he had better Pictures, & other rarities: A more debonaire brave Gentleman I never saw, nor could possibly expect to find in this rude Country & among the blunt Swisse: Wherefore the next morning, having presented his daughter (a pretty Virgin, & well fashion'd) a small rubie ring, we parted somewhat late from our generous Host: Passing through the same pleasant valy, continue'd betweene the horrid mountaines on either hand, & lying like a

Gallery for many miles in length, & so got to *Martigni* where we were also well entertain'd: The Houses in this Country are all built of firr boards plain'd within, low & seldom of above one storie: The People very Clownish, & rustickly clad, after a very odd fashion, for the most part in blew cloth, very whole & warme, nor with almost any variety or distinction, twixt the gentlemen & common sort, by a law of their Country, being exceedingly frugal: so as I saw not one begger among them; add to this their greate honestie & fidelitie, though exacting enough for what they part with: We paied the value of 20 shill: *English* for a days hire of one horse: Every man gos with a sword by his side, & the whole Country well disciplind, & indeede impregnable, which made the *Romans* have so ill successe against them; one lusty Swisse, at their narrow passages sufficient to repell a Legion: 'Tis a frequent thing here for a Young Trades man, or fermor to leave his Wife & Children for 12 or 15 Yeares, and seeke his fortune in the Warrs abroad in Spaine, France, Italy or Germanie & then returne againe to Work: I looke upon this Country, to be the safest spot of all *Europ*, neither Envyed, nor Envying, nor are any of them rich, nor poore; but live in greate Simplicity & tranquilitie, & though of the 14 *Cantons* halfe be *Roman Catholics*, the rest Reformed; yet they mutualy agree, & are confederate with *Geneva* & its onely security against its potent Neighbours: as their owne is, from being atack'd by the greater Potentates, by the Jealosie of their neighbours, who would be over balanc'd, should the *Swisse* (who now are wholy mercenarie, & Auxilliaries) be subj(e)cted to France or Spaine:

We were now ariv'd at St. *Maurize*, a large & handsome Towne, & residence of the President, where Justice is don: To him we presented our letter from *Sion*, and made known the ill usage we receiv'd for the killing of a wretched Goate; & which so incens'd him, as he sware, if we would stay, not onely to helpe us to our mony againe, but most severely to punish the whole rabble: but we were by this time past our revenge, & glad we were gotten so neere France, which we reckon'd as good as home: He courteously invited us to dine with him, but we excus'd ourselves, & returning to our Inn, whilst we were eating something before we tooke horse, the Governor had causd two pages to bring us a present of two huge Vessels of Cover'd Plate full of Excellent Wine, which we drank his health in, & rewarded the Youthes;

The Plate were two vast boules, supported by 2 Swisses handsomly wrought after the German manner: This Civilitie, & that
of our hosts at *Sion*, perfectly reconcild us to the hig⟨h⟩landers, &
so proceeding on our journy, we passd this afternoone through
the Gate which divides the *Valois* from the Dutchy of *Savoy*, into
which we now were entering, & so thro *Montei* ariv'd that
evening to *Beveretta*, where being extreamely weary, & com-
plaining of my head, & little accommodation in the house,
I caus'd one of our Hostesses daughters to be removed out of her
bed, & went immediately into it, whilst it was yet warme, being
so heavy with paine & drowsinesse, that I would not stay to have
the sheetes chang'd; but I shortly after pay'd dearely for my impatience, falling sick of the Small Pox so soone as I came to
Geneva; for by the smell of franc Incense, & the tale the good-
woman told me, of her daughters having had an Ague, I afterwards concluded she had ben newly recoverd of the Small Pox:
The paine of my head & wearinesse making me not consider of
any thing, but how to get to bed so soone as ever I alighted, as
not able any longer to sit on horseback: Notwithstanding this,
I went with my Company the next day, hiring a bark to carry us
over the Lake [*Lacus Lemanus*], & indeede, sick as I was, the
Weather was so serene & bright, the Water so Calme, & aire
temperate, that, never had Travelers a sweeter passage: Thus we
saild the whole length of the Lake, for about 30 miles, The
Countries bordering on it, *Savoy* & *Bearne*, affording one of the
most delightfull prospects in the World, the *Alps*, cover'd with
Snow, though at greate distance, yet shewing their aspiring tops:
[They speake of Monsters & *Tritons* often seene in this *Lake*.]
Through this Lake, the River *Rhodanus* passes with that velocity
as not to mingle with its exceeding deepe waters, which are very
cleare, & breedes the most celebrated Troute, for largenesse
& goodnesse of any in all *Europ*: I have ordinarily seene one of 3
foote in length, sold in the Merket for a small Price: & such we
had in the Lodging where we abode, which was at the *White
Crosse*: All this while I held up tollerably, & the next morning
(having a letter for Signor *John Diodati* the famous *Italian Minister*, & Translator of the *Holy Bible* into that Language) I went
to his house, & had a greate deale of discourse with that learned
person: He told me he had ben in England, droven by Tempest
into *Deale*, sailing for Holland, had seene London, & was

exceedingly taken with the Civilities he receivd: He so much
approv'd of our Church Government by Bishops; that he told
me, The French Protestants would make no Scruple to submitt
to it, & all its pomp, had they a King of the reform'd Religion, as
we had: he exceedingly deplord, the difference now betweene
his Majestie & his Parliament: After dinner came one *Monsieur
Saladine* (with his little Pupil the Earle of *Carnarvon*) to visite
us, offering to carry us to the Principal places of the Towne: But
being now no more able to hold up my head, I was constrain'd to
keepe my Chamber, imagining that my very eyes would have
droped out, & this night felt such a stinging all about me that
I could not sleepe: In the morning I was very ill: yet for all that,
the *Doctor* (whom I had now consulted, & was a very learned old
man, & as he sayd had ben Physition to *Gustavus* the greate
King of Sweden, when he pass'd this way into Italy, under the
name of Monsieur *Garse*, the *Initial* letters of *Gustavus Adolphus
Rex Sueciæ*, & of our famous *Duke of Boukingham* returning out
of *Italy*) perswaded me to be let bloud, which he accknowledg'd
to me he should not have don, had he suspected the Small-Pox,
which brake out a ⟨day⟩ after; for he also purg'd me, & likewise
applied *Hirudines* ad *anum*, & God knows what this had produc'd if the spots had not appeard: for he was thinking of bloud-
ing me againe: Wherefore now they kept me warme in bed for
16 daies, tended by a vigilant Swisse Matron whose monstrous
Throat, when I sometimes awake'd out ⟨of⟩ unquiet slumbers
would affright me: After the pimples were come forth, which
were not many, I had much ease, as to paine, but infinitly
afflicted with the heate & noysomenesse; But by Gods mercy,
after five weekes keping my Chamber, being purg'd, & visited by
severall of the Towne: espec⟨i⟩aly Monsieur Saladine & his
Lady, who sent me many refreshments, during my sicknesse:
Monsieur Le Chat (my *Physitian*) to excuse his letting me bloud,
told me it was so burnt & vitious, as it would have prov'd the
Plague or spoted feavor, had he proceeded by any other method:
     The next day after my going abroad, I din'd at Mr. *Saladines*,
& in the afternoone, went crosse the Water on the side of the
Lake, to take a Lodging that stood exceeding pleasantly, about
halfe a mile off the Citty, for better ayring; but I onely stayd one
night, having no Company there save my Pipe; so as the next
day, I causd them to row me about the *Lake*, as far as the greate

Stone, which they call *Neptunes* rock, on which they say, Sacrifice was antiently offer'd to him: Thence I landed at certaine
Chery-Gardens, & pretty *Villas* situate on the rivage, & exceedingly pleasant: Returning I visited their Conservatories of Fish,
in which were Trouts of 6 & 7 foote long as they affirm'd: The
River *Rhone*, which parts the Citty in the midest, dips into a
Cavern under ground, about 6 miles from it, & afterwards rises
againe, & runns its open Course, like our *Mole* or *Swallow* by
Darking in *Surrey*. Next morning (being *Thursday*) I heard
Dr. *Diodati* preach in *Italian*, many of that Country, especialy of
his native *Lucca* being Inhabitants at *Geneva*, & of the Reformd
religion: And now I was intent about seeing the Towne, which
lies betweene *Germanie*, *France*, & *Italy*, so as those three
Tongues are familiarly spoken by the Inhabitans: 'Tis a strong,
well fortified Citty, part of it built on a rising ground; The
houses are not despicable, but the high pent-houses (for I can
hardly call them Cloysters) being all of wood; thro which the
people passe drie, & in the shade winter & summer, exceedingly
deforme the fronts of the buildings: Here are aboundance of
Booke-Sellers, but Ill Impressions: These with Watches (of
which store are made here), Chrystal, & excellent Screw'd
Gunns, are the staple commodities: & all Provisions are good
& cheape: One of the first things I went to see after I was gotten
abroad, was the *Towne-house*, fairely built of stone. The *Portico*
has foure black-marble Columns; & on a *Table* of the same this
Inscription.

Post Tenebras, Lux.

(which is the motto under the Citty Armes, which are a demie
Eagle, & a *Crosse* betweene the *Crosse Keys*).

The Territories about the Towne are not so large as many
ordinary gentlemen have about their Country farmes; for which
cause they are in continual watch, especialy on the *Savoy* side;
but in case ⟨of⟩ any seige the Swisse are at hand, They shew'd us
in this Senat house 14 antient Urnes, dug up as they were removing Earth in the fortifications:

Hence we walked a little out of Towne, to a spacious field,
which they call *Campus Martius*, & well it may so be term'd,
with better reason, than that of *Rome* at present, (which is no
more a field, but all built into streetes) for here on every *Sonday*

after the Evening devotions, this precise people, permitt their Youth to exercise Armes, & shoote in Gunns, & in the long & Crosse bowes, in which they are exceedingly expert, as reputed to be as dextrous as any people in the world; To encourage which, they yearely elect he that has won most prizes at the mark, to be their King: as the King of the Long bow, Gun, or Crosse-bow who weares that weapon in his hat in gold, with a crowne over it, made fast to the hatt like a broach: There is in this fild a long house wherein in severall presses, are kept their Armes, & furniture very neately; to which joynes a Hall, where on certaine times they meete & feast, & in the glasse windos, are the Armes & names of their Kings: At the side of the fild is a very noble Pall-Mall, but it turnes with an elbow; Also a bowling Place, a Tavern, and a True-table, & here they likewise ride their menag'd Horses; and it is the usual place of publique Execution, who suffer here, for any capital crime, tho committed in another Country, by which Law, divers fugitives have ben put to death, who have repaird hither for protection: amongst other severe punishments, Adultery is death: Having seene this field, & playd a game at Mall, I supp'd at Mr. *Saladines*. On *Sonday*, I heard *Dr. Diodati* preach in *French* & after the French mode in a Gowne with a Cape, & his hat on: The Church Government is severely *Presbyterian*; after the discipline of *Calvine* & *Beza*, who set it up; but nothing so rigid, as either our Scots, or English Sectaries of that denomination: In the afternoone *Monsieur Morise* a Young most learned person, & excellent Poet, chiefe Professor of the University: This was in St. *Peters*, heretofore a Cathedral, & a reverend pile: I⟨t⟩ has 4 Turrets, on which stands a continual Sentinel, on another Cannons mounted: The Church within is very decent, nor have they at all defac'd the painted windows, which are full of Saints pictures, nor the Stalls, which are all carved with the Historie of our *B: Saviour*: a Spacious Church, of *Gotic* fabric:

In the afternoone I went to see the young townes men exercise in Mars field, where the Prizes were pewter plates, & dishes: 'Tis said that some have gain'd competent Estates, by what they have thus won: Here I first saw huge *Balistæ* or Crosse bows (such as they formerly us'd in wars, before Greate guns were known) shot in: They were placed in frames, & had might⟨y⟩ screws to bend them, doing execution an incredible distance:

They are most accurate at the long-bow, and Musquet, very rarely missing the smalest mark; & I was as buisy with the *Carbine* I brought with me from *Bressia* as any of them: After every shot, I found them go into the long house & clense their guns before they charg'd againe.

On Moneday I was invited to a little Garden without the Workes, where were many rare *Tulips*, *Anemonies* & other choice flowers: The ⟨*Rhodanus*⟩ running 'thwart the Towne out of the Lake, makes halfe the Citty Suburbs, ⟨which⟩ (in imitation of *Paris*) they call *St. Germans fauxbourg*, and it has a church of the same name: On Two Wooden bridges that go Crosse the river, are severall water Mills, & shops of Trades, especialy Smiths & Cuttlers, & betweene the bridges an Iland, in the midst of which a very antient Tower, said to be built by *Julius Cæsar*, at the end of the other bridge is the Mint, & a faire sun-dial.

Passing againe by the Town-house, I spied a large *Crocodile* hanging in chaines, and against the wall of one of the Chambers seaven *Judges* painted without hands, all excepting one in the middle who has but one; I know not the storie—: The *Arsenal* is at the End of this building, & is exceedingly well furnished & kept.

After dinner Monsieur *Morice* led us to the Colledge, which is a faire structure, underneth are the Scholes, which consist of 9 *Classes*, & an hall above, where the students assemble: & a good Library. They shewd us a very antient Bible, of about 300 yeares in vulgar *French*, a MSS: in the old munkish Character: Here have the Professors their Lodgings: I also went to see the *Hospital*, which is very commodious: But the Bishops Palace is now a Prison.

Whilst we thus linger'd in this famous Towne, not very much celebrated for beauties, (for even at this distance from the *Alps*, the gentlewomen have something full Throates,) our Captaine *Wray*, (afterwards Sir Will: Wray, eldest son to that Sir *Christopher*, who had ben both in armes against his Majesty for the Parliament) fell so mightily in love with one of Monsieur *Saladines* daughters, that with much perswasion, could he be gotten to think of his journey, into *France*, the season now coming on extreamely hot: My sicknesse and abode here cost me 45 pistols of gold to my Host, & 5 to my honest Doctor, who for 6 Weekes attendance & the Apothecarie, thought it so generous a reward, that at my taking leave, he presented me with his advice for the regiment of my health, written with his own hand in Latine.

FRANCE AGAIN AND MARRIAGE
(1646-1647)

BUT I BLESSE God, I pass'd this *Journey* without any of these inconveniences, yet much observing the regiment prescribed me: It was an extraordinary hot, unpleasant season, & journey by reason of the Craggie Waies: The morning after we tooke, or rather purchased a boate, for it could not be brought back againe, because of the streame of the *Rhodanus* running here about. Thus were we two days going to Lions, passing by many admirable Prospects of Rocks & Cliffs, and neare the towne, down a very steepe declivitie of Water, for a full mile: From *Lions*, we proceeded the next morning, taking horse to *Rohan*, & lay that night at *Tarrara*: At *Rohan* it was we indulged our-selves, with the best that all *France* affords; for here the provisions are choice & plentifull: so as the supper we had, might have satisfied a Prince: We lay that night in Damask beds (at *Monsieur de Loups*) & were treated like Emperours:

This Town is one of the neatest built in all France, on the brink of Loire & here we agreede with an old fisher, to row us as farr ⟨as⟩ Orleans:

The first night came we to *Nevers*, early enough to see the Towne, the Cathedral St. *Cyre*; the *Jesuits Colledge*, the Castle, or Palac of the Dukes, with the bridge to it is nobly built. Next day we past by *La Charite*, a pretty towne somewhat distant from the River, & here it was I lost my faithfull *Spaniel* (*Piccioli*) who had follow'd me from *Rome*; it seemes he had ben taken up by some of the *Governors* pages or foote-men, without recovery, which was a greate displeasure to me, because the curr, had many use-full qualities: The next day we ariv'd at *Orleans*, taking our turn to row through all the former passages, & reckoning that my share amounted to little lesse than 20 legues; sometimes footing it through pleasant fields & medows, sometimes we shot at fouls & other birds, nothing came amisse, sometimes we play'd at

Cards, whilst other sung, or were composing Verses; for we had the greate Poet Mr. Waller in our Companie, & some other ingenious Persons: At *Orleans* we abode but one day, the next (leaving our mad Captaine behind us) I arived at *Paris*, strangely rejoyc'd, after so many dissasters, & accidents, of a tedious Peregrination, that I was gotten so neere home, & therefore resolved to rest myselfe before I set on any farther Motion.

It was now *October*, & the onely time that in my whole life I spent most idly, tempted from my more profitable recesses; but I soone recovered my better resolutions, & fell to my study, & learning of the high-dutch & Spanish tongues, & now & then refreshing my Dauncing, & such exercises as I had long omitted, & which are not in such reputation among the sober *Italians*.

1647. *January* 28, I chang'd my Lodging in the Place *de Monsieur de Metz* neere the Abby of St. *Germains*, & thence on the 12 *feb:* to another in *Rüe Collumbiers*, where I had a very faire Appartment, which cost me 4 pistols per Moneth: The 18 I frequented a Course of *Chymistrie*, the famous Monsieur *Le Febure* operating upon most of the Nobler processes: 3 March, *Monsieur Mercure* began to teach me on the *Lute*, though to small perfection.

In *May* I fell sick & had very sore Eyes, for which I was 4 times let blood. The 22d: My *Valet* de Chambre *Hebert* robbed me of the value of threescore pounds in *Clothes* & *plate*; but through the dilligence of Sir *Richard Browne* his Majesties Resident at the Court of France & with whose Lady & family I had contracted a greate Friendship (& particularly set my affections on a Daughter)[1] I recoverd most of them againe; obtaining of the *Judge* (with no small difficulty) that the processe against my Theife, should not concerne his life, being his first fault:

June 10th: We concluded about my Marriage, in order to which on 26: I went to *St. Germans*, where his Majestie (then *Prince of Wales*) had his Court, to desire of *Dr. Earles*, then one of his Chaplaines, & since, Deane of Westminster, Clearke of the Closset & Bishop of Salisburie, to come with me to *Paris*.

So on *Thursday* 27 June 1647 the Doctor Married us in Sir *Richard Browne* Knight & Baronet My Wifes fathers Chapell, twixt the houres of 11 & 12; some few select friends being present: And this being *Corpus Christ* feast, solemn(l)y observ'd in

1 Mary, *c.* 1635–1709, whom Evelyn married.

these Countries, the stretes were sumptuously hung with Tapissry, & strew'd with flowers.

July 13, I went with my Wife, & her *Mother*, to St. *Cloud*, where we collation'd, and were serv'd in Plate:

September 10th, being call'd into England to settle my affaires, after about 4 yeares absence (my Wife being yet very Young, and therefore dispensing with a temporarie & kind separation, whilst left under the care of an excellent Lady, & prudent Mother) I tooke leave of the Prince, & *Queene*:

Octob: 4: I seald & declard my Will: & that morning went from *Paris* taking my journey thro *Rouen*, *Dieppe*, *Ville-Dieu*, *St. Vallerie*, where I staied one day, with Mr. *Waller*, with whom I had some affaires, & for which cause I tooke this Circle to *Calice*, where I ariv'd on the 11th and that night Imbarking in the Paquet-boate, was by one aclock gott safe to *Dover*; for which I heartily put up my Thankes to God, who had conducted me safe to my owne Country, & ben mercifull to me through so many aberrations: Hence taking *Post*, I ariv'd at *London* the next day at Evening, being the 2d of October *New-style*.

THE DEFEATED ROYALIST
(1647–1649)

ON THE 4TH my *Bro: George* hearing where I was sent me horses & a kind Invitation, so on the 5t I came to *Wotton* the place of my Birth, where I found his Lady, my Sister, & severall of my friends and relations, amongst whom I refresh'd my selfe & rejoyc'd 'til the 10th, when I went to *Hampton Court*, where I had the honour to kisse his Majesties Hand, and give him an Account of severall things I had in charge, he being now in the power of those execrable Villains who not long after mu⟨r⟩der'd him: Here I lay at my Co: Searjeant *Hattons* at *Thames Ditton* whence on the 13 I went to *London*, the next day to *Sayes*-Court (now my house) at *Deptford* in *Kent*, where I found Mr. *Prety-man* my Wifes *Unkle*, who had charge of it, & the Estate about it during my F in Laws Residence in *France*: on the 15th I went to lodge in my owne Chambers at the *Middle Temple* about the

dispatch of my particular concernes. *November* the 7th I return'd
againe to *Wotton* to visite my brother, & on the 9th my Sister,
opened to me her Marriage with Mr. *Glanvill*: *December* 3: I
went back to *Deptford*, and the next day to *London*, where I
staied till [1648] *January* 14th when I went to *Wotton* to see my
young *Nephew*, & thence to *Baynards* to visite my *Bro: Richard*,
who came back with me on the 18th & stayd 'til 29, before my
returne to *London*.

Feb: 5 I saw a *Tragie Comedie* acted in the *Cock-pit*, after there
had ben none of these diversions for many Yeares during the
Warr.

28 I went to *Thistleworth* (with my noble friend Sir *William
Ducy*, afterwards Lord Downe) where we dined with Sir
Clepesby Crew, and afterwards to see the rare Miniatures of *Peter
Oliver* [and rounds of plaster] & then the curious flowers of Mr.
Barills garden: Sir *Clepesby* has fine *Indian* hangings, and a very
good chimny-piece of Water Colours don by *Breugle* which
I bought for him: Mr. *Barill* has also some good *Medails* &
Pictures.

Aprill 3. I went to *Wotton*, thence to a place neere *Henly* cald
Boyne, belonging to one Mr. *Elmes*, which I thought to have
purchas'd & settled in; but we did not accord: So on the 5t
I return'd, & the 10th to *Lond*:

26. There was a greate up-rore in *Lond*, that the *Rebell* Armie
quartering at *Whitehall* would plunder the *Cittie*, who publish'd
a proclamation for all to stand on their guard:

May: 4 Came-up the Essex petitioners for an agreement
'twixt his Majestie & the Rebells. 16 The *Surry* men addressd to
the Parliament for the same, of which some were slayne & murder'd by *Cromwells* guards in the new Palace yard.

I now sold, the Impropriation of *South Malling* neere *Lewes*
in Sussex to Mr. *Kemp* & *Alcock* for 3000 pounds:

23 I went to *Deptford*, & 30: to *Lond*: 29: to Dept: 30: Lond:
about buisinesse:

There was a rising now in *Kent*, my Lord of *Norwich* being in
the head of them and their first rendezvous in *Broome-fild*, next
my house at *Says-Court* whence they went to *Maidstone*, & so to
Colchester where there was that memorable siege:

June 27: I purchas'd the Manor of *Hurcott* in *Worcestershire* of
my Bro: *Geo:* for 3300 pounds: on the 29 I return'd to *Deptford*.

July 1. I sate for my *Picture* (the same wherein is a *Deaths head*) to Mr. *Walker* that excellent Painter: The 10th Newes was brought me of my Lord *Francis Villiers* being slaine by the rebells neere Kingston: 13th I returnd to *Deptford*: 17th I went to hunting at my *Lady Lees*, where we kill'd a buck: 25 I return'd & went to *Ebsham* to meete my Bro: *Richard* & so return'd: 28: I went to *Eltam*, to visite my Lady *Gerrard*.

Aug: 10th To Lond, return'd: 16 To *Woodcoat* to the Wedding of my *Bro: Richard* who married the Daughter & Coheire, of Esquire *Minn* lately deceased: by which he had a greate Estate both in Land & monie, upon the death of a Brother &c: *Memorandum* that the Coach in which the Bride & Bridegroome were, was overturn'd in coming home, but no harme: 19 I return'd to *Sayes-Court* &: 22: to *Lond:* 25 return'd: 28 To Lond, & went to see the celebrated follies of *Bartholomew* faire.

September 8. I returnd to *Deptford*: 16 Came my lately married Bro: *Richard* & his Wife to visite me: 17 I shewed them Greenewich & her Majesties Palace, now possessd by the *Rebells*: 18 Went my Unkle *Pretyman* into *France*, & my Bro: return'd home. 25 I went to *Lond:* & next day to *Wotton*: 28 to *Alburie* to visite the Countesse of *Arundel*, return'd to *Wotton*. 30th To *Woodcot* & the 3d of *Octob:* to *Lond:* 7 to *Says Court*: 13 To *Lond:* 20 Return'd, next day came my *Bro: Richd:* with whom I went to *Woodcot* & on 26: To *Lewes*, in which journey I escaped a strange fall from my horse in the dark, from an high bank & deepe way about *Chaylie:* 31 I went to see my Mannor of *Preston Beckhelvyn*, & the Cliff *house*:

1 *November* we return'd with my Bro: R: & *Glanvill* by *Shoreham, Bramber* (where is a ruinous Castle) *Billingshurst* where we lay that night, & next day at *Woodcot*, & on the 6 to *Says-Court*: 7: to *Lond:* 11: returned: 14: To *Lond.* 29 Myselfe, with Mr. *Tho: Offley*, & Lady *Gerrard* Christned my Nieece Mary, Eldest daughter of my Bro: Geo: Evelyn by my *Lady Cotton* his second *Wife*: I presented my *Niepce* a piece of *Plate* which cost me 18 pounds.

Decemb: 2: I lent 1000 pounds to Esquire *Hyldiard* on a statute: & this day sold my *Mannor* of ⟨Hurcott⟩ for 3400 pounds to one Mr. *Bridges* & on the 4th acknowlegd the fine.

4th I lent 1000 pounds to my Lord *Vicount Montague*, on a ⟨Mortgage⟩ of *Horslay*, in Surry: 10 I went to *Deptford*: 13 to

Lond: The Parliament now sat up the whole night, & endeavord to have concluded the Ile of *Wight* Treaty, but were surprizd by the rebell Army, the Members disperssd, & greate confusion every where in expectation what would be next: I now also gave Mr. *Christmas* a Receipt for 5000 pounds which being deposited in his hands, had ben repay'd me at severall times.

14. I visited the Countesse of *Arundell*: 17 I heard an *Italian* Sermon in *Mercers* Chapell, one Dr *Middleton* an acquaintance of mine preaching:

18. I gott privately into the Council of the rebell *Army* at White-hall, where I heard horrid villanies: 20: I return'd to Sayes-Court: 28 my Bro: *George* came & dined with me: *Memorand* This was a most exceeding wett yeare, neither frost or snow all the winter for above 6 days in all, & Cattell died of a Murrain every where:

1649. *January* 1. I went from *Sayes Court* (my Fa: in *Laws howse* in *Deptford* where I had a Lodging, & some books) to *Lond*, & on the 2d to see my old friend & fellow Traveller Mr. *Henshaw*, who had two rare pieces of *Steenewicks* perspectives: 3d I din'd at Sir *Cl: Crews*, where was old Sir *Arthyr Gorge*, after dinner I visited my *Lord Montague* where was the Marquis of *Winchester*, Sir Jo: *Winter* & his Lady: 13. I returned to *S. Court*: 17: [To Lond:] I heard the rebell *Peters* incite the Rebell powers met in the Painted Chamber, to destroy his Majestie & saw that Arch Traytor *Bradshaw*, who not long after condemn'd him. On the 19 I return'd home, passing an extraordinary danger of being drown'd, by our *Whirries* falling fowle in the night, on another vessell there at *Anker*, shooting the Bridge at 3 quarter Ebb, for which his mercy, God Almighty be prais'd.

21. was published my Translation of *Liberty* & *Servitude*, for the Preface of which I was severely threatn'd: 22d I went through a Course of *Chymistrie* at *S. Court* & now was the *Thames* frozen over, & horrid Tempest of Winds, so different was this part of the Winter from the former:

The Villanie of the Rebells proceeding now so far as to Trie, Condemne, & *Murder* our excellent King, the 30 of this Moneth, struck me with such horror that I kept the day of his *Martyrdom* a fast, & would not be present, at that execerable wickednesse; receiving that sad ⟨account⟩ of it from my Bro:

Geo: & also by Mr. *Owen*, who came to Visite this afternoone, recounting to me all Circumstances.

31 Came to see me my good & deare Friend Mr. *Phil: Packer*, with whom after dinner, I walked on foote to Lond, it being an hard frost:

Feb: 1. I entertaind my *Bro: G:* & his *Lady* with other friends at my Lodgings in the *Temple*: Now were *Duke Hamilton*, E: of *Norwich*, L: *Capell* &c at their *Trial* before the Rebells: New Court of Injustice: 15. I went to see the Collection of one *Friars* a rich Merchant, who had some good Pictures, especialy a rare Perspective of *Stenewicke*, a faire *Organ* for the Voice: from whence to other Virtuosos, the Paynter *La Neve*, who has an *Andromeda*, but I think it a Copy after *Vandike* from *Titian*, for the Orig⟨i⟩nal is in *France*.

Web, at the Exchange has some rare things in miniature of *Breugls*, also *Puti* in 12 Squares, that were plunderd from Sir *James Palmer*: At *Du Bois* we saw 2 Tables of Puti, that were gotten I know not how, out of the Castle of St. *Angelo* by old *Petit*, thought to be *Titians*, he has some good heads of Palma, & one of *Stenewick*:

Bellcan shewd us an excellent Copy of his Majesties Venus Sleeping, & the Satyre, with other figures; for now they had plunderd sold & dissipat⟨e⟩d a world of rare Paintings of the Kings & his Loyall Subjects: After all Sir William *Ducy* shewd me some excellent things in Miniature, & in Oyle of *Holbeins* Sir Tho: *Mores* head, & an whole figure of *Ed: the Sixt*: which were certainly his Majesties; also a Picture of Q: *Elizabeth*, the Lady *Isabella Thynn*, a rare painting of *Rotenhamer* being a *Susanna*, & a *Magdalena* of *Quintine* the black-smith. Also an *Hen:* 8th of *Holben*, & *Francis* the first rare indeede, but of whose hand I know not:

16: *Paris* being now streitly besieged by the Pr: of *Condy*, my wife being with her Father & Mother shut up, I writ to comfort her: next day went back to *Says-Court*: 20: To *Lond:* 22. return'd, having recomended *Obadiah Walker* [*since Apostate*], a Learned & most ingenious Person, to be Tutor, [to,] & to Travell with Mr. *Hyldiards* two sonns; 25 Came to visie me Dr. *Joyliffe* inventor of the *Lymphatic Vessells*, & an excellent *Anatomist*. 26: Came to see me Cap: *George Evelyn* my kindsman, the greate Travellor, & one who believed himselfe a better *Architect* than realy he was, witnesse the *Portico* in the *Garden* at *Wotton*; yet the greate roome at *Alburie* is somewhat better understood: he had a large mind, but over built every thing:

27 Came out of *France* my Wifes Unkle, (Paris still besieg'd): being rob'd by sea of the Dynkirk Pyrats, I lost among other goods my *Wifes Picture* painted by Monsieur *Bourdon*: 28: *Lond:*

Mar: 2: To S. *Court* with my Bro: G: thence with him to *Wotton*; 3d to *Horsley* to visite the V: *Countesse Montague*, return'd by *East Horsley* to see Mr *Hyldyard* & Lady: 5. I returnd home by Woodcot. Now were the Lords Murdered in the *Palace Yard*: 9 Came my Bro: in Law *Glanvill* to visite me.

18 Mr. *Owen* a sequesterd, & learned Minister, preach'd in our Parlor, & gave us the *Blessed Sacrament*, which was now wholy out of use: in the *Parish Churches* on which the *Presbyterians* & *Fanatics* had usurped: 21 I went to Lond:

21 I receiv'd letters from *Paris* from my *Wife* & Sir *Richard*, with whom I kept a political Correspondence, with no small danger of being discover'd:

23 I sealed my Tennant *Harris* his lease of the Farme at *Preston* in *Sussex* for II. yeares at 100 pounds per Ann: 25. I heard Common-prayer (a rare thing in these dayes) at St. *Peters Paules* Wharfe Lond: & in the Morning the Arch-Bishop of *Armagh* that pious person & learned man *Usher* in *Lincolns Inn* Chapell. 29 I tooke preventing Physick: & 31 return'd to S. *Court*:

Aprill 2. To Lond, & Inventoried my Moveables, that had hitherto ben dispers'd for feare of Plundering: & writ into *France* touching my suddaine resolutions of coming over to them: 5. I visited Sir *Charles Lee*: 8: heard *Archbish: Usher* againe, on 4 *Eph:* 26. 27.

My *Italian* Collection being now ariv'd, came *Moulins* the greate Chirurgion to see & admire the Tables of *Veines* & *Arteries*, which I purchasd, & causd to be drawne out of several humane bodys at *Padua*: 11 I receiv'd newes out of *France* that the Peace was concluded, & din'd with Sir Jo: Evelyns at *Westminster*: 13 I saw a private *dissection* at *Moulin's*. 14 I heard the AB: of *Armagh* on *15. Pro: 18* against the passion of Wrath: 16 I writ into *France* treating with my F in Law about *Warley*: 17 I fell dangerously ill of my head, was blisterd, & let blood, & behind the Eares and forehead: & 23d began to have Ease, by using the fumes of Cammomile on Embers applied to my Eares, after all the *Physitians* had don their best: 28 Went abroad: 29. I saw in *Lond:* an huge *Oxe* bred in *Kent* of 17 foote in length, & higher by much than I could reach:

May 9: I din'd at Eltham with my La: *Gerrard*: 10th Visite my Lo: *Montague* &c:

12 I bought, & seald the Conveyances for *Warley Magna* in Essex a *Mannor*, [Payd 2500 pounds.] This afternoone went to see *Geldrops* collections of Payntings, where I found Mr. *Endymion Porter* of his late Majesties *Bedchamber*, where we had collation: 15 I returnd to S. *Court* & 16 to Lond: 17: To *Putney* by Water in barge with divers Ladys, to see the *Schooles* or *Colledges* of the Young Gentlewomen: 19. to see a rare Cabinet of on⟨e⟩ *Delabarrs*, he had some good *Paintings* especialy a *Munk* at his beades: 21 I seald my Tennant *Raynolds*, Lease of Ripe in Sussex at the rent of 48 pounds, for 21 yeares: 22. Return'd to S. Court: & 24. Lond: & back at night. 30 was Un-king-ship, pro-claim'd, & his Majesties Statues throwne downe at St. *Paules* Portico, & Exchange: 31 I went to Lond:

7. *June* I visited Sir *Arthyr* Hopton (bro: to Sir Ralph Lord Hopton that noble Hero) who having ben *Ambassador* extr: in *Spaine*, sojourn'd some time, with my F. in Law, at *Paris*, a most excellent Person: Also: *Signora Lucretia* a *Greeke* Lady, whom I knew in *Italy*, now come over with her husband an Eng: Gent: also the Earle & Countesse of *Arundel* taking leave of them & other friends now ready to depart for *France*: This night was a scuffle betweene some rebell Souldiers & Gentlemen about the Temple:

10: Preach'd the A.B.: of *Armagh* in Lincolns Inn, I receiv'd the B: *Sacrament* preparatory to my Journey: his text was 5 *Rom:* 13.

13 I din'd with my worthy friend Sir John *Owen* newly freed from Sentence of Death among the Lords that Sufferd: here was with Sir John one *Carew* who playd incomparably on the *Welsh Harp*. 13. I treated divers Ladys of my relations in *Spring Garden*: This night was buried with greate pomp *Dorislaw* slaine at the *Hague*, the villain who menag'd the Triall against his Sacred Majestie. 16 I kept Court at *Warley* my late *Purchas*. I receivd of a debt, 320 pounds from my Bro: *Ge: Evelyn*: 17: I got a *Passe* from the Rebell *Bradshaw* then in greate power: & visited Mr. *Lewes*: 19: to S. *Court*, & back that Evening. 20 I went to ⟨*Puttny*⟩ & other places on the Thames to take

prospects in Crayon, to carry into *France*, where I thought to have them Engrav'd.

24 I went to Mr. *Lewes's* Wedding, & that Evvening Seald another Will & return'd home. 28 I went to *Wotton* to take leave of my Bro: &c. passing by *Woodcot*: 29 We went all to be merry at *Guildford*, returnd that evening:

30 Riding out my Brothers stonehorse struck me dangerously on the leg: but it soone healed God be blessed:

July 2. I went from *Wotton* to *Godstone*, where was also Sir *Jo: Evlyn* of Wilton, where I tooke leave of both Sir *Johns*, & Ladys: *Memorand*, the prodigious memory of Sir Jo: of Wilts's daughter, since married to Mr. W: *Pierepoint* & mother of the present Earle of Kingston: I return'd to S. Court this night. 3. To Lond. 4th Visited *Lady Hatton*, her Lord sejourning at *Paris* with my F. in Law:

5 I went to see my God-daughter Evelyn at *Chesewick* at Nurse. 6 home: 7 *Lond*. dind at a Merchants, who furnishd me with bills for France. 9. din'd with Sir *Walter Pye* & my good friend *Mr. Eaton* (afterwards a *Judge*) who corresponded with me in *France* & return'd to *S. Court*. 11 Came *Old Alexander Rosse* the Divine, Historian, & Poet: Mr. *Henshaw*, *Scudamor* & other friends to take leave of me: The next day about 3 in the Afternoone I tooke Oares for *Gravesend*

EXILE: FRANCE, ENGLAND AND FRANCE AGAIN
(1649–1652)

12 ACCOMPANIED BY my *Co: Stephens*, & my *Sister Glanvill*, who there supp'd with me, & return'd: Whence I tooke post immediately to *Dover*, where I arived by 9 in the morning, & about 11 that night went on board in a bark, Guarded by a Pinnace of 8 gunns, this being the first time the Pacquett boate had obtain'd a Convoy, having severall times before ben pillag'd: I carried over with me my Servant *Ri: Hoare* an incomparable writer of severall hands, whom I afterwards preferrd in the Prerogative Office, at returne of his Majestie. We had a good passage, though chased by a *Pyrate* for some houres, but he Durst not attaque our fregat & so left us: But we then chased them, til they got under

the protection of the Castle at *Calais*: The vessell was a small *Privateere* belonging to the *Prince of Wales*: I was very sick at *Sea*, till about 5 in the morning that we landed, before the Gates were open: & so ⟨did⟩ my Lady *Catherine Scot* daughter to the *Earle* of *Norwich*, that follow'd us in a Shallop, with one Mr. *Arth: Slingsby*, who came out of England *Incognito*. At entrance of the Towne, the Lieutennant Governor being on his horse with the Guards let us passe Courteously: I went to visite Sir Richard Lloyd an English Gent: in the Towne, & walked in the Church, where the Ornament about the high Altar of black-marble is very fine, & there is a good picture of the Assumption: The Citadell seemes to be impregnable, & the whole Country about it, to be laied under Water by sluces for many miles.

16 We departed for Paris, in company with that pleasant Lady, Scott, one Slingsby, and a Spanish don call'd *Sanchez* whom I found to be a very good Schollar, and one that had seen the World: The 2d days Journey passing through *Marquise* there being a Faire that day, I lost a Spaniel which I brought with me out of England, taken up I suppose by the Souldiers: We were in all this Journey greately apprehensive of Parties, which caused us to alight often out of our Coach, & walke separately on foote with our Guns ready, in all suspected places.

1. August 3 afternoone we came to *St. Denis*, saw the rarities of the Church & Tresury & so to *Paris* in the Evening: The next day, came to Wellcome me at dinner my *Lord High Treasure⟨r⟩ Cottington, Sir Edw: Hide Chancellor*, Sir *Ed: Nicholas Secretary of State*, Sir *Geo: Cartret Governor* of Jersey, Dr. *Earles*, having now ben absent from my Wife above a Yeare & halfe, & were very cherefull.

The rest of the Weeke was taken up with visites from, & to my friends: On the 18 I went to St. Germains to kisse his Majesties hands; In this Coach (which was my Lord Willmots), went *Mrs. Barlow*, the Kings Mistris & mother to the Duke of *Monemoth*, a browne, beautifull, bold, but insipid creature: 19, I was to salute the French *King*, & Q: Dowager: 21. I returnd in one of the queenes Coaches with my L: German, Duke of Buckingham, Lord Wentworth, & Mr. Crofts, since Lord Crofts:

September 5. Dr. *Earles* preached in our Chapell on 22. Psal: 15, & my Wife received with me the H: Sacrament the first

time: 7th We went with Deane *Cousin* to St. *Germans*, kissed
Queene-Mothers hand: Din'd with my L: Keeper, Lord *Hatton*.
10 Saw the Duke of *Rohan*, *Del Boeuf*, *D'Allenson* & divers
greate Monsieurs, that came to visite his Majestie. The next day
the Pr: of Condy came to see the King: & so returning, went to
see *Maisons*, a noble pile built by a President of that name, 'tis
invirond in a dry, but sweete moate, the offices underground,
the Gardens very magnificent, with extraordina⟨r⟩y long
Walkes set with Elmes, & a noble Prospect on the *Sienne*
towards Paris, but above all, what best pleas'd me, the Artificial
Harbour cut out of the River: The house is well furnish'd, & it
may compare with any Villa about Rome: 12: Dr. *Crighton* (the
Scotch man & on⟨e⟩ of his Majesties Chaplains, a learned
Gretian, who set out the Council of Florence) preach'd. 13 The
King invited the Pr: of Condy to supper at *St. Clo's*: There I
kiss'd the duke of *Yorks* hand in the Tennis Court, where I saw a
famous match 'twixt Monsieur *Saumeurs* & Coll: Cooke, & so
return'd to *Paris*: 'Twas nois'd about I was knighted, a dignity I
often declind: 1 Octob: I went with my *Co: Tuke* (afterwards Sir
Samuel) to see the fountaines of St. *Cloe*, & *Ruel*, & after dinner to talke with the poore ignorant & superstitious
⟨Anchorite⟩ at *Mont Calvarie* & so to *Paris*. 2: Came Mr.
William *Coventrie* (afterwards Sir William & the Dukes Secretary, &c) to visite me. 5. I receiv'd the B: Sacrament, Dr.
Crowder the Dukes Chaplain, preaching on 91. Psal. 11. & din'd
with Sir *Geo: Radcliffe*, that greate favorite of the [late] *Earle of
Straffords*, formerly L: Deputy of Ireland, decapitated. 7th. To
the Louvre to Visie the *Countesse* of *Morton* Governesse to
Madame. 15 Came newes of *Droghedas* being taken, by the
Rebells & all put to the Sword, which made us very sad, fore-
running the losse of all *Ireland*. 21. I went to heare Dr. D'Avin-
sons Lecture in the Physical Garden, & see his Laboratorie: he
being *Prefect* of that excellent *Garden* & professor *Botanicus*: 30
I was at the funerall of one *Mr. Downes* a sober *English* Gent,
we accompanied his Corps to *Charenton*, where he was interr'd
in a Cabbage-Garden, yet with the Office of our Church,
which was said before in our Chapell at *Paris*: Here I saw also
where they buried the Greate Souldier *Gassion*, who had a
Tomb built over him like a Fountaine, the designe & materials
meane enough: I returnd to *Paris* in Coach with Sir *Phil:*

Musgrave, & Sir *Marmaduk Langdal*, since Lord *Langdale*: *Memorandum*: this was a very sickly, & mortal Autumne:

5 *November* I received divers letters out of England, requiring me to come over about settling some of my Concernes: 7 Dr. *Geo: Morley* [officiating] (since Bishop of Winchester) [& Cousin] preaching on 4 Matt: 3. I received the B. Sacrament: in our Chapell.

18 I went with my F. in Law to his Audience at the French Court, where next the *Popes Nuncio*, he was introduc'd by the Master of Ceremonies, & after delivery of his Credentials (as from our King, since his Fathers murder) he was most graciously receivd by the King of France & his Mother, with whom he had a long audience: This was in the *Palais Cardinal*: After this, being presented to his Majestie & the Queene Regent, I went to see the house, built by the late greate *Cardinal* de *Richlieu*: The most observable thing is, the Gallerie painted with the portraicts of the most Illustrious Persons, & signal actions in *France*, with innumerable Emblemes twixt every table: In the middle of the Gallery is a neate Chapell, rarely paved in works & devices of severall sorts of marble, besides the Altarpiece, & 2 statues of white marble, one of St. *John*, the other of the *Virgin Mary* &c: of *Bernini*: The rest of the Apartments are rarely Gilded & Carved, with some good modern Paintings: In the Presence hung 3 huge branches of Chrystal: In the French Kings Bed-chamber, was an *Alcove* like another Chamber, set as it were in a Chamber like a moveable box, with a rich embroidred bed: The fabric of the *Palace* is not magnificent, being but of 2 stories, but the *Garden* is so spacious, as to containe a noble basin, & fountaine continualy playing, & there is a Mall, with an Elbow or turning to protract it: so I left his Majestie on the *Terrace* buisie in seeing a Bull-baiting, & return'd home in *Prince Edwards* Coach with Monsieur Paule, the Pr: Electors Agent.

19 I went to visie Mr. *Waller*, where meeting Dr. Holden (an English Sorbonne divine) we fell into some discourse of Religion:

29: I christned Sir *Hugh Rilies* child (with Sir Geo: Ratcliffe) in our Chapell, the Parents being so poore, that they had provided no Gosships; so as severall of us drawing lotts it fell on me: the Deane of *Peterborow*, Dr. Cosin, officiating: We nam'd it Andrew, being on the Eve of that *Apostles* day:

⟨December⟩ 5. I receiv'd the B: Comm: in our Chapell: Dr. *Morley* preaching on 12: Heb. 5. The like also on 25: Dr. *Cosin* preaching on: 18 Gen: 12. where were (besides all the English) divers *French* it being *Christmas* Day:

28 Going to visite Mr. *Waller*, I considered St. *Stephens* church, the building though *Gotic*, is full of Carving, especialy the Lapidation; within it is beautifull, especialy the *Quire* & winding Staires: The Glasse is well painted, & the Tapissry hung this day up about the Quire were of the Conversion of Constantine exceeding rich. 31 I went to that excellent Ingraver *Du Bosse* for his instruction about some difficulties in *Perspective* deliverd in his booke: Concluded this yeare in health, for which I gave solemn Thanks to Almighty God:

1650. 1 I begun this *Jubilie* with the Publique Office in our Chapell: Dind at my Lady *Herberts*, wife of Sir Ed: Herbert, afterwards Ld: Keeper:

8 I kept in some dayes for a hurt in my foote: till the 12th:

18 This night were the Pr: of *Condie* & his brother carried Prisoners to the *Bois* de *Vincennes*. 4 Feb: I write to my Sister *Glanvill* congratulating the birth of her son: 6: I receiv'd the B: Sacrament, Dr. *Morley* preaching on 12: *Heb:* 5 an excellent discourse touching the danger of fainting & back-sliding in these times:

After Evening prayer came Signor *Allessandro* one of the *Card: Mazarinis* Musitians, & a person of greate name for his knowledge in that Art, to visite my Wife, & sung before divers persons of qualitie in my Chamber:

20: I went to the Course & *Thuillieres* with my Wife &c: where there was much Gallantry.

1 *March* I went to see the *Masquerados*, which was very fantastic, but nothing so quiet & solemn as I found it at *Venice*. 4th Came to take leave of me Sir Geo: *Radcliffe*. 6. Deane Cousin preach'd on 4. Mat: 2. 3. on the duty of Fasting: I received the Bl: Sacrament. 10th Came Dr. *Morley* to take his leave of me:

13 I went to see a Triumph in *Monsieur del Camps* Academie, where divers of the French & English Noblesse, especially my *Lord of Ossorie*, & Richard, sonns to the Marquis of Ormon'd (afterwards Duke) did their Exercises on horsback in noble Equipage, before a World of Spectators, & greate Persons, men & Ladies: it ended in a Collation.

17: *Aprill Easter* day preached the Deane, on 24 *John*: 46, & I receivd the H: Communion.

25 I went out of Town, to see *Madrid* a Palace so cald built by Fr: the first to salve his oath equivocating, that he would not go out of *Madrid* without leave, when he was Prisoner in *Madrid* in Spaine: 'Tis observable onely for its open manner of Architecture, being much of Tarraces & Galleries one over another to the very roofe; & for the materials which are most of Earth painted like *Porcelain* or China ware whose Colours appeare very fresh, but is very fragile: There are whole Statues & relievos of this potterie, Chimnypieces & Collumns, both without, & within: Under the Chapell is a *Chimny* in the midst of a roome, parted from the *Sale des Guards*: The House is fortified with a deepe ditch, & has an admirable *Vista* towards the *Bois de Boulogne* & River.

30 I went to see the Collection of the famous Sculptor Steffano de la Bella, returning now into Italy, & bought some prints: & visited *Perelle* the Landskip Graver.

3 of *May*, at the *Hospital* of the *Charitie*, I saw the whole operation of *Lithotomie* namely 5 cut of the stone: There was one person of 40 years old had a stone taken out of him, bigger than a turkys Egg: The manner thus: The sick creature was strip'd to his shirt, & bound armes & thighs to an high Chaire, 2 men holding his shoulders fast down: then the Chirurgion with a crooked Instrument prob'd til he hit on the stone, then without stirring the probe which had a small chanell in it, for the Edge of the Lancet to run in, without wounding any other part, he made Incision thro the *Scrotum* about an Inch in length, then he put in his forefingers to get the stone as neere the orifice of the wound as he could, then with another Instrument like a Cranes neck he pull'd it out with incredible torture to the Patient, especially at his after raking so unmercifully up & downe the bladder with a 3d Instrument, to find any other Stones that may possibly be left behind: The effusion of blood is greate. Then was the patient carried to bed, & dress'd with a silver pipe accomodated to the orifice for the urine to passe, when the wound is sowed up: The danger is feavor, & gangreene, some Wounds never closing: & of this they can give shrewd conjecture by the smothnesse or ruggednesse of the stone: The stone pull'd forth is washed in a bason of water, &

wiped by an attendant *Frier*, then put into a paper & writen on,
which is also entred in a booke, with the name of the person,
shape, weight &c of the stone, Day of the moneth, & Operator:
After this person came a little Child of not above 8 or 9 yeares
age, with much cherefullnesse, going through the operation
with extraordinary patience, & expressing greate joy, when he
saw the stone was drawn: The use I made of it, was to give
Almighty God hearty thankes, that I had not ben subject to
this Infirmitie, which is indeede deplorable:

7. I went with my *Lady Browne*, & my *Wife*, together with the
Earle of Chesterfield, Lord *Ossorie* & his *Bro:* to *Vamber*, a place
neere the Citty, famous for the butter, when comming homewards (for we were on foote) my Lord Ossorie stepping into a
Garden, the doore open; There step'd a rude fellow to it, and
thrust my Lord, with uncivil language from entering in: upon
this our young Gallants struck the fellow over the pate, & bid
him aske pardon; which to our thinking he did with much submission, & so we parted: but we were not gon far, but we heare a
noise behind us, & saw people coming with gunns, swords,
staves & forks, following, & flinging stones; upon which we
turn'd and were forc'd to engage, & with our Swords, stones
& the help of our servants, (one of which had a pistol), make our
retreate for neere a quarter of a mile, when an house receiv'd us:
by this time numbers of the baser people increasing, we got up
into a turret, from whence we could discover their attempts,
& had some advantage: however my L: *Chesterfield* was hurt in
the face & back with a stone, his servant in the Eye & forehead,
& Sir R: Bro: protecting his Lady with his Cloake, on the shoulder, & his Lady with such a blow on the head & side of her neck
as had neere fell'd her: I myselfe was hurt on the shoulder: my
servant La Roch (a stoute Youth) much hurt on the reines:
'Twas a greate mercy that though they were so many, they durst
not come neere us with their hookes, & that their gunns did no
Execution amongst us, tho fir'd: In the Scuffle one of them was
thrust through the arme, another wounded, in his elbow, with
his owne Gun, with which one of our Company struck him; We
discharged one among them with our *Pistol*, what hurt it did ⟨I⟩
know not, & we had no more amunition: Being got up into the
Turret & battail below over, they beset the house, but durst not
attempt to come up, where they knew we had a trap-doore

betweene us, whence we could easily repell them: At last, with
much adoe, & making them understand the occasion of the
quarell, we came to parlie, and the conclusion was, that we
should all be that angry fellows prisoners: This we absolutely
refuse'd: upon which they fell to attacque the house; but coming
at last to consider that we might be persons of qualitie (for at
first they tooke us for Burgers of *Paris*) the company began to
slink away, & our Enemie to grow so mild, upon intercession of
the Master of the house, & that we might come downe into the
next chamber: I obtain'd leave also to Visite my *Lord Hatton*
(comptroller of his Majesties Household) who with some others
of our Companie, were taken prisoners in the flight, whom
I found under 3 locks & as many doores one within another, in
this rude fellows Masters house, who pretended to be steward to
one *Monsieur St. Germains* one of the first *Presidents* of the *grand
Chamber* de *Parliament* & a Canon of Notre Damme: In this
Interim one of our *Laquais* escaping to *Paris* during the Scuffle;
went & caused the *Bailife* of St. *Germains* to come with his
Guard & rescue us, which he did, accompanied with Sir Rob:
Welch, Mr. Percy *Church*, & others, with Weapons, & immediately after Monsieur St. Germains himselfe, newes being
brought him to *Paris* that his housekeeper was assaulted, upon
which he expressd mighty revenge: But when he saw the Kings
Officers, the Gentlemen & noblemen, with his Majesties Resident, & better understood the occasion, he was asham'd of the
Accident, begging the fellows pardon, & desiring the Ladys to
accept of their Submission, & a Supper at his house, whilst we
found for all that, it grieved him to the heart, we had not ben
some inferior persons, against whom he might have taken some
more profitable advantage: The *Bailife* in the meanetime exaggerated the affront, (& indeede it was a greate one upon no
manner of occasion offer'd on our part:) & would have fallen on
the little towne, striking downe as many as he mett about the
streetes & way. It was 10 a clock at night ere we got to *Paris*,
guarded by *Prince Griffith* (a certaine Welch Hero, going under
that name, & well knowne in England, for his extravagances)
together with the Scholars of *two Academies* who came forth to
assist & meete us on horseback; & would faine have alarm'd the
Towne we received the affront from, which with much ado we
prevented.

8: Deane *Cousin* preached on 5: *Matt*. 34. against using unlawfull meanes to escape persecution, applied to the calamity of our Nation.

12 Complaint being come to the Queene & Court of *France* of the affront we had receiv'd at *Vamber*, The President was ordred to aske Sir R: Bro: his Majesties Resident, Pardon, & the fellow to make submission & be dismissd: There came along with him President *Thou*, the greate *Thuanus's* sonn & so all was composd: But I have often heard, that gallant Gent: my Lord Ossorie, affirme solemnly, that in all the Conflicts he was ever in at sea, or land (in the most desperate of both which he had often ben) he believed he was never in so much danger, as when these people rose against us: He was usd to call it the *Bataill de Vambre*, & remember it with a greate deale of Mirth, as an Adventure *en Cavaliere*.

22: Preached on⟨e⟩ Mr. *Castillian* on 16. John: 33.

24. We were invited by the noble *Academists* to a running at the ring, where were many brave horses, Gallants, & Ladys; my Lord *Stanhop*, entertaining us with a collation. 29 preach'd the *Deane* on 4: *Mat:* 4 concerning the Ceasing of Miracles.

June 5, being *Whit-Sonday* the Deane of *Peterborow* on *Luke ult*. 47 out of which he had this note, That no Religion save the *Christian* had Preaching: In the afternoone was buried a Young Gent: one Mr. *Hide*. I receiv'd the B: Sacrament, as likewise on the 12th *Trinity* Sonday purposing now to make a step into *England*. The *Deanes* Text was 20: Joh: 21. 22. Observing that no man might assume of himselfe the ministry, but was to receive it: for 'tis said *receive ye*, not Take the *Holy Ghost*: & from Christs breathing on the *Apostles*, the use of Ceremonies on severall occasions, & how the imposition of hands succeeded this act of our B: Saviour: and this discourse was apposite, there being after Sermon an Ordination of Two *Divines*, *Durell* & *Brevent*, [Since one is Deane of *Winsor* the other of *Duresme* both very Learned persons] The Bishop of *Galloway* Officiating, with greate Gravity after a pious & learned Exhortation, declaring the weight & dignitie of their function, especially now, in a time, ⟨of⟩ the poor Church of Englands affliction: He exaggerated the sublimitie of the calling, from the object, *viz*. the Salvation of mens Soules, the Glory of God &c: producing many humane Instances of the transitorienesse & vanity of all other dignities: That of all the

Triumphs the Roman Conquerers made, none was comparable
to that of our B: Saviours when he lead Chaptivity Captive, &
gave Gifts to men, namely that of the H: Spirit, by which his
faithfull & painefull Ministers Triumph'd over Satan that great
Enemy of Soules, as oft as they reduc'd a sinner from the error of
his Wayes: Then proceeded to the *Ordination*: They were presented by the *Deane* in their surplices before the Altar, the
Bishop sitting in a chaire at one side—& so were made both
Deacons & *Priests* at the same time, in reguard of the necessitie
of the times, there being so few *Bishops* left in *England* & consequently danger of a faileur of both functions: Lastly, they
proceeded to the *Communion*: This was all perform'd in Sir *R:
Browne* ⟨s chapel⟩ at *Paris*.

13 I sate to the famous Sculptor *Nanteuil* [afterwards made a
knight by the French King for his Art:] who engraved my Picture in Coper:

19, The *Deane* preach'd on 4 Matt: 4.

21. I went to see the *Samaritan* or Pumpe at the End of *Pont
Noeufe*, which though to appearance promising no greate matter,
is besides the Machine, furnished with innumerable rarities
both of Art & Nature; Especialy the costly *Grotto*, where are the
fairest Corals, growing out of the very rock, that I have seene,
also huge morsels of Chrystals, Ametheists, & Gold in the mine
& other mettals & marcasites, with two huge Conchas, which
the owner told us, cost him 200 Crounes at Amsterdam: He
shew'd us a world of landscips & prospects very rarely painted in
miniature, some with the Pen & Crayon, with divers antiquities
& Relievos of Rome, above all that of the inside of the
Amphitheater of Titus incomparable drawne by Monsieur ⟨*Lin-
clere*⟩ himselfe, two boys, & 3 *Sceletons* moulded by *Fiamingo*, a
Booke of Statues with the *pen* made for *Hen* the 4th rarely executed, & by which one may discover many errours in that of *Per-
riere*, who has added divers conceits of his owne that are not in
the Originals. He has likewise an infinite collection of *Taille
douces*, richly bound in *Marroquin*: He led us into a stately
Chamber, furnished to have entertaind a Prince, with Pictures
of the greatest masters, especialy one of *Perin del Vagas*, a *Venus*,
the *Puti* carv'd in the Chimny piece by the Fleming, The Vasas
of Porcelan, & many Vasas designd by *Raphael*, some paintings
of *Pussine* & *Fiorevanti*, Antiques in brasse, the looking-glasse

& stands rarely carved; in a ⟨word⟩ all was greate, choice & magnificent, & not to be pass'd by, as I had often don, without the least suspicion that there were such rare things to be seene, in that place:

27 I seald my *Will* in presence of my Lord *Stanhop* & Mr. *Radcliff*, &c & taking leave of my *Wife* & other friends, tooke horse for *England*, paying the *Messager* 8 *pistols* for me & my servant to *Calais*, seting out with 17 in Company well arm'd, some Portugezes, *Swisse* & *French*, whereof 6 were Captaines & Officers: We came the first night to *Beaumont*, next day to *Baovais* & lay at *Poiz*, & the next, without dining reach'd *Abbeville*, next din'd at *Montrell*, & proceeding met a Company of foote (being now within the inroades of the Parties, which dangerously infest this days Journey, from *St. Omers* & the Frontiers) which we drew very neere to, ready, & resolute to Charge through, & accordingly were ordered & led by a Captaine of our traine; but as we were on the speede, they cald out, & prov'd to be *Scotch*-men, newly landed & raisd men & few arm'd among them. This night we were well treated at *Bollogne*: Jun: 21 we march'd in good order, the passage being now exceeding dangerous, & got to *Calais* by a little after two: The sun did so scorch my face in this journey, as made all the Skin peele off: The 22d I din'd with Mr. *Booth* his Majesties Agent, & about 3 in the afternoone imbark'd in the Packet-boat (hearing there was a *Pirate* then also setting saile, we had security from molestation), & so with a faire S.W. Wind, in 7 houres we lande'd safe at *Dover*: The buisy Watch-man would have us to the *Major* to be searched, but the gent being in bed, we were dismiss'd: Next day being *Sonday*, they would not permit us to ride post, so that afternoone our Trunkes were visited, after which one Mr. *De la Vall* collation'd us: Next morning by 4 we set out for *Canterbury*, where I met with my La: *Cathrine Scot* whom that very day twelve moneth before, I met at Sea, going for *France*; she had ben visiting Sir *Tho: Peyton*, not far off, & would needes carry me in her Coach as far as *Gravesend*, with one Mr. *Kingstone*, that had long served the *Venetian*, & *Duke* of *Parma*: so dining at *Sittinburne*, we came late to *Gravesend*, & so to *Deptford*, taking leave of my Lady about 4 the next morning extreamly weary. 27th I went to *Lond*; & was visited by severall friends: 1 *July* I paied 45 pounds to my *Lady Hatton*, so much taken up by me at

Paris of my *Lord* her husband: 5. I supped in the *Citty* with my
Lady K. Scot, at one *Monsieur du bois's*, where was a ⟨Gentle-
woman⟩ cald *Everard*, that was a great *Chymist*: on the 7. I heard
a Sermon at the *Rolles* Chapell on 1. *Pet:* 2. 7., relating to the
Excellences of *Christ*. In the afternoone having a mind to see
what doings was among the *Rebells* now in full possession at
White-hall, I went thither, & found one at Exercise in the
Chapell, after their Way, & thence to St. *James's*, where another
was preaching in the *Court* abroad: having finish'd my businesse
at London I return'd home where I found severall of my *Wifes*
relations.

17th I went to *Lond:* to Visite my Bro: & *Lady* & to obtaine a
Passe, intending but a very short stay in *England*: returning, my
Bro: & severall friends were to visite me: Received letters from
my *Wife*, in answer to my Bills of Exchange, lately sent: 23d
Went to Lond about my Accompts, & tooke order about my
journey: 25. I went to *Wotton*, & passing by *Epsom*, saluted Sir
Robert *Cook*, & visited my sister *Glanvill*: The Country was now
much molested by Souldiers, who tooke away Gentlemens
horses for the Service of the State as then call'd: 28 The *Minister*
of *Wotton* preach'd on 6 *Matt* 13. on part of the Lords Prayer: 30
I din'd at Mr. *Duncombs* where I met many Gent: & Ladys, especialy one of them, viz. the Lady *Ford*, who was observ'd to Eate
most prodigiously: After dinner I went to visite my Lord
Vicount *Montague*, and returning to *Wotton* bath'd this Evening
in the pond, after I had not for many years ben in cold Water:
Aug: 1. I went to see my *Bro: Richard* at Woodcot, & after dinner
at *Durdens*, meeting my former acquaintance Mr. *Pierson* [since
L. Bishop of Chester], I had good Conversation: Sir *Rob: Cooke*
invited me next day to dinner: Next day, I visited my *Sister
Glanvill* & saw her little Child my Nephew, & so return'd to
Says-*Court*, next day to *London*: 4th at the *Rolls* heard a Sermon
on 1. *Sam.* 12 *ult.* & in the afternoone wander'd to divers
Churches, the pulpets full of novices & novelties: 6t I tooke
leave of my friends in Towne, & passing by Mr. *Walkers* a good
painters, he shew'd me an excellent Copie of *Titians*: thence
home till the 12th when I set out towards *Paris*, taking post at
Gravesend, & so that night to *Canterbury*, where being Surpriz'd
by the Souldiers, & having onely an antiquated passe, with some
fortunate dexterity I got clear of them; though not without

extraordinary hazard, having before counterfaited one, with successe, it being so difficult to procure one of the Rebells without
entering into oathes, which I never would do, & at *Dover* Mony
to the Searcher & officers was as authentique as the hand &
Seale of *Bradshaw* himselfe. 13 I came to *Dover*, where I had not
so much as my Trunk open'd: so at 6 in the Evening we set saile,
the wind not favorable I was very sea-sick, coming to anker
about one a Clock: about 5 in the morning we had a long-boate
to carry us to land, though at good distance; this we willingly
enter'd, because two *Vessels* were chasing us: but being now
almost at the harbours mouth, through inadvertancy, there
brake in upon us two such huge seas, as had almost sunk the
boate, I being neere the middle up in Water: our steeres man, it
seemes, apprehensive of the danger was preparing to leape into
the sea, and trust his swimming: but seeing the vessell emerge,
put her into the peere, & so God be thanked we got wet to
Calais, where I went immediately to bed, sufficiently discompos'd: here I was visited by Sir *Richard Lloyd*. Next day (15: old. 25
New style) attending Company, (the passages towards *Paris*,
being so infested with *Volunteeres* from the Spanish frontieres)
I visited Collonel *Fitz Williams* & his Lady, who had ben the
day before to see me: Then my Lord *Strafford*: I was also visited
by Monsieur *Zanches d Avila* an acquaintance of mine. Next
morning, the regiment of *Picardy* consisting of about 1400 horse
& foote, & among them a Cap: whom I knew, being come to
Towne; I tooke horses for myselfe & servant, and march'd under
their Protection to *Boulogne*: 'Twas a miserable spectacle, to see
how these tatter'd souldiers, pillag'd the poore people of their
Sheepe, poultry, Corne, Catell, & whatever came in their Way:
but they had such ill pay, that they were ready themselves to
sterve: 27: I din'd at *Montreull*, & lay at *Abb-Ville* now past
danger, and warning the poore people (infinitely inquisitive
& thankfull) how the Souldiers treated their neighbours, & were
marching towards them: The 28 we got to *Pois*, a Village belonging to the *Mareshall de Crequey*, it stands in a bottome, here we
lay, dind next day at *Bovais*, lay at *Beaumont*, & so the 30, to
Paris. As we pass'd *St. Denis* the people were in up-rore, the
Guards doubl'd, & every body running with their goods
& moveables to *Paris*; upon an *Alarm'e* that the Enemy was
within 5 leagues of them; so miserably expos'd was even this part

of *France* at this time: I lay this night at my old Hosts, in *Rue Dauphine*, & next morning went to see my *Wife* at her *Fathers* after 2 monethes absence onely.

1 *September* my *Lady Herbert* (for now was Paris, & indeede all France, full of Loyall fugitives,) invited me to dinner: Next day, I spent in visiting divers friends, & great persons: 4. Preached in our Chapell the D. of *Peterborow* on 4: *Matt.* 8. 5. shewing how *Satan* began his Temptation on our B: Lords necessities, then with Subtilties, & lastly false promises: That some interpreted this Mountaine prospect as visionarie: He apply'd it much to the present times of Englands Calamity: & then to the *Auditors*, who though not likely to be tempted with the glory of Kingdoms, in their necessities & banishment, lay yet expos'd to other dangers. The Communion follow'd:

5 I carried my Wife, & others to see the *President Maisons* Palace, & to take a more exact view of a place formerly so pleasant to me: Tis built of a milk white fine free stone; the body of the house not vast, but neate, & well contriv'd, especialy the staire Case, & ornament of *Puti* about it: The prospect on the river, & towards the forest is incomparable: tis built castle wise, in a deepe dry, cleane Moate, which serve as Courts to the Offices under ground: The Court spacious, the bass-Court Theaterlike, opening towards the Wood, & long walk of *Elmes*: The *Citronario* is verry noble, & the Gardens incomparable towards the Inlet of the river or *Naumachia*, so as take it alltogether, the Meadows, Walkes, River, forest, Corne-grounds & Vineyards, I hardly saw anything in *Italy* exceed it: The Yron ⟨Cast⟩ Gates to ⟨the⟩ Courts & Gardens are very magnificent: The *President* has pull'd downe a whole Village to make roome for his pleasures about it: 9 I spent in writing letters into *England*. 11. The *Deane* on *Psal.* 129. shewing upon what occasions Cursing was lawfull: whereever prohibited in Scripture, related to private revenge onely: also the various significations of *Sion* in Scrip: referring to *God* & the *King*, whose Palace was contiguous to the Temple:

15 Came *Mr. Waller* the greate Poet, to visie me, about a Child of his, which the Popish Mid-wife had baptiz'd. ⟨18⟩ Mr. *Crowder* (the *Dukes* Chaplain) preachd on 56 *Psal.* 8. 9, Against *Atheists*: This Gent: has not the Talent of Preaching.

24. Came Mr. *Coventrie* [Sir William], & Sir *R: Fanshaw* to see me, & a Knight of *Malta*, with Mr. Ratcliff: We had the sad

newes of the *Scots* defeated. 25. Dr. *Duncan* preach'd on 6: *Matt*. 33. That contrary to other things, here the *Act* præceedes the *Object*, according to Chr⟨is⟩t: by how much the more a thing is greate & good, by so much the greater zeale it were to be prosecuted: That the best way to recover any thing, is to consider how it was lost: The Kingdom of Grace first lost, that of Glory should chiefly be sought: That hence *David* aptly termes the Children of God, a generation of seekers: that many desyre to seeke the K⟨ing⟩dome of God, but without its Righteousnesse, & therefore come short, & faile of the promise annex'd of having all other things (viz. necessaries of life) into the bargain.

27 I went to see Dr. *Davison* (sick of a fevor,) where I met Sir *Kenelme Digby* &c.

1 *October* I writ letters into England: 2d Dr. *Stewart* (deane of St. *Paules*) preach'd, his Majesty present: On 18 *Luke*: 8, admirably, upon the Parable of the Unjust-Judge: That God would certainly avenge his *Saints*, however deferr'd: The difficulty was our unfittnesse for such a blessing: Men had no faith; for though we praid for the restitution of our Estates, & defeate of our Enemys: yet we must not think of selfe revenge, or go on in luxurie. In such cases, how mild a Judge soever the *Almighty* is; he would be inexorable even to *Moses*, *Samuel* & *Jobe*, were they interceding: That such Tentations might come, as to stagger the strongest Faith: Thus *Davids* feete had once well nigh slip'd. The B: Communion follow'd, at which I participated.

4 I went againe to see *Monsieur Lincleres* collection, to which was added, a new Grotto, & Bathing-place, hewe'd thro the buttments of the Arches of *Pontnoeuf*, into a wide vault, at the intercolumniation; so as the Coaches & horses thunder over on⟨e⟩s head: He assur'd me he found Batts as big as catts, & Ratts of a strange size:

I went this Evening to the *Thuylleries*, thence to the *Palace* of *Orleans*, in which I now tooke notice of that rich gilded & carved roofe in the Dukes Presence, with the *Parquette'd* floore: I had seldom seene a looking glasse of so large a size; The frame had a tree of Ivy twisted about it, in silver curiously wrought, & severall Tablets of historie enamell'd: Two fine Clocks on the table, & so returned home:

9 The *Deane* preach'd on 4: *Matt*: 9. shewing that the Devils promises are all presumptions & things future; for gifts should be free without duty or service &c.

15 We came from our old House in *Ruë Tarane*, to that in the *Ruë Saint Pierre*. 16 Dr. *Duncan* on 26: Matt: 27. This was spoken against those who thought outward Service sufficient: Spiritual exercises ever the most gratefull: &c: 22 I din'd at my Lord *Stanhop* where we drank too liberaly. 23. The *Dean* on 4. *Matt:* 10. That some Temptations may be admitted for trial of our faith in Scripture the best weapon some sentence of Scriptures:

28 Sir *Thomas* Osborn [afterwards L. high *Treasurer*] & I shot for a wager of five Loises to be spent in a Treatement at St. Clos, with my Lord *Stanhop*: Memoran'd, It was so just shot, that it proved a drawne Match. 29 I visited my Lord *Hatton*. 30 Dr. *Duncan* preached on 22 *Mal:* 3. That according to the Fathers Gr: & Lat: this King is affirmed to be *God Almighty*, the Wedding of his Sonn, the union of Christ to the Spouse; The feast all the Spiritual graces.

1 *November* I took-leave of my *Ld: Stanhop*, going on his Journey towards *Italy*. 3 I visited my L. *Hatton* (Comptroller of his Majesties household) being sick; also the Countesse of *Morton*, Governesse to the Lady *Henrietta*: & Mrs. *Garder* one of the Queens Maides of honour & Mr. William *Coventry*:

6 The *Deane* preach'd on 20 *John*: 29. Obser: That all *Sermons* should begin & end with blessings: That some have neither seene nor believed, others have not seen & yet believed, & some both: That it was not to be positively affirm'd that all the Gentiles were accursed, that had lived moral lives; many of the Fathers judging favorably; since they might be extraordinarily inlightned, though none saved without *Christ*: The H. Comm: follow'd, I received:

This night Sir *Tho: Osborn* [since Ld: *Treasurer* of *England*], supping with us, his groome was set upon in the streete before our house, & received two wounds, but gave the other nine, who was carried off to the *Charite* hospital. 7: Sir Tho: went for *England*, & carried divers letters for me to my friends:

8 Monsieur *Nanteuils* presented me with my owne Picture, don all with a *pen*, an extraordinary curiosity: 13 The *Deane* on 17: *Act* 19. Blaming that *Attic* humor & itch of hearing novelties,

especialy ⟨such⟩ as are ever hearing never profiting: St. *Paules*
doctrine was as new to the *Athenians* as the *Protestant* to the
Papists, though nothing was older, & so it was to the *Jewes*: How
new then is much of the Romish superstition & additions: halfe
Communion, Masse in an unknowne tongue: &c:

15. Came the *French* King from *Bordeaux* which had ben in
disorder: 16 Newes of the Pr: of *Oranges* death of the Small pox:
I went in the afternoone to a Consort of French Musick
& Voices, consisting of 24: 2 *Theorbas* & but one bass viol: at one
Monsieur *Visse's* house a *Secretaire* du *Roy*; being repetition of
what was to be sung at *Vespers* at St. *Cicilias* on her feast: she
being patronesse of the *Musitians*. 20 One Mr. *Hammilton*
(a *Scotch*-man) preached on 8 *Rom*. 28. Applied to the present
sufferings of the Church, & necessitie of it, as proving our
legitimation.

27 The *Deane*, on 1 *Corinth:* 10. 3. 4. 5. shewing how the *Jewes*
had from the first the Symbols of the spiritual foode.

2 *December* I heard a *Jesuite* preach (at their Greate & magnificent Church) on their Patron *Xaveriu's* day, on: 1. Cor: 9. 19:
Eloquently shewing, how he became all things to all men, to
gaine some; the chiefe discourse of his whole Sermon, was Elogies on their Saints: representing their owne patron to be one of
the most flattering timeservers that ever was: There succeeded
excellent Musik. 4. The Deane of *Peterborou⟨g⟩h* pursu'd his former Text, concerning the *Sacraments*. St. *Aug:* calling them
Gemina excludes the 5 remaining: The danger of Interpreting
Scriptures after the literal sense: illustrated by many Instances.
⟨11th⟩ Dr. *Duncan* preached. 11. *Matt*. 10 being *Advent*, a
preparatory to the H: Communion:

14 I went to visite Mr. *Ratcliffe* in whose Lodging there was
an Impostor that had like to have impos'd upon us, a pretended
seacret of Multiplying gold: 'Tis certaine he had lived in *Paris*
some time before in extraordinarie Splendor; but I found him to
be an egreageous Cheate.

18 Mr. *Hamilton* preached on his former subject: That
Solomon for want of Affliction, fell into Idolatry: I dined with
the *Deane* at my L. *Hattons*: 22 Came the Learned Dr. *Boet* to
visite me:

25. Christmas day. The Deane preach'd 1. *Tim:* 3. 16. applied to
the Solemnity: 31 I gave God thanks for his mercys & protection

the past yeare, made up Accompts, which came this yeare to 7075 livers french, neere 600 pounds *sterling*.

1651. 1. *Jan:* Dr. *Duncan* preached on 2 *Luk:* 21: Shewing the use of interpreted names, especialy in the Scriptures, & among holy men. I receiv'd the B: Sa: 3 I wrot to my Bro: directing him concerning his Garden at *Wotton* & Fountaines: 8. The Deane: 2 *Luke*. 42. Explaining the *Epiphanies* &c: note: our B:S. first appearing was about his fathers buisinesse: applied to young persons: After Evening Prayer came Mr. *Wainsford* to visite me, he had long ben Consul at *Aleppo* and told me many strange things of those Countries, the Arabs especialy: he affirm'd, that though they allowd common places of sinn; yet if any man of reputation had his daughter corrupted, he cutt her throat with his owne hands: That though the *Arabs* were poorely arm'd, they were capable of destroying the greatest powers of the Earth; by knowing how to cover, & conceale their Springs in those Sandy Deserts: That when their ⟨Chief⟩ will shew himselfe in State, all his greate men sit on their armour cover'd with a red Cloth: Their safty is their Excellent horses, ⟨they⟩ ride without Stirrops: dwell in long black Tents, made of a wooll like felt, that resists all weather: Their riches is in Catell and Camels: Sometimes ⟨they⟩ threaten the Cities about them: *Damascus* itselfe pays them Contribution:

15 The *Deane* on 2. *Luke* 34. How our B: S. was received by persons of all sorts: how a *signe* to be spoken against: an active signe, but we made him a passive: in severall Instances.

20 There was a greate inundation that overflow'd a greate part of *Paris*, much harme don, many houses fell:

22 ⟨*Jan:*⟩ Dr. *Duncan* on 8 *Matt*. 11. The *Gospell* of the day: sitting downe in heaven, how it signified its joyes: The Text, imported the Calling of the *Gentils*, this *Centurion* one of the first: The East & West in scriptures ever signifying the whole world: 27: I had letters of my Grandmother in Laws death Mrs. *Newton*, for which I was very sorry, though by it I was eased of a rent charge of 60 pounds per ann: she had a most tender care of me during my childhood, & was a Woman of Extraordinary charity & piety, spending most of her time in devotion. 29: Dr. *Duncan* on 8: *Matt*. 34. shewing the mischiefe of Covetousnesse: My L: *Marq:* of *Ormond* & *Inchequeen* come newly out of *Ireland*, were this day at Chapell:

1 Feb: I was surpriz'd with a violent fit of an *Ague*, which held me within 4 dayes onely, blessed be God. 4. Came my L. *Hatton* to visite me. 5. The *Deane* on his former Text: Condemning the *Romanists* halfe Communion: 9. *Cardinal Mazarini* by *Arrest du Parliament* was proscrib'd, & greate commotions began in *Paris*: The *Deane* preach'd on 3. *Gen:* 13 shewing the greate antiquitie of the *Septuagessima* it being the Gospel of the day. Gods question to *Eve*, usefull in examining ourselves: 15 The *Deane* brought his Son (newly come out of *England*) to see me: 19 Dr. *Duncan* 18. *Luke* 39: The efficacy of that short prayer, & virtue of Faith:

21 I went to see the *Bonnes hommes* a Convent that has a fayr Cloister painted with the Lives of the *Eremites*, a glorious Altar now erecting in the Chapell: The Garden on a rock with divers descents, with a fine Vyneyard, & a delicate prospect towards the Citty: 24 I went to se a *Dromedarie*, a very monstrous beast, much like the Camel, but larger, & with tufts of haire on the neck, knees, & thighs; & two bunches on its back about 3 foote one from the other: There was also dauncing on the rope; but above all surprizing (to those who were ignorant of the addresse) was the Water Spouter, a fellow that drinking onely fountaine water, rendred out of his mouth in severall glasses, all sorts of Wine, & sweete Waters &c: This seacret was so strange, that for a piece of mony the *Montebanc* discover'd it to me: ⟨26 Feb.⟩ The *Deane* preached on 4 *Mat:* 2 Concerning the duty of Abstinence, it being now *Lent*: The Cheate of the *Papists*, by saying *Vespers* before dinner:

⟨Mar:⟩ 5. The *Deane* on his former Text, That the sin of our first Parents was the most haynous of all their posterity, as being the most obliged, & most perfect: of the alegorical sense, of the Poetic fictions: I received the B: Communion:

7 I went to visite Frier *Nicholas* at the Convent at *Challiot*, who being an excellent *chymist* shew'd me his *Laboratorie*, & rare collection of *Spagyrical* remedies: He was both Physitian & Apothecarie of the Convent, & insteade of the names of his *drogues* painted his boxes & potts with the figure of the *drug* or *simple* containe⟨d⟩ in them: he shew'd me as a raritie some ☿ of *Antimonie*: he had cur'd Monsieur *Seneterre* of a desperate sicknesse for which there was building a monumental Altar, that was to cost 1500 pounds.

II This morning I went to the *Chastlett* or prison, where a Malefactor was to have the *Question* or Torture given to him, which was thus: They first bound his wrists with a strong roope or smalle Cable, & one end of it to an iron ring made fast to the wall about 4 foote from the floore, & then his feete, with another cable, fastned about 6 foote farther than his uttmost length, to another ring on the floore of the roome, thus suspended, & yet lying but a slant; they slid an horse of wood under the rope which bound his feete, which so exceedingly stiffned it, as severd the fellows joynts in miserable sort, drawing him out at length in an extraordinary manner, he having onely a paire of linnen drawers on his naked body: Then they question'd him of a robery, (the *Lieutennant* Criminal being present, & a clearke that wrot) which not Confessing, they put an higher horse under the rope, to increase the torture & extension: In this Agonie, confessing nothing, the Executioner with a horne (such as they drench horses with) struck the end of it into his mouth, and pour'd the quantity of 2 boaketts of Water downe his throat, which so prodigiously swell'd him, face, Eyes ready to start, brest & all his limbs, as would have pittied & almost affrited one to see it; for all this he denied all was charged to him: Then they let him downe, & carried him before a warme fire to bring him to himselfe, being now to all appearance dead with paine. What became of him I know not, but the Gent: whom he robbd, constantly averrd him to be the man; & the fellows suspicious, pale lookes, before he knew he shold be rack'd, betraid some guilt: The *Lieutennant* was also of that opinion, & told us at first sight (for he was a leane dry black young man) he would conquer the Torture & so it seemes they could not hang him; but did use in such cases, where the evidence is very presumptuous, to send them to the *Gallies*, which is as bad as death. There was another fat Malefactor to succeede, wh⟨o⟩ he said, he was confident would never endure the Question; This his often being at these Trials, had it seemes given him experience of, but the spectacle was so uncomfortable, that I was not able to stay the sight of another: It represented yet to me, the intollerable suffering which our B: S: must needes undergo, when his blessed body was hanging with all its weight upon the nailes on the Crosse.

12 Mr. *Hamilton* preached on 6. *John*: 14. That our Lord, did this Miracle on his birth-day, as that at Cana: & the aparition of the H. Spirit at his Baptisme, by antient Tradition: That all his miracles were mercies, two onely excepted, the cursing of the barren tree, and falling backward of his apprehenders.

20 I went this night with my Wife to a Ball at our neighbours the Marquis de *Creve Coeurs*, where were divers Princes, dukes & greate persons; but that which I found very meane & extravagant, it began with a *pupet play*.

25 The *Deane* preached on his former Text: That good Angels never appeard in evil or hideous shapes; The Sophisme of the Devils Syllogisme: The doctrine of Independents like that of his:

28 Dr. *Duncan* going now into *Italy*, came to take leave of me. First Sonday of Passion Weeke, 2 *Aprill*. The Deane on   describing the unjust & malicious procedure of the *Sanedrym*. 9: Easter day The *deane* on 2. *Cor*. 15. 4. upon the subject of the day. The B: Sa: follow'd at which I did communicate.

11 I went to visite the Earle of *Strafford*: 16 The *Deane* on 20 *Joh:* 9, he shewd by what Scriptures, & types, the Resurrection was proved: Especialy that of Isaaks devoted to sacrifice, & escape:

17 I was much indisposd, with a sore throate, & let out 10 ounces of bloud, & tooke Physick.

23. The *Deane* preached on 10. *Joh:* 11. on the property of a good Shepherd, repugnant to that of one that calls himselfe the universal Shepherd: he pursud the same subject the next Sonday 16 verse: In what sense the Catholic Church to be taken, by *Vincentius Lirinensis's* rule:

⟨May⟩ 2 My Wife miscarried, of which she was extreamely ill, proceeding from some Physick prescribd, not believing she was with Child:

6 I went with the *Ambassadors* to a Masque at Court, where the *French King* in person daunc'd five enteries: but being ingaged in discourse, & [better] entertaind with one of the Queene regents Secretaries I left the entertainement.

7 The *Deane* preach'd on 5. *Gal:* 13. He shew'd how *Schismatics* did wrest Christian Liberty & that *Luther* who writ an excellent Tract on this Epistle, was faine to retract in a manner, what he had written *de servo arbitrio*, foreseeing the consequences: No liberty for the flesh &c.

8 Came one Mr. *Elois* & *Godfery* to visite me, newly coming out of *Spaine*.

11 I went to the *Palas Cardinal* where the Master of Ceremonies plac'd me to see the royal *Masque* [Opera]: The first sceane represented a Charriot of Singers, composd of the rarest voices to be procur'd, representing *Cornaro* & Temperance: This was overthrowne by *Bacchus* & his Revellers, the rest consisted of severall enteries, & pageants of Excesse, by all the Elements: A Masque representing fire was admirable: Then came a *Venus* out the Clouds &c. The Conclusion was an heaven whither all ascended. But the glory of the Masque was the greate persons performing it, namely the *French* King & his brother the Duke of *Anjou*, D: of *Joyeuse*, de *Mercoeure*, *Compt d'Agnan*, de *Vivonne*, de *Guich*, *Marq*. de *Mongelas*, de *Villequere*, *Chevalier* de *Guize*, *Compt* de *Villebonne*, *Marq:* de *Richlieu*, de *Humieres*, *Duc: de Candale*, Mar. de Pisy: Com: de *Frould*, *de la Tour*, *Roqulaux*, *Marq:* de *S. Martin*, de *Charmazel*, *Com: de Carces, et de Bergy*, *Prince d'Harcourt*, *Duc: de Roüannez*, *Le gran Maistre* de *l'Artillerie*, & a number of Gentlemen, with all the grander of the Court: The King performing to the admiration of all: The *Musique* was 24 Violins, vested al'antique; but the habites of the Masquers were stupendiously rich & glorious:

14: Preached the Deane, on 16: Joh: 23. To keepe time with *Rogation*: shewing how sad a time it was with the Disciples when this was pronounced by our Saviour, applied to the calamity on the Church of England, & that she was not to despond, but be more & more devout:

There was a Communion for the Ld: *Ambassadors* & their followers, who were going for *Spaine*, who all dined with us:

21: The *Deane* on 1. *Acts* 9. 10. 11. describing the *Ascension*. That since our B: Saviour was to be received into the Heavens til his 2d Comming; how vaine it was to fancy a corporal presence in the B: Sacrament, as the *Romanists* would impose: 23. I went to take leave of the Ambassadors for Spaine, which were my L. *Treasurer Cottington* & *Hide* Sir Edw: & as I return'd visited Monsieur *Morines* Garden, & other rarities, especialy Coralls, Minerals, Stones, & other natural Curiosities: particularly Crabs of the red-sea, the body no bigger than a small birds egg, but flatter, & the 2 leggs or claws a foote in length: he had aboundance of incomparable shells, at least 1000 sorts which furnish'd a Cabinet of greate price, & a very curious collection of Scarabies & Insects, of which he was compiling a natural historie; also the pictures of his Choice flowers & plants in miniature: he told me there were 10000 sorts of *Tulips* onely: he had also *Tallie douces sans nombre*: he had also the head of the *Rynoceros* bird, which was indeede very extravagant; & one butterflie resembling a perfect bird:

25 I went to Visite *Mr. White* a learned Priest, & famous Philosopher, author of the booke *De Mundo*, with whose worthy brother I was well acquainted at *Rome*.

27 I was shew'd this morning a Cabinet of *Maroquine* or *Turky* leather so curiously inlaied with other leathers, & guilding, that the Workman demanded for it 800 *livers*.

28 The *Deane* preached on 2. *Act:* 1. Insisting much on the time of the antient celebration of *Pentecost* 50 daies after the *Israelites* first deliverance, from M: Sion when the Law ⟨w⟩as promulg'd, Then at the *harvest*, then this of the Text, how venerable the number 50: perstringing those of *Geneva*, for their ireverence of the *B: Virgin*:

3 *June.* Dr. *Croydon* coming out of *Italy* & from *Padoa*, came to visite me in his returne to *England*.

4: The *Deane* on 20: *Joh:* 21. 22. being *Trinity* Sonday: Concerning the antiquity of the Feast: That peace & agreement dos ever precede the coming of the H: Spirit: Christ sent none to domineere but to Preach all of the same power: of the ceremonie of breathing: That it was not the H: Ghost in Substance, but Virtue: *Christus semper res loquitur non verba*: Then followd a Communion: I was absent in the afternoone upon a charitable affaire for the *Abesse* of *Boucharvant*, who but for me had ben abused by the chymist *du Menie*: Returning I stept into the grand *Jesuites* who had this high day exposd their *Cibarium*, made all of solid Gold, & imagerie, a piece of infinite cost:

5: I accompanied my L: *Strafford* & some other noble persons to heare Madame *Lavaran* sing, which she did both in *french* & *Italian* especialy, excellently well; but her voice was not strong:

7. There was this day a grand Procession, all the streetes tappissri'd: & severall Altars erected in the Streetes, full of Images & other rich furniture, especialy that before the Court, of a rare designe & *Architecture*: There were aboundance of excellent Pictures, & huge *Vasas* of silver. It was Corpus Christis day:

11. The *deane* on 16: *Luke*: 27: That 6 of the Fathers held this to be a real history & no Parable:

13 I went to see the Collection of one Monsieur *Poignant*, which for variety of *Achates*, *Chrystals*, *Oxyxes*, *Porcelain*, *Medails*, *Statues*, *Relievos*, *Paintings*, *Tailes douces* and Antiquities might compare with the *Italian Virtuosos*:

16 Came my Lord *Stafford* to visite me.

18 The *Deane* on his former subject: Concerning *Poena damni & sensus*, &c:

21 Came my *Co: Keightly* to visite me newly made a *Proselyte* at *Rome*, which did not a little trouble me: 25 The *Deane* preach'd on 15 *Luke*: the I seaven verses: of the returne or finding of the lost sheepe:

I came acquainted with Sir *William Curtius* a very learned & Judicious Person, of the *Palatinate*, he had ben Scholar to *Alstedius* the *Encyclopædist*, & well advanc'd in yeares; and now Resident for his Majestie at *Frankfort*: The next day I brought the Deane of *Peterborow* & Dr. *Earle*, cleark of his Majesties Closet &c: to Conferr with my Cousen, touching his change of Religion: In the afternoone came Sir Geo: Radcliffe to se⟨e⟩ me, who was newly come out of *Holland* with the *D: of York*:

28: My *Co: Keightly* came to me with one of his Perverters (as since I understood) who cal'd himselfe Mr. *Paynter*; but was indeede a Frier whose name was *Conyers*, who seem'd to desire some conference with the *Deane*, that had exceedingly perplexed my Cousin some days before: I write a letter to the *Deane* that it might be at the *Louver* (where his library was) but he fearing it would be resented by the Queene Mother of England, who there had now her Court, he chose rather to come to my lodging: So a formal Dispute began, which held many houres, to the very manifest conviction of the *Frier*; & consequently of my Kindsman; but so had they wrought with ⟨him⟩, as he tooke his leave of me unsatisfied, & went shortly after into England: He insisted wonderfully on a miracle he had seene at *Rome*, but had by no meanes, any solid arguments to defend his change; abating the pretended visibilitie of the Church, which he would needes have understood the present Church of Rome.

2 July Mr. *Crowder* preached in our Chapell on 2. Tim: 4. 3. as a Prophecy of the later daies: The Duke was present: We all received the H: Sacrament.

Came to visie me in the afternoone the Earle of *Strafford*, Lord *Ossory* & his Brother, Sir *Jo: Southcott*, Sir *Edw: Stawell*; Two of my Lord *Spencers* Sonns, & Dr. *Steward* deane of *St. Paules* a learned & pious man, where we entertained the time upon Severall subjects, especialy the affaires of *England*, & the lamentable condition of our Church.

5 Came my *Lord Gerrard* to see my Collection of Seiges & Battailes: Mr. Baker came to take leave of me:

⟨9⟩ *Dr. Earles* preached on 119 *Psal:* last part: *Greate is the peace which they have, who love thy Law, & are not offended* at it: Concerning: That the want of Peace in *England* was, our making slight of the Law of *God* &c. I hardly in my whole life heard a more excellent discourse. His highness the *Duke* was present:

11 I let bloud, for my often infirmitie of the *Eemeroides*.

16 The *Deane* of *Peterborow* preach'd ⟨on⟩ 4: *Matt:* 3d. The drift of Satans bold Tentation was to have made our B: *Saviour* doubt his *filiation*: & that he still exercises the same stratagem, when ever we are in affliction & straites:

21 Was an extraordinary Fast celebrated in our Chapell where *Deane* of *Paules* Dr. *Steward* preach'd on: 1. *Cor:* 11: 31. That men ought to erect a Judicial, & Legislative Tribunal in their owne Consciences, to bring every sin to Trial & punishment.

30 Mr. *Crowder* preach'd on 66 Psal: 17: Concerning Vowes. This good meaning Man, was not for the *Pulpet*, yet he was well learn'd:

31 The *Deane* of *Peterborow* Mr. *Maxfield* & my selfe went to Collation & reconcile an unkindnesse which pass'd betweene Sir *R: Bro:* & my Lord *Hatton*:

1 *Aug:* Came Mr. *Eloizes* to take leave of me, & his companion Mr. *Godfery* now both going for *England*; they were both pretty Gent: & well improv'd:

2 I went with my Wife to *Conflance*, where were aboundance of Ladys & others bathing in the River: The Ladys had their Tents spread on the Water for privacy: it being exceeding hot weather, we also bathed, & return'd next day by boate to *Paris*:

6 The Dr. Clare on 12: *Rom:* 1: shewing what was ⟨meant⟩ by reasonable Sacrifice: I received the B: Sacrament.

11 I visited the E: of *St⟨r⟩afford*, being indispos'd.

13 *Dr. Earles* preached on 107 *Psal:* 11: That it was better to be humble & penitent Malefactors, than profane & wicked

Loyalists, inveighing against the vicious lives of severall of the Kings party: He wished Confession had ben retain'd: The Discourse was so passionate, that few could abstaine from teares, at his description of our abuse of Gods infinite mercys:

20 The *Deane* of *Pet:* on 4: *Matt:* 4: *It is written:* [*Scriptum est:*] This answer of our B: Lords, was so effectual against all *Satans* Tentations, that St. Aug: would have this part of the storie written on the Wall of his bed-chamber, that when he should be speechlesse he might have it ready to repell him.

I this day received safe, divers books & other things I had sent for out of *England*, which were reported to have ben taken by the *Pyrates*: but God be thanked it was otherwise:

27 *Mr. Crowder* preach'd on: 6: *Mich:* 8. That God requires no impossibilities, the doing justice, humility, & loving mercy, being duties of greate pleasure & Ease:

29 Was kept a solemn fast, for the Calamities of our poore Church, now trampl'd on by the Rebells:

Mr. *Waller* (being at *St. Germains*) desired me to send him a Coach from *Paris* to bring my Wifes *Godaughter* to *Paris*, to be buried by the Comm: Prayer:

31 I visited Deane *Cousins*:

⟨3⟩ *September*: Dr. *Earles* preach'd on 4: *Pet:* 17. That they were onely transitory Judgements, not permanent, which afflicted the house of God: which he prosecuted according to his excellent talent:

I received the blessed Communion; to which was added a Prayer extraordinary, for the afflicted *Church* of *England* & the King.

6 I went with my *Wife* to St. *Germaines*, to Condoule Mr. *Wallers* losse: I carried with me, & treated at dinner, that excellent & pious person, The *Deane of Pauls* Dr. *Steward*, & Sir *Lowes Dives*, halfe brother to the *Earle* of *Bristol*, who entertain'd us with his wonderfull Escape out of Prison in *White-hall*, the very evening before he was to have ben put to death, leaping down out of a *jakes* 2 stories high into the *Thames* at high-Water, in the coldest of Winter, & at night: so as by swiming he got to a boate that attended for him: tho' he was guarded with six musqueteeres: That after this he went about in Womens habits, & then in a Small-Coalemans; Then travell'd 200 miles on foote, Embarkd for *Scotland*, with some men he had raised, who

coming on shore were all surpriz'd & imprison'd on the *Marq:* of
Montrosses score, he not knowing any thing of their barbarous
murder of that *Hero*: This he told us was his 5 Escape, & none
lesse miraculous, with this note, That the charging through 1000
men arm'd, or whatever danger could possibly befall a man in his
whole life, he believed could not more confound, and distract a
mans thoughts, than the execution of a premeditated Escape,
The passions of hope & feare being so strong: This Knight was
indeede a valiant Gent: but not a little given to romance, when
he spake of himselfe. I return'd to Paris the same Evening:

The 7th of *September* I went to Visite Mr. *Hobbs* the famous
Philosopher of Malmesbury, with whom I had long acquaintance:
from whose Window, we ⟨saw⟩ the whole equipage & glorious
Cavalcade of the Young *French Monarch Lewis* the XIVth passing to *Parliament*, when first he tooke the Kingly Government
on him, as now out of *Minority* & the *Queene* regents pupilage:
First came the ⟨Captain⟩ of the King's *Aydes*, at the head of 50
richly liveried: Next the *Queene* Mothers light horse an hundred: The Lieutennant being all over cover'd with Embroiderie
& ribbans, having before him 4 Trumpets habited in black velvet, full of Lace, & Casques of the same:

Then the Kings light horse 200: richly habited, with 4 Trumpets in blew velvet embrodred with Gold, before whom rid the
Count d'*Olonne* Coronet, whose belt ⟨was all⟩ set with Pearle:
next went the grand *Prevosts* Company on foot, with the Prevost
on horseback, after them, the *Swisse* in black Velvet *toques* led by
2 gallant Cavalieres habited in scarlet colour'd Sattin after their
Country fashion, which is very fantastick: he had in his cap a
pennach of *heron*, with a band of *Diamonds*, & about him 12
little *Swisse* boyes with halebards, which was very pretty: Then
came the *Ayde des Ceremonies*; next the grandees of Court, &
Governors of Places, Lieutenants Gen: of Provinces magnificently habited & mounted, among ⟨them⟩ one, I must not forget, the *Chevalier Paul* famous for many Sea-fights & signal
exploits there, because 'tis said, he never had ben an *Academist*,
& yet govern'd a very un-rully horse, & beside his rich suite, &
Malta Crosse esteem'd at 10 thousand Crownes: These were
headed with 2 Trumpets, & indeede the whole Troup cover'd
with Gold and Jewells, & rich Caparisons were follow'd by 6
Trumpets in blew Velvet also, præceeding as many *Heraulds* in

blew Velvet Semé'd with *floeur de lys*, & *Caduces* in their hands,
velvet caps: Behind them came one of the *Masters* of the *Ceremonies*, then divers *Marishalls*, & of the Nobility exceeding
splendid, behind them *Count d'Harcourt Grand Escuyr* alone
carrying the Kings Sword in a Scarf, which he held-up in a blew
sheath studded with *flor de lyss*; his horse, had for reines two
Scarfs of black Taffata: Then came The foote-men & Pages of
the King aboundance of them, new liveried, & with white & red
feathers: Next the *Guard de Corps* & other officers, & lastly
appear⟨d⟩ the King himselfe upon an *Isabella Barb*, on which a
housse seméd with Crosses of the Order of the H.G. & *floure de
lyces*: The King himselfe like a young *Apollo* was in a sute so
coverd with rich embrodry, that one could perceive nothing of
the stuff under it, going almost the whole way with his hat in
hand saluting the Ladys & Acclamators who had fill'd the Windos with their beauty, & the aire with *Vive Le Roy*. Indeede he
seem'd a Prince of a grave, yet sweete Countenance, now but in
the 14th yeare of his Age: After the king followd divers Greate
persons of the Court exceeding splendid, also his *Esquire*, Masters of horse on foote, Then the Company d'*Exempts des Gards*,
& six Guards of *Scotch*, 'twixt their files divers *Princes* of the
bloud, *Dukes* & Lords: After all these the *Queenes* guard of
Swisse, Pages & *foote-men*, Then *Queene Mother* herselfe in a rich
Coach, with *Monsieur* the Kings brother, The *Duke* of *Orleans* &
some other Lords and Ladys of honour: about the Coach
march'd her *Exempts de gards*, Then the Company of the Kings
Gens d'Armes well mounted 150 with 4 Trumpets and as many of
the Queenes, Lastly an innumerable many Coaches full of
Ladys and Gallants, & in this Equipage passed this Monarch to
the *Parliament*, henceforth exercising his Kingly Government.

10 Dr. *Steward* preach'd in our Chapell on 5. *Matt:* 10, shewing the blessednesse resulting from a right use of Persecution.

14 Came old Sir *Geor: Ratcliffe* (that greate favorite of the
Lord *Deputy* of *Ireland* who lost his head) to visite me:

15 I accompanied Sir R: *Bro:* my F. in Law to the *French*-
Court, who had a favourable *Audience* of the *French King* &
Queene [his] Mother, congratulating the one his coming to the
exercise of his royal charge, & the others prudent, and happy
Administration during her late Regency, desiring both their
Majesties to conserve the same Amitie for his Master, our King,

they had don: which they both promis'd, with many civil expressions & words of Course upon such occasions: We were accompanied both going, & returning, by the Introductor of
Ambassadors, & *Ayd* of *Ceremonies*: I also saw the *Audience* of the
Ambassador of *Venice Morosini*, and divers other Ministers of
State, from *German Princes*, *Savoy*, &c: Afterwards I tooke a
walk in the *Kings Gardens*, where I observ'd that the Mall gos the
whole Square thereof next the Wall, & bends with an angle so
made as to gla⟨n⟩ce the ball, which angle is of stone: Ther's a
basin at the end of the Garden fed by a noble fountaine & high
jetto very plentifully: There were in it two or three boates in
which the K. now & then rowes about: In another part is
a Compleate fort, made with Bastions, Graft, halfe moones,
ravelins & furnishd with great Gunns, cast up on purpose
to in⟨s⟩truct the K. in Fortification:

17 Dr. Wolly preach'd on: 44. Psal. 17. referring to the Afflictions of the Church:

22 Arived the newes of the fatal Battail at *Worcester*, which
exceedingly mortified our expectations.

24 Mr. Crowder on. 56 *Psa:* 8. Applied to the deplorable Condition of our Nation.

25 I went to see *Deane Stewart*, & *Dr. Earles*. 28 I was shew'd
a Collection of Books & Prints, made for the D: of York.

29 I discharg'd my *Valet de Chambre La Roch*, perfected my
Accompts, & set all my Concernes in order.

1 Octob: Preach'd the Deane of *Peterborow* on 13. Job 15.
Encouraging our trust in God upon all events, & extremities,
& for the establishing & comforting some *Ladys* of greate
Qualitie, who were then to be discharg'd from our Q. Mothers
service unlesse they would come-over to the *Romish* Masse:
The H: Sacrament follow'd which I receiv'd: The Deane, dining
this day at our house, told me the occasion of Publishing those
Offices, which among the *Puritans*, were wont to be call'd
Cousins Cousning Devotions, by way of derision: That at the first
coming over of the *Queene* into *England* she, & her *French*
Ladys, were often up-braiding our Religion, that had neither
appointed, nor set forth, any *Houres* of Prayer, or *Breviaries*,
which Ladies & Courtie⟨r⟩s (that have much spare time) might
edifie by, & be in devotion, as they had: Our Protestant Ladys
scandaliz'd it seemes at this, moved the matter to the *King*,

whereupon his Majestie, presently call'd *Bishop White* to him, and asked his thoughts of it, & whither there might not be found some formes of Prayer, proper on such occasions, collected out of some already approved formes? that so the Court-Ladys &c (who spend much time in trifling) might at least appeare as devout, and be so too, as the new-come-over *French* Ladys, who tooke occasion to reproch our want of zeale, & Religion: Upon which the *Bish⟨o⟩p* told his Majestie that it might be don easily, & was very necessary: Whereupon the K. commanded him to employ some Person of the *Cleargy* to compile such a Work, & presently the *Bishop* naming *Dr. Cosin*: & the King injoynes him to charge the Doctor in his name to set about it immediatly: which *Mr. Deane* told me he did, & 3 monethes after bringing the book to the *King*, he commanded the *Bishop* of *London* to reade it over, & make his report: which was so well liked; that (contrary to former customs [by Chaplan]) he would needes give it a warrant [& Imprimatur] under his owne hand: upon this, there were [at first] onely 200 printed, nor said he, was there anything in the whole book of my owne Composure (nor did I set any name or Author to it) but those necessary *Præfaces* &c: out of the *Fathers*, touching the *Times* & *Seasons* of *Prayer*, all the rest being intirely translated & collected out of an Office publish'd by Authority of Q. *Elisabeth* Anno *1560*, & our owne *Liturgie*: This note, I the rather mention to justify that industrious & pious *Deane*, who had exceedingly sufferd by it, as if he had don it of his owne head, to *introduce Popery*, from which no man was more averse: & one who in this time of temptation, & Apostacy held, & confirm'd many to our Church.

6 *Deane Steward*, wanting 100 pounds, I procur'd it for him, no small difficulty at this time:

8 Dr. *Earle* preachd on 1: Pet: 4. 7. according to his costome, making a most pious discourse, upon the last times:

13 My Lord of *Ossorie* & his bro: my L. *Richard Butler* (sonnes of the Marq: of Ormond) came to take leave of me, going to *Caën*.

⟨15⟩ Dr. Clare on: 83. Psa: 1. 2. speaking of the Calamitie under which our Church groan'd & the unjustice & impiety of the *Covenant*:

20 Mr. *Spencer* & *Radcliff* tooke their leaves of me now going into *England*.

⟨22⟩ Dr. *Wolley*, on 11. *Heb:* 24. 25: shewing what strange things were brought about by Faith, exceeding all expectation: this good Doctor was no greate Preacher:

25 I tooke Physick preventingly.

29 Mr. *Crowder* on: 123. Psal: 2. 3. Perswading to Patience in our affliction, upon assurance of undoubted deliverance &c:

This morning came newes & Letters to the *Queene*, & Sir *Richard Bro:* (who was the first had intelligence of it) of his Majesties miraculous Escape after the fight at *Worcester*, which exceedingly rejoic'd us.

30 I was 31 *yeares of Age*:

4: *November* I receivd Bills of Exchange:

5 The *Deane* preachd on: 2 *Sam:* 22, shewing the extraordinary care which God has of his Church, & those who depend upon him: a Congratulatory *Sermon*, & *Anniversarie* of the *Powder Conspiracy*, The B: Communion followd, I receiv'd:

7 I visited *Sir Kenholm Digby* with whom I had much discourse of chymical matters, I shew'd him a particular way of extracting oyle of ♃ & he gave me a certaine powder with which he affirm'd he had fixed ☿ before the late *King*, which he advised me to try and digest a little better, & gave me a Water, which he said was onely raine water of the Autumnal *æquinox* exceedingly rectified, very volatile, it had a tast of a strong vitriolique, and smelt like *aqua fortis*, he intended it for a disolvant of ☉. But the truth is, Sir *Kenhelme*, was an arrant Mountebank:

Came newes of the gallant Earle of *Derby's* execution by the Rebells:

12 *Dr. Clare*, preach'd on 28. *Gen:* 20. 21. 22. Upon *Jacobs* vowe, which he appositely applied: it being the first Sonday his Majestie came to Chapell, after his Escape: I went in the afternoone to visite the Earle of *Norwich*, he lay at the Lord *Aubignies*:

16 Deane *Stewart* I went to visite, who had ben sick about 2 daies before, when going up to his Lodging, I found him dead, which exceedingly surpriz'd me, as being a person that besides his particular affection & love to me, was of incomparable parts, & greate learning, of exemplary life, & a very greate losse to the whole Church: He was buried the next day with all our Churches Ceremonies, many noble persons accompanying the Corps.

17 I went to visite and congratulate the marriage of Mrs. Gardner, maid of honor, lately married to that odd person, Sir H: Wood: but riches dos all things.

⟨19⟩ Dr. *Earles* on 116. *Psal:* 11. 12, raising an excellent discourse upon his Majesties deliverance, and ending with a pious Commemoration of Dr. *Steward* lately deceased.

20 I went to see Monsieur *Feburs* course of *Chymistrie*, where I found Sir K. *Digby*, and divers Curious Persons of Learning & quality: It was at his first opening his Course and præliminarys in order to operation: 26 Dr. *Wolly* preach'd on 2. Sam: 25. 26. shewing the Care that *Kings* should have of the Church &c: 28 I visited the D: of *Peterborow* now indisposd:

1 December I receiv'd a Bill of Exchange being now resolv'ed to returne into *England*.

3 Mr. *Crowder* on 49 *Isa:* 2. 3. That the Protections of God, were the greatest incitements to praise him, apply to the occasion: his *Majestie* Present.

⟨Sir⟩ Lew: Dives din'd with us, who amongst other his Adventures, shew'd me divers pieces of broad Gold, which being in his pocket in a fight, preserv'd his life, by receiving a Musket bullet upon them, deaded the violence of it, so as it went no farther, but made such a stroake on the Gold, as fix't the Impressions upon one another, battering & bending severall of them, the bullet it selfe flatted, & retaining on it the colour of the Gold; and assurd us that of an hundred of them which he then it seemes had in his pocket, not one of them scaped without some blemish, He affirm'd that his being protected by a *Neapolitan* prince, who conniv'd at his bringing some Horses into *France*, contrary to the permission of the *Vice-Roy*, by assistance of some *Banditi*, was the occasion of a difference betweene those greate men, & consequently of the late Civil Ware in that Kingdom, The *V: Roy* having killed the Prince standing on his defence, at his owne Castle. He told me, that the second time of the *Scots* coming into *England*, the *King* was six-times their number, & might easily have beaten them, but was betraied, as were all other his designes & Counsels, by some even of his *Bed-Chamber*, meaning *M: Hammilton*, who coppied out *Montroses* letters from time to time, when his Majestie was a sleepe.

10 Deane *Cousin* preach'd on 11: *Matt.* 6: Upon the nature of Scandals &c:

12 Came to visite me Mr. *Obadiah Walker* of University Coll: with his two Pupils, the Sonns of my worthy friend Hen: *Hyldiard* Esquire, whom I had recommended to his care:

My Sister *Glanvill* sent to desire I would substitute my *Proxie*, to stand Godfather to her Child, but my intended journey home-ward was so soone to follow, that there was no neede of it:

⟨17⟩ Dr. *Clare* preached on 1. Joh: 48, shewing what a true Christian was &c:

21 Came to Visite my Wife *Mrs. Lane*, the Lady who conveied the King at his Escape from Worcester to the sea-side.

22 Mr. *Jo: Cosin* (sonn to the *Deane*) debauch'd by the Priests, writ a letter to me, to mediate for him to his father &c:

24. Dr. *Earle* preach'd *coram Rege*, 6 *Rom:* 13 shewing the possibilitie of our own selves to keepe our bodys from many actual sinns; patheticaly moving to purity of life: The *B: Communion* follow'd at which I received: [25] *Deane Cousin* preaching the next day on. 1. *John*. 9. Concerning false lights, & the greate, & true light of the Gentiles: The *King* & *Duke* receivd first by themselves, the *Lord Biron* & *Willmot* holding the long Towell all along the Altar.

26 Newes came of the Death of that Rebell *Ireton*:

31 Preached Dr. Wolly—after which was celebrated the H: Communion, which I receivd also preparatorie to my Journey, & to returne God Almight⟨y⟩ thanks for his gracious Protection of me this past yeare:

1652. 1 *Jan:* After publique prayers in the Chapell, making up all Accompts, I prepard for my last Journey, being now resolved to leave France ⟨for⟩ alltogether.

2 Came Dr. Cousen to see me, & acquaint me what the Priests had contriv'd & dispersd in the *Queene Mothers* bed-chamber, as if I had drop't his Sonns letter there upon designe, which was utterly false. Came to me this Evening the newes of my *Sister Glanvills* death in Child-bed, which exceedingly afflicted me:

3 I went to one *Marc Antonios* an incomparable Artist in Enamailing, he wrought by the lamp figures in bosse of a large size, even to the life, so as nothing could be better moulded. He

told us greate stories of a *Genoveze* Jeweller, who had the greate *Arcanum*, and had made projection before him several times: He mett him at *Cyprus* travelling into *Ægypt*, & that in his returne he died at Sea, & the Seacret with him, that else he had promis'd to have lef⟨t⟩ it to him: That all his Effects were seiz'd on & dissipated by the *Greekes* in the Vessel to an immense value: He also affirm'd that being in a Goldsmiths shop at *Amsterdam*, a person of very low stature came in & desired the Goldsmith to mealt him a pound of lead, which don, he unscrew'd the pummel of his sword, & taking out of a little box, a small quantity of pouder, casting it into the Crucible, pourd an ingot out, which when cold, he tooke up, saying, Sir you will be paied for your lead in the Crucible, & so went out immediately; when he was gon, the Goldsmith found 4 ounces of good Gold in it; but could never set eye againe on the little man, though he sought all the Citty for him: This *Antonio* asserted with greate obtestation nor know I what to think of it, there are so many Impostors, & people who love to tell strange stories, as this *Artist* did; who had ben a greate rover, & spake 10 severall Languages:

6 After *Epiphanie* Service in the Chapell, his Majestie & Duke offered according to Costome.

7 Next day Mr. *Crowder* preach'd on 123 *Psal.* 3. 4. shewing how all were servants to God, & therefore oblig'd to obedience: & patience:

13 I tooke leave of Mr. *Waller*, who having now obtain'd leave of the Rebells (who had proscrib'd him) to returne, was going into *England*.

14 I was so hindred by providing & putting up my things, to part with the Carriages to *Calais*, that I could not be present at Morning Sermon:

16 I sent away my Goods for England by the Way of *Rouen*:

21 Dr. *Lloyd* preach'd on 4. *Philip* 11 & made an excellent discourse concerning Contentednesse.

22 Invited to *Monsieur Feburs to dinner*, where was hard drinking:

25 I visited my L: *Hatton*, Lady *Herbert*, Deane of *Peterborow*, Dr. *Earle*, Countesse of *Morton*, Mrs. *Lane* & tooke leave of divers friends:

28 Dr. *Earle* preach'd on Psal: *Teach me so to number my daies* &c: That it was an Art of *Arithmetique* which God onely could teach us: The wisdome here meant, was a holy & religious life: Mr. *Hyliards* two sonns din'd with us, [and Obadiah Walker:]

29 Came aboundance of my *French* & *English* Acquaintance, & some Germans to take leave of me, & conducted me to the *Coach* & *Horses*; So about 12 a Clock (in an extraordinary hard Frost, that had continud a good while before,) we set forth & got that night to B⟨e⟩aumont. 30, at *Beau⟨v⟩ais*, 31 we found the wayes very deepe with Snow, & exceeding cold; din'd at *Pois*, lay at *Berneè*, a miserable Cottage, of miserable people in a Wood, & wholy unfurnish'd, but in a little time, we had sorry beds & some provision, which they told me they hid in the wood, for feare of the frontier Enemy, the Garisons neere them continualy plundering what they had: They told us they were often infested with Wolves: I cannot remember that I ever saw more miserable Creatures:

1 *Feb:* I din'd at *AbbeVille*—afterward we met 2 Capuchin friers marching towards *Paris*. 2 din'd at *Montreuill*, lay at *Bollogne* 3 & came next day to *Calis* by 11 in the Morning; so I thought to have embarq'd in the Evening, but feare of *Pyrates* plying neere the Coast, I durst not trust our small *Vessel*, 'til *Moneday* following, when 2 or 3 lusty vessels were to depart:

I brought with me from *Paris*, Mr. *Chr: Wase*, sometime before made to resigne his *Fellowship* in *Kings Coll: Camb:* because he would not take the Covenant; he had ben a Souldier in Flanders, came miserable to *Paris*, where both ⟨h⟩is excellent learning & some relation he had to Sir R: Browne, made me beare his Charges into *England*: I also clad, & provided for him, 'till he should find some better Condition, for he was worthy of it, both for his exceeding greate Erudition & no lesse modesty. There came with us also on⟨e⟩ *Cap: Griffith*, *Mr. Tyrell*, brother to Sir Timothy *Terryll* of *Shotover*, a prety Gentleman: Sonday, the wether chang'd to Wett: so I went to Mr. *Booths* (his Majesties *Agent* here) to Morning Prayer; [invited to] dine with My *Lord Wentworth* who was now in *Calais*; Writ Letters to *Paris*: 5. It continud so ill weather as no Vessels put to sea; This Evening therefore I met Mr. *Heath*, Sir *Rich: Lloyd*, *Cap: Paine*, & divers of our banish'd Company &c: of whom understanding that the *Count de la Strade*, Governor of *Dynkirk*, was in the Towne, who before at *Paris*, my *Lord of Norwich* had inform'd me, bought my Wifes

Picture of certaine Pyrates, that had plunder'd it at *Sea*, the yeare
before, that she sent it me into England: I made my addresse to
him, who frankly told me that indeede he had such a Picture in his
owne bed-chamber, amongst other Ladys, & how he came by it;
seeming well pleas'd that it was his fortune to preserve it for me, &
so generously promising to sende it to any friend I had at Dover,
I mentiond a French Merchand there, & so tooke my leave:

THE RETURN TO ENGLAND
(1652–1654)

6 I EMBARK'D early in the *Packet-boat*, but put my goods in a
Stouter Vessell: 'twas dark, but exceeding Calme weather, so as
we got not to *Dover* till 8 at night; The other vessell out sailing
us an houre & more:

Next morning came the *Cleark* of the *Passage* & *Monsieur De
la Vall* to visite me, we supped together: 29: *English* style (having
desir'd Mr. *De la Valle* to convey a letter to Monsieur *Le Compt de
Strade*, to put him in mind of his promise, & that he would con-
signe the Picture to him) I tooke horse for *Canterbury*, thence to
Sittenburne, thence, lying at *Rochester*, 30th to *Gravesend*, thence,
in a pair of Oares, & so landed at *Says-Court* about 2 in the
Afternoone, where I stayed Friday, Sat: & Sonday, to refresh, &
looke after my packetts, & goods I brought:

⟨Feb.⟩ 1 I went to *Lond:* visited my Bro: his Lady & severall
friends: 2: Came *Mr. Davie* Walker (one of his Majesties Bed-
chamber) to visite me: 3 My *Bro: Richard*, La: Cath: *Scott*, Mr.
Waller; at whose house I din'd. 4: I went to Visite my Co: Rich:
Fanshaw, & received divers visites from friends: 5: My *Bro:
Glanvill* came to see me, with whom I condold the death of my
deare sister, a most ingenious & virtuous woman, & whom I
exceedingly loved: Next day he sent me Mourning: & this day
I saw the Magnificent Funeral of that arch-Rebell *Ireton*, carried in pomp from Somerset house to *Westminster*, accompanied
with divers regiments of Souldiers horse & foote; then marched
the Mourners, Generall *Cromewell* (his father in Law) his Mock-
Parliament men: Officers, & 40 poore-men in gownes, 3 led
horses in housses of black-Cloth: 2 horses led in black-Velvet, &

his Charging horse all coverd over with embrodery & gold on crimson *Velvet*: Then the *Guidons, Ensignes, 4 Heraulds*, carrying the armes of the State (as they cald it) namely the red Crosse, & *Ireland*, with the Casque, Wreath, Sword, Spurrs &c: next a 〈Charriot〉 Canopied, all of black Velvet, & 6 horses, in this the Corps, the Pall held up by the Mourners on foote: The *Mace & Sword* with other marks of his Charge in *Ireland* (where he died of the Plague) carried before in black Scarfs; Thus in a grave pace, drums coverd with cloth, souldiers reversing their armes, they proceeded thro the streetes is a very solemn manner. This *Ireton* was a stout rebell, & had ben very bloudy to the Kings party, witnesse his severity at Colchester; when in cold blood he put those gallant gent: Sir *Charles* Lucas & G. *Lisle* to death:

6. I dind at my Bro: Evelyns, & visited divers friends: Sir *Hen: Herbert* presented me with his bro: my *L: Cherberies booke de Veritate*.

8 I writ into *France*. My Co: R: *Fanshaw* came to visite me, & to informe me of many considerable affaires.

9 I went to visite my Lady *Elouis* & her sonn, who had ben so civill to me at *Paris*:

10 I went to *Deptford*; where having prety well settld my buisinesse in *Lond:* I made preparation for my settlement, no more intending to go out of England, but endeavor a settled life, either in this place, or some other, there being now so little appearance of any change for the better, all being intirely in the rebells hands, and this particular habitation, & the Estate contiguous to it (belonging to my F in Law, actualy in his Majesties service) very much suffering, for want of some friend, to rescue it out of the power of the Usurpers; so as to preserve our Interest, & to take some care of my other Concernes, by the advise, & favour of my Friends, I was advis'd to reside in it, and compound with the Souldiers; being besides, authoriz'd by his Majestie so to do, & encourag'd with a promise, that what was in Lease from the Crowne (if ever it pleas'd God to restore him), he would secure to us in Fee-ferme: I had also addresses, & Cyfers, to Correspond with his Majestie & Ministers abroad; upon all which inducements, I was persuaded to settle hence forth in England, having now run about the World, most part out of my owne Country neere 10 yeares: I therefore now likewise meditated of sending over for my Wife, whom as yet I had left at Paris:

⟨15⟩ I went to *Leusham* where I heard an honest sermon on: 2 *Cor:* 5. 7. shewing that the universal practise of the *Church*, was the Surest Interpreter of H. Scripture: This was the first Sonday I had ben at *Church* since my returne, it being now a very rare thing to find a *Priest* of the *Church* of *England* in a Parish pulpet, most of them fill'd with Independents & *Phanatics*:

15 I saw the *Diamond* & *Rubie* Launch'd, in the Dock at *Deptford*, carrying 48 Brasse Cannon Each: ⟨*Cromwell*⟩ & his Grandees present, with greate acclamations:

16 Came to see, & dine with me my Bro: Geo: & Mr. Needham, my deare friend.

18 Came that worthy divine Mr. *Owen* of *Eltham*, a sequesterd person to visite me:

19 Invited by my *Lady Gerrard*, I went to *Lond*, where we had a greate supper, & all the Vessels, which were innumerable, of *Porcelan*, which was very extraordinarie, she having the most ample & richest collection of that curiositie in England:

22 I went with my *Bro: Evelyn* to Wotton, to give him what directions I was able about his Garden, which he was now desirous to put into some forme: but for which he was to remove a mountaine, that ⟨was⟩ over-growne with huge trees, & thickett, with a moate, within 10 yards of the very house: This my Brother immediately attempted, & that without greate Cost for more than an hundred yards South, by digging downe the Mountaine, & flinging it into a rapid streame, which not onely carried the Land &c away, but filled up the moate, & leveld that noble arëa where now the Garden & fountaine is: The first occasion of my Bro: making this alteration, was my building of a litle retiring place betweene the greate wood East ward, next the Meadow, where some time after my *Fathers* death I made a triangular Pond or little stew, with an artificial rock, after my coming out of *Flanders*: 26: I went to visite *Mr. Hylyard*, to whose sonns I had ben serviceable in *France*: 28 I returned, visiting my Bro: *Richard* & Wife at Woodcot.

29 I heard that excellent Prelate, the Primate of *Ireland* (*Jacob: Usher*) preach in *Lincolns Inn* Chapell on 4: *Heb:* 16, encouraging of penitent Sinners; dined at my Bro: *Evelyns*:

⟨Mar:⟩ 1 I return'd to *Says-Court*: 5. Came my Bro: G. to visite me, brought *Cromwells* Act of *Oblivion*, to all that would submit to the Government: returnd that Evening: I also receivd Letters from my *Wife*: 6. I went to Lond: 7: at *St. Gregories*, Mr. *Godard* preached on 2. *Joel*: 3 Concerning the real mortification of the Spirit &c: I receivd the Holy Comm: dind at my Bro: Visited in the Evening my L: *Vicount Montague*, where I met divers of my friends, My *Lord Arundell* of *Wardour*, & that ingenious gent: Sir William *Godolphin*, who kept me there late at night: 8: I wrot to my Wife, & my L: of *Norwich*:

9. Consulting with *Dr. Stanley*, I went home, & tooke *Physick*: 10: Came my *Bro*: Rich: *Glanvill* & divers of my friends to visite me, & staied all night: I was still in my Course of *Physick*, being much indisposed in my Stomache: 13 Newes was brought me that my *Lady Cotton* (my Bro: Georges Wife) was deliverd of a *Sonn*, my Brothers return'd: I was moved by a letter out of *France* to publish the Letter which sometime since, I sent *Deane Cousins* proselyted sonn; but, I did not conceive it convenient, for feare of displeasing her *Majestie* the Queene: I had also newes of the safe arivall of some goods I expected out of *France*:

15 This night was an *Ecclipse* of the *Moone*, I writ Letters to my Wife &c: concerning my resolution of settling; also to the *Deane* touching my buying his Library, which was one of the choicest collection⟨s⟩ of any private persons whatsover in England:

I had now also newes that Monsieur the *Count de Strade* had sent me my Wifes Picture from *Dynkirk*, which he most generously & handsomely did in a large tin case, without any charge: The Picture is of Mr   and is that which has the dog in it; & is to the knees, but has ben something spoild by washing it ignorantly with sope-sudds:

16 I let bloud 9 ounces. 17 Sweate, & bathed, & went to Lond, to take order about my goods ariv'd out of France: I had ben exceedingly troubld with a swelling in my throat & neck, which fore-ran the *Piles*, & had now for 2 Springs indisposd me, but now prevented, by the Course I tooke & greate evacuations:

23 I was at the Christning of my Bro: Eldest sonn, by my *Lady Cotton* who was named Richard (after the name of his Grandfather) my Bro: Rich: Glan: & *La: Herbert* Susceptors &c:

25 I went to visite *Ald: Kendrick* a Fanatic *L. Mayor*, who had married a relation of ours, where I met with a Cap: that had ben

13 times at the *E. Indias*, & was full of strange stories, & so return'd:

27 Came Mr. Radcliffe (sonn of Sir Geo:) to visie & dine with me.

29 Was that celebrated Eclipse of the Sun, so much threatned by the *Astrologers*, & had so exceedingly alarm'd the whole Nation, so as hardly any would worke, none stir out of their houses; so ridiculously were they abused by knavish and ignorant star-gazers.

30 Came my Bro. Geo: & Bro: Rich: with his wife to dine with me, & my little *Nephew Geo: Evelyn* brought to abide some time with me, if possible to reclaime him of his fondnesse to home, where he miserably lost his time: We went this afternoon to see the *Queenes* house at *Greenewich*, now given by the Rebells to *Bolstrood Whittlock* one of their unhappy Counselors, keeper of pretended *Liberties*.

2 Aprill, I went to Lond: to dispatch divers affaires, return'd that Evening:

9 I went againe to Lond: & next day, passing by Smithfield, there was a miserable Creature burning who had murder'd her husband: I returnd: 17 I went to Lond: to receive the blessed Sacrament, at the Church in *East-Cheape*, hoping to have heard Mr. *Pierson* [Since Bishop of *Chester*], but a stranger preach'd on 3. *Phil:* 10, applying it to the Resurrection:

21 I went to see some workmanship of that admirable Artist *Reeves*, famous for Perspectives, & turning curiosities in Ivorie: 24 return'd. 26: To Lond: to prepare some things against my Wifes coming over, return'd 28. I went next day againe to take order about a Coach, to be made against her Coming, being ⟨my⟩ first *Coach*, the pattern whereof I brought out of Paris, returnd in the Evening: Next day I went to obtaine of my Lord of Devonshire, that my Nephew ⟨George⟩ might be brought up, with my Young Lord his sonn to whom I was recommending Mr. *Wase*:

May 4 I kept a Court *Leete* & Baron at *Greate Warley* in *Essex* & so to Lond: thence to Rittington the next day, dining at one Mr. *Walkers*, returnd the 6 to Lond.

7 I had Letters from Paris, dated 11th *May* of my Wifes being with Child of her first, and returnd to Saies Court: 14 I went to *Lond*, & *returnd*: 17 came my Bro: to see me: 19 my Wife

confirm'd to me her being quick: 20 To Lond, about my parting
with my house in the *Cliffe* neere *Lewes* in *Sussex*: The next day I
went to see the manner of chambletting silk & *Grograns* at one
Monsieur La Dorees in *Morefields*; & thence to Coll: *Morley* (one
of their Council of State, as then calld) who had ben my Schole-
fellow, to request a Passe for my Wifes safe landing & the goods
she was to bring with her out of *France*, which ⟨he⟩ courteously
granted, & did me many other kindnesses, which was a greate
matter in those daies: 22 return'd home: 25 Came Mr. *Ja: Scudamor* Unkle to my Lord *Vicount Scudamore* of *Homlacy* in *Herefordshire* & a most worthy Gent: to consult with me about
reclaiming a relation of his in *Paris*; 30 In the afternoone, at
Charleton Church, I heard a *Rabinical* Sermon on 1. *Gen:* 2: And
that since God was able to educe all things out of nothing, men
were not to despaire of his power, or distrust him. Here is a faire
Monument of *Sir Adam Newton* in black Marble, who built that
faire House neere it for *Prince Henry*, & where my noble friend
Sir *Henry Newton* succeeded him.

3 *June* I went to Lond, received Letter⟨s⟩ from Coll: Morley
to the Magistrates & Searchers at Rie to assist my Wife at her
Landing, & shew her all civility: returned:

4 I set out for *Rie* to meete my Wife, now upon her journey
from *Paris*, after she had obtain'd leave to come out that Citty,
which had now ben besieged some time, by the Pr: of *Condys*
armie, in the Time of the Rebellion: & after she had now ben
neere 12 Yeares from her owne Country, that is since 5 yeares of
age, at which time she went over: 5 I lay this night at *Sennock*,
ariv'd the next at *Rie*, where was an *Embargo*, upon occasion of
the late Conflict with the *Holland Fleete*, the two Nations being
now in Warr; & which made sailing very unsafe: 6: Whitsonday, I went to *Church* (which is a very faire one) ⟨heard⟩ one of
their Canters, who dismiss'd the Assembly rudely, & without
any blessing: I was displeased when I came home, that I was
present at it, having hitherto kept my Eares incontaminate
from their new fangled service: Here I stayed til the 10th with
no small impatience, when I walked over to survey the ruines of
Winchelsea, that antient *Cinq*-port, which by the remaines &
ruines of ample Streetes, & publique structures, discovers it
to have formerly ben a considerable & large Citty, There are
to be seene vast Caves & Vaults, Walls, & Towers, ruines of

Monasteries, & of a sumptuous Church in which some handsom monuments, especialy of the *Templars* buried just in the
manner of those in the Temp: at Lond: This place being now all
in rubbish, & a few despicable hovells & cottages onely standing, hath yet a *Major*: The sea which formerly renderd it a rich
& commodious port, having now forsaken it: so we walked
back to Rie:

11 About 4 in the after-noone, being at bowles on the Greene,
we discoverd a Vessel, which proved ⟨to⟩ be that in which my
Wife was, & got into harbour about 8 a clock that Eveni⟨n⟩g to
my no small joy: They had ben 3 days at Sea, & hardly Escaped
the whole Dut⟨c⟩h Fleete, through which the⟨y⟩ pass'd taken for
Fishers; which was a greate good fortune; there being 17 bailes of
furniture, & other rich plunder, which I blesse God came all safe
to land, together with my *Wife*, & my *Lady Browne* her mother,
accompanying her Daughter: But my Wife discompos'd with
being so long at sea, we set not forth towards home 'til the 14th,
when hearing the Small-pox was very rife in and about *Lond:*
and that my *Lady* had a greate desire to drink Tunbridge Waters;
I carried them thither, where I staied in a very sweete place, private & refreshing, and also tooke the Waters my selfe a few
daies, 'til the 23d when buisinesse calling me homewards, & to
prepare for the reception of my little family (leaving them for
the present in their Cottage by the Wells) The morning growing
excessivly hot, I sent my footman some hours before, and so rod
negligently, under favour of the shade, 'til being now come to
within three miles of *Bromely*, at a place called the procession
Oake, started out two Cutt-throates, & striking with their long
staves at the horse, taking hold of the reignes, threw me downe,
& immediately tooke my sword, & haled me into a deepe
Thickett, some quarter of a mile from the high-way, where they
might securely rob me, as they soone did; what they got of mony
was not considerable, but they tooke two rings, the one an
Emrald with diamonds, an ⟨Onyx⟩, & a pair of boucles set with
rubies & diamonds which were of value, and after all, barbarously bound my hands behind me, & my feete, having before
pull'd off my bootes: & then set me up against an *Oake*, with
most bloudy threatnings to cutt my throat, if I offerd to crie out,
or make any noise, for that they should be within hearing, I not
being the person they looked for: I told them, if they had not

basely surpriz'd me, they should not have made so easy a prize,
& that it should teach me hereafter never to ride neere an hedge;
since had I ben in the mid way, they durst not have adventur'd
on me, at which they cock'd their pistols, & told me they had
long guns too, & were 14 companions, which all were lies: I
begg'd for my *Onyx* & told them it being engraven with my
armes, would betray them, but nothing prevaild: My horses bridle they slipt, & search'd the saddle which they likewise pull'd
off, but let the horse alone to grace, & then turning againe
bridld him, & tied him to a Tree, yet so as he might graze, & so
left me bound: The reason they tooke not my horse, was I suppose, because he was mark'd, and cropt on both Eares, & well
known on that roade, & these rogues were lusty foote padders,
as they are cald: Well, being left in this manner, grievously was I
tormented with the flies, the ants, & the sunn, so as I sweate
intollerably, nor little was my anxiety how I should get loose in
that solitary place, where I could neither heare or see any creature but my poore horse & a few sheepe stragling in the Coppse;
til after neere two houres attempting I got my hands to turne
paulme to paulme, whereas before they were tied back to back,
and then I stuck a greate while ere' I could slip the cord over my
wrist to my thumb, which at last I did, & then being quite loose
soone unbound my feete, & so sadling my horse, and roaming a
while about, I at last perceiv'd a dust to rise, & soone after heard
the rattling of a Cart, towards which I made, and by the help of
two Country fellows that were driving it, got downe a steepe
bank, into the highway againe; but could heare nothing of the
Villains: So I rod to *Colonel Blounts* a greate justiciarie of the
times, who sent out *hugh* & *Crie* immediately: and 25, The next
morning weary & sore as I was at my wrists & armes, I went
from *Deptford* to *Lond*, got 500 ticketts printed & dispers'd, by
an officer of *Gould Smiths-hall*, describing what I had lost, and
within two daies after had tidings of all I lost, except my Sword
which was a silver hilt, & some other trifles: These *rogues* had
paund my Rings &c for a trifle to a Goldsmiths Servant, before
the tickets came to the shop, by which meanes they scap'd, the
other ring was bought by a Victualer, who brought it to a Goldsmith, that having seene the ticket, seiz'd upon him; but whom I
afterwards discharg'd upon the mediation of friends, & protestation of his innocency: Thus did God deliv⟨e⟩r me from these

villains, & not onely so, but restor'd to me what they tooke, as twise before he had graciously don, both at sea & land, I meane, when I had ben rob'd by *Pyrates* and was in danger of a considerable losse at *Amsterdam*, for which & many, many signal preservations I am eternaly obligd to give thanks to God my Saviour.

There fell this 25t day (after a drowth of neere 4 monethes) so violent a Tempest of haile, raine, wind, Thunder & lightning, as no man alive had seene the like in this age: The haile being in some places 4 & 5 Inches about, brake all the glasse about Lond: especialy at Deptford, & more at Greenewich, where Sir Tho: *Stafford, Vice-Chamberlaine* to the *Queene*, affirm'd some had the shape of Crownes: others the order of the Gartyr about them; but these were fancies: it was certainely a very prodigious Storme: 26: I return'd to *Says Court*. 29 I went back in Coach to see my Wife at Tunbridge after my late disaster, & began againe to drink the Waters til the 10th of July, that is I ariv'd to 20 *Glasses* each glasse containing 8 *Ounces*:

1 *July*, We went to see the house of my Lord *Clainrichards* at Summerhill (now given to the villain *Bradshaw* who condemned the King): 'tis situated on an eminent hill with a park, but has nothing else extraordinary: 4th I heard a *Sermon* at Mr. *Packers* Chapell at Groomebridge, a prety Melancholy seate, well wooded & watred: on 10 *Luk* 4: In this house of my worthy friend Mr. Packer, was one of the French Kings kept prisoner: The *Chapell* was built by his Father, in remembrance of K: Charles the 1. his safe return out of *Spaine*.

The 9th we went to see *Pensherst* being the E. of *Licesters*, famous onc⟨e⟩ for its Gardens & excellent fruit: and for the noble Conversation which was wont to meete there, celebrated by that illustrious person Sir *Phil: Sidny*, who there composd divers of his pieces: It stands also in a park, is finely waterd: & was now full of Company, upon the marriage of my old fellow-Collegiate, Mr. Robert Smith, who married my L: Dorothy Sidny, widdow of the Earle of *Sunderland*.

10 I had newes of the taking of one of the knaves who robbd me, & was summon'd to appeare against him: so as on the 12, I was in *Westminster Hall* but not being bound over (nor willing to hang the fellow) I did not appeare, comming onely to save a friends baile who appeard for me; however the man being found ⟨guilty⟩, was turn'd over to the old bailey:

13 My Wife & her Mother came first to *Deptford*: next day her Bro: John Pretyman & severall friends to congratulate. 15 We all went to *Lond:* to returne Visites: In the meane time, I received a letter from *Sir Tho: Peyton*, & a petition from the Prisoner (whose father I understood was an honest old fermor in Kent) to be favourable which I was; not withstanding, others comming in, about a Rape, & that he had ben in Goaile before, he was condemn'd, but repriv'd by Sir Tho: I was told he was a bloudy rascal, & had murderd severall of his Majesties Subjects being a souldier in Ireland, & that had it not ben for his companion, a younger fellow, 'twas ten to one, but he had knock'd me on the head: This I came to know afterwards & that in the End, upon some other Crime, he being obstinate & not pleading, was press'd to death: one thing I remember, that he was one of the worst look'd fellows I ever saw.

23 Came my old friend Mr. *Spencer* to visie me.

27 Came to visite me both my Bro: & their Ladys, L: Gerrard, two Coach fulls of friends to rejoice & welcome us, who staid tw⟨o⟩ daies with us; returnd the next day.

30 I went to Lond, return'd in the Evening, & the next day againe to take advise about purchasing Sir Richards Interest of those who had bought *Sayes Court*, returning that night:

1 *Aug:* Came Old *Jerome Lennier* (a man greatly skill'd in Painting & Musique) and another rare Musitian, cald *Mell*: 2: Came Mr. Robinson & brother in Law to see me; & I went to see *Jer: Lenniers* rare Collection of Pictures, especialy those of *Julio Romanos*, which surely had ben the Kings, & an *Egyptian* figure &c: there were also excellent things of *Polydor, Guido, Raphael, Tintoret* &c: 20 Came Mr. Henshaw to visite me.

23 I went to Lond, to treate with Sir *N: Crisp*, concerning some Improvements, returned with my new & first Coach:

24 Aug: precisely at one a clock, was my Wife brought to bed of my first Child & son:

26 Went to Lond, return'd. 29 At Greene-Wich one *Abbot* preach'd on 4: *Mal:* 2 shewing how Christ was ⟨the⟩ Sunn of righteousnesse: &c with the signes & effects of his healing sinners: In the afternoone on 2 *Coloss* 6. shewing how we ought to be carefull after our cure: I now gave God thanks for his Mercy to my Wife & family:

31 I went to Lond: receivd congratulations from severall friends:

2d *September Mr. Owen*, sequestred Parson of *Eltham* christned my Son, by the Name of *Richard* (my F. *Evelyns* & Sir R: *Brownes* names) Susceptors my *Bro: Geo:* & *sister Evelyn*, about 4 in the afternoone, in the little drawing roome, next the Parlor in Says Court, many of my Relations & neighbours present: The Goships return'd that Evening:

3 I was bound with *Mr. W: Pretyman* to my *Co: Steephens* in behalfe of Sir R: B: in a penal bond of 1500 pounds, for the setting out Lands to pay him a debt Sir R: owed him, within 6 moneths.

5 At *Deptford* church one preachd on 15 *Matt:* 26. That by the bread of Children, was ment the Gospel: & on the 19th upon the same Text: In what capacitys *Christians* were Children.

21 My Wife was Churched at home by *Mr. Owen*: I had divers friends Eng: & french at dinner:

23 I went to *Lond:* to visite the Marquesse of *Ormond*, La: *Montague* & severall Ladys returnd:

25 I went to see Dr. *Masons* house, so famous for the Prospect (for the house is a wretch⟨e⟩d one) & description in Barkeleys *Icon Animorum*.

26 A stranger preach'd at *Deptford* on 13 *Osea*: 14, of the ransome paied by our *B: Saviour*.

29 I went to *Woodcot* intending thence to *Wotton* & thence into *Wiltshire* &c with my Wife & Mother in Law, to have visited & rejoiced with my Brothers, & severall of both our Relations, so desirous of our Company; but being gotten to *Woodcott* it pleased God to visite my *Lady* with a Scarlet feavar, the Thursday following, of which she died the Wednesday following, which not onely interrupted that designe, but fill'd us with excessive sorrow: so as on the 6: of *Octob*: we carried her in an hearse to *Deptford*, & interr'd her in the Church neere Sir Richards Relations, upon the 9th following, accompanied with many Coaches of Friends, & other persons of qualitie; with all decent Ceremonie, & according to the Church Office, which I obtain might be permitted, after it had not ben usd in that Church of 7 yeares before, to the greate satisfaction of that innumerable multitude who were there: Thus ended an Excellent & Virtuous Lady, from a disconsolate Husband (now beseigd &

Calamitous in *France*) & a sad *Daughter*, but newly return'd into *England*: Indeede she was universaly lamented, having ben so obliging upon all ocasions to those who continualy frequented her house in *Paris*, which was not onely an *Hospital*, but the *Asylum* to all our persecuted & afflicted Countrymen during her 11 yeares residence there, in that honarable Station:

11 Came Mr. *Salvage* a sonn of my L: *Rivers's* to see me. 16 I let bloud, to prevent a pleurisie: 19 I went to Lond, about my Nep: George, return'd next day: 21, came severall Ladys & friends to Condole: 24. I tooke Physick: 26 I went to my Wifes Unkle *Mr. Pretymans* Wedding to *Greenewich*.

28 I received condoling letters from *Sir Ed: Hide* (since Lord High Chancellor) & Sir *Geo: Radcliff* &c: 30 being the Eve of my Birth-day, I made my Will, & all accompts Even, being 31. *Thirty two years old*: Blessed be God for all his mercies:

5 *November* I went to *Lond*, to visite severall friends, but the insolensies were so greate in the streetes, that I could not returne till the next day: 8. I went againe, returnd at night:

10 I went to *Lond:* to the Christning of my *Bro: Richards daughter* Ann, return'd next day: Dr. *Scarbrough* was instant with me to give the Tables of *Veines* & *Arteries* to the Colledge of *Physitians*, pretending he would not onely reade upon them but celebrate my curiositie, as having ben the first who caus'd them to be compleated in that manner, & with that cost; but I was not so willing yet to part with them as to lend them to the Colledge during their *Anatomical* Lecture, which I did accordingly: 15. Went againe, returnd that Evening.

20 Came to Visite us, my *Co: Edgecomb* of Mount *Edgecomb* in Cornewall neere *Plymoth*. 22 I went to *Lond:* where was proposd to me the promoting of that greate Work (since accomplishd by *Dr. Walton* (*Bishop* of Chester) *Biblia Polyglotta*), by *Mr. Pierson* that most learned divine.

3 *Decemb:* Came divers friends to visite me: 4. I went to Lond: about repairing my Chambers in the *Midd: Temple*. 12. At *Lewsam* I heard one preach on 21 *Matt*. 5: being Advent, Concerni(n)g our B: Saviours meekenesse: 20 Came My Brothers & Ladys to dine with me: 21, My Wife & I went to Lond: to returne visites & dispatch some buisinesse:

25 *Christmas day* [no sermon anywhere, so observd it at home, the next day] we went to *Lewsham*, where was an honest

divine preach'd on 21. *Matt*: 9. celebrating the Incarnation, for on the day before, no Churches were permitted to meete &c: to that horrid passe were they come: 31 I adjusted all accompts, & renderd thanks to God for his mercys to me the yeare past.

1653. 1 *Jan:* I set a part, in preparation for the B: *Sacrament*, which the next day *Mr. Owen* administred to me & all my family in *Says-Court*, preaching on: 6: *John* 32. 33. shewing the exceeding benefits of our B: Saviours taking our nature upon him.

14 I went to *Greenewich* to see againe *Mr. Lenniers* Collection, who shewed me *Q: Elizabeths* head an Intaglia in a rare *Sardonyx*, cut by a famous *Italian*, *Mr. Lennier* who had ben a domestic Servant of that *Queene*, assured me it was exceedingly like her:

17 I began to set out the *Ovall Garden* at Says Court, which was before a rude *Ortchard*, & all the rest one intire fild of 100 *Ackers*, without any hedge: excepting the hither holly-hedge joyning to the bank of the mount walk: & this was the beginning of all the succeeding *Gardens*, *Walkes*, *Groves*, *Enclosures* & *Plantations* there:

21 I went to Lond: & sealed some of the Writings of my Purchase of *Sayes-Court*, returnd next day:

23 At *Leusam* a Sermon on 26. *Act*. 26. 27. 28. Concerning the notion of the word Sacrament, against *Transubstantiation*, refusing the Cup to the Layitie; instructing us in the duties of Love & Charity:

30. At our own *Parish Church*, a Stranger preachd on 1. *Apoc*. 5. 6. describing the greate benefits don us by our B: Lord: Note, that there was now & then, an honest orthodox man gotten into the *Pulpet*, and though the present *Incumbent* were somewhat Independent; yet he ordinarily preachd sound doctrine, & was a peaceable man, which was an extraordinary felicity in this age:

1 February, Old *Alex: Rosse* (Author of *Virgilius Evangelizans* & many other little bookes) presented me with his Book against Mr. *Hobbs's Leviathan*.

19 I planted the *Ortchard* at *Says-Court*, *new Moone*, *wind West*.

22 Was perfected the *sealing*, *livery & sesin* of my Purchase of *Says Court* My Bro: Geo: *Glanvill*, Mr. *Scudamor*, Offley, Co: William *Glanvill*, sonn to Serjeant Glanvil (sometime Speaker

of the H: of Commons) Co: Steephens, & severall of my friends dining with me, it being also Shrove Tuesday; I paid for it 3500, my bargaine being 3200 pounds: [cost *3500* pounds 300 pounds more than I bargain'd for:]

A bloudy fight now with the *Dut(c)h*: 24. I was surprizd with a severe fit of an *Ague* which held me neere 12 houres:

3 *March*, my *Ague* accompanied with a feavor, treated me so rudely, that with much difficulty escaped I with my life, but by the goodnesse of God, & plying with Physick, by advise of Dr. *Wilson* my *Physitian*, I began to recover, & was out of danger, after 4 or 5. fitts: but was not cleeare till the 15th: Severall of my Relations & friends coming daily to visite me.

25 Came to see me that rare graver in *Tallie douce Monsieur Richett*, he was sent over by Card: *Mazzarini*, to make Collections of Pictures: 30 I was able to go abroad:

3 *Aprill* I went first to Church, the Minister preaching on 2. *Cor:* 5. 17, somewhat mysteriously about predestination, & such high points, as the manner was: his drift was to shew in what sense the *Elect* were one with *Christ*.

7 Came divers of my Relations to Visite me, & congratulate my recovery:

9 I went with my family to Lond: to receive the *B: Sacrament*, at St. *Mary Mag:* in old *Fish-streete* where a *Scotch-man* preach'd on 20. Jo. 1. 2. the *Gospel* of the day: din'd at my Brothers & afternoone heard at *East-Cheape* Mr. *Pierson* on 28 *Matt:* 6. most excellently handld on the *Resurrection:* he shewed how our B: S: was then properly Lord, after he had vanquishd death.

11 I went to take the aire in *Hide-Park*, where every Coach was made pay a shill: & horse 6d. by the sordid fellow who had purchas'd it of the State, as they were cald: Collation'd at Spring Garden, returning back met the *Portugal* Ambassador in a glorious Charriot; dined next day at my Physitians, & so home to *Says-Court*:

12 Went againe to a *Treate* at Esquire *Abdys*, & to meete Severall Relations, & so Home:

13 Came My Co: *Edgecom* & his Lady, with Mr. *Ducie*, to visite us.

17 The first time I went with my Wife to our Parish-Church, since she had ben in England: the Minister preaching on 2. *Cor:* 5: 17: shewing how the new Creation was wrought.

29 Went to *Lond*, return'd:

1 *May*. Our Parson, proceeded on his former subject. 6 came friends to visite:

8 A Young man, on⟨e⟩ *Johnson* on 3. *Phil:* 8 a practical discourse:

10 I kept Court at *Warley magna* in *Essex*.

12 Came my *Bro: Glanvill*, brought me his little Sonn, whom I so much longed to see, being the onely child of my deare sister; a very fine, & hopfull boy:

15 A Stranger preachd on 5. *Matt*. 8. That to see God, was to be transcendently happy: In the afternoone the *Minister* of the Parish on his former text:

17 My Servant *Hoare* (who writ those exquisite severall hands) fell of a fit of an *Apoplexie* caus'd as I suppose, by tampering with ☿ about an experiment on Gold:

18 My Wife perceivd herselfe quick with her 2d Child: 22 Our Parson on his old Text:

24 I went to *Lond:* to take my last leave of my honest friend *Mr. Barton* now dying: it was a greate losse to me, & my affaires:

29 Our Minister proceeded on his Subject: & so 3. *June* A greate batall at sea, with the Hollanders: we heard the gunns plainly to my house:

5 June, I went to Charleton, where on⟨e⟩ *Pemberton*, a young man preached very well on 6. *Amos* 6 Concerning the duty of Christians in times of Publique Calamity.

6 I went to *Mr. Bartons* funeral.

8 Came my Bro: Geo: Cap: Evelyn (the greate *Travellor*) Mr. *Muschamp*, my Co: *Tho: Keightly* and a *Virtuoso* fantastical *Symons* (who had that talent of Embossing so to the life) to visite me:

9 I went to visite my Worthy neighbour *Sir H: Newton*, & consider the Prospect, which (after *Constantinople*) is doubtlesse for Citty, river, Ships, Meadows, hill, Woods, & all other distinguishable amenities, the most noble the whole World has to shew: so as had the house running water, it were a princely seate:

12 Our Parson proceeded on 19 Ver:

14 Went to Lond, to take leave of my bro: he now going into the Country, & this day paied all my debts to a farthing, ô blessed day!

18 Mr. *Henshaw* & his brother in Law came to visite me, & he presented me with a *Selene-scope*.

19 The Minister proceeded. So on the 26:

27 Mr. *Philips* going Consul to *Venice* came to take his leave of me, I had this day ben six-yeares married:

⟨3⟩ *July*, I went to church to *Charleton*, where on⟨e⟩ Dr. Stoakes (Chaplaine to the late King) preachd on 10 *Deut:* 12, in an excellent incitement of our Love to God: In the afternoone to our Parish Church, proceeding on that *Chapter*, as also he did on the 10th & 17th:

21 Came to Visite us my *Lady Gerrard*, & one *Esquire Knight* a very rich *Gent:* of N.hamptonshire with his Lady: 23 Monsieur *Lombart* a ⟨famous⟩ Graver came to see my Collections:

24 Our *Minister* on a new *Text*: 10. *Luke*: 20, shewing that there could be no true joy, without assurance of eternal joy:

Dick had an accesse of an *Ague*, which greately afflicted us: but it last⟨ed⟩ not above 3 fits:

29 *Monsieur Roussel* sent me a small *phiole* of his *Aurum potabile*, with a letter shewing the way of administring it, & the stupendious cures it had don at *Paris*, but ere it came to me, by what accident I know not, it was all of it run out.

31 Our Parson proceeded, shewing that the Bookes recording the *Elects* names, was onely Gods Owne remembrance &c:

1 *Aug:* I went to visite some friends at *Greene-wich* where I met La: *Newton* & *Peto*.

7 Our Parson on his former Text:

The *Hollanders* shrewdly beaten in another fight at sea:

9 My Lord Strafford, Earle of Ossorie, & Mr. Seymor came to visite us:

13 I first began a Course of yearely washing my head with Warme Water, mingld with a decoction of Sweete herbs, & immediately, with cold Spring water, which much refreshd me, & succeeded very well with me divers yeares:

14 Extreame ill weather kept us from Church this day:

15 I went with my Wife the first time to *Wotton*, & to divert her after her Mothers death, the sorrow whereof long hung upon her.

17 We went to visite *Mr. Hyliard* at his house at Horsley: formerly, the greate Sir *Wal: Raleighs*, where met me Mr. *Oughtred*, the famous *Mathematician*: ⟨he⟩ shewed me a box or golden case, of divers rich & aromatic *Balsoms*, which a *Chymist* a Scholar of his, had sent him out of *Germanie*.

21 I heard, that good old man, *Mr. Higham*, the parson of the Parish of *Wotton* where I was born, & who had baptizd me, preach after his very plaine way on *Luke*, Comparing this troublesome world to the Sea, the Ministers to the fishers, & Saints to the Fish:

22 We all went to Guildford, to rejoice at the famous Inn the Red Lion, & went to see the Hospital, & Monument of *Geo: Abbot*, late A: Bish: of Canterbury, who lies buried in that Chapell of his Endowment, & so returnd:

23 We went to *Albury* to see Mr. *Howard*: & 26t returnd home to *Says Court*: where we found most of our Servants sick:

28 At *Greenewich* preachd that *holy Martyr*, Dr. *Hewet* on 90 Psal: 11. Magnifying the grace of God to penetents; and threatning the Extinction of his Gospel light for the prodigious impiety of the age:

1 *September* I went to Lond, to visite a sick Person, return'd.

4 Our M: preach'd on 19 *Matt:* 25. 26. The paucity of the Saved, & exceeding difficulties:

9 Came my Bro: Richard to visite us: ⟨11⟩ our M: proceeded on his Text: 13 Came Dr. *Joylife*, indagator of the *Lymphatic veines*, & a famous *Anatomist* to see me, this day my Bro: went home:

⟨18⟩ Our Minister proceeded: 20 I went to Warley to see my Woods, return'd at night:

25 Mr. *Owen* preached in my Library at Says Court on, 18 *Luke.* 7. 8. an excellent discourse on the un-just Judge, shewing why Almight⟨y⟩ God, would sometimes be compard by such similitudes; He administred to us all the Holy Sacrament:

6 *October* I sent to Wotton to ⟨congratulate⟩ my Bro: & Lady, on the birth of their Son, John:

9 Our Minister pr: of. 2. *Cor:* 13. 5, about Christian Examination before the H. *Sacrament.*

11 of *October* at 10 $\frac{1}{2}$ houre night, my Sonn *John Standsfild* was borne, being my second child, & christned on 17th by the name of my *Mothers Father*, that name now quite extinct, being of *Chesshire*: Susceptors, my *Bro: Glanvill*, Wives Unkle *Jo: Pretyman*, & Aunt *Hungerford* of *Cadenham* in *Wiltshire*: Christned by Mr. *Owen* in my Library at Says Court:

23 Our parson on his former subject.

28 I went to Lond, to visite my *Lady Gerard*, where I saw that cursed woman cald the Lady *Norton*, of whom it was reported,

that she spit in our Kings face, as he went to the Scaffold, indeede her talke & discourse was like an impudent woman: I returnd that Evening.

30 a stranger preachd in our Church on 2. *Tit:* 12: The scope was to shew how disagreable a disorderly conversation was to the principles of the Gospel: also cleared the necessity of good works, & the assurance of reward, not as of worth, but by grace & promise:

5 ⟨November⟩ I went to *Lond:* on foote, returnd that evening: next day our Minister on his former subject:

7 My Wife was Churched by Mr. *Owen,* whom I allways made use of on these occasions, because the *Parish Minister* durst not (or perhaps would not) have officiated according to the forme & usage of the Church of England, to which I allwayes adhered: 13 our Parson [10 Zach: 12] proceeded: 18 I went to Lond, came back that day with my friend & old fellow Traveller Mr. *Hensheaw,* who stayed all night with me, & return'd next day:

20 Our Minister pr: on 11 *Isa:* 10, shewing how Christ was the roote of *Jesse,* & an Ensigne:

21 I went to *Lond:* to speake with Sir Jo: Evelyn my kindsman: about the Purchase of an Estate of Mr. *Lambards* at *Westram,* which afterwards Sir Jo: himselfe bought for his son-in Law Leech: return'd that Evening:

27 My son: *J. Standsfild* fell into Convulsion fitts, which not long after carried him away:

4 *December*: 'Til now I had met with no Phanatical Preachers, but going this day to our Church, I was surprizd to see a Tradesman, a Mechanic step up, I was resolv'd yet to stay, & see what he would make of it, his Text was 2. Sam. 23. 20 *and Benaiah sonn of Jehoiada—went downe also & slew a lion in the midst of a pit, in the time of Snow.*

That no danger was to be thought difficult, when God call'd for sheading of blood, inferring that now, the Saints were calld to destroy, temporal Governments, with such truculent, ⟨anabaptisticall⟩ stuff: so dangerous a *Crisis* were things growne to:

8 I went to visite my L: *Strafford,* E: of Ossory, Mr. Seymour, where was my Lady *Ross-Common* & *Madamoiselle La Varenne,* who sung so finely to the *Guittar*: I lay this night in my Lodging at the M: Temple: Next day visited Mr. *Radcliffe* & Cap: *Forster,* the next day returnd home:

11 Our Minister on his former Text:

12 I causd an *Issue* to be made in my little Boy Standfilds neck: which abated his fitts:

14 I kept Court at *Warley*, lay at *Brentwood*, return'd next day: 18 Our Parson, proceeds:

20 I went to welcome my Bro: *G. Evelyn* to *Lond*, who was come now up to passe the rest of Winter in Towne: returnd that Evening:

25 *Christmas-day*, no Churches ⟨or⟩ publique Assembly, I was faine to passe the devotions of that blessed day with my family at home: 29. Came my Bro: E: & divers friends to dine with me:

31 I made up all my Accompts, blessed God for his protection of me the past yeare:

1654 2 *Jan:* I went to Woodcot to visite my Bro: where meting severall friends, we pass'd the time very cherefully, & returnd home on Saturday 7th.

11 I went to *Lond*, visited my Lady *Radcliff* return'd in the Evening:

15 Our *Parson* preach'd on his former subject: next day came my Bro: to see me:

20 Came to see me my old acquaintance & most incomparable player on the Irish-Harp, Mr. Clarke after his Travells: He was an excellent Musitian, a discreete Gentleman, borne in Devonshire, as I remember: such musique before or since did I never heare, that Instrument neglected for its extraordina⟨r⟩y difficulty; but in my judgement far superior to the Lute it selfe, or whatever speakes with strings:

⟨22⟩ Our Minister proceedes: concerning the Rest of Gods people:

25 Died my Son, *J. Standsfield* of Convulsion fits, buried at *Deptford* on the East Corner of the Church, neere his mothers greate Grandfather &c: the Thursday after, being a quarter old, & little more, as Lovely a babe as ever I beheld. 27 a Court was kept at Warley, but I was absent:

29 A very youth preach'd on 1. Pet: 22. very well, about the necessity of regeneration:

5 Feb: our Minister proceeded on the last part of 11. Esay: 10.

8 In Contradiction to all Costome & decency, the Usurper *Cromwell* feasted at the L. Majors on Ash-Wednesday, riding in

T⟨r⟩iumph through the Citty: 12 our Parson proceeded to describe the glory of the Church:

13 My Bro: *Richard* paied me 1000 pounds, which I went to Lond: to receive, return'd next day when I saw a tame *Lion* play familiarly with a *Lamb*: The *Lion* was a huge beast, I thrust my hand into his mouth, & felt his tongue rough like a Catts: A sheepe also that had 6 leggs and made use of 5 of them to walke: A *Goose* that had 4 leggs, two Cropps, & as many Vents, voyding excrement by both, which was strange:

19 Our Minister tooke a new Text. 1. *Cor:* 6. 11. Of the causal clensing of sin: &c:

25 I went to Lond: return'd with my Aunt *Hungerford*:

26 Our Minister on 11: *Hosëa* 4. of the Compulsorie love of God:

3 *March* came to visite me my Lady *Newton*, Sir Jo: Hammilton, & Mr. *Cranes*.

5 Our Parson preach'd on 2. *Ephes:* 22 shewing how the Mysterie of the Trinity was wraped up in the 2 first Words:

11 I went to Lond: to bespeake a new Coach, return'd:

12 Our Parson: on 55 *Isa:* 1. Christs gracious Invitation:

13 I had some grudging of an Ague, & thence forwards a Tertian. 18 Came my Bro: and Lady to visite me: next day, being *Palme* sunday, I op'ne'd a veine, & was in Physick til the 26. when it pleased God to restore me, being even in this short time extreamely weakned, so as I could not go to Church.

29 Mr. *Owen* preach⟨ed⟩ in my Library on 28 *Matt.* 6. a Resurrection Sermon, & after it we all receiv'd the blessed Communion.

2 *Aprill* I went to the Parish Church: The Minister preachd on 50 *Psal:* 5. 6. Preparatory to the Sacrament, which was a very rare thing in these daies:

6 Came my *Lord Herbert*, Sir *Kenhelme Digbie*, *Mr. Denham* & other Friends to Visite me.

⟨9⟩ Our Minister proceeded: 15 I went to Lond: to heare the famous Dr. *Jer: Taylor* since Bish: of *Downe* & *Connor:* but in the Morning preachd Dr. *Reeves* at *Lincolns Inn* on: 1. *Tim:* 6. 10. excellently against the sin of Avarice: In the afternoone at St. *Greg:* Dr. *Taylor* on 6: *Matt:* 48, concerning evangelical perfection, & how few were realy sinns of Infirmity:

17 I returnd: 23. Our Minister proceeded, & so he did the Sonday following: & then Celebrated the H. Sacrament, at

which considering, the Vastnesse of the Parish, were very few Communicants, in so divided a State was the Church at this Period: 30 on the same.

5 *May*. I bound my ⟨Laquay⟩ *Tho: Heath* Apprentise to a Carpenter, giving with him 5 pounds, and new Cloathing: he thriv'd very well & became rich: I went to Lond, to visite many relations, & return'd not til the 12th, lying at the Temple:

7 At Milk-streete Chur⟨c⟩h preach'd Dr. *Taylor* on. 5. *Matt:* 19. of the Danger of the Contempt of small sinns: In the afternoone the same, at my Lord Rutlands Chapel: 3. *Act:* 19. against deferring of Repentance:

8 I went to *Hackny* to see my Lady *Brooks* Gardens, which was one of the neatest, & most celebrated in England: The House also well furnish'd, but a despicable building: returning visited on⟨e⟩ Mr. *Tomb's's Garden*, it has large & noble Walks, some modern statues; but what was pretiest was the Vine-yard planted in Strawberry-borders, staked at 10 foote distance: Also the Banqueting house of Cedar, where the Couch & seates were carv'd *a l'Antique*: Some good Pictures in the House, especialy one of *Van dykes* being a Man in his Shirt; also some of *Steenewich*: I also call'd at Mr. *Ducies*, who has indeede a rare Collection of the best Masters, & one of the largest Stories of H. *Holben*: I also saw Sir T. *Fowlers* Aviarie which is a poore buisinesse:

9 My Bro: in law Glanvill entertaind me & my Wife (who was now come to Lond) at an handsome Collation:

10 My Lady *Gerrard* treated us at Mulbery-Garden, now the onely place of refreshment about the Towne for persons of the best quality, to be exceedingly cheated at: *Cromwell* & his partisans having shut up, & seiz'd on Spring Garden, which 'til now had ben the usual rendezvous for the Ladys & Gallants at this season: 11: My Bro: Evelyn treated us in the same manner:

11 I now observed how the Women began to paint themselves, formerly a most ignominious thing, & used onely by prostitutes. I return'd this evening home:

14 There being no such thing as Church Anniversaries in the Parochial Assemblies, I was forc'd to provide at home for *Whitsonday*: In the Afternoone a stranger preachd on 57 *Isa:* 14. The fruite of the Lipps:

15 My Bro: & their wives all din'd with me. 16 Came Sir Robert *Stapleton*, the Translator of *Juvenal* to visite me.

⟨21⟩ Our Parson, on former Text: 55 *Isa:* 2d & so on the 28, necessity of hearing the Word: &c.

26 My second new-Coach was brought home:

2 *June* I went to [Lond] ⟨to⟩ take leave of severall Relations & friends, resolving to spend some monethes amongst my Wifes friends &c in *Wiltshire* & other parts, to whom we had ben so uncessantly invited. 4: our Minister proceeded, to shew the difference 'twixt the animal & spiritual life.

THE TOUR OF ENGLAND
(1654)

8 MY WIFE & I set out on our Journey, in Coach & 4 horses &c: din'd at *Windsore*, and saw the Castle, the Chapell of *St. George*: where they have laied our blessed *Martyr* K. Charles in the Vault, just before the Altar: The Church & Workmanship in stone (though *Gotic*) is admirable: The Castle it selfe, large in Circumference, but the roomes Melancholy & of antient magnificence: The keepe (or mount) hath besides its incomparable Prospect, a very profound Well, & the *Terrace* towards *Eaton*, with the Park, meandring *Thames*, swete Meadows yeilds one of the most delightfull prospects in the World; So that night we lay at *Reading*, saw my Lord *Cravons* house at *Causam* now in ruines, his goodly Woods felling by the Rebells: [9] Din'd at *Marlborow*, which having lately ben fired, was now new built: At one end of this Towne we saw my Lord *Seamors* house, but nothing observable save the Mount, to which we ascend winding for neere halfe a mile: It seemes to have ben cast up by hand: Then we passd by *Coll: Pophams*, a noble Seate, Park & River; Thence by *Newbery*, a Considerable Towne, & *Dennington Castle*, famous for the Battail, seige, & that this last had ben the possession of old *Geofrie Chaucer*: Then *Aldermaston*, a house of Sir *Humphry Forster* built *a la moderne*: Also that exceedingly beautiful seate of my *L: Pembrocks* on the ascent of an hill, flank'd with woods &

reguarding the river, & so at night [11] to *Cadenham* the Mansion of Ed: Hungerford Esquire, Unkle to my Wife where we made some stay:

11 On the *Sonday* preached Dr. *Hungerford*, brother to my *Unkle*, Text: 12 Heb. 2. and after dinner one Mr. *Fly*. 4. *Amos* 12, without any thing extraordinary and [18] The Sonday following Mr. *Hill* upon 22. *Luke* 62; shewing how not onely the *Jewes*, but all men had ben Crucifiers of Christ. In the afternoone the former poore *Curate* upon the Judgements of God against sinners: The rest of the Weeke daies we did nothing but feast, & make good cheere, to wellcome my Wife &c: 25 on⟨e⟩ Mr. *Hopkins* made an excellent discourse on 2. Jam: 12. describing the final Judgement, & especialy for the sinns of the Tongue, by detraction, lying, perjurie, common swearing, and even for jeasting: In the afternoone vindicated the opinion & arguments of the Church of England against the notion of free Grace, as preach'd by the Sectaries: of the true nature of the Law of Liberty, & the servil Law of sinn:

27 We all went to see *Bathe*, where I bathed in the Crosse bathe; amongst the rest of the idle diversions of the Towne, one *Musitian* was famous for acting a Changling; which indeede he personated strangely: The *Faciate* of this Cathedrall is remarkable for the Historical Carving: The *Kings Bath* is esteemed the fairest in *Europe*; The Towne is intirely built of stone, but the streetes narrow, uneven & unpleasant: Here we trifled & bath'd, & intervisited with the company who frequent the place, for health &c: till 30th & then went to *Bristoll* a Citty emulating *London*, not for its large extent, but manner of building, shops, bridge: Traffique: Exchange, Market-place &c. The Governor shew'd us the Castle, of no greate concernment: The City wholy Mercantile, as standing neere the famous *Severne*, commodiously for *Ireland* & the Western world: Here I first saw the manner of refining Suggar, & casting it into loaves, where we had collation of Eggs fried in the suggar furnace, together with excellent Spanish Wine; but what was most stupendious to me, was the rock of St. *Vincent*, a little distance from the Towne, the precipice whereoff is equal to any thing of that nature I have seene in the most confragose cataracts of the *Alpes*: The river gliding betwene them after an extraordinary depth: Here we

went searching for *Diamonds*, & to the hot Well of Water at its
foote: There is also on the side of this horrid Alp, a very roman-
tic seate: & so we returned that Evening to *Bathe*, & on the 1 of
July to *Cadenam*, where on the Sonday, preachd Dr. *Hayward*
Chaplaine to the late *A: Bish: Lawde*, on 15: *Luke* 7 describing the
Joyes of Heaven at the conversion of a sinner:

4 Upon a Letter of my Wifes Unkle *Mr. Pretyman*, I waited
back on her to London, passing by *Hungerford* towne (famous
for its Troutes) I ariv'd at *Deptford* the next day, which was 60
miles, in the extreamity of heate:

6 I saw ⟨my⟩ pretty boy, return'd early to Lond, & the next day,
met my Wife and company at *Oxford*, which being on the 7th
was the Eve of the Act: [8] Next day was spent in hearing severall exercises in the *Scholes*, & after dinner the *Procter* opened the
Act at *St. Maries* (according to custome) & the *Prævaricators*
their drolery, then the *Doctors* disputed, & so we supp'd at *Waddum* Coll: The 9th Dr. *French* preechd at St. *Maries* on 12: *Matt:*
42, advising the Students the Search after true Wisdome, not to
be had in the books of *Philosophers*, but *Scriptures*: in the afternoone the famous Independent Dr. *Owen*, perstringing *Episcopacy*: he was now *Cromwells* Vice-Chancellor: We din'd with Dr.
Ward, Mathematical Professor [since Bish: of *Salisbury*], & at
night Supp'd in *Balliol Coll:* Hall, where I had once ben student
& *fellow Commoner*, where they made me extraordinarily wellcome, but I might have spent the Evening as well.

10 On Monday I went againe to the Scholes to heare the severall facultics, & in the Afternoone tarried out the whole Act in
St. Maries. The long speeches of the Proctors: The V: *Chancelors*,
the severall Professars, Creation of Doctors, by the *Cap*, *ring*,
Kisse &c: those Ceremonies not as yet wholy abolish'd, but
retaining the antient Ceremonies & Institution: Dr. *Kendal*
(now Inceptor amongst others) performing his Act incomparably well, concluded it with an excellent Oration, abating his
Presbyterian animositie, which he withheld not even against
that Learned & pious divine Dr. *Hammond*: The Act was closd,
with the Spech of the V: *Chancellor*. There being but 4 In *Theologie*, 3 in *Medicine*, which was thought a considerable matter,
the times consider'd: I din'd at on⟨e⟩ *Monsieur Fiats*, a student at
Excester Coll: & supped at a magnificent Entertainment in

Waddum Hall, invited by my excellent & deare Friend *Dr. Wilkins*, then Warden [now Bishop of *Chester*]: on the Eleventh was the *Latine Sermon* which I could not be at, invited, being taken-up at *All-Soules*, where we had Music, voices & *Theorbes* perform'd by some ingenious Scholars, where after dinner I visited that miracle of a Youth, Mr. *Christopher Wren*, nephew to the *Bishop* of Elie: then Mr. *Barlow* [since Bishop of *Lincoln*] *Bibliothe⟨c⟩arius* of the *Bodlean* Library, my most learned friend, who shewd me, together with my *Wife*, The rarities of that famous place, *Manuscrip⟨t⟩s*, *Medails* & other Curiosities. Amongst the *MSS* an old English *Bible* wherein the Eunuch mention'd to be baptizd by *Philip*, is cald the *Gelding*, & *Philip* & the *Gelding* went down into the Water &c, also the Original Acta of the *Council* of Basil, 900 years since, with the Bulla or *leaden* Affix, which has a silken Chord, passing thro every parchment: likewise a MS: of *Ven: Beades* of 800 years antiquity: together with the old *Ritual secundum Usum Sarum*, exceeding voluminous: Then amongst the nicer curiosities: The Proverbs of *Solaman* written in *French*, by a Lady every Chapter of a severall Character, or hand, the most exquisitely imaginable: An *Hieroglypical* Table, or *Carta* folded up like a Map, I suppose it painted on *Asses hide*, extreamely rare: but what is most illustrious, were the no lesse than 1000 MSS: in 19 Languages, espe⟨c⟩ialy Oriental, furnishing that new part of the Library, built by *A: Bishop Lawd*: some of *Sir Kenhelme Digby*, & the Earle of *Pembroch*: In the Closset of the Tower, they shew *Josephs* parti colourd Coate, A Muscovian Ladys Whip, some Indian Weapons, *Urnes*, *Lamps*: &c: but the rarest, is the Whole *Alcoran* written in one large sheete of *Calico*, which is made up in a Priests Vesture or Cape after the *Turkish*, & the *Arabic* Character so exquisitely written, as no printed letter comes neere it: Also a rolle of Magical Charmes or *Periapta*, divers *Talismans*, some *Medails*: Then I led my Wife into the Convocation house finely Wainscoted: The *Divinity* Schole & gotic Carv'd roofe; The *Physick* Or Anatomie Schole, adorn'd with some rarities of natural things; but nothing extraordinary, save the Skin of a *Jaccal*, a rarely Colour'd *Jacatroo*, or prodigious large *Parot*, two humming birds, not much bigger than our *humble bee*: which indeede I had not seene before that I remember. &c.

12 We went to *St. Johns*, saw the Library, & the 2 *Skeletons*, which are finely clense'd, & put together: observable are also the store of Mathematical Instruments, all of them chiefly given by the late A: Bishop *Lawd*, who built here an handsome Quadrangle: Thence we went to *New Coll:* where' the Chapell was in its antient garb, not withstanding the Scrupulositie of the Times: Thence to *Christ-Church*, in whose Library was shew'd us an Office of *Hen:* 8, the writing, Miniature & gilding whereof is equal if not surpassing any curiosity I had ever seene of that kind: It was given by their founder, the Cardinal *Wolsy*: The Glasse Windos of the Cathedral (famous in my time) I found much abused: The ample Hall, & Columne that spreads its *Capitel* to sustaine the roofe as one gos up the Stayres is very remarkable: Next we walked to *Magdalen* Coll: where we saw the *Library* & *Chapell*, which was likewise in pontifical order, the *Altar* onely I think turn'd *Table*-wise: & there was still the double *Organ*, which abominations (as now esteem'd) were almost universaly demolish'd: Mr. *Gibbon* that famous *Musitian*, giving us a tast of his skill & Talent on that Instrument: Hence we went to the *Physick* Garden, where the Sensitive [& humble] plant was shew'd us for a greate wonder. There Grew *Canes*, *Olive Tres*, *Rhubarb*, but no extraordinary curiosities, besides very good fruit, which when the Ladys had tasted, we return'd in Coach to our Lodging.

13 We all din'd, at that most obliging & universaly Curious Dr. *Wilkins's*, at Waddum, who was the first who shew'd me the *Transparant Apiaries*, which he had built like *Castles* & *Palaces* & so ordered them one upon another, as to take the *Hony* without destroying the *Bees*; These were adorn'd with variety of *Dials*, *little Statues*, *Vanes* &c: very ornamental, & he was so aboundantly civill, as finding me pleasd with them, to present me one of these *Hives*, which he had empty, & which I afterwards had in my Garden at *Says-Court*, many Yeares after; & which his Majestie came on purpose to see & contemplate with much satisfaction: He had also contrivd an hollow Statue which gave a Voice, & utterd words, by a long & conceald pipe which went to its mouth, whilst one spake thro it, at a good distance, & which at first was very Surprizing: He had above in his Gallery & Lodgings variety of *Shadows*, Dyals, Perspe⟨c⟩tives, places to introduce the *Species*, & many other artif⟨i⟩cial, mathematical,

Magical curiosities: A Way-Wiser, a *Thermometer*, a monstrous *Magnes*, *Conic* & other *Sections*, a Balance on a demie Circle, most of them of his owne & that prodigious young Scholar, Mr. *Chr: Wren*, who presented me with a piece of *White Marble* he had stained with a lively red very deepe, as beautifull as if it had been naturall. Thus satisfied with the Civilities of Oxford: Dining at Farington a Towne which had newly ben fir'd, during the Warrs, & passing neere the seate of Sir *Walter Pies*, we came on the 13th to *Cadenam*, where on the 16 The *Curate* preach'd on his former Subject, like a Country parson, that tooke no greate paines: 16 We went to another Uncle & relation of my Wifes, Sir *John Glanvill*, a famous Lawyer formerly Speaker of the House of Commons; His Seate is at *Broad-hinton*, Where he now lived but in the Gate-house, his very faire dwelling house, having ben burnt by his owne hands, to prevent the *Rebells* making a Garison of it: Here my Co: *Will: Glanvill* (his eldest sonn) shewed me such a lock for a doore, that for its filing, & rare ⟨contrivances⟩, was a masterpiece, yet made by a Country *Black-Smith*: But we have seene *Watches* made by another, with as much curiositie, as the best of that Profession can brag off; & not many yeares after, there was nothing more frequent, than all sorts of Iron-Work, more exquisitely wrought & polish'd, than in any part of *Europ*; so as a dore lock, of a tollerable price, was esteem'd a Curiositie even among forraine *Princes*: We went back this Evening to *Cadenham*, & on the 19 to Sir *Ed: Bayntons* at *Spie-Park*, a place capable of being made a noble seate; but the humorous old knight, has built a long single house of 2 low stories, upon the precipice of an incomparable prospect, & landing on a bowling-greene in the Park; The house is just like a long barne, & has not a Windo, on the prospect side: After dinner they went to bowles, & in the meane time, our Coachmen made so exceedingly drunk; that returning home we escaped incredible dangers: Tis it seemes by order of the Knight, that all Gentlemens servants be so treated: but the Custome is barbarous, & much unbecoming a Knight, much lesse a *Christian*:

On the 20th We proceede to *Salisbury*; We went to see the Cathedral, which I take to be the compleatest piece of *Gotic*-Worke in *Europe*, taken in all its uniformitie; a neate fabric, but the pillars (reputed to be cast) are of stone manifestly cut out of the cuarry: Most observable are those in the Chapter-house:

There are some remarkable Monuments, particularly the antient Bishops founders of the church; Knights Templars, the Marques of *Hartfords*: Also the Cloysters of the Palace & Garden to it, & greate Mural dial.

In the afternoone we went to *Wilton*, a fine house of the E. of *Penbrochs*, in which the most observable are the Dining-roome in the modern built part towards the Garden, richly gilded, & painted with story by *De Creete*, also some other apartments, as that of Hunting Landskips by *Pierce*: some magnificent chimny-pieces, after the *French* best manner: Also a paire of artificial winding-stayres of stone, & divers rare Pictures: The Garden (heretofore esteem'd the noblest in all *England*) is a large hand-some plaine, with a *Grotto* & Waterworks, which might be made much more pleasant were the *River* that passes through, clensed & rais'd, for all is effected by a meere force: It has a flower Gar-den not inelegant: But after all, that which to me renders the Seate delightfull, is its being so neere the downes & noble plaines about the Country & contiguous to it. The stables are well order'd, & yeild a gracefull front, by reason of the Walks of limetrees, with the Court & fountaine of the stable adorn'd with the *Cæsars* heads:

We return'd this evening by the Plaine, & 14 mile-race, where out of my Lords Hare-Waren we were entertain'd with a long course of an hare for neere 2 miles in sight: Neere this a *Pergola* or stand, built to view the Sports; so we came to *Salisbury*, and view'd the most considerable parts of that Citty, the Merket place, which together with most of the streetes are Watred by a quick current & pure streame, running through the middle of them, but are negligently kept, when with small charge they might be purged, & rendred infinitely agreable, & that one of the sweetest Townes in *Europe*; but as 'tis now, the common buildings are despicable, & the streetes dirty.

22 We departed & dined at a ferme of my *U. Hungerfords* cald *Darneford magna*, situate in a Vally under the Plaine, most sweetly water'd, abounding in Trowts and all things else requi-site, provisions exceeding cheape: They catch the Trouts by Speare in the night, whilst they come wondring at a light set in the sterne: There were Pigeons, Conys, & foule in aboundance, & so we had an excellent dinner at an houres warning: After dinner continuing our returne we passd over that goodly plaine

or rather Sea of Carpet, which I think for evennesse, extent, Verdure, innumerable flocks, to be one of the most delightfull prospects in nature and put me in mind of the pleasant lives of the Shepherds we reade of in *Romances* & truer stories: Now we were ariv'd at *Stone-henge*, Indeede a stupendious Monument, how so many, & huge pillars of stone should have ben brought together, erected some, other Transverse on the tops of them, in a Circular *arëa* as rudly representing a Cloyster, or heathen & more natural Temple: & so exceeding hard, that all my strength with an hammer, could not breake a fragment: which duritie I impute to their so long exposure: To number them exactly, is very difficult, in such variety of postures they lie & confusion, though they seem'd not to exceede 100, we counted onely 95: As to their bringing thither, there being no navigable river neere, is by some admir'd; but for the stone, there seemes to be of the same kind about 20 miles distant, some of which appeare⟨s⟩ above ground: About the same hills are divers mounts raisd, conceiv'd to be antient intrenchments, or places of burial after bloudy fights: We now went by the *Devizes* a reasonable large Towne, so passing over *Tan-hill* (esteemed one of the highest in *England*) we came late to *Cadenam*: We had in this journey some disasters by a stonehorses getting loose: *Stonhenge* app⟨e⟩ares like a Castle at a distance.

23 Mr. *Flea* preachd on his former Text, still describing what ornaments a Christian should put on, to meete our B: Lord in.

27 I went to Hunting of a Sorel deare, & had excellent chase for 4 or 5 houres: The venison little worth, we expecting it should have ben a male:

28 I went next day to *Langford* to see my *Co: Stephens*, & return'd by the old Towne, *Greekelade* of old an University, but now shewing no appearence of it: I also saw *Dryfield* the house heretofore of *Sir Jo: Pretyman*, Grandfather to my Wife, & sold by her Unkle: both the seate & house very honorable & well built, much after the modern:

30 Mr. *Flea* at *Cadenam* preachd on: 1. *Cor:* 11.30, shewing how we might prevent many Sinns even of infirmity: In the afternoone one Mr. Brides 8 *Luke*: 15 in a very meane discourse.

31 Taking leave of *Cadenam* (where we had ben long & very nobly entertain'd) we went a Compas into *Licestershire*, where dwelt anoth⟨er⟩ relation of my Wifes, for I indeede made these

excursions to shew her, the most considerable parts of her native Country, who from her childhood had lived altogether in France, as well as for my owne curiosity & information: First we came to *Glocester*, an handsome Citty, considerable for the Church, monuments, new Librarie, very noble though a private designe; but for nothing so famous as the Whispering place, which is indeede very rare, being thro a passage of 25 yards, in a many-angl⟨e⟩d Cloister, & was I suppose, either to shew the skill of the *Architect*, or some invention of a Cunning Priests, who might (standing in a Chappell un-seene in the middle) heare whatever was spoken at either end: This is above the *Quire*, in which lies buried *K. Stephen* under a Monument of *Irish* Oake, not ill carved considering the age: This *Minster* is a noble fabric: I was also pleasd with the *Severne* gliding so sweetely by it, The Dukes house, Castle, Workes, now almost quite dismantl'd; nor yet without sad thoughts did I see this Towne, considering how fatal the siege had ben (few yeares before) to our good King: About two miles e'er we came to *Glocester*, we have a prospect from woody hills into a most goodly Vale & Country.

August 1 We set out towards *Worcester*, by the way (thick planted with Cider-fruit) we deviate to the holy Wells trickling out of a Vally, thro a steepe declivity toward the foote of greate-*Maubern* hills: They are said to heale many Infirmities, As Kings-evil, Leaprosie &c: sore Eyes: Ascending a greate height above them, to the Trench dividing *England* from South *Wales* we had the Prospect of all *Hereford* shire, *Radnor*, *Brecknock*, *Monmouth*, *Worcester*, *Glocester*, *Shropshire*, *Warwick*, *Derby*-shire, & many more: We could discern *Tewxbery*, *Kings-rode* towards *Bristol* &c so as I esteeme it one of the goodliest Vista's in *England*.

2 This evening we ariv'd at *Worcester*, The Judges of Assise, & Sherifs just entering as we did: Viewing the Towne the next day, we found the Cathedral extreamely ruin'd by the late Warrs, otherwise a noble structure: The Towne is neately pav'd and very cleane, The goodly river *Severne* runing by it: It stands in most fertil Country:

3 We pass'd next thro *Warwick*, & saw the Castle, which is built on an eminent rock, which gives prospect into a most goodly greene: a Woody & plentifully Watred Country; the river running so delightfully under it, that it may passe for one of

the most surprizing seates one should meete with: The Gardens are pretily confus'd, & might be much improv'd; The *Castle* is the dwelling-house of the *Lord Brook*, of a Castle-like fabric, the furniture noble: Here they shew us Sir Guys greate two-handed Sword, Staff, horse-armes, Pott, & other reliques of that famous Knight errant. Warwick is a faire old Town, rocky, & hath one Church full of antient Monuments: having view'd these, I went to visite my worthy friend Sir H: *Puckering* at the Abby, & though a melancholy old Seate, yet in a rich soile: Hence to Sir *Guys Grott*, where they say he did his penances, & dyed, & 'tis certainely a squalid den made in the rock, croun'd yet with venerable Oakes, & respecting a goodly streame, so as were it improv'd as it might ⟨be⟩, 'twere capable of being render'd one of the most roma⟨n⟩tique & pleasant places imaginable: neere this we were shewd his Chapell, and gigantic statue hewn out of the solid rock, out of which there are likewise divers other Caves cut, & some very capacious:

The next place was *Coventry*, where most remarkeable is the Crosse, for *Gotic* worke, & rich gilding, comparable to any I had ever seen, excepting that of Cheape side in *Lond*, now demolish'd: This Citty, has many handsome Churches, a very beautifull Wall, a faire free-Schole & Librarie to it: the streetes full of greate Shops, cleane & well pav'd: At going forth the Gate they shew us the bone or rib of a Wild-boare said to have ben kild by Sir *Guy*, but which I take to be the chine of a Whale: [4] Hence riding through a considerable part of *Licestershire*, an open, rich, ⟨but⟩ unpleasant Country, we came late in the Evening to *Horninghold* a seate of my Wifes Unkle.

6 One Mr. *Waybright* preached on Jude 20, 21 touching the love of God, very excellently well.

7 I went to *Upingham* the Shire-towne of *Rutland*, pretty & well built of stone, which is a rarity in that part of *England*, where most of the rural parishes are but of mud, and the people living as wretchedly as in the most impoverish'd parts of *France*, which the⟨y⟩ much resemble being idle & ⟨sluttish⟩: The Country (especialy Licester shire) much in Commune, the Gentry greate drinkers:

9 I went on the ninth, to the old & raged Citty of *Licester*, large, & pleasantly seated, but despicably built; the Chimnies flues like so many smiths forges: however famous for the Tombs

of the Tyrant *Rich:* the Third, which is now converted to a Cistern at which (I think) catell drink: also here in one of the Churches lies buried the magnificent *Cardinal Wolsey*: *John* of *Gaunt* has here also built a large, but poore Hospital, neere which a Wretch, has made him an house out of the ruines of a stately Church: We were shew'd also the ruines of an old Roman Temple, thought to be of *Janus*: Entertain'd at a very fine Collation of Fruite, such as I did not expect to meete with so far north, (especialy very good Melons) we return'd to my Unkles.

12 Came to see me, my Co: *R: Fanshaw* &c:

13 Preached on⟨e⟩ Mr.   on 2 Luke. 28. concerning the obedience of Wives; in the afternoone on the necessity of finding Christ, by the example of Marys grieving 'til she found him.

14 I tooke a Journey into the Northern parts: riding thro *Ockham*, a pretty Towne in *Rutlandshire*, famous for the Tenure of *Barons Harrington*, who hold it by taking off a shoe, from every noble-mans horse that passes with his Lord thro the streete: unlesse redeem'd at a certaine piece of mony: a toaken of this, are severall gilded shoes, nailed-up on the Castle Gate; which seemes to have ben large and faire: Hence we went by *Brook*, a very sweete seate & Parke of the old Lady *Camdens*: Next *Burleigh*-house belonging to the Duke of *Bouckingham*, & worthily reckon'd among the noblest seates in England, situate on the brow of an hill, built *a la modern* neere a Park Waled in, & a fine Wood at the descent. Now we were come to *Cottsmore* a pretty seate belonging to Mr. *Health*, sonn, to the late L. C. Justice of that name; here after dinner parting with the Company that conducted us thus far, I pass'd that Evening by *Belvoir Castle* built on a round Mount, at the point of a long ridge of hills, which afords a stately Prospect, & is famous for its strenuous resistance in the late Civil Warr; also neere *Newark* upon *Trent*, a brave Towne, & Garison; next by *Wharton* house, belonging to the L: *Chaworth*, an handsom seate; Then by *Home* a noble place of the Marq: of *Dorchesters*, and pass'd the famous River *Trent*, which divides the South, from the North of England, & so lay that night ⟨at⟩ *Notingham*. This whole *Towne* & County seemes to be but one intire rock as it were, an exceeding pleasant shire, full of Gentry: here I observ'd divers to live in the rocks, & Caves, much after the manner as about *Tours* in *France*: The Church is well built on an Eminence: a faire house of the

L. *Clares*, another of *Pierepoints*, an ample Merkeat place, large
streetes full of Crosses: The reliques of an antient Castle,
holow'd beneath with many Caverns, especialy that of the *Scots-
king* & his work there; but above all for being the place where
his Majestie first erected his standar'd at the beginning of our
unhappy differences. The Prospects from this Citty towards the
river, & meadows is most delightfull. [15] We passd next thro
Sherewood forest, acounted the most extensive of *England*: Then
Paplewich, a⟨n⟩ incomparable *Vista* with the pretty Castle neere
it. Thence we saw *Newstead Abby* belonging to the *Lord Biron*
situated much like *fontaine Beleaw* in *France*, & capable of being
made a noble seate, accommodated as it is with brave Woods, &
streames: It has yet remaining the front of a glorious Abby
Church: Next by *Mansfield* Towne, Then *Wellbeck* the house of
the *Marquis* of *New-Castle*, seated in a botome in a Park, & invirond with Woods, a noble, yet melancholy seate: The *Palace* is an
handsom & stately building: Next, *Worksop Abby* almost demolish'd, The Church has a double flat towre intire, & a pretty Gate.
The *Mannor* belongs to the *Earle* of *Arundel* & has to it a faire
house at the foote of an hill in a Park that afords a delicate
prospect. *Blith* a Towne: ⟨*Tickel*⟩ a Towne & Castle and very
noble Prospect, all these in *Notingham*-shire: [16] so we ariv'd at
Doncaster where we lay this night, a large & faire Towne, famous
for greate Wax-lights, & good stockings. The next day we pass
thro *Pontfract*, as the Castle (famous for many seiges both of
late, & antient times, & the death of that unhappy King murder'd in it) was now demolishing by the Rebells: It stands on a
Mount, & makes a goodly shew at distance: The *Queene* has an
house here, & many faire seates neere it: Especialy Mr. *Pier-
points*, built at the foot of an hill out of the Castles ruines: We
now all alighted in the high Way, to drink at a Christal Spring,
which they call *Robinhoods* Well, neere it is a Stone Chaire, & an
Iron Ladle to drink out of Chain'd to the ⟨Seate⟩. Hence we rod
to *Todcaster* at the side of which we have prospect of the *Archbishops* Palace, which is a noble seate, & in sight of divers other
faire Gentlemens houses: This tract is a goodly, fertile, well
water'd and Wooded Country, abounding with Pasture & plenty
of all Provisions.

17 To YORK the 2d Citty of *England*, fairely Waled, of a Circular forme, Waterd by the brave river *Ouse*, bearing Vessels of

Considerable burdens, over which a stone bridge, emulating
that of *London*, & built on: The Middle Arch larger than any I
have seene in all *England*, with a rivage or Wharfe all of hewn
stone which makes the river appeare very neate: but most
remarkeable & worthy seeing, is *St. Peters* Cathedrall, which
alone of all the greate Churches in *England*, had best ben preserv'd from the furie of the sacrilegious, by Composition with
the Rebells, when they tooke the Citty, during the many incursions of *Scotch* & others: It is a most intire, magnificent piece of
Gotic Architecture: The Skreene before the *Quire* is of stone,
carv'd with flowers, running work & statues of the old Kings:
The Monuments (many of them) very antient: Here as a greate
rarity in these dayes, & at this time, they shew'd me a *Bible* &
Common-prayer book cover'd with Crimson Velvet, & richly
emboss'd with silver gilt: Also a Service for the *Altar* of Guilt
wrought Plate, flagons, Basin, Eure, Chalices, Patins &c: with a
gorgeous covering for the Altar, Pulpet &c: carefully preserv'd in
the Vestrie: in the holow Wall whereof rises a plentifull Spring
of excellent Water: I got up to the Toure, where we had Prospect
towards *Duresme*, & could see *Rippon*, part of *Lancashire*, & the
famous & fatal *Marston Moore*, the Spaus of *Knarsbrough*, & all
the invirons of that admirable Country.

    Sir *Ingoldsby* has here a large house, Gardens & Tennis-
Court; Also the Kings house; & church neere the Castle which
was modernly fortified with a *Palizad* & bastions: The Streetes
narrow, ill pav'd, the shops like London. [18] We went next day
to *Beverly*, a large Towne, Two stately Churches, St. *Johns* &
St. *Maries* not much inferior to the best of our Cathedrals. Here
a very old Woman shew'd us the Monuments, and being above
100 yeares of age, spake the language of Q: *Maries* daies in
whose time she was born, being the Widdow of a Sexton that
had belonged to the Church, an hundred yeares. Hence we passe
through a fenny-Country (but rich) to *Hull*, situate like *Calais*,
modernly & strongly fortified with three Block-houses, of Brick
& Earth: It has a good harbour for ships, & Mercat Place: The
Water-house is worth seeing: famous also is this Town, (or
rather infamous) for *Hothams* refusing enterance to his Majestie:
and here ends the South of *Yorkshire*, so now we passe the *Hum-
ber*, which is an arme of the Sea, of about 2 leages breadth; [19]
the weather was bad, but we cross'd it in a good barque over to

Barton the first Towne in that part of *Lincoln-shire*, all Marsh ground 'til we came to *Briggs* famous for the plantations of *Licoris*, & then brave pleasant riding to Lincoln, much resembling *Salisbury* Plaine.

LINCOLN an old confusd towne, very long, uneven & confragose, steepe & raged, but has formerly ben full of good houses, especialy Churches & *Abbies*, especialy the Minster, comparable to that of York it selfe, abounding with marble pillars, a faire front: Here in was interrd Q. *Elianor*, loyal & loving Wife to her Husband out of whose wound she succked the poisond arrow: The *Abbot* founder, with rare carving in the stone: The Greate Bell or *Tom* as they call it: I went up the steeple to view the Countrie: The Cloyster & Bish: Palace: but the Souldiers had lately knocked off all or most of the Brasses which were on the Gravestones, so as few Inscriptions were left: They told us they went in with axes & hammers, & shut themselves in, till they had rent & torne of some barges full of Mettall; not sparing the monuments of the dead, so helish an avarice possess'd them.

I went to see a Tall woman, that was six foote & 2 Inches high, a comely middle ag'd & well proportiond woman, kept a very neate & cleane Ale house, & got most by peoples coming to see her: The malicious Souldiers had besides the Sacred places and Churches, exceedingly ruined this Citty: from which the Minister yeilds a goodly prospect all over the Country:

20 From hence we had most pleasant riding over a large heath (like that of Salisbery plaine) to *Grantham*, a pretty Towne, so well situated on the side of a botome; which is large, & at distance inviron'd with ascending grounds, that for pleasure I think it comparable to most [inland] places of *England*: famous is the Steeple for the exceeding height of the Shaft, which is of stone: About 18 miles South we passe by a noble seate, & see *Boston* at distance; here we came to a parish of which the *Parson* has Tith Ale: Thence through Rutland we brought night [21] to *Horninghold*: Mr. *Leake* a poore ⟨preacher⟩ to the Impropriation, made a meane discourse about Gods care to preserve his Vineyard the Church, upon that of the *Canti⟨c⟩les*: But in the afternoone one Mr. *Cradock* mended the matter somewhat on. 3. *John*: 9th: shewing how all men were trees, sative, native, how well the doctrine became the Eremetical life of the Baptist &c.

22 I went a setting, & Hauking, where we had tollerable Sport:

25 I went to see *Kirby* a very noble house of my *Lord Hattons* in N. ha⟨m⟩pton-shire; built a la moderne: Garden, & stables agreable, but the avenue ungracefull, & the seate naked; return'd that Evening:

27 Mr. *Allington* preached ⟨on⟩ 6. *Rom:* 19 shewing the absolute necessitie of altering the Service of our sinfull Members in a most excellent discourse: This was he who published those bold Sermons of the Members warring against the mind, or the *Jewes* Crucifying *Christ*: applied to the wiccked *Regicides* for which he was ruin'd: We had no Sermon in the Afternoone:

30 Taking leave of my Friends, who had now feasted me more than a Month, I now with my Wife &c: set our faces toward home, & got this Evening to *Peterborow*, passing by a stately Palace of ⟨*St. Johns*⟩ (one deepe in the bloud of our good King) build out of the ruines of the Bishops Palace & Cloyster: The Church of this Citty is exceeding faire, full of monuments of greate antiquity: Here lies Queen *Catharine* the unhappy Wife of Hen: 8: & the no lesse unfortunate *Mary* Q: of *Scots*: On the steeple we viewed the fenns of *Lincolnshire*, now much inclosd, & drained with infinite expense, and by many sluces, cutts, mounds, & ingenious Mills & like inventions: at which the Citty & Country about it consisting of ⟨a⟩ poore & very lazy sort of people, were much displeas'd: *Peterborow* is an handsome Towne, & hath another well build church to it: [31] The next morning through a part of *Huntington* shire, we passe that Towne, which is a faire antient Towne, a sweete river running by it, and the Country about it so abounding in Wheate, that when any King of England passe thro it, they have a costome to meete his Majestie with an hundred plows: and so this Evening we came early to

1 *September Cambridg*, & went first to see *St. Johns* Colledge & Librarie, which I think is the fairest of that Universitie: one Mr. *Benlous* has given it all the ornaments of *Pietra Commessa*, whereof a Table, and one piece of Perspective is very fine, other trifles there also be of no greate value, besides a vast old song book or Service, & some faire *Manuscripts*: This Coll: is well built of brick: There hangs in the Library the Picture of *Williams* ABishop of York, & sometime Ld: Keeper, my Kindsman, and

their greate benefactor. Next we saw *Trinity* Coll, esteemed the fairest Quadrangle of any University in Europ, but in truth far inferior to that of *Christ-Church Oxford*: the Hall is ample, & of stone, the fountaine in the Quadrangle is gracefull, The Chapell & Library faire, there they shew'd us the prophetic *MS.* of the famous *Grebner*; but the passage & Emblem which they would apply to our late King, is manifestly relating to the Swedish; in truth it seemes to be a meere fantastic rhapsody, however the Title bespeake strange revelations: There is an Office finely miniatur'd MS, with some other antiquities given by the Countesse of *Richmond* mother of Hen: 7: and the for-mention⟨ed⟩ Bishop *Williams* when *Bishop* of *Lincoln*: The Library is pretty well stor'd: Here the *Greeke* Professor had me into another halfe Quadrangle, cloistred & well built, and gave us an handsome Collation in his owne Chamber: Then we went to *Caius*, then to *Kings* Coll, where I found the Chapel alto-gether answerable to expectation, especialy the roofe all of stone, which for the flatnesse of its laying & carving may I conceive vie with any in Christendome; The contignation of the roofe (which I went upon), weight, and artificial joyning of the stones is admirable: The lights are also very faire: The library is too narrow: here in one Ile, lies the famous Dr. *Collins* so celebrated for his fluency in the Latine Tongue: from this roofe we could discry Elie, and the Incampment of Sturbridge faire now beginning to set up their Tents & boothes: also Roys-ton, *New-Market* &c: houses belonging to the King. Thence we walked to *Clare-hall* of a new and noble designe, but not fin-ish'd: hence to *Peterhouse* formerly under the charge & gover⟨n⟩ment of my worthy friend Dr. Jo: *Cosin*; deane of *Peter-borow*, a pretty neate Coll: & delicate Chapell: next to *Sidny*, a fine College, *Kathrine*-hall, though meane structure, yet famous for the learned *B: Andrews* once Master: then to *Emanuel* Coll: that zealous house, where to the Hall, they have a Parler for the fellows: The Chapell is reform'd *ab origine*, built N. & South, meanely built, as is the Librarie: Thence to *Jesus* Coll: one of the best built, but in a Melancholy situation: next to *Christ Coll*. very ⟨nobly⟩ built, especialy the modern part, built without the Quadrangle towards the Gardens, of exact Architecture: The Schooles are very despicable, & publique Librarie but meane though somewhat improved by the

Wainscoting and Books lately added by the *Bishop Bancrofts* Library & *M.SS*: They shew'd us little of antiquity: onely K: *Jamess* Works, being his owne gift, and kept very reverently and was the onely rarity shewd us. The Mercat place of Chambridg is very ample and remarkable for old *Hobsons* the pleasant Carriers beneficence of a fountaine: But the whole Towne situated in a low dirty unpleasant place, the streetes ill paved, the aire thick, as infested by the fenns; nor are its Churches (of which St. *Maries* is the best) anything considerable in compare to *Oxford* which is doubtlesse the noblest Universitie now in the whole World. From *Chambridge* we went to *Audley End* and spent some time in seeing that goodly Palace built by *Howard* E. of *Suffolck*, & once Lord *Treasurer* of *England*: It is a mixt fabric, 'twixt antique & modern, but observable for its being compleately finish'd, & without comparison one of the statliest Palaces of the Kingdome, consisting of two Courts, the first very large, Wingd with Cloisters: The front hath a double Entrance: The Hall is faire, but somewhat too smale for so august a pile: The *Kitchin leaded* & Cellars very large & arched with stone, Celars I never saw any so neate & well dispos'd: These Offices are joynd by a Wing out of the way very handsomely: The Gallery is the most cherefull, & I thinke one of the best in England: a faire dining-roome, & the rest of the Lodgings answerable with a pretty Chapell: The Gardens are not in order, though well inclosed: It has also a Bowling ally, a nobly well walled, wooded & watred Park, full of fine collines and ponds, the river glides before the Palace, to which an avenue of lime-trees; but all this much diminishd by its being placed in an obscure bottome; for the rest a perfectly uniforme structure, & sh(e)wes without like a diademe, by the decorations of the Cupolas & other ornaments on the Pavilions: I observ'd that instead of railes and balusters, there is a bordure of Capital letters, as was lately also on *Suffolck* house neere Charing Crosse, built by the same L: Tress: This house stands in the Parish of *Saffron Walden* famous for the aboundance of Saffron there Cultivated and esteem'd the best of any forraine Country.

Having dined here, we passe thro *Bishop Stratford* a pretty waterd Towne, and so by *London* late home [3] to *Sayes-Court* after a parerration of 700 miles, but for the variety an agreable refreshment after my Turmoile & building &c.

THE LAST YEARS OF THE PROTECTORATE
(1654–1659)

⟨SEPTEMBER 3⟩ OUR *Minister* preached on 55 *Isay* upon the difficult points of Prædestination &c after the Independent sort, as also on [10] the next *Sonday*, with no greate edification.

12 I went to see my Bro: at *Wotton* who had ben sick:

14 I went to visie my noble friend Mr. *Hyldiard*, where I met that learned Gentleman my *Lord Aunger* & Dr. *Stokes* one of his Majesties Chaplaines: 15: To Bechworth Castle to visite Sir Abr: Browne: &c: other Gent: of my sweete & native Country:

17 ⎫ The good old Parson *Higham* preached at Wotton Church
24 ⎭ on:

8: *Rom:* 15, shewing the benefits of Adoption: &c: a plaine preacher, but innocent & honest man.

Octob: 4 I came home to my house.

8. *Mr. Mallorie* on his former Text, shewing how men Glorifie God but imputatively &c:

9. Went to Lond, return'd that evening:

13. I was let bloud 9 ounces: 16: Went to *Lond.* return'd that evening.

22: The Minister on the same chap: v. 6, concerning redeeming the time, & the losse of opportunities, that God was to be wearied, & would not always be neglected: The danger of procrastination.

23 I went to Lond, to visite my Co: *Fanshaw*, & this day saw one of the rarest collections of *Achates, Onixes* & *Intaglias* &c collected by a conceited old Hat-Maker in Black Friers, that ever I had seene either at home or abroad, especialy one *Achat* Vase her⟨e⟩tofore the greate E: of *Licesters*: returnd that evening:

28 Came my *Lady Langham* a kindswoman of mine to visie us; also one Cap. *Cooke* esteem'd the best singer after the *Italian* manner of any in *England*: he entertain'd us with his voice & *Theorba*.

29: The Minister proceeding—That though none fell into more enormouse sinns, than some Saints themselves, yet it was by surprize, not designingly, & for want of Caution, nor did they repeate them, but repent them, & take greate care afterward.

31 Being my Birth-day & 34th of my Age; blessing God for his Providence, I went to Lond, to visie my Brothers &c: return'd next day.

November 5. *Gunpouder* Plot Anniversarie, a stranger preach'd 4. Amos. 13. of Gods Judgments on sinners.

11. To Lond: return'd. 12 our *parson* on his former *Theame*, the extreame danger of evil Thoughts, sometimes exceeding evil actions.

23 To Lond: about buisinesse, returnd the 25:

December 3 *Advent* Sonday, there being no Office at the *Church* but extemporie prayers after the *Presbyterian* Way, for now all formes were prohibited, & most of the Preachers Usurpers, I seldome went to *Church* upon solemn *Feasts*; but either went to *Lond:* where privately some of the orthodox sequestred Divines did use the Common Prayer, administer Sacraments &c: or else procured one to officiate in my house: Where fore on the 10th Dr. Rich: Owen (the sequesterd Minister of Eltham) preached to my Family in my Library: on 1: St. *John*: 10. concerning Christs *Advent*, in an excellent discourse & then gave the H. Communion to me & my family:

17 At the P. Church *Mr. Mallorie* on his former Text 55 *Isaiah*: concerning remission of sinns, the manner of it, how they became debts:

19 To Lond, return'd next day: 24: the Preacher proceeded to shew how God remitted sinn, as to the act, subject, adjunct: of his stock of Pardons &c:

25 *Christmas-day*, were no public offices in Churches, but penalties to the observers: so as I was constraind to celebrate it at home:

27: One Mr. Pemberton preach'd at Greenewich on 7: *Esay:* 14. boldly asserted the reasonablenesse of the feastivity &c: &c: an excellent discourse:

28 Came my Bro: E. to visite me: & the next day my *Lady Newton*:

31 By Gods special Providence we went not to Church, my wife being now so very neere her time: for my little *sonne Richard* now about 2 yeares old as he was fed with broth in the morning, a square but broad & pointed bone of some part of a ract of Mutton, stuck so fast in the Childs Throate & crosse his Weason, that had certainely choaked him, had not my Wife & I ben at home; for his mayd being alone with him above in the Nurserie, was fallen downe in a swone, when we below (going to Prayers) heard an unusual groaning over our head, upon which we went up, &

saw them both gasping on the floore, nor had the Wench any
power to say what the Child ail'd, or call for any help: At last she
sayd, she believed a Crust of bread had choak'd her little Master, &
so it almost had, for the eyes & face were s⟨w⟩ollen, & clos'd, the
Mouth full of froath, and gore, the face black—no Chirurgeon
neere: what should we doo?, we cald for drink, power it downe, it
returnes againe, the poore babe now neere expiring. I hold its head
down, incite it to Vomite, it had no strength, In this dispaire, &
my Wife almost as dead as the Child, & neere despaire, that
so unknown & sad an accident should take from us so pretty a
Child: It pleased God, that on the suddaine effort & as it were
strugling his last for life, he cast forth a bone of this shape &

forme I gave the child some *Lucotellus Balsome*

for his Throat was much excoriated. Ô my Gracious God out of
what a tender feare, & sad heart, into what Joy did thy goodnesse
now revive us! Blessed be God for this mercy: Wherefore beging
pardon for my sinns, & returning Thanks for this grace, I implord
his providential care for the following yeare.

165⅘. *January*: 1 Having with my Family perform'd the Pub:
Offices of the day, & begged a blessing on the Yeare I was entering &c: not forgetting his late deliverance &c:

[2] I went the next day to keepe the rest of Christmas at my
Bro: R: *Evelyns* at *Woodcot*: 7: one Mr. *Vowel* on 1 Joh: 4. 9.
preached, or rather read a *Sermon* apposite to the festival &c: 8th
I returned home: 10th went to *Lond*, returnd: and so on the 12:
about buisiness concerning *Warley*.

14 About ½ after 10 in the Morning, was my Wife delivered of
another Sonn, being my Third, but 2d living: *Benedictus sit deus in
donis suis*: 16th I went to *Lond:* returnd the 18th & the same on
foote, returning by Water 20th: I saw a live *Camelion*.

21 Mr. *Malorie* still pursued his 55 *Esay* 8. describing the
incomprehensibility of Gods free Grace, to exceede both faith &
reason, nay our very sinns, in a very pious discourse:

26 Was Christned my Sonne *John* by Sir *Jo: Evelyn, Lady
Gerrard*, & his Unkle *Will: Pretyman* susceptors, Mr. *Owen*

officiating at *Says-Court*, according to the rite of the Church of England:

28 A stranger preached 3. Coll: 2. Inciting our affections to the obtaining heavenly things: I understood afterwards, that this man had ben both Chaplaine & *Lieutennant* to Admiral *Pen*, using both swords, whither ordain'd or no I cannot say; Into such times were we falln!—29 I went to *Lond*, returnd:

Feb: 1. I went to *Lond*. 'til the 3d & on the 8th til the 9th.

11 Dr. *Owen* officiating in my family, Churched my Wife:— 13 I went to *Lond:* returnd: also on the 20th: returnd the 24th: I was shew'd a Table Clock whose balance was onely a Chrystall ball, sliding on paralell Wyers, without being at all fixed, but rolling from stage to stage, till falling on a Spring conceald from sight, it was throwne up to the upmost chanell againe made with an imperceptible declivity, in this continual vicissitude of motion prettily entertaining the eye every halfe minute, and the next halfe minute giving progresse to the hand that shew'd the houre, & giving notice by a small bell; so as in 120 halfe Minuts or periods of the bullets falling on the ejaculatorie Spring The Clock-part struck: This very extraordinary piece (richly adorn'd) had ben presented by some German Prince to our late King, & was now in possession of the Usurper: valued 200 pounds:

27 Shrovetide, my Wife & I went to *Lond:* lay at my Bro: in *Covent Garden*:

2 *Mar:* Mr. *Simson* (the *Kings* Jeweler) shew'd me a most rich *Achat* cup of an Escalop shape, & having a figure of *Cleopatra* at the Scroll, her body, haire, smock, mantle & vaile of the severall natural Colours: It was underpropp'd by an halfe *M: Antony*, the Colours as rarely natural, & the work truely antique: but I conceiv'd they were of severall pieces, & not all of one stone; which had it be(en), were invaluable—3 I went home:—9. went againe to *Lond:* return'd, likewise on the 18 on purpose to heare that excellent preacher Dr. *Jer: Taylor*: on: 14: *Mart:* 17 shewing what were the conditions of obtaining Eternal life, also concerning abatements for unavoidable infirmities, how cast on the accompts of the Crosse &c:—I dined at Mr. *Cottyles*: In the afternoone a stranger preached at St. *Gregories* on 105 Psal: 4. the importance of early seeking God: &c:—I went home on foote as I went:—31. I made a visite to Dr. *Taylor* to conferr with him about some spiritual matters; using him thenceforward as my Ghostly Father

&c: I beseech Almighty God, to make me ever mindfull, of, & thankful for his heavenly Assistances:

Aprill Mr. *Gataker* at St. Greg: on: 3. *Rom:* 24 & 25, a Lenten Sermon, & excellent penetentiary discourse &c:—2 I returned home: This being the first Weeke, that (my U: Pr: being parted with his family from me), I began housekeeping, 'til now sojourning with him in my owne house.—7 to *Lond:*—8: D. *Throcknorton*—2. Tim. 3. 5. shewing the perill of hypocrisie; but his voice so low, I could heare little: In the afternoone Dr. *Taylor* on 51 *Psal.* 17. touching the degrees of Penetentiary Sorrow: that no remanent affection to sin, consistent with true repentance.— 9th I return'd home, my Bro: dining with me, we went to see the greate Ship newly built, by the Usurper *Oliver*, carrying 96 brasse Guns, & of 1000 tunn: In the *Prow* was *Oliver* on horse-back trampling 6 nations under foote, a *Scott*, *Irishman*, *Dutch*, *French*, *Spaniard* & English as was easily made out by their several habits: A *Fame* held a laurell over his insulting head, & the word *God with us*:

15 I went to *Lond:* with my family, to celebrate the Feast of *Easter*: Dr. Wild preaching at *St. Gregories* on 20: John: 13. a Resurrection Sermon, the H. Sacrament follow'd: The ruling powers, conniving at the use of the *Liturgie* &c in this Church alone: In the afternoone Mr. Pierson [since Bishop of *Chester*] preach'd at *East-cheape*, touching the verity of Christs Resurrection—but was disturbed by an alarme of Fire, which about this time were very frequent in the Cittie.

20 I was invited to dine at the Sherifs of Lond: where was extraordinary cheere & Musique, returned:—22: our Minister on his worn-out Text: 55 Esa: 13.—& so on the 29: shewing the difference of signes, & peculiar names of Distinction of the Elect—30 I went to *Lond:* return'd—

May 4. I went to keepe Court at *Warley*, return'd that night:— 6. A stranger at our Church, on 3 *Coll:* 2. in an *Enthusiastic* style: I heard since he was a *Trooper*, & I minded him but little:—12 I went to Lond:—13 to St. *Gregories* where Dr. Wild preach'd 3: *Phil:* 10: a Resurrection Sermon.—In the afternoone at *st. Peters* East-cheape one Mr. Harris 7: *Matt:* 19 in a most admirable discourse on the Barren Tree: I came home the 14th:—17 To *Lond:* return'd—21 To *Lond:* returnd the 22, also 25t: return'd: 26: to *Lond:* with my Wife, to passe a fine about *Preston*: return'd:

27 Our Parson—on 6 *Eph:* 24. magnifying the Love of God to Christ, the treasure & felicity in mans love to him, though there were no other collateral incentives to it &c:

29 I receivd 500 pounds of Coll: *Morly* in part of the sale of *Preston*: Lent 1500 pounds to my L: Chesterfild. 31 Came my Brothers & their wifes to dine with me:

June: I celebrated *Whitsonday* at home:—5: to *Lond:* to visite my Bro: Gl: sick of a *Tertian*: return'd:—10 To *Lond:* intending to receive the H. Sacrament but none was celebrated. Dr. Wild preaching at st. Greg: on 2. *Acts*: 37, of the nature & necessity of Repentance &c: he usd this similitude, Speaking of the hearing of many Sermons: That though we forget them, they were profitable, & did us good, like Water passing through a Cive, albeit it stayed not there, yet in passing through it clensed:—In the afternoone Dr. *Gillingham* on 2 *Eph:* 3. perswading to holinesse & humility:—12 To *Lond:* about the Commission of Sewers—return'd: 17 one *Mr. Martine* on 1 John. 3. 2d: The priveledge of filiation & dignitie of being the Sonns of God; fell into magnifying the discipline & doctrine of the Church of *England*, which he did very boldly &c:—There was now a Collection for the Persecuted Churches & Christians in *Savoy*, remanents of the antient *Abbigenses*.—18 To *Lond:* returned: also on the 22d, returnd next day:—24 Our Parson on: 11. *Rom:* 36, magnif⟨y⟩ing the worke of Creation, especialy of Man &c: In the afternoone at Greenewich: Dr. *Viccars* on 11 *Heb:* 37. The Exercise, & benefit of Suffering, its comforts & reward: very passionately bewayling the persecution in *Savoy*, & calling it their funerall Sermon:

26 To *Lond*. til Tuesday: also on: 29th: returnd that evening:

July. To *Lond:* Dr. *Gillingham* 2. *Tit:* 12. on the Effects of Righteousnesse &c: The H. Sacrament follow'd, I communicated:—In the afternoone at *Lincolne* In: Chapell, where a young preacher made an excellent Sermon on: 6. *Gall*. 1 shewing the mildnesse which ought to be in Christian correptions & reprehension, by the Example of God, & holy Persons.—return'd this Evening.—3. To *Lond:* about L. Stanhops buisinesse:—I was shew'd a pretty *Terrella* describ'd with all the Circles, & shewing all the Magnetic deviations, &c:—returnd the 7th.

8: our Minister on former Text, of Gods glory in the Creatures, how exalted in his Sonn the truer Image of the Glory of the father. Afternoone at Greenewich a stranger. 22 *Esa:* 13. In an admirable discourse against Carnal Security; how unreasonable even Lawfull & innocent Pleasures in times of publique Calamity (as were now in England, in reguard of the sad oppressions, Tyrannies, frequent & lamentable fires so frequently happning, & universal neglect of Piety &c):—9: *Lond:* to finish my Mortgage of L: *Stanhop*, returnd next day—12: To Lond: about the same, returnd: 13:

14 Came Mr. Prat my old acquaintance at *Rome* &c. with other Gent: to dine with me.

15 Mr. *Mallory* on former Text, shewing how Gods mercys lead to Repentance.

17 I went to take leave of Mrs. Earles, wife of *Dr. Earle*, now going into Flanders to him: Return'd.

19 To the Commissioners of the Sewers: *return'd*: 22 our parson on 2. Cor: 5. 6. describing the gracious Communications of God to us in the face & incarnation of Christ: &c: 24 Came my Lord *Stanhop* to take leave of me, now going into *France*: There came also sir Ed: *Hales*, & sir Jo: *Tufton*: with Mr. *Seamour*.—29 At Charleton Mr. *Owen* on 2 *Gal:* 6 That God is no excepter of Persons, applying the Justice of God in it: 31 I went to *Wotton* to see my Bro: & Lady, now brought to bed of a Sonn, whom my wife (as one of the Go(s)hips) named *Standsfield*.

August I went to *Darking* to see Mr. Charles Howards Amphitheater Garden, or Solitarie recesse, being 15 Ackers, invirond by an hill: he shew'd us divers rare plants: Caves, an Elaboratory:

5 Preached in the morni⟨n⟩g Dr. *Offley* on 14 John: 6 in an honest discourse: In afternoone Mr. *Higham* on 14 *Hosea ult:* without much edification:—10 I went to *Abburie* to visite Mr. *Howard*, who had begun to build, and alter the Gardens much, he shewed me many rare Pictures, particularly the *Moore* on horseback; & *Erasmus* as big as the life of *Holbein*: also a *Madona* in miniature by *Oliver*; but above all the Skull carved out in wood by *Albert Durer*, he assur'd me his father was offered 100 pounds for it; Also Alberts head by himselfe, with divers rare Achats, Intaglia, & other Curiosities.

12 The good old parson at *Wotton* preach'd on 3. Col: 6:

13 I went to *Woodcot* to condole with my Bro: R: upon the death of his Sonn.

17 Was the Christning at Wotton. 20 Came Mrs. *Eliz: Carew* upon my letter, upon my proposal to her of Sir *Edw: Hales* &c:—19 Mr. Offly preached on 2. *Chro:* 20. 12.

21 I went to *Rygate* to visite Mrs. *Cary* at my Lady *Peter-borows*, in an antient Monastery well in repaire, but the Parke much defac'd, the house nobly furnish'd: The Chimny piece in the greate Chamber carv'd in wood was of Hen: 8th & was taken from an house of his in *Bleching-Lee*: Here was now the Arch Bishop of *Armagh*, the learned *James Usher*, whom I went to Visite, he receive'd me exceeding kindly; In discourse with him, he told me how greate the losse of time was to study much the Eastern languages, that excepting *Hebrew*, there was little fruite to be gatherd of exceeding labour; that besides some *Mathematical* bookes, the *Arabic* itselfe had little considerable: That the best *Text* was the *Heb: Bible*, That the *Septuagint*, was finish'd in 70 daies, but full of Errors, about which he was then writing: That *St. Hieroms* was next the *Hebrew* to be valued: also that the 70 translated the *Pentateuch* onely, the rest finish'd by others: That the *Italians* at present understood but little *Greeke*, & *Kirker* a Mountebank; That Mr. *Seldens* best Book was his *Titles of Honer*; That the Church would be destroied by *Sectaries* who would in all likliehood bring in *Poperie*; In conclusion recommended to me the study of *Philologie*, above all humane studies, & so with his blessing I tooke my leave of this excellent Person, return'd to Wotton.

26 I went to *Horsley* to visite Mr. *Hyldiard*, return'd—27 to *Box-hill* to see those rare natural bowers, cabinets & shady walkes in the box-coppses; & went to view the *Swallow* famous for the diving of the river of *Darking* there, & passing under ground at the foote of a huge white Cliffe or precipice, looking West-ward, the Channell where the water sinks in, being full of holes; It not rising til some miles distance about *Lether-head*: Hence we walked to *Micklame*, & saw sir Fr: *Stidolphs* seate invi-rond with *Elme Trees*, & Wallnut innumerable, & of which they told us he receivd a considerable revenue, & here are such goodly walkes & hills shaded with *yew* & *Box*, as render the place extreamely agreable, it seeming to be summer all the winter for many miles prospect:

28 Came that renowned *Mathematitian Mr. Oughtred* to see me, I sending my Coach to bring him to *Wotton*, being now very

aged: Amongst other discourse, he told me he thought *Water* to be the *Philosophers* first matter; & that he was well perswaded of the possibility of their Elixir: He believed the *Sunn* to be a material fire, the *Moone* a Continent as appeares by the late *Selenographer*: He had strong apprehensions of some extraordinary event to happen the following yeare from the *Calculation* of coincidence with the *Diluvian* period; & added that it might possibly be to convert the *Jewes* by our Saviours visible appearance or to judge the world, & therefore his word was *parate in occursum*: He said *Original* Sin was not met with in the *Greeke* Fathers: yet he believd the thing; this was from some discourse upon Dr. *Taylors* late booke which I had lent him.

29 I returned with my Wife to *Sayes-Court*: 31 I went to *Lond*, concluded with Mr. *Hart* about Warley, return'd the next day ⟨home⟩:

September 5 Came Mrs. E. *Cary* to my house & staied the 7th.—9 our Parson preach'd on 1. Tim: 2: 5. That A. God, set *Christ* a part for Mediator, as being the middle Person of the H. Trinity. The *Father* proper to send, The H. *Spirit* to anoynt & consecrate &c:

15 To *Lond*: 16 preached at St. Greg: one *Darnel* on. 4. *Psal* 4. concerning the benefit of selfe examination, more learning in so short a time as an houre, I seldome heard: In the afternoone one *Dukeson* on Pro: 28. 13: of the danger of hiding sinn, as *Adame*— The *Patriarchs*—*Saule*—

17 Received 2600 pounds for the *Mannor* of *Warley Magna* in *Essex*, purchased by me some time since: The *Taxes* were so intollerable, that they eate up the *Rents* &c: surcharged as that County had ben above all others during our unnatural War:—18 returnd home.

19 Came Sir *Ed: Hales*, Mr. *Ashmole*, Mr. *Harlakinton*, Mr. *Thornhill* &c to see us:

20 I visited Sir *Hen: Newton* at *Charleton* where I met the Earle of *Winchelsea*, Lady *Beauchamp* Daughter to my *L: Capel* &c:—21 To *Lond*, return'd home:

23 Preached a stranger on 73. *Psal: ult:* concerning the infinite blessednesse of Communion with God, to exceede all other enjoyments.—27 To *Lond:* visited friends, & return'd.

29 I made my *Will* again. 30: a stranger—on. 29: *Pro:* 1. of the mercy of God in reproving sinners by whatever methods &c:

October 7 to *Lond*, to receive the *B: Sacrament* at St. *Gregories*, Dr. *Wild* on, 1. *Jer:* 4 shewing the natural condition of Man, & Gods infinite mercy &c: In the afternoone Dr. *Gillingham* on 2. *Tit:* 14.—⟨Infinitely⟩ magnifying the price of our Redemption &c: I went home this Evening—14. To *Lond:* a *Scotch-man* preach'd on 11. *Luke.* 31 (in *Eastcheape* Church) concerning the different states of Glory in heaven, from all the greatnesse & pompous enjoyments of this world: In the Afternoone to the *French* Church, where after usual Chatchising—Monsieur *Le Franc* preach'd on 11: *Matt:* 12. That the price was of a value, that well deserv'd the Combate: This person, had ben a late *Proselyte*, formerly a *Frier* &c: I return'd & the 16. To *Lond* againe:

21 A young stranger preach'd on 8: *Luke* 18. shewing our greate concerne to take care of what we heard: That the Word was our pardon, our portion, & that by which we should be judg'd. In the Afternoones I frequently stayd at home to Catechize & Instruct my Familie, those exercises universaly ceasing in the parish churches, so as people had no Principles, & grew very ignorant of even the common points of Christianity, all devotion being now plac'd in hearing Sermons and discourses of Speculative & notional things: & our owne *Viccar* very tedious in repeating.

26 I went to see Coll: *Blounts* Subterranean Warren, & drank of the Wine of his Viniard, which was good for little. 28: The Minister on 1. *Pet:* 2. 24. about the necessity of mortification, to sin, as soone as justified from sin: That in the Regenerat sin had still a being, but no dominion:

31 I was this day 35 yeares of Age: The Lord be praised for all his mercies: Sir *Nic: Crisp* came to Treate with me, about his vast designe of a Mole or Sasse to be made for ships in part of my Grounds &c:

November 3. To *Lond:* to visite my Bro: & his Lady: I had accidentaly discourse with a *Persian* and a *Greeke*, concerning the devastation of *Poland* by the *Swedes* late incursion:

7 To Lond: to visite friends & return'd:—11 our *Parson* on his former *Text* concerni⟨n⟩g the difference twixt speculative & actual righteousnesse; pregnant, and barren Faith &c:—15 came to dine with me my Co: Hungerford. 18, Mr. *Ma:* on his for-mer—That a man may leave enormous sinns, & yet be voide of Grace. Such were the *Pha⟨r⟩isees*: Moral Virtue a negative Reli-gion without faith:

22 A storme of terrible Lightning & Thunder with an exceeding cold night:

23 Came my Bro: *Richard* to visite us:—26 I dined at *Charleton*:

27 To *Lond* about Sir N: *Crisps* designs: I went to see York-house & Gardens belonging to the former greate *Buckingham*: but now much ruin'd thro neglect. Thence to visite honest & learned Mr. *Hartlib*, a Publique Spirited, and ingeni⟨o⟩us person, who had propagated many Usefull things & Arts: Told me of the *Castles* which they set for ornament on their stoves in *Germanie* (he himselfe being a Lithuanian as I remember) which are furnishd with small ordinance of silver on the battlements, out of which they discharge excellent Perfumes about the roomes, charging them with a little Powder to set them on fire & disperse the smoke: & intruth no more than neede; for their stoves are sufficiently nasty: He told me of an Inke that would give a dozen Copies, moist Sheetes of Paper being pressed on it, & remaine perfect; & a receit how to take off any Print, without injury to the original in the least: This Gent: was Master of innumerable Curiosities, & very communicative. I returnd home that evening by water, & was afflicted for it with a Cold, that had almost kil'd me. This day came there also forth the *Protectors* Edict or Proclamation, prohibiting all ministers of the Church of England from Preaching, or Teach any Scholes, in which he imitated The *Apostate Julian*: with the *Decimation* of all the Royal parties revenues thro-out England.

December 9 *Mr. Mal:* on 106 *Psal:* 4.5. how Christ redeemed his Elect: &c: 13 to Lond: 14: I visited Mr. *Hobbs* the famous Philosopher of *Malmesbury*, with whom I had ben long acquainted in *France*.—return'd that Evening—Now were the *Jewes* admitted—

16 our *Minister* proceeded, shewing how one peculiare People were chosen, & sanctified to God, by the ceremonie of oyle, a *Type* of a more universal Call, & invitation, from its diffusive nature. 23d The use of it, was to perswade a Seeking for this signe in our selves, which were holinesse & spirituality: &c.

25 There was no more notice taken of Christmas day in Churches; wherefore

30 I went to *Lond:* where Dr. *Wild* (at St. *Greg*) preached the funeral Sermon of Preaching, this being the last day, after

which *Cromwells* Proclamation was to take place, that none of the Ch: of England should dare either to Preach, administer Sacraments, Teach Schoole &c. on paine of Imprisonment or Exile; so this was the mournfullest day that in my life I had seene, or the Church of *Eng:* her selfe, since the *Reformation*: to the greate rejoicing of both *Papist* & *Presbyter*: The Text was 2. Cor: 13. 9. That however persecution dealt with the Ministries of Gods word, They were still to pray for the flock, & wish their perfection, as it was the flocks, to pray for & assist their Pastors, by the example of St. *Paule* &c: So pathetic was his discourse, as drew many teares from the auditory: My selfe, Wife, & some of our family received the H. *Communion*, God make me Thankfull, who hath hithertoo provided for us the foode of our Soules, as well as bodys. So return'd home the Evening: The Lord *Jesus* pitty our distressed Church, & bring back the Captivity of *Sion*.

31 I made up my Accompts of the past yeare, giving Thanks to Almighty God for his mercifull protection, & supplicating the continuance of it, the following yeare.

January 1 celebrating the Anniversarie with my family &c: the 2d, & 3d, I invited divers of my Neighbours.

5 Came to visite me, my Lord *Lisle* sonn to the Earle of Leycester, with Sir Charles *Ouseley*, tw⟨o⟩ of the Usurpers Council; Mr. Jo: *Hervey*, & Jo: *Denham* the Poet &c.

6 *Epiphanie*, said Prayers at home, *Afternoone* at Church, the Preachers Text was 106 *psal:* 4. 18 I went to *Eltham* on foote, being a greate frost, but a Mist falling as I return'd gave me such a *Rheume*, as kept me within neere a whole Moneth after:—31. To Lond: *Feb:* 3. I went to a place, where Dr. *Hewet* preached—on—shewing through how many sad persecutions, & dangers God still preserv'd his *Church*: &c:—5. was shew'd me a pretty Perspective & well represented in ⟨a⟩ triangular Box, the greate Church at *Harlem* in Holland, to be seene thro a small hole at one of the Corners, & contrived into an ⟨handsome⟩ Cabinet: It was so rarely don, that all the Artists & Painters in Towne, came flocking to see & admire it:

10 I heard Dr. *Wilkins* Preach in *St. Paules* before the L. *Mayor*, shewing how Obedience was preferrable to Sacrifice &c: He was a most obliging Person, but had married the *Protectors* sister, to preserve the *Universities* from the ignorant Sacrilegious

Commander & Souldiers, who would faine have ben at demolishing all both places & persons that pretended to Learning:

11 I adventurd to go to *White-Hall*, where of many yeares I
had not ben, & found it very glorious & well furnish'd, as far as I
could safely go, & was glad to find, they had not much defac'd
that rare piece of *Hen* 7th & 8 &c. don on the Walles of the
Kings Privy Chamber. 14th I dined with Mr. *Barckley* Son to my
Lord *Berckley* of Ber: Castle, where I renewed my Acquaintance
with my *Lord Bruce*, my fellow Tra: in *Italy*:

16 At *Greenewich* I was Godfather to My *U: Prit:* Eldest
daughter, & first child:—18 Went to Lond—19. Went with Dr.
Wilkins [since Bishop of *Chester*] to see Barlow the famous
Paynter of fowle Beasts & Birds. 23. Returned home with my A:
Hungerford & severall friends, who christn'd one of my servants
children, borne the night before in my House, & who had married one of my servants: 24. Preached *Mr. Mal:* on a verse of the
Canticles, touching the Garden of the Spouse, which he interpreted to be the *Catholic Church*, & every particular Christian
Gods Privy *Garden*, filled with all the fruites of the Spirit: That
all Family assemblies were so many Churches, and might have
all Essentials of a church, though no Ceremonies: Much of this
discourse savor'd of the Conventicle: 29 I went to Lond: 29 Dr.
Hewet preached on 1. *Sam:* 2. 9. shewing who were the Saints:
There was a Communion, at which I received.

Mar: 4: This night I was invited by Mr. *Rog: L'Estrange* to
heare the incomperable *Lubicer* on the Violin, his variety upon a
few notes [& plaine ground] with that wonderfull dexterity, as
was admirable, & though a very young man, yet so perfect &
skillfull as there was nothing so crosse & perplext, which being
by our Artists, brough⟨t⟩ to him, which he did not at first sight,
with ravishing sweetenesse, & improvements, play off, to the
astonishment of our best Masters: In Summ, he plaid on that
single Instrument a full Consort, so as the rest, flung-downe
their Instruments, as acknowl⟨e⟩dging a victory: As to my owne
particular, I stand to this houre amaz'd that God should give so
greate perfection to so young a person: There were at that time
as excellent in that profession as any were thought in Europ:
Paule Wheeler, Mr. *Mell* and others, 'til this prodigie appeared &
then they vanish'd, nor can I any longer question, the effects we
read of in *Davids* harp, to charme maligne spirits, & what is said

some particular notes produc'd in the Passions of *Alexander* &
that King of *Denmark*—5. I return'd home:

9 Mr. M: Preached on his former Subject, shewing the divers
acceptions of Nation in Scripture, how the Saints were the
nation of God, & their distinctions: That the holy Nation had
its original in *Adame*, thence to the Patriarchs, & were select out
of all people & tongues: &c:

13 Came my Bro: & Mr. *Triplet* to visite me.—16 on the
same—of the joy of the Saints, & difference from worldly joy; of
the Joy of the Father himselfe, illustrated by the reception of the
Prodigal.

20 Came my Lady *Newton* & Mr. *Murrey* & other persons of
quality:—21 To *Lond*. about a Commission concerning my Lord
of *Kildare*, returnd: 22: was a tirrible storme. 23, our Parson proceedes—how particularly the church was *Christs* Inheritance, of
his household, utensils, C⟨h⟩apel, Crowne, Garden, field fruit,
Jewels, Spouse &c:

27 I went to *Lond:* thence to *Hackney* to see L: *Brooks* garden
which was both well furnished & kept: returnd 28:—31 dind at
Charleton:

Aprill. 6. To *Lond:* to Celebrate *Easter*—so greate a snow fell as
seldome had I seene a greater, it fell as I was on the way, with two
new stone-horses to the Coach, which made them unruly, but we
got safe to Lond:—where preach'd Dr. *Hewet* on 28 *Matt:* 5. 6.
magnif⟨y⟩ing the piety & devotion of Women: of the knowledge
of Angels, that nothing carnal might touch Christ⟨s⟩ glorified
body after his resurrection &c: we pass'd to the H. Communion. I
din'd at Mr. *Cotyles*, In the Afternoone Dr. *Wild* on 20: *John* 19 a
Resurrection excellent discourse: I returnd home:

11 To Lond: returned 12. *Mr. Barkley*, & Mr. *Rob: Boyle* that
excellent person, & greate *Virtuoso*, Dr. *Taylor* & Dr. *Wilkins*
dined with me at *Sayes* Court, when I presented Dr. *Wilkins* with
my rare Burning-glasse; Afternoone we all went to Coll: *Blount*
to see his new invented Plows: & so went with them to Lond:

13 Our Preacher on: 25 *Matt* 1. concerning the wise Virgins: so
on the 20th on the same: 21 To Lond: returnd: 23: Came Mr.
Henshaw & Sir William Pastons son [since Earle of *Yarmouth*]
to see mee. 26 I went to see his Majesties House at *Eltham* both
Palace & Chapell in miserable ruines, the noble woods & Park
destroied by Rich the Rebell: 27 Went on foote to Lond:

Dr. *Hewet* preaching on. 20 *John*: 19. *Pax vobis*, shewing the different beginni⟨n⟩g of the Gospel from the Law, the one with gentlenesse, the other in *Thunder* & fire; the Ease of our B: Saviour⟨s⟩ Yoake; The Sword never planted true Religion: No peace yet to the Wicked &c: Afternoone: Dr. *Wild* on. 15 *Luke*: 18 On the Prodigals returne—I went home in the Eveni⟨n⟩g:

28 I made up my grand Accompt with my *U: Pretyman* being 10376 pounds: 16s. 04d, which this day after long calling on him, was finish'd & mutualy discharged: 30: Came to dine with me my Bro: & their Wives, with severall other Relations.

May: 1 Came to visite me Monsieur *Cisner* pastor of the *French*-Church *Lond*:

6 I brought Monsieur *Le Franc* a young *French Sorbonist*, proselyte, to converse with Dr. *Taylor*: The⟨y⟩ fell to dispute concerning original sinn *in Latine*, upon a booke newly published by the Doctor: Who was much satisfied with the young man: Thence to se *Mr. Dugdale* our learned Antiquarie & Herauld: Returning, I was shewd the 3 vast Volumes of Father *Kirchers Obeliscus Panphilius*, in the 2d *volume*, I found the *Hieroglypic* I first communicated & sent him to *Rome*, by the hands of Mr. *Henshaw*, who⟨m⟩ he mentions; I design'd it from the stone it selfe brought me to *Venice* from *Cairo*, by Cap: Powell: returnd home—

4 Our Preacher on his former Text: The privileges of the Saints, at Christs second app⟨e⟩ari⟨n⟩g.

6: went to Lond, lay at my Lodging in Mid: Temple. 7th. Visited Dr. *Taylor*, & procur'd him to propose Monsieur *Le Franc* to the *Bishop*, that he might have Orders, I having some time before brought him to a full consent to the Church of England her doctrine & discipline, in which he till of late made difficulty: so he was this day Ordaind by the Bish: of *Meathe*, both Deacon & Priest.—I paying the Fees to his Lordship, who was very poore, & in Want, to that necessit⟨i⟩e were our Cleargy reduc'd: In the Afternoone I met with Alderman *Robinson* to treate with Mr. *Papillion* about the settlement of my Co: *Geo: Tukes* marriage with Mrs. *Fontaine*.

8 I went to visite *Dr. Wilkins* at *Whitehall*, where I first met with Sir *P: Neale* famous for his optic-glasses:—*Greatorix* the Mathematical Instrument maker, shew'd me his excellent Invention to quench fire, & returnd home.

11 Our preacher proceeded—That the numbers of appearing Professors were almost equal, but should be separated from the real ones (who should be very few in comparison) at the last day: &c:

12 Was published my Essay on *Lucretius*—with innumerable *Errata* &c; ⟨by⟩ the negligence of Mr. *Triplet* who undertook the Correction of the Presse in my absence: [little of the Epicurean Philosophy was known then amongst us:]

18 Our Preacher proceeds in the Alegorie of the Virgins: Afternoone I went to *Charleton* where a stranger preached on 25 *Matt*. 13. Inciting to Watchfullnesse and Prayers upon the uncertaintie of *Christs* coming:

20 To *Lond:* about buisinesse, return'd: 25. our Preacher proceedes.

26 Came Sir *Jo: Evelyn* & *Lady*, my Co: Hales & his, newly married to Visite me &c:

27 To *Lond* to see my *Bro:* returnd: 28 Againe, to dine with *Nieupoort* the *Holland Ambassador*, who received me with extraordinary courtesie: I found him a judicious Crafty & wise man: Gave me excellent cautions as to the danger of the times and Circumstances our Nation was in &c:—remember the Observation he made, upon the ill successe of our former Parliaments, by their private animosities, & little care of the publicque: so taking the aire in *Hide-parke* I went home:

30 I went to *Lond:* to Take leave of my Bro: now returning into the Country.

June 1 our Preacher proceeds:

6 Came *Mr. Needham* to see me, now newly return'd out of France:

8 A stranger preached on. 4. Hosea: 6 condemning mens blindnesse & ignorance in midst of so greate light:—12: To Lond, about affaires, visited the *Dut⟨c⟩h* Ambassador, returnd.

14 Came to visie me the old *Marquis* of *Argyle*, [since executed;] the Lord *Lothain* & some other Scotch noblemen all strangers to me. Note, the Marqu⟨i⟩s, tooke the *Turtle-Doves* in the Aviary for *Owles*.

15 Our Preacher proceedes:

17 Came to visite us, Mr. *Spencer*, Bro: to the E. of *Sunderland*, & my Co: T. *Keightly*:

20 Came to see my Garden &c: the Earle of Southampton [since *L. Treasurer.*]

22. Our Preacher proceedes concerni⟨n⟩g Christs comming to Judgement:—25 I went to *Lond*, to treate with old *Sir Charles Harbord* about a match betweene his Eldest Sonn & my Co: *Eliz: Hungerford*, return'd that evening. ⟨29⟩ Our Preacher proceedes:

July 1 Came Sir Hen: *Herbert* & Lady *Gerrard* to visite us: 6: our Preacher gos on.

7 I began my journey to see some parts of the North East of England; but the weather so excessive hot & dusty, I shortned my progresse—I lay this night at *Ingulstone*, [8] the next day to *Colchester*, a faire Towne but now wretchedly demolished by the late Siege; espe⟨c⟩ialy the suburbs all burnt & then repairing: The Towne is built on a rising, having faire meadows on one side, & a river, with a strong antient Castle, said to have ben built by *K. Coilus* father of *Helena* mother of *Constantine* the *Greate* of whom I find no memory, save at the pinacle of one of their Woolstaple houses, where *Coilus* has a statue of wood wretchedly carvd: The walles are exceeding strong, deeply trenched & fill'd with Earth. It has 6 gates & some Watch toures; & some handsome Churches; but what was shew'd us as a kind of miracle, at the outside of the Castle, the Wall where (Sir *Charles Lucas* & *Sir Geo: Lisle* those valiant persons who so bravely behav'd themselves in the late siege, & were barbarously shot to death & murderd by *Ireton* in cold blood & after rendission upon articles) the place was bare of grasse for a large space, all the rest of it abounding with herbage: For the rest, this is a raged, factious Towne, & now Swarming in Sectaries. Their Trading Cloth with the *Dutch*, & *Baies* & saies with Spaine; & is the only place in *England* where these stuffs are made unsophisticated. Famous likewise will this Place ever be for the strenuous resistance of those most Loyal Gent: &c: against the Rebells, when neere all the strong places & Townes in England had given up to the Conquerors, what time, they expected reliefe from the Scotch Army, defeated with his Majesty at Worcester: It is also famous for *Oysters*, & Erringo of rootes here about growing & Candied: Henc we went to *Dedham* a pretty Country Towne, & very faire Church, finely situated, the vally well watred: Here I met with *Dr. Stokes* a young Gent: but an excellent Mathematician: This is (as most are in Essex) a Clothing Towne, and lies in the unwholsome hundreds. [9] Hence to *Ipswich* in *Suffolck*, which is doubtlesse one of

Sweetest, most pleasant, well built ⟨Towns⟩ in England. It has
12 faire Churches, many noble houses, especialy the Lord
D'evorixe's &c—a brave Kay & commodious harbor, being
about 7 miles from the maine: an ample Mercat-place, & here
was born the greate *Cardinal* Woolsey, who began a palace here,
which was not finish'd &c: I returnd to *Dedham*: At *Ipswich* I
had the curiosity to visite some *Quakers* there in Prison, a new
phanatic sect of dangerous Principles, the⟨y⟩ shew no respect to
any man, magistrate or other & seeme a Melancholy proud sort
of people, & exceedingly ignorant: one of these was said to have
fasted 20 daies, but another endeavoring to do the like perish'd
the 10th, when he would have eaten, but could not: 10: I returnd
homeward, passd againe thro *Colchester*, & by the way saw neere
the antient Towne of *Chelmsford*, saw *New-hall* built in a parke
by *Hen:* 7th & 8, & given by Q: *Eliz:* to the Earle of *Sussex* who
sold it to the late greate *Duke* of ⟨*Buckingham*⟩ and since seiz'd
on by O. *Cromwell* (pretended *Protector*) a faire old house, built
with brick, low & but of 2 stories, as the manner then was: The
Gate-house better: The Court large & pretty: The staire case of
extraordinary widenesse, with a piece representing Sir F: *Drakes*
action in 88, an excellent Sea-piece: The galleries are trifling,
the hall noble, Garden a faire plot, & the whole seate well
accommodated with water; but above all the Sweete & faire
avenue planted with stately Lime-trees in 4 rowes for neere a
mile in length: It has 3 descents which is the onely fault, & may
be reformed: There is another faire walk of the same at the *Mall*
& wildernesse, with a Tenis-Court, & a pleasant *Terrace*
towards the Park, which was well stored with deere, & ponds:
From the Towne we saw the antient *Maldon* (*Camelodunum*)
suppd at *Chelmsford*, ⟨lay⟩ at *Ingolstone* & came home by
Greenewich ferry, where I saw Sir Jo: *Winters* new project of
Charring Sea-Coale, to burne out the Sulphure & render it
Sweete: he did it by burning them in such Earthen-pots, as the
glassemen, mealt their Mettal in, so firing the Coales, without
Consuming them, using a barr of Yron in each crucible or Pot,
which barr has an hooke at one end, that so the Coales being
mealted in a furnace, with other crude sea Coales, under them,
may be drawn out of the potte, sticking to the Yron, whence
they beate them off in greate halfe exhausted Cinders, which
rekindling they make a cleare pleasant Chamber fires with,

depriv'd of their Sulphury & Arsenic malignity: what successe it may have time will discover:

There had ben to visie me in absence Mr. Ducy [since L: of *Downe*] a greate Travellor & curious, Mr. *Spencer*, & *Needham*: 13 our Preacher proceeded on his long exhausted subject: & so on the 20th. 21, I went to *Lond:* returnd that Evening:

Aug: 3 to *Lond*, to receive the B: *Sacrament*, & was the first time that ever the *Church* of *England* was reduced to a Chamber & Conventicle, so sharp was the Persecution; The Parish churches filld with sectaries of all sorts, Blasphemous & Ignorant *Mechanics* usurping the Pulpets every where. In a private House in *Fleetestreete* Dr. Wild preachd on 14. Luke. 23: The B: Communion succeeded & we had a greate meeting of zealous *Christians* who were generaly much more devout & religious, than in our greatest prosperity: Afternoone, I went to the *French-Church* in the Savoy, where I heard Monsieur *D'Espagne* Catechize: & so returnd to my house:

8 I was invited to My Co: G. Tukes wedding at Greenewich: ⟨10⟩ our Preacher proceedes:

11 Came to visite me my Co: *R: Fanshaw*, when I propos'd Mr. *Woodhead* to him, for Governor to my Lord of *Corkes Sonns*, requesting me to recommend some learned person &c: This Mr. *Woodhead* was a monkish solitary person (as afterwards I learned) and by some suspected for popish, but doubtlesse a most heavenly man:

12 To *Lond*, visited Sir *Rich: Edgecomb* now sick, & a relation of ours, & return'd. ⟨17⟩ Our *Preacher* had now for a while don with his long breath'd Text & chose 89: Psal: 15: In the afternoone a stranger, I think a *German* 1. *John*. 16.

20 Was a confused Election of Parliament cald by the Usurper: 24: our Preacher proceeds on his new subject: My son *Richard* a child of most prodigious hopes was now 4 years old: *Deo gratias*. 29 I went to take leave of my excellent neighbour Sir H: ⟨Newton⟩ & lady, now going to dwell at *Warwick*. 31 our Preacher proceedes.

September My *Wife* went with her *Co: Tuke* to divert in the Country for some daies in Essex:

7 our Preacher proceedes &c: Mr. Needham my deare & learned friend came to keepe me company: 13 Came Mr. *Packhurst* & others to visite me: 14: our Preacher proceedes—In the Afternoone a young man on 3: *Mal*. 18:

Now was old *Sir Hen: Vane* sent to *Carisbrook Castle* in *Wight* for a foolish booke he publish'd: The pretended Protector fortifiying himselfe exceedingly, & sending many to Prison: My deare boy, was sick of an *Ague*: ⟨21⟩ our Preacher proceedes:

28 I had Prayers & Sermon at home. 30: To Lond, to visite *Dr. Clark* an ingenious Physician, now in a dangerous feavor: returnd home:

October 2. To Lond againe, returnd that evening: 4. Came to Visie me my Co: Steephens and Mr. Perce [since head of *Magdalen Oxon:*] a learne'd Minister of *Brighton* in *Northamptonshire*, & Cap: Cooke both excellent *Musitians* also:

5 I went to Lond, with my wife now returnd, heard Dr. Hewet on 10. *Pro:* 5: I came home to dinner &c: 12: our Preacher is againe in the *Canticles* (as these halfe *Independents* & *Presbyters* delighted to be). 5. Cap: v: 1. shewing the Spiritual presence of *Christ* with the Saints in the Ordinances, the same on 26. 30: I was 36 years of age. Blessed ⟨be⟩ God for all his patience & mercys.

November 2 our Preacher now on 8. *Rom:* 31. 32 magnif⟨y⟩ing the Grace of God, & benefit of justification, made sure of thro faith: &c: note that there was now nothing practical preached, or that pressed reformation of life, but high & speculative points & straines, that few understood, which left people very ignorant, & of no steady principles, the sourse of all our sects & divisions; for there was much envy, & uncharity in the world: God of his mercy, amend it.

7 I went to Lond, to treate againe with Sir *Ch: Harbord*, returnd:

9 Had prayers at home to my family, by reason of the weather: 15 To Lond. to buy some things, retur⟨ne⟩d: 16 our Preacher proceedes, concerning the benefit of Son-ship of our *B: Saviour*, & our accesse therby to the throne of Grace:

21 Came my Co: R: *Fanshaw* his lady & Mr. *Fanshaw* of Fenchington to visie us:

22 Came my Co: *Verney* &c: to dinner:

23 A very wet day, had the Church office & sermon read to my Family, my Wife not well.

30 An accident keept me at home from Church also: Now indeede that I went at all to Church whilst these usurpers possess'd the *Pulpet*, was that I might not be suspected for a Papist,

& that though the Minister were Presbyterianly affected, he yet was as I understood duly ordaind, & preachd sound doctrine after their way, & besides was an humble harmelesse & peaceable man.

December 1 I went to *Lond*, returnd next day: 7: our Minister proceeds, shewing that the first thing God gives is himselfe. 12 Came Doctor Clark to visite me, now recoverd of his long sicknesse. 13 To Lond: returnd: 14: our Preacher proceedes. 20: The deepe & greate Snow kept us from Church, but not from the publique Office at home:

22 I went to the funerall of Mr. *Russell* a neighbour at Charleton, where was neere 100 *Coaches:* one *Tailor* preachd on 2: *Cor:* 5. 2, making an heavenly meditation apt for the occasion—he had this note on the word ἐπενδύσασθαι: That the Saints, & St. *Paule* in their behalfe, desired (if possible) to have gon to heaven clothed in glory, & without dying at all.

25 I went to Lond, to receive the B: Communion this holy Festival, at Dr. Wilds lodging, where I rejoiced to find so full an assembly of devout & sober Christians, he preached on 2: *Matt.* 2. but I was not able to come so neere the doore for the presse, as to heare the Doctor, coming from home this morning: I received the blessed Sacrament, the Lord make me Thankfull: returnd home:

26 I invited some of my Neighbours & Tennants according to Costome, & to preserve hospitality & Charity: 28 A stranger preachd on 18 *Luke* 7. 8. on which he made a confused discourse, with a greate deale of *Greeke* & ostentation of Learning, to no purpose.

30 Dined with me Sir William *Pastons* sonn, Mr. *Henshaw* & Mr. Clayton:

31 I beged Gods blessing & mercys for his goodnesse to me the past yeare, & set my domestic afaires in order:

1657. *Jan:* 1 Having praied with my Family & celebrated the *Anniversarie*, I spent some time in imploring Gods blessing the yeare I was entred into.

2 I invited some neighbours: 3. Came *Mr. Bovey* to see me: 4th our Preacher proceedes, concerning the right which the faithfull have to the Creature, by their Interest in *Christ*, & that they onely do truely enjoy those Comforts.

7 Came Mr. *Mathew Wren*, [since Secretary to the *Duke*

slaine in the Dut⟨c⟩h War] eldest sonn to the Bish: of Ely (now a
Prisoner in the Tower) and a most worthy, & learned Gent: to
visite me. (11) Being not well, could not go to the Parish Church.
18, my Indisposition continued: Dr. *Joylife* that famous Physitian
(& Anatomist, first detecter of the *lymphatic* veins) came to
visite me.

24 Came againe the old *Marquis* of *Argile* & another Scotch
Earle: 25. My sore Eyes hindred me from going to Church:
31 I was let bloud:

Feb: 3 Came my Bro: *Geo:* & Mr. *Needham* to visite me. 5, I
din'd at the *Holland* Ambassadors: he told me the E. *India*
Comp: of *Holland* had constantly a stock of 400000 pounds in
India, 48 Men of Warr there: of their exact & just keeping their
books, Correspondence &c: so as no Adventure⟨r⟩s Stock could
possibly be lost or defeated: That it was a Vulgar Error of the
Hollanders furnishing their Enemies with powder & ammunition for their mony, though ingaged in actual warr; but that they
usd to merchandize indifferently, & were permitted to sell to the
friends of their Enemies: He laugh'd at our Commitèe of Trade,
as compos'd of men wholy ignorant of it, & how they were the
ruine of Commerce, by gratifying some for private ends: Sir
Geo: Wentworth, Bro: to my Lord Deputy *Strafford* & his lady
dined with us &c:

8 Dr. *Gauden* [since Bish: of *Excester*] preachd at St. *Greg:* an
Eloquent discourse touching the dignity of the Crosse of our
Lord; how we should embrace it; he said that *Jacobs* interchanging & crossing his armes to blesse *Josephes* two sonns *Eph:* &
Manasses was to denote the blessing that should come by it:
That all foundations & contignations in buildings, all contrivement of natural things were full of those figures & signatures;
these were pretty curiosities but the application of the use of it,
was profitable & pious:

10 I went to visite the Governor of *Havana*, a brave sober,
valiant Spanish Gent: taken by Capt: Young of Deptford, when
after 20 yeares being in the *Indias* & amassing greate Wealth, his
lady, & whole family (excepting two ⟨Sonns⟩) were burnt,
destroyed, & taken within sight of *Spaine*: His Eldest Son,
daughter and Wife perishing with immense treasure: One
Sonn, with his brother of one yeares old were the onely saved:
The young Gent: about 17: was a well complexion'd Youth, not

olive colourd: he spake latine handsomly, was extreamely well bred, & borne in the ⟨*Charcas*⟩ 1000 miles south of the *Equinoxial* neere the mountaines of *Potisi*: had never ben in *Europe* before: The Governor was an antient Gent: of greate Courage, of the order of *S: Jago*: sore wounded, his arme & rib broken & lost for his owne share 100000 pounds sterling, which he seem'd to beare with exceeding indifference, & nothing dejected; after some discourse I went with them to *Arundel* house where they dined: They were now going back into *Spaine*, having obtaind their liberty from *Cromewell*. An example of human Vicissitude:

11 I went home: 14: To *Lond:* return'd: where I found Mrs. *Cary*; next day came Mr. *Mordaunt* [since Vicount *Mordant*] (younger son to the Countesse of *Peterborow*) to see his Mistris; bringing with him two of my Lord of *Dovers* daughters: so after dinner they all departed.

Mar: 1. To *Lond:* to receive the B: Comm: Dr. *Hewet* preaching on 7: *Luke:* 37, on the Efficacy of teares.

5 Dr. *Rand* a learned *Physitian*, dedicated to me his Version of *Gassendus's Vita Peireskij*:

8 Our Preacher on 4: *Eph:* 17: 18: That all sinn, was the product of Ignorance: 15 on the same subject: 16. Came my Bro: *Richard*, Wife & family to visite us, & staied all this Weeke: 19, I went with my Bro: to *Lond:* to seale some Writings, wherein I was a *Trusteè* for my Co: Tuke, & return'd: 21: My Bro: & lady &c: went home to *Woodcot*:

22 Our *Viccar* preached on the same Text, of Gods infinite grace to the Gentiles. 25. I went to *Lond:* to celebrate the feast of *Annuntiation*: Dr. Gunning preaching at a private house, on: 11: *Phil:* 6. 7. shewing the stupendious humility & exinanition of Christ, in his Incarnation: I visited Dr. *Taylor*, who shewed me his MSS: of Cases of Conscience, or *Ductor dubitantium* now fitted for the presse: I return'd next day: 29 I went to *Lond:* to keepe *Easter*, in the morning preach'd Dr. *Gillingham* on 1. *Cor:* 15. 20, a Resurrection sermon: The Communion follow'd: In the afternoone Mr. *Gunning* on 60: *Esay.* 20. 21. &c: shewing how the Christian Faith spread abroad, under the dominion of *Christ*: I returned home:

The Protector *Oliver*, now affecting *King-ship*, is petition'd to take the Title on him, by all his new-made sycophant Lords &c:

but dares not for feare of the *Phanatics*, not thoroughly purged out of his rebell army:

 Aprill: 1 Came Sir Tho: *Hanmer* of *Hanmer* in *Wales* to visite me: 2: I went about buisinesse to the Commissioners of the *Sewers*. 5: our Parson—on 4: *Eph:* 19. 20: as formerly, & on the 12th, proving the Scriptures to be the Word of God, so on the ⟨19th⟩ That Truth made us most to resemble God: 21 I went to *Lond:* to consult *Dr. Bate* about taking preventing Physick: Thence to Visite my *Lord Hatton*, with whom I dined; at my returne I step'd into *Bedlame*, where I saw nothing extraordinarie, besides some miserable poore Creatures in chaines, one was mad with making Verses: & also visited the *Charter-house*, formerly belonging to the *Carthusians*; now an old neate, fresh solitarie Colledge for decaied Gent: It has a grove, bowling-greene, Garden: Chapell, hall &c where they eate in common: I likewise saw Christ-Church & Hospital, a very goodly building, Gotic: also the Hall, Schoole, Lodgings, in greate order, for the bring⟨ing⟩ up many hundreds of poore Children of both sexes, & is a⟨n⟩ exemplary Charity: There is a large picture at one end of the *Hall*, representing the Governors, founders, & Institution: so on the 23d I returned home: 25. To *Lond*, return'd that Evening. I had a dangerous fall out of the Coach in Covent Garden, going to my Bro: but without harme, The Lord be praised: 26: our *Viccar* on his former subject: shewing how the old man, dwelt even in the regenerate:

 27 I tooke preventing *Physick*.

 May: 1 Divers Souldiers quarter'd at my house, but I thank God, went away the next day towards *Flanders*: 2: I tooke *Physick*. The next-day (lying at *Greenewich* on the 4th) I went into *Surrey* with my Co: G: *Tuke*, to see *Baynards*, an house of my *Bro: Richards*, which he would have hired: We going in a Charriot drawne with unruly young horses, one of which (they said) had already killed two keepers, were often in very greate danger; so as after 20 ⟨miles⟩ riding, we were forced to change our horses. This is a very faire & noble house of my Bro: built in a park, & having one of the goodliest avenue⟨s⟩ of Oakes up to it, that ever I saw: There is also a pond of 60 Ackers neere it: The Windos of the chiefe roomes are of very fine painted glasse: but the situation excessively dirty & melancholy: We return'd next day, dining by the way at Wotton: 8: I went to

Lond: to congratulate Mr. *Hyldiards* sonns, newly returned from their Travells: came home at night: 11. To Lond: to visite my Bro: Richard: returnd. 13 To *Lond:* to treate againe with Sir *Cha: Harbord* about a Match with my Co: *Hungerford*, of which formerly: return'd at night: There had ben at my house this afternoone *Laurence* president of *Olivers* Council, & some other of his Court Lords to see my Garden & plantations: 14. Came my *Aunt* Hungerford to dinner:

16 I went to *Lond:* to keepe *Whitsonday*. 17: I received at *St. Greg:* where now againe Dr. *Hewet* preached on 2: Act: 4: in the Afternoone Mr. Gunning on part of the *Creede*, I believe in God the H: Ghost: shewing what it was to believe, *onely*, & to believe *in*: & spake something of the Controversy with the *Greeke-Church*: I visited *Mr. Mordaunt* & returned. 22d, I went to see Sir *Tho: Hanmer*. 24: our Preacher on his former text: 30 To Lond: lay at the Midle *Temple*: 31: at *Serjeants Inn* preached Doctor *Gauden* on 27: *Psal:* 9. how we are to seeke the face of God &c: In the Afternoone Mr. *Gunning* expounding the Gospel of the day. 16 *Luke*, declaiming against un-mercifullnesse to the poore, & voluptuousnesse of Life: 1 *June* I returned home, having dined at the Countesse of *Peterborows*, & brought Mr. *Mordaunt* & new married *Lady* my deare friend, to my house, who returned also that Evening back to Lond:

3 *June* Came my Lady *Glanvill* (⟨my⟩ Wifes Aunt) to visite us: 6: Came my Bro: Richard & his Wife:

7 *June* My Wife fell in *Labour* from 2 in the morning till 8¼ at night, when my fourth Sonne was borne, it being Sonday: he was Christned on Wednesday on the 10th & named George (after my Grandfathers name) my Bro: *Rich: Evelyn*: Co: *George Tuke* & *Lady Cotton* susceptors &c: Dr. *Jer: Taylor* officiating in the withdrawing-roome at *Says-Court*:

14: A stranger preached on 32: Psal: 11, shewing the danger & insecurity of the Wiccked.

16 To Lond, returned: 18 I saw at *Greenewich* a sort of Catt brought from the *East Indies*, shaped & snouted much like the *Egyptian Ratoone*, in the body like a *Monkey*, & so footed: the eares & taile like a Catt, onely the taile much longer, & the Skin curiously ringed, with black & white: With this taile, it wound up its body like a Serpent, & so got up into trees, & with it, would also wrap its whole body round; It was of a wolly haire as

a lamb, exceedingly nimble, & yet gentle, & purr'd as dos the Cat.

21 Our Minister preached on 4: *Eph:* 23. concerning the soules renovation: 25 I went to *Lond* to visite friends, return'd. 28: our Preacher on his former *Text*: That putting on the new man, was induing of Christian graces &c:—29 a stranger:

July: 3 A ship blown-up at *Wapping*, shooke my whole house, & the chaire I was sitting & reading in ⟨in⟩ my study. 5. Dr. *Owen* preached at my house on. 128 Psal: 1. 2. ad. 5. upon occasion of now *Churching* my Wife: he also gave us the H: Sacrament:

12 Our *Viccar*, on his former: afternoone at *Greenewich* Mr. *Hardy* on 84 *Psal.* 11. shewing in how many Instances God was both Sun & shild, light, & defence to the Righteous: 16 on Dr. *Taylors* recommendation I went to *Eltham* to helpe one *Moody* a young man, to that living, by my Interest with the *Patron*: return'd:

19 Preachd a stranger: on 5: Eph: 2: concerning the necessitie & want of charity: In the afternoone our Parson, shewing how holinesse was in God the *Archtype*, in us as in the *Ectype*.

26: on the same &c:

August 2: Our Minister on the same Text: 6: I went to see Coll: *Blount* who shewed me the application of the Way-Wiser to a Coach, exactly measuring the miles, & shewing it by an Index as one rid along: It had 3 Circles, one point⟨e⟩d to the number of rods: The other to the miles by 10, to 1000: with all the subdivisions of quarters &c: very pretty, & very usefull: 6: Our Viccar 18 Joh: 36 declaiming at the folly of a sort of Enthusiasts & desperat Zealots, cald the fift Monarchy-men, pretending to set up the Kingdome of *Christ* with the Sword: to this passe was this age arivd, when we had no king in *Israel*: 7: Came Sir *Edm: Bowyer* & Lady to visite us.

21 Fell a most prodigious raine at *Lond:* & the yeare very sickly in the Country. Our *Viccar*, on 3: *Psal:* 8. An anniversary, commemorating Gods infinite mercys to this nation, in continuing the purity of his Gospel, notwithstanding the many troubles & alterations in State; which was true but in part: for never was Religion so perverted: 30:—on 1. *Rom:* 6: shewing the benefit of a true faith. A most unseasonable, wett, sickly Summer: my son: *Richard* ill of a Feavor:

September: I visited Sir *Ed: Bowyer* at his melancholy Seate at *Cammerwell*: he has a very pretty grove of Oakes, & hedges of yew in his Garden, & a handsom row of tall Elmes before his Court: 6: To Lond: to receive the B: Comm: Dr. *Taylor* preaching on 1. Corr: 11. 27. piously discoursing of the signes of a worthy Communicant: The afternoone, a grave old man at *Woolchurch* on. 102 *Psal:* 6 shewing the ignominie of Christs suffering: I returnd home. 13 our Viccar on 45 Isa: 22. how *Christ* was the onely object of our Faith:

15 Going to *Lond:* with some Company, who would needes step in to see a famous *Rope-daunser* call'd the *Turk*, I saw even to astonishment the agilities he perform'd, one was his walking bare foote, & taking hold by his toes onely, of a rope almost perpendicular & without so much as touching it with his hands: also dauncing blindfold on the high-roope: & with a boy of 12 yeares old, tyed to one of his feete about 20 foote beneath him dangling as he daunced, & yet moved as nimbly, as it had ben but a feather: Lastly he ⟨stoode⟩ on his head, upon the very top of a very high mast, daunced on a small roope that was very slack, & finaly flew downe the perpendicular, with his head foreward on his breast, his legs & armes extended: with divers other activities, to the admiration of all the Spectators: I also saw the hairy Maid, or Woman wh⟨om⟩ 20 years before I had also seene when a child: her very Eyebrowes were combed upward, & all her forehead as thick & even as growes on any womans head, neately dress'd: There come also tw⟨o⟩ lock⟨s⟩ very long out of Each Eare: she had also a most prolix beard, & *mustachios*, with long locks of haire growing on the very middle of her nose, exactly like an Island Dog; the rest of her body not so hairy, yet exceeding long in comparison, armes, neck, breast & back; the ⟨Colour⟩ of a bright browne, & fine as well dressed flax: She was now married, & told me had one Child, that was not hairy, [as] nor were any of her parents or relations: she was borne at *Ausburg* in *Germanie*, & for the rest very well shaped, plaied well on the Harpsichord &c: I returnd home:

17 I went to see Sir *Rob: Needham* at *Lambeth*, a relation of mine, and thence *John Tradescants Musæum*, the chiefest rarities were in my opinion, the antient *Roman*, *Indian* & other Nations Armour, shilds & weapons; Some habits also of curiously

colourd & wrought feathers: particula⟨r⟩ly that of the *Phoenix* Wing, as tradition gos: other innumerable things there were too long here to recite, & printed in his Catalogue by Mr. *Ashmole*, to whom after death of the widdow, they are bequeathe'd: & by him designd a Gift to *Oxford*:

Dunkirk was now beseig'd by our *Fleete* joynd with the *French*.

19 I went to see divers Gardens about *London*, returnd home: 20: our *Viccar* on his former subject: 22: To *Lond:* to visite the *Holland Ambassador* with whom I had now contracted much friendly corresponden⟨c⟩e: usefull to the Intelligence I constantly gave his Majestie abroad: returning, I saw at Dr. *Joylifes*, two *Virginian* rattle-snakes a live: they exceeded a yard in length, small heads, & slender tailes but as big as my leg in the middle; when vexed or provoked, swiftly vibrating & shaking theire tailes, they rattled as looud as a childs rattle, or as if on⟨e⟩ heard a jack going: & this by the collision [or atrition] of certaine gristly Skinns curiously joynted, yet loose, like the *Vertebra* or back bone; & transparant as parchment; by which they give warning, a providential caution for other creatures to avoid them: They leape cruely: the Doctor tried their biting on ratts & mice which they immediately killed; but their vigour must needes be much exhausted here, where they had nothing to eate, & were in another Climate, kept onely in a barill of bran &c: 27: the *Viccar* proceedes. 30: To *Lond:* to pay 100 pounds which I had borrowed, returnd: Now ⟨w⟩as *Mardyke* taken by the *English*:

Octob: 4: Our *Viccar* proceedes. 10: I dind at *Lond:* with the *Dutch* Ambassador, now taking his leave, I return'd. 11: The *Viccar* on his former: 18 he preached on: 1 *John:* 1. 1 about *Christs* humane-nature. 21: Came Mr. *Henshaw* & Lady to visite us, with his Bro: in Law Mr. *Dorrell:* 25 The Viccar proceedes how our B: S. was the *Word:* 31: I was ⟨now⟩ 37 yeares of age: *Lord* so teach me to number my dayes, that I may apply my heart to Wisedome:

Nov. 1 I went to *Lon:* to receive the *H. Sacrament:* Dr. *Taylor* preaching on 1. Cor: 11. 16 concerning *Charity:*

15 Our Viccar on 1. *Jo:* 1. 2. How *Christ* was eternal life: 16 To *Lond:* about buisinesse with the E. of *Chesterfield* 'til the 20th. 22: Our *Viccar* proceedes: of the felloship of Believers:

26 I went to *Lond*: to a Court of the E. *India Comp;* upon its new Union: where was much dissorder by reason of the *Anabaptists*, who would have the Adventurers obliged onely by an Engagement, with out Swearing, that they might still pursue their private trade; but it was carried against them: & that Wednesday should be a Generall Court for Election of Officers; after Sermon, & prayers for good successe: The stock resolv'd on was 800000 pounds: (27) I tooke the Oath, at the E. *India house*, subscribing 500 pounds: & so returnd: (29): our Vicc: persu'd his former Text.

December 1 To *Lond*. 2: Dr. *Raynolds* [since *Bishop* of *Norwich*] preached before the *E. India* Comp: at St. *Andrews undershaft* on 13 *Nehem:* 31. shewing by the Example of *Nehemiah* all the Perfections of a trusty person in publique affaires, with many good precepts apposite to the occasion; ending with a prayer for Gods blessing on the Comp: & Undertaking:

3 Mr. *Gunning* preached on: 3. *John*: 3 against the Anabaptists, shewing the effect, & necessity of the Sacrament of *Baptisme*: This Sect was now wonderfully spread: 6: Dr. *Taylor* on 26 *Psal:* 6: concerning the preparation before the H. Sacrament, but chiefly insisting on care, & perseveration afterwards, also the necesity of restitution in case of wrongs &c:—In the afternoone at the *Savoy Monsieur D'Espagne, Cathechizing*: why God makes use of Wicked Instruments to execute his designes, as the Devil himselfe: That very impious men, commonly die by their owne hands, as being the worst to be found; by the Example of *Judas, Achitophel, Saule*, &c:

9 I paied in my fi⟨r⟩st payment to the *E. Ind: stock*: There being a Court in *Merchant-Taylors hall*: 10 returned home: ⟨13⟩ Our *Viccar* on 1. Jo: 4 that the plenitude of the Saints Joy consisted in his Communion with God. 17 Came to dine with me my Bro: R. *Evelyn*, & Mr. *Needham*.

20 Viccar: proceeded: 25, I went with my Wife &c: to *Lond:* to celebrate *Christmas day*. Mr. *Gunning* preaching in *Excester* Chapell on 7: *Micha* 2. Sermon Ended, as he was giving us the holy Sacrament, The Chapell was surrounded with Souldiers: All the Communicants and Assembly surpriz'd & kept Prisoners by them, some in the house, others carried away: It fell to my share to be confined to a roome in the house, where yet were permitted to Dine with the master of it, the Countesse of

Dorset, *Lady Hatton* & some others of quality who invited me: In the afternoone came *Collonel Whaly*, *Goffe* & others from *Whitehall* to examine us one by one, & some they committed to the *Martial*, some to Prison, some Committed: When I came before them they tooke my name & aboad, examind me, why contrarie to an Ordinance made that none should any longer observe the superstitious time of the *Nativity* (so esteem'd by them) I durst offend, & particularly be at *Common prayers*, which they told me was but the *Masse* in *English*, & particularly pray for *Charles stuard*, for which we had no Scripture: I told them we did not pray for *Cha: Steward* but for all *Christian Kings*, *Princes* & *Governors*: The⟨y⟩ replied, in so doing we praied for the K. of *Spaine* too, who was their Enemie, & a *Papist*, with other frivolous & insnaring questions, with much threatning, & finding no colour to detaine me longer, with much pitty of my Ignorance, they dismiss'd me: These were men of high flight, and above Ordinances: & spake spitefull things of our B: Lords nativity: so I got home late the next day blessed be God: These wretched miscreants, held their muskets against us as we came up to receive the Sacred Elements, as if they would have shot us at the Altar, but yet suffering us to finish the Office of Communion, as perhaps not in their Instructions what they should do in case they found us in that Action: 27: Our *Viccar* proceeded:

28 I invited some of my Neighbours according to Costome.

31 Praised God for his mercies the yeare past, & set all things in order in my family:

1658 *Jan:* 1. Celebrating the *Anniversarie* & implor'd the blessing of God for the yeare to come, I invited severall Neighbours &c—3. our *Viccar* on his former Text, & so 10:—upon the 6: verse: who were yet in darknesse, & the degrees of it: 17 a Stranger preachd on 1. Jo: 3. 2. shewing how every true believer was a Sonn of God: In the afternoone on 2 *Cor:* 13. 5: How we should examine our faith: &c: 24: our *Viccar* on his old Text: v: 7. To Walke in the light was to walk with God:

27 After six fitts of a *Quartan Ague* it pleased God to visite my deare Child *Dick* with fitts so extreame, especiale one of his sides, that after the rigor was over & he in his hot fitt, he fell into so greate & intollerable a sweate, that being surpriz'd with the aboundance of vapours ascending to his head, he fell into

such fatal Symptoms, as all the help at hand was not able to recover his spirits, so as after a long & painefull Conflict, falling to sleepe as we thought, & coverd too warme, (though in midst of a severe frosty season) and by a greate fire in the roome; he plainely expird, to our unexpressable griefe & affliction. We sent for Physitians to Lond, whilst there was yet life in him; but the river was frozen up, & the Coach brake by the way ere it got a mile from the house; so as all artificial help failing, & his natural strength exhausted, we lost the prettiest, and dearest Child, that ever parents had, being but 5 yeares & 3 days old in years but even at that tender age, a prodigie for Witt, & understanding; for beauty of body a very Angel, & for endowments of mind, of incredible & rare hopes. To give onely a little tast of some of them, & thereby glory to God, (who out of the mouths of Babes & Infants dos sometimes perfect *his* praises) At 2 yeares & halfe old he could perfectly reade any of the *English*, *Latine*, french or *Gottic* letters; pronouncing the three first languages exactly: He had before the 5t yeare or in that yeare not onely skill to reade most written hands, but to decline all the *Nounes*, Conjugate the verbs, regular, & most of the irregular; learned out *Puerilis*, got by heart almost the intire Vocabularie of Latine & french primitives & words, could make congruous *Syntax*, turne English into Lat: & *vice versa*, construe & prove what he read & did, the government & use of Relatives, Verbs *Transitive*, *Substantives* &c: Elipses & many figure & tropes, & made a considerable progresse in *Commenius's Janua*; began himselfe ⟨to⟩ write legibly, & had a strange passion for *Greeke*: the number of Verses he could recite was prodigious, & what he remembred of the parts of playes, which he would also act: & when seeing a *Plautus* in ones hand, he asked what booke it was, & being told it was *Comedy* &c, & too difficult for him, he wept for sorrow: strange was his apt & ingenious application of Fables & Morals, for he had read *Æsop*, & had a wonderfull disposition to *Mathematics*, having by heart, divers propositions of *Euclid* that were read to him in play, & he would make lines, & demonstrate them: As to his Piety, astonishing were his applications of Scripture upon occasion, & his sense of God, he had learn'd all his Catechisme early, & understood the historical part of the Bible & N. Test: to a wonder, & how Christ came to redeeme Mankind &c: & how comprehending these necessarys, himselfe, his Godfathers &c were discharged of their promise: These and the like illuminations, far exceeding his age & experience, considering the prettinesse of his addresse & behaviour, cannot but leave impressions in me at the memory of him: When one told him how many dayes a certaine *Quaker* had fasted in *Colchester*, he replied, that was no wonder; for Christ had sayd, That Man should not live by bread alone, but by the word of God: He would of himselfe select the most pathetical *Psalmes*, & Chapters out of Jobe, to reade to his Mayde, during his sicknesse, telling her (when she pittied him) that all Gods Children must suffer affliction: He declaim'd against the Vanities of the World, before he had seene any: often he would desire those who came to see him, to pray by him, & before he fell sick a yeare, to kneele and pray with him alone in some Corner: How thankfully would he receive admonition, how soone be reconciled! how indifferent, continualy cherefull: Grave advise would he be giving his brother *John*, beare with his impertinences, & say he was but a Child: If he heard of, or saw any new thing, he was unquiet till he was told how it was made, & brought us all difficulties that he found in booke, to be expounded: He had learn'd by heart divers Sentences in *Lat:* & *Greeke* which on occasion he would produce even to wonder: In a word he was all life, all prettinesse, far from morose, sullen, or childish in any thing he said or did: The last time he had ben at Church, (which was at *Greenewich*) according to costome, I asked him what he remembred of the Sermon: Two good-things Father, replys he: *Bonum Gratiæ*, & *bonum Gloriæ* with a just account of what the preacher said: The day before he died, he cald to me, & in a more serious manner than usualy, Told me, That for all I loved him so dearely, I would give my house, land & all my fine things to his Bro: Jack, he should have none of them, & next morning when first he found himselfe ill, & that I perswaded him to keepe his hands in bed, he demanded, whither he might pray to God with his hands un-joyn'd, & a little after, whilst in greate agonie, whither he should not offend God, by using his holy name so oft, calling for Ease: What shall I say of his frequent pathetical ejaculations utter'd of himselfe, Sweete *Jesus* save me, deliver me, pardon my sinns, Let thine *Angels* receive me &c: so early knowledge, so much piety & perfection; but thus God having dressed up a Saint fit for himselfe, would not permit him longer with us, unworthy of the future fruites of this incomparable hopefull blossome: such a Child I never saw; for such a child I blesse God, in whose boosome he is: May I & mine become as this little child, which now follows the Child Jesus, that Lamb of God, in a white robe whithersoever he gos. Even so Lord *Jesus*, *fiat Voluntas tua*, Thou gavest him to us, thou hast taken him from us, blessed be the name of the Lord, That I had any thing acceptable to thee, was from thy Grace alone, since from me he had nothing but sinn; But that thou hast pardon'd, blessed be my God for ever Amen:

30 On the *Saturday* following, I sufferd the Physitians to have him opened: Dr. *Needham* & Dr. *Welles*, who were come three days before, & a little time ere he expired, but was past all help, & in my opinion he was suffocated by the woman & maide that tended him, & covered him too hott with blankets as he lay in a Cradle, neere an excessive hot fire in a close roome; for my Wife & I being then below & not long come from him, being come up, & I lifting up the blanket, which had quite cove(re)d the Cradle, taking first notice of his wonderfull fresh colour, & hardly hearing him breath or heave, soone perceived that he was neere overcome with heate & sweate, & so doubtlesse it was, & the Child so farr gon, as we could not make him to heare, or once open his eyes, though life was apparantly in him: we gave him some thing to make him *neeze* but ineffectivly: Being open'd they found a membranous substance growing to the cavous part of the *liver*, somewhat neere the edge of it for the compasse of 3 Inches, which ought not to be; for the Liver is fixed onely by three strong ligaments, all far distant from that part, insomuch as it could not move in that part; on which they confidently affirm'd, the Child was (as tis vulgarly cald) *livergrowne*, & thence that sicknesse & so frequent complaint of his side: & indeede both *Liver* & *Splen* were exceedingly large &c: After this I caused the body to be Cofin'd in Lead, & reposited him that night, about 8 a clock in the Church of Deptford, accompanied with divers of my relations & neighbours, among whom I distributed rings with this—*Dominus abstulit*: intending (God willing) to have him transported with my owne body, to be interrd at our Dormitorie in *Wotton* chur(c)h in my deare native County Surry, & to lay my bones & mingle my dust with my Fathers, &c: If God be so gracious to me; & make me as fit for him, as this blessed child was: Here ends the joy of my life, &

for which I go even mourning to the grave: The *L. Jesus* sanctifie this & all other my Afflictions: *Amen*:

Feb: 7 Our viccar preached on his former subject, shewing the wonderfull efficacy of *Christs* blood: 14 so on the 18: That none of the Saints, were without sinn: In the afternoone stepped up a young stripling, making a very sorry discourse ⟨on⟩ those sweete words of our B. Lord: 11: *Matt.* 28.

15 The afflicting hand of God being still upon us, it pleased him also to take away from us this morning my other youngest sonn *George* now 7 weekes languishing at Nurse, breeding Teeth, & ending in a Dropsie: Gods holy will be don: he was buried in *Deptford* Church the 17th following:—21 our Viccar proceedes. 25 Came Dr. *Taylor* & my Brothers to visite & Condole with me. 28: The Viccar proceedes, shewing the nature of a sincere Confession: &c:

Mar: 6 to *Lond:* [7] to hear Dr. *Taylor* in a private house on: 13. *Luke.* 23. 24, how few were likely to be saved, by reason of the many lusts & tentations men are expos'd to, & little concurrence of their wills to the aide of Gods *H. Spirit*: That we ought not censure the inevitable decrees of his sovraine Majestie & fancy the *Idea* & sourse of all Justice, mor⟨e⟩ cruel & unjust then man him-self: After this follow'd the H. Comm: of which I partici-patd: In the Afternoone Mr. *Gunning* at Excester-house, expounding part of the Creede: *Credo Remissionem Peccatorum*: The 9th I returnd home. This had ben the severest Winter, that man alive had knowne in *England*: The *Crowes* feete were frozen to their prey: Ilands of Ice inclosd both fish & foule frozen, & some persons in their boates:

11 Sir Ed: Bowyer & Lady came to visite us: 14 our *Viccar* on his former Text. That where God forgives sinn, he obliges his faithfullnesse & justice: 21: That those who pretend they have no sinn, are of all others the greatest sinners: exhorting to a true Confession: 28: on 14 *Joh*: 1. concerning saving Faith: 29 To Lond, to visite my Bro: return'd:

Aprill 4. Vicc: on his former, concerning the Faith of Believers under the N.T. 10 To *Lond*, to celebrate *Easter*. 11 Dr. *Taylor* in his owne house on: 15. *Cor:* 12: shewing how we should attaine the fruits of *Christs* resurrection: Afternoone at Wool-Church, a stranger on 20: John: 19. 20. showing the truth of the resurrection: I walked home this Evening on foote: 12. 13. Tooke

Physick: 15 Let bloud. 18 our Curate on his former: what the Faith of the Fathers in the old Test: was:

21 Being greately afflicted with the *Hemerhoids* ⟨bleeding⟩ very much, by reason of the purges which I tooke, stoping this day on a suddain taking cold, I was so ill, that I was not far from death, & so continud to the 23. when being let bloud in the foote, it pleas'd God to restore me after some time; Blessed ⟨be⟩ God.

May 15 I went to *Lond:* to divert myselfe from my sadnesse, lay at my Bro: 16 The Minister at *Covent-Garden* Chapell 2. *Act:* 41 shewing how the World became the ordinary meanes of Salvation, faith wrought by it alone, & therefore preferrable to all other meanes, w⟨h⟩ither reading, Tradition, Conference or whatever &c: In the Afternoone St. *Clements* by M. *Masterson* on 4. *Gal:* 19: That *Christ* without us, profets nothing, but *Christ* within us; & to be form'd after his similitude requires a new Creation. 17: I went to take the aire in *Hide-park* &c, with Sir *Ch: Lee,* my Lady Seamor & others. ⟨19⟩ was a publique Fast, to avert an Epidemical sicknesse, very mortal this Spring: [19] Mr. *Marsterson* at St. *Greg:* On 18 *Luke*: 13. In commendation of short & pathetical prayers, their power with God, that they make all places Consecrate: 20: I went to see a Coach-race in H. Park, & collationd with my Bro: ⟨in⟩ Spring Garden: 21. To visite Sir *Jo: Evelyn* & other friends. 23 *Dr. Manton* the famous Presbyterian at *C. Garden* on 6: *Matt* 10. shewing what the Kingdom of God was, how pray for it &c: Afternoone Dr. *Reeve* incomparably on 1. *Pet.* 2. 29. concerning living unto righteousnesse, namely, by a life of grace & vertue, mortifying corruptions, the bent & inclinations to holinesse, & the Love of God were the best of signes, with a severe discourse of Death-bed Repentance: There was now a Collection for Persecut⟨e⟩d & sequestered Ministers of the Ch: of *England*, whereof dive⟨r⟩s in Prison: a sad day: The Church now in Dens & Caves of the Earth. 24 supped at my La: Gerrards:

30 Was *Whitsonday* at St. *Greg:* Mr. *Massam* 2. *Act:* 4. The benefit of Tongues, & the miracle at this time for Conversion: The Prudence of it: The benefit of pub: meetings & their union for the obtaining the H: *Spirit*: That we should come early, & empty that God may fill us: The H. Sacrament followd: Dr. *Griffith* in the Afternoone 3: *Matt:* 11 shewing the difference 'twixt the water, & firie Baptisme; why like fire the Spirit, by Symbolical

Types from the zeale, purity, penetration, separation, that therefore all who will be saved must passe this Babtisme &c.

31 I went to visite my La: *Peterborow* whose sonn (Mr. *Mordaunt*) prisoner in the Tower, was now on his Tryal, & acquitted
but by one voice, but that holy *Martyr* Dr. *Hewet* condemned to
die, without Law, Jury, or Justice, but by a mock Council of State
as they calld it: A dangrous tretcheros time:

June 2. An extraordinary storme of haile & raine, cold season
as winter, wind northerly neere 6 moneths.

3 A large *Whale* taken, twixt my Land butting on the *Thames*
& *Greenewich*, which drew an infinite Concourse to see it, by
water, horse, coach, on foote from *Lond*, & all parts: It appeared
first below *Greenewich* at low-water, for at high water, it would
have destroyed all the boates: but lying now in shallow water,
incompassd with boates, after a long Conflict it was killed with
the harping yrons, & struck in the head, out of which spouted
blood & water, by two tunnells like Smoake from a chimny: &
after an horrid grone it ran quite on shore & died: The length
was 58 foote: 16 in height, black skin'd like Coach-leather, very
small eyes, greate taile, small finns & but 2: a piked snout, & a
mouth so wide & divers men might have stood upright in it: No
teeth at all, but sucked the slime onely as thro a greate made of
that bone which we call Whale bone: The throate ⟨yet⟩ so narrow, as would not have admitted the least of fishes: The
extreames of the *Cetaceous* bones hang downewards, from the
Upper ⟨jaw⟩, & was hairy towards the Ends, & bottome within-

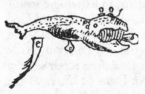

side: all of it prodigious, but in nothing more wonderfull then that an
Animal of so greate a bulk, should be
nourished onely by slime, thro' those
grates: a) The bones making the
grate. b) The Tongue, c. the finn: d
the Eye: e) one of the bones making
the grate (a) f the Tunnells through which, shutting the mouth,
the water is forced upward, at least 30 foote, like a black thick
mist. &c:

5. I returnd:

6. *Trinity Sonday* our *Viccar* on 14: *John*: 6 That *Christ* is the
Way of God to the Creature, & of the Creature to God: all other
ways are deviations.

7. To *Lond*, leaving my Wife with my sick La: *Cotton*. 9: I went to see the Ear⟨l⟩e of *Northumberlands* Pictures, whereoff that of the *Venetian* Senators was one of the best of *Titians*, & another of *Andrea de Sarta*, viz, a *Madona*, *Christ*, St. *John* & an old Woman &c: a St. Catharine of *Da Vinci*, with divers Portraits of *V. Dyke*, a Nativity of *Georgioni*: The last of our blessed Kings, & D: of *Yorke* by *Lilly*: A rosarie of flo: by the famous *Jesuite* of *Bruxells* & severall more: This was in Suffolck house: The new front towards the Gardens, is tollerable, were it not drown'd by a too massie, & clowdy pair of stayers of stone, without any neeate Invention.

8 Was that excellent Preacher & holy ⟨Man⟩, Dr. *Hewet* Martyr'd, for having Intelligence with his Majestie by the L. Marq: of *Ormond* &c.

10 I went to see the Medical Garden at *Westminster*, well stored with plants, under *Morgan* a very Skillfull *Botanist*, & so 11 went home: 13. our *Viccar* on his former: How *Christ* the Truth to believers in his promises, his word, the Effects of it &c:

17 *Dynkirk* now taken by the *English*. 20: former Text: how *Christ* was the life of Grace & Glory:

21 To Lond: returnd: 26: To *Eltham* to visite honest Mr. *Owen*: 27: our Viccar as formerly: [*Pomerid*:¹ Mr. *Day*. 1 *Joh*: 4. 19:]

30 Came Mr. *Henshaw* & Mr. *Dorill* to visite me.

July 3 I went to *Lond*, din'd with Mr. *Henshaw*, Mr. *Dorell* & Mr. *Ashmole* founder of the *Oxford* repository of rarities, with divers Doctors of Physick & Virtuosos: returnd that evening.

4 A stranger preached on 17 *Jo:* 3. shewing how an ignorant man is in as much danger as a wicked: that the knowledge of God is requisite in all our actions to temper our zeale. Afternoon on the 6. Rom: 23. shewing what a death entred by sinn &c:

5 I went to *Woodcot* to my Brothers, to be *Godfather* to his sonn & heire George, with my Bro: G. Evelyn & Mrs. Lewknor, he was christned the 6t, & on the 7th I came home. Next day I fell ill of the Coliq: Sir Ed: Bowyer came to visite me in the afternoone with Dr. Needham next day: on the ⟨11⟩: *Mr. Hinchman* preachd on 5. *Ephes:* 1. perswading to the Imitation of *Christ*, from our relation to him as Children: Afternoone on 7:

1 In the afternoon; from the Latin adjective *pomeridianus*.

Rom: 22: of the greate delight & complacency the⟨y⟩ had within themselves from the testimony of a good Conscience:

15 Came to see me my Lord *Killmurrey* & Lady, Sir Rob: Nee⟨d⟩ham, Mrs. Offley, & two daughters of my Lord Willogby of Parrham: 16 Came to visite, the Lady Gerrard: I also went to Lond, & return'd. 18: our Viccar on 14 Jo: 7: That those who go to the *Father*, must proceede from the Father: Afternoone a stranger on 8. *Rom:* 33. shewing how freely God justifies sinners.

22 To *Lond:* returned, & the next day with my Wife & son *John* to *Wotton*, by the way dining at my Bro: at *Woodcot.* 25. preachd Mr. *Higham* on 15 *Luke* 27, afternoone the Learned Mr. *Gataker* on 39 *Gen:* 9. 27: I returnd to *Woodcot*, where I found them all in sorrow for the death of my late Godson, so went back to *Wotton* that evening. 30 I went ⟨to⟩ visite Mr. *Mordaunt* at *Rygate*, at my L. *Peterborows*, & returning calld in to see Mr. *Thurland* &c:

August 1 Mr. *Higham* on 15 *Luke* 28. 3 I went with my Wife to visite Sir *John Evelyn* at *Godstone* where we staied three dayes, and exceedingly well received: The place is not excellent, but might be very sweete, by turning some offices of the house, & removing the Garden, The house being a noble fabric, though not comparable to what was first buil⟨d⟩ed by my Unkle who was Master of all the Powder mills: 5 We went to *Squirrills* to visie my Co: *Leech* daughter to Sir *John* a pretty finely wooded & watred seate: The stables good, the house old but convenient. 6. return'd to *Wotton.* 8 Mr. *Higham* on 3. *Titus* 10. 9 My *Lord Chesterfield* sent me a Buck. 10. I din'd at Mr. *Carew Raleighs* at *Horsley*, son to the famous *Sir Walter* &c: 14. We went to a challeng'd match to *Durdens* to Bowles for 10 pounds, which we wonn. 15 Mr. *Cosin* of *Darking* preachd on 6. *Mat:* 24. Afternoone Mr. Higham on 14 *Job.* 14. 16 I went againe to Mr. *Raleighs*: The 10th to Sir *Ambros Brown* at *Betchworth Castle* in that tempestious Wind, which threw-downe my greatest trees at *Says Court*, & did so much mischiefe all *England* over: It continued all night, till 3 afternoone next day, & was *S. West*, destroying all our winter fruit. 22: Mr. *Higham* on 8. *Rom* 12. ⟨29⟩: on the same Text:

September 3 Died that archrebell *Oliver Cromewell*, cal'd Protector. 5 Mr. *Higham* on former Text:

5 I fell sick of a sore throat & feavor, which made me keepe my bed 4 or 5 dayes: on the 9 let bloud, & my Bro: *Richard* came to visite me. 16 I tooke a Vomite of ☿ *vitæ*. And this day was published my Translation of *St. Chrysostomes Education* of *Children*, which I dedicated to both my Brothers, to comfort them upon the losse of their Children:

19 Mr. *Higham* on 13. *Rom:* 12. afternoone Mr. *Gere* at *Abinger* on 4. *Hosea.* 1. 2. 20 I went to returne my Bro: Visite. 21 My Lord *Berkeley* of *Berkeley Castle* invited me to dinner: 26 Mr. *King* preached at *Ashsted* on 15. *Pro:* 24. a *Quaker* would have disputed: in the afternoone we went to he⟨a⟩re Dr. *Haccket* [since Bishop of Lichfild] [on 21 *Matt:* 38] at Cheme: [here (at Cheme) lie buried the *Lumlies*.] 27: To *Bedington* that antient Seate of the Carews, a faire old hall, but a scambling house: famous for the first *Orange* garden of *England*, being now over-growne trees, & planted in the ground, & securd in winter with a wooden tabernacle & stoves: This seate is rarely watred, & lying low invirond with sweete pastures &c: The pomegranads beare here: here is also a fine parke: from hence we went to *Cassalton* incomparably watred, & capable of being made a most delicious seate being upon the sweete downes, & a champion about it full planted with Walnuts & Chery trees, which afford a considerable rent: riding over these downes & discoursing with the shepherds, I found that digging about the bottome neere Sir *Christopher Buckles* neere *Bansted*, divers *Medails* have ben found both Coper & silver, with foundations of houses, urnes &c: & here indeede antiently stood a famous Citty of the *Romans*, se *Itinerarium Antonini* &c: 29 I returned home after 10 weekes absence.

October 2 I went to *Lond:* to receive the H: *Sac:* on the 3d. Dr. *Wild* [*sinc* Bish: of   ] preachd in a private place on 1 *Esay:* 4. shew⟨ing⟩ the Paralells twixt the sinns of *Israel* & those of *England*: In the afternoone Mr. *Hall* (sonn to *Joseph* B: of *Norwich*) on 1. *Cor:* 6. 2. of the dignitie of the Saints, & in what manner they should be judges with Christ at the last day, an excellent sermon: 4. I went to visite Mr. *Madox* now come newly out of *France* & dined with the *Holland* Ambassador at *Derby*-house: returning I diverted to see a *White Raven* & indeede very white, bred in *Cumberland*, also a *Porcupine*, of that kind that shoots its quills: of which *Claudian* Ep: it was headed like a Rat, the fore-feete like a *badger*, the hindfeete like a Beare: I returned:

10 Preached one Mr. *Simson* a famous Independent on 14. *Rom.* 12, on the Judgement to come. 17: Our *Viccar* on 14. *Joh:* 10. 11: 18 I was summoned to Lond. by the Commissioners for new buildings, returnd: 19 To the *Commissioners* of *Sewers*, but because there was an Oath to be taken of fidelity to the Government as now constituted without a *King*: I got to be excus'd, & returned home:

November 1 I went to dine with the *Fefees* of the poores stock: 3. Came *Coll: Tuke* to me out of France: 7. My sore throte much incommoded me: 14 Our *Viccar*: on 14 *Joh.* 12. 13. What work Believers do through faith: 15 To Lond. about buisinesse, returnd the next day. 21. *Viccar* on former Text: That one of fruits of our B: *Saviours* going to his father, was to obtaine the effect of our Prayers: 22 To *Lond*, to visite my Bro: & the next day saw the superb Funerall of the *Protectors*: [22] He was carried from *Somerset-house* in a velvet bed of state drawn by six horses houss'd with the same: The Pall held-up by his new Lords: *Oliver* lying in Effigie in royal robes, & Crown'd with a Crown, scepter, & *Mund*, like a King: The Pendants, & Guidons were carried by the Officers of the Army, The Imperial banners, Atchievments &c by the *Heraulds* in their Coates, a rich caparizon'd Horse all embroidred over with gold: a Knight of honour arm'd *Cap a pè* & after all his Guards, Souldiers & innumerable Mourners: In this equipage they proceeded to *Westminster* μετ᾽⟨πολλῆς⟩ φαντασιας &c: but it was the joyfullest funerall that ever I saw, for there was none that Cried, but dogs, which the souldiers hooted away with a barbarous noise; drinking, & taking *Tabacco* in the streetes as they went: I went not home til the 17th.

December 3 I was summoned againe to appeare before the Commissioners about new foundations erected within such a distance of Lond: In the afternoone I heard Mr. *Gunning* on 59 of *Isay*, an *Advent* exhortation, & perstringing the now sinfull abrogation of *Christian* Anniversaries & feastivals: 5. Dr. *Reeve* preached on 1. *Pet:* 2. 14. magnifying the infinite Love of *Christ* in dying for us: That the Sacrifice being but once, one, & sufficient, That of the *Masse* for quick & dead was a grievous innovation &c: the rest was preparatory to the holy Communion at which I participated. 6 I returnd: Now was publishd my *French Gardiner* the first & best of that kind that introducd the use of the *Olitorie* Garden to any purpose:

23 I went with my Wife to keepe Christmas at my *Co: Geo: Tukes* at *Cressing Temple* in *Essex*, lay that night at *Brentwood*: 25 Here was no publique Service, but what we privately us'd: 31 I blessed God for his Mercys the yeare past, & 1. Jan: beged the Continuance of them: Thus for 3 *Sundayes*, by reason of the incumbents death, here was neither praying nor preaching: Tho there was a Chapell in the house: where we had good cheere & well come, so as on the 10th I returned home, having ben robbd during my absence of divers things of value, some plate, 20 pounds in mony &c: I also lost a Coach-horse in the journey: lay at *Ingulstone* & got to *Says Court* on the 11th: ⟨16⟩ our *Viccar* preach'd on the 17. verse of his former Text, shewing that the H. *Ghost* would never come to those as a Comforter, to whom I first did not come as a Sanctifier. 23 proceeded, shewing how the Spirit dwells in the Saints & so concluded with a pathetical Speech, taking leave of the *Parish* to go to a Living in the Citty.

Feb: 3 to *Lond*, to prepare: kept solemn fast on the 4th with Mr. *Gunning* who preachd on 1 *John* 4. 8. describing what was the Love & knowledge of God: 7. I returned home:

21 To *Lond*, about my erections at *Deptford*, return'd: 27 A stranger preached on 5. *Matt:* 47. exhorting to the service of God with more exactnesse, & the preeminence of the knowledge of God, above all other things:

Aprill 3 I went to *Greenewich* to receive the B: Comm: with my Wife & family (our parish yet destitute) where Mr. *Plume* preach'd on 130 *Psal:* 61.

5 Came the Earle of *Northampton*, & the famous Painter Mr. Write to visite me: 7: To Lond: about buisinesse, din'd at Mr. *Slingsbys*, return'd:

10 One Mr. *Littler* being now presented to the Living of our Parish, preached on 6. Joh: 55 a sermon preparatory to the H: Sacrament. 17: on 1. *Jo:* 2, concerning regulating our Love to the World.

18 To *Lond*, return'd: 24: our Viccar on 1. *Sam*. 30. 6. shewing in times of Calamity, the Soules comfort was trust in God.

25 A wonderfull & suddaine change in the face of the publique: The new *Protector Richard* slighted, severall pretenders, & parties strive for the Government, all *Anarchy* and confusion; Lord have mercy on us.

May: Our new Viccar preach'd on: 21: Matt: 23. shewing the Causes, & misery of Gods depriving a people of the Gospel.

5 I went to visite my Bro, & next day to see a new *Opera* after the *Italian* way in *Recitative Music* & *Sceanes*, much inferior to the Italian composure & magnificence: but what was prodigious, that in a time of such a publique Consternation, such a Vanity should be kept up or permitted; I being ingag'd with company, could not decently resist the going to see it, though my heart smote me for it: I returnd home:

7 Came the *Ambassador* of *Holland* & Lady to visite me, & staid the whole afternoone:

8 Our Viccar preachd on. 5. *Matt:* 8. of the happinesse of the pure in heart. 12 I returned the Dutch *Ambassadors* visite, discoursing much of the revolutions &c: returnd next day.

15 Our Viccar on 45 Isa: 19. 19 Came to dine with me my Lord *Gallowy* & his son, a Scotch Lord, & learned: Also my Bro: & his Lady: Lord *Berkeley* & his Lady, Mrs. *Sherley*, and the famous Singer Mrs. *Knight*: with other friends.

21 I went to *Lond:* to celebrate Whitsontide: 22 Mr. Gunning preached on 14. Joh: 13. shewing we have by the spirit, *Christ* ascending, that the spirit might descend &c: The Communion follow'd: In the afternoone Mr. *Chamberlaine* on: 20 *Jan:* 21, about the mission of the Apostles, & Successors: 23 I went to Rookwoods & din'd at Sir William Hicks's, where was a greate feast, & much company: 'Tis a melancholy old house invirond with Trees & rooks: returnd the evening: 26: came to see me my Lord *Geo: Berkeley*: 28: Sir *Will: Ducy*, another knight: Sir Jo: *Potts's* son of *Norfolck*:

29 Preached Mr. *Hienchman* on 143 *Psal:* 10. 11. shewing how we should direct our Prayers, submitt our wills &c: & that being in covenant with God, 'twas sufficient argument to move him to heare us: That we should pray the Conduct of the H: *Spirit* in the Church, raise & quicken our devotion, & thereby engage the heavenly power to deliver us from our Calamities: The Nation was now in extreame Confusion & unsetled, betweene the Armies & the Sectaries: & the poore *Church* of *England* breathing as it were her last, so sad a face of things had over-spread us:

June: ⟨5⟩ Preachd at our Church a stranger on. 103 *Psal:* 3. wonderfully celebrating the Mercies & long suffering of God: In the Afternoone. 1. *Thess:* 5, 19. of the danger in quenching the

motions of Gods holy *Spirit*. 7. To *Lond*. to take leave of my Bro:
& to see the foundations now laying for a long Streete, & buildings in *Hatton Garden* design'd for a little Towne: lately an ample
Garden: 12 our Viccar preach'd on 45 *Esay*: 19, his former subject:
23 Came to see us, my Lady *Strangford*, Daughter to the Earle of
Lycester. 26: *Viccar* on 5. Matt: 8. concerning the Vision of God.

July: 1 To *Lond:* return'd the 2d. 3: the *Viccar* on 1. Joh: 5. 20.
concerning the *deity* of *Christ*.

10: On 2. *Tim:* 3. 15. of the dignitie of the Scriptures, & benefit of Learning it in Youth: 17: on 7: *Matt:* 14. of the difficulty of
Salvation, & paucity of true believers: 24: on 3 *Heb:* 7: shewing
the danger of unprofitably living under the meanes:

August 6: To *Lond:* ⟨7⟩: a stranger at Excester-house on 19
Luke. 41, of the miseries that comes on a people for sin: [the
Communion followd:] In the afternoone on 13 *Rom:* 13—I
returned home: 14: our *Viccar* on 1. *Sam:* 30. 6. of our recourse to
God in time of trouble: My sonn *John* was falln very ill of a
feavor, & so continued in greate danger, 'til towards the 21:

September 1 Came Mr. *Rob: Boyle* (son to the Earle of Corke) to
visite me: I communicated to him my proposal to Errect a [Philo-
sophic] *Mathematical College*: &c: 5. Went to *Lambeth* to visite Sir
Robert *Needham*. 8: To *Lond:* to visite Mr. *Boyle* &c: return'd the
10th. 11: our *Viccar* on his former Subject: 15 Came to see me *Mr.
Brereton*, a very Learned Gent: sonn to my Lord *Brereton*, with
his, & divers other Ladys: 18: our *Viccar* as above concerning the
markes of sin pardon'd, & effects of Confession: 20: Came to visite me *Hen: Howard* of Norfolck. [Since *Duke of Norfolck*:]

25 Viccar: on: 1. *Coloss:* 14. of the infinite obliquity of sinn, &
benefit of the bloud of Christ.

26 To *Lond:* to see Lodgings against winter, my sonn being
yet un-recoverd, & now sick of an Ague: return'd the Evening:
30: I went to visite Sir *William Ducie*, & *Coll: Blount*, where I
met Sir *Henry Blount* the famous Travellor, & water-drinker:

October 2: Our *Viccar* preachd on 1. *John*: 5.20. of the veracity
of Christs Godhead, & benefit by it:

8 To *Lond* to the monethly Communion. 9: Mr. *Gunning*
excellently on: 4. *Mark* 3. 4. 5. 6. 7. 8. &c: concerning the Parable
of the Seede: That the seede the Devil sowed was those Heresies
& *Schismes* that sprung up in the Church, whilst the *Bishops* &
Pastors slept: & that therefore it was not necessarie to tell the

precise time when these errores first came in: so long as we certainely know, ther once were none of them, namely before this universal negligence: &c: I receivd the B: *Sacrament*.

THE RESTORATION
(1659–1660)

OCT 10 I CAME WITH my Wife & family to Lond: tooke Lodgings at the 3 feathers in *Russel-streete Covent Garden* for all the *Winter*: 11. Came to Vis⟨it⟩e me Mr. *William Coventrie*, [since *Secretary to the Duke*] son to L: Keeper Coventrie: a wise & witty Gent: The Armie now turn'd out the *Parliament*. 12 I went home, returnd the 15th. 16 Mr. *Gunning* as above: That the reaping was not to be here, but at the end of the World: In the afternoone Mr. *Pierce* Chaplaine to the Count: of *Sunderland*. 5 *Gal*: 24 of the Superiority of the Spiritual part: Man a creature of different Composure from the rest of *Animals*, as both to Soule & body; how the one was to be subject to the other. We had now no Government in the Nation, all in Confusion; no Magistrate either own'd or pretended, but the souldiers & they not agreed: God Almight⟨y⟩ have mercy on, & settle us. 17 I visited Mr. *H Howard* at *Arundel*-house, who gave me a faire *onyx* set in Gold: shew'd me his designe of a Palace there. 18 Mr. *Gunning* preachd on St. *Lukes* day. 21: Was our private Fast kept by the *Church* of *England* Protestants in Towne, to beg of God the removal of his Judgements; with devout Prayers for his mercy to our Calamitous Church: 23: Mr. *Gunning* on 1 Tim: 19. 20, shewing the difference of Consciences, the danger of Excommunication, & Heresie: In the Afternoone Mr. Chamberlaine on 119 Psal: 92. shewing what a comfort in Affliction, Purity, Religion, & delight in God, is: I went afterwards to Mr. *Gunnings* Chamber, where we discoursed concerning severall points &c: 30: He preach'd on his former Text, & then Mr. *Chamberlaine*. 31. I was now 39 yeares of age: blessed be the Lord &c:

November Mr. *Chamb:* on 14. *Apoc:* 13. of the blessednesse of those who die in *Christ*: That since they rest from their Labours, there can be no Purgatorie: 4. I went to *Says-Court*, return'd next day:

5 A stranger—on. 124. *Psal:* 1. 2: of the greate deliverances of Gods Church, That its present sufferings were no marks of his displeasure or dereliction: 6: Mr. *Gunning* also on his former. Concerning Excommunicasion, an historie of its dire effects: In the Afternoone a stranger, on 16. *Matt:* 25. shewing the benefit of taking-up the Crosse: &c:

7 Was published my bold *Apologie* for the *King*, in this time of danger, when it was capital to speake or write in favour of him: It was twice printed, so universaly it tooke: 9: We observ'd our solemn fast, for the Calamitie of our Church: Mr. Gunning preachd on 2. *Phil:* 12. Concerning mans Free-Will, affirmatively:

12 I went to see the severall *Drougs* for the confection of *Treacle*, *Diascordium* & other *Electuaries* which an ingenious *Apothecarie* had not onely prepard, & ranged upon a large & very long table, but coverd every ingredient with a sheete of paper, on which was very lively painted the thing, in miniature very well to the life, were it plant, flower, Animal, or other exotic drough: 13: Mr. *Gunning* preached on: 1. Tim: 1: concerning *Ecclesiastical Censures*: That since we had endeavord to abolish *Episcopacy*, God had abandon'd us to *Heresies*, *Schismes* & dangerous doctrines &c: I receivd the B: Comm: In the afternoone one Mr. *Clarke* a very eloquent man: 14 I went to visite Sir Jo: *Evelyn*. 15 dind with the *Dutch Ambassador*: he did in a manner acknowledge, that their Nation mind onely their profit, do nothing out of Gratitude, but collateraly, as it relates to their gaine, or security: for which reason it was they gave ayde to the K. of Denmark, & that therefore the *English* were to looke for nothing of assistance to the banish'd King: which was to me no very gratefull discourse, though an ingenuous confession. I went home: 18: Mr. *Gunning* celebrated the wonted fast, & preach'd on 2. Phil: 12. 13. That the Spirit of God first ⟨wrought⟩ holy motions, & then mans part was to cooperate, his will being free, & not determin'd irresistably. The same on: 5. *Jam:* 12. of the danger of comon swearing: how the holy *Angels* revere the name of God, prefacing the *Trishagion* before they dare name it &c: In the Afternoone Mr. *Chamberlaine* 13 *Matt* 1 ad 9th. The parable of the Sower: shewing the danger, & prevention of the stony ground, how to cultivate it for fruit:

24 Sir *Jo: Evelyn* invited us to the 41th Wedding-day feast, where was much company of friends:

25 Mr. *Gunning* on his former text, pursuing the doctrine of Mans free Will &c:

26 I was introduc'd into the acquaintance of divers learned & worthy persons, Mr. *Massham*, Mr. *Dugdale*, Mr. *Stanley* &c: 27: Mr. *Gunning* on his other Text, against Swearing: Mr. *Chamberlaine* afternoone on his former subject: shewing the necessity of cleansing the heart, to render it fruitfull:

December 2 Fast, at Mr. *Gunning* on his former subject: Illustrates *Pharoahs* example &c. touching *Gods Election*, Reprobation &c: 4: as before: against swearing: In the Afternoone *Dr. Wild* at the *Temple* on 4: Phil: 5. recommending moderation in all our actions; how *summum jus*, was *injuria* &c: 9: Mr. *Gunning* on 14 Job: from 11. ad. 16. shewing the happy death of the Just &c: I supped with Mr. Gunning (it being our fast-day) Dr. *Fearne*, Mr. *Thriscoe*, Mr. Chamberlaine, Dr. Hienshaw, Dr. *Wild*, & other devout and learned divines, firme Confessors & excellent persons: [most of them *Bishops since*:]

10 I treated privately with Coll: Morley (then Lieutenant of the Tower, & in greate trust & power) concerning delivering it to the King, and the bringing of him in, to the greate hazard of my life; but the Colonel had ben my Schole-fellow & I knew would not betray me: 11 Mr. *Gunning* on 94. *Psal:* 9, shewing the folly of *Atheists* & wicked men. Afternoone a stranger on: 8: *Matt.* 2: Sin the Cause of Sickness:

12 I spent in publique concernes for his Majestie pursuing the point to bring over Coll: Morley, & his Bro: in Law Fay, Governor of Portsmouth &c:

16 Mr. *Gunning* on 8: Jer: 7. 8. 9. 10. The Effects of Repentance, the possibility of willfull falling from Grace &c: 18 preached that famous divine *Dr. Sanderson* [Sinc B: of *Lincoln*] now 80 years old on 20 Jer: 13. concerning the evil of forsaking God: Afternoone Mr. *White* on 2. *Tim:* 2. 19. concerning the Baptismal vowe &c:

23 Mr. *Gunning* at our solem⟨n⟩ fast on 9: *Dan.* 20, The fullfilling of the proph⟨e⟩sy of the *Messias* & effects of humiliation & prayers &c:

25 *Christmas* day, Mr. *Gunning* on 45 Isa: 7.8. of the Mysterie of the Incarnation: The H. *Sacrament* followd: In the Afternoone *Mr. Chamberlaine* on 1. *Jho:* 4. upon the same subject: 26. St. *Stephens* day, Mr. *Gunning* on 20: *Apoc:* 4 touching the

Martyrs that died in the first persecution: A greater Impostor yet to come then had ben.

27—on: 21 *Jo:* 21. 22. 23. concerning the life & sufferings of St. *John* a *Martyr* in intention. 28: on: 31 *Jer:* 15, of the cruelty of *Herod* &c:

29 Came my Lord Count *Arundel* of *Wardoer* to visite me: I went also to visite My Lord *V-count Montague.*

31 Settling my domestic affaires in order, blessed God for his infinite mercies and preservations the past Yeare:

ANNUS MIRABILIS:

1660. *January* 1. Begging Gods blessing for the following Yeare, I went to Excester Chapell, where Mr. *Gunning* began the Yeare on 4: *Gal:* from 3. to 7th, shewing the Love of *Christ* in sheding his bloud so early for us: That Circumcision was in detestation of impurity: Afternoone Mr. *Chamberlaine* on the same Text.

5 Came to Visite & sup with me, my Lord *Howard* of the North, & divers Ladys &c:

8 On 1. *John* 29. shewing how *Christ* was the Lamb of God: The Sacrament followd: which I receivd with my Wife: Afternoone Dr. *Burgh* deane of *Worcester.* 1. *Matt:* ult a sententious discourse, in honour of the *B: Virgin*, & virginitie:

12 I wrot⟨e⟩ to Colonel *Morley* againe to declare for his Majestie: see your book of *Letters.*

22 Dr. Hensman [Since Bishop of *London*] preach'd on 1. Apoc: 9. of Christian meekenesse, by the example of *John.* I went this afternoone to visite Colonel *Morley*, then Lieutennant of the Tower: of Lond. In the Chapell, a young man preach'd, on 7 Eccles: 9: against the passion of Anger very well: After dinner, I discoursd the Colonel, but he was very jealous, & would not believe *Monk* came in to do the King any service. I told him he might do it without him, & have all the honour: he was still doubtfull, & would resolve on nothing yet: so I tooke leave, and [23] went home, to see a sick person at my house at S. Court, & returnd the 26:

Feb: 2 A stranger on 2: *Luke* 22. shewing the history & reason of the purification: Instituted in the time of *Justinian*, in stead of an heathnish Costome to carry Candles, whence its name, though it had other; but the Superstition of blessing these candles came in by *popery*. I went home after Sermon to bury an antient & faithfull servant of my F. in Laws, that was his *Secretary* in *France*, & made me his Executor for what he left:

3 I returnd to Lond, & kept the Fast: Mr. Gunning preaching on 31 Jer: 21. concerning Gods infinite mercy to penitents:

Generall Monke came now to *Lond:* out of *Scotland*, but no man knew what he would do, or declare, yet was he mett on all his way by the Gent: of all the Counties which he pass'd, with petitions that he would recall the old long interrupted Parliament, & settle the Nation in some order, being at this time in a most prodigious Confusion, & under no government, every body expecting what would be next, & what he would do. 5. A stranger made an excellent discourse on 1. *Joh.* 3. 1. concerning the greate Love of God, to Man. In the afternoone M: *Chamberleyne* on 1. *Cor:* 9. 26. of the active, & contending life of a *Christian*. 10: *Mr. Gunn:* on the fast. 31. *Jer:* as before: Now were the Gates of the Citty broken-downe by *Gen: Monke*, which exceedingly exasperated the Citty; the Souldiers marching up and downe as triumphing over it, and all the old Army of the phanatics put out of their posts, & sent out of Towne. 11 I visited Mr. *Boyle*, where I met the *Earle* of *Corke*. A signal day: Monk perceiving how infamous & wretched a pack of knaves would have still usurped the Supreame power, & having intelligence that they intended to take away his commission, repenting of what he had don to the Citty, & where he & his forces quarterd; Marches to White hall, dissipates that nest of robbers, & convenes the old Parliament, the *rump-parliament* (so cal'd as retaining some few rotten members of the other) being dissolved; and for joy wheroff, were many thousands of rumps, roasted publiquely in the Streetes at the Bonfires this night, with ringing of bells, & universal jubilee: this was the first good omen.

12 Mr. *Gunning* made an admirable sermon on the effects of Gods chastisements, & gracious returnes on 94. *Psal:* from v. 8. ad 15. I received the *B: Sacrament*. Afternoone Mr. Chamberlaine on 18. *Ezek ult*. 17: I fell sick, & that very dangerously of a malignant feavor:

From *Feb:* 17th to the 5 of *Aprill* I was detained in Bed, with a kind of double *Tertian*, the cruell effects of the *Spleene* & other distempers, in that extremity, that my *Physitians* Dr. *Wetherborn*, *Needham*, *Claud*, were in greate doubt of my recovery, & in truth I was brought very low; but it pleased God to deliver me also out of this affliction, for which I render him hearty thanks: going to church the 8th & receiving the B: *Eucharist*, Mr. *Gunning* preaching on 20 *Exod:* against the sinn of Swearing:

During this Sicknesse came innumerable of my Relations & friends to visite me, and it retarded my going into the Country longer than I intended: however I writ, and printed a letter in defence of his *Majestie* against a wicked forged paper, pretended to be sent from *Bruxells*, to defame his Majesties person, Virtues, & render him odious, now when every body were in hopes & expectation of the Gen: & Parliaments recalling him, & stablishing the Government on its antient and right basis: In doing which towards the decline of my sicknesse, & setting-up long in my bed, had caused a small relapse, out of which it yet pleased God also to free mee, so as by the 14th I was able to go into the Country, which the *Physitians* advisd me to, which I accordingly did to my Sweete & native aire at *Wotton*. 20: I receivd there the B: Sacrament being good friday, in the house, by reason of my Indisposition, officiating Mr. *Higham* Minister of the Parish. & 22: preaching on 1. *Cor:* 10. 16. preparatory to the Sacrament on *Easter day* &c: also 29: on 18 *Jer:* 9. 10. concerning Gods Judgements against nations and kingdomes, when not prevented by repentance, applicatory to the time. 30. I was able to ride abroad & went often to take the aire.

May. 3 Came the most happy tidings of his *Majesties* gracious *Declaration*, & applications to the Parliament, Generall, & People &c and their dutifull acceptance & acknowledgement, after a most bloudy & unreasonable Rebellion of neere 20 yeares. Praised be forever the Lord of heaven, who onely dost wondrous things, because thy mercys indure forever.

6 The *Minister* preached on his former Text: 8. I returned home to *Says-Court*, my Wife meeting me at *Woodcot* where I dined: This day was his Majestie Proclaimed in London: &c.

9 I was desired & designed to accompany my *Lord Berkeley* with the publique Addresse of the Parliament Gen: &c: & invite him to come over, & assume his Kingly government, he being

now at *Breda*; but being yet so weake & convalescent, I could not make that journey by sea, which was not a little to my detriment &c: so I went to *Lond* to excuse my selfe, returning the 10th, having yet received a gracious message from his *Majestie*, by *Major Scot* & Colonel *Tuke*. 13 our Viccar [Mr. Litler] preached on 4: *Matt:* 10. Shewing the necessity of giving God bodily worship:

14 To *Lond:* lay at my *Lord Gorings* my old acquaintance:

⟨20⟩ Mr. *Gunning* on 20 *Exod* 8: concerning the Lords day. Afternoone Mr. Chamberlaine on 45 *Psal.* 7.

24 Came to me *Colonel Morley* about procuring his pardon, & now too late saw his horrible error & neglect of the Counsel I gave him, by which he had certainly don the greate Work, with the same ease that *Monk* did it. Who was then in *Scotland*, & *Morly* in a post to have don what he pleasd, by which he had made himselfe the greatest person in England next the King: but his jealosie & feare kept him from that blessing, & honor. I addressd him to my L: *Mordaunt*, then in greate favour, for his pardon, which he obtain at the cost of 1000 pounds, as I heard: ô the sottish omission of this gent: What did I not undergo of danger in this negotiation, to have brought him over to his Majesties Interest when it was intirely in his hands: 27: Mr. *Gunning* on 91. *Psal:* 11. 12. 13. of *Guardian Angels*: Afternoone Mr. Chamberlaine on 45 Psal: 7: of the dominion of Christ:

29 This day came in his Majestie *Charles* the 2d to London after a sad, & long Exile, and Calamitous Suffering both of the King & Church: being 17 yeares: This was also his Birthday, and with a Triumph of above 20000 horse & foote, brandishing their swords and shouting with unexpressable joy: The wayes straw'd with flowers, the bells ringing, the streetes hung with Tapissry, fountaines running with wine: The Major, Aldermen, all the Companies in their liver⟨ie⟩s, Chaines of Gold, banners; Lords & nobles, Cloth of Silver, gold & vellvet every body clad in, the windos & balconies all set with Ladys, Trumpets, Musick, & ⟨myriads⟩ of people flocking the streetes & was as far as *Rochester*, so as they were 7 houres in passing the Citty, even from 2 in the afternoone 'til nine at night: I stood in the strand, & beheld it, & blessed God: And all this without one drop of bloud, & by that very army, which rebell'd against him: but it was the Lords doing, *et mirabile in oculis nostris*: for such a Restauration was never seene in the mention of any history,

antient or modern, since the returne of the *Babylonian* Captivity, nor so joyfull a day, & so bright, ever seene in this nation: this hapning when to expect or effect it, was past all humane policy.

31 Mr. *Gunning* preach'd on 24. *Psal*. 7, being Ascention day apposite to the occasion, & to Gods miraculous mercy in *Convertendo*. Also 1 *June* on 1. Eph: 21:

3 On—24. Psal: 7. on the *Ascention*, as before, I received the B: Comm:

4 I received letters of Sir *R: Brownes* landing at *Dov⟨e⟩r*, & also Letters from the *Queene*, which I was to deliver at *Whitehall*, not as yet presenting my selfe to his Majestie by reason of the infinite concourse of people: It was indeed intollerable, as well as unexpressable, the greedinesse of all sorts, men, women & children to see his Majesty & kisse his hands, inso much as he had scarce leasure to Eate for some dayes, coming as they did from all parts of the Nation: And the King on the other side as willing to give them that satisfaction, would have none kept out, but gave free accesse to all sorts of people: Wherefore addressing my selfe to the *Duke*, I was carried to his *Majestie* when he was alone, & very few noble-men with him, & kissed his hands, being very gratiously receivd: which don I return'd home to meet [5] *Sir R: Browne*, who came not 'til the Eight, after a 19 yeares Exile, during which yet, he kept up in his Chapell, the Liturgie & offices of the Church of England, to his no small honour, & in a time, when it was so low & as many thought utterly lost, that in many Controversies both with *Papists* & Sectaries, our divines used to argue for the visibility of the Church from his Chapell & Congregation: I went to *Lond:* this Evening, the 9., when on *Whitsonday* Mr. *Gunning* preached on 59. *Esay* 20. 21. Mr. *Chamberlaine* in Afternoone on 20 Joh: 22: I was all this Weeke too & froo at Court, about buisinesse.

15 Mr. *Gunning*, on 16 Joh: 7. 11. 16 The *French*, *Italian* & *Dutch* Ministers came to make their addresse to his Majestie, one Monsieur *Stoope* pronouncing the *harange* with greate Eloquence. 17 *Trinity* Sonday Mr. *Gunn:* on 16 Jo: 12 ad 15. Afternoone Mr. *Sameis* on 1 Cor: 16: 22.

18 I proposed the Ambassy of *Constantinople* for Mr. *Henshaw*, but my Lord *Winchelsea* struck in: Goods that had ben pillag'd from *White-hall* during the Rebellion, now daily brought in & restor'd upon proclamation: as plate, Hangings, Pictures &c:

20 I saw the Audience of the Duke of Brandenburg: 21 The *Warwick-shire* Gentlemen (as also did all the shires & chiefe Townes in all the three Nations) present their Congratulatory Addresse to his Majestie. This was carried by my L. of *Northampton*. I went home this Evening:

29 St. *Peters* day to Lond: 30 The *Sussex* Gent presented their Addresse to which was my hand; I went with it, & kiss'd his Majesties hand; when his Majestie was pleasd to owne me more particularly, by calling me his old Acquaintance, & speaking very graciously to me:

July. Dr *Gauden* at the *Temple* Church in 16 Act: 24: Afternoone on⟨e⟩ *Heardman* at St. *Clements*, on 49. Gen: 6.

3 I went to *Hide-park* where was his *Majestie* & aboundance of *Gallantrie*:

4 I heard Sir Sam: Tuke harangue to the house of *Lords*, in behalfe of the *Ro: Catholicks*: & his account of the transaction at *Colchester* about the Murdering of my *Lo: Capel*, and the rest of those brave men, that sufferd in cold bloud, after Articles of reddition &c:

5 I saw his Majestie go with as much pompe & splendor as any Earthly prince could do to the greate Citty feast: (The first they invited him to since his returne) but the exceeding raine which fell all that day, much eclips'd its luster: This was at *Guild-hall*, and there was also all the Parliament men, both Lords & Comm: the streetes adorn'd with Pageants &c: at immense cost:

6 His *Majestie* began first to Touch for the Evil according to costome: Thus, his Majestie sitting under his State in the *Banqueting* house: The *Chirurgeons* cause the sick to be brought or led up to the throne, who kneeling, the King strokes their faces or cheekes with both his hands at once: at which instant a *Chaplaine* in his formalities, says, *He put his hands upon them, & he healed them*, this is sayd, to every one in particular: when they have ben all touch'd, they come up againe in the same order, & the other *Chaplaine* kneeling & having Angel gold, strung on white ribbon on his arme, delivers them one by one to his *Majestie*: Who puts them about the neck of the Touched as they passe: whilst the first *Chaplaine* repeates: *That is the true light who came into the World*: Then followes an *Epistle* (as at first a *Gospell*) with the Liturgy prayers for the sick with some alteration: Lastly the blessing, And

then the Lo: *Chamberlaine* & *Comptroller* of the household, bring basin, Ewer & Towell for his Majestie to wash:

The King received a Congratulatory Letter from the Citty of *Collogne* in Germany, where he had ben sometime in his Exile: his Majestie saying they were the best people in the world: the most kind & worthy to him that ever he met: His two Bro: D. of *York* & *Gloucester* din'd With his *Majestie*. I recommended *Monsieur Messeroy* to be *Judge Advocate* in Jersey by the Vice-chamberlaines mediation with the Earle of *St. Albans*, & saluted my excellent & worthy noble friend my Lord *Ossory*, sonn to the *Marquesse* of *Ormond*, after many yeares absence: returnd home:

8 *Mr. Hinchman* on 5: *Ephes:* 15: From hence forth was the *Liturgie* publiquely used in our Churches, whence it ⟨had⟩ ben for so many Yea⟨r⟩es banish'd: 10: Came Sir *Hen: Blount* & Lady to visite us: 12 Came to visite us my Bro: Sir Tho: Spencer, & Lady Gerrard &c:

15 our *Viccar* on 22. *Matt:* 39. exhorting to mutual Charity. 16 Came Sir *Geo: Carterett* & Lady to visite us, he now *Treasurer* of the *Navy:* 17 I was let bloud 7 ounces, being not well: 22: our *Viccar* on 1. *Jam:* 22: 26 Came my L: *Howard*, Mrs. *Sherley* & other Ladys to dine with me, I went in the Evening with them to *Lond:*

28 I heard his *Majesties* Speech in the *Lords* house, passing the bills of *Tunnage* & *poundage*, Restauration of my L. *Ormond* to his Estate in *Ireland*, concerning the Commission of the Sewers, and Continuance of the Excise. In the afternoone I saluted the *Æbish: of Armagh* my old friend, formerly of *London Derry*: he presented severall Irish Divines &c: to his Majestie (This was Dr. *Bramall*): to be promoted *Bishops* in that Kingdome, most of the *Bishops* in all the 3 Kingdome, being now almost worne out, & *Sees* vacant: I went home this Evening: 29 our *Viccar* on 5: *Matt:* 43. 31 I went to visite *Sir Phil: Warwick* now Secretary to the Lord Treasurer at his house in *North-Cray*.

August 5 Our *Viccar* on 5. *Matt.* 44. 8 Came *Lady Puckering* to visite us: 9: To *Lond:* return'd next day:

12 Mr. *Rowland* preached on 19. *Luke* 42. That there was a set time for the returne of Sinners, & magnifying the restauration of the *Church* of *England*. 16 I went to visite my Bro: at *Woodcot*, return'd at night: 19 Our *Viccar* read the 39 *Articles* to the Congregation, (the National Assemblies beginning now to settle, &

wanting Instruction) & preached on 19 *Levit:* 17. 23. Came *Duke Hamilton*, Lord *Lothein* & severall *Scotish* Lords, to see my Garden: 25. Coll: *Specer*, Coll: of a Regiment of horse in our Country of *Kent*, sent to me, & intreated that I would take *Commission* for a *Troope* of *Horse*, & that I would nominate my *Lieutennant* & *Ensigns*: but I thanked him for the honour intended me, & would by no meanes embrace the trouble. 26: our *Viccar* on 28 *Esa:*

Sept 2. *Viccar* on 11. 2. Cor: 26. a preparatory Sermon, the holy Sacrament follow'd: I received. 3 To *Lond:* 4. I was invited to an *Ordination* by the Bish: of *Bangor*, in *Hen:* 7th Chapell: Westminster: & afterwards saw the Audience of an *Envoyeè* from the *D: of Anjou*, sent to complement his Majesties returne: Return'd home: 5: Came to visite and dine with me, The *Envoyeè* of the *King of Poland*, & Resident of the K: of *Denmark* &c:

7 I went to *Chelsey* to visite Mr. *Boyle*, & see his *pneumatic Engine* performe divers Experiments. Thence to *Kensington* to visite Mr. *Henshaw* returning home that Evening:

9 *Viccar* on former *Text*:

13 I saw in *Southwark* at St. *Margarites* faire, a monstrous birth of Twinns, both femals & most perfectly shaped, save that they were joyn'd breast to breast, & incorporated at the *navil*, having their armes throwne about each other thus: It was reported quick in *May* last, & producd neere Turne-style *Holborn*: well exent⟨e⟩rated & preserved till now: We saw also a poore Woman, that had a living Child of one yeare old, who had its head, neck, with part of a Thigh growing out about *Spina dorsi*: The head had the place of *Eyes* & nose, but none perfected. The head monstrous, rather resembling a greate Wenn; & hanging on the buttocks, at side whereoff, & not in the due place, were (as I remembred) the excrements it avoided, we saw also *Monkyes* & Apes daunce, & do other feates of activity on the high-rope, to admiration: They were galantly clad *alamode*, went upright, saluted the Company, bowing, & pulling-off their hatts: They saluted one another with as good grace as if instructed by a Daimcing Master. They turned heales over head, with a bucket of Eggs in it, without breaking any: also with *Candles* (lighted) in their hands, & on their head, without extinguishing them, & with vessells of

water, without spilling a drop: I also saw an *Italian* Wench daunce to admiration, & performe all the Tricks of agility on the high rope, all the Court went to see her: ⟨likewise⟩ here was ⟨her⟩ *Father*, who tooke up a piece of Yron *Canon* of above 400 pounds weight, with the haires of his head onely; So I returnd that Evening. 16 our *Viccar* on 10 *Luke* 42.

17 I went to *Lond:* to see the Splendid *Audience* of the Prince *de Lignis Ambassador* extraord: from *Spaine*, who was accompanied with 17 Coaches 6 horses of his owne, besides a very greate *Corteggio* of *English* &c: greater bravery, in my whole life ⟨had⟩ I ⟨never⟩ seene: He was Gen: of the Span: Kings horse in *Flanders*, accompanied with divers greate persons of *Flanders*, & an innumerable retinue: The King receivd him in the Banqueting house in exceeding state, all the greate Officers of Court &c: attending &c:

13 In the middst of all the joy & jubilie, dies the *Duke of Gloucester* of the Small-pox, which put all the Court in Mourning: died the 13th in prime of youthe, a Prince of extraordinary hopes &c: I return'd home: 20 Came Sir Ro: *Needham* & much other Company to visite us. 23: A stranger preached on 3: *Jer:* Afternoone came to take leave of me Monsieur *D'avison*, the K: of *Polands Envoyè*, going now to *France*, with divers persons of quality.

26 To *Lond:* about affaires: 27. The Merchands Addresses to his Majestie in his Closset: giving them assurance of his persisting to keepe *Jamaica*: Choosing Sir Ed: *Massy Governor*. In the Afternoone was the Danish Ambassadors Condolences presented. And this Evening I saw the *Princesse* Royal Mother to the Pr: of *Orange* now come out of *Holland* in a fatal period: I returnd home: ⟨30⟩ A stranger preach'd on 8 *Rom:* 8.

Octob: 6. I paied the greate *Tax* of Pole-mony, levied for the disbanding of the Army, 'til now kept up; I paid as Esquire 10 pounds & 1s: for every Servant in my house &c:

7 Our *Viccar* on 2. *Cor:* 11. 26: There dind with me this day a *french Count* with Sir S: Tuke, who came to take leave of me, being now sent over to the Queene-Mother to breake[1] the Marriage of the *Duke* with the Daughter of *Chancellor Hide*; which the *Queene* would faine have undon; but it seemes matters were reconcild, upon greate offers of the Chancellor to befriend

---

1 To divulge.

the Queene, who was much indebted, & was now to have the settlement of her affaire go thro his hands:

11 I went to *Lond:* to be sworn a Commissioner of the Sewers; & this day were those barbarous *Regicides*, who sat on the life of our late King, brought to their Tryal in the old baily, by a Commission of *Oyer & terminer*: I return'd at night.

14 Our *Viccar* on 28 *Esay* 1: 17 To *Lond:*

17 This day were executed those murderous Traytors at Charing-Crosse, in sight of the place where they put to death their natural Prince, & in the Presence of the King his sonn, whom they also sought to kill: take⟨n⟩ in the trap they laied for others: The Traytors executed were *Scot, Scroope, Cook, Jones*. I saw not their execution, but met their quarters mangld & cutt & reaking as they were brought from the Gallows in baskets on the hurdle: ô miraculous providence of God; Three days before suffered *Axtel, Carew, Clements, Hacker, Hewson & Peeters* for reward of their Iniquity: I returnd:

18 My Wife receiving a fall from a stoole, miscarried of a fine boy, to our greate trouble: 21. A stranger preachd on 42 *Esay:* 1: Afternoone the *Viccar* on 19 *Psal:* 9: Against some Phanatics, who held we were not to feare, but onely to love & praise God.

28 His Majestie went to meete the *Queene Mother*:

29 Going to Lond: about my affaires, My *Lord Majors* shew stop'd me in cheape-side: one of the Pageants represented a greate Wood, with the royal Oake, & historie of his Majesties miraculous escape at *Bosco-bell* &c:

31 Arived now to my 40th yeare, I rendred to Almighty God my due & hearty thanks:

November I went with some of my Relations to Court, to shew them his Majesties Cabinet and Closset of rarities: The rare miniatures of *Peter Oliver* after *Raphael, Titian* & other masters, which I infinitely esteeme: Also that large piece of the *Dutchesse* of *Lennox* don in Enamaile by *Petito*; & a vast number of *Achates, Onyxes,* & *Intaglios,* especialy a *Medalion* of *Cæsar,* as broad as my hand: likewise rare Cabinetts of *Pietra Commessa*: A Landskip of Needle-worke, formerly presented by the *Dutch* to K Char: I. Here I saw a vast book of Mapps in a Volume of neere 4 yards large: a curious Ship modell, & amongst the Clocks, one, that shewed the rising & setting of the son in the Zodiaque, the Sunn, represented in a face & raies of Gold, upon an azure skie, observing the diurnal & annual motion, rising & setting behind a landscap of hills, very divertisant, the Work of our famous *Fromantel*, & severall other rarities in this royal *Cimelium*.

3 Arived her *Majestie Queene Mother* in to England, whence she had ben now banished almost 20 years; together with her illustrious daughter the Princesse *Henrietta*, divers other Prin⟨c⟩es & noblemen accompanying them. I return'd home.

4 *Viccar* on 34. *Psal:* 9. 11: on the same: 14: To Lond: 15 I kiss'd the *Q: Mothers* hand. 18, preached at the Temple Ch: Dr. *Gauden* on 3: *Phil:* 9: 19 I din'd at my *Lord Mordaunts*. 20 at the Cleark *Comptrollers* of the *Greenecloth*, being the first day of reestablishment of the Court *Diet*, & settling of his Majesties household:

23 Being this day in the *Bed-Chamber* of the *Princesse Henrietta* (where were many great beauties, & noble-men) I saluted divers of my old friends & acquaintance abroad; his *Majestie* carying my Wife to salute the *Queene* & *Prin⟨c⟩esse*, & then led her into his Closet, & with his owne hands shew'd her divers Curiosities.

25 Dr. Rainbow preach'd *coram Rege* on 2. Luk: 14. of the Glory to be given God for all his mercys, especialy for restoring the Church, & government: & now ⟨w⟩as perform'd the service with Musique, Voices &c: as formerly: I returnd in the Evening: 27 came downe the *Cleark Comptroller* (by the Lord *Stewards* appointment) to survey the land at *Says-Court*, on which I had pretence, & to returne his report: 28: The rest of this week I was indisposd: till 5t when I went to *Lond:* 6, din'd at L. *Mordaunts*:

December 6 I waited on my Bro: & sister *Evelyn* to Court: Now were presented to his Majestie those two rare pieces of Drolerie, or rather a Dutch Kitchin, painted by *Douce*, so finely as hardly to be at all distinguished from *Enamail*: I was also shewed divers rich jewells, and Christal Vasas; The rare head of *Jo: Belino*, *Titians* Master, The *Christ* in the Garden by *Hanib: Carraccia*, Two incomparable heads of *Holbein*: The Q: *mother* in a *Miniature* as big as the life: an exquisite piece of Carving, 2 *Unicorns* hornes, &c: This in the *Closset*: 9 Dr. *Gauden* (now made Bish: of *Exon*) preach'd at St. *Greg:* by S: *Paules* on 22: *Matt:* 21. 13 I presented my Son *John* to the *Queene Mother*: who kissed him, talked with, & made extraordinary much of him. 14 I visited my *Lady Chancellor*. 15 We visited, my Lady Marchionesse of *Ormond*, & Countesse of *Guildford*, all whom we had knowne abroad in Exile:

16 Dr. *Pierce* preach'd at S. *Paules* on. 5. *Ephes*. 15. 16. incomparably: Afternoone a stranger at *Westminster* on 12 *Esay:* 3. 18. I carried Mr. *Spellman*, a most ingenious Gent (& Grandchild to the learned *Sir Henry*) to my *L. Mordaunt*, to whom I had recommended him for his *Secretary*:

21 The Marriage of the *Chancellors Daughter* being now newly owned, I went to see her: she being Sir R: *Browne* (my father in laws) intimate acquaintance, when she waited on the Princesse of Orange: She being now at her fathers, at Worcester house in the strand, we all kissed her hand, as did also my Lord *Chamberlaine* (*Manchester*), and Countesse of *Northumberland*: This was a strange change, can it succeed well! I spent the Evening at St. *Jamess* whither the *Princesse Henrietta* was retired during the fatal sicknesse of her Sister the *Princesse* of *Orange*, now come over to salute the King her brother: The Princesse gave my Wife an extraordinary complement, & gracious acceptance, for the *Character* she had presented her the day before, & which was afterwards printed: 22. I went to *Lambeth* to visite my kinds-man Sir *Rob: Needham*: This day died the Princesse of *Orange* of the Small-pox, which wholy alterd the face & gallantry of the whole Court: 23 Dr. *Bull* preached at St. *Greg:* on 5 *Ephes:* 15. 16. I return'd home. A robbery attempted at my house, but God deliverd us:

25 Preached at the Abby, *Dr. Earles*, (clearke of his Majesties Closet, & my deare friend, Deane of Westminster) on 2: *Luke* 13. 14. Condoling the breach made in the publique joy, by the lamented death of the *Princesse*: I receivd the B: Sacrament the *Deane* officiating: The Service was also in the old Cathedrall Musique: In the afternoone preachd a ⟨Chaplaine⟩ of my L. *Chamberlaine* on 7: *Esay:* 14. 27 I returned home; my sonn, not well, & next day to *Lond:* againe. ⟨30⟩ At the *Abby* Dr. *Heywood* on 7: *Esay:* 14. I dined at the *Deanes*, where was a greate Entertainment: Afternoone pre: a Stranger on 1. *Matt*. 22.

30 I dined at Court, with *Mr. Crane* Clerk of the *Greene-Cloth*: 31: I gave God thankes for his many signal mercies to my selfe Church & Nation this wonderfull Yeare:

THE CREATION OF THE ROYAL SOCIETY
(1661–1664)

1661. JAN: 1 After Prayers, & Gods blessing implor'd, I din'd with some friends in *London*.

2 The *Queene-mother* with the *Princesse Henrietta* began her journey to Portsmouth in order to her returne into *France*. 4: I dined at Mr. *Boltons* one of the *Sherifs* of Lond: where we had a Citty feast: 5. I visited my Lord *Chancellor*, with whom I had ben well acquainted abroad: 6: Dr. *Alestree* preached at the *Abby* on 13. *Act:* 3: there succeeded the Consecration of 4 *Bishops Hereford, Norwich*   Afternoone Dr. *Fuller* on 22 *Luke* 24. This night was a bloudy Insurrection of some fift-monarchy *Enthusiasts*, suppressd, & next day examin'd at *Council*; where the wretchedly abused people could say nothing to extenuate their madnesse, & unwarantable zeale:

I was now chosen (& nominated by his Majestie for one of that *Council*) by Suffrage of the rest of the Members, a Fellow of the *Philosophic Society*, now meeting at *Gressham* Coll: where was an assembly of divers learned Gent: It being the first meeting since the returne of his *Majestie* in Lond: but begun some years before at *Oxford*, & interruptedly here in *Lond:* during the Rebellion: This morning was another rising of the *Phanatics* in which some were slaine: his *Majestie* being absent; til the 10th. 12 I returnd home:

16 I went to the *Philosophic* Club: where was examin'd the *Torricellian* experiment: I presented my Circle of *Mechanical* Trades, & had recommended to me the publishing what I had written of *Chalcography*: 17 returned: 20: our *Viccar* preache'd on 5. *Eph:* 1. 23. To Lond, at our *Society*, where was divers Exp: on the *Terrella* sent us by his *Majestie*. 25. After divers yeares, that I had ⟨not⟩ seene any Play, I went to see acted the *Scornfull Lady* at a new *Theater* in *Lincolns-in fields*. 26 returnd home.

27 our *Viccar* on 66. *Esay* 2: 24 Came *Mrs. Sherley* with some other to visite us, & s⟨t⟩ayd some days:

30 Was the first Solemn Fast & day of humiliation to deplore the sinns which so long had provoked God against this Afflicted Church & people: orderd by *Parliament* to be annualy celebrated, to expiate the Gilt of the Execrable Murder of the late *King Char:* I, our *Viccar* preaching on 21. *Deut:* 7. 8. on which he

made a very pious, & proper discourse: This day (ô the stupendious, & inscrutable Judgements of God) were the Carkasses of
that arch-rebell *Cromewell*, *Bradshaw* the Judge who condemn'd
his Majestie & *Ireton*, sonn in law to the Usurper, draged out of
their superbe Tombs (in Westminster among the Kings), to
Tyburne, & hanged on the Gallows there from 9 in the morning
til 6 at night, & then buried under that fatal & ignominious
Monument, in a deepe pitt: Thousands of people (who had
seene them in all their pride & pompous insults) being spectators: looke back at November 22: 1658, & be astonish'd—*And
⟨ fear⟩ God, & honor the King, but meddle not with them who are
given to change.*

   Feb: 3. Our *Viccar* on 2. *Cor:* 5. 15, applied to the B. *Sacrament*,
at which I was participant: Afternoone the *Curate* on 118 *Psal:* 8.

   6 To *Lond*, to our *Society*: where I ⟨gave notice of⟩ [the] visite
of the *Dane Ambassador Extraordinary* & was ordered to returne
him their acceptance of that honour, & to Invite him the next
meeting day: This was the L: *Guildenlow* [son of the 2d wife or
Concubin] a very accomplished Gentleman & General [&
Governor] of the K: of *Denmark* in *Norway*.

   7 I dined at Mr. *Booreman Comptroller* of the *Greene-cloth* at
Court, & afterward went to see my Lord *Hatton*. 8: Dined with
my Lord *Goring*:

   10 Dr. *Baldero* preached at *Ely-house* on 6: *Matt:* 33: After Sermon, The Bishop (which was Dr. *Wren*) gave us the Blessing very
Pontificaly: Afternoone Dr. *Buck* on 19. *Luke*. 17 at St. *Gregories*:

   13 I conducted the Danish *Ambassadour* to our Meeting at
Gressham Coll: where were shew'd him divers Experiments in
Vaccuo, & other Curiosities: &c:

   14 I returned home: 17 Our *Viccar* on 1. *Cor:* 9. 24.

   20 To Lond: about buisinesse: & to our *Meeting*, trying severall Exp: about refining Metalls. 21 *Prince Rupert* first shewed
me how to Grave in *M⟨e⟩zzo Tinto*. 24 Dr. *Johnson* preachd on
43. Psal: 5 *coram Rege*. I dined with my Lord *Chancelor*, with
whom I had buisinesse after dinner, concerning Says-Court: 26:
I went to Visite my Lord *Mordaunt* at *Parsons Greene*, return'd:

   27 Ashwednesd⟨a⟩y, preach'd *coram Rege*: the *Bish:* of *London*,
(*Dr. Sheldon*) on 18 *Matt*. 25, concerning Charity, & forgivenesse:
I returned home:

   March 3. Our *Viccar* on 5. *Matt*. 33:

6 To *Lond:* to our *Society*, whether his *Majestie* had sent a small piece of Glasse made in this forme which though strock with an hamer at the oval end would not breake, but breaking the taile or small part with your hand, & which was not much bigger than ⟨a⟩ small pin, the whole would crumble to dust in your hand: The reason was considerd, but so many objections made, as was hard to solve:

8 I went to my L. *Chancelors* & deliverd him the state of my Concernement at *Says-Court*:

9 I went with that excellent person & Philosopher Sir *Rob: Murray* to visite Mr. *Boyle* at Chelsey, & saw divers effects of the *Eolipile*, for weighing the aire:

10 At St. *Greg:* preache'd one, upon 4. *Matt:* 1. 2: Afternoone at the *Abby* a *Scotch-man* on 15. *Matt.* 21. ad. 29: 11. To our Society: where were experimented divers ways of the rising of water in glasse tubes, above the Super ficies of the stagnant water: either by uniting one part of the water to the other by a kind of natural appetite to joyne its like; or rather by the pressure of the subjacent water by the super stantial aer, to an *æquilibrium* of Cylinder of the *Atmosphere*: &c:

13 I went to *Lambeth* with *Sir R: Brownes* pretence to the Wardenship of *Merton Coll:* in *Oxford*, to which (as having about 40 years before ben student of that house) he was unanimously elected, one fellow onely excepted: now the statutes of that house being so, that unlesse every fellow agree, the election devolves to the *Visitor*, who is the *A: Bish: of Canterbury*, his Grace gave his vote to *Sir T. Clayton* resident there, & the Physick Professor; for which I was not at all displeas'd; because though Sir Rich: miss'd it, by much ingratitude & wrong of the *Arch-Bishop* (Clayton being no fellow) yet it would have hindred Sir Richard from attending at Court, to settle his greater Concernes, & prejudicd me: he being so much inclined to have pass'd his time in a Collegiate life, very unfit for him at that time for many reasons. So I tooke leave of his Grace, who was *Dr. Juxon*, formerly *L: Treasurer* in the reigne of *Charles* I.

This after noone his hig⟨h⟩nesse *Prince Rupert* shewed me with his owne hands the new way of Graving call'd *Mezzo Tinto*, which afterwards I by his permission publish'd in my Historie of *Chalcographie*, which set so many artists on Worke, that they soone arived to that perfection it is since come, emulating the tenderest miniature.

Our *Society* now gave in my *Relation* of the *Pic* of *Tenariffe* in the Greate *Canaries*, to be added to more *quæries*, concerning divers natural things, reported of that Iland: I return'd home with my *Co: Tuke*, now going for *France*, as sent by his *Majestie* to Condole the late death of the greate *Minister* & *Polititian* Card: *Mazarine*.

17 Our Viccar preachd on 23. *Pro:* 16: Afternoone, 5. *Matt.* 34. concerning the Unlawfullnesse of the Rebellious Leage & Covenant, to reforme without the Chiefe Magistrate &c. 18 To *Lond:* 21 at our *Society*, Exp: touching the compression of aire & water, and order given the Curator for Engines: 24. *Dr. Hylin* (Author of the Geography) at the *Abby*, preachd on 5 *Cant*. 25: the Doctor was I think at this time quite darke, & so had ben some yeares before: In the afternoone a stranger, on 12 *Jobe* 21: 25. A prebend at the Abby also on 1. *Luke*. 26. ad 39.

30 I went with L: *Mordaunt* to *Parsons Greene*. 31 Dr. Heywood at the *Abby* on. 9. Heb: a. v. 4. ad. 16.

31 This night his *Majestie* promis'd to make my Wife Lady of the *Jewels* (a very honorable charge) to the future *Queene* &c: [but which he never performd, bribd by the Lady Scroope.]

Aprill: 1 I din'd with that great Mathematicia⟨n⟩ & virtuoso Monsieur *Zulecum*, Inventor of the *Pendule* Clock and *Phænomenon* of *Saturns anulus*; he was also elected into our *Society*: 4. I return'd home:

8. To *Lond:* 11 returnd: 12 Our *Viccar* on 2. *Phil*. 8. 13 I went to *Parsons Greene* to visite Mr. *Rowland* Chap: to my L. *Mordaunt*, now sick to death: 14 our Viccar on 4. *Rom:* 24, I receivd the H. Communion: 19 To *Lond:* about *Says-Court* buisinesse: Saw the *Bathing* & rest of the Ceremonies of the *Knights* of the *Bath* preparatory to the *Coronation*, it was in the Painted Chamber in *Westminster*: I might have received this honour, but declined it: The rest of the ceremony was in the chapell at White-hall where their Swords being laid on the Altar, the *Bishop* deliverd them &c: 21. I heard part onely of a Sermon at *St. Martines*:

22 Was the splendid *Cavalcade* of his Majestie from the Tower of *Lond:* to *White Hall*: Where I also saw the *King* in the *Banqueting house* Create six *Earles*, & as many *Barons* viz: Ed: *L. Hide L. High Chancellor* created Earle of *Clarendon*, supported

by the Earles of *Northumberland* & *Sussex*: The Earle of *Bedford* carried the *Cap* & *Coronet*, E: of *Warwick* the *Sword*: E: of *Newport* the *Mantle*. Next was *Capel* created Earle of *Essex*: *Brudnell Cardigan*: *Valencia Anglesea*, *Greenevill Bath*, *Howard Caerlisle*: The *Barons* were *Denzill Holles*, *Cornwallis*, *Booth*, *Townsend*, *Cooper*, *Crew*, who were all led-up by severall *Peeres*, with *Garter* & Officers of Armes before them, where after Obesience on their severall approches to the Throne, their *Patents* were presented by *Garter* K. at Armes, which being received by the L. *Chamberlaine* & deliver'd his *Majestie* & by him to the Secretary of State, were read, & then againe delivred to his Majestie & by him to the severall Lords Created, then were they robed, their *Coronets* & *Collers* put on by his *Majestie*, then were they placed in rank on both sides the State & Throne: but the *Barons* put of their caps & circles and held them in their hands, The *Earles* keeping on their *Coronets* as *Cousins* to the King:

I spent the rest of the Evening in seeing the severall *Arch Triumphals* built in the streetes at severall Eminent places thro which his Majestie was next day to passe, some of which though tem⟨p⟩orarie, & to stand but one Yeare, were of good Invention & architecture, with Inscriptions:

23 Was the *Coronation* of his *Majesty Charles* the *Second* in the *Abby*-Church of *Westminster* at all which Ceremonie I was present: The *King* & all his *Nobility* went to the *Tower*, I accompanying my *L: Vicount Mordaunt* part of the Way: This was on Sunday: 22: but indeede his *Majestie* went not 'til Early this morning, & proceeded from thence to Westminster in this order: first went the *Duke* of *Yorks* Horse guards, Messengers of the Chamber. 136 Esquires to the *knights* of the *Bath*, each having two: most richly habited: The knight *Harbinger*, Searjeant *Porter*, *Sewers* of the *Chamber*, *Quarter* Waiters, Six-Clearks of *Chancery*, Cler: of the *Signet*, *Cler:* of the *Privy-Seale*, *Clearks* of the *Council*: Cler: of the *Parliament*, Cler: of the *Crowne*: *Chaplaines* in *ordinary* having *dignities* 10: Kings *Advocats* & *Remembrancer*, *Cou⟨n⟩cil* at Law: Masters of the *C⟨h⟩ancery*: *Puisne Serjeants*, Kings *Attourney* & *Soliciter*: Kings *eldest Serjeant*; *Secretaries* of the *French* & *Latine Tongue*: *Gent: Ushers* daily *Waiters*: *Sewers*, *Carvers* & *Cupbearers* in Ordinary, *Esquires* of the *body* 4. Masters of *standing Offices* being no *Councellers viz.* of the *Tents*, *Revells*, *Ceremonies*, *Armorie*,

Wardrob, *Ordnance*, Masters of *Requests*, *Chamberlaine* of the *Exchequer*, Barons of the *Exchequer* & *Judges*: *Lord Ch: Baron*, L.C. Justice of the Common pleas, Master of the *Rolls*, L.C. *Justice* of *England*: *Trumpets*, Gent: of the *Pr: Chamber*, *Knights* of the *Bath* 68 in Crimson robes exceeding rich, & the noblest shew of the whole *Cavalcade* (his Majestie Excepted) Knight *Marishall*: Treasurer of the Chamber, Master of the *Jewells*, Lords of the *Privy Council*: *Comptroller* of his Majesties *Household*: *Treasurer* of the *Household*: *Trumpets*, *Searjeant Trumpeter*: *Pursuivants* at *Armes* 2: *Barons*: 2 *Pursuivants* at *Armes*: *Viscounts*, *Heraulds* 2: *Earles*. L. *Chamb:* of the *Household*. 2 *Heraulds*: *Marqu⟨i⟩ses*, *Dukes*: Her: ⟨*Clarencieux*⟩ and ⟨*Norroy*⟩: Lord *Chancellor*: L.H. Steward of Eng: Two Persons representing the *Dukes* of *Normandy* & *Aquitain* (viz. Sir *R: Fanshaw* & Sir *Herb: Price*) in fantastique habits of that time: *Gent: Ushers*, *Garter*: Lord *Major* of *Lond:* The *Duke* of *York* alone: (the rest by twos) L.H. *Conestable* of *Eng:* L: Gr: *Chamb:* of *England*: The Sword born by the *Earle Marishall* of Eng: Lastly the *KING* in royal Robes, & Equipage: Afterwards followd *Equerries*, *Foote-men*, Gent: *Pensioners*, *Master* of the *horse* leading an horse richly caparisond: *Vice-Chamberlaine*: Cap: of the *Pensioners*: *Cap:* of the *Guard*: The *Guard*, Horse-*Gard*, The *Troope* of *Voluntieres* &c with many other officers, & Gent: This magnificent Traine on horseback, as rich as *Embroidery*, *velvet*, *Cloth* of *Gold* & *Sil:* & Jewells could make them & their pransing horses, proceeded thro the streetes, strew'd with flowers, houses hung with rich *Tapissry*, Windos & *Balconies* full of Ladies, The Lond: Militia lining the ways, & the sevrrall Companies with their Banners & Loud musique ranked in their orders: The Fountaines runing wine, bells ringing, with Speeches made at the severall Triumphal Arches: At that of the Temple Barre (neere which I stood) The *Lord Major* was received by the *Baylife* of *Westminster* who in a Scarlet robe made a Speech: Thence with joyfull acclamations his Majestie passed to *White-hall*: [Bonfires at night] & the next day being *st. Georges* he went by Water to Westminster *Abby*: when his *Majestie* was entered, the *Deane* & *Prebends* brought all the *Regalia*, & deliverd them to severall Noble-men, to beare before the *King*, who met them at the West dore of the *church*, singing an *Antheme*, to the *Quire*: Then came the *Peres* in their *Robes* & *Coronets* &c in their hands, til his Majestie was placed in a Throne elevated before the Altar: Then the Bish: of *Lond* (the *A Bishop* of *Canterbury* being sick) went to every side of the Throne to present the *King* to the *People*, asking if they would have him for their *King*, & do him homage, at which they shouted 4 Times *God Save K. Ch: the 2d*: Then an *Anthem* sung: Then his Majesty attended by 3 *Bishops* went up to the *Altar*, & he offerd a pall, & a pound of Gold: Then sate he downe in another chaire during the sermon, which was preachd by Dr. *Morley* then B: of *Worcester* on   after *Sermon* the K: tooke his *Oath* before the Altar, to ⟨mainetaine⟩ the *Religion*, *Mag: Charta* & Laws of the Land: Then the Hymn *Veni S. Sp.*, then the *Leitany* by 2 Bish. Then the L: AB: of Cant (present but ⟨much⟩ indisposd & weake) said, Lift-up your hearts: Then rose up the *King*, & put off his robes & upper garments; & was in a Wastcoate so opened in divers places as the A: Bishop might commodiously anoint him, first in the palmes of his hands, then was sung an *Anthem* & prayer, Then his breast, & twixt the shoulders, bending of both armes, & lastly on the crowne of the head: with apposite hymns & prayers at each anoynting: Then closed & buttned up the *Wastcoate*, which was don by the *Deane*: Then was a *Coyfe* put on & the *Colobium*, *Syndon* or *Dalmatic*, & over this a *Supertunic* of Cloth of Gold, with *buskins* & *sandals* of the same, *Spurrs*, The *Sword*, a prayer being first saied over it by the *A.Bish.* on the *Altar* before 'twas girt on: by the *L: Chamberlain*: Then the *Armill, Manteles* &c: Then the A: B: placed the *Crowne Imperial* on the *Altar*, prayed over it, & set it on his Majesties Head, at which all the *Peres* put on their *Coronets* &c. Anthems & rare musique playing with *Lutes, Viols, Trumpets, Organs, Voices* &c. Then the A B: put a ring on his *Majesties* finger: Then the K. offered his Sword on the Altar: which being redeemed, was drawn & borne before him: Then the AB: deliverd him the *Scepters* with the Dove in one hand, & the other in the other with the *Mond*: Then the K. kneeling the *A: Bish:* pronounc'd the blessing: Then ascending againe his Regal *Throne* & *Te Deum* singing all the *Peeres* did their *Homage* by every one touching his Crowne: The *ArchBish* & rest of the Bish: first kissing the King: Then he received the *H: Sacrament*, & so disrobed, yet with the Crowne Imperial on his head, accompanied with all the nobility in the former order, he went on foote upon blew cloth, which was spread & reachd from the West dore of the *Abby*, to *Westminster Stayres* where he tooke Water in a Triumphal barge to *White-hall*. where was extraordinary feasting:

24 I presented his Majestie with his *Panegyric* in the Privy Chamber, which he was pleasd most graciously to accept: &c. also to the L. *Chancelor* & most of the noble men who came to me for it, & dined at the *Marq:* of *Ormonds* now made *Duke*, where was a magnificent feast, & many greate persons:

25 I went to the *Society* where were divers Experiments in Mr. *Boyls Pneumatique* Engine. We put in a *Snake* but could not kill it, by exhausting the aire, onely made it extreamly sick, but the chick died of Convulsions out right, in a short space:

28 A sermon at *White-hall* but his voice so low, I could heare nothing: I dined with Sir G. *Lane*, secretary to the D: of *Ormond* whom I had known long in *France*.

May 1 I went to *Hide Park* to take the aire, where was his *Majestie* & an inumerable appearance of Gallantry & rich Coaches &c: it being now a time of universal festivity & joy: &c:

2 I had audience of my L. *Chancellor* about my Title to *Says-Court*:

3 I went to see the wonderfull Engine for weaving silk-stockings, said to have ben the Invention of an *Oxford* Scholler 40 years since: return'd by *Fromantel* the famous Clock maker to see some *Pendules*: Monsieur *Zulichum* being with us: This evening I was with my L: *Brouncker*, Sir Rob: *Morray*, Sir *Pa: Neill*, Monsieur de ⟨*Zulicum*⟩ & Mr. Ball (all of them of our *Society*, & excellent Mathematicians) to shew his *Majestie* (who was also present) *Saturns Ansatus* as some thought, but as *Zulicum* affirmd with his *Balteus* (as that learned Gent: had published), very neere *eclipsed* by the *Moone*, neere the *Mons Porphyritis*: Also *Jupiter* & *Satelites* through the greate *Telescope* of his Majesties, drawing 35 foote: on which were divers discourses:

4 I returned home to my house: 6: To *Lond* &c:

8 His *Majestie* rod in state, with his Imperial Crowne on, & all the Peeres in their robes in greate pomp to the *Parliament*, now newly chosen (the old one disolv'd) & that evening declard in *Council* his intention to marry the *Infanta* of *Portugal*:

9 At Sir *Rob: Morrays* I met Dr. *Wallis* professor of Geomet. in Oxon: where was discourse of severall *Mathematical* subjects:

11 My *Wife* present⟨e⟩d his *Majestie* the *Madona* she copied in Miniatur after P: *Olivers* painting after Raphael, which she wrought with extraordinary paines & Judgment. The K. was infinitely pleas'd with it, & caus'd it to be placed in his Cabinet amongst his best Limmings:

12 Dr. *Phil: King* preached at the *Abby* on 16. Jo: 7: Afternoone Dr. *Hill* of *Christ-Chur* ⟨c⟩ *h* Oxon:

13 I heard, & saw such Exercises at the Election of *Scholars* at *Westminster Schoole*, to be sent to the Universitie, both in *Lat: Gr:* & *Heb: Arabic* &c in Theames & extemporary Verses, as wonderfully astonish'd me, in such young striplings, with that readinesse, & witt, some of them not above 12 or 13 years of age: & pitty it is, that what they attaine here so ripely, they either not retaine, or improve more considerably, when they come to be men: though many of them do: & no lesse is to be blamed their odd pronouncing of *Latine*, so that out of *England* no nation were able to understand or endure it: The Examinants or Posers were Dr. *Duport Greek* professor at *Cambridge*: Dr. *Fell*: Deane of Christchu⟨rc⟩h, Oxon: Dr. *Pierson*, Dr. *Alestree, Deane* of *Westminster* & any that would:

14 His *Majestie* was pleased to discourse with me concerning severall particulars relating to our *Society*, & the *Planet Saturne* &c: as he sat at Supper in the withdrawing roome to his Bed-Chamber.

15 We made sevverall experiments on *Vipers*, & their biting of *Dogs* & *Catts*, to make tryall of a stone presented us from the *E: Indias* a pretended cure: 16. I dined at Mr. *Garmus* the Resident of *Hamburg*, who continud his feast neere 9 whole hours, according to the Custome of his Country; though no greate excesse of drinking, no man being obligd:

19 A *Scotch Doctor* at Westminster on 16: *Joh:* 33.

22 Was the *Scotch-Covenant* burnt by the common hangman in divers places of Lond: ô prodigious change! This after ⟨noone⟩ at our *Society* were severall discourses concerning poisons. Sir *Jo Finch* told us of an exquisite poyson of the D: of Florences that kill'd with a drop: That drawing a threit & needle dipt in it thro a hens thigh it perish'd immediatly, but if an hot needle were thrust after it, it cured the wound. This was tried also on a dog, successfully: That any thing thus killed, the limb affected being suddainly cut off the rest eate most delicately and

tender, without any detriment to the Eater: Hereupon *Dr. Charleton* affirm'd that having killed a Linnet with *Nux Vomica* suddainly: a *Sea-Gull* eating that bird died also immediately, & some other animal that prey'd on that *Gull* the Venume in force after the third Concoction: I return'd home this Evening: 26 Our *Viccar* on 7: Mat: 21.

29 This was the first *Anniversary* appointd by *Act* of *Parliament* to be observ'd as a day of gen: Thanksgiving for the miraculous Restauration of his *Majestie*: our *Viccar* preaching on 118 *Psal:* 24. Requiring us to be Thankfull & rejoice, as indeede we had Cause:

June 2 A stranger on 2 *Cor:* 5. 14. 15: I received the B: *Sacrament*. Afternoone a young man on 8 *Pro:* 14. 4. Came Sir Ch: *Harbord* his *Majesties Surveior* to give an accompt, of what grounds I challengd at *Says-Court*. 5 To *Lond:* went to our *Society*, where was admitted the Duke of Bouckingham: 7: I dined at Sir Hen: *Newtons*: 8 returnd home: 9: our Viccar on 2. Jo: 5. 7. learnedly. 12. Went to *Lond:* dined at *Parsons Greene*: 13 visited my Bro: *Evelyn*:

16 Preachd *Dr. Wood coram Rege* on 30. Esay: 23. concerning Gods Mercy to the Church: &c:

19 Discourses at our Society about poysons againe. We gave *Nux Vom:* to birds that killed them out-right, afterwa⟨r⟩ds, because some writers affirmed Sublimate was its *conterpoyson*, we tried it on other birds, but it succeded not:

23 Preached on⟨e⟩ *May* at St. *Margarits* on 6. *Luke:* 24: Afternoone a stranger in the Abby on 4. *Matt:* 1: returnd home, to see *Jack*, now falln sick of the *Measles*: 24. Came to visite us Sir H. *Newton*, & Sir T. *Holt* with divers Ladys &c: 25. To *Lond:* 26: we tried more *Vipers* & poysond arrows to dogs &c: but they succeeded not: 27. I saw the *Portugal Ambassador*, at dinner with his *Majestie* in state: where was excellent Musique. 30: Dr. *Wollsal* preachd in the *Abby* on 14 *Joh:* 27: I dined at my *Bro: Evelyns* & heard a Sermon read:

July: 2 I went to see, the new Spring-Garden at *Lambeth* a pretty contriv'd *plantation*: 5: We continued many Experiments about compressing of Water: &c. 6 I returnd home. 7: *Viccar* on 1. *Cor:* 10. 3. 4: I receivd this day: Afternoone the *Curate* on 26: *Matt:* 39.

11 I went to *Epsom* to visite my Bro: Rich: 14: My Lord *Berkeley* invited me to dinner to *Durdens* the Sweete *Villa*: 17 I went to

Lond. at our Assembly: we put a *Viper* & *slow-worme* ⟨or⟩ *Aspic*
to bite a *Mouse*, but could not irritate them to fasten at all: Mr.
Boyle brought 2 polishd Marbles 3 inch diameter: which first
well rubb'd, then with a drop of *oyle olive*, which was afterwards
cleane wiped off, the stones claped together stuck close, even so
close, that the nether stone having a hook insert⟨e⟩d, & the
uppe⟨r⟩ a ring, tooke up 42 pound weight, by the power of contiguity, before they separated: The oyle was added to fill up any
possible porositie in the polishd Marbles: 19 We tried our *Diving* bell, or *Engine* in the Water Dock at *Deptford*, in which our
Curator contin⟨ue⟩d halfe an houre under water: It was made of
Cast lead: let downe with a strong Cable: 21 *Viccar* on 3. *Coloss:* 4:
I din'd with the *Vice-Chamberlaine*.

22 My *Wife* went to the Waters at *Tunbridge* for her health: 24
I went to *Lond:* about buisinesse, return'd in the Evening: our
Viccar on 3: *Coloss:* 4: There was a *Camel* shewen in our Towne,
newly bro⟨u⟩ght from the *Levant*, which I saw, as I had others.
31. To our Society, where a bladder blowne up onely raised a
weight of 24 pound; it was at first flaxid & welted on purpose, &
the weight hanged at its bottome, then the wind conveyd thro a
pipe that had a valve &c:

August 3 Came my *L: Hatton Comptroller* of his Majesties
Household to visite me: 4 our *Viccar* on 1. *Cor:* 3. 4: I receivd: In
the Afternoone on 1. *Sam.* 3. 18:

7 Repeating the Experiment of the bladder was raisd 142
pounds & my Laquay, who was an heavy looby of 17 years old
&c: A pouder of a plant was brought, which thrown into the fire
⟨flashed⟩ like Gun-powder: 8. I visited my L: *Mordaunt*:

15 I went to *Tunbridge* wells, to visite my Wife, who was there
drinking the Waters. 17 Walking about the solitudes ⟨not⟩ far
from our Lodging, I greately admired at the extravagant turn-
ings, insinuations, & growth of sertaine birch trees among the
rocks: 18 the Curate of *Speld-herst* preached on 12: *Rom:* 1. who
made so weake a discourse, as I was griev'd to find that so ignorant a man should undertake the Cure of Soules, or be placed
where so many people of quality frequent it, at the season of taking those medicinal Waters: This afternoone as I was at church
and Dr. *Burgh* going into the Pulpet, I was called out, one of my
horses having struck my Coach-man so as he remain'd as dead
for a while; I caus'd him to be let bloud, & laying a *Cere-cloth* to

his brest (much brused) & so after a weeke he recovered: 22 I
returned:

September 13 To *Lond:* 14. I presented my *Fumifugium* dedicated to his Majestie who was pleased I should publish it by his
special Command; being much pleasd with it:

15 I went to Ludgate Church *St. Martins*, where a *Doctor*
preachd on: 3. *Coloss:* 3: Afternoone St. *Gregories* by S. *Paules*—
on 16 Luke: 25: 16. I returned: Dr. *Wren* & Dr. Needham came to
visite & dine with me: 18: To *Lond:* This day was our *Petition*
to his Majestie for his royal Graunt authorizing our *Society* to
meete as a Corporation &c: with severall privileges, was read:
An Experiment of flame in flame was tried: I went home:

22 Our *Viccar* on 26. *Matt:* 39: An exceeding sickly wet
Autumne after a very wet summer:

October 1 I sailed this morning with his *Majestie* ⟨on⟩ one of
his Yaachts (or Pleasure boates) Vessells newly known amongst
us, til the *Dut*⟨*c*⟩*h* [E. India Comp.] presented that curious piece
to the King, & very excellent sailing Vessels. It was on a Wager
betweene his other new *Pleasure boate*, built fregate-like, & one
of the *Duke* of *Yorks*, the wager 100 pounds. The race from
Greenewich to *Gravesend* & back: The King lost it going, wind
Contrary, but sav'd stakes returning: There were divers noble
Person⟨s⟩ & Lords on board: his Majestie sometimes steering
himselfe: There attended his *Barge* & Kitchin boate: I brake fast
this morning with the king, at returne in his smaller Vessell, he
being pleasd to take me & onely foure more who were Noble-
men with him: but dined in his *Yacht*, where we all Eate together
with his *Majestie*. In this passage his *Majestie* was pleasd to discourse to me about my Book inveing against the nuisance of the
Smoke of Lond: & proposing expedients how by removing
those particulars I mention'd, it might be reformd; Commanding me to prepare a Bill, against the next session of Parliament;
being (as he said) resolved to have something don in it: Then he
discoursd to me of the improvement of Gardens & buildings
(now very rare in England, comparatively to other Countries)
and then commanded me to draw-up the *Matter* of *fact* happning at the bloudy Encounter which then had newly happn'd
betweene the *French* & *Spanish Ambassador* neere the *Tower*, at
the reception of the *Sweds* Ambassador contending for pre-
cedency; giving me order to consult Sir *William Compton* (Master

of the Ordnance) to informe me what he knew of it; & with his
favorite Sir *Char: Berkeley* [after: Earle of *Falmoth*:] (Cap: of the
Dukes life-guard) then present with his Troope, & 3 foote
Companies; with some other reflections and Instructions; to be
prepard for a Declaration to take off the reports which went
about of his Majesties partiality in this affaire, & of his Officers
&c: Spectators rudenesse whilst the conflict lasted: So I came
home that night: & went [2] next morning to *Lond*, where from
the Officers of the *Towre*, Sir *William Compton*, Sir *Ch: Berkeley*
and others, who were attending at this Meeting of the Ambassadors 3 dayes before, having collected what I could; I drew up a
narrative in vindication of his Majestie & carriage of his officers,
& standersby &c: on Thursday, his Majestie sent one of the
Pages of the *Backstayrs* for me, to waite on him with my papers,
in his Cabinet, where was present onely Sir *Henry Bennet* (privy
purse) [since Secretary of State & E. of *Arlington* & Lord
Chamb:] when I read to his Majestie what I had drawn up: by
the time I had read halfe a page, came in Mr. *Secretary Morice*
with a large paper, desiring to speake with his *Majestie* who told
him that he was now very buisy, & therefore order'd him to
come againe some other time: The Secretary replyd, what he
had in his hand was of extraordinary importance: So the King
rose up, & commanding me to stay, went aside to a Corner of
the roome with the *Secretary*: after a while, the Secretary dis-
patchd, his Majestie returning to me at the Table, a letter was
brought him from *Madame* out of *France*, this he read, & then
bid me proceede where I left off, which I did 'til I had ended
all the narrative, to his majesties greate satisfaction, and after
I had inserted one or 2 more *Clauses*, in which his *Majestie*
instructed me, commanded that it should that night be sent to
the post-house, directed to the Lord Ambassador at *Paris*,
which was the Earle of St. *Albans*: and then at leasure to prepare
him a Copy, which he would publish: This I did, & immediately
sent my papers to the *Secretary* of *State*; with his *Majesties*
expresse command of dispatching them that night for France:
Before I went out of his *Majesties* Closet, he cal'd me back, to
shew me some *Ivorie Statues*, and other Curiosities that I had
not seene before: 3: Next day Evening, being in the withdrawing
roome next the *Bed-chamber*, his Majestie espying me came to
me from a greate crowde of noblemen standing neere the fire, &

asked me if I had don: told me, he fear'd it might be a little to sharp (on second thoughts) for he had that morning spoken with the *French Ambassador* who it seemes had palliated the matter, & was very tame; & therefore directed me where I should soften a period or two, before it were publish'd &c [(as afterward it was)]. This night also spake to me to give him a sight of what was sent, and to bring it to him in his *Bed Chamber*, which I did, & received it againe from him at dinner next day: By *Saturday* having finish'd it with all his Majesties notes, the King being gon abroad, I sent the papers to Sir *Hen: Bennet* (*privy-Purse*, & a greate favorite) and slip'd home, being my selfe much indisposs'd & harrass'd, with going about, & sitting up to write, &c:

6 Our *Viccar* preachd on 3. *John*: 3. 13: our pious *Viccar* being taken away by death, the *Curate* preachd on 3. *Cant:* ult. 19 I went to *Lond:* to visite my *Lord of Bristoll*, having before ben that day with Sir *Jo: Denham* (his Majesties *Surveyor*) to consult with him about the placing of his Palace at *Greenewich*; which I would have had built betweene the *River* & the *Queenes* house, so as a large Square Cutt, should have let in the *Thames* like a Baye &c: but Sir Jo: was for seting it on Piles at the very brink of the water, which I did not assent to, & so I came away, knowing Sir *John* to be a better *Poet* than *Architect*, though he had Mr. Webb (*Inigo Jone's* Man) to assist him:

20 Dr. *Killegrew* preached at the Abby on. 4: *Ephes:* 25: 21 I din'd at *Arundel* house: next day went home: 26: To *Lond:* where now was my *Wife*.

27 Preachd Dr. *Alestree* at Court on 73. *Psal*: 1: 29 I saw the *Lord Major* passe in his Water Triumph to *Westminster* being the first solemnity of this nature after 20 yeares: 30. Taking our *Society* in the way (who were upon Examination of universal disolvants) I returnd home:

31 I was this day ⟨41⟩ years of age: for which I render thanks to Almighty God, & implore his favour for the yeare to come.

November 2 Came Sir *Henry Bennet* [sinc L. Arlington] to visite me, and to acquaint me that his Majestie would do me the honor to come himselfe & see my Garden; but it then being late, 'twas deferrd &c:

20 To *Lond:* the discourse was about a *Vernish* that should resist all Weathers, & preserve yron from rust; but fire would not

dry it, nor boyling water fetch it off: Sir *William Petty* produced his excellent discourse of the Manufacture of *Wollen-Cloth*, & proposd divers things concerning the improving of shipping, & a versatile keele that should be on Hinges: also concerning sheathing ships with a thin lead: 24. *Coram Rege* Dr. *Rainebow* on 14 *Psal*. 1. This night his Majestie fell into discourse with me Concerning *Bees* &c: 26: I saw *Hamlet* Pr: of Denmark played: but now the old playe began to disgust this refined age; since his Majestie being so long abroad: 27. I din'd at *Arundell* house: 28: I din'd at Thom: *Chiffings* house warming in St. Jam: Park, he was his Majesties *Closet-keeper* & had his new house full of good pictures &c: there dined with us *Russell* popish *Bishop* of *Cabo Verde*, who was sent over to negociate his Majesties match with the *Infanta* of *Portugal*, after the Ambassador was returned: 29 I dined at the *Countesse* of *Peterborows* and went that evening to *Parsons greene* with my Lord *Mordaunt*, with whom I staied that night.

December 1. Preached at *Fullham* the Minister on 21. *Matt:* 5: This evening I went back to *Lond*, with my Lord to take leave of my L: *Peterborow* going now to *Tangier*, that was to be deliv⟨ere⟩d to the English on our Match with Portugal: &c:

3 By universal suffrage of our Philosophic Assembly, an order was made, & registred, that I should receive their Publique Thanks for the honorable mention I made of them by the name of *Royal Society*, in my Epistle Dedicatory to the Lord Chancellor, before my Traduction of *Naudeus*: Too greate an honour for a trifle:

4 I had much discourse with his highnesse the *Duke* of *York* concerning strang Cures. He affirmed that a Woman who swallow'd a whole Eare of Barly, had it worke out at her side. I told him of the knife swallow'd, & the pinns: &c: I tooke leave of the Bish: of Cap-*Verde* now going in the fleete to bring over our new *Queene*: 7: I din'd at *Arundell* house, the day when the greate contest in *Parliament* was concerning the restoring the *Duke* of *Norfolck*; however 'twas carried for him. I also now presented my little trifle of *Sumptuary Laws* intitld *Tyrannus*: 9 I went home, & next to *Lond* againe: 14: I saw *Otter hunting* with his Majestie & killed one:

31 Setting my domestique affaires in order, & beging a blessing for the future Yeare I ended the present.

1662 *Jan:* 1. After Prayers I went to *Lond:* invited to the solemn foolerie of the *Prince de la Grange* at *Lincolne Inn*: where came also the King, Duke &c: beginning with a grand Masque and a formal Pleading, before the mock-princes ⟨Grandees⟩, Nobles & knights of the *Sunn*: He had his L. Chancelor, Chamberlaine, Treasurer, & other royal officers gloriously clad & attended, which ended in a magnificent Banquet: one Mr. *Lort*, being the young spark, who maintaind the Pageantrie:

⟨5⟩ In the *Abby* preach'd a stranger on: 10: *Deut:* 12:

6 *Epiphanie* on⟨e⟩ Dr. Lamb (a prebend) on 1. *Matt:* 1: I din'd at the Comptrollers. This evening (according to costome) his Majestie opned the Revells of that night, by throwing the Dice himselfe, in the Privy Chamber, where was a table set on purpose, & lost his 100 pounds: the yeare before he won 150 pounds: The Ladys also plaied very deepe: I came away when the Duke of *Ormond* had won about 1000 pounds & left them still at passage, Cards &c: at other Tables, both there and at the *Groome-porters*, observing the wiccked folly vanity & monstrous excesse of Passion amongst some loosers, & sorry I am that such a wretched Custome as play to that excesse should be countenanc'd in a Court, which ought to be an example of Virtue to the rest of the kingdome.

9 I saw acted the ⟨2⟩d part of the Seige of *Rhodes*: In this acted the faire & famous Comœdian call'd *Roxalana* for that part she acted, & I think it was the last; then taken to be the E. of *Oxfords* Misse (as at this time they began to call lew'd women) it was in *Recitativa* Musique.

10 Being call'd into his Majesties Closet, when Mr. Cooper (the rare limmer) was crayoning of his face & head, to make the stamps by, for the new *mill'd* mony, now contriving, I had the honour to hold the Candle whilst it was doing; choosing to do this at night & by candle light, for the better finding out the shadows; during which his Majestie was pleasd to discourse with me about severall things relating to Painting & Graving &c:

11 I dined this day at *Arundell*-house, where I heard excellent Musique, perform'd by the ablest Masters both French & Eng, on *Theorba*, *Viols*, *Organs* & Voices as an Exercise against the comming of the *Queene*, as purposly composd for her chapell &c: After which my *Lord Aubignie* (her Majesties Almoner to

be) shewed us his elegant Lodging; & his wheele-chaire for Ease & motion, with divers other Curiosities, especialy a kind of artificial Glasse or *Purcelan* adorn'd with relievo's of Past, hard & beautifull: My *L: Aubigny*, bro: to the Duke of Lenox, was a person of good sence, but wholy abandon'd to Ease & effeminacy &c. I received of Sir *Peter Ball* (the Queenes Attourney) a draught of an Act, against the nuisance of the Smoke of Lond, to be reformed by removing severall Trades, which are the cause of it, & indanger the heal⟨t⟩h of the K: & his people &c: which was to have ben offered to the Parliament, as his Majesty commanded:

12 Dr. *Killegrew* preached in the *Abby* on: 4: *Matt.* 7. afternoone at St. *James's* Chapell preached or rather harrangued the famous Orator *Monsieur Morus* (on   *all things operate for the best to those who love God*, &c.) in *French*: At which was present the *King, Duke, French Ambassador*, L. *Aubignie, Earle of Bristol* & a world of *Roman Catholics*, drawne thither to heare the eloquent Protestant.

15 Was Indicted a generall *Fast* through the whole Nation, & now celebrated at *Lond:* to avert *Gods* heavy judgment on this *Land*, there having falln so greate raine without any frost or seasonable cold: & not onely in England, but in *Sweden* & the most northern parts; it being here neere as warme as at *Midsomer* some yeares: The wind also against our *Fleete* which lay at greate expenses, for a gale to carry it to Portugal for the new *Queene*; and also to Land the *Guarnison* we were sending with the *Earle* of *Peterborow* at *Tangier*, now to be put into our hands, as part of the Q: portion: This solemn Fast was held for the *House of Commons*, at St. *Margarites*: Dr. *Reeves* (deane of *Windsore*) preaching on 7. *Joss:* 12. shewing how the neglect of exacting Justice on offenders (by which he insinuated such of the old *Kings* murderers, as ⟨were⟩ yet reprievd, & in the Tower) was a maine cause of Gods punishing a Land &c: he brought in that of the Gibeonites, as well as Achan & others, concluding with an *Elogie* of the *Parliament*, for their Loyaltie in restoring the *Bishops* & *Cleargie* & vindicating the Church from *Sacrilege*; Afternoone in the same place, Dr. *Bolton* an eloquent man, on: 2. *Titus.* 11. 12. shewing how our living contrary to that holinesse & righteousnesse recommended in the *Text*: was the occasion of all our publique Calamities, & present judgement: The effect of this fast

appeard, in an immediate change of wind, & season: so as our Fleete set-saile this very afternoone, having laine wind-bound a moneth &c:

16 Having notice of his R: *Highnesse* the *Duke* of *Yorks* intention to visite my poore habitation and Garden this day, I returned; where he was pleasd to do me that honour of his owne accord: and to stay some time viewing such things as I had to entertaine his curiosity; after which he caused me to dine with him at the *Treasurer* of the *Navys* house, & to sit with him coverd at the same table: There were with his Highnesse The *Duke* of *Ormond* & severall Lords: Then they viewed some of my Ground, about a project of a *Sasse* or receptacle for ships to be moored in; which was laied aside, as a fancy of Sir *Nic: Crisp* &c: After this I accompanied the *Duke* to an *East India* vessel that lay at *Black-Wall*, where we had Entertain⟨me⟩nt of several curiosities: among other spiritous drinks, as *Punch* &c, they gave us *Canarie* that had ben carried to, & brought back from the *Indies*, which was indeede incomparably good: So I returned to *Lond*, with his *highnesse*. This night was acted before his Majestie the *Widow*, a lewd play:

18 I came home to be private a little, not at all affecting the life & hurry of Court. 22: To Lond: at our *Society* divers tryals about the declination of the Needle; & discourses concerning the reduction of *time* and *Measures* to a certaine standard, as by *Vibration* of *Pendules* & other proportions.

24 His Majestie entertaind me with his intentions of building his *Palace* of *Greenewich* & quite demolishing the old; on which occasion I declard him my thoughts. 25. I dined with the *Trinity Company* at their house, that Corporation being by Charter fixed at Deptford: 26. At the *Abby* preachd Dr. *Goade* on: 4. *Deut:* 7. I din'd at my L: *Chancelors*: & 28. returned home, & the morrow to Lond: againe, where on 29: at our *Society*, we received the Ambassador of *Genöa*, & Dr. *Wren* produced his ingenious *Thermometer*. 30. Preached on the *Anniversary* of the old *Kings Martyrdome* at St. *Margarites* before the *Commons* Dr.   on   In the *valy* of *Hadadrimmon was greate Mourning*: apposite to the season & occasion: Afternoone Dr. *Alsop* on: 5: *Matt:* 11. 12. in an excellent discourse, so as making it appeare, that his Enemies had indeede made our *Royal Martyr*, the most glorious King in the World:

Feb: 2. *Candlemas* day, preachd at S. *Margarits* the Minister of the Parish on 5. Joh. 4: In the Afternoone, a stranger on: 53. *Esay:* 4: 3. I went to *Chelsey* to see Sir *Arthyr Gorges* house: 5 our *Society* prosecuted former Experiments. 6 I went to *Parsons greene* to visite my La: *Vicountesse Mordaunt.* 9: Preachd at St. Mar: the Parson, on his former Text. Afternoone, on 5. *Joh:* 40. a young man at the Abby-Church: 11: I saw a Comedy acted before the *Dutchesse* of *York* at the Cock-pit: The *king* was not at it: 16: at St. *Marg:* a stranger on 13. *Heb:* 16: Afternoone a stranger on 1. *Cor:* 7. 24, concerning abiding in our calling, applied to holding to the disciplin of the Church & Liturgie as we found it reformed: 17 I went with my *Lord* of *Bristol* to see his house at *Wimbledon* (newly bought of *Queene Mother*) to help contrive the Garden after the moderne. It is a delicious place for Prospect, & the thicketts, but the soile cold & weeping clay: returned that evening with Sir *Hen: Bennet.*

17 This night was buried in *Westminster* the *Queene of Bohemia* (after all her sorrows & afflictions being come to die in her Nephews armes the King) & this night, & the next day fell such a storme of Haile, Thunder & lightning, as never was seene the like in any mans memorie; especialy the tempest of Wind, being South-west, which subverted besids huge trees, many houses, innumerable Chimnies, among other that of my parlor at *Says Court,* & made such havoc at land & sea, as severall perish'd on both: Divers lamentable fires were also kindled at this time: so exceedingly was Gods hand against this ungratefull, vicious Nation, & Court. 19. at our Assembly, discourses of Vegetation without Earth, for which I was ordered to prepare some experiments: It was there affirmed of an *English* Lady, who sweate so excessively, that a quart of water, might at any time be taken out of the Palmes of her hands, not smelling ill, & proportionably from the rest of her body: Also of a little Woman at *Rome* who pissed about 200 weight of Water every 24. hours and dranke nothing, upon which were divers discourses & conjectures of the resolution of aire.

20 I returned home to repair my miserably shatt⟨er⟩ed house by the late Tempest: 16: *Jan:* 23 our new *Viccar* Mr. *Breton,* preached on 15. Rom: 29:

May 7 I waited on *Prince Rupert* to our Assembly, where were tried severall experiments in *Mr. Boyles* Vaccuum: a man thrusting

in his arme, upon exhaustion of the ayre had his flesh immediatly swelled, so as the bloud was neere breaking the vaines, &
unsufferable: he drawing it out, we found it all speckled: I
returned next day:

11 Our *Viccars* Curate, on 16: *Mal:* 26: 12. To *Lond*, about
buisinesse with Sir *N: Crispe*. 13 Returned: 14 To *Lond*, being
chosen one of the *Commissioners* about reforming the buildings,
wayes, streetes, & incumbrances, & regulating the Hackny-
Coaches in the Citty of Lond: taking my Oath before my Lord
Chancelor, & then went to his Majesties Surveyors Office in
Scotland Yard, about naming & establishing officers, adjourning
til: 16: when I went to view, how St. *Martines Lane* might be
made more passable into the strand. There were divers Gent: of
quality in this Commission: [17] I returnd:

20 Came *Dr. Earles* Deane of Westminster & *Cleark* of his
Majesties *Closet* to dine with me:

25 Our *Curate* on 1. John: 5. 7: Afternoone, on 1. Cor: 12. 9. I
went this Evening to *Lond*. in order to our journey to *Hampton-
Court* to see the new *Queene*, being now landed at *Portsmouth*, &
married to the *King* a weeke before by the *Bishop* of *Lond:* 27: I
came to H: Court: lodged with my Wife in the house at the
Vice-Chamberlains appartment: by whom we were most civily
treated all our stay:

30 The *Queene* arived, with a traine of Portugueze Ladys in
their mo⟨n⟩strous fardingals or *Guard-Infantas*: Their complex-
ions *olivaster*, & sufficiently unagreable: *Her majestie* in the same
habit, her foretop long & turned aside very strangely: She was
yet of the handsomest Countenance of all the rest, & tho low of
stature pretily shaped, languishing & excellent Eyes, her teeth
wronging her mouth by stiking a little too far out: for the rest
sweete & lovely enough: This day was solemnly kept the
Anniversary of his Majesties Birth, & restauration: Dr. *Alestree*
preaching in the Chapell:

31 I saw the *Queene* at dinner: The *Judges* came to Complement her arival, and after them the *Duke* of *Ormond* brought me
to kisse her Majesties hand:

June: 1 Dr. *Carleton* preached: 2: The L: *Mayor* & Aldermen
made their Addresses, presenting her 1000 pounds in Gold:
Now saw I her Portuguesse Ladys, & the *Guarda Damas* or
mother of her maides; & the old knight, a lock of whose haire

quite covered the rest of his bald-pate, bound on by a threit, very oddly:

I had newes sent me from home, that a *Swarme* of my *Bees* tooke flight, & hived them selves betweene a Cabine in his Majesties ship, the Oxford fregat; which telling the King of he tooke for a good omen; desiring me that none should disturb them.

I saw the rich *Gudola* sent his Majestie from the state of *Venice*, but it was not comparable for swiftnesse to our common wherries, though managed by Venetians: &c: 4. Went to visite the Earle of *Bristol* at *Wimbledon*. 8: Dr. *Wood* preachd: I saw her Majestie at supper privately in her Bed-chamber. 9 I heard the Q: Portugals Musique, consisting of *Pipes*, *harps* & very ill voices.

Hampton Court is as noble & uniforme a Pile & as Capacious as any *Gotique* Architecture can have made it: There is incomparable furniture in it, espe⟨c⟩ialy hangings design'd by *Raphael* & very richly with gold: also many rare Pictures, especialy the *Cæsarian* Triumphs of *Andr: Mantegna*: formerly the Duke of *Mantuas*; & of the *Tapissrys* the story of *Abraham*, & Tobit: than which I believe the whole world shews nothing nobler of that kind: The Gallery of Hornes is very particular for the vast beames of staggs &c: *Elks, Antelops* &c: The *Queenes* bed was an Embrodery of silver on Crimson Velvet, & cost 8000 pounds, being a present made by the states of *Holland*, when his Majestie returned, & had ben formerly given by them to our Kings sister, the Princesse of *Orange*, & being bought of her againe, now presented to the King: The greate looking-Glasse & Toilet of beaten & massive Gold was given by the Q: Mother &c: The *Queene* brought over with her from Portugal, such *Indian Cabinets* and large trunks of Laccar, as had never before ben seene here: The Greate hall is a most magnificent roome: The Chapell roofe incomparably fretted & gilt: I was also curious to visite the Wardrobe, & Tents, & other furniture of State: The *Park* formerly a flat, naked piece of Ground, now planted with sweete rows of *lime-trees*, and the Canale for water now neere perfected: also the hare park: In the Garden is a rich & noble fountaine, of Syrens & statues &c: cast in Copper by *Fanelli*, but no plenty of Water: The Cradle Walk of horne-beame in the Garden, is for the perplexed twining of the Trees, very observable &c: Another

Parterr there is which they call *Paradise* in which a pretty banqueting house, set over a Cave or Cellar; all these Gardens
might be exceedingly improved, as being too narrow for such a
Palace: 10: I returned to Lond: &: presented my *Historie* of
Chalcographie[1] (dedicated to Mr. *Boyle*) to our *Society*: where was
shewed a Bird of *Paradise* or *Manucodiata* that had both large
wings and feete, confuting the vulgar error: Also two *death-
Watches* as those *Insects* are cald, which were nothing but small
betels as big as flesh flies, that get into old timber, and make that
noise which frights the Superstitious: also a Moth of 4 Wings
beamed & featherd, like the wings of a white dove: Also 2 puppies, no bigger than the top of ons fingers, perfectly shaped both
within & without: which were preserved in Spirit of Wine: Also
the Model of a perpetual motion, where a Circular motion carried another body in straite lines: & a new model of a ship: some
discourse about refining Gold &c: 12 I returned: my *Lady
Cartaret*, wife to the *Vice-Chamberlaine* and *Treasurer* of the
Navy, dined with me: 15 our *Viccar* on. 16. Matt. 26: 19. I went to
Albury in *Surrey*, to visite Mr. *Henry Howard* [since *Duke* of
Norfolk], soone after he had procured the *Dukedome* to be
restored &c: This Gent: had now compounded a debt of neere
200000 pounds, contracted by his Grandfath(e)r: I was much
obliged to that greate *virtuoso* and to this young Gent: so as I
staied a fortnight with him. ⟨22.⟩ Preachd at *Albury* a *Prebend* of
Paules on 4: *Amos* 12. 28 I went to visite my *Bro:* at *Wotton*, dined
with Sir *Adam Browne*. 29: preachd the Minister of *Albury* on 5.
Eph: 14. *July.* 2: We hunted and killed a *Buck* in the Park, Mr.
Howard inviting most of the Gent: of the Country neere him.
3. The 3d my Wife meeting me at *Woodcot*, whither Mr. *Howard*
accompanied me, to see my sonn *John*, who had ben much
brought up amongst Mr. *Howards* Children at *Arundel* house, 'til
for feare of their perverting him, in the popish religion, I was
forc'd to take him home; where I came late at night: 6: Our *Viccar* preachd on 16: *John* 8. 9. 10. 11: 8: To *Lond:* about my *Says-
Court* affaire; having ben in the morning to take leave of the L:
Duke and *Dutchesse* of *Ormond*, going then into *Ireland* with an
extraordinary retinue: 9: was given in to the *Society* the historie
of making *Pitch* & *Tarr* &c: 11. I returnd, & received at dinner

---

1 *Sculptura: or the history, and art of chalcography and engraving in copper.*

Mr. *Vice-chamberlaine*, his *Lady*, & *daughters*. 13 our Viccar preachd on 16. *Joh:* 9: To *Lond:* to speake with my L. *Chancelor*, where I had discourse with my Lord *Willogby* Governor of *Barbados*, concerning divers Particulars of that *Colonie*: I went to the *Heraulds* office, and then over to *Lambeth*, to see a new vessel building there by some of our Society:

16 I went to my Lord *Tresurers*, din'd at Mr. *Poveys*, where dined the Earle of *Peterborow* newly arived from *Tangier* &c: 17 I sate Commissioner about the highwayes & streetes of Lond, returnd in the Evening: 20: our *Viccar* on his former Text. v. 10: 23: To *Lond:* our *Society*, Mr. *Boyle* in the Chaire, divers discourses on the *Torricellian* experiment: returnd: 24. Dined divers Neighbours at my house: 26 I went to Visite Sir *Phil: Warwick* Secretary to my L: of *Southampton* Lord *high Treasurer*: 27: our *Minister* on his former text: 28: His Majestie going to sea to meete *Queene-mother* (now coming againe for England), met with such ill weather, as greately indangerd him. I went to *Greenewich* to waite on the *Queene* now landed. 30: To *Lond:* at our Society, where was a meting about *Charitable Uses*, & particular to enquire how the Citty had dispos'd of the revenues of *Gressham Colledge*; & why the *Salaries* of the Professors there was no better improv'd: I was of this *Commission*, & so were divers *Bishops* & Lords of the *Council*, but little was the progresse we could make. 31. I sate with the Commissioners about reforming the buildings & streetes of *London*, & we ordered the Paving of the Way from st. *James's* north, which was a quagmire, & also of the *Hay-market* about *Piqudillo*, and agreed upon Instructions to be printed & published for the better-keeping the Streetes cleane: so returnd home:

August 1. *Mr. H: Howard*, his Bros charles, Edward, Bernard, Philip the priest (& now the Queenes Almoner) [Since *Cardinall at Rome*] (all Brothers of the *Duke* of *Norfolck* still kept in Italy, as not Compos) came with a greate traine & dined with me; leaving with me his Eldest & younger son, Henry and Thomas for three or foure daies, my son *John* having ben some time bred up in their fathers house: 2: Came my L. VC. *Mordaunt* to visite us, & his Lady: 3: our Viccar preached on 1. *Cor:* 11. 26. I received the B: *Sacrament*. 4. Came to see me, the old Countesse of *Devonshire*, with that worthy & excellent pirson my *Lord* her Sonn, from *Rowhampton*: 5. To *Lond:* and [6] next day to *Hampton-Court* about my purchasse: & tooke leave of Sir R: *Fanshaw* now going *Ambassador* into *Portugal*: I dined with Mr. *Pinkney* Clearke of the Kitchin, and return'd this Evening, & next day home. 10: our *Viccar* on 1. Pet: 2. 5; taking occasion to perstring the audacious usurpation of the ministerial function by the *Sectaries*. 13 To *Lond*. Our *Charter* being now passed under the *Broad-Seale*, constituting us a Corporation under the Name of the *Royal-Society*, for the Improvement of naturall knowledge by Experiment: to Consist of a President, Council, Fellows, Secretaries, Curators, Operators, Printer, Graver & other officers, with power to make laws, purchasse land, have a peculiar Seale & other immunities & privileges &c: as at large appears in our Graunt, was this day read, & was all that was don this afternoone, it being very large:

14 This After-noone her Majestie *Queene-Mother* (with the Earle of St. *Albans*, & many greate Ladys & persons) was pleased to honour my poore *Villa* with her presence, & to accept of a Collation, being exceedingly pleased, & staying 'till very late in the Evening: [15] The day following Came also my Lord Chancellor Earle of Clarendon (& Lady) his purse, & Mace borne before him, to Visite me, who likewise Collation'd with us, & was very merry: They had all ben our old acquaintances in Exile, during the Rebellion; & indeede this greate person was ever my friend &c: his sonn, my L: *Corneberry* was here too:

17 Being the *Sonday* when the Common-prayer-booke reformed, was ordered to be used for the future, was appointed to be read: & the *Solemn League & Covenant* to be abjured by all the Incumbents of England, under penalties of loosing their Livings &c: our *Viccar*, accordingly read it this morning, and then preachd an excellent Sermon on 1. *Pet:* 2. 13. pressing the necessity of obedience to *Christian Magistrates*, & especialy *Kings*: There were strong Guards in the Citty this day, apprehending some Tumult, many of the *Presbyterian* Ministers, not conforming:

I din'd at Mr. *V. Chamberlaines*, & then went to see the Q: Mother, who was pleased to give me many thanks for the Entertainement she receiv'd at my house, after which she recounted to me many observable stories of the Sagacity of some Dogs that she had formerly had.

20: To *Lond:* I was this day admitted, & then Sworne one of the present Council of the Royal Society, being nominated in his Majesties Original Graunt, to be of this first *Council*, for the regulation of ⟨the⟩ Society, & making of such Laws & statutes as were conducible to its establishment & progresse: for which we now set a part every *Wednesday* morning, 'till they were all fin-ished: My Lord *Vicount Brounchar* (that excellent *Mathematitian* &c) being also, by his *Majestie*, our Founders, nomination, our first ⟨*President*⟩: The *King* being likewise pleas'd to give us the armes of England, to beare in a *Canton*, in our *Armes*, & send us a Mace of Silver guilt of the same fashion & bignesse with those carried before his Majestie to be borne before our President on Meeting-daies &c: which was brought us by Sir *Gilbert Talbot*, Master of his Majesties *Jewelhouse*.

22d. I dind with my L. *Brounchar* our President, & Sir *Rob: Morray*, & then went to consult about the new modeld-ship at *Lambeth*, the intention being to reduce that art to as certaine a Method as any other part of *Architecture*:

23 I this day was spectator of the most magnificent Triumph that certainly ever floted on the *Thames*, considering the in-numerable number of boates & Vessels, dressd and adornd with all imaginab⟨l⟩e Pomp: but above all, the Thrones, Arches, Pageants & other representations, stately barges of the Lord Major, & Companies, with vari⟨o⟩us Inventions, musique, & Peales of Ordnance both from the vessels & shore, going to meete & Conduct the new Queene from *Hampton Court* to White-hall, at the first time of her Coming to Towne, ⟨far⟩ exceeding in my opinion, all the *Venetian Bucentoro's* &c on the *Ascension* when they go to Espouse the *Adriatic*: his *Majestie* & the Queene, came in an antique-shaped open Vessell, covered with a State or Canopy of Cloth of Gold, made in forme of a Cupola, supported with high Corinthian Pillars, wreathd with flowers, festoones & Gyrlands: I was in our new-built Vessell, sailing amongst them.

29. The *Council* & Fellows of the R: Society, went in Body to White hall, to accknowledge his Majesties royal grace, in granting our Charter, & vouchsafing to be himselfe our Founder: when our President, my L: *Brounchar* made an eloquent Speech, to which his Majestie gave a gracious reply, & then we all kissed his hand: [30] Next day, we went in like manner with our addresse to my Lord *High-Chancelor*, who had much promoted our Patent &c: who received us with extraordinary favour: In the

Evening I went to Queene-Mothers Court & had much discourse with her Majestie & so returnd home late.

September 3 At our *Society* were experiments of the weight
of ☿: There was presented for the Repository a piece of *Elephants*
skin, which was about inch-thick. 4. Commission for Charitable
Uses, my L. *Mayor* & Aldermen being againe summond, & the
improvements of Sir T. *Gressham* examin'd: There was present
the L. *Bish:* of *Lond:* L. C. *Justice*, & Kings *Attourney*: I went
home: 6. Dind with me Sir *Edw: Walker Garter* King at *Armes*,
Mr. *Slingsby* Master of the *Mint* & severall others:

10 To *Lond:* to our Councel, where we passed divers Statutes:
Afternoone were examind some tryals, & a discourse concerning *Echos* was read. 11. I sat in Commission about the Streetes
&c: and return'd that Evening: 14: Mr. LLoyd [since *Bish:* of
Peterborow] now our *Curate* preached on 1. *Cor:* 1. 10. 17 I went to
our Councel to passe severall other statutes: We had now
resolved upon the Armes of the Society: that it should be a field
Argent, with a Canton of the armes imperial of England: the
Supporters two Talbots, argent: The Crest an Eagle or, holding
a Shield with the like armes of England, viz: 3. Lions: The
Word, *Nullius in Verba*, which was presented to his Majestie for
approbation, & orders Given to Garter K. at Armes to passe the
Diploma of their office for it. I returned home:

20 To Lond: I presented a Petition to his Majestie about my
owne concerne: & afterwards accompanied his Majestie to
Monsieur Febure his *Chymist* (& who had formerly ben my Master in *Paris*) to see his accurate preparation for the composing of
Sir *Walter Raleighs* rare *Cordial*, he making a learned discourse
before his Majestie in French on each Ingredient: I went home
to dinner: 21. our Doctor on 16. Acts. 30. 31: I received the B:
Sacrament. 24. To *Lond:* to waite on L. *Chancelor*: & returned,
having also this morning met in Council at the *R. Society*.

27 Came to visite me Sir George Savell [since Marques of
Hallifax], grandsonn to the Learned Sir Hen: Savell, who publishd St. *Chrysostome*: Sir Geo: was a witty Gent, if not a little
to⟨o⟩ prompt, & daring: 28 our *Curate* on: 1. *Cor:* 16: 22. Afternoone 4. *Phil.* 11.

October 1 To Lond: There were *Vipers* brought to the Society,
Mr. *Boyle* produced 2 cleare liquors, which being mingled
became a hard stone: There was also brought the *Hippomanes* or

Mare-poyson: I returned home: 3. To *Lond.* invited to the *Colledge* of *Physitians*, where Dr. *Meret* a learned man, and Library-keeper shewed me the Library, Theater for *Anatomies*, & divers natural Curiosities, especialy the *Devil* Fish (as he call'd it) which being very strong, had when taken nothing in its head save sheere water, & no other braine: There were also divers *skelletons*: I much admired the thigh bone of an *Ostridge*: The Statue & epigraph under it of that renouned *Physitian* Dr. *Harvey*, inventor of the *Circulation* of blood: There I saw Dr. *Gilberts*, Sir Will: *Paddys*, & other famous mens Pictures in their faculty. Thence went to visite one *Mr. Wright* a *Scots-man*, who having lived long at *Rome* was esteemed a good Painter. The Pictures of the *Judges* in Guild-hall are of his hand, & so are some pieces in White hall, as the roofe in his Majesties old Bed-chamber, being *Astrea*, the St. *Catharine*, a Chimney piece in the *Queenes* Privy Chamber: but his best in my opinion is *Lacy* the famous *Rossius* or Comedian, whom he has painted in three dresses, a Gallant, a Presbyterian Minister, and a *Scots* high-lander in his plod: It is in his Majesties *Dining* roome at *Windsor*: yet ⟨was⟩ this man no good painter; but had at his house an excellent collection, especialy that small piece of *Correggio*, *Scotus* of *de la Marca*, a Designe of *Paulo*, & above all those ruines of *Polydore*, with some good *Achates* & *Medaills*, especialy a *Scipio*, & a *Cæsars* head of Gold: I return'd this Evening: 5. our Doctor on 16: *Acts*: 31. 6. Came *Monsieur Herauld* the Minister of the *French* Church in *Lond:* a learned old man, & sonne to the greate *Desiderius Heraldus*, to visite me: ⟨12⟩, a stranger preached on 3 *Malachy* 14. Afternoone our *Curate* on 2. *Pet.* 2. 9. 10: 14. To *Lond:*

15 I this day delivered my Discourse concerning *Forest-trees* to our *Society* upon occasion of certaine *Queries* sent us by the Commissioners of his Majesties *Navy*: being the first Booke that was Printed by Order of the Society, & their Printer, since it was a Corporation:

16 I saw *Vulpone* acted at *Court* before their Majesties &c: 17: I visited my L. *Mordaunt.* 18. returned.

19 our *Doctor* on: 11: *Matt:* 28. 20 To Lond: 21. To Q: Mothers Court: where her Majestie related to us divers Passages of her Escapes during the Rebellion & Warre in *England*: I dined at Court: 22d I went to my L. *Tressurers*, & then to our *Society*,

where Dr. *Charleton* brought in his discourse of *Birds*, relating to the names of such, as being mention'd in divers Authors, were reduced to known birds, for the rectifying the defects in most *Dictionaries*: Also the jaw of a *Pike*, wherein 'twas observed that every-other tooth was moveable upon a *Muscle*, the rest fix't: Dr. *Whistler* shewed, that the wormes breeding in Timber, were the very same with mites in *cheese*, onely much leaner; which produced a discourse concerning æquivocal generations, and some experiments ordered to be made about it. Next day I went home.

26 A stranger preached on 4. *Esay.* 6. 28: To *Lond:* & that evening at Court, where Q: *Mother*, his *Majestie* & Q: *Consort* being advertis'd of some disturbances forbore to go to the *L: Majors* shew & feast, appoint:⟨e⟩:d next day: the new *Queene* having never yet seene that Triumph: 29 Was my L. *Majors* shew with a number of sumptuous pageantry, speeches & Verses: I was standing in an house in *Cheape side*, against the place prepared for their *Majesties*. The *Prince* & *heire* of *Denmark* [after: *King* of *Denmark*] was there, but not our King: There were also the *Maids* of honor: I went to Court this Evening and had much discourse with Dr. *Basiers* one of his *Majesties Chaplains* the greate *Travellor*, who shewed me the *Syngraphs* & original subscription of divers Eastern *Patriarchs* & *Asian* Churches to our Confession &⟨c⟩: I returnd the next day: 31 I was now 42 years of Age: blessed be God:

November 1 Rendring God thanks for his protection the yeare past, I went to Church wher our Doctor preachd on 34. *Psal:* 3: Being one of the *Fefees* for the poores stock, I went to the meeting. 2: our Doctor preach'd on his former subject: 11. *Matt:* 28: I receivd the B: *Communion*.

4 I was invited to the Wedding of Sir Geo: *Carteret* the *Tressurer* of the *Navy*, & *Kings* Vice-*Chamberlains* Daughter married to Sir Nich: *Slaning* knight of the *Bath*, married by the Bish. of London in the *Savoy* chapell, after which was an extraordinary feast &c: 5. The Council for the R: So: met to make an end of the statute, & dined together: afterward meeting at *Gressham Coll:* there was discourse suggested by me, about planting his Majesties *Forest* of *Deane* with *Oake* now so much exhausted of the choicest ship-timber in the World: 6. din'd with my L: *Treasurer*: 6: went to my L: *Chancelor* who set his hand to my report, concerning ⟨my⟩ Interest in *Sayes-Court*. 7: gave my

petition to Sir H: *Bennet* now *Secretary* of State: dined with his Majesties *Carvers*, had some discourse with his R: Highnesse. 8. Invited by my Lord *Haully* to dine at his Quarters in *Southwark* in my way home: 9: Curate preachd on: 2. Pet: 2. 9: 11. Came to dine with me The two Sonns of Mr. *Howard* of Norfolck, heires to the *Duke*: 16: a stranger on: 14: Joh: 3.

27 I went to *Lond:* to see the Enterance of the *Russian Ambassador*, whom his Majestie ordered should be received with much state, the *Emperor* his Master having not onely ben kind to his Majestie in his distresse, but banishing all Commerce with our Nation during the Rebellion: & first then the Citty Companies & Traind bands were all in their stations, his Majesties *Army* & Guards in greate order: his Excellency came in a very rich Coach, with some of his chiefe attendants; many of the rest on horse back, which being clad in their Vests, after the Eastern manner, rich furrs, Caps, & carrying the present, rendred a very exotic and magnificent shew: Some carrying Haukes, furrs, Teeth, Bows, &c:

28 I dined at Mrs. Howards at Court: 30 St. *Andrews* day, invited by the Deane of *Westminster* to his Consecration dinner & ceremonie, now made *Bishop* of *Worcester*: Dr. Bolton preaching in the *Abby Church* on 4: *Eph:* 11, in an excellent discourse of the various Guifts in the Church of *Christ*, & of their use: then followd the Consecration by the *Bishops* of *London*, *Chichester*, *Winchester*, *Salisbery* &c: after this to one of the most plentifull & magnificent dinners, that in my life I ever saw; it cost neere 600 pounds, as I was assurd: & here were the Judges, Nobility, Clearg⟨i⟩e & Gent: innumerable this *Bishop* being universaly beloved for his gentle & sweete disposition: he was the Author of those *Characters* which go under the name of *Blount*: he translated his late Majesties *Ichon* into Latine, was Clearke of his Closet, Chaplaine, Deane of Westminster, & yet a most humble, meeke, but cherefull man, an excellent Schol⟨a⟩r & rare preacher; I had the honour to be loved by him, he marrying me at Paris, during his Majestie & the Churches Exile: when I tooke leave of him he brought me to the cloysters in his Episcopal habite: I then went to Evening prayer to White hall, where I passd that Evening:

December 1. Having seene the strange, and wonderfull dexterity of the sliders on the new Canall in St. *James's* park, perform'd

by divers Gent: & others with *Scheets*, after the manner of the
Hollanders, with what pernicitie & swiftnesse they passe, how
sudainly the⟨y⟩ stop in full carriere upon the Ice, before their
Majesties: I went home by Water but not without exceeding dif-
ficultie, the *Thames* being frozen, greate flakes of yce incompassing our boate: 7: Our *Doctor* now made one of his *Majesties
Chaplaines*, preachd on his former *Text*: 11: *Matt:* 28: 14 The
Curate on 2: Cor: 5. 17. 17 To *Lond:* to our Society: 18 I saw acted
the *Law against Lovers; coram rege.* 21: ⟨one⟩ of his Majesties
Chaplains preachd: after which, instead of the antient grave and
solemn wind musique accompanying the *Organ* was introduced
a Consort of 24 Violins betweene every pause, after the *French*
fantastical light way, better suiting a Tavern or Play-house than
a Church: This was the first time of change, & now we no more
heard the *Cornet*, which gave life to the organ, that instrument
quite left off in which the English were so skilfull: I dined at Mr.
Poveys, where I talked with *Cromer* a greate *Musitian.* 23, I went
with Sir *S: Tuke* to heare the Comedians con, & repeate his new
Comedy, the *Adventures of 5 houres*: a play whose plot was taken
out of the famous *Spanish Poet Calderon.* 24. Visited the Bish: of
Worcester & went home:

25 our *Curate* on 4: *Phil:* 4:

26 Some of my Parish Neighbours dined with us. 27. I visited
Sir *Theoph: Biddulph.* &c.

29 To *Lond:* Saw the Audience of the *Moscovy Ambassador*,
which was with extraordinary State: for his retinue being
numerous, all clad in vests of several Colours, & with buskins
after the *Eastern* manner: Their Caps of *furr*, & *Tunicks* richly
embrodr⟨e⟩d with gold & pearle, made a glorious shew: The
King being sate under the Canopie in the banqueting house,
before the *Ambassador* went in a grave march the Secretary of
the Embassy, holding up his Masters letters of Credence in a
crimson-taffaty scarfe before his forehead: The Ambassador
then deliverd it, with a profound reverence to the King, the King
to our Secretary of State; it was written in a long & lofty style:
Then came in the present borne by 165 of his retinue, consisting
⟨of⟩ Mantles & other large pieces lined with Sable, Black fox,
Ermine, Persian Carpets, the ground cloth of Gold and Velvet,
Sea-morce teeth aboundance, *Haukes*, such as they sayd never
came the like; Horses, said to be *Persian*, Bowes & Arrows &c:

which borne by so long a traine rendred it very extraordinary:
Wind musick playing all the while in the Galleries above: This
finish'd & the Ambassador conveyed by the Master of Ceremonies to York house, he was treated with a banquet, that cost
200 pounds, as I was assured: &c: I returned home.

30 Some of my neighbours dined with me, amongst which
was that most ingenious Gent: Mr. *Tindal* Secretary to the
Bishop of *London.* 31 Setting my domestique affaires in order, I
gave God thanks for his goodnesse to me the past yeare:

1663. January 1 our *Doctor* preached on 1. Malac: 21: I now
humbly begd Gods blessing for the following yeare: The last
having ben so very Wett, but both fruitfull & healthfull:

20 A *Commiteè* of some of our *Society* to consider of the
improvements of Fruit-trees in the Nation: [21] another Experi-
ment for diving: 23. Dind at Mr. Treasurers of the houshold Sir
Ch: *Berkeleys* where were the *Earle* of *Oxford*, Lord *Belasis*, L.
Gerard, Sir Adr: *Scroope*, Sir William *Coventry*, Dr. *Frasier*, Mr.
Windham &c:

24 I went home. 25 A stranger on 1. *Cor:* 4. 7. Afternoone, on
2. *Thess:* 1. 7. 8. 27 Come Mr. Howard &c to dine with me: 30 A
stranger preached on the Ks *Martyrdom* on: 18 *Ezek.* 30. no ruine
to the true penitent.

Feb: 1 Our Doctor on his former Text: 11: *Matt:* 29: The
Communion followd: 4: To *Lond.* an Experiment concerning
the velocity of motion. 5. I saw the Wild Gallant, a Comedy; at
the greate ball at Court, where his Majestie, Queene &c
daunced: 6. I dined at my L. *Majors* Sir Jo: *Robinson* Lieutennant of the Tower: returnd home. 8. our *Curate* on 24. *Act:* 16:
Pomeridiano 2. Cor: 13. 11. 12 I tooke possession in his *Majesties*
name of a certaine place cald the slauter-house in Deptford by
Commission directed from his Majesties Surveyor Generall: 15
our Doctor preached on 11: Mat: 29. as formerly: This night
some villans brake into my house & study below & robb'd me to
the Value of 60 pounds in plate, mony & goods.

18 To *Lond:* when I brought his *Majestie* a Copy of what
pass'd at *Tower-hill* at the reception of the *Sweeds* Ambassador,
to assert the reasons why for the future his Majestie would have
that Ceremonie of the Coaches of foraine Ministers to be of the
Introducers: 19. Din'd with Sir P: *Warwick.* 20 at *Arundel* house
Mr. *Howard* being newly come out of *France.* 21. Din'd at my L.

Chamberlaines to the *Queene* with whom I had buisinesse: 22: Dr.——preachd on 119. *Psal:* 96. I din'd at the K's carvers table, & had discourse with his *Majestie*: 23. Came home:

Mar: 1 Our Doctor on 3. Coloss: 5. preparatory to the *Lenten* fast: I received the B: Sacrament: 8. A. young stranger on: 3 *Col:* 2: *Pomerid:* 2. Cant: 16.

10 To *Lond.* 11. Dr. *Alestree* on   *Ezek:*   *why will ye die ô house of Israel, coram rege,* an excellent discourse of Gods kind expostulation, & unwillingnesse that men should perish: 14. home: 15. our Doctor as before: 18. To *Lond:* our Council of R: So: ordered their Printer to print my *Sylva*, & was the first printed by their order: I returnd: 22. our Curate on: 2. Mar: 27: *Pomerid.* 16. Jo. 23.

24 To Lond: 25. After pub: prayers to our Society, where was an account of severall Experiments made lately at *Sea* by our President & other members a fortnight before: 26. I sat at the Commission of *Sewers*, where was a greate case pleaded by his Majesties Counsel, who having build⟨ed⟩ a wall over a Water Course denyed the Jurisdiction of the Court: The Verdict went for the plaintif: 27. I visited severall friends & Relations in Town: 28 returned home: 29. Doctor on former Text.

April 30 Came his Majestie to honor my poore Villa with his presence, viewing the Gardens & even every roome of the house; & was then pleased to take a small refreshment: There was with him the Duke of Richmont, E: of St. Albans, L: Lauderdail & severall Persons of quality:

May 3. Our Doctor preachd on 2. *Phil:* 9. The H: Comm: follow'd. 4: To Lond: & to take leave of Mr. *Howards* & bring home my sonn *John*, who had ben the whole winter with the *Gent:* his sonns at *Arundel house*, & for feare he might be perverted with their religion: returned the 7th: 10 our *Curate* on 4. *Psal:* 6: 13. To *Lond:* where some laws passed: 14: Din'd at my L: *Mordaunts*, and thence went to *Barnes* to visite my excellent & ingenious friend *Abraham Cowley*: 15 Din'd at the *Comptrollers*:

16: With the *Treasurer:* 17: preachd a Doctor *Coram rege* on   *straite is the gate &c:* I saluted the old Bishop of *Durham*, Dr. *Cosin*, to whom I had ben kind & assistant in his exile, but which he little remembred in his greatenesse: I din'd with the Secretary *Bennet:* 18 with the Clerk of the *Kitchin:* 19 Visited my Bro: & Lady: 21 went home, & returnd in the evening, my buisinesse requiring it: 22. Din'd with the Carver: 24 The Curate at St. *Margarets* on   Not many rich &c: Dind at my L: *Chancelors* where dined my Lord Treasurer, E: of *Southampton*, E. of St. *Albans*, L: Winchester & E. of Cleavland:

30 This morning was pass'd My Lease from the Crowne of *Says-Court*, for the finishing whereof I had ben obligd to such frequent journeys to Lond: I returnd this Evening, having seene the Russ: Ambassador take leave of their Majesties with greate solemnity: 31 our Doctor as formerly:

June 3. I came home ill from *Lond*: & so continued: 10: Let bloud: 11. Came my Bro: to visite me: 15. To Lond: return'd not till 18. ⟨21⟩: our new *Curate* preached on. 2: Act: 28: *Pomerid*: on 73. *Psal:* 27.

July 1 To Lond: To our Society were brought severall *Insects* describd by Mr. *Hooke* with the *Microscop* and reduced to a scale, which we ordered should be cut in Brasse in order to his print-ing his industrious description of them: 2: I saw the greate Masque at Court: & lay that night at *Arundel* house: 4: I saw his Majesties Guards being of horse & foote 4000 led by the Gen-erall, The *Duke* of Albemarle, in extrordinary Equipage & gal-lantrie, consisting of Gent: of quality, & *Veterane* Souldiers, excellently clad, mounted & ordered, drawn up in batallia before their Majesties in Hide-parke, where the old *Earle* of *Cleavela⟨n⟩d* trailed a Pike, & led the right-hand file in a foote Company commanded by the Lord *Wentworth* his sonn, a worthy spactacle & example, being both of them old & valiant Souldiers: This was to shew the *French Ambassador* Monsieur *Cominges*: There being a greate Assembly of Coaches &c in the Park: In the Evening I went home: 5. our Curate on his former Text, *Pomerid*: on 11. Matt 28.

6 To Counsel: to take order concerning some Experiments to be shew'd his Majestie when he came to visite: 7: Din'd at the *Comptrollers*, after dinner we met at the Commission about the streetes, & to regulate Hackny Coaches, also to make up our *Accompts* to passe the Exchequer: I return'd: 12. Doctor as formerly on *Joshua*: I r⟨e⟩ceivd the B: Communion: 16. A most extraordinary wet & cold season: My Brothers & their Wives with much other company dined with me: 19 our Curate on 3. John: 6: *Pomerid*: 1 Jo: 1. 7: This evening came Mrs. *Bennet* (sister to Mr. Secretary) to vis-ite us: we all sup'd at Sir Geo: Carterets Tressurer of the navy, who

had now maried his daughter *Caroline* to Sir *Tho: Scot* of *Scots* hall: This Gent: thought to be begotten by *Prince Rupert*.

Aug: 2. *Curate* on 6: *Matt*. 12. This Evening, I accompanied Mr. *Tressurer* & *Vice Chamberlaine* Carteret to his lately married Son in Laws Sir *Tho: Scot* to *Scots hall* in Kent; wee tooke barge as far as *Grays-in*,[1] thence by Post to *Rochester*, whence in Coach & six horses to *Scots hall*, a right noble seate, uniformely built, handsome Gallery, it stands in a Park well stored, fat & good land: we were exceedingly feasted by the young knight & in his pretty Chapell heard an excellent sermon by his *Chaplaine* on   *Let me a lone*. &c. shewing the force of prayer: *Pomerid*: preached the L⟨e⟩arned Sir Norton Knat⟨c⟩hbulls (who has a noble seate hard by, & a plantation of stattly fir-trees) Chaplaine on.   *Whereof I am chiefe* &c. In the Churchyard of the Parish-Church I measurd an over-grown Yew-tree that was 18 of my paces in compasse out of some branches of which, torne off by the Winds, were divers goodly planks sawed: 10: We returnd by Sir *Nortons*, whose house is likewise in a park: This gent: is a worthy person and learned Critic espe⟨c⟩ialy in the Gr: & Heb: Passing by *Chattam* we saw his *Majesties* Royal Navy, dined at Commissioner *Pets* Master builder there, who shewed me his study & Models, with other curiosities belonging to his art, esteemed for the most skillfull *Naupægus*[2] in the World: he has a prety Garden & banqueting house, potts, status, Cypr⟨e⟩sses, resembling some villa about *Rome*; after a greate feast we rod post to *Graves-End*, & sending the Coach to *Lond*, came by barge home that night:

14 I went to accompany my Neece & God-daughter *M: Evelyn* (who had now ben some days at my house) to Wotton, where I staied two dayes: 16 The Parson preachd on 3 *Jam* 17: *Pomerid*: 20 Exod: 14. &c: 17 I returned: 18 To *Lond* to see my L. *Chancellor*, where I had discourse with my Lord Æ**B** of *Canterbury*, & Winchester, who injoyned me to write to Dr. *Pierce* President of Magd: in Oxon: about a Letter sent him by Dr. *Goff* a *Romish Oratorian*, about an Answer to Deane *Cressys* late book: &c:

20 I din'd at the Comptrollers, with the *Earle* of *Oxford* & Mr. *Ashburnham*; It was saied it should be the last of the publique

1 Gravesend.
2 Ship-builder.

Diets or Tables at Court, now determining to put downe the old hospitality, at which was greate murmuring, considering his Majesties vast revenue, and plenty of the Nation: hence I went to sit in a Committè of which I was one, to consider about the regulation of the *Mint* at the *Tower*, in which some small pro-gresse was made, & so return'd that Evening:

25 To *Lond:* having severall affaires at Court; where I saw her Majestie take leave of the greate-men & Ladys in the Circle, being the next morning to set out towards the *Bath*: 26: At our *Society* some Experiments: 27: din'd at Sir Ph: *Warwicks* Sec-retary to my L: *Tressurer*, who shewed me the Accompts & other private matters, relating to the Revenue: Thence to the Com-missioners of the *Mint*, particularly about Coynage, & bringing his *Majesties* rate from 15 to 10 shill: for every pound weight of Gold: &c: & went home next day: 30: Mr. *LLoyd* our Curate on 24. *Act:* 16: In the Afternoone I walked to *Greenewich* & heard Mr. Plume Expound on the *Catechisme*.

31 I was invited to the Translation of *Dr. Sheldon* Bish: of *London* from that *see* to *Canterbury*; the Ceremonie perform'd at *Lambeth*: First went his Graces Mace-bearer, Steward, *Tressurer*, *Comptroller* all in their Gownes & with white-staves; next the Bishops in their habites, eight in number: next Dr. *Sweat* Deane of the *Arches*, Dr. *Exton* Judge of the Admiralty, next Sir William Merick, Judge of the Prerogative Court, with divers Advocates in Scarlet: After divine service in the Chapell per-form'd with Musique extraordinary: Dr. *Franck* & D. *Stradling* (his Graces Chaplaines) saied prayers: The *A Bish*: in a private roome looking into the Chapel, the Bishops who were Commis-sioners went up to a Table plac'd before the *Altar* & sat about it in chaires: Then Dr. *Chawworth* presented the Commission under the broad-seale to the Bish: of *Winchester*, which was read by Dr. *Sweat*; Then the *Viccar-Generall* went to the *Vestery*, & brought his *Grace* into the *Chapell*, his other officers marching before, he, being presented to the Commissioners, was seated in a greate arm'd Chaire at one end of the Table: Then was the Definitive Sentence read by the Bishop of Winchester, & sub-scribed by all the *Bishops* & Proclamation three-times made at the Chapell dores, which were then set-open for any to enter, & give their exceptions, if any they had: This don, we all went to dinner in the Greate hall to a mighty feast of 500 pounds

expense. There were present all the Nobility in Towne, the Lord Maior of Lond: Sheriffs, Duke of Albemarle &c: My Lord *A Bishop* did in particular most civily welcome me &c. So going to visite my *Lady Needham* who lived at *Lambeth* I went over to *Lond:*

September 2. I went home. 6: our Doctor preached on 2. *King:* 18. 9. against a new sect, that cal'd them selves Perfectionists: I received the B: *Sacrament*. 10. I dind with Mr. Tressurer of the Navy, where sitting by Mr. *Secretary Moris* we had much discourse about Bookes & Authors, he being a learned man, & had a good collection: Now was *Christned* Sir N: Slanings daughter: 13 A stranger on. 2. *Eph:* 10: 16. To *Lond:* 17 Dined at the Bish: of *Salisberies* with whom I had buisinesse that concernd Dr. *Pierce*. 18 I dined with Dr. *Wilkins*: Lord Mordaunt & his Lady came to visite us: 19: At a neighbours funerall our Doctor preachd on 1. *Pet:* 9. of the Accompt to be given at the last day: 20 he preachd as formerly on 2: Reg: I dined at the Treasurers of the Navy.

Octob 18 Our Doctor on 34. Exod: 6. 7. 20: To *Lond:* To waite on L: *Chancellor*: 21 return'd. 24 Mr. *Edw: Philips*, came to be my sonns præceptor: This Gent: was Nephew to *Milton* who writ against *Salmasius's Defensio*, but not at all infected with his principles, & though brought up by him, yet no way taint⟨e⟩d: 25. *Curate* on his former Text:

November 30 Was the first Anniversary our Society for the Choice of new Officers, according to the Tenor of our Patent, & Institution; it being *St. Andrews* day, who was our *Patron*, each fellow wearing a *St. Andrews* Crosse of ribbon on the crowne of his hatt, after the Election was over, we all dined together, his Majestie sending us Venison:

December 1 I return'd. 6 our Curate as formerly. 13 our *Doctor* as formerly: 16 To *Lond:* To our Society, where Mr. P: *Balle* our Treasurer on this Election, presented the Society with an Iron Chest with 3 Locks, & in it an hundred pounds as a Gift & benefactor:

18 I dined with the Gent: of his Majesties Bed-Chamber at *Whitehall*; 19 returnd: 20: our Curate on: 1. *Tim:* 1.15. 25. Curate on 7: *Esay:* 14.

28 Divers Neighbours din'd with me according to Costome: 29: my sonn John was let bloud 3 ounces, for his feavour: 31. Setting our domestique affaires in order, I gave God thanks for his providence hithertoo: &c:

1664 *Jan* 1 our Doctor preached on 1. *Psal:* 10: My *Aunt Hungerford* & several Relations din'd with us:

2 I went to visite my L: *Mordaunt* at Parsons greene; thence to *Barne Elmes* to see *Abr: Cowley* after his sicknesse, return'd that Evening to *Lond:* 3: Dr. *Breton* our *Viccar* preachd on 2. *Luke* 14 at St. *Martines Ludgate*, then was Married my Co: *Eliz: Hungerford* to Mr. *Moore*: In the Afternoone Dr. *Breton* (as Prebend of S: *Paules*) in St. *Paules* on 1. John: 20: in an excellent discourse. I went home next morning.

10 Our Doctor on his former Text in *Luke:* ⟨17⟩: our Curate on 1. *Thess:* 4.16: Pomerid: on: 1 *Pet:* 1.5: And this day was my Wife brought to bed of a sonn borne exactly at 2 in the afternoone: blessed be God for this mercy to her, who had ceased from bearing some yeares: 20: To Lond: at our Society: 21 Din'd at Sir *Phil: Warwicks* & return'd: 24: our doctor on former Text:

27 Was Christned my sonn *Richard* [2d. of that name] by his Grandfather Sir *Rich: Browne*, my *Lord Vicount Mordaunt* & my *Lady Warwick* being Sponsors &c: Dr. *Breton* officiating in the greate Chamber at *Says Court*. 30: he preachd on the Kings Anniversarie Martyrdom 1. *Jonah*: 14. shewing how fearfull a thing it was for a people to draw on them the gilt of Innocent-blood: [31] our *Curate* on: 3. *Titus* 1. on the necessity of obedience to superiors:

Feb: 3 To Lond: At our Society: 4: Din'd at Sir Ph: *Warwicks*, thence to Court: I had discourse with his Majestie about an invention of *Glasse Granados* & severall other subjects: 5. I saw acted the *Indian Queene* a Tragedie well written, but so beautified with rich Scenes as the like had never ben seene here as happly (except rarely any where else) on a mercenarie *Theater*: I went to Q: *Mother's* Court, & next day home: 7: our *Viccar* on his former text. 10 To *Lond:* my *Sylva*[1] being now in the *presse*: 12 returnd: 14 *Curate* on 5: *Mal:* 6.

16. I went to *Lond:* presented my *Sylva* to the *Society*. & 17: To his Majestie to whom it was dedicated, to my *Lord Treasurer*, & *Lord Chancellor*: 20: came home: 21. our *Viccar* on. 3. Act: 19: 23. Came my Brothers to dine with us, it being *Shrove tuesday*: 24: My Lo: *Geo: Berkeley* of *Durdens* & Sir Sam: *Tuke* to visite me: We went on board Sir William Petties double

1 *Sylva, or a Discourse of Forest-Trees, and the Propagation of Timber in His Majesties Dominions.*

bottom'd Vessel: & so went with my Lord to *Lond:* 26: Din'd at my Lord *Chancellors* who invited me. Thence to Court, where I had greate thanks for my *Sylva* & long discourse with him of divers particulars. 27: returned: 28 our Curate on: 2: *Joel* 12. 13: 29 I was *Godfather* to Dr. *Breton* (our Vicca⟨r⟩s) sonn *John*, & was the same day sent to, to be Godfather also to Mr. *Chr: Wases* sonn, which I did by proxie:

Mar: 2 I went to Lond, to distribute some of my Books amongst friends, return'd: 4: Came to visite & dine with me the E: of *Lauderdail* his Majesties greate favorite, & Secretary of Scotland, the *Earle* of *Tivedale*; My Lord Vicount Brouncher (president of the Ro: Society) Dr. *Wilkins* deane of *Rippon*, Sir Robert *Morray* & Mr. *Hooke* Curator to the Society:

6 our *Viccar* as before:

This Spring I planted the home field & West field about Says-Court, with Elmes; being the same Yeare that the Elmes were also planted by his Majestie in *Greenewich park*.

9 I went to the *Tower* of Lond, to sit in Commission about regulating the Mint, & now it was the fine new Milled Coyne both of White-mony & *Ginnies* was established: returnd:

16 To Lond: at our Society: 17 return'd: 19: To Lond: to my Co: Halls funerall, returnd:

20 Our Doctor as formerly: 24: To *Lond*. about buisinesse, returnd 24: 26: It pleased God to take-away my sonn *Richard*, being now a moneth old, yet without any sicknesse of danger perceivable, being to all appearance a most likely child; so as we suspected much the *Nurse* had over-layne him to our extreame sorrow, being now againe reduc'd to one: Gods will be don:

27: our Curate on: 11: *Matt:* 28: After evening prayer was my child buried neere the rest of his brothers, my deare children: 31. I went to Lond: about severall affaires.

Aprill: 2: returned. 3. our *Viccar* as formerly:

3 Came the Earle of *Essex*, & *Lord Cornberry* to visite me: 8. *Viccar* on 12: *Heb:* 3: I received the B: Sacrament:

10 *Easter-day* he preached on 3. *Act:* 26: 16: To *Lond:* return'd: 17: *Curate* on 3. *Coloss:* 1. 24. *Viccar:* as before: In the afternoone I went with Sir *Sam. Tuke* to *Epsam*, & staied with my Bro: at Woodcot 'til tuesday, when Sir R: Browne & my Wife fetched me home in the Coach: 27: To *Lond* about buisinesse: supp'd at

Mr. *Secretary* Bennets; saw a facecious Comedy Cald Love in a Tub, returnd on the 30th.

May. 1 Our *Curate* on 11: *Matt.* 28. as before, *Pomerid*: on 1. *Thess*. 5.23. The *Fefeès* for the poore met according to Costom & dined together: 3: Came the *Earle* of Kent (my kindsman) & his Lady to visite us. 4: To Lond: supped at Mr. *Sec: Bennets*:

5 I went with some company a journey of Pleasur on the Water, in barge, with *Musick* & at *Mortlack* had a greate banquet, returning late: The occasion was *Sir Robert Carr* now Courting Mrs. *Bennet*, sister to the secretary of state, &c:

6 Went to see Mr. *Write* the Painters Collection of rare shells &c: returned.

19 To Lond about affaires. 21 *returnd*. 22. our Doctor as formerly. 29 Mr. *Woodward* on 15 *Joh:* 26.

June 5. Our *Viccar*, concerning the *Mysterie* of the *H: Trinity* 1. *Jo:* 5: 7. I received the B: *Comm*.

8 I went to our Society, to which his Majestie had sent that wonderfull horne of the fish, which struck a dangerous hole in the keele of a ship, in the *India* Sea, which being broake off with the violence of the fish, & left in the timber, preserv'd it from foundring: 9. returnd.

9 Sir *Samuell Tuke* being this morning married to a Lady kinds-woman to my Lord *Arundel* of *Wardoer*, by the Queenes Lord *Almoner* L. *Aubignie* in St. *Jame's Chapell*, solemniz'd his Wedding night at my house with much companie.

12 our *Curate* on 6 *Matt:* 33: 21. To *Lond:* To visite & take leave of Sir S: Tuke & Lady, now going for France with the young Mr. *Howards*.

22 One *Tomson* a *Jesuite* shewed me such a ⟨Collection⟩ of rarities, sent from the *Jesuites* of *Japan* & *China* to their order at *Paris* (as a present to be reserved in their *Chimelium*, but brought to Lond; with the East *India ships* for them) as in my life I had not seene: The chiefe things were very large *Rhinoceros's* hornes, Glorious Vests, wrought & embrodered on cloth of Gold, but with such lively colours, as for splendor & vividnesse we have nothing in Europe approches: A Girdill studdied with achats, & balast rubies of greate value & size, also knives of so keene edge as one could not touch them, nor was the mettal of our Couler but more pale & livid: *Fanns* like those our Ladys use, but much larger, & with long handles curiously

carved, & filled with Chineze Characters: A sort of paper very broad thin, & fine like abortive parchment, & exquisitely polished, of an amber yellow, exceeding glorious & pretty to looke on, & seeming to be like that which my L: *Verulame* describes in his *Nova Atlantis*; with severall other sorts of papers some written, others Printed: Also prints of Landskips, of their Idols, Saints, Pagoods, of most ougly Serpentine, monstrous & hideous shapes to which they paie devotion: Pictures of Men, & Countries, rarely painted on a sort of gumm'd *Calico* transparant as glasse: also Flowers, Trees, Beasts, birds &c: excellently wrought in a kind of sleve-silk very naturall. Divers Drougs that our Drougists & physitians could make nothing of: Especialy, one which the *Jesuite* called Lac *Tygridis*, it look'd like a fungus, but was weighty like metall: yet was a Concretion or coagulation of some other matter: Also severall booke MSS. A grammar of the Language writen in *Spanish*, with innumerable other rarities: We sate in the *R: Society* as a Commiteè about improvement of Husbandry: I went home:

29 To *Lond:* about buisinesse: 30 To see my L: *Mordaunt* at parsons-Greene, return'd.

July 1. Went to see Mr. *Povey's* elegant house in Lincolns-Inn field, where the Perspective in his Court, painted by *Streeter*, is indeede excellent, with the *Vasas* in Imitation of *Porphyrie*; & fountaine; The Inlaying of his Closet; but, above all his pretty Cellar, & ranging of his Wine-bottles &c: I returnd: 3: our *Viccar* as formerly: 6: To Lond: 7: To Court, where I subscribed to Sir *Arthyr Slingsbys* loterey, a desperate debt owing me long since in Paris: 8: din'd at *Arundell* house, & returned home. 10. our Curate on 5. *Matt:* 7: 11 Mr. *Charles Howard* & Lady came to dine with me. 14: I went to take leave of the two Mr. *Howards* now going to *Paris* & brought them as far as *Bromely*, thence to *Eltham* to see Sir *John Shaws* new house now building, the place is pleasant, if not too wett, but the house not well contrived, especialy the roofe, & roomes too low pitch'd, & *Kitchins* where the Cellars should be: The *Orangerie* & *Aviarie* handsome, & a very large plantation about it. 17: our Doctor on his former subject: 19. To *Lond.* to see the event of the *Lottery*, which his Majestie had permitted Sir *Arth: Slingsby* to set up for one day in the Banqueting house at whitehall: I gaining onely a trifle, as well as did the *King*, *Queene Consort*, & *Q: Mother* for neere 30 lotts: which was thought to be contriv'd very un-handsomely by the master of it, who was in truth a meer shark:

20 I dined with my L: *Treasurer* at *Southampton* house, where his Lordship used me with singular humanitie: I went in the afternoone to *Chelsey* to waite on the Lord *Duke* of *Ormond*, return'd to *Lond:* 22 My Sister *Evelyn* brought to bed of a *Sonn*: my Wife was God-mother, & christned it *Richard*: next day I went home. 24: our Curate preach'd on 1. *Pet:* 1. 1: *Pomerid:* on. 60 *Psal:* 11: 28. Came old Monsieur *Zulichem* (Secretary to the *Prince* of *Orange* & an excellent Lat: Poet, & now neere 80 years of age, a rare Lutinist) with Monsieur *Oudart*, to see me: 31. our Doctor on his former subject: I received the B: *Sacrament*:

Aug 9: I went to *Lond:* & thence with my *Bro: Richard* to *Wotton* to visie & comfort my disconsolate Bro: I called in at *Durdens*: 13. Visite⟨d⟩ Mr. *Charles Howard* at *Dipden* neere *Darking*. 14: The Parson of *Wotton* preached on 1. *Pet*. 5. 5:

15 Returned home. 16 Came to see me the *Earle of Peterborow* & Lord *Mordaunt* with whom I went to see Sir *William Ducies* house at *Charleton*, which he purchased of my excellent neighbour Sir Hen: *Newton*, now nobly furnish'd. 17: To *Lond*, about buisinesse; & returned: 21. A stranger on 6: *Matt:* 20, a vehement but hearty Preacher: 22. I went back to *Wotton* to assist at the Funerall of my *sister*-in Law, the Lady *Cotton* buried in our Dormitorie there, she being put up in Lead: Dr. *Owen* preaching on   *Isaiah*   Cease from man &c: on which he made a profitable & pathetic discourse, concluding with an Elogie of that virtuous, pious, & deserving Lady &c: it was a very solemn funerall of about 50 mourners: I came back next day: with my Wife to *Lond:* 25. To *Deptford*: my foote-man lingering at some distance behind the Coach, was robb'd, & bound being night: 28: our Doctor on: 2. *Pet:* 5. 6. 7:

October 2d. Our *Curate* as above: 8: v. 5. To *Lond:* at our *Society* Experiments on severall bodys descent in Water, by vibrations of a pendule, also was brought a new invented Instrument of Musique, being an *harpsichord* with gut-Strings, sounding like a Consort of *Viols* with an *Organ*, made vocal by a Wheele, & a *Zone* of parchment that rubb'd horizontaly against the Strings: 6: I heard the *Anniversary* oration in praise of Dr. *Harvy* in the *Anatomie Theater* in Col: of *Physitians*; after which I was invited

by Dr. *Alston* the *Præsident* to a magnificent feast: 7: I dined at
Sir Nic: *Stroods* one of the *Masters* of *Chancery* in greate St.
Bartholomews; passing the Evening at *Whitehall*, where I had
discourse with the *Queene* &c. 8, Dined at the *Vice Chamber-
lai⟨n⟩es* & returned home: 9 our Doctor as formerly: Sir *William
Cursius* his Majesties *Resident* in Germany came to visite me, he
was a Wise, & learned Gent: & as he told me Scholar to *Henry
Alstedius* the *Encyclopædist* &c:

   To Lond, to sit in Commission about regulating the *Hackney
Coaches* of Lond: & highways:

   15 Dined, at L: *Chancelors*, where was also the Duke of
Ormond, *Earle of Cork*, and Bishop of *Winchester*: After dinner
my Lord *Chancellor* & *Lady* carried me in their Coach to see
their Palace (for now he lived at Worcester-house in the Strand)
building at the upper end of St. *James's Streete*; & to project the
Garden: Then went with my Lady to St. James's house to see her
Grand-Children, the Lady *Mary* & a sonn, &c, children of the
Dutchesse of Yorke; & this Evening presented his Lordship
with my booke of *Architecture*,[1] as before I had don to his
Majestie & Queene Mother, both whom were pleasd to say it
was the usefullest booke on that subject of any extant: My L:
Chamberlaine caused me to stay with him in his bed chamber,
discoursing of severall matters, very late, even 'til he was going
into his bed:

   16 Dr. *Crofts* deane of Norwich preachd *Coram Rege* at
Whitehall on   Lord, Teach us how to pray: dind at Sir *Ph:
Warwicks*. 17. I went with my L: *V. Count Cornbury* to *Cornebury*
in *Oxford-shire*, to assist the Planting of the *Park* & beare him
company, with Mr. *Belin*, both virtuous & friendly Gent: also
with Mr. May, in Coach & six horses, din'd at *Uxbridge*, lay at
Wicckam: 18 at *Oxford*, went through *Woodstock* where we beheld
the destruction of that *Royal Seate & Park* by the late Rebels; &
ariv'd that Evening at *Cornbury*, an house built by the Earle of
Denby, in the midle of a Sweete dry Park walled with a Dry-
wall: The house of excellent free stone, abounding in that park, a
stone that is fine, but never swets or casts any damp: tis of ample
receite, has goodly Cellars, the paving of the hall admirable, for

1 *A Parallel of the Antient Architecture with the Modern*. Translated by Evelyn
from the French of Roland Fréart, sieur de Chambray.

the close laying of the Pavement: We design'd an handsome Chapell that was yet wanting, as Mr. *May* had the stables which indeede are very faire, having set out the Walkes in the *Park*, & Gardens: The Lodge is a prety solitude, and the Ponds very convenient; The Parke well stored. Hence on the 20: we went to see the famous Wells natural, & artificial Grotts & fountains calld Bushells Wells at Ensham: this *Bushell* had ben Secretary to my L. *Verulam*: It is an extraordinary solitude: There he had two *Mummies*, a *Grott* where he lay in an *hamac* like an Indian: Hence we went to *Dichley* an antient seate of the *Lees*, now Sir *Hen: Lees*, a low antient timber house, with a pretty bowling greene: My Lady gave us an extraordinary dinner: This Gent: Mother was Countesse of *Rochester*, who was also there, & Sir *Walt: Saint Johns*: There were some Pictures of their ancesters not ill Painted; the Gr: *Grandfather* had ben *Knight* of the *Gartyr*, also the Picture of a Pope & our Saviours head: so we returned to Cornbury:

23 Mr. *Nash* (formerly Præceptor to my Lord) preachd at Charlbery the Parish-Church, on 18 *Luke* 18: 24: We dined at Sir *Tim: Tyrills* at *Shotover*: this Gent: married the daughter & heyre of *Bishop Usher* A:B: of *Armagh* that learned *Prælate*: th⟨e⟩y made a greate entertainement: There is here in the Grove, a fountain of the coldest water I ever felt: 'tis very cleere, his plantations of Oakes &c is commendable: so we went this Evening to *Oxford*, lay at Dr. *Hides* Principal of *Magdalen Hall* (related to my L:) bro: to the Lord *Ch: Justice*, and that Sir *Henry Hide* that lost his head for his Loyalty: we were handsomly entertaind two dayes.

25 Came to visite my Lord *Cornbery* (whose father my L: H: *Chancelor* of England, was also now Chancelor of the University) the *Vice-Chancellor*, who with the Dr. *Fell*, Deane of *Christ-Church*, Warden of Queenes, the learnd Dr. *Barlow*, & severall heads of houses came to visite my Lord, & next day Invited him & us all to dinner:

I went to visite Mr. *Boyle* now here, whom I found with Dr. *Wallis* & Dr. *Chr: Wren* in the *Tower* at the *Scholes*, with an inverted *Tube* or *Telescope* observing the *Discus* of the *Sunn* for the passing of ☿[1] that day before the *Sunn*; but the *Latitude* was

1 Mercury; the symbol also used for the metal.

so greate, that nothing appeared: So we went to see the rarities in the *Library*, where the Library keepers, shewed me my name, among the Benefactors: They have a Cabinet of some *Medails*, & Pictures of the Muscular parts of Mans body: Thence to the new *Theater*, building now at an exceeding & royal Expense by the L: A: B: of *Canterbury*, to keepe the *Acts* in for the future, 'til now being in St. *Maries* church: The foundation being but newly laied & the whole, Design'd, by that incomparable genius, & my worthy friend Dr. *Chr: Wren*, who shewed me the Model, not disdaining my advise in some particulars: Thence to see the Picture on the Wall over the *Altar* at *All-Soules*, being the largest piece of Fresco painting (or rather in Imitation of it, for tis in oyle [of *Terpentine*]) in England, & not ill design'd, by the hand of one *Fuller*: yet I feare it will not hold long, & seemes too full of nakeds for a Chapell: Thence to New-Coll: & the Painting of Magdalens Chapell, which is on blue Cloth in *Chiaro Oscuro* by one Greeneborow, being a *Cæna Domini*, & Judgement ⟨on⟩ the Wall by Fuller, as is the other, somewhat varied: Next to *Waddam*, & the *Physi⟨c⟩k Garden* where were two large *Locust Trees*, & as many *Platana*, & some rare Plants under the Culture of old *Bobart*. 26: We came back to *Beaconsfield*, next day to *Lond.* where we dined at my L: *Chancelors* with my L: *Belasis* & divers greate persons:

⟨28⟩ Being casualy in the Privy Gallery at *White-hall*, his Majestie gave me thanks (before divers Lords & noble men) for my Book of *Architecture* & *Sylva* againe: That they were the best designd & usefull for the matter & subject, the best printed & designd (meaning the *Tallè doucès*[1] of the *Paralelles*) that he had seene: then caused me to follow him alone to one of the Windows, he asked me if I had any paper about me un-written, & a *Crayon*; I presented him with both, & then laying it on the Window stoole, he with his owne hands, designed to me the plot for the future building of *White-hall*, together with the Roomes of State, & other particulars, which royal draft, though not so accurately don, I reserve as a rarity by me: After this he talked with me of severall matters, & asking my advice, of many particulars, in which I find his Majestie had an extraordin⟨ar⟩y

1 Engravings.

talent, becoming a magnificent Prince: The same day, at Council (there being Commissioners to be made, to take care of such
sick & Wounded, & Prisoners at War, as might be expected
upon occasion of a succeeding Warr, and Action at sea; a War
being already declared against the Hollanders) his *Majestie* was
pleasd to nominate me to be one; amongst three other Gent: of
quality, Parliament Men: viz: Sir *William D'oily* knight &
Baronet, Sir *Tho: Clifford* [since L: *Tressurer* of *England*], &
Bullein Rhemys Esquire, with a Sallary of 1200 pounds
amongst us, besides extraordinares &c: for our care & attendance in time of Action, each of us appointed his particular
District, & mine falling out to be *Kent*, [&] *Sussex*: with power
to constitu⟨t⟩e *Officers*, *Physitians*, *Chirurgeons*, *Provost Martials*
&c: dispose of halfe of the Hospitals thro England: after which
I kissed his *Majesties hand*, as did the rest of my *Collegues* when
the Council was up: At this Council, I heard *Mr. Solicitor Finch*
[since *L: Chan*] plead most elegantly the Merchants Cause,
trading to the *Canaries*, that his *Majestie* would grant them a
new Charter. 29 Was the most magnificent triumph by Water
& Land of the *Ld: Major*, I dined at *Guild-hall*: the feast said to
cost 1000 pounds: at the upper Table, placed next to Sir *H: Bennet Secretary* of *State*, just opposite to my L: *Chancelor* & the
Duke of *Buckingham*, who sate betweene Monsieur *Comminges*
the Fr: *Ambassador, Lord Tressurer*, Dukes of *Ormond*, of *Albemarle*, E: of *Manchester* Lord *Chamberlaine* & the rest of the
greate officers of State: My Lord *Major* came twice up to us,
first drinking in a Golden Goblett his *Majesties* health, then the
French Kings (as a Complement to the Ambassador). Then we
return'd my L: *Majors* health, the Trumpets, Drumms sounding: for the rest, the Cheere was not to be imagind for the
Plenty & raritie, an infinitie of Persons at the rest of the Tables
in that ample hall: so I slip'd away in the crowd & came home
late:

    November 24: His Majestie was pleasd to tell me what the con-
ference was with the *Holland Ambassador* which (as after I found)
⟨was part of⟩ the heads of the Speech he made at the reconven-
tion of the *Parliament*, which now began: 24: I dined with the
Commissioners for Sick & Wounded, & sate at Painters hall:

    25 I din'd at Sir *Edw: Stroodes* & returned hom⟨e⟩ 26: 27: our
Curate on 3. *John:* 3: 29 To *Lond:* about our Commission, which I

received sign'd by all the Lords of the Council, together with our Instructions: 30: We met at the Ro: Society, and chose Officers according to our new establish'd Statu⟨t⟩es:

December 1. State at *Painter hall*. 2. Sir William D'Oylie & myselfe deliverd the Pr: Councils letters to the Governors of St. *Thomas Hospital* in Southwark, that a mo⟨ie⟩tie of the house should be reserved for such sick & wounded as should from time to time be sent from the Fleete, during the War: This being dellivr⟨e⟩d at their Court, the President & severall Aldermen Governors of that Hospital invited us to a greate feast in Fishmong⟨e⟩rs hall: I return'd hom that Evening:

6 Went to *Lond:* din'd at Sir Robert *Pastons*. 8: Spake with the King, concerning some Prisoners at Warr, committed to my Martial. 9 dind at Mr. Vice Chamberlains, came home. 11 our Curate on 3: *John* 3: *Pomerid*: 11: *Matt:* 10: 13 To *Lond:* Sate at Painters hall, where we perfected the Method for disposing of the sick. 14: met at the *R: Society*, where we had severall letters read, from correspondents beyond sea, about the *Comet* which now appeared: orders were given for accurate observations to our Curator &c: 15 Dined at the V. *Chamberlains*: 16. returned home: 18 our Doc: on: 4. *Gal:* 5: 20: To Lond: our last sitting taking order for our personal visiting our several Districts: 21. I dined at Cap: Cocks (our Treasurer) with that most ingenious Gent: *Math: Wren*, sonn to the Bish: of *Ely*, Mr. Joseph *Wiliamson* [since Sec: of State], Mr. *Bolteele*: then went to Gr: Coll: 22: I went to the Launching of a new ship of two bottomes, invented by Sir *William Petty* by a Modell of Sir *William Petty* on which were various opinions: his Majestie present, gave her the name of the Experiment: so I came home, where I found Sir *Humphrie Winch*, & Mr. *Phil*. Packer who dined with me: This yeare I planted the Lower grove next the Pond:

Now was the *Comet* very visible. 25. our *Curate* on: 1. *Tim:* 1. 15. being Christmas day:

26: To *Lond:* about buisinesse, return'd. 28 Some of my poore Neighbours dined with me: & others of my *Tennants* with some Company from Lond: The Comet appears 'twixt *Aries* & *Cete* north-west of the *Pliades*: 29: To *Lond:* returnd: 31. Set my Affaires in order, Gave God praise for his Mercys the past yeare, & prepard for the reception of the holy Sacrament: It was now exceeding cold, & a hard long frosty season:

1665. JAN: 1 Our *Doctor* preached on 4: *Gal:* 4. 5: I received the B: Sacrament: &c:

2 [To Lond] This day was publishd by me that part of the *Mysterie of Jesuitisme* translat⟨e⟩d & collected by me, though without name, containing the Imaginarie Heresy with 4 letters & other Pieces. I dind at my L: *Chancelors*, to whom I recomended Sir Roger Langlys my kindsmans contest with Sir Tho: Osborne [since L. *Tress.* of *England*] about being knight for Yorkshire: Then, my Lord Chiefe Justice recommended a relation of his to be one of my officers, so I returnd.

3 Dined with me severall neighbours:

4 I went in Coach (it being excessive sharp frost & snow) towards *Dover*, & other parts of *Kent*, to settle Physitians, Chirurgeons, Agents, Martials & other offices in all the Sea-Ports, to take Care of such as should be set on shore, Wounded, sick or Prisoner &c in pursuance of our Commission, reaching from the North foreland in Kent, to *Portsmouth* in hampshir: the rest of the Ports in England, from thence, to Sir Will: D'oily, to Sir *Tho Clifford* [afterward L: *Tress:* of *England*], *Bulleyn Rhemes*: so that evening I came to *Rochester*, where I delivered the Privy Councils letter to the *Major* to receive orders from me: 5. I arived at *Canterbury*, [6] being *Epiphanie*, when I went to the *Cathedral*, exceedingly well repaired since his Majesties returne: ⟨7⟩: To *Dover*, where Col: *Stroode* Lieutennant of the Castle, (having receiv'd the Letter I brought him from the *Duke of Albemarle*) invited me, and made me lodge in the *Castle*, & was splendidly treated, assisting me from place to place: here I settled my first Deputy: 8: I heard an excellent sermon in the chiefe Church on⟨e⟩ Dr. *Hynd*, on 12: *Rom:* 6. The Major, & Officers of the Costomes were very civel to me:

9 To *Deale*, settled Agent, & matters there: 10: To *Sandwich*, a pretty towne about 2 miles from the sea, a river: The country sandy: here the *Major* also very dilligent to serve me: I visited the forts in the way: Thence that night back to *Canterbury*, 11 To *Rochester*, where I tooke order to settle Officers at *Chatham*. 12 To graves end, where having dispatch'd with the Governor of the Block-house, & Major, relating to my Instructions, I

426 JANUARY-2 MARCH 1665

returned home, a Cold, buisy, but not unpleasant Journey: 15 our
Viccar as formerly on: 4: Gal: 4. 5: 17: To *Lond:* to meete my Bro:
Commissioners & give accompts what we had don in our severall districts: 18: At the R: *Society* came in severall schemes &
observations about the Comet: Mr. *Hooke* produc'd an Experiment of fire, shewing that the aire was but a certaine disolving
menstrue: ⟨19⟩ I din'd at the L: *Majors*, a prodigious feast, it
being a day when the Companies were receivd &c: I waited on
Q: Mother: 20: Din'd at my L: *Chancelors* & went home: 22: our
Curat continued his discourse on 1. *Tim:* 1. 15: 24: I was of a committe selected out of our Ass⟨e⟩mbly, for the Improvement of
our English tongue. 25 We met also to receive the *Duke of
Brunswick* Lunenburg as a Fellow: 26: Met at Commission for
Sick & Wounded: This night being at *White hall*, his Majestie
came to me standing in the Withdrawing roome, & gave me
thanks for publishing the *Mysterie* of *Jesuitisme*, which he said he
had carried 2 days in his pocket, read it, & encouragd me, at
which I did not a little wonder; I suppose Sir *Robert Morray* had
given it him.

27 Dind at L: Chancelors who caused me after dinner to sit 2
or 3 houres alone with him in his Bed-Chamber: I return'd: 29:
our *Viccar* as formerly. 30 The *Anniversary* of the old Kings
Martyrdom our Doctor preached on 4. *Lam:* 20. how the King
was the breath of our Nostrills &c: 31 To *Lond.*

Feb: 1. I din'd at Mr. Sec: *Benets*, thence to the R: So: more
Schemes of the *Comets* progresse:

8 *Ashwednesday* I visited our Prisoners at *Chelsey Colledge*, &
to examine how the Martial & Suttlers behaved themselves:
These were Prisoners taken in the Warr; They onely complain'd
that their bread was too fine: I din'd at Sir *Hen: Herberts* Master
of the *Revells*:

9 Dined at my L: Treasure⟨r⟩s the Earle of Southampton in
Blomesbury, where he was building a noble Square or Piazza &
little Towne: his owne house stands too low, some noble roomes,
a pretty Cedar Chapell, a naked Garden to the north, but good
aire: I had much discourse with his Lordship whom I found to
be a person of extraordinary parts, but *Valetudinarie*:

I went to St. *Ja: Parke*, where I examin'd the Throate of the
Onocratylus or *Pelecan*, the tongue scarce appearing, the Peake
above 2 foote long, crooked at the very point & a little red at the

tip: the neck rough, a fowle betweene a Stork & Swan & neere as big as a Swan; a Melancholy water foule: brought from *Astracan* by the Russian Ambassador: it was diverting to see how he would tosse up & turne a flat-fish, plaice or flounder to get it right into its gullet, for it has one at the lower beake which being filmy stretches to a prodigious widenesse when it devours a greate fish &c: Here was also a small Water-fowle that went almost quite erect, like the *Penguin* of *America*: It would eat as much fish as its whole body weighed, I never saw so unsatiable a devourer, I admir'd how it could swallo⟨w⟩ so much & swell no bigger: I believe it to be the most voracious creature in nature, it was not biger than a *More hen*: The *Solan-Geece* here also are greate devourers, & are said soone to exhaust all the fish of a pond: Here were a curious sort of Poultry, not much exceeding a tame pidgeon, with legs so short, as their crops seem'd to touch the Earth: also a milk-white Raven, a good⟨l⟩y bird: here was also a *Stork*, which was a raritie at this season, seing he was loose, & could flie loftily: Also 2 Balearian *Cranes*, one of which having had one of his leggs broken and cut off above the knee, had a wodden or boxen leg & thigh with a joynt for the ⟨knee⟩ so accurately made, that the poore creature could walke with it, & use it as well as if it had ben natural: It was made by a souldier: The *Parke* was at this time stored with infinite flocks of severall sorts of ordinary, & extraordinary Wild foule, breeding about the Decoy, which for being neere so greate a Citty, & among such a concourse of Souldier⟨s⟩, Guards & people, is very diverting: There were also Deere of severall countries, W⟨h⟩ite, spotted like Leopards, Antelope: An Elke, Red deeres, Robucks, Staggs, Guinny Goates; Arabian sheepe &c: The supporting the Withy potts or nests for the Wild foule to lay in, a little above the surface of the water was very pretty. 10. I returned home:

Mar. 1. Dr. Bathu⟨r⟩st præs: of *Trin:* Col: *Oxon Coram Rege* on 1 Joh: 30 The Easy Yoake, an incomparable sermon, as that ingenious & excellent man, can do no other: This day I introduc'd Mr. *Phil: Carteret* sonn to the Vice-Chamb: & Sir Nic: Slaning to our Society. 2. I went with his Majestie into the Lobbie behind the house of Lords, where I saw the King & rest of the Lords robe themselves, & getting into the *Lords house* in a corner neere the Woolsackes, that on which the L: Chancelor sate next below the Throne, The King sate in all the ⟨*Regalia*⟩, the Crown Imperial on his head, Scepter & Mond &c: The D: of *Albemarle* bare the sword, the D: of Ormond the Cap: of dignity: The rest of the Lords rob'd & in their places, the Lords spiritual &c. A most splendid & august convention: Then came in the Speaker & H: of Comm: & at the barr made a speech, after which he presented divers bills, read by the Cleark, the King by a nod onely passing them, the Cleark saying *le Roy le veult*, this to the Publique bills, the Private bills, *Soit fait comme il est desirè*, being in all 26 bills, Then his *Majestie* made a very handsome, but short speech, commanding my Lo: *Privy-Seale* to prorogue the Parliament, which he did, my L: *Chancelor* being absent & ill: so all rise: I had not before seene the manner of passing Laws &c:

3 I went to waite on the Duke of York about buisnesse: din'd at Sir N: Strood's, returnd home:

4 Dined with me Sir William D'Oily. 5. our *Curate* on *Tim:* as formerly:

7 To *Lond:* at *Painter hall*: 8: Dind at V: *Chamb:* 9 Went to receive the poore burnt Creatures that were saved out of the *London* fregat in which were blowne up above 200 men by an axident and so perish'd on⟨e⟩ of the bravest ships in *Europe*: returning this evening I saw a pillar of Light, of a very strange Colour, & position, being to appearance upright from the body of the setting sunn 7 or 8 yards long & 2 foote broade. 12 our *Viccar*, on former text: I received the H. Comm: 14: To Lond: to discharge some *Dutch* Prisoners: 15 At Court, Dr. *Alestreè* on   *crucified with Christ*: an excellent serm: It was now Lent: Afternoone at our *Society*, where was tried some of the Poysons sent from the King of *Macassar* out of E. *India*, so famous for its suddaine operation: we gave it a wounded dog, but it did not succeede. 16 went home, having taken leave of Sir *Jo: Lawson* the V. *Admiral*:

17 I sent Dr. *Clarke* (Phys: to his Majestie in ord: of the household) to visite the Chirurgions and sick in my district, in order to my following.

23 I tooke leave of his R: Highnesse & kissed his hand, now going to the fleete: returned home:

28 To Lond: at our Commiss: 29 Dined at Sir Ph: Warwicks, went to *Goring-house*, now Mr. Secretary *Benets*: ill built but the

place capable of being made a pretty Villa: his Majestie was now finishing the Decoy in the Park: 30: returnd home:

Aprill: 2: our *Curate* on 20 *Joh*: 19. 20: 4: Lond: Comiss: to take order about some Prisoners sent from Cap: *Allens* ship, taken in the *Solomon*, viz. the brave Man who defended her so gallantly. 5. return'd, which was a day of humiliation pub: & for successe of this tirrible Warr, begun doubtlesse at seacret instigation of the *French* &c to weaken the States, & Protestant Interest &c: prodigious preparations on both sides: our Doctor preached on 4. *James* 10. concerning the effect of true humiliation &c: 6 To our Commiss: In the afternoone saw acted *Mustapha* a *Tragedy* written by the E. of *Orary*: 7 came home: 9: our Doctor on his former 3. *Coloss:* 1: 11: To Lond: being now left alone & onely Commissioner to take all necessary orders here to exchange, remove, & keepe Prisoners, dispose of *Hospitals* &c: the rest of my Bro: Commissioners being all gon to their several districts in expectation of a suddaine Engagement:

19 Invited to a greate dinner at *Trinity house* in *Lond:* where I had buisinesse with the Commissioners of the Navy, & to receive the second 5000 pounds imprest for his Majesties Service of the Sick & Wounded & Prisoners: &c: Thence to our *Society* where were divers poisons experimented on Animals:

20: To White-hall, to the King, who call'd me into his Bed-Chamber as he was dressing, to whom I shew'd the Letter written to me from his R: Highness the *Duke of York* from the *Fleete*, giving me notice of Young *Evertse*, & some other considerable Commanders (newly taken in fight with the *Dartmouth* & *Diamond* fregats) whom he had sent me as Prisoners at Warr: I went to know of his *Majestie* how he would have me treate them: who commanded me to bring the Young Cap: to him, &, to take the Dutch Ambassadors Word (who yet remained here) for the other, that he should render himselfe to me when ever I cald, & not stir without leave: Upon which I desired more Guards, the Prison being Chelsey house: I went also to my L: *Arlington* (viz. Mr. Secretary Bennet, lately made a Lord) about another buisinesse; dined at my L: *Chancelors*, none with him but Sir *Sackvill Crow* (formerly Ambassador at ⟨*Constantinople*⟩) where we were very cherefull, & merry: 21 Went home, having taken order with my *Martial* about my Prisoners; & with the Doctor & Chirurgeon to attend the Wounded, both Enemies, & others of our owne: Next day to Lond: againe I visited my Charge, severall their leggs & armes off, miserable objects God knows:

24 I presented Young Cap: *Everse*, eldest sonn of Cornelius, Vice-Admirall of *Zealand*, & Nephew of John now *Admiral*, a most valiant person, to his Majestie, being in his bed-chamber: the K. gave his hand to kisse, gave him his liberty, asked many quest: concerning the fight (it being the first bloud drawne) his Majestie remembring the many civilities he had formerly received from his relations abroad, and had now so much Interest in that Considerable Province: Then I was commanded to go with him to the *Holl: Ambassador*, where he was to stay for his pass-port, & ordered me to give him 50 pieces in broad gold: next day I had the Ambassadors Parole for the other Cap: taken in Cap: Allens fight ⟨before⟩ *Cales* &c: 26: I gave his Majestie *Accompt* of what I had don, & desired the same favour for another Cap: which his Majestie gave me:

14 *Whitsonday Curate* on 14. *Joh:* 26. 16: To Lond to consider of the poore *Orphans* & *Widdows* made by this bloudy beginning, & whose Husbands & Relations perished in the *London* fregat: whereof 50 Widdows, & of them 45 with child:

18 Din'd with Mr. V: *Chamberlaine*, tooke leave of his Majestie preparing for *Dover*, returned home.

22 *Trinity* monday, election of a *Master* of the *Trinity* fraternity at *Deptford*: our Doctor preachd on 2: *Chro:* 15. 2. Admonitorie to union & Concord: We went in Barge to *Lond:* (after Election of *Cap: Hurleston*) where dined the Duke of *Albemarle* L. *Gen:* & divers greate persons, after which I returned home: 25 Lond: 26: To treate with the Holl: *Ambassador* at Chelsey, for the release of divers Prisoners at Warr, in Holland, upon Exchange here. After dinner, being calld into the Council Chamber at White hall, I gave his Majestie an accompt what I had don, informing him of the vast charge upon us, being now amounted to no lesse than 1000 pounds weekely; desiring our *Treasurer* might have another Privy-Seale for 500 pounds speedily, then went home:

29 I went (with my little boy) to visite my District over Kent, & to make up Accompts with my Officers; & so by Coach to *Rochester*, lay at *Sitingburne*, [30] din'd at *Canterbury*, next to *Dover*, visited the Governor at the Castle where I had some Prisoners: My son went to sea but was not sick. 31 To *Deale*:

June 1 finished my Accompts at *Deale*: visited the small forts: 2. returnd to *Canterbury*. 3. Through *Roch: Sittingh: Grave⟨s⟩end*, & the Fleete being just now Engaged gave special orders for my Officers to be ready to receive the Wounded & Prisoners: returned late home by boate:

⟨4⟩ Our *Doctor* on 1: *Pet:* 2: 5. 5 To *Lond:* to speake with his *Majestie* & D: of *Albemarle* for Horse & foote Guards for the Prisoners at War committed more particularly to my Charge, by a Commission a part, under his Majesties hand & seale: 8: I went againe to his Grace, thence to the Council, and moved for another Privy-seale for 20000 pounds: That I might have the disposal of the *Savoy Hospital* for the sick & Wounded: all which was granted: hence to our R: *Society* to refresh among the *Philosophers*:

8: Came newes of his Highnesse Victory over the Enemie, & indeede it might have ben a compleate one, & at once ended the Warr, had it ben pursued: but the Cowardize of some, Tretchery, or both frustrated that: we had however bonfires, bells, & rejoicing in the Citty &c. 9: Next day I had instant orders to repaire to the *Downes*; so as I got to *Rochester* this evening, dind next day at *Canterbury*, [10] lay at *Deale* where I found all in readinesse: but the fleete hindred by Contrary winds, I came away: having staied there the 11: where the *Mini⟨s⟩ter* preached on 37 *Psal:* 21. 5, *Pomerid*: 15 *Jam:* 17. 18. 12: I went back to *Dover*, din'd with the Governor at the Castle, returnd to Deale: next day, hearing the Fleete was at *Sold-bay*, I went homeward, lay at *Chattham*, in which journey, my Coach, by a rude justle against a Cart, was dangerously brused: 14 I got home: 15 Came Monsieur *Brizasiere* eldest sonn to the Pr: Sec: of State to the *French* King, with much other companie to dine with me: After dinner I went with him to *Lond* to speake to my *Lord* Gen: for more Guards, [16] & gave his Majestie an account of my journey to the Coasts, under my inspection: I also waited on his *R: Highness* now come triumphant from the fleete; goten in to repaire: See the whole history of this Conflict in my Hist: of the Dutch Warr: so on Saturday got home being 17: June.

18 Our *Doctor* on his former Text: 20: To Lond: represented the state of the S. & Wo: to his Majestie being in Council; for want of mony, who orderd I should apply to my *L: Tressurer* & Chan: of Exchequer upon what fonds to raise the mony promised: at which time we also presented to his Majestie divers

expedients for retrenchment of the charge: This Evening making my Court to the *Duke*, I spake with Monsieur *Cominges* the *French Ambassador* & his highnesse granted me six Prisoners *Embdeners*, who were desirous to go to the *Barbados* with a Merchant: 22: We waited on the *Chancellor* of the *Exchequer*, & got an order of Council for our mony, to be paied to the Tressurer of the navy to our Receiver: I dind with Sir Rob: Paston [since Earle of *Yarmouth*]. 23 Saw the *Duke* of *Verneuille* base-bro: to Q: *Mother* an handsome old man, & a greate hunter: &c:

23 The *Duke* of *Yorke* told us, that his dog sought out absolutely the very securest place of all the vessel, when they were in fight: In the afternoone I saw the pompous reception & audience of el *Conde de Molino* the Spanish Ambassador in the Banqueting house: both their Majesties siting together under the state: returned home: 28: To Lond: to R: *Society*, the Assembly now prorogued to *Michaelmas*, according to costome; & the sooner, because the *Plague* in *Lond* much increased: 29 went home, &c:

30 I went to *Chattam*: 1 *July* downe to the fleete, with my Lord San⟨d⟩wich now *Admiral*, with whom I went in a *Pinnace* to the Buy of the *Noore* where the whole fleete rod at anker: went on board the *Prince* a vessel of 90 brasse ordnance, (most whole canon) & happly the best ship in the world both for building & sailing: she had 700 men: They made a greate *huzza* or shout at our approch 3 times: here we dined with many noble men, Gent: and Volunteeres; served in Plate, and excellent meate of all sorts: after dinner came his *Majestie* & the *Duke* & Prince *Rupert*; & here I saw him knight Cap: *Cuttance*, for behaving himselfe so bravely in the late fight: & was amaz'd to ⟨behold⟩ the good order, decency, & plenty of all things, in a vessell so full of men: The ship received an hundred Canon shot in her body: Then I went on board the *Charles*, to which after a Gun was shot off, came all the flag-officers to his Majestie, who there held a generall Council, determining his R: Highness should adventure himselfe no more this summer: I spake with Sir *Geo: Ayscogh*, Sir William Pen &c: & Sir William Coventry (secretary to the Duke) about buisinesse, and so came away late, having seene the most glorious fleete, that ever spread saile: here was also among the rest the *Royal Sovraigne*: we returned in his Majesties *Yacht* with my L: *Sandwich* & Mr.

V: *Chamberlaine* landing at *Chattam* on Sunday morning: In the afternoone I went to Church at Chatt: where the Minister preached on   Redeeming the time, because the daies are evil &c: 3. I tooke order for 150 men to be carried on board, (who had ben recovered of their wounds & sicknesse) the *Clove-tree*, *Carolus quintus* & *Zeland*, ships that had ben taken by us in the fight: & so returnd home.

4 I was invited by Sir *William Ducy* to dine at *Charleton*. 7: To *Lond:* to Sir *William Coventrie* & so to *Sion*, where his Majestie sat at Council (during the Contagion): when my buisines was over I viewed that seate, belonging to the E. of *Northumberland* built out of an old *Nunnerie*, of stone, & faire enough, but more celebrated for the Garden than it deserves; yet there is excellent Walle fruit, & a pretty fountaine, nothing else extraordinarie: returnd that day: 9: I went to *Hampton Court* where now the whole Court was: my buisinesse was to solicite for mony, to carry letters intercepted, to conferr againe with Sir W: *Coventrie*, the Dukes *Secretary*, & so home, having dined at Mr. *Sec: Morice*. 16. To *Hampton-Court* againe, hearing a fragment of a sermon there by Dr. *Turner*: There died of the *Plague* in *Lond:* this Weeke 1100: 23. our Curat on 8 Rom: 18: There perished this weeke above 2000, & now were two houses shut up in our parish: 30: our Doctor as formerly 1. *Pet.* 2. 5.

Aug: 2. Was the Solemn Fast through England to deprecate Gods displeasure against the Land by *Pestilence* & *War*:

3 Came his *Grace* the *Duke* of *Albemarle* L: Gen: of all his Majesties forces &c: to Visite me, & carried me to dine with him &c: 4: The next I went to *Wotton* to carry my sonn & his Tutor Mr. *Bohune*, a fellow of *New Coll:* (& recomended to me by Dr. *Wilkins* & the President of Trinity Coll: in Oxford) for feare of the Pestilence still increasing both in *Lond:* & invirons: 6: Mr. *Higham* preached on: 4: *Jam:* 4: 7. I returned home, calling at *Woo⟨d⟩cot*, & *Durdens* by the way: where I ⟨found⟩ Dr. *Wilkins*, Sir William *Pettit*, & Mr. *Hooke* contriving Charriots, new rigges for *ships*, a Wheele for one to run races in, & other mechanical inventions, & perhaps three such persons together were not to be found else where in Europ, for parts and ingenuity: 8: To *Lond:* where I waited on the D: of *Albemarle*, who was resolv'd to stay at the Cock-pit in St. James Parke: who had sent me a Letter about buisinesse for his Majesties service: There dying this Week in

Lond: 4000: 13 was so tempesteous that we could not go to church: 13. There perished this Weeke 5000: 20 our *Doctor* on 1. *Cor:* 11. 28: The Plage still increasing:

28 The Contagion growing now all about us, I sent my *Wife* & whole family (two or three of my necessary Servants excepted) to *Wotton* to my Brothers, being resolved to stay at my house my selfe, & to looke after my Charge, trusting in the providence & goodnesse of God.

September 5 I went to ⟨*Chattam*⟩ to inspect my Province, carrying in my Coach 900 pounds. 6: I went to a place cald *Bobing* neere *Sittinburne*, to see my *Lady Smith* where I dined.

7 Came home, there perishing now neere ten-thousand poore Creatures weekely: however I went all along the Citty & suburbs from *Kent streete* to St. *James's*, a dismal passage & dangerous, to see so many Cofines exposd in the streetes & the streete thin of people, the shops shut up, & all in mournefull silence, as not knowing whose turne might be next: I went to the D: of *Albemarle* for a Pest-ship, to waite on our infected men, who were not a few: 10: Dr. *Plume* at Greenewich, on 3. Coloss: 5. 6. shewing how our sinns had drawne downe Gods Judgements: I dined with the Commissioners of the Navy, retreated hither, & with whom I had buisinesse:

14 I went to *Wotton*, to see my *Wife* & family: 16: To visite old Secretary *Nicholas* being now at his new Purchase of West *Horsley*, once Mortgaged to me by my L: VC. Montague: a pretty drie seate on the downe: returned to Wotton. 17: Receiving a Letter from his Excellency my L. *Sandwich* of a defeate given to the *Dut*⟨*c*⟩*h*, I was forc'd to travell all Sonday, when by the way calling in to see my other Bro: at *Woodcot*, as I was at dinner, I was surpriz'd with a fainting fit: which much a'larm'd the family, as well it might, I coming so lately from infected places; but I blesse God it went off, so as I got home that night; but was exceedingly ⟨perplex'd⟩, to find that there were sent me to dispose of neere 3000 Prisoners at Warr; so as on the 18, I was forc'd to go to *Lond*; & take orders from my Lord Gen: what I should do with them, they being more than I had places fit to receive & guard, he made me dine with him, & then we consulted about it:

19 next day I din'd with my L: *Brounchar*, & so return'd home: 23. My L: *Admirall* being come from the *Fleete* to *Greenewich*, I went thence with him to the Cock-pit to consult with the *Duke*

of *Albemarle*: I was peremptory, that unlesse we had 10000 pounds immediately, the Prisone⟨r⟩s would sterve, & 'twas propos'd it should be raised out of the East India Prises, now taken by my L: *Sandwich*: They being but two of the Commissioners & so not impower'd to determine, sent an expresse to his Majestie & Council to know what they should do: In the meane time I had 5 Vessels with Competent Guards to keepe the Prisoners in for the present, & to be placed as I should think best: After dinner (which was at the Generals) I went over to visite his Grace, the A: Bish: of *Canterbury* at Lambeth, who was not gon from his Palace, whence I returned home:

24: Mr. *Plume* at Greenewich (for our Parish was exceedingly infected) preached on 8. *John*: 51.

28 To the L: Generall to acquaint him againe of the deplorable state of our men, for want of provision, return'd with orders: 29. To *Erith* to quicken the Sale of the *Prizes* lying there, by orders, to the Commissioners who lay on board, til they should be disposed of, 5000 pounds being proportiond for my quarters: Then I also deliverd the Dut⟨c⟩h *Vice Admirall*, who was my Prisoner, to Mr. Lo, of the *Marshallsea* he giving me bond of 500 pounds to produce him at my call: I exceedingly pittied this brave, unhappy person, who had lost with these Prizes 40000 pounds, after 20 yeares negotiation in the *East Indies*: I dined in one of these Vessels of 1200 tunn, full of riches, and return'd home:

October 1. At *Greenewich* Mr. *Plume*, on *Luke*,   *are there few shall be saved*? I received the H: Comm: & din'd with Mr. *Cottyles*:

This afternoone as I was at Evening prayer, tidings were brought me, of my *Wifes* being brought to bed at *Wotton* of a *Daughter* (after 6 sonns) borne this morning 1. *Octob:* in the same Chamber, I had first tooke breath in, and at the first day of that moneth, in the morning, as I was on the last: 45 yeares before: & about the very same houre, being $\frac{1}{3}$ aft⟨e⟩r 4: *Sonday*:

4 Was the monethly fast, Mr. *Plume* on: 16: *Numb:* 46, of the sinn of rebellion against Magistrates & Ministers: 7: I went to see my Wife. 8: The Parson of *Wotton* Mr. *Higham* on 15 Luke 18. 19. 20: & then before Dinner, was my Daughter Christnd *Mary* in the Chamber cald the red chamb⟨e⟩r, where borne, Her Grandfath⟨e⟩r Sir *R: Bro:* my Aunt *Hungerford* of *Cadenam* (by

proxy) & my *Neepce* Mary (& God-daught⟨e⟩r) being Gossips:
10 I returned to Lond: I went thro the whole *Citty*, having occasion to alight out of the Coach in severall places about buisinesse of mony, when I was invironed with multitudes of poore
pestiferous creatures, begging almes; the shops universaly shut
up, a dreadfull prospect: I dined with my L: Gen: was to receive
10000 pounds & had Guards to convey both my selfe & it, & so
returned ⟨home⟩, through Gods infinite mercy: 15. Mr. *Plume* at
Greenewich on 6. *Gal:* 10.

17 I went to *Gravesend*, next day to *Chattam*, thence to *Maidstone*, in order to the march of 500 Prisoners to *Leeds-Castle*
which I had hired of my Lord *Culpeper*, and [19] dined with Mr.
Harlakingdon, a worthy Gent: of *Maidstone*, being earnestly
desired by the Learned Sir *Roger Twisden* & Deputy *Lieutenants*, to spare that towne from quartering any of my sick
flock: Here Sir Ed: *Brett* sent me some horse to bring up the
rere, which returned that night to *Rochester*: 20: This Country
from *Rochester* to *Maidstone* by the *Medway* river, is very agreable, the downes & prospect: 21 I came from *Gravesend*, where
Sir *Jo: Griffith* the Governor of the fort, entertaind me very
handsomly: 22. Mr. *Plume* as formerly: 23. To *Lond:* to the D: of
Albemarle, returnd:

29: 31 I was this day 45 yeares of age, wonderfully preserved,
for which I blessed his infinite goodnesse:

November 3 I dined with the *Duke* of *Albemarle* having much
buisinesse with him. 5. Mr. *Plume* on. 106. *Psal:* 42. The wonderfull deliverances God had given his Church. I received the B:
Sacrament.

23 I went home, the contagion beginning now to decrease
considerably: 26: Mr. *Plume*   on feare not, *little flock, tis
your fathers will to give you a Kingdome.* 27: I went to the D: of
Albemarle having buisinesse to recommend to his grace, going
now to *Oxford*, where both Court, K & Parliament had ben most
part of the summer: There was no small suspicion of my Lord
Sandwiches permitting divers Commanders that were in the fight
& action, at the taking the E. India prizes, to break bulk, and take
to their owne selves many rich things, Jewels, Silkes &c: though
I believe some whom I could name, fill'd their pockets, my
L: *Sandwich* himselfe had the least share: however he underwent
the blame of it, & it created him Enemies, & prepossessed the

L: Generall, for he spake to me of it with much zeale & concerne, & I believe laied load enough on *Sandwich* at *Oxford*.

December 3 Our Doctor Preached at Deptford (nor had that good man stirred from his charge) on 2: Hab: 1: I received the bless⟨e⟩d Comm: the contagion now abated also in this Parish: 6: was the monethly fast: our Doctor on 1. Reg: 8. 37:

8 To my L: of *Albemarles* (now return'd from *Oxon*) who was also now declared Generall at Sea, to the no small mortification, of that Excellent Person, the *Earle* of *Sandwich*: Whom the Duke of *Albemarle*, not onely suspected faulty about the prizes, but lesse Valiant: himselfe imagining how easie a thing it were to confound the *Hollander*, as well now, as when heretofore he fought against them, upon a more disloyal Interest:

10 A stranger preached at Greenewich on 13 *Luke*. 1. 2. ad 5. not to judge uncharitably of others, for our owne Escape: applied to those who survived the Contagion &c: a seasonable discourse: 15 I din'd at the *Sherifs* of *Lond*. with the *Duke* & *Dutchesse* of *Albemarle*, & Lieutennant of the *Tower*, where was a mighty feast: 17: Mr. *Plume* as formerly:

23. To *Wotton* to see my Wife, & kept *Christmas* with my hospitable *Brother*:

25 on the same, I received the B: *Eucharist*. 26. on the same. 30: To *Woodcott*, where I supped at My Lady *Mordants* at *Ashley*; here was a roome hung with *Pintado* full of figures, greate & small, pretily representing sundry Trades and occupations of the Indians, with their habits &c: very extraordinarie: here supped also Dr. *Duke* a learned & facetious Gent:

Now blessed be God, for his extraordinary mercies & preservations of me this Yeare when thousands & ten thousands perish'd & were swept away on each side of me: There dying in our Parish this yeare 406 of the Pestilence:

1666 *January* 1 I beged the Protection of Almighty God, for the ensuing yeare: &c:

2 I supped in *None-such* house (whither the Office of the Exchequer was transferrd, during the Plague) at my good friends Mr. *Packer*: & tooke an exact view of the Plaster Statues & *Bass-relievos* inserted twixt the timbers & *poincons* of the outside walles of the Court, which must needes have ben the work of some excellent *Italian*: admire I did much how it had lasted so well & intire as since the time of *Hen:* 8, exposd, as they are to

the aire, & pitty it is they are not taken out, & ⟨preserved⟩ in some dry place, a gallerie would become them: there are some *Mezzo relievi* as big as the life, & the storie is of the heathen Gods, Emblems, Compartiments, &c.

The Palace concists of two Courts, of which the first is of stone Castle like, by the Lord *Lumlies* (of whom 'twas purchas'd) the other of Timber a Gotique fabric, but these walls incomparably beautified: I also observed that the appearing timber *punchions*, *entretices* &c were all so covered with Scales of Slate, that it seemed carved in the Wood, & painted, the Slat fastned on the timber in pretty figures, that has preserved it from rotting like a coate of armour: There stand in the Garden two handsome stone *Pyramids*, & the *avvenue* planted with rows of faire *Elmes*, but the rest of those goodly Trees both of this & of *Worcester*-Park adjoyning were fell'd by those destructive & avaritious Rebells in the late Warr, which defac'd one of the stateliest seates his Majestie had.

After much, & indeede extraordinary mirth & cheere, all my Brothers, our Wives & Children being together, & after much sorrow & trouble during this Contagion, which separated our families, as well as others, I returned to my house, but [12] my Wife went back to *Wotton*, I not as yet willing to adventure her, the Contagion, though exceedingly abated, not as yet wholy extinguish'd amongst us:

29 I went to waite on *his Majestie* (now return'd from *Oxford* to *Hampton Court*) where the *Duke* of *Albemarle* presenting me to him, he ran towards me, & in most gracious manner gave me his hand to kisse, with many thanks for my Care, & faithfullnesse in his service, in a time of that greate danger, when every body fled their Employments; he told me he was much oblig'd to me, & said he was severall times concern'd for me, & the peril I under-went, & did receive my service most acceptably: Though in truth I did but what was my duty, & ô that I had perform'd it as I ought: After this his Majestie was pleas'd to talke with me alone neere an houre, of severall particulars of my Employment, & ordred me to attend him againe the thursday following at *White-hall*: Then the *Duke* came towards me & embrac'd me with much kindnesse, & told me, if he had but thought my danger would have ben so greate, he would not have sufferd his *Majestie* to employ me in that Station: then came to

salute me, my L. of *St. Albans*, L. *Arlington*, Sir *William Coventrie* & severall greate persons, after which I got home, not being very well in health. The Court was now in deepe Mourning for the *French Queene-mother*. 30. our Doctor (being the Anniversary of the Ks. *Martyrdome*) preach'd on 4. *Threnæ*. 20, describing the vile tr⟨e⟩atchery of his late Majesties Enemies, through the simple meaning of some, & abominable treason & malice of others: That no pretence of doing good, by evil meanes was justifiable, this he proved exceedingly well:

Feb 2 To *Lond*, his Majestie now come to *W. hall*, where I heard & saw my *L: Major* & breathren make his Speech of wellcome, & the two sherifs knighted:

6 My *Wife* & family return'd to me now out of the Country, where they had ben since *August* by reason of the Contagion, now almost universaly ceasing: Blessed be God for his infinite mercy in preserving us; I having gon through so much danger, & lost so many of my poore officers, escaping still my selfe, that I might live to recount & magnifie his goodnesse to me: 7: our Doctor on 1. *Reg:* 8. 38. on occasion of the monethly fast: 8 To *Lond*. had another gracious reception of his *Majestie* who call'd me into his bed-chamber, to lay-before, & describe to him my project of an *Infirmarie*, which I read to him, with greate approbation, recommending it to his R: *Highnesse*, & so I returned home.

11 Our Doctor as formerly on *Esay:* 16 To Lond, to meete my fellow *Commissioners* now returnd from their dwellings: & went home this Evening:

20: To the *Commissioners* of the *Navy*, who having seene the project of the Infirmary, encouragd the worke, & were very earnest it should be set about speedily: but I saw no mony, though a very moderate expense, would have saved thousands to his Majestie and ben much more commodious for the cure & quartering our sick & wounded, than the dispersing of them into private houses, where many more Chir⟨ur⟩giones, & tenders were necessary, & the people tempted to debaucherie &c: 21. I went to my *L: Tress:* for an assignement of 40000 pounds, upon the two last quarters, for the support of the next yeares Charge: next day to the D: of *Albemarle*, & Sec: of State: to desire them to propose it at the next *Council:* 24. I waited on the Council, return'd home:

Mar: 1 To *Lond:* presented his *Majestie* with my booke, intituled, The Pernicious Consequences of the new *Heresy* of the *Jesuites*, against Kings & States: 2: Dr. *Sandcroft* [since A: *Bish*: of *Cant:*] preachd *Coram Rege* on 102. *Psal* 27: I returnd home:

Ap⟨ri⟩ll: 1 Our *Curate* on: 4: *Rom:* 25. 2: To *Lond:* to bespeake a new Coach: & consult about ordering the natural rarities belonging to the Repositorie of the R: Soc: referr'd to a Committè: return'd: 8: Our Doctor as formerly: 10. To *Lond:* to visite Sir W: *D'Oylie*, surpriz'd with a fit of *Apoplexie* & in extreame danger: 11: Dr. *Bathirst coram Rege* on   what I say, I *say unto* you all, *watch*, in a seasonable & most excellent discourse: As his Majestie came from Chapell, he call'd to me in the lobby, & told Me he must now have me Sworn for *Justice of Peace* (having long since made me of the Commission) for preventing some dissorder in our parish at this time; I replied, that it was altogether inconsistent with the other service I was ingag'd in, during this hostility with *Dutch* & *French* and humbly desired to be excus'd, notwithstanding he persisted: After dinner waiting on him I gave him the first notice of the *Spaniards* referring the umpirage of the Peace 'twixt them, & the *Portugal* to the *French King*, which came to me in a letter from *France* before the *Secretaries* of *State* had any newes of it: After this againe his Majestie asked me, if I had found out any able person about our Parts, that might supplie my place of *Justice* of Peace (the thing in the world, I had most industriou⟨s⟩ly avoided to act in hitherto, in reguard of the perpetual trouble theroff in this numerous Parish &c) on which I nominated one, whom his *Majestie* commanded me to give immediate notice of to my *L: Chancellor*, & I should be excus'd: for which I rendred his *Majestie* many thankes: After dinner, I went to the D: of *Albemarle* about some complaints I had against the Cleark of the Passage at *Dover*: Thence to my *L: Chancellors* to do his Majesties Command: Thence to the R: *Society* where I was chosen by 27 Voices to be one of their Council for the ensuing yeare, but upon my earnest suite, in respect of my other affairs, I got to be excused, & so home:

13 Doctor on   good friday, when I received the B: Comm: The Lord make me mindfull of his mercy, & my promises: 15. our Doctor on 15. [1]. *Cor:* 20. *Easter day*: Our Parish now was more infected with the Plague, than ever, & so was all the Countrie

about, though almost quite ceased at *London*: 18. I went to *Lond*: to propose the Sale of *Cressing Temple* (in which I was a Trustee for my late Co: G. Tuke) to the Duke of *Albemarle*, when also I tooke leave of his Grace, now preparing to go *Generall* of the *Fleete*: so returnd: & that night my poore Wife *Miscarried* of a Sonn, being but young with Child:

22 Our *Curate* on 28 *Matt:* 6: 24: To Lond: about our *Mint Commiss:* and sate in the inner Court of Wards: Din'd at the Comptrollers: 26: Sate at *Painters hall*: as formerly, returned home: At the *R: Society*, was tried a Saddle on Springs, to make a Trotting ho⟨r⟩se go Easie to the rider. 29: our Doctor as formerly:

May 1. To *Lond:* to sit in Commiss. 2: *Deane* of *Rochester* coram rege on the fast: Afternoone to the R: So: where were some experiments on the Load-stone: 3. went home: 6. our Curate as formerly:

7 I went to *Rochester*: 8 To *Queenborow* where finding the *Richmond* fregate I sailed to the Buy of the *Noore* to my L: *Gen:* & *Prince Rupert* where was the Rendezvous of the most glorious Fleete in the World, now preparing to meete the *Hollander*: having received orders & settled my buisinesse there, I return'd on the 9th to Chattham at night: next day I went to visite my *Co: Hales* at a sweetely watred place neere *Bochton* at *Chilston*: The next morning to *Leedes-Castle*, once a famous hold &c. now hired by me of my *Lord Culpeper* for a Prison: here I flowed the drie moate and made a new draw bridge, brought also Spring Water into the Court of the Castle to an old fountaine, & tooke order for the repaires: 10: returnd to *Rochester*, & next day home:

22 To Lond: dined with my Bro: Richard: thence waited on my L: Chancellors new Palace, & Lord *Berkeleys* built next to it; & so to Court: 24: din'd with my L: *Cornbury* now made L. *Chamberlaine* to the *Queene*, who kept a very honorable table, & so home.

June: 1. Being in my Garden & hearing the Greate gunns go thick off: I immediately tooke horse, & rod that night to *Rochester* it being 6 at Evening when I set out: [2] Thence next day towards the *Downes* & Sea-Coast: but meeting with the *Lieutennant* of the *Hantshire* fregat, who told me what pass'd, or rather not pass'd, I returned to *Lond:* (there being no noise, nor appearance at Deale or that Coast of any engagement) this recounting to his Majestie (whom I found at St. *Jams's* [*Park*] impatiently expecting) & [I] knowing that Prince Rupert was loose, about 3 at St. *Hellens* point at N. of *Wight*, it greately rejoic'd him; but was astonish'd when I assur'd him they heard nothing of the Gunns in the *Downes*, nor the *Lieutennant* who landed there by five that morning.

3: Whitsonday: Dr. *Cartwrite coram rege*   *if ye love me keepe my Commandments*: after sermon came newes, that the *Duke* of *Albemarle* was still in fight & all Saturday; & cap: *Harmans* ship (the Henrie) like to be burnt: Then a letter from Mr. *Bertie* that *Pr: Rupert* was come up with his *Squadron* (according to my former advice of his being loose & in the way) & put new courage into our fleete now in a manner yeilding ground; so as now we were chasing the chacers: That the D: of *Alb:* was slightly wounded, & the rest in greate danger 'til now; so having ben much wearied with my journey, I slip'd home, the Gunns still roaring very fiercely:

5 I went this morning to *Lond:* where came severall particulars of the fight: 6: came Sir *Dan: Harvey* from the Generall & related the dreadfull encounter, upon which his *Majestie* commanded me to dispatch away an extraordinary *Physitian*, & more *Chirurgions*: 'Twas on the solemn fast day, when the newes came, his Majestie being in the Chapell made a suddaine Stop, to heare the relation, which being with much advantage on our side, his Majestie commanded that Publique Thanks should immediately be given as for a Victory; The *Deane* of the Chapell going downe to give notice of it to the other Deane officiating; & so notice was likewise sent to St. *Paules* and *Westminster* abby: But this was no sooner over, but newes came that our losse was very greate both in ships & men: That the *Prince* fregat was burnt & so a noble vessel of 90 brasse Guns lost: together with the taking of Sir Geo: *Ayscue* & exceeding shattring of both *fleetes*, so as both being obstinate, both parted rather for want of amunition & tackle than Courage, our Generall retreating like a *Lyon*, which exceedingly abated of our former jolitie: There was however order given for bone-fires & bells, but God knows, it was rather a deliverance than a Triumph: so much it pleased God to humble our late over Confidence, that nothing could withstand the *Duke of Albemarle*: who in good truth made too forward a reckoning of his successe, now, because he had once beaten the Dutch in another quarrell: & being ambitious to

out-do the Earle of *Sandwich*, whom he had prejudice ⟨to⟩ as defective of Courage:

7 I sent more Chirurgions, linnen, medicaments &c: to the severall ports in my District: din'd at my *L: Cornburies*, returned home with my Wife: 8. Dined with me Sir *Alex: Frasier* (prime Physitian to his Majestie) after dinner went on board his Majesties pleasure-boate where I saw the *London* fregate launched (a most statly ship built by the Cittie, to supply that which was burnt by accident some time since) The *King*: L. *Major* & *Sherifes* being there, with a greate Banquet: I presented my Sonn to *his Majestie*:

10 our *Viccar* on: 8 Rom: 11. The effects of Prayer by the Spirit, how that gift differ'd from the common presbyters extemporaries: I received the H: Comm: 11. *Trinity Moneday* he preached before the fraternity on   *Psal: Blessed are they who put their trust in him* &c applied to the remeeting of that Corporation after the late raging & wasting Pestilence: I dined with them in their new roome in *Deptford*, the first time after it was new built:

12 To *Lond:* to our Commission. 13 To the R: Society, where was brought the new Pendulum:

14 Went home: 15 I went to *Chattham*: 16 in the Jemmy Yach't (an incomparable sailer) to sea, arived by noone at the *Fleete* in the B of *Nore*, dined with *Pr: Rupert* & *Generall*: 17: came his *Majestie*, *Duke*, & many Noblemen; after Council, we went to Prayers: having dispatch'd my buisinesse, I return'd to *Chattham* having layne but one night at sea, in the *Royal Charles*, we had a tempestuous sea; I went on shore at *Sheere-Nesse*, where they were building an *Arsenal* for the Fleete, & designing a royal Fort, with a receptable for greate ships to ride at *Anker*; but here I beheld that sad spectacle, namely more than halfe of that gallant bulwark of the Kingdome miserably shatterd, hardly a Vessell intire, but appearing rather so many wracks & hulls, so cruely had the *Dutch* mangled us: when the losse of the Prince (that gallant Vessell) had ben a losse to be universaly deplor'd, none knowing for what reason we first ingagd in this ungratefull warr: we lost besids 9 or 10 more, & neere 600 men slaine, & 1100 wounded 2000 Prisoners, to balance which perhaps we might destroy 18 or 20 of the Enemies ships & 7 or 800 poore men: 18 weary of this sad sight I returned home: 19 came Sir

Rob: Cotton, my Lady *Morice* (wife to the Secretarie of State) to dine with me. 20: Came to visite me my old *Italian* acquaintance Dr. *Croydon*, Waldrond, Clark, Quartermaine to dine with me: 24: Our *Viccar* as formerly: 26: To Lond: 27: To Our Society: 28 Din'd at my L: *Chancelors*: 30: returned home:

July 2. Came Sir Jo: *Duncomb* & Mr. *Tho: Chichley* both Privy Councellers & Commissioners of his Majesties Ordinance to give me a visite, & to let me know his Majestie had in *Council* nominated me to be one of the Commissioners for regulating the farming & making of *Salt-peter* through the whole King-dome, & that we were to sit in the Tower the next day &c: When they were gon, came to see me Sir *Jo: Cotton* (heire to the famous Antiquarie Sir Robert) a pretended greate *Gretian*, but had by no meanes the parts or genius of his Grandfather: with him were severall other knights & Gent:

3 I went to sit with the Commissioners at the *Tower* of Lond, where our Commiss: being read, we made some progresse in buisinesse: Sir G: *Wharton* being our Secretary, that famous *Mathematitian*, & who writ the yearely Almanac, during his Majesties troubles:

Thence to Painter hall to our other *Commiss:* & dined at my L: *Majors*: 4: Doctor *Megot* preach⟨ed⟩ the solemn fast day *coram rege* on 26: *Esay:* 8 an excellent discourse on the terror of Gods Judgements: After Sermon I waited on my L: A: Bish: of *Cant* and B: of *Winchester*; where the *Deane* of *Westminster* spake to me about putting into my hands the disposal of 50 pounds which the Charitable people at *Oxford* had sent to be distributed among the sick & wounded seamen &c: since the battaile: Thence I went to my L: *Chancellor* to joy him of his *Royal High-nesse* second sonne now born at St. *James's*, and to desire the use of the *Star-chamber* for our Commissioners to meete in, painters hall not being so convenient. 5. I met at *Painters hall*, thence went home. 8. our *Viccar* on 17: Gen: 1: Afternoone to *Greene-wich* where Dr. *Harding* deane of *Rochester* on 4. *Amos* 11: 10. To the *Tower* about the *salt-peter* Commiss: thence to the Court of Wards: &c: 11. To Sir William *Coventrie* to explaine certaine orders of his R: Highnesse: din'd at my Lord *Fitz Hardings*, Afterwards to the R: Society, where was an experiment of vibrating two [concave] Globes fill'd with sand, of severall dimensions, to represent the motion of the Earth & Moone about it, which the sand issuing out of the bottome described on the floore: Triall againe of the saddle Charriot, & fountaine to water Gardens & tops of tallest trees: &c: 12: We sate the first time at the Star-Chamber: There was added to the Commission now Sir *Geo: Downing* (one that had ben a greate   against his Majestie but now insinuated into favour, & from a pedagoge & fanatic preach⟨e⟩r, not worth a groate, becoming excessive rich) to inspect the Hospitals, & treate about Prisoners: so I return'd this night:

14 To Lond: Sat at Tower, with Sir J: *Duncomb* & L *Berkeley* to signe Deputations for Undertakers to furnish their proportions of Salt-peter, returnd: 15 our *Curate* on 8: *Matt:* 26. *Pomerid:* 68. *Psal:* 1. 17. To Lond: to prepare for the next Engagement of the Fleetes now gotten to sea againe: Sir *Robert Murray* brought in severall *Minerals* & *Marcasites* to the R: So: out of Walles, with divers *Medailes*: 18: home: 20: sat at the *Tower*.

22 I went to *Greene wich* to Prayers: our Parish still exceedingly infected with the Contagion:

24 To *Lond:* 25 The Fleetes ingaged: I din'd at L. *Berkeleys* at St. *James's* where dined my Lady *Harriette Hyde*, L: *Arlington*, Sir Jo: *Duncomb* &c: 26. returned:

28 At The *Tower* about the *Salt-peter* Commiss: & immediately returnd home:

29 The Pestilence now a fresh increasing in our *Parish*, I forbore going to Church: In the ⟨Afternoon⟩ came tidings of our Victorie over the Hollanders, sinking some, and driving others on ground, & into their ports: 31. To Lond: to the Star-Chamber:

Aug: 1 Being pub: fast: Dr. *Gunning* on *Psal:*   shewing how the Angels had the custody of Good men: &c: In the afternoone I went to Dr. Keffler who married the daughter of the famous *Chymist* Drebbell inventor of the ⟨Bow-dyed⟩ *Scarlet*: I went to see his Yron *Ovens* made portable formerly for the Pr: of *Oranges* Armie &c: I supped at the Rhenish Wine-house with divers Scots Gentlemen: 2: return'd home. ⟨5⟩ our *Viccar* on former text: I received the H: Sacrament.

6. To *Lond:* din'd with Mr. *Povy*, & then went with him, to see a Country house he had bought neere *Brainford*, returning by *Kensington*, which house I saw standing to a very gracefull avenue of trees; but tis an ordinary building, especialy one part. I returnd to *Lond:*

8 Dined at Sir Stephen Foxes, & came home: 10 To *Lond*: din'd with Mr. *Odart* Secretary of the Latine tongue: 12 The pestilence still raging in our Parish, I durst not go to Church. 14 came with my Wife to Lond: sat with the Commissioners: passd the Evening at Hide-park. 10 Went to *Parsons greene*. 17: Din'd with L: Chancellor whom I intreated to visite the Hospital of the Savoy, & reduce it (after the greate abuse had ben continued) to its original institution, for the benefit of the poore, which he promised to do: 18 din'd at Sir *Arthyr Ingrams* in the Citty at a greate feast, & returnd home: 19: went not to church by reason of the Contagion. 21. To star-Chamber. 22. Din'd at Sir Will: *Morices* (sec: of state) having ben in the morning at Sir W: Coventries about baile for some Captaines my Prisoners: Afternoone at our Society: 23. Sat at Star-Chamber, Din'd at Sir William *D'Oylies* now recovered as it were miraculously: In the afternoone Visited the *Savoy* Hospital, where I staied to see the miserably dismembred & wounded men dressed & gave some necessary orders: Then to my L: *Chancelor*, who had (with the Bish: of *Lond* & others in Commission) chosen me one of the three Surveyors of the repaires of *Paules*, & to consider of a model for the new building, or (if it might be) repairing of the Steeple, which was most decayd: & so I returned home.

26 Contagion still continuing, we had the Church Office at home &c:

27 I went to St. *Paules Church* in *Lond:* where with Dr. *Wren*, Mr. Prat, Mr. *May*, Mr. Tho: Chichley, Mr. Slingsby, the Bish: of Lond., the Deane of S. Paule, & severall expert Workmen, we went about, to survey the generall decays of that antient & venerable Church, & to set downe the particulars in writing, what was fit to be don, with the charge thereof: giving our opinion from article to article: We found the maine building to receede outward: 'It was Mr. Chichleys & *Prats* opinion that it had ben so built ab origine for an effect in Perspective, in reguard of the height; but I was with *Dr. Wren* quite of another judgement, as indeede ridiculous, & so we entered it: We plumbed the Uprights in severall places: When we came to the Steeple, it was deliberated whither it were not well enought to repaire it onely upon its old foundation, with reservation to the 4 Pillars: This Mr. *Chichley* & Prat were also for; but we totaly rejected it & persisted that it requird a new foundation, not onely in reguard

of the necessitie, but for that the shape of what stood was very meane, & we had a mind to build it with a noble *Cupola*, a forme of church building, not as yet knowne in England, but of wonderfull grace: for this purpose we offerd to bring in a draught & estimate, which (after much contest) was at last assented to, & that we should nominate a Committè of able Workemen to examine the present foundation: This concluded we drew all up in Writing, and so going with my L: *Bishop* to the Deanes, after a little refreshment, went home.

28 To Lond: Sate at *Star-Chamber*: next day to the R: So: where one *Mercator* an excellent Mathematician produced his rare Clock & new motion to performe the æquations, & Mr. *Rooke* his new Pendulum: 30: Went home: 31: Mr. *Henshaw* came with one Mr. *Garret* to dine with me.

September 2: This fatal night about ten, began that deplorable fire, neere Fish-streete in Lond: 2: I had pub: prayers at home: after dinner the fire continuing, with my Wife & Sonn took Coach & went to the bank side in Southwark, where we beheld that dismal speectaccle, the whole Citty in dreadfull flames neere the Water side, & had now consumed all the houses from the bridge all Thames Streete & up-wards towards Cheape side, downe to the three Cranes, & so returned exceedingly astonishd, what would become of the rest: 3 The Fire having continud all this night (if I may call that night, which was as light as day for 10 miles round about after a dreadfull manner) when consp⟨ir⟩ing with a fierce Eastern Wind, in a very drie season, I went on foote to the same place, when I saw the whole South part of the Citty burning from Cheape side to the Thames, & all along Cornehill (for it likewise kindled back against the Wind, as well ⟨as⟩ forward) *Tower-Streete*, *Fen-church*-streete, *Gracious Streete*, & so along to Bainard Castle, and was now taking hold of St. *Paules-Church*, to which the Scaffalds contributed exceedingly: The Conflagration was so universal, & the people so astonish'd, that from the beginning (I know not by what desponding or fate), they hardly stirr'd to quench it, so as there was nothing heard or seene but crying out & lamentation, & running about like distracted creatures, without at all attempting to save even their goods; such a strange consternation there was upon them, so as it burned both in breadth & length, The Churches, Publique Halls, Exchange, Hospitals,

Monuments, & ornaments, leaping after a prodigious manner from house to house & streete to streete, at greate distance one from the other, for the heate (with a long set of faire & warme weather) had even ignited the aire, & prepared the materials to conceive the fire, which devoured after a⟨n⟩ incredible manner, houses, furniture & everything: Here we saw the Thames coverd with goods floating, all the barges & boates laden with what some had time & courage to save, as on the other, the Carts &c carrying out to the fields, which for many miles were strewed with moveables of all sorts, & Tents erecting to shelter both people & what goods they could get away: ô the miserable & calamitous speectacle, such as happly the whole world had not seene the like since the foundation of it, nor to be out don, 'til the universal Conflagration of it, all the skie were of a fiery aspect, like the top of a burning Oven, & the light seene above 40 miles round about for many nights: God grant mine eyes may never behold the like, who now saw above ten thousand houses all in one flame, the noise & crakling & thunder of the impetuous flames, the shreeking of Women & children, the hurry of people, the fall of towers, houses & churches was like an hideous storme, & the aire all about so hot & inflam'd that at the last one was not able to approch it, so as they were force'd ⟨to⟩ stand still, and let the flames consume on which they did for neere two whole mile⟨s⟩ in length and one in bredth: The Clowds also of Smoke were dismall, & reached upon computation neere 50 miles in length: Thus I left it this afternoone burning, a resemblance of Sodome, or the last day: It call'd to mind that of 4 *Heb: non enim hic habemus stabilem Civitatem*: the ruines resembling the picture of *Troy*: *London* was, but is no more: Thus I return'd:

4. The burning still rages; I went now on horse back, & it was now gotten as far as the Inner Temple; all *Fleetestreete*, old baily, Ludgate hill, Warwick Lane, Newgate, Paules Chaine, Wattling-streete now flaming & most of it reduc'd to ashes, the stones of *Paules* flew like granados, the Lead mealting downe the streetes in a streame, & the very pavements of them glowing with fiery rednesse, so as nor horse nor man was able to tread on them, & the demolitions had stopped all the passages, so as no help could be applied; the Easter⟨n⟩ Wind still more impetuously driving the flames forewards: Nothing but

the almighty power of God was able to stop them, for vaine was the help of man: on the fift it crossed towards *White-hall*, but ô the Confusion was then at that Court: It pleased his *Majestie* to command me among the rest to looke after the quenching of fetter-lane end, to preserve (if possible) that part of *Holborn*, whilst the rest of the Gent: tooke their several posts, some at one part, some at another, for now they began to bestirr themselves, & not 'til now, who 'til now had stood as men interdict, with their hands a crosse, & began to consider that nothing was like to put a stop, but the blowing up of so many houses, as might make a ⟨wider⟩ gap, than any had yet ben made by the ordinary method of pulling them downe with Engines; This some stout Seamen proposd early enought to have saved the whole Citty; but some tenacious & avaritious Men, Aldermen &c. would not permitt, because their houses must have ben ⟨of⟩ the first: It was therefore now commanded to be practised, & my concerne being particularly for the *Hospital* of st. *Bartholomeus* neere Smithfield, where I had many wounded & sick men, made me the more diligent to promote it; nor was my care for the *Savoy* lesse: So as it pleased Almighty God by abating of the Wind, & the industrie of people, now when all was lost, infusing a new Spirit into them (& such as had if exerted in time undoubtedly preserved the whole) that the furie of it began sensibly to abate, about noone, so as it came no farther than the Temple West-ward, nor than the enterance of Smithfield North; but continued all this day & night so impetuous toward Cripple-Gate, & The Tower, as made us even all despaire; It also brake out againe in the Temple: but the courage of the multitude persisting, & innumerable houses blown up with Gunpowder, such gaps & desolations were soone made, as also by the former three days consumption, as the back fire did not so vehemently urge upon the rest, as formerly: There was yet no standing neere the burning & glowing ruines neere a furlongs Space; The Coale & Wood wharfes & magazines of Oyle, rozine, [chandler] &c: did infinite mischiefe; so as the invective I but a little before dedicated to his Majestie & publish'd,[1] giving warning what might

---

1 *Fumifugium.*

probably be the issue of suffering those shops to be in the Citty, was lookd on as prophetic: but there I left this smoking & sull-try heape, which mounted up in dismall clowds night & day, the poore Inhabitans dispersd all about St. Georges, Moore filds, as far as higate, & severall miles in Circle, Some under tents, others under miserab⟨l⟩e Hutts and Hovells, without a rag, or any necessary utinsils, bed or board, who from delicat-nesse, riches & easy accommodations in stately & well furnishd houses, were now reduc'd to extreamest misery & poverty: In this Calamitous Condition I returnd with a sad heart to my house, blessing & adoring the distinguishing mercy of God, to me & mine, who in the midst of all this ruine, was like *Lot*, in my little Zoar, safe and sound:

6 Thursday, I represented to his Majestie the Case, of the French Prisoners at War in my Custodie, & besought him, there might be still the same care of Watching at all places contiguous to unseized houses: It is not indeede imaginable how extraordi-nary the vigilanc⟨e⟩ & activity of the King & Duke was, even labouring in person, & being present, to command, order, reward, and encourage Workemen; by which he shewed his affection to his people, & gained theirs: Having then disposed of some under Cure, at the Savoy, I return'd to white hall, where I dined at Mr. *Offleys*, Groome-porter, who was my relation, together with the *Knight Martial*, where I also lay that night.

7 I went this morning on foote from White hall as far as *London* bridge, thro the Late fleete streete, Ludgate hill, by St. Paules, Cheape side, Exchange, Bishopsgate, Aldersgate, & out to Morefields, thence thro Cornehill, &c: with extraordinary difficulty, clambring over mountaines of yet smoking rubbish, & frequently mistaking where I was, the ground under my feete so hott, as made me not onely Sweate, but even burnt the soles of my shoes, & put me all over in Sweate. In the meane time his Majestie got to the *Tower* by Water, to demolish the houses about the Graft, which being built intirely about it, had they taken fire, & attaq'd the white Towre, where the Magazines of Powder lay, would undo⟨u⟩btedly have not onely beaten downe & destroyed all the bridge, but sunke & torne all the vessels in the river, & rendred the demolition beyond all expression for severall miles even about the Country at many miles distance: At my returne I was infinitly concern'd to find that goodly

Chur⟨c⟩h St. *Paules* now a sad ruine, & that beautifull Portico (for structure comparable to any in Europ, as not long before repaird by the late King) now rent in pieces, flakes of vast Stone Split in sunder, & nothing remaining intire but the Inscription in the *Architrave* which shewing by whom it was built, had not one letter of it defac'd: which I could not but take notice of: It was astonishing to see what imense stones the heate had in a manner Calcin'd, so as all the ornaments, Columns, freezes, Capitels & proje⟨c⟩tures of massie Portland stone flew off, even to the very roofe, where a Sheete of Leade covering no lesse than 6 akers by measure, being totaly mealted, the ruines of the Vaulted roofe, falling brake into St. Faithes, which being filled with the magazines of bookes, belonging to the Stationer⟨s⟩, & carried thither for safty, they were all consumed burning for a weeke following: It is also observable, that the lead over the Altar at the East end was untouch'd; and among the divers monuments, the body of one *Bishop*, remaind intire. Thus lay in ashes that most venerab⟨l⟩e Church, one of the ⟨antientest⟩ Pieces of early Piety in the Christian World, beside neere 100 more; The lead, yronworke, bells, plate &c mealted; the exquisitely wrought Mercers Chapell, the Sumptuous Exchange, the august fabricque of Christ church, all the rest of the Companies Halls, sumptuous buildings, Arches, Enteries, all in dust. The fountaines dried up & ruind, whilst the very waters remained boiling; the Voragos of subterranean Cellars Wells & Dungeons, formerly Ware-houses, still burning in stench & dark clowds of smoke like hell, so as in five or six miles traversing about, I did not see one loade of timber unconsum'd, nor many stones but what were calcind white as snow, so as the people who now walked about the ruines, appeard like men in some dismal desart, or rather in some greate Citty, lay'd wast by an impetuous & cruel Enemy, to which was added the stench that came from some poore Creaturs bodys, beds, & other combustible goods: Sir *Tho: Gresshams* Statue, though falln to the ground from its nich in the Ro: Exchange remain'd intire, when all those of the Kings since the Conquest were broken to pieces: also the Standard in Cornehill, & *Q: Elizabeths* Effigies, with some armes on Ludgate continud with but little detriment, whilst the vast yron Chaines of the Cittie streetes, vast hinges, barrs & gates of Prisons were many of them mealted, & reduc'd

to cinders by the vehement heats: nor was I yet able to passe
through any of the narrower streetes, but kept the widest, the
ground & aire, smoake & fiery vapour, continud so intense, my
haire being almost seinged, & my feete unsufferably surbated:
The bielanes & narrower streetes were quite fill'd up with rubbish, nor could one have possibly knowne where he was, but by
the ruines of some church, or hall, that had some remarkable
towre or pinacle remaining: I then went towards Islington, &
high-gate, where one might have seene two hundred thousand
people of all ranks & degrees, dispersed, & laying along by their
heapes of what they could save from the *Incendium*, deploring
their losse, & though ready to perish for hunger & destitution,
yet not asking one penny for reliefe, which to me appeard a
stranger sight, than any I had yet beheld: His *Majestie* & Council indeeade tooke all imaginable care for their reliefe, by
Proclamation, for the Country to come in & refresh them with
provisions: when in the middst of all this Calamity & confusion, there was (I know not how) an *Alarme* begun, that the
French & *Dutch* (with whom we were now in hostility) were not
onely landed, but even entring the Citty; there being in truth,
greate suspicion some days before, of those two nations joyning, & even now, that they had ben the occasion of firing the
Towne: This report did so terrifie, that on a suddaine there was
such an uprore & tumult, that they ran from their goods, & taking what weapons they could come at, they could not be stop'd
from falling on some of those nations whom they casualy met,
without sense or reason, the clamor & perill growing so excessive, as made the whole *Court* amaz'd at it, & they did with infinite paines, & greate difficulty reduce & appease the people,
sending Guards & troopes of souldiers, to cause them to retire
into the fields againe, where they were watched all this night
when I left them pretty quiet, & came home to my house, sufficiently weary and broken: Their spirits thus a little sedated, &
the affright abated, they now began to repaire into the suburbs
about the Citty, where such as had friends or opportunit(i)e got
shelter & harbour for the Present; to which his Majesties
Proclamation also invited them. Still the Plage, continuing in
our parish, I could not without danger adventure to our
Church. 10: I went againe to the ruines, for it was now no
longer a Citty: 11 Sat at Star Chamber, on the 13, I presented his

Majestie with a Survey of the ruines, and a Plot for a new Citty, with a discourse on it, whereupon, after dinner his Majestie sent for me into the Queenes Bed-chamber, her Majestie & the Duke onely present, where they examind each particular, & discoursd upon them for neere a full houre, seeming to be extreamly pleasd with what I had so early thought on: The *Queene* was now in her *Cavaliers* riding habite, hat & feather & horsemans Coate, going to take the aire; so I tooke leave of his Majestie & visiting the *Duke* of *Albemarle*, now newly return'd from Sea, I went home. 15 To *Lond:* & dined with my L: *Brounchar* president of our Society, where was also the Earle of *Clancarne*, Sir *Rob: Murray*, & Dr. *Christopher Wrenn*. 16 *Pomeridiano* I went to Greenewich church, when Mr. *Plume* preached very well on *Pet: Seing therefore all these things must be disolvd* &c: 19: To *Star-Chamber*, returnd at night; 23: To *Greenewich*, where the Minister proceeded on his former Text: 25 To *Lond:* to Star: cha: 26. Din'd at Sir W: *Boremans*. 27: at Sir William *D'Oylies* with that worthy Gent: Sir *Jo: Holland* of Suffolck, & Mr. *Scaven*, sat with our Commissioners for sick & Wounded, & returned home. 29 *Michaelmas-day*, I went to visite my *Bro: Richard*, who was now indisposd in his health:

October 2: I gave my Bro: of *Wotton* a Visite, being myselfe also not well, & returnd the 4th, so as I entred into a Course of Steele, against the *Scorbut*:

10 This day was indicted a Generall fast through the nation, to humble us, upon the late dreadfull Conflagration, added to the Plage & Warr, the most dismall judgments could be inflicted, & indeede but what we highly deserved for our prodigious ingratitude, burning Lusts, disolute Court, profane & abominable lives, under such dispensations of Gods continued favour, in restoring Church, Prince, & people from our late intestine calamities, of which we were altogether unmindfull even to astonishment: This made me resolve to go to our Parish Assemblie, where our Doctor preached on 19 Luke: 41 &c: piously applying it to the occasion, after which followd a Collection for the poore distressd loose⟨r⟩s in the late fire, & their present reliefe. 14: He preached on 9: *Dan:* 14:

18 To *Lond:* Star-Chamber: thence to Court, it being the first time of his *Majesties* putting himselfe solemnly into the *Eastern fashion* of Vest, changing doublet, stiff Collar, [bands] & Cloake

&c: into a comely Vest, after the *Persian* mode with girdle or shash, & Shoe strings & Garters, into bouckles, of which some were set with precious stones, resolving never to alter it, & to leave the French mode, which had hitherto obtained to our greate expense & reproch: upon which divers Courtiers & Gent: gave his Ma⟨jesty⟩ gold, by way of Wager, that he would not persist in this resolution: I had some time before indeede presented an Invectique against that unconstancy, & our so much affecting the french fashion, to his Majestie in which ⟨I⟩ tooke occasion to describe the Comelinesse & usefullnesse of the Persian clothing in the very same manner, his Majestie clad himselfe; This Pamphlet I intituled *Tyrannus* or the mode, & gave it his Majestie to reade; I do not impute the change which soone happn'd to this discourse, but it was an identitie, that I could not but take notice of: This night was acted my Lord *Brahals* Tragedy cal'd *Mustapha* before their Majesties &c: at Court: at which I was present, very seldom at any time, going to the publique *Theaters*, for many reasons, now as they were abused, to an atheisticall liberty, fowle & undecent; Women now (& never 'til now) permitted to appeare & act, which inflaming severall young noble-men & gallants, became their whores, & to some their Wives, wittnesse the *Earle* of *Oxford*, Sir R: Howard, Pr: Rupert, the E: of Dorset, & another greater person than any of these, who fell into their snares, to the reproch of their noble families, & ruine both of body & Soule: I was invited to see this Tragedie, exceedingly well writ, by my Lord Chamberlain, though in my mind, I did not approve of any such passe time, in a season of such Judgements & Calamitie: 19 I return'd home;

21 Our *Viccar* on his former subject: This season (after so long & extraordinary a drowth in September, & Aug: as if preparatory for the dreadfull fire) was so very wett & rainy, as many feared an ensuing famine: 23. To Star-Chamber.

24 I din'd at my *L. Corneberies*; 25 at *Star-chamb*. return'd: 28 our *Viccar* as before: *Pomerid*: 1. *Rom:* 18: The Pestilence now through Gods mercy, began now to abate in our Towne considerably. 30 To *Lond*. to our Office, & now had I on the Vest, & Surcoate, or *Tunic* as 'twas cald, after his Majestie had brought the whole Court to it; It being a comely, & manly habite: to⟨o⟩ good to hold, it being impossible for us to leave the Monsieurs Vanitys in good earnest long: 31 I heard pleaded the signal Cause

of my L: *Cleavelands* pleaded by the *Solicitor* before the House of Lords, & was this day 46 yeares of age, wonderfully protected by the mercies of God, for which I render him immortal thanks: & return'd to my house:

November 4 our Doctor as formerly on the 1. *Rom*: I received the blessed Communion; & went in the afternoone to *Greenewich* to prayers: 5. our Viccar on 116 Psal: 1: 8. I went to *Woodcot*, to visite my Bro: who having now a sore leg, was much indisposd, my Wife accompanying me, returned that evening: 9: To *Lond:* & returnd: 10. Came my Bro: in Law *Glanvill* to visite us: 11 our Viccar as formerly: In the afternoone to *Greenewich* wher Mr. *Plume* on 91 Psal: 11.

14 I went my Winter Circle through my district, Rochester & other places wher I had men quartered & in Custody: 15. To *Leedes Castle*. 16 I musterd them being about 600 *Dutch* & *French*, ordred their proportion of Bread to be augmented, & provided cloths & fuell: *Monsieur Colbert* Ambassador at the Court of *England*, having also this day sent mony from his Master the French King to every Prisoner of that nation under my Guards: I lay at *Chilston* at my *Co: Hales's*. 17: I return'd to *Chattham*, my Charriot overturning on the steepe of Boxley-hill, wounded me in two places in the head, but slightly, my sonn Jack being with me, & then but newly out of long Coates, was like to have ben Worse cutt, by the Glasse, of the Charriot dores, but I thank God, we both escaped without much hurt, though not without exceeding danger. 18. one of the Prebends of *Rochester* preach'd in the Cathedral on 13. Gen: 8. & in the Afternoone Mr. *Loton* (who had formerly ben Curate at our Parish) on: 11. *Matt*. 12: 19 I got home:

22 To *Lond:* 23. I heard an extraordinary Case before a Comitteè of the whole house of Commons, in the Commons house of Parliament, betweene one Cap: *Taylor*, & my Lord *Vicount Mordaunt*; where after the Lawyers had pleaded, & the Witnesses examin'd, such foule & dishonorable things were producd against his *Lordship* of *Tyrannie* during his goverment of Windsore Castle, of which he was Constable, Incontinence & suborning, of which last one Sir Rich: Breames was most concerned, that I was exceedingly concernd for his *Lordship*, who was my special friend, and husband of the most virtuous Lady in the world: We sate 'till neere ten at night, & yet but

halfe the Council had don, on behalfe of the plaintife: The question then was put, for the bringing in of lights to sit longer, which lasted so long a time before it was determind, & raisd such a confused noise among the Members, that a stranger would have ben astonished at it: & I admire, that there is not a *Rationale* to regulate such trifling accidents, which yet I find consume a world of time, & is a reproch to the gravity of so greate an Assembly of sober men: 24 I went home. 26 To Lond: 27: Sate in Star: cha: 27: Sir *Hugh Pollard* Comptroller of the household died at W: Hall, & his Majestie Conferred the *White-Staffe* on my bro: Commissioner for Sick & Wounded, on Sir *Tho: Clifford*, [since Lord high Tressurer of *England*] a bold young Gent: of a meane fortune in *Devon*: but advanc'd by my L: *Arli⟨n⟩gton* Sec: of State: to the greate astonishment of all the Court: This gent: was some what related to me, by the marriage of his mother, to my neerest Kindsman Greg: *Coale*, & was ever my noble friend; a valiant & daring person, but by no meanes fit for a soupple & flattering Courtier: I dined at my L: *Jo: Berkeleys*. 28 Sate at star-Chamber: din'd with L. *Cornberie*, afterward went to see *Clarendon house* [since *quite demolished*] now almost finish'd, a goodly pile to see too, but had many defects as to the Architecture, though placed most gracefully: After this I waited on my L: *Chancellor* who was now at *Berkshire* house since the burning of *London*. 30 I returned home.

December ⟨2⟩ our *Viccar* as formerly: 2 dind with me Monsieur *Kiviet*, a *Dut⟨c⟩h Gent: Pensioner* of *Roterdam*, who came over hither for protection, being of the Prince of Oranges party, now not wellcome in Holland: The King knighted him for some merit in the princes behalfe: he should (if caught) have ben beheaded with Monsieur *Buat*, & was brother in Law to *Van Tromp*, the Sea Generall &c: with him came downe Mr. *Gab: Sylvius*, & Mr. Williamson, Secretarie to my L. *Arlington*: Sir *Kiviet* came downe to examine, whither the soile about the river of Thames would be proper to make *Clinkar* brick with & to treate with me about some accommodations in order to it: 9: To Lond: & returned the 14: 16 our Doctor as before: 17 To Lond: about severall affaires. 20 Visited my L. Duke of Albemarle, returned home:

25 Our Doctor on 2. *Cor:* 8. 9: I received the blessed Comunion, being Christmas day: 26 Divers Neighbours dined with me, according to costome: & so the next day:

30: Dr. *Dolben* deane of *Westminster*, & now made Bishop of Rochester our *Diocesse*, preached at our Parish-Church his first sermon on 1. *Tim:* 3. 16, of the wonder of our B: S: Incarnation &c: after sermon Confirmed many young children, solemnly prepar'd the weeke before, among whom my *sonn John* was bro⟨u⟩ght, and then his Lordship dined at my house. 31. Blessed God for his Protection of me & mine this past yeare:

THE FALL OF CLARENDON
(1667–1670)

1667. JANUARY 1 Beging Gods protection for the ensuing yeare, our Doctor pr: on 2. *Chro:* 1. 10: 2: I went to *Woodcot* to see my yet sick brother, 4. returned, it being an exceeding cold Snow: 6: Our Viccar on: 2. *Matt:* 11, after which I received the B: Comm: 8 To *Lond:* 9 To the *R: Soc:*, which since the sad Conflagration, were now invited to sit at *Arundel* house in the strand, by Mr. *Howard*; who upon my instigation likewise bestowed on the *Society* that noble *Library*, which his Grandfath⟨er⟩ especialy, & all his *Ancesters* had collected: this Gent: having so little inclination to bookes, that 'twas the preserving them from imbezilment: We had divers Experiments for improving Pendule Watches: & for winding up huge Springs by the force of powder; with an invention for the letting down, & taking up any Earth, Corall, or what ever it met with at the bottome of the sea &c: This Evening I heard *Finch* an Eloquent Lawyer [since L: *Chancelor*: & *Earle* of *Notingham*], plead the Case of my Lord Roberts sonn, concerning the Will of Mr. *Bodvill* his Ladys father: this was befor the King in Council, & returned home:

13 Dr. *Breton* (our *Viccar*) preach'd on 2 Cor: 8. 9: 15 To *Lond:* Dined with my Bro: *George*, where was Sir *Jo: Munson*, Sir Tho: Woodcock, Sir John Pellham, all Parliament men. 16: To Arundell house, where were some Experiments, to answer an Appeale of some learned French Virtuosi to our Society. 17. I went home: 20: our *Viccar: Pomeridiano* to *Greenewich* wher Mr. Plume on . . . *whosoever breaketh one of the least of these Com:* 21 To *Lond:* 22. Returned home for writings I had use of. 23. To *Arundell* house. 24 Din'd at Sir Ph: *Warwicks*, visited my L: Chancelor, &

presented my son *John* to him, now preparing to Go to *Oxford*, of which his Lordship was *Chancelor*: This Evening I heard rare *Italian* voices, 2 *Eunuchs* & one Woman, in his Majesties greene Chamber next his Cabinet: 25 I returned home: 27: our Doctor as formerly: 29 To *Lond:* in order to my sonns *Oxford* Journey, who being very early entered both in the Lat: & Greeke, & prompt to learne beyond most of his age, I was perswaded to trust him under the tutorage of Mr. *Bohune* fellow of New Coll: who had ben his Præceptor in my house some years before; but at Oxford, under the inspection of Dr. *Batthurst* President of *Trinity* where I placed him: My son not as yet 13 years old: 30: being the kingly *Martyrs* anniversarie fast, Dr. *Beaumont* preached *coram Rege* at White-hall, but the Chapell was so crowded, that I could not possibly approch to heare &c: *Jack* set out this day to *Oxford* with his Tutor: 31 My Wife brought me home in the Coach.

Feb: 3 Our Doctor on his former Text: & I received the holy Communion.

12 To Lond: Star: cha: 13: *Arundel* house where Dr. *Croone* produced his *Calesh* or new invented Charriot, the Carriage a single deale board onely instead of the Pearch: his Majestie was well pleas'd with it as he told me this Evening: As to the Lamp: it was a Globe so order'd as just to conterpoise the oyle in it, so as it never sunk: The Globe shewing also by its revolution (as the oyle Wasted) the houre of the night &c.

14 I saw a Comedy acted at Court: 15 My little booke in answer to Sir *Geo: Makenzys Solitude*, was now published:[1] in the evening I returnd: 17 our *Viccar* as before &c:

19 *Lond:* star: cha: in the afternoone I saw a Wrestling-match for 1000 pounds in St. *James's* Parke before his *Majestie* &c: twixt the Western & Northern men: Mr. Secr: *Morice* & Lo: *Gerard* being the Judges; befor a world of Lords, & other Spectators. The Western-men won: ⟨many⟩ greate summs were abetted: 18 I saw a magnificent Ball or Masque in the *Theater* at Court, where their Majesties & all the greate Lords & Ladies daunced infinitely gallant: the Men in their richly imbrodred, most becoming Vests: 22 I began to be very feavorish, & so continued til the 24th, when letting blood, I grew better.

---

1 *Publick Employment and an Active Life prefer'd to Solitude.*

Mar: 3 our Doctor on his former: restor'd to health, I receiv'd the holy *Eucharist*:

6 To *Lond:* I proposed to my L: *Chancelor* Monsieur *Kiviets* undertaking to wharfe the whole river of Thames or Key, from the Temple to the Tower (as far as the fire destroied) with brick, without piles, both lasting & ornamental: Sate at star: cha: &: *Arundel* house, & this evening had discourse with his Majestie concerning some Experiments: 8. Dined at our Treasure⟨r⟩s Cap: *Cock* having Accompts with him: 9. returned home: 10: our *Viccar* as before: Greate frosts, snow & winds, prodigious at the vernal æquinox; indeede it had hitherto ben a yeare of nothing but prodigies in this Nation: Plage, War, fire, raines, Tempest: Comets:

13 To Lo: star: cha: 14 Saw the *Virgin Queene* a play written by Mr. *Dryden* &c:

22 Dined at Mr. *Secretarie Morices*, who shewed me his Librarie, which was a well chosen Collection: I had this afternoone audience of his Majestie concerning the proposal I made of building the Key: & so return'd: 24: Our Doctor as before. 26 *Sir John Kiviet* dined with me, we went to search for brick-Earth, in order to a greate undertaking. 28: To Lond. at Ar: house the Society experimented the transfusion of bloud, out of one animal into another; it was successfuly don out of a sheepe into a dog, 'til the sheepe died, the dog well, & was ordered to be carefully looked to. 30 Din'd with the *Vice-Chamberlaine*: returned home: 31 Our Viccar as formerly.

Aprill: 4 The cold so intense, as hardly a leafe on a tree. 5. *Good-friday* our *Doctor* excellently, on 14. *Rom:* 9: I received the B: Comm: 7: Came *Kiviet* &c: 14: our Doctor as before: &c:

18 I went to make Court to the Duke & Dutchesse of *New-Castle* at their house at *Clarkenwell* (being newly come out of the north) they received me with extraordinary kindnesse, & I as much pleasd, with the extraordinary fancifull habit, garb, & discourse of the *Dutchesse*: returnd home:

21 Our Doctor preached as before: 22: To *Lond:* saw the sumptuous Supper in the banqueting house at *Whitehall* on *St. Georges day*, where were all the Companions of the Gartir: [23] In the morning his Majestie went to Chapell, with the Knights all in their habits, & robes, ushered by the Heraulds: After the first service they went in Procession, the youngest first, the

Sovraigne last, with the Prelate of the Order, & Deane, who had about his neck the booke of the Statutes of the Order, & then the Chancelor of the Order, (old Sir H: De Vic.) who wore the Purse about his: then Heraulds & Gartyr King at Armes, ⟨Clarenceux⟩, Black-rod: but before the Prælate & Deane of Winsor, went the Gent: of Chapell, Choristers &c. singing as they marched, behind them two *Doctors of Musick* in damask robes: This proceeding was about the Courts of White-hall, then returning to their Stalles & Seates in the Chapell, placed under each knights coate armour, & Titles: Then began Second Service, then the *King* Offered at the *Altar*, an Anthem sung, then the rest of the knights offerd, & lastly proceeded to the Banqueting house to a greate feast: The King sate on an elevated Throne at the uper end, at a Table alone: The Knights at a Tab: on the right-hand reaching all the length of the roome; over against them a cuppord of rich gilded Plate &c: at lowere end the Musick; on the balusters above Wind musique, Trumpets & kettle drumms: The King was se⟨r⟩ved by the Lords, & pension-ers, who brought up the dishes: about the middle of dinner, the *Knights* drank the Kings health, then the King theirs: Then the trumpets, musique &c: plaied & sounded, the Gunns going off at the Tower: At the banquet came in the *Queene* & stood by the Kings left hand, but did not sit: Then was the banqueting Stuff flung about the roome profusely: In truth the crow'd was so greate, that though I staied all the supper the day before, I now staied no longer than this sport began for feare of disorder: The Cheere was extraordinary, each knight having 40 dishes to his messe: piled up 5 or 6 high: The roome hung with the richest Tapissry in the World &c:

24. Sate at *Star: chamber*: 25. Visited againe the Duke of *New-Castle*, whom I had ben acquainted with long before in France, & had obligation to my *Wives mother*, for his marriage, there, That is his *Dutchesse* had, who was Sister to my *L: Lucas*, & maide of honor then to Q: Mother; married in our Chapel at Paris, & in gratitude had often & solemnly promis'd to give my wife 1000 pounds: but now all was forgotten of that nature: My Wife being with me, the *Duke* & *Dutchesse* both would needes bring her to the very Court. 26. My *Lord Chancellor* shewed me all his newly finished & furnished Palace, & Librarie; Then we went to take the aire in Hide-park:

27 I had a greate deale of discourse with his Majestie at dinner. Afternoone I went againe with my Wife to the Dutchesse of *N. Castle*, who received her in a kind of Transport: suitable to her extravagant humor & dresse, which was very singular; Then came in the *Bish:* of *Winchester*, my Lo: *Percy*, & so we came away, & returned home:

28 Our *Viccar* on his former: 30. To Lond: about Commission buisinesse & returned:

May 1 It being the day for the *Feefeès* of the poore, our *Viccar* preached on 25 *Matt:* 16: I dined with the fefeès, doing Parish buisinesse.

5 Our Doctor as formerly on the *Romans*: I received the B: Sacrament: 7: To *Lond: Star: chamber*. 8 Made up Accompts, with our Receiver, which amounted to 33936 pounds: 01: 04: 9. dined with L. *Cornbery* with Don *Francisco de Melos* Portugal Ambassador & kindred to the Queene; here also dined, Mr. *Henry Jarmine*, Sir *Hen: Capell*, & severall persons of qualitie: afterwards I went to *Arundel* house to salute Mr. *Howards* Sonns newly returned out of *France*, & so went home, having buisinesse with the Commissioners of the *Navy*: 11 To Lond. dined at the *Duke of New Castle*, & sate discoursing with her Grace in her bed-chamber after dinner, 'til my Lord *Marquis* of *Dorchester* came in with other company, & then home: 12 our *Vicc:* as before:

23 To *Lond:* din'd at my *Bro: Evelyns*, did buisinesse: 25: home: 26: our Doctor on: 2 *Act: 1. 2. 3. 4:* afterward to the Sacrament: 27: Came my Bro: G: E: to visite me & staied this weeke with me. 30. To *Lond:* to waite on the *Dutchesse* of *New-Castle* (who was a mighty pretender to Learning, *Poetrie* & *Philosophie*, & had in both published divers bookes &c) to the *Royal Society*, whither she came in greate pomp, & being received by our L: President, at the dore of our Meeting roome, the Mace &c carried befor him, had severall Experiments shewed before her: I returned home, having conducted her Grace to her Coach: 31 both my Bro: & severall of my relations came to visite & dine with me:

June 1 I went to *Greenewich* where his *Majestie* was trying divers *Granados* shot out of *Cannon* at the Castle hill, from the house in the Park: which broke not till they hit the mark; the forged ones brake not at all, but the Cast ones very well: The inventor was a Germane there present: At the same time was a

ring shewed his Majestie pretended to be a projection of ☿ &
maleable, & said by the gent: to be fixed with the Juice of a
Plant: 2: Doctor on his former Text. 3. on 12: *Rom:* 1: I dined with
the Trinity fraternity Sir *William* Pen *Master*: on which occasion
(as of Costome) the Sermon was preached: 4: To Lond: 6: Was
cal'd before the Lords Commissioners of the Treasury, concerning a fon'ds to be assign'd for the maintenance of our charge: 7:
Dined in the Citty: 8. home: 9: our *Viccar* as formerly on *Whitsonday* &c: 11: To *Lond:* alarm'd by the *Dutch*, who were falln on
our Fleete, at Chattam by a most audacious enterprise entering
the very river with part of their fleete, doing us not onely disgrace, but incredible mischiefe in burning severall of our best
Men of Warr, lying at Anker & Moored there, & all this thro
the unaccountable negligence of our delay in setting out our
fleete in due time: This alarme caused me (fearing the Enemie
might adventure up the Thames even to Lond, which with ease
they might have don, & fired all the Vessels in the river too) to
send away my best goods, plate &c: from my house to another
place; for this alarme was so greate, as put both County and
Citty in to a pan⟨i⟩que feare & consternation, such as I hope I
shall never see more: for every body were flying, none ⟨knew⟩
why or whither: Now then were Land forces dispatched with
Lord Duke of *Albemarle*, L: *Midleton*, Pr: Rupert & the *Duke* to
hinder the *Dut⟨c⟩h* comming to *Chattham*, fortifying Upnore
Castle, & Laying chaines & bombs, but the resolute Enemy
brake through all, & set fire on our ships, & retreated in spight,
stopping up the Thames, the rest of their Fleete lying before the
mouth of it: 14: I went to see the Work at Woolwich, a batterie
for to defend them from coming up to Lond: which Pr: Rupert
comanded, & sunk some ships in the river. 16: Our *Viccar* on 13.
Hosea. 9.

   17 This night about 2 a clock, some chipps & combustible
matter prepared for some fireships, taking flame, in *Deptford*
yard, made such a blace, and caused such an uprore in the
Towne, it being given out that the *Dutch fleet* were come up, &
had landed their me⟨n⟩, & fired the Towne, as had like to have
don much mischiefe before people would be perswaded to the
Contrary, & believe the accident: every body went to their
armes, & all my family alarm'd with the extraordinarie light, &
confusion &c: These were sad, & troublesome times.

18 To *Lond*, & returned the 20th: 23: our Doctor as formerly. 24 I was before the *Council* (the *Dutch fleete* still continuing to stop up the river of Thames, so as nothing could stirr out, or come in) and commanded by his Majestie that I with some others, should search about the invirons of the Citty, now exceedingly distressed for want of fuell, whither there could be any *Peate* or turfe, fit for use, could be found: & the next day I went, & found enough, & made my report, that there might be found a greate deale, &c: but nothing was now farther don in it: so on the 28 I went to *Chattham*, and thence to view not onely what Mischiefe the Dutch had don, but how triumphantly their whole Fleete, lay within the very mouth of the Thames, all from *North-foreland*, Mergate, even to the Buoy of the Noore, a Dreadfull Spectacle as ever any English men saw, & a dishonour never to be wiped off: Those who advised his *Majestie* to prepare no fleete this Spring, deserv'd I know what! but—

Here in the river of Chattam, just before the Towne lay the Carkasse of the *Lond:* (now the 3d time burnt) the *Royal Oake*, the *James* &c yet Smoking, & now when the mischiefe was don, we were making trifling forts on the brink of the river: Here were yet forces both of horse & foote with *Gen: Midleton*, continualy expecting the motions of the Enemys fleete: I had much discourse with him, an experien⟨c⟩'d Commander: I told him I wondered the King did not fortifie Sheerenesse, [since *don*:] & the Ferry, both abandon'd: and so returned home:

July: 1 To Lond: to star: *Chamber*: 2: Cald upon by my L: Arlington, as from his Majestie, about the new fuell; the occasion why I was mention'd, was from something I had said about a sort of fuell, for a neede, printed in my *Sylva* 3 yeares before, which obstructing a pattent my Lord Carlingford had ben seeking for himselfe; he was seeking to bring me into the project, & proferred me a share: I met my *Lord*, & on the 4th by an order of Council, went to my *Lord Major*, to be assisting: In the meane time, they had made an experiment of my receite of *Houllies* which I mention in my booke, to be made at *Maastricht*, with a mixture of charcoale dust & loame, which was tried with Successe at Gressham Colledge (which then was the Exchange, for meeting of the Merchants, since the fire of London) for every body to see: This don, I went to the Lords Commissioners of the *Tressury* about a supply of 12000 pounds for the Sick &

Wounded yet on my hands: next day we met againe about the Fuell, at Sir *Ja Armorers* in the *Mewes*, & thence home. 7: our Doctor preached on his former: I received the B: Communion. 8 My Lord *Brereton* & severall gentlemen dined at my house, where I shewed them profe of my new fuell; which was very glowing, & without Smoke or ill Smell: 9: to Lond: 10: I went to se Sir *Samuel* Morelands inventions & Machines, Arithmetical Wheele: Quench-fires, new harp: &c: returned home. 11: The Master of the *Mint* & his Lady, came to dine with me, Mr. *Williamson*, Sir *Nic: Armorer* & others.

13 Came my Kindsman Sir *Sam: Tuke* out of *France*: ⟨14⟩ Our *Viccar* as formerly:

17: dined with Sir Ed: Bowyer, Sir Anth: *Auger* & other friends: Then to *Lond*, returnd next day. 21. our *Viccar* finished his text: 23. To Lond: returned: 24 I went to *Gravesend*, (The *Dutch fleete* at anker still before the *River*) where I saw 5 ships of his Majesties men of Warr, encounter above 20 of the Dutch, in the bottome of the *Hope*, chacing them with many broad sides given & retur⟨n⟩ed, towa⟨r⟩ds the buoy of the *Noore*, where the body of their Fleete lay, which lasted til about midnight: There was one of their ships fired, suspected as don by the Enemie, she being run on ground: having seene this bold action, & their braving us so far up the river, I went home the next day, not without indignation at our negligence & nations reproch: 'Tis well knowne who of the Commissioners of the Treasury gave advice that the charge of setting forth a Fleete this yeare, might be spared: Sir W: C: by name: 28: our Doctor on 5: *Eph:* 15. 16.

30 To *Lond:* 31 had buisinesse in the Citty where I dined:

Aug: 1 To Arundell house, thence home: where I received the sad newes of *Abraham Cowlys* death, that incomparable Poet, & Virtuous Man, my very deare friend and greately deplored &c: 2: I dined at Sir *Edm: Bowyers* at *Camberwell*: 3. Went to Mr. *Cowleys* funerall, whose Corps Lay at Wallingford house, & was thence conducted to Westminster Abby in an *Hearse* with 6 horses, & all funebral decency, neere an hundred Coaches of noble men & persons of qualitie following, among these all the Witts of the Towne, Divers Bishops & Cleargy men: &c. He was interred next *Jeofry Chaucer* & neere *Spencer* &c: [a goodly Monument since erected.] I returned home:

6 The King discoursed with me much about swimming &c:
7: proceeded on my Accompt in Star-chamber: Dined at the
middle Temple invited by my old friend Serjeant *Barton*, now
Reader: Now did his Majestie againe dine in the Presence, in
antient State, with Musique & all the Court ceremonies, which
had ben interrupted since the late warr: 8: Home, by the way visiting Mr. *Oldenburg* now close Prisoner in the *Tower*, for having
ben suspected to write Intelligence &c: I had an order from my
L: *Arlington* secr: of state, which made me be admited: this
Gent: was Secretary to our *Society*, & will prove an innocent person I am confident: [Soon after *released*.]

⟨11⟩ *Viccar* as before. 13 To *Lond:* finish'd my Accompt
amounting to 25000 pounds: 14 dined with Sir Sam: Tuke, thence
to *Grays Inn* about his buisinesse: 15 Din'd at Mr. Sec: *Morices*,
thence to Sir *Rob: Carr:* 17: Dined with Sir William *D'Oylie* &
that afternoone to the funerall of Mr. *Farringdon* a kindsman of
my Wifes, & so home with her: ⟨18⟩: our *Viccar* as formerly: 20:
To *Lond:* about the Executor ship of my *Co: Geo: Tuke*: There was
now a very gallant horse to be baited to death with doggs, but he
fought them all, so as the fiercest of them, could not fasten on
him, till they run him thro with their swords; This wicked and
barbarous sport, deserv'd to have ben published in the cruel Con-
trivers, to get mony, under pretence the horse had killed a man,
which was false: I would not be perswaded to be a Spectator: 21 I
dined at the *V: Chancellor* & afterwards attended the Lords
Commissioners for mony: saw the famous *Italian* puppet play,
for 'twas no other. 22 at *Star Chamber*: thence home: There was
also now an *Hermaphrodite* shew'd both *Sexes* very perfectly, the
Penis onely not perforated, went for a woman, but was more man,
of about 21 years of Age: divers curious persons went to see her,
but I would not: 24. I was appointed with the rest of my brother
Commissioners to put in Execution an order of *Council*, for the
freeing of the Prisoners at War in my Custody at *Leedes Castle*, &
taking off his Majesties extraordinary charge, having called
before us the *French* & *Dutch* Agents: I returned, the Peace being
now proclaimed according to usual forme by the *Heraulds* at
Armes: Sir *Sam: Moreland*, Sir *Jo: Kiviet* & some others dining
with me this joyfull day:

25 Doctor on former subject: after evening prayer, I went
to visite Mr. *Vaughan* [Since L. Chief *Justice*] who lay at

Greenewich, a very Wise, and learned person, one of Mr. *Seldens* Executors & intimat friends; 26: *Lond* Star Cha:

27: Visited L: Chancellor to whom his Majestie had sent for the Seales a few daies before: I found him in his bed Chamber very Sad: The Parliament had accused him, & he had enemies at Court, especialy the boufoones & Ladys of Pl⟨e⟩asure, because he thwarted some of them & stood in their way, I could name some of the chiefe, The truth is he made few friends during his grandure among the royal Sufferers; but advanced the old rebells, that had mony enough to buy places: he was however (though no considerable Lawyer,) one who kept up the forme & substance of things in the nation with more solemnity than some would have, & was my particular kind friend on all occasions: but the Cabal prevailed, & that ingredient in Parliament: Greate division at Court concerning him, & divers greate persons interceeding for him: 28 I dined with my Late *L: Chancellor* where dind also Mr. As⟨h⟩burnham, Mr. W: Leg of the *Bed Chamber*, & his Lordship pretty well in heart, though now many of his friends & *Sycophants* abandon'd him: Afternoone I went againe to the Lords Comm: for mony; & thence to the Audience of a *Russian* Envoyè in the *Queens Presence chamber*: introduced with much State, the *Souldiers*, *Pensionars*, *Guards* in their order; his letter of Credence brought by his Secretary in a Scarfe of *Sarsenett*; their vests Sumptuous much embroid⟨er⟩ed with pearle. He delivered his Speech in the *Russe language* alowd, but without the least action or motion of his body (besides his tongue) which was immediately interpreted alowd also by a *German* that Spake good *English*; halfe of it consisted in repetition of the *Zarrs* titles which were very haughty & oriental; & the substance of the rest, that he onely sent to see the *King* & *Queene* & know how they did &c: with much compliment & froth of Language, then they kissed their Majesties hands, & went as they came: but their real errand was to get mony:

Sept: 13 'Twixt the houres of 12 and one at night, was borne my second daughter.

16 Came my Bro: & Sister of Woodcot to us. 17: My Daught⟨e⟩r was Christned *Elizabeth* by my Sister Evelyn, A: Pretyman, & Sir R: Bro: her Grandfather by Dr. *Breton* our Viccar, in my house at Says Court: 18 my Bro: & Sister returned home:

19 To Lond: & with Mr. *Hen: Howard* of *Norfolck*: of whom I obtained the gift of his Arundelian Marbles, Those celebrated & famous Inscriptions Greeke and Latine, with so much cost & Industrie gathered from *Greece*, by his illustrious Grandfather the magnificent *Earle of Arundel*, Thomas E. Marishall of *England*, my noble friend whilst he lived: These precious Monuments, when I saw miserably neglected, & scattred up & downe about the Gardens & other places of Arundell-house, & how exceedingly the corrosive aire of *London* impaired them, I procured him to bestow on the *Universite* of *Oxford*; This he was pleased to grant me, & now gave me the Key of the Gallery, with leave to marke all those stones, Urnes, Altars &c: & whatever I found had Inscriptions on them that were not Status: This I did, & getting them removed & piled together, with those which were incrusted in the Garden walles, I sent immediately letters to the *Vice-Chancelor* what I had procured, & that if they esteemed it a service to the University (of which I had ben a Member) they should take order for their transportation: This don, 21. I accompanied Mr. *Howard* to his Villa at *Alburie*, where I designed for him the plat for his Canale & Garden, with a *Crypta* thro the hill &c:

22 I went to Prayers at *Albury Church*; ⟨23⟩. I went to visite & dined with my Bro: at *Wotton*. 24 returned to *Lond:* where I had order to deliver the possession of Chelsey Coll: (hither⟨to⟩ my Prison During the Warr with ⟨Holland⟩, for such as were sent from the fleete to Lond) to our Society, as a gift of his Majestie our founder. 27: home: 29: our Doctor as formerly: after Evening Pray⟨e⟩r, I went againe to visite Mr. *Vaughan*: at *Greenewich*, whither he was retired during the Contagion:

October 6 our Vicc: on 24. *Act.* 16, I received the bless: Sacrament:

8 Came to dine with me Dr. *Bathurst* Deane of Wells, Pres: of Trinity Coll, & sent by the Vice-Chancelor of *Oxon:* in the name both of him, & whole University, to thanke me for procuring the Inscriptions, & to receive my directions what was to be don, to shew their gratitude to Mr. *Howard* &c. 10: To *Lond:* dined with the *Swedish Resident*: where was a disection of a dog, the poore curr, kept long alive after the *Thorax* was open, by blowing with bellows into his lungs, & that long after his heart was out, & the lungs both gashed & pierced, his eyes quick all

the while: This was an experiment of more cruelty than pleased me: 11 I visited Lo: *Arlington*, ill of a fall: Afternoone I went to see my Lord *Clarendon* (late *L: Chancelor*, & great⟨e⟩st Officer in England) in continual apprehension what the Parliament would determine concerning him, upon divers Articles exhibited of his *mal-Administration*: returned home: 13 our Doctor as before. 15 To *Lond:*

17 Came Dr. *Barlow Warden* of *Queens* Coll: & *Protobibliothec* ⟨ari⟩us of the *Bodlean* Library, from the University of *Oxford*, to take order about transportation of the Marbles &c: 18 I returned home: 20: our *Viccar* ⟨as before⟩: 21: To *Lond* in the evening: next day din'd with the Vice Chamberlain: 24. To the R: Society at *Arundell* house:

25 Were delivered to me two Letters, from the *Vice-Chancelor* of *Oxford* with the Decre of the Convocation, attested by the Publique Notarie, ordering fower *Doctors* of *Divini⟨t⟩y* & *Law* to accknowledge the obligation the Universite had to me (the originals whereoff I keepe) for procuring the *Marmora Arundeliana*, which was solemnly don, by Dr. Barlow Provost of Queens: [since B: of *Lincoln*] Dr. *Jenkins* Judge of the Admiralty, [since *Secretary* of *State*] Dr. Lloyd, & *Obadia Walker* of University Coll: [since head of that *Coll:*] who having made me a large Compliment from the University, delivered me the Decree, fairely written

Sir

We intend also a noble Inscription, in which also honorable mention shall be made of your selfe: But Mr. V. Chancellor commands me to tell you, that that was not sufficient for your merite, but that if your occasions would permitt you to come down at the Act (when we intend a dedication of our new Theater) some other Testimonie should be given both of your owne worth, & affection to this your old Mother; for we are all very sensible of this greate addition of Learning, and Reputation to the Universitie is due as well to your industrious care for the Universitie, and interest with my Lord Howard, as to his greate noblenesse & generositie of Spirit: I am Sir Your most humble servant *Obadia Walker*

Univ: Coll: Sep: 24. 1667

The *Vice-Chancellors* Letter to the same effect, were too vaine-glorious to insert: with divers copies of Verses that were also sent me &c: and their mentioning me in the Inscription I totaly declined, when I directed the Titles of Mr. *Howard* now made Lord: &c: upon his Ambassage to *Morocca* &c:

These fower *Doctors* having made me this Complement, desired me to carry, and introduce them to Mr. *Howard* at *Arundel* house, which I did, Dr. *Barlow* Provost of Queenes delivering after a short speech, a larger Letter of the Universitys thankes which was writen in *Latine*, expressing the greate sense they had of the honour don them, after which Complement handsomly performed & as nobly received Mr. *Howard* accompanied the Doctors to their Coach: That evening I supped with them. 26: My late *L: Chancellor* was accused by Mr. *Seamor* in the house of Commons, & in the Evening I returned home:

27: our *Viccar* as formerly: 31. I was this day 47 years of age: Blessed ⟨be⟩ God for his mercys: I went to Lond: dined with my Bro: made the *Royal Society* a present of the Tables of *Veines, Arteries & Nerves* which with greate Curiositie I had caused to be made in Italy, out of the natural humane bodies, by a learned Physit: & the help of *Vestlingius* professor at Padoa, from where I brought them *1646*, for which I received the publique thanks of the Society, & are hanging up in their Repositary; with an Inscription; I lay this night at *Arundell* house:

November 1 I heard solemn Prayers in his Majesties Chapell, & saw him Offer &c: returnd home:

3 our Doctor as before, applying it to the B: Sacrament which I received. ⟨5⟩. the Gunpowder Anniversary our *Viccar* preached on 121 *Psal:* 4 shewing the gracious effects of Trusting in God. &c: his universal Vigilancy for his Church:

December 1 our Doctor as before: 8: as before: 9: To Lond: to visite my late Lord Chancelor, I found him in his *Garden* at his new built Palace sitting in his Gowt wheele chayre, & seeing the Gates towards the North & fields setting up: he looked & spake very disconsolately, after some while deploring his condition to me, I tooke my leave, & the next morning heard he was gon: though I am perswaded had he gon sooner, though but to *Cornbery* & there lay quiet, it would have satisfied the Parliament: That which exasperated them was his presuming to stay, & contest the Accusation as long as twas possible, & that they were upon the point of sending him to the Tower &c:

12 I saw the Experiment repeated, of transfusing bloud out of a sheepe into a Man, celebrated at *Arundel* house, according to the particulars entred in the journal, and Register: Thence home: 15. A stranger on 23 Pro: *My son, give me thine heart: Pomeridiano* on: 10: John: 27. 28.

19 Went to Lond: about affaires, din'd at Sir *Geo: Carterets*. 20: With Sir *W: Boreman* Cleark of the *Kitchin* to his Majestie, thence to Arundel house. 21 I saw one *Carr* Piloried at Charing-Crosse for *libelling*, which was burnt before him by the *Hangman*, dined in the Citty, returned home: 22. Our Doctor as before.

25 *Christmas* day our *Viccar* on 3 *Joh:* 6: I received the *H: Communion*. 26: Divers of my Neighbours dined with me according to Costome. 29 our *Viccar* as above.

31 I gave solemn Thanks for the Almighties mercies this yeare past:

1668. January 1 Beging the Almighties assistance for the yeare to come, our Doctor preached 2: *Luke* 21:

7 To *Lond:* about Sir *Sa: Tukes* buisinesse, dined at Mr. *Howards*. 8: Wednesday I saw deepe & prodigious gaming at the *Groome-porters*, vast heapes of Gold squandered away in a vaine & profuse manner: This I looked on as an horrid vice, & unsuitable to a *Christian Court*: 9: met at the R: So: went to see the Revells at the Middle Temple, which is also an old, but riotous Costome, & has relation to neither Virtue nor policy: 10: To visie *Mr. Povey* where were divers greate Lords to see his conceited Cellar, & other Elegancies: home.

15 Petition'd the Lords Commissioners of the Treasury, about the Enlargement of my Back-yard at Sayes Court. 16: went to *Arundel house*. 17: I visited Monsieur *Ruvigny* the *French Ambassador*, thence home: 19: our Doctor proceedes: 23. I went to Lond, about buisinesse: 24: We went to stake out ground for the building a Colledge for the *R: Society* at *Arundel* house but did not finish it, which we shall repent of: ⟨25⟩: I returned home:

26 our Doctor preached as before. 30: on 119 *Psal:* 136 the Solemne Anniversary of the late Kings *Martyrdom*: how the faithfull should lament the sinns of others as well as their owne:

Feb: 2: as before: I received the blessed Sacrament: 4: To *Lond:* This Evening I saw the Trajedie of *Horace* (written by the

virtuous *Mrs. Philips*) acted before their *Majesties*: 'twixt each act
a Masque & *Antique*: daunced: The excessive galantry of the
Ladies was infinite, Those especialy on that . . . Castlemaine
esteemed at 40000 pounds & more: & far out shining the
Queene &c: 5. Ash-wednesday I was hindred from going so
early to the publique service as I intended. 6: din'd at *Arundel*
house, saw severall Experiments: 7: returned: 9 our *Viccar* as formerly. 13. To *Lond:*

14 I saw the Audience of the *Swedishe* Ambassador *Count
Donna*, in greate State in the Banqueting house, a goodly person: returned home: 16 our Doctor as formerly: 18 To Lond:
about buisinesse, 21 returned. 23. our *Viccar* as above: 25.
Mr. *Vice-Chamberlaine*, his Lady, Sir *Philip Cartrite* & Lady
dined with me: & my sonn *John* went back to Oxford the second
time, having ben long at home with his Tutor:

March 1 Our *Viccar* as before: 3. Was launched at *Deptford*
that goodly Vessel the *Charles*: I was now neere his *Majestie*, she
is longer than the *Sovraine*, & carries 110 brasse Canon: built by
old *Shish*, a plaine honest Carpenter (Master builder of this
Dock) yet one that can give very little account of his art by discourse, as hardly capable to reade, yet of greate abilitie in his
calling: They ⟨have⟩ ben Ship-Carpenters in this Yard above 100
yeares: ⟨8⟩ Our Viccar ⟨as before⟩:

11 To *Lond.* 12 Went to visite Sir *Jo: Cotton* who had me into
his Library, full of good MSS: Gr: & Lat: but most famous for
those of the *Saxon* & English Antiquities collected by his
Grandfather:

Aprill: 2 To the R: *Society* where I subscribed 50000 bricks,
towards the building of a Coll: Amongst other Libertine
Libells, there was now printed & thrown about a bold Petition
of the poore Whores, to the Lady *Castlemaine* &c: I came home.
⟨5⟩ Our *Viccar* as above. I received the holy Comm: 9: Lond:
about buisinesse, namely the finishing my grand Accompt of the
Sick & Wounded & Prisoners at War, amounting to above
34000 pounds. 11. returned home: 12: ⟨our Vicar⟩ as before. 15
Lond: with my wife, 18 returned: 19 our *Viccar* as before: 22:
To Lond: 24 I transferred 500 pounds to *Signor Palavicini* in the
East India Comp: as part of his Wifes *Portion*, in which I was a
Trusteè: for her Mother: I heard Sir R: *Howard* impeach Sir
William *Pen* in the H. of Lords, for breaking bulk, & taking a

way rich goods out of the *E. India Prizes* formerly taken by my L: *Sanwich*: 25. home: 26. our *Viccar*: as before: *Pomerid:* at *Greenewich* Mr. *Plume*, on 20. Joh: 29: 28 Lond: being now about the Purchase of *Ravensbourn Mills* & Land, about it in upper Deptford, of one Mr. *Beecher* &c.

30 *Ascention* day, when we sealed the Deedes &c: in Sir Ed: Thurlands Chamber *Inner Temp:* I pray God blesse it to me, it being a deare penyworth, but the passion Sir *R: Browne* had for it engaged me, & that it was contiguous to other grounds:

May: 2. I went home, about an Inventory of my Co: *Tukes* goods, which I gave in to the Probate office:

3 Our *Vicc:* as above: 6. To *Lond:* to transfer a *Mortgage* to my Bro: *Geo: Evelyn*, returned next day: ⟨10⟩: Our Doctor on 14. Joh. 16. *Whitsonday opus diei*: The blessed Sacrament followed: which I participated with more than ordinary resignation, & resolution &c:

13 Invited by that expert Commander Cap: Cox (Master of the lately built *Charles* the 2d, & now best vessell of the fleete) design'd for the Duke of York; I went to *Erith*, where we had a greate dinner: I return'd in the Evening: 16: Sir *Rich: Edgecome* of Mount *Edgecome* by Plymouth, my Relation, came to visite me; a very virtuous, & worthy gent: 17 our *Viccar* as above. 18. I dined with the Trinity Companie:

July 2. To *Lond.* 3 return'd: ⟨5⟩: our Doctor on 17: *Gen:* 7: The holy *Eucharist* follow'd: Sir *Sam: Tuke Baronet* & the Lady he had married but this day came & beded her at night at my house, many friends accompanying the Bride: 10: I went to Lond: 11 about petitioning his Majestie to enlarge my Court with a small slip of Land out of the brick-Close: returned: 12 our *Viccar* as before. 16. To *Lond:* returnd: 19 our Doctor as before. 23. Went to R: Society, where were presented divers *Glossa Petra's*, & other natural Curiosities, found in digging to build the fort at *Sheere-Nesse*, they were just the same, ⟨as⟩ what the⟨y⟩ bring from *Malta*, pretending them to have ben Vipers teeth, whereas in truth they are of a Shark: as we found by comparing them to one in our *Repository*: home this Evening:

Aug: 14 His Majestie was pleased to grant me a lease of a slip of ground out of *Brick*-Close, to enlarge my fore Court; for which I now gave him thanks; & then entering into other discourse, he talked to me of a new Invention of a Vernish for ships, instead of Pitch, and of the Guilding with which his new Yacht was beautified with all: I also shew'd his Majestie the Perpetual motion sent me by Dr. *Stokes* from Collen, and then came in Monsieur *Colbert* the *French Ambass:* &c: [15] I returned home: 16 our *Viccar* as formerly; against the *Anabaptists*, now swarming: 18 To Lond: about my Lease: 19 I saw the magnificent Entrie of the Fr: Ambassador *Colbert* received in the Banqueting house: I had never seene a richer Coach than what he came in to Whitehall. Standing by his Majestie at dinner in the Presence, There was of that rare fruite called the *King-Pine*, (growing in *Barbados* & W. Indies), the first of them I had ever seen; His Majestie having cut it up, was pleasd to give me a piece off his owne plate to tast of, but in my opinion it falls short of those ravishing varieties of deliciousnesse, describ'd in *Cap: Liggons* history & others; but possibly it might be, (& certainely was) much impaired in coming so farr: It has yet a gratefull accidity, but tasts more of the Quince and Melon, than of any other fruite he mentions: 20 I went home.

23 Our *Viccar* as above. 28 To Lond: Publishd my booke of the Perfection of *Painting*, dedicated to Mr. *Howard*: after other buisinesse, return'd the 29: 30: Our *Vicc:* finish'd his text: 31. To *Lond*, came home that evening:

September 13 Our Doctor as above: 17: I entertained *Signor Muccinigo* The *Venetian* Ambassador & one of the noblest families of that State, this being the day of making his Publique Enterie, setting forth from my house, with severall Gent: of Venice & others in a very glorious traine: With me he staied til the Earle of *Anglesea*, Sir *Cha: Cotterell* (Master of the Ceremonies) &c came with the Kings Barges to Carry him to the Tower, where the Gunns went off at his Landing, & then entered his Majesties Coach, follow'd by many others of the nobility: I accompanied him to his house, where there was a most noble Supper to all the Companie of six Courses: After the extraordinarie Compliment to me & my Wife for the civilities he receiv'd at my house, I tooke leave of his Excellency & return'd: he is a very much accomplish'd person: [since *Ambassador* at *Rome*.]

Now was *Candia* in exceeding danger. 18 To *Lond*, return'd next day:

20 our *Viccar* as above: 22. To *Lond:* about buisinesse: 25. returned: 27: *Viccar*, as above. 28. To Lond: on the Hospitals accompt: 29, I had much discourse with Signor *Pietro Cisij* a *Persian* Gent: about the affaires of *Turky* to my infinite satisfaction: I went to see Sir *Elis Leighto⟨n⟩s* project of a Cart, with yron Excle-trees: return'd home:

October 4: Our Doctor as before inlarging: The Holy Sacrament followd: 7: To *Lond*, returned the 9th: 11. Our *Bishops* Chaplaine preached on: 5: *Matt:* 20: I was much indisposed this Weeke: 22. To Lond: return'd next day: 25 our Vicc: as formerly: 28 To Lond: til 30.

31 Being now my birth day & 48th yeare of age I rendered Almighty God my hearty accknowledgements, & supplicate his blessing & protection &c:

November 1 Doctor as above: I receiv'd the B: *Sacrament*, beseeching Gods assistance the yeare now entred: 4. To *Lond.* 5: Viccar preached before his Majestie at W: hall on I besech ye therefore that you yield your members a living, holy & acceptable Sacrifice &c: on which he made a most excellent discourse, shewing that Sacrifices were as well for *Thanksgiving* and Eucharistical, as well as for Pardon; & that both were to be pure, & none so acceptable to God, as man himselfe, so qualified: Then went through the severall parts of this purity, which he applied so personaly, & yet so decently, as shew'd him to be an excellent Orator, as well as a sincere Preacher: 7: home: 8: Our Doctor   Blessed are they who *consider* the poore, being an *Anniversarie* at meeting of the *Fefees* (though it should have ben on the first day) shewing how we are oblig'd to relieve them not transitorily onely, but deeply, ponder, & *consider* it, how to relieve & comfort them: Being now at Dinner, My Sister Evelyn sent for me to come up to *Lond*, to my continuing sick Bro: fallen into a more surprising distemper: I staied with him til the 13th: 12 There was presented to the *Royal Society* the hand & arme of a *Syrene*, by a *Portugal*, & killed by a Portugueze Cap: about *Brasile*. 13 Went home.

14 To *Lond:* againe invited to the Consecration of that excellent Person the *Deane of Rippon* Dr. *Wilkins*, now made *Bish:* of *Chester*; it was at *Elie house*: Officiating The A: *Bish:* of *Canterbury*, *Bish:* of *Durham Cousin*, Bish: of Ely, *Salisbery*, *Rochester* & others: Dr. *Tillotson* preaching on   Go Teach all Nations:

baptizing &c, which he learnedly applied to the function, answering that pretence [Infallibil⟨it⟩y] of the Ch: of *Rome*, by the later clause of the *Text* &c: most learnedly: Then we went to a most sumptuous dinner in the hall, where was the *Duke* of *Buckingham*, Judges, Secretaries of *State*, Lord Keeper, Counsell, Noblemen, & such an infinity of other Companie, as were honourers of this incomparable man, the most universaly beloved of all that knew him: This being her Majesties Birthday, greate was the galantrie at White-hall, and the night celebrated with very fine fireworks &c: My poore Bro: continuing ill, I went not from him til the 17th: when dining at the *Groome Porters*, I heard Sir *Edw: Sutton* play excellently on the *Irish-harp*: & indeede plaies gentily, but not approching my worthy friend Mr. *Cleark* a Gent of Northumberland, who makes it exceede *Lute*, *Viol*, & all the harmonie an Instrument is capable of, pitty 'tis that is not more in use: but indeede to play well, it takes up the whole man, as *Mr. Clark* has assur'd me, who tho a Gent: of Quality & parts, was yet brought up to that Instrument from 5 Yeares old, as I remember he told me: 22d: our Doctor preached on 1. *Luke* 6. 25 To *Lond:* to visite my *Brother*: I waited on my Lo: *Sandwich*, who presented me with the *Sembrador* he brought me out of *Spaine*, shewing me his two bookes of the observation he made during his Ambassy, & stay at *Madrid*, in which were severall rare things, which he promis'd to impart to me: 27. I dined at my Lord *Ashleys* [since *Earle* of *Shaftsbury* & *L. Chan:*] where the Match of my *Niepce* was proposed, for his onely sonn, in which my assistance was desired for my Lord: ⟨29⟩: Dr. *Patrick* at *Covent-Garden* on 17: *Act:* 31. 30: St. Andrews Day we chose Officers at the *R: Society*, & I of the *Council* for this yeare; We dined together, the *King* sending us Venison:

December 2. Home. 6 Our *Doctor* as before, I receivd: 9. To *Lond:* to visite my Bro: 10: return'd: 13: our Viccar as formerly: 15 To *Lond:* with my *Wife* to visite my sick Bro: We lay in Somerset house &c:

17 At the Ro: *Society*, some experiments about the Principle of Motion, viz. *Elastic*, & that where was not spring, there could be no motion; tried by a pendule ball of solid Glasse, vibrating against wyre strings & catts-gutts; it making a much greater & quicker rebound from the Wyre, than from the fiddle strings, t⟨h⟩o equaly stretched: & died suddanly against wood, or Yron,

where there was no Spring: 19. I went to see the old play *Cataline* acted, having ben now forgotten 40 yeares almost: 20: Dr. *Patrick* at *Co: Gard:* on 15 *Rom:* 12: I dined with my *Lord Cornbury* at *Clarendon house*, now bravely furnish'd; especialy with the Pictures of most of our Antient & Modern *Witts*, *Poets*, *Philosophers* famous & learned English-men, which Collection of my L: Chancelors, I much comended, and gave his Lordship a Cataloge of more to be added: 21 return'd: 25: Our *Viccar* on 7: *Esay:* 14: I received the H: Comm: 27: on the same:

29: 30: 31. I entertained my kind Neighbours according to Costome, giving Almighty God thanks for his gracious mercys to me the past yeare:

166⅞ *January*: 1: Imploring his blessing for the yeare entring, I went to Church, where our Doctor preached on 65 *Psal:* 12. apposite to the season, & beginning a new yeare: 3: on his former: of the veracity of *Christs* Godhead: note, that about this time, one of Sir W: *Pens* sonns, had publish'd a blasphemous booke, against the *Deity* of our B: *Lord*: I now received the bl: Sacrament. 10: A stranger on: 8: Joh: 32:

28 More Exp: at R: Soc: about Motion: 29 I went to see a tall gigantic Woman, that measured 6 foote 10 Inches hight, at 21 years old, the rest proportionable, borne at the Busse in the Low Countries: 30: I return'd home early enough to celebrate the Late Kings Anniversarie, our Doctor pr: on 5. *Threnæ*: 16 shewing the greate losse of a People, when a good Prince is taken away: & that our sinns are cause of it, exemplified in *Josiah*: & paralleld: 31: on his former text.

February 3. To Lond: 4: At the Society about motion: 5 home by Water, & our Whirrie running ⟨thwart⟩ an hauser, I was like to be drawne over board: but blessed by God, I scaped:

13 I presented his Majestie with my Historie of the foure Impostors,[1] he told me of other like cheates: gave my booke to L: *Arlington* to whome I dedicated it &c: It was now he began to tempt me about writing the Dutch-Warr &c: 14. Dr. *Duport* (Greeke Professor of Cambridge) preached *coram Rege* on   Consider what I say, & the Lord &c:

---

1 *The History of the Three late famous Impostors.*

March 1 Dined at L. *Arlingtons* at Goring house, with Bishop of *Hereford*: 3 home: having ⟨heard⟩ in the morning at W. hall Dr. *Doughty*   on Whosoever shall speake a word &c: 4: To Lond: at the Council of the R: Soc: about the disposing of My L: H. *Howards* Librarie now given to us: I return'd. 7 Our Doctor as before: 10: To *Lond:* 11 returned: 14: Vicc: as before. 16: To *Lond:* to place *Mr. Wase* about my L: *Arlington*. 18, I went with my L: Howard of *Norfolk* to visite Sir William *Ducy* at *Charleton*, where we dined: The servants made our Coach-men so drunk, that they both fell-off their boxes upon the heath, where we were faine to leave them, & were droven to Lond: by two Gent: of my Lords: This barbarous Costome of making their Masters Well-come, by intoxicating the Servants had now the second time happn'd to my Coachman: My sonn came from *Oxon*: for altogether: 19 I return'd home: 21 our Doctor as formerly:

Aprill: 1 At R: Soc: an handsome discourse touching the pulse of the bloud &c: There was a Lobster discected: 2 Din'd at Mr. *Tressurer* where was my L: *Newport* Comptroller, L. *Asshley*, *Lauderdaill*, Bishop of *Chester*, Coll: *Titus* of the bedchamber (author of that famous piece against *Cromwell*, *Killing no Murder*) & other greate persons: I now placed Mr. Wase, with Mr. *Williamson* Secretary to the secretary of state, & Cleark of the Papers: 3 home:

May: 19 To *Lond:* next day at a Council of the *R: Society* our Graunt was finished in which his Majestie gives us *Chelsey Colledge* & some Land about it: & it was ordered that five should be a *quorum* for a Council: There were then also Sworne the *Vice-President* the first time: & It was also then proposed how we should receive the *Prince* of *Tuscanie*, who desired to visite the Society.

20 This Evening returning, I found my Wife in Labour, but was delivered within an houre at 10 a clock at night, being *Ascension* day, when was borne my third *Daughter*. 23. Our Doctor finished his former Text:

25 Was baptisd my Daughter *Susanna* (by the name of her *Godmother* her *Aunt Hungerford* of *Cadenam*): Godfather her Grandfather Sir *R: Browne* &c:

26 To *Lond*, returnd next day: 29: The Kings birth-day our *Viccar* preached on: 1. *Tim* 2. 1. 2 describing the duty to Kings & Magistrates; That one of the chiefe causes ⟨why⟩ they were many times greate sinners, was from the neglect of their subjects

prayers for them, instead of censuring them: That our duty in this was so important, that the *Apostle* had reckon'd up more sorts of devotion, which we were obliged to performe for them (as considering their greate needes above others) than for any other duty, or person whatsoever.

June 2 To *Lond:* to see my Brothers: 3. At the R: Soc: a Council, then went to take leave of my Lord *Howard*, now going Ambassador to *Morocco*: 4. din'd at L. *Arlington*, where was Mr. *Tressurer, Earle of Berk-shire*, Lord *St. Johns*, Sir Rob: *Howard*, Sir R: *Holmes* &c: I went home: 6: our *Viccar* on *Gall*: as before: 10: Came my Lord *Cornbery*, Sir *William Poultny* & others to visite me; I went that evening to *Lond:* to carry Mr. *Pepys* to my Bro: (now exceedingly afflicted with the Stone in the bladder) who himselfe had ben successfully cut; & carried the Stone (which was as big as a tenis-ball) to shew him, and encourage his resolution to go thro the operation. 12 home: 16 To *Lond:* & tooke leave of my Bro: going out of towne: 17: home: 20 our *Viccar* as formerly: 25 To *Lond* returnd next day. 27: our *Viccar* as above:

July. 28 To *Lond:* & 30 return'd: My Wife being gon a journey of Pleasure downe the River as far as the Sea, with Mrs. *Howard*, & her daughters the Maids of Honor, amongst whom, that excellent creature *Mrs. Blagge*: I now built the long wall which separates my Court from the brick-close, newly granted me of the King:

July. 7 I went towards *Oxford*, lay at little *Wicckam*, 8: at *Oxford*, lay at one of the *Beadles*.

9 In the morning was celebrated the *Encenia* of the New Theater, so magnificently built by the munificence of Dr. *Gilbert Sheldon* Arch-Bishop of *Canterbery*, in which was spent 25000 pounds, (as Sir *Chr: Wren* the Architect as I remember told me) & yet was never seene by the Benefactor, my L: *A Bish:* having upon occasion told me, that he never did, nor never would see it. It is in truth a fabrique comparable to any of this kind of former ages, and doubtlesse exceeding any of the present, as this Universitie dos, for Colledges, Libraries, Scholes, students & Order all the Universities in the World:

To the *Theater* is ⟨joined⟩ the famous [*Sheldonian*] Printing-house: This being at the Act, and the first time of opening the *Theater* (Acts being formerly kept in St. *Maries-Church*, which might be thought undecent, as being soly set a part for the

immediate worship of God, & was the inducement of building
this noble Pile) it was now resolv'd, to celebrate its dedication
with the greatest splendor & formalitie that might be, & therefore drew a world of strangers & other Companie to the University from all parts of the Nation: The *Vice-Chancelor* then,
Heads of Houses, & Doctors being seated in magisterial seates,
the *Vice-Chancellors* Chaire & Deske, Proctors &c: covered
with *Brocatell* & Cloth of Gold: The Universitie Register read
the Founders Grant & gift of it to the Universitie, for their
Scholastic Exercises upon these solemn occasions: Then follow'd Dr. *South* the Universities Orators Eloquent Speech upon
it; it was very long, & not without some malicious & undecent
reflections on the *Royal Society* as underminers of the University, which was very foolish and untrue, as well as unseasonable,
(but to let that passe, from an ill natured man) the rest was in
praise of the Arch Bish: and the ingenious Architect: This
Ended, after loud Musique, from the Corridor above, (where
was placd an Organ) there follow'd divers Panegyric Speeches
both in Prose & Verse interchangeably pronounc'd by the
young students, plac'd in the *Rostrum*, *Suggestum*, *Plutea's* &c
Some in *Pindarics*, *Ecclogas*, *Heroics* &c: mingled with excellent
Musique both vocal, & Instrumental to entertaine the Ladys
&c: then was a spech made in praise of Academical Learning;
all which lasted from 11 in the morning till 7 at night, which was
likewise concluded with Bells ringing, & universal joy &
feasting:

10 The next day began the more solemn Lectures in all the
Faculties which were perform'd in their several Scholes, where
all the Inceptor Doctors did their Exercises, the Professors having first ended their reading: The Assembly now return'd to the
Theater, the *Terræ filius* or Universitie bouffoone, entertaind the
Auditorie with a tedious, abusive, sarcastical rhapsodie, much
unbecoming the gravity of the Universitie, & that so grossly, as
that unlesse it be suppress'd, will be of ill consequence, as I
plainly expressed my sense, both to the *Vice Chancelor* and severall heads of houses afterwards, who were perfectly ashamed of
it, and resolv'd to take care of it for the future, for they had left
the facetious old way of raillying upon the *Questions*: &c & fell
wholy upon persons; so as in good earnest, 'twas rather licentious lying, & railing than genuine & noble witt: In my life was I

never witnesse of so shamefull entertainement. After this rib-
auldry, The *Proctors* made their Speeches: Then began the
Musick Act, Vocal, & Instrumental, above in the Balustred Corridore, opposite to the *Vice-Chancelors* seate: Then Dr. Wallis
the *Mathematical* Professor made his Oration, and created one
Doctor of Musique, according to the usual Ceremonies, of
Gowne (which was white Damask) Cap: Ring, kisse &c: Next
follow'd the *Disputation* of the *Inceptor* Doctors in *Medicine*, the
Speech of their Professor *Dr. Hyde*, & so in Course their respective Creations: Then Disputed the Inceptors of Law, the Speech
of their Professor & Creation: Lastly, Inceptors in *Theologie*, Dr.
Compton (bro: to the Earle of Northampton) being *Junior*
began, with greate modesty, & applause: & so the rest: After
which Dr. *Tillotson*, Dr. *Sprat* &c: & then Dr. *Alestreès* (the
Kings Professors) Speech, & their respective Creations: Last of
all the Vice-Chancelors shuting up all in a Panegyrical Oration
celebrating their Benefactor, & the rest apposite to the occasion:
Thus was the *Theater* Dedicated by the Scholastic Exercises in
all the faculties with infinite solemnity, & the night (as the former) entertaining the new Doctors friends, in feasting &
Musique: I being invited by *Dr. Barlow*, the worthy & learned
Provost of Queenes Coll:

   11 The Act Sermon was this forenoone preach'd by Dr. *Hall* in
St. *Marie's* in an honest practical discourse against *Atheisme* on
Rom.   In the afternoone, the Church was so crowded, that
coming not so early, I could not approch to heare: 12 *Moneday*
was held the *Divinity* Act in the *Theater* againe, where pro-
ceede⟨d⟩ 17 Doctors in all the Faculties some: 13 I dined on Tuesday at the *V. Chancelors*, & spent the afternoone in seeing the
rarities of the Pub: Librarie, & visiting the noble Marbles &
Inscriptions now inserted in the Walles that compasse the *Area*
of the *Theater*, which were 150 the most antient, and worthy
treasure in the Learned World of that kind, procur'd by me for
them some time before: now observing that people, approaching
them too neere, some Idle people began to Scratch and injure
some of them, I advis'd that an hedge of holly, should be planted
at the foote of the wall, to be kept breast-high onely, to protect
them, which the *V: Chancelor* promisd to see don the next season:

   14 Came Dr. Fell (Deane of Christchurch) *Vice-Chancellor*,
[now *Bish:* of *Oxon*] with Dr. *Alestree*, K⟨ing⟩s Professors;

Beadles & Maces before them, to Visite me at my Lodging:
Then I went to Visite My L: *Howards sonns* at *Magdalen Coll:*
who also repaied me theirs: [15] Having two daies before notice
that the Universitie intended me the honor of Doctor-ship,
I was this morning attended by the *Beadles* belonging to the
Law, who carried me to the *Theater*, where I found the *Duke*
of *Ormond* (now Chancelor of the Universitie,) with the Earle of
Chesterfild, & Mr. *Spencer* brother to the late Earle of *Sunderland*: Thence we marched to the Convocation house, a Convocation having ben cald on Purpose: Here being all of us rob'd in
Scarlet, with Caps & hoods &c: in the Porch, we were led in by
the Professor of Laws, & presented respectively by name & a
short elogie &c: to the *Vice-Chancelor* who sate in the Chaire,
with all the Doctors & heads of houses & Masters about the
roome, which was exceeding full: Then began the Publique
Orator, his speech, directed chiefly to the *Chancelore*, the *Duke*
of *Ormond*, in which I had also my Compliment in Course: This
ended, we were called up, and Created Doctors according to the
forme, and seated by the *Vice-Chancelor* amongst the Doctors,
on his right hand: Then made the Vice-Chancelor a short
spech, & so saluting our Bro: Doctors the Pageantry concluded,
& the Convocation desolved: So formal a Creation of
Honorarie *Doctors*, had seldome ben seene, that a Convocation
should be cald on purpose, & Speeches made by the *Orator* &c:
But they could do no lesse, their *Chancelor* being to receive, or
rather do them this honour: I had ben made *Doctor* with the rest
at the Publique *Act*; but their expectation of the *Duke* their
Chancelor made them deferr it; & so I was led with my Bro:
Doctors, to an extraordinary Entertainement at *Dr. Mewes*,
head of St. *Johns Coll:* & after aboundance of feasting & complements, having visited the V: Chancelor & other Doctors & given
them thanks for the honours don me, [16] I went towards home
the next day, & got as far as *Windsor*, & to my house [17] the next.
    Aug: 4. I was invited by Sir Hen. *Peckham* to his Reading feast
Mid: Temp: a pompous Entertainement: where was the A Bish:
of Cant: all the greate Earles & Lords &c: I had much discourse
with my Lo: *Winchelsea*, a prodigious talker; and the *Venetian*
Ambassador Signor *Moccinigo*, whom I was acquainted with, a
very fine *Gent:* at night I went home: 8: our *Vicc:* as before. 10 To
Visite my Bro: againe at *Woodcot*, return'd: 12. Came the Earle of

Norwich to dine with me. 15 The Bishop of *Rochester* (our Diocesan Dr. Dolben & Deane of Westminster) preached at our Church on 19. *Luke* 41 ad: 44 in a practical discourse: 17: To Lond: spending almost the intire day in surveying what progresse was made in rebuilding the ruinous Citty, which now began a little to revive, after its sad calamatie: 18 din'd with the *Duke* of *Ormond*, & had some discourse with his Majestie this evening at W: hall: 19 I went to my L: *Arlingtons* about affaires.

20 I saw the most splendid Audience of the *Danish Ambassador* in the banqueting house: returned home: 22 Our *Viccar* as formerly: 23 I went to visite my most excellent & worthy neighbour, the L. *Bish: of Rochester* at *Bromely*, which he was now repairing, after the dilapidations of the late rebellion, returned after dinner:

29 A stranger preach'd on 6: *Mic:* 9: I was this day very ill, of a paine in my limbs: which continued most of this weeke, & was increased, by a visite I made [*September*] to my old acquaintance the *Earle of Norwich*, at his house in Epping forest: There are many very good pictures, put into the Wainscot of the roomes, which Mr. *Baker* his Lordships predecessor there, brought out of Spaine: especialy the Historie of *Joseph*: The Gardens were well understood, I meane the *Pottagere*: here is also an excellent picture of the pious & learned *Picus Mirandula* &c & one of old *Breugle* incomparable: I return'd late the Evening, ferrying over at *Grenewich*:

⟨5⟩ My Indisposition hindred me from Church, & B: Sacrament to my greate sorrow.

7 I let bloud, purged, drew blisters, but Leaches did me most good exceedingly pa⟨i⟩ned with my Teeth: 22. I was able to go to Lond: where I had much buisinesse.

26 To *Church* to give God thanks for my recovery: our *Viccar* preaching on 10: *Heb:* 21. 22. very solidly. 27 I visited my still afflicted deare Bro: at *Woodcot*, return'd next day: 30: To Lond: returned:

Octob: 3 our Doctor on his former text, I received the bl: *Eucharist* to my unspeakable joy:

10 Our Viccar proceeded, & so on the 17th. 19. To Lond, on buisinesse: 21. To the R: *Society* meting now the first time after a long recesse during Vaccation, according to costome: where were red many letters from our Philosophical Correspondents; also a Map, and description of the prodigious irruption &

Incendium of *Ætna*, together with a large box of the severall materials, mettals, cinders, salts, &c: throwne out of that mountaine which burnt in a flowing river of Sulphur 30 miles in Length & 12 in bredth, as far as Catanea & even into the sea it selfe, a greater eruption never was recorded in any historie: Sir *Geo: Southwell*[1] likewise presented Balsomes & other Curiosities out of *Portugal*: & our *English Itinerant* an account of his Autumnal peregrination about England (for which we hired him) of dried foules, *Fish*, *Plants*, *Animals* &c: 23 I returned home: 24 our Viccar as before:

26 To Lond: 27: Dind at L: *Arlingtons*, where was Sir *Jo: Trevor*, one of the Secretaries of State, the E: of *Sandwich* & others: 29: Afternoone at the *R: Society*, where was produc'd Mr. *Hooks* pendule Clock going 12 moneths to a second as affirm'd: proposals were now made, for the more accurate measuring a *Degree* in the Earth, from that in the heavens: There was shew'd also a stain'd Wollan Cloth in imitation of *Tapissry*, as also a relation of the Salt-pits at *Namptwich*: My deare Brother continued extreamely full of paine: the Lord be gracious to him: 29 I returned home:

November 14: went home (having ben the night before at the funeral of Mrs. Pepys: &c:) In the Afternoone our Doctor as formerly. 18 To Lond, where my buisinesse staied me the whole weeke: 21. A stranger at Co: Garden on 24 *Matt* 14: *Pomerid:* Dr. *Patrick* of the Resurrection: I went then to Visite the Countesse of Kent my Kindswoman:

25 At R: So: an Experiment about mensuration: 26: returned: 28: our *Doctor* as before:

30 To *Lond*, it being St. Andrews, & our Anniversarie choosing Officers at the *R: Society*, din'd together: &c:

December 3 I waited on the Lords of the *Tressury* about Deale quarters in arrere, returned:

1670. Jan: 1 Beging Gods protection I went to Church, Our Doctor preaching on 68 *Psal:* 19:

2: Our Viccar: on his former days text: In the Afternoone on his other in *Tim:* 7: so extraordinary a storme of wind, as had seldome ben known, that did much harme: all over the nation almost: 9: our Doctor as above: 10: To Lond: 13. To the *R: Society*:

1 Evelyn's error for Sir Robert Southwell.

returned: 16: our Doctor as above: 18 To *Lond:* about selling *Cressing Temple* for Sir *Sam: Tuke*, returned: 23 Our Doctor as before. 24 To *Lond:* about *Cressing Temple*.

26 I had much discourse with the *Venetian* Ambassador concerning the excessive Cold weather they often had in Italy, & especialy this Winter &c: 27: home.

30 Our *Viccar* on 51. *Psal:* 14, of the crying sin of sheding innocent blood, applyd to the Murder of our late King, whose Anniversarie it was: but the fast was to be celebrated the next day, which was moneday:

Feb: 4: To *Lond:* about Deale: return'd: 6: Dr. *Jo: Breton* Master of *Emanuel* in *Cambridge* (Unkle to Our *Viccar*) on 1. Joh: 27: *whose shoos Latchet I am not worthy to unloose* &c. The Lawfullnesse, decentnesse & necessitie of subordinate degrees & ranks of men & servants, as well in the Church as State, against the late *Levellers* & others of that dangerous rabble, who would have all alike: The B: Sacrament followd: Pomerid: Our Viccar proceeds on his former subject: out of *Timothy*: 13 & so on the 13th now finishing his Text: 17 To Lond, to visite my continualy afflicted *Brother*. 20 Dr. *Patric* on   *Least there be any roote of bitternesse* &c a practical & monitory sermon; Then went home to Says-Court: Afternoone our *Viccar* on 8. *Rom:* 13. 21 To Lond: to meete the Countesse of *Huntington* about Sir *Samuell Tukes* buisinesse, return'd next day: 27 our *Viccar* as before.

March: 3 Finding my brother in such exceeding torture, & that he now began to fall into Convulsion fits, [4] I solemnly set the next-day a part, to beg of God to mitigate his sufferings, & prosper the onely meanes which yet remained for his recovery; or if otherwise; that it would please Almighty God to prepare him for himselfe, he not onely being very much wasted, but exceedingly, & all along averse from being cut, which he was advised to undergo from time to time, with extraordinary probability of successe: but when it came to the operation, & all things prepared, his spirit & resolution failed, & there was now lesse hopes than ever. 5. I went to visite my poore afflicted brother, whom I found almost in the last agonies:

6 Dr. *Patric* in *Covent Garden* Church, on his former Text. I participated of the blessed Sacrament, recomending the deplorable condition of my bro: his agonies still increasing: In the Afternoone, a stranger made an excellent sermon against

Atheists: &c. I watched late with my Bro: this night, yet not imagining his end to be so neere; but so it pleased God, to deliver him out of this miserable life, towards five this moneday morning, to my unspeakeable griefe & sorrow, being a Bro: whom I most dearely loved for many Virtues; & that was but two yeares Younger than my-selfe, a sober, prudent, & worthy Gent: he had married a greate fortune, and left one onely daughter, & a most noble seate, at Woodcot neere, Epsom in Surrey &c: 7: I staied all the next day to comfort my sister in Law, his Wife: 8 On Tuesday he was ordred to be opened; but it was not a specctacle I desir'd to be present at; & therefore returned home this evening full of sadnesse, & to bemoane my losse: 10: To Lond: My Bro: being opened, a stone was taken out of his bladder, not much bigger than a nutmeg, somewhat flatt, & oval, not sharp, one part excepted, which was a little rugged: but his *Livar* so faulty, that in likelyhood ⟨it could not⟩ have lasted much longer, and his kidnis almost quite consum'd: all of this doubtlesse the effects of his intollerable paine proceeding from the stone; & that perhaps by his drinking too excessively of Epsom Waters, when in full health, & that he had no neede of them, being all his lifetime of a sound & healthy constitution, &c: I returnd, & came up againe to visite my sister, & being one of the *Overseeres* of the Will, to take order about the funeral, which kept me in towne 'til the 12th. 13. a stranger on 27: *Psal:* 13: *Pomerid:* our *Doctor* proceeding on his former subject: 18 To *Lond:* In order to my deare Bro: funeral. 20: A stranger preached at the *Savoy* French Church, the *Liturgie* of the *Church* of England, being now used altogeth⟨e⟩r, as translated into French by *Dr. Durell*. The Text was in   Peter   *Cast all your Care on God, for he Careth for you:* 21. We all accompanied the Corps of my deare Bro: to *Epsome Church*, where he was decently interred in the Chapell belonging to Woodcot his house: There were a greate number of Friends & gent: of the Country & innumerable people, about 20 Coaches of six-horses; so as yet we return'd to *Lond:* that night, somewhat late. 22: I went to Westminster where in the house of *Lords*, I saw his Majestie sit on his Throne, but without his robes; all the Peeres sitting also with their hatts on: The buisinesse of the day being about the Divorce of my Lord *Rosse*: such an occasion & sight had not ben seene in England since Hen: 8th. 23. I returned.

May ⟨1?⟩ Our *Viccar* on 68 *Psal:* 18. I received the holy Communion. 8 on the former Text: 10: Mr. *Slingsby* Master of the *Mint*, Mr. Jos: *Williamson* Secretary of my L. Arlington Prin: Sec: of State, came to dine with me. 11. To Lond: about a buisinesse in Chancery of my Lady Tukes: home:

22 our *Doctor* on 8: *Rom:* 11 Whit-sonday, a sermon fitted for that solemnity: The blessed Sacrament follow'd, of which I participated: 26: Came my Bro: *G: Evelyn* & Niepce *Marie* my *Goddaughter* to dine with me. This afternoone receiving a letter from *Phil: Howard* [since *Cardinal* of *Norfolk*] *Lord Almoner* to the *Queene* that *Monsieur Evelin* (first *Physitian* to *Madame*, who was now come to *Dover* to visite the King her brother) was come to *Lond:* greately desirous to see me, & his stay so short, that he could not come to me; I went with my Bro: to meete him at the Toure of Lond: where he was seeing the Magazine and other Curiosities, having never ben before in England: There was with him the Marishal de *Plessis Prasline*, & the Bishop of Tournon his Bro: where we re-newed our aliance & friendship, with much regret on both sides that being that Evening to returne towards Dover, we could enjoy one another no longer: How this french Familie *Ivelin of Eveliniere*, their familie in Normandie, & of a very antient & noble house is grafted into our Pedegree; see in your Collection, brought from Paris 1650. &c: 29 Trinity Sonday our Doctor on: 8 Rom: 11. as before.

June 3: To *Lond:* return'd. 5. *Viccar* as before, I receiv'd the B: Comm: My son *John*, having ben at *Dover* to see the intervieu of *Madame* & his *Majestie* & accompanied that Court at her returne into *France*, as far as *Calais*, was now come home:

9 To *Lond:* return'd: There was this day produced in the R: Society, an invention by intromitting the Species into a dark large box, to take the profile of ones face as big as the life; which it did performe very accurately: 12 A young man on 1. *Cor:* 6. 19: *Pomerid* on 2 *Cor:* 5. 4. full of sentences & without much connexion: 15 To Lond: 16 I was forc'd to accompanie some friends to the Bear-garden &c: Where was Cock *fighting*, Beare, *Dog-fighting*, Beare & *Bull baiting*, it being a famous day for all these butcherly Sports, or rather barbarous cruelties: The Bulls did exceedingly well but the Irish Wolfe dog exceeded, which was a tall Gray-hound, a stately creature in deede, who beate a cruell Mastife: One of the Bulls tossd a Dog full into a Ladys lap, as

she sate in one of the boxes at a Considerable height from the *Arena*: There were two poore dogs killed; & so all ended with the Ape on horse-back, & I most heartily weary, of the rude & dirty passetime, which I had not seene I think in twenty yeares before:

17 I dined at my Bro: & made Visites: 18 at Goring-house whither my L: *Arlington* carried me from W: hall, with the *Marquis* of *Worcester*; there we found my L. *Sandwich*, Vicount *Stafford* [since beheaded], The Lieutennant of the Tower & others:

After dinner, my Lord, communicated to me his Majesties desire, that I would undertake to write the Historie of our Late War with the *Hollander*, which I had hitherto declin'd; This I found was ill taken, & that I should disoblige his Majestie who had made choice of me to do him that service, & that if I would undertake it, I should have all the Assistance the Secretarie Office & others could give me, with other encouragements, which I could not decently refuse: Note, that at Dinner, my *Lord Vicount Stafford* rose from Table in some Disorder, because there were roses stuck about the fruite, when the Discert came in & was set on the table: such an *Antipathie* it seemes he had to *Roses*, as once my Lady Selenger also had, & to that degree, that, as Sir *Kenhelme Digby* tells us, laying but a rose upon her Cheeke, when she was a sleepe it raisd a blister: but Sir *Kenhelme* was a teller of strange things. I went home this evening.

26. In the Afternoone at *Greenewich* Mr. *Plume*, on 4: *Gal:* 26: 29 To Lond: in order to my *Niepce* Evelyns Marriage, daughter to my Late Brother of Woodcot, with the Eldest Son of Mr. *Attourney Montague*, which was celebrated at *Southampton* house Chapell, after which a magnificent Entertainement, Feast & dauncing, diner & supper in the greate roome there; but the bride &c was bedded at my Sisters Lodging in Drurie-Lane &c:

July: 1 I returned home. ⟨3⟩: our Viccar as before: 6. Came Mr. *Stanhop Gent: Usher* to her Majestie (& Unkle to the Earle of Chesterfield) a very fine Gent: came to visite me, with my Lady Hutchison &c: 10: Dr. *Lloyd* on 4: Ephes: 1. in the afternoone on: 14: *Pro:* 34: he had ben our Curate, & was now preacher at Grays-Inn: [since Bishop of *Peterborow*:] 17 our *Viccar* on 6: Mich: 8.

18 I went to *Lond*, to accompany my worthy friend, that excellent man (Sir *Rob. Morray*) with Mr. *Slingsby* Master of the

Mint, to see his Seate & Estate at *Burrow Greene* in *Cambridg-shire*: desiring our advice for the placing a new house Mr. *Slingsby* was resolv'd to build: 19 We set out in a Coach & six horses, with him & his Lady: dined about midway at one Mr. *Turners*, where we found a very noble dinner, Venison, Musique, and a circle of Country Ladys & their Gallants: so after dinner we proceeded, and came to *Borrow Greene* that night: This had ben the antient seate of the *Cheekes* (whose daughter Mr. Slingsby married) for-merly Tutor to K: Edw: the Sixt: The old house large & ample & built for antient hospitalitie, ready to fall down with age; plac'd in a dirty hole, a stiffe Clay, no Water &c: & next a *Church-Yard* adjoyning, & other inconveniences: so we pitch'd upon a spot, on a rising ground, & adorn'd with venerable woods, a dry & sweete prospect E: & West, & fit for a Parke, at some mile distant, but no running water to be found:

⟨21⟩ We went to dine at my Lord *Allingtons*, who had newly built a house of greate cost, (his Architect Mr. Pratt) I believe little lesse than 20000 pounds, seated in a Parke, with a Sweete Prospect & stately avenue, water still defective: The house has also its infirmities; thence we went back to Mr. *Slingsbies*: my Lord *Allington* [since Conestable of the Tower] having very nobly entertaind us. 22 We rod out to see the greate *Meere* or Levell of recoverd fenland not far off: In the way we met my Lord *Arlington* going to his house in *Suffolk* accompanied with Count *Ogniati* (the *Spanish* Minister) & Sir *Bernard Gascoigne*: My Lord was exceedingly importunate with me to go with him to *Euston*, being but 15 miles distant: but in reguard of my Com-panie I could not: so passing through New-Market, we alighted, to see his *Majesties* house there now new building, the arches of the Cellers beneath, are exceedingly well turned, by the *Architect Mr. Samuel*, the rest meane enough, & hardly capable for a hunt-ing house: Many of the roomes above had the Chimnies plac'd in the angles & Corners, a Mode now introduc'd by his Majestie which I do at no hand approve of, & predict it will Spoile many noble houses & roomes if followed; it dos onely well in very Small & trifling roomes, but takes from the state of greater: besids this house is plac'd in a dirty Streete; without any Court or avenue, like a common Burgers: whereas it might & ought to have ben built at either end of the Towne, upon the very Carpet, where the Sports are Celebrated; but it being the purchase of an

old wretched house of my Lord *Tumonds*, his Majestie was perswaded to set it on that foundation, the most improper imaginable for an house of Sport & pleasure: We went to see the Stables
and fine horses, of which many were here kept, at vast expense,
with all the art & tendernesse Imaginable: Being ariv'd at *Some
meeres*, we found my Lord *Wotton* & Sir *Jo: Kiviet* about their
draining Engines, having it seemes undertaken to do wonders,
on a vast piece of March-ground, they had hired of Sir *Tho:
Chichley*, Master of the Ordinance: They much pleasd themselves
with the hopes of a rich harvest of Hemp & Cole-seede, which
was the crop expected: Here we visited the Engines & Mills,
both for Wind & Water, draining it thro two rivers or grafts cut
by hand, & capable of considerable barges, which went thwart
one the other, discharging the water into the Sea, such as this
Spot had ben the former winter, which was now drie, & so exuberant & rich as even astonish'd me to see what increase there
was; Weedes grew as high as horse & man almost upon the
bankes: Here my Lord & his Partner had built two or 3 roomes
with flanders white brick, very hard; one of the greate Engines
was in the *Kitchin*, where I saw the fish swimm up even to the
very Chimny hearth, by a small cut derived thro the roome, &
running within a foote of the very fire: having after dinner rid
about that vast levall, pesterd with heate & swarmes of *Gnatts*,
we returnd over *New-market-heath*, the way being most of it a
sweete Turfe, & down, like *Salisbery* plaine, the *Jockies* breathing
their fine barbs & racers, & giving them their heates. Having ben
very much made ⟨of⟩ at Borrow-Greene on 23 we return'd to
Lond: staying some time at *Audlie End* to see that fine Palace: It
is indeede a cherefull piece of Gotic-building, or rather *antico-
moderno*, but placed in an obscure bottome: The Cellars, & Gallerie are very stately; It has a river by it, a pretty avenue of Limes,
& in a parke: This is in *Saffron Walden* Parish famous for that
usefull plant, with which all the Countrie is covered: so dining at
Bishops Stratford we came late to London:

24. I din'd at the Vice-Chamberlains: after dinner to heare
preach a French Frier (that was now a *Proselyte*,) in the *French-
Church* at the *Savoy* his Text 4: *John*: 7: on which he made a most
eloquent, & practical discourse, shewing, what small (& to vulgar
opinions) circumstances, our B: S. tooke hold of to convert men;
exaggerating Gods infinite love to man, & how indefatigable our

Saviour was to gaine their Soules. I went to *White-hall* to speake with Mr. *Treasurer*, & next morning home: 31. Our Doctor on his former subject:

August 5 There was sent me by a Neighbour, the Servant-maid of a friend of hers, who the last moneth as she was sitting before her mistris at work (I think 'twas sewing) felt a seacret stroke upon her arme a little above her wrist, the upper part for a pretty height, the smart of which as if she had ben strock with another hand, caus'd her to hold her arme a while, 'til it was somewhat mittigated; but so it put her into a kind of convulsion fit, or rather Hysteric: A gentleman coming casualy in, looking on her arme, found that part poudred with red Crosses, set in most exact & wonderfull order

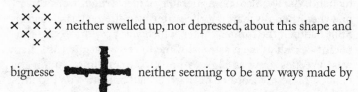 neither swelled up, nor depressed, about this shape and

bignesse   neither seeming to be any ways made by

artifice; of a redish colour, not so red as bloud, the skin over them smooth, but the rest of the arme livid & of a mortified hue with certaine prints as it were of the stroke as of fingers: This had hapned three severall times in *July* at about 10 days intervall, the Crosses beginning to ware out, but the successive ones set in other different (yet uniforme) order: The Maid seem'd very modest, no *Phanatic*, but well disposd to the Church established: she was borne northward and came from *Lond:* to *Dept-ford* with her *Mistris* to avoid the discourses & importunity of curious people; made no gaine by it, pretended no religious fancies, had never any commerce with the *Popish* Priests &c but seemed to be a plaine, ordinary, silent working wench, some-what fat, short, & high colour'd: she told me divers *Divines* & *Physitians* had seene her, but were unsatisfied; That she had taken some remedies against her fits, but did her no good, that she never had any fits 'til this happn'd; but that she once since seemed in her sleepe, to heare one say to her, that she should tamper no more with them, nor trouble herself with any thing that happn'd; but put her trust in the Merits of *Christ* onely: This being the substance of what she told me, & of what I saw, & curiously examin'd (being formerly acquainted with the impostorious *Nunns* of *Loudune* in France, which made such noise in the World amongst the Papists,) I thought worth the notice: I remember *Monsieur Monconis*, (that curious Travellor & a *Roman* Catholick) was by no meanes satisfied with the *stigmata* of those *Nunns*, because they were so shie of letting him scrape the Letters, which were *Jesus, Maria, Joseph*, (as I think) observing they began to scale off with it: whereas this poore Wench was willing to submit to any trial; so as I professe, I knew not what to think of it; nor dare I pronounce it any thing supernaturall; though (as I told her) I did by no meanes conceive it to have ben sent, as any mark to encourage her to change her Religion; which I told her might probably be the temptation of subtile priests; but rather engage her to a constancy in the *Christian* Profession, & particularly of the *Church* of *England* who have respect to the Crosse, & beare it on their foreheads as soone as made *Christians*, & that this might be a seasonable admonition, now in a time of so many *Heresies, Sects*, & *Atheistical* men: &c:

7 Our Viccar as formerly: 14: on his former, The same on the 21: 24. To Lond: Thence to *Windsore*: 26, I supped with the *Duke* of *Monmoth*; & the next day, invited by my Ld: *Arlington* dined with the same Duke & divers Lords: After dinner my Lord & I had conference of more than an houre alone in his Bed-chamber, to engage me in the Historie, I shew'd him some thing that I had drawn up, to his greate satisfaction, & then he desired me to shew it to the *Tresurer* also &c:

28 One of the *Prœbends* preached on   The ambitious demand of the Mother of *Zebedeus's* children: Then followed the Offering of the knights of the Order [of the garter] *Secundum Consuetudinem*: first the poore-knights went ⟨in⟩ procession, Then the Canons in their formalities, Deane, & Chancelor; Then his Majestie (the sovraine) then the *Duke* of *york*, Pr: *Rupert*, lastly the Earle of *Oxford*, who was all that was then at Court, the *D:* of *Monmouth* being gon the night before to *Hampton-Court*: I din'd with the *Tressurer*, consulted with him, what pieces I was to add &c. & in the afternoone his *Majestie* toke me aside into the *Balconie* over the *Tarice*, extreamely pleased with what had ben told him I had begun in order to his commands, & enjoyning me to proceede vigorously in it; & told me he had ordered the Secretaries of state to give me all necessary assistance of papers & particulars relating to it, & enjoyning

me to make it a little keene, for that the *Hollanders* had very unhandsomely abused him, in their pictures, books & libells. &c:

I went in the Evening to *Eaton* to visite the *Provost* Dr. *Alestrie Professor Regius Oxon:* 29 returned home. Note, that Windsor was now going to be repaired, being exceedingly ragged and ruinous: *Prince Rupert Constable* had begun to trim up the *Keepe* or high round Tower, & handsomly adorn'd his hall, with a furniture of Armes, which was very singular; by so disposing the Pikes, Muskets, Pistols, Bandilers, [holster⟨s⟩], Drumms, Back, brest & head pi⟨e⟩ces as was very extraordinary: & thus those huge steepe stayres ascending to it, had the Walls invested with this martial furniture, all new & bright, & set with such study, as to represent, Pillasters, Architraves, Cornishes, Architraves, Freezes, by so disposing the bandalliers, holsters, & *Drums*, so as to represent festoones, & that with out any Confusion, Trophy like: from the Hall, we went into his *Bedchamber* & ample roomes which were hung with tapissrie, curious & effeminate Pictures, so extreamely different from the other, which presented nothing but Warr & horror, as was very Surprizing & Divertissant. The *King* passed most of his time in hunting the *Stag*, & walking in the *Parke* which he was now also planting with walks of Trees, &c:

Sept: ⟨4⟩ Our *Viccar* on his former subject: The holy Comm: follow'd:

6 I went to the Wedding of my neighbour Mrs. *Jeakel* married to Colonel Midleton, one of the Commissioners of the Navy; at *Grays-Inn* Chapell, & dined in *Suffolck-streete*, returned:

8 I went with my Wife & Children to visite my Bro: at Wotton in *Surrey*: 11: Mr. *Higham* preached on 24. *Luke*. 43: In the afternoone to *Abinger* to heare Dr. *Offley* on   *a brand plucked out of the fire*. 13 I went to visite Sir Rich: Lachford my kindsman, & Mr. *Charles Howard* at his extraordinary Garden at *Dip-den*. 15 To visite Mr. *Arthyr Onslow* at *West-Horseley*, a pretty dry seate on the Downes, where we dined in his greate roome:

17 To visite Mr. *Hussey*, who (being nigh Wotton) lives in a sweete vally deliciously watered: 18 *Mr. Higham* preached as before: in the afternoone at *Abinger* a Young man chaplaine to Sir *Jo: Nicholas* on 16: *Acts*: 30. 31.

23 to *Alburie* to see how that Garden proceeded, which I found exactly don according to the Designe & plot I had made, with the *Crypta* through the mountaine in the parke, which is 30

pearches in length, such a *Pausilippe* is no where in England besides: The Canals were now digging, & Vineyards planted.

October 14 I conferr'd againe with the *Tressurer* &c: & dined with the *Earle of Norwich.* 15. I spent the whole afternoone in private with the *Treasurer*, who put into my hands those seacret pieces and Transactions concerning the *Dutch* war, & particularly the Expedition of *Bergen* in which he had himselfe the chiefe part; & gave me instructions &c 'til the *King* arriving from *New market,* we both went up into his Majesties Bed-Chamber, it being now almost night, after which I went home, the weather uncomfortable: 16 our *Viccar* on 7: *Matt* 21: of the Danger of formal Professors: 20 To Lond: to consult the Tressurer & Earle of *Arlington* Secretary of state. 21. Din'd at the *Tressurers* & after dinner were shut-up together, I received other advises, & ten paper-bookes of Dispatches & Treaties, to returne which againe, I gave a note under my hand to the Master of the Paper Office Mr. *Jos: Wiliamson* & so return'd home. ⟨23⟩ our *Vicc:* as before. 26: To *Lond:* din'd with Mr. *Vice-Chamberlaine*, return'd next day, having caled at the *Ro: Society*, it being the first time of meeting since their recesse; where were several Curiosities of nature sent us from *New England*, & a learned discourse from *Bolognia* of some starrs disappearing in the *Constellation* of the Ship, starrs of the *2d Magnitude*, which were wont to be conspicuous with the bare Eye; Also was presented a noble Piece of Chrystal from *Iseland* sent from *Copenhagen* with a book: 30. our *Doctor* as above: 31. I was this morning fifty-yeares of Age: The Lord teach me to number my daies so, as to apply them to his glory *Amen*:

November 1. Our *Viccar* on 10: *Heb:* 22: We met this day as *Foefeès* for the poore, according to Costome: 3: *Lond:* at our *Society* where there was an Experiment about cracking a thin & ordinary bell glasse with the shrillnesse of the voice onely. 4. Dined at the *Groome-porters*, return'd that Evening, having seene the *Prince* of *Orange*, newly come to see his Unkle the *King*: he has a manly couragious wise Countenance, resembling both his Mother, & *Duke* of Glocester both deceased: I now also saw that famed beauty (but in my opinion of a childish simple & baby face) *Madamoiselle Quirreval*, lately maide of honour to *Madame*, & now to be so to the *Queene*:

5 Our Doctor preaches on his former, against instability, with some small reflections on the Solemnity of the day. 6: on 7: *Matt*: 21: The Communion follow'd: 10. To *Lond*. returnd at night:

23 Dined with the E. of *Arlington* where was the *Venetian* Ambassador, of whom I now tooke solemn leave, being now he told me on his returne: There were also L: *Howard, Wharton, Winsore,* & divers other greate persons: 24 I din'd with the *Treasurer* where was the *Earle* of *Rochester* a very prophane Wit: Thence to our *Society.* 25 Dined in *Hatton Garden.*

26 I had a Tryall in *Guild-Hall* against on⟨e⟩ *Cock* who had exceedingly wronged me in an Accompt of monies going through his hands; but there being many Causes, 'twas respited til Wednesday following: 27: returned home in the morning it being *Advent Sonday,* our *Viccar* still on his former Text. 29, To *Lond:* in order to our *Tryal;* but by perswasion of *Judge Hales* (that excellent good Man) I was willing to put it to arbitration &c: 30: St. *Andrews* day we proceeded to Elections in the *Society,* where I was chosen of the *Council* for the following yeare, then dined all together according to costome, his Majestie & Lord *Howard* sending the Venison:

December 11 Dr. *LLoyd* (preacher of *Grays Inn* & now *Chap:* to his *Majestie*) on 11: *Matt:* 3. 4. 5. 6. 15 To *Lond:* It was the thickest, & darkest fogg on the *Thames,* that was ever know⟨n⟩ in the memory of man, & I happned to be in the middst of it: I supped with Monsieur *Zulestein* late Governor to the Young Pr: of Orange, with severall other greate persons, & had a greate entertainment: next day, at the Ro: *Society,* where was present⟨ed⟩ from *Pr: Rupert* an Inscription in a stone found on the *Keepe* at *Winsore,* which covered the *Skelleton* of a child; with an Urne full of old Coynes &c:

18 Our *Doctor* now finished his Text:

20 To *Lond* about buisinesse til 23d. 25 Our *Viccar* on 2. Luke 10. 11. in an excellent discourse apposite to the Occasion, being *Christmas day.* 26 I entertain'd my Neighbours *more solito.* 31. Humbly giving God praise for his most mercifull protection &c:

THE DISCOVERY OF GRINLING GIBBONS – NELL GWYN – COLONEL BLOOD – THE COUNCIL OF PLANTATIONS – THE DUTCH WARS
(1671–1674)

167$\frac{0}{1}$ JAN: 1. New Years day, our *Viccar* continues his former discourse: I received the holy Comm: which follow'd, with extraordinary resolutions, God of his mercy sanctifie them to me. 2. & 3. Invited my Neighbours:

5 My long Consumptive Servant J: *Smith* died, a faithfull honest servant:

8 Our Doctor as above:

10 Mr. *Bohune* my sonns *Tutor*, having now ben 5 yeares in my house, & now Batchelor of Laws & Fellow of New Coll: went from me to Oxford to reside there, having well & faithfully perform'd his Charge &c: 15 our Doctor on his former: 16 To Lond: about buisinesse, dined in Hatton Garden at the first-fruits Office: 18 Dined with the *Groomes* of his Majesties *Bed Chamber*.

18 I this day first acquainted his Majestie with that incomparable young man, *Gibson*,[1] whom I had lately found in an Obscure place, & that by meere accident, as I was walking neere a poore solitary thatched house in a field in our Parish neere *Says-Court*: I found him shut in, but looking into the Window, I perceiv'd him carving that large *Cartoone* or *Crucifix* of *Tintorets*, a Copy of which I had also my selfe brought from *Venice*, where the original Painting remaines: I asked if I might come in, he opned the doore civily to me, & I saw him about such a work, as for the curiosity of handling, drawing, & studious exactnesse, I never in my life had seene before in all my travells: I asked why he worked in such an obscure & lonesome place; he told me, it was that he might apply himselfe to his profession without interruption; & wondred not a little how I came to find him out: I asked if he were unwilling to be made knowne to some Greate men; for that I believed it might turne to his profit; he answerd, he was yet but a beginner; but would yet not be sorry to sell off that piece; I asked him the price, he told me 100 pounds. In good earnest the very frame was worth the mony, there being nothing even in nature so tender, & delicate as the flowers & festoones about it, & yet the worke was very strong; but in the Piece above 100 figures of men &c: I found he was likewise *Musical*, & very Civil, sober & discreete in his discourse: There was onely an old Woman in the house; so desiring leave to visite him sometimes, I tooke my leave: Of this Young *Artist*, together with my manner of finding him out, I acquainted the *King*, and beged of his *Majestie* that he would give me leave to bring him & his Worke to White-hall, for that I would adventure my reputation with his

1 Grinling Gibbons.

Majestie that he had never seene any thing approch it, & that he would be exceedingly pleased, & employ him: The *King* sayd, he would himselfe go see him: This was the first notice his Majestie ever had of Mr. *Gibbons*.

20: His Majestie ⟨came⟩ to me in the *Queenes* Withdrawing roome, from the Circle of *Ladies*, to talke with me what advance I had made in the *Dutch Historie*: I dined with the *Tressurer* & after we went to the Secretaries Office, where we conferred about divers particulars: 21. I was directed to go to Sir *Geo: Downing* who (being a pub: Minister in Holland, at the beginning of the War) was to give me light in some material passages: so returned home with my *Lady Tuke* who gave my Wife a Visite for some daies:

30 Was our late good Kings Anniversary & *Martyrdome*, our Doctor preached on 7: *Act: ultimo*: He shew'd the antiquity & duty of kneeling at Prayers, reprehending the late irreverenc: The Examples of Praying for, & forgiving Enemies: The sinn of Cursing them, clearing those Texts in some of the Prophetical *Psalmes*, as against the *Children* mocking Elias, Judas, Simon Magus & others; as being predictions rather then maledictions: Then exaggerated the monstrousnesse of the Crime of Murdering the King, so good a king, & how it became the sinn of the whole nation, which was yet to expiate it by serious Repentance, to prevent the ruine threatned &c and in truth the leudnesse of our greatest ones, & universal luxurie, seemed to menace some yet more dreadfull vengeance: we have had a plague, a Warr, & such a fire, as never was the like in any nation since the overthrow of *Sodome*, and this very yeare so Wett, Stormy & unseasonable, as had not ben knowne in many yeares: The Lord be gracious to us, we that are yet the most happy, are withall the most unthankfull & undeserving people of the Universe:

Feb: 5 Our *Doctor* on 12. *Heb:* 14: The blessed Sacrament followed.

6 To *Lond:* 7: din'd at the Tressurers. 9: I saw the greate *Ball* danced by the *Queene* & greate Ladies at White hall Theater: & next day was acted there the famous Play, cald the Siege of *Granada* two days acted successively: there were indeede very glorious scenes & perspectives, the worke of Mr. *Streeter*, who well understands it:

12 I heard a sermon in the *French Church* 23 Pro: 13
home: 19 our *Doctor* as above: This day dined with me Mr. Surveyor Dr. Chr: *Wren*, Mr. *Pepys* Cleark of the Acts, two extraordinary ingenious, and knowing persons, and other friends;
I carried them to see the piece of Carving which I had
recomended to the King. 25 Came to visite me one of the Lords
Commissioners of *Scotland* for the Union: 26: our *Viccar* as
above: 27 To *Lond:* to the funerall of Sir *Jo: Minnes* Comptroller
of the Navy, a pleasant man:

28: The *Treasurer* acquainted me his Majestie was graciously
pleased to nominate me one of his Council of forraine Plantations, & ⟨had⟩ given me a salarie of 500 pounds per Annum to
encourage me. 29: I went to thanke the *Tressurer* who was my
greate friend, and loved me; I dined with him, & much company
there: Thence to my Lord *Arlington* Secretary of state, in whose
favour I likewise was: upon many occasions, though I cultivated
neither of their friendships with any meane submissions: I kissed
his *Majesties hand*, upon his making me one of that new Establish'd Council:

Mar: 1. I caused Mr. *Gibbon* to bring to *Whitehall* his excel-
lent piece of Carving where being come, I advertised his
Majestie who asked me where it was, I told him, in Sir R:
Brownes (my F. in Laws) Chamber, & that if it pleased his
Majestie to appoint whither it should be brought (for 'twas
large, and though of Wood, yet heavy) I would take care for it:
No says the King; shew me the Way, Ile go to Sir *Richards*
Chamber: which his Majestie immediately did, walking all
along the Enteries after me as far as the *Ewrie* til he came up
into the rome where I also lay: & no sooner was he entred, &
cast his eye on the Worke but he was a stonish'd at the curiositie
of it, & having considred it a long time, & discours'd with
Mr. *Gibbon*, whom I brought to kisse his hand; he commanded
it should be immediately carried to the *Queenes* side to shew her
Majestie, so it was carried up into her bed-chamber, where she
and the King looked on & admired it againe, the King thus leaving us with the Queene being now caled away, I think to Council, believing that she would have bought it, it being a Crucifix;
but when his Majestie was gon, a French pedling woman, one
Madame de boord, that used to bring peticoates & fanns &
baubles out of France to the Ladys, began to find faults with

severall things in the worke, which she understood no more
than an Asse or Monky; so as in a kind of Indignation, I caused
the porters who brought it, to carry it to the Chamber againe,
finding the Queene so much govern'd by an ignorant french
woman: and this incomparable *Artist* ⟨had⟩ the labour onely for
his paines, which not a little displeased me; so he was faine to
send it downe to his cottage againe, though he not long after
sold it for 80 pounds, which was realy, (even without the frame)
worth an hundred: Sir *Geo: Viner* buying it of him, as his first
Essay, and his Majesties Surveyor *Mr. Wren* faithfully promising
me to employ him for the future; I having bespoke his *Majestie*
also for his Worke at *Windsore* which my friend *Mr. May* (the
Architect there) was going to alter and repaire universaly: for on
the next day, I had a faire opportunity of talking to his *Majestie*
about it, in the *Lobby* next the Queenes side, where I presented
him with some Sheetes of my historie, & thence walked with
him thro St. *James's* Parke to the *Garden*, where I both saw and
heard a very familiar discourse betweene — & *Mrs. Nellie* as
they cal'd an impudent Comedian, she looking out of her Garden on a Tarrace at the top of the Wall, & — standing on the
greene Walke under it: I was heartily sorry at this scene: Thence
the King walked to the *Dutches* of *Cleavelands*, another Lady of
Pleasure & curse of our nation: It was on a Council day, & so I
went back & on the 4th to my house.—

    5 Our *Viccar* on his former subject: The holy Sacrament
follow'd, I dined at *Greenewich* to take leave of Sir *Tho: Linch*
now going Governer of *Jamaica* &c:

    10 To *Lond:* about passing my Grant for my *sallarie* of 500
pounds per ann: as one of the standing Council for Plantations;
a considerable honour: There being now added in my pattent
onely the *Duke of York*, D: of *Bukingam*, the Earle of *Lauderdall*
& my selfe: I dind at the *Treasurers*, visited my Lord *Arlington*,
& thence to my *Lord Keepers* & *Attourney* Generals & next day
to Says-Court: 12 Our *Viccar* as above: so also on the 19th: 20:
To *Lond:* passing the whole weeke in buisinesse, returnd the 25
being our Lady-day. 26 our *Viccar* as above: 29 To *Lond*, returnd:
To *Lond* againe next morning & returned the day after:

    Aprill 2: Our *Doctor* on his former: 9: he preached on 3.
Lament: 40. 10 To *Lond:* to condole with the Treasurer Sir *Tho:*
Clifford upon the losse of his eldest sonn dying at *Florence*: so

return'd: 15 To *Lond:* returnd: 16: our Doctor as above: 18 To *Lond:* returned: 21 *Good-friday* on 12 Heb: 2. The holy Sacrament.

23 *Easter day* our Doctor on 1. *Apoc:* 10. 30: on the same subject:

May: Was our yearly meeting for the Poore, our Doctor preaching on 17 Act: 28: 2. To *Lond:* The *French King* being now with a greate Army of 28000 about *Dynkirk* divers of the grandees of that Court, & a vast number of Gentlemen & *Cadets* in fantastical habites, came flocking over to see our Court, & complement his *Majestie*. I was present when they first were conducted into the *Queenes* withdrawing roome where saluted their Majesties The *Duke* of *Guise*, The D: of Longuville, of *Ballion*, Marq: *Arignie*, *Monsieur* Le *Grand*, Monsieur *Le Premiere* & innumerable more of the first sort: so I went home: 7 Our *Viccar* on his former: The Communion follow'd:

10 To *Lond:* din'd at Mr. *Treasurers* where dined Monsieur de *Gramont* & severall French noblemen: & one *Bloud* that impudent bold fellow, who had not long before attempted to steale the Imperial *Crowne* it selfe out of the *Tower*, pretending onely curiositie of seeing the *Regalia* there, when stabbing (though not mortaly) the keeper of them, he boldly went away with it, thro all the guards, taken onely by the accident of his horses falling. How he came to be pardoned, & even received to favour, not onely after this, but severall other exploits almost as daring, both in *Ireland* and here, I could never come to understand: some believed he became a spie of severall Parties, being well with the Sectaries & Enthusiasts, & did his Majestie services that way, which none alive could so well as he: But it was certainely as the boldest attempt, so the onely Treason of this nature that was ever pardon'd: The Man had not onely a daring but a vilanous un-mercifull looke, a false Countenance, but very well spoken, & dangerously insinuating: 11 I went to *Eltham* to sit as one of the Commission about the subsidie now given his Majestie by Parliament: returnd: ⟨14⟩ our *Viccar* as above.

17 To Lond: 18 dined at Mr. *Tressurers* with the E: of *Arlington, Ca⟨r⟩lingford*, Lord *Arundel* of *Wardoer*, Lo: *Almoner* to the *Queene*; a *French Count*, and two *Abbots* with severall more of French nobility: And now by something I had lately observed of Mr. *Treasurers* conversation & discourse on occasion I suspected him a little warping to *Rome*: 21 Our *Doctor* on 2: *Pet:* 3. 10: 23: To

Lond, in order to my being sworne of the Council of Pl: but our meeting was deferred by the Duke of York.

24 Dined with the Groomes of the *Bed-chamber*. 25. I dined at a feast made for me & my Wife by the *Trinity Company*, for our Passing a fine about the Land, Sir R: Bro: my Wifes Father, freely gave to found & build their Colledge or *Almes houses* on, at *Deptford*; it being my Wifes after her Father: It was a good & a Charitable Worke & gift, but much better bestowed on the poore of that Parish, than on the seamens Widdows, the Trinity Company being very rich, & the rest of the poore of the Parish exceedingly Indigent:

26: Meeting all at *Queenes streete* at the Earle of Bristols house (which we had lately taken, & furnish'd with rich hangings of the Kings, 7 roomes on a floore with a long Gallery, Gardens &c:) The Duke of *Buckingham*, E: of *Lauderdail*, L: *Culpeper*, Sir *Geo: Carteret Vice-Chamberlaine* & my selfe, had our Oathes given us by the Earle of *Sandwich* our *President*: To *Advise* & Counsel his *Majestie* to the best of our abillities &c: for the well Governing of his Majesties forraine Plantations &c. The forme very little differing from what is given the *Privy Council*: Then we tooke all our Places in the Council Chamber at the board: The roome very large, & furnished with the *Atlases*, Mapps, Charts, Globes &c: Then came the *Lord Keeper* Sir *Orlando* Bridgeman, E: of *Arlington* Pr: Secretary of State: Lord *Ashley*, Mr. *Treasurer*, Sir *Jo: Trevor* the other Pr: Secretary, Sir Jo: *Duncomb*, Lord *Allington*, Mr. *Grey*, sonn to the Lord *Grey*, Mr. Hen: *Broncher*, Sir *Humfry Winch*; Sir *John Finch*, Mr. *Waller*, Coll: *Titus* of the Bed chamber, Mr. *Slingsby* the Secretary to the Council, & two Clearks of the Council, who were all Sworne some dayes before: being all set, our Patent was read, & then the additional Patent, in which was recited this new establishment: Then was delivered to every one of us a Copy of the Patent, & of our Instructions: after which we fell to debate matters; & first agreed on a forme for Circulating Letters to be immediately dispatched to all his Majesties Plantations & Territories in the West Indies & Ilands thereof; to give them notice to whom they should apply themselves on all occasions, & to render us an account of their present state, & Government; & therefore the Letters were directed to the respective Governors: but most we insisted on, was to know in what condition

New-England was; which appearing to be very independent as to their reguard to old England, or his Majestie, rich & strong as now they were, greate were the debates, in what style to write to them: for the Condition of that Colonie was such, as they were able to contest with all our Plantations about them, & feare there was, of their altogether breaking from all dependance on this nation: His *Majestie* therefore recommended this afaire more expressly: We therefore thought fit, in the first place, to acquaint our selves as well as we could of the state of that place, by some who we heard of, that were newly come from thence, & to be informed of their present posture & Condition; because some of our Council were for sending them a menacing Letter which those who better understood the touchy & peevish humor of that Colonie, were utterly against. Then a letter was red which came from Sir *Tho: Modiford* Governor of *Jamaica*, & then the Council brake up: My agreement with *Cock* not succeeding, I went to take advise of that famous Lawyer Mr. Jones of Grays Inn: & 27: had a Trial before the *L: C. Justice Hales* for a summ of mony owing me; so after the Lawyers had wrangled sufficiently, It was againe referred to a new *Arbitration*: This being the very first Suite at Law, that ever I had with any Creature before and ô that it might be the Last: from hence I returned to my house:

28 Our *Viccar* preached on his former Text & subject: 29 was his Majesties Nativity and restauration Anniversary, our Doctor preaching on 14 *Rom:* to obey not onely for feare, but Conscience &c: in an excellent & pertinent discourse:

June 1 I went to London to Council, but our meeting was put off, by reason of an Installation at Windsore; so dining at my *Bro: Evelyns* (now in Towne) I returned home.

4 Our Doctor preached as on the former Sonday: 6: I went to Council, where was produc'd a most exact and ample Information of the state of *Jamaica*, and of the best expedients to reduce *New-England*, on which there was a long debate, & whether it were fit ⟨to⟩ send a Letter & certaine curious *Queries* relating to the seacrets of the Government: but 'twas concluded in the negative, & that if any, it should be onely a conciliating paper at first, or civil letter 'til we had better information of the present face of things; since we understood they were a people al most upon the very brink of renouncing any dependance of the Crowne:—I din'd at

my Brothers, & went home. 9: My Bro: Geo: & Sister Evelyn of
Woodcot, my *Niepce Montague* &c came to dine with me, &
return'd this evening: 11 *Whit Sonday* our *Viccar* on 4: *Ephes:* 30:
The B: Sacrament follow'd: 18 on the same Text. 19 *Trinity Moneday* was the meeting of that Society; on which the Doctor proceeded on the *Mysterie*, applying the unitie of the persons, to our
Union as christian breathren: hence to a greate dinner at the greate
roome in *Deptford* Trinity house, Sir Tho: Allen chosen Master &
succeeding the Earle of *Cravon*. 20: To carry Coll: *Midleton* to
White hall to my L: *Sandwich* our President, for some information
he was able to give the *Council* of the state of the *Colonie* in
N. *England*, & return'd: Next day to *Council* againe, where one
Coll: *Cartrite* a Notingham-shere man, (formerly in Commission
with Coll: *Nichols*) gave us a considerable relation of that Country.
Upon which the Council concluded, that if policy would not
reduce the disaffected there, force should: that yet in the first
place, a letter of amnestie should be dispatch'd, with an intention
to fortifie a certaine Iland in the mouth of the chiefe river; & to
purchase the maine of that part of the Plantation belonging to
Ferdinando Gorges, which would inable the King to curb *Boston*: I
went home: 23 Came the Lord Vic: *Mordaunt* to see me.

24 Came *Constantine Hugens* S⟨e⟩igneur of *Zulechom*,
that excellent learned man, *Poet* & *Musitian*, & now neere
80 yeares of age a vigorous brisk-man, to take leave of me
before his returne into Holland, with the *Prince*, whose Secretary he was:

26 To *Lond:* to Council, where my Lo: Arlington being present, acquainted us that it was his Majesties Proposal, we should
every one of us contribute 20 pounds a piece, towards the building of a Council-chamber and conveniences some where in
White-hall, to the end, that his Majestie himselfe might come
and sit amongst us & heare our debates; The mony we laied out
to be reimbours'd us out of the contingent monies already set
apart for us, viz: 1000 pounds yearley: To which we unanimously
consented. There came also an uncertaine brute from *Barbados*,
of some disorder there: so I went home, steping in at the Theater, to see the new Machines for the intended scenes, which
were indeede very costly, & magnificent:

29 To *Lond:* & Council; where were letters from Sir *Tho:
Mudyford* of the Expedition and Exploit of Coll: Morgan &

others of *Jamaica* on the *Spanish* Continent at *Panama*: but there being not a quorum of us, we rose & went home: I dined at Mr. *David* Walters, a groome of the Bed-chamber & Lieuten: of the Ordinance &c: & steped in at the *Ro: Society* where we had letters from Dr. *Sylvius del Boe* Professor at *Leyden*, with a present of his Booke ⟨newly⟩ published, with others from *Hevelius* of *Dantzique* &c.

July ⟨2⟩ our *Doctor* on his former: I received the H: Comm: 4: To *Lon:* to *Council*: where we drew up & agreed to a letter to be sent to N: England & made some proposals to *Mr. Gorges* for his Interest &c: I went home. 9: our *Viccar* as above: 16 I was not well: 18: To *Lond:* to *Council*, dind at the *Vice-Chamberlaines.* 23. our *Viccar* on 15. *Luke*: 11 on the *Parable* of the *Prodigal.* 24: To Lon: *Council:* Mr. Surveyor brought us a plot for the building of our *Council*-Chamber to be erected at the end of the *Privy-Garden* in *White-hall* which was all was don: I returned. 30. A stranger on 5. *Jer:* 4:

Aug: 1 To *Lond:* Council, which being put off, I returnd immediately home:

3 To Lond: & to *Council* where was a full appearance: viz, The *Lo: Keeper*, Secretaries of State, Mr. *Treasurer*, & many of the Lords of the Privy Council: The matter in debate was, whether we should send a Deputy to *New England* requiring them of the *Massachusets* to restore such to their limits, & respective possessions, as had petitioned the Council: This to be the open Commission onely, but in truth with seacret Instructions to Informe the Council of the condition of those *Colonies*; & whether they were of such power as to be able to resist his Majestie & declare for themselves as Independent of the Crowne, as we were told, & which of late yeares made them refractorie: Coll: *Midleton* being called in assured us they might be curbed by a few of his Majesties 5t rate fregats, to spoile their Trade with the *Ilands*: but though of this my L: *President* was not satisfied, the rest were, & we did resolve to advise his Majestie to send Commissioners with a formal Commission for adjusting boundaries, &c: but under hand with seacret Instructions &c: I return'd home: 4 To *Parsons Greene* to visite my Lo: *Mordaunt*, return'd the Evening:

6 our *Viccar* as formerly: The blessed Sacrament follows:

10 Came Sir *Geo: Lane* (Secretary to the D: of Ormond, & Cl: of the Pr: Council) [since made a Viscount] to dine with me:

19 To *Lond:* & *Council:* The letters of Sir T: *Mudiford* were read, giving relation of the Exploit at Panamà, which was very brave: They tooke & burnt, and pilag'd the Towne of vast Treasures, but the best of the booty had ben ship'd off, & lay at anker in the South Sea, so as after our Men had ranged the Countriy 60 miles about, they went back to *Nombre de Dios* & embarq'd to *Jamaica*; Such an action had not ben don since the famous *Drake*: I dined at the *Resident* of *Hambroghs*, & after dinner at the *Christning* of Sir Sam: *Tukes Son Charles* which was don at *Somerset* house by a *Popish Priest* with many odd Ceremonies, Spittle & anointings: *Godfathers* the *King*: L: *Arundell* of *Wardoer*, &c *Countesse* of *Huntington*: after which I went home. 20: *Viccar* as above: 24: To *Lond:* returned.

27: Our Vicc: as above: 29 To *Lond:* with some more papers of my progresse in the *Dutch* Warr, delivered to the Treasurer: on 1. *September* when I dined with him, my L: *Arlington, Halifax*, Sir *Th: Strickland*, & next day went home, [2] being the *Anniversarie* of the late dreadfull fire of *London*. 3: our *Viccar* on his former: The holy Communion followed &c.

10 Our *Viccar* proceeded. 12. To *Lond:* The *Council* adjurn'd to my L. *Sandwiches*. 13. This night fell a dreadfull tempest. 14. I spent this morning privately with Mr. Tres: and 15 Afternoone at *Council*, where leters were read from Sir *Ch: Wheeler* concerning the resigning his Government of St. *Christophers*: There was a very warme contest betweene my L: *Sandwich* our President, & Mr. Slingsby our *Secretary*, about some unkind expressions, wherein I think the Latter was to blame: I returned home: ⟨17⟩ our *Viccar* proceedes. In the afternoone to *Greenewich*, Mr. *Plume*. 18. *Luke*: 15. 20 To *Lond* about buisinesse: 21. I dined in the Citty, at the fraternity feast in yron-mongers hall, where the 4 stewards chose their successors of the next yeare with a solemn procession, garlands about their heads & musique playing before them, so coming up to the uper Tables where the gentlemen sate, they drank to the new ⟨stewards⟩ &c: and so we parted. 22 I dind at the *Tressurers* where I had discourse with Sir *Hen: Jones* (now come over to raise a regiment of horse) concerning the *French* Conquests in *Lorraine*: He told me the King sold all things to the Souldiers, even to an handfull of hay: My L:

Sunderland was now nominated Ambassador for *Spaine*. After dinner the Tressurer carried me to *Lincolns Inn* to one of the *Parliament Clearks*, to obtaine of him that I might carry-home, with me and peruse some of the *Journals*, which I had delivered to me to examine about the late Dutch war &c: Returning home I went on shore to see the Costome-howse now newly rebuilt since the dreadfull Conflagration. 24. our Viccar as above:

Octob: 1 our Doctor proceede⟨s⟩ to ver: 18: The holy Sacrament followd: 8: on the same: I went after Evening Service to *Lond:* in order to a journey of refreshment with Mr. Treasurer to *Newmarket* &c where his *Majestie* was &c:

9 We set out on the 9th in his Coach of 6 brave horses, which we changed thrice: & first at *Bishop Stratford*, & last at *Chesterford* so as by night we got to *N. Market*, where Mr. *Henry Jermin* (Nephew to the Earle of St. *Albans*) lodged me very Civily: We went immediately to Court (the King & all the English Gallantes being here at their autumnal sports) supped at my L: *Chamberlaines*, & next day after dinner went on the *heath*, where I saw the greate match run betweene *Wood-cock* & *Flat-foot* the Kings, & Mr. *Eliots* of the Bedchamber, many thousands being spectators, a more signal race had not ben run of many yeares: This over, I went that night with Mr. *Tressurer* to *Euston*, a palace of my L: ⟨*Arlingtons*⟩ [10] where we found Monsieur *Colbert* (the French Ambassador) & the famous new *french* maid of honor, *Mademoisell Quierovil* now comeing to be in greate favour with the K—: here was also the *Countesse* of *Sunderland*, & severall Lords & Ladies more who lodged in the house: during my stay here with my Lord *Arlington* neere a fortnight; Came his Majestie almost every second day with the Duke, who commonly returnd againe to New-market; but the King lay often here, during which time I had twice the honor to sit at Dinner with him, with all freedome: It was universaly reported that the faire Lady — was bedded one of these nights, and the stocking flung, after the manner of a married Bride: I acknowledge she was for the most part in her undresse all day, and that there was fondnesse, & toying, with that young wanton; nay 'twas said, I was at the former ceremonie, but tis utterly false, I neither saw, nor heard of any such thing whilst I was there, though I had ben in her Chamber & all over that appartment late enough; & was my selfe observing all passages with curiosity enough: however

twas with confidence believed that she was first made a *Misse* as they cald these unhappy creatures, with solemnity, at this time &c:

16 Came all the greate Men from *N: Market* & other parts both of *Suffolck*, & *Norfolck* to make their Court; the whole house fill'd from one end to the other, with Lords, Ladys & Gallants, and such a furnished Table had I seldome seene, nor any thing more splendid & free: so as for 15 dayes there were entertain'd at the Least 200 people, & halfe as many horses, besids Servants, Guards, at Infinite expense: In the mornings we went a hunting & hauking; In the afternoone 'til almost morning to Cards & dice &c yet I must say without noise, swearing, quarell or Confusion of any sort: I who was no Gamster, had often discourse with the *French Ambassador* Colbert, & went sometimes abroad on horse back with the *Ladys* to take the aire, & now & then to hunting; thus idly passing the time, but not without more often recesse to my prety apartment, where I was quite out of all this hurry, & had ⟨leasure⟩, when I would to converse with bookes; for there is no man more hospitably easy to be withall than my L: *Arlington*, of whose particular friendship & kindnesse I had ever a more than ordinary share:

My Lord Chamberlaines house is a very noble pile consisting of 4 greate pavilions after the french, beside a body of a large house, & though not built altogether, but form'd of additions to an old house (purchasd by his Lordship of one Sir *T Rookwoods*) yet with a vast expence, made not onely capable & roomesome, but very magnificent & commodious, as well within as without, nor lesse splendidly furnish'd: The Stayre case is very elegant, the Garden handsome, the Canale beautifull, but the soile drie, barren, & miserably sandy, which flies in drifts as the wind sets: Here my Lord was pleasd to advise with me about the ordering his Plantations of firs, Elmes, limes &c up his parke, & in all other places & Avenues; I perswaded him to bring his Park so neere, as to comprehend his house with in it, which now he resolved upon; it being now neere a mile to it: The Water furnishing the fountaines is raised by a pretty Engine or very slight plaine Wheele, which likewise serves to grind his Corne, from a small cascade of the Canale, the invention of Sir *Sam: Moreland*: In my Lords house, & especialy above the Stayre Case, the greate hall & some of the Chambers & roomes of State, is painted in fresca, by the hand of *Signor Virrio* [the same who has painted all *Winsor*] being the first worke which he did in *England*.

17 My Lord: *Henry Howard* coming this night to visite my Lord *Chamberlain*, & staying a day, would needes have me go along with him to *Norwich*; promising to convey me back againe after a day or two; This as I could not refuse, so I was not hardly perswaded to, having a desire to see that famous Scholar & Physition Dr. T. *Browne* author of *Religio Medici* & *Vulgar Errors* &c: now lately knighted: Thither then went my Lord & I alone in his flying Charriat with 6 horses; & by the way discoursing to me of severall of his Concernes, he acquainted me of his going to marry his Eldest sonn to one of the Kings natural daughters, by the Dutchesse of *Cleaveland*; by which he reckon'd he shall come into might⟨y⟩ favour: he also told me that though he kept that idle Creature & common — Mrs. B— & would leave 200 pounds a yeare to the sonne he had by her; he would never marry her, & that the King himselfe had caution'd him, against it: All the world knowes, how he kept this promise; & I was sorry at heart to hear what now in confidence he confessed to me; & that a person & a family (which I so much honou⟨re⟩d, for [the sake of] that noble & illustrious friend of mine, his Grandfathers) should dishonour and polute them both, with those base, & vicious Courses he of late had taken, & was falln into, since the death of Sir *Sam: Tuke*, & that of his owne virtuous Lady my L: *Ann Somerset* (sister to the Marquesse) who whilst they lived, preserv'd this Gentleman by their example & advice, from those many extravagances that impaird both his fortune & reputation:

Being come to the *Ducal Palace*, my Lord made very much of me, but I had little rest, so exceedingly desirous he was to shew me the contrivances he had made, for the entertainement of their Majesties & whole Court not long before, & which, though much of it, but temporary appartments fram'd of boards &c onely, were yet standing: As to the Palace, tis an old wretched building, & that part of it, newly built of brick, is very ill understood; so as I was of opinion, it had ben much better to have demolish'd all, & set it in a better place than to proceede any farther; for it stands in the very Market place, & though neere a river, yet a very narrow muddy one & without any extent: here before we went to bed, my Lord fell-out with his Carpenter,

about measuring of a roome, & grew into such a passion, as in my
life, I had never seene any mortal man; so much beneath his dignitie, & for so wretched a trifle; my Lord saying the dimension
was so many foote, the Workman so many: This conflict lasting
from 8 till 1 at night, was grievous to me:

Next morning I went to see Sir *Tho: Browne* (with whom I
had sometime corresponded by Letters tho never saw before)
whose whole house & Garden being a Paradise & Cabinet of
rarities, & that of the best collection, especialy Medails, books,
Plants, natural things, did exceedingly refresh me after last nights
confusion: Sir Thomas had amongst other curiosities, a collection of the Eggs of all the foule & birds he could procure, that
Country (especialy the promontorys of Norfolck) being (as he
said) frequented with severall kinds, which seldome or never, go
farther into the Land, as Cranes, Storkes, Eagles &c: & variety of
Water-foule: He likewise led me to see all the remarkeable places
of this antient Citty, being one of the largest, & certainely (after
London) one of the noblest of England, for its venerable Cathedrall, number of Stately Churches, Cleanesse of the streetes; &
buildings of flint, so exquisitely headed & Squared, as I was
much astonish'd at; Sir Tho: told me they had lost the art, of
squaring the flint, which once they ⟨were⟩ so excellent in: & of
which the Churches, best houses, & Walls are built: The Castle is
an antique extent of ground, which now they call *marsfield*, &
had ben a fitting area to have placed the *Ducal* Palace in: The
suburbs are large, the prospect sweete, & other amoenities, not
omiting the flower-gardens, which all the Inhabitans excell in of
this Citty, the fabric of stuffs, which it affords the Merchants, &
brings a vast trade to this populous Towne: Being return'd to my
Lords, who had ben with me all this morning, he advis'd with me
concerning a plot to rebuild his house, having already (as I said)
erected a front next the streete, & a left wing, and now resolving
to set up another wing, & pavilion next the Garden, & to convert
the bowling greene into Stables: In summ, my advise was to
desist from all, & to mediate wholy on the rebuilding an handsome Palace at *Arundell* house in the *Strand*, before he proceeded
farther here; & then to place *this* in the *Castle*, that ground
belonging to his *Lordship*: One thing I observ'd of remarkable in
this Citty, that most of the Church-yards (though some of them
large enough) were filled up with earth, or rather the congestion

of dead bodys on⟨e⟩ upon another, for want of Earth &c to the very top of the Walls, & many above the wales, so as the Churches seem'd to be built pitts:

18 I return'd to *Euston* next day (leaving my Lord Howard at Norwich) in my Lords Coach, & in company with a very ingenious Gent: one Mr. *White*, whose *Father* & Mother (daughter to the late Lord *Treasurer Weston* [Portland]) I knew at *Rome*, where this gent: was borne, & where his Parents lived & died with much reputation, During their banishment in our Civil broiles:

In this journey my *L: Howard* told me he would go to Church & become Protestant & recover his title of *Earle Martial* of England; & at another time, that he would have his sonn *Harry* go to *Church* &c: (for he thought most Religions alike) but that being the head of his family, it would not so well become himselfe to change: 'Tis greate pitty, that a person, not onely of so eminent birth, but of such excellent natural parts, & smo⟨o⟩th a tongue; should have so little Judgement, & be so very inconstant, for he has fits of good resolutions, greate generositie, &c, & then of things quite contrary &c: my time now being short

⟨19⟩ Leaving *Euston*, I lodged this night at Newmarket, where I found the jolly blades, Racing, Dauncing, feasting & revelling, more resembling a luxurious & abandon'd rout, than a Christian Court: The *Duke* of *Buckingam* was now in mighty favour, & had with him here that impudent woman, the Countesse of *Shrewsbery*, with his band of fidlars &c.

Next morning (in Company with Sir *Bernard Gascoyne* & my L: Hawly) I came in the *Tressurers* Coach, to *Bish: Stratford*, where the Tressurer gave us a noble supper, and next day to London & so home:

22 Our Doctor preached on his long text: 29 on the same: Afternoone Mr. *Plume* at *Greenewich* on 2: *Pet:* 3. 10:

31 I was now arived to my 51 yeare of age, giving God thanks for his many many mercys: and went to Lond: about buisinesse:

November: 2. Was a Council, & in the afternoone at the *R: Society* a full meeting after a long recesse: 3: I dind at the *Tressurers* & return'd that evening: 5. Our *Viccar* on 27: *Isa:* 2. 3: *Pomerid.* a stranger at Greenewich on: 1. Tim: 2. 13. 14 &c: 6: To *Lond:* being sent for by the Lords Commissioners about an accompt: return'd the Evening: 12 our *Viccar* as before:

13 To *Lond:* to Council: dind at the *V: Chamberlaines*, return'd: ⟨19⟩: our *Viccar* as before: Next day to Council, where Sir *Cha: Wheeler* (late Governor of the *Lee-ward Ilands* in *America*) having ben complained of, for many indiscreete managements; it was resolv'd (upon the Scanning many of the particulars &c), to advise his Majestie to remove him; & consult what was to be don to prevent those inconveniencys he had brought things to: This buisinesse staied me in *Lond*, almost a weeke, being either in Councill, or Committe every Morning til the 25.

⟨26⟩ Our *Doctor* as formerly. 30: To *Lond:* to our Election at *R: Society*: There was also a Council of forrain *Plantations* againe, where were divers Lords of the Privie Council; We ordered that a Proclamation should be presented his Majestie to signe, against what Sir *Charles Wheler* had acted in *St. Christophers*: I din'd with the R: Society: & thence home:

December 1. Came my Bro: Evelyn to visite me: 3: our *Viccar* on his former Text: The holy Sacrament follow'd:

6 Came Sir *William Haywood* to visite me, a greate pretender to English antiquities &c: my Bro: returned to *Lond*, whom I accompanied; there being next day a Council, where was finished the Proclamation to prohibite, what had been indiscreetly ordered by Sir *Char:* Wheeler at *St. Christophers* since the war, upon the articles of Peace at Breda: In the afternoone at the *R: Society* were examind some draughts of arches to sustaine a *Cupola*: 8: I went home: 10: our *Viccar* proceedes: 13. To *Lond:* at Council next morning, where was present the *Duke* of *Ormond*: upon the buisinesse of the *Ilands*.

14 At the R: *Society*, whence to see the *Duke* of *Buckingams* ridiculous farce & ⟨Rhapsody⟩ called the *Recital*, bouffoning all Plays yet prophane enough—15 I returned home:

17 Our Viccar as formerly. 19 To *Lond:* Council, when we adjourn'd til the next Terme, unlesse any extraordinary buisinesse interven'd; having finished the Instructions for the new Governor of the *Lee-ward Ilands*, & recalld Sir C. *Wheeler*: and then went to see a play. 21: I din'd with the Gent: of the Kings Bed-chamber, thence to the *R: Society*, where Mr. *Hooke* read his new method of the Art of *Musique*, and part of *Malphigiu's* Anatomie of Vegetables, sent us in MS; from *Bolognia*, which we intended to have published: next day home: 24. our Doctor as

above, & so ending his long exhausted subject on the 25. preached on 1. *John:* 4. 9: The holy communion followed.

27 To *Lond:* to dine with [some of] the rest of our bro: Counsilers, as agreed upon at our Recesse this Vaccation: where met the Earle of *Sandwich* our President, Lord *Ashley* [since E: of *Shaftsbery* & *Chancellor*]: E: of *Arlington*, Lo: *Gorges*, Coll: *Titus* of the *Bed-chamber*: Mr. *Slingsby* our *Secretary*: Mr. *Brouncher* at the *Cock* in *Suffolck* streete: Afterwards visiting Mr. *Treasurer* I returned home for the rest of the holy daies: 30: Invited some of my neighbours according to costome. 31. Our Doctor made an end of his Text, admonishing to the Love of God, for sending his sonn &c: & for all his preservations the yeare past, for which I also return'd my solemn acknowledgements for his mercys to me in particular &c:

167½ *Jan:* 1 Our Doctor preached on 3 *Joh:* 3: I beged Gods protection & guidance for the new yeare following: 4: I invited some Neighbours. 7: Our *Viccar* as before; of the Costome of Saluting, against the surly rudenesse of our new Sectaries: 9 To *Lond:* about severall affaires: 11. Dined with Mr. Tressurer where was the Duke of *Buckingam*, L: *Ashley*, *Arlington*, *Ossorie*, *Lauderdaile* & severall greate persons.

12 His *Majestie* renewed us our Lease of *Says-Court* Pastures for 99 yeares &c: but ought according to his solemn promise (as I hope he will still performe) have passed them to us in Fee-farme. 13 I returned: 14 our *Viccar* as above:

23 To *Lond:* in order to Sir *R: Bro:* my F. in Laws resigning his Clerke of the Councils Place to Sir *Joseph Williamson*, which he did in the Council Chamber in his Majesties Presence, according to the usual forme of taking the *Oathes* of *Supr:* & *Alegiance* & then that of the Cl: of the Council, after which his *Majestie* knighted him: This Place his *Majestie* had promised me many yeares before, but upon consideration of 1000 pounds; and our lease of 500 pounds per ann: at fourty shill⟨ings⟩ rent, without fine for 99 yeares, I chose to part with it to Sir *Joseph* who gave us, & the rest of his bro: Clearkes an handsome supper at his house, & after supper, a Consort of Musique:

25 To the *R: Society*; where were produc'd new invented Perspectives, a letter from *Grene-Land*, of recovering men that had ben drown'd, we had also presented us from *Iseland* some of the Lapis *Obsidialis*. 26: The *Council* of *Plantations* now meeting

againe, we resum'd the buisinesse of *New England*; & so I went home: 28: Our *Viccar* as before: 30: Being our Late Kings *Martyr-dome Anniversary* our Doctor preached on 7: *Act:* ult.; being almost but a repetition of what we had the last yeare on this occasion.

Feb: 3: I went to *Lond*: an extraordinary Snow. ⟨4⟩: At the Abby preached Dr. — on 17: *Jer:* 10: the holy Sacrament follow'd; & then dined with the *Bishop* of *Rochester* who is Deane of *Westminster: Pomerid*,[1] a young man on 17: *Act:* 31. The rest of the Weeke was taken up in consulting about the Commission, & Instruction to our Officers, in order to a second War with the Hollanders, his Majestie having made choice of [some of] the former Commissioners & amongst them my selfe againe. 9: We met also at the *Council* of *Plantations* upon the buisinesse of *Jamaica* under our Inspection on certaine letters writen from that Governor, but we not being a ⟨quorum⟩, there was nothing don: 11: Dr. *Perinchiefe* at *White-hall* (*Coram Rege*) preached on 17: *Act:* 31 on the same subject I had heard at the *Abby* the Sonday before: I din'd at the *Vice-Chamberlaines. Pomerid*: at the *Abby* preached that famous *Proselyte* (Monsieur *Brevall*) in English on 2. *Cor:* 6. 15, extreamely well & with much eloquence; he had ben formerly a *Capucine*, but much better learned than most of that Order. 12. At the *Council of Plant*: we entred upon enquiries about improving his Majesties American Dominions by *Silk, Galls, Flax, Senna* &c & considered how *Nut-megs* & *Cinamon* might be obtain, & brought to *Jamaica*, that Soile & Climat promising successe; upon this Dr. *Worsley* being called in spake many considerable things to encourage it: We also tooke order to send to the Plantations, that none of their ships should adventure homeward single, but stay for company & Convoyes, in reguard of the late indicted War &c: we also deliberated of sending some fit Person to goe as Commissioner to Inspect their actions at New-England, & from time to time to make report by Letters, & to give us information how that Nation stood affected: This we had formerly in deliberation: Then adjourn'd for the future to meete at *White-hall*, & 13 I returned home.

18 Dr. *Breton*, our excellent Minister, & my good friend unhappily dying, the young Curate preached on 4: *Gal:* 4. 5.

20 Dr. Parr (of Camerwell) made a most pathetical funebral discourse, & *Panegyric* at the Interrment of our late Pastor

1 i.e., in the afternoon

on   *Happy is that servant whom when his Lord cometh* &c:
this good man (among other expressions) professed he had never
ben so touch'd & concern'd at any losse, as at this, unlesse it were
the death of K. *Charles* our *Martyr*, & that of the Archbishop of
Armagh, *Usher*, whose Chaplaine he had ben: he shewed how
suddain Death (such as was our Doctors) was no malediction to
the prepared, & those who die in the Lord: for on friday, having
fasted all that day, making his provisionary Sermon for the Sonday following, he went well to bed, & being suddenly surpriz'd,
expir'd before help could come to him, being of a plethoric habit
of body, & seemingly over full, even of health it selfe: Never had
Parish a greater losse, not onely as he was an Excellent Preacher,
and fitted for our greate & vulgar Auditory, but for his excellent
life & Charity, his meekenesse, & obliging nature, Industrious,
help-full, & full of good workes; leaving neere 400 pounds to the
poore in his Will, & that what children of his should happen to
die in minority, their portion should be so employed: I lost in
particular a special friend, & one that had an extraordinary love
to me & mine: Gods will be don.

24 To *Lond* to speake with our *Bishop* & Sir *John Cuttler* our
Patron, to present Mr. *Frampton* [since Bishop of *Worcester*:], &
returned: 25. our *Curate* on Psal: 95. *ver:* 8: Pomerid to *Grenewich*
Mr. *Plume* on 20: *Apoc:* 12.

Mar. 1 To Lond: at our *Council* of *Plant:* where was present
his Royal Highnesse the Duke: Pr: *Rupert*, D: of *Buckingham*,
both the Secretaries of state &c: divers Lords of the Privy
Council: Debating of our saving the *Lee-ward Ilands*, now in
danger of the *French*, who had taken some of our Ships, & began
to interrupt our trade; as also about the power of the new Governor of st. *Christophers*, whither he should be Subordinate to
the Governor of *Barbados* &c: The Debates were serious & long:

3 Dr. *Clark* deane of *Winchester* [(coram rege)] on St. Jude
          concerning the Judgement to come &c: an eloquent
preacher: The B: Comm: followed: *Pomerid*: at St. *Margarits* Westminster preached a stranger on   The Devils believe & tremble: to the reproch of Atheists, now Swarming &c: 7: I went home.

12 To Lond: Now was the first blow given by us against
the *Dutch* Convoy of the *Smyrna* fleete, by Sir *Robert Holmes* &
my *Lord Ossorie*, in which we received little save blows, & a
worthy reproch, for atacquing our neighbours ere any war was

proclaim'd, & then pretending the occasion to be, that some time before, the *Merline Yacht* chancing to saile thro the whole *Dutch fleete*, their Admiral did not Strike to that trifling vessel: Surely this was a quarel slenderly grounded, & not becoming Christian neighbours, & of a Religion: and we are like to thrive accordingly: My Lord Ossory several times deploring his being ingaged in it to me, & he had more justice & honour than in the least to approve of it, though he had ben over perswaded to the expedition, & there is no doubt, but we had surpriz'd this exceeding rich fleete, had not the avarice and ambition of Holmes & Sprag, separated themselv⟨e⟩s & willfully divided our fleete, on presumption that either of them were strong enough to deale with the *Dutch Convoy*, without joyning & mutual help; whilst the *Dutch Convoy* so warmly plied our divided fleete, that whilst they were in Conflict, the Merchants saild away & got safe into Holland: It was a few daies before this that the Treasurer of his Majesties Howsehold (Sir Tho: Clifford) hinted to me (as a Confident) that his Majestie would shut up the Chequer, & accordingly his Majestie made use of infinite Treasure there to prepare for an intended rupture; but says he, it will soone be open againe, & every body satisfied: for this bold man (who had ben the sole adviser of the *King*), to invade that sacred stock, though some pretend it was my Lord *Ashleys* counsel (*Chancelor* then of the chequer) was so over confident of the successe of this unworthy designe against the Smyrna Merchants; as to put his Majestie on an action which not onely lost the hearts of his subjects, & ruined many *Widdows* & *Orphans* whose stocks were lent him, but the reputation of his Exchequer for ever, it being before in such Credit, that his Majestie before this seizure, might have commanded halfe the wealth of the nation: The Credit of this bank being thus broken, did exceedingly discontent the people, & never did his Majesties afaires prosper to any purpose after it, for as it did not supply the expense of the meditated war, so it mealted away I know not how. And to this succeded his Majesties declaration for an universal Tolleration; Papists & Swarmes of sectaries now boldly shewing themselves in their publique meetings; & this was imputed to the same Council, *Clifford* warping to *Rome*, as was believe'd, nor was my Lord *Arlington* cleare of suspicion, to gratifie that partie, but, as since it has prov'd & was then evidently

fore-seene, to the extreame weakning the Church of England &
its Episcopal Government; as 'twas projected: I speake not this
as my owne sense, but what was the discourse & thoughts of
others, who were lookers on: for I think, there might be some
relaxations without the least prejudice to the present Establishment, discreetely limited, but to let go the reines in this manner,
& then to imagine they could take them up againe as easily, was
a false politique, & greately destructive; The truth is our *Bishops*
slipt the occasion; since had they held a steady hand upon his
Majesties restauration, as easily they might have don, The
Church of England had emerg'd & flourish'd without interruption; but they were then remisse, & covetous after advantages of
another kind, whilst his Majestie suffer'd them to come into an
harvest, which without any injustice he might have remunerated
innumerable gallant Gentlemen with for their services, who had
ruin'd themselves for him in the late rebellion: 15. preached
(*Coram Rege*) the *Bishop* of *Carlisle* on 11 *Heb:* 18: home: 20: To
Lond: & return'd: 21. I went to the Co⟨a⟩sts in my *District* of
Kent, lay this night at *Gravesend*, where I visited divers wounded
& langwishing poore men that had ben in the *Smyrna* conflict: I
went over to see the new begun *Fort* of *Tilbery*, a Royal work
indeede, & such as will one day bridle a greate Citty to the purpose, before they are aware: 22, To *Rochester.* ⟨23⟩: *Cap: Cox* one
of the *Commissioners* of the *Navy*, furnishing me with a *Yacht*, on
the 23, I sailed to *Sheere Nesse* to see that fort also, now newly
finished; severall places on both sides the *Swale* & *Medway*
to *Gillingham* & *Upnore* being also provided with redouts &
batteries, to secure the station of our Men of War at Chatham,
& shut the doore when the steedes were stollen, & so returned
to *Rochester*. 24: I din'd with Mr. *Commissioner Cox* having seene
that morning my *Chirurgeon* cut off a poore creaturs Leg, a
little under the knee, first cutting the living & untainted flesh
above the *Gangreene* with a sharp knife, and then sawing off the
bone in an instant; then with searing & stoopes stanching the
blood, which issued aboundantly; the stout & gallant man,
enduring it with incredible patience, & that without being
bound to his chaire, as is usual in such painefull operations, or
hardly making a face [or crying oh]: I had hardly courage
enough to be present, nor could I endure to se any more such
cruel operations.

The leg was so rotten & gangreen'd, that one might have run a straw through it; but neither did this the cure, for it not being amputated high-enough, the gangreene prevaild upon the knee, & so a second amputation of the Thigh, cost the poore Creature his life, to my very greate sorrow: I do not remember that ever in my life I smelt so intollerable a stink as what issu'd from the part was cut off, & which I ordered should immediately be buried in the Garden: Lord, what miseries are mortal men obnoxious to, & what confusion & mischiefe dos the avarice, anger, and ambition of Princes cause in the world, who might be happier with halfe they possesse: This stoute man, was but a common sailer.

25 I proceeded to *Canterbery*, said my Prayers at the *Cathedral*, & next morning to *Dover*, saluted the Governor of the Castle, 27 To Deale: next to the Isle of *Thannet* by *Sandwich* & so to *Margate* where I was handsomely entertain'd & Lay at my Deputies *Cap: Glovers*: here we had aboundance of miserably wounded men, his Majestie sending to meete me, Serjeant Knight, his Majesties chiefe *Chirurgeon*, & Dr. *Waldrond* who attended me all this journey, so having taken such order for the accommodation of the Wounded as was requisite, I came back through a Country the best cultivated of any that in my life I had any where seene, every field lying as even as a bowling greene, & the fences, plantations, & husbandrie in such admirable order, as infinitely delighted me, after the sad & afflicting specctacles & objects I was come from: observing almost every tall tree, to have a Weather-cock on the top bough, & some trees halfe a dozen, I learned, that on a certain holy-day, the Farmers feast their Servants, at which solemnity they set up these Cocks in a kind of Triumph &c:

Being come back towards *Rochester*, I went to take order about building a strong & high Wall about an house I had hired of a Gent: at a place called *Hartlip*, for a Prison, paying 50 pounds yearely rent: here I settled a Provost Martial, & other officers, returning by *Feversham*, and on the 30 heard a Sermon at the Cathedral of *Rochester* on *Palme Sonday*, a young man preaching very well on 1. *Cor:* 11. 28, preparatory to *Easter*, & so got to Says-Court by the first of *Aprill*.

Aprill: 2: To *Lond:* to give his Majestie an account of my Progresse. 4: I went to see the fopperies of the Papists at Somerset house, & York-house, where now the *French Ambassador* had

caused to be represented our B: Saviour, at the Pascal Supper, with his Disciples, in figures & puppets made as big as the life, of wax work, curiously clad, & sitting round a large table, the roome nobly hung, & shining with innumerable Lamps & Candles, this exposed, to the whole world, all the Citty came to see; such liberty had the *Roman Catholicks* at this time obtained.
5. Good frid⟨a⟩y, Dr. *Patric* at *Covent Garden* Church, preached on the Gospel of the day; that evening returning home &c:

16 I went to Lond: sate in Council, preparing my L: *Willogbies* Commission & Instructions for Governor Generall of the Barbados & Caribbe Ilands &c:

17 I din'd with the Bed-Cha: men, sate about buisinesse in the star-chamber. 19 at Council, preparing Instructions for Collonel Stapleton now to go Governor of St. *Christophers*; & heard the Complaints of the *Jamaica* Merchants against the Spaniard hindring them from cutting Log-Wood on the maine land, where they have no pretence, & reserved it to next meeting.

20 Met at the Middle Temple to umpire a difference & so returned home:

21 Our Curat preached as before: 23 I went to visite my Lord of Canterbery, & to entreate him to ingage Sir Jo: Cuttler (Patron of our Viccaridge) to provide us a grave and learned man, in opposition to a Novice &c:

May: 2: My sonne *John* was specialy admitted of the *Middle Temple* by Sir *Fra: North*, his Majesties Solicitor general [Since Lord *Chancelor*]: I pray God blesse this begining, my intention being he should seriously apply himselfe to the study of the Law:

5 A young man preached at the Abby &c: where I received the B: Sacrament: & dined with the *Bishop* of *Rochester*, *Pomerid*: Dr. Stradling on 2. *Philip:* 7: 6. I went home. 10. To Lond: din'd with Sir *W: D'Oylie* when came a Letter from the Council, that I was forthwith to repaire to his Majestie whom I found in the *Pal-Mal* in St. *Ja: Park*, where his *Majestie* coming to me from the companie, he commanded me to go immediately to the Sea-Coast, & to observe the motion of the Dutch Fleete & ours, the *Duke*, & so many of the flower of our Nation being now under saile coming from Portsmouth thro the *Downes*, where 'twas believed there might be an encounter; so as I went on the next day (11) to *Chatham*: 12 heard a sermon at the Cathedrall of *Rochester*, din'd at *Coll: Midletons*: 13 To *Canterbury*, Visited

Dr. *Bargrave* my old fellow Travelor in Italy & greate Virtuoso.
14: To *Dover* where I staied in attendance of the Fleete from
Portsmouth, but which appear'd not til the 16: *Ascention day*,
when the *Duke* of *York* with *his*, & the *French* Squadron, in all
170 ships, of which above 100 Men of War, sailed by after the
Dutch, who were newly withdrawn: Such a gallant & formidable
Navy never I think spread saile upon the seas, it was ⟨a⟩ goodly,
yet tirrible sight, to behold them as I did passing by the straits,
twixt Dover & *Calis* eastward, in a glorious day: The wind was
yet so high, that I could not well go on board, & they were soone
gotten out of sight: So the next day having visited our Prisoners
at the Castle & saluted the Governor, I tooke horse [17] for
Margate, where from North-foreland lighthouse top (which is a
pharos built of Bricque, having on the top a Cradle of yron, in
which one attends a greate Sea-Coale fire, all the yeare long
when the nights are darke, for the safe-guard of Sailers) we
could see our fleete as it lay at *Anker*; & the next morning
weighing, sailed out of sight to the N: East: 19: I went to *Margate* church, where one Mr. *Chunie* the minister made an excellent sermon on 14: *Apoc:* 7:

20 I was carried to see a gallant Widow a Farmoresse, & I
think of *Gygantic* race, rich, comely, & exceedingly Industrious:
She put me in mind of *Debora*, and *Abigal*; her house was so
plentifully stored with all manner of Countrie provisions, all of
her own groth, & all her conveniences so substantiall, neate &
well understood; She herselfe so jolly & hospitable, & her land,
so trim, & rarely husbanded, that it struck me with a kind of
admiration at her Oeconomie:

21 This towne much consists of Brewers of a certaine heady
Ale; & deale much in mault &c: for the rest tis raggedly built, &
an ill haven, with a small fort of little concernement, nor is the
Iland well disciplin'd, but as to the husbandry & rural part, far
exceeding any part of England, & I think of the whole world for
the accurate culture of their ground, in which in truth they
exceede even to Curiosity & emulation: We passed by *Richborow*,
& in sight of Reculvers, & so came thro a sweete garden as it were
to *Canterbery*, hearing no noise from the sea: [22] at *Canterbery*
after Prayers and Sermon I came to *Rochester*, & [23] next day to
my house: 24 I went to *Lond*, gave his Majestie an account of my
Journey, and that I had put all things in a readinesse, upon all

events, & so returned home sufficiently wearied: 26: our Curate
on 15. *John*: 26: The holy Communion followd: *Pomerid*: to
Greenewich a stranger on 1. Cor: 15. The last Enemy &c: not very
pertinently chosen for a *Whitsonday*: 29: being the *Anniversary*
of our Kings birth & Restauration, Our *Curate* on 118. *Psal*: 1.
inciting to praise Almighty God for his blessings &c: 31. I
received another Command to repaire to the seaside againe, so
I went to *Rochester*, where I found many both Wounded, sick,
and Prisoners newly put on shore, after the Engagement of the 28,
in which the Earle of *Sandwich*, that incomparable person, &
my particular friend & divers more whom I loved, were lost: My
Lord (who was *Admiral* of the ⟨Blew⟩) in the *Prince* which was
burnt, being one of the best Men of War, that ever spread canvas
on the sea: Lost likewise with this brave man, was Sir Charles
Coterell('s) Sonn, whose Father was Master of the Ceremonies,
& Sir *Ch: Harbord* sonn of his Majesties Surveyor generall, two
valiant, & most accomplish⟨ed⟩ youths, full of virtue &
Courage, & that might have saved themselves, but would perish
with my Lord, whom they honor'd & loved above their owne
lives: And here I cannot but make some reflection upon things
past: Since it was not above a day or two, that going at *White-
hall* to take my leave of his *Lordship* (who had his Lodgings in
the Privy Gardens) shaking me by the hand bid me *god buy*, he
should he thought see me no more, & I saw to my thinking
something boading in his Countenance; no says he, they will not
have me live: Had I lost a Fleete (meaning on his returne from
Bergen, when he tooke the E. India prise) I should have fared
better; but be it as please God; I must do I know not what, to
save my reputation; something to this effect, he had hinted to
me; but thus I tooke my leave: and well I remember, that the
Duke of *Albemarle*, & my now Lord *Clifford*, had I know not
why, no greate opinion of his Courage, because in former Conflicts, being an able & experienc'd sea-man (which neither of
them were) he allwayes brought of his Majesties ships, without
losse, though not without as many markes of true Courage as
the stoutest of them; & I am witnesse, that in the late War, his
owne ship was pierced like a Culender: But the buisinesse was,
he was utterly against the War from the beginning, & abhor'd
the attacquing of the Smyrna fleete; He did not favour the
brutish & heady expedition of Clifford at Bergin; nor was he so

stupidly furious, & confident as was the D: of *Albemarle*, who
believed he could vanquish the Hollander with one Squadron:
My L: *Sandwich* was prudent as well as Valiant, & allways govern'd his afairs with successe, and little losse, he was for deliberation, & reason, they for action & slaughter without either; & for
this, whisperd it, as if my L: of Sandwich were not so Gallant,
because he was not rash, & knew how fatal it were to loose a
Fleete, such as was that under his Conduct, & for which these
very persons would have censurd him on the other side: This it
was which I am confident griev'd him, & made him enter like a
Lion, & fight like one too, in the middst of the hottest service,
where the stoutest of the rest, seing him ingagd, & so many
ships upon him, durst not, or would not, come into his succour,
as some of them, whom I know, might have don: Thus this gallant Person perish'd to gratifie the pride & envy, of some I
named: & deplorable was the losse, of one of the best accom-
plish⟨ed⟩ persons, not onely of this Nation but of any other: He
was learned in the Mathematics, in Musique, in Sea affaires, in
Political: Had ben divers Embassies, was of a sweete obliging
temper; Sober, Chast, infinitly ingenious, & a true noble man,
an ornament to the Court, & his Prince, nor has he left any that
approach his many Virtues behind him: He had I confesse serv'd
the *Tyrant Cromwell*, when a young man, but 'twas without malice, & as a souldier of fortune, & readily submitted & that with
joy, bringing an intire fleete with him from the Sound, at the
very first tidings of his *Majesties* restauration: nor praise I him
for what he did then amisse, but for the signal services he since
had don, & verily believe him as faithfull a Subject as any that
were not his Friends: I am yet heartily griev'd at this mighty
losse, nor do I call it to my thoughts without emotion.

June 2 Trinity Sonday I passd at *Rochester*, & on the 5, was
buried in the *Cathedral Monsieur Rabiniere tres le bois*, *Reare
Admiral* of the *French Squadron* (a very gallant person) of his
Wounds received in the fight: I went to visite him languishing
some time before, & now this Ceremonie lay on me, which
I perform'd with all the decency I could; inviting the Mayor &
Aldermen to come in their formalities: Sir *Jonas Atkins* there
with his Guards, the Deane & Prebends; one of his Countriemen,
pronouncing a funeral Oration, at the brink of his Grave, which
I caused to be in the *Quire*, with all decent solemnity, as it was

more at large describd in the *Gazzet* of that day, *Colonel Reymes*, (my Collegue in Commission) assisting, who was so kind as to accompany me from Lond: though it was not his district: for indeede, the stresse of both these Warrs, lay more on me, by far, than on any of my breatheren, who had little to do in theirs:

7 I went to see *Upnore Castle*, which I found pretty well defended, but of no greate moment: Nex⟨t⟩ day I sailed to the Fleete now riding at the buoy of the Noore, where I met his *Majestie*, the *Duke*, L. *Arlington* & all the greate men in the *Charles*, lying miserably shatterd; but the misse of my Lord *Sandwich* redoubled the losse to me, as well as the folly of hazarding so brave a fleete, & loosing so many good men, for no provocation in the World but because the Hollander exceeded us in Industrie, & all things else but envy: Here at *Sheere-nesse*, I gave his Majestie [& R: Hig⟨hn⟩esse] an account of the Charge under my inspection, & so returnd that night to *Quinborow*, & the next day (being Sonday) din'd at *Major Dorels* Governor of Shere Nesse, at his Country house, who treated me with greate Civility, thence to *Rochester*, & [10] next day home. 12: To *Lond:* to solicite his Majestie for Mony for the Sick & Wounded, which he promisd me: 13 I dind at Mr. *Poveys*, & thence to Condole my L: *Sandwich*. 14: To visite my *Sister Evelyn*. 15 Waited on the L: *Treasurer* & so to *Says-Court*. 16 our *Curat*, on his former Text, & in the afternoone on 2 *Ephes:* 7. 17: Came my bro: & severall friends to visite me. 19 To *Lond:* to solicit againe for mony. 21. At a *Council* of Plantations: I dined at the Resident of *Hamborgs* Monsieur *Garmus*. 23. a stranger at *White-hall* preached. I was most of this weeke buisied for the Wounded &c: 28: at the Council of Pl: & got home this evening: 30: our *Curate* on 2: *Eph:* 5, in the afternoone Mr. *Plume* at *Greenewich* on 16: *John*: 8: &c:

July: 3: To *Lond:* din'd at my *Sister Evelyns*, & then to my L: Sandwiches funerall, which was by Water in solemn pomp to Westminster: 5: At Council, & so home:

7 our *Curate* on 1. Cor: 11. 28: The B: Sacrament follow'd, *Pomerid*: on 2: *Eph*: 5 as before:

31 I entertaind the *Maids* of *honour*, (among whom there was one whom for her many & extraordinary virtues, I did infinitely esteeme) at a Comedy, this afternoone, & so went home:

August 1. I was at the Marriage of my L: *Arlingtons* onely Daughter, (a Sweete Child, if ever there was any) to the *Duke* of *Grafton*, natural sonn, of the King, by the *Dutchesse* of *Cleaveland*, The *Archbishop* of Cant: officiating, the King & all the grandees present: I had a favour given me by my Lady, but tooke no greate joy at the thing for many reasons: 3: I went home: 4: A stranger on 3: *Apoc:* 20, I receiv'd the holy Sacrament: &c: 5. I went twice this Weeke to Council, & the last Council, we adjourn'd for a short recesse: ⟨11⟩ our Curate proceeded upon the *Beatitudes* as formerly: 11: Came to see my Wife, the Queenes Maides of honour, and amongst them my particular *Devota*, Mrs. *Blagge*, they returned late in the Evening. 13: To *Lond* about buisinesse with his *Majestie* whom I found at Goring house, & so return'd. 15 To see my Sister *Evelyn* at *Woodcot*, & after dinner to *London*: 17 home where I found Sir *Rob: Morray* & Sir John *Colidon*:

18 our *Curate* on Meekenesse &c: 25. on the next beatitude: Sir *James Hayes* Secretary to *Prince Rupert*, dined with me; after dinner, I was sent for to *Gravesend*, to dispose of no fewer than 800 sick men &c: That night I got to the Fleete in the *Buoy* of the *Noore*, where I spake with the *King* & *Duke*, & after dinner next day return'd to *Gravesend*: 26. Thence to *Rochester* & thence on 28 to my house: 29: To *Lond*: for mony: ⟨31.⟩ I kept a fast.

Sept: 1. Dr. *Perinchiefe* preached to the household[1] in White-hall on: 5. *Eph:* 2. the Communion follow'd: *Coram Rege* preached Dr. *Crighton* on: 2. Tim: 15. an honest discourse but not approching his Fathers talent which was extraordinarie: I spent this weeke in soliciting for monies, & in reading my papers of the first *Holland War* to my *Lord Clifford* &c: And now our Council of Plantations met at my Lord *Shaftsberys* (chancelor of the Exchequer) to reade, and reforme the draght of our new Patent, joyning the *Council* of *Trade* to our political capacities: after which I returned home, in order to another Excursion to the sea side, to get what recovered men on board the fleete was possible; so as 8: I lay at *Gravesend*, thence to Rochester, returning on the 11th.

⟨22⟩ A stranger at *White-hall*. 25. I dined at my Lord John *Berkeleys*, newly arive'd out of *Ireland* where he had ben *Deputy*:

---

1 The members of the royal household, as distinguished from the king and his attendants; also called the family, and the services are held *coram dom.*, i.e. *domesticis*.

It was in his new house, or rather Palace, for I am assured it stood him in neere 30000 pounds: & truely is very well built, and has many noble roomes in it, but they are not so Convenient, because it consisting of but one *Corps de Logis*, there are no Clossets, all are roomes of State, The furniture is princely, The Staire Case *Cedar*; The Kitchin & Stables are ill placed, & the *Corridors* worse, having no report to the wings they joyne to; for the rest the fore Court is noble, so are the Stables, & above all the Gardens which are incomparable, by reason of the inequalitie of the ground, & prity Piscina: The holy hedges on the Terrace I advis'd the planting of: note that the *Porticos* are in imitation of an house described in *Paladio*, but it happens to be the very worst of his booke, how ever my good friend Mr. *Hugh May* his Lordships *Architect* affected it: [26] I carried with me to dinner my Lord: H: *Howard*, now to be made Earle of Norwich, and L: *Marishal* of *England*, to Sir *Rob: Claytons* now *Sherif* of *Lond:* where we had a greate feast: in his new House, built indeede for a greate Magistrate at excessive cost: The Cedar Dining roome is painted with the Historie of the Gyants War, incomparably by Mr. *Streeter*; but the figures are too neere the Eye: 28 I returned home:

October 8 My Lord *Sunderland* now *Ambassador* at Paris, I went to take my Leave of my Lady, who was now going over to him: she made me stay dinner at *Lycester* house, & after dinner sent for *Richardson* the famous *Fire-Eater*, who before us devourd *Brimston* on glowing coales, chewing and swallowing them downe; he also mealted a beere glasse & eate it quite up: then taking a live Coale on his tongue, put on it a raw oyster, which coale was blown on with billows till it flam'd & sparkled in his mouth, & so remain'd til the Oyster gaped & was quite boiled: Then he mealted pitch & Wax with Sulphure, which he drank downe as it flamed; I saw it flaming in his Mouth a good while: he also tooke up a thick piece of Yron, such as Laundresses use to put in their Smoothing boxes, & when 'twas fiery hot, he held it betweene his teeth, ⟨then⟩ in his hand, & threw it about like a stone: but this I observed he car'd not to hold very long: Then he stood on a small pot, & bending his body, tooke a glowing Yron with his mouth from between his feete, without ⟨touching⟩ either pot or ground with his hands; with divers other prodigious feates: 9 I returned home: 11: To *Lond:*

13 Dr. *Thisteltwhait* to the Household at *W:hall*, on our B: S: Passion: 1: *Galat:*   *Coram Rege* Dr. *Ball*, very elegantly on 8: *Matt: Pomerid*: to *Covent Garden* Dr. *Patrick* on   *Let the dead bury the dead: follow thou me*: After sermon (being summon'd before) I went to my *Lord Keepers* Sir *Orlando Bridgeman* at Essex-house, where our new *Patent* was opened & read, Constituting us that were of the *Council* of Plantations to his Majestie to be now of the *Council* of *Trade* also, both now united into one: after the Patent was read, we all tooke our *Oathes* & departed:

16 My Devout, & deare Friend declaring her condition to me for want of one she could trust, to govern & manage her competent stock; and earnestly desiring my poore assistance; I promised to do my best to serve her, & from that time forwards, I reckond her as my Child; for none did ever shew greater esteeme for a Father, than did this incomparable Creature to me, worthy of all the returnes I could ever make, for the many lasting obligations I received from her; a rare example of so much piety, & Virtue in so greate a Witt, beauty & perfection; This Miracle of a young Lady in a licentious Court & so deprav'd an age: She now delivered me the ☆ under her owne hand, & it shall be *Inviolable*. 17: I returnd home. 20: Dr. *Par* preached at our Church on 2. *Thess:* 3. 5: he din'd at my house:

24: To *Lond:* next day met at Council: the Earle of *Shaftsbery* now our *President*, swearing our Secretarie & his Clearkes which was *Mr. Lock* an excellent learned Gent: & student of Christ-Church: [*Mr. LLoyd*] *Mr. Frowde* &c: after this we dispatch'd a letter to Sir *Tho: Linch Governor* of *Jamaica*, giving him notice of a designe of the *Du⟨t⟩ch* on that *Iland*: 27: A young man preached at *W:Hall* on 12: *Rom:* 3. Then I went to heare that famous Preacher Dr. *Frampton* at St. *Giles's* on 39 *Psal:* 6. This divine had ben twice at *Jerusalem*, & was not onely a very pious & holy man, but excellent in the Pulpet; for the moving affections:

30 My Lord of *Ossory*, having newly received the *Order* of the *Garter* carried me in his Coach with him to *Clarenden house* where I dined with my Lord *Duke* his father. &c: In the afternoone we met at the *R: Society*, where were made divers *Microscopic* observations on Plants &c:

31 I was now full 52 yeares of age: The Lord be praised for all his goodnesse, hitherto hast thou brought me.

November 3 A stranger preached at W:hall to the household; That before the King, by Dr. *Benson* Deane of *Hereford* on 2. *Phil:* 15 an excellent discourse about exemplarily walking: The holy Communion follow'd: 4 I returned home: 5. We had onely prayers at our Church, our Patron not having as yet resolved whom he would present. 8 To *Lond:* to *Council*, Where being present the Duke of *Ormond*, E. of Shaftsbery, Arlington, Lo: *Halifax*, L: *Gorges*, L. *Culpeper* we debated the buisinesse of the Consulage of *Ligorne*, & some other matters relating also to *Jamaica*. 9. I was of the Committè with Sir *Humph: Winch* (the Chaire man) to examine the Lawes of his *Majesties* severall Plantations & Colonies in the W. Indies &c: 10: Preached a stranger at Whitehall on 2. *Coloss:* 11. 12.

13 A *Council*, but little don for want of a quorum: 15 Was a Council, many Merchants being summond about the Consulage of *Venice*, which caused greate dispute; the most considerable thought it Uselesse; but it was dismiss'd to another hearing on friday when they were to produce their proposals: This being the *Queen Consorts* birth day, There was an extraordinary appearance of Gallantrie & a Ball danced at Court: 16 I went home. 17: A stranger on 10. *Gen:* 21, making a *Cabalistic* discourse, turning all those names into Mystical sense, not much to Edifying: 22: To *Lond:* We had the Merchants againe about the Consul of *Venice*, but they could not agree. 24 Dr. *Tomkins* chapl: to the *A: Bish:* preached to the household on 1. *Jo:* 5. 3. *Coram Rege* Dr. *LLoyd* on 23 Jer: 5: *Pomeridiano* Dr. *Turner* [since Bishop of *Rochester*] at St. *Jamess* on: 1. *Pet:* 4. 8: I dind at Barkly house: 26. returned home: 28 To Lond: 30: St. Andrews Day at our Election at R: Society, I was chosen Secretary.

1673. *Jan:* 1. After pub: Prayers in the Chapell at *W:hall*, & my humble supplication to God for his blissing the Yeare now entering, I went to see ☆ not well,[1] & so returned home, having my lately deceased Servant to bury, & some neighbours to entertaine: ⟨5⟩ To *Lond:* Dr. *Colebrand* Sub-deane of his *Majesties Chap:* preaching on   *meeke*, & *sitting on an Asse* &c: I received the *B: Sacrament*: I presented the *Turcois Locket* & 16 *Diamonds* cum Symbolo &c.

1 The pentacle signifies Margaret Blagge.

My *Sonn* now publish'd his version of *Rapinus Hortorum* &c dedicated to the Ear: of *Arlington*:

7 I went to Councel in the morning; din'd at my L: *Treasurers*, where dined also my L: *Chancellor*: 8: ☆ went first from Court to *Berkeley house* whither I conducted her, after she had obtained a favourable dismission from their Majesties. Thence to the *R: Society*: 9 Dined at L: *Berkeleys* where ☆ was to reside some time. 10: To *Parsons-Greene* to visite my L: *Mordaunt*: return'd that Evening with my Lord & Lady *Cornbery* to Lond: 12 Dr. *Bredox* deane of *Salisbury* preached on 2. *Luke* 49, Then *coram rege* the Sub-deane on   *Psal:*   Thy Word is a lantern &c: and I dined at the *Duke* of *Lauderdalls*. 14: Visited ☆ & dind at *Berkley-house*, Thence to Council, & next day home:

Feb: 2. A stranger at W:hall on 2: *Luke*: 34, being purification, The holy Sacrament follow'd &c: In the aftersermon Dr. *Pierce* (Deane of *Sarum*) coram rege, on 21. *Matt:* 31, excellently: 4: visited ☆ din'd at *Bark: house*, & in the afternoone went with my *Lady* to see Pictures at *Remeès*: 5. I went to waite on my L: *Treasurer*.

6 To *Council* about reforming an abuse of the *diers* with *Saunders* & other false drogues, exam⟨in⟩ing divers of that trade &c: 7: I return'd home. 9. A stranger preach'd on 2. *Rom* 7. I stayed at home all this Weeke. 16. Mr.   Preached on 2. *Cor:* 6. 3. 4. *Gospel* of the day. 17. To *Lond:* 18 Visited ☆ & dined with her, thence to *Council*. 19 Dr. *Castillion* preached on   *be Carefull for nothing* &c. and

23 (It being now *Lent time*) Dr. *LLoyd* (my L: Tressurers *Chaplaine*) on *Acts* ⟨xvii. 30⟩: on which he made a profitable discourse: he had ben formerly Curate of our Parish at *Deptford*: & coram rege the Bish: of *Chichester* on 2. *Coloss:* 14. 15. admirably well, as he can do nothing but well: 25. To *Council*, thence to visite ☆:

Mar 9 Our new *Minister* Mr. *Holden* preached 4: Psal: 6.7. shewing the difference of the Choice which the men of the world make, different from that of the Saints: This Gent: a very excellent & universal Scholar, a good & a wise man, but he had not the popular way of preaching, nor in any measure fit for our plain & vulgar auditorie, as had ⟨been⟩ his predecessor; though there were no comparison 'twixt their parts for profound learning &c: but time, & experience, may forme him to a more practical way, than that I find he now is in of university lectures, &

erudition, which is now universaly left off, for a much more profitable: *Pomeridiano* one Mr. *Holland* on. 4. *Coloss*: 1: 12: Dr. *Littleton* preached at Lond: W:hall: on   *Aske and ye shall have* &c *seeke & ye shall find* &c. very excellently: ⟨14⟩ *Coram rege* Dr. *Thomas* on 13. *Luke*: 3. 15. I heard the Speech made to the *Lords* in their house by Sir *Sam: Tuke*, in behalfe of the *Papists*, to take off the *Penal Laws*; and then dined at Coll: *Norwoods* with severall Lords &c: 16 Dr. Littleton to the family, on   that Love the *L: Jesus in sincerity* &c a pathetical discourse: Then *coram Rege* Dr. *Pierson* Bish: of *Chester* on 9: Heb: a most incomparable sermon, from the most learned Divine of our Nation. I dind at my L: *Arlingtons* with the *Duke*, & *Dutchesse* of *Monmoth* who is certainly one of the wisest & craftiest of her sex; she has much witt: here was likewise the learned *Isaac Vossius*. 17: At *Council* about the *Barbados* buisinesse: 18 home: 23: our *Viccar* on 1. *Cor:* 6. 20: *Pomerid*: the Curat. 1. *Cor:* 11. 28. 24 To *Lond:* to solemniz the Passion-Weeke & heare the excellent Preaching which there constantly is by the most eminent Bish: & Divines of the Nation, during lent &c:

26 I was sworn a Younger-brother of the *Trinity Company* with my most worthy & long acquainted noble friend My *Lord Ossorie* Eldest sonn to the Duke of *Ormond*: Sir *Richard Browne* my F. in *Law*, being now Master of that Society; after which there was a greate Collation &c:

29 I carried my Sonn to the *Bishop* of *Chichester* that learned & pious man, Dr. *Peter Gunning*, to be instructed by him before he received the holy *Sacrament*, when he gave him most excellent advise, which I pray to God may influence, and remaine with him as long as he lives; and ô that I had ben so blessed, and instructed, when first I was admitted to that Sacred Ordinance! 30: Easter-day preached in the Morning one Mr. *Field* . . . a Resurrection sermon with much eloquence: The Blessed *Communion* followd, at which both my selfe, & my Sonne received, it being his first time, & with that whole weekes more extraordinary preparation, I besech God make him a sincere good Christian, whilst I endeavor to instill into him the feare & love of God, & discharge the Duty of a Father: The Sermon *Coram Rege* this day, was by Dr. *Sparrow* Bishop of *Excester*; but he spake so very low, & the crowde so greate, that I could not heare him: however I staied to see whither (according to custome) the *Duke of York* did

Receive the Communion, with the *King*, but he did not, to the amazement of every body; This being the second yeare he had forborn & put it off, & this being within a day of the *Parliaments* sitting, who had Lately made so severe an *Act* against the increase of *Poperie*, gave exceeding griefe & scandal to the whole Nation; That the heyre of it, & the sonn of a Martyr for the *Protestant Religion*, should apostatize: What the Consequence of this will be God onely knows, & Wise men dread: 31 I went home.

Aprill: 6 There being no Communion at our Church, I went to *Greenewich* where a Chaplain of my L: *Ossories* preached on 4. *Hosea*. 14 in a pious discourse: The Communion follow'd: *Pomerid*: our Curate on 1. *Cor:* 5.8. &c: 7 to *Lond*: to visite Mrs. *Blagg* at my *Lord Berkeleys*. 10 To Council, and thenc to thank Mr. Secretary, for a kindnesse don my *Lady Tuke*: 11 I dined with the *Plenepotentiaries* Designed for the Treaty of *Nimegen*, where was a greate feast, & thence home: ⟨13⟩ Our *Minister* on 12 *Rom:* 17: Not to render Evil for Evil &c: *Pomerid*: our *Curate* on 2. *Jam:* 19:

14 I went to *Lond:* with my Wife. 15 We both visited Mrs. Blagg, & 17th: I carried my *Lady Tuke* to visite, & thank the Countesse of *Arlington*, for speaking to his *Majestie* in her behalfe about being one of the *Queene Consorts* Women: she carried us up into her new dressing roome at Goring house, where was a bed, 2 glasses, silver jarrs & Vasas, Cabinets & other so rich furniture, as I had seldom seene the like; to this excesse of superfluity were we now arriv'd, & that not onely at Court, but almost universaly, even to wantonesse, & profusion:

19 I went to *Parsons Greene* to visite the Vicountesse Mordant, that virtuous Creature, & our long & intimate acquaintance abroad:

20 Dr. *Stillingfleete* made an incomparable sermon on 6: Matt: 33. before the family: *Coram rege* Dr. *Compton* (bro: to the E: of *Northampton*) on: 1. *Cor:* 11.16: This worthy Persons Talent is not preaching; but he is like to make a grave & serious good man:

This Evening Mrs. *Thornhill*, sister to the Earle of Bath, & a relation of ours, shewed my Wife and me her Majesties rich *Toylet* in her Dressing roome, which being all of Massie Gold, & presented her by the King, was valued at 4000 pounds.

22 I visited my *Lord Tressurer* (who had lately ben my bro: Commissioner for the sick & Wounded) who was ever more than ordinarily kind to me, even to intimacy & friendship:

⟨27⟩ Dr. *Compton* pr: at W.hall to the household on: 10: *Luke* 42, Thence at St. *Martines* the *Minister* on 1. *Cor:* 11. 29 the holy *Sacrament* following: which I partooke of upon Obligation of the Late *Act* of *Parliament*, injoyning every body in Office Civil or Militarie, under penalty of 500 pounds, to receive the holy Sacrament within one moneth, before two authentique Wittnesses: so as I had besides Dr. *Lamplughs* the Viccars hand, the two *Church-Wardens* also ingrossed in parchment to be afterwards producd in the Court of *Chancery* or some other Court of Record: which I did at the *Chancery* barr, as being one of the *Council* of *Plantations* & *Trade*, [*May* 3] taking then also the *Oath* of *Allegiance* & *Supremacy*, signing the clause in the said Act against *Transubstantiation*. Dined at Mr. *Herveys* the Queens Tressurer with Mr. *Sid: Godolphin*. 4 A stranger at *White hall*, first sermon on 10: *Heb:* 21 & *Coram Rege* Dr. *Fell* Deane of Christ-Church *Oxford*: on 1. Cor: 13. ult. when I also received the *B: Sacrament*: it being the first Sonday in the Moneth: 6: I dined with Mrs. *Blagg* at *Berkeley* house: 7: At *Council*, my L: Chancelor being our President, being present: 8: Ascension—pr: at St. *Martines* Dr. *Lam⟨p⟩lugh* on 1. *Heb:* 13: The holy Comm: follow'd, & so home to my house: 11: I had a greate swelling in my face, & could not go to Church: 13: Buisinesse caled me to Lond: where I stayed til the 16: 18 Mr. *Plume* at *Greenewich* (there being no Communion at our Church) on: 2: *Acts*: 1.2. a very choice discourse (*opus diei*) the Bl: Sacr: followed: *Pomerid*: our Curate on 16. Joh: 8: ⟨19⟩ I went to *Lond:* with Mr. *Bernard Greenevill* bro: to the *Earle* of *Bath* & one of the *Groomes* of his *Majesties Bedchamber*: who with his Lady, & Lady Catharin *Morley*, Mrs. *Howard*, one of the *Maids* of honour, came to dine with us: 20: I visited ☆ & returned home: 21: Came to see us & Dine with me, my Lord Jo: *Berkeley* and his Lady, my deare Friends Mrs. Blagg, Mr. *Sidny Godolphin* (a *grome* of the Bedchamber) Sir Robert Morray, Mr. *Lucie Gore*, & Sir *Elis Leighton* &c:

25 Our Viccar on 19 *Psal:* 13: *Pomerid*: the *Curate* Mr. *Holland* on 16 St. Joh: 8. as the Sonday before: 26: Trinity Moneday The *Bishop* of *Rochester* at our church: before the *Trinity Comp:* on 107: *Psal:* 23. 24 of usefull matter: My F: in Law Sir *Rich: Bro:* being *Master*, Sir *Jer: Smith* (one of the Commissioners of the Navy & a stout sea-man, who had interposed & saved the Duke from perishing by a fireship in the late Warr) succeeding: My

Sonn, was now sworn a Younger brother, there was a mighty feast: 28. I carried one *Withers* an ingenious *Shipwright*, to the *King*, to shew his Majestie some new method of building &c: 29: preached Mr. *Woodruffe coram rege*, it being his Majesties Birthday, on 126. *Psal:* 1.

I saw the *Italian* Comedie act at the Court this afternoone.

June 1: At St. *Martines* a stranger on   *In the last days perilous times shall come &c: men shall be lovers of Pleasures* &c: The holy communion follow'd: 3. I dined with my deare friend at *B: house*: 5. I went to my *L: Tressurer* for Mony, & then to Says-Court: 8: Both *Viccar* & *Curate* preached on their former Text. 10 To *Lond:* return'd the next day: 12 Came to Visite and dine with me, my Lord V: Count Cornbery & his Lady, My Lady *Francis Hyde* Sister to the *Duchesse* of *York*, Mrs. *Dorothy Howard* Mayd of *Honour*: We all went after dinner to see the formal, & formidable Camp, on Black-heath, raised to invade Holland, or as others suspected for another designe &c—: Thence to the *Italian Glasse-house* at *Greenewich*, where was Glasse blowne of finer mettal, than that of *Muran* &c:—

13 Came to visite us my *Lady Carr* (sister to my *L: Chamb:* & Wife to the *Chancelor* of the *Dutchy*) Lady *Scroope*, Lady *Stanhop*, Mrs. *Baron*, & Mrs. *Sidly*, daughter to Sir *Charles*, who was none of the most virtuous, but a Witt &c: 15 our *Viccar* on: 11: *Matt* 30: *Pomerid*: Curat: on: 1. *Pet:* 5.9. 16 To *Lond:* to our *Council*. 17 Din'd with Mrs. *Blagg*, at *B: house*, thence to Mr. *Dicksons* the Painters, to whom she sate the first time for her picture, which I desired her to give me:

19 I din'd at my Bro: *Evelyns*, Visited my *Sister*, Congratu-lated the new Lord Tressurer Sir Tho: *Osborn*, a Gent: whom I had ben intimately acquainted with at *Paris*, & who was every day at my F in *Laws* house & Table there; on which account I was too Confident of succeeding in his favour, as I had don in his Predecessors; but such a friend never shall I find, & I neg-lected my time, far from believing that my *Lord Clifford* would have so rashly laied down his staffe as he did, to the amazement of all the World; when it came to the Test of his receiving the Communion; which I am confident he forbore, more for some promise he had entered into, to gratifie the *Duke*, than for any prejudice to the *Protestant* Religion, though I found him waver-ing of a prety while: 20 I returned home, where I found my

Nephew Geo: & his *Lady*. 22: our *Viccar* as above. 23. To *Lond*, to accompanie our Council, who went in body to congratulate the new L: *Treasurer*, no friend to it, because promoted by my L: *Arlington* whom he hated: 24: Dind with Mrs. Blagg: 25. her Picture was finished &c: 25 Visited my L: *Clifford* late Lord Tressurer: returned home. 26: Came my *Bro: Evelyn*, my *Sister* of *Woodcott*, my *Niepce Montague* & severall persons of quality from Court, to dine with me, and see the army, still remaining Encamp'd on Black-heath: next day came & din'd with me my *Lady Blount*, her sonn, & two Daughters: together with my Lord *Manchester*: 29: our *Viccar* preach'd on 8: *Matt:* 30: In the afternoone our *Curate* on the Gospel of the day, &c:

July to *Lond* about buisinesse, supped with Mrs. *Blagg*: 6: Dr. *Durell* (*Deane* of *Winsor*) preached on 7: *Joh:* 37.38: The 2d Serm: *Coram rege* by Dr. Parry on   *Except your righteous-nesse exceede* &c: This evening I went to the funerall of my deare & excellent friend, that good Man & accomplish'd Gent: *Sir Rob: Moray*, Secretary of Scotland: he was buried by his Majestie in *Westminster* Abby: 7: I went to Council:

8 To visite ☆, and in the afternoone with my *Lady Berkeley* in the Dutchesse of *Albemarls* Coach, to *Twicknam* to see Mrs. *Talbot*, the next day I returned home:

13 Our *Viccar* as formerly: *Pomerid*. Curate on 39. *Psal:* 5. concerning preparation to Death: The minister himselfe so weake, that I was expecting when he himselfe should faint away. 14 To *Lond:* to sp⟨e⟩ake with my L. *Arlington*, and returned: ⟨20⟩ our *Viccar* as before: *Pomerid*: the Curate of *Greenewich* there, on: 118 *Psal* 18.

⟨21⟩ To *Lond:* Council: 21 I spake with his *Majestie* about the sick & Wounded & returned home.

25 I went to *Tunbridge* Wells, to visite my *Lord Clifford*, Late *L: Tressurer*, who was ther to divert his mind, more than body, that he had so engag'd himselfe to the Duke (as was believed) that rather than take the *Test*, without which he could be capable of no office, he would resigne that greate & honorable station; This, I am confident grieved him to the heart, & at last broke it; for though he carried with him musique & people to divert him, & when I came to see him, Lodged ⟨me⟩ in his owne appartmen⟨t⟩, & would not let me go from him, I found he was struggling in his mind, & being of a rough & ambitios nature,

could not long brooke the necessitie he had brought on himselfe
of submission to this conjuncture; besides that he saw the
Dutch-Warr, which was made much by his advise, as well as the
shutting up of the Exchequer, very unprosperous: These things
his high spirit could not support. 26. I went to the *Wells* with my
Lord, & visited my *Lady Henrietta Hyde*: 27: Sonday, was no
[pub:] prayers in the morning: but in the afternoone I heard
Prayers at my Lady *Henriettas*: so having staied here two or 3
daies I obtain'd leave of my Lord, that I might returne, by the
way I saw my Lord of *Dorsets house* at *Knowle* neere *Sevenock* a
greate old fashiond house &c.

30 To *Lond:* to Council, where the buisinesse of Transporting
Wooll was brought before us: I dined at the *Countesse* of *Suffolcks*
in her Lodging, groome of the *stole* to her Majestie, who used
me with greate respect. 31 I went home, turning in, as I went
through Cheape side to see the Pictures of all the Judges &
Eminent men of the Long robe newly painted by Mr. *Write*,
& set up in *Guild-hall* costing the Citty 1000 pounds: most
of them are very like the Persons they are made to represent,
though I never tooke *Write* to be any considerable artist.

Aug: 3 our *Viccar* on 1. *Sam:* 3. 18: I received the holy Sacrament:

10 Our *Viccar* as before; Pomerid, at *Grenewich* the *Curate* on
5. *Mat:* 4: 13 I rid to *Durdens* where I dined at my L: *Berkeleys* of
Berkely Castle my old & noble friend; it being his Wedding
Anniversarie where at a mighty feast, I found the Dutchesse of
Albemarle, my Sister Evelyn, N: Montague & much companie,
& so return'd home that evening late:

18 To Lond: to speak with his Majestie: My *Lord Clifford*
being about this time returned from *Tunbridge* where I left him,
& now preparing for Devonshire, I went to take my Leave of
him at Wallingford house, where he was packing up of Pictures,
most of which were of hunting wild beasts, & vast pieces of bull-
baiting, beare baiting &c: with other furniture: I found him in
his study, & restored to him several papers of state, & other
importances, which he had furnished me with, upon ingaging
me to write the historie of the Holland War; with other private
letters of his acknowledgements to my L: *Arlington*, who of a
private Gent: of a very noble family, but inconsiderable fortune,
had advanc'd him from almost nothing: The first thing was his

being a Parliament man, then knighted, then made one of the *Commissioners* of the Sick & Wounded, upon which occasion we sate long together: then on the death of Hugh Pollard, he was made Comptroller of the Household & Privy Counselor, yet still my bro: Commissioner: after the death of my *L: Fitzharding Treasurer* of the Houshold, which (by letters of his my L: Arlington has shew'd me) he beging of his Lordship to obtaine for him as the very height of his ambition, with such submissions, & professions of his patronage, & being totaly his creature, as I had never seene more accknowledging: The Earle of *Southampton* then dying, & he with others made one of the Commissioners of the *Treasury*, his Majestie inclining to put it into one hand, my L: *Clifford* under pretence of making all his Interest for his Patron my L: *Arlington*, cutt the Grasse under his feete & procur'd it for himselfe, assuring the King, that my L:A: did not desire it, & indeede my Lord A: has himselfe protested to me, that his Confidence in my L: *Clifford*, made him so remisse, & his affection to him so particular that was absolutely minded to devolve it on my L: Clifford, that was his Creature, all the world knowing how himselfe affected Ease & quiet, now growing into Yeares, but yet little thinking of go-by: This was the onely greate ingratitude which my L: *Clifford* shew'd, keeping my Lord *Ar:* in ignorance, whom he ⟨continualy⟩ assurd, he was pursuing his Interest, which was the *Duke*, into whose greate favour *Clifford* was now gotten, but which did certainly cost him the losse of all; namely his going so irrevocably far in his Interest: &c: For the rest my Lord *Clifford* was a valiant, uncorrupt gent: ambitious, not Covetous, generous, Passionate, and a most constant sincere friend to me in particular; so as when he lay'd downe his office, I was at the end of all my hopes, and endeavors; which were not for high matters, but to obtaine what his *Majestie* was realy indebted to my F. in law, which was the uttmost of my ambition, and which I had undoubtedly don, if this friend had stood; he who succeeded him, Sir *Thomas Osborn*, though much more obliged to my F in Law & his family, & my long & old acquaintance; being of a more haughty & far lesse obliging nature, & from which I could hope for little; a man of excellent natural parts, but nothing generous or gratefull: Well, thus taking Leave of my L: *Clifford*, wringing me by the hand, & earnestly looking on me, he bid me *god buy*, adding, Mr. E: I shall never see thee more; no ⟨said⟩ I my L: whats the meaning of this? I hope I shall see you often, and as greate a person againe; No Mr. E: do not expect it, I will never see this Place, this Citty or Court againe, or words of this sound: In this manner, not without mutual tears almost I parted from him: nor long was it after, but the newes was, that he was dead; and as I have heard from some that I believe knew, made himselfe a way, after an extraordinary Melancholy: This is not confidently affirm'd; but a servant who lived in the house, & afterward with Sir *Ro: Clayton* L: Mayor, did report it, as well as others; & when I hinted some such thing to Mr. *Prideaux* one of his *Trustees*, he was not willing to enter into that discourse: but tis reported with these particulars, That causing his Servant to leave him one morning unusualy, locking himselfe in, he strangled himselfe with his Cravett, upon the bed *Tester*: His Servant not liking his manner of dissmissing, & looking through the *key hole* (as I remember) & seeing his Master hanging, brake in before he was quite dead, & taking him downe, vomiting out a greate deale of bloud, was heard to utter these words; Well, let men say what they will, there is a God, a just God above, after which he spake no more &c: This if true, is dismal, and realy, he was the chiefe occasion of the *Dutch Warr*, & of all that bloud which was lost at *Bergen*, in attaquing the Smyrna fleete, & that whole quarell &c: which leads me to the calling to mind, what my Lord Chancellor affirm'd not to me onely, but to all my brethren (the Councel of forraine *Plantations*) when not long after, this accident being mention⟨ed⟩, as we were one day sitting in Council; his Lordship told us this remarkeable passage; That being one day discoursing with him, when he was onely Sir Tho: *Clifford* and a Parliament man: speaking of mens advancement to greate Charges in the Nation: Well says he, my *Lord*: I shall be one of the greatest men in England; don't impute what I say, either to fansy, or vanity; I am certaine that I shall be a mighty man, but it will not last long, I shall not hold it, but dye a bloudy death: What says my L: your *horoscop* tells you so: 'tis no matter for that, it will be as I tell you: Well says my L: Chancelor *Shaftsbery*, if I were of that opinion, I either would be no greate man, but decline preferrment, or prevent my danger &c: This my Lord, affirmed in my hearing, before severall Gent: & noble men sitting in Council together at *Whitehall*: And I the rather am confident of it; remembring what Sir Ed: Walker *Gartyr* K. at *Armes*, had likewise affirmed to me long time before, even when he was first made Lord: Sir Ed: told me, that carrying to him his Pedegreè, & finding him buisy, he bid him go into his study, & divert himselfe there, till he was at Leasure, to discourse with him about some things relating to his family: There lay says Sir Ed: on his Table, his *Horoscope* & *Nativity* calculated, with some writing under it, where he read, That he should be advanc'd to the highest degree in the state could be conferred upon him, but that he should not long Enjoy it, but should Die, or expressions to that sense, & I think (but cannot confidently say) a bloudy death: This Sir Edw: affirmed both to me and Sir *Rich: Browne*: nor could I forbere to note this extraordinary passage in these memoires: &c:

19 I dined with my L: *Arlington*, & then went with him to see some Pictures in Lond: & returned home: 24: A *stranger* on 22: *Matt:* 39: our Viccar in the afternoone as formerly: 2 Pet: 1. 16.

26 I went to *Twicknam* Park with my deare friend Mrs. *Blagg.* 27: We dined at *Coll:* Talbots, & next day I returned home: 31. Our viccar as above: & Curat on 118 Psal: 18. A thanks giving to God, for restoring him after a long indisposition: & it was a usefull sermon:

September Came my deare friend ✮ to visite & dined with us. 6 I was to attend the Lords *Commissioners* of the Admiralty about the sick & wounded: & so returned: 7: our *Minister* preached on 13. *Luke* 24: I received the holy *Sacrament*. Afternoone an excellent serm: by a young man, on 6. Rom: 21:

15 I procurd 4000 pounds of the Lords of the *Tress:* & rectified divers matters, about the sick & wounded: 16 Visited my ✮, thence to *Council*, about choosing a new Secretary &c: 17: I went with some friends to visite Mr. Bernard *Grinvill* at *Abs-Court* in *Surrey*, an old house in a pretty parke, & next day home:

23 To *Lond*; dining with Mrs. Bl: we went to see *Paradise*, a roome in *Hatton Garden* furnished with the representations of all sorts of animals, handsomely painted on boards or cloth, & so cut out & made to stand & move, fly, crawll, roare & make their severall cries, as was not unpretty: though in it selfe a meere bauble, whilst the man who shew'd, made us Laugh heartily at his formal *poetrie*. 24 I went home. 27 To *Lond:* to the Admiralty &c: return'd: 28 our Curate did very well on 4. *Eph:* 3:

Pomerid, our *Viccar* proceeded on his former. 30 To Lond. 31 Visited my ☆, returned:

Octob: 15 Council, & sware Mr. *Lock* Secretary, Dr. *Worsley* being deceased: 16 I went home. My Lord *Brounker*, L: *Cornbery*, Mr. *Harvey* & Mr. *Newport* came to visite me. *Anniversary*, I writ to a friend: 19 Mr. *Mills* preached on 14 Joh: 21:

21 To *Lond*: 23: home: 26: Mr. *Bohune* late Tutor to my sonn, preached on. 1 *Cor*: 22. 23 very excellently well: *Pomerid*: a stranger on 7: *Matt*: 21. 27. To Lond *Council*, about sending succours to recover *New-York*; & then we read the Commission & Instructions to the new Governor of *Barbados* Sir *Jonathan Atkins*.

28 I dined at My L: Berkeleys with ☆, & then to visite a poore sick person.

30 I sat with the Commissioners of Sewers in *Southwark*, & returned home:

31 Was my birth-day *Anniversarie*, now the 53d: it being also a preparation day for the blessed Sacrament.

November 2 Our *Viccar* on 10. *Heb*: 25 of the antiquitie of Church Assemblies, in opposition to sectaries & separatists &c: The holy Communion followd: *Afternoone* Mr. *Holland* on: 11. *Ecclesiast*: 1.2.: 3. To Lond: to Council. 4: To visite ☆, fainting at Pr: reviv'd: 5. Dr. *Stillingfleete* on 7: *Matt*. 15 of the hypocrisie of the Popish Emissaries, preach'd before the house of Commons at St. *Margarits*: This night the youths of the Citty burnt the *Pope* in *Effigie* after they had made procession with it in greate triumph; displeased at the D: for altering his Religion, & now marrying an *Italian Lady* &c:

30 It being St. *Andrews* day I saw first the new *Dutchesse* of *York*, and the *Dutchesse* of *Modena* her mother, newly come over & married &c:

December 1 In the morning to the *Council* of *Plant*: & thence to *Gressham Coll*: whither the Citty had invited the *Royal Society*, by severall of their chiefe Aldermen & Magistrates and gave us a Collation, to wellcome us to our first place of Assembly, from whence we had ben driven to give place to the Citty to make it their Exchange upon the dreadfull Conflagration, 'til their new exchange was now finished: the *Society* having til now ben entertaind & met at *Arundel* house: This day we also Chose Officers, St. *Andrews* day being on the Sonday & day before:

2 I dined with ♎¹ & visited the sick, thence to an Almeshouse, where was prayers, & reliefe, some very sick & miserable: returning prayers, and it was one of the best daies I ever spent in my life: There was this day at Dinner my Lo: *Lockart* design'd Ambassador for France, a gallant & a sober person &c: 3. To the Council of Plant: & so home. 4: To Lond: & next morning to the L: of the *Tress:* soliciting for monies; Thence to our *Council* about this yeares *Accompts*: Thence home:

7: Our *Viccar* on his former text: The Communion follow'd, at which my Sonn & I participated: *Pomerid*: *Curate* on 8 Nehem: 1:

9 I saw againe the two *Italian* Dutchesse⟨s⟩ & her bro: the Prince *Reynaldo*, supped [11] at Berkley house with Mrs. *Blagg*. 14: pre: Dr. *Lamplugh* coram rege on 1. *Cor:* 6. 11 very practicaly, according to his manner: Din'd at the V. *Cham:* 16: Dined and supp'd with ♎ pr: & next day returned home: 19 To *Lond:* to the Lords of the *Admiralty*, and to signe things at our Council.

20 I had some discourse with certaine strangers, not unlearned, who had ben born not far from the old *Niniveh*: They assur'd me the ruines being still extant, & vast, wonderfull was the buildings, Vaults, Pillars, & magnificent fragments now buried, & remaining: but little could they say of the Toure of *Babel* that satisfied me: but the description of the amœnitie & fragrancy of the Country for health, & cherefullnesse, did almost ravish me; so sensibly the⟨y⟩ spake of the excellent aire & climat, in respect of our cloudy & splenetic Country:

21 Dr. *Patrick* preached the first serm: to the Houshold at W:hall on 4. *Phil:* 4: Before the *King*, a Stranger on 5. *Gall:* 11. 22. To Council:—dind, ♎ Pr: Went to see a poore Creature had poyson'd herselfe by accident, but recovered: Made Court at St. *James's* to see the new *Dutchesse*. 24. *Christmas* Eve, *jejun*, returning home visited some prisoners at *Ludgate*, taking order about the releasing of some &c: for ♎ &c: 25. our *Minister* on 1. *Heb:* 1, apposite to the festivity: when I received the bl: Sacrament: 26. Invited some *Neighbours more solito*:

1674 *January*: 1 Beseeching Gods mercy & protection for the yeare following: severall neighbours dined with me. 2. To Lond:

1 The sign of the zodiac Libra, the scales, also signifies Margaret Blagge.

on buisinesse: 4: A chaplaine, in the morning on 5: *Matt*. 22: The holy Sacrament followed: blessed be God: *Coram Rege* Dr. *Bredoy* on 17: *Joh*: 4: 5, I saw an *Italian Opera* in musique, the first that had ben in *England* of this kind:

6 Came Mrs. *Blagge* to see us —pr: I supp'd at my L: *Cornberies*, where at a Ball divers greate Ladys daunced: 7 I dind with my L: *Berkeley*: This night there was a greate Supper and Ball, at my L: *Chamberlaines*, the *King, Duke, Dutchesses* &c:

8 Home: 9 Sent for next morning to *Lond:* by his Majestie to write some thing against the *Hollanders*, about the Duty of the flag & fisherie: so returned with some papers. 11. our *Viccar* on 37: *Psal:* 37: 12 Sent for againe to Lond: 13 Din'd with ☆ :

June 27: Mr. *Dryden* the famous Poët, & now *Laureat* came to give me a Visite: It was the *Anniversarie* of my *Marriage*, & the first day I went into my new little *Cell*, & *Cabinet* which I built below towards the South Court, at East end of the Parlor: 28: a stranger on 32. *Deut:* 19: *Pomerid*. the Curate as before:

July 4. To *Lond: Council*, home: 5. one Mr. *Fletcher* a pathetical orator, on 32 *Deut:* the former Text: The H. *Sacrament* followd: *Pomerid: Curat* on 7: *Matt:* 21: 7: *Lond: Council*, returnd the next. 9: To *Lond:* to pay Dr. *Jacomb* 360 pounds for his sonn now of age: for his part of the purchase of the Mill & Land, I bought of the *Beechers* in Deptford: returned the 10: 12: The same preached on: 23. *Luke*: 24: *Pomer*: Curat as before:

16 To *Lond:* Sent for by ♎, return'd that evening, not well pleas'd, upon an unjust report: 19. Lond: Mr. *Fletcher* againe on 7: Heb: 19: *Pomer: Curate* of *Greenewich* on 19. *Job*: 25:

22 I went to *Winsore* with my Wife & sonn, to see my Daughter *Mary* who was there with my *Lady Tuke*; & to do my Duty to his Majestie: next day to a greate entertainement at Sir *Robert Holmes's* at *Cranburne* Lodge in the forest: There were his *Majestie, Queene, Duke, Dutchesse* & all the Court: I returned in the Evening with Sir Jos: *Wiliamson* now declared Secretary of state: Sir *Jos:* was sonn of a meane Clergyman some where in Cumberlandshire, brought up at Queenes Coll: [Oxon:] of which he came to be a fellow; Then traveled with . . . & returning when the King was restord, was received as a Cleark under Mr. Secretary Nicholas: Sir *Hen: Bennet* (now *L. Arlington:*) succeeding, *Williamson* is transferred to Sir Henry: who loving his ease more than buisinesse, (though sufficiently able had he

applyed himselfe to it) remitted all to his man *Williamson*, & in a short time let him so into the seacret of affaires, that (as his Lordship himselfe told me) there was a kind of necessity to advance him; & so by his subtilty, dexterity & insinuation, he got now to be principal Secretary; absolutely my L: *Arlingtons* Creature, and ungratefull enough; for so it has ben the fate of this obliging favorite, to advance those who soone forgot their original: Sir *Joseph* was a Musitian, could play at *jëu de Goblets*, exceeding formal; a severe Master to his Servants; but so inward with my *Lord Obrian*, that after a few moneths of that Gent: death, he maried his *Widdow*, who being daughter & heire of the *Duke* of *Richmond*, brought him a noble fortune; but, twas thought, they lived not so kindly after marriage as they did before: & she was infinitely censur'd for marrying so meanely, being herselfe alyed to the royal family: 24 I came home. 26 The same person preached mor: on his former Text, & afterwards the Curate on 6. *Rom:* 11. 27: To *Lon:* returned 28:

Aug: 2: Our *Viccar* on 130 *Psal:* 3. 4: The Comm: followed: *Pomer: Curate* on 23: *Exod:* 2. not to follow a multitude to do evil, applyed to those who left the Church assemblies for Conventicles: 6 I went to *Groomebridge* to see my old friend Mr. *Packer*, the house built within a Moate & in a woody Valy: The old house had ben the place of Confinement of that duke of *Orleance* taken by one *Waller* (whose house this then was) at the Bataile of *Agencourt*; but now demolish'd, a new ⟨w⟩as built in its place; though a far better had ben on the south of the wood on a graceful ascent: At some small distance is a large *Chapell* not long-since built by Mr. *Packers* father, upon a *Vowe* he made to do it, upon the Returne of *Charles* the first, out of Spaine 1625. & dedicated it to *St. Charles*: but what saint there was then of that name, I am to seeke; for being a Protestant, I conceive it was not *Borrhimeo*. 7: I went to the Wells, but did not drink the waters: 8 I went to see my farme at *Ripe* in *Sussex* neere *Lewes*, return'd the same day:

9 Mr. *Pogton*, preached at a church neere *Chafford* the seate of the *Rivers's* on   *My Yoake is easy* &c; in the afternoone at Mr. *Packers* Chapell, on: 3. *Apoc:* against hypocrisy, & did excellently well on both: I went to the Wells at *Southborrow* to visite my deare friend Mrs. *Blagg*, then drinking the Waters with my Lady *Berkeley*: 11 passing againe by the Wells, I went home:

16 our *Viccar* on 12: *Luke* 47: 48: *Pomerid Curate* on 23 *Pro*: 18
To *Lond*, and next day to *Winsore* about buisinesse with my *Lord
Tressurer*: next day his *Majestie* told me how exceedingly the
Dutch were displeased, at my Treatise of *historie* of *Commerce*;[1]
That the *Holland Ambassador* had complained to him of what
I had touch'd of the *flag*, & *fishery* &c: & disired the booke
might be caled in: whilst on the other side, he assur'd me he was
exceedingly pleased with what I had don & gave me many
thanks: However it being just upon conclusion of the *Treaty at
Breda*, (for indeed it was designed to be published some moneths before, & when we were at defyance) his Majestie told me,
he must recall it formaly, but gave order that what Copies
should be publiquely seiz'd to pacifie the Ambassador should
immediatly be restord to the Printer, & that neither he nor the
Vendor should be molested: The truth is, that which touch'd the
Hollander, was much lesse, than what the *King himselfe* furnish'd
me with, & oblig'd me to publish, having caus'd it to be read to
him 'ere it went to the presse: but the error was, it should have
ben publish'd before the peace was proclaim'd: The noise of this
books suppresion, made it be presently bought up, & turn'd
much to the Stationer⟨'s⟩ advantage: Nor was it other, than the
meere preface, prepard to be præfix'd to my Historie of the
whole *Warr*; which I now pursu'd no farther.

21 There was approches, & a formal seige, against a Work
with *Bastions*, Bullwarks, Ramparts, Palizads, ⟨Graft⟩, horn-
works, Conterscarps &c: in imitation of the Citty of *Maestrict*,
newly taken by the *French*: & this being artificialy design'd &
cast up in one of the Meadows at the foote of the long *Terrace*
below the Castle, was defended against the *Duke of Monmouth*
(newly come from that real seige) who [with the Duke of York]
attaqu'd it with a little army, to shew their skill in *Tactics*: so on
Saturday night, They made their approches, opened trenches,
raised batteries, [took] the Conterscarp, Ravelin, after a stout
Defence. Greate Gunns fir'd on both sides, Granados shot,
mines Sprung, parties sent out, attempts of raising the seige,
prisoners taken, Parlies, & in short all the Circumstances of a
formal seige to appearance, & what is most strange, all without disorder, or ill accident, but to the greate satisfaction of a

1 *Navigation and Commerce, their original and progress.*

thousand spectators, when being night it made a formidable shew, & was realy very divertisant: This mock seige being over, I went with *Mr. Pepys* back to Lond: where we arived about 3 in the morning: & at St. *Martines* heard a sermon [⟨23⟩] on 26: *Matt:* 74: The very same sermon, by the same preacher, I happn'd to heare againe at St. *Jamess* this Afternoone: 25 I return'd home. 30: our *Viccar* as before: *Curate* on 12: *Luke:* 5: 31 our Vicc: on: 2: *Luke: 29: 30* at the funerall of Mr. *Uttart* a neighbour of mine: The Song of *Simeon:* That therefore he wished to die for that having seene the *Lord*, there was no other object, that he ever desired to see in this world: so St. *Paule* wished to be disolv'd: that it was sometimes profitable to dwell among the Tombs:

September 3. I went to Lond: about sealing writings in Trust for Mrs. *Blagge*, & then home. 6: our *Viccar* on 12: *Luke* 47. 48: The holy Sacr: follow'd. *Pomerid:* our Curate on 6: *Matt:* 15: 8 To Council: 9 returnd:

15 To *Council*, about the fetching off the English left at *Syrenam* &c since our reconciliation with *Holland:* I visited ☆, gave her the deedes about the 500 pounds I had disposed of for her &c. —pr: 16 I went to Congratulate our new Secretary of state: &c: 20: To Lond: Ember Weeke Dr. *Lamplugh* preaching on 119 *Psal:* 60: The holy Comm: followed: I din'd at *White-hall: Pomerid:* stranger at *Covent Garden* on 1. *Cor:* 15. ult: I went home on foote. 22: To *Lond*, dind with ☌ —pr: having ben at Council: 23. I went to ⟨see⟩ the greate losse that my Lord *Arlington* had received by fire, at *Goring-house*, now this night consum'd to the ground, with exceeding losse of hangings, plate, rare pictures and Cabinets, in a word, nothing almost was saved, of the best & most princely furniture that any subject had in England: My Lord & Lady being both absent at the *Bathe*; so returned home full of astonishment at the uncertaintie of worldly enjoyments: 27 Our *Vicc:* on 40: *Isa.* 6. 7. *Pomerid. Curate* on 28 *Pro:* 13: 29: To *Lond:* to *Council*, passd the Evening with ☆ —pr: and returnd next day home.

Octo: 1 To *Lond: Council:* return'd. 4 Viccar on the same Text; the holy Comm: followed: Curate as before: 6 To *Lond: Council:* dind with ☆ return'd: 8: Lord *Chief Barron Turner*, and *Serjeant Wild Recorder* of Lond: came to visite me: 11: our Doctor on his former: *Pomerid. Curate* on 4. *Phil:* 11: 13 To *Lond: Council:* spent the Evening with ☌ —pr: next day having buisinesse with Sir *Den: Gauden*, I din'd with him, & 15 home:

16 Anniversarie ≏ inviol: 18. *Viccar* as above: *Pomer*: *Curate* of *Greenewich* on 19 *Job*: 26: 20: *Lond:* Council, dind with ☆ at my L: *Berkeleys* where I had discourse with Sir *Tho: Modiford*, Late *Governor* of *Jamaica*, & with *Coll: Morgan* who undertooke that gallant exploit from *Nombre de Dios* to *Panamà* on the Continent of *America*: he told me 10000 men would easily conquer all the *Spanish Indies*, the⟨y⟩ were so secure: greate was the booty they tooke, & much, nay infinitly greater had it been, had they not ben betraied & so discovered before their approch, as they had time to carry on board the vast Treasure, which they put off to sea, in sight of our Men, that had no boates to follow &c: They set fire of *Panamà*, and ravag'd the Country 60 miles about. The⟨y⟩ were so supine, & unexercis'd, that they were afraid to give fire to a greate gun &c: 22 To *Council*, return'd:

25 Our *Viccar* on the same &c: Afternoone Wett, had prayers at home: 27: To ☆ —pr: To *Council*, next day home: 31 My Birthday 54th yeare Blessed be God: It was also now preparation day for the holy Sacrament on ⟨Sunday⟩.—I sent *Memoria Sard.* ≏.

Nov 1 *Viccar* on 23. *Luke*. 31: The bl: *Communion* followed, at which I participated, imploring Gods protection for the yeare following, & confirming my resolutions of a more holy life, even upon the holy booke: The Lord assist, & be gracious to me. *Pomer*: *Curate* 1. *Pet:* 3. 15.

2 Was the annual meeting of the foefeès for the Poore, when our *Viccar* also preached on 12: *Heb:* 14. 3. Lond: Council, visited ☆. 5: Dr. *Littleton coram Rege* 13 Rom: 1. of Obedience to Magistrates: dined with Mrs. *Howard*: 6 Council, The *Surenam* buisinesse: I visited my L: *Chamb:* 7 returned home:

8 A Stranger Mr. Flet⟨c⟩her preached on: 23: *Psal:* 4, pathetically describing the terrors of Death to some men, & how differently religious men entertain'd it: exhorting to prepare for it: That God seldome or never take⟨s⟩ those a way who realy turne from their sinns, 'til they have wrought out their Salvation: A comfortable Text for me: *Pomerid* Mr. *Mills* on 14 *Pro:* 16: To Lond:

15 The *Anniversary* of my *Baptisme* I first heard that famous & Excellent Preacher *Dr. Burnet* (Author of the *Historie* of the *Reformation*) on: 3 Coloss: 10: with such a floud of Eloquence, & fullnesse of matter as shew'd him to be a person of extraordinary parts: The B: Comm: followed: & din'd with my friend

Dr. *Needham*: This night being her Majesties Birth-day: the Court was exceeding splendid, in Clothes & Jewells to the height of excesse:

17 A Council in the morning, din'd with ✰, & Council also in the afternoone still about the buisinesse of *Surenam*, where the *Dutch* had detained some *English* in prison, ever since the first War *1665*.

19 I heard that stupendious Violin Signor *Nicholao* (with other rare Musitians) whom certainly never mortal man Exceeded on that Instrument: he had a stroak so sweete, & made it speake like the Voice of a man; & when he pleased, like a Consort of severall Instruments: he did wonders upon a note: was an excellent Composer also: here was also that rare *Lutinist* Dr. *Wallgrave*: but nothing approch'd the *Violin* in *Nicholas* hand: he seem'd to be *spiritato'd* & plaied such ravishing things on a ground as astonish'd us all: 20 I went home after Council:

26 With Mr. [Bap] May *Privy Purse to his Majestie* & Mrs. *Blagg* christned Mrs. *Wattsons* sonn, *Baptist*: Mr. *Leake* officiated in its mothers Lodging *Kings-streete*:

30 Anniversarie of Electing Officers at the *R: Society*, we all din'd together a greate appearance of Noble men &c:

December 1 To Visite ☉. There was a *Council*. 2: heard Signor *Francisco* on the *Harpsichord*, esteem'd on⟨e⟩ of the most excellent masters in Europe on that Instrument: then came *Nicholao* with his *Violin* & struck all mute, but Mrs. *Knight*, who sung incomparably, & doubtlesse has the greatest reach of any English Woman: she had lately ben roming in *Italy*: & was much improv'd in that quality: There was other Musique, & this Consort was at Mr. *Slingsbys* Master of the Mint, my worthy friend, & greate lover of Musique: 4 A *Council*. 5 home:

8 To *Lond* to *Council*: visited ✰—pr: I spent this whole weeke in affaires chiefly with my L: *Tresurer*. 12 went home:

15 To *Lond:* to *Council*: Saw a Comedie at night, at Court, acted by the Ladys onely, viz: The Lady *Mary* & *Ann* his R: hignesses two Daughters, & my deare friend Mrs. *Blagg*, who having the principal part, perform'd it to admiration: They were all covered with *Jewels*:

17 Mrs. Blagg, with the two Maids of honor, Mrs. Howarde, & my Wife, came to house warming to my new Lodging: 19 I went home: 20 *Viccar* on his former. The *Curate* on: 1. *Tim:* 3. ult.

22 *Lond:* to *Council*, & for the poores mony: was at the repetition of the *Pastoral*, on which [occasion] my friend Mrs. Blagg, had about her neere 20000 pounds worth of *Jewells*, of which one she lost, borrowed of the Countesse of Suffolck, worth about 80 pounds, which the *Duke* made good; & indeede the presse of people was so greate, that it was a wonder she lost no more: 23 I visited ☌ —pr: 24 home:

25 *Christmas day* our *Viccar* on 24. *Num:* 17: I received the blessed *Communion*:

28 I invited Neighbours: 31 Gave almighty God thanks for his Mercys: the Yeare past.

SIR WILLIAM PETTY – VISITS TO OXFORD AND NORTHAMPTON – THE MARRIAGE OF MARGARET BLAGGE
(1675–1677)

167$\frac{4}{5}$ JANUARY 1 I implored Gods protection for the yeare following: & divers of my Neighbours came to dine with us:

3 Our *Viccar* as above. 5 To Lond: visited ✫—pr: 6. return'd, din'd at a friends:

11 To *Lond*, dind at *B: house*: 17: At St. *Martins* Dr. *Beaumont* on 2. *Phil:* 14: I received the holy *Sacrament*: Then a stranger on 16 *Luke*: 31: spent the evening with ☌—pr: 19 I carried Mrs. *Blagg*, & other Ladys to heare the famous *Nicholaos* Violin at Mr. *Slingsbys*:

20 Visited ✫—pr: & to see Mr. *Streeter* that excellent Painter of Perspective &c: & *Landscip*, to comfort, & encourage him to be cut for the stone, with which that honest man was exceedingly afflicted: 21 returned home:

29 All the Queenes Mayds of honor came to dine with mee: 30 *Vicc:* on 2: Sam: 11. 9. of the Sacrednesse of Kings, being K. Charles the firsts Martyrdome Anniversarie:

31 Our Viccar as before: *Curate* on: 1. *Jacob*: 15.

Feb: 3 To Lond: in the Evening to visite ✫—pr: returned on the 6:

9 To *Lond* about severall affaires, but especialy to begin the Lent: 11. Dind at L: *Berkeleys* with Mrs. *Blagg*, returned next day. 14 *Lond:* Dr. *Duport* at W. hall preached on 14 *John*: 21: To the King Dr. *Pierce* on   *Let him that standeth take heede* &c excellently pursued: 15 I received the blessed Communion at a sick persons with ⌒ Dr. *Leake* officiating.

24 Dr. *Stillingfleete coram Rege* on 3. *Heb:* 13: excellently pressed: 26: Dr. *Tillotson Coram Rege* on 119 *Psal:* 59. I supped with ⟨Mrs.⟩ B: at B: house —pr: ⟨28⟩ Dr. *Glanvill* W. hall 1 serm: 17 *Act:* 31: Then I heard a stranger at *Covent Garden* Church how shall they preach unlesse they be sent, excellently well perstringing the bold sectaries, exhorting to an esteeme of the Lawfull Ministrie &c: To this succeeded an Ordination of about 30 *Deacons* & *Priests* by Dr. *Pierson* Bishop of *Chester*, very solemn & the B: Sacrament follow'd of which I communicated with greate Comfort; Din'd at a poore widdows with ⌒.

Mar: 6. I return'd home. 3. To *Lond:* Dr. *Pierce coram Rege* on 12: *Heb:* 13, shewing the perill of dissobedience. I supped with ☆ —pr: at B: house: 4 I went to the *R: Society*, where was read a paper from Monsieur *Isa: Vossius* concerning an appearance in ☾, & *Archimedes's Speculum Ustorium*: I supped at Mr. Secretarie Williamsons with severall of our *Society*: among whom Mr. *Sheeres* Sonn of *Cap: Sheres* of our *Parish*, who undertooke and best succeeded in the Mole of *Tanger*, affirmed, that if a *Scorpion* were placed within a Circle of fire, or so invirond with danger as no way to escape, he would sting himselfe to death: he spake of the prodigious bignesse of *Locusts* in *Africa*: That all the Teeth of *Elephants* grew downewards, & not as commonly painted: That the *Camelion* preied chiefly on *flys* by a violent *Suction*, first so exhausting its owne body of breath & aire as to reduce itselfe to as thin as the edge of a knife in appearance, & then sudainly relaxing and violent suction of the aire, filling himselfe againe drew in with it, the flies that were within it⟨s⟩ Spheare & opposite to him:

22 To *Lond:* 24: A Stranger W:hall on 26 *Matt:* 43: I supped at Sir *William Pettys*, with The Bish: of *Salisbury*, & divers honorable persons: we had a noble entertainement, in a house gloriously furnished; The *Master* & *Mistris* of it extraordinary Persons: Sir *Will:* being the sonn of a meane man some where in *Sussex*, was sent from Schole to *Oxon:* where he studied Philos:

but was most eminent in Mathematics & Mechanics, proceeded
Doctor of *Physick*, & was growne famous as for his Learning, so
for his recovering a poore wench that had ben hanged for
felonie, the body being beged (as costome is) for the *Anatomie*
lecture, he let bloud, put to bed to a warme woman, & with
spirits & other meanes recovered her to life; The Young Scholars
joyn'd & made her a little portion, married her to a Man who
had severall children by her, living 15 yeares after, as I have ben
assured: He came from *Oxon:* to be ⟨pedagogue⟩ to a neighbour
of mine; Thence when the Rebells were dividing their Conquests in Ireland, he was employed by them to measure & set
out the Land, which he did upon an easy contract so much per
Acker: which he effected so exactly, & so expeditiously, as not
onely furnish'd him with a greate summ of mony, but enabled
him to purchas an Estate worth 4000 pounds a yeare; he afterwards married the Daughter of Sir *Hardresse Waller*, she an
extraordinary witt, as well as beauty, & a prudent Woman: Sir
William amongst other inventions author of the Double-bottom'd
ship; which though it perishd, & he censur'd for rashnesse; yet it
was lost in the bay of *Biscay* in a storme when, I think 15 more Vessels misscarried: The Vessell was flat-bottom'd, of exceeding
use to put into shallow Ports, & ride over small depths of water;
It consisted of two distinct *Keeles* crampt together with huge
timbers &c: so as a violent streame ran betweene: It bare a monstrous broad saile; & he still persists it practicable & of exceeding use, & has often told me he would adventure himselfe in
such another, could he procure sailors, and his Majesties Permission to make a second Experiment, which name the King
gave it at the Launching: The Map of *Ireland* made by Sir
William is bilieved to be the most exact that ever was yet made
of any Country: he did promise to publish it: & I am told it has
cost him neere 1000 pounds to have it ingrav'd at *Amsterdam*.
There is not a better Latine pöet living, when he gives himselfe
that Diversion; nor is his Excellency lesse in Counsil, & prudent
matters of state: &c: but is so extraordinary nice in scifting, &
examining all possible contingences, that he adventures at nothing, which is not Demonstration: There were not in the whole
world his equal for a superintendent of Manufacturs, &
improvement of Trade; or for to govern a Plantation: If I were a
Prince, I should make him my second Counselor at least: There

is nothing difficult to him; besids he is Coragious, on which
account I cannot but note a true storie of him: That when Sir
Aleyn Brodrick sent him a Challenge, upon a difference twixt
them in *Ireland*: Sir Will: though, exceedingly *purblind*,
accepted the challenge, & it being his part to propound the
Weapon, defied his Antagonist, to meete him with an hatchet or
Axe in a darke Cellar; which he refusing, was laught at, for
challinging one whom every body knew was so short sighted:
Sir William was with all this facetious, & of Easy Conversation,
friendly, & Courteous & had such a faculty to imitate others,
that he would take a Text, and preach now like a grave orthodox
Divine, then fall-into the Presbyterian way, thence to the Phanatical, the Quaker, the Moonk, & frier, the Popish Priest, with
such admirable action, & alteration of voice & tone, as it was not
possible to abstaine from wonder, & one would sweare, to heare
severall persons, or think he were not in good earnest an Enthu-
siast & almost beside himselfe, when he would fall out of it in to
a serious discourse &c which was very divertisant: but it was
very rarely he would be courted to oblige the company with this
faculty, unlesse among most intimate friends: My Lord *Duke* of
Ormond once obtain'd it of him, & was almost ravished with
admiration of it; but by & by he fell upon a serious reprimand of
the faults & miscarriages of some Princes & Governors, which
though he named none, did so sensibly touch my L: *Duke*, who
was then *Lieutenant* of *Ireland*; that my Lord began to be very
uneasy, & wish'd the spirit alayed: for he was neither able to
indure such truths, nor could he for his heart but be delighted;
so at last he mealted his discourse to another more ridiculous
subject & came done from the joyne stoole; but my Lord, would
heare him preach no more. He could never get to be favoured at
Court; because he outwitted all the projecturs that came neere
him: In my life having never know⟨n⟩ such a Genius, I cannot
but mention these particulers, among multitude of others,
which I could produce: When I have ben in his splendid Palace,
who knew him in meaner Circumstances, he would be in admiration himselfe how he ariv'd to it; nor was it his value ⟨or⟩ inclination to splendid furnitur & the curiositie of the age: but his
Elegant Lady, who could indure nothing meane, & that was not
magnificent; whilst he was very negligent himselfe & of a Philosophic temper: Lord, would he say, what a deale of do is here;

I can lie in straw with as much satisfaction: & was indeede rather negligent of his person &c: Sir *William* is the Author of the ingenious deductions from the bills of Mortality which go under the name of Mr. Graunt: also of that usefull discourse of the manufactur of Wooll, & severall other, in our Register of the R: Society: The Author of that Paraphrase on 104 Psal: in Latin Verse, which gos about in MSS: & is inimitable: In a word, there is nothing impenetrable to him.

Aprill: 29 I read my first discourse of *Earth* & *Vegetation* before the *Royal Society*, as a lecture in Course after Sir Rob: *Southwell* had read his the weeke before on Water: I was commanded to print it by our President & the Suffrage of the *Society*: returned home that Evening:

May: 1 Our *Viccar* on   keeping the unity of the Spirit in the bond of Peace: Meeting of the foefeès for the poore, who dined together &c: 2: On: 12: *Heb*: 1: The holy Communion follow'd: *Curate* on: 2: *Tim*: 16. 17: 8 To *Lond*: 9: at St. *Martines* the *Bish*: of *Oxon* on 18 Joh: 36: The Communion follow'd, 'twas Rogation Sonday, I dined at B: house with Mrs. *Blagg*: 13: A stranger (*Ascention day*) at St. *Mart*: on 24. Luke 51. 52. apposite to the solemnity & very well: The holy Sacrament follow'd, dind with ☿ at B: house:

This day was my deare friend Mrs. *Blagg* maried to Mr. *Sidny Godolphin* Groome of the *Bed-Chamber* to his Majestie at the *Temple Church* by Mr. *Leake* Chap: to the *Duke*:

18 To *Lond*: invited by Mrs. *Blagg* to a Collation with my Lady *Yearbrow*, Mrs. Howards, my *Wife* & other friends; & returned next day. 20: My pious friend Mrs. *Godolphin*, my Lady *Berkeley*, La: *Yarborow*, Mrs. *Howard* came all downe to my house & return'd in the Evening. ☿ —pr: 23. A stranger on 8 *Rom*: 9. *Whitsondy*: The blessed Communion follow'd: *Pomerid*: at Greenwich the *Curate* on 3. *Joh*: 8. I went then to visite one Mr. *Bathurst* a *Spanish Merchant* &c: a Neighbour:

27: *Ember-Weeke*, I went to *Lond*: 29: his Majesties Birth day at W:hall, By the Bish: of *Bath* & Wells on: 2: *Hebb*: 23. 30: Trinity *Sonday* a stranger on   *prove your selves whether ye be in the faith* &c: Thence to St. *Martines*, where a Chaplain of the *Bish*: of *Caerliles* on   *In this I exercise my selfe, to have a Conscience voide of offence* &c. The holy Communion followed: I went in the afternoone to visite my sick Lady *Vicountesse*

Mordaunt. 31. I went with my *L. Ossorie* to *Deptford* where we chose him Master of the *Trinity Companie*; our *Viccar* preaching on 4: *Eph:* 30 very excellently & appositely to the occasion: Thence by barge, to *Lond:* where at the Trinity house we had a magnificent feast, & divers greate persons: I thence went with his Lordship to his Lodging in White-hall:

June 1 I supped at Berkeley house with ☆ —pr:

2 At a Conference of the Lords & Comm: in the painted Chamber upon a difference about imprisoning some of their Members I was present: Din'd at the *Duke* of *Ormonds*, with the *Duke* of *Munmoth* & severall greate men. 3: I was at another Conference, where the Lords accused the Commons for their transcended misbehaviour, breach of Privelege, *Magna Charta*, Subversion of *Government*, & other high & provoking & diminishing Expressions; shewing what duties & subjections they owed to the Lords in Parliament by record *Hen:* 4th &c. which was like to create a notable disturbance: I din'd at the Master of the *Mints*, went to R: Society: The discourse being of Fountaines &c & so to my owne house:

6 our *Viccar* on 12: *Heb:* 1. There follow'd the blessed Sacrament. The Lord make me thankfull & vigilant. *Pomer: Stranger* on 9. *Heb:* 27:

8 To *Lond:* about buisinesse, dined with ☆ at B: house, where also din'd the young Prince of *Nieuburg:* 10: I was upon an Evidence at *Guild-hall* & thence went home: 13 Our *Vicc:* on his former & subject, little added: *Pomerid*: the *Curate* on: 4: John: 24:

14 Came divers *Ladys* to dine at my house, with whome I went to Lond:

15 Came Mrs. *Godolphin* to see me —pr: 18 home: 20: *Viccar* on 7: *Job:* 20.

This afternoone came Monsieur *Quierwill* & his *Lady* Parents to the famous beauty & . . . favorite at Court, to see Sir Rich: Bro: my F. in Law, with whom they were intimately acquainted in *Bretagne*, what time Sir Richard was sent to *Brest*, to supervise his Majesties sea affaires during the later part of his Majesties banishment abroad: This Gent: house being not a mile from *Brest*; Sir *Richard* made an acquaintance there, & being used very Civily, was oblig'd to returne it here, which we did in a Collation: after which they returned to Lond: He seem'd a souldierly person, & a good fellow, as the *Bretons* generaly are,

his *Lady* had ben very handsom, & seem'd a shrew'd understanding woman: Conversing with him in our *Garden*, I found
severall words of the *Breton* language the same with our *Welch*:
His daughter was now made *Dutchesse of Portsmouth* and in the
height of favour; but we never made any use of it: &c:

22 To *Lond:* stayed most of the weeke upon buisinesse:

27: At *Ely-house* I went to the Consecration of my worthy
friend the Learned *Dr. Barlow*, Warden of *Queenes Coll: Oxon:*
now made Bishop of *Lincoln*, Dr. *Hamilton* preaching in that
Chapell on Tim: an excellent discourse of the *Episcopal* Office
&c: after which succeeded a magnificent feast, where were the
Duke of *Ormond*, E: of *Lauderdail*, Lord *Tres: Keeper* &c severall
other Lords, & *Bishops*:

28 My F in Law had a Tryal before the *L: Chancelor*, to
advantage; but the Register prevaricated in the minutes, which
is a shamefull abuse: & ought to be reform'd, by causing them to
be read in Court: I visited Mrs. G — pr:

29 I went with Mrs. *Godolphin* to my house at Says-Court,
where she staied a Weeke with us: *pr:*

July: 4: our *Viccar* on his former *Text* in *Job*: The holy Comm:
follow'd which we all rec'd: In Afternoone at *Grenewich* the
Curate on Eccles: 1 Remember thy Creator &c.

5 Came to dine with us Mr. *Sidny Godolphin* to see his Lady,
with the two *Howards Ma: of honour*, & returned that Evening:
6: I carried Mrs. *Godolphin* to *Lond:* & set her downe at my Lord
Sunderlands.

8 I went with Mrs. *Howard* & her two daughters towards
Northampton Assises about a *Tryal* at *Law*, in which I was Concerned for them as a *Trusteè*. We lay this night at *Henly* on the
Thames at our *Attourney* Mr. ⟨*Stephens's*⟩ who entertain'd us very
handsomely: Thenc next day dining at *Shotover* at Sir *Tim: Tyrills*
a sweete place, we lay at Oxford it being the *Act*: when Mr. *Rob:
Spencer* Unkle to the *Earle* of *Sunderland* & my old acquaintance
in *France*, entertain'd us at his appartment in *Christ-Church*
(where he had hired one of the Canons Lodgings,) entertain'd us
all the while, with exceeding generosity: 10: The *Vice-Chancelor
Dr. Bathurst*, (who had formerly taken particular care of my
Sonn) President of *Trinity*, invited me to Dinner, & did me
greate honour all the time of my stay: The next day he also
invited me & all my Company, though strangers to him, to a very

noble Dinner: I was at all the *Academique* Exercises: *Sondy*, at St. *Maries* preached a fellow of *Brasen nose* on 2: *Tit*: 15., not a little magnifying the dignity of Church-men: In the afternoone one of New Coll: but the heate and presse was so greate I could not hear &c: & was faine to go out:

We heard the Speeches & saw the Ceremonie of Creating Doctors in Divinity, *Law*, *Physique* &c: I had in the morning early heard Dr. *Morison Botanic Professor*, reade on divers Plants in the Physic Garden; & saw that rare Collection of natural Curiosities, of Dr. *Plots* of *Magdalen* hall: *Author* of the Natural hist: of *Oxford-shire*; all of them collected in that shire, & indeede extraordinary, that in one County, there should be found such varietie of Plants, Shells, Stones, Minerals, Marcasites, foule, Insects, Models of works &c: Chrystals, Achates, Marbles: he was now intending to Visite *Staffordshire* & as he had of Oxfordshire to give us the *Natural*, *Topical*, *Political*, *Mechani⟨c⟩al* history: & pitty it is, more of this industrious mans genius were not employed so to describe every County of England, since it would be one of the most usefull & illustrious Workes that was ever produc'd in any age or nation: I visited also the *Bodlean* library & my old friend the Learned *Obadia Walker* head of Universitie Coll: which he had now almost quite rebuilt or repair'd: So taking leave of the V: Chancelor, Dr. *Alestree* the Kings Professor in Divinity, Deane of *Christ Church* Dr. *Fell*, we proceeded to *Northampton* where we arived next day:

In this journey went part of the way Mr. *Ja: Grahame* [Since *privy purse to the Duke*], a Young Gent: exceedingly in love with Mrs. *Dorothy Howard* one of the *Mayds of honor* in our Company: I could not but pitty them both: The Mother not much favouring it: This Lady was not onely a greate beauty, but a most virtuous & excellent Creature, & worthy to have ben Wife to the best of men: My advice was required, & I spake to the advantage of the young gent: more out of pitty, than that I thought she deserv'd no better; for though he was a gent: of a good family, yet there was greate inequalitys &c:

14 I went to see my Lord *Sunderlands* seat at *Althorp*, 4 miles from the ragged Towne of Northampton [Since burned & well rebuilt]: tis placed in a pretty open bottome, very finely watred & flanqued with stately woods & groves in a Parke with a

Canale, yet the water is not running, which is a defect: The house a kind of modern building of Free stone: within most nobly furnishe'd: The Apartments very commodious, & Gallerie & noble hall: but the *Kitching* for being in the body of the house, & Chapell too small were defects: There is an old, yet honorable Gate house standing a wry, & out-housing meane, but design'd to be taken away: It was Moated round after the old manner, but it is now dry & turf'd with a sweete Carpet: above all are admirable & magnificent the severall ample Gardens furnish'd with the Choicest fruite in England, & exquisitely kept: Great plenty of *Oranges*, and other Curiosities: The Parke full of Fowle & especialy Hernes, & from it a prospect to *Holmby* house, which being demolished in the late Civil Warre, shews like a Roman ruine shaded by the trees about it, one of the most pleasing sights that ever I saw, of state & solemne:

15 Our Cause was pleaded in behalfe of the Mother Mrs. *Howard* & *Daughters* before baron *Thurland*, who had formerly been Steward of Courte for me: We carried our Cause, as there was reason; for here was an imprudent as well as disobedient sonn, against his Mother by instigation doubtlesse of his Wife, one Mrs. *Ogle* (an antient Maid) whom he had clandestinly married, & who brought him no fortune, he heire aparent of the Earle of *Berkshire*. After dinner we went toward *Lond:* Lay at *Brickhill* in *Bedfordshire* & came late next day to our journeys end.

This was a journey of Adventure & knight errantry, one of the Ladys servants being as desperatly in love with Mrs. *Howards* Woman, who riding on horsback behind his *Rival*, the amorous & jealous Youth, having a little drink in his pate, had certainly here killed himselfe, had he not ben prevented; for alighting from his horse & drawing his sword, he endeavored to fall upon it twise or thrice, but was interrupted; ⟨by⟩ our Coachman & a stranger that passed by, after which running to his rival, & snatching another sword from his side (for we had beaten his owne out of his hand) & on the suddaine pulling downe his Mistriss, would have run both of them through; but we parted them, though not without some blood: This miserable Creature Poyson'd himselfe for her not many daies after they came to Lond:

18 Came to visite me Mrs. *Godolphin* — pr. ⟨18⟩: I received the B: *Sacrament* at St. *James* in the morning with ⌒: Thence to my

L: Tressurers whose Chaplain preached at *Wallingford-house* excellently well on 31 *Psal: 31:* I dined at a poore Widdows with ☍: *Pomerid*: Dr. *Leake* at St. *Jame's* on: 24. *Matt* 42: 20 I returned home, where I had the un-wellcome newes of my sonns being falln ill of the Small-pox: but *God* was mercifull to him in all his sicknesse.

25 St. Jam: day our *Viccar* absent, preached a stranger on 34. *Psal:* 14: Afternoone on the same: 26 Lond: returned not till 29: My Sonn recovers blessed be God.

August 1 A stranger made a pathetical, & very tedious discourse on 13 *Jer*: ult. *When shall it once be?* The holy Comm: followed: *Pomerid*: another stranger on 73. Psa: 24.

9 My Coach-house was broken open this night, & the Glasses & Damaske Cushions, Curtaines &c: taken away: Went to *Wimbledon* to see my Lord of *Bristoll* & return'd in the Evening: 10 To *Lond:* 11: Dind with my Lady *Sunderland* at my owne Lodging. 12 Went to *Twicknam* to visite Mrs. *Godolphin*, return'd: 15. our *Viccar* on his former Text in *Job*:

24 I went with my Wife to see my L: *Arch-bishop* of *Canterbery* where we dined & were exceedingly kindly received: returned from *Croydon* in the Evening:

29 our *Viccar* on his old beaten Text: Afternoone the *Curate* on 9: *Pro:* 8: 30: To *Lond:* return'd next day; found Mrs. *Blagge* there, she gave me a letter of *Attourney* about her Concernes & return'd to *Twicknam* that evening, my Wife bringing her a good part of the way:

September 2 I went to see *Dullwidge* Colledge, being the pious foundation of one *Allen* a famous *Comoedian* in K. *James's* time: The Chapell is pretty; The rest of the *Hospital* very ill contriv'd; it yet maintaines divers poore of both sexes, 'tis in a melancholy part of *Camerwell* Parish; I came back by certaine Medicinal *Spâ Waters* at a place called *Sydname* Wells in *Lewisham* Parish; much frequented in Summer time:

5 Our *Viccar* as formerly: The holy Communion followed; & it was I hope a blessed day to me.

9 I went to *Lond:* to see a sick [poore] person taken suddenly ill of a dumb Palsy.

10 I was Casualy shewed the *Dutchesse* of *Portsmouths* splendid Appartment at *Whitehall*, luxuriously furnished, & with ten times the richnesse & glory beyond the *Queenes*, such massy

pieces of Plate, whole Tables, Stands &c: of incredible value &c: 11 returned home: 12 our *Viccar* as before: *Curat* on 1 *Joh:* 5: 7: My Lord *Brounchar* coming to visite me, interrupted my going this afternoone to church:

⟨14⟩ To *Lond:* din'd at B: house with Mrs. Bl:— pr: 19 *Ember* weeke & *Ordination* Sonday, I receiv'd the bl: Comm: at St. *James's*, heard a serm: at W hall on   the *Burden of Dumah*, concerning Repentance: 21 Rec'd with ✵ at a poore sick persons. 22. returned home. 23: *Lond:* To visite my L: *Berkeley* falln ill. 26: Received the B: Sacrament at St. *Jamess*, Then *Coram Rege* at W:hall Dr. *Standish* on: 2: *Cor:* 5. 20: *Pomer:* Dr. Lake on 3. *Gen:* 13: 29: I went to *Parsons Greene* to visite my Lady *Mordaunt* with my Wife & Mrs. *Godolphin*: saw the Italian *Scaramucchio* act before the King at *White-hall*; People giving monye to come in, which was very Scandalous, & never so before at Court Diversions: having seene him act before in *Italy* many yeares past, I was not averse from seeing the most excellent of that kind of folly:

Octob: 1 I went home. 3: *Curate* as formerly: The holy Sacrament follow'd, with greate resolutions &c: God make me mindfull: *Pomerid*: a stranger on 3: *Matt* 8: a very excellent sermon: 6 To *Lond:* dind at *Ber: house.* 7: At Sir *Step: Foxes.* 8. Supp'd at *Ber: house*: 9 home:

10 *Viccar* on 12 *Pro:* 5: *Pomerid*: Curate on his former Text:

11 To *Lond:* din'd at *B: house.* 14. Went on foote to *Kensington*, din'd with my old acquaintance Mr. *Henshaw*, newly returnd from *Denmark*, where he had ben left *Resident* in that *Court* after the Death of the *Duke* of Richmond who died there Ambassador:

15 I got an extreame cold, such as was afterwards so epidemical, as not onely afflicted us in this Iland, but was rife over all Europe, & raged like a Plague; note that it was after an exceeding dry Summer & Autumn. 16: *Anniver:* ⇌ pr: when I settled affaires my sonn being to go into france with my Lord *Berkeley*, designed Ambassador Extraordinary for *France*, & Plenipotentiary for the gen: Treaty of Peace at *Nimegen*:

17 Preached *coram Rege* Mr. *Barnes* on 2. Pet. 3. 16: I received the holy Comm: the morning at St. *James's. Pomerid*, at my requeste preached at St. *Jamess* Mr. *Bohune* my sonns *Tutor* before the La: Mary & an illustrious Auditorie excellently well on: 6: *Rom:* 12:

24 At St. *James'* I received the bl: *Sacrament*, then *Coram Rege* Dr. *Thisteltwhait* on 1. *Gal:* 4. *Pomerid* at St. *James*, a stranger on 15. *Rom:* 4. din'd at L: *Chamberlains* with the *Holland* Ambassador: L: Duras [since E: of *Faversham*] nephew to the *Duke* of *Bullion* [Marshal Thuren] a Valiant Gent: whom his Majestie made an Eng: Baron, of a *Cadet*; & gave his seate of *Holmeby* in *Northampton* shire &c:

27 My Lord *Berkeley* now in precinct for his departure into France, coming to the *Council* fell downe in the Gallery at *White*-hall of a fit of *Apoplexie*, & being carried into my L: *Chamberlaines* Lodgings employed all that night severall famous Doctors & with much adò was at last recovered to some sense by applying hot firepans & Spirit of *Amber* to his head, but nothing was found so effectuall as cupping on the shoulders: an almost miraculous restauration: The next day he was carried to *B: house*. This stopped for the present his journey, & caused my stay in Towne, into whose hands he had put all his Affaires & whole estate in *England* during his absence, which though I was very unfit to undertake, in reguard of ⟨many⟩ buisinesses then which tooke me up; yet upon the greate importunity of my *Lady*, & Mrs. *Godolphin* (to whom I could refuse nothing) I did; It seemes when he was Deputy (not long before in Ireland) he had ben much wronged by one he left in trust with his affaires, & therefore wished for some unmercenary friend, who would take that trouble on him; which was to receive his Rents, looke after his Houses & Tennants, solicite for Supplies from the *L: Tressurer* &c: Correspond weekely with him, more than enough to employ any drudge in *England*: but what will not friendship & love make on⟨e⟩ do!

31 The *Anniversary* of my *Birthday* & 55th of my Age being Sonday likewise I received the holy Sacrament at St. *James's*: *Coram Rege* preached one Mr. *May* on 7: *Jer:* 4: I din'd at my *L: Chamb:* with my sonn; there were divers persons of quality, and the learned *Isa: Vossius* & *Spanhemius* sonn of the famous man of *Heidelburg*, nor was this gent: lesse learned being a generall Schol: amongst other pieces, Author of that excellent Treatise concerning *Medails* &c: here were also the E: of *Northampton* Constable of the *Towre* & the E: of *Westmorland*: *Pomerid* at St. Jam: preached Dr. *Turner* (sometime Tutor to my sonn at *Trinity Coll:* Oxon) on: 7: *Matt:* 14.

November 2 I went home: 7 our *Viccar* on: 7: *Matt:* 1. 2, the holy Sacrament followd: *Curate* on 1. *Joh:* 5. 8: 8. To *Lond:* in order to my *Sonns* journey, & to provide bills of Exchange for Mrs. *Godolphin*, whose whole Concernes were still in my hands:

9 I din'd at *B: house*, & went late home: the next day being the time appointed for my L: Ambassador to set forth, [10] I met them with my *Coach* at *New-Crosse*: There was with him my Lady his Wife, & my deare friend *Mrs. Godolphin* who, out of an extraordinary friendship, would needes accompany my Lady to *Paris* & stay with her some time, which was the chiefe inducement of my permitting my *Sonn* to Travell; but I knew him safe under her inspection, & in reguard my Lord himselfe had so promis'd me to take him into his special care, who had intrusted all he had to mine: Thus we set out 3 *Coaches*, 3 Wagons, and about 40 horse besides my *Coach*: It being late and my Lord but *valetudinarie* yet, we got but to *Dartford* the first day, & [11] the next to *Citinburne*; by the Way the *Major* of *Rochester Mr. Cony*, who was then an Officer of mine for the Sick & Wounded of that place &c, entertain'd the Ladys with an handsome present of refreshments, as we came by his house: 12 We came to *Canterbery*, where next morning *Mrs. Godolphin* & I went to the *Cathedrall* to prayers, and thence to Dover: There was in my Lady Ambassadors Company also my *Lady Hammilton*, a Spritefull young Lady, who was much in the good-graces of that family, & wife of that valiant & worthy Gent: *Geo: Hammilton* not long after slaine in the Warrs; she had ben a *Maid* of Honor to the *Dutchesse*, & now turn'd *Papist*:

13 At *Dover* Mrs. *Godolphin* delivered me her *Will*, which her *Husband* had given her leave to make, & absolutely to dispose of all her fortune, which was in value better than 4000 pounds: then after prayers, [14] the next morning my Lord having delivered me before his Letters of Attourney, Keyes, Seale, & his Will, (it being *Sonday*-morning and a glorious day) We tooke solemn leave of one another upon the *Beach*, the Coaches carrying them into the sea to the *Boats*, which delivered them to Cap: *Gunmans Yacht* the *Mary*: & so I parted with my Lord, my sonn, & the person in the world whom I esteemed as my owne life Mrs. *Godolphin*; being under saile, the Castle gave them 17 Gunns, & Cap: *Gunman* answered with 11: Hence I went to Church to beg a blessing on their Voyage: The Ministers text

was 1. Joh: 5. 4: I dined at the *Majors*, who was also an Officer of mine in this port: & lay that night at his house: 15. being the *Anniversary* of my *Baptisme* after prayers, I went back to *Canterbery* where I went to the *Cathedral* service:

16 To *Rochester*, lay at the *Majors*. 17 returned home Blessed be God: 19 *Lond*: return'd:

22 *Lond*: buisinesse at the Doctor Commons for my *Lady Tuke*. 28: *Coram Rege* Dr. *LLoyd* on 53 *Psal:* 11: 28 Communion at St. Jame's Advent Sonday: 30 Royal Society *Anniversary* Ellection, the fellows all dining together *more solito*.

December 2 I visited my La: Mordaunt at P: Greene, my Lord her sonn being sick: After dinner this pious woman delivered me 100 pounds to bestow as I thought fit for the release of poore Prisoners, & other Charitable Uses: I returned home:

16 *Lond:* about releasing Prisoners with the Charities given me by my L: *Mordant*: din'd at Sir R: *Claytons*. 19 Dr. *Outram* on 130 *Psal:* 3. 4: 20 I received the holy Comm: at St. *Jamess* Ember Weeke & Ordination Sonday: 21 Visited my *Lady Mordaunt* at Par: Gr: where I found the *Bish:* of *Winchester* whom I had long knowne in *France*: he invited me to his house at *Chelsey*. I returned home: 23 To Lond: return'd: My *Lady Sunderland* gave me ten *Ginnies*, to bestow in Charities: 25 our *Viccar* on 2: *Heb:* 17: apposite to the day: The holy *Commun:* followed: 26: A stranger on 37: *Psal:* 4: 31 I gave God thanks for his mercys the yeare past:

1676 *Jan:* 1 Imploring the blessing of God for the ensuing yeare. 2: *Viccar* on 2: *Heb:* 17. The holy Sacrament follow'd: 3 we had divers Neighbours to dinner. 6 I was invited to one. 9 *Viccar* as above. *Pomer: Curate* on 1. Gen: 1: To *London*.

Febr: 18 Dr. *Sancroft* D: of S. *Paules* Friday *Coram Rege*. 2. *Act:* 40. How few should be saved &c: 19 At the R: *Society* Experiments to prove that the force of gun-powder was from the compression of aire in the Cornes. 20 Dr. *Gunning* Bish: of *Elie* (*Coram Rege*) 20 *Joh:* 21. 22. 23. Chiefly against an *Anonymous Booke* called *Naked Truth*, a famous & popular Treatise against the Corruption in the Cleargie, but not sound as to its quotations; supposed to have ben the Bish: Herefords: & was answered by Dr. *Turner*: I received the B: Com: at St. *Jamess* in the morning. 21. I went home. 23. To *Lond:* 25 Dr. *Tillotson* at *Whitehall* on 1. Joh: 3. 10: I received the B: Sacrament at a sick persons: 27: *Bish:* of *Glocester* Dr. *Pritchard* at

Whall: on 5 *Isa:* 5 Very *Alegoricaly* (according to his manner) yet very gravely & wittily: That the Christian Church was a Vineyard, how in particular God had planted & cultivated that of England; how the true & generous Vine was to be known; with the danger of not answering the Cost & paines of the dresser or *Vigneroon*, applied to the wickednesse of the age: I tooke leave of my young *Lo: Mordaunt* going into France, & sent a recommendatary letter to Mrs. *Godolphin*, to have some eye over him: 29 I dind with Mr. *Povie* on⟨e⟩ of the Masters of *Requests*, a nice contriver of all Elegancies, & exceedingly formall: supped at Sir *Jos: Williamsons*, where were of our Society, Mr. *Rob: Boile*, Sir *Chr: Wren*, Sir *W: Petty*, Dr. Holder (Subdeane of his Majesties Chapell), Sir *James Shaen*, Dr. *Whistler* and our Secretary Mr. *Oldenburg*:

 Mar: 1 At *White-hall* Dr. *Megot* incomparably on *Psal:* Thou thoughtest me such a one as thy selfe but—&c: 3: Dr. *Lamplugh* Deane of *Rochester*, on 1. *Sam:* 15. 2. 3: 4 I din'd at Sir *Tho: Linches* late Governor of *Jamaica*, with the Countesse of *Sunderland* & *Mordaunt*. 5: Dr. *Smallwood* on: 4. Job: 31. 32, an ordinary Sermon: The holy Communion follow'd: *Coram Rege* Dr. *Bredox* B: of *Chichester* 22 Job: 26. 27; a very meane discourse for a *Bishop*: I visited my La: *Mordaunt* at Parsons Greene. 6: returned home:

 9 To *Lond:* about Accompts: 10: *Coram Rege* Dr. *Frampton* Deane of Glocester on 25 *Psal:* 11. That no sinn was so greate but *God* for *Christs* sake did pardon: & therefore exhorting earnestly to Repentance: That it was a greater King than any on Earth who thus humbled himselfe to death; & therefore no shame for the greatest potentate on Earth to Repent & beg pardon: applying to us all & especialy to—12: Dr. *Littleton* on 51 *Psal:* 9: A sermon of greate encouragement: *Coram Rege*, Dr. *Fleetewood* Bish: of *Worcester* on 26 *Matt:* 38: This *Bish:* no greate preacher &c: 13 I went to see *Coll: Talbot* & Lady at *Twicnam* where I dined, afterwards Mrs. *Davis* sister to my *L:* Ambassador *Berkeley*, Then to *Twicknam-Parke* my Lords Country seate, to examine how the *Baylife* & Servants ordered matters &c: return'd to *Lond:* 15 Dr. *James* on 4: *Heb:* 11. 16 my Lady the Countesse of *Sunderland* & I went by water to *Parsons Greene* to Visite my Lady Vic: *Mordaunt*: & to consult with her about my Lords *Monument*: we return'd by Coach: 17 Dr. *Ashley* De: of *Norwich* on 27: Matt: 46: 19 Dr. *Lloyd* [now *Bish.* of *Landaf*] (late *Curate*

at *Deptford*), *Coram Rege* on 1. *Cor:* 15. 57: I din'd at the *Bish: of Rochesters*: I received the B: Sacrament.

⟨20?⟩ Dining at my *La: Sunderlands*, I saw a fellow swallow a knife, & divers greate pibble stones, which shaking his stomach, would make a plaine rattling one against another: The Knife was in a sheath of horne to bend in: 22: Dr. *Ironside* on 14. *Proverbs*: 10: 24 *Goodfriday* St. *Martines* Dr. *Doughty* (the *Dukes Chap:*) 1. *Pet.* 2. 21. incomparably describing the incomparable sorrows of our Saviours: Exhorting imitation: The bl: Sacrament follow'd: *Pomerid*: *Coram Rege*: W:hall: Dr. *North*, sonn to my Lord *North*, a very young, but learned, & excellent person on 53 *Isa:* 57: Note, this was the first time the *Duke* appeared no more in the Chappell, to the infinite griefe and threatned ruine of this poore Nation: I went to *Says-Court*.

26 *Easter-day* our *Viccar* on 3 *Exod:* 3: The holy *Commun:* follow'd: *Pomerid*: *Curate* on 1. *Tim:* 2. 5: I went againe to *London* this Evening to speake to my *L: Tressurer*: returned on the 28:

Aprill 2: *Viccar*, as before, & so the *Curate* with much repetition: The blessed Communion followed. 4 I went to Lond: Visited my L: *Marshall*, Lord *Shaftsbery* where I found the *Earle* of *Burlington*: I had now notice that *Mrs. Godolphin* was returning from *Paris* & landing the 3d at *Dover*, so I din'd with my L: *Sunderland* expecting her:

6 Came my dearest Friend to my greate joy; whom after I had welcom'd, I gave accompt to of her buisinesse, & return'd home. 9: our *Viccar* on his former Text: Pomerid: a stranger on 33 *Luke*: 34:

10 To *Lond* about buisinesse & see my friend: return'd: 13 Came Mrs. *Godolphin*, Countesse of *Sunderland*, Mrs. *Graham*, Mrs. *Howard* one of the Q: Maids of honor to see & dine with us: I went back to Lond: with them.

14 I supped with Mrs. *Godolphin* at my Lady *Sunderlands* [returned.] ⟨16⟩ A stranger on 4 *Matt:* 17: *Pomer: Greenewich* Dr. *Plume*, 6: *Rom:* 8. 9. 10.

17 To *Lond:* 23 St. *Geo:* day *W:hall* first ser: Dr. *Stillingfleete* 112 *Psal:* 7:

26 Din'd with ☆, discovered her Marriage by her sister:

27 My Wife entertaind her Majestie at *Deptford*, for which the *Queene* gave ⟨me⟩ thanks in the Withdrawing roome at White-hall.

28 The University of *Oxford* presented me with the *Marmora Oxon: Arundell:* the *Bish:* of *Oxford* writing to me, that I would introduce Mr. *Prideaux* the *Editor* (a most learned young man in *Antiquities*) to the *Duke* of *Norfolck*, to present another, dedicated to his *Grace*, which I did, & we both din'd with the Duke at *Arundel* house: & supped at the *Bish:* of *Rochesters* with *Isa: Vossius*.

May: 1 The meeting for the *Trustees* of the poore, we din'd together. 2: To *Lond*:

3 Visited Mrs. *Godolphin* expostulated with her about the concealement, & was satisfied, it was not her intention: 4: *Ascension day* [com: at landladys then] At St. *Martines* a stranger on 68: *Psal*: 18: The bl: Comm: followed. 6 Returned home with my Wife:

7 our *Viccar* on 5. *Psal*: 8: the Communion followed; *Curate* on 1. *Tim*: 2. 5. 9: To *Lond* to visite ☆: —pr: I spake to the *Duke* of *Yorke* about my L: *Berkeleys* going to *Nimegen* &c: Thence to the *Queenes* Council at *Somerset house* about my friend Mrs. G: lease of *Spalding* in *Lincolnshire*. 11. I din'd with Mr. *Charleton*; went to see Mr. *Montagues* new Palace neere *Bloomesbery*, built by Mr. *Hooke* of our Society, after the French manner: Spake with my Lord *Treasurer* about Mony &c.

12 Dind with my L: *Arlington*. 13 returned home, & found my sonn returned out of *France*, praised be God; for my deare friend Mrs. *Godolphin* coming thence I had no desire he should stay there any longer for many reason⟨s⟩:

14 *Viccar* as before: It was *Whitsonday* & the holy Sacrament, I received: *Pomerid*: a stranger on 6. *Rom*: 23:

21 *Trinity Sonday* our *Viccar* as before: *Pomerid*: a stranger on 2. *Cor*: 5. 10: 22. *Trinity Monday* preached a Chaplaine of my L: *Ossories*, after which we tooke barge to *Trinity* house in Lond, where was a greate feast, Mr. *Pepys* (Secretary of the Admiralty) chosen *Master*, & succeeding my *Lord*.

29 His Majesties Birth & Anniversarie returne, Bish: of *Rochester* on 118 Psal: 22. 23. 24. of his Majesties miraculous Restauration: How *Christ* & *Kings* were head stones, & especialy ours, as rejected, & yet set on the top, for the union of the whole building:

30 I dind at my L: *Chamberlains* with the Dutch *Ambassador* & divers Lords &c. Visited ☆ —pr:

June: 2 I went with my L: *Chamberlaine* to see a Garden at *Enfield* towne; Thence to Mr. *Secretary Coventries* Lodge in the

Chace, which is a very prety place, the house commodious, the Gardens handsome, & our entertainement very free; there being none but my Lord & my selfe: That which most I admir'd at, was, that in the compasse of 25 Miles (yet within 14 of Lond) there is never an house, barne, Church, or building, besides three Lodges: To this Lodge are 3 greate ponds, & some few inclosures, the rest a solitarie desert, yet stored with no lesse than 3000 deare &c: These are pretty retreates for Gent: especialy that were studious & a lover of privacy: We return'd in the Evening by Hamsted, where we diverted to see my Lord Wottons house & Garden; built with vast expense by Mr. *Oneale* an *Irish* Gent: who married his Mother, the Lady Stanhop: The furniture is very particular for Indian Cabinets, Porcelane, & other solid & noble moveables, The Gallery very fine: The Gardens very large, but ill kept; yet Woody & chargeable; the mould a cold weeping clay, not answering the expense:

12 I went to Sir *Tho: Bonds* new & fine house by *Pecham*, the place is on a flat, yet has a fine Garden, & prospect thro the meadows towards *Lond:* 13 To *Lond:* about Mrs. *Godolphins* Lease at the Queenes Council: 14 Visited ☍ —pr: 16 home: 18 *Viccar* as formerly: *Curat* as before: 20 To *Lond:* to the *Council* at Somerset house againe: 21. To the *Duke* about the sick & Wounded under my inspection:

23 din'd at Mr. Sec: *Williamsons*, 24. Return'd home. 25 *Vicc:* as formerly: 26: To *Lond:* 27 My Marriage *Anniversarie*, I din'd with Mrs. *Godolphin* at *Berkeley*-house, being the first day of her house-keeping since her Marriage & returne into *England*.

July 3 din'd with my *Lo: Chamberlaine*, & sealed the Deedes of Mortgage for security of 1000 pounds lent by my friend Mrs. *Godolphin* to my Lord *Sunderland*. 4 I dind at B. house with ☆: 6 at Sir *Stephen Foxes*: 7: Went to *Parsons Greene*, dind with the *Vicountesse Mordaunt*: 8: with my Wife at L: *Chamberl:* where was the *Duke* of *Monmoth*, Lord *Ossorie*, Dut⟨c⟩h *Ambassador*, and returned home that evening: 9 a stranger on 1. *Luke* 77. 11. To *Lond* dind with ☆: Afternoone went to visite L: *Mordaunt*:

19 dind at L: *Chamb:* Went to Sir *William Sandersons* funerall (husband to the Mother of the Maides, & author of two large, but meane Histories of KK. *James* & *Charles* the first): he was buried at *Westminster*: 20 returned home: 23 A stranger on 23: *Pro:* 23: *Pomerid*, the *Curat* on his former Text: 25 To *Lond:* dind with ☆:

28 Went to the Navy Office about my Accompt: Supp'd with L: *Chamberlaine*: 29 went to *Par: Greene* to visite my Lady V. C. *Mordaunt*, where was Mrs. *Godolphin*, & after dinner we went to *Wimbledon* to see the Countesse of *Bristoll*. 30: I received the bl: *Communion* in the morning at St. *James*: To the household at *Whitehall* preached a stranger on 3. *Matt* 8, dind at L. *Chamb:*

Aug: 1. I din'd with Mrs. *Godolphin*: In the afternoone after prayers at St. *Jame's Chapell* was christned a Daughter of Dr. *Leakes*, the Dukes Chaplaine: Godmothers were *Lady Mary*, daughter of the *Duke* of *Yorke*; *Dutchesse* of *Monmoth*, Godfather the *Earle of Bathe*: I went home this Evening: 6: our *Viccar* on 6: *Heb:* 19: 20: The B: Sacrament follow'd: *Pomerid: Curate* on 5 *Ephes:* 15: 8: To *Lond:* dind with ☆: Next day my L:V: *Countesse Mordaunt* and Mrs. *Godolphin* called me to go to my house, where we dined, & I waited on them to *Lond* againe: 13. I received at St. *Jame's*, in the morning: Din'd at *Cap: Grahams*, Serm: *Coram Rege* on 8 Joh: 9: by the *Bish:* of *Ossory*: Supp'd at L: *Chamberlaines* with the *Portugal Ambassador*, & Earle of Ossorie &c: 14 din'd with ⌒ —pr: returned home, &c: Came the *Bishop* of *Rochester* to visite me:

15 Came to visite & dine with me my *Lord Halifax*, Sir Tho: *Meeres*, one of the *Commissioners* of the *Admiralty*: Sir *John Clayton*; Mr. *Slingsby* (Master of the Mint), Mr. *Henshew*, & Mr. *Bridgeman* &c: 17: I tooke preventing *Physick*: 20: A stranger on 4. *Philip:* 11: *Pomerid* at *Greenewich* on 90 *Psal:* 10: the same person. 21 Came my Lady *Tuke* to visite us: I went to *Lond:* with her: 22: Dind with ⌒ —pr:

25 Din'd with Sir *Jo: Banks's* at his house in *Lincolns Inn* fields: upon recommending Mr. *Upman* to be Tutor to his sonn going into France: This Sir Jo: *Bankes* was a Merchant, of small beginnings, but by usurie &c: amass'd an Estate of 100000 pounds &c.

26 I din'd at the Admiralty, with Sec: *Pepys*: Supp'd at L: Chamberlaines, here was Cap: *Baker*, who had ben lately on the attempt of the Nor-west passage: he reported prodigious depth of yce, blew as a *Saphire* & as transparant: That the thick mists was their chiefe impediment, & cause of returne: [I went home.] 27: A stranger preach'd on 17: *Act:* 30: 29 To Lond: dind with ⌒ pr—

September 2 I paied 1700 pounds, to the *Marquis* de *Sissac*, which he had lent to my L: *Berkeley* &c: which I heard the *Marqu*⟨*i*⟩*s* lost at play ⟨within⟩ a night or two:

3. The *Deane* of *Chichester* preached coram Dom on 24. *Act:* 16. The holy *Sacrament* follow'd: Din'd at *Cap: Grahams*, where I came acquainted with Doctor *Compton* (bro: to the Earle of Northampton) now *Bishop* of *London*, & Mr. *North*, sonn to the Lord *North*; bro: to the L.C. *Justice*: & clerke of the Closet, a most hopefull young man: The Bishop had once ben a *Souldier*, had also traveld *Italy*, & became a most sober, grave and excellent *Prelate*: The 2d sermon (*Coram rege*) Dr. *Crighton* on 90 *Psal:* 12: 5. dind with ⌢ —pr: 6. Supp'd at L: *Chamberlains*, where also supped the famous beauty & errant Lady, the *Dutchesse* of *Mazarine* (all the world knows her storie) the Duke of *Monmouth*, Countesse of Sussex, both natural Children of the Kings, by that infamous Adulteresse the Dut: of *Cleaveland*: & the Countesse of *Derby* a vertuous Lady, daughter to my best friend, the Earle of *Ossorie*: I returned next day:

12 To *Lond:* to take order about the building of an house, or rather an appartment, which had all the conveniences of an house; for my deare friend Mr. *Godolphin* & Lady: which I undertooke to Contrive, & Survey, & employ workmen in, til it shold be quite finished: It being just over against his Majesties *Wood-yard*, by the *Thames* side, leading to Scotland yard: I din'd with ⌢ pr: [returned.] 17: *Viccar* on 3. *Joh:* 16: There dined with me Mr *Flamested* the learned *Astrologer* & *Mathematitian*, whom now his Majestie had established in the new *Observatorie* in *Greenewich* Park, & furnish'd with the choicest Instruments: an honest, sincere man &c: *Pomerid: Curate*, as before: 18 To *Lond*, to survey my Workemen, dind with ⌢ —pr: and [19] then with Mrs. *Godolphin* to *Lambeth*, to that rare magazine of Marble, to take order for chimny-pieces &c: The Owner of the workes, had built him a pretty dwelling: This *Dutchman*, had contracted with the *Genoezes* for all their Marble &c: We also saw the *Duke* of *Bouckingams Glasse worke*, where they made huge *Vasas* of mettal as cleare & pondrous & thick as Chrystal, also *Looking-glasses* far larger & better than any that come from *Venice*: I dined with Mr. *Godolphin* & his Wife:

20: I went to visite also ⌢ —pr: 21 home: 24: *Viccar* as above: The *Curate* as before, with small addition:

27 I went to *Twicknam* to see how the *Bailife* & housekeeper looked after their charge, that house & land, &c being wholy under my care for my L: *Berkeley* &c: upon the importunity of my friend:

28 Came Mrs. *Godolphin* to visite & stay with us some time:

October 1 Our *Viccar* as before, The holy Communion follow'd, of which we all received: I went to *Lond:* to looke after the workmen, with my friend, & [3] came back. 8: *Viccar* as above.

9 I went with Mrs. *Godolphin* & my Wife to *Black-wall* to see some *Indian* Curiosities, & as I was walking thro a streete, the way being s⟨l⟩ipperie & misty, I fell against a piece of Timber, with such violence, as quite beate the breath out of my body, so as being taken up, I could not speake, nor fetch any breath, for some space, & then with greate difficulty, coming to my sense, after some applications, being carried into an house, & let bloud: I was carried to the water side, & so home, where after a daies rest, I recovered, though my bruse was not quite healed: This being one of the greatest deliverances that ever I had, The *Lord Jesus* make me ever mindfull, & thankfull: 11 I went to *Lond:* with Mrs. G: 13: supped with ☆:

15 Mindfull of Gods infinite mercy to me, I received at St. *James's* in the morning with ⌣: A stranger preaching at *W-hall* on *Jude*. v. 3. I dind with ☆:—16 *Anniver* ⌣ pr:

17 I din'd with my Wife at *B:house* & carried Mrs. *Godolphin* to our house that Evening: where she staied till 19. when I waited on her to Lond: 22: In the Morning *Comm:* at St. *James's.*

29 A stranger on 23: Pro: 26. *Pomeridiano* our *Viccar* on 6. *Rom:* 23: 30 To *Lond:* about the building; Mrs. *Ann Howard* Mayd of honor to the *Queene*, whom I went to Visite, related to me the strang⟨e⟩ *Vision* she saw: which was thus: One of her maides being lately dead & one whom I well knew, had in her life time told her *Mistris*, that when she died she would certainly appeare to her: This Wench, being deepely in love with a young man, dying, a little while after appeared to her Mistris, as she lay in ⟨bed⟩, drawing the Curtaine, siting downe by her, & beckning to her; her Mistris being broad awake, & sitting up at the affright, called alow'd for her maid to come to her, but no body came; The *Vision*, now going from her, she still continued to call her Maid, who lying in another chamber next to her, rose & came at last to her Mistris: begging her pardon that she did not come at her first call; for said

shee, I have ben in a most deadly fright, & durst not stirr for Mistress *Maundy* (for so was her name) who has appear'd to me, and looked so wistly on me, at the foote of my bed, that I had not the power to rise or answer: These two, Mistris *Howard* & her *Woman Davis*, affirming it so positively, & happning to see it, neere the same time, & in severall chambers, is a most remarkable thing: & I know not well how to discredit it, Mrs. *Howard* being so extraordinary a virtuous & religious *Lady*.

31 Being my Birth-day, & 56 yeare, I spent the morning in Devotion, surveying my accompts & imploring Gods protection, with solemn thanksgiving for all his signal mercys to me, especialy for that escape which concern'd me this Moneth at *Blackwall*: I din'd with *Mrs. Godolphin* & return'd home the Evening, thro a prodigious & dangerous Mist &c:.

November Beging the blessing of *God*, for the ensuing yeare, I went to Church, when [1] our *Viccar* preached on his former subject, yet introducing something apposite to the [5] solemnity. The blessed *Sacrament* follow'd: The L. *Jesus* assist my resolutions &c: *Pomerid, Curat* on 9. *Heb:* 27. 28. The obligation we had in this *Kingdome* especialy, to thanke God for this delivrance of his Church &c: 7: To *Lond:* dined with ☆. 8: at my L: *Chamb:* 9: I sealed & finished the Lease of *Spalding* for Mrs. *Godolphin* at her Majesties *Council* at *Somerset* house. 10 returned home:

16 My *sonn* & I dining at my *Lo: Chamberlaines*, he shewed us, amongst others that incomparable piece of *Raphaels*, being a *Minister* of *state* dictating to *Guicciardine*, the earnestnesse of the Secretary looking up in expectation of what he was next to write, is so to the life, & so naturall, as I esteeme it for one of the choices⟨t⟩ pieces of that admirable Artist: There was an other womans head of *Leonardo da Vinci*; a Madona of old *Palma*, & two of *Van-Dykes*, of which one was his owne picture at *length* when young, in a leaning posture, the other an *Eunuch* singing; but rare pieces indeede: 17: I returned: 19 Our *Viccar* as before, with little addition &c: 21. To *Lond*, returned next day:

23 Came to dine with me my Lord *Chamberlaine Earle of Arlington*, the Earle of *Derby*, and their Countesses, The *Dutchesse* of *Grafton, Countesse* of *Ossory, Mademoiselle Beverward*; & Sir *Gabriel Sylvius*, & return'd to Lond: in the Evening:

27 I went to *Lond:* 28 dind with ☆. 30: Was our *Anniversarie* Elections at the *R: Society*, where I was againe chosen of the

Council: having in the morning before ben to visite & Com: with a poore sick person:

December 3 *Advent Sonday* Dr. *Patric* to the household excellently on 13 *Rom:* 12: The holy *Sacrament* follow'd, the *Bishop* of Lon: Officiating. *Coram Rege* Dr. *Doughty* on 7: *Matt:* 6: I din'd at Sir *Steph: Foxes*. 4. I saw the greate *Ball* daunced by all the *Gallants* and *Ladys* at the *Dut⟨c⟩hesse* of *Yorks*. 5. Supped with ⌒ pr: 6: I visited my L: *Vic: Mordaunt* at P: Greene with my Wife, & returned to *Says-Court* next day:

10 Fell so deepe *a Snow*, as hindred us from Church &c: 12: To *Lond:* in so greate a snow, as I remember not to have ever seene the like: supped with Mrs. *Godolphin*:

13 Din'd with Lo: *Chamber:* & Duke of *Ormond*: supp'd at L: *Ossories* &c: 15 at ☆: 16 Went againe to my La: *Mordaunt* about buisinesse: dind with Lo: *Clarendon*,[1] Lady *Henrietta Hyde*, Mr. *Andr: Newport*, & with much a doe got home through the snow:

17 More Snow falling, I was not able to get to church &c: 19: To *Lond* about buisinesse: dind at Mrs. *Godolphins*; fell ill of a feavorish distemper &c: which confin'd me to bed two daies: 23 I returned home: 24. The extreame cold kept me within:

1677 January I implor'd Gods protection & blessing for the yeare following: had divers Neighbours dined with me:

25 I return'd home, not very well disposed; yet din'd at Mr. *Gaudens*, & then kept in.

30 Our *Viccar* on 13: *Rom:* 2: on which this observation on the original ἀντιτασσομενος signifying not onely a disobedience; but as if the *Apostle* had seene before hand that which those wicked *Rebells* would alledge in defence of their taking armes against their King: using that *very word*, prohibiting it in expresse termes: He also proved that κρῖμα imported Eternal damnation; & that the Kings person could not be separated from his right & power, as not obnoxious to any tribunal but Gods, to answer for what he dos amisse: 31. I went to *Lond:*

Feb: I supped with ☆: 4: Dr. *Craddock* to the house on: 26: *Matt:* 41: The H: Comm: followed: *Cor: Reg:* by Dr. *Pierce* on 1. *Pet:* 2. 11. shewing the danger of sensual lusts. 5 I din'd at the Holl: *Ambassadors* Mr. *Beverning* with my Lady *Ossory, Arlington, Derby* & La: Mary *Cavendish* daughter to the *Duke* of *Ormond*.

1 The former Lord Cornbury.

6 Din'd with ✩——7: with my Lo: *Ossory* at my Lord *Brounck-
ers*: 8 Went to *Rohampton* with my Lady *Dutchesse* of *Ormond*:
The Garden & perspective is pretty, the Prospect most agreable,
I went home that Evening: 11: our *Viccar* as above &c: I went this
evening to *Lond*, to passe a fine early next day in Westminster at
the *Comm: Pleas* barr about my Trust for Mr. William Howard,
sonn to the Earle of *Berkshire*, which concerned his Daughters
the two Maids of honor &c: dind with Sec: Williamson.

March 31 Mrs. *Godolphin* remov'd to the Buildings I had finished in *W:hall* from *Berkeley house*:

April: 1 at *White-hall Synaxis*: din'd at Mrs. *G:* at her *new*
lodging:

May: 1. Meeting of the *Foefees* for the poore: our *Viccar* on 12
Luke 21 against *Covetousnesse* &c. I din'd with the Foefees & did
Parish buisinesse: 6: at *Grenewich* Dr. *Plume* on: 5: *Joh:* 14 on the
duty of Gratitude: That the restored man went immediately to
the Temple: reproved those who made any excuses to abstaine
from the publique worship, & that frequently take Physick on
the Lords day: recommended above all publique & Congrega-
tional worship, as most acceptable, the danger of *Schismatical*
meetings where the publique was protected & incourag'd: The
holy Sacrament followd: *Pomerid* a young preacher on 2: *Apoc:* 5:

8 I went to Lond: dined with Mrs. *Godolphin*, visited the
Countesse of *Hammilton*, supp'd at Lord *Chamberlaines*. 10
Dined at my Lady Tukes with the *Dutchesse* of *Grafton*: Supped
at the Earle of *Derbies*. 12 returned home: put 100 fish into the
pond &c:

June 12 I went to *Lond:* to give the L: *Ambassador Berkeley*
(now return'd from the Treaty at *Nimegen*) an accompt of the
greate Trust repos'd in me during his absence, I having received
& transmitted to him no lesse than 20000 pounds: to my no
small trouble, & losse of time, that during his absence, & when
the *Lord Tressurer* was no greate friend, I yet procurd him greate
Summs, very often soliciting his Majestie in his behalfe, looking
after the rest of his Estate & concernes intirely; without once so
much as accepting any kind of acknowledgement, purely upon
the request of my deare friend Mrs. *Godolphin*.

13 I din'd with Mrs. *Godolphin* & return'd, with aboundance of
thanks & professions [16] from my Lord *Berkeley* & *Lady* &c: 17:
Viccar as before & so the Curate.

24 My Lord *Berkeleys* troublesome buisinesses being now at an end & I delivered from that intollerable servitude & Correspondence; I had leasure to be somewhat more at home, & to myselfe: Our *Viccar* preached on his former, with little addition: Dr. *Trumbal* Doctor of Laws, & a Learn'd Gent: Chancellor to the B: of *Rochester* &c: din'd with me:

July 1 our *Curate* (the *Viccar* being absent) on 6: *Rom:* 21: The holy Communion follow'd: *Pomerid*, a stranger on 21. *Job:* 7. 2: To *Lond:* & 3d: Visited ☆ & dind: I sealed the deedes of Sale of the Mannor of *Blechinglee* to Sir *Rob: Clayton*, for payments of my Lord *Peterborows* debts, according to the trust by Act of Parliament: Then visited ♎—pr: & so home: 8: A stranger preached on 2: *Ephes:* 8: *Curat* as above, a weake preacher: 12: I went to Cap: *Johnsons* funerall, Dr. *Mills* preaching on 25 *Matt*. 21, describing the joys of heaven &c:

15 Our *Curate* on 10. *Luke*. 25. 26. 27.—*Pomerid*, a stranger on 3. *Coloss:* 12: 16 I went to *Wotton* to see my deare Brother. 22: Mr. *Evans Curate* at *Abinger*, preach'd an excellent sermon on 5. *Matt:* 12. In the Afternoone Mr. *Higham* at *Wotton* Catechiz'd: 23. I went to see *Albury*, a sweete Villa of the *Duke* of *Norfolcks*, the plot of which Garden & *Crypta* through the mountaine, I had first design'd &c:

26 I din'd at Dr. *Duncombs* at *Sheere* whose house stands inviron'd with very sweete & quick streames: 29 Mr. *Bohune* my sonns late Tutor at *Abinger* on 4: *Phil:* 8 very elegantly, & practicaly: 30 I returned home: next day to *Lond:* to speake to my Lo: Duke of *Ormond*, now passing through Oxfor'd (where he was Chancelor) towards *Ireland*, to make Mr. *Cary* a Doctor &c: supp'd at my La: *Ossories*, my Lord having ben to visite me, as he tooke shipping for *Holland. Aug:* 2: I return'd home:

August 5 *Viccar* on 7: *Jer:* 12. The holy *Sacrament* follow'd: *Curate* on: 10: *Mark*: 7. I went this Evening to visite my Lo: *Brounker* now taking the waters at *Dullage*.

7 I came to *Lond:* to excuse my not accompanying the *Portugal Ambassador* to *Euston*, as I promised, but it did not comply with my buisinesse: I supp'd at my Lady *Ossories*: &c:

9 Dined at the Earle of *Peterborows*, the day after the *Marriage* of my Lord of Arundell, to my Lady Mary Mordaunt, daughter to the E: of P: & so return'd home:

12 *Viccar* as before: *Pomerid*: a stranger on 27: *Psal:* 4: a pious discourse: 16 I went to visite my La: V. C. *Mordaunt* & return'd:

19 Our *Viccar* as above adding little: *Curate* on 4: *Eph:* 14. 21. To *Lond*, to meete with one about a proposal of a Match for my Sonn: 24. home: 26: our *Viccar* as above. *Curate* on 4: *Eph:* 29:

COUNTRY TOUR AND THE DEATH
OF MARGARET GODOLPHIN
(1677–1678)

27 TO LON: designing to Visite my *Lord Chamberlaine* in *Suffolck*: 28 whither I came on *Tuesday*, his *Lordship* sending his Coach & 6 horses, to meete me at, & bring me from St. *Edmondsbury* to *Euston*: 29, We went a hunting in the Park, & killed a very fat *Buck*: 31 I went a *Hauking*:

September 2: Preached one Mr. *Clegett* on 6. *John:* 44: There din'd this day at my Lords, one Sir Jo: *Gaudy* a very handsome person, but quite *dumb*: yet very intelligent by signes, & a very fine Painter: so civil, & well bred he was, as it was not possible to discerne any imperfection by him; his Lady & children were also there, & he was at church in the morning with us: 4: I went to visite my Lord *Crofts*, now dying at St. *Edmonsbery*, and tooke this opportunity to see this antient Towne, & the remaines of that famous *Monasterie* & Abby; There is little standing intire save the *Gate-house*, which shews it to have ben a vast & magnificent Gotique structure, & of greate extent: The Gates are Wood, but quite plated over with jron: There are also two stately Churches, one especialy. 5. I went to *Thetford* the *Borrogh Towne*, where stands likewise the ruines of another religious house; & there is a round mountaine artificialy raised, either for some Castle or Monument, which makes a pretty *Landscape*: As we went & return'd a *Tumbler* shew'd his extraordinary addresse in the Warren: I also saw the Decoy, much pleased with the stratagem &c: 9: A stranger preach'd at *Euston* Church on 1. *Thess:* 5. 21. Prove all things, that is examine your faith, your life, your actions, & that of others, to imitate the best; & then fell into an handsome *Panegyric* on my Lords new building the Church, which indeede for its Elegance and cherefullnesse is absolutely the prettiest Country Church in England: My Lord told me that his heart smote him, after he had bestow'd so much on his magnificent Palace there he should see Gods-house in the ruine it lay; he has also rebuilt the Parsonage house all of stone, very neately & ample:

10 My *Lord*: to divert me, would needes carry me to see *Ipswich*, where we dined at one Mr. *Manns* by the way, *Recorder* of the Towne: There was in our Company my Lord *Huntingtore*, sonn to the *Dutchesse* of *Lauderdail*, Sir *Ed: Bacon*, a learned Gent, of the family of the greate Chancellor *Verulame*, & Sir Jo: *Felton* with some other knights & Gent: After dinner came the *Baylifs*, & *Magistrates* in their formalitie⟨s⟩ & Maces, to Complement my Lord, & invite him to the Towne-house, where they presented us a noble Collation of dried Sweetemeates & Wine, the Bells ringing &c: Then we went to see the Towne, & first the *L: Vicount Herefords* house which stands in a Park neere the Towne, like that at *Bruxelles* in *Flanders*: The house not greate, yet pretty, especialy the Hall: & the stewes of fish succeeding one anoth⟨e⟩r & feeding one the other, all paved at bottome: There is a good Picture of the B: *Virgin* in one of the parlours, seeming to be of *Holbein*, or some good Masters. Then we saw the Haven, 7 miles from *Harwich*: There is no River, but it dies at the Towne running out every day with the tide; but the bedding being soft mudd, it is safe for ships, & a station: The Trade of *Ipswich* is for most part, *New-Castle Coales* which they supply *London* with; but was formerly Cloathing: There is not any beggar dos aske any Almes in the whole Towne; a thing very extraordinary; so ordered by the prudence of the Magistrates: It has in it 14 or 15 very beautifull Churches, in a word 'tis for building, cleanesse & good order, one of the sweetest Townes in England: *Cardinal Wolsey* was a butchers sonne of this Towne, but there is little of that magnificent Prælates foundation here besides a *Schole*, &, I think a *Library*: which I did not see; but his intentions were to build some greate thing &c: Thus we return'd late to *Euston*, having travelled above 50 miles this day:

Since first I was at this place, seated in a bottome betweene two gracefull swellings, I found things exceedingly improvd: The maine building being now made in the figure of a Greeke Π with 4 pavilions two at each corner & a breake in the front, rail'd & balustred at the top, where I caused huge jarrs of Earth to be plac'd full of Earth to keepe them steady ⟨on⟩ their ⟨Piedestalls⟩, betweene the statues, which make as good a shew, as if they were of stone; and though the building be of brick & but two stories, besides Cellars & Garrets, covered with blew Slate, yet there is roome enough for a full Court, the Offices & out-houses being so ample & well disposed: The Kings appartment is both painted a fresca, & magnificently furnish'd: There are many excellent Pictures in the roomes of the greate Masters: The Gallery is a pleasant noble roome, & in the breake or middle, a *Billiard* Table; but the Wainscot being of firr, & painted dos not please me so well as Spanish Oake without painting: The Chapell is pretty, & Porch descending to the Gardens: The Orange-Garden is very fine, & leads into the Greene-house, at the end whereoff is a sall to eate in, & the Conservatory very long (some hundred feete) adorn'd with Mapps, as the other side is with the heads of *Cæsars* ill cut in alabaster: over head are severall appartments for my Lord, Lady, & Dutchesse, with Kitchins & other offices below in a lesser volume, with lodgings for servants, all distinct, for them to retire to when they please, & that he would be in private & have no communication with the Palace, which he tells me he will wholly resigne to his Sonn in Law, & Daughter, that Wise, & charming young Creature: The *Canale* running under my Ladys dressing chamber window, is full of Carps, & fowle, which come & are fed there with greate diversion: The Cascade at end of the Canale turnes a Cornemill which finds the family, & raises water for the fountaines & offices: To passe this Chanal into the opposite Meadows, Sir *Sam: Moreland* has invented a Skrew Bridge, which being turned with a Key land⟨s⟩ you 50 foote distant, at entrance of an ascending Walke of trees for a mile in length: as tis also on the front into the Park, of 4 rows of Ashes & reaches to the Parke Pale which is 9 miles in Compas, & the best for riding & meeting the game that ever I saw, There were now of red & fallow deere almost a thousand, with good Covert, but the soile barren & flying sand in which nothing will grow kindly: The Tufts of Firr & much of the other wood were planted by my direction some yeares before: In a word, this seate is admirably placed for field sports, hauking, hunting, racing: The mutton small, but sweete: The stables are capable of 30 horses & 4 Coaches: The out offices make two large quadrangles, so as never servants liv'd with more ease & convenience, never Master more Civil; strangers are attended & accomodated as at their home in pretty apartments furnish'd with all manner of Conveniences & privacy: There are bathing roomes, Elaboratorie, Dispensatorie, what not: Decoy & places to keepe & fat foule &c: He had now in his new Church (neere the Garden) built a Dormitory or Vault with severall repositories to burie in for his family: In the expense of this pious structure, I meane the church, exceedingly laudable, most of the houses of God in this Country resembling rather stables & thatched Cottages than Temples to serve God in: He has also built a Lodge in the Park for the Keeper, which is a neate & sweete dwelling, & might become any gentleman of quality, the same has he don for the Parson, little deserving it, for his murmuring that my Lord put him for some time out of his wretched hovell, whilst it was building: he has also built a faire Inn at some distance from his Palace, a bridge of stone over a River neere it, and repaired all the Tennants houses, so as there is nothing but neatenesse, and accomodations about his estate, which yet I think is not above 1500 pounds a yeare: I believe he had now in his family 100 domestic servants. His Lady (being one of the *Bredrodes* daughters; grandchild to a natural sonn of Henry Fred: Prince of Orange) is a good natured, & obliging woman. They love fine things, & to live easily, pompously, but very hospitable; but with so vast expense as plunges my Lord into debt exceedingly; My Lord himselfe is given to no expensive vise but building & to have all things rich, polite, & Princely: he never plays, but reades much, having both the Latine, French & Spanish tongues in perfection: has traveled much, & is absolutely the best bred & Courtly person his Majestie has about him; so as the publique Ministers more frequent him than any of the rest of the nobility: Whilst he was secretary of state & prime Minister he had gotten vastly, but spent it as hastily, even before he had established a funds to maintaine his greatenesse, & now beginning to decline in favour (the Duke being no greate friend of his) he knows not how to retrench: He was the sonn of a Doctor of Laws whom I have seene, & being sent from *Westminster* Schole to *Oxon:* with intention to be a divine, and parson of *Arlington* a Village neere *Brainford*, when Master of Arts, the Rebellion falling out, he followd the Kings Army, & receiving an honorable wound in the face, grew into favour & was advanc'd from a meane fortune at his Majesties restauration, to an Earle, & knight of the Garter: L: Chamb: of the Household, & first favorite for a long time, during which the King married his Natural Sonn the Duke of Grafton, to his onely Daughter & heiresse: worthy for her beauty & vertue of the greatest Prince in Christendom: My Lord is besids all this a prudent & understanding person, in buisinesse, speakes very well: Unfortunate yet in those he has advanc'd, proving ungratefull most of them: The many obligations & civilities I have to this noble gent: exacts from me this Character, and I am sorry he is in no better Circumstances. Having now pass'd neere three weekes at Euston, to my greate Satisfaction, with much difficulty he sufferd me to looke homewards; being very earnest with me to stay longer, & to engage me, would himselfe have carried & accompanied me to *Lynn regis*, a Towne of important Trafique about 20 miles beyond, which I had never seene, as also the *Travelling Sands*, about 10 miles wide of *Euston*, that have so damaged the Country, rouling from place to place, & like the Sands in the desarts of *Lybia*, quite overwhelmed some gentlemens whole Estates, as the relation extant in print, and brought to our Society describes at large:

The 13 of *September* my Lords-Coach conveyed me to *Berry*: & thence baiting at *New Market*, stepping in at Audly end, to see that house againe, I lay at *Bishops Stratford*, & the next day home, accompanied in my Jorney with one Major *Fairfax* of a Younger house of the Lord Fairfax, a Souldier, a Traveller, an excellent Musitian, good natured, well bred gent:

16 Our *Viccar* preach'd on 5. *Matt:* 20: Curat on 4: *Eph:* 29: I preferred Mr. Philips to the service of my L. Chamb: who wanted a *scholar* to reade to & entertaine him some times: My Lord has a library at *Euston* full of excellent bookes: 18 To Lond: dind with Mrs. *Godolphin*. 20 with my *Lord Treasurer*. 23: I received the holy Comm: at St. *James's*, heard Dr. *Burnet* on 2. Titus 13: visited ⁓—pr: 24 home.

Octob: 3 To Lond: returned next day: 7: *Viccar* on his former subject, the holy Communion follow'd: *Curat* on 22: *Pro:* 6, a profitable discourse: 11. To Lond: 12 With Sir *Robert Clayton* to *Marden*, an estate he had lately bought of my *kindsman* Sir *John Evelyn* of *Godstone* in Surry: which from a despicable farme house Sir Robert had erected into a Seate with extraordinary expense: Tis seated in such a solitude among hills, as being not above 16 miles from Lond, seemes almost incredible, the ways also to it so winding & intricate: The Gardens are large & walled nobly, & the husbandry part made so convenient, & perfectly understood, as the like I had not seene: The barnes, the stacks of Corne, the Stalls for Cattell, Pidgeon house, &c of most laudable example: Innumerable are his plantations of Trees, espe⟨c⟩ialy Wallnuts, the Orangerie & Gardens very curious; large & noble roomes in the house. He & his Lady (very curious in Distilling &c) entertain'd me 3 or 4 dayes very freely: I earnestly suggested to him, the repairing of an old desolate delapidated Church, standing on the hill above the house, which I left him in good disposition to do, & endow it better, there not being above 4 or 5 inhabitants in the Parish besids this prodigious rich Scrivenor: This place is exceeding sharp in Winter, by reason of the serpenting of the hills, & wants running water, but the solitude exceedingly pleased me: all the ground is so full of wild Time, Majoram & other sweete plants, as is not to be overStock'd with Bees, so as I think he had neere 40 hives of that industrious Insect: 14. I went to Church at *Godstone*, where on 30 *Psal.* 4 the *Minister* made a good sermon: After sermon I went to see old Sir Jo: Evelyns Dormitory, joyning to the Church, pav'd with Marble, where he & his Lady lie on a very stately Monument at length, in Armor &c: white Marble: The *Inscription* (being onely an account of his particular branch of our family) is on black Marble.

15 I went back with my Lady to *Lond:* leaving Sir Robert behind: This Evening I saw the Prince of Orange, & supp'd with my Lord Ossory.

16 I dind with Mr. *Godolphin* it being Anniver &c: 17 at my L: Chamberlaines, went home in the Evening. 21 our Viccar pursues his former subje⟨c⟩t.

23 To *Lond:* dind with ☆. I saw againe the Prince of *Orange*: his Marriage with the Lady Mary (eldest Daughter to the Duke by Mrs. Hyde the late Dutchesse) was now declared. 24 dind with ☆. 25 at L: *Chamber:* returned at night:

31 Being my Birth day & 57th yeare, I blessed God for his protection &c:

November 1. Beging the favour of God for the yeare entering, I went to Church, where our *Viccar* preached on 12 *Luke* 21, the

Text of the former yeare: Then dined with the Foefees of the Poore according to Costome.

11 I received at St. *Jamess*, *Coram Rege* Dr. *Glanvill* on   Acts, *Felix trembled* &c: I was all this Weeke in composing matters betweene old Mrs. *Howard*, and Sir *Gabriel Sylvius*, upon his long & earnest addresses to Mrs. Ann, her second daughter Mayd of Honor: my friend *Mrs. Godolphin* (who exceedingly loved the young Lady) was most industrious in it, out of pitty to the languishing Knight; so as (though there were greate difference in Yeares) it was at last effected, & they married on the 13. in Hen: 7th Chapell, by the Bish: of Rochester, there being besides my wife & Mrs. Graham her sister with Mrs. *Godolphin* very few more: We din'd at the old Ladys, & supp'd at Mr. Grahame's at St. *James's*: I likewise dined there the next day, & supp'd at Sir Jos: Williamsons among severall of our Society.

15 The *Queenes* birth-day, & of my *Baptisme*; a greate Ball at *Court*, where the Prince of *Orange* & his new *Princes* daunc'd: I dind with ☆.

17 I din'd with Mr. *Godolphin* & his Wife, at which time he sealed the Deedes of settlement on his Lady, in which I was a Trustee: &c: 18. Dr. *Alestree* on 17: *Psal:* Then shall I be satisfied, when thy Glory dos appeare &c: I received the B: *Sacrament* at *St. Jamess*, dind at Sir St: *Foxes*.

19 The *Prince* & *Princesse* of *Orange* went away, and I saw embarqued my *Lady Sylvius* who went now also into *Holland* with her *Husband*, made *Hoffmaester* to the *Prince* a considerable Charge: We parted with greate sorrow, for the greate respect and honour I bore to the Lady, a most pious and virtuous creature &c: I dind with my *Lord Berkely* at his house.

20 At Mrs. *Godolphins*, then visited Mr. *Rob: Boyle*, where I met *Dr. Burnet* & severall *Scots* Gent: Mr. *Boyle* now shewing us his new Laboratorie:

27: I dind at *Lo: Tress:* with *Prince Rupert*, Vicount *Falkenberg*, Earle of *Bath*, Lo: *O Brian* &c: & went home in the Evening. 29 To *Lond:* din'd at Sir *Rob: Claytons*. 30: To the R: Society, it being our Anniversary Election day, where we chose Sir *Joseph Williamson* (now prin: Secretary of state) *President* for the next yeare, after my Lord Vicount *Brounchar* had possessed the Chaire now 16 yeares successively: & therefore now thought fit to change &c: that prescription might not prejudice &c: we had a greate Entertainment this night.

December 2: A *stranger* at *White-hall* on 2: *Cor:* 5. 15: The holy Comm: follow'd, Bish: of *Lond:* Officiating: *Coram Rege* Dr. *Ball* on 5. Eph: 20: 4: Dind with ☆, having in the morning ben with our new *President*, as one of the *Council* to administer his *Oath*, & this being the first day of his taking the chaire, he gave us a magnificent supper. 8 home:

20 To *Lond:* din'd at *Lo: Chamb:* Carried my *Lord Treasurer* an account of the *Earle* of *Bristols Librarie* at *Wimbleton*, which my Lord thought of purchasing, til I acquainted him, it was a very broken Collection, consisting much in books of Judicial Astrologie, Romances & trifles &c: Thence to our *Society*, where were experiments of the incumbency & gravitation of the Aire on ☿ for the *Barometer*. Peper wormes were first shewed us in the Microscope &c: 21 I return'd home:

23 Our *Viccar* as before. *Pomerid*: a stranger on 26: *Matt:* 26. a logical dry discourse, not at all fit for our Congregation:

I gave my *Sonn* an *Office*,[1] with Instructions how to govern his Youth, I pray God give him the Grace to make a right use of it &c: 25 our *Viccar* on 3: *Gen:* 15: The holy Sacrament follow'd: I entertain'd our neighbours this Weeke according to ⟨Custome⟩. 30: our *Viccar* as above, nothing extraordinary, nor the Curate: who preached in the afternoone on 20: Cor: 5: 10:

31 Blessed be *God* for his mercys & protection &c:

1678. *January* 1. Imploring the blessing of Almighty God for the yeare following: divers Neighbours din'd with me.

4 My Lord *Ossory* going now Into *Holland*, sent his Barge to bring me to his *Yacht*, now under saile; I went with him a good part of the way towards Gravesend, & after dinner returned with my *Lord*, it beginning to be stormie &c: 6: our *Viccar* on his former Text: The holy *Sacrament* follow'd: *Pomeridiano* a stranger on 1. *Tim:* 2: 5: 7: To *Lond:* waited on the Bish: of Lond, to give him Thankes for bestowing *St. Helens* on *Mr. Evans* upon my sole recomendation: I din'd with my Lo: *Chamb:* 8 with Mrs. *Godolphin*: return'd home next day: 11 My L: of *Ossorie* pursuing his Voyage, sent againe his barge for me &c: so having conducted him as before I return'd: 13 A stranger preach'd on 5.

1 A book of devotions.

Eph: 14. 20 Also a stranger on 4: Phil: 14: *Pomer:* Curat, as before: 21. To *Lond:* about severall affaires: Din'd 22 with Mrs. *Godolphin*, and next day with the *Duke* of *Norfolck*; being the first time I had seene him since the Death of his elder *Bro:* who died at *Padoa* in *Italy* where as being *lunatic*, he had ben kept above 30 yeares: The *Duke* had now newly declard his *Marriage* to that infamous Woman his Concubine, whom he promised me he never would marry: I went with him to see the *Duke* of *Buckingam*, thence to my Lord *Sunderlands* now *Secretary* of State, to shew him that rare piece of *Vostermans* (sonn of old *Vostermans*) which was a View or *Landscip* of my Lords Palace &c: at Althorp in *Northampton*-shire.

24 I dind at my L: *Treasurers* with the *French Ambassador* Monsieur *Barillon* & severall other Lords &c: Thence to the *R: Society*, where in absence of the President it was voted I should take the Chaire, which I did: The experiments were Microscopical, particularly the motions of certaine particles, or rather *Animalculs* in *Milk*, & another in *Bloud* upon which some excellent discourses: I Supped at one *Monsieur Obloors* a French Merchant with my Lord Obrian &c: next day home; after Prayers, it being the feast of St. *Paule*:

Feb: ⟨3⟩ Dr. *Cradock White-hall* on 4: *Joh:* 21: (Coram *Rege*) Dr. Pierce on: 4: Eph: 30: The holy Sacrament follow'd: B: of Lond Officiated:

5 Dind at ☆: 6. I had a private audience of the Duke in his Closet about my pretence to the Fee of *Sayes-Court*: Being in some dispute with my Lord *Gerhard* of *Brandon*, concerning the Corporal presence of Christ in the holy Sacrament, & that I told him, the impossibility of it, for that his body as man was after his Ascension to be & remaine in Heaven, my Lord desiring to see the Text: (we being both in the little privat chapell at White-hall) we went to the desk, & asked *Dr. Pierce* who ⟨was⟩ then officiating to shew us the words; he said, such a Text there was, but he could not readily turne to it; upon which I opning the greate Bible at adventure put my finger exactly on 3. *Acts*: 21: which did both exceedingly astonish & satisfie my Lord: 8: Supping at my Lord Chamberlaines I had a long discourse with the *Conde de Castel Melior*, lately the prime Minister in Portugal, who taking part with his Master *King Alphonso*, was banished by his Brother *Dom Pedro* now Regent; but had behav'd himselfe so

uncorruptly in all his ministrie, that though he was acquitted & his estate restored, yet would they not suffer him to returne: he is doubtlesse a very intelligent, & worthy Gentleman.

13 *Ashwednesday* to *Lond*, to begin the solemnity of Lent: *B: of Lond* preached W:hall on 13 *Luke* 3: it was the best sermon I ever heard him make: *Except ye repent, ye shall all likewise perish*.

17 I received the B: Sacrament at St. *James* in the morning, afterwards at Wh:hall, preached the B: of *Excester* for the Bish: of *Sarum* on 24. *Act:* 16, a little to critical about Words at first, the rest very well: I din'd with ☆.

18 My *Lord Treasurer* sent to me that I would accompanie him to Wimbledon which he had lately purchased of the Earle of Bristoll, so breaking fast with him privately in his Chamber (at what time he was very like to be choaked in drinking too hastily) I accompanied him, with two of his daughters, my L: Conway, & Sir *Bernard Gas⟨c⟩ogne* & having surveied his Gardens & alterations, returned late at night:

22 Dr. *Pierce* on 2. *Thessal:* 3. 6. Against our late Schismatics in a very rational discours but a little over sharp, & not at all proper for the Auditory at White-hall:

I had a private *Audience* of his *Majestie* in his *Bed-chamber* &c. went home:

23 I was at the Funerall of my kind neighbour *Cap: Tinker*, our *Viccar* preaching on 1. *Phil:* 23:

March 22 I went to *Graves-end* about a Pay & Accompt, for the quarte⟨r⟩s of men, during the late Warr, where to my extraordinary affliction, I found my Agent there had missbehaved himselfe; I returned home next day: 24. our Viccar on his former: The holy Sacrament follow'd; Now was our Comm: Table placed Altar wise, The Church Steeple, Clock & other reparations finish'd: *Curate* on 21. *Mat.* ⟨8. 9.⟩ Rhetoricaly describing our B. Saviours Triumphal entrie into *Jerusalem*, previous to his passion. 25 To Lond: 26 dind with Mrs. *Godolphin*. 27: Dr. *Alestree* on 2. *Cor.* 2. 6: 29 I received the B: Sacrament at *St. Martines* in the Morning: *Coram Rege* Dr. *South* (for the Lord *Almoner* the B: of Rochester) on   A Wounded spirit who can beare? an incomparable discourse: I supped with Mrs. *Godolphin*, & next day home:

Aprill 4 Came to dine with me Sir *Will: Godolphin*, his Bro: *Sidny*, his *Lady* (my deare friend,) and their Sisters: 7: Mr. *Bohune* on 33. *Isa*: 14: 10 To *Lond*: Dr. *Pettus* at W:hall on 14. *Rom*: 10: I received in the morning at St. *Jamess*:

16 I went to shew Dom: *Emanuel de Lyra* (Portugal Ambassador) & the *Count de Castel Mellor* the Repository of the R: Society, & Coledge of *Physitians*: 18 I went to see New *Bedlam* Hospital, magnificently built, & most sweetely placed in *Morefields*, since the dreadfull fire of *Lond*: dind with ☆: 20: Din'd at Lo: *Treasurers*. 21 Dr. *Stillingfleete* (*Deane of St. Paules*) on 6. *Gal*: 14. admirably: To the *King*: Dr. *Tillotson* (Deane of *Canterbery*) on 16 *Luke* ult: I received the holy Sacrament at St. *Martines* after the Court sermons were don: 28: Synax. at St. *James's*: Then at *W:hall* (*Coram Rege*) The Deane of St. *Paules* on 16 *Joh*: 33: I never heard him do better: 30 I dind at my Lord *Berkeleys*:

May 16 Being the Wedding *Anniversarie* of my excellent friend Mrs. *Godolphin*, *she*, with my Lady *Sylvius* & her sister *Grahame* came to visite, & dine with me; returning in the Evening, & was the last time, that blessed Creature ever came to my house, now being also greate with Child, & seldome stirring abroad:

19 Our *Viccar* on 1. *Thess*: 5. 19. *Whitsonday*: The holy *Sacrament* followd: *Pomer*: *Curate* on 16: *John*. 13 describing the coming of the H: *Ghost* historicaly onely: 23. To *Lond*: 26: At St. *Jam*: *Synax*, being *Trinity Sonday*: *Coram Rege* at *W:hall* Dr. *Hayward* on 1. 13 *Cor*: 12: I dind with ☆: 27: At L. *Chamb*: 28 At Mrs. *Godolphins* & went home. 29: *Anniversary* of his Majesties Birth &c. our *Viccar* on 8: *Pro*: 15 shewing by very learned & excellent readings, The reasons of the preference of *Monarchical* above all other formes of Government: & that from *Adam* (to whom God had given the *Empire* of all things & Persons) that it seemed to be not onely of divine, but most natural Institution: how it was at first, in the Eldest of each Family, where the first borne was King & Priest, & therefore had a double portion above his breathren to sustaine the Charge of sacrifices & the pub: worship: The weaknesse of all other Constitutions; concluding in an Exhortation to be obedient, & thankfull &c:

June 2: Our *Viccar* on 1. *Thess*: 5. 19: The Monethly *Communion* followd: *Pomer*: *Curate* on 19 *Matt*: 21. 6 Came my Lady *Hungerford*, & her Mother in Law (my wifes *Aunt*) to visite us: 9 our *Viccar* as above: *Pomer*: The exceeding raine hindred my going to church.

28 I went to *Windsor* with my *Lord Chamberlain* (the Castle now new repairing with exceeding Cost &c) to see the rare Worke of *Virrio*, & incomparable Carving of *Gibbons*: 29 returned with my Lord &c: by *Hownslow* heath where we saw the new raised *Army* encamp'd, designed against France, in pretence at least, but gave umbrage to the Parliament: his Majestie & a world of Company in the field, & the whole Army in Batallia, a very glorious sight: now were brought into service a new sort of souldier called *Granadiers*, who were dextrous to fling hand granados, every one having a pouch full, & had furr'd Capps with coped crownes like Janizaries, which made them looke very fierce, & some had long hoods hanging down behind as we picture fooles: their clothing being likewise py bald yellow & red: so we returned to Lond:

30 A stranger at W:hall: on: 10: *Luke*: 30: Thence to St. *Martins* where Dr. *Lloyd* preached on 3. *Rom:* 20.

July 1 I return'd home to *Says-Court*. 7: Our *Viccar* on 1. *Thess:* 5. 19: the holy *Comm:* followd:

8 Came to dine with me my Lord *Longford* Tressurer of *Ireland*, & nephew to that learned gent, my *L: Angier*, with whom I was long since acquainted &c: also the Lady *Stidolph* & other Company:

10 Came to take his leave of me the *Earle* of *Ossory*, going into *Holland* to Command the English forces &c:

20 I went to the *Tower* to try a Mettal at the Say-Masters, which onely proved *Sulphur*: then saw *Monsieur Rotiere* that incomparable Graver belonging to the Mint, who emulates even the Antients in both mettal & stone; he was now moulding of an Horse for the *Kings statue* to be cast in silver of a Yard high: I dined with Mr. *Slingsby* Master of the Mint. Visite⟨d⟩ *L: Brouncker*:

23 Return'd, having ben to see Mr. *Elias Ashmoles* Library & Curiosities at *Lambeth*, he has divers *MSS*, but most of them *Astrological*, to which study he is addicted, though I believe not learned; but very Industrious, as his history of the Order of the Gartir shews, he shewed me a Toade included in Amber: The prospect from a Turret is very fine, it being so neere Lond: & yet not discovering any house about the Country. The famous *John Tradescant*, bequeath'd his Repositary to this Gent: who has given them to the University of Oxford, & erected a Lecture on

them &c: over the Laboratorie, in imitation of the *R: Society*: My deare friend *Mrs. Godolphin* & my Wife were with us: I think it was the last of her going abroad:

25 I went to *Lond:* to the wedding of my Bro: in Law Glandvills Niepce, married to *Cap: Fowler* &c: Thence to R: *Society*: supp'd with Mrs. *Godolphin* whose husband was now made Master of the Robes to the *King*.

There was now sent me 70 pounds from some ⟨one⟩ whom I knew not to be by me distributed among poore people at my discretion; I came afterwards to find it was from that heavenly creature my deare friend: who had frequently given me large Summs to bestow on Charities &c:

August 2 To *Lond:* 4: Dr. *Offley* at *W:hall*, on 7: *Joh:* 37, an honest pious, discourse: *Coram Rege*, a young Chaplain on 22. *Psal:* 6. I din'd with Mrs. *Godolphin* & La: *Mordaunt*:

16 I went to my La: *Mordaunts*, who put 100 pounds into my hands, to dispose ⟨of⟩ for pious uses, reliefe of Prisoners &c: poore &c: & many a summ had she sent me on the same occasion; for a blessed Creature she was, one that feared & loved God exemplarily: ⟨18⟩ *Synax* St. Jamess: home: &c a stranger: 3 *Jude*:

23 Upon Sir *Rob: Readings* importunity, I went to Visite the *Duke of Norfolck* at his new Palace by *Way bridge*; where he has laied out in building neere 10000 pounds, on a Copyhold, & in a miserable barren sandy place by the streete side, never in my daies had I seene such expense to so small purpose: The roomes are Wainscoted, & some of them richly parquetted with *Cedar, Yew,* Cypresse &c. There are some good Pictures, especialy, that ⟨incomparable⟩ painting of *Holbens* where The Duke of Norfolck, Charles Brandon, & Hen: the 8: are dauncing with the three Ladys, such amorous countenances, & spritefull motion did I never see expressed: 'Tis a thousand pitties (as I told my Lord of Arundel his sonn) that Jewell should be given away to the present broode, & not be fixed to the incontaminate issue:

24 I went to see my L: ⟨St. *Albans's*⟩ house at *Byfleete*, an old large building; and thence to the *Paper-mills*, where I found them making a Course white paper: First they cull the raggs (which are linnen for White paper, Wollen for browne) then they stamp them in troughs to a papp, with pestles or

hammers like the powder mills: Then put it in a Vessel of Water, in which they dip a frame closely wyred, with wyer as small as an haire, & as cloose as a Weavers reede: upon this take up the papp, the superfluous water draining from it thro the wyres: This they dextrously turning shake out like a thin *pan-cake* on a smoth board, betweene two pieces of flannell; Then presse it, betweene a greate presse, the ⟨flannel⟩ sucking out the moisture, then taking it out ply & dry it on strings, as they dry linnen in the Laundry, then dip it in allume water, lastly polish, & make it up in quires: &c: note that the⟨y⟩ put some gumm in the water, in which they macerate the raggs into a pap: note that the marks we find in the sheetes is formed in the wyres.

25 The *Minister* preached on 19. *Gen:* 26: After Evening prayer Visited *Mr. Sheldon* (Nephew to the late *Archbish:* of *Cant:* where I found the Bish: of *Rochester*) and his pretty melancholy Garden, I tooke notice of the largest *Arbor Thuyæ* I had ever seene: The place is finely water'd, & there are many curiosities of India which we were shew'd in the house: There was at *Way-bridge* the Dutchesse of *Norfolck*, My *Lord Thomas* Howard (a worthy & virtuous gent, with whom my sonn, was sometime bred up in Arundel house) who was newly come from *Rome* where he had ben some time; also one of the Dukes Daughters by his first Lady: My Lord leading me about the house, made no scruple of shewing me all the *Latebræ* & hiding places for the popish Priests, & where they said Masse, for he was no bigoted *Papist*: He told me he never trusted them with any seacret; & used *Protestants* onely in all buisinesses of importance: I went with my *L. Duke* this evening to *Windsore*, where was a magnificent Court, it being the first time of his Majesties removing thither, since it was repaired: 26: I din'd with Mr. *Secretary Coventrie*, & then returned with the Duke of *Norfolck*. 27: I tooke leave of him, & dined at Mr. *Hen: Brounchers* at the Abby of Sheene formerly a *Monastery* of *Carthusians*, there yet remaining one of their solitary Cells with a Crosse: within this ample inclosure are severall pretty Villas, and fine Gardens of the most excellent fruites, Especialy Sir William *Temples*, lately Ambassador into Holland, & the *Lord LIles* sonn to the Earle of Licester, who has divers rare Pictures, above ⟨all⟩ that of Sir *Brian Tukes* of *Holbein*: After dinner I walked to *Ham*, to see the House & -

Garden of the *Duke* of *Laderdaile*, which is indeede inferiour to few of the best Villas in Italy itselfe, The House furnishd like a greate Princes; The Parterrs, flo: Gardens, Orangeries, Groves, Avenues, Courts, Statues, Perspectives, fountaines, Aviaries, and all this at the banks of the sweetest river in the World, must needes be surprizing &c: Thence I went ⟨to⟩ my worthy friends Sir *Hen: Capels* (bro: to the Earle of *Essex*) it is an old timber house, but his Garden has certainely the Choicest fruite of any plantation in England, as he is the most industrious, & understanding in it: from hence To Lond: & [28] next day to Says-Court; after a most pleasant & divertisant Excursion, the weather bright & temperate:

29 I was cald againe to *London* to waite againe on the *Duke of Norfolck* who having at my request onely, bestow'd the *Aru⟨n⟩-delian Library* on the *Royal Society*, sent to me to take charge of the Bookes & remove them; onely that I would suffer the *Heraulds* Chiefe Officer Sir W: *Dugdale* to have such of them as concernd Herauldry & Martials Office As bokes of Armorie & Geneologies; the *Duke* being Earle *Marishal* of England: I procured for our Society besides Printed bookes, neere 700 MSS: some in Greeke of greate concernement; The Printed books being of the oldest Impressions, are not the lesse valuable; I esteeme them almost equal with MSS: Most of the Fathers printed at *Basil* &c: before the *Jesuites*, abused them with their Expurgatorie *Indexes*: There is a noble MSS: of *Vitruvius*: Many of these Bookes had ben presented by Popes, Cardinals & greate Persons to the Earles of Arundell & Dukes of Norfolck; & the late magnificent Tho: E: of *Arundel* bought a noble Library in Germanie, which is in this Collection; nor should I for the honour I beare the family, have perswaded the Duke to part with these, had I not seene how negligent he was of them, in suffering the Priests, & every body to carry away & dispose of what they pleased: so as aboundance of rare things are gon, & irrecoverable:

Having taken Order here, I went to the *R: Society*, to give them an *account* of what I had procured, that they might call a Council, & appoint a day to waite on the *Duke* to thank him for this munificent gift:

There were this afternoone also severall Experiments shewn, and divers learned & curious discourses: as first, Concerning a Woman that in *Lions* had ben 24 yeares with Child, which had

ben dead 7 yeares before the Mother, who lived to 60: Also that
this Child was found out of the Womb: Also of another Conceiv'd out of the Womb, lying in the hollow of the body, during
which the Mother conceiv'd & brought forth another Child; the
first coming forth by piecemeale, bones, & putrid flesh, through
severall ulcers in severall parts below: This was in *England*: An
other (abroad) who went divers yeares with an *Embrio* in her
body, at last brought forth, a Child whose head and limbs were
halfe *petrified*: Divers learned *Physitians* now present held, that
these *extra-Utrine* Conceptions happn'd through the Eggs passing out of the *Ovarium* or *Fallopian Tubes*, by some occult *meatus*,
besides that into the womb: There being a discourse of *Iseland*; It
was affirm'd, that the bodys of men when dead, are piled up for
severall monethes without corruption, frozen as hard as marble;
till the Thaws come, & then buried: the ground being 'til then
too hard to dig: The same is sayd of *Muscovy*, & that they commonly remaine so expos'd til about mid-*May*: Dr. *Croone*
affirmed that *Freezing* is not by any ⟨gradual⟩ conjelation of the
Water, but an instantaneous action or operation, so as listning
attentively, one may heare a kind of obscure sharp frizling noise
when it shoots the Icy skin or first *Epidermis* which is swift as
thought: This he tried by a glasse of Water. Also ⟨that⟩ all water
shoots into the shape of branches infinitely multiplied at right
angles, & resembling the veines in the Leafe of a Vegetable: That
Snow by accression did grow when falling, & shot like a tree, at
right angles also, besides the Stellifying of every individual atome
of it ✳. It was by some there also assured us, that the *Greeneland*
Whale when struck hastens to the shore, a Vast fish in Thicknesse with a huge head & jawes: That the *Bermudas* is longer &
more slender, with a sharp snout, & he being smitten contrarie to
the other, hastens out to sea, for they find them at a certaine season, among the rocks neerer the Iland; & being gotten out no
rope is long enough to fasten to their harping Irons; so as it was
so difficult to kill them, that the trade (which is very Considerable) had certainly failed there, had not an halfe drunken fellow,
after he had flung his speare & wounded a Whale, desperately
hoped out of his boate upon the fishes back, where he so hacked
him, as killed him before he could get to sea; & this is now familiarly practised by those of the Bermudas ever since. This story
was affirmed me for a certaine truth by Sir *Rob: Clayton* who has

one of the most considerable Plantations in that fertil Iland: I returned home this evening:

September 1. Our *Viccar* preached on 4: *Heb:* 1: The blessed Sacrament follow'd: *Pomerid*: *Curate* on 5 *Hosea*: 15.

3 I went to *Lond:* to dine at Mrs. *Godolphins* according to my custome every Tuesday, and found her in Labour; & staye'd 'til they brought me word the infant was borne, a lovely boy, the Mother exceeding well laied to all appearance, Mr. G: (the *Father*) being at *Windsore* with the Court: 5 It was christned, The *Susceptors* being Sir Will: *Godolphin* (head of the family) Mr. Jo: Hervey Tresurer to the Queene, & Mrs. *Boscawen* (sister to Sir William & the Father); and named after the Gra⟨n⟩dfathers name *Francis*: *It was baptiz'd* in the Chamber where it was borne, in the mothers presence, at *White-hall*, by the Chaplaine who used to officiate in her pretty family; so I returned this evening home with my Wife, who was also come up to see her & congratulate. 8: our Curate (in absence of the *Viccar*) preaching on his former Text, whilst I was at Church this morning, came a Letter from Mr. *Godolphin* (who had ben sent for from *Winsore* the night before) to give me notice that my deare friend, his Lady, was exceedingly ill, & desiring my Prayers & assistance, his affliction being so extreme: so my Wife and I tooke boate immediately, & went to *White-hall*, where to mine unexpressable sorrow I found she had ben atacqu'd with the new feavor then reigning, this excessive hot *Autumne*, which being of a most malignant nature, & prevailing on her now weakned & tender body, eluded all the skill & help of the most eminent Physitians; and ⟨surprizing⟩ her head, so as she fell into *deliriums*, & that so vilontly & frequent, that unlesse some (almost mira⟨c⟩ulous) remedy were applied, it was impossible she should hold out; nor did the *Doctors* dare prescribe such remedies as might have ben proper in other cases, by reason of her condition, then so lately brought to bed; so as the *paroxysmes* increasing to greater height, it was now despair'd that she should last many houres, nor did she continue many minutes, without repeated fitts, with much paine & agonie, which carried her off [9] the next day, being moneday, betweene the houres of one & two in the afternoone, in the 26t yeare of her Age: to the unexpressable affliction of her deare Husband, & all her Relations; but of none in this world, more than my selfe, who lost the most excellent, & most estimable Friend, that ever liv'd: I cannot but say, my very

Soule was united to hers, & that this stroake did pierce me to the
utmost depth: for never was there a more virtuous, & inviolable
friendship, never a more religious, discreete, & admirable creature; beloved of all, admir'd of all, for all the possible perfections of
her sex: But she is gon, to receave the reward of her signal Charity,
& all other her Christian graces, too blessed a Creature to converse with mortals, fitted (as she was) by a most holy Life, to be
receiv'd into the mansions above: But it is not here, that I pretend
to give her *Character*, who have design'd, to consecrate her worthy
life to posterity: I must yet say, she was for witt, beauty, good-
nature, fidelitie, discretion and all accomplishments, the most
choice & agreable person, that ever I was acquainted with: & a
losse to be more sensibly deplord by me, as she had more particularly honord me with a friendship of the most religious bands, &
such, as she has often protested she would even die for with
cherefullnesse: The small services I was able to do her in some of
her secular concernes, was immensly recompenc'd with her
acceptance onely; but how! ah how! shall I ever repay my obligations to her for the infinite good offices she did my soule, by so
o'ft ingaging me to make religion the termes & tie of the friendship which was betweene us: She was certainly the best *Wife*, the
best *Mother*, the best *Mistris*, the best *friend* that ever *Husband*,
Child, *Servant*, *friend* [or] that ever any creature had, nor am I able
to enumerate her vertues: Her *husband* fell downe flat like a dead
man, struck with unspeakeable affliction, all her Relations partooke of the losse; The King himselfe & all the Court express'd
their sorrow, & to the poore and most miserable it was irreparable;
for there was no degree, but had some obligation to her memorie:
So virtuous & sweete a life she lead, that in all her fitts, (even
those which tooke away her discernement); she never was heard
to utter any syllable unbecoming a Christian, or uninnocent,
which is extraordinary in *delirious* persons: So carefull, & provident she was to prepare for all possible accidents, that (as if she
fore-saw her end), she received the heavenly *Viaticum* but the
Sunday before, after a most solemn recollection; & putting all her
domestic Concerns in the exactest order, left a Letter directed to
her Husband (to be opened in case she died in Child-bed) in
which, with the most pathetic and indearing expressions of a most
loyal & virtuous wife, she begs his kindnesse to her Memorie,
might be continu'd; by his care and esteeme of those she left

behind, even to her very domestic servants, to the meanest of
which she left considerable Legac⟨i⟩es, desiring she might be
buried in the Dormitorie of his family neere 300 miles from all
her other friends; And as she made use of me to convey innumerable & greate Charities all her lifetime, so I paied 100 pounds to
her chiefe woman, 100 to a kindswoman in declining circumstances: To her sister⟨?s⟩ the value of 1000 pounds: In *diamond*
rings to other of her friends, 500 pounds: & to severall poore
people, widows, fatherlesse, Prisoners & indigents, *pensions* to
continue: ô the passionate, humble, mealting disposition of this
blessed Friend; how am I afflicted for thee! my heavenly friend; It
was now seaven yeares since she was maid of *Honor* to the *Queene*
that she reguarded me as a *Father*, a *Brother*, & (what is more) a
Friend: we often prayed, visited the sick & miserable, received,
read, discoursed & communicated in all holy Offices together
without reproch: She was most deare to my *Wife*, affectionate to
my *Children*, intrested in my Concernes, in a word, we were but
one Soule, as aboundance of her professions & letters in my hands
testifie: But she is gon, & the absence so afflicting to me, as I shall
carry the sense of it to the last: This onely is my Comfort, that she
is happy, & I hope in Christ, I shall shortly behold her againe in
the boosome of our deare Saviour, where she is in blisse, &
whence we shall never part:

   The excessive affliction of this losse did so exceedingly affect
her husband, and other neere Relations, that knowing in what
profession of a most signal Friendship, she ever own'd me; The
Fees to the *Physitians*, The intire Care of her funeral, was wholy
comitted to me; so as having closed the Eyes, & drop'd a teare
upon the Cheeke of my blessed Saint, Lovely in death, & like an
Angel; I caused her Corps to be embaulmed, & wrap'd in Lead,
with a plate of Brasse sothered on it, with an *Inscription* & other
Circumstanc⟨e⟩s due to her worth, with as much dilligence &
care as my grieved heart would permitt me; being so full of sorrow, & tir'd with it, that retiring home for two daies, I spent it in
solitude, & sad reflections:

   15 our *Viccar* preach'd on 4: *Heb:* 1: *Pomerid*: *Curate* 11. *Eccles:* 1:
   16 I went to *Lond:* in order to the funeral of my deare Friend:
so as on the 17th in an *herse* with 6 horses, & two other *Coaches* of
as many, & with about 30 people of her relations & servants, we as
privately, & without the least pomp (as expressly required by her)

proceeded towards the place, where she would be buried: There accompanied her *hearse* her husbands Bro: Sir Will. & two more of his Bro: & 3 Sisters: Mr. G: her husband, so surcharg'd with griefe, that he was wholy unfitt to Travell so long a journey 'til he should be more composed, & for this reason, after I had waited on the companie as far as *Hounslow* heath, with a sad heart, I was oblig'd to returne, upon some indispensable affaires: The Corps was ordred to be taken out of the *hearse* & decently placed in the house, with tapers about it, & her servants attending, every night during all the way to the foote of Cornewell, neere 300 miles, & then as honorably interred in the Parish Church of *Godolphin*. This funerall, as private as it was, costing her deare husband not much lesse than 1000 pounds; and ô that ten thousand more might have redeemed her life! Returning back, I caled in to visite & Condole with my *Lady Berkeley*, my *Lord*, being also newly dead, which repeated sorrowes:

18 I spent most of the afternoone with disconsolate Mr. *Godolphin*, in looking over & sorting his Ladys Papers, most of which consisted of Prayers, meditations, Sermon-notes, Discourses & Collections on severall religious subjects, & many of her owne happy Composing, & so pertinently digested, as if she had ben all her life a student in *Divinity*: There we found a Diarie of her solemn resolutions, all of them tending to Institution of life, & practical virtue; with some letters from select friends &c all of them put into exact method; so as it even astonish⟨ed⟩ us to consider what she had read, & written, her youth considered, few *Divines* having taken halfe that paines, or to better purpose; for what she read, or writt, she liv'd, full of Charity, and Good works which she did. 19 I return'd home to my house:

TITUS OATES AND THE POPISH PLOT
(1678–1680)

22: OUR VICCAR & Curate, on their former Texts: My Family being also this crazy season, much discomposed with sicknesse.

23 I went to waite on my L: *Arch Bish*. of *Canterbery* Dr. *Sancroft* late *Deane* of *Paules*, who was exceedingly civil to me, There

din'd with us the *Bishops* of *Lond:* & *Rochester*: I went back: 26: To *Bromely* to Visite the *Bishop* of *Rochester*, but found him not at home:

Octob: 1 I went with my *Wife* to *Lond:* The Parliament being now alarm'd with the whole Nation, about a conspiracy of some Eminent Papists, for the destruction of the King, & introducing Popery; discovered by one *Oates* and Dr. *Tongue*, which last, I knew, being the Translator of the *Jesuites Morals*: I went to see & converse with him, now being at *White-hall*, with Mr. *Oates*, one that was lately an *Apostate* to the Church of Rome, & now return'd againe with this discovery: he seem'd to be a bold man, & in my thoughts furiously indiscreete; but everybody believed what he said; & it quite chang'd the genius & motions of the Parliament, growing now corrupt & intrested with long sitting, & Court practises; but with all this Poperie would not go downe: This discovery turn'd them all as one man against it, & nothing was don but in order to finding out the depth of this &c: *Oates* was encourag'd, & every thing he affirm'd ⟨taken⟩ for Gospel: The truth is, The *Roman* Chath: were Exceeding bold, & busy every where, since the D: forbore to go any longer to the Chapell &c: 2: I went to *Parsons Greene* to visite my *Lady Mordaunt*, & condole with her for my Deare Mrs. G: 4: I returned home:

⟨6⟩ Our *Viccar* on his former Text: The blessed Communion follow'd: *Curate* as before:

13 our *Viccar* proceedes: & *Curate* on 14. *Luke*: 16: ad: 20: 17: I went to Lond: to make up *Accompts* with Mr. *Godolphin*, as on the 16, I was constantly wont to do with his Lady, when she lived: He then requested me to continue the trust she reposed in me, in behalfe of his little sonne, & would by no meanes alter anything; conjuring me to transferr the kindnesse & friendship I had for his deare wife, on him & his:

20 Dr. Ball preached (*Coram Rege*) on   *Seacret things belong to God, things revealed to us & our Children*: I din'd with Sir *Gab: Sylvius* & his *Lady* at St. *James's*.

21 The barbarous murder of Sir *Edmund Bery-Godfry*, found strangled about this time, as was manifest by the Papists, (he being a Justice of the Peace, and one who knew much of their practises, as conversant with *Coleman*, a Servant of the . . . now accus'd) put the whole nation in a new fermentation against

them:—I din'd with my *Lady Tuke*. 22 At the Countesse of *Sunderlands*. 23 Supp'd at my L: *Chamberlaines*. 24: Din'd at Mrs. *Boscawens*. 25 went home:

27 Our *Viccar* as above. 31. Being the 58th of my age, requir'd my humble addresses to Almighty God, & that he would take off his heavy hand still on my family, and restore comforts to us, after the losse of my Excellent friend: I also now review'd & new made my Will:

November 1 Imploring Gods mercy for the Yeare entering, I went to Church, where our *Viccar* proceeded on his former yeares *Anniversa⟨r⟩y* Text, concerning works of Charity: I din'd with the foefees: 3: *Vicc:* on 1, *Pet:* 5. 7: The holy *Sacrament* follow'd: *Pomerid*: Sir Tho: *Clutterbooks* Chaplaine made a pious & eloquent discourse on: 1. *Tim:* 2: 8:

4 To *Lond:* 5. Dr. *Tillotson* before the house of *Commons* at St. *Margarits*: 'Tis since Printed: 'Twas now he sayed, the *Papists* were ariv'd to that impudence, as to deny there was ever any such thing as the Gun-powder Conspiresy: To this he affirm'd, he had himselfe severall letters written by Sir *Everard Digby* (one of the *Traytors*) in which he glories that he was to suffer for it; & that it was so contriv'd, that of the *Papists*, not above 2 or 3 should have ben blown-up, & they such, as were not worth the saving:

10 I went to St. *Jamess* in the morning *Synax: Cor: Rege* at *W:hall* Dr. *Butler* on 5. *Gal:* 1, shewing by way of Paralell, the Case of the *Protestants*, wavering betweene us & the *Papists*: he spake very home to his *Majestie*, exhorting to stedfastnesse in the Faith, & Liberty, in which Christ had made us free in this Land especialy, reckning up the heavy Yoake of *Popish* bondage &c.

13 Was an Universal Fast; That God would avert his Judgements, & bring to naught the Conspirators against the K: & Government: In the morning preach'd to The *Lords*, the A: *Bishop* of Cant: in the *Abby* on 57: *Psal:* 1. shewing how safe the Church & People of God were in the midst of the most iminent dangers, under the wings of the Almighty: This was also Printed.

15 The *Queenes* birthday &c: I never saw the Court more brave, nor the nation in more apprehension, & Consternation &c: It was also my *Baptismal Anniversary*:

17 Dr. *LLoyd* at *Whitehall* on 10: Heb: 24. *Cor: Rege*: Dr. *Allestry* on   *Luke*   shewing how much wiser the Children of this world were, as to the end they pursued, than the Children of Light &c: 18 I returned home: 23 To *Lond:* 24: Dr. *Allestry W:hall*, on 26 Isa: 20: Elegantly shewing, the greate benefit, & privileges of Private Prayer: Retirement, & Meditation. *Coram Rege* the Deane of Bangor Dr. *Lloyd*: on 2: *Act:* 46.

Now had *Coleman* ben try'd, & one *Staly*, both Condemn'd & Executed: *Oates* on this grew so presumptuous as to accuse the *Queene* for intending to Poyson the *King*; which certainly that pious & vertuous Lady abhorred the thought off, & *Oates* his Circumstances, made it utterly unlikely in my opinion: 'Tis likely he thought to gratifie some, who would have ben glad his Majestie should have married a more fruitfull Lady: but the King was too kind an husband to let any of these make impression on him. However, Divers of the Popish Peres sent to the *Toure*, as accused by Oates, all the Ro: Cath: Lords were by a new Act, for ever Excluded the Parliament: which was a mighty blow: The *Kings*, *Queenes* & *Dukes* servants banished, & a *Test* to be taken by every body, who pretended to enjoy any Office of publique Trust, or not be suspected of Popery: This was so Worded That severall good Protestants scrupuled; & I went with Sir W: *Godolphin* (a Member of the Commons house) to *Bish:* of *Ely* (Dr. *Pet: Gunning*) to be resolved, whether *Masse* were *Idolatry*, as the *Test* expressed it: for Sir *William* (though a most *learned Gent:* & excellent *Divine* himselfe) made some doubt of it: but the *Bishops* opinion was he might take it, & that the *Papists* could not excuse themselves from Idolatry; though he wished it had ben otherwise worded in the Test:

30 Dining at *Gressham* Coll. (being the *Anniversary* for Elections at the R: Society) I returned home:

December 1 Dr. *Patric* at Whitehall preached to the family on   *God forbid that I should glory save-in the Crosse* &c which according to his manner he handled most profitably: *Coram Rege* Dr. *Owtram* on 6 *Matt:* 11, that by the tenor of our lives & dispositions, our *Love* to God might easily be known: 5 I din'd at my L: *Chamb:* & returned to my house.

8 I tooke *Physick* being indisposed, & stirr'd not out all this weeke:

15 Preach'd Mr. *Saunders* on 5. Eccles: Shewing the reverence
due to the house of God: a seasonable discourse there being some
in our Congregation not so reverent at prayers, as they should be.

16 To *Lond:* the nation exceedingly disturb'd at the publique
commotions: for now was also the Lo: Treasurer *Danby* impeach'd
&c: 21 I return'd:

29 Being very ill of Gripings I was faine to keepe my bed:
Divers of my Neighbours invited &c: according to Costome: 31
I gave God thanks for his goodnesse to me the yeare past, &
begg'd that I might make a sanctified use of those Afflictions I
had pass'd thro for the losse of a deare friend.

1679. *Jan:* 1 I implord Gods blessing for the Yeare now entred:
5. our *Viccar* as before: The holy Comm: followed: *Pomerid*: *Curate*
on 21 *Luke* 27: 28: 12: *Viccar* on his former; When so strange a
Clowd of darknesse came over, & especialy, the Citty of *London*,
that they were faine to give-over the publique service for some
time, being about 11 in the forenoone, which affrited many, who
consider'd not the cause, (it being a greate Snow, & very sharp
weather,) which was an huge cloud of *Snow*, supposed to be
frozen together, & descending lower than ordinary, the Eastern
wind, driving it forwards:

13 I went to *Lond*: on foote: 14 Din'd with Mr. *Godolphin* now
newly return'd from the funeral of his deare Wife, which he follow'd after some daies of its setting forth from *London*, he being
then not able to ⟨have⟩ accompanied ⟨it⟩ on the way, for very griefe:

15. I went with my ⟨Lady⟩ *Sunderland* to *Chelsey* & din'd with
the *Countesse* of *Bristol*, in the greate house formerly Duke of
Buckinghams, a spacious & excellent place for the Extent of
Ground & situation, in a most sweete aire; The house large, but ill
contriv'd, though my L: of *Bristol*, who purchased it after he sold
Wimbledon to my Lord *Tressurer*, expended much mony on it:
There were divers pictures of *Titian* & *V:Dyke* and some of *Bassano* very excellent: Especialy an *Adonis & Venus*, a *Duke* of Venice,
a Butcher in his Shambles, selling Meate to a Swisse: &c: and of
V: Dykes My Lord of *Bristols* picture with the Earle of *Bedfords* at
length in the same table. There was in the Garden a rare collection of *Orange trees*, of which she was pleased to bestow some
upon me: 16 To the R: *Society*, Mr. *Sec: Williamson* president, the
Exper: of the *Lamp*, describ'd in Mr. *Hooks Lampas*; a letter from
Germany read, of a *Menstrue* to preserve dead bodys: I supp'd this

night with Mr. *Secretary* at one Monsieur *Houblons* a french Merchant, who had his house furnish'd *en Prince* & gave us a splendid entertainement. 17: I din'd at Lo: *Chamb:* & went home:

25 Was the Long *Parliament* (which now had sate ever-since his Majesties restauration) disolv'd by perswasion of the *L: Tressurer*: though divers of them were believed to be his Pensioners; at which all the polititians were at a stand: they being very eager in pursuite of the late plot of the *Papists*: 26 Our *Viccar* as before, *Curat* as before: 29 To *Lond:* 30. *Cor: Rege* his late *Majesties Anniversary*, Dr. *Cudworth* on 2. *Tim:* 3. 5. reckoning up the perils of the last times, in which amongst other wickednesse *Treasons* should be one of the greatest, applying it to the occasion, as committed under a forme of Reformation & Godlinesse; concluding that the prophecy did intend more particularly the present age, as one of the last times, the sinns there innumerated more aboundantly reigning than ever &c:

Feb: *White-hall, Candlemas day* Dr. *Durell* D: of Winsore preach'd to the household on: 1: Cor: 16. 22: The Doctor read the whole sermon out of his notes, which I had never seene *Frenchman* (he being of *Jersey*, & altogether bred at Paris &c) do before. The holy *Communion* follow'd. *Coram Rege* Dr. *Pierce* D: of *Salisbury* on 1. *John*: 4: 1. *Try the Spirite*—there being so many delusorie ones gon forth of late into the world, he inveied against the pernicious doctrines of Mr. *Hobbs*:

11 To *Lond:* 16 W:hall a *stranger* on 5. *Eph:* 6: *Coram Rege* Dr. *Pierce*, 12: *Luke*: 4. 5: 23: Dr. *Cradock Coram Rege*: 3. *Matt:* 8: I received the holy *Sacrament* in the Morning at St. *Jamess*: ⟨25?⟩ Went home: My *Bro: Evelyn* of *Wotton* was now chosen knight for the County of *Surrey*, carying it against my Lord *Longford* and Sir *Adame Browne* of *Bechworth* Castle; The Country coming-in to give their suffrages for my bro: were so many, that I believe they eate & dranke him out neere 2000 pounds by a most abominable costome:

Aprill 16 *White hall*, Dr. *Sprat* 7: *Matt* 21: That all Religion consisted in practical obedience, not in verbal profession, eloquently & excellently: after which the Bishop of *Lond:* Confirm'd many Children & others, & amongst them my *Daughter Mary*, now about 14 yeares old:

18 Dr. *LLoyd* at St. *Martines* on 1. *Cor:* 5 & 7: The holy *Sacrament* followed: & went home in the evening, having heard the

B: of *Bath & Wells* on 19 *John*: 30 *Coram Rege* upon our B: Saviours last Words, It is *finishd*:

20 *Easter-day* our Viccar exceeding well on the same Text as Dr. *LLoyd*: The holy Communion followd; at which I & my Daughter *Received* for the first time: The holy *Jesus* continue his grace to her, & improve this beginning:

Afternoone the *Curate* on 1. *Cor:* 15. 19. &c: very indiferently, as he used to do:

27 His Royal highnesse the *Duke*, *Voted* against by the *Commons* for his Recusancy, went over into *Flanders*, which made much discourse among the Politicians: &c:

May ⟨18⟩ To Lond: at St. *Jamess Synax*, at St. Martines a stranger on 24. *Matt.* 21: I din'd at my *Bro: Pomerid*: the *Bish:* of *Rochester* in *Covent Garden* on 16 *Matt:* 3 signes of the weather discern'd by the Clowds, and not the signes of the Times? applying it to the Nation &c:

16 I went to chelsey, & din'd with the *Countesse* of *Bristoll*. 25 Dr. *Onely* at *White-hall* on: 2: *Cor:* 5. 20: Then went with my Lord the Earle of *Ossory* to the *French church*, where one preached on 16 *John*: 7. 8: I din'd with my *Bro:* & heard the B: of *Exon* at *Co: Garden* on 19 John: 41. 42. on Christs Weeping over the Citty *Jerusalem*, comparing our time of Visitation, with a pathetical discourse: &c:

29 *Ascension* & his Majesties *Birth-day*, Dr. *Pettus* at St. *Mart:* on 2 *Sam:* 14.19, of Obedience to Princes &c: 31 Dining at L: Chamberlains I returned home:

June: 1. Our *Viccar* on 2: *Tim:* 3. 16: The ho: Sacrament followed. *Curate* on 42: *Gen:* 21:

4. To *Lond:* Din'd with Mr. *Pepys* at the *Tower*, whither he was committed by the house of Commons, for misdemeanors in the *Admiralty*, where he was Secretary; but I believe unjustly: Here I saluted my *Lord Stafford* & *Peters* who were also committed for the *Popish* Plot: 7: I saw the magnificent Cavalcade and Entery of the Portugal Ambassador: din'd at L: Chamberlaines: 7: *went home*.

14 To *Lond:* 15 Being *Trinity-Sonday* at St. *Martins* Dr. *LLoyd*, on 2: *Cor:* 13. 14. All the Persons of the holy Trinity being mentiond in that Text, he made an excelent sermon, with divers arguments against the *Socinians*: the holy Communion followed.

17 I was *Godfather* to a *Sonn* of Sir *Chr: Wren* Surveyor of his Majesties building⟨s⟩, that most learned & excellent person; with Sir William *Fermor* & my Lady *Vicountesse Newport* wife of the Treasurer of the household: Thence to Chelsey with Sir *Step: Fox* and my *Lady*, in order to his purchas of the Co: of Bristols house ther, which she desired me to procure a Chapman for: 19 I din'd at Sir *R: Claytons* & Sir *Rob: Viner* (the greate *Banquers*): thence to our *Society*, where was read Dr. *Grews* discours on the *Salts* of severall *Waters* about the Citty, Extracted, and produc'd before us, & examin'd: Then our *Curator* M: *Hooke* shew'd us his *Weather Clock* describing the winds, Weather & severall other curious motions, by night and day: &c: 21 I return'd hom⟨e⟩ in my New Coach: 22: Our *Viccar* as before: The *Curate* on 16: Psal: 12: There were now divers *Jesuites* executed about the Plot; & a Rebellion in *Scotland* of the Phanatics there; so as there was a sad prospect of publique affaires: ⟨24⟩ To *Lond:* returned next day to meete the new Commissioners of the Admiralty, who came to Visite me, viz: Sir *Hen: Capel* bro: to the Earle of *Essex*, Mr. *Finch* eldest sonn to the L: Chancelor, Sir Humphry *Winch*, Sir Tho: *Meeres*; Mr. *Hales*; with some of the Commissioners of the *Navy*. I went with them to *Lond:* 29: *Whitehall* a young Chaplaine on 6: *Matt:* 18. 19 St. *Peters* day, concerning his Supremacy, confuted very well by the ordinary arguments: After this his Majestie Offered: I din'd at the Master of the Mints. 30 Went to take leave of my L: *Chamberlaine*, now removing with the Court to *Winsore*:

July 1 I din'd at Sir *William Godolphins*, & with that most learned Gent: to take the aire in *Hyde-park*; where was a glorious *Cortege*: 3. Sending a piece of *Venison* to Mr. *Pepys* Sec: of the Admiralty, still a *Prisoner*, I went & dined with him; Thence to the *R: Society*, where was both a discourse, & experiment of innumerable wormes or Insects in the *Sperme* of an *horse* by the *Microscope*: And also of a Liquor, in which flesh, or fish being boiled, the bones were rendred as soft as marrow, yet neither over boiled, or ill relished, all by the Contrivance of a Digestorie, with very inconsiderable expense as to fire: This by Dr. *Papin* of our *Society*: I went home in the Evening. 5: Sir *Denis* Gauden & his sonn dined with me:

6: our *Viccar* as before; The holy *Comm:* follow'd: *Pomerid.* a Fellow of *Trinity* Coll: *Camtab:* on 15 *John*: 4. 5. Now were there Papers, Speeches, Libels, publiquely cried in the streetes against the *Duke* of *York*, & Lauderdail &c obnoxious to the Parliament, with too much, & indeede too shamefull a liberty; but the People & Parliament had gotten head, by reason of the vices of the greate ones:

There was now brought up to *Lond.* a Child (sonn of one Mr. *Wotton* formerly *Amanuensis* to Dr. *Andrews* Bish: of Winton) who both read & perfectly understood Heb: Gr: Latine, Arab: Syriac, & most of the Modern Languages; disputed in Divinity, Law, all the Sciences, was skillfull in Historie both Ecclesiastical & Prophane, in Politic &c, in a word so universaly & solidly learned at 11 yeares of age, as he was looked on as a Miracle: Dr. *LLoyd* (one of the most deepe learned Divines of the nation, in all sorts of literature) with Dr. *Burnet* who had severely Examin'd him, came away astonish'd and told me, they did not believe there had the like appeared in the world since *Adame* to this time: He had onely ben instructed by his Father, who being himselfe a learned person, confessed that he knew all that he knew to a tittle: but what was more admirable was not so much his vast memorie, but his judgement & invention, he being tried with divers hard questions which required maturity of thought & experience: he was also dextrous in Chronologie, Antiquities, in the Mathematics &c: in summ a⟨n⟩ Intellectus Universalis beyond all that we reade of Picus Mirandula & other precoce witts: &c: with all this a very humble Child: 10 To *Lond:* dind at *Sir Ro: Claytons*, went home on friday evening: 13 A stranger on: 14: *Joh:* 6 & In the Afternoone Mr. *Evans* whom I had holpen to a Competent living in Lond, having casualy heard him preach in an obscure place in Surry, where he was but *Curate*: his Text was 139 *Psal:* 7: My buisinesse called me this Evening to Lond: 14: To see how things stood at Parsons Greene, my *Lady V. Countesse Mordaunt* (now sick in Paris, whither she went for health) having made me a *Trustee* for her Children, an office I could not refuse this most excellent, pious & virtuous Lady, my very long acquaintance &c:

15 I dind with Mr. *Sid: Godolphin* now one of the Lords Commissioners of the Treasury: 17 I din'd with my Wife at Sir R: *Claytons* where dined also the Marquis of *Winchester*:

18 I went early to the *old-Baily* Sessions-house to the famous Trial of Sir *Geo: Wakeman* (one of the *Queenes Physitians*) &

3 *Benedictine Monkes*; The first (whom I was well acquainted with, & take to be a worthy gent: abhorring such a fact) for intending to poyson the King: The other as complices to carry on the Plott, to subvert the Government, & introduce *Poperie*: The Bench was crowded with the Judges, Lo: Major, Justices, & innumerable spectators: The chiefe Accusers Dr. *Oates* (as he called himselfe) ⟨and⟩ one *Bedlow*, a man of inferior note; but their testimony were not so pregnant, & I feare much of it from *heare-say*, but sworne positively to some particulars, which drew suspicion upon their truth; nor did Circumstances so agree, as to give either the bench or Jurie so intire satisfaction as was expected: After therefore a long & tedious tryal of 9 houres, the Jury brought them in not guilty to the extraordinary triumph of the *Papists*, & not without sufficient disadvantage & reflections on the Witnesses, especialy *Oates* & *Bedlow*: And this was an happy day for the *Lords* in the *Tower*, who expecting their Triall (had this gon against the Prisoners at the barr) would all of them ⟨have⟩ ben in uttmost hazard: For my part, I do looke on *Oates* as a vaine, insolent man, puff'd up, with the favour of the Commons, for having discovered something realy true; as more especialy detecting the dangerous intrigue of Coleman, proved out of his owne letters: & of a generall designe, which the *Jesuited* party of the Papists, ever had, & still have to ruine the Church of England; but that he was trusted with those greate seacrets he pretended, or had any solid ground for what he accused divers noble men of, I have many reasons to induce my contrary beliefe; That amongst so many Commissions as he affirm'd he delivered to them from *P: Oliva* & the *Pope*, he who made no scruple of opening all other Papers, letters & seacrets, should not onely, not open any of those pretended Commissions, but not so much as take any Copy, or Witnesse, of any one of them, is ⟨almost⟩ miraculous: But the Commons (some leading persons I meane of them) had so exalted him, that they tooke for Gospell all he said, & without more ado, ruin'd all whom he nam'd to be Conspirators, nor did he spare whomsoever came in his way; But indeede the Murder of Sir *Ed: Godferie* (suspected to have ben compassed by the *Jesuite* party, for his intimacy with *Coleman* (a buisy person whom I also knew) & the feare they had he was able to have discovered some thing to their prejudice) did so exasperate, not onely the

Commons, but all the nation; That much of these sharpnesses against even the more honest *Ro: Catholicks* who lived peaceably, is to be imputed to that horrid fact: The *Sessions* ended I dined, or rather indeede supped, (so late it was) with the Judges, in the large ⟨roome⟩ annexed to the Place, & so returned to my house: And though it was not my ⟨Custome⟩ or delight, to be often present at any *Capital Trials*, we having them commonly, so exactly published, by those who take them in short hand; Yet I was inclined to be at this signal one, that by the occular view of the carriages, & other Circumstances of the Manegers & parties concerned I might informe my selfe, and regulate my opinion of a Cause that had so alarm'd the whole Nation, & filled it with such expectations:

21 To Lond: 22 Dind at *Clappham* at Sir *D: Gauden*, went thence with him to *Winsore*, to assist him in a buisinesse with his Majestie. I lay that night at Eaton Coll: in the Provosts Lodging (Dr. Craddock) where I was courteously entertained: 23. To Court, after dinner I visited that excellent Painter *Verrio* whose worke in *Fresca*, the Kings Palace at *Winsor*, will celebrate as long as those walls last: Signor *Verrio* shewed us his pretty Garden, choice flowers & curiosities, he himselfe being a skillfull Gardner; after an herty Collation with him, I went to *Clifden* that stupendious natural Rock, Wood, & Prospect of the Duke of *Buckinghams*, & building of extraordinary Expense: The Grotts in the Chalky rock are pretty, 'tis a romantic object, & the place alltogether answers the most poetical description that can be made of a solitude, precipice, prospects & whatever can contribute to a thing so very like their imaginations: The ⟨house⟩ stands somewhat like *Frascati* as to its front, & on the platforme is a circular View to the uttmost verge of the Horison, which with the serpenting of the *Thames* is admirably surprising: The Staire Case, is for its materials, singular: The *Cloisters*, Descents, Gardens, & avenue through the wood august & stately: but the land all about wretchedly barren, producing nothing but ferne: & indeede, as I told his Majestie that evening, (asking me how I liked *Clifden*?) without flattery: that it did not please me yet so well as Windsore, for the Prospect & the Park, which is without compare; There being but one onely opening, & that but narrow, which let one to any Variety, where as That of Winsore is every where greate & unconfin'd:

Returning I called in at my Co: Evelyns, who has a very pretty seate in the Forest, 2 miles behether Cliffden, on a flat, with sweete Gardens, exquisitly kept though large, the house a stanch good old building; & what was singular some of the roomes floor'd Dovetailed wise without a naile; so exactly cloose, as I was exceedingly pleas'd with the manner of it, one of the Closets being parquetted,

with plaine deale set in Diamond thus exceeding

stanch & pretty: but my Kindsman & Lady being from home, I went back to Winsor, & next morning followed the King to *Hampton Court*, where was a *Council*, at which I had affaires: thence dining at *Kingstone* I returned that night to Says-Court: not at all displeased at the journey: 27: our *Curate* on 16 *Psal:* 12: *Pomerid:* a Stranger on: 55 Esay: 7:

Aug: 1. I went on board his Majesties Yach't, his Majestie saling towards *Portsmouth*, Mr. *Henry Thynn* & Mr. *Brisbane*, the one Secretary to *Mr. Coventry* Sec: of state, & the other, to the Admiralty, dining with me: afterwards to *Lond:* to see my deare friend, Mr. *Godolphins* little sonn, who was sick, & with my Wife came back at night.

3 A stranger on 90: Psal: 12: The blessed Sacrament follow'd: *Pomerid*: *Curate* on 11: *Matt.* 28. 29. but nothing of much note: 6: Came Sir *William Godolphin* & other Company to dine with me, his Sisters bringing with them that deare child, now almost a yeare old, & next day to be weaned:

7. To *Lond:* Dined at the *Sherifs*, when the Company of Drapers & their Wives being invited, there was a sumptuous entertainement according to the formes of the Citty, with Musique &c: comparable to any Princes service in Europ:

8 I went this morning to shew My L: Chamberlaine, his Lady, & the Dutchesse of Grafton, the incomparable work of Mr. *Gibbons* the *Carver* whom I first recommended to his Majestie, his house being furnish'd like a Cabinet, not onely with his owne work, but divers excellent Paintings of the best hands: Thence to Sir *St: Foxes* where I dined with my Lord, & all our Company, & so home:

12 To *Lond:* about buisinesse, & return'd not 'til the 15th: 17: Mr. *Bohune* preached at *Lee* (whither I went this morning) on 1.

Phil: 27. *Curate* on: 1. *Jam:* 27 against the *Atheisme* of the times: 24. our Vicc: as before, with small addition, nor more the *Curate*: Dr. *Needham* came to see my Sonn, now indispos'd, & next day was sent for to *Windsore* the King being sick, & he one of his *Physitians* in Ordinarie:

25 I went to meete the Countesse of *Sunderland* at *Parsons Greene* to see the children. Thence to *Chelsey* the *Countesse of Bristols* (her mother) thence to Lond: 27 I dined with Sir Ro: *Clayton* having buisinesse: 29 home: 31. *Viccar* as before: In the afternoone to *Lee*, & after evening service, to see a neighbour one Mr. *Bohune* (related to my sonns late Tutor of that name) who being a rich Spanish Merchant, lives in a most pretty place, which he has adorn'd with all maner of curiosities, especialy Carvings of Mr. Gibbons, & a Cabinet of his *Wives* (a most ingenious Lady) furnished with many rarities, some paintings of Mr. *Streeters* &c & so home:

September 6 To *Lond:* 7: Mr. *Blagrave* at White-hall 1 *Jam:* 14. 15: The bl: Comm: follow'd: In the afternoone Dr. *Meriton*, at a temporary Chapell, (caled the Tabernacle) whilst *St. Albans* Church was building: on: 11 *John*: 9: a tedious Preacher: 11 I returned home: 13: To *Lond:* thence to Winsore to congratulate his Majesties recovery; I also kissed the *Dukes* hand, now lately returned from *Flanders* to visite his Brother the King, of which there were various, & bold & foolish discourses, the *Duke* of *Monmoth* being sent away.

14 Dr. *Stradling* (*Deane* of *Chichester*) preached to the household excellently on 1. *Thess:* 22: *Coram rege*, Dr. *Crighton* on 7: *Matt:* 16, shewing by what fruites a True Christian was to be known: much perstringing the *Jesuites*: My *Lord Sunderland* (one of the principle Secretarys of State) invited me to dinner, where was the Earle of *Shrewsbery*, Earle of *Essex*, E: of *Mulgrave*, & (the Kings natural sonn) the E: of *Plymoth*: Mr. *Hyde*, Mr. *Godolphin* &c: After dinner, I went to Prayers at *Eaton*, & visited Mr. *Hen: Godolphin* fellow there, & Dr. *Cradock*: 15 Dined with my *Lady Tuke* (one of the *Women* of the Queenes *Chamber*, & my relation). The Lord Major, & Aldermen came this morning to congratulate his Majesties recovery; I return'd with them to Lond: & next day home: ⟨21⟩: A *stranger* on 36: Ezek: 26: *Pomeridiano Curate* as before 1 *Jam:* 27.

25 Came to visite & dine with me Mr. *Slingsby* Master of the *Mint* & Signor *Verrio* the famous *Painter*, to whom I gave China oranges of my owne trees, as good as were ever eaten I think, to Signor Verrios no small admiration: 28 our *Viccar* on 8: *John*: 36 That Christian Liberty did not qualifie any to Rebell against Magistrates: excellen⟨t⟩. The *Curate* on 4: *Phil:* 11:

Octob: 1 To *Lond:* 3. Dined at Sir *Rob: Claytons*, now *Lord Major Elect*: Thence to the R: Society: 5. I went with the *L: Major* to dine with the Bish: of *London* at *Fullham*, where also I met Dr. *Stillingfleete*: I called at Parsons *Greene*, visited the Countesse of *Bristoll* at *Chelsey*, & so to *Lond:*

5 Dr. *Bell* (of *St. Sepulchres*) preach'd at W:Hall on 1. Tim: 2: 1: The holy *Sacrament* followed: *Bish:* of *Lond:* officiating: din'd at Mr. *Slingsbys.*

6 I return'd home, a very wett, & sickly season:

12 our *Viccar* as before, & so the Curate: 16 to *Lond:* made up my first Accompts with Mr. *Godolphin*, as intrusted for his little *sonn* &c: 19 A stranger at *W:hall* to the household on: 5: *Matt:* 34. ad 38: *Coram rege*, one of his *Chap:* on: 2: *Tim:* 1. 13: 23: I din'd with my L: *Chamb:* the King being now newly return'd from his *Newmarket* recreations: 24 I went home:

26 Our *Viccar* on 73: *Psal:* 25: *Pomerid: Curate* 1. John: 5. 3:

31 My *Birth* day: & 59th of my age, I spent in recollection of my life, especialy of the yeare past, & prepare for the Communion the following moneth, beseeching Almighty God to be gracious to me the Yeare entering, & giving him thanks for the past:

November 1 I met with the *foefees* of the poore about their buisinesse, our *Viccar* (according to *Costome*) preaching on 51 *Psal:* 19, by way of *Paraphrase* &c: That God would be gracious to the Publique, Spiritual & temporal Concernes &c:

2 Being the first *Sunday* the *Viccar* prosecuted his former text: The holy *Communion* followed; of which almost all my familie participated: blessed be God:

4. To *Lond:* din'd at *Lo: Majors*, & in the Evening went to the funerall of my pious, deare & antient learned friend *Dr. Jasper Needham*; he was buried at St. *Brides Church*; he was a true & holy Christian, & one who loved me with greate affection: Dr. *Dove* preached on   *Psal*, with an Elogie due to his memorie: I lost in this person one of my dearest remaining sincere friends.

5 I was invited to dine at my *Lord Tividales* (a Scotch Earle of my acquaintance, a learned & knowing noble man) we afterwards went to see *Mr. Montagues* new Palace neere Blomesbery, built by our *Curator* Mr. Hook, somewhat after the French; it was most nobly furnished, & a fine, but too much exposed Garden:

6 Dind at the Co: of *Sunderlands*, & was this evening at the remarriage of the *Dutchesse* of *Grafton* to the *Duke* (his Majesties natural son) she being now 12 yeares old: The Ceremonie was perform'd in my *Lord Chamberlaines* (her fathers Lodgings) at *Whitehall* below, by the Bish: of *Rochester*, his Majestie Present: a suddaine, & unexpected thing (when every body believed the first marriage, would have come to nothing:) But the thing being Determined, I was privately invited by my *Lady* her mother, to be present: but I confesse I could give her little joy, & so I plainely told her; but she told me, the *King* would have it so, & there was no going back: & this sweetest, hopfullest, most beautifull child, & most vertuous too, was Sacrific'd to a boy, that had ben rudely bred, without any thing to encourage them, but his Majesties pleasure: I pray God the sweete Child find it to her advantage; who if my augurie deceave me not, will in few yeares be such a paragon, as were fit to make the Wife of the greatest Prince in Europe: I *staied Supper*, where his Majestie sate betweene the *Dutchesse of Cleaveland* (the incontinent mother of the Duke of *Grafton*) & the sweete *Dutchesse* the Bride, with severall greate Persons & Ladies, without Pomp; my Love to my Lord *Arlingtons* family, & the sweete Child made me behold all this with regret: Though as the *Duke* of *Grafton* affects the *Sea*, to which I find his father intends to use him; he may emerge a plaine, usefull, robust officer; & were he polish'd, a tollerable person, for he is exceedingly handsome, by far surpassing any of the Kings other naturall Issue: 7: I dind at my *Lady Sylvius*.

8 At Sir *St: Foxes*, & was agreeing for the Countesse of Bristols house at Chelsey, within 500 pounds. 9: Dr. Smith to the household on: 2: Coloss: 13. very Well: To the *King* a Chaplain, on 13 *Jer:* 16:

18 I dined at my *Lo: Majors*, being desired by the *Countesse* of *Sunderland* to carry her thither on a Solemn Day, that she might see the pomp & ceremonie of this Prince of Citizens, there

never having ben any, who for the statlinesse of his Palace, prodigious feasting & magnificence exceeded him: This *Lord Majors* acquaintance had ben from the time of his being Apprentice to one Mr. *Abbot* (his Unkle) who being a Scrivenor, & an honnest worthy man, (one who was condemn'd to die [(but escaped)] at the beginning of the Troubles 40 years past, as concerned in the Commission of Aray, for K. Char: 1:) I often used his assistance in mony matters: Rob: Clayton (now *Major*) his Nephew, then a boy, became after his Unkle *Abbotts* death, so prodigiously rich & opulent, that he was reckoned on⟨e⟩ of the welthiest Citizens: he married a freehearted Woman, who also became his hospitable disposition, & having no Children, with the accession of his Partner & fellow Apprentice, who also left him his Estate; he grew Excessively rich, was a discreete Magistrate, & though, envied, I thinke without much cause: some believ'd him gilty of hard-dealing, especialy with the Duke of *Buckingham*, much of whose estate he had swallow'd: but I never saw any ill by him, considering the trade he was off: The reputation, & known integrity of his Unkle Abbot, brought all the Royal party to him, by which he got not onely greate credite, but vast riches; so as he passed this Office with infinite magnificence & honor:

20 I dind at the Master of the Mints with my Wife, invited to heare Musique which was most exquisitely performed by 4 the most renoun'd Masters, *Du Prue* a *French-man* on the *Lute*: Signor *Batholomeo* Ital: on the *Harpsichord*: & *Nicolao* on the Violin; but above all for its swetenesse & novelty the *Viol d'Amore* of 5 wyrestrings, plaied on with a bow, being but an ordinary *Violin*, play'd on *Lyra* way by a *German*, than which I never heard a sweeter Instrument or more surprizing: There was also a *Flute douce* now in much request for accompanying the Voice: Mr. *Slingsby* Master of the house (whose Sonn & Daughter played skillfully) being exceedingly delighted with this diversion, had these meetings frequently in his house: 21 I din'd at my *Lord Majors*, to accompany my worthiest & generous Friend, the *Earle* of *Ossorie*; it was on a *Friday*, a private day; but the feast & entertainement, might have become a *King*: such an hospitable costome, & splendid Magistrature, dos no Citty I believe in the world shew. 23: Dr. *Allestree* before the household on: 11: Luke: 2: *Coram Rege, Dr. LLoyd* on 28

Matt: 20: shewing with how little reason the *Papists* applied those words of our B: *Saviors* to maintaine the pretended Infallibility they boast of: I never heard a more Christian & excellent discourse: Yet were some offended that he seemed to say, the Church of *Rome* was a *true Church*; but 'twas Captiously mistaken; for he never affirmed any thing that could be more to their reproch: His Instances were, That a Man may be a *true man*, though full of sores, & botches, yea of a mortal plague; & an house a *true house*, though infected & *leaprous*; and that such was the present Church of *Rome*; shewing at large how frequently, and desperately it had erred; as by adopting false & doubtfull Articles into the *Creede*, to be believed on paine of *Damnation*, by which meanes the *Council* of *Trent* exclude all possible reconciliation &c: But men were now very angery with the *papists*, & violently transported, by reason of the late plot, & especialy the *Murder* of Sir E: *Godfery*, which so exasperated, that they would endure nothing which was not carried with the uttmost Violence against all persons of that church: but here was in this Sermon, not so much as any shadow for censure, no person of all the Cleargy, having testified greater zeale against the errors of the Papists, than this pious & most learned person:—I din'd at the *Bish:* of *Rochesters*, & then went to heare that greate *Wit* Dr. *Sprat*, now newly succeding Dr. *Outram* in the *Cure* of St. *Margarits*, who preached an incomparable sermon on: 1. *Thess:* 4: 11: Dr. *Sprats* talent was, a greate memorie, never making use of notes, a readinesse of Expression, in [a] most pure and plaine style, for words & full of matter, easily delivered:

26 I met the *Earle* of *Clarendon* with the rest of my fellow Executors of the Will of my late Lady *Vicountesse Mordaunt*, namely with Mr. *Laurence Hyde* one of the Lords Commissioners of The *Treasury*, & lately *Plenepotentiary Ambassador* at *Nimegen*; also *Andrew Newport*, & Sir *Charles Wheeler*; for the Examining, Auditing, & Disposing of this yeares Accompt, of the Estate of this Excellent Lady, according to the directions of her Will &c:—I din'd at Mr. *Boscawen*: 27: I went to see Sir *John Stonehouse*, with whom I was treating a Marriage, betweene my Sonn, & his Daughter in Law: & dined with Sir *James Shaen*, & thence to the *R: Society*, where there was excellent Conversation. 28: Came over the *Duke of Munmoth* from *Holland*

unexpectedly to his Majestie whilst the *D: of Yorke* was on his Journey to Scotland, whither the *King* sent him to *preside*, & governe &c: The Bells & Bone-fires of the Citty at this arival of D:M: publishing their joy to the no small regret of some at Court; This Duke (whom for distinction they cal'd the *Protestant Duke*, though the sonn of an abandoned woman) the people made their *Idol* of: I returned home: 30: *Viccar*: on 73: *Psal*: 25 as before: &c:

December 1. Being the day after St. *Andrews*, was the *Anniversarie* of choosing Officers at the R: *Society*, when continuing our former President, I was chosen & sworn of the *Council*: for this yeare: After Elections were over, we (as, usual) din'd together, his Majestie having sent us in two *Does*: &c:

4 I dined (together with my *L: Ossorie* & *E:* of Chesterfild) at the *Portugal* Ambassadors now newly come, at Cleaveland house: a noble Palace, too good for that infamous————: The Staire Case is sumptuous & Gallerie: with the Garden: but above all the costly furniture belonging to the *Ambassador*, especialy the rich ⟨*Japan*⟩ *Cabinets* of which I think there were a dosen; & a *Billiard* table with as many more hazards as ours commonly have: the game being onely to prosecute the ball til hazarded, without passing the port or touching the pin: If one misse hitting the ball every time, the game is lost, or if hazarded: & 'tis more difficult to hazard a ball though so many, than in our Tables, by reason the board is made so exactly Even, & the Edges not stuff'd: The balls also bigger, & they for the most part use the sharp & small end of the billiard-stick, which is shod with brasse or silver: The Entertainement was exceeding Civile, but besids a good *olio*, the dishes were trifling, hash'd & Condited after their way, not at all fit for an English stomac, which is for solid meate: There was yet good fowle, but roasted to Coale; nor were the sweetemeates good: I had much discourse with the Secretary, who seem'd an understanding person.

5 I din'd with my L: *Major*: 7: To the house—preached at *W:hall*, Dr. *Patrick* on 1. *Tim*: 6. 3: The B: Sacrament follow'd: (*Cor: Rege*) Dr. *Leake* on 119 *Psal*: 34. I din'd at the *Earle* of *Ossories* who had before invited all the Company who dined with him at the *Portugal* Ambassadors, that is, the *Ambassador* himselfe, a *Portugal* knight, the Secretary, Duke of *Grafton*, Earle of *Chester-*

field, Earle of Bath, Lo: *Cavendish*, son to the Earle of *Devon-shire*: & severall other noble persons.

10 I was summond to meete at a Council of the R: *Society* at Sir Jos: Williamsons, for the reforming divers things out of order, & carrying on the Experiments to be prosecuted this following yeare, after which we had a noble supper:

11 I introduc'd the *Conde de Castell Melior* (late prime Minister & favorite to the King of Portugal) & a Portugal Gent: with him, into our Society: where he saw severall experiments: &c:

12 I supped with the Countesse of Sunderland at White-hall & next day got home.

14 Our *Viccar* on 23. *Luke*: 31: I was ill this afternoone:

18 To Lond: to our Society: 19 Din'd with the E: of ⟨*Ossorie*⟩ and the Earle of Clarendon: at my *Lord Majors*: 21. A stranger preach'd at *W:hall* on 1. *Pet:* 4: 18. *Coram Rege*. Dr. *Sprat* on: 3: Jam: 13.

24 I returned home, & [25] on Christmas day our *Viccar* on: 1. Heb: 1. after which the holy Sacrament &c: The [three following] days after divers of my neighbours dined with mee according to Costome:

30 I went to Lond, to meete Sir *John Stonehouse*, and give him a particular of the settlement on my Sonn, who now made his addresses to the Young Lady his Daughter in Law; & so returned home:

31 Recollecting the passages of the Yeare, I gave thanks to Almighty God &c:

1680. Jan: 1 Imploring the blessing of God on me & mine [&c]: Divers Neighbours din'd with us.

4 our *Viccar* preached on his former text: the Com: follow'd: some friends dind with us; *Pomerid*: one Mr. *Burton* on 3: *John*.

11 I tooke *Physick* my face & eye swelled by a Cold: 13 Came to Visite me Sir *W: Godolphin*: *La: Sylvius* &c: 18 The Minister of Lee on: 133: *Psal*. 3: I went in the afternoone to *Lond:* about special buisinesse, heard evening prayer at *W:hall*. 23. Supp'd at *La: Sylvius* with Mr. *Laurence* Hyde & Lady, Sid: *Godolphin* &c.

25 Dr. *Cave* (Author of *Primitive Christianity*, a learned & pious man) at W:hall to the household on 3: *Jam:* 17: *Coram Rege* Dr. *Pellin*, 49 Isa: 23. a Prerogative discourse, but very honestly shewing what obedience is due from Subjects to their Princes; it being in a Conjuncture when there was a very ill understanding

'twixt the Court & Countrie upon his Majesties unwillingnesse to let the *Parliament* sit. &c: 26 I went to Counsel for the set-tling my Estate on my Sonn, now in treaty about a marriage, with my Lady *Stonehouse's* Daughter:

30 Being the *Anniversarie* fast of K: *Charles* the 1. his *Martyr-dom*, the B: of *Rochester* preached very patheticaly, as his costome ⟨was⟩, on 27: *Matt:*   noting that that lesson (describing the suffering of our *B: Saviour*) was the proper lesson for the day of old apointed; & paralelling his sufferings in a very pertinent manner:

I supp'd at Sir *Steph: Foxes*, now made one of the Lords Com-missioners of the Treasury: &c:

Feb: 9 To *Lond* about my sonns *Marriage*. 15 Dr. *Durell* D: of *Winsore* to the household on 1. *Eph: 7: Cor: Rege*, Dr. *Thisteltwhait* on 16: *Matt:* 27: Afternoone at St. *Jame's* Dr. *Leake* on 84. *Psal*: 10:

19 Were the Writings for the Settling Joynture, & other Con-tracts of Marriage of my Sonn finish'd and sealed &c: at *White-hall* Mr. *Thursby* & *Melldecot* being our Counsel, Sir *John Stonehouse* & *Nephew Glanvill* being *Trustees*: The Lady was to bring 5000 pounds in consideration of a settlement of 500 pounds a yeare present maintenance,—Which was likewise to be her joynture, & 500 pounds, after myne & my Wifes decease: though with Gods blessing it will be at the least 1000 pounds a yeare more in few yeares; I pray God make him worthy of it, and a Comfort to his excellent Mother, who deserves much from him: 20: I dined at a Servant of my Wifes, with the Earle of Ossory, whose servant had married her, & so home: 22: *Viccar* on 5. *Eph:* 15: I went in the Evening againe to Lond:

24 It being *Shrove tuesday* was my *Sonne Married* to Mrs. *Martha Spencer* Daughter to my Lady *Stonehouse* by a former Gent: at St. *Andrews* in *Holborn* by our *Viccar*, (borrowing the Church of Dr. *Stillingfleete* Deane of *St. Paules* who was the present incumbent) & afterward dined ⟨at⟩ an House in *Hol-born*; & after the solemnity & Dauncing was don, They were beded at Sir *Jo: Stonehouses* Lodging in *Bow streete* Covent gar-den: I would very faine have had the marriage deferr'd til after the Lent; but severall accidents requiring it now, it was left to the disposall of her friends, & their convenience:

25 *Ashwednesday Coram Rege* preach'd the B: of *Lond* on 119 *Psal:* 71: 26: To the *R: Society*, where I met an *Irish Bishop* with his Lady, who was Daughter to my worthy & pious friend

Dr. *Jer: Taylor* late Bish: of *Downe* & *Conner*, they came to see
the *Repositorie*; she seemed to be a knowing Woman beyond the
ordinary talent of her sex: 27: first friday in Lent. *Coram Rege*, D:
of S. *Paules* preached: a buisinesse of Charity keeping me from
all but a fragment of his sermon: 29 Dr. *Tailor* before the household on 6. *Gal:* 10: *Co: Rege* the *Bish:* of *Excester* (Dr. *Lamplugh*)
incomparably on 39: *Psal:* I din'd with Sir Jo: *Stonehouse* (my
Sonns-Wifes Father in Law) at his Lodging: Afternoone heard
a stranger at Co: Garden Church on 23. *Luke:* 43:

Mar 3 Preached Dr. *Tenison Coram Rege*, on 119 *Psal:* 106: I
dind at L: *Majors* in order to the meeting my *Lady Beckford*,
whose Daughter (a rich heyresse) I had recommended to my
Bro: of *Wotton* for his onely sonn: she being the daughter of this
Lady by *Mr. Ersfield* a *Sussex Gent*.

4 I went home, to receive my new *Daughter* in *Law* & her
husband my sonn, with his Wifes Relations, who all dined with
us, & returning to *Lond:* in the Evening, left my Daughter in
Law with us for altogether.

7 Our *Viccar* on 1. Pet: 5. 8: The H: Sacrament follow'd:
Pomer: Curat, on 16 *Matt* 26:

16 To *Lond:* to receive 3000 pounds of my Daughter in Laws
Portion, which was paied in Gold: 17: Dr. *Cradock* at *W:hall* on 2:
Phil: 13: an excellent discourse, as his allways are, pious & cleare
& very sound divinity.

18 At the *Ro: Society* was a letter from *Surenam* of a certaine
small *Eele* that being taken with hooke & line at 100 foote
length, did so benumb, & stupifie the limbs of the Fisher, that
had not the line suddainly beene cutt, by one of the Iland (who
was acquainted with its effects) the poore man had immediately
died: There is a certaine wood growing in the Country, which
put into a *Waire* or *Eele-pot*, dos as much intoxicate the fish as
Nux Vomica dos other fish, by which this *mortiferous Torpedo* is
not onely caught, but becomes both harmelesse, & excellent
meate: I this day introduc'd Mr. *Bridgeman* (Secretary to the E:
of *Sunderland* now Pr: Sec: of *state*) to be a member of the R:
Society, he being a very ingenious Person: 19 Dr. *Megot* on 12:
Rom: 17: 20 Din'd with my L: *Chamb:* & so went home: 21. our
Viccar on his former, & *Curat* on 9: *Matt* 15.

26 To *Lond:* the D: of *Sarum* on a Text he entred on 5. *Feb:*
viz: 45 *Jer:* 5. Not to seeke great things to our selves, Gods

counsel to *Baruc*, in the time of distresse: In which he assembled
so many Instances out of heathen histories, & greate persons,
who had quitted the Splendor & opulence of their births, fortunes, & grandures, that he seemed for an houre & halfe to do
nothing else but reade *Common-places*, without any thing of
Scripture almost in his whole sermon, which was not well: I
went home next day:

28 Our *Vicc:* & *Curate* both on their former Texts.

Aprill: 1 Din'd at *L. Majors*, thence to the R: *Society*: 2: Dr.
Tillotson on 24 Josh: 15, shewing upon occasion of speaking of
the *Israelites* worshiping false Gods, both before, and after Abra-
hams time; that the objections made to us of the *Papists*, concerning the novelty of the Reformation, lay as much against all
the people of God, in all times of their Reformation: The whole
discourse was incomparable, I return'd home this Evening:

4 our *Viccar* on 4: *Rom:* 25: *Pomerid*: Curate: 24: *Luke* 25: 26.

7 Being holy *Weeke*, I went to *Lond:* Dr. *Littleton* on 10: *Heb:* 5
(*Coram rege*):

9: Being *Goodfriday* at St. *James*, where the *Dukes* Chap: on
12: *Joh:* 27: the holy Communion follow'd: *Pomerid*: Dr. *Goodman*, an excellent *Divine*, on: 13. *Heb* 11. 12: I return'd home this
Evening:

11 *Easter-day* our *Viccar* on 4: *Rom: ult*: The bl: *Sacrament* follow'd, of which I participated with my family: *Pomer*: *Curate* on
24: *Luke*: 45. 46. with usual application &c:

VISIT TO CASSIOBURY – THE TRIAL OF
LORD STAFFORD – THE ROYAL LIBRARY
(1680)

17 I WENT TO LOND. and the next day, upon the earnest invitation of the *Earle* of *Essex* went with him to his house of *Cas-
sioberie* in Hartford-shire: It was on *Sunday*, but going early
from his Lordships house in the Square of St. *Jamess* we ariv'd by
ten a clock; but my Lord, thinking it too late to go to Church,
we had prayers in his Chapell: The House is new, a plaine fabric,
built by my friend Mr. *Hugh-May*; there are in it divers faire &
good roomes, excellent Carving of *Gibbonss*, especialy the

chimny ⟨piece⟩ of his Library: There is likewise a painting in the porch or Enterance of Signor *Virrios*, *Apollo* & the *Illiberal* Arts: One roome parquetted with yew which I liked well: The Chimny mantles are some of them of a certaine *Irish Marble* (which his *Lordship* brought with him when he was *Lieutennant* of Ireland not long before) not much inferior to *Italian*: The *Tympanum* or Gabel at the front is a *Bass-relievo* of *Diana* hunting cut in Portland stone handsomely enough: The middle Dores being round I did not approve of: but when the Hall is finishd as his Lordship designs it, being an Oval *Cupol'd*, together with the other wing, it will be a very noble Palace: The Library is large, & very nobly furnish'd, & all the books richly bound & gilded: No *Manuscripts*, except of the *Parliament Rolls*, and Journals, which his Lordship assured me cost him 500 pounds transcribing & binding: No man has ben more industrious than this noble Lord in Planting about his seate, adorn'd with Walkes, Ponds, & other rural Elegancies; but the soile is stonie, churlish & uneven, nor is the Water neere enough to the house, though a very swift & cleare streame run within a flight-shot from it in the vally, which may fitly be cald cold-brook, it being indeede excessive Cold, yet producing faire Troutes: In a word, 'tis pitty the house was not situated to more advantage; but it seemes it was built just where the old one was, & which I believe he onely meant to repaire at first, which leads men into irremediable errors, & saves but little: The Land about it is exceedingly addicted to Wood, but the coldnesse of the place hinder⟨s⟩ their growth: onely *Black-Cherry* trees prosper even to Considerable Timber, some being 80 foote long: The⟨y⟩ make also very handsome avenues: There is a pretty *Oval* at the end of a faire Walke, set about with treble rows of Spanish firr-trees: The Gardens are likewise very rare, & cannot be otherwise, having so skillfull an Artist to governe them as *Mr. Cooke*, who is as to the *Mechanic* part not ignorant in Mathematics, & pretends to *Astrologie*: Here is an incomparable Collection of the choicest fruits: As for my *Lord*, he is a sober, wise, judicious & pondering person, not illiterate beyond the rate of most noble-men in this age, very well Versed in our English Histories & Affaires, Industrious, frugal, Methodical, & every way accomplished: His Lady (being sister to the late Earle of *Northumberland*) is a wise [yet somewhat] melancholy woman, setting her heart too much upon the little *Lady* her daughter, of whom she is over fond: They have a hopefull sonn, at the *Academie*: My Lord was now not long since come over from his *Lieutenancy* of *Ireland*, where he shew'd his abillities in Administration & government there; as well as prudence in considerably augmenting his Estate, without reproch: He had also ben Ambassador Extraord: in *Denmark*; & in a word, such a person as becomes the sonn of that worthy *Hero* his Father, the late *Lord Capel*, who lost his life for K: *Charles* the first: We spent our time in the mornings in Walking or riding about the Grounds & Contriving; The Afternoones in the Library among the Books; so as I passed my time for 3 or 4 daies with much satisfaction: He was pleased also during this Conversation, to impart to me divers particulars of state relating to the present times; but being no greate friend to the D——was now laied aside; his integritie & abillities being not so sutable in this Conjuncture: 21 I came back in my Lords Coach with him to *Lond:*

22 I din'd at my L: *Arlingtons*, & thence to the R: *Society*, where was read a letter out of *Germanie*, with some *haire* inclos'd, that had ben taken from a *Corps* long buried, that was totaly covered with it, of an Inch in length, exceeding thick, and somewhat harsh & reddish: It seem'd to grow on the skinn like *Mosse* upon a *Tree*, the rest of the *Cadaver* being totaly consum'd. Then a *Physitian* present, shew'd us a *Tooth*, or rather a *trebble Grinder*, with its roote, which he affirmed to have ben found in the *Testicle* of a *Woman* whom he Discected:

30 To *Lond:* about buisinesse, to meete the *Earle* of *Peterborow*, E: of *Clarendon*, Mr. *Laur: Hyde* (his brother), Mr. *Newport* to take & adjust this halfe-yeares Accompts of my Lady V: *Countesse Mordaunts* Estate as *Executors*, & to consider of the Sale of *Parsons Greene*, &c: being in treaty with Mr. *Loftus*: Then returned home:

May: 1. Was a meeting of the *Foefees* for the Poore of our Parish, our Doctor (according to *Costome*) preach'd on   Let your Conversation be without Covetousnesse &c. I this yeare would stand one of the Collectors of their rents; to give Example to others: My *Sonne* was also now added to the *Foefees* &c:

There came to visite me this *Afternoone* Sir *Edw: Deering* of *Surrenden* in *Kent*, one of the Lords of the *Treasury*, with his daughter, married to my worthy friend Sir *Rob: Southwell*,

Cleark of the Council; now extraordinarie Envoyè to the Duke of *Brandenburg* & other Princes in *Germanie*, as before he had into *Portugal*; being a *sober*, *wise* & virtuous Gent:

2 Our *Viccar* preach'd on 3: Revel: 20: The bl: *Sacrament* follow'd: *Pomeridiano*, our *Curate* on the same Text, as before: 3: Buisinesse with the LL Commiss: of the Treasury cald me to *Lond:* but returned that Evening: 9: our *Viccar* as before: 13: I was at the funerall of old Mr. *Shish* Master *Shipwrite* of the *Kings Yard* here in this Parish, an honest and remarkable man, & his death a publique losse, for his excellent successe in building Ships, (though illiterate altogether) & for the breeding up so many of his Children to be able Artists: I held up the *Pall*, with three *knights* who did him that honour, & he was worthy of it: our *Viccar* preaching on a Text of the good-mans choice out of 12 *Isa:* 2. shewing his Trust, and faith in God, & thankfullnesse for his mercies: It was the Costome of this good man, to rise in the night, and to pray kneeling in his owne Cofin; which many yeares he had lying by him: he was borne that famous yeare of the *Gunpowder Plot 1605*:

16 The morning wet stayed us at home: Afternoone *Curate* on his former Text:

18 To *Lond:* 20 *Ascention* day, a stranger at St. *Mart:* on 8. *Rom:* 12: There was no *Communion*, as I thought there might have ben: return'd: 23: Mr. *Bohune* on 2: *Rom:* 15:

Pomerid: *Curate* on 11: *Matt:* 28:

29 His Majesties Birth & returne; but there was so thin a Congregation, that our Viccar who came prepar'd to Preach, omitted it: so soone do we slight & forget Gods benefits:

30 *Whitsonday Viccar* on 2: *Act:* 2. 3. 4: the holy *Sacrament* followed: The excessive raine in the afternoone confin'd me to home, where we used the Office of the Day &c:

June 14 Came to Dine with us the *Countesse* of *Clarendon*, Dr. *Lloyd Deane* of *Bangor* [since Bish: of St. *Asaph*.] and Dr. *Burnet* author of the Hist: of *Reformation*, & my old friend Mr. *Henshaw*. After dinner we all went to see the Observatory & Mr. *Flamsted*; where he shewed us divers rare Instruments, especialy, the greate *Quadrant*:

20 Our *Viccar* pr: on his former Text in the *Apocalypse*: *Curat* as above:

24 To *Lond:* R: Society, a Council summon'd to meete at the

presidents next day, which [25] we did; & made an order, that the next experiments to be examin'd, should be my L: *Verulams*, & an account to be given of them to the publique from yeare to yeare 'til we had gon through them:

July: 4 our *Viccar* on: 1: *Sam*: 3: 8: The holy Com: followed: *Pomerid*: *Curate* went on with his parable:

6 To *Lond*: 8. To our *Society* on the first Exp: of my L: *Bacon*: 9 home:

24 Sir *Will*: *Godolphin* lending me his six-horses, I went with my Wife & Daughter to *Winsore*, to see that stately Court, now neere finished: there was now erected in the Court, the *King* on Horse-back lately cast in Coper, & set upon a rich Piedestal of white Marble, the worke of Mr. *Gibbons* &c: at the expense of *Toby Rustat*, a *Page* of the *Back stayres*, who by his wonderfull frugality had arived to a greate Estate in Mony, & did many works of Charity; as well as this of gratitude to his Master; which cost him 1000 pounds: he is a very simple, ignorant, but honest & loyal creature: We all dined at the *Countesse* of *Sunderlands*, afterwards to see Signor *Virios* garden; thence to *Eaton* Coll to salute the *Provost*, & heard a Latine Speech of one of the *Alumni* (it being at the Election) were invited to supper, but tooke our leaves, and got to *Lond*: that night in good time: 25 A stranger at *W:Hall* on 9: *Eccl*: 11.

26 my most noble & illustrious friend, the *Earle of Ossorie* espying me this morning after sermon, in the Privy-Gallerie, calling to me, told me he was now going his journey; (meaning to *Tangier*, whither he was designed Governor, & Generall of the *Forces*, to regaine the losses we had lately suffer'd from the *Moores*, when *Inchequeene* was *Governor*): I asked his *Lordship* if he would not call at my house (as he allways did when ever he went out of *England* on any exploit) I feare I shall not said his *Lordship*, for I foresee I must embarque at Portsmouth; wherefore I pray, let you & I dine together to day, I am quite alone, and have something to impart to you: I am not well, & have taken a little Physick this morning; & so shall be private, & I desire your Company: Being retird to his Lodgings & sat downe on the Couch, he sent to his *secretary* for the Copy of a Letter, which he had written to my Lo: *Sunderland* (secretary of state) wishing me to reade it; and it was to take notice, how ill he resented it, That he should tell the *King* before my L: *Ossories* face, That

Tangier was not to be kept, but would certainly be lost; & yet added, that twas fit, my L: *Ossorie* should be sent, that they might give some account of it to the world, meaning (as supposed,) the next *Parliament*, when all such miscarriages would probably be examin'd, This my L: O: tooke very ill of my L: S. & not kindly of his *Majestie*, who resolving to send him with an incompetent force, seem'd (as his *Lordship* tooke it) to be willing to cast him away upon not onely an hazardous Adventure, but, in most mens opinions Impossible; seing there was not to be above 3 or 400 horse & 4000 foote, for the *Garison* & all, both to defend the Towne, forme a Camp, repulse the Enemie, & fortifie what ground they should get in: This touch'd my Lord deepely, that he should be so little consider'd, as to put him on a buisinesse, in which he should probably, not onely loose his reputation, but be charg'd with all the miscarriages & ill successe; where as at the first they promis'd him 6000 *foote* & 600 *horse effective*: My *Lord*, being an exceeding brave & valiant person, & that had so approv'd himselfe in divers signal batailes, both at Sea, & Land; so beloved, so esteem'd by the people, as one they depended on upon all occasions worthy such a Captaine; looked on this as too greate an indifference in his Majestie after all his services (& the merits of his father the Duke of *Ormond*) & a designe of some who envied his Virtue; And it certainly, tooke so deepe roote in his mind, that he who was the most voide of feare in the world (and assur'd me he would go to *Tangier* with ten men, if his Majestie Commanded him) could not beare up against this unkindnesse: Having disburdned himselfe of this to me after dinner, he went with his *Majestie* to The *Sherifs*, at a greate supper in Fishmongres Hall; but my Lord, finding himselfe ill, tooke his leave immediately of his Majestie & came back to his Lodging, without staying at all at the *Sherifs*: Not resting well this night, he was perswaded to remove to *Arlington* house for better accommodation; where being no longer able to sustaine his indisposition, it manifestly turn'd to a *Malignant* feavor; which increasing to violence, after all that six of the most able *Physitians* could do to save him, beginning now and then to be somewhat delirious, at other times with intervalls of better sense: Dr. *LLoyd*, (now Bish: of St. *Asaph*) administring then to him the holy *Sacrament*, (of which I also participated) he died the friday after, about 7 in the Evening, being the 30th of *July*, to the universal griefe of all that either knew, or ever heard of his greate worth: nor had any a greater losse than my selfe, he being so much my friend; Oft would he say I was the oldest acquaintance he had in England (when, his Father was in Ireland) it being now of above 30 yeares, contracted abroad, when he rid at the *Academie* in *Paris*, & that we were seldome asunder: Surely his Majestie never lost a worthier Subject; nor Father, a better, & more dutifull sonn, a loving, goodnatured, generous and perfectly obliging friend, & one who had don innumerable kindnesses to severall persons, before they so much as kn⟨e⟩w it; nor advanc'd he any but such as were worthy; None more brave, more modest, none more humble, sober, & every way virtuous: Ô unhapy *England*! in this illustrious persons losse: Universal was the Mourning for him, the Elogies on him, nor can I sufficiently deplore him: I staied night & day by his bedside to his last gasp to close his deare Eyes: ô sad Father, Mother, Wife & Children! What shall I add? he deserved all that a sincere friend, a brave Souldier, a Virtuous Courtier, a Loyal Subject, an honest man, a bountifull Master, & good Christian could merit of his Prince & Country: One thing more let me note, That he often expressed to me, the abhorrance he had, of that base & unworthy action, which he was put upon, of Engaging the *Smyrna* fleete in time of Peace, which, though he behaved himselfe like a greate Captaine; yet he told me was the onely blot of his life, & troubled him Exceedingly: for though he was commanded, & niver examin'd it farther, when he was so: yet allways spake of it with regret, & detestation:

30 I went home very sad: & then write his *Countesse* a letter giving her an Account of what pass'd in his sicknesse, she being then at her Daughters the Countesse of *Derby*, at his seate almost 200 miles off:

Aug: 1 A *stranger* on 23: *Psal:* 4: The holy Sacrament follow'd: *Curate* on 30: *Pro:* 8: indifferently: 5 Sir Jo: *Stonehouse*, his *Lady*, and other Company came from *Lond*. to dine with us. 8 our *Curate* as before, with the usual *Common places*: *Pomerid*: Mr. *Jackson* on 11. *Eccles:* 9.

17 Went to *Bromely* to visite the Bish: of *Rochest* ⟨e⟩r wher I met Dr. *Alestrie* provost of Eaton, who having lately received a fall, appeared to me, as if he would not overcome, the indis⟨pos⟩ition it put him into:

24 Came Mr. ⟨*Boscauen*⟩ & his Lady, & my sweete Child Godolphin, to dine with us:

27 To *Lond:* return'd that Evening: 29 *Viccar* as before: 30: Lond: I went to visite a French Stranger, one Monsieur *Jardine* [1] [since Knighted by his Majestie & made Denison of *England*] who having ben thrice at the *East Indias*, *Persia* & other remote Countries, came hither in our returne ships from those parts; and it being reported he was a very curious man, & knowing, I was desir'd by the *Ro: Society* in their name, to salute him, & to let him know how glad they should be to receive him, if he pleased to do them that honour: &c. There were appointed to accompanie me Sir *Jo: Hoskins* & Sir *Chr: Wren* &c. We found him at his lodging, in his Eastern habite, a very handsom person, extreamely affable, not inclin'd to talke Wonders, but exceedingly modest, & a well bred man: It seemes he traveld in search of *Jewels*, & was become extreamely rich: He spake *Latine*, understood the *Greeke*, *Arabic* & *Persian* by 11 yeares Conversation in those Parts, yet seem'd he not to be above 36 years of age: After the usual Civilities, we told him, we much desired an account of the extraordinary things he must have seene; having (as we understood) trav⟨e⟩ld over land, those places, where few, if any *northern Europeans* used to go, as about the Black & Caspian Sea, *Mingrelia*, *Bagdat*, *Ninive*, ⟨*Persepolis*⟩ &c: He told us the things most worthy of our sight, would be, the draughts he had caused to be made of some noble ruines &c: for that (besides his little talent that way) he had carried two very good Painters along with him, to draw Landskips, Measure, and designe the remainders of the *Palace* which *Alexander* burnt in his frolique at *Persepolis*, with divers Temples, Columns, Relievos, & statues, yet extant, which he affirm'd were Sculptures far exceeding, any thing he had observ'd either at *Rome*, [Greece] or any other part of the World, where Magnificence was in estimation: That there was there an Inscription, of Letters not intelligible, though exceedingly intire; but was extreamely sorry he could not gratifie the Curiosity of the *Society*, at present, his things, not being yet out of the ship; but would take the first opportunity to waite on us with them, at his returne from Paris, whither he was hastning the very next morning, but with intention, to be suddenly back againe, & stay

1 Chardin, later Sir John Chardin.

longer in our Country, the persecution in *France* not suffering
Protestants, & such he was, to be quiet: so we failed of seeing his
Papers; but it was told us by others, that he durst indeede not
open or shew them, 'til he had first shew'd them to the French
King; though of this he himselfe said notthing: On farther dis-
course, he told us that *Nineveh* was a vast Citty, all now buried in
her ruines, and the Inhabitants building on the subterranean
Vaults, which were (as appeared) the first stories of the old Cittie;
That there were frequently ⟨found⟩, huge Vasas of fine Earth,
Columns, & other Antiquities &c: That the straw which the
Egyptian *Pharoah* so tyrannicaly requir'd of the *Israelites*, was not
to burne, or Cover their rowes of brick, as we use; but being
chopp'd small, to mingle with the *Clay*, which drying in the Sunn
(for they bake not in the furnaces) would else cleave asunder:
That in *Persia* are yet a race of *Igniculi*, that still Worship the
Sunn, & the fire as Gods: That the Women of *Georgia* & *Mingrelia* were Universaly, & without any compare, the most beautifull Creatures for shape, features, & figure in the whole world, &
that therefore The *Grand Signor*, & *Bashaws* &c had thence most
of their Wives & Concubines: That there had within these 100
yeares ben *Amazons* amongst them (that is) a sort or race of
Valiant Women, given to Warr: That *Persia* was infinitely fertile.
He spake also of Japon, & China, & of the many greate errours of
our late Geographers &c: as we suggested occasion to discourse;
& so we tooke our leaves, & made report to our *Society*: & I
returned home:

September 2: I went to *Lond:* because of an Opportunity I had
of his Majesties being yet at *Winsor*, to see his private Library at
Whitehall, which I now did at my full Ease; and went with
expectation of finding some Curiosities: But tho there were
about a thousand Volumes, there were few of any greate importance, or which I had not perused before; they consisting
chiefely of such books as had from time to time ben dedicated,
or presented him: Few Histories, some Traveles, & french
bookes, Aboundance of *Mapps* & Sea-⟨Charts⟩: Entertainements, & Pomps; buildings, & Pieces relating to the Navy: some
Mathematical Instruments &c: But what was most rare were 3 or
4 Romish *Breviaries* with a greate deale of *Miniature* & Monkish Painting & Gilding; one of which is most exquisitely don,
both as to the figures, *Grotescs* & Compartiments, to the uttmost

of that curious art: There's another in which I find written by
the hand of *Henry* the 7th, his giving it to his deare Daughter
Margarite, afterwards *Queene* of *Scots* ([Greate] mother of our
K. *James*, & greate greate Grandmother to the successive Kings,
uniting the two Kingdomes) in which he desires her to pray for
his soule, subscribing his Name at length: There is also the
Processe of the Philosophe⟨r⟩s greate *Elixir*, represented in
divers pieces of incomparable miniature; but the Discourse is in
high-Dut⟨c⟩h & a MSS: Also another MS. in quarto of above
300 yeares old in *French*, being an *Institution* of *Physic*, & in the
Botanical part, the Plants are curiously painted in Miniature:
There is likewise a *Folio Manu-script* of a good thicknesse, being
the severall exercises, as *Theames*, *Orationes*, *Translations* &c: of
K. *Edward* the *sixt*, all written & subscrib'd by his owne hand,
& with his name very legibly, & divers of the Greeke, interlin'd,
& corrected, after the manner of Schole-boys exercises, & that
exceedingly well & proper, with some Epistles to his *Præceptor*
&c, which shews that Young Prince to have ben extraordinarily
advanc'd in learning, & as *Cardan* that greate Wit &c (who had
ben in Englan'd) affirmed, stupendiously knowing for his age:
There is likewise his Journal, no lesse testif⟨y⟩ing his earely
ripenesse & care about the affaires of state: [Dr. *Burnet* has tran-
scribd many remarks out of this in his *Hist* of the *Reformation*.]

There are besides many other pompous Volumes, some
emboss'd with Gold, & Intaglios on *Achats*, *Medailes* &c: I spent 3
or 4 intire daies locked up, & alone amongst these bookes &c:
There is in the rest of the Private Lodgings contiguous to this,
divers of the best pictures of the greate *Masters*, *Raphael*, *Titian*
&c (& in my esteeme) above all the *Noli me tangere* of our *B: Saviour* to M: *Magdalen*, after his *Resurrection*, of *Hans Holbeins*,
than which, in my life, I never saw so much reverence & kind of
Heavenly astonishment, expressed in Picture: There are also
divers Curious *Clocks*, *Watches* & *Penduls* of exquisite work, and
other Curiosities: An antient Woman, who made these lodgings
Cleane, & had all the Keyes, let me in at pleasure, for a small
reward, by the meanes of a friend:

5 I found our late affected fantastical *Curate* Mr. Al——
preaching in the Chapel at *W:hall* on 119 Psal: 175 ver: that mens
soules were certainly immortal, distinct from the animal life
&c: It was not ⟨possible⟩ to heare him without astonishment at

his Confidence & formalitie: He was a boy of our *Parish*, that from a poore grammar schole, turn'd Preacher; & at last got the degree of Batchelor of Art, by a Mandamus, at *Cambridge*, where he had ben 2 or 3 daies, in his whole life: when he came back, that people might take notice of his degree, he ware his lamb-skin not onely two whole Sundays in the Church, but going all over the Towne, and Every streete, with a wonderfull traine of boys & girles running after him, (as they do when the Beares are led about) came to give me a visite in his formalities, at which I could not ⟨possibly⟩ containe my Countenance: This yet I must say of Mr. A. . . . that he has together with a vast stock of Confidence, a prodigious Memorie, & strong lungs, & some are taken with his Preachment, that know not the man out of the Pulpet: In a word he is a most singular person, & exceedingly conceited of his abillities: The blessed Sacrament follow'd: *Pomerid*: Co: *Garden* the Lecturer, on 1. Joh: 2. 23. an heavenly discourse:

6 I din'd with Sir *St: Fox*, now one of the Lords Commissioners of the *Treasury*: This Gent: came first a poore boy from the Quire of Salisbury, then was taken notice of by Bish: *Duppa*, & afterwards waited on my Lord Percy (bro: to *Algernon* E: of Northumberland) who procured for him an inferior place amongst the Clearks of the *Kitchin* & *Greene-Cloth* side: Where he was found so humble, dilligent, industrious, & prudently to behave himselfe, that his Majestie being in Exile, & Mr. Fox waiting, both the *King* & Lords about him, frequently Employed him about their affaires, trusted him both with receiving and paying the little mony, they had: Returning with his *Majestie* into England after greate Wants, & greate sufferings: his Majestie . . . so honest & industrious, & withall so capable & ready; that being advanced, from Cl: of the *Kitchin* to that of the Greene-Cloth &c: he procured to be pay-Master to the Whole Army, & by his dexterity, & punctual dealing ⟨obtained⟩ such credit amongst the Banquers, that he was in short time, able to borrow vast summs of them, upon any exigence; The continud Turning thus of mony, & the souldiers moderate allowance to him, for his keeping touch with them, did so inrich him; that he is believed to be worth at the least 200000 pounds honestly ⟨gotten⟩, & unenvied, which is next to Miracle, & that with all this he still continues as humble, & ready to do a Courtesie, as ever he was; nay he

is generous, & lives very honorably, of a sweete nature, well spoken, & well bred, & so very highly in his Majesties Esteeme, &
usefull, that being long-since made a Knight, he is also advanc'd
to be one of the Lords Commissioners of the *Treasury*: & has the
reversion of the Coferers place after Harry Brounckar: He has
married his Eldest Daughter to my Lord Cornwallis, & gave her
12000 pounds & restored that intangled family besides: Match'd
his Eldest Sonn to Mrs. *Trallop* who brings with her (besides a
greate summ) neere, if not altogether 2000 pounds per annum:
Sir Stephens Lady (an excellent Woman) is sister to Mr. *Whittle*
one of the Kings Chirurgions: In a word, never was man more
fortunate than Sir Stephen; & with all this he is an handsom person, Vertuous & very religious, & for whom I have an extraordinary esteeme:

9 Solemnly remembred a deare deceased Friend, whose
memory is never by me to be forgotten on this day:

11 I went with my *Wife* to see my deare *Bro*: at *Wotton*. 12: one
Mr. *Wye* the *Curat* of *Ábinger* preach'd at Wotton, on 1. Sam: 3.
18: *Pomerid*: were Prayers at my Brothers:

13 My Lord the Earle of *Chesterfield* now *Justice in Iyre*; sent
me a fat Buck out of *New-Park*, which I presented to my Bro: &
we eate among severall good friends & gent: of the neighbour-
hood:

23 Came to my house some German strangers, & *Signor
Pietro* a famous *Musitian*, who had ben long in *Sweden* in *Queene
Christinas* Court: he sung *admirably* to a *Guitarr* & has a perfect
good tenor & base &c: & had set to *Italian* composure, many of
Abraham Cowleys Pieces which shew'd extreamely well: He told
me the heate [some part] in summer was as excessive as the Cold
in winter in Sweden; so cold he affirm'd, that the streetes of all
the townes are desolate, no creature stirring in them for many
moneths, all the inhabitans retiring to their stoves: He spake
high things of that romantic *Queene*, her Learning, skill in Languages, the Majestie of her behaviour, her Exceeding Wit, & that
the Histories she had read of other Counteries, especialy of *Italy
& Rome* made her despize her owne: That the real occasion of
her resignation of the Crowne to her *Cousin*, was the Noblemens
importuning her to Marie, and the Promise which the Pope had
made her of procuring her to be *Queene* of Naples, which also
caused her to change her Religion, but she was cheated by his

crafty holinesse, working on her ambition: That the reason of her *Killing* her secretarie at *Fontain Beleaw*, was his revealing that Intrigue with the Pope: But after all this, I rather believe it was her mad prodigality & extreame Vanity, which had Consum'd all those vast treasures, the greate *Adolphus* (her father) had brought out of Germany, during his enterance there, & wonderfull successes; & that if she had not voluntarily resign'd (as forseeing the Event) the States of her Kingdome would have compell'd her.

October 3 our *Viccar* on 12 *Luke* 47: 48: The holy Sacrament follow'd: *Pomer*: a stranger on 4. Psal: 6 To Lond.

9 I was *Godfather*, with the Earle of *Fevershame* Monsieur Duras (of the family of *Turen*;) Lord Chamberlaine to the Queene, together with the *Dutchesse* of *Grafton* & *Mademoiselle* de *Beverward* to *Signor Del Campos Twinns*, a Boy & a Girle; Christend at *White-hall*: *Del Campo*, was one of the Pages of the back-stayres to her *Majestie*. 10: Dr. *Goodman* pre: on 119 *Psal*: 96. *Coram Rege*: Dr. *Bell* on: 1: *Eccles*: 16: *Pomeridiano* to St. *Martines*, where I saw Christned, by the Bish: of St. *Asaph* a *Jewesse* of quality come out of *Holland*, her *Susceptors* were Sir *Lionel Jenkins* pr: *Secretary* of state, The Countesses of *Thannet* & *Clarendon*. 16 I returned home:

17 Our *Viccar* as before: *Pomerid*: a young man on 22: *Matt*: 12: 24 I was wonderfully indispos'd by a Cold, so as I could not - stirr out:

30 I went to *Lond*: [to be private:] My Birth-day being the next; & I now arived to the sixtieth yeare of Age; [31] upon which, I began a more solemn survey of my whole Life, in order to the making, and confirming my peace with *God*, by an accurate Scrutinie of all my actions past, as far as I was able to call them to min'd: And oh, how difficult, & uncertaine, yet most necessarie worke; The Lord be mercifull to me & accept me. Who can tell how oft he offendeth? Teach me therefore so to Number my daies, that I may apply my heart to wisdome, make my calling & election sure: *Amen Lord Jesus*: I spent this whole day in Exercise &c: A *stranger* preaching at *White-hall* on 16 *Luke* 30. 31: I thence went to St. *Martines*, where the Bish: of St. *Asaph* preach'd on 1. *Pet*: 3. 15. How necessary it was every *Christian* should be able to render an account of their Faith & Religion, applying it to the present Conjuncture: The holy *Communion* follow'd, at which I participated, humbly imploring

Gods Assistance in the greate Work I was entering into. *Pomerid*: I heard Dr. *Sprat* at St. *Margarites* on 17: Act: 11, shewing how Religion & Holinesse, & Dexterity in the Scriptures dos truely enoble, from the Example of the *Bereans* &c:

November 1. I began, and spent this whole Weeke in examining my life, beging pardon for my faults, Assistance & blessing for the future, that I might in some sort be prepared for the time that now drew neere, & not have the greate worke to begin, when one can worke no longer: The Lord *Jesus* help & assist me: I therefore stirred little abroad til the 5t, when I heard Dr. *Tenison* the now *Viccar* of St. Martines (Dr. *LLoyd*, the former incumbent, being made Bishop of St. Asaph): his Text was on   They will thinke they do God good service, whosoever killeth you, applied to the solemnity of the day, which was the *Papists* Conspiracy: On the

7 Dr. *Patrick* at *Covent Garden* on 1: *Phil:* 9, excellently setting-forth the Love we ought to have to our fellow *Christians*, & to all man-kind: after which succeded the blessed *Communion*, at which I participated finishing, & confirming my Resolutions, of giving my-selfe up more intirely to God, to whom I had now most solemnly devoted the rest of my poore remainder of life in this World; The *Lord* inabling me, who am an unprofitable servant, a miserable sinner, yet depending on his infinite goodnesse & mercy, accepting my endeavors: I dind at my Bro: now come up to the Parliament, being Knight of the Shire for *Surrey*: In the afternoone a stranger on 1. *Eccles:* 2, & on the 12, returned to my house, finding my Daught⟨e⟩r *Mary* (whom I left very ill) well recovered, for which Almighty God be praised. 15 Came to Visite & dine with us Sir Ri: *Anderson*, his Lady, Sonn & Wife sister to my Daughter in Law:

30 The Anniversary Elections at the R: Society brought me to Lond: where was chosen Præsident, that excellent person, & greate Philosopher Mr. *Robert Boyle* who indeed, ought to have ben the very first; but neither his infirmitie, nor modestie could now any longer excuse him: I desir'd I might for this yeare be left out of the *Council*, by reason my dwelling was in the Country; The *Society*, according to Costome, din'd together: This signal day, began the *Trial* of my Lord *Vicount Stafford* for conspiring the Death of the King, and was likewise his *Birth-day*.

December 2. I was curious to see & heare the famous Triale of my *L: Stafford* [second] sonn to my Lord *Thomas Howard*, Earle

of *Arundel* & Surry, *Earle Marishall* of England, & Grandfather
to the present Duke of Norfolck, whom I so well knew, & from
which excellent person, I received so many favours: The Trial was
in *Westminster Hall*, before the *King, Lords* & *Commons*, just in
the same manner as just 40 yeares past, the greate & wise Earle of
Strafford (there being but one letter differing their names)
received his Tryal (for pretended ill government in Ireland) in
that famous *Parliament* [and same place]: This Lord *Staffords*
Father being High-Steward &c: Onely the Place of sitting was
now exhalted some considerable height from the Paved flore of
the Hall, with a stage of boards, His Majesties Throne or state, the
Woolsacks for the Judges, long formes for the Peeres, Chaire of
the Lord Steward *pro tempore*, exactly ranged as in the house of
Lords: All the sides on both hands Scaffolded to the very roofe,
for the Members of the H: of Commons: At the uper end, &
right side of the *Kings* state, was a box for his *Majestie*, others for
the Greate Ladys on the left hand; and over head a gallerie for
Ambassadors & Pub: *Ministers*: At the lower-end or Enterance
was a Barr, & place for the Prisoner, The *Lieutennant* of the *Toure*
of *London*, the *Axe-bearer* & Guards, My Lord *Staffords* two
Daughters, the Marchionesse of Winchester being one. There
was likewise a Box for my Lord to retire into; At the right hand
in another box some what higher, stood the *Witnesses*, at the left,
the *Manegers*, who were to produce & manege the Evidence &
whole processe in the name of the *Commons* of *England*: viz: Serjeant *Maynard*, (the greate lawyer, the same who prosecuted the
Cause against the Earle of Strafford 40 yeares before in the same
place, being now neere 80 yeares of age) Sir *William Jones*, (late
Attourney Gen:) Sir *Fran: Winnington* (a famous Pleader) & Mr.
Treby (now Recorder of Lond:) not appearing in their gownes as
Lawyers, but in their cloakes & swords, as representing the
Commons of *England*. To these were joyn'd *Mr. Hamden, Mr.
Sechevarell, Mr. Poule, Coll: Titus, Sir Tho: Lee* all Gentlemen of
Qualitie & noted Parliament men: The two first dayes (in which
was read, the *Commission*, & Impeacchment) was but a very
tedious enterance into Matter of fact, the Charge, at which I was
little present: But on *Thursday* being commodiously seated
amongst the *Commons*, when the wittnesses were sworn, &
deposed, of which the principle were Mr. *Oates* (who cal'd himselfe *Doctor*) Mr. *Dugdale* & *Turberville*: Oates tooke his *Oath*,

that he delivered a Commission to V. Count *Stafford* from the *Pope*, to be *Pay-Master Generall*, to an Army intended to be raised &c: *Dugdale*, that being at my Lord *Astons*, the ⟨*Prisoner*⟩ dealt with him plainely to Murder his *Majestie*, & *Turbervile*, that at *Paris* also he proposed the same to him &c.

3 *Friday* was spent in Depositions of my *Lords* Wittnesses, to invalidate the Testimonie of the *Kings Witnesses*, which being very slight persons, though many, viz, 15 or 16: tooke up all that day: and in truth they rather did my Lord injurie than service, & made but little for him. 4: *Saturday* came other Witnesses of the Commons, to corroborate the *Kings*, of which some were *Peeres*, & some *Commons*, with other of good qualitie, who tooke off all the former days objections, & set the Kings *Witnesses recti in Curia*, & then adjourn'd 'til *moneday*:

5 Preach'd to the Household at *White-hall* Dr. *Calamie* (sonn to the famous *Presbyterian*, but of quite other Principles) on 5: *Matt* 24. Against taking Gods sacred-name in vaine; an excellent discourse & highly seasonable, the people of all degrees being ariv'd to a most dredfull excesse of that prophanatie, in such oathers & execrrations, as would make a *Christian* tremble to recite or heare: Also of the Lawfullnesse of *Oathes* in Judicial cases: &c: The holy Sacrament follow'd: *Coram Rege* preached Dr. *Patric Deane* of *Peterborow* on: 2: *Pet:* 3. 16: I din'd at my Bro: After dinner I heard prayers, & a good sermon at *Co: Garden* church on 5. *Luke* 25. 26.

6 *Moneday*, being the 6 of December I went againe to the Trial, where I heard the Evidences summ'd up by Sir *William Jones*, which was very large; and when he had don, & said all he could to exaggerate the charge succeded all the rest of the *Lawyers* Manegers; Then began Mr *Hen: Poule* in a vehement Oration, as to the profes of the *Jesuitical* doctrine, of holding it not onely *lawfull*, but meritorious to Murder an Heretic King; which my Lord, had in his plea denyed: After this my *Lord* (as upon all occasions, & very often he did during the whole Trial) spake in his owne defence, denying the Charge altogether; that he never in his life saw either *Turbervile* or *Oates* at the time, and manner affirmed; & in truth their Testimonie did little weigh with me; *Dugdales* onely seemed to presse hardest: To which my *Lord* spake a greate while, but without any method, & confus'dly: One thing my Lord said, which I confesse did exceedingly affect

me, as to *Titus Oates*, That a Person, who, during his depositions, should so vauntingly as he did, brag that though he went over to the Church of Rome, yet he was never a Papist, nor of their Religion, all the time that he seem'd to *Apostatize* from the Protestant; but onely as a spie; Though he confess'd he tooke their Sacraments, Worship'd Images, went through all the Oathes & discipline of their Proselytes, swearing seacrecy, & to be faithfull, but with intention to come over againe & betray them: That such an Hypocrite, that had so deeply prevaricated, as to turne even Idolater, (for so we of the *Church* of *England* esteem'd it) attesting God so solemnly, that he was intirely theirs, & devoted to their interests, & consequently (as he pretended) trusted; I say that the Witnesse of such a proflygate wretch should be admitted, against the life of a Pere; This my Lord, looked upon as a monstrous thing, & such as must needes redown'd to the dishonor both of our Religion & Nation: And verily, I am of his *Lordships* opinion; Such a mans Testimonie should not be taken against the life of a Dog: 'Tis true, many Protestants had defected, & return'd againe; but we know of none, (nor if any, can approve them) who when they turned *Papists*, did not heartily believe they were in the right, 'til they were convinc'd to the Contrary: But this is not *Oates* his case, he went thro all the mysteries of their Religion, thro all their Oat⟨h⟩es, Execrations on himselfe, Sacraments &c, whilst by his owne Confession, he disembl'd all; This he affirmed & I know not on what occasion it escaped from him, no lesse impiously: than foolishly: From this moment foreward, I had quite lost my opinion of Mr. *Oates*. But the merite & service of something material which he discovered against *Coleman* at first, put him in such esteeme with the Parliament &c: that now I fancy, he stooke at nothing, & thought every body was to take what he said for *Gospel* afterwards: The Consideration of this, and some other Circumstances began to stagger me; particularly, how 'twas possible, that one who went amongst the *Papists* with such a designe, & pretended to be intrusted with so many letters, & Commissions from the *Pope* & *party*, nay & delivered them to so many greate Persons, should not reserve one of them to shew, or produce, nor so much as one Copie of any Commission; which he who had such dexterity in opening letters &c, might certainly have don, to the undenyable Conviction of those whom he accus'd: But, as I said, he gained

Credit upon *Coleman*, but as to others whom he so madly flew
upon, I am little inclined to believe his testimonie; he being so
slight a person, so passionate, ill-bred, & [of] impudent behaviour: nor is it at all likely, such piercing politicians as the *Jesuites*
should trust him with so high, & so dangerous seacrets. [7] On
Tuesday I was againe at the *Trial*, when Judgement was
demanded, and after my Lord had spoken what he could in
denying of the fact &c: The *Manegers* answering the objections
&c: The Peeres adjourned to their House, & within two houres,
return'd againe: There was in the meane time this farther question put, whither there being but one witnesse to any single
Crime or act, it could amount to convict a man; upon this, the
Judges being cald on to give their opinion, unanimously
declar'd, that in case of *Treason* they all were overt acts; for
though no man should be condemn'd by one witnesse for any
one act, yet for severall acts to the same intent, it was valid,
which was my Lord Staffords Case; for one sware he practised
him to Kill his Majestie at *Paris*, another at my L: *Astons*, a
Third that he delivered him a Commission from *Rome*, but to
neither of these were ⟨there⟩ above one Witnesse, so it was over-
ruled: This being past, and The Peres in their seates againe, my
Lord [Chancelor] *Finch* (who was this day *High Steward*)
removing to the *Wool-sack* next his Majesties state, after summoning the *Lieutennant* of the *Tower* to bring forth his Prisoner,
and Proclamation made for silence; demanded of every Peere
(who were in all 86) whither William *Lord Vicount Stafford*
were Guilty of the Treason Laied to his Charge, or not Guilty:
Then the Peere (spoken to) standing up, & laying his right hand
upon his breast, sayed *Guilty*, or *Not Guilty* Upon his honour;
& then sate downe: & so another 'til all were asked: the L: *Steward*
noting their severall Suffrages as they answered upon a paper:
When all had don, the number of not Guilties being but 31, the
Guiltys 55, after *Proclamation* for silence againe; The *Steward*
directing his speech to the Prisoner (against whom the Axe was
turn'd edge ways towards him, & not before) in aggravation of
his Crime, he being enobled by his *Majesties Father*, & since
received many favours & graces from his present Majestie: That
came of such a stock, & noble family, had appeared in his
defence in time of the late rebellion &c: & all that could signifie
to the charge of his ingratitude & disloyalty: Then inlarged on

the honor & justice of their Proceedings against him with a *Christian* exhortation to Repentance, & Confession, deploring first his owne unhapinisse, that he who never Condemned any man before, should now be necessitated to begin with him, &c: & then Pronounced Sentence of Death, by *Hanging, Drawing & Quartering* (according to forme) with greate solemnity, and dreadfull gravity; last of all, after a short pause; Told the *Prisoner*, That he believed the *Lords* would interceede with his *Majestie* that some Circumstances of his sentence, might be omitted, beheading onely excepted & then breaking his Whitestaff, the Court disolved. My *Lord Stafford* during all this later part spake very little, & onely Gave their Lordships thanks, after the sentence was pronounc'd; & indeede behav'd himselfe modestly, and as became him: 'Twas observ'd, that all his owne Relations, & of his Name & family Condemn'd him, excepting onely his *Nephew* the *Earle* of *Arundel*: sonn to the D: of *Norfolck*: and it must be acknowledg'd that the whole Trial was carried on from first to last, with exceeding gravity, & so stately and august appearance I had never seene; for besides innumerable spectators of Gent: & forraine Ministers &c: who saw & heard all the proceedings, the Prisoner had the Consciences of all the Commons of England for his Accusers, and all the *Peeres* to be his *Judges* & *Jury*: He had likewise the assistance of what Counsel he would to direct him in his plea, that stood by him: And yet I can hardly think, a person of his age & experience, should engage men, whom he never saw before, (& one of them that came to visite him as a stranger, at *Paris*), *point blanque* to Murder the *King*: God onely, who searches hearts, can discover the Truth, & to him it must be left: My Lord *Stafford*, was not a man belov'd, Especialy of his owne family, & had ben suspected, & in danger to by it, of a Vice in Germanie, which neede not be nam'd, and I doubt not but he had seriously repented.

11 I returned home:

12 Our *Viccar* & *Curate* proceeded on their former Texts: This Evening looking out of my Chamber Window towards the West, I first saw a Meteor, (or what ever other *Phœnomenon* it was) of an obscure bright Colour (if so I may call it without a solecisme) resembling the brightnesse of the *Moone* when under a thin Clow'd, very much in shape like the blade of a sword, whose point to the starre in appearance, bending Northwards

towards London, not seeming at the *Horizon* to be above a yard in bredth, & so pyramidal, the rest of the skie, very serene & cleere; The Moone new, but not appearing, the Weather exceeding sharp, hard frost with some snow falling 2 daies before: What this may Portend (for it was very extraordinarie) God onely knows; but such another *Phænomen⟨on⟩* I remember I saw, which went from *North to South*, & was much brighter, & larger, but not so *Ensiforme* in the yeare *1640*, about the Triall of the greate Earle of *Strafford*, præceeding our bloudy Rebellion: I pray God avert his Judgements; we have had of late severall *Comets*, which though I believe appeare from natural Causes, & of themselves operate not, yet I cannot despise them; They may be warnings from God, as they commonly are for-runners of his Annimadversions: After some daies this plainly appeared to be headed with a small hazy-starr distant from *Venus* 23°–'58 & the bright st: of *Aquila* 28–15– $\frac{1}{2}$ –5°–90 *Latitude*-9°–44 South, the taile or point extending to the middle of Sagitta above a *degree* broad, & was 35 *deg:* long.

17 This day being friday, at exactly halfe an ⟨houre⟩ after one at noone, was my Daughter in Law brought to bed of a *Sonn*, a very fine babe; for which I gave God Thanks:

18 Came the *Duke of Norfolck* to visite me, and lay this Night at my house, being the next day going towards *Dover* & Embark for Flanders: he did not seeme to be at all Concern'd for his Unkle Stafford: but We were discoursing & talking of other matters 'til it was neere one a Clock at night: After his Grace was gon, who kept me from church all the Morning, [19] being the last Sonday of Advent; was Christned my little Grandsonn, by the name of *Richard*: his Grandfather *Sir Rich: Browne* & my Bro: *Geo: Evelyn* being Susceptors with my *Lady Stonehouse* mother of my Daughter in Law:

22 Was the solemn Publique Fast thro out England, that God would prevent all popish plotts, avert his Judgements, & give a blessing to the proceedings of the *Parliament* now assembled, & which struck at the *Succession* of the *Duke of York* &c: our *Viccar* preached on 122 *Psal:* 7 pray for the peace of *Jerusalem*. 25 *Chr:mas day*, on 1 *Tim* 1. 15: The holy Sacrament follow'd. 26: on the same Text: I had neighbours dined with us. 29, was the unhappy Vi-Count *Stafford* beheaded on *Tower* hill. 31 After recollection &c: I humbly gave thanks to God, for his mercies to me this past Yeare:

EXOTIC EMBASSIES – THE FOUNDING
OF THE ROYAL HOSPITAL, CHELSEA
(1681–1682)

1681. JAN: 1, I beged the blessing of Almighty God upon me & mine the yeare now entered:

2 Our *Viccar* as before: The holy Communion follow'd: *Pomerid*: *Curate* on 4: *Phil*: 4. 9: our *Vicc*: as above: *Curate* on his former also:

After many daies & nights of Snow, Clowdy & dark weather, the *Comet* was gotten as far as the head of *Andromeda* & not above 23 deg: long, much wasted:

12 I went to *Lond*: about buisinesse, returned the 15. 16 our *Viccar* sick, a stranger, on 50 *Psal*: 15: This day was my Daughter in Law *Churched*: *Pomerid*. on 16: Matt: 26: 17: I went to *Lond*, return'd immediately:

23 Our *Viccar* on his former, with no greate addition: *Pomerid*: a *stranger* on 85 *Psal*: 10: 30 *Viccar* on 24. *Act*: 16: *Curat* on his former, nothing very observable. 31 To *Lond*: Dr. *Turner Coram Rege*, (being the *Anniversarie* of his fathers *Martyrdom*) on 4: *Threnæ* 20. describing the Tretcherie of his Enemies, & in what sense a good Prince & Governor, is the life of his People &c:

Feb: ⟨6⟩: Dr. *Patrick* at *Co*: *Gard*: 10 *Heb*: 38: The holy Sacrament follow'd: I dind at my Bro: & afternoone heard the *Curate* on 23 Pro: 17.

10 I was at the Wedding & Marriage of my Nephew *Jo*: *Evelyn* of Wotton, married by my L: *Bish*: of *Rochester* at *Westminster* (in *Hen*: 7th *Chapell*) to the daughter & heyre of Mr. *Erskin* of *Sussex*, her portion 8000 pounds: I wish it may ⟨prove⟩ happy to him, & the familie, having first proposed it to my Bro: & that she is like to be a proper beautifull young Lady, & of an honourable familie: The solemnity was kept with a few select friends only, at My *Lady Beckfords* mother of the Lady: ⟨13⟩: Dr. *Thistletwhait coram Rege*, on 8 *Eccl*: 11: I din'd with my Bro: *Pomerid*: Dr. *Sprat* at St. *Margarits* on 2: *Tit*: 14. 18: Dr. *Stillingfleete* excellently on 18 *Luke* 13: 19 I returned home: ⟨20⟩ our *Viccar* on 24 Act: 16 his former Text. *Curate* on 19: Luke: 41.

Mar: 7 To *Lond*: din'd at the *Earle* of *Sunderlands*. 8 Visited, & din'd at the *Earle* of *Essexes*, with whom I spent most of the

Afternoone alone in his study: Thence to Visite my (yet living) *Godmother* & kindswoman Mrs. Keightly (Sister to Sir *Tho:* Evelyn & niepce to my Father,) being now 86 yeares of age, a spritfull woman & in perfect health, her Eyes yet serving her as well as ever, & she of a Countenance very Comely, one would not take her to be above 50 at most:

27 Our Viccar on his former Text: holy Sacrament followed: *Pomerid*: *Curate* on 1. *Cor:* 2. 2. The *Parliament* now conven'd at *Oxford*: Greate expectation of his *Royal Highnesses* Case, as to Succession, against which the house was set:

An extraordinary sharp, cold Spring, not yet a leafe on the trees, frost & snow lying: whilst the whole nation was in a greate ferment. 30 To *Lond:* in order to preparation against Easter:

Aprill 1. At. St. *Martines Dr. Tenison* on 2: *Tit:* 14: the holy Comm: follow'd. *Pomerid* Dr. *Smith* of Chr: *Church Oxon* (*coram rege*) on 2. *Heb:* 17. I supp'd at my L: Chamberlains. 2 went home: 3 *Easter-day* a stranger on 24 *Luke* 34: The holy *Sacrament* follow'd: I received with my family: *Pomer*: *Curate* on: 1. *Cor:* 15. 20: 9: To *Lond:* 10: Dr. *Stillingfleete* first serm: on 1. *Jam:* 12. (*Coram Rege*) Dr. *Tillotson* on 13 *Jer:* 23. The exceeding difficulty of reforming habitual sinns & making it next to impossible, from that of the *Ethiops* changing his skin, ⟨*Leopard*⟩ his spotts: like the Camels going through the needles Eye, which our *B: Saviour* makes onely possible with God; to expresse the Rich-mans difficulty &c: It was a tirrible & severe discourse, shewing how it concerned sinners to serious repentance: 11 I went to Visite the Bish: of *Rochester*, & tooke my leave of Dr. *Lloyd* now Bish: of St. *Asaph*, at his house in Licester fields, now going to reside in his Diocesse: 12 I din'd at Mr. Brisbans Secretary to the Admiralty, a learned & industrious person: whither came Dr. *Burnet* to thank me for some Papers I had contributed towards his excellent *Historie* of the *Reformation*: Thence to the R: *Society*, next day home: 17: Our *Viccar* on his former *Text. Curate* on 3 *Zech:* 2 of Obedience to *Magistrates*, not much to the Text: 22: To Lond about my Accompts: 24. at *W:hall*: Dr. *Pettus* on 1. *Pet:* 48: (*Cor: Rege*) Dr. Hall on   Iniquity shall not be your ruine: *Pomerid*: B: of St. *Asaph*, at the *Tabernacle* (neere St. *Martines*) on 1. *Pet:* 3. 6:

26 I dined at *Dom Piedro Ronquillos* the Spanish *Ambassador* at *Wild house*, used me with extraordinarie Civility: After dinner (which was plentifull, halfe after the Spanish, & halfe after the

English way) he led me into his Bed-chamber, where we both
fell into a long discourse about *Religion*; in which, though he
was a learned man in Politiques, & an Advocate; I found him
very ignorant, & unable to defend any point of Controversy,
blindly recurring at every foote, to the Churches *Infallibility*, &
Tradition—he was however far from being fierce; onely at parting earnestly wishing that I would humbly apply my selfe to the
Blessed Virgin to direct me, & that he had know⟨n⟩ divers that
had ben averse from the *Roman Catholique* religion, be wonderfully inlightned & convinced by her Intercession. This was a
pretty *Postulatum*; he would have one be a *papist*, that he might
be a *Papist*: They have not a weaker tenet in all their Religion,
than this error of Invocation of Saints & Adoration: so I tooke
leave of the *Ambassador*, who importun'd me to come & visite
him offten:

29 I gave in my grand Accompt to the Lords *Commissioners*
of the Treasury, & so home, but one showre of raine all this
Moneth, the whole yeare dry &c:

May 1 *Viccar* on 11 *Heb:* 17: The ho: sacrament followed &c:
Curate Pomerid: on: 2: Phil. 1. 7. of Charity & Union &c, it being
Mr. Smith our Curates valedictory Sermon, now going to a living
in the Country: a good man, but had not the talent of Preaching:
2 The Foefees of the poore mett according to Costome:

5 Came to visite & dine with me Sir *William Fermor*, of
N:hamptonshire, & Sir *Chr: Wren*, his Majesties *Architect* &
Surveyor, now building the Cathedrall of St. Paules, & the
Columne in memorie of the Citties Conflagration, & was in
hand with the building of 50 Parish Churches: a ⟨wonderfull⟩
genius had this incomparable Person:

9 To *Lond:* about my *Accompt* with the *Auditor* of the Exche-
quer. ⟨12⟩ *Ascension* day, a stranger at St. *Martins* on 3 *Jonah*: 4.
The holy com: followed: 15 At the Abby church, Dr. *Brevall* a
French Proselyte (now a prebend there) on 14 *John* 16. 17:

I dined at Sir *James Shaens*, who had married my Lady
Frances, daughter to the Earle of *Killdare* a relation of ours,
where was also her sister, the Countesse of *Clancarne*, virtuous
& most religious Ladys, *Niepces* to *Boyle* Earle of *Corke* &
Burlington &c: *Pomerid*: we all went to St. *Margarites* where
Dr. *Tillotson*; shewing the danger of deferring Repentance 'til
old age:

16 Came my Lady the *Countesse* of *Sunderland*, to desire me, that I would propose a Match to Sir *Stephen Fox*, for her sonn, my *Lord Spencer*, to Marry Mrs. *Jane* Sir *Stephens* daughter: I excused it all I was able; for the truth is, I was afraid he would prove an extravagant man; for though a youth of extraordinary parts, & that had all the Education imaginable to render him a worthy man; yet his early inclinations to vice made me apprehensive I should not serve Sir *St: Fox* in it, like a friend: This being his now onely Daughter, so well bred, & who was like to receive a large share of her fathers kindnesse, as far as opulence & mony could expresse it: For Sir *Stephen* is my Friend, & for whom I have much esteeme; & I consider'd that My Lord *Sunderland*, being much sunke in his Estate, by Gaming & other prodigalities, it could not at this time answer Sir *Stephens* expectations; for my *Lord*, was now no longer secretary of state, but was falln in displeasure with the King, for his siding with the Commons &c: about the Succession; but which, I am very well assured he did not do, out of his owne inclination, or for the preservation of the *Protestant* religion; but by mistaking a party, which he believed would have carried it, & perhaps had good reason to think so: For otherwise Sir *Stephen* did not stand so much upon a rich fortune for his Favorite daughter, but was willing to marry her to a noble familie, both to fortifie his interests, & better his allyance: However so earnest & importunate was the *Countesse* that I would use my interest, & breake it to him; that I was over come, and did accordingly promise it: so next day, I tooke an opportunitie to introduce the proposal: Sir *Stephen* (who knew nothing of the young gallants inclinations, but that he was as to appearance, one of the loveliest & spiritous Youths in England) professed to me, that no man in England's recomendations should be sooner receiv'd than mine; but told me That it was too greate an honour to him, that his Daughter was very Young, as well as my Lord, & he was fully resolv'd never to marry her, without the parties mutual liking, which she could not judge of 'til more advanc'd in age, with other difficulties and objections that I neither could, nor would contradict: I told him how I was ingag'd, & that I would serve them both, if he thought good to proceede, and take what measures he should give me in this matter; I onely told him that I was my Lady *Sunderlands* friend, one that she trusted with many ⟨of⟩ her concernes, & did Confesse their condition as

to *Estate* was impair'd; but that I verily believ'd, that if it were set-free, they would husband things better for the future, & that he would do an act of greate Generositie, & as already he had, (by marrying his Eldest Daughter with a vast Portion,) redeem'd my Lord *Cornwallis's* intangled estate, (& who proved a very worthy gent:) so it would be his glory to set up the Earle of Sunderlands family againe; with how great an obligation it would be to those who sought his Alyance: This did a little worke upon *Sir Stephens* good nature, who I am sure might have had his choice in any of the best families in England: However he desired me to write to the Countesse, & to expresse the greate sence he had of the honour don him; that his Daughter & her sonn were too Young, that he would do nothing without her liking, which he did not think her capable of expressing judiciously, 'til she should arive to the age of 16 or 17: of which she now wanted 4 yeares; & in short, that I would put it off as civily as I could for the present; which indeede I did: But my Lady, (now that I had broken the ice,) continues to conjure my assistance, & that I would not leave it in this posture:

20 I went home. 22: our *Viccar* on *Whitsonday* pr: on: 4: Eph: 30: The Bl: Sacrament followed: *Pomerid*: the new *Curate*, a pretty hopefull young man, yet somewhat raw, & newly come from the Colledge, full of latine sentences &c: which in time will weare off: He read prayers very well, & preached on 6: *Matt*. 33 of the preference of Heaven before Earthly fruitions; &c:

There had scarce fallen yet any raine since *Christmas*:

25 There came to visite me Sir *William Walter* & Sir *Jo: Eloues*: 26: and next day the Earle of Kildare, (a young gent related to my Wife) and other company to dinner: 29 His Majesties Birthday &c. & *Trinity Sonday*, our *Viccar* on 13: Rom: 1. of the duty of subjects, very well &c: *Curate* on 11: *Matt*: 28.

30 *Trinity* Monday, (a festival day with the *Society* in our Parish, where the Elections are made by Graunt from H: 8:) my *Lord Berkeley* being chosen *Master*, his Chaplaine preach'd on 1. *Jonah* 6: shewing the greate reason sea-men (of all others), have of being well prepared for death, & most exposed to danger &c: I went up to Lond, with my Lord, & din'd at the *Trinity* house:

June: 1 Din'd at Sir R: *Claytons*, thence to the R: *Society*. 2: To *Hampton-Court* where the Surry Gentlemen presented their Addresses to his Majestie whose hand I kissed, introduc'd by the

Duke of *Albemarle*: but my chiefe affaire was with some of the privy Council about my greate accompt: I tooke likewise another occasion of discoursing with Sir *Steph: Fox* about his daughter, & to revive that buisinesse, & at last brought it to this, That in case the young people liked one the other, after 4 yeares, (he first desiring to see a particular of my Lords present estate, if I could transmitt it to him privately, & not 'til then acquaint them with what now past betweene us) he would make her Portion 14000 pounds: though to all appearance, he may likely make it 50000 pounds as easily: his Eldest son, having no child, & growing very fatt: &c: So I went back to Lond: & the 4th home:

12 Our *Viccar* on 4 *Eph:* as before: *Curate* on 5. *Matt:* 3. My exceeding drowsinesse hindred my attention, which I feare proceeded from Eating too much, or the drinesse of the season & heate, it still continuing so greate a drowth, as was never knowne in Eng: & was said to be universal: 13 To *Lond:* 14: about my Accompt with the Lords Commiss: of the *Tres:*

16 returned home: 19 our *Viccar* proceeded: The *Curate* also went on: The dry weather had now withered every thing, & threatned some universal dirth &c:

21 To *Lond:* againe about my Accompts, return'd next day:

24 Came to dine with us the Earle of *Kildare*, Countesse of *Clancartie*, and some other persons of qualitie: I went to *Lond* with them returned next day.

26 our *Viccar* on 18 *Luke* 9. *Curate* on 5 *Matt*: 4. Some raine now fell:

July To *Lond*, about my Accompts: was very ill of gripings, & went home:

3 our *Viccar* absent; the Minister of *Roderith* supplied 5: Judg: 8: The holy Commu: followed: *Curate* on 2: *Act:* 37:

6 To *Lond:* to the R: *Society*, an Exper: of the effect & reason of impressed force, by the appulses of severall magnitudes: There were present two *Italian* Gent: recomended by Signor *Malphigi* of *Boulogna*: 8 I returned home:

10 Mr. *Saunders* on 73. *Psal:* 25: *Pomeridiano* on 19 *Luke* 42 The sad condition of a People, when no warning reformes them: Perstring'd the wanton temper of the Nation, the *schisme* & sedition in Church & state: &c: 11 To *Lond:* returnd that evening. 17: our *Curate* on 4: *Pro:* 23: *Pomerid:* a young *Scotch-man* on 1. *Eph:* 7: 20 To *Lond*, returned that evening.

21 My *Wife* & *Daughter* Mary &c: went to *Tunbridge* to
drinke the Waters: &c:

24 A stranger preached on 5: *Eph:* 1: *Pomer.* Curate on his for-
mer subject very well, and in good Method, of which the former
Curate had none: 31. The *Minister* of *Roderith* on 21 *Isa:* 11:
Curate on 19 *Luke*: 41. 42.

Aug: 4. To *Lond:* about severall affaires: Went to the *R: Society*
where was produced by Dr. *Slaer* (one of the Members) an
extraordinary Experiment: He prepared a matter, which without
exposure to the Sunn, or light, (as other *Phosphorus's* were)
shoone as bright as the flame of a Candle: It was a substance of
the Colour of mouth glew; had an urinous smell; with this he
wrote on a sheete of paper, ⟨nothing⟩ in the least appearing, but
being put into a dark place, shoone forth in a bright & delicate
stroke these two words *Vivat Rex Carolus*, which remain'd above
halfe an hour, & longer than we were willing to stay: A beame of
the Sunn was not more perspicuous, it did not flame up, but
remained close to the paper, in a neate stroake about the bignesse
⟨of⟩ Text letters, so as to give a pretty light about it; The very
motion of drawing it on a paper, (as one would write with a
black-lead pen) seting it on this lambent fire: & when it was
almost quite spent, rubbing it a little with ones hand or finger, it
would rekindle, yet without taking hold of, or leaving any track
on the paper, when exposed to the day againe: Many *Phosphorus*
had I seene, as that famous *Lapis illuminabilis* of *Boulogna*, which
I went there to see being in *Italy* many years since; but never
did I see any comparable to this: Washing my hands & face with
it, I appeared in the darke like the face of the moone, or rather
like some spirit, or strange apparition; so as I cannot but attribute
it to the greate providence of God, that it was not first found out
by the *Papists*; for had they the *seacret* onely, what a miracle might
they make it, supposing them either to rub the Consecrated
Wafer with it, or washing the Priests face & hands with it, &
doing the feate in some darke Church or Cloyster, proclaime it to
the Neighbour hood; I am confident the Imposture would bring
thousands to them, & do an infinity of mischiefe, to the establishing of the common error about Transubstantiation; all the
world would ring at the miracle &c: This matter being rubbed
very hard on paper or board, set it in a devowring flame, which
I never saw any *Phosphorus* do but this, & it being of a nature to

spend it selfe, or if a little warmed either by the fire or the Sunn, would flame out right, & burne most fiercely, but being kept continualy in a glasse of water, lasted without impaire: He affirm'd it to be *chymicaly* & with extraordinary preparation, composed of Urine & humane bloud: which gives greate light to Dr. *Willis* &c notions of the *flamula Vitalis* which animates the bloud, & is, for ought we know, the animal life it selfe of all things living: It is certainely a most noble Experiment; first excogitated & hinted (as this Doctor Confessed) by Mr. *Boyle*, with whom this industrious young Physitian, some time wrought in his Laboratory: He tooke a small portion, not bigger than a small peper Corne, layed it on a dry piece of fir board, & with the flatt of a knife bruised it, as one would spread a *Plaister*, & it immediately rose up in a fierce flame, & consum'd the board: Then he had a *Phiol* of *Liquor*, which he said was made of a disolution of this, which dropping into a beere glasse of *Ale*, conceived a flame, so soone as it touched & mingled with the *Ale*: of this I drank, & seem'd to me to be of an agreable amber scent, with very little altering the tast of the *Ale*: The Doctor pretends to bring it into a useful & precious *Medicine* or *Panaceam*: This liquor was *red*: This noble Experiment, exceeded all that ever I had seene of this nature, unlesse that which my learned Friend, & fellow Traveler *Mr. Hensheaw* & I accidentaly beheld a certaine *Mountebank* at *Rome* in the *Piazza Navona* (formerly Circus Maximus) now the Market place; here, whilst the other *Charlatans*, invited people to their stages, by Monkies, Jack-puddings & *Pantomimes*; This Fellow onely tooke from his finger a *Ring* (w⟨h⟩ither gold, brasse or silver, I could not examine, nor did I mind) which seem'd to have a lump of a blackish wax upon it, about the bignesse & of the shape, of those we call *Toade stones*, (which are indeede, but the grinders of the shark-fish). This he no sooner touched with the tip of his finger, which he seemed to wet with spittle at his mouth onely (though perhaps dip'd in some oyle or other *menstrue* before) but it immediately rose into a flame, as big & bright as any Wax light; This we saw him two or three times blow out, & accend againe, with the least touch of his finger, & then put the ring on his finger, & having by this surprizing trick, gotten Company about him, he fell to prating for the vending of his pretended Remedies &c: But a thousand times have we deplored, that whatever it Cost, we had not purchased this rare receit; Tis mention'd how to make the like both in Wecker & *Jo: Bap: Porta* &c: but on many tryals, it did not succeede: & what stupidity should seaze & possesse us, that all the time we were in *Rome*, we should never think of this, 'til some yeares after we were nearer home, We have both admir'd: The matter of fact is true, & I wish I knew how to make the like for a greate summ of mony; since, ⟨if⟩ it could be made without exceeding Cost, it would be an expeditious way to kindle any fire, light a Candle, & use upon a thousand occasions, abroad or at home:

4. I din'd at the E: of *Sunderlands*, the Countesse of Bristol, & Mr. *Sidney*, sonn to the Earle of *Licester* who had ben Ambassador in Holland: & returned home in the Evening:

7 A stranger preached on 3: *Lam:* 26: The holy Communion follow'd: &c: Afternoone the *Curate* on his former subject, with little addition of moment: 14: Our *Viccar* still indisposed, the Curate preached on 3: Apocalyps. 19. No *Sermon* this afternoone, which I think did not happen twice in this *parish* these 30 yeares; so gracious had God ben to it, & indeede to the whole Nation: God Grant, we abuse not this greate privelegdge: either by our wantonesse, schismes, or Unfruitfullnesse under such meanes, as he has not favoured any nation with under heaven besides:

16 To Lond: din'd next day at the Earle of Arlingtons: returned the 18:

23 I went to visite my deare Bro: at *Wotton*, the place of my birth: & Country:

24 I was invited to Mr. *Denzil Onslows* at his seate at *Purford*, where was much company, & such an extraordinary feast, as I had hardly ever seene at any Country Gent: table in my whole life; but what made it more remarkeable was, that there was not any thing, save what his Estate about it did not afford; as Venison, Rabb⟨i⟩ts, hairs, Pheasants, Partridge, [pigeons,] Quaile, Poultrie, all sorts of fowle in season (from his owne Decoy neere his house) all sorts of fresh fish: so Industrious is this worthy Gent: After dinner we went to see sport at the decoy, I never saw so many herons &c. The seate stands on a flat, the ground pastures, rarely watred, & exceedingly improved; since Mr. Onslow bought it of Sir *Rob: Parkhurst*, who spent a faire Estate &c: The house is Timber, but commodious, & with one ample dining roome, & the hale adorned with paintings of fowle, & huntings

&c: the work of Mr. *Barlow*, who is excellent in this kind from
the life: It stands neere part of Guildford river, within 12 or 14
miles of Lond: we returned to Wotton in the Evening: 28 A
stranger preached at Wotton on 4: Eph: 4: no Sermon after
noone:

30 I went to visite *Mr. Hussey* a neere neighbour of my Bro:
who has a very prety seate, delicately watred, & he certainely the
neatest husband for curious ordering his Domestic & field
Accomodations, & what pertaines to husbandry, that in my life I
have ever seene, as to his severall Graneries, Tackling, Tooles &
Utensils, Ploughs, Carts, Stables, Woodpiles, Woork house,
even to the hen rosts & hog troughs: so as mithought I saw old
Cato or Varro in him: all substantial, all in exact order, which
exceedingly delighted me: The sole inconvenience he lies under,
is the greate quantities of sand, which his streames bring along
with them, which fills his chanales & receptacles of fish too
soone: The rest of my time of stay at *Wotton* was spent in walking about the grounds & goodly Woods, where I have in my
Youth entertained my solitude &c: & so on the 2d of *September*
I returned to my home, being two daies after my Wife &c was
returned from *Tunbridge*, where they had ben, I blesse God,
with good successe, now neere five weekes:

6. Died my pretty Grand-child at Nurse of the gripes. 8. My
good neighbour Mr. *Turner* was buried, our *Viccar* preached on
126. *Psal.* 7: when ⟨likewise⟩ was interred our little Child: 9:
I sadly remembred the losse of another deare friend: This afternoone came the Bish: of *Rochester* & his Lady to visite us:

11 our *Viccar* as formerly; & *Curate* likewise. 12 Came my *La:
Sylvius* & other Ladys to Visite us, with whom I went to Lond:
that evening: 14. Din'd with Sir *Step: Fox*: Who proposed to me
the purchasing of *Chelsey Coll*; which his Majestie had some
time since given to our *Society*, & would now purchase it of us
againe, to build an *Hospital* [Infirmary] for Souldiers there; in
which he desired my assistance as one of the Council of the R:
Society: 15 I had another opportunity of perusing his Majesties
private Library at White-hall: I dined at Mr. *Chichleyes*: thence
to see Sir *Sam: Morelands* house, & Mechanics: supp'd at L: *Syl*:
17: I went with Monsieur *Faubert* about the taking of the
Countesse of *Bristols* house &c: for an *Academie*, he being lately
come from *Paris*, for his Religion, & resolving to settle here:

I dind at Sir *Bernard Gas⟨c⟩oynes*, & home in the Evening: ⟨18⟩ *Viccar* & Curat as above, with the usual applications:

23 I went to see Sir *Tho: Bonds fine house* & *Garden* at *Peccham*: 25 our *Viccar* on 3. *Jam:* 18: Curat as before:

Octob: 2 As above: The holy Sacrament followd: *Pomeridiano* I went to *Camerwell* where that good man Dr. *Par* (late Chapl: to the Primate of Ireland *Bishop Usher*) preached on 16 *Act:* 30: 4: To *Lond:* about severall affaires &c:

11 I went to *Fullham* to visite the *Bish:* of *Lond:* in whose Garden I first saw the *Sedum arborescens* in flowre, which was exceeding beautifull: I called in at *Parsons Greene* to see our Charge, my L: Vic: *Mordaunts* Children: 13. I went to visite my worthy friend Mr. *Boyle*:

16 *Cor: Rege* preached Dr. *Ball* on 13 *John:* 17. 18 My *Coach-house* was robbed, they ript off the Velvet &c: There was this day a meeting with the rest of the *Trustees*, upon my Young *Lord Vicount Mordaunts* offer to procure 20000 pounds for the payment of his Bro: & sisters portions, in consideration that we would possesse him of *Parsons Greene*, & the *Coale-farme*, which were worth 3000 per Annum: This tooke up long debates with our Council, who were for us Sir *William Jones* late *Attourney* Gen: and Mr. *Keck*: There were with me the *Earle* of *Clarendon*, Mr. *Newport*, & Mr. *Herbert*: but nothing concluded. 19 I dind at *Somerset-house* with my L. *Clarendon*; thence to The *R: Society*, where in absence of our *President*, I was faine to take the Chaire: There was much Company, it being the first day of meeting after our summers accostom'd Recesse:

21 Dr. *Tenison* Cat⟨e⟩chiz'd at St. *Martines*, very profitably on that article of the *Creede*: *I believe the forgivenesse of sinns* &c: I supp'd with my L. *Chamberlaine*, 21 returned home:

23 *Viccar* on his former: Curate on 3: *Apoc:* 19: 30: *Viccar* as before: *Pomerid:* a *stranger* on 2: *Heb:* 3. 31 Being my Birth-day and 61 yeares of my age, I spent in recollection of the yeare past, giving God thankes for his many signal mercys, & imploring his blessing on the yeare now entering:

November 1 Met the foefoès for the poore, the *Viccar* (as usualy) on 73 *Psal:* 1. 2. Concerning the Providential care of God over his Creatures &c: &c: 3 To *Lond:* 5. *Coram Rege* preached Dr. *Hooper* on 12. *Mar:* 16. 17. of the Usurpations of the *Chur⟨c⟩h* of Rome: this is one of the first rank of pulpet men in the Nation.

6 To the household a *stranger* on 1. *Jam*. 27: The B: *Sacrament* follow'd: Bish: of *Lond:* officiating: *Coram Rege* Dr. *Jane* 2: Tim: 3. 2. of the prodigious defecction & vices of the last times, an excellent discourse: 13 A chaplain on 23 *Pro* 17. 18:

15 I went to Visite, & dined with the *Earle* of *Essex*, who after dinner in his study sitting alone with him by the fire, related to me how much he had ben scandaliz'd & injur'd in the report of his being privy to the Marriage of his Ladys Niepce, the rich young Widdow of my late Lord *Oagle*, sole daughter of the Earle of *Northumberland*; shewing me a letter of *Mr. Thinns* excusing himselfe for his not communicating his Marriage to his Lordship; acquainting me also with the whole storie of that unfortunate Ladys being betraied by her Grandmother the Countesse of *N-humb:* & Coll: *Bret* for mony; and that though upon the importunitie of the *Duke* of *Monmoth*, he had delivered [to the Grandmother] a particular of the Joynture, which *Mr. Thynn* pretended he would settle on the Lady; yet he totaly discourag'd the proceeding, as by no meanes a competent Match, for one that both by her birth, & fortune might have pretended to the greatest Prince in Christendome: That he also proposed the Earle of *Kingston* (a kinds man of mine) or the Lord *Cranborn*; but was by no meanes for Mr. *Thynn*:

19 I din'd with & visited my worthy friend Mr. *Aerskin* Master of the *Charterhouse*, a Wise & learned *Gent:* ⟨fitter⟩ to have ben a Privy Councelor & Minister of state than laied aside: he is likewise Unkle to the *Dutchesse* of *Monmoth*.

20 D⟨r⟩. *Jane* on *Heb:*   concerning the infinite value of *Christs* Sacrifice: *Cor: Rege* Dr. *Smith* on 112. *Psal:* 7. 23 To the *R: Society*. 24. I was at the Audience of the *Russia Ambassador* which was before both their Majesties in the Banqueting-house: The presents were carried before them, held up by his followers standing in two rankes towards the Kings state, & consisted of Tapissry (one suit of which was doubtlesse brought from France as being of that fabric, this *Ambassador* having passed through that *Kingdom* as he came out of *Spaine*) a large *Persian* Carpet, Furrs of *Sable* & *Ermine* &c: but nothing was so splendid & exotick, as the *Ambassador* Who came soone after his Majesties restauration: This present *Ambassador* was exceedingly offended that his Coach was not permited to come into the Court; til being told that no *Kings* Ambassadors did, he was pacified, yet

requiring an attestation of it under Sir *Ch: Cotterells* the Master
of the Ceremonies hand; being it seemes afraid he should offend
his Master if he omitted the least *puntillo*: 'Twas reported he
condemn'd his sonn to loose his head, for shaving off his beard,
& putting himselfe in the *French* mode at *Paris*, & that he had
executed it, had not the french *King* interceeded: of this *quære*:

28 Several Fellows of our *Society* met at diner in the Citty, to
consult about Electing a fit Secretarie, & to regulate some other
defects: This Evening I got Dr. *Slaer* to shew my Lord Chamberlaine, the Duke & Dutchesse of Grafton, the Earle of
Chesterfild, *Conde de Castel Melior* & severall others, that
admirable and stupendious experiment of both the liquid & drie
Phosphorus, at which they were all astonish'd: 30 Being *St.
Andrews* day, we continued Sir *Chr: Wrenn* our President, elected
a new Council according to the Statute, of which I was one; &
chose *Mr. Austine* secretary with Dr. *Plott*, the ingenious Author
of the Natural *Hist.* of Oxfordshire: There was a most illustrious
appearance:

December 1 I went home to my house, after neere a Moneths
absence upon buisinesse with Sir *Denis Gauden*, & Commissioners of the Navy: 4: our *Viccar* on 8: Joh: 36: *Pomer:* a stranger,
on: 2: *Phil:* 13. 11: our *Viccar* as before: Curate on: 6: *Rom:* 21: 11.
To Council of the R: So: about letting a lease of some Lands
belonging to the Society: Din'd at Mr. *Ben: Bathursts*. 15 The
Duke of *Grafton* invited me to a magnificent Feast at the Trinity
house: 17. home:

18 Mr. *Bohune* preached on 25 *Matt* 25. perstringing *Phare-
saical* Hypocrisie of the present age: That Religion consisted not
in the *minutiæ*, but greater lines of *Christian* duty, *Faith, Love,
Justice* &c: not in refusing to receive indifferent Ceremonies of
Ornament, Edification & Order, in the poure of the Magistrate
to impose, so long as there was nothing repugnant or unagreable
to the life of the Gospel: such as the Crosse in Baptisme, Sur-
plice &c: at which precise people are scandalized without cause:
Pomer: a stranger, on: 11: *Psal:* 11.

21 To *Lond:* to a Council of the Society: 22 return'd home:

25 *Christmas day* our *Viccar* on 2. *Heb:* 17 apposite to the day:
The holy Comm: followed: *Pomer: Curate* 2: *Luke* 14, on the
same subject: 31 I gave thanks to God for the past yeares protection, & his gracious dealing with me:

1682. *Jan:* 1 Our *Viccar* preached on his former subject 2. Heb: 27: The holy Sacrament *followd*, at which I implored the blessing of Almighty God for the yeare now entering:

Some Neighbours dined with us according to Costome: *Pomerid*: Curate on 6: *Rom:* 21: with no greate addition, it being on his former Text: 8: our *Viccar* as above: & so the *Curate*:

11 To Lond: Saw the *Audience* of the *Morroco Ambassador*: his retinue not numerous, was receivd in the Banqueting-house both their Majesties present: he came up to the Throne without making any sort of Reverence, bowing so much as his head or body: he spake by a *Renegado English* man, for whose safe returne there was a promise: They were all Clad in the *Moorish* habite Cassocks of Colourd Cloth or silk with buttons & loopes, over this an *Alhaga* or white wollan mantle, so large as to wrap both head & body, a shash or small *Turban*, naked leg'd & arm'd, but with lether socks like the *Turks*, rich *Symeters*, large Calico sleev'd shirts &c: The Ambassador had a string of Pearls odly woven in his Turbant; I fancy the old Roman habite was little different as to the Mantle & naked limbs: The Ambassador was an handsom person, well featur'd, & of a wise looke, subtile, and extreamely Civile: Their Presents were *Lions* & *Estridges* &c: Their Errant, about a Peace at Tangire &c: But the Concourse & Tumult of the People was intollerable, so as the Officers could keepe no order; which they were astonish'd at at first; There being nothing so regular exact & perform'd with such silence &c, as [in] all these publique occasions of their Country, & indeede over all the Turkish dominions: 12 I din'd at Sir *Gab: Sylvius* with the Countesses of *Bristol* & *Sunderland* & supped at the Earle of *Arlingtons*. 13 din'd At Sir St: *Foxes*. 14 At the *Bish:* of *Rochesters* at the *Abby* it being his Marriage day after 24 yeares: He related to me after dinner, how he had ben treated by Sir *William Temple* forseeing he might be a Delegate in the Concerne of my Lady *Ogle*, now likely to come in Controversy, upon her Marriage with *Thynn*: Also howe arnestly the late *E:* of *Danby* L: Tressurer sought his frie⟨n⟩dship, and what plaine & sincere Advice he gave him from time to time about his mis-carriages & Partialities; particularly, his outing Sir *Jo: Duncomb* from being *Chancelor* of the Exchequer, & Sir *St: Fox* above all from Pay-Master to the Armie: The *Treasurers* excuse & reason was that *Foxes* Credit was so over-greate with the *Bankers* &

monied men, that he could procure none, but by his meanes: For that reason (replied the Bishop) I would have made him my Friend: Sir *Steph⟨en⟩* being a person both honest & of credit: he told him likewise of his statlinesse, & difficulty of Accesse & severall other miscarriages, & which indeede made him hated &c: & so I returned home: 15 *Vicc:* & *Cur:* as before, & so on the 22d:

24 To *Lond:* where at the Council of the *R: Soc:* we passed a new Law, for the more accurate consideration of *Candidates* before admission, as whither they would realy be Usefull: & also concerning Honorarie Members, that none should be admitted but *per diploma*: An exper: for the describing any *Parabola line* whatsoever. This Evening I was at the Entertainement of the *Morroco ⟨Ambassador⟩* at the Dut: of *Portsmouths* glorious Appartment at W. hall, where was a greate banquet of *Sweete-meates*, & *Musique* &c but at which both the *Ambassador* & *Ret-inue* behaved themselves with extraordinary Moderation & modestie, though placed about a long Table a Lady betweene two Moores: viz: a Moore, then a Woman, then a Moore &c: and most of these were the Kings natural Children, viz: the Lady Lichfield, Sussex, DD of *Portsmouth*, *Nelly* &c: Concu-bines, & catell of that sort, as splendid as Jewells, and Excesse of bravery could make them: The *Moores* neither admiring or seeming to reguard any thing, furniture or the like with any earnestnesse; and but decently tasting of the banquet: They dranke a little Milk & Water, but not a drop of Wine, also they drank of a sorbett & Jacolatte: did not looke about nor stare on the Ladys, or expresse the least of surprize, but with a Courtly negligence in pace, Countenance, & whole behaviour, answer-ing onely to such questions as were asked, with a greate deale of Wit & Gallantrie, & so gravely tooke leave, with this Compli-ment That *God* would blesse the D: of P: and the Prince her sonn, meaning the little Duke of Richmon'd: The *King* came in at the latter end, just as the Ambassador was going away: In this manner was this Slave (for he was no more at home) entertained by most of the Nobility in Towne; & went often to *Hide-Park* on *horse back*, where he and his retinue shewed their extraordinary activity in Horsmanship, and the flinging & Catching their launces at full speede; They rid very short, & could stand up right in full speede, managing their speares with incredible

agility. He also went sometimes to our *Theaters*, where when upon any foolish or fantastical action he could not forbeare laughing, he endeavored to hide it with extraordinary modesty & gravity: In a word, the *Russian Ambassador* still at Court behaved himselfe like a Clowne, compar'd to this Civil *Heathen*:

27 I went to heare Dr. *Tenison* at St. *Mart:* Expound on the Church Catechisme:

This Evening Sir *St. Fox* acquainted me againe with his Majesties resolutions of proceeding in his Erection of a *Royal Hospital* for Emerited Souldiers on that spot of ground The *Ro: Society* had sold his Majestie for 1300 pounds & that he would settle 5000 pounds per Annum on it, & build to the value of 20000 pounds for the reliefe & reception of 4 Companies, viz. 400 men, to be as in a Coledge or Monastrie: I was therefore desired by Sir *Stephen* (who had not onely the whole menaging of this, but was (as I perceiv'd) himselfe to be a grand benefactor, as well it became him, who had gotten so vast an Estate by the Souldiers &c) to assist him & Consult what Method to Cast it in, as to the Government: So in his Study, we set downe the Governor, Chaplaine, Steward, Housekeeper, Chirurgion, Cooke, Butler, Gardner, Porter & other Officers, with their severall salaries & entertainements: I would needes have a Librarie, & mentioned severall books &c. since some souldiers might possibly be studious, when they were at this leasure to recolect: Thus we made the first Calculations, & set downe our thoughts to be considered & digested better to shew his *Majestie* & the *Archbishop*: He also engaged me to consider of what Laws & Orders were fit for the Government, which was to be in every respect as strickt as in any religious Convent &c: After supper, came in the famous Trebble *Mr. Abel* newly return'd from *Italy*, & indeede I never heard a more excellent voice, one would have sworne it had ben a Womans it was so high, & so well & skillfully manag'd: being accompanied with Signor *Francesco* on the *Harpsichord*:

28 Mr. *Pepys* (late Sec: to the Admiralty) ⟨shewed me⟩ a large folio containing the whole Mechanic part, & art of Building royal ships & Men of Warr; made by Sir *Anth: Deane*, being so accurate a Piece, from the very keele to the lead block, rigging, Gunns, Victualing, Manning, even to every individual Pin & naile, in a Method so astonishing & curious; with the draughts

both Geometrical, & in Perspective, & severall sections; That I do not think the Whole World can shew the like; I esteeme this one booke above any of the *Sybillas*, & it is an extraordinary Jewel: hence I returned home.

⟨29⟩ *Viccar* on 8: *Joh:* 26: *Curate* on 5: *Matt* 5: 31. To *Lond:* but tooke such a cold that the next day returning from our *Society* (where we had the *Phosphorus* experimented in *Vaccuo Boyliano* which greately surprized me) to my Lodging at *White-hall*, I was attaq'd with a fit of an *Ague Tertian* for 3 fitts, which so exceedingly weakn'd me, that I was not able to stirr out til Sonday when

Feb: 5 I went to Chapell a Young Divine on 90. *Psal:* 12: The blessed Sacrament followed: B: of *Lond:* officiating: *Cor: Rege* Dr. *Perce* out-doing himselfe in an incomparable discourse on: 18 *Luke*: 8: when the Sonn of man cometh, shall he find faith on the Earth? Shewing by the deprav'dnesse of mankind, & especialy among Christians, particular⟨l⟩y England more than had ever ben known, the end of the world could not now be long, & that it would come surprizingly, none minding:

My fitts continuing with much violence I sent to my Wife to fetch me home in the Coach: There came & sent to Visite me my L: *Chamberlaine*, Dutchesse of *Grafton*, Countesse of *Bristol* & *Sunderland*, Sir William *Godolphin*, & severall of my friends almost daily:

7. I went home: My Daughter *Mary* now first began to learne Musick of Signor *Bartholomeo*, & Dauncing of Monsieur *Isaac*, both reputed the best Masters &c: I continu'd ill for 2 fitts after, and then bathing my leggs to the knees in *Milk* made as hott as I could endure it, & sitting so in it, in a deepe *Churn* or Vessell, Covered with blanquets & drinking *Carduus* posset, then going to bed & sweating, I not onely missed that expected fit, but had no more; onely continued so weake that I could not go to church 'til *Ash-wednesday*, which I had not missed I think so long in twenty yeares, so long had God ben gracious to me:

After this Warning & admonition, I now began to looke-over & methodize all my *Writings*, *Accompts*, *Letters*, *Papers* &c: Inventoried the goods &c of the house, & to put things into the best order I could; & also new made my Will: That growing now in yeares, I might have none of these secular things & Concernes, to distract me, whensoever it should please Almighty *God* to call me from this transitorie life: And with this prepared

me some special Meditations & devotions for the time of sicknesse: The Lord *Jesus* grant them Salutary for my poore Soule at
that day, that I may obtaine Mercy & acceptance.

March 1 Was my second Grand-child borne, exactly at Sun-
rising; & Christned the next day by our *Viccar* at *Sayes-Court*, his
Susceptors being My Selfe with my *Nephew* Jo: *Evelyn* of *Wotton*, by the Name of *John*: his God-mother was Mrs. *Anderson*,
sister to his Mother: I beseech God to blesse him.

⟨1⟩ *Ashwednesday* I went to our Church Office &c: 5: Our *Viccar* on   Pro: shewing what care and vigilancy was
required for the keeping of the heart upright: the holy Comm:
followd: on which I gave God thanks for his gracious dealing
with me in my late sicknesse, & affording me this blessed
opportunity of praising him in the Congregation, and receiving
the Cup of Salvation, with new & serious resolutions:—The
Curate on 73. *Psal:* 24. 9: Came to see & congratulate my recovery Sir *John Lowther*, Mr. *Herbert*, Mr. *Pepys*, Sir *Anth: Deane*, &
Mr. *Hill*, which last gave me a hopefull account of the successe
my Letter was like to have (which I lately sent to Mr. *Dan: Call-
well*) in behalfe of the *Royal Society*: See a *Copy* of the Letter in
my book of Letters: 10: To *Lond:* to a Master of *Chancery*, about
our Answer of the L: V: *Mordaunts* bill &c: I return'd, having
return'd my Visites to the L: *Chamberlain*, Sir *Ste: Fox* and other
my kind friends: There was this day Executed *Coll: Vrats* & some
of his Complices, for their Execrable Murder of *Mr. Thynn*, set
on by the Principal *Koningsmarke* ⟨who⟩ went to Execution like
an undaunted Hero, as one that had don a friendly office for
that base Coward C. *Coningsmark*, who had hopes to marry his
Widdow the rich Lady Ogle; & was quitted by a Corrupt Jury,
& so got away: *Vrats* told a friend of mine, who accompan⟨y⟩ing
him to the Gallows & gave him some advice; That dying he did
not value a rush, & hoped & believed God would deale with
him like a Gentleman; never man went so gallant, & so uncon-
cern'd to his sad fate:

12 Our *Viccar* on his former *Text*: with little addition: *Curate*
5. *Matt:* 7: 19 A *stranger* on 122: *Psal:* 6: The same in the After
noone: I was this day exceedingly paind in both my kidnies,
which gave me apprehension of some farther evil, which *God* in
mercy avert: 21, I went to *Lond*, to ⟨meete⟩ the rest of the
Trustees, viz. the *Earle* of *Clarendon*, Lo: *Hyde*, Mr *Newport* &c

to my L: *Chancelor*, where was severall of the most learned
Council on both sides, to consider what security we might
expect, in Case we relinquich'd our Trust for the payment of the
Portions to my Lady V: C. *Mordaunts* Children, & that my L:
Chan: would settle it by decree &c. I dind at the C: of *Sunderlands*. 22: I dined with severall of the *R: Society* (as frequently we
did on the meeting daies) & the *President* being absent, I was
voted into the *Chaire*: Severall *letters* from abroad were red, &
answers ordered to them: There was shewed a live *Scorpion*
found in an Oyle-shop in *Lond:* Also were presented divers faire
pieces of *Amber* from the *Duke* of *Brandenburg*, in one of which
was a large spider, in another a gnat, both very intire & rare: The
experiment for the day, was the *Anatomical* demonstration of Dr.
Tysons, of the *decussations* of the *optic-nerves*, so as to cause the
sight to be single, & not double, from the paralelle fibers on the
Retina, exactly answering one-the other, which being by any
accident distorted, caused *Squinting*, & indirect Vision &c:
Then follow'd a discourse in *Latine*, endeavoring to shew how
much wider the pores of *Gold* were than *Silver*, & affirm'd to be
the occasion of the operation of *Aqua regalis* upon it, insinuating
more easily, which being reasoned upon, was rejected: Also there
was a discourse of the tinging of *Glasse*, especialy with red, & the
difficulty of finding any red colour effectual, to penetrate glasse
among the *glasse-painters*; That the most diaphanous as blew,
yellow &c did not enter into the substance of what was ordinarily painted, but very shallowly, unlesse incorporated in the mettal itselfe, other redds & whites, not at all farther than to the
superficies onely: &c:

I went hence to see the Corps of that obstinate creature, Coll.
Vratz the *German* murderer of Mr. *Thynn* (set on by the Principal Count *Koningsmark*) the King permitting his body should be
transported to his owne Country, (being it seemes a person of a
good family) it being one of the first, which was *embaulmed* by a
particular art invented by one *Will: Russell* a Coffin Maker;
which preser⟨v⟩ed the body without disboweling or using to any
appearance any bituminous matter; The flesh florid, soft & full,
as if the person were onely sleeping: The *Cap:* having now ben
dead neere 15 daies: He lay exposed in a very rich Coffin, lined
with lead: &c to⟨o⟩ magnificently for so daring, & horrid a
Murderer: 23 I visited severall friends, dind at Sir *St: Foxes*: 23.

24: Both these daies were spent in a most anxious attendance of my *Lady Tukes* Cause, at the *Assizes* in *Southwark*: I dined with the high *Sherif* & *Judges* &c where was a mighty feast, & returned home on our Lady day. 26 Our *Viccar* on 57. *Isa:* 10. *Pomer: Curate* on 9 *Eccles:* 10:

Apr⟨i⟩ll 2: Our *Viccar* on his former, much repetition: The *Curate* on: 2: *Phil:* 8, preparatory to the solemne time approaching, for which reason there was no Communion this Sunday (as there ought to have ben) there being three to succeede the weeke following:

My Daughter in Law was Churched this day, after the birth of my *Grandson* John, whom I pray God to blesse:

5: To Lond: our *Society*, where at a Council, was regulated what *Collections* should be monethly published, as formerly the *Transactions*, which had of late ben discontinued; but were now much desired & called for by the Curious both from abroad, & home:

12 I went this Afternoone to a Supper, with severall of the R: Society, which was all dressed (both fish & flesh) in Monsieur *Papins Digestorie*; by which the hardest bones of Biefe itselfe, & Mutton, were without water, or other liquor, & with lesse than 8 ounces of Coales made as soft as Cheeze, produc'd an incredible quantity of Gravie, & for close, a Gellie, made of the bones of biefe, the best for clearnesse & good relish, the most delicious that I had ever seene or tasted; so as I sent my Wife a glasse of it, to the reproch of all that the ladys ever made of the best Hartshorne &c: We Eate Pick & other fish with bones & all without any impediment: but nothing exceeded the Pigeons, which tasted just as if baked in a *pie*, all these being stewed in their owne juice, without any add⟨i⟩tion of water, save what swam about the ⟨digester⟩, as in balneo: The natural juice of all these provisions, acting on the grosser substances, reduct the hardest bones to this tendernesse: but it is best described (with infinite more particulars for extracting tinctures, preserving & stewing fruite &c, & saving fuel) by Dr. *Papins* booke, published & dedicated to our Society, of which he is a member, though since gon to *Venice* with Signor   late Resident for that State here, & a member also of our Society, who carried this excellent Mechanique Philos: & Physitian, to set up a Philos: meeting in that Citty: By this Experiment it is plaine, that the most obdurate

bones are but the more compacted & closer parts of the same matter (by *juxtaposition*) which composes the tenderest flesh & Muscular parts; & reduces them to a friable, rather than glutinous substance, which disolves into gravy, or composes the Gelly: These bones then, breaking as it were into crumbs, one may strew on bread & eate without harme: This Philosophical Supper, raised much mirth amongst us, & exceedingly pleased all the Companie:

14 *Good Friday* (at St. *Martins*) preached Dr. *Tenison* on 1. *Threnæ* 12: The blessed Communion followed: I suppd at my old & worthy friends Mr. P: Packers: This afternoone *Coram Rege* preached Dr Sherlock on 1. Cor: 1. 22. 23: which I also heard.

15 I returned home: 16 *our Viccar* (*Easter day*) on 28 *Matt:* 5. 6. with the ordinarie Topics on this beaten text: &c: The holy Comm: followed, at which I with my family participated: *Pomerid: Curate* on 1. Cor: 15. 20. As now I grew in yeares, I becam much subject to sleepe in the Afternoones, which I formerly censured in some others, and believed impossible; I beseech God to pardon & help me: Seldome & rarely did I sleepe in the morning Exercises &c:

23 Our *Viccar* on his former: *Curate* of *Greenewich* on 1. *Cor:* 15. 10: I stirr'd not forth this Weeke, but tooke *Physick*, the season unusualy wet, with such stormes of Raine & Thunder, as did greate damage:

May: 6 I went to *Lond:* about buisenesse. 7: A stranger at *W:hall* on 1. *Pet.* 3. 18: The holy Sacrament follow'd: 11 I returned home:

19 To *Lond:* in order to a *Trial*, with the *Legatie⟨s⟩* of *Geo: Tuke*, in which I was a *Trustee*, but which was put off, 'til my *Lady Tuke*, could obtaine leave of her Majestie to come from Winsore, where the Court now was:

25 *Dies Ascentionis*: I was desired by Sir St: *Fox*, & Sir Chr: *Wren*, his Majesties Surveior, and *Architect*, to accompanie them to *Lambeth*, with the plot, & designe of the College to be built at *Chelsey* for emerited Souldiers, to have the *Archbishops* approbation: It was a quadrangle of 200 foote square, after the dimensions of the larger quadrangle of *Christ Church* in *Oxon* for the accommodation of 440 Persons with Governor & Officers: This being fix'd, & agreed upon, we went to dinner, & then returned: 27: As a *Trustee* of *Geo: Tuke*, in behalfe of my Lady, we had a

Trial before my L: Chancelor, against the Plaintifs, who being of the Kindred, expected Legacies before the debts were paied, and that there were *assets*: After many yeares charge & trouble, the Accompts were referred to a Master to be examin'd, which was just, & what we desired: I din'd at Mr. *Sheldons*: The *Duke* & *Dutchesse* of York were just now come to *Lond:* after his Escape & shipwrack by sea, as he went for *Scotland*. 28: Sonday, At the *Rolls*-Chapell preached the famous Dr. *Burnet* on 2: *Pet:* 1. 10, excellently well describing what was meant by Election &c:— I din'd at Sir Tho: *Beckfords* to visite my Niepce Evelyn of Wotton, who had miscarried of a *sonn* in the Coach as she came up to lie-In at *Lond:* This afternoone I went to St. *Laurences* where the *Minister* (naming his Text 18 *Ezek:* 27) spake so very low, & was so feeble an old man, that I could by no meanes hear what he saied: The church is new & a cherefull pile: 29. I din'd [Sir S: Foxe] at the B: of *Rochesters*: congratulated his eldest sonns Marriage: He is a good scholar & studying the Law, like to make a worthy & usefull gent: I gave notice to the Bish: what *Maimburg* had published, about the motives of the late Dutchesse of *Yorks* Perversion, in his *Historie* of *Calvenisme*; & did my selfe write to the Bish: of *Winchester* about it, who being concernd in it, I urged to set forth his *Vindication*: 30: The Kings *Anniversarie*, I was hindred from going to the pub: Office: 31: To our *Society*, where the *Morocco Ambassador* being honorarily admitted, & subscribing his Name & Titles in *Arabic*, I was ⟨ordered⟩ by the *Council*, to go and complement him, &c.

Jun 1. I din'd at my Lord *Sunderlands* with Mr. *Sidny* & so home: 4: *Whitsonday* our *Viccar* on 4: *Heb:* 1. Text formerly begun, not much agreable to the festival: The holy *Sacrament* followed: *Curate* on 2: *Act:* 1. against the *Dissenters* choosing barnes, & obscure places to meete in, rather than the Church; so as they were not together like the Assemblies of the *Apostles*, which was in a Conspicuous well known place & house, where so many of all nations came to heare them, & were all of one accord:

19 About buisinesse to *Lond*. 20 To our *Society*, where Mr. *Hook* read to us his ingenious *Hypothesis* of Memorie, which he made to be an Organ of sense, distinct from any of the five; placed somewhere in the braine, which tooke notice of all *Ideas* & reposited them; as the rest of the senses do of their peculiar objects:

The *Bantame* or *East India* Ambassadors (for we had at this time in Lond together The *Russian*, *Morrocan*, & *Indian* Ambassador) being invited to dine at my Lord Geo: Berekeleys (now created Earle) I went to the entertainement, to Consider the exotic guests: They were both very hard favour'd, & much resembling in Countenance to some sort of *Munkeys*: We eate at two Tables, The Ambassador & Interpreter by themselves: Their Garments were rich Indian silks flowred with gold, viz, a Close *Wast-Coate* to their knees, Drawers, Naked leggs; and on their heads Capps made just in fashion like fruit baskets; They Ware poison'd Daggers at their boosome, the haft carved with some ougly serpents or devils head, exceeding keene, & of dam-asco mettal: they wore no sword: The second *Ambassador* (sent it seemes to succeede, in case the first should die by the Way in so tedious a journey) having ben at *Méca* (for they were *Mahumetans*) ware a Turkish or rather *Arab Shash*, a little part of the linnen hanging downe behind his neck, With some other diference of habite; & was halfe a negro; bare legg'd & naked feete; esteem'd a very holy man: They sate Crosse-legd like Turks, & sometimes in the postures of *Apes* & *Munkys*; Their nailes & ⟨Teeth⟩ black as any jeat & shining, which being the effect of perpetual chewing *betell*, to preserve them from the *Toothatch* more raging in their Country, is esteem'd beautifull: The first *Ambassador* was of an Olive hue, had a flatter face & narrow eyes, squat nose & morish lips, haire none appeared: Wore severall rings of silver, gold, coper on their finger, which was a toaken of Knighthood or nobility: They were of *Java major*, whose Princes have ben turn'd *Mahumetans* not above 50 yeares since, The Inhabitans stil *Pagans* & Idolaters: They seem'd of a dul & heavy Constitution, not wondering at any thing they saw; but exceedingly astonish⟨ed⟩ to understand, how our *Law's* gave us propriety in our Estates, & so thinking we were all Kings; for they could not be made to Comprehend, how subjects could possesse any thing but at the pleasure of their Prince, they being all slaves, but infinitly surprized at it, & pleased with the notion, & admiring our happinesse; They were very sober, & I believe subtile in their way: Their meate was cook'd, carried up, & they attended on, by severall fat slaves, who had no Covering save drawes, their whole body from the girdle upward stark naked, as well as their leggs, which appeared very uncouth, & lothsom; They eate their *pilaw* & other spoone-meate without spoones, taking up their pottage in the hollow of ⟨their⟩ fingers, & very dextrously flung it into their mouthes, without spilling a drop:

25 Preached at *W:hall*. Dr. *Comber* on 7: *Joh:* 17: *Pomerid*: at St. Margarets a stranger on 71 Psal: 12.

28 home, having ben in the morning to heare *Dr. Tenison* on our Church Cat⟨e⟩chisme:

July: 1 Sir Jo: Stonehouse & Lady &c dined with us:

2 Mr. *Fowler* preached on 6: *Jam:* 10: The *B: Sacrament* follow'd &c: 5. To *Lond:* Society, where I met those two excellent persons *Monsieur Justell*, & Monsieur *Azoule* that greate Mathematician & Virtuoso: 6: Din'd at my L: *Sunderlands*: 8 home.

9 Our *Viccar* on 53: *Psal:* 3. *Curate*: 1 *Cor:* 2. 2: 11 I went to *Lond:* to have seene againe the ⟨*Morocco*⟩ *Ambassador*, but he was gon to *New-hall* invited by the *Duke* of *Albemarle*, so I return'd:

17 Came to dine with me the *Duke* of *Grafton*, & young Earle of *Ossorie*, sonn to my most deare deceased friend: 18: Came Sir St: Fox, his Lady, Sonn and Daughter to Visite us: 22: Came Mr. *Onslow* of Surrey, & Lady to Visite us:

23 A stranger: on 1. *Jam:* 22. of the necessity of practise, and doing, as well as hearing: That in the Easter⟨n⟩, & *African* Churches was much preaching heretofore, but in no nation under heaven more than in ours, even to the nauseating of Prayers, & placing all religious duties in sermons &c: The danger of our being given-up to barbarizme, as they were, for our neglect of practise. *Pomerid*: a stranger on 2. *Tit:* 2.

27 I went to *Bromely* to visite the Bish: of *Rochester*:

30 A stranger on the 5t of *Matt:* 20: *Pomerid* at *Lee* the Lecturer on: 1. *Pet:* 55, of the grace of humility, danger of traducing of this age: spiritual pride & prejudices among the *dissenters* &c:— We went after to visite our good neighbour Mr. *Bohune*, whose whole house is a Cabinet of all elegancies, especialy *Indian*, and the Contrivement of the ⟨*Japan*⟩ Skreenes instead of Wainscot in the *Hall*, where an excellent *Pendule*-Clock inclosed in the curious flower-work of Mr. *Gibbons* in the middst of the *Vestibule*, is very remarkable; and so are the Landskips of the Skreenes, representing the manner of living, & Country of the *Chinezes* &c: but above all his Ladys Cabinet, adorn'd on the fret, Ceiling & chimny-piece with Mr. Gib: best Carving; there is also some of

Streeters best painting, & many rich Curiosities of Gold & sil: growing in the Mine: &c: Besides the *Gardens* are exactly kept, & the whole place very agreable & well watred: The *Owners* good and worthy neighbours, & he has also builded, & endowed an Hospital for Eight poore people, with a pretty Chapell, & all accommodations:

Aug: 1 To *Lond:* to see my Charges the late V: C: Mordaunts Children at Chelsey, & thence to *Fulham* to visite the *Bish:* of *London*, & review againe the additions which *Mr. Marshall* had made of his curious booke of flowers in miniature, and Collection of Insecta: 2: I din'd with Sir *Ja: Shaen.* 3: At Mr. *Boscawens*: 4: With *Sir St:* Fox to survey the foundation of the *Royal Hospital* begun at Chelsey, and 5. home: 6: Mr. *Saunders* preach'd on 1. Cor: 11. 28: The bl: Communion follow'd: *Pomerid:* 13: Matt: 45:

9 To *Lond:* R: *Society*, where Dr. *Tyson* produced a *Lumbricus Latus*, which a Patient of his voided, of 24 foote in length, it had severall joynts, at lesse than one inch asunder, which on examination prov'd so many mouthes & stomachs in number 400 by which it adhered to & sucked the nutrition & juice of the Gutts, & by impairing health, fills it selfe with a white Chyle, which it spewed-out, upon diping the worme in spirit of Wine; nor was it otherwise possible a Creature of that prodigious length should be nourish'd, & so turgid, with but one mouth at that distance: The part or joynt towards the head was exceeding small: We ordered the Doctor to print the discourse made upon it: The Person who voided it, indured such torment in his bowels, that he thought of killing himselfe: There were likewise the Anatomies of other Wormes bred in humane bodys, which, *though* strangly small, were discoverd apparently to be *male* & *female*, had their *Penis, Uterus, Ovaries* and seminal Vessels &c: so as no likely hood of æquivocal generations: There was also produced *Millipedes* newly voided by Urine, *per penem*, it having it seemes stuck in the neck of the blader & yard, giving a most intollerable itching to the patient; but the difficulty was, how it could possibly passe-through the bloud and the *Heart*, & other minute *ductus's* & strainers through the kidnies to the blader; which being looked on as impossible, was believed to be produced by an Egg in the bladder; The person who voided it, having ben prescribed *Millipedes* against suppression of Urine: &c: Then Dr. *King* presented a sharp pointed *stone* that a day or two

before had ben taken out of the *Ureters* of a Gent, who ⟨had⟩ no kidney at all: The *Council* this day had recomended to them the being *Trusteès* & Visiters or Supervisers of the *Academie* which *Monsieur Faubert* did hope to procure to be builded by the sub-scription of worthy Gent: & noblemen, for the Education of Youth, & to lessen the vast expense the nation is yearely at, by sending their Children into *France*, to be taught these militarie Exercises: We thought therefore good, to give him all the Encouragement our recommendation could procure: After this we *Adjourned* our meetings 'til *Michaelmas* according to *Costome* at this season: so I went home, where I found my Aunt *Hunger-ford* come to Visite us:

15 Came to visite me Dr. *Rogers* an acquaintance of mine long-since at *Padoä*, he was there *Consul* of the English Nation students in that Universitie, where he proceeded Doctor in *Physic*; presenting me now with the *Latine Oration* he lately made upon the famous Dr. *Harveys Anniversarie* in the Coll: of *Physitians* at *Lond:*

18 Came to Visite me the LL: Bishops of *London* & *Rochester:* My A: *Hungerford* went away: 20 Our *Viccar* proceeded:—*Curat* as above.

This night I saw another *Comet* neere *Cancer*, very bright, but the streame not so long: 24 Came to Visite us, Dr. *Parr* of *Camerwell* that good man—

27 our *Viccar* on his former Text.—*Curate* of *Greenewich* on 5: *Matt ult*. A *Metaphysical* discourse of the Perfections of God, altogether unintelligible to most of our plaine Auditores. 29 Came to see me very much Company, as indeede there had, all this whole summer: &c:

September ⟨3⟩ Our *Viccar* on his former text: the holy *Sacra-ment* follow'd:—*Curate* on 10: *Pro:* 9.

This weeke continual Companie to my house from *Lond:*

9 Being the Anniversarie of a deare friend, I was not a little affected: & the Evening, I was at the funeral of my Neighbour Mr. *Sheeres*, our *Viccar* preaching on a part of *Eccles:* concerning the transitorienesse of all worldly things:

24 Our *Bishop* preached on 6 *Matt* 24. a very profitable dis-course of the impossibility of serving two Masters: Of the Choice we have, of the Vile servitude of One, the freedome, & easy Conditions of the other: Concluding with an exhortation

to hold fast the choice we had made at our *Baptisme*; & such especialy as now came to be Confirmed, addressing his speech both to the Young who were not yet Confirm'd, & to the rest who were: After this, he laied his hands on about 600 young Children &c: There was also an Adult Young man baptized: Also my two Daughters, *Elizabeth* & *Susanna* were now Confirmed. I dined with the *Bishop* at our *Viccars*; *Pomerid*: Curat on his former: &c:

Octob: 25 To *Lond*, din'd with the R: *Society* (now againe ⟨meeting⟩ after recesse). After dinner a *French-man* produced some experiments for the raising of Water: Also we found, that Water put in *Vaccuo Boyliano* & the glasse hermeticaly sealed, if jogged & shaken, made the same noise as if so many pibble stones had ben in the glasse, or some solid body beaten against the bottom & sides of it: The reason; because the aire being exhausted both out of the water & the Vessel, the Contact of the water, was more immediate, & the body more solid; for it had ben easie to have broken the bottle with the water onely.

27 I suppd at the *Earle* of *Clarendons*, with my L: *Hide* his bro, now the greate favorite, who now invited himselfe to dine at my house the tuesday following:

29 I receiv'd the *B: Comm:* at St. *James's*, having some daies before ben in no small trouble & sorrow for the unkindnesse & ungratitude of one I deserved better from: Dr. *Tenison* preach'd at St. *Martin's*, on 11: *Rom:* 20 against *Atheisme* with the usual *Topics*, in which twas believ'd he met with a greate *Marques* there present.

30 Being my Birth-day, and I now entering my greate *Climacterical* of 63, after serious Recollection of the yeares past, giving Almighty God thankes for all his mercifull preservations & forbearance; beging pardon for my sinns & unworthinesse, & his blessing & mercy on me the Yeare entering: I went with my Lady *Fox*, to survey her Bu⟨i⟩lding, and give some direction for the Garden at *Chiswick*: The Architect is *Mr. May*, somewhat heavy & thick; & not so well understood: The Garden much too narrow, the place without water, neere an high way, & another greate house of my Lord *Burlingtons*; little Land about it; so as I wonder at the expence; but Women will have their Will.

November 1 The Meeting of the *Foefees* for the poore of *Deptford*, cald me home &c:

5 The *Anniversarie* of the *Pouder-plot* Mr. *Bohun* preaching on 1. *Cor:* 10. 7. Comparing Popish Idolatrie, to that of the Heathen: The peril of their doctrine; Their wicked & pernicious Conspiracys, The danger of our late *Dissenters* least they bring us againe into that corrupt religion, by provoking God to take away the light we have so long abused: The holy Comm: follow'd: *Pomer: Curate* on 3 *Coloss:* 2. 12 our *Viccar* on his former Text: *Pomeridiano* the *Greenewich Curate* on 147: *Psal:* 5.

25 I was invited by Monsieur *Lionberg* The *Swedish* Resident, who made a magnificent Entertainement it being the *Birth-day* of his *King*: There dined the Duke of *Albemarle*, D: *Hamilton*, *Earle of Bathe*, E: of *Alesbery*, Lord *Arran*, Lord *Castlehaven*, the sonn of him who was executed 50 yeares before for Enormous Lusts &c: & sevveral greate persons: I was exceedingly afraide of *Drinking*, (it being a Dutch feast) but the *Duke* of *Albemarle* being that night to waite on his *Majestie* Excesse was prohibited; & to prevent all, I stole away & left the Company as soone as we rose from Table: 26: At St. *Mart:* Dr. *Tenison* on 1. *Gal:* 10. 28: I went to Council of *R: Society*, for the Auditing the last yeares Accompts, where I was surpriz'd with a fainting fit, that for the present tooke away my sight; but God being mercifull to me, I recovered it after a short repose: 30: St. *Andrews* day, being our *Anniversar⟨i⟩e* for the Choice of new President; I was exceedingly indangr'd & importuned, to stand this Election, having so many Voices &c: But, by favour of my friends & reguard of my remote dwelling, & now frequent Infirmities, I desired their Suffrages for me, might be transferr'd on Sir *John Hoskins*, one of the Masters of the Chancery, a most learned virtuoso, as well as Lawyer, who accordingly was elected; & then we all dined together according to Costome:

December 7 I was this whole Weeke transacting buisinesse with Mr. *Brent*, about my *Arrere* due from his Majestie & made severall Visites: 17: A stranger at *W:hall* on   *Judge not before the time* &c & before his *Majestie* Dr. *Patrick* on   *Greate is the Mysterie of Godlinesse* &c: on which he made an incomparable discourse: I went to Visite, & Congratulate my Lord *Hyde* (the greate favorite) newly made *Earle of Rochester*, & lately marrying his Eld: Daughter to the Earle of *Ossorie*:

18 I sold my East India Adventure of 250 pounds, Principal for 750 pounds after it had ben in that Companie 25 yeares, to

my extraordinary Advantage: & by the blessing of God: 20: To our *Society*, where was an Experiment of the puritie of the *Æther* and a learn'd Discourse of Dr. *Tysons* red: proving that according to the newest & most accurate *Anatomists*, The *Embrio* was Nourish'd onely by the Mouth, of the liquor in the *Amnion* (not by the navil onely as the vulgar error) for that there was onely that liquor found in its Stomack & Intestines: & that the *Umbilical* Vessells carried blood onely, impregnated with *nitrous* aire for the supplie of life, but not at all for nourishment &c: 21 I supp'd with the new *Earle* of *Rochester* and much other Companie: & went home next day to my house:

24 Our *Viccar* on 5. *Jam:* 15. of the Antiquity & preference of Publique & set formes of Prayer in the Congregation; now much neglected by the Discenters &c: *Pomerid*: The *Curate* on 5: *John*: 14:

25 *Christmas day*, our *Viccar* on 4: *Malachie* 2: a discourse apposite to the festival, &c: The holy Communion followed:

29 I went to *Lond:* invited to dine with my good friend Mr. *Packer*, & returned the next day. 31. A stranger on 1. *Pet:* 2. 21, & in the *Afternoone* on 116 *Psal:* 4: This Evening recollecting the Passages of the former yeare, I gave Almighty God thanks for his gracious preservation hitherto, being now advancing in yeares apace.

WINDSOR CASTLE TRANSFORMED – A NEW PLOT – WINCHESTER PALACE (1683)

AND ON THE [1683 *January*] first, besought the continuance of his mercy & protection for the yeare now entering & which was my grand *Climacterical*. 3. I went to *Lond:* about my E: *India stock*, which I had sold to the *Royal Society* for 750 pounds: it being not to be paied 'til the 25 of *Mar:* returned that evening: & Entertained severall of my Neighbours, according to costome:

7 our *Viccar* on 4: *Mal:* 2. The holy Sacrament followed. *Pomerid: Curate* on 5: *John* 14. 14. *Viccar* on his former.—*Curate*, the peril of indulging the least sinn. 16 To *Lond:* dind with some of the *R: Soc*: 21. Sir *Jonathan Trelany* Baronet, preached *Cor:*

Rege on   Rom: very handsomely & well: he
became Baronet, by the death of his Bro: sonn, who I think was
slaine at *Tangier*, when the *Moores* besieged it. 23: Sir *Fran:*
North, sonn to the Lord *North* & L:C. Justice, being upon the
Death of the Earle of *Notingham* late L. Chancelor, now made
Lord Keeper, and my former Acquaintance, I went now to see,
& Congratulate: He is a most knowing, learned, ingenious gent,
& besides an excellent person, of an ingenuous sweete disposition, very skillful in Musick, Painting, the new Philosophie &
politer studies: He received me with all respect:

28 Dr. *Cave* (Author of severall usefull bookes, as Primitive
Christianity, the life of the *Fathers* for the first 400 yeares &c)
preached on 16 *Luke* 25, very excellently: I dind at the Bish: of
Rochesters, & then heard a sermon in the *Abbey Church*. 29
Supped at Sir *Jos: Williamsons*, where was a select companie of
our *Society* Sir *Will: Petty*, Dr. *Gale* (that learned scholemaster
of St. *Paule*) Dr. *Whistler*, Mr. *Hill* &c: & the intire Conversation was *Philosophical* & Cherefull, upon divers Considerable
questions propounded: as of the hereditaire succession of the
Roman Empp: The *Pica* mention'd in the Præface to our *Comm:*
Prayer, which signifies onely the *Greeke Kalendarium*: of facetious things, The name of *Ninehamer*, viz, *Anent-hammer*, he
that holds the hammer at the opposite point of a naile to
clinch it, being a thing of no art or skill, but such as any dull
fellow may do: This was upon an action at *Law*, against one
that calld a Greate Person, a *Ninehammer*, & interpreted by a
Smith in Dublin, upon which the Controversy fell, & no damage recovered: Then we discoursed of *Rebus's* & *Anagramms*;
That this sort of Trifling was seldom used by the *Romans* or
Greekes: The most natural being that which usualy fell from
Words, without literal Transpositions; such as that which was
made upon *John Bishop of Tuam* in *Ireland*: by one who asked
him   *Jo-an-es Tu amens is*? &c: in truth the discourse
was perfect *Deipno-sophisme* & very harmelesse; nor without
Salt, & instruction.

30 The Anniversary of *Charles* the first his *Martyrdom*: The
B: of Rochester preached on 2: *Apoc:* 10. cor: *Rege*, appositely to
the Occasion:

Feb: 1 Returning with Sir *William Godolphin* from Visiting
Dr. *Burnet* & P: Church-Yard among the Bookes, being stop'd

in *Fleetestreete*; a *Paver*, or inferior Labourer, working in a deepe Channell, by St. *Dunstans* in *Fleetestreete* flung in a greate stone to the Coach, and brake a greate glasse in pieces, which was drawn up, without doing either of us other harme, we being on the brink of the pit:

2 I made my Court at St. *Jamess* where I saw the Sea *Charts* of Cap: *Collins*, which that industrious man now brought to shew the Duke, having taken all the Coastings from the mouth of the *Thames* as far as *Wales*, & exactly measuring every Creeke, Iland, Rock, Soundings, harbors, Sands, Tides & intending this next Spring, to proceede til he had finish⟨ed⟩ the ⟨whole⟩ Iland: & that measured by Chaine, & other Instruments: a most exact & usefull undertaking: He affirmed, that of all the Mapps, put out since, there are none extant, so true as those of *Jo: Norden*, who gave us the first in Q: Eliz: time &c: all since him erroneous: hence I returned home:

6 I went to *Lond:* 7 Dined with some of our *Society*, we had a very usefull Experiment how to describe any Spirals by a Counterpoise upon *Mercurie*, which rising & falling the *Axis* after a new manner of motion of the poles describ'd the figure upon paper &c. 11: Morning [at *Whitehall*] I came to the fragment of a sermon preached by Dr. *Cradock* Provost of Eaton on   perstringing the *Papists*, seeking to maintaine some erroneous conclusions by incompetent Arguments:

Coram Rege preached Dr. *Cann*[1] on 138 *Psal:* 1. copiously & learnedly shewing, that by Gods were ment *Princes* & Kings, *Angels* &c:

12 This morning being at Mr. *Packers*, I received the newes of the death of my *Father* in Law, Sir *Rich: Browne* knight & Baronet, who dyed at my house at Says-Court this 12th of *Feb:* at 10 in the morning, after he had labour'd under the Gowt, and Dropsie for neere 6 monethes, in the 78th yeare of his Age, upon which I returned home to comfort my disconsolate Wife; & take order about his Funerall.

18 I went not to *Church*, obeying the Custome of keeping at home 'til the Ceremonies of the Funerall were over: which were solemniz'd, on the 19th at *Deptford* with as much Decency, as the Dignity of the Person, & our Relation, required: There being

1 Thomas Ken, later Bishop of Bath and Wells.

invited the *Bishop* of *Rochester*, severall Noble Men, knights, & all the fraternity of the *Trinity Companie* (of which he had ben *Master*) & others of the Country &c: The *Viccar* preaching on 39: *Psal:* 10, a short, but Proper discourse upon the frailty of our mortal Condition, Concluding with an ample, & well deserving Elogie upon the Defunct, relating to his honorable Birth, & Ancestors, Education, Learning in Gre: & Latin, Modern Languages, Travells, Publique Employments, Signal Loyaltie, Character abroad, & particularly the honour of supporting the *Church* of *England* in its publique Worship, during its pers(e)cution by the late Rebells Usurpation, & Regicide, by the Suffrages of divers Bishops, Doctors of the church & others, who with it, found such an *Asylum* in his house & family at *Paris*, that in their disputes with the *Papists* &c (now triumphing over it, as utterly lost) they us'd to argue for its Visibility & Existence from Sir *R: Brownes* Chapell & Assembly there: Then he spake of his greate & loyal sufferings during 19 yeares Exile with his present Majestie, his Returne with him, the signal yeare 1660; his honourable Employment at home, his timely Recesse, to recollect, his greate Age, Infirmity, Death; He gave that land, to the *Trinity Corporation* in Deptford, to build upon it, those *Almes houses*, now standing for 24 Widdows of Emerited Seamen &c: He was borne the famous yeare of the Gun-powder Treason *1605*; & being the last of his Family, left my Wife his onely Daughter heire: His Grandfather Sir *Rich: Browne* was the greate Instrument under the greate Earle of Licester (favorit to Quene *Eliz*,) in his government of the Nether-Lands: He was Master of the household to King James; & Coferer; (I think) was the first who regulated the Compositions through all England, for the Kings household provisions, Progresse &c, which was so high a service & gratefull to the whole Nation, as he had accknowledgements & publique thanks sent him from all the Counties; finaly he died by the rupture of a Veine in a vehement speech he made about the Compositions, in a Parliament of K. James's. By his Mothers side he was a *Gunson*, Treasurer of the Navy in Hen: 8th: Q: *Marys*, Q: *Eliz:* reigne; & as by his large & noble Pedegree appeares, related to divers of the *English* peeres & nobility: too tedious here to reherse: &c: Thus ended this honorable Person after infinite Changes & tossing too & froo, in the same house and place where he was borne: Lord teach us so to number our daies, that we may apply our hearts to Wisdome, & sit so loose to the things & employments of this world, as to be ready & prepared for a better: *Amen*: By an especial Clause in his last Will, he ordered to be buried in the Church-Yard under the South-East Window of the Chancel, joyning to the burying places of his Ancestors, since they came out of *Essex* to Says-Court: being much offended at the novel Costome of burying every body within the body of the *Church* & chancel, as a favour hertofore granted onely to Martyrs, & greate *Princes*, this excesse of making *Churches Charnel-houses* being of ill & irreverent example, & prejudicial to the health of the living: besides the continual disturbance of the Pavement, & seates, the ground sinking as the Carcases consume, & severall other undecencies: Dr. *Hall*, the pious *Bish:* of *Norwich* would also so be interr'd, as may be read in his Testament:

23 I went to *Lond:* about severall buisinesses & return'd next day: 25 The morning being bitter weather, I went not to Church til the Afternoone—Curate on 24 *Matt:* 42.

28 I went to *Lond*, about proving Sir R: *Brownes Will.*

Mar. 2. I heard Dr. *Tillotson* at St. *Michaels* in *Cornehill*, but his Text I could not guesse what: his argument was the infinite goodnesse & mercy of God &c: It was not on a *Sunday*, but *lecture* & I steped in but casualy, as I was going by to the R: *Society*.

3 I returned home: 4: our *Viccar* on 17: *Act:* 30: the holy Sacrament followd: *Pomer:* stranger on 1. *John* 1. 3: 11. our *Viccar* on his former subject:—Po: *Curat* 24. Matt: 42. 14. To Lond: about buisinesse & probate of Sir R: Br: Will:

16 I went to see Sir *Josiah* Childs prodigious Cost in planting of Walnut trees, about his seate, & making fish-ponds, for many miles in Circuite, in Eping-forest, in a Cursed & barren spot; as commonly these over growne & suddainly monied men for the most part seate themselves: He from an ordinary Merchants Apprentice, & managements of the E. *India Comp:* Stock, being arived to an Estate of (tis said) 200000 pounds: & lately married his daughter to the Eldest sonn of the Duke of *Beaufort*, late Marques of Worcester, with 30000 pounds portion at present, & various expectations: This Merchant, most sordidly avaricious &c: I dined at one Mr. *Houblons* a rich & gentile french Merchant, who was building an house in the Forest neere *Childs*, in the place where the Late Earle of *Norwich* dwelt some time, &

which came from his Lady, the Widow of Mr. Baker: & where I had formerly ben with his Lordship: It will be a pretty Villa, about five miles from *White-Chapell*:

18. I received the *holy Comm:* at St. *James's* in the morning, then preached a stranger at Court on 51 *Psal:* 3: In the afternoone I went to the *Savoy-Church* to heare Dr. *Horneck* on 2: *Phil:* 5: This Dr. *Horneck* (being a German borne) is a most pathetic preacher, a person of a sai⟨n⟩tlike life; & hath written an excellent Treatise of *Consideration*: [20] I supped, at Sir Jos: *Williamsons*: Din'd at *Dr. Whistlers* at the Physitians Coll: with Sir *Tho: Mellington*, both most learned men, Dr. *Wistler* the most facetious man in nature; & now *Censor* of the Colledge. I was here consulted, where they should erect their Librarie: 'Tis pitty this Colledge is bu⟨i⟩lt so neere newgate Prison, & in so obscure an hole, a fault in placing most of our Publique buildings & Churches in the Citty, through the avarice of some few men, & his *Majestie* not over-ruling it, when it was in his powre after the dreadfull Co⟨n⟩flagration &c:

21. Preached at W:hall: *Dr. Tenison* on 1. *Cor:* 6. 12, shewing the lawfullnesse of the Use of every thing that God has created, even our passions & appetites, Recreations, Oathes, Actions, [Riches, Garments] &c: in a most incomparable discourse: in what Circumstances safe, & how perverted by bringing our selves under their dominion, & becoming Vassals, to our Servants &c: concluding in a most heavenly exhortation, almost rapturous: I esteeme this Doctor to be absolutely one of the most profitable preachers in the Church of England, being likewise of a most holy Conversation, very learned, & ingenious; but the insuperable paines he takes & care of his Parish, will I feare weare him out, which were an unexpressable losse.

24, I went to heare Dr. *Charletons* Lecture in the *Anatomie Theater* at the *Physitians Colledge*, upon the *heart*; & returned home:

25 Our *Viccar* as before: *Curate* as above: 30. I went to *Lond:* in order to my passing the previous weeke for the Celebration of the *Easter* now approching; there being in the holy-Weeke, so many eminent Preachers, officiating at the *Court* &c:

30: Dr. *Tillotson* at *Whitehall* (*coram Rege*) on 1. *John*: 47. on the Testimonie *Christ* gave of *Nicodemas*, to recommend the grace of Truth & Sincerity in all our actions; perstringing the vaine & servile Complements crept in in this late ⟨depraved⟩ age, in this nation, from the Imitation of the *French* and other Nations; their submisse & servile expressions, when they intend nothing lesse, but shew their passions & revenges on every slight occasion: whereas we ought to be plaine, & intire in all our words & transactions, expressive of the simplicitie of our hearts &c:

Aprill: 17 I was at the Launching of the last ship of the 30, ordred to be new built, by Act of Parliament, & named the *Neptune*, a 2d rate, one of the goodliest vessels of the whole Navy, & of the world, & built by my kind neighbour [young] Mr. *Shish*, his *Majesties Master Ship-Wright* of this Dock: 21. Came to Visite & Dine with me Sir *Joseph Williamson*, late *secretary* of state, & Plenepotentiary Ambassador at *Nimeghen*, with my old fellow-Traveller Mr. *Henshaw* & Mr. *Hill*:

26 To *Lond:* To our *Society*, return'd home. 29: The morning exceeding wett; Pomerid: *Curate* 23. *Pro*: 23.

May: 1. Our *Viccar* on 7: Matt: 21: The Foefees for the Poore met, with whom I was, & then went to *Black-heath*, to see the new *faire*, being the first, procured by the L: *Dartmoth*, this being the first day, pretended for the sale of Cattell; but, I think in truth to inrich the new *Tavern* at the bowling-greene, erected by *Snape* his Majesties farrier, a man full of projects: There appeared nothing but an innumerable assemblie of drinking people from *Lond*, Pedlers &c: & I suppose it too neere *Lond*; to be of any greate use for the Country: *March* was unaccostomably hott & drie this spring & all *April* hitherto, excessively Wet; I planted all the out limites of the Garden, & long Walks, with Holly:

7 To *Lond:* about affaires. 8. To our *Society*. 9: Din'd at Sir *Gab: Sylvius*, & thence went to visite the *Duke* of *Norfolck*, & to know whither he would part with any of his *Cartoones* & other Drawings of *Raphael* & the greate masters: He answered me, he would part with & sell any thing for mony, but his *Wife* (the *Dutchesse* &c) who stood neere him; & I thought with my selfe, That if I were in his condition, it should be the first thing I would be glad to part with: In conclusion he told me, if he might sell them altogether, he would; but that the late Sir *Peter Lely* (our famous painter) had gotten some of his best: The person who desir'd me to treate with the *Duke* for them was *Van der*

Douse, (Grand-son to that greate Scholar, Contemporarie, & friend of *Jos: Scaliger*,) a very ingenious *Virtuoso*: &c.

⟨10?⟩ I dined at my *Lord Keepers* who treated me with extraordinary kindnesse, setting me the very next to him, & after dinner carrying me into his Withdrawing roome, we discoursed together of divers Philosophical subjects, as the Nature of Water, especialy, that of *Thames*, *That* onely, and the water of a River neere Bantam in the *East Indies* being of the same nature, to putrifie, & grow sweete againe, & is for all purposes the best we have in England: That the most *dulcorus* & milky tasted were not the best: There was here at dinner, my kindsman Sir *Humph: Forster* a pretty Gent: newly come out of Spaine: I went home this Evening:

Curate on his former Text: I was so exceeding drowsy (as usualy I now am in the decline of my age) that I could hardly hold mine Eyes open: The Lord be gracious to me.

16 Came to dinner & Visite Sir Rich: *Anderson* of *Pendley* & his Lady, with whom I went to Lond:

17 *Ascention* day I received the holy Comm: at St. *Martins*, The Reader preaching on 68 *Psal:* 18: I return'd home this Evening: 20: our *Viccar* on his former, with little addition: *Pomerid*: the *Curate* on 4: *Eph:* 14. 15, shewing (very well) the peevishnesse of our present dissenters, & that private opinions, though in themselves innocent & Indifferent, when they come to whart, & set-up against the judgement of the *Church*, & Legal Authority, become occasions of great Scandal, & instruments of evil Consequence, disagreable to Christian Charity, & Condescention. 23 To Lon: R: *Society*, when Mr. *Baker*[1] (a most ingenious young man) that had ben at St. *Helenas*, shewed us some Experiments of the Variation of the *Needles* plac'd betweene t⟨w⟩o equal *Magnets*, and Dr. *Tyson* brought in the *Anatomie* of a greene *Lizard*: I return'd that Evening.

June 1 Came the Duke of *Grafton* to see me: 3. our *Viccar* as before. The holy Comm: follow'd, of which with my wife I participated.

Curate on his former &c: ⟨4⟩: *Trinity Moneday*, was elected Master of that fraternity, the Lord *Dartmouth* (sonn to Geo: Legg [late] Master of the Ordinance & one of the Groomes of

1 An error for Edmond Halley.

the bedChamber) a greate favorite of the Dukes, an active & understanding Gent in sea affaires &c: our *Viccar* (as of costome) preaching on 11: *Heb:* 7: shewing how *Noach* was saved by faith, a sermon apposite to the occasion, being before sea-men:

6 To *Lond:* our *Society*: an Experiment on the *Magnes*, which immersed in filings, they so sated it, that it would take up nothing more, 'til it was perfectly clensed from them: Mr. *Hake* brought a small *Magnes*, that being formerly of great activity, being laied a side for severall yeares, lost all its Virtue, as if sterv'd for want of foode; which being by little & little applied to steele, from 2 ounces weight that it would hardly take up, now suspended an yron of six pound, still augmenting in power, as it recovered strength, he applying weight after weight, & by degrees, not at once, as they treate famished people, to whom if at first, they give their fill of Victuals, it indangers their lives: This we recorded as a noble experiment: 8 I returned home where I found Mr. *Wilbraham*, a young gent: of *Chesshire*, &c—

10 our *Viccar* on 9: *Luke* 62: *Curate* on 33: *Ezek:* 11: 13 *Lond:* our *Society*, where we received the ⟨Count⟩ de *Zinzendorp Ambassador* from the *Duke* of *Saxonie*, a very fine young Gent: we shew'd him divers Experiments on the *Magnet* on which subject the *Society* were upon:

16 I went to *Windsore*, dining by the way at *Chesewick* at Sir St: *Foxes*, where I found Sir *Robert Howard*, (that universal pretender) and Signor *Virrio* who brought his draught & designe for the painting of the Staire Case of Sir *Stephens* new house: &c: That which now at *Winsore* was new & surprizing to me since I was last there, was that incomparable fresca painting in St. *Georges Hall*, representing the Legend of *St. George*, & Triumph of the *black-Prince*, and his reception by *Edw:* the 3d, The *Volto* or roofe not totaly finished: Then the *Chapell* of the *Resurrection*, where the figure of the *Ascention*, is in my opinion comparable to any paintings of the most famous *Roman* Masters: The Last-Supper also over the *Altar* (I liked exceedingly the Contrivance of the unseene Organs behind the Altar) nor lesse the stupendious, & beyond all description, the incomparable Carving of our *Gibbons*, who is (without Contraversie) the greatest *Master*, both for Invention, & rareness of Worke, that the world ever had in any age, nor doubt I at all but he will prove as greate a Master in the statuary Art: *Virio* the Painters Invention is likewise

admirable, his Ord'nance full, & flowing, antique & heroical, his figures move; and if the Walls hold (which is the onely doubt, by reason of the Salts, which in time, & in this moist ⟨climate⟩ prejudices) the Work will preserve his name to ages: There was now the *Terraces* almost brought round the old *Castle*: The Grafts made cleane, even, & curiously turf't, also the *Avenues* to the New-Park, & other Walkes planted with *Elmes* & limes, and a pretty Canale, & receptacle for fowle: nor less observable, & famous is the exalting of so huge a quantity of Excellent Water, to the enormous height of the *Castle*, for the Use of the whole house, by an extraordinary invention & force of Sir *Samuell Moreland*:

17 A Chaplaine preached in this glorious Chapell on 19: *Pro:* 11. [&] Concerning the danger of prosecuting worldly pleasures by Dr. *Woodroff* on 16 Matt 26 *Coram Rege*: I was invited, and dined at the *Earle* of *Sunderlands* where was the *Earles* of *Bath*, Castlehaven, L. V: Falkonberg: *Faulkland, Bish:* of *London*: The *Grand Maistre* of *Malta* brother to the Duke of *Vendosme* (a young wild spark) Mr. *Dryden* the Poet &c: After Evening Prayer I walked in the Park with my L. *Clarendon*, where we fell into discourse of the Bish: of *Salisbury* Dr. *Seth Ward*, his subtiltie &c—Dr. *Durell* being now dead, late Deane of *Winsore*, Dr. *Turner* (one of the Dukes *Chaplaines*) was made *Deane*: I visited my Lady *Arlington* Groome of the *Stoole* to her *Majestie*, who being hardly set downe to supper, word was brought her, that the *Queene* was going into the Park, to walke, it being now neere *Eleaven* at night; The *alarme* caused this *Countesse* to rise in all hast, leave her supper to us; by which one may take an estimate of the extreame slavery & subjection that Courtiers live in, who have not time to eate & drinke at their pleasure; & put me in mind of *Horac⟨e⟩'s* Mouse, & to blesse God for my owne private Condition. Here was Monsieur *Del Angle* the famous *Minister* of *Charenton* (lately fled from the persecution in *France*) concerning the deplorable Condition of the Protestants there:

18 I was present, & saw & heard the humble Submission & Petition of the *Lord-Major Sherifs* & *Aldermen* in behalfe of the Citty of *London*, upon the *Quo Warranto* against their *Charter*, which they delivered to his *Majestie* in the presence Chamber: It was delivered kneeling; & then the *King* & *Counsel*, went into the *Council-Chamber*, the *Major* & his Brethren attending still in the

Presence: After a short space, they were called in, & my *Lord Keeper* made a speech, to them, exaggerating the dissorderly & royotous behaviour in the late Election & polling for *Papillon* & *Du Bois*, after the Common hall had been formaly disolv'd, with other misdemeanors, Libells on the Government, &c for which they had incurr'd upon themselves his Majesties high displeasure; and that but for this submission, and under such *Articles* which the *King* should require their obedience to: he would certainely, *Enter Judgement* against them; which hitherto he had suspended: which were as follows: That they should neither Elect *Major*, *Sheriff*, *Alderman*, *Recorder*, *Common Serjeant*, *Towne-Cleark*, *Coroner* or *Steward of Southwark*, without his Majesties approbation; and that if they presented any, his Majestie did not like, they should proceede in wonted manner to a second choice, if that were disapprov'd, his Majestie to nominate them; & if within five daies they thought good to assent to this, all former miscarriages should be forgotten &c: & so they tamely parted, with their so antient priveleges, after they had dined & ben treated by the *King* &c: This was a signal & most remarkable period; what the Consequence will prove time will shew, whilst there were divers of the old & most learned Lawyers & Judges, were of opinion that they could not forfaite their *Charter*, but might be personaly punish'd for their misdemeanors; but the pluralitie of the younger Judges, & rising Men, judg'd it otherwise:

The *Popish Plot* also (which had hitherto made such a noise) began now sensibly to dwindle, through the folly, knavery, impudence & giddynesse of *Oates*; so as the *Papists* began now to hold up their heads higher than ever, & those who were fled flock'd to *Lond:* from abroad: Such suddaine Changes & eager doings there had ben, without any thing of steady, or prudent for these last seaven yeares: 19: I returned in Coach with the *Earle* of *Clarendon*, when passing by the glorious Palace his father built, but few years before, which they were now demolishing, being sold to certaine undertakers &c: I turn'd my head the Contrary way til the Coach was gon past it, least I might minister occasion of speaking of it, which must needes have grieved his Lordship that in so short a time, their pomp was fallen &c: I went [20] next day to my house:

24 Our *Viccar* on his former *Text*, shewed the danger of Apostacie:—*Curat*, on his former:

26 I went to *Lond:* with my Bro: *Evelyn*, who came to visite me, & next day to the *Society*, where the *Curator* shew'd an Experiment how to Calculate the *Saliences* & altitude of Water, by the pressure of a small portable Pump which crowding a small quantitie of Water, caused it to rise in a slender *Tube* of Glasse, seal'd at the extreame, & marking by the gradations on the Tube, what weight of Water was requisite to any height given, an exceeding usefull Instrument: My affaires kept me in Towne 'til the end of the moneth.

28 After the *Popish*-plot &c there was now a new (& as they call'd it,) *Protestant-Plot* discover'd, that certaine Lords, & others should design the Assacination of his *Majestie* & Duke, as they were to come from New-Market, with a general rising of several of the Nation, and especialy the Citty of *Lond:* disafected to the present Government &c: Upon which were committed to the *Tower* the *Lord Russel*, Eldest sonn of the *Earle* of *Bedford*: Earle of Essex, Mr. *Algernon Sydnie*, sonn to the old Earle of *Licester*; Mr. *Trenchard, Hambden*: Lord Howard of *Eskrick* & others; with Proclamation out against my Lord *Grey*, the Duke of *Munmouth*, Sir *Tho: Arme-Strong*, and one *Ferguson* who had escaped beyond sea &c: of which some were said to be for the Killing of his Majestie, others for onely seasing on him, & perswading him to new Counsils, on pretence of the danger of Poperie, should the *Duke* live to succeede &c: who was now admitted to the Councils, & Cabinet seacrets againe &c: Much deplor'd were my Lords *Essex* & *Russell*, few believing they had any evil Intention against his Majestie or the *Church*, & some that they were cunningly drawn in by their Enemies, for not approving some late Councils, & manegement of affaire(s), in relation to France, to Popery, to the prosecution of the Dissenters &c. They were discovered by the *Lord Howard*, & some false breathren of the Clubb, & the designe happily broken; since had all taken effect; it would in all appearance have indangered the Government to unknowne & dangerous Events: *which God avert*:

28 Was borne about 3 in the Afternoone, my *Grand-Daughter* at *Says* Court, & Christned by the name of *Martha Maria*, by her two Grand-mothers, the *Lady Stonehouse* & my *Wife* &c: our *Viccar* Officiating:

July: 4 Was my *Grand-daughter* christned: The two Godmothers & Sir *Gabriel Roberts* Susceptors, by the Name of

Martha Maria, I pray God blesse it, & may she choose the better part: 7: Came Sir *Tho: Bellot* to treate about Mr. *Wilbraham* proposed to my Daughter Mary:

8 Our *Viccar* pursues his Text: *Curat* as above &c: 11: To *Lond:* din'd with a Club of our *Society*: Divers Experiments: one by *Dr. Slaer* attempting to demonstrate the several fermentations in our bodies, viz that of our bloud in *Paroxysmes* of Agues & Feavors: He put an *extract* of humane *blood* & spirit of *Vinegar* drawn thro *Veredigreece* into fountain Water in a *Vescica* of Glasse, which all remained very cold: Then a pretty quantity of *sal armoniac*, which set it all a boiling like a pot, whilst in the meane time it grew more cold than before; which sayd the Doctor is the cold fit of the *Ague*, the *Pulse* being then higher by much: Then with a few drops of Spirit of *Sulphure*, the *fermentation* & cold quite ceasing, it became hot immediately: This says he is the hot fit, succeeding the rigor of the Cold: A most *luciferous* & ingenious *Experiment*: It was then by Mr. *Waller* a young modest, & most ingenious Gent: Suggested that the experiment should be repeated the next meeting, with a preparation of the *Cortex* (or *Jesuits Powder* as cald so famous for *Talbors* curing Agues with it) to trie whither it would hinder both Ebulition & Fermentation: Then Mr. *Hooke* brought in his new *Pump* that moved by Vanes or Wings, so contriv'd as best to receive the full power of the wind, shewing the defects of the ordinary way of ordering them: This did allways turne of it selfe the whole Mill, & tooke the Wind backward: & how it was applicable to all sorts of Millworke, for grinding, sawing, drawing Water &c: He also shewed, how by the help of a small, but strong rope, to stop the fall of any ponderous weight, in case of breaking the line which holds it; by help of a small & simple piece of yron, fastned to the Weight & running at the other end with an Eye *parallel* to the descending weight, upon the lines breaking, by altering the Center of gravitation, which would stop at the other line or stronger chord: by this slight device he securd the vast weight of 2000 pounds which setts the *Chimes* of the R: *Exchange* a going, which before sometimes falling, had almost beaten-down the *Tower*. 12. I dind at my L: Chamberlains with the *Duke* of *Grafton* &c:

13 ⟨*Friday*⟩, as I was visiting Sir Tho: *Yarbrow* & Lady in Covent Garden, that astonishing newes of the *Earle* of *Essex*

having Cut his owne Throat was brought to us, having now ben but three dayes prisoner in the Tower, & this happning on the very day & instant that the Lord *Russel* was on his Trial, & had sentence of death: This accident exceedingly amaz'd me, my Lord of *Essex* being so well know⟨n⟩ by me to be a person of so sober & religious a deportment, so well at his ease, so much obliged to the *King*. It is certaine the *King* & *Duke* were at the *Tower* & pass'd by his Window about the same time this morning, when My Lord asking for a rasor he shut himselfe into a closet, & perpetrated the horrid fact: It was wondred yet by some how it was possible he should do it, in the manner he was found; for the wound was so deepe & wide, as being cut through the Gullet, Wind-pipe, & both the jugulars, it reached to the very *Vertebræ* of the neck, so as the head held to it by a very little skin as it were, which tack'd it from being quite ⟨off⟩; The gapping too of the rasor, & cutting his owne fingers, was a little strange, but more, that having passed the Jugulars he should have strength to proceede so farr, as an Executioner could hardly have don more with an axe, and there were odd reflections upon it: This fatal newes coming to *Hicks-hall* upon the article of my L: *Russels Trial*, was said to have no little influenc'd the *Jury*, & all the bench, to his prejudice: Others said, he had himselfe upon some occasions hinted, that in case he should ⟨be⟩ in danger of having his life taken from him, by any publique misfortune, those who thirsted for his Estate, should misse of their aime, & that he should long since speake favourably of that D: of *Northumberland* & some others who made away themselves: But these are discourses so very unlike his sober & prudent Conversation, that I have no inclination to credit them: what might instigate him to this develish fact I am not able to conjecture; since (as my Lord Clarendon his bro: in Law, who was with him but the day before assur'd me) he was then so very cherefull, & declared it to be the Effect of his innocence & loyalty: & most believe his *Majestie* had no severe intentions against him; however he was altogether inexorable as to my *Lord Russell* & some of the rest: For my owne part I believe the crafty & ambitious Earle of *Shaftsbery* had brought them into some dislike of the present carriage of matters at Court, not with any designe of destroying the *Monarchy* (which *Shaftsbery* has in Confidence & for unanswerable reasons, told me, he would support, to his last breath, as having seene & felt the miserie of being under [a] Mechanic Tyrannie &c) but perhaps of seting up some other, whom he might govern, & frame to his owne *Platonic* fancie, without much reguard to the *Religion* establish'd under the *Hierarchie*, for which he had no esteeme: But when he perceiv'd those whom he had engag'd to rise, faile of his expectations, & the day past, reproching his Complices, that a second day for an Exploit of this nature, was never successfull, he gave them the slip, & got into *Holland*, where the fox died, three moneths before these unhappy Lords & others were discovered or suspected: Every creature deplored *Essex*, & *Russell*, especialy the last, as being thought to be drawn in on pretence onely of endeavoring to rescue the King from his present Counselors, & secure Religion, from Popery, & the Nation from Arbitrary government, now so much apprehended; whilst the rest of those who were fled, especialy *Ferguson* & his gang, had doubtlesse some bloudy designe, set up a Commonwealth, & turne all things topsie turvy; of the same tragical principles is Sidney &c:

I had this day much discourse with *Monsieur Pontaque* son to the famous & wise Prime President of *Bourdeaux*: This gent, was owner of that excellent *Vignoble* of *Pontaque* & *Obrien*, whence the choicest of our *Burdeaux*-Wines come and I think I may truely say of him (that was not so truely said of st. Paule) that much learning had made him madd: he had studied well in Philosophie, but chiefly the *Rabbines*, & was exceedingly addicted to Cabalistical fancies, an eternal *hablador*,[1] & halfe distracted with reading aboundance of the extravagant Eastern Jewes: For the rest he spake all Languages, was very rich, an handsome person, & well-bred; aged about 45.

14 I visited this morning Mr. *Frazier*, a learned Scots Gent: whom I had formerly recommended to my Lord Berkeley, for the Institution & government of his sonn, since dead at sea: he had now ben in Holland, at the sale of the learned *Hiensius's* Library, & shewed me divers very rare & curious bookes, & some *Manuscripts* he had purchas'd to good value: There were Three or foure Herbals in *Miniature* accurately don, divers *Roman* Antiquities, & of Verona &c: very many books of *Aldus's* Impression &c: hence I went home:

1 Chatterer.

15 A stranger preached on 6. *Jer:* 8: The old man preached much after Bish: *Andrews's* method, full of *Logical* divisions, in short, & broken periods, & latine sentences, now quite out of fashion in the pulpet: grown into a far more profitable way, of plaine & practical, of which sort this *Nation* nor any other ever had greater plenty, & more profitable (I am confident) since the *Apostles* time: so much has it to answer for thriving no better on it: Pomerid: our *Curate* on 11: *Matt:* 28.

The whole Nation was now in greate Consternation, upon the late Plot & Conspiracy; his *Majestie* very Melancholic, & not stirring without redoubled Guards, all the Avenues & private dores about White-hall & the Park shut up; few admitted to walke in it: The *Papists* in the meane while very jocond, & indeede they had reason, seeing their owne plot brought to nothing, & turn'd to ridicule & now a Conspiracy of *Protestants*, as they cald them: The Turk likewise in hostility against the German Emperor, almost Master of the upper *Hungarie* & drawing towards *Vienna*; on the other side the *French* (who tis believed brought in the Infidel) disturbing their Spanish, & Dutch Neighbours, & almost swallowed, all *Flanders*, pursuing his ambition of a fift [& Universal] Monarchy; & all this blood, & dissorder in *Christendome* had evidently its rise from our defections at home, in a Wanton peace, minding nothing but Luxurie, Ambition, & to procure Mony for our Vices: To this add our *irreligion* & *Atheisme*, greate ingratitude & selfe Interest: the Apostacie of some, & the Suffering the *French* to grow so Greate, and the Hollanders so Weake. In a word we were Wanton, madd, and surfeiting with prosperity, every moment unsettling the old foundations, & never constant to any thing. The *Lord* in mercy avert the sad *Omen*; & that we do not provoke him farther, 'til he beare it no longer:

This summer did we suffer 20 *French*-men of *Warr* to passe our Chanell towards the Sound, to help the Dane against the Swede, who had ⟨abandoned⟩ the ⟨French⟩ Interest; we having not ready sufficient to guard our Coasts, or take Cognizance of what they did; so as though the Nation never had more, or better Navy, the *Sea* never had so slender a Fleete:

19 *George Prince* of *Denmark*, who landed this day, came to Mary the Lady *Anne* daughter to the *Duke*: so I return'd home; having seene the Young Gallant at dinner at *Whitehall*.

20 Severall of the Conspirators, of the lower forme, were Executed at *Tyburn*—

21 And the next day was the *Lord Russell* decapitated in *Lincolns in fields*, the Executioner giving him 3 butcherly strokes: The Speech he made & Paper he gave the Sherif, declaring his Innocence, the noblenesse of the family, the piety & worthynesse of the unhappy Gent: wrought effects of much pitty, & various discourses on the plot &c:

22: A stranger on II: *Pro:* 18. 19: with reflections on the late *plot*:

25 I went to Lond: saw againe *Prince George*, he had the Danish Countenance, blound; a young gent of few words, spake French but ill, seemed somewhat heavy; but reported Valiant, & indeede had bravely rescued & brought off his brother the K. of *Denmarke* in a battaile against the Swede, when both those Kings, were engaged very smartly:

At the R: *Society* was repeated Dr. *Slaers* Experiment, which shewed the Cause of the Fitts in Agues & intermittent feavers; & the Effects of the *Cortex* mingled with a little *Chalk*, which qualified the Ebulition: After this we adjourn'd 'til October, according to Costome, & I returned home.

28 Prince Geo: was *married* to the *Lady Ann* at White-hall: Her Court & household to be moduled just as the Dukes her fathers &c: & to continue in England:

August: 1 Came to see me Mr. *Flamested* the famous Astrologer from his Observatorie at Greenewich, to draw the Meridian for my *Pendules* &c:

2 Came to Visite me the Countesse of *Bristol*, & *Sunderland*, Aunt & Co: Germ: to the late Lord *Russell*; & to Condole his sad fate:

5 Mr. *Saunders* preached on 1. *Hagg:* 7, a most excellent discourse: *Pomeridiano* on 2 *Psal:* 6. Paralleling the preservation of his Majestie to that of K. *David* &c: a Politique discourse relating to the Plot &c:

8 A Woman, who came from *Lond:* to speake with my Wife, was Arested for debt in my Hall, by one who pretended to be a Porter, & to deliver her a letter; but I rescued her from the Insolence &c:

17 Came all the daughters of the late *Vicountesse* Mordaunt to visite & dine with us &c:

19 Mr. *Bohune* preached on 33. *Isay* 14. a most profitable discourse: *Pomerid*: our *Curate* on 33 Ezek. his former subject: 23d I went to *Bromely* to visite our *Bishop* our excellent neighbour, & to Congratulate his now being made *Arch-bishop* of York, returnd that evening: 24 Dr. *Par*, Dr. *Bradford* and some other friends dined with me; Came to visite me Colonel Jo: *Russell* unkle to the ⟨Late⟩ *Lord Russell*, & bro: to the Earle of *Bedford*, & with him Mrs. *Midleton* that famous, & indeede incomparable beautifull Lady; Daughter to my Relation Sir Robert Needham.

28 Died my sweete little Grand-child *Martha Maria* of Convulsion fitts, an extraordinary pretty & foreward child: *Gods will be don*:

Came also this morning to take his leave of us his Grace the Archbishop of Yorke now preparing for his Journey: & reside in his Province. 29 Was buried our Grand-child, amongst the rest of our sweete Infants in the *Parish-Church*:

September 2 This morning was read in the Church after the Office was don, the *Declaration* setting forth the late Conspiracy against his *Majesties Person* &c: after which Dr. *Jackson* preach'd on 2: *Phil*: 1. 2. of the Nature of Love, friendship & Charity, very eloquently ending with an exhortation to Unitie. The holy Comm: followed: *Pomerid*: the *Curate* 3: *Coloss*: 2.

3 I went (together with my Wife &c) to Chelsey, to see my Charge, the Daughters, and Children of my deare friends, the late V. Countesse *Mordaunt*: After dinner I walked to survey what had ben don as to repaires &c, by the *Duke* of *Beaufort* upon his late purchased house at ⟨Chelsey⟩, of which I had once the selling for the Countesse of *Bristol*: I found he had made greate alterations, but might have built a better house with the Materials & that cost: at my returne to our Company, I found the Countesse of *Monte Feltre*, whose husband I had formerly known, & was a subject of the *Popes*, but Changing from his Religion, & become Protestant, resided here in England, & married into the familie of the *Savells* of York-shire: The Count (her late husband) was a very learned Gent: a greate Polititian; a goodly man: she was accompanied with her Sister, exceedingly skild in painting; nor indeede did they seeme to spare for Colour on their owne faces: They had a greate deale of Wit, one of them especialy, who talked of a sparrow she had at home not inferior to *Lesbias*.

9 It being the day of publique Thanksgiving for his Majesties late preservation, the former Declaration read the 2d time, there was a publique Office used compos'd expressly for the occasion; & then our *Viccar* preached on 144 *Psal:* 10. Thou has⟨t⟩ preserved *David from the perill of the sword* &c, very learnedly seting forth the providence of God over Kings &c: & proving they were never set up, nor ought be pull'd downe by the *people*: he shew'd how the father of the Family was Monarch of his Tribe ab origine, that therefore the Eldest sonn, had a double portion, to sustaine the government, & as being Priest, the expense of Sacrifices: That from *Tribes* they grew to Nations, & that this patriarchal dominion continued 'til God himselfe chose the *Kings* &c so by divine right, The blessing of Monarchical Government above any other: That not one of all the murderers of J. *Cæsar* but came to untimly periods, or made themselves away: remarke on the late Regicides: The strange discovery of plots against Q: Eliz: K: James, his present Majestie &c: & exhorting to obedience & loyalty, from the example & doctrine of the primitive Christians, & Church of England &c: with much more:—*Curate* 21. *Psal:* 1. chiefly consisting of the severall deliverances of his Majestie & that we should continue to pray for his preservation: My little Grand-Child was very ill all yesterday, so as we feared his life, 'til this day, that God was pleas'd to give us hopes: 15 Came to visite & dine'd with us Sir W: *Godolphin* and my sweete charge, little *Francis*: also his Unkle *Henry* & Aunt Boscawen; came also ⟨to⟩ visite me the learned Anatomist *Dr. Tyson* with some other fellows of our Society:

16 Our *Viccar* on 5. *Psal:* 8: a former Text: In the Afternoone at *Lee*, the *Lecturer* on 34: *Psal:* 9: I passed the Evening in a Visie of my excellent neighbour Mr. *Bohun* at his elegant Villa, and *Gardens*; where upon sight of the *Zinnar Tree* or *Platanus*, he told me that since their falling to plant this Tree about the Citty of *Ispahan* in *Persia*, the Plague (which formerly much infested that place) has exceedingly abated of its mortal effects, & rendered it very healthy; & that they impute it to the salutarie shade of this Tree.

18 I went to Lond: to visite & waite on the *Dutchesse* of *Grafton* now greate with Child, a most vertuous & beautifull Lady, & dining with her at my Lord Chamberlains met my Lo: of *St. Albans*, now growne so blind, that he could not see to the taking his meate: It is incredible how easy a life this Gent: has

lived, & in what plenty even abroad, whilst his Majestie was a sufferer; nor lesse, the immense summs he has lost at play, which yet at about 80 yeares old he continues, having one that sets by him to name the spot in the Chards: He eate & dranke with extraordinary appetite. He is with all this a prudent old Courtier, & much inrich'd since his Majesties returne.

After dinner I walked to survey the sad demolitions of *Clarendon* house that costly & onely sumptuous Palace of the late *L. Chancelor* Hydes, where I have often ben so cherefull with him, & so sad; hapning to make him a visite but the day before he fled from the angry Parliament, accusing him of maladministration, & envious at his grandure, who from a private lawyer, came to be fatherinlaw to the *Duke* of *York*; &, as some would suggest, designing his Majesties marriage with the Infanta of Portugal, not apt to breede: To this they imputed much of our unhapinesse, & that being sole Minister & favorite at his Majesties Restauration he neglected to gratifie his Majesties suffering party, for the rewards he received of his richer, & disloyal subjects, who were the cause of our troubles: But perhapps as many of these were injuriously laied to his charge; so he kept the Government far steadier than since it has proved: I could name some others who I thinke contributed greately to his ruine, The bouffones, and the *Misses* to whom he was an Eye sore: 'Tis true he was of a jolly temper, after the old English fashion; but *France* had now the ascendent, & we become quite another nation. The C⟨h⟩ancellor gon, & dying in *Exile*, the Earle his successor sold that which cost 50000 pounds building to the Young Duke of *Albemarle* for 25000, to pay his debts, which how contracted remaines yet a Mysterie, his sonn being no way a prodigal; some imagine the *Dutchesse* his daughter had ben chargeable to him; however it were, this stately *Palace* is decreede to ruine, to support the prodigious Wast the D: of *Albemarle* had made of his Estate, since the old man died; so as selling it to the highest bidders, it fell to certaine inferior people, rich bankers & Mechanics, who gave for it & the ground about it 35000 pounds; who designing a new Towne as it were, & the most magnificent *Piazza* in Europ, 'tis said have already materials toward it, with what they sould of the house alone, more worth than what they paied for it: See the Viccissitude of earthly things: I was plainely astonish'd as at this demolition, so noe lesse, at the little armie of Labourers, & Artificers in levelling ground, laying foundations, & contriving greate buildings at an expense of 200000 pounds, if they perfect their designe:

19 I din'd at *Mrs. Boscawens*, visited Sir St: *Fox*: 20 did some buisinesse among the *Lawyers*, having a troublesome suite of an Accompt, with Mr. *Pretiman* my Wifes *Unkle*, pretending bills of Exchange not paied, during her Fathers Residence in *France*: This Controversie having now lasted for many Yeares, coming now to be defended by me, upon My Fa: in Laws decease, as executor in right of my Wife (whose land was engag'd, & Writings ⟨kept⟩ from us, on an imaginary debt) to put it to a final Issue, I was now to commence all a new; & for that end, did this day (among other Council) retaine Mr. *North*, brother to my L: *Keeper*, & so referr the issue to the good providence of God, & return'd home to my house: Note, that by the way, I stepped in to a *Gold-beaters* work-house, who shewed me the wonderfull ductilitie of that spreading & oylie *Metall*: he said it must be finer than the standard; such as was old *Angel* gold: & that of such he had once to the value of 100 pounds, stamp'd with the Agnus Dei, & coyn'd at the time of the *holy-War*, which had ben found in a ruin'd Wall some where in the north, neere to *Scotland*: some of which he beate into leaves, & the rest sold to the *Curiosi* of Antiquities & *Medails*.

23 Our *Viccar* pursu'd his former subject, & so the *Curate* 33: *Ezek:* 11. We had now the wellcome tidings of the K: *of Polands* &c raising the siege before *Vienna*, which gave terror to all Europe, & uttmost reproch to the *French*, who 'tis believed brought him in, for diversion, that he might the more easilie swallow Flanders, & pursue his unjust conquests on the Empire &c, whilst we sate unconcerned, & under a deadly charme from somebody: There was this day a Collection for the rebuilding of *New-Market* Consum'd by an accidental fire, which removing his *Majestie* thence sooner than was intended, put by the Assassinates, who were dissapointed of their *Rendezvous* & expectation, by a wonderfull providence: This made the *King* more earnest to render *Wi⟨n⟩chester* the seate of his *Autum⟨n⟩al* field diversions for the future, designing a Palace there, where the antient Castle stood, infinitely indeede preferrable to *New-Market*, for Prospect, aire, pleasure, & provisions; The Surveior having already begun the foundations for a palace of 35000 pounds & his *Majestie* purchasing ground about it, to make a Parke &c:

My right arme of late yeares becoming very cold & weakened, it passed now into my left, with paine, & such weakenesse, that I had little force left in it, yet without the least appearance of any thing outwardly:

Octob: 4: I went to *Lond:* on buisinesse, having receiv'd a note from the Countesse of *Arlington*, of some Considerable Charge, or advantage I might obtaine, by applying my selfe to his Majestie on this signal Conjuncture, of his Majesties entering Judgement against the *Citty Charter*: The ⟨proposal⟩ made me, I wholy declin'd, not so well satisfied with these violent transactions, & not a little sorry, his *Majestie* was so often put upon things of this nature, against so greate a *Citty*, the Consequences wheroff might be so much to his prejudice: so I return'd home againe: It was at this time the L: C. Justice *Pemberton* was displac'd, held the very learnedst of the Judges, & an honest man: Sir *Geo: Geoffries* advanc'd, reputed the most ignorant, though the most daring: Sir *Geo: Treby*, Recorder of Lond: also put by, & one *Genner*, an obscure lawyer set in his place: Eight of the richest & prime Aldermen remov'd, & all the rest made onely *Justices* of the Peace, & wearing no more Gownes or Chaines of Gold: The *Lord Mayor* holding now his place & two Sherifes by new Grants, as *Custodes*, at the Kings pleasure; the pompe & grandure of the most august Cittie in the World chang'd face in a moment, & gave much occasion of discourse, & thoughts of heart, what all this would end in, & prudent men were for the old foundations.

Following his Majestie this morning through the Gallerie, ⟨I⟩ went (with the few who attended him) into the Dutchesse of Portsmouths dressing roome, within her bed-chamber, where she was in her morning loose garment, her maides Combing her, newly out of her bed: his Majestie & the Gallants standing about her: but that which ingag'd my curiositie, was the rich & splendid furniture of this woman's Appartment, now twice or thrice, puld downe, & rebuilt, to satisfie her prodigal & expensive pleasures, whilst her Majestie dos not exceede, some gentlemens Ladies furniture & accommodation: Here I saw the new fabrique of *French Tapissry*, for designe, tendernesse of worke, & incomparable imitation of the best paintings; beyond any thing, I had ever beheld: some pieces had *Versailles*, St. *Germans* & other Palaces of the French King with Huntings, figures, & Landscips, Exotique fowle & all to the life rarely don: Then for *Japon Cabinets*,

Skreenes, Pendule Clocks, huge *Vasas* of wrought plate, *Tables, Stands, Chimny furniture, Sconces, branches, Braseras* &c they were all of massive silver, & without number, besides of his Majesties best paintings: Surfeiting of this, I din'd yet at *Sir Steph: Foxes,* & [5] went contentedly home to my poore, but quiet *Villa.* Lord what contentment can there be in the riches & splendor of this world, purchas'd with vice & dishonor:

10 I went to *Lond:* with my Wife, to put in our Answer to the Suite in *Chancery:* Visited, the *Dutchesse* of *Grafton,* not yet brought to bed, & Dining with my *Lord Chamberlain* (her Father) went with them to see *Montague-house,* a Palace lately built, by that *Gent:* who had married the most beautifull Countesse of *Northumberland:* It is within a stately & ample Palace, *Signor Virios* fresca Paintings, especialy the funeral Pile of Dido, on the Stayre Case & Labours of *Hercules,* fight with the *Centaures, Effeminacy* with *Dejanira,* & *Apotheosis* or reception amongst the Gods, on the walls & roofe of the Greate roome above, I think exceeds any thing he has yet don, both for designe, Colouring, & exuberance of Invention, comparable certainely to the greatest of the old Masters, or what they so celebrate at Rome: There are in the rest of the Chambers some excellent paintings of Holbein & other Masters: The Garden is large, & in good aire, but the fronts of the house not answerable to the inside: The Court at Entrie, & Wings for Offices seeme to neere the streete, & that so very narrow, & meanely built, that the *Corridore* [is] unproportionable to the rest, to hide the Court from being overlook'd by neighbours, all which might have ben prevented, had they plac'd the house farther into the ground, of which there was enough to spare: But in summ, 'tis a fine Palace, built after the *French* pavilion way; by Mr. *Hook,* the *Curator* of our Society: There were with us my *Lady Scroope,* the greate Witt: & *Monsieur Jardine* the greate Traveller; & so we came late to Says Court:

13 Came to Visite me, my old & worthy friend Mr. Packer, bringing with him his Nephew *Berkeley,* Grandsonn to the honnest Judge; a most ingenious virtuous & religious Gent: seated neere *Worster,* & very Curious in Gardning &c:

I accompanied my friends after dinner to *Greenewich,* where we heard the fragment of a sermon preached by a stranger, encouraging an holy life:

15 Mr. *Packer* & his *Nephew,* return'd to *London:*

17 I was at the Court Leete of this *Mannor*: my L: Arlington his Majesties high steward:

21 Our *Viccar* on his former: *Pomeridiano*, the *Curate* as before on 33: Ezek: 11. Sleepe exceedingly surpriz'd me.

26 Came to visite, & dined with me Mr. *Brisbane* Secretary to the Admiralty, a learned, & knowing person:

28 Our Viccar on his former subject, with little addition, concerning the unreasonablenesse of Dissenting from the church communion: &c: *Pomeridiano* the Curate of *Greenewich* 1 *Sam:* 12: 24: Sleepe surprizing me, I was not so attentive as I ought to have ben, The Lord *Jesus* pitty me:

30 I went to *Cew* to visite Sir *Henry Capell* bro: to the late Earle of Essex, but he being gon to *Cassioberry*, after I had seene his Garden, & the Alterations therein, I returned home. He had repaired his house, roofed his Hall with a kind of Cupola, & in a niche an artificial fountaine; but the roome seemes to me over-melancholy; yet might be much improved by having the walls well painted a *fresca* &c: The two Greene-houses for Oranges & Myrtils communicating with the roomes below are very well contriv'd: There is a Cupola made with pole work betweene two Elmes at the end of a Walk, which being covered by plashing the trees to them, is very pretty: for the rest, there ⟨are⟩ too many fir-trees in the Garden.

31 Being determin'd to passe this winter in London with my family, by reason of many important affaires; I invited divers of our Neighbours to dinner: ⟨it⟩ was likewise my Birth-day & the 63d or *greate Climacterical*, to w⟨h⟩ich through Gods infinite goodnesse I was now arived, & for which his holy name be praised.

November 1 Was a meeting of the fœfees for the poore, & according to Costome a sermon by our *Viccar*: on 2. I invited divers Neighbours, being purposed to spend the rest of the winter in London:

4: Our *Viccar* on his former Text, with little addition: The holy Sacrament followed, of which I was participant, the Lord make me thankfull: *Pomeridiano*, our Curate as before: Sleepe also surprizing.

5 Our *Viccar* on 48 *Psal:* ult: (being the powder conspiracy) shewing how God alone gives all deliverances; & particularly how signaly he is our God, as to the many deliverances of this Church: He suppos'd the *Psalme* to have ben indited by

Hezekiah, after the slaughter of *Senacharibs* host: Praysing God that though the danger was so iminent & greate, there was not the least detriment to the Citty, not an house, nor a tower beaten downe: This applied to the hellish powder plot, which intended to have laied all the Citty in ruinous heapes &c ending with an exhortation to prayse God, & to keepe the day in better remembrance, than of late we had don, as if we were not concerned with a thing so long since, & before we were borne, which was greate Ingratitude: That the Israelites were from one age to another put in mind of their fathers deliverances out of Egypt, & other Calamities, as if not onely their fathers, but they themselves so many hundred yeares after had themselves ben the persons: This was the summ:

11 our *Viccar* proceedes: Afternoone at *Greenewich* the *Curate* on 51 *Psal: 7*:—I visited Sir William *Hooker*: whose Lady related to us of a Child laied to sleepe, & [that] whilst the Nurse was a little absent, a Monkey had bitten out its Eyes, torne the face, & eaten the head into the brain: Those mischievous animals should not be kept by Ladies that have young children, this being the second accident of that nature I have ben told of, one of which happned in this Parish, a vile Monkey had killd a Nurse child in the cradle almost after the same manner, whilst the nurse went but out to draw a bucket of water: & what was most deplorable, it was the onely child remaining of one who had lost severall.

17 I came with my whole Family (except my little Grandson, & his Nurse & some servants to looke after the house) to be in London the rest of this Winter, having many important concernes to dispatch which I could not so well attend at home [& for the education of my daughters]: I tooke therefore the house of one Mr. Dive's, in Villars streete in Yorke-buildings in the Strand.

23 I went home to Says Court, to see my little family, and return'd next day: The Duke of Monmoth 'til now proclaim'd Traytor upon the pretended plot, for which my L: Russell lately was be headed: Came this evening to white-hall & rendered himselfe, [24] upon which were various discourses:

Mr. *Forbus* shew'd me the plot of the Garden making at Burleigh at my L: of *Exesters*, which I looked on as one of the most noble that ever I had seene: The whole Court & Towne in solemn mourning for the death of the K. of Portugal, her Majesties Brother.

26 I went to complement the *Dutchesse* of *Grafton* now laying in of her first child, which was a sonn, which she cald for me to see with greate satisfaction: She was become more beautifull (if it were possible) than before, & full of vertue & sweetenesse, discoursed with me of many particulars with greate prudence, & gravity beyond her yeares:

30 Being St. Andrews, & our Anniversary at the R: Society: Sir *Cyrill Wich* was elected President. We din'd together according to Costome &c: The King sent us two does.

December ⟨2⟩ Dr. Tenison, on 13 Hosea 8. The holy Sacrament followed, at which I participated: I went to Court this Evening, visited my L: Chamb: &c:

[4 I was invited to dinner by my Lady Sunderland, wher was a most elegant entertainement:]

5 I was this day invited to a Weding of one Mrs. Castle, to whom I had some obligation, & it was to her fift Husband, a Lieutennant Coll: of the Citty: The woman was the daughter of one Burton a Broome-man & of a Mother who sold Kitchin stuff in Kent Streete, Whom God so blessed, that the Father became a very rich & an honest man, was Sherif of Surrey, where I have sat on the bench with him: Another of his daughters was Married to one Sir Jo: Bowles; & this Daughter a jolly friendly woman: There was at the Wedding the Lord Major, the Sherif, severall Aldermen and persons of quality, & above all Sir Geo: Jeoffries newly made Lord Chiefe Justice of England, with Mr. Justice Withings, daunced with the Bride, and were exceeding Merrie: These greate men spent the rest of the afternoone til 11 at night in drinking healths, taking Tobacco, and talking much beneath the gravity of Judges, that had but a day or two before Condemn'd Mr. Algernoon Sidny, who was executed on the 7th on Tower hill upon the single Wittnesse of that monster of a man the L: *Howard* of Eskrick, and some sheetes of paper taken in Mr. Sidnys study, pretended to be writen by him, but not fully proov'd, nor the time when, but appearing to have ben written before his Majesties restauration, & then pardon'd by the Act of Oblivion: So as though Mr. Sidny was known to be a person obstinately averse to government by a Monarch (the subject of the paper, in answer to one of Sir E: Filmer) yet it was thought he had very hard measure: There is this yet observable, that he had ben an inveterate enemy to the last King, & in actual rebellion against

him: a man of greate Courage, greate sense, greate parts, which he shew'd both at his trial & death; for when he came on the scaffold, in stead of a speech, he told them onely, that he had made his peace with God; that he came not thither to talk but to die, put a paper into the Sherifs hand, & another into a friends, sayed one prayer as short as a grace, laied downe his neck, & bid the Executioner do his office: The Duke of Monmouth now having his pardon, refuses to accknowledge there was any Treasonable plot, for which he is banish'd White-hall: This was a greate dissappointment to some, who had prosecuted the rest, namely Trenchard, Hampden &c: that for want of a second wittnesse were come out of the Tower upon their *Habeas Corpus*. The King had now augmented his guards with a new sort of dragoons, who carried also granados & were habited after the polish manner with long picked Caps very fierce & fantastical; & was very exotic:

I went to The Tower & (after 4 years Imprisonment,) gave a visite to the Earle of Danby, late Lord H. Tresurer, who received me with greate kindnesse, I dined with him, & staied with him til night: we had discourse of many things, his Lady railing sufficiently at the keeping her husband so long in prison: Here I saluted the L: ⟨Dunblaines⟩ Wife, who before had ben married to *Emerton*, & about whom was that Scandalous buisinesse before the Delegates:

12 At our Society Dr. *Slaer* (an excellent chymist) having read a learned discourse concerning the production of the stone in the Kidnies, produced two very cleare liquors which being mingled together & shaken, turn'd into a curdled stone, so as none of the liquor (now all turnd to a white stone) would come out of the glasse, to shew the nature of some liquids, & that possibly there might be some such mixtures in the body, that produced the stone, the Experiment was universaly approv'd, & he was desired to ⟨improve⟩ the experiment: These two liquors were a sort of Spir: of Urine, & Spirit of Wine. Here was the famous Naturalist Dr. Lister, & some discourses concerning subterraneous shells &c:

20 I went to Deptford, return'd the 22d in very cold & severe weather: My poore Servant *Humphry Prideaux* being falln sick of the small-pox some days before:

23 At White-hall *Coram Rege*, a Chaplaine of my L: *Manchesters* preached a most excellent sermon on 21 *Luke* 27: *Pomerid* Dr. *Meriton*, as before: This night died my poore excellent

servant of the small pox, that by no remedies could be brought out, to the wonder of the Physitians: It was exceedingly mortal at this time; & the season was unsufferably cold. The Thames frozen, &c:

25 *Christmas day* I received the Bl: Sacrament at St. James's chapel, with the Princesse of *Denmark*, The Dutchesses of Monmouth, & Grafton & severall others of quality: the Bishop of *Rochester* (Dr. Turner) preaching on 9 *Isa:* 6. 7. I went to visite the L: Chamberlaine this evening, where I met with a *Milaneze* Count, of a very pleasant humor.

26 I dined at my Lord *Clarendons* where I was to meete that most ingenious and learned Gent: Sir Geo: Wheeler, who has publish'd that excellent description of Attica & Greece, and who being a knight of a very faire estate & young had now newly entred into holy Orders: I also now kissed the Princesse of Denmarks hand, who was now with Child.

27 I went to visite Sir *J. Chardin* that *French* gent, who had 3 times travelled into *Persia* by Land, and had made many curious researches in his Travells, of which he was now setting forth a relation. It being in England this yeare one of the most severe frosts that had happn'd of many yeares, he told me, the Cold in *Persia* was much greater, the yce of an incredible thicknesse: That they had little use of *Iron* in all that Country, it being so moist (though the aire admirably cleare & healthy) that oyle would not preserve it from rusting immediately, so as they had neither clocks nor Watches, some padlocks they had for doors & boxes &c:

30 Dr. *Sprat*, now made Deane of *Westminster* preached to the King at White-hall on 6: *Matt:* 24: Afternoone a Chaplaine of the Bish: of *Elys*, on 36 *Job*: 24:

THE THAMES FROZEN – A RHINOCEROS, AND A CROCODILE – THE DEATH OF THE KING
(1684–1685)

31 RECOLLECTING THE passages of the past yeare, I gave God thanks for his Mercys, beging his blessing for the future &c:

1683/4 January 1 Beseeching the Continuance of Gods mercy & protection the yeare now entred, after publique Prayer at *St. Martines*, preached a young divine on 2. *Luke* 21, after which the Communion, at which I also participated; The Lord make me thankfull:

My Daughter *Susan* had some few small pox come forth on her, so as I sent her out of the Family; The Weather continuing intollerably severe, so as streetes of Boothes were set up upon the Thames &c: and the aire so very cold & thick, as of many yeares there had not ben the like: The small pox being very mortal, many feared a worse Contagion to follow &c:

2 I dined at Sir *St: Foxes*, after dinner came a fellow that eate live charcoale glowingly ignited, quenching them in his mouth, & then champing & swallowing them downe: There was a dog also that seemd to do many rational actions.

⟨6⟩ A stranger at St. Martines on 2 *Philip:* 7. 8: The holy Commun: follow'd at which I received. *Pomerid:* Dr. *Meriton* on 3 Colossians 18.

6 I went home to Says-Court to see my Grandson, it being extreame hard weather, and return'd the next-day by Coach the river being quite frozen up:

8 Came Sir *Geo: Wheler* and Mr. *Ottwood* to visite me. 9 I went crosse the *Thames* upon the Ice (which was now become so incredibly thick, as to beare not onely whole streetes of boothes in which the⟨y⟩ roasted meate, & had divers shops of wares, quite crosse as in a Towne, but Coaches & carts & horses passed over): So I went from *Westminster* stayers to *Lambeth* and dined with my L. *Archbishop*, where I met my *Lord Bruce*, Sir *Geo: Wheeler*, Coll: *Coock* and severall Divines; after dinner, and discourse with his Grace 'til Evening prayer, *Sir Geo:* and I returnd, walking over the Ice from *Lambeth* stayres to the Horse Ferry, and thence walked on foote to our Lodgings: 10: I visited Sir *Rob: Reading*, where after supper we had musique, but none comparable to that which Mrs. Bridgeman made us upon the Gittar, which she master'd with such extraordinary skill, and dexterity, as I hardly ever heard any lute exceede for sweetenesse.

13 Dr. *Pellin coram Rege* at Whitehall: on 1. *Pet:* 5. 7: Against solicitude & over anxiety or despondency of the Gods assistance in all dangers & extremities, with the special care he had of *Princes* and his Church; in which he much insisted on the late

Conspiracys; There was much of the Court in this sermon, calculated for the present conjuncture: &c: *Pomeridiano* Dr. *Meriton* on 3. *Coloss:* 19, a plaine honest discourse & usefull.

After sermon, came to Visite us, the *Dutchesse* of *Grafton*, & a
daughter of my late Earle of Ossory, my antient & deare friend:

14 I dined with my Lord Chamberlaine. 15 We had Mr.
Hooks new balances produc'd and much approved of. 16 Was my
first tryal befor my L: Keeper at the Chancery for a rehearing of
my Cause: I went thence to the Bishops of Lond, with whom
I dined: endeavouring to procure some of his Majesties Charity
for the poore of our Parish, the severe weather still continuing, &
now the *Thames* was filled with people & Tents selling all sorts of
Wares as in the Citty it selfe: 16 I tooke a little Physick: 20 At
white-hall *coram Rege*, preached a Chaplaine of the L: Keepers
on 10 *Matt:* 16: *Pomeridiano* at *St. Mertines* Dr. *Meriton* on 3.
Coloss: 20, Catechisticaly:

24 The frost still continuing more & more severe, the
Thames before London was planted with bothes in formal
streetes, as in a Citty, or Continual faire, all sorts of Trades
& shops furnished, & full of Commodities, even to a Printing
presse, where the People & Ladys tooke a fansy to have their
names Printed & the day & yeare set downe, when printed on
the *Thames*: This humour tooke so universaly, that 'twas estimated the Printer gained five pound a day, for printing a line
onely, at six-pence a Name, besides what he gott by Ballads &c:
Coaches now plied from Westminster to the Temple, & from
severall other staires too & froo, as in the streetes; also on sleds,
sliding with skeetes; There was likewise Bull-baiting, Horse
& Coach races, Pupet-plays & interludes, Cookes & Tipling,
& lewder places; so as it seem'd to be a bacchanalia, Triumph or
Carnoval on the Water, whilst it was a severe Judgement upon
the Land: the Trees not onely splitting as if lightning-strock, but
Men & Cattell perishing in divers places, and the very seas so
locked up with yce, that no vessells could stirr out, or come in:
The fowle [Fish] & birds, & all our exotique Plants & Greenes
universaly perishing; many Parks of deere destroied, & all sorts
of fuell so deare that there were greate Contributions to preserve
the poore alive; nor was this severe weather much lesse intense
in most parts of *Europe* even as far as *Spaine*, & the most southern tracts: London, by reason of the excessive coldnesse of the

aire, hindring the ascent of the smoke, was so filld with the fuliginous steame of the Sea-Coale, that hardly could one see crosse the streete, & this filling the lungs with its grosse particles exceedingly obstructed the breast, so as one could scarce breath: There was no water to be had from the Pipes & Engines, nor could the Brewers, and divers other Tradesmen work, & every moment was full of disastrous accidents &c:

26 I visited Mr. *Berkeley* at St. *Johns*, his wives sister paints very finely in Oyle: In the Evening I went to see Sir Geo: Wheeler.

27 Dr. *Dove Coram Rege* on 1 John: 3. v: 3. in a very plaine & honest discourse setting forth the necessity of purity, in reference to a well-grounded hope, & how most men deceived themselves with a notional faith & opinion, that the bare profession of Religion would carry them to heaven, however they lived, as to interior purity, & righteousnesse, which being the unsound doctrine of the *Gnosticks*, was the occasion of St. *Johns* writing against them.

Pomeridiano Dr. *Meriton* proceeded:

30 The frost still raging as fircely as ever, the River of *Thames* was become a Camp, ten thousands of people, Coaches, Carts, & all manner of sports continuing & increasing: miserable were the wants of poore people, Deare universaly perished in most of the parks thro-out England, & very much Cattell:

February 4 I went to Says-Court to see how the frost & rigorous weather had dealt with my Garden, where I found many of the Greenes & rare plants utterly destroied: The Oranges & Myrtils very sick, the Rosemary & Lawrell dead to all appearance, but the Cypresse like to indure it out: I came to Lond: the next day when it fir(s)t of all began to Thaw, and pass'd-over without alighting in my Coach from Lambeth to the Horseferry at Mill-bank at Westminster; the Weather growing lesse severe, it yet began to freeze againe; but the boothes were allmost-all taken downe; but there was first a Map or Landskip cut in copper representing all the manner of the Camp, & the several actions, sports and passe-times thereon in memory of this signal Frost:

6 I presented a Petition to his Majestie in Council, in behalfe of our Parish for reliefe of the poore: [7 Invited by the Swedish Resident, I dined at his house with the publique Minister of the

Emperor, Venetian, Genoan and other strangers, all persons of quality.]

⟨8⟩ I dined with my *L: Keeper*, in order to some further informing him concerning the state of our Parish, & then walking alone with him some time in his Gallery, we had discourse of Musique, his Lordship told me he had ben brought up to it from a Child, so as to sing his part at first sight: Then speaking of painting, of which he was also a greate lover, & other ingenious matters, I tooke leave of him, desiring me to come oftner to him &c:

I went this Evening to visite that greate & knowing Virtuoso Monsieur *Justell*: The weather now was set to an absolute Thaw & raine, but the Thames still hard:

10 The *Bishop* of *Cork Coram Rege* made an excellent practical sermon at *White-Hall* on 119 *Psal:* ver: 6: *Pomeridiano*, at St. *Martines*, the Lecturer on 8 *Rom:* 13.

After 8 weekes missing the foraine posts, there came aboundance of Intelligence from abroad: ⟨13⟩ Ash-Wednesday, an excellent sermon in the afternoone at St. Martins by Dr. L. On 119 *Psal:* 60.

11 I visited Dr. *Tenison* viccar of St. *Martins* newly recovered of the smal pox.

12 The E: of *Danby* late L: *Tressurer* together with the Rom: Cath: Lords impeach'd of high Treason in the popish-plot, had now their *Habeas Corpus*, and came out upon Baile, after 5 years Imprisonment in the Toure: Then were also Tried and deeply fin'd Mr. *Hambden* & others, for being supposed of the late Plot, for which my L: ⟨*Russell*⟩ and Coll: ⟨*Sidney*⟩ suffered: As also the person, who went about to prove that the E: of ⟨Essex⟩ had his Throat Cut in the Tower by others: likewise Mr. *Johnson*, the Author of that famous piece cald *Julian*.

13 Newes of the P: of Oranges having accus'd the Deputies of *Amsterdam* of *Crimen Læsæ Majestatis*, & being Pensioner to France.

Dr. *Tenison* communicating to me his intention of Erecting a Library in St. *Martines* parish, for the publique use, desird my assistance with Sir *Chr: Wren* about the placing & structure thereof: a worthy & laudable designe: He told me there were 30 or 40 Young Men in *Orders* in his Parish, either, Governors to young Gent: or Chaplains to Noble-men, who being reprov'd by him upon occasion, for frequenting Taverns or Coffè-houses, told him, they would study & employ their time better, if they had books: This put the pious Doctor upon this designe, which I could not but approve of, & indeede a greate reproch it is, that so great a Citty as *Lond:* should have never a publique Library becoming it: There ought to be one at S. *Paules*, the West end of that Church, (if ever finish'd), would be a conven-ient place: 15. Dr. *Stillingfleete Dean* of *Paules Coram Rege* on 23 *Job* 15 an incomparable discourse against *Atheisme*: see sermon printed:

19 I went to visite the Countesses of *Ossory*: 21 I had a tryal at the *Chequer* before the L: Chiefe *Barron* against my Lady *Michelthwaite* about an Accompt of Rent & asserted my Cause: This & other buisinesse on Friday hindred my hearing two *Lenten sermons*. [20 I went to visite & congratulate my Lo: *Danby*, after his coming out of Tower:]

23 I went to Sir John *Chardins*, who desired my Assistance for the ingraving of the plates, the translation & Printing of his his-torie of that wonderfull *Persian* monument neere *Persepolis*, & other rare Antiquities, which he had Caus'd to be drawne from the originals, at his 2d journey into *Persia*: which we now con-cluded upon: And afterwards I went to Dr. *Tenison* (with Sir *Chr: Wren*) where we made both the draught & estimate of the *Library* to be begun this next spring, neere the *Mewes*:

Greate expectations of the *Prince* of *Oranges* attempts in Holland, to bring those of *Amsterdam* to consent to the *new Levies*; to which we were no friends by a *Pseudo*politic adherence to the French Interest:

24 *Coram Rege* preached Dr. *Lloyd: Bishop* of *Peterborow*, once Curate of our Parish of Deptford; on 1. *Thessal:* 2: 12. shewing in a most elegant, & practical discourse, what itt was to walke Worthy of the Glory to be revealed, namely to live religiously & holily, & such a life as becomes the Ends & designe of God, to exhalt us to his heavenly Kingdome: *Pomeridiano* Dr. *Meriton* at St. *Martins* proceeding in his former lecture.

26 Came to visite me Dr. *Turner* our new *Bishop* of *Rochester*:

27 *Coram Rege* preached Dr. *Hooper* Parson of *Lambeth*, on 19: *Psal:* 13: it was a quaint & excellent discourse:

I went this Afternoone to the R: *Society*, where there were read severall learned discourses upon Experiments of Cold &c:

of Optics, & Acoustics &c: Mr. Boyle presented me his booke or Natural historie of humane blood:

28 I din'd at my *Lady Tukes*, where I heard Dr. *Wallgrave* (physitian to the Duke & Dutchesse) play most incomparably on the Lute; I know not that ever I heard any to exceede him.

29 *Coram Rege* &c: *Dr. Sharp* on. 2. *Cor:* 6. 2. Convincingly shewing the danger of deferring our Repentance 'til our old age or death-bed:

March 2 Dr. *Tillotson* at St. *Martins* on 24 *Josh:* 15: I had heard him twice on This Text before; but it could not be preached too often; The holy *Communion* follow'd at which I participated, The Lord be praised:

5 I went to visite Mr. *Ro: Boyle*, who had presented me with his History of Experiments upon humane Blood: &c:

6 I went home to Says Court, returned the next day.

7 Dr. *Megot Deane* of *Winchester* preached an incomparable sermon (the King being now gon to New-Market) on 12: *Heb:* 15.

8 I went to visite Dr. *Tenison* at *Kensington* whither he was retired to refresh after he had ben sick of the small-pox:

12 At White-hall preached *Mr. Hen: Godolphin* a preb: of S. Pauls Bro: to my deare friend Sydnie, on 55 *Isa:* 7. very excellently:

15 I dined at my L. *Keepers* and brought to him *Sir John Chardin*: who shewed him his accurate draughts of his travels in Persia &c:

28 *Good-friday*, at St. *Martines*, a Chaplaine of my L. Manchesters excellently on 12: *Heb:* 3 in a very ample & profitable discourse. The holy *Sacrament* follow'd at which I participated, the Lord accept me: *Pomeridiano coram Rege* at *Whitehall* (Dr. *Sprat, deane* of *Westminster*) on 4: *Rom:* 25.

There was so greate & eager a concourse of people with their children, to be touch'd of the *Evil*, that 6 or 7: were crush'd to *death* by pressing at the *Chirurgions* doore for Tickets. &c. The weather began now onely to be more mild & tollerable, but there was not the least appearance of any Spring.

30 Easter-day, I received the B: Sacrament at *white-hall* early, with the Lords & household: the B: of *Lond:* officiating: Then went to St. *Martines* wher Dr. *Tenison* (now first coming abroad after his recovery of the small-pox) preached on 16: *Psal:* 11:— Hence I went againe to *White Hall*, where *coram Rege*, preach'd

the *B: of Rochester* on a Text out of *Hosea* 6. 2. touching the subject of the day: After which his *Majestie*, accompanied with 3 of
his natural Sonns, (viz. the Dukes of *Northumb: Richmond* & *St.
Albans*, base sonns of *Portsmouth*, *Cleaveland*, *Nelly*, prostitute
Creatures) went up to the Altar; The three Boyes entering
before the King within the railes, at the right hand, & 3 Bishops
on the left: viz: *Lond:* (who officiated) *Durham*, *Rochester*, with
the sub-Deane Dr. Holder: The King kneeling before the Altar,
making his offering, the Bishops first received, & then his
Majestie, after which, he retir'd to a Canopied seate on the right
hand &c: note, there was perfume burnt before the office began:
Pomeridiano, preached at St. *Mart:* the Lecturer Dr. *Meriton* on
6: *Rom:* 4:

Aprill 4 After 5 monethes being in *Lond:* this severe winter,
I return'd home with my family this day: My sonn with his wife
&c: continuing behind, upon pretence of his applying himselfe
more seriously to his studying the Law, but wholy without my
approbation:—hardly the least appearance of any Spring.

6 Our *Viccar* preach'd on 14. *Rom:* 9. *Pomerid*: The *Curate* on
6 *Mich:* 8:

12 Being much indispos'd this weeke, I tooke Physick, & a
Vomite, which did greately restore me, blessed be God:

13 A young stranger preached on 4: *Phil:* 5, in a very solid discourse, onely a little too full of his *Greeke* for our Auditorie &c.
Pomerid: The same person on 6. *Matt:* 12: Sleepe surpriz'd me:

30 I went to *Lond:* To the *R: Society*, a letter of mine to it concerning the tirrible effects of the past Winter being read, they
desire it might be publish'd in the next transactions.

May 1 Being the meeting of the *Foefeès* for the poore, our *Viccar* preached on 7 *Matt:* 21. [the same as on the last yeare.]

May 10th. I went to visite my Brother in Surry, caled by the
Way at Ashstead where Sir Robert Howard Auditor of the
Exchequer entertain'd me very civily at his newly built house,
which stands in a very sweete-park upon the downe, the avenue
south though downe hill to the house exceedingly pleased me:
The house is not great but with the outhouses very convenient: The staire Case is painted by *Verrio* with the storie of
Astrea, amongst other figures is the picture of the Painter himselfe, and not unlike him; The rest well don; only the Columns
did not at all please me; There is also Sir Roberts owne picture

in an Oval, the whole in fresca: there is with all this one greate defect, that they have no Water save what is drawne with horses from an exceeding deepe Well. Hence I went to Wotton that night:

11 One Mr. Crawly preached in the Morning at *Abinger* on 13 *Heb:* 18: In the Afternoone I went to visite Mr. *Higham* now sick in his Climacterical, whereof he died [about] 3 days after: his Grandfather & Father (who Christn'd me) with himselfe had now ben 3 generations Parsons of the Parish an hundred and foure years this *May*: viz: from 1584.

12 I returned to Lond: where I found the Commissioners of the Admiralty abolished, & the Office of Admiral restord to the *Duke*, as to the disposal & ordering all sea buisinesse: But his Majestie signing all the Petitions, Papers, Warrants & Commissions, that the Duke not acting as Admiral by Commission, or Office, might not incurr the penalty of the late Act against Papists & Dissenters holding Office or refusing the Oath & Test: &c: every body was glad of this Change: Those in the late Commission being utterly ignorant of their duty, to the greate damage of the Navy royal:

Now was also the utter ruine of the *Low-Countries* threatn'd, by the Seige of *Luxemburge* (if not timely reliev'd) & the Obstinacy of the Hollanders not to assist the Prince of Orange: Corrupted (as appear'd) by the French &c:

16 I received 600 pounds of Sir *Charles Bickerstaff* for the Fee farme of Pilton in *Devon*: & payed my Bro: 500 pounds which I owed him:

18 Being W⟨h⟩itsonday, I received the B: Sacrament at St. Margarites, a stranger preaching on 15 *John* 26: against *Socinus* & other heretics: *Pomerid*: another stranger on: 16: *John*: 17:

19 At St. *Martines* my L: *Manchest⟨er⟩s* chaplain excellently on 14 *John*: 26 on the former subject:—I return'd home this Evening: Praysed ⟨be⟩ God.

An excessive hot & dry Spring after so severe a Winter:

21 I visited the Bish: of Lond; & din'd with him at Fullham, return'd that evening:

26 Being Trinity monday *Dr. Can*, preached before the Trinity Company (my L: *Dartmouth* being first chosen and continued Master for the Ensuing Yeare, now newly return'd with the fleete from blowing up, & demolishing Tangier) Text 107

Psal: 31. After a very learned discourse about the dimensions of
the Ark, compar'd with other Vessells of antient & later times, to
obviate severall objections of Atheistical persons; he shewed the
prophanesse of others, in the usual sarcasme, of calling an ignorant sayler on⟨e⟩ of St. *Paules* seamen, for that description in 27
St. Luke *Acts Apost:* where 'tis said they cast Ankers out of the
fore-ship, to proceede from utter ignorance, that because we do
not so in our seas, in stresse of Weather, & as our Vessels are
built; so they did in other seas; whereas it is at this day, and allways has bin the practise so to do in the Mediterranean seas, as
St. Luke describes it: he also most rhetoricaly inlarg'd on the
severall perils of sea Adventurers, and Mariners, by Tempests,
leakes, casual fires, Wracks; fights, [slavery], diseases &c:
thereby exciting those sort of men, to be above all others most
religious, who were found usualy the most prophane: & what
cause they had also above all others, to praise God for their
deliverances; [He preached with much action:] Then we went to
Lond: where we were magnificently feasted at the Trinity house,
My L: of Dartmouth, Earles of Cravon & Berkely &c to the
number of at the least of 100 at one table as I conjectur'd &c:

28 I paied my Bro: G: Evelyn 500 pounds more of the Mortgage: Dined with severall of our Society of Gressham Coll,
where after some Experiment: viz: by putting yron with A: fortis
in *pleno*, & another piece of yron in *Vaccuo*, That in pleno, was
rusted & eaten through twenty times sooner than that in *vaccuo*,
by w⟨h⟩ich was shew'd what a corrosive spirit there is in the
common aire &c: especialy about the Citty, so infected with
steams of the seacoale &c: Now was *Luxemburg* rendered to the
Conquering French, which makes him Master of all the Nei-
therland, gives him entrance into Germanie; & a faire game for
an universal Monarchy: which that we should suffer (who onely,
& easily might have hindred) all the world were astonish'd at:
But thus is the poore P: of *Orange* ruin'd, & this Nations, & all
the Protestant Interest in Europ following, unless God of his
infinite mercy (as by a Miracle) interpose; & that our Greate
ones alter their Counsels.

29 Being his Majesties Birth-day & restauration, I went to
the Temple Church where a stranger preached before all the
Judges & that Society on 1. 4. *Pet:* 15, a Theologo-political sermon, in order to obedience & Union; greately celebrating the

moderation of our first reformers, & perstringing our present
dissenters; after which I returned home, & found my Daughter
much mended of her feavor, God be blessed:

The *French fleete* were now beseiging *Genöa*: [burnt much of
that beautiful Citty with their bombs most maliciously, & went
off with disgrace.]

1 *June* Our Viccar, & Curate, upon the same subject & Text
with no greate addition. The B: Communion I receiv'd &c:

8 Little improvement of either Text: My daughter now wholy
freed of her feavor and myselfe of an Indisposition, for which
God be ever praised.

10 I went to Lond, about my Law buisinesse, 11: At the
R: Society where was an experiment of the adhesion of a plaine
flat ground glasse to a Cucurbit emptyed in *Vaccuo
Boyliano*; & that so close, as to beare the weight of
almost 50 pound hanging on the plate, nor did it separate 'til aire was againe let in: 12 I went to advise &
give directions about the building of two streetes in
Berkeley Gardens, reserving the house, & as much of the Garden
as the breadth of the house; in the meane time I could not but
deplore that sweete place (by farr the most pleasant & noble
Gardens Courts and Accommodations, [statly] porticos &c any
where about the Towne) should so much of it ⟨be⟩ streitned &
turn'd into Tennements; but that magnificent pile & Gardens
contiguous to it (built by the late L. Chancellor Hyde with so
vast cost) being all demolish'd, & design'd for *piazzas* & buildings, was some excuse for my Lady Berkleys resolution of leting
out her ground also, for so excessive a price as was offerd,
advancing her revenue neere 1000 pounds per Ann: in meere
Ground rents; to such a mad intemperance the age was come of
building about a Citty, by far too disproportionat already to the
Nation, I having in my time seene it almost as large more than it
was within my memorie. I return'd home this evening.

15 Our *Viccar* his former subject, most of it repetition:
Pomerid: the Curate of *Greenewich* on 10 *Pro:* 9: My Co: *Verney*
(to whom a very greate fortune was fallen) came to take his leave
of us; going into the Country: a very worthy, and virtuous young
Gent:

22 The last friday was Sir Tho: Armstrong executed at
Tyburn for Treason, as outlaw'd and apprehended in Holland,

upon the Conspiracy of the D. of Monmoth, Lord Russell &c: without any Tryal, which gave occasion to people & Lawyers of discourse, in reguard it being on an outlawry, Judgement was given & execution don thereon:

27 Hearing my good & deare friend *Mr. Godolphin* (now Secretary of state) was very ill of a feavor, I went immediately to Lond: in order to visite him at Windsore, where the Court now was: 29 I got to Windsor by nine in the morning, where after I had visited my sick & deare friend, I went to the morning service, one Dr. Fuller Deane of Lincoln preaching an excellent sermon on 10 *Matt:* 28: I din'd with the Earle of Sunderland, where was my L: Keeper, earle of Sussex, young E. of Essex, L. Alington Constable of the Tower &c: after dinner I stayed with Mr. *Godolphin* now somewhat better; Visited my Lady Bristol, & Arlington, & came back to Lond: before nine at night; [30] returned next day home to my house.

July: 2 I went to the Observatorie at Greenewich, where Mr. Flamstead tooke his observations of the Ecclipse of the sunn, now hapning to be almost 3 parts obscur'd: So greate a drowth still continu'd, as never was since my memorie:

6 Our Viccar being now absent, Mr. Meriton supplied on 1. Pet. 4. 8: The holy Comm: follow'd of which I participated: *Pomeridiano* the *Curat* as above: I was exceedingly drowsy; the Lord pardon me:

Some small sprinkling of raine, never so dry a season in my remembrance, the leaves droping from the Trees as in Autumn.

20 A stranger preach'd on 1 *Tim:* 3. 4: *Pomeridiano* our Curate on 2. *Matt:* 37.

23 I went to Lond. to congratulate the recovery of my Friend Mr. Godolphin, now made principal Secretary of state:

25 St. Jam: day Dr. *Meriton* Lecturer at St. *Martines* preach'd on the 3d of S. *James*: 13. I din'd at my Lord Falklands, Tressurer of the Navy, where after dinner we had rare Musique, there being amongst others Signor *Pietro Reggio* and Signor Jo: Battist bothe famous, the one for his Voice, & the other his playing on the Harpsichord, few if any in Europe exceeding him, there was also a Frenchman who sung an admirable base.

26 I return'd home, where I found my Lord Chiefe Justice, the Countesse of Clancartie, & the Lady Catharine Fitz Gerald, who dined with me & went back in the Evening to Lond: late:

Aug: 3 Our Viccar on 5 Mat: 5. The Curat afternoone on the former Text: I received the holy Sacrament this Morning, the Lord make me mindfull of my purposes:

8 Came my Lord Falkland to Visite me:

10 Both Viccar & Curate proceeded on their former Texts:

We had now raine after such a drowth as no man living had known in England, to the greate refreshing of the ground.

15 Dined with us My L. Faulkland, & his Lady:

17 Feavors being now very rife, my Daughter & severall of my family fell sick:

18 I went to see Mr. *Bohune* at Lee my excellent neighbour:

19 I dined at my L: Falklands at the Tressurers house in Deptford: the next day I went to Lond: about buisinesse, returned 22d:

24 St. Bartholomews day our Viccar & Curate preached on their former Text, much of it repetition onely: I was exceedingly drowsy this afternoone it being most excessively hot: we having not had above one or two considerable showres (& they stormes) these eight or nine moneths so as the trees lost their leafe like Winter, & many of them quite died for want of refreshment.

31 Our Viccar proceeded, Pomerid. a stranger on 20 *Exod:*

Now was my deare friend Mr. Secretary Godolphin made Baron of Godolphin:

September 7 Viccar as before: I received the B: Sacrament: Curat 1. Cor: 11. 28.

14 Our Viccar finished his Text this day against Common Swearing, a Vice greately prevailing: The Curat proceeded.

The sister of my deare friend Mrs. Godolphin died on the same day of the moneth of the same distemper six-years after.

21. The Viccar being absent, the Curate preached on 18 *Pro:* 8: against Tale bearers, in which 'tis believed, he reflected upon one who had reproved the scandalous life of his Wife: pomerid: 1. Thess: 4: 11. much to the same effect: [22 I dined at Dr. Parrs, visited Mr. Bowyer.] 23: Lord & Lady Falkland came & dined with us:

26 I went to Lond, to Congratulate my deare friend Mr. Sidny Godolphins being created a Baron of England, the King being now returned from Winchester, there was a numerous Court at White-hall where I saluted divers of my acquaintance: There was at this time a remove of the Earle of Rochester from

the Treasury to the presidentship of the Council, & my L: Godolphin made first Commissioner of the Treasury in his place, my Lord Midleton a Scot, made Secretary of state. These Alterations (being very unexpected & mysterious) gave greate occasion of discourse among the Politicians: I supped this night at my *La: Sylvius*, with *Dr. Tenison*, & the afternoone taking the aire in Hide Parke, saw two bucks encounter each other very fiercely for a long willes 'til one was quite vanquished:

There was now an Ambassador from the King of *Siam* from the *E. Indias* to his Majestie.

27 I returned home:

28 Our *Viccar* preach'd on 2: *Mar:* 17: The *Curate* on 55. *Isay* 6. I was much oppress'd with sleepe:

29 I was let bloud about 8 ounces for the dizzinesse of my head.

Octob: 5 A stranger preached on 1. *Cor:* 11: 28: Concerning preparation to the H: Sacrament, at which I was participant: The Afternoone was so extreamely wet, that we had the Office, & a sermon at home:

6 I tooke a little preventing physick:

⟨12⟩ Our Viccar on his former Text, with no greate addition: In the Afternoone the *Curate* of Greenewich on 6. *Luke* 36. I afterward visited some friends:

14 I went to Lond: din'd at my Lord Falklands, made visits, & return'd: Mr Boile had now produced his Invention of dulcifying Sea-Water, like to be of mighty consequence:

18 I went againe to Lond: about my suite in Chancery, returned in the Evening:

19 Mr. Bohune preached on a former Text: 29: 30, shewing very pressingly the necessity of repentance, from the assurance of an approching Judgement to come, a learned Philosophico Theological discourse:

Afternoone the Curate on 9th *Heb:* 27: 28. upon almost the former subject, the necessity of preparation, from the frequent burials hapning at this time, by reason of much sicknesse in these quarters:

21 I went to Lond: about buisinesse at this Terme:

22 Sir William Godolphin and I went to see the Rhinocerous (or Unicorne) being the first that I suppose was ever brought into England: It more ressembled a huge enormous Swine, than

any other Beast amongst us; That which was most particular &
extraordinary, was the placing of her small Eyes in the very center of her cheekes & head, her Eares in her neck, and very much
pointed: her Leggs neere as big about as an ordinarie mans wast,
the feete divided into claws, not cloven, but somewhat resembling the Elephants, & very round & flatt, her taile slender and
hanging downe over her Sex, which had some long haires at the
End of it like a Cowes, & was all the haire about the whole
Creature, but what was the most wonderfull, was the extraordinary bulke and Circumference of her body, which though very
Young, (they told us as I remember not above 4 yeares old) could
not be lesse than 20 foote in compasse: she had a set of most
dreadfull teeth, which were extraordinarily broad, & deepe in
her Throate, she was led by a ring in her nose like a Buffalo, but
the horne upon it was but newly Sprowting, & hardly shaped to
any considerable point, but in my opinion nothing was so
extravagant as the Skin of the beast, which hung downe on her
hanches, both behind and before to her knees, loose like so
much Coach leather, & not adhering at all to the body, which
had another skin, so as one might take up this, as one would do a
Cloake or horse-Cloth to a greate depth, it adhering onely at the
upper parts: & these lappets of stiff skin, began to be studdied
with impenetrable Scales, like a Target of coate of maile, lori-
cated like Armor, much after the manner this Animal is usualy
depicted: she was of a mouse Colour, the skin Elephantine;
Tame enough, & suffering her mouth to be open'd by her
keeper, who caus'd her to lie downe, when she appeared like a
[greate] Coach overthrowne, for she was much of that bulke, yet
would rise as nimbly as ever I saw an horse: T'was certainly a
very wonderfull creature, of immense strength in the neck, &
nose especialy, the snout resembling a boares but much longer;
to what stature she may arive if she live long, I cannot tell; but if
she grow proportionable to her present age, she will be a Mountaine: They fed her with Hay, & Oates, & gave her bread.

She belonged to Certaine E. *Indian Merchants*, & was sold
for (as I remember) above two-thousand pounds:

At the same time I went to see a living Crocodile, brought
from some of the W: Indian Ilands, in every respect resembling
the Egyptian Crocodile, it was not yet fully 2 yards from head to
taile, very curiously scaled & beset with impenetrable studds of a

hard horny substance, & most beautifully ranged in works especialy on the ridge of the back & sides, of a dusky greene Colour,
save the belly, which being tender, & onely vulnerable, was of a
lively & lovely greene, as lizards are, whose shape it exactly kept:
The Eyes were sharp & piercing, over which it could at pleasure
draw up a thin cobweb skinn: The rictus was exceeding deepe
set with a tirrible rank of sharp & long teeth: We could not discerne any tongue, but a small lump of flesh at the very bottome
of its throate, which I suppose helped his swallowing: the feete
were divided into long fingers as the Lizards, & he went forward
wadling, having a chaine about the neck: seemed to be very
tame; I made its keeper take up his upper jaw which he affirmed
did onely move, & so Pliny & others confidently report; but it
did not appeare so plaine to me, whither his keeper did not use
some dexterity in opening his mouth & placing his head so as to
make it seeme that the upper chap, was loose; since in that most
ample & perfect sceleton in our Repositarie at the R: Society, it
is manifestly fixed to the neck & Vertebræ: the nether jaw onely
loose: They kept the beast or Serpent in a longish Tub of warme
Water, & fed him with flesh &c: If he grow, it will be a dangerous Creature.

Octob: 23 I dined at Sir Stephen Foxes with the Duke of
Nor⟨t⟩humberland another of his Majesties natural sonns, by
that strumpet Cleaveland: He seemed to be a Young gent, of
good capacity, well bred, civile, & modest, had ben newly come
from Travell, & had made his Campagne at the siege of Luxemburg: Of all his Majesties Children, (of which he had now
6 Dukes) this seemed the most accomplished, and worth the
owning; he is likewise extraordinary handsome & perfectly
shaped: what the Dukes of Richmond, & *St. Albans*, base sonns
of the Dutchesse of Portsmouth a French Lasse, and of *Nelly*,
the Comedian & Apple-woma⟨n⟩s daughter, will prove their
youth dos not yet discover, farther than that they are both very
pretty boys, & seeme to have more Witt than [most of] the rest:

25 I visited Mr. Rob: Boyle with whom I staied most part of
the afternoone, discoursing of various Philosophical subjects:

26 At White-hall, *Coram Rege*, preached Dr. *Goodman*, on 2:
James 12: It was an excellent discourse, & in good Method: This
Doctor is Author of the Prodigal son; a Treatise worthy reading,
[and another of the old Religion.]

I dined at my sonns, now newly being come to his new house & house-keeping: My Daughter in Law ready to lie-in of her 4th Child: Thence I went to *St. Clements* (that prettyly built & contrived Church) where a Young Divine gave us an eloquent sermon on 1. *Cor:* 6. 20:

26 I attended the Chancery in Westminster Hall, where I had a Cause pleaded, giving reasons for the changing of the Master who had made an injurious Accompt, in the difference betwixt me & Mr. Pretyman: my L: Chan: was pleas'd to grant our plea:

27 I din'd & went to Visite my Lord Chamberlaine now returned from the Countrie, where dined the black Baron, & Monsieur Flamerin, who had so long ben banish'd France for a duel:

28 Being S. Sim: & Judes, I carried my Lord Clarendon through the Citty amidst all the Squibbs & barbarous bacchanalia of the Lord-Majors shew, to the *R: Society*, where he was proposed a Member, and then Treated him at dinner:

30 I returned home to Says-Court:

[31 I was this day 64 yeares of Age: Lord teach me to number my daies &c—]

November 1 Was a meeting of The Trustees for the poore: who dined together &c:

2 Our *Viccar* proceeded on his former Text: the holy Comm: followed at which I was participant: So suddaine an alteration from temperate warme weather to an excessive cold, raine, frost, snow & storme, as had seldome ben knowne, this Winter weather beginning as early & firce, as the past did late, & neere christmas, till which there had hardly ben any winter at all: *Buda* in *Hungary* yet besieg'd: by the DD: of Lorrain & Bavaria, to the losse of many brave commande⟨r⟩s & men:

4. I went to *Lond:* 5t Dr. Turner now translated from Rochester to Ely upon the death of Dr. Peter Gunning, preached *coram Rege* at W.hall on 3. *Rom:* 8, a very excellent sermon, vindicating the Church of England against the Church of Roomes pernicious Doct⟨r⟩ines, of the lawfullnesse of doing evil upon a good intent, proving that to be no ways justifiable in the least instance: one thing very observable, in reguard of the common imputation of the Episcopal Cleargies being inclin'd to Popery; He challenged the producing but of 5 Cleargy-men, ⟨who⟩ forsooke our church, & went over to Roome, during all the troubles & Rebellion in

England, which lasted neere 20 yeares, among 10000 of them: And this was to my certaine observation a greate truth:

6 I delivered my Petition to his Majestie for reliefe against my grand suite, who referr'd it to the Lords Commissioners of the Treasury: Supped with L: Clarendon &c:

15 Being the Queenes Birth-day, there was such fire works upon the Thames before White-hall, with pageants of Castles, Forts, & other devices of Gyrandolas, Serpents, The King & Queenes Armes & mottos, all represented in fire, as had not ben seene in any age remembred here: but that which was most remarkable was the several fires & skirmishes in the very water, which actualy moved a long way, burning under the water, & now and then appearing above it, giving reports like Muskets & Cannon, with Granados, & innumerable other devices: It is said this sole Triumph cost 1500 pounds: which was concluded with a Ball, where all the young Ladys & Gallants daunced in the greate Hall: The Court had not ben seene so brave & rich in apparell since his Majesties restauration:

16 I received the B: Sacrament at St. James: & then at White hall Dr. Jeane (Regius professor Oxon:) preach⟨ed⟩ incomparably on 17: *Act:* 30: I din'd at Sir W: Godolphins: returned home the 18: having made a Visite in the morning to The Arch-bishop of Canterbury at Lambeth &c:

26 Was my Sons Wife brought to bed of a Daughter at hir house in Arundel streete neere *Norfolck house*, & Christned by the Curate of St. Clements in the Chamber, the Godfather my Nephew Glanvil, Godmother the Lady Anderson, & my Niepce Mary Evelyn, who named it Elizabeth, the name of my Lady Anderson: [30] St *Andrews Day*. It was Christned on *Sonday* 30: November:—In the morning cor: Rege at ⟨White-hall⟩ preached *Dr. Finnes* sonn of the L: Say & Seale, on 21 *Joshua* 11:

December. St. Andrews day being on the Sonday, our Election & meeting of the R: Society was on [1] Moneday, when I brought the Duke of Norfolck & Earle of Clarendon to the Society, who being first ballotted & chosen, tooke their places, & were after chosen also of the Council for this yeare, as was also myselfe: Mr. *Pepys*, Secretary of the Admiralty elected President.

3 I carried Monsieur *Justell*, & *Slingsby* Master of the Mint to see Mr. Sheldons collection of Medaills; The series of *Popes* was

rare, & so was among the Moderns several, especialy that of *John Husses* Martyrdome at Constance; of the Roman Emp: Consulars; some Greeke, &c both Coper, Gold, Sil: not many of truely antient; a Medalion of *Otho*, *P: Æmil:*   , &c, hardly antient. They were held a thousand pound price, but not worth I judge above 200 pound, [there being many not truely antique:]

7 To the House-hold at W.hall preached *Dr. Calamy* on 1. *Cor:* 11. 29. The holy Communion follow'd at which I was partaker: Then to his Majestie preached Dr. Patrick, on 15 *Rom:* 5: *Pomeridiano* I went to see the new church St. *James*', elegantly indeede built, especialy adorn'd was the Altar, the white Marble Enclosure curiously & richly carved, & the flowers & Garlands about the Walls by Mr. *Gibbons* in Wood, a *Pelican* with her young at her breast just over the Altar in the Carved Compartment and bordure, invironing the purple-velvet, richly frenged, with H̅I̅S̅ richly embrodred, & most noble Plate were given by Sir R: Geere—to the value (as was said) of 200 pounds: such an Altar was no were in any Church in England, nor have I seene any abroad more handsomly adorn'd: Dr. *Etcher* preached an Excellent Sermon on: 119 *Psal:* 165 ver: I went to visite my Lady Berkeley, & Yarborow:

14 Dr. *Patrick* deane of Peterboro, preach'd before the household on 24 *Act:* 16: *Coram Rege*: Dr. *Calamie*, on 10: *Act:* 38, of the virtue of Charity, and obligation of Doing good, from the example of our B: Saviour: That there was yet little hope of profiting by Preaching the duty &c. so long as Greate persons, Magistrates & men in high place lived ill lives, & gave so ill example, which was very boldly, but seasonably & truely said.

17 Early in the morning I went into St. James's Park to see three Turkish or Asian Horses, brought newly over, and now first shewed his Majestie: There were 4 of them it seemes in all, but one of them died at sea, being 9 weekes coming from Hamborow: They were taken from a Bashaw at the seige of *Vienna* in Austria, the late famous raising that Leaguer: & with mine Eyes never did I behold so delicate a Creature as was one of them, of somwhat a bright bay, two white feete, a blaze; such an head, [Eye,] eares, neck, breast, belly, buttock, Gaskins, leggs, pasterns, & feete in all reguards beautifull & proportion'd to admiration, spiritous & prowd, nimble, making halt, turning with that sweiftnesse & in so small a compase as was incomparable, with

all this so gentle & tractable, as called to mind what I remember
Busbequius speakes of them; to the reproch of our Groomes in
Europ who bring them up so churlishly, as makes our horse most
of them to retaine so many ill habits &c: They trotted like Does,
as if they did not feele the Ground; for this first Creature was
demanded 500 Ginnies, for the 2d 300, which was of a brighter
bay, for the 3d 200 pound, which was browne, all of them
choicely shaped, but not altogether so perfect as the first. In a
word, it was judg'd by the Spectators, (among whom was the
King, Prince of Denmark, the Duke of Yorke, and severall of
the Court Noble persons skilled in Horses, especialy Monsieur
Faubert & his sonn & Prevost, Masters of the Accademie and
esteemed of the best in Europe), that there were never seene any
horses in these parts, to be compared with them: Add to all this,
the Furniture which consisting of Embrodrie on the Saddle,
Housse, Quiver, bow, Arrows, Symeter, Sword, Mace or Battel
ax a la *Tur⟨c⟩isque*: the Bashaws Velvet Mantle furr'd with the
most perfect Ermine I ever beheld, all the Yron worke in other
furnitur being here of silver curiously wrought & double gilt,
to an incredible value: Such, and so extraordinary was the
Embroidery, as I never before saw any thing approaching it, the
reines & headstall crimson silk, covered with Chaines of silver
gilt: There was also a Turkish royal standard of an horses taile,
together with all sorts of other Caparison belonging to a Generals horse: by which one may estimate how gallantly & ⟨magnifi-
cently⟩ those Infidels appeare in the fild, for nothing could
certainely be seene more glorious, The Gent: (a German) who
rid the horse, being in all this garb: They were shood with yron
made round & closed at the heele, with an hole in the middle
about as wide as a shilling; the hoofes most intire:

   I dined with severall Gent: of the R: Society, going to
Gr: Colledge after, where was the experiment of *Dr. Papins*
Syphon: &c:

   18 Mr. *Faubert* having newly railed in a Manage & fitted it for
the Academy, I went with my Lord *Cornwallis* to see the Young
Gallants do their Exercise: There were the Dukes of Norfolck &
Northumberland, Lord Newburge, and a Nephew of the Earle
of Feversham: The exercises were first running at the ring, next
flinging a Javlin at a Mores head, 3d, discharging a Pistol at a
Mark, lastly, the taking up a ⟨Gauntlet⟩ with the point of the

Sword, all these ⟨Exercises⟩ performed in full speede: The D: of Northumberland, hardly miss'd succeeding in every one a douzen times as I think: Next the D: of Norfolck did exceeding bravely: *Newburge* & *Duras* seemed to be nothing so dextrous: here I saw the difference of what the French call *bell-homme a Cheval*, & *bonn homme a Chevall*, the D: of Norfolck being the first, that is rather a fine person on an horse; The D: of Northumberland being both, in perfection, namely a most gracefull person, & excellent rider: But the Duke of *Norfolck* told me he had not ben at this exercise this twelve yeare before: There were in the fild the Prince of *Denmark* & the L: Landsdown, sonn of the Earle of Bath, who had ben made a Count of the Empire last summer for his service before Vienna.

20 I returned home to my house to keepe Christmas now approching:

A villanous Murder perpetrated by *Mr. St. Johns*, (eldest sonn to Sir Walter, a worthy Gent:) on a knight of quality in a Tavern: The Offender being Sentenced, & Repriv'd, so many horrid murders & Duels about this time being committed (as was never heard of in England) gave much cause of complaint & murmure universaly.

21 St. *Thomas's* day & *Sonday*, my Rheume & cold was so greate, that it kept me from Church:

25 *Christmas-day*, o⟨u⟩r *Viccar* preach'd on 11: *Matt:* 3. 4. 5: I received the B: Communion:

28 In the afternoone it was such terrible weather that we heard prayers at home: 29. I entertained my Neighbours: as accostom'd:

31 I spent this day (as usualy) in recollecting the passages of the yeare now past, making up all my Accompts, & giving God thanks for his greate mercys the last yeare &c:

168$\frac{4}{5}$ *Jan:* 1 I implord the continuance of Gods mercy & providence for the yeare now enter'd; & went to the Publique Prayers &⟨c⟩. It proved so sharp weather and so long & cruel frost that the Thames was frozen crosse, but the frost often dissolved, & froze againe:

4 Our *Viccar* altogether repeated, shewing the danger of the now universal neglect of the Lords Supper, of which I this day communicated, the Lord improve it to me: *Amen*.

There happn'd nothing this weeke worthy of note:

14 To Lond: about my tedious Chancery suit: 18th Dr. *Cave* preach'd before the King on 4: *Psal:* 8: 23. I dind at my L: *Sunderlands*: 24 at my L: Newports, who has some excellent pictures, especialy that of Sir Tho: Hanmers of V: Dyke, one of the best he ever painted: another of our English Dobsons painting: but above all, that *Christo* in gremio of *Pussine*, an admirable piece, with something of most other famous hands: 25. Dr. Dove preached *coram Rege* on 16. *Act:* 4: 5. [I saw this evening such a sceane of profuse gaming, and luxurious dallying & prophanesse, the King in the middst of his 3 concubines, as I had never before:]

27 I dind at my Lord *Sunderlands* invited to heare that celebrated voice of Mr. *Pordage* newly come from *Rome*, his singing was after the Venetian Recitative, as masterly as could be, & with an excellent voice both Treble & base: Dr. Wallgrave accompanied it with his *Theorba Lute* on which he perform'd beyond imagination, and is doubtlesse one of the greatest Masters in Europ on that charming Instrument: *Pordage* is a *Priest* as Mr. *Bernard Howard* told me in private:

There was in the roome where we din'd, & in his bedchamber Those incomparable pieces of Columbus, a flagellation, The Grammer schoole, The *Venus* & *Adonis* of *Titian*, & of Van Dykes That picture of the late Earle of Digby (father of the Countesse of Sunderland) & E: of Bedford, Sir Kenhelme Digby, & 2 other Ladys, of ⟨incomparable⟩ performance, besides the Moses & burning bush of *Bassano*, & several other pieces of the best Masters: a Marble head of *M: Brutus* &c:

28 I was solemnly invited to my L: Arundel of Wardour, (now newly releas'd of his 6 yeares confinement in the Tower, upon suspicion of the plot, called Oates's plot) where after dinner the same Mr. *Pordage* entertained us with his voice, that excellent & stupendious Artist Signor Jo: Baptist, playing to it on the Harpsichord: My Daughter Mary being with us, she also sung to the greate satisfaction of both Masters, & a world of people of quality present: as she also did at my Lord Rochesters the Evening following, when we had the *French boy* so fam'd for his singing: & indeede he had a delicate voice, & had ben well taught:

I also heard Mrs. Packer (daughter to my old friend) sing before his Majestie & the Duke privately, That stupendious

Base *Gosling*, accompanying her, but hers was so lowd, as tooke away much of the sweetenesse: certainely never woman had a stronger, or better ⟨voice⟩ could she possibly have govern'd it: She would do rarely in a large Church among the Nunns:

30 Being the day of K. *Charles* Is Martyrdom, The Bish: of Ely preached on 5 *Matt:* 28. being an historical Oration, perstringing now & then the severall dangerous Tenents of those pretended Reformists, who in divers of their Writings have favour'd the Killing of Kings, whom they found not complying with their discipline; among these (after he had deduced that wicked doctrine of divers Popes & their Doctors &c) he reckoned *Calvine* ⟨who⟩ implicitly verges that way; & observed that not one of all the Regicides executed for the Murder so barbarously perpetrated this day, shewed any signes of remorse. After Sermon I returned home.

Feb: 1 Our Viccar proceeded on his former Text 11: *Matt:* The bl: Sacrament follow'd of which I was partaker:

4 I went to Lond, hearing his Majestie had ben the moneday before surpriz'd in his bed chamber with an Apoplectical fit, & so, as if by Gods providence, Dr. King (that excellent chirurgeon as well as Physitian) had not ben accidentaly present [to let him bloud] (with his lancet in his pocket) his Majestie had certainely died that moment, which might have ben of direfull consequence, there being no body else with the King save this doctor & one more, as I am assured: It was a mark of the extraordinary dexterity, resolution, & presentnesse of Judgment in the Doctor to let him bloud in the very paroxysme, without staying the coming of other physitians, which regularly should have ben don, & the not doing so, must have a formal pardon as they tell me: This rescued his Majestie for that instant, but it prov'd onely a reprieve for a little time; he still complain'd & was relapsing & often fainting & sometimes in Epileptical symptoms 'til Wednesday, for which he was cupp'd, let bloud againe in both jugularies, had both vomit & purges &c: which so relieved him, that on the Thursday hops of recovery were signified in the publique Gazett; but that day about noone the Physitians conjectur'd him somewhat feavorish; This they seem'd glad of, as being more easily alaied, & methodicaly to be dealt with, than his former fits, so as they prescrib'd the famous *Jesuits* powder; but it made his Majestie worse; and some very able Doctors

present, did not think it a feavor, but the effect of his frequent
bleeding, & other sharp operations used by them about his
head: so as probably the powder might stop the Circulation, &
renew his former fitts, which now made him very weake: Thus
he pass'd Thursday night with greate difficulty, when complain-
ing of a paine in his side, the⟨y⟩ drew 12 ounces more of blood
from him, this was by 6 in the morning on friday, & it gave him
reliefe, but it did not continue; for being now in much paine and
strugling for breath, he lay doz'd, & after some conflicts, the
Physitians desparing of him, he gave up the Ghost at halfe an
houre-after Eleaven in the morning, being the 6 of Feb: in the
36t yeare of his reigne, & 54 of his age: [*Feb:* 6] 'Tis not to be
express'd the teares & sorrows of Court, Citty & Country:
Prayers were solemnly made in all the Churches, especialy in
both the Court Chapells, where the Chaplaines relieved one
another every half quarter of an houre, from the time he began
to be in danger, til he expir'd: according to the forme prescribed
in the Church office: Those who assisted his Majesties devotion
were the A: Bish: of Cant: of London, Durrham & Ely; but
more especialy the B: of Bath & Wells. It is sayd they exceedingly urged the receiving the H: Sacrament but that his Majestie
told them he would Consider of it, which he did so long, 'til it
was too late: others whispered, that the Bishops being bid withdraw some time the night before, (except the Earls of Bath, &
Feversham), *Hurlston* the Priest, had presum'd to administer the
popish Offices; I hope it is not true; but these buisie emissaries
are very forewarde upon such occasions: [See September 16:] He
gave his breeches & Keys to the Duke, who was almost continualy kneeling by his bed side, & in teares; he also recommended
to him the care of his natural Children, all except the D: of
Monmoth, now in Holland, & in his displeasure; he intreated
the Queene to pardon him, [(nor without cause)] who a little
before had sent a Bishop to excuse her not more frequently visiting him, in reguard of her excessive griefe, & with all, that his
Majestie would forgive it, if at any time she had offended him:
He spake to the Duke to be kind to his Concubines the DD: of
Cleveland, & especialy *Portsmouth*, & that *Nelly* might not
sterve; I do not heare he said any thing of the Church or his
people, now falling under the government of a Prince suspected
for his Religion, after above 100 yeares the Church & Nation

had ben departed from Rome: Thus died K. Charles the 2d, of a Vigorous & robust constitution, & in all appearance capable of a longer life. A prince of many Virtues, & many greate Imperfections, Debonaire, Easy of accesse, not bloudy or Cruel: his Countenance fierce, his voice greate, proper of person, every motion became him, a lover of the sea, & skillfull in shipping, not affecting other studys, yet he had a laboratory and knew of many Empyrical Medicines, & the easier Mechanical Mathematics: Loved Planting, building, & brought in a politer way of living, which passed to Luxurie & intollerable expense: He had a particular Talent in telling stories & facetious passages of which he had innumerable, which made some bouffoones and vitious wretches too presumptuous, & familiar, not worthy the favours they abused: He tooke delight to have a number of little spaniels follow him, & lie in his bed-Chamber, where often times he suffered the bitches to puppy & give suck, which rendred it very offensive, & indeede made the whole Court nasty & stinking: An excellent prince doubtlesse had he ben lesse addicted to Women, which made him uneasy & allways in Want to supply their unmeasurable profusion, & to the detriment of many indigent persons who had signaly serv'd both him & his father: Easily, & frequently he changed favorites to his greate prejudice &c: As to other publique transactions and unhappy miscarriages, 'tis not here I intend to number them; but certainly never had King more glorious opportunities to have made himselfe, his people & all Europ happy, & prevented innumerable mischiefs, had not his too Easy nature resign'd him to be menag'd by crafty men, & some abandoned & prophane wretches, who corrupted his otherwise sufficient parts, disciplin'd as he had ben by many afflictions, during his banishment: which gave him much experience, & knowledge of men & things; but those wiccked creatures tooke him [off] from all application becoming so greate a King: the History of his Reigne will certainly be the most wonderfull for the variety of matter & accidents above any extant of many former ages: The [sad tragical] death of his father, his banishment, & hardships, his miraculous restauration, conjurations against him; Parliaments, Warrs, Plagues, Fires, Comets; revolutions abroad happning in his time with a thousand other particulars: He was ever kind to me & very gracious upon all occasions, & therefore I cannot without ingratitude [but]

deplore his losse, which for many respects (as well as duty) I do
with all my soule: [See 2. *Octob:* 1685:]

A NEW KING AND A CHANGED COURT –
A DAUGHTER DIES
(1685)

HIS MAJESTIE DEAD, The Duke (now K. *James* the 2d) went
immediately to Council, & before entering into any buisinesse,
passionately declaring his sorrow, Told their Lordships, That
since the succession had falln to him, he would endeavor to follow the example of his predecessor in his Clemency & tendernesse to his people: That however he had ben misrepresented as
affecting arbitrary power, they should find the contrary, for that
the Laws of England had made the King as greate a Monarch as
he could desire; That he would endeavour to maintaine the Government both in Church & state as by Law establish'd, its Principles being so firme for Monarchy, & the members of it shewing
themselves so good & Loyal subjects; & that as he would never
depart from the just rights & prerogative of the Crown, so would
he never Invade any mans propriety: but as he had often adventured his life in defence of the Nation, so he would still proceede,
& preserve it in all its lawfull rites & libertyes:

This being the substance of what he said, the Lords desired it
might be published as containing matter of greate satisfaction to
a jealous people, upon this change: which his Majestie consented to: Then were the Counsel sworn, & a proclamation
ordered to be publish'd, that all officers should continue in their
station; that there might be no failure of publique Justice, 'til his
farther pleasure should be known: Then the King rose, the
Lords accompanying him to his bed Chamber, where, whilst he
reposed himselfe (tired indeede as he was with griefe & watching) They immediately returned againe into the Council-
Chamber to take order for the Proclayming of his Majestie
which (after some debate) they consented should be in the very
forme, his Grandfather K. *James* the first was, after the death of
Q: *Elizabeth*, as likewise that the Lords &c: should proceede in
their Coaches through the Citty for the more solemnity of it;

upon this was I and severall other Gent: (waiting in the privy Gallerie), admitted into the Council Chamb: to be wittnesse of what was resolv'd on: & Thence with the Lords (the Lord Martial & the Herraulds & other Crowne Officers being ready) we first went to Whitehall gate, where the Lords stood on foote beareheaded, whilst the Herauld proclaimed His Majesties Titles to the Imperial Crowne, & succession according to the forme: The Trumpets & Kettle drumms having first sounded 3 times, which after also ended with the peoples acclamations: Then an Herauld called the Lords Coaches according to ranke, my selfe accompanying the solemnity in my Lord Cornwallis Coach, first to Temple barr, where the Lord Major & his breathren &c met us on horseback in all their formalities, & proclaymed the King; Thence to the Exchange in Cornhill, & so we returned in the order we set forth: being come to White-hall, we all went and kissed the King & Queenes hands, he had ben on the bed, but was now risen, & in his Undresse. The Queene was in bed in her appartment, but put forth her hand; seeming to be much afflicted, as I believe she was, having deported herselfe so decently upon all occasions since she came first into England, which made her universally beloved: Thus concluded this sad, & yet Joyfull day: [I am never to forget the unexpressable luxury, & prophanesse, gaming, & all dissolution, and as it were total forgetfullnesse of God (it being Sunday Evening) which this day sennight, I was witnesse of; the King, sitting & toying with his Concubines Portsmouth, Cleaveland, & Mazarine: &c: A french boy singing love songs, in that glorious Gallery, whilst about 20 of the greate Courtiers & other dissolute persons were at Basset round a large table, a bank of at least 2000 in Gold before them, upon which two Gent: that were with me made reflexions with astonishment, it being a sceane of uttmost vanity; and surely as they thought would never have an End: six days after was all in the dust.]

Feb. 8: Preached in the Chapell of W:hall *Mr. Horne*, a fellow of Eaton Coll: on 1. Thess: 5. 19: he tooke occasion to speake of the prayers & office used, during his late Majesties sicknesse, & indeede they were most solemnly perform'd & with extraordinary & passionate devotion:

I dined at Sir W: *Godolphins*, & then heard *Dr. Patrick* in St. *James's* new Church: on 1. *Thess:* 5. 3, describing the nature of

Spiritual Sacrifices, and necessitie of puritie: with a pathetical exhortation to holinesse, constancy & perseverance in the true faith, & concluded in the Collect of the day, being the 5 *Sonday* after *Epiphanie*, That God would keepe the church continualy in his true Religion: &c:

9 I went home the next day to refresh, it being injoyned, that those who put on mourning, should weare it as for a father, in the most solemn & lugubrous manner:

10 Being sent to by the Sherif of the County, to appeare, & assist the Proclayming the King; [11] I went the next day to *Bromely*, where I met the Sherif, and the Commander of the Kentish Troope, with an appearance of (I suppose) above 500 horse, & innumerable people: Two of his Majesties Trumpets, & a searjeant, with other officers, who having drawn up the horse in a large field neere to towne, march'd thence [with swords drawn] to the Market place, where making a ring, after sound of Trumpets, & silence made, the high Sherif read the Proclaming Titles, to his Bailife, who repeated it alow'd, & then after many shouts of the people &c: his Majesties health being drunk in a flint glasse of a yard-long, of the Sherif, Commanders, Officers & chiefe Gent: they all disperc'd and I returned:

13 I went to Lond: to passe a fine upon the selling of Honson-grange in Stafford-Shire, being about 20 pounds per ann: which lying at so greate distance I thought fit to part with, to one *Buxton* a farmor there, it came to me as part of my Daughter in Laws portion, this being but a 4th part of what was divided betweene the Mother & 3 sisters:

14 The King was [this night] very obscurely buried in a Vault under Hen: 7th Chapell in Westminster, without any manner of pomp, and soone forgotten after all this vainity, & the face of the whole Court exceedingly changed into a more solemne and moral behaviour: The new King affecting neither Prophanesse, nor bouffonry: All the Greate Officers broke their white-Staves on the Grave &c: according to forme:

15 Dr. Tenison preach'd to the Household on 42. *Psal:* ult:

The 2d sermon (which should have ben before the King, who to the great griefe of his subjects, did now the first time go to Masse publicly in the little Oratorie at the Dukes lodgings, the doores set wide open) was by Mr. Fox, a young quaint Preacher, who made a very profitable sermon on Pro: *Fooles make a mock at sin*, against prophanes & Atheisme; now reigning more than ever through the late dissolutenesse of the Court:

I dined at my Friend Mr. Packers, & went in the afternoone to St. Margarites, where a stranger preached on 1. *Isa:* 26.

16 I din'd at Sir Rob: *Howards Auditor* of the Exchequer, a Gent: pretending to all manner of Arts & Sciences for which he had ben the subject of Comedy, under the name of Sir Positive; not ill-natur'd, but unsufferably boosting: He was sonn to the late Earle of Berkshire:

This morning his Majestie restored the staffs & Key, to my Lord Arlington L: Chamberlaine, to Mr. Savell Vice-Cham: to my L: Newport, & Mainard Tressurer & Comptroller of the Household: [18] And made my Lord Godolphin Chamb: to the Queene, L. Peterborow Groome of the Stoole in place of the Earle of Bath: Gave the Treasurers Staff to the E: of Rochester, & made his bro: the E: of Clarendon, Lord Privie-Seale, in place of the Marques of Hallifex, who was made President of the Council: The Secretarys of State remaining as before:

18 I was carried by my Lord Privy-Seale to congratulate my Lord Tressurer who [19] the next day, together with the other new Officers, were all sworne at the Chancery barr, & at the Chequer: I return'd home in the Evening.

The late King having the revenue of Excise, Costomes, & other late duties granted for his life onely; were now farmed & let to severall persons upon an opinion that the late K: might let them for 3 yeares after his decease (some of the old Commissioners refusing to act) The major part of Judges, (but as some think, not the best lawyers) pronounced it legal; but 4 dissenting: The lease was made but the day before his Majesties death; which seemes by the words of the statute to be invalid:

Note that the Clearke of the Closset, had shut-up the late Kings private Oratory next the Privy-Chamb: above; but the King caus'd it to be open'd againe, & that Prayers should be said as formerly: The Papists now swarmed at Court. &c:

22 Severall most usefull tractates against Dissenters, Papists & Fanatics, & resolutions of Cases, were now publish'd by the London divines:

Our Viccar preach'd on 13 *Luke* 24: I was hindred from Church this evening. I stayed at home all this weeke:

March 1 Our ⟨Viccar⟩ proceeded with small addition, the holy Comm: followed. I participated together with my daugh⟨t⟩er Mary:

The Curate on ⟨1⟩ Jac: 27:

3 My daughter complain'd of her indisposition.

4 After Evening prayer Ash-wednesday I went to Lond: about my buisinesse:

5 To my griefe I saw the new pulpet set up in the popish oratory at W—hall, for the Lent preaching, Masse being publiqly saied, & the Romanists swarming at Court with greater confidence than had ever ben seene in England since the Reformation, so as every body grew Jealous to what this would tend; A Parliament was now also summond, and greate industry used to obtaine Elections which might promote the Court Interest: Most of the Corporations being now by their new Charters in power to make what returnes of members they pleased: Most of the Judges likewise having given their opinions that his Majestie might still take the Costomes, which to foure Judges (⟨esteem'd⟩ the best Lawyers) seemed against the Act of Parliament which determines it with the Kings life:

Now came over divers Envoyès & greate Persons to condole the Death of the late King: The Q: Dowager received them on a bed of mourning, the whole Chamber seiling & floore hung with black, tapers lighted; so as nothing could be more Lugubrous & solemn: The Q: Consort sat out under a state on a black foot-cloth, to entertaine the Circle as the Q: used to do, & that very decently:

6 Lent Preachers continuing as formerly in the Royal Chapell, The Deane of S. Paule preached on 1. *Pet:* 3. 14: shewing that what ever Changes happn'd in the state or Government, an holy, & innocent life, was the greatest security; but in the meane time, Christians should endeavor to informe themselves in the faith they profess'd, and (behaving themselves thus inoffensively, & obediently to their Governers) when it came to suffering go through it with courage & meekenesse &c: I supp'd this night at my Lady Sylviu's with Dr. Tenison & other friends:

7 Newes coming to me that my Daughter Mary was falln ill of the Small Pox, I hastned home full of apprehensions, & indeede found her very ill, still coming-forth in aboundance, a wonderfull affliction to me, not onely for her beauty, which was

very lovely, but for the danger of loosing one of extraordinary parts & virtue. &c: Gods holy will be don.

8 A stranger preach'd at our Parish on 4. *Gal:* 18, very solidly.

My Deare Child continuing ill, by reason of the Disseases fixing in the Lungs, it was not in the power of physick without more plentifull expectoration to recover her, insomuch as [9] Dr. Short (the most approved & famous Physition of all his Majesties Doctors) gave us his opinion, that she could not escape, upon the Tuesday; so as on Wednesday she desired to have the B: Sacrament given her (of which yet she had participated the Weeke before) after which disposing her selfe to suffer what God should determine to inflict, she bore the remainder of her sicknesse with extraordinary patience, and piety & with more than ordinary resignation, and marks of a sanctified & blessed frame of mind, rendred [up] her soule to the Lord Jesus on Saturday the 14 of March, exactly at halfe-an houre after Eleeaven in the fore noone, to our unspeakable sorrow & Afflic-tion, and this not to ours (her parents) onely, but all who knew her, who were many of the best quality, greatest & most vertuous persons: How unexpressable losse I and my Wife sustain'd, the Virtues & perfections she was endow'd with best would shew; of which the justnesse of her stature, person, comelinesse of her Countenance and gracefullnesse of motion, naturall, & unaf-fected (though more than ordinaryly beautifull), was one of the least, compar'd with the Ornaments of her mind, which was truely extraordinary, especialy the better part: Of early piety, & singularly Religious, so as spending a considerable part of every day in private devotion, Reading and other vertuous exercises, she had collected, & written out aboundance of the most usefull & judicious periods of the Books she read, in a kind of Common place; as out of Dr. Hammonds *N. Test:* and most of the best practical Treatises extant in our tonge: She had read & digested a considerable deale of History, & of Places, the french Tongue being as familiar to her as English, she understood Italian, and was able to render a laudable Account of what she read & observed, to which assisted a most faithfull memory, & discernement, & she did make very prudent & discreete reflections upon what she had observe'd of the Conversations among which she had at any time ben (which being continualy of persons of the best quality), she improved: She had to all this an incomparable sweete Voice,

to which she play'd a through-base on the Harpsichord, in both
which she ariv'd to that perfection, that of all the Schollars of
those Two famous Masters, Signor *Pietro* and *Bartolomeo*: she
was esteem'd the best; [for] the sweetenesse of her voice, and
manegement of it, adding such an agreablenesse to her Countenance, without any constraint and concerne, that when she sung,
it was as charming to the Eye, as to the Eare; this I rather note,
because it was a universal remarke, & for which so many noble
& judicious persons in Musique, desir'd to heare her; the last,
being at my Lord Arundels of Wardours, where was a solemn
Meeting of about twenty persons of quality, some of them greate
judges & Masters of Musique; where she sung with the famous
Mr. *Pordage*, Signor *Joh: Battist* touching the Harpsichord &c:
with exceeding applause: What shall I say, or rather not say, of
the cherefullnesse & agreablenesse of her humor, that she con-
descending to the meanest servant in the family, or others, she
kept still her respect without the least pride: These she would
reade to, examine, instruct and often pray with, if they were sick;
so as she was extreamely beloved of every body: Piety was so
prevalent an ingredient in her constitution (as I may say) that
even amongst superiors, as equals, she no sooner became intimately acquainted; but she would endeavour to improve them
by insinuating something of Religious, & that tended to bring
them to a love of Devotion; and she had one or two Confidents,
with whom she used to passe whole dayes, in fasting, reading
and prayers, especialy before the monethly Communions, &
other solemn occasions: She could not indure that which they
call courtship, among the Gallants, abhorred flattery, & tho she
had aboundance of witt, the raillery was so innocent and ingenuous, as was most agreable; She sometimes would see a play, but
since the stage grew licentious, tooke greate scandal at them, &
express'd her being weary of them, & that the time spent at the
Theater was an unaccountable vanity, nor did she at any time
play at Cards, without extreame importunity & for the Company; but this was so very seldome, that I cannot number it
among any thing she could name a fault: No body living read
prose, or Verse better & with more judgement, & as she read,
so she writ not onely most correct orthography, but with
that maturitie of judgement, and exactnesse of the periods,
choice expressions, & familiarity of style, as that some letters of

hers have astonish'd me, and others to whom she has occasionaly written: Among other agreablenesses she had a talent of rehersing any Comical part or poeme, as was to them she might decently be free with, more pleasing than the Theater: She daunc'd with the most grace that in my whole life I had ever seene, & so would her Master say, who was Monsieur *Isaac*; but she very seldome shew'd that perfection, save in the gracefullnesse of her Carriage, which was with an aire of spritefull modestie, not easily to be described: Nothing of haughty, nothing affected, but natural and easy, as well in her deportment, as her discourse, which was allways material, not trifling, and to which the extraordinary sweetenesse of her tone, even in familiar speaking, was very charming: Nothing was so pretty, as her descending to play with little Children, whom she would caresse, & humor with greate delight: But she most of all affected to be [with] grave, and sober men, of whom she might learne something and improve herselfe: I have my selfe ben assisted by her, both reading & praying by me; and was comprehensive of uncommon notions, curious of knowing every thing to some excesse, had I not indeavor'd to represse it sometimes: Nothing was therefore so delightfull to her, as the permission I ever gave her to go into my Study, where she would willingly have spent whole dayes; for as I sayd, she had read aboundance of History, & all the best poets, even to Terence, Plautus, Homer, Vergil, Horace, Ovide, all the best Romances, & modern Poemes, and could compose very happily, & put in her pretty Symbol,[1] as in that of the *Mundus Muliebris*, wherein is an enumeration of the immense variety of the Modes & ornaments belonging to the Sex: But all these are vaine trifles to those interior vertues which adorn'd her Soule, For she was sincerely Religious, most dutifull to her parents, whom she lov'd with an affection temper'd with greate esteeme, so as we were easy & free, & never were so well pleased, as when she was with us, nor needed we other Conversation: She was kind to her Sisters, and was still improving them, by her constant Course of Piety: Ô deare, sweete and desireable Child, how shall I part with all this goodnesse, all this Vertue, without the bitternesse of sorrow, and reluctancy of a tender Parent! Thy Affection, duty & love to me

1 Contribution (properly to a feast).

was that of a friend, as well as of a Child, passing even the love
of Women, the Affection of a Child: nor lesse dearer to thy
Mother, whose example & tender care of Thee was unparalleled;
nor was Thy returnes to her lesse conspicuous: Ô how she
mourns thy losse! ô how desolate hast Thou left us, Sweete,
obliging, happy Creature! To the grave shall we both carry thy
memory—God alone (in whose boosome thou art at rest &
happy) give us to resigne Thee, & all our Contentments (for
thou indeede wert all in this world) to his blessed pleasure: ô let
him be glorified by our submission, & give us Grace to blesse
him for the Graces he implanted in thee, thy vertuous life, pious
& holy death, which is indeede the onely remaining Comfort of
our soules, hastning through the infinite love and mercy of the
Lord Jesus, to be shortly with Thee deare Child, & with Thee
(and those blessed Saints like thee,) glorifie the Redemer of the
World to all Eternity. Amen:

It was in the nineteenth yeare of her Age, that this sicknesse
happn'd to her, at which period *Dr. Harvy* somewhere writes, all
young people should be let blood; and to this we advised her;
whilst to all who beheld her she looked so well, as her extraordinary beauty was taken notice of, the last time she appeared at
Church: but she had so greate an aversion to breathing a veine,
as we did not so much insist upon it as we should: being in this
exceeding height of health, she was the more propence to
change, & had ever ben subject to feavors; but there was yet
another accident that contributed to the fixing it in this dissease;
The apprehension she had of it in particular, & which struck her
but two days before she came home, by an imprudent Gentlewomans telling my Lady Faulkland (with whom my daughter
went to give a Visite) after she had entertained them a good
while in the house, that she had a servant sick of the small pox
above, who died the next day; This my poore Child accknowl-
edged made an impression on her spirits, it being with all [of] a
mortal & spreading kind at this time about the towne:

There were now no lesse than foure Gent: of Quality offering
to treate with me about Marriage; & I freely gave her her owne
Choice, knowing she was discreete: One (against which I had no
exceptions) and who most passionately lov'd her, but was for a
certaine natural blemish that rendered him very disagreable, she
would in complyance to me have married, if I did injoyne her;

but telling me she should never be happy with him (observing it seemes a neerenesse in his nature, and a little under-breeding) I would not impose it; for which she often expressed her satisfaction, & thanks to me in the most obliging & respectfull manner: The other was one *Weston* a Stafford shire Gent: of the family, & I thinke heire (within one) to the Earles of Portland: This was but now just beginning: But the person who first made love to her, was Mr. *Wilbraham* a Chesshire Gent: of a noble Family, whose extreamely rich & sordid Fathers demands of Portion, I could by no meanes reach, without injury to the rest of my daughters, which this pious, & good natured Creature, would never have suffered, and so that match stood in suspense; I say in suspense, for the young Gent: still pursu'd, & would have married her in private, if either my Daughter, or We had don so disingenuously: She & we had principles that would by no meanes suffer us to harken to it: At last he's sent for home, continues his Affection, hop⟨e⟩s to bring his father to reasonable termes: My Child is taken with his Constancy, his Virtuous breeding, and good nature, & discretion, having beene a fortnight together in my house: This, made us not forward to embrace any other offers, together with the extraordinary indifferency she ever shewed of Marrying at all; for truely says shee to her Mother, (the other day), were I assur'd of your lives & my deare Fathers, never would I part from you, I love you, & this home, where we serve God, above all things in the world, nor ever shall I be so happy: I know, & consider the vicissitudes and changes of the world, I have some experience of its vanities, & but for decency, more than inclination, & that You judge it expedient for me, I would not change my Condition, but rather add the fortune you designe me to my Sisters, & keepe up the reputation of our family: This was so discreetely & sincerely utter'd as, could not proceede but from an extraordinary Child, & one who loved her parents without example:

At London then it was she doubtlesse tooke this fatal disease; and the Occasion of her being there at all was this:

My Lord Viscount Falklands Lady having ben our Neighbours (as he was Treasurer of the Navy) she tooke so greate an Affection to my Daughter, that when they went back in the Autumn to the Citty, nothing could pacifie their uncessant importunity, but the letting of my ⟨daughter⟩ accompany my

Lady, & the staying some time with her; so with the greatest
reluctancy (as all can wittnesse) I ever refused any thing, I was
almost forc'd to let her be with this Young Lady: Whilst she was
there, my Lord being musical, and [that] I saw I could not prevaile with my Lady to part with her til ⟨Christmas⟩, I was not
unwilling she should improve the opportunity of learning of
Signor Pietro, an Italian who had an admirable way both
of Composure & teaching; & when Christmas came, it was
the end of February ere I could obtaine my Lady to part with
her; But hearing she was to make a Step into Oxfordshire (when
my Lord stood for knight of that County) my Daughter (who
now longed to come home) expressed her wearisom⟨n⟩esse of
being in a Family, not so regular as to the due service of God, &
religious duties, though otherwise exceedingly well govern'd, &
where they were all of them infinitely fond, & pleased with her
generous & obliging Way, sent to her mother, that she had
obtained of my Lady, she should come home; upon condition of
returning to her againe, when she came out of the Country, hoping to prevaile with us, to continue with them 'til the Spring,
when their family usualy lived at their house in Deptford: To
this my Wife & I resolved not to Consent, finding likewise so
greate a desire in my daughter to remove no more from her
deare Parents, & which she expressed with a more than ordinary earnestnesse: quite tired, as she confessed, with the vaine
& empty Conversation of the Towne, the Theaters, the Court,
& trifling visites which consum'd so many precious moments,
and made her sometimes (unavoidably) misse of that regular Course of piety, which gave her the greatest satisfaction:
But this was the truth, that where ever she came, every body
was taken with her way, something appeared so charming in
her Conversation, & that modest freedome, which she knew
how to govern, & was indeede natural to her: This made her
contin⟨u⟩aly sought to [by] severall persons of the first rank,
especialy my Lord Treasurers Lady, my Lady Rochester, Sunderland, Burlington, Clarendon, Arlington, Dutchesse of
Grafton; besides other Ladys & persons lovers of Musick, her
two Italian Masters having (for their own-sakes) spread the Talent she had: but the Child was starke weary of this life, and went
seldome, & I thinke not thrice to Court all this time, except
when her Mother, or my selfe carryed her thither, when we came

sometimes to Towne, whither my occasions often brought me; for with all this she, did not affect the shewing & producing of her-selfe, she knew the Court well, passed one whole Summer at Windsore in it, with my Lady Tuke (one of the Queenes Women of the Bed-chamber) a most vertuous Relation of hers: so as she was not fond of that glittering scene, now become abominably licentious: though there was a designe of my Lady Rochester & Clarendon to make her Mayd of ⟨honour⟩ to the Queene, so soone as there was a place empty: but this she did not in the least set her heart upon, nor indeede upon any thing so much as the service of God, a quiet regular life, & how she might improve her selfe in the most necessary accomplishments, & to which she was arived in so greate a measure, as I acknowledge (all partiality of relation layed aside) I never saw, or knew her equal, considering how universal they were; save in *one onely Creature* of her Sex, Mrs. *Godolphin*, (late the wife of my *Lord Godolphin*, whose life for the singular piety, Vertue & discretion, (& that she was to me a Friend, in all the peculiar transcendencys of that relation) I have written at large, and consign'd to my Lady *Sylvius* (whom she loved above all her Sex) & who requested it of me: And this I mention here, because the Example of that most religious Lady: made I am assured deepe impressions in my deare Child; and that I was told, she caused it to be read to her, at the very beginning of her sicknesse, when She had taken that bed, out of which she never risse, to my insupportable griefe & sorrow; though never two made more blessed ends: But all this sorrow is selfe-love, whilst to wish them here againe, were to render them miserable who are now in happinesse, and above: This is the little History, & Imperfect Character of my deare Child, whose Piety, Virtue, & incomparable Endowments, deserve a Monument more durable than brasse & Marble: *Precious is the Memorial of the Just*—Much I could enlarge on every period of this hasty Account, but thus I ease & discharge my overcoming passion for the present, so many things worthy an excellent Christian & dutifull Child, crowding upon me: Never can I say enough, ô deare, my deare Child whose memory is so precious to me.

   This deare child was born at Wotton in Surry, in the same house and roome where I likewise first drew breath, (my wife being retir'd to my bro: there, the greate sicknesse yeare) upon the first of that moneth, & neere the very houre, that I was borne, upon the last: viz: October:

16 Was my deare Daughter interr'd in the south east end of the church at Deptford neere her Grand mother & severall of my Younger Children and Relations: my desires were she should have ben carried & layed among my owne Parents & Relations at Wotton, where our Family have a Vault, where she was born, & where I have desire to be interred my selfe, when God shall call me out of this uncertaine transitory life; but some Circumstances did not permit it; & so she was buried here. Our Viccar Dr. Holden preaching her Funerall Sermon on: 1. Phil: 21. *For to me to live is Christ, & to die is gaine*, upon which he made an apposit discourse (as those who heard it assure me, for griefe suffer'd me not to be present) concluding with a modest recital of her many vertues, and especialy her signal piety, so as drew both teares, & admiration from the hearers, so universaly was she beloved, & known to deserve all the good that could be sayd of her: & I was not altogether unwilling something of this should be spoken of her, for the edification & encouragement of other young people: There were divers noble persons who honor'd her Obsequies, & funerall, some in person, others in sending their Coaches, of which there were 6 or 7. of six horses viz. Countesse of Sunderland, Earle of Clarendon, Lord Godolphin, Sir St. Fox; Sir William Godolphin, Vis⟨c⟩ount Falkland &c [following the hearse of 6 horses &c] there were (besides other decenc⟨i⟩es) distributed among her friends about 60 rings: Thus lived, died, & was buried the joy of my life & ornament both of her sex & my poore family: God Almighty of his infin⟨i⟩te mercy grant me the grace thankfully to resigne my selfe & all I have, or had, to his divine pleasure, & in his good time, restoring health & Comfort to my Family, teach me so to number my days, as I may apply my heart to Wisdome, & be prepared for my dissolution, & that into the hands of my blessed Saviour I may recomend my Spirit. Amen:

Having some days after opened her Trunks, & looked into her Closset, amazed & even astonished we were to find that incredible number of papers and Collections she had made of severall material Authors, both Historians, Poets, Travells &c: but above all the Devotions, Contemplations, & resolutions

upon those Contemplations, which we found under her hand in
a booke most methodicaly disposed, & much exceeding the talent & usage of [so] young & beautifull women, who consume so
much of their time in vaine things: with severall prayers, Meditations, & devotions on divers occasions; with a world of pretty
letters to her confidents & others savoring of a greate witt, &
breathing of piety & honor: There is one letter to some divine
(who is not named) to whom she writes that he would be her
Ghostly Father & guide, & that he would not despise her for the
many errors & imperfections of her Youth, but beg of God, to
give her courage, to acquaint him with all her faults, imploring
his assistance, & spiritual direction: & well I remember, that she
often desired me to recommend her to such a person, but
(though I intended it) I did not think fit to do it as yet, seeing
her apt to be scrupulous, & knowing the greate innocency &
integrity of her life; but this (it seemes) she did of her selfe:
There are many other books, offices & papers thus written by
her selfe, so many indeede, as it is plainly astonishing how one
that had acquired such substantiall & practical knowledge in
other the ornamental parts of (Especialy) Music vocal & Instrumental, Dauncing; paying, & receiving visites, necessary Conversation, & other unavoidable impertinences of life could find,
much more employ, her time to accomplish a quarter of what
she has left: but as she never affected Play, Cards &c: (which
consumes a world of precious time) so she was in continual exercise, which yet abated nothing of the most free & agreable Conversation in the world: But as she was a little miracle whilst she
lived, so she died with out Example:

26 I was invited to Cap: Gunmans Funerall, that excellent
Pilot, & sea-man, who had behav'd himselfe so valiantly in the
Dut⟨c⟩h-Warr: taken away by the gangreene which happn'd in
his cure, upon his unhappy fall from the peere of Calais: This
was the Cap: of the yacht, whom they accused for not giving
timely warning, on the Dukes (now the King) going into Scotland, when his ship split upon the Sands, when so many perished: But of which I am most confident, the Cap: was no ways
guilty, either through negligence, or designe; as he made appeare
not onely at the Examination of the matter of fact; but in the
Vindication he shewed me some time since, which must needes
give any-man of reason satisfaction: Our Doctor Preach'd the

funerall sermon on   He was a sober, frugal, cherefull
& temperat man; we have few such sea-men left:

There ⟨came⟩ to Condole the death of my deare Daughter
this Weeke moneday, & friday: The Countesses of Bristoll, Sunderland, La: Sylvius, Mrs. Penelope Godolphin: Sir Stephen
Fox & his Lady &c:

29 A servant mayd of my Wifes fell sick of the very same disease, of the same sort of S:pox, & in all appearance in as greate
danger, though she never came neere my daughter: we removed
her into the Towne with care:

Aprill: 5 Our Viccar proceeded: & the Curate on 2: Phil: 8:
Drowsinesse much surpriz'd me: The Lord be gratious to me:

The mayd, by Gods greate mercy, but with extraordinary difficulty, recovered: Blessed be God:

7 Being now somewhat compos'd after my greate affliction,
I went to Lond: to heare Dr. Tenison (it being [8] a Wednesday
in Lent) at Whitehall: who preached on 3. *Gen*: 3: I returned in
the Evening: I observ'd that though the King was not in his
seate above in the Chapell, the Doctor made notwithstanding
his three congèes, which they were not us'd to do, when the
[late] King was absent, making then one bowing onely: I asked
the reason; it was sayd, he had a special order so to do: The
Princesse of Denmarke yet was in the Kings Closset, but sat on
the left hand of the Chaire, the clearke of the Closset standing
by his Majesties Chaire as if he had ben present: [I met Q:
Dowager going now first from W.hall to dwell at Somerset
house.] This day was my Bro: of Wotton [& Mr. Onslow] (candidates against Sir Adam Bro: & my Co: Sir Edward Evelyn)
circumvented of their Elections standing for knights of *Surry* for
the ensuing Parliament by a trick of the Sheriffs, taking advantage of my brother &c: partys going out of the small village of
Letherhead to seeke shelter & lodging, the afternoone being
very tempestious; to proceede to the Election when they were
gon, expecting the next morning: where as before, & then they
exceeded the other party by (I am assured) many hundreds: The
Duke of Norfolck lead Sir Ed: E: & Sir Adam Browns party:
but this Election was very unfaire: Indeede I writ to my Bro:
earnestly not to stand, finding the Court was unwilling he
should, & that I had observ'd by the account we had weekly,
what very meane & slight persons (some of them Gent:

Servants, Clearks, persons neither of reputation nor Interest) were set up; but the Country would choose him whether he would or no: but thus he miss'd it, by an indirect trick, as appeared; the other Candidate Sir Adam Browne, was so deafe, that he could not heare one word: But Sir Ed: Evelyn, an honest Gent: & much in favour with his Majestie, & it had ben but decent in my Bro: to have transferred his Votes to him, as I advised:

10 Friday I went early to W:hall to heare Dr. Tillotson deane of Cant: preaching on 9: *Eccl:* 18: a very usefull discourse: I return'd in the Evening: I visited my Lady Tuke, and found with her Sir Geo: Wakeman the Physitian, whom I had seene tried & acquitted amongst the plotters, about empoys'ning his late Majestie upon the accusation of the famous *Oates*: & surely, I believ'd him guiltlesse: Se 18 July:—79:

12 A stranger preach'd very well for-noone on 5. *Gall.* 24: *pomeridiano* The Comm: followed: at which I was participant: The Lord be praised:

The same person in the Afternoone on 24: *Act:* 25. Drowsinesse so exceedingly surpriz'd me, that I could hardly hold up my head, at the sermon: The Lord pardon me:

14 According to my costome, I went to *Lond:* to passe the *Holy Weeke*:

15 Dr. *Craddock* Provost of *Eaton* preach'd at W:hall: on 1: *Heb:* 8, most excellently shewing That *Christ* is *God* against the *Arrians* of old & *Socinians* of late:

17 *Good Friday*, preach'd at the new Church (St. *Jame's*) Dr. *Tenison* on 1: *Cor:* 16: 22: The holy Sacrament follow'd at which I participated: The Lord make me thankfull:

In the Afternoone preached in *W:Hall:* Chap: (the Auditory very full of Lords; The two Arch-Bish: & many others, now drawn to Towne upon the occasion of the *Coronation* & ensuing *Parliament*) Dr. *Sprat* Deane of *Westminster* & *Bish:* of *Rochester*: on: 2. *Titus* 14: shewing That *Christs* giving him-selfe for us was the most invaluable Gift not onely that ever was given; but that God could Give: He tooke occasion (speaking of the necessity of *Good-Works*, not as *meritorious*, but signes of our Faith & other Graces) to shew, that there had ben more Works of Munificent Charity of all degrees & kinds (bating [the] superstitious pomps, & ostentation among the Papists) within 100 yeares since the Reformation; than in all the ages which went before: & this was very well justified & applyed:

I supped with the Countesse of Sunderland & Lord Godolphin, & so returned home:

23 Was the day of his Majesties Coronation, the Queene was also crown'd, the solemnity very magnificent, as the particulars are set forth in print: The Bish: of Ely preached, but (to the greate sorrow of the people) no Sacrament, as ought to have ben: However the King beginns his reigne with greate expectations and hopes of much reformation as to the former vices, & prophanesse both of Court & Country:

Having ben present at our late Kings Coronation, I was not ambitious of seing this Ceremonie; nor did I think fit to leave my poore Wife alone, who was yet in greate sorrow:

26 Hearing that my good neighbour, [the] painefull & charitable Dr. Par, minister of *Peccham* was dangerously ill, We went first to church ther where the *Curate* preached on   Phil:

29 I went to Lond: about my yet troublesome suite &c: returned 2d of May:

5 To Lond: 7th: I was in Westminster Hall when *Oates* (who had made such a stirr in the whole Kingdome, (upon his revealing a plot of the Papists) as alarm'd several Parliaments, & had occasion'd the execution of divers persons, priests, noble men &c:) was tried for Perjurie at the Kings-bench; but it being exceedingly tedious, I did not much endeavor to see the issue of it, considering that it would certainly be publish'd: Aboundance of R: Cath: were now in the Hall, in expectation of the most gratefull conviction & ruine of a person who had ben so obnoxious to them; & as I verily believe had don much mischiefe & greate injurie to several by his violent & ill grounded proceedings, whilst he was at first so unreasonably blowne-up, & encourag'd, that his insolence was no longer sufferable:

[6 I went to the R: Society, Dr. Wallis presenting his booke of *Algebra* &c:]

7 ⟨I⟩ went this Evening to visite my L. Arch: Bishop of Yorke: *Roger Le Strange* (a gent: whom I had long known, & a person of excellent parts, abating some affectations) appearing first against the Dissenters, in severall Tractates; had now for some yeares turn'd his style against those whom (by way of hatefull distinction) they called Whiggs & Trimmers; under the title of

Observator, which came out 3 or 4 days every weeke: In which sheets, under pretence to serve the Church of England, he gave suspicion of gratif⟨y⟩ing another party, by severall passages, which rather kept up animosities, than appeased, especialy now that nobody gave the least occasion: [8] I return'd home:

10 The *Scots*, valuing themselvs exceedingly to have ben the first Parliament called by his Majestie gave the Excise Costomes &c: forever to the K. & successors; the Duke of *Queenesborow* &c making eloquent speeches, & especialy minding them of a speedy suppression of those late desperate fild Conventiclers, who had don so unheard of assasinations &c: In the meane time Elections for the ensuing Parliament in England, were thought to be very indirectly carried on in most places, and persons chosen who had no interest in the Country & places for which they served: God grant a better issue of it, than some expect:

12 To Lond: about my petition: 13. R: *Society*. Earle of Pembroque was admitted:

16 Was sentenc'd *Oates* to be whip'd & pilloried with uttmost severity: &c:

20 To *Lond:* R: Soc: 21. Din'd at my Lord Privy-Seales, with Sir *Will: Dugdale* the ⟨Garter⟩ K: at Armes, Author of the *Monasticon*, & greate Antiquarie; with whom I had much discourse: he told me he was 82 yeares of age, had his sight & memory perfect &c: There was shew'd a draght of the exact shape & dimensions of the Crowne the Queene had ben crown'd withall, together with the Jewells & Pearles, their weight & value, which amounted to 100650 pounds sterling, an immense summ: attested at the foote of the paper by the Jeweller and Gooldsmith who set the Jewells &c:

22 In the morning, I went (together with a French gent, a person of quality) with my Lord Pr: Seale to the house of Lords, where we were both plac'd by his Lordship next the barr just below the Bishops very commodiously both for hearing and seeing: After a short space came in the Queene & Princesse of Denmark, & stood next above the Arch-Bishops, at the side of the house on the right hand of his Majesties *Throne*: In the interim divers of the Lords (who had not finish'd before) tooke the Test, & usual Oathes, so as her Majestie (Spanish Ambassador & other forraine Ministers who stood behind the state)

heard the Pope, & worship of the Virg: Mary &c: renounc'd very
decently, as likewise the following Prayers, standing all the
while: Then came in the King, the Crowne on his head &c and
being sate, The Commons were let in, so the house being fill'd,
he drew forth a Paper, containing his speech, which he ⟨read⟩
distinctly enough to this effect: That he resolved to call a Parliament from the moment of his brothers decease, as the best
meanes to settle all the concernes of the Nation so as might be
most easy & happy to himselfe & his subjects: That he would
confirme what ever he had said in his declaration at the first
Council, concerning his opinion of the principles of the Church
of England, for their Loyaltie, & would defend & support it,
and preserve its government, as by Law now establish'd: That as
he would Invade no mans property, so he would never depart
from his owne prerogative: & as he had ⟨ventur'd⟩ his life in
defence of the nation so he would proceede to do still: That having given this assurance of his Care of our Religion (his word
was *your* Religion) & propertie, (which he had not said by
chance, but solemnly) so he doubted not of suitable returnes of
his subjects duty & kindnesse, especialy as to the settling his
Revenue for life for the many weighty necessities of the government which he would not suffer to be precarious: That some
might possibly suggest that it were better to feede & supply him
from time to time onely, out of their inclination to frequent Parliaments; but that that, would be but a very improper Method to
take with him; since the best way to engage him to meete
oftener, would be allways to use him well; & therefore expected
their compliance speedily, that this session being but short, they
might meete again to satisfaction: *At every period of this, the house
gave lowd shouts* &c: Then he acquainted them with that mornings news of *Argiles* being landed in the West-highlands of *Scotland* from Holland, and the Treasonous declaration he had
published, which he would communicate to them, & that he
should take the best care he could it should meete with the
reward it deserv'd, not questioning of the parliaments Zeale &
readinesse to assist him, as he desired: *At which There followed
another Vive le roy*, & so his Majestie retired: &c: & I went into
the Court of Requests &c:

So soone as the Commons were return'd, & put themselves,
into a grand Committè, they immediately put the Question, &

unanimously voted the Revenue to his Majestie during life: Mr. *Seamour* made a bold speech against many Elections, and would have had those Members who (he pretended) were obnoxious, to withdraw, 'til they had cleared their being legaly return'd, but no body seconded him: The truth is there were very many of the new Members, whose Elections & returnes were universaly censur'd; being divers of them persons of no manner of condition or Interest in the nation, and places for which they served, especialy in the Counties of Devon, Cornwell, Norfolck, &c, said to have ben recommended from the Court, and effect of the new charters, changing the Electors: It was reported my L: of Bath, carried-down with him no fewer than 15 Charters, so as some cald him the Prince Elector: whence *Seaymor* told the house in his speech, that if this were digested, they might introduce what Religion & Lawes they pleased, & that though he never gave heede to the feares & jealosies of the people before, he now was realy apprehensive of Popery &c: The truth is, by the printed List of Members of 505, there did not appear to be above 135 who had ben in former Parliaments, especialy that lately held at Oxon:

In the Lords house, my Lord Newport made but an impertinent exception against two or three [young] Peeres, who wanted some moneths, & some onely 4 or 5 daies of being of age:

The Popish Lords (who had some time before ben released from their Confinement about the Plot) were now discharg'd of their Impeachment: of which I gave my L. Arundel of Wardoer joy:

Oates, who had but two days before ben pilloried at severall places, & whip't at the Carts taile from New-gate to Algate; was this day placed in a sledge (being not able to go by reason of his so late scourging) & dragd from prison to Tyburn, & whip'd againe all the way, which some thought to be very severe & extraordinary; but in case he were gilty of the perjuries, & so of the death of many innocents, as I feare he was; his punishment was but what he well deserv'd: I chanc'd to passe in my Coach, just as Execution was doing on him: *A strange revolution.*

Note, that there was no speech made by my *Lord Keeper*, after his Majesties as usualy: It was whispered, he would not long be in that station; & many believing the bold Chiefe Justice *Jeofries* (now made Baron of Wem in Yorkshire, & who went through-stitch in that Tribunal) stood faire for that Office: I gave him joy

the morning before of his new honor, he having always ben very
civil to me &c:

23 I supped this Evening with much Company at my
L. Privy-Seales, & return'd home next morning:

24 Our *Viccar* having lost his onely sonn, & one of his daughters, (who died I think both in the same week of feavors, but at
some greate distance each from the other), a stranger supplied the
pulpet, on 2. *Cor:* 4. 17. shewing the little proportion betweene all
our sorrows, losses & suffering in this life, compar'd to the exceeding weight of glory & reward in the life to come; by many
instances & proofes: &c: The *Curate pomerid*: &c on 12: *Matt:* 20.

I fell into an exceeding drowsinesse after prayers:

We had hithertoo [not] any raine for many monethes, insomuch as the Caterpillar had already devoured all the Winter
fruite through the whole land, & even killed severall greate &
old trees; such two Winters, & Summers I had never known:

27 I went to Lond: There was newes of *Argiles* being landed
in Scotland, having published a treasonous Declaration: 29.
A Loyal Sermon at St. *Martines* on 124: *Psal:* 8. rememorating
the signal deliverances of the late & present King, & exhorting to thankfullnesse & obedience: The Office for the day being
now newly fitted for the occasion since his late Majesties
Restoration & death: After Sermon I returned home.

My Lord Clarendon L. Privy-Seale was so obliging, as to
give me the use of his intire Lodgings in White-hall, he having
accommodation in another part of the house:

30 I went againe to Lond: to resigne a Trust which concerned
Mrs. *Thayre* & her husband; return'd that evening:

June 4. Came to visite, and take leave of me Sir *Gab: Sylvius*
now going Envoyè Extraordinary into Denmark: with his secretary, & chaplaine, a french-man who related the miserable
persecution of the Protestants in Fr: not above ten Churches left
them, and they threatned to be also demolish'd: That they were
commanded to christen their children within 24 houres after
birth, or else a Popish priest was to be call'd, & then the Infant
brought-up in popery: and that in some places they were 30
leagues from any Minister or opportunity: That this persecution
had dispeopled the most industrious part of the nation and dispers'd them into Swisse, Burgundy, Hollond, Ger: Denmark,
England, Plantations & where not. There were with Sir Gab:

his Lady, Sir William Godolphin, and sisters, & my Lord Godolphins little son, (my Charge): I brought them to the water side, where Sir *Gab:* embarked for his Voyage, & the rest return'd to Lond:

THE MONMOUTH REBELLION –
A DAUGHTER ELOPES – VISITS TO
WINCHESTER AND PORTSMOUTH
(1685–1687)

THERE WAS NOW certaine Intelligence of the Duke of Monmoths landing at Lyn in Dorset shire, & of his having set up his standart, as K. of England: I pray God deliver us from the confusions which these beginings threaten:

Such a drowth for want of raine, was never in my memory:

17 To *Lond:* at which time the D: of Monmoth invaded this nation landing with but 150 men at *Lyme* in Dorsetshire, which wonderfully alarm'd the whole Kingdome, fearing the joyning of dissafected people; many of the train'd bands flocking to him: he had at his landing publish'd a Declaration, charging his Majestie with Usurpation, & severall horrid crimes, upon pretence of his owne title, and the calling of a free-Parliament: This Decl: was condemn'd to be burnt by the hang-man, the Duke proclaim'd Traytor, a reward of 5000 pounds to him that should kill him &c: Now were also those words in the Inscription about the *Pillar* (intimating the Papists firing the Citty) erased and cut out &c:

The exceeding Drouth still continued: God grant a successfull conclusion to these ill-boding beginnings: I tooke the Chaire as Vice-President at the R: *Society*.

18 I dined at my L: Sunderlands: 19: I heard the Appeale of my worthy friend Mr. Ch: Howard (against the Duke of Norfolck his brother) pleaded in the house of Lords, &c: and in the afternoone returned home, where I met a Warrant to send out an horse with 12 dayes provision &c:

21 Our Doctor proceeded on the later part of his former Text: *Pomeridiano*, the Curate of Greenewich on 80 *Psal:* 4: Drowsinesse surpriz'd me:

28 We had now plentifull Raine after two yeares excessive drowth, & severe winters. A stranger preached on 1: *Jam:* 25:— Argile taken in Scotland and executed; his party desperssed:

July 2 Came to Dine with me the Countesses of Bristoll, Sunderland, & little Clancartie with Mrs. Boscauen, her sister, & the deare Child Godolphin: No considerable account of the forces sent against the D: of Mon: though greate forces sent: there was a small ski⟨r⟩mish, but he would not be provok'd to come to an encounter, but still kept in the fastnesses: The Parliament prorogu'd til 4: Aug: Dangerfild whip'd & like *Oates* for perjurie:

8 To Lond: Came now the newes of Monmouths Utter defeate, and the next day of his being taken by Sir William Portman & Lord Lumley, with the Militia of their Counties. It seemes the horse commanded by my Lord Grey, being newly raised, & undisciplin'd, were not to be brought in so short a time to indure the Fire, which exposed the foote to the Kings: so as when Monmoth had led the foote in greate silence and order thinking to surprise my Lord Feversham Lieutenant Generall newly incamped, and given him a smart charge, interchanging both greate & small shot; The horse breaking [theire owne] ranks; monmoth gave it over, and fled with *Grey*, leaving their party to be cut in pieces: to the number of 2000: the whole number reported to be about 8000: The Kings but 2700: The slaine were most of them Mendip-miners, who did greate Execution with their tooles, and sold their lives very dearely: whilst their leaders flying were pursu'd and taken the next morning, not far from one another: Mon: had walked 16 miles on foote changing his habite with a poore coate, & was found by L. Lumley in ⟨a⟩ dry-ditch cover'd with fern-braken, but neither with sword, pistol, or so much as any Weapon, and so might happly have passed for some country man, his beard being grown so long, & so gray, as hardly to be known, had not his George discovered him, which was found in his Pocket: Tis said he trembled exceedingly all over not able to speake: Grey was taken not far from him: Most of his party were Anabaptists, & poore Cloth-workers of the Country, no Gent: of account being come into him: The Arch-*bouttefew* Ferguson, Mathews &c: were not yet found: The 5000 pounds to be given to whomsoever should bring Monmouth in by Proclamation, was to be distributed among the Militia by agreement twixt Sir William Portman & Lumley:

The battail ended, some words first in jeast then in heate [pass-
ing] twixt Sherrington Talbot a worthy Gent, (son to Sir Jo: Talbot, & who had behav'd himselfe very handsomly) and one
Capt: *Love*, both commanders of the Militia forces of the Country, whose souldiers fought best: both drawing their Swords, &
passing at one another Sherrington was wounded to death upon
the spot; to the greate regrett of those who knew him, being also
his fathers onely son:

9 Just as I was coming into the Lodgings at Whitehall a little
before dinner my Lord of Devonshire standing very neere his
Majesties bed-Chamber-doore in the lobby: came *Coll: Culpeper*
& in a rude manner looking my Lord in the face, Asked whether
this were a time and place for Excluders to appeare, my Lord
tooke little notice of what he said at first, knowing him to be a
hot-headed fellow; but reiterating it againe, Asked Culpeper
whether he meant him? he said, yes, he meant his Lordship: My
Lord told him he was no Excluder (as indeede he was not) the
other affirms it againe: My Lord told him he Lied; on which
Culpeper struck him a box o'th'Eare, my Lord him another and
fell'd him downe; upon which being soone parted: Culpeper was
seiz'd and commanded by his Majestie (who was all the while in
the B: chamber) to be carried downe to the Greenecloth Officer,
who sent him to the Martialsea, as he deserv'd: My L: *Devon*
had nothing said to him.

I supped this night at Lambeth at my old friends Mr. Elias
Ashmole with my Lady Clarendon, the Bish: of St. Asaph, and
Dr. Tenison rector of St. Martines, &c: when we were treated at
a greate feast:

10 The Count of *Castel Melior*, that greate favorite and prime
Minister of *Alphonso* late King of Portugal, after several Yeares
banishment; now being againe received to grace & called home
by *Dom Pedro* the present King (as having ben found a person of
the greatest integrity after all his sufferings) desired me to spend
part of this day with him, and assist him in a Collection of
books, & other curiosities, which he would carry with him into
Portugal: Mr. *Hussey* a young Gent: who made love to my deare
Child, disseased of the small-pox in March-last; but whom she
could not bring her selfe to answer his affection: died now of the
same cruel dissease; for which I was extreamly sorry; because it
is apparent, he never enjoy'd himselfe after my daughters death,

nor was I averse to the Match, could she have overcome her inclinations:

11 I returned home:

12 Our *Viccar* proceeded on his former Text and subject: The *Curate* on: 3. *Titus* 1: concerning subjection to Magistrates: I was surpriz'd with *sleepe*:

15 I went to Lond: to see Dr. *Tenisons* Library, returned in the Evening:

This day was Monmoth brought to Lond: examin'd before the King to whom he made great submission, accknowledg'd his seduction by Fergusson the Scot, whom he named the bloudy Villain: thence sent to the Tower, had an enterview with his late Dutchesse, whom he received coldly, having lived dishonestly with the Lady Hen: Wentworth for two yeares; from obstinatly asserting his conversation with that debauched woman to be no sin, seing he could not be perswaded to his last breath, the Divines, who were sent to assist him, thought not fit to administer the holy Communion to him: for the rest of his faults he professed greate sorrow, and so died without any apparent feare, would make use of no cap, or other circumstance, but lying downe bid the fellow do his office better than to my late Lord Russell, & gave him gold: but the wretch made five Chopps before he had his head off, which so incens'd the people, that had he not ben guarded & got away they would have torne him in pieces: He made no Speech on the Scaffold (which was on Tower-hill) but gave a paper (containing not above 5 or 6 lines) for the King, in which he disclaimes all Title to the Crowne, accknowledges that the late King (his Father) had indeede told him, he was but his base sonn, & so desire'd his Majestie to be kind to his Wife & Children: This Relation I had from the Mouth of Dr. Tenison *Rector* of St. Martines, who with the Bishops of *Ely* & *Bath* & *Wells*, was one of the divines his Majestie sent to him, & were at the execution: Thus ended this quondam Duke, darling of his Father, and the Ladys, being extraordi⟨na⟩rily handsome, and adroit: an excellent souldier, & dauncer, a favorite of the people, of an Easy nature, debauched by lust, seduc'd by crafty knaves who would have set him up onely to make a property; tooke this opportunity of his Majestie being of another Religion, to gather a party of discontented; failed of it, and perished: He was a lovely person, had a vertuous & excellent Lady that brought him greate riches & a second Dukedome in Scotland; Was Master of the Horse, Gen. of the K. his fathers Army, Gent: of the Bed chamber: Knight of the Garter, Chancellor of Camb: in a Word had accumulations without end: Se what *Ambition* and want of principles brought him to. He was beheaded on Tuesday the 14th *July*: His mother (whose name was Barlow, daughter of some very meane Creatures) was a beautifull strumpet, whom I had often seene at *Paris*, & died miserably, without anything to bury her: Yet had this *Perkin* ben made believe, the King had married her: which was a monstrous forgerie, & ridiculous: & to satisfie the world the iniquitie of the report, the King his father (if his Father he realy were, for he most resembld one *Sidny* familiar with his mother) publiquely & most solemnly renounced it, and caused it to be so entred in the Council booke some yeares since, with all the Privy Counsel(o)rs attestation.

17 Came my Lord Hatton Governor of Gurnsey (a Worthy person) to Visite me:

19 Our Viccar absent, preached a stranger on 1: *Cor:* 16. 13 shewing the necessity of Armour & Christian vigilancy, with a long narrative of the Disloyaltie of our late Rebellions & the mischiefe of their principles:—

In the *Afternoone*, another stranger on 20: *Exod:* 8:

I went the Saturday before to see the Muster of the 6 Scotch & Eng: Regiments, whom the Pr: of Orange had lately sent his Majestie out of Holland, upon this rebellion, but were now returning, having had no occasion to make use of them: They were all excellently clad, and perfectly disciplined, and were incamped on Black-heath most formaly with their Tents: The King & Queene &c: being come to see them exercise & the manner of Encamping, which was very neate & magnificent.

By a grosse mistake of the Secretary of his Majesties forces, they had ben ordred to quarter in private Houses (which was contrary to an Act of Parliament) but upon my informing his Majestie timely of it, it was prevented:

The two horse-men which My Son & myselfe sent into the County Troopes, were now come home, after neere a moneths being out, to our extraordinary charge:

20 The Trinity Company met this day, as it should have indeede don on the moneday after Trinity Sonday, which was put off til now, by reason of the royal Charter, which being

exceeding large could not be ready before: some other immunities superadded: Mr. *Pepys* (Secretary of the Admiralty) was a second time chosen Master: present the Duke of Grafton, & Lord of Dartmouth Master of the Ordnance, the Commissioners of the Navy & breathren of that Corporation: Then we went to Church according to costome when preached Dr. Hicks, on 72 Psal. v: 8. a most learned, excellent & instructive sermon, of the antiquity, usefullnesse & other benefits of shipping and Navigation: The parallel between the Catholic Church & a ship was very handsome: but the sermon (I suppose) will be printed, as it deserves:

Then we tooke barge to the Trinity house in Lond: where we had a most plentifull & magnificent feast, There being above 80 at one Table; & so I return'd:

26 Being the day of Thanksgiving for his Majesties late victory over the Rebelles, Argyle in Scotland, & Monmouth in the West, according to a forme of Prayers composed for the Occasion; one Mr. *Hutchins* preached in the morning on 72 *Psal:* 10: shewing from what signal dangers, God had in all ages delivered his church: In the Afternoone the Curate on 64 *Psal:* 9. 10. relating much of the particulars of the late rising, and both concluding in Eucharistical exhortations: And most certain it is, that had not it pleased God to dissipate their beginnings, they had in all appearance gathered by an irresistable head, and desperately proceeded to the ruine of Church, & Government; so ⟨general⟩ was the discontent, and expectation of the opportunity: For my owne part, I looked upon this deliverance as absolutely most signal; such an innundation of Phanatics and men of impious principles, must needes have caused universal dissorder, cruelty, injustice, rapine, sacrilege & confusion, an unavoydable Civilwar, and misery without end: but blessed be God, the knot was happily broken, and a faire prospect of Tranquilitie for the future likely to succeede if we reforme, be thankfull, & make a right use of this Mercy:

27 This night when we were all asleepe went my Daughter Eliz: away, to meete a young fellow, nephew to Sir Jo: Tippet (Surveyor of the Navy: & one of the Commissioners) whom she married the next day being Tuesday; without in the least acquainting either her parents, or any soule in the house: I was the more afflicted & ⟨astonish'd⟩ at it, in reguard, we had never

given this Child the least cause to be thus dissobedient, and being now my Eldest, might reasonably have expected a double Blessing: But it afterward appeared, that this Intrigue had ben transacted by letters long before, & ⟨when⟩ she was with my Lady Burton in Licester shire, and by private meetings neere my house: She of all our Children had hitherto given us least cause of suspicion; not onely for that she was yet young, but seemed the most flattering, souple and observant; of a silent & particular humor; in no sort ⟨betraying⟩ the levity & Inclination which is commonly apparent in Children who fall into these snares; having ben bred-up with the uttmost Circumspection, as to principles of severest honour & Piety: But so far it seemes, had her passion for this Young fellow made her forget her duty, and all that most Indulgent Parents expected from her, as not to consider the Consequence of her folly & dissobedience, 'til it was too late: This Affliction went very neere me & my Wife, neither of us yet well compos'd for the untimely losse of that incomparable & excellent Child, which it pleased God to take from us by the small pox a few moneths before: But this farther Chastizement was to be humbly submitted to, as a part of the burden God was pleased to lay farther upon us; in this yet the lesse afflictive, That we had not ben wanting in giving her an Education every way becoming us: We were most of all astonish'd at the suddainesse of this action, & the privatenesse of its manegement; the Circumstances also Consider'd & quality, how it was possible she should be flattered so to her dissadvantage: He being in no condition sortable to hers, & the Blessing we intended her: The thing has given us much disquiet, I pray God direct us, how to govern our Resentments of her dissobedience; and if it be his will, bring good out of all this Ill:

Aug: 2 So had this Affliction descompos'd us, that I could not be well at Church the next Lords day; though I had prepared for the B: Sacrament: I hope God will be more gracious to my onely remaining Child, whom I take to be of a more discreete, sober and religious temper: that we may have that comfort from her, which is deny'd us in the other:

This Accident caus'd me to alter my Will; as was reasonable; for though there may be a reconciliation upon her repentance, and that she has suffer'd for her folly; yet I must let her see what her undutifullnesse in this action, deprives her of; as to the provision she else might have expected; solicitous as she knew I now was of bestowing her very worthily:

6 I went to Lond: next day to see Mr. Wats, keeper of the Apothecaries Garden of simples at Chelsey: where there is a collection of innumerable rarities of that sort: Particularly, besids many rare annuals the Tree bearing the Jesuits bark, which had don such cures in quartans: & what was very ingenious the subterranean heate, conveyed by a stove under the Conserveatory, which was all Vaulted with brick; so as he leaves the doores & windowes open in the hard⟨e⟩st frosts, secluding onely the snow &c: I returned home by Clapham:

14 [15] came to visite us Mrs. Boscawen, with my Lord Godolphi⟨n⟩s little son, with whose Education hitherto his father had intrusted me:

16 Came newes to us that my undutifull daughter was visited with the small-pox, now universaly very contagious: I was yet willing my Wife should go visite & take care of her:

⟨16⟩ A stranger preached on 10. Rom: 6. 7. 8. 9. 10. 11: Pomerid: Curate on: 1. *Cor:* 2. 2.

22 I went to Lond, to see my unhappy Child, now in greate danger, and carried our Viccar with me, that according to her earnest desire, (being very sensible & penitent for her fault) he might administer to her the H: Sacrament, which he did; & after some time, and her greate submissions & agonies, leaving her to the mercys of God, & her mother with her I returned in the Evening: We had now the newes of Newhausels being taken by the Christians: There was also this day an universall appearance of the Kings forces at Brainford:

28 My poore unhappy Daughters sickness increasing, a violent feavor succeeding when her other distemper appeared to be past danger; I went up againe to see, & comfort her, together with our Minister: My disconsolate Wife I left with her, who had ben almost all her sicknesse with her; so I return'd home in greate doubt how God would deale with her, whom the next morning he was pleased to take out of this vale of misery, I humbly trust, to his infinite mercy, though to our unspeakeable affliction, loosing another Child in the flower of her age, who had never 'til now given us cause of any displeasure, but many hopes of Comfort: & thus in lesse than 6 moneths were we depriv'd of two Children for our unworthinesse, & causes best

known to God, whom I beseech from the bottome of my heart that he will give us grace to make that right use of all these chastisements that we may become better, and intirely submitt [in] all things to his infinite wise disposal. She departed this life on ⟨Saturday⟩ 29: Aug: at 8 in the Morning: fell sick [& died] on the same day of the weeke, that my other most deare & dutifull daughter did, and as also one of my servants (a very pious youth) had don the yeare before: I beseech God of his mercy Sanctifie this and all other Afflictions & dispensations to me. His holy will be don *Amen*.

30 This sad accident kept me from the publique service this day being Sonday.

My Child was buried by her sister on 2d September in the Church of Deptford:

The 3 of Sep: I went to Lond, being sent to by a Letter from my Lord Clarendon (Lord privy-seale) to let me know that his majestie being pleased to send him *Lord Lieutennant* into *Ireland*, was also pleased to Nominate me one of the Commissioners to execute the office of *Privy-Seale* during his *Lieutenancy* there: It behoving me [4] to waite upon his Majestie & to give him thanks for his greate honor (returning home that Evening) I accompanied his Lordship [5] the next morning to *Windsore* (dining by the Way at Sir *Hen: Capels* at *Cue*) where his Majestie receiving me with extraordinary kindnesse, I kissed his hands: I told him how sensible I was of his Majestie gracious favour to me: that I would endeavour to serve him with all sincerity, dilligence & loyalty, not more out of my duty, than Inclinations: He said, he doubted not of it, & was glad he had this opportunity to shew the kindnesse he had for me: After this came aboundance of the greate Men to give me Joy, particularly L: *Tressurer*, L: *Sunderland*, L: *Peterborrow*, L: *Godolphin*, L: *Falkland* & every body at Court who knew me: [6] The next day being *Sonday*, I went to Church in the Cathed: where preached Dr. Standish on   after which follow'd the H: Communion of which I participated, beseeching God to be gracious to me &c: The 2d sermon was preached by Dr. *Creighton* on 1: *Thess:* 4: 11: Then I went to heare a *French* man, who preached before the *King* & *Queene* in that splended *Chapell* next St. *Georges Hall*, his discourse was on the Gospel of the day, describing the leaprosies of sin &c: Their Majesties going to *Masse*, I withdrew, to consider the stupendious painting of the

Hall, which both for the Art & Invention deserves the Inscription, in honor of the Painter *Signior Verrio*: The History is Edw: the ⟨3rd's⟩ receiving the black-prince, coming towards him in a Roman Triumph &c. The whole roofe, the Hist: of St. George, The Throne, the Carvings &c are incomparable, & I think equal to any & in many Circumstances exceeding any I have seene Abroad:

I was invited to Dinner by the *Duke* of *Norfolck*, but had ben engaged before to dine at my L: *Sunderlands*, where also dined my L: Clarendon, L: Arran, L: *Middleton*, & Sir W: *Soames*, design'd Ambassador to Constantinople; After dinner, I visited the Countesse of *Bristol*, & then went to Evening prayers. About 6 a Clock came Sir *Dudley* & his Bro: *Roger North* & brought the *Greate* Seale from my *L: Keeper*, who it seemes died the day before at his house in *Oxfordshire*: The King went immediately to *Council*, and everybody guessing who was most like to succeede this greate officer; most believing it could be no other than my L: Ch: Justice *Jeoffries*, who had so vigorously prosecuted the late Rebelles, and was now gon the Western-Circuit, to punish the rest that were secured in the severall Counties; and was now neere upon his returne: I tooke my leave of his Majestie who spake very graciously to me; & supping that night at Sir Stephen Foxes; promising to dine at his house [7] the next day: [which I did] on Moneday, returning with my Lord Clarendon, thro Cheesewick, and [9] the next day home to my house:

13 Our Viccar preached on 12: Heb: 1: The *Curate* proceeded on his former: I was exceedingly sleepie: The Lord pardon me:

15 I went to Lond: accomp⟨a⟩nied Mr. *Pepys* (Secretary of the *Admiralty*) to *Portsmouth*, Whither his Majestie was going the first time since his coming to the Crowne, to see in what state the Fortifications were. Wee tooke Coach & 6 horses, late after din⟨n⟩er, yet got to *Bagshot* that night: whilst supper was making ready I went & made a Visite to Mrs. Grahames, some time Maide of honor to the queen Dowager, now wife to Ja: Gr: Esquire of the Privie-purse to the King: her house being a Walke in the Forest, within a little quarter of a mile from Bagshot Towne: very importunate she was that I would sup, & abide there that night; but being oblig'd by my companion, I return'd to our Inn, after she had shew'd me her house which was very commodious, & well furnish'd, as she was an excellent housewife, a prudent & vertuous Lady: There is a parke full of

red deare about it: Her eldest son, was now sick there of the small pox, but in a likely way of recovery; & other of her Children ran about, & among the infected, which she said she let them do on purpose that they might whilst young, passe that fatal dissease, which she fancied they were to undergo one time or other, & that this would be the best: The severity of this cruel dissease so lately in my poore family confirming much of what she affirm'd:

16 The next morning early seting out, we ariv'd early enough at *Winchester* to waite on the King, who was lodg'd at the Deanes, (Dr. Megot) I found very few with him besides my Lord *Feversham*, *Arran*, *Newport*, & the *Bishop* of *Bath* and *Wells* to whom his Majestie was discoursing concerning Miracles, & what strange things the *Saludadors* would do in *Spaine*, as by creeping into [heated] ovens with[out] hurt &c: & that they had a black Crosse in the roofe of their mouthes: but yet were commonly, notorious & prophane wretches: upon which his Majestie farther said, that he was so extreamely difficult of Miracles, for feare of being impos'd on, that if he should chance to see one himselfe, without some other wittnesse, he should apprehend it some delusion of his senses: Then they spake of the boy who was pretended to have had a wanting leg restor'd him, so confidently asserted by *Fr: de Santa Clara*, & others: To all which the Bishop added a greate Miracle happning in that Citty of Winchester to his certaine knowledge, of a poore miserably sick & decrepit Child, (as I remember long kept un-baptized) who immediately on his Baptisme, recover'd; as also of the sanatory effect of *K. Charles* his Majesties fathers blood, in healing one that was blind: As to that of the *Saludador* (of which likewise I remember Sir *Arthir Hopton*, formerly Ambassador at Madrid had told me many like wonders) *Mr. Pepys* passing through *Spaine*, & being extreamely Inquisitive of the truth of these pretended miracles of the *Saludadors*; found a very famous one of them at last, whom he offered a considerable reward to, if he would make a trial of the *Oven*, or any other thing of that kind, before him: The fellow ingenuously told him, that, finding he was a more than ordinary curious person, he would not deceive him, & so accknowledg'd that he could do none of those feates, realy; but that what they pretended, was all a cheate, which he would easily discover, though the poore superstitious people

were imposed upon: yet have these Impostors, an allowance of the Bishops, to practise th⟨e⟩ir Juggleings: This Mr. *Pepys* affirm'd to me; but said he, I did not conceive it fit, to interrupt his Majestie, who told what they pretended to do, so solemnly: Then there was something said of the second-sight, happening to some persons, especialy *Scotch*: Upon which both his Majestie & (I think) my Ld: *Arran*, told us, that Monsieur   a French Nobleman lately here in England, seeing the late Duke of Monmoth, come into the Play-house at Lond: suddainly cryed out to some sitting in the same box: *Voila Messieurs comme il entre sans tete* After this his Majestie speaking of some Reliques, that had effected strange cures, particularly a *Thorne* of our B: S: Crosse; that healed a Gentlewomans rotten nose by onely touching; & speaking of the Golden Crosse & Chaine taken out of the Coffin of St. *Edward the Confessor* at *Westminster*, by one of the singing-men, who as the scaffolds were taking-down, after his Majesties Coronation, espying an hole in the Tomb, & something glisten; put his hand in, & brought it to the Deane, & he to the King: his Majestie began to put the Bishop in mind, how earnestly the [late] King (his brother) call'd upon him, during his Agonie, to take out what he had in his pocckett: [See Feb: 6:] I had thought (says the King) it had ben for some keys, which might lead to some Cabinets, which his Majestie would have me secure; but (says he) you well remember that I found nothing in any of his pockets but onely a Crosse of Gold, & a few insignificant papers; & thereupon shewed us the Crosse, & was pleased to put it into my hand; it was of Gold about 3 Inches long, having on one side a Crucifix enameled & embossed, the rest was graved & garnished with gold-smith worke & two pretty broad table Amethists (as I conceived) & at the bottome a pendant pearle; within was inchas'd a little fragment (as was thought) of the true Crosse: & a latine Inscription, in Gotic & roman letters: How his Majestie came by it I do not remember; for more company coming in this discourse ended: Onely I may not forget, a Resolution which his Majestie there made, & had a little before entered upon it, at the Counsel board at Windsor or White-hal: That the Negros in the Plantations should all be Baptized, exceedingly declaiming against that impiety, of their Masters prohibiting it, out of a mistaken opinion, that they were then *ipso facto* free: But his Majestie persists in his resolution to have them Christn'd, which piety the *Bishop*, deservedly blessed him for; and so I went out, to see the New Palace his late Majestie had began, and brought almost to the Covering: It was placed on the side of the Hill, where formerly stood the old Castle; a stately fabrique of 3 sides, & a Corridor, all built of brique, & Cornished, windoes, Columns at the break & Entrance, of freestone: intended for a Hunting House, when his Majestie came to those parts, & having an incomparable prospect: I believe there had already ben 20000 pounds and more expended; but his now Majestie did not seeme to encourage the finishing of it; at least for a while; & it is like to stand: Hence I went to see the Cathedrall, a reverend pile, & in good repaire: There is still the Coffines of the 6 Saxon kings, whose bones had ben scattered by the sacrilegious Rebells of 1641, in expectation (I suppose) of finding some valuable Reliques: & afterward gather'd-up againe & put into new chests, which stand above the stalls of the Quire: Here lies the body of their Founder, of Card: & severall other Bishops &c: & so I went to my Lodging, very wett, it having rained the whole day:

17 Early next morning we went to *Portsmouth*, some thing before his Majestie arived: we found all the way full of people, the Women in their best dresse, multitudes of all sorts, in expectance of seeing his Majestie passe by, which he did, riding on horse-back, a good part of the way: We found the Major, his Aldermen with their Mace, & in their formalities standing at the Entrance of the Fort, a Mile on this side the Towne, where he made a speech to the King, & then went off the Guns of the fort, as did all those of the Garison, so soone as he was come into *Portsmouth*, all the souldiers (which were neere 3000) drawn up, and lining the streetes, & platforme to *Gods-house* (which is the name of the Governors house) where (after his Majestie had viewed the new Fortifications, & Ship-yard) he was Entertained at a Magnificent dinner, by Sir   Slingsby, the Lieutenant Governor; all the Gent: of any quality, in his traine setting downe at Table with him, & which I also had don, had I not ben before engag'd to *Sir Robert Holmes* (Governor of the *Isle of Wight*) to dine with him at a private house, where likewise we had a very sumptuous & plentifull repast of excellent Venison, Fowle, Fish, fruit, & what not: After dinner I went to waite on his Majestie againe, who was pulling on his boots in the Towne

hall joyning to the house where he dined, & then having saluted some Ladys &c: that came to kisse his hand; he tooke horse for Winchester, whither he returned that night: This hall is artificialy hung round, with Armes of all sorts, like the Hall & keepe of Windsor, which looks very finely:

I went hence to see the Ship-yard, & Dock, the Fortifications, and other things; What I learned was, the facility of an armies taking the Ile of Wight, should an attempt be made by any Enemy, for want of due care in fortifying some places of it, & the plenty of the Iland, able to nourish 20000 men, besides its inhabitants: *Portsmouth* when finished will be very strong, & a Noble Key: There were now 32 Men of war in the Harbour: I was invited by Sir R: Beach, the ⟨Commissioner⟩ where after a greate supper, Mr. Secretary and my selfe lay-all that night: & the next morning set out for Gildford [18] where we arived in good houre, & so the day after to Lond: whence [19] taking leave of Mr. Pepys, I came home to my house, after a journey of 140 miles:

I had twice before ben at *Portsmouth*, Ile of Wight &c: many yeares since: I found this part of *Hampshire* bravely wooded; especialy about the house and estate of *Coll: Norton*, who (though now in being, having formerly made his peace by meanes of Coll Legg) was formerly a very fierce Commander in the first Rebellion: His house is large, & standing low, as one goes from Winchester to ⟨Portsmouth⟩:

By what I observed in this Journey; I find that infinite industry, sedulity, gravity, and greate understanding & experience of affaires in his Majestie, that I cannot but predict much happinesse to the Nation, as to its political Government, & if he so persist (as I am confident he will) there could nothing be more desired, to accomplish our prosperity, but that he were of the national Religion: for certainly such a Prince never had this Nation since it was one:

Octob: 1: This day I din'd at Mr. Slingsbys: Visited the *Dutchesse* of *Grafton*: Came in my absence to see me The *Duke* of *Norfolck*, neither my wife nor my selfe being at home; There were with him   and much company:

2 I spent this morning in Devotion, preparing for the Communion, when having a letter sent me by Mr. P[epys], with this expression at the foote of it: *I have something to shew you, that I may not have againe another time*: &c & that I would not faile to

dine with him: I went accordingly: After dinner he had me, and
one Mr. *Houblon* (a very rich & considerable Merchant, whose
Fathers had fled out of *Flanders* upon the persecution of the
Duke of *Alva*) into a private roome: & being sate downe, told us
that being lately alone with his Majestie and upon some occasion
of speaking concerning my late Lord *Arlingtons* dying a *R: Cath*,
who had all along seemed to professe himselfe a Protestant,
taken all the Tests &c: 'til the day (I think) of his death: His
Majestie say'd, that as to his inclinations he had known him long
wavering, but ⟨for⟩ feare of loosing his places [he] did not think
convenient to declare himselfe: There are (says the King) who
believe the Ch: of R: gives Dispensations, for going to church, &
many like things; but that it was not so; for if that might have ben
had, he himselfe had most reason to make use of it: Indeede he
said, As to some Matrimonial Cases, there are now & then Dispensations, but hardly in any Cases else: This familiar discourse
encourag'd Mr. P: to beg of his Majestie (if he might aske it,
without offence, and for that his Majestie could not but observe
how it was whispered among many), [whither] his Late *Majestie*
had ben reconcil'd to the *C. of Rome*: He againe humbly besought
his Majestie to pardon his presumption, if he had touch'd upon a
thing, did not befit him to looke into &c: The *King* ingenuously
told him, That he both was, & died a *R: Cath:* & that he had not
long since declared it was upon some politic & state reasons, best
known to himself [(meaning the King his Brother)] but that he
was of that persuasion, he bid him follow him into his Closett,
where opening a Cabinet, he shew'd him two papers, containing
about a quarter of a sheete on both sides, written in the late
Kings owne hand, severall Arguments opposite to the Doctrine
of the *Church of Eng:* Charging her with heresy, novelty, & [the]
phan⟨tas⟩ticisme of other Protestants: The chiefe whereoff (as
I remember) were, our refusing to accknowledge the Primacy
& Infallibility &c of the Church of Rome, how impossible it was
so many Ages should never dispute it, til of late; how unlikely our
B: Saviour would leave his Church without a Visible Head &
guide to resort to during his absence, with the like usual *Topics*; so
well penn'd as to the discourse, as did by no means seeme to me,
to have ben put together by the Late King: Yet written all with
his owne hand, blotted, & interlin'd, so as if indeede, it were not
given him by some Priest; they happly might be such Arguments

and reasons as had ben inculcated from time to time, & here rec-
ollected, & in the conclusion shewing his looking on the Protestant Religion, (& by name the Church of Eng:) to be without
foundation, & consequently false & unsafe: When his Majestie
had shew'd him these *Originals*, he was pleas'd to lend him the
Copies of those two Papers, attested at the bottome in 4 or
5 lines, under his owne hand: These were the papers I saw & read:
This nice & curious passage I thought fit to set downe; Though
all the Arguments, and objections were altogether weake, & have
a thousand times ben Answerd irreplicably by our Divines;
though such as their Priests insinuate among their Proselytes, as
if nothing were Catholique but the C. of Rome, no salvation out
of that, no Reformation sufferable &c: botoming all their Errors
on *St. Peters* Successors unerrable dictatorship; but proving nothing with any sort or Reason, or the taking notice of any Objection which could be made against it: Here was all taken for
granted, & upon it a Resolution & preference implied: I was
heartily sorry to see all this; though it were no other, than what
was long suspected, by his late Majesties too greate indifference,
neglect & course of Life, that he had ben perverted, & for secular
respects onely, profess'd to be of another beliefe; [See 6: *Feb*
168$\frac{4}{5}$;] & thereby giving infinite advantage to our Adversaries,
both the Court, & generaly the Youth, & greate persons of the
nation becoming dissolute & highly prophane; God was
incensed to make his Reigne very troublesome & improsperous,
by Warrs, plagues, fires, losse of reputation by a universal neglect
of the publique, for the love of a voluptuous & sensual life, which
a vitious Court had brought into credit. I thinke of it with sorrow
& pitty, when I consider of how good & debonaire a nature that
unhappy prince was, what opportunities he had to have made
himselfe the most renouned King, that ever sway'd the British
Scepter; had he ben firme to that Church, for which his Mar-
tyred & Bl: Father suffer'd; & gratefull to Almighty God, who so
miraculously Restor'd him, with so excellent a *Religion* had he
endeavored to owne & propagate it, as he should, not onely for
the good of his Kingdomes, but all the Reformed Churches in
Christendome, now weaken'd, & neere utterly ruind, through our
remissnesse, & suffering them to be supplanted, persecuted &
destroyed; as in *France*, which we tooke no notice of: The Consequence of this time will shew, & I wish it may proceede no

farther: The Emissaries & Instruments of the C. of R: will never rest, 'til they have crush'd the Church of Eng: as knowing that alone able to cope with them: and that they can never answer her fairely, but lie aboundantly open to ⟨irresistible⟩ force of her Arguments, Antiquity, & purity of her doctrine: so that albeit it may move God (for the punishment of a Nation so unworthy) to eclipse againe the profession of her here; & darknesse & superstition prevaile; I am most confident the Doctrine of the *Church of Eng:* will never be extinguish'd, but remaine Visible, though not Eminent, to the consummation of the World: I have innumerable reasons that confirme me in this opinion, which I forbeare to mention here: In the meane time, as to This discourse of his Majestie with Mr. Pepys, & those Papers; as I do exceedingly preferr his Majestie free & ingenuous profession, of what his owne Religion is, beyond all Concealements upon any politique accounts what so ever; so I thinke him of [a] most sincere, and honest nature, one upon whose word, one may relie, & that he makes a Conscience of what he promises, to performe it: In this Confidence I hope, the Church of England may yet subsist; & when it shall please God, to open his Eyes, & turne his heart (for that is peculiarly in the Lords hands) to flourish also: In all events, whatever do become of the C. of Eng: It is certainely of all the Christian Professions on the Earth, the most Primitive, Apostolical, & Excellent:

I returned home this Evening.

15 Being the Kings birth-day, was a solemn Ball at Court; And Musique of Instruments & Voices before the Ball: At the Musique I happen⟨ed⟩ (by accident) to stand the very next to the Queene, & the King, who ta⟨l⟩ked with me about the Musick:

18: The King was now building all that range from East to west by the Court & Garden to the streete, & making a new Chapel for the Queene, whose Lodgings this new building was: as also a new Council Chamber & offices next the South end of the Banqueting-house:

20. I returned home: [21] Next morning againe to *Lond:*

22 I accompanied my Lady Clarendon to her house at Swallow-field in *Berkeshire*, dining by the way at Mr. *Grahams's* Lodge at *Bagshot*: Where his Lady (my excellent & long acquaintance when maide of honour) entertain'd us at a plentifull dinner: The house, new repaired, and capacious of a good

family, stands in a Park: Hence we went to Swallow-fild the
house is after the antient building of honourable gent: houses
where they kept up the antient hospitality: but the Gardens
& Waters as elegant as 'tis possible to make a flat, with art &
Industrie and no meane Expenses, my Lady being so extraordinarily skilld in the flowry part: & the dilligence of my Lord in
the planting: so that I have hardly seene a seate which shews
more toakens of it, then what is here to be found, not onely in
the delicious & rarest fruits of a Garden, but in those innumerable & plentifull furniture of the grounds about the seate of timber trees to the incredible ornament & benefit of the place:
There is one Ortchard of a 1000 Golden & other cider Pepins:
Walks & groves of Elms, Limes, Oake: & other trees: & the
Garden so beset with all manner of sweete shrubbs, as perfumes
the aire marvelously: The distribution also of the Quarters,
Walks, Parterre &c is excellent: The Nurseries, Kitchin-garden,
full of the most desireable plants; two very noble Orangeries
well furnish'd; but above all, The Canale, & fishponds, the one
fed with a white, the other with a black-running water, fed by a
swift & quick river: so well & plentifully stor'd with fish, that for
Pike, Carp, Breame, & Tench; I had never seene any thing
approching it: We had Carps & Pike &c of size fit for the table
of a Prince, every meale, & what added to the delight, the seeing
hundreds taken in the drag, out of which the Cooke standing by,
we pointed what we had most mind to, & had Carps every
meale, that had ben worth at London twenty shill a piece: The
Waters are all flag'd about with Calamus arromaticus; of which
my Lady has hung a Closset, that retaines the smell very perfectly: Also a certaine sweete willow & other exotics: There is to
this a very fine bowling-greene; Meadow, pasture, Wood, in a
word all that can render a Country seate delightfull:

25 The minister preached on 1. *Cor:* 6. ult a very honest &
excellent sermon, after which the holy Sacrament, at which I was
particip⟨a⟩nt: There is also a well furnished library in the house.

26 We return'd to Lond, having ben treated with all sorts of
Cheare, & noble freedom, by that most religious & vertuous
Lady, whom I beseech God to blesse & prosper: She was now
preparing to go for Ireland with her husband; now made Lord
Deputy, & went to this Country house, and antient seate of her
Fathers & family, to set things in order during absence, but

never were good peopl⟨e⟩ & neighbour⟨s⟩ more concern'd, than
all the Country (the poore especialy) for the departure of this
Charitable woman; every body were in teares, & she as unwilling to part from them: There was amongst them a Maiden of
primitive life: The daughter of a poore labouring man who sustain'd her parents (sometimes since dead) by her labour; & has
for many yeares continued a Virgin (though sought by severall
to marriage) & refusing to receive any assistance of the Parish
(besides the little hermitage my Lady gives her rent-free) lives
on foure pence a day which she getts in spinning: She says she
abounds, & can give almes to others, living in strange humility
and contentednesse, without any apparent affectation or singu-
larity; she is continualy working, or praying, or reading; gives a
good account of her knowledge in Religion; Visites the sick; is
not in the least given to talke; is wonderfull modest, & of a
simple, not unseemly behaviour; is of a Comely countenance,
clad very plaine, but cleane & tight; in summ, appeares a *Saint*
of an extraordinary sort, in so religious a life as is seldom met
with in Villages now a daies:

27 I was invited to Sir St: Foxes, with my L. Lieutennant,
where was such a dinner for variety of all things, ⟨as⟩ I had seldome seene, & it was so, for the triall of a Master-Cooke, which
Sir Stephen had recommended to go with his Lordship into
Ireland: There was all the Dainties not onely of the season, but of
what art could add: Venison, & plaine solid Meate, Foule, Baked
& boiled meates; banquet &c in exceeding plenty, & exquisitely
dressed: There also din'd my Lord Ossory & Lady the Duke of
Beauforts daught⟨e⟩r, my Lady Treasurer, Lord Cornbery &c:

28 I went to the R: Society, being the first meeting after our
Summer recesse, & was very full: An Urn full of bones, was presented, for the repository, dug up in an high way, by the repairers
of it: in a field in *Camberwell* in *Surry*: This Urn & cover was
found intire among many others; believed to be truely Roman &
antient: Sir Ri: Bulkeley, described to us a model of a Charriot he
had invented, which it was not possible to overthrow, in whatsoever uneven way it was drawn: giving us a stupendious relation,
of what it had perform'd in that kind; for Ease, expedition, &
Safty: There was onely these inconveniences yet to be remedied;
that it would not containe above one person; That it was ready to
fire every 10 miles, & being plac'd & playing on no fewer than 10

rollers, made so prodigious noise, as was almost intollerable: These particulars the Virtuosi were desir'd to excogitate the remedies, to render the Engine of extraordinary Use: &c:

31 I dind at our greate Lord Chancellors, who us'd me with greate respect: This was the late L: C. Justice Jeofries, who had ben newly the Western Circuite, to trie the Monmoth Conspirators; & had formerly don such severe Justice amongst the obnoxious in Westminster Hall &c for which his Majestie dignified him with creating him first a Baron, & now L. Chancellor: He had some yeares past, ben conversant at Deptford: is of an assur'd & undaunted spirit, & has serv'd the Court Interest upon all the hardiest occasions: [of nature cruell & a slave of this Court.]

I had now accomplish'd the 65t yeare of my Age: Lord teach me to Number my daies so, as to employ their remainder to thy glory onely. Amen:

November 3 I returned home: The *French* persecution of the Protestants, raging with uttmost barbarity, exceeding what the very heathens used: Innumerable persons of the greatest birth, & riches, leaving all their earthly substance & hardly escaping with their lives, dispers'd thro' all the Countries of Europe: The Fr: Tyrant, abrogating the Edicts of Nants &c in favour of them, & without any Cause on the suddaine, demolishing all their Churches, banishing, Imprisoning, sending to the Gallies all the Ministers: plundring the common people, & exposing them to all sorts of barbarous usage, by souldiers sent to ruine & prey upon them; taking away their children; forcing people to the Masse, & then executing them as Relapsers: They burnt the libraries, pillag'd their goods, eate up their filds & sustenance, banish'd or sent to the Gallies the people, & seiz'd on their Estates: There had now ben numbred to passe through *Geneva* onely, from time to time by stealth onely (for all the usual passages were strictly guarded by sea & land) fourty thousand, towards Swisserland: In Holland, Denmark, & all about Germany, were dispersed some hundred thousands besids here in England, where though multitude of all degrees sought for shelter, & wellcome, as distressed Christians & Confessors, they found least encouragement; by a fatality of the times we were fall'n into, & the incharity & indifference of such, as should have embrac'd them: and I pray, it be not laied

to our Charge: The famous Claude fled to Holland: Alex &
severall more came to Lond: & persons of mighty estates came
over who had forsaken all: But France was almost dispeopled,
the bankers so broaken that the Tyrants revenue exceedingly
diminished: Manufacture ceased, & every body there save the
Jesuites &c. abhorring what was don: nor the Papists themselves approving it; what the intention farther is time will
shew, but doubtlesse portending some extraordinary revolution: I was now shew'd the Harangue that the *Bishop* of *Valentia* on Rhone, made in the name of the Cleargie, celebrating
the Fr: King (as if he were a God) for his persecuting the poore
protestants; with this Expression in it: That as his Victories
over Heresy was greater than all the Conquests of Alexander
& Cæsars &c: it was but what was wished in England: & that
God seem'd to raise the French King to this power & magnan-
imous action, that he might be in capacity to assist the doing
of the same here: This paragraph is very bold & remarkable;
severall reflecting on *Æ*: *Ushers Prophecy* as now begun in
France, & approching the orthodox in all other reformed
Churches: &c: One thing was much taken notice of, That the
Gazetts which were still constantly printed twice a weeke, &
informing us what was don all Europ over &c: never all this
time, spake one syllable of this wonderfull proceeding in
France, nor was any Relation of it published by any, save what
private letters & the persecuted fugitives brought: Whence
this silence, I list not to conjecture, but it appeared very
extraordinary in a Protestant Countrie, that we should know
nothing of what Protestants suffered &c: whilst greate Collections were made for them in forraine places more hospitable &
Christian to appearance.

5 It being an extraordinary wett morning, & I indisposed by a
very greate rheume, I could not go to Church this day, to my
greate sorrow, it being the first Gunpouder conspiracy Anniversary, that had ben kept now this 80 yeares, under a Prince of the
Roman Religion: Bonfires forbidden &c: What dos this portend?

9 Began the Parliament; The King in his Speech requiring
continuance of a standing force in stead of a *Militia*, & indemnity & dispensation to Popish Officers from the Test; Demands
very unexpected & unpleasing to the Commons; He also

requir'd a Supply of Revenue, which they granted; but returned no thanks to the King for his Speech 'til farther consideration:

10 I dined at my L. *Arch-Bishops* of *York*, w⟨h⟩ere were The *Bishops* of *London*, & St. *Asaph* &c:

12 The Commons postpon'd the finishing the bill for the Supply, to consider of the Test, & popish Officers: this was carried but by one voice:

14 They voted an Addresse to the King about it:

I dined at Lambeth my Lord *Arch Bish:* carrying me with him in his barge: there were my L: Deputy of Ireland: The *Bishops* of Ely, & St. Asaph, Dr. Sherlock & other divines, Sir William *Hayward*, Sir Paule Rycot &c: The Dinner was for cheere extraordinary.

I returned home this Evening:

15 This day 65 years, was I Baptized: &c: Blessed be God:

20 Was the Parliament adjourn'd to ffeb: Severall both of Lords & Commons, excepting against some passage of his Majesties Speech, relating to the Test, & continuance of Popish Officers in Command: This was a greate surprize to a Parliament, which people believed would have complied in all things:

Popish pamphlets & Pictures sold publiqly: no books or answers against them appearing &c: [till long after:]

21 I returned home, having ben at a Triall of my La: Tukes Cause in Chancery the morning, with doubtfull successe; and also resigned my Trust for the Composing of a difference betweene Mr. Thayre & his Wife:

December 3d: I din'd at Lord *Sunderlands*, where din'd L: *Chancellor*, L: *Midleton*, *Abergavenie* &c: 4th Lord *Sunderland* was declar'd President of the Counsel, & yet to hold his *Secretaries* place &c: The forces disposed into severall quarters through the Kingdome, are very insolent, upon which greate Complaints: Lord *Brandon* (tried-for the late conspiracy) condemn'd & pardoned; so was L: Grey his accuser: & wittnesse: Persecution in France raging: The French insolently visite our Vessels, & take away the fugitive protestants: Some escape hidden in barills &c:

5 I return'd home:

6 Our Viccar & Curate prosecuted their former subjects: The H: Sacrament follow'd, of which I participated: The Lord make me Thankfull & carefull:

10 I went to *Greenewich* being put into the new Commission of Sewers, where I tooke the Oathes of Alegeance &c: din'd with the Commissioners:

13 Dr. Patric Deane of *Peterborow* preached at W:hall before the Princesse of Denmark, who since his Majestie came to the Crown, allways sate in the Kings Closset, (and had the same bowings & Ceremonies applied to the place where she was, as if his Majestie had ben there in person) on 1. Tim: 3. 9:

15 Dining at Mr. *Pepyss* Secretary of the Admiral⟨ty⟩, & still president of our Society: Dr. *Slayer* shew'd us an Experiment of a wonderfull nature; pouring first a very cold liquor into a Matras, & superfusing on it another (to appearance) cold & cleare liquor also, it first producd a white clowd, then boiling, divers Corruscations & actual flames of fire mingled with the liquor, which being a little shaken together fixed divers sunns & starrs of real fire perfectly globular upon the walls of the Glasse to our greate astonishment, & which there stuck like so many Constellations burning most vehemently, & exceedingly resembling starrs & heavenly bodys, & that for a long space: It seem'd to exhibite a Theorie of the eduction of light out of the *Chäos*, & the fixing or gathering of the universal light, into luminous bodys: This matter of *Phosphorus*, was made out of human blood & Urine, elucidating the Vital flame or heate in Animal bodys: a very noble Experiment:

16 I accompanied my L: Lieutennant as far as St. Albans, there going out of Towne with him neere 200 Coaches, of all the Greate Officers & Nobilitie:

17 Next morning taking leave, I return'd to Lond.

18 I dind at the greate entertainement his Majestie gave the Venetian Ambassadors Signors *Zenno* & *Justiniani*, accompanied with 10 more Noble *Venetians* of their most illustrious families *Cornaro, Maccenigo* &c, who came to Congratulate their Majesties coming to the Crowne &c: The dinner was one of the most magnificent & plentifull that I have ever seene, at 4 severall Tables with Music, Trumpets, Ketle-drums &c which sounded upon a whistle at every health: The banquet was 12 vast Chargers pild up so high, as those who sat one against another could hardly see one another, of these Sweetemeates which doub⟨t⟩lesse were some dayes piling up in that exquisite manner, the Ambassadors touched not, but leaving them to the Spectators who came in

Curiosity to see the dinner, &c were exceedingly pleas'd to see in what a moment of time, all that curious work was demolish'd, & the Comfitures &c voided & table clear'd: Thus his Majestie entertain'd them 3 dayes, which (for the table onely) cost him 600 pounds as the Clerk of the Greene-Cloth Sir W: Boreman, assur'd me: Dinner ended, I saw their procession or Cavalcade to W:hall, inumerable Coaches attending: The 2 Ambassadors had 4. Coaches of their owne & 50 footemen, as I remember, besides other Equipage as splended as the occasion would permitt, the Court being still in mourning, Thence I went to the Audience which they had in the Queenes presence Chamber: The ban-queting-house being full of goods & furniture til the Galleries on the Garden side, Council Chamber & new Chapell, were fin-ish'd, now in building: They went to their Audience in those plaine black Gownes, [& Caps] which they constantly weare in the Citty of Venice: I was invited to have accompanied the two Ambassadors in their Coach to supper that night, returning now to their owne Lodgings, as no longer at the Kings expense, but being weary, I excus'd my selfe:

19 My Lord Tressurer made me to dine with him, where I came acquainted with Monsieur *Barillon*, the French Ambas-sador, a learned & crafty Advocate:

20 Dr. *Turner* bro: to Bishop of Ely, & sometime Tutor to my Son, preached at W.hall on 8: *Mar:* 38: concerning the submission of Christians to their persecutors, in which were some passages indiscreete enough, considering the time, & the rage of the inhumane French Tyrant against the poore protestants:

22 Our pattent for executing the Office of the Lord Privy-Seale, during the absence of the L: Lieutennant of Ireland, being this day sealed by the L: Chancellor: We went afterwards to St. *Jame's*, where the Court then was, upon occasion of the building at White-hall; where his Majestie deliverd *The Seale* to My L: *Tiveat* & myselfe (the other Commissioner being not come) and then, gave us his hande to kisse: There was the 2 *Venetian Ambassadors* & a world of Company, amongst the rest, The first *Popes Nuntio* Signor that had ever ben in England since the Reformation; so wonderfully were things chang'd, to the univer-sal jealosie &c:

24 We were all three Commissioners sworn on our knees by the Cleark of the Crowne before my Lord Chancellor, 3, severall

Oathes, Allegeance, Supremacy, & the oath belonging to the
L: Privy-Seale, which we onely tooke standing: After which the
L. Chancellor invited us all to dinner; but it being Christmas
Eve, we desir'd to be excus'd; at 3 in the afternoone intending to
Seale divers things which lay ready at the Office: So attended by
three of the Clearks of the Signet, we met, & sealed; amongst
other things, one was a Pardon to *West*, who being privy to the
late Conspiricy, had reveald the Complices, to save his owne
neck: There was also another pardon, & two Indenizations: & so
agreeing to a fortnights vaccation, I return'd home to my house:

31 Recollecting the passages of the yeare past [I] made up
Accompts, humbly besought Almighty God, to pardon those
my sinns, which had provok'd him to discomposse my sorrowfull
family, that he would accept of our humiliation, & in his good
time restore comforte to it: I also blesse God for all his unde-
served mercys & preservations, beging the continuance of his
grace & preservation: The winter had hitherto ben extraordinarily wett, & mild:

1 *Jan: 1685/6*. Imploring the continuance of Gods Mercy, &
providential care for the yeare now entred, I went to the
publique Devotions: some neighbours din'd with us. The Deane
of the Chapell, & Clerk of the Closset put out, viz. Bishop of
Lond: and & Rochester & Durham put in their places; They
had opposed the Tolleration intended, &c & shew'd a worthy
zeale for the reformed religion established:

3 Our *Viccar* proceeded: The holy Communion follow'd, at
which I participated, in order to the *Test*, as a Commissioner of
the Sewers, by a late Commission now renew'd &c: The *Curat*
preach'd on 1. *Joh:* 4. 9, drowsinesse surprizing me:

6 I went to Lond: to our Office, din'd with the L. Arch-Bish:
of Yorke, where was Peter-Walsh that Romish Priest, who was
so well known for his moderation; professing the Ch: of England to be a true member of the Catholique Church; he is used
to go to our publique prayers without scrupule, did not acknowledge the Popes Infallibility, & onely primacy of Order &c. I
returned this Evening:

19 I went to Lond: pass'd the Privie Seale amongst others, the
Creation of Mrs. *Sidly* (concubine to . . .) Countesse of Dorchester, which 'tis certaine the Queene tooke very grievously: so as
for two dinners, standing neere her, she hardly eate one morsel,

nor spake one word to the King, or to any about her, who at all other times was us'd to be extreamely pleasant, full of discourse & good humor: The Roman Cath: were also very angrie, because the⟨y⟩ had so long valu'd the Sanctite of their Religion & Proselytes &c:

Dryden the famous play-poet & his two sonns, & Mrs. *Nelle* (Misse to the late . . .) were said to go to Masse; & such purchases were no greate losse to the Church. This night was burnt to the Ground my Lord Montagues Palace in Bloom⟨s⟩bery; than which for Painting & furniture, there was nothing more glorious in England: This happen'd by the negligence of a servant, airing (as they call it) some of the goods by the fire, in a moist season; for indeede so wett & mild a Winter had scarce ben ever seene in mans memory:

At this *Seale* there also passed, the creation of Sir *H: Walgrave* to be a Lord: He had married one of the Kings natural Daughters, begotten on Mrs. *Churchil*: These two Seales, my Bro: Commissioners pass'd in the morning before I came to Towne, at which I was not at all displeas'd; We likewise pass'd privy seales for 276000 pounds upon severall accounts, Pensions, Guards, Wardrobes, Privie purse &c, besids divers Pardons: & one more which I must not forget (& which by providence, I was not present at) one Mr. *Lytcott*, to be Secretarie to the Ambassador to *Rome*: we being three Commissioners [any] two were a *Quorum*.

24 Our *Viccar* proceeded to the Application: & the Curate to his former text: Unheard of Cruelties to the persecuted protestants of France, such as hardly any age has don the like even amongst the pagans.

It began to freeze sharply:

Feb: 3 A Seale: 6: Being his Majesties day, on which he began his Reigne; By Order of Council, it was to be solemniz'd with a particular Office, & sermon, which the Bis: of *Ely* preached at W:hall: on 11: *Numbers*: 12: a Court-*Oration*, upon the Regal Office &c: It was much wonder'd at; that this day which was that of his late Majesties death, should be kept as festival, & not the day of the present Kings Coronation: It is said, that it had formerly ben the costome, though not 'til now, since the Reigne of K. James. 1.

7 The Dutchesse of *Munmoth* being in the same seate with me, appeared with a very sad & afflicted countenance:

8 I tooke the Test, in *Westminster Hall* before the *L: C. Justice* &c: [I now came to Lodge in White hall, in the Lord privy-seals Lodging]

12 My greate Cause was heard by my Lord Chancellor, who granted me a Rehearing: I had 6 Eminent Lawyers, my Antagonists 3. whereof one the smoth tong'd Soliciter, whom my Lord Chancellor reprov'd in greate passion for a very small occasion: Blessed be God for his greate goodnesse to me this day:

March 1 Came Sir Gilb: Gerrard to treate with me about his sonns marying my Daughter *Susanna*; The father being obnoxious, & in some suspicion & displeasure of the King, I would receive no proposal, 'til his Majestie had given me leave, which he was pleas'd to do: but after severall meetings, we brake off, upon his not being willing to secure any thing competant for my daughter(s) Children: besides that I found his estate to be most of it in the Coale-pits as far as N. Castle, & leases from the *Bishop* of Durrham, who had power to make concurrent Leases with other difficulties, so as we did not proceede to any conclusion:

7 Dr. Frampton [2d sermon] Bish: of Glocester on 44: Psal: 17: 18. 19: shewing the severall afflictions of the Church of Christ, from the primitives to this day, and her Constancy & deliverance, applyed exceedingly to the present conjuncture, when many were wavering in their minds, & greate temptations appearing, through the favour the Papists now found; so as the people were full of jealosies, & discouragement; The Bish: magnified the Ch: of England exhorting to constancy & perseverance, &c:

I din'd at the Lord *Treasurers*.

10: At Council of the R: Society, about disposing of Dr. Rays book of fishes, which was printed at the charge of the Society &c: I was at morning Pr: but heard not the sermon:

11 I din'd at Mr. Pepys Secretary of the Admiralty:

12 There was a doquett to be sealed importing a Lease of 21 yeares to one Hall, who styled himselfe his Majesties Printer (& lately turn'd Papist) for the printing Missals, Offices, Lives of Saints, Portals, Primers &c: books expressly forbidden to be printed or sold, &c by divers Acts of Parliament: which I refused to put the seale to, & made my exceptions against, so it was laied by:

14 The Bish: of Bath & Wells[1] preach'd on 6: Joh: 17: (being the Gospel of the day) in a most excellent & pathetical

1 Ken.

discourse, ⟨after⟩ he had recommended the duty of fasting, & other penetential dutys; he exhorted to Constancy to the protestant religion, detestation of the French unheard of Cruelty, & stirring up to a liberal contribution: This sermon was the more acceptable, as it was unexpected, from a Bish: who had gon through the censure of being inclin'd to popery; the contrary whereoff no man could more shew, as ⟨indeede⟩ did all our Bishops, to the disabusing & reproch of all their delators, none more zealous against popery than they:

16 I was at the [review of the] Army about Lond: which was in Hide-parke, the whole consisting of about 6000: horse & foote in excellent order &c: his Majestie & an infinity of people present:

17 I went to my house in the Country, refusing to be present at what was to passe the next day at the Privy-Seale:

This morning preached at W:hall, Dr. *Tenison* on 2: *Tim:* 3. 4. in an incomparable discourse:

29 I return'd home:

The Duke of Northumberland (a Natural sonn of the late King, by the Dutchesse of *Cleaveland*, an impudent woman) marrying very meanely, with the helpe of his bro: *Grafton*, attempted to spirit away his Wife &c:

A Briefe was read in all the Churches for Relieving the French Protestants who came here for protection, from the unheard-off, cruelties of their King:

Aprill 15 The Arch-Bish: of Yorke now died of the small-pox, aged 62 yeares, a Corpulent man; My special loving Friend, & whilst our Bish: of *Rochester* (from whence he was translated) my excellent Neighbour, an unexpressible losse to the whole Church, & that Province especialy, he being a learned, Wise, stoute, and most worthy Prelate; so as I looke on this as a greate stroke to the poore Church of England now in this defecting period:

18 Afternoone I went to Camberwell to visite *Dr. Par*: but sate so inconveniently at Church, that I could very hardly heare his Text, which was 5. *Heb:* 9: After sermon I went to the Doctors house, where he shew'd me The life and Letters of the late learned Primate of *Armagh*, *Usher*, and among them that letter of *Bish: Bramhals* to the Primate, giving notice of the popish practises to pervert this nation, by sending an hundred priests &c into England, who were to conforme themselves to all Sectaries,

and Conditions for the more easily dispersing their doctrine amongst us: This Letter was the cause of the whole Impressions being seiz'd on, upon pretence, that it was a political or historical account, of things, not relating to Theologie, though it had ben licenc'd by the Bish: &c: which plainely shewe'd what an Interest the Popish now had, that a Protestant Booke, containing the life, & letters of so eminent a man was not to be publish'd. There were also many letters to & from most of the learned persons his correspondents in Europ: but The Booke will, (I doubt not) struggle through this unjust impediment.

20 To Lond: a seale—& to see little Godolphin now, I blesse God, in an hope full way of Escape: Severall Judges put out, & new complying ones put in.

24 I returned home, found my Coach-man dangerously ill of vomiting greate quantities of blood:

25 St. *Mark*: this day was the Briefe for a collection of reliefe to the Persecuted French Protestants (so cruely, barbarously & inhumanly oppressed, without any thing laied to their charge) read in our Church; but which had ben so long expected, & difficulty at last procur'd to be publish'd, the interest of the French Ambassador & cruel papists obstructing it:

May 1. Being the day the foefees for the poore of Deptford met, our Viccar (according to custom) preached, the Text, as on the last Sunday, with little alteration:

Hitherto a very wett Spring.

5 To Lond: There being a Seale, it was feared we should be required to passe a Doquett, Dispensing with Dr. Obadia Walker & 4 more, whereoff one an Apostate Curate at Putney, the other Master of University Coll: Ox: to hold their Masterships, fellowships & Cures, & keepe pub: schooles & enjoy all former emoluments &c. notwithstanding they no more frequented, or used the pub: formes of Prayers, or Communion with the Church of England, or tooke the Test, & oathes of Allegeance & Supremacy, contrary to 20 Acts of Parliaments &c: which Dispensation being likewise repugnant to his Majesties owne gracious declaration at the begining of his Reigne, gave umbrage (as well it might) to every good Protestant: nor could we safely have passed it under the Privy-Seale: wherefore it was don by Immediate warrant, sign'd by Mr. Soliciter &c at which I was not a little glad: This *Walker* was

a learned person, of a munkish life, to whose Tuition I had more than 30 years since, recommended the sonns of my worthy friend *Mr. Hyldiard* of Horsley in Surry: believing him to be far from what he proved, an hypocritical concealed papist, by which he perverted the Eldest son of Mr. *Hyldyard*, Sir *Ed. Hales's* eld: son & severall more [&] to the greate disturbance of the whole nation, as well as the University, as by his now publique defection appeared: All engines being now at worke to bring in popery amaine, which God in mercy prevent:

This day was burnt, in the old Exchange, by the publique Hangman, a booke, (supposed to be written by the famous Monsieur Claude) relating the horrid massacres & barbarous proceedings of the Fr: King against his Protestant subjects, without any refutation, that might convince it of any thing false: so mighty a power & ascendent here, had the French Ambassador: doubtlesse in greate Indignation at the pious & truly generous Charity of all the Nation, for the reliefe of those miserable sufferers, who came over for shelter:

About this time also, The Duke of Savoy, instigated by the Fr: King to exterpate the Protestants of *Piemont*, slew many thousands of those innocent people, so as there seemed to be a universal designe to destroy all that would not Masse it, thro⟨ugh⟩ out Europ, as they had power, *quod avertat D.O.M.*

I procur'd of my L. president of the Council, the nomination of a son of Mrs. Cock, a Widdow (formerly living plentifully, now falln to want) to be chosen into the Charter-house Schoole, which would be a competent subsistence for him:

7 I return'd home:

8 Died my sick Coachman of his feavor, to my greate griefe, being a very honest, faithfull servant: I beseech the Lord, to take-off his afflicting hand, in his good time.

9 The Duke of Savoy, instigated by the French ⟨king⟩, put to the sword many of his protestant subjects: No faith in Princes.

12 To Lond: Memorand, I refus'd to put the P: Seale to Dr. Walker⟨s⟩ licence for the printing & publishing divers Popish Books &c: of which I complain'd both to my L: of Canterbury (whom I went to advise with, which was in the Council-chamber) and to my Lord Treasurer that evening at his lodging: My Lord of Cantorburies advise was that I should follow my owne

Conscience therein; my L: Tressurer, that if in Conscience I could dispence with it; for any other hazard, he believed there was none: Notwithstanding which I persisted not to do it:

16 A stranger on: 2: *Zeph:* 1. 2. 3. Afternoone, on: 2. *Tit:* 11. 12 &c: both practical sermons exhorting to Repentance upon prospect of the ruines threatning the Church, & drawing on for our prodigious Ingratitude, & doubtlesse Never was England so perverted, through an almost universal face of prophanesse, perjury, luxurie, unjustice, violence, hypocrisie, Atheisme, & dissolution: A kingdome & people so obliged to God, for its long prosperity, both in Church & state: so signaly delivered, and preserved: & now threatn'd to be destroyed, by our owne folly & wickednesse: How strangely is this nation fallen from its antient zeale & Integritie! ô unhappy, unthankfull people!

June 2 To Lond: passing divers Pardons & other doquetts:

Such stormes, ⟨raine⟩ & foule weather hardly ever know⟨n⟩ at this season: The Camp now on Hounslo-Heath forc'd for sicknesse and other inconveniences of Weather to retire to quarters:

9 To Lond: a Seale, most pardons, & discharges, of Knight Baronets fees; which having ben pass'd over for so many yeares, did greately dissoblige several families who had serv'd his Majestie.— The Camp now at *Brainford* [Hounslow] after exceeding ⟨wet⟩ & stormy weather, now as excessively hott; many grew sick: greate feasting there, especialy in my L: Dunbarton⟨s⟩ quarters: many jealosies & discourse what the meaning of this incampment of an army should be:—L: Terconell gon to Ireland with greate powers & commissions—giving as much cause of talke as the other: especialy 19 new Pr: Councelors being now made & Judges, among which but three protestants: & Terconell made [L.] Generall: New-Judges also here, among which *Milton* a papist, & bro: to the Milton who wrot for the Regicides, who presum'd to take his place, without passing the Test:—Scotland, refuse to grant Liberty of Masse to the Papists in Scotland:—The French persecution more inhumane than ever &c: The Protestants in Savoy, successfully resist the French Dragoons, perfidiously murdering them.— The booke written by *Monsieur Claude* to informe the world of the cruel persecution in France: Translated here burnt by the hang man, so greate was the Interest of the Fr: Ambassador, as was said: It seem'd to relate onely matter of fact, very modestly: & was thought a severe treatement; his

Majestie having both given protection, & reliefe to the Refugies: It was thought hard, the people should not know for what & to whom they gave so bountifully.—The Kings chiefe physitian in Scotland, Apostatizing from the protestant Religion, dos of his owne accord publique Recantation at Edenbrugh.—

11 I went to see Midletons—receptacle of Waters at the New River: & the new Spà wells neere it.

24 The New [very] young L. C. Justice Herbert, declared these positions on the bench for Laws viz:

at which every body were astonished; by which the Test was abolished. Times of great Jealosies, where these proceedings would end.

27 Our Viccar proceeded on his former Text: The afternoone wet, Dr. Bohune read the Office & a sermon (to the family) out of Dr. Barrow:

I had this day ben married 39 yeares: Blessed be God for all his mercys.

July: 3 To Lond: 4: Dr. Megot preach'd on & I received the holy Sacrament in St. Georges Chapell:[1] returning next day to Lond: my buisinesse being with my L: Godolphin &c: By the way saw the Camp, was in the Generals Tent &c.

6 I supp'd with the Countesse of Rochester where was also the Dutchesse of Bouckingham & *Madame de Governè* whose daughter was married to the Marq(u)esse of Halifax's son. She made me a Character of the French King, & Dauphine, & of the Persecution: That they kept much of the cruelties from the Kings knowledge: That the Dauphine was so afraid of his Father, that he durst let nothing appeare of his sentiments; that he hated letters and Priests, spent his time in hunting, & seem'd to take notice of nothing that passed &c:

This Lady of a greate family & fortune, was now fled for refuge hither:

12 I went to visite Dr. Godolphin vice-Provost of Eton, & dined with him in the Colledge: among the Fellows: It is an admirable foundation:

13 I return'd to Lond: Note, that standing by the Queene at Basset (Cards) I observ'd that she was exceedingly concern'd for

1 At Windsor, where the court was at this time.

the losse of 80 pounds: her outward affability much changed to statelinesse &c since she has ben exalted:

The season was very rainy, & inconvenient for the Camps: his Majestie cherefull:

14 Was sealed at our Office the Constitution of certaine Commissioners to take upon them the full power of all Ecclesiastical Affaires, in as unlimited a manner, or rather greater, than the late High-Commission Court, abbrogated by Parliament: for it had not onely faculty to Inspect & Visite all Bishops diocesses, but to change what lawes & statutes they shold think fit to alter, among the Colledges, though founded by private men; to punish [suspend] fine &c give Oathes, call witnesses, but the maine drift was to ⟨suppresse⟩ zealous Preachers &c—In summ, it was the whole power of Viccar General, note the Consequence—The Commissioners were of the Cleargy, the *A Bish of Cant: Bishops of Duresme*, *Rochester*:—of the Temporal: L: Tressurer, Chancellor (who alone was ever to be of the quorum) Chiefe Justice, L: President:

19 To Lond: to a Seale. Came this morning to visie me Sir W: Godolphin, L. Sylvius: Mrs. Boscawen; Dr. Tenison, with divers Ladys & Gent: After dinner, I went to Lond, to a *Seale*. &c. Return'd 21: Evening, having ben at the R: Society, where was a Wind Gun brought & tried, which first shot a bullet with a powder Charge, & then discharged 4 severall times with bullets, by the wind onely, every shoote at competent distance piercing a thick board: The Wind-Chamber was fastned to the barrill through the stock, with Valves to every ⟨charge⟩ so as they went off 4 successive times: I⟨t⟩ was a very curious piece, made at Amsterdam, not bigger than a pretty Birding piece: Note, that the drawing up of the Cock alone ⟨admitted⟩ so much aire into a small receptacle at the britch of the piece out of the Chamber or magazine of aire underneath as suffic'd for a charge, which was exploded by pulling downe the Cock by the Triccker: (a) the wind Chamber [of brasse], to scrue into the barrell thro the stock, at (b): note, that it was fill'd with an [aire] pumpe.

27 This day was bound Apprentice to me, & serve as a Gardner, *Jonathan Mosse*, to serve from 24 June 1686: to 24 June-92, being six yeares:

28 I went to Lond, to a Seale, return'd by the R: Society: having seen the ⟨e⟩xperiment of a bullet droven out of a gun, by the

external aire, the barill of the piece having a perforation by which the aire within it was sucked out by the Boylean pump, the two extreames shut close with corks: Then one of the ends, viz, the breech part suddainly opned, the aire in the roome rushed in with that extreame ⟨swiftnesse⟩ as forced out the bullet to a greate distance:

Aug: ⟨1⟩ Our Viccar proceeded on his Text: The holy *Comm:* follow'd at which I participated:

Afternoone the Curate on 6 *Gal:* 7: Sleepe surpriz'd me: Came my Lady Tuke to be some time with us, being in an ill state of health.

4 I went to *Lond*, to a seale, din'd at Signor *Verrios* the famous Italian Painter, & now settled in his Majesties Garden of St. ⟨James's⟩, which he had made now a very delicious Paradise: I return'd in the Evening:

8 Our Viccar being gon to dispose of his country living in Rutlandshire, & now having an addition of St. Dunst: East, given him by the Arch Bishop of Cant: Dr. *Bohune* supplied his place here, preaching on 14: Rom: 17: In the Afternoone a young Stranger on: 4: *John*: 22: I went to visite the *Marquis de Ruvignie* now my Neighbour at Greenewich, he had ⟨been⟩ 'til this cruel persecution in France (whence he was now retir'd) the Deputy of all the Protestants of that Kingdome in the Parliament of Paris, & severall times Ambassador in this & other Courts; a Person of greate Learning & experience:

Sept: 1 to Lond: There was nothing at our Office ready to passe the Seale, so I immediately returned home.

8. I went to Lond: to a Seale: The Bish: of Lond was on Monday suspended on pretence of not silencing Dr. Sharp of St. Giles's, for something of a sermon, in which he zealously reprov'd the Doctrine of the R.C. The Bish: having consulted the Civilians, who told him, he could not by any Law proceede against Dr. Sharp, without producing wittnesses, & impleading according to forme &c: But it was over-ruled by my L: Chancelor & the Bishop sentenc'd, without so much as being heard to any purpose: which was thought a very extraordinary way of proceeding, & universaly resented; & so much the rather, for that 2 Bish: Durham, & Rochester, sitting in the Commission, & giving their suffrages: The AB: of Cant: refusing to sit amongst them: What the issue of this will be, Time will shew:

12 Both our *Viccar* & *Curate*, preached on their former subject:

Budâ now taken from the Turks; A forme of Thanksgiving was ordered to be used in the (as yet remaining) protestant Chapells, & Church of White-hall & Winsor:

The K. of Denmark, was now besieging Hambrow: no doubt but by the French contrivance, to embroile the protestant princes in a new warr, that Holland &c being ingag'd, matter for new quarrell might arise: The unheard persecution against the poore Prot: still raging more than ever:

22 To Lond, to a Seale, return'd that Evening: My deare Bro: came from Wotton to visite me. The Dane Troops retire from Hambrow, The Protestant Princes appearing for their succor, & the Emperor sending his Minatories to the K: of *Denmark*, & also requiring the Restauration of the D: of Sax-Gottorp: thus it pleas'd God to defeate the French designes, which was evidently to kindle a new warr:

25 Receiving a Letter from the Secretary of my Lord President; that the two Bishops Elect Oxford & Chester could not have the Royal assent for the *Conge d'elire* without a privy Seale: I made a step to Lond: & return'd immediately:

28 My Brother went home: My La: Tuke (who had ben most of this summer with us [for her health]) went away.

30 To Lond, a Seale; little buisinesse: The King returned from Windsor to White-hall. I went home in the Evening:

October 3 Our *Viccar* proceeded as before: Communion follow'd, I received: Blessed be God: Curate of *Grenewich* Afternoone: 5. *Eccl:* 1:

14: His Majesties Birth day, I was at his Majesties rising in his Bed-Chamber: Afterwards in the [Hide] Parke where his Majesties 4: Comp: of Guards were drawn up: Such horse & men as could not be braver: The Officers &c: wonderfully rich & gallant: They did not head their troops, but their next officers; the Colonels &c: being on Horse ⟨back⟩ by the King, whilst they marched: The Ladys not lesse splendid at Court, where was a Ball that night; but small appearance of qualitie: This day all the shops both in Citty & suburbs shut up, and kept as solemnly as any holy-day: Bone-fires at night in Westminster &c: but forbidden in the Citty:

17 Dr. *Patric* Deane of *Peterborow* preach'd at Co: Garden Ch: on 5: *Eph:* 18. 19:

In the Evening I went to prayers at W:Hall:

I visited my L: Chiefe Justice of Ireland, with whom I had long & private discourse concerning the Miserable condition that Kingdome was like to be ⟨in⟩ if Tyrconnells Counsels should prevaile at Court: I also waited on the Countesse of Clancartie, & return'd home on [18] Moneday, St. *Lukes* Day.

22 To Lond: the next day with my Lady the Countesse of Sunderland, I went [23] to Cranburne, a Lodge & walke of my Lord Godolphins, in Windsor parke: there was one roome in the house, spared in the pulling-downe the old one, because the late Dutchesse of York, was borne in it, the rest was build & added to it by Sir Geo: Carteret, Tressurer of the Navy: & since the whole purchased by my Lord Godolphin, who spake to me to go see it, and advise what trees were fit to be cut downe, to improve the dwelling, it being invironed with old rotten pollards, which corrupt the aire: It stands on a knowle, which though insensibly rising, gives it a prospect over the keepe of Windsore, which is about three miles north-east of it: The ground is clayy & moist, the water stark nought: The Park is pretty; The house tollerable & gardens convenient: after dinner we came back to Lond, having 2 Coaches both going and coming, of 6 horses a-piece, which we changed at Hounslow:

29 Was a Triumphant shew of the Lord Major, both by land & water with much solemnity, when yet his power was so deminish'd, by the losse of their former charter:

31 Was my Birth-day, which I kept fast: in order to my receiving the holy Sacrament on [November 1] the next day, which I did at St. James's Chapel: It being the 66t yeare of my age; dining at Sir William Godolphins; after I had heard Mr. Branston (grand-son of the late Judge) preach excellently on 15. Rom: 1. before the Princesse of Denmark at White-hall: Thence I went [2] to visite the Countesse of Clancartie & the 3d home, [4] The next day dined with us the Countesse of Sunderland & other company: whom I left to waite on my Lord Tressurer at the Treasury Chamber about my long processe, where appear'd against me the Attorney Generall; but my Cause was comitted to Referrees:

5 I went to St. *Martines* in the Morning, where preached Dr. Birch on 16 *Joh:* 2 very boldly, Laying open the wiccked stratagemms, & bloudy proceedings of the Papists in that devlish

conspiracy: a more pertinent discourse could not be: In the afternoone I heard Dr. *Tillotson* in Lincolns-In Chapell on the same Text, but more cautiously: I din'd at the Countesse of Clancarties:

16 I went with part of my family to passe the melancholy winter in Lond: at my sonns house in Arundel Buildings:

17 I was at the Seale: In the afternoone I went to Gressham Coll: where was shew'd the *pineal glandule* taken out of a mans head, petrified, on which the *Cartesians* fell to reasoning about it:

26 I din'ed at my L. Chancelors, where being 3 other Serjants at Law, after dinner being cherefull & free, they told their severall stories, how long they had detained their clients in tedious processes, by their tricks, as [if] so many highway thieves should have met & discovered the severall purses they had taken: This they made but a jeast of: but God is not mocked:

December 2 At white-hall *Dr. Patric*: on: 2. *Heb:* 3. 4. as I remember: The holy Sacrament to the household, among whom I received: Dr. *Tenison* at St. *Martins* on: 6. *Gal:* 14:

5 I dind at my Lady *Arlingtons* Groome of the Stole to the Q. Dowager at Somerset-house, where dined Divers French Noble men driven out of their Country by the Persecution: In the Afternoone I went to the French-Church in the Savoy, where a young man preached on: 26. *Act:* 29 Concerning *Paules* bonds, & Apologie before Agrippa, much relating to the Persecution &c: & encouraging the Sufferers: &c:

16 I carried the Countesse of Sunderland to see the rarities of one Mr. Charleton at the Middle Temple, who shewed us such a Collection of Miniatures, Drawings, Shells, Insects, Medailes, & natural things, Animals whereoff divers were kept in glasses of Sp: of wine, I think an hundred, besids, Minerals, precious stones, vessels & curiosities in Amber, Achat, chrystal &c: as I had never in all my Travells abroad seene any either of private Gent: or Princes exceede it; all being very perfect & rare in their kind, espec⟨i⟩aly his booke of Birds, Fish: flowers, shells &c drawn & miniatured to the life, he told us that one book stood him in 300 pounds: it was painted by that excellent workeman whom the late Gastion duke of Orleans emploied: This Gent:'s whole Collection (gathered by himselfe travelling most parte of Europe) is estimated at 8000 pounds: He seem'd a Modest and obliging person:

This Evening I made a step to my house in the Country, where I stayed some dayes:

Jan 3 A Seale to confirme a gift of 4000 pounds per ann for 99 years to L. Tressurer out of the post office, and 1700 per Ann for ever out of L. Greys Estate—

Now was there another change of that greate Officer The *L. Treasurer*: It being now againe put into Commission, two professed Papist(s) among the rest, viz, the Lord *Bellasis* & Dover, joyned with the old ones, L: *Godolphin*, Sir *S. Fox*: and Sir J. Earnley:

5 The French K. now sayd to be healed or rather patch'd up of the fistula in *Ano*, for which he had ben severall times cutt: &c: The persecution still raging:

TOWARDS REVOLUTION
(1687–1688)

* I WAS TO heare the Musique of the Italians in the new Chapel, now first of all opned at White-hall publiquely for the Popish Service: Nothing can be finer than the magnificent Marble work & Architecture at the End, where are 4 statues representing st. Joh: st. Petre, st. Paule, & the Church, statues in white marble, the worke of Mr. Gibbons, with all the carving & Pillars of exquisite art & greate cost: The history or Altar piece is the Salutation, The Volto, in *fresca*, the Asumption of the blessed Virgin according to their Traditions with our B: Saviour, & a world of figures, painted by *Verio*. The Thrones where the K. & Q: sits is very glorious in a Closset above just opposite to the Altar: Here we saw the Bishop in his Miter, & rich Copes, with 6 or 7: Jesuits & others in Rich Copes richly habited, often taking off, & putting on the Bishops Miter, who sate in a Chaire with Armes pontificaly, was adored, & censed by 3 Jesuits in their Copes, then he went to the Altar & made divers Cringes there, censing the Images, & glorious Tabernacle placed upon the Altar, & now & then changing place; The Crosier (which was of silver) put into his hand, with a world of mysterious Ceremony the Musique pla⟨y⟩ing & singing: & so I came away: not believing I should ever have lived to see such things in the K. of Englands palace, after it had pleas'd God to inlighten this nation; but our greate sinn, has (for the present) Eclips'd the Blessing, which I hope he will in mercy & his good time restore to its purity. This was on the 29 of December:

Little appearance of any Winter as yet:

17 We had a Private Seale: & I open'd my buisinesse againe to my L. Godolphin, now againe made one of the Lords Commissioners of the Treasury; My Lord of Rochester being layd aside:

Greate expectations of severall greate-mens declaring themselves Papists: and L: Tyrconell gon to succeede my Lord Lieutennant in Ireland, to the astonishment of all sober men, & to the evident ruine of the Protestants in that Kingdome, as well as of its greate Improvement: Much discourse that all the White-staff-Officers and others should be dismissed for adhering to their Religion: Popish Justices of Peace established in all Counties of the meanest of the people: Judges ignorant of the Law, and perverting it: so furiously does the Jesuite drive, & even compell Princes to violent courses, & distruction of an excellent Government both in Church & State: God of his infinite mercy open our Eyes, & turne our hearts, Establish his Truth, with peace: the *L: Jesus* Defend his little flock, & preserve this threatned church & Nation.

24 I din'd at the Duke of Norfolcks: where was my L. Yarmoth &c: I saw the Queenes new appartment at W-hall with her new bed, the embrodery cost 3000 pounds: the carving about the Chimny piece is incomparable of Gibbons:

27 I had an hearing of my buisinesse before the Lords of the Treasury.

Feb: 2: Candlemas-day, a stranger preached at St. Martins on shewing the inconsistence of sin, with the service of God:

Mar: 2 Came out now a Proclamation for Universal liberty of Conscience in Scotland and dispensation from all Tests & Lawes to the Contrary; as also capacitating Papists to be chosen into all Offices of Trust: &c. *The Mysterie operats*.

[3 I went out of Town to meete my Lord Clarendon returning from Ireland, &c:]

10 His Majestie sent to the Commissioners of the Privy-Seale this morning into his bed-chamber, & told us that [tho] he had thought fit to dispose of the Seale, into a single hand, yet he

would [so] provide for us, as it should appeare how well he accepted of our faithfull & loyal service, with many gracious expressions to this effect: upon which we delivered the Seales into his Majesties hands—It was by all the world both hoped & expected his Majestie would have restor'd it to my Lord Clarendon againe; but they were astonish'd to see it given to my L. Arundel of Wardour, a zealous Rom: Catholique: & indeede it was very hard, and looked very unkindly, his Majestie (as my L: Clarendon protested to me, going to visite him & long discoursing with him about the affaires of Ireland) finding not the least failor of duty in him during all his government of that Kingdome: so as his recalling, plainely appeared to be from the stronger Influence of the Papists, who now got all the preferments:

Most of the greate officers both in the Court, [& Country,] Lords & others, dismissed, who would not promise his Majestie their consent to the repealing the Test, & penal statutes against the Romish recusants: There was to this end most of the Parliament men, spoken to in his Majesties Closset, & such as refused, if in any place or office of Trust, Civil, or military, put out of their Employments: This was a time of greate trial: Hardly one of them assenting, which put the Popish Interest much backward: The English Cleargy, every where very boldly preaching against their Superstition & errors, and wonderfully follow'd by the people, not one considerable proselyte being made in all this time. The party so exceedingly put to the worst by the preaching & writing of the Protestants, in many excellent Treatises, evincing the doctrine & discipline of the Reformed Religion, to the manifest disadvantage of their Adversarys: & to which did not a little contribute [13] the Sermon preached now at W-hall before the Princesse of Denmark, & an innumerable crowde of people, & at least 30 of the greatest nobility, by Dr. Ken: Bish: of Bath & Wells, upon 8: *John*: 46 (the Gospel of the day) all along that whole discourse describing the blasphemies, perfidie, wresting of Scriptures, preference of Traditions before it, spirit of persecution, superstition, Legends & fables, of the Scribes & pharisees; so as all the Auditory understood his meaning of paralleling them with the Romish Priests, & their new Trent Religion: Exhorting the people to adhere to the Written-Word, & to persevere in the Faith tought in the Church of England, whose doctrine for Catholique &

soundnesse, he preferr'd to all the Communit⟨i⟩es & Churches of Christians in the whole-world; & concluding with a kind of prophesy, that whatsoever it suffer'd, it should after a short trial Emerge to the confusion of her Adversaries, & the glory of God:

I went this Evening to see the order of the Boys & children at Christs hospital, there was neere 800 of them, Boys & Girles: so decently clad, cleanely lodged, so wholesomly fed, so admirably taught, some the Mathematics, Especialy the 40 of the late Kings foundation; that I was plainly astonished to see the progresse some little youths of 13 & 14 years of age, had made: I saw them at supper, visited their dormitories, admired the order, Oeconomie, & excellent government of this most charitable seminary: The rest, some are tought for the Universitie, others designed for seamen, all for Trades & Callings: The *Girles* instructed in all such worke as became their Sex, & as might fit them to make good Wives, Mistresses, & a blessing to their generation: They sung a Psalme before they sat downe to supper in the greate hall, to an Organ which played all the time, & sung with that cherefull harmony, as seem'd to me a vision of heavenly Angels: & I came from the place with infinite Satisfaction, having never in my life seene a more noble, pious, & admirable Charity: All these consisting of Orphans onely: The foundation (which has also had & still has many Benefactors) was of that pious Prince, K. Edward the 6: whose picture, (held to be an Original of Holbeins) is in the Court, where the Governors meete to consult of the affairs of the Hospital, & his stat⟨u⟩e in White-marble stands in a Nich of the Wall below, as you go to the Church which is a modern noble & ample fabric.

16 I made a step home, 10th Saw the trial of those devlish murdering mischiefe-doing engines *Bombs*, shot out of the Morter piece on black-heath: The distance that they are cast, the destruction they make where ever they fall is most prodigious:

20. The Bish: of Bath & Wells *Dr. Ken*, preached at St. *Martines*; the Crowd of people is not to be expressed; nor the wonderfull Eloquence of this admirable preacher: The Text: 26: Matt: from ver: 36 ad 40: upon all which he made most pathetical discourses: The Communion follow'd, at which I was participant: And afterwards din'd with the Bishop, & that young, most learned, pious & excellent Preacher *Mr. Wake*, at

Dr. Tenisons, who invited me: In the Afternoone, I went to
heare Mr. *Wake*, at the New-built Church *St. Anns*: on 8: *Mar:*
34: upon the subject of taking up the Crosse, & strenuously
behaving our selves in times of persecution: such as this now
threatned to be: His majestie having againe prorogu'd the Parliament, forseeing it would not remitt of the Laws against
Papists, by the extraordinary, zeale & bravery of its members, &
[free] renuntiation of greate officers both in Court & State, who
would not be prevailed with for any temporal concerne:

Aprill: 8 Had a tryal of re-hearing my greate Cause at the
C⟨h⟩ancery in Westminster hall, I had 7. of the most learned
Council, my Adversary five, among which the Attourney Gen:
& late Soliciter Finch son to the L: Chancellor Earle of Notingham: The Accompt was at last brought to one Article of the
Surcharge, & referr'd to a Master, the Cause lasting two houres
& more:

9 After 5 monethes Absence, of my Family, wintering at my
Sons in Lond: we all returned home, (I thank God) in health:
for which the Lord be blessed:

10 There having the last weeke ben issu'd forth a dispensation
from all Obligations and Tests, by which dissenters & Papists
especialy, had publique liberty of exercising their severall ways of
Worship, without incurring the penalty of the many Laws, &
Acts of Parliament to the Contrary ever since the Reformation;
& this purely obtained by the Papists, thinking thereby to ruine
the C. of England, which now was the onely Church, which so
admirably & strenuously oppos'd their Superstition; There was a
wonderfull concourse at the Dissenters meeting house in this
parish, and the Parish-Church left exceeding thinn: What this
will end in, God Almighty onely knows, but ⟨it⟩ lookes like confusion, which I pray God avert:

11 To Lond: about my Suite, some termes of Accommodation
being proposed:

19 I heard the famous Singer the Eunuch *Cifacca*, esteemed
the best in *Europe* & indeede his holding out & delicatenesse in
extending & loosing a note with that incomparable softnesse, &
sweetenesse was admirable: For the rest, I found him a meere
wanton, effeminate child; very Coy, & prowdly conceited to my
apprehension: He touch'd the Harpsichord to his Voice rarely
well, & this was before a select number of some particular

persons whom Mr. Pepys (Secretary of the Admiralty & a greate lover of Musick) invited to his house, where the meeting was, & this obtained by peculiar favour & much difficulty of the Singer, who much disdained to shew his talent to any but Princes:

24 I staied to heare the *French* sermon, which succeded (in the same place, & after use of the English Liturgie translated into French) the congregation consisting of about 100 French Protestants refugiès from the Persecution, of which Monsieur de *Rouvigny* (present) was the chiefe, & had obtain'd the use of the Church after the Parish had ended their owne Service &c: The Preachers text was 16: *Psal:* 11, patheticaly perswading to patience, constancy & relyance on God, for the comfort of his Grace, amidst all their Sufferings, & the infinite reward to come:

2 *May* I dined at Myn heere *Dickvelts* the Holland Ambassadors: a prudent and worthy person: There din'd, my Lord Middleton Prin⟨ci⟩pal Secretary of state; Lord Pembrock, L: Lumly, L. Preston, Coll Fitz-Patrick, Sir J: Chardin: After dinner the Ambassador discoursed [of] & deplored the stupid folly of our Politics, in suffering the French to take Luxembourg: it being a place of the most concerne to have ben defended for the Interest of not onely the Netherlands, but of England also:

11 Lond: 12 I came downe with the Countesses of Bristol & Sunderland, whose husband being Lord President [& Secretary of state] was made knight of the Gartir, & prime favorite: The two Countesses &c: dined at my house: Memorandum: this day was such a storme of wind as had seldome happened in an age for the extreame violence of it, being as was judged a kind of Hurocan: It also kept the floud out of the Thames that people went on foote over several places above bridge, the tide was so low. I return'd this evening with the Ladys:

17: Lond: about my P: Seale &c: stayed all this weeke: An Earthquake in severall places of England about the time of the great storme 11th past:

26: To Lond: about my Agreement with Mr. Pretyman after my tedious suit:

June: 2: I went to Lond: it having pleas'd his Majestie to grant me a Privy-Seale for 6000 pounds, for the discharging the Debt, I had ben so many yeares persecuted for. It being indeede for Mony drawne over by my F. in Law Sir R: Browne during his Residence

in the Court of France, & so (with a much greater summ, due to
Sir Richard from his Majestie & now this part of the Arrere
payed) there remaining yet due to me (as Excecutor to Sir
Richard) about 6500 more: But this determining a tedious &
expensive Chancery suite, has ben so greate a mercy & providence
to me (through the kindnesse & friendship of my L. Godolphin
one of the Lords Commissioners of the Treasury), that I do accknowledge it, with all imaginable thanks to my gracious God:

6 I visited my Co: Pierpoint, Daughter to Sir Jo: Evelyn of
Deane, now widdow of Mr. Pierpoint, & mother of the Earle of
Kingston: she was now marrying my Cousen Evelyn Pierpoint
her 2d son.

I also visited my Co: Hales & her Daughter, & severall other
of my Relations, now happning to be in Towne:

7 My Lord Clarendon (late Lord Lieutennant of Ireland)
inviting himselfe & Lady &c to dinner to my house, I returned
home this evening:

12 There was about this time brought into the Downes, a Vast
treasure which after 45 yeares being sunk in a Spanish Galioon,
which perish'd somewhere neere Hispaniola [or B⟨a⟩hama
Ilands] coming home; was now weighed up, by certaine Gentlemen & others, who were [at] the Charge of Divers &c: to the
suddaine enriching of them, beyond all expectation: The Duke
of Albemarles share came (tis believed) to 50000, & some private Gent: who adventured but 100 pounds & little more, to ten,
18000 pounds, & proportionably; [his Majesties tenth to 10000
pounds:]

The Camp was now againe pitch'd at Hounslow, The Commanders profusely vying in the expense & magnificence of
Tents:

16 I went to Lond: thence to Hampton-Court to give his
Majestie thanks for his late gracious favour, though it was the
granting but what was a due debt to me, [18] & so return'd
home: Whilst I was in the Council-chamber came in a formal
person, with a large roll of Parchment in his hand, being an
Addresse (as he said, for he introduc'd it with a Speech) of the
people of Coventry, giving his Majestie their greate Acknowledgements for his granting a liberty of Conscience: He added,
that this was not onely the Application of one party, but the
unanimous Addresse of C. of England men, Presbyterians,

Independents, & Anabaptists, to shew how extensive his
Majesties Grace was, as taking in all parties to his Indulgence &
protection, had also taken a way all dissentions & animosit⟨i⟩es,
which would not onely unite them in bonds of Christian Charity, but exceedingly incourage their future Industry to the
Improvement of Trade in his Majesties dominions, & spreading
of his Glory through out the world, & that now he had given to
God his Empire, God would establish his, with Expressions of
greate loyaltie & submission: and so gave the King the roll:
which being return'd him againe, his Majestie caused him to
reade: The Addresse was short, but much to the substance of the
speech of their foreman: To whom the K. (pulling off his hatt,)
sayed; That what he had don in giving liberty of Conscience,
was, what was ever his judgement ought to be don, & that as he
would preserve them in their injoyment of it during his reigne;
so he would indeavor so to settle it by Law, that it should never
be alter'd by his successors: After this he gave them his hand to
kisse: It was reported the subscribers were above 1000: But this
is not so remarkeable as an Addresse of the Weeke before (as I
was assured by one present) of some of the Family of Love; His
Majestie asked them what their Worship consisted in, & how-
many their party might consist of: They told him, their costome
was to reade the Scriptures, and then to preach, but did not give
any farther account, onely sayed, that for the rest, they were a
sort of refined *Quakers*, but their number very small, not consisting (as they sayed) of above threescore in all, and those chiefly
belonging to the Ile of Ely:

I din'd this day at Mr. Blathwaites (two miles from Hampton); the Gent: is Secretary of Warr, Cl: of the Counsel &c having raised himselfe by his Industry, from very moderate
Circumstances: He is a very proper handsome person, and very
dextrous in buisinesse, and has besids all this married a very
greate fortune, his incomes [alone] by the Army, & his being Cl:
of the Counsel, & Secretary to the Committeè of Foraine Plantations brings him in above 2000 pounds per Annum:

23 I went to Lond: which day was his Majesties grant of 6000
pounds part of the debt due to me, passed to me by Privy-Seale,
so as that tedious affaire being dispatched & the Privy-Seale
Inrolled, I returned home the 25: Giving thankes to God for his
gracious mercy in delivering me at last from my ruinous suite:

July. 19 I went to Wotton [with wife, daughter, son, daughter in law &c:] to visite my deare Bro: in the way dined at Ashsted with my Lady Mordant:

24: At *Wotton* church preached one Mr. *Lucas* on 5. *Eph:* 16: a very trim preacher & though very young, likely to make a good preacher:

3. Aug: I went to see *Albury* now purchased by Mr. Finch, son to the late L. Chancelor & Kings Soliciter: I found the Garden (which I first designed for the L. Duke of Norfolck) nothing improved:

4: I went to Clandon to visite Mr. Onslow, where we dined:

7 Mr. *Duncomb*, Parson of Wotton, preached on 18 *Ezek:* 30, very indifferently & buisily, a very ill choise of my Bro: for that excellent living: In Afternoone at *Abinger* I heard Mr. Lucas on: 13. *Rom:* 13.

8 I went from Wotton to Bagshot, a house [in a desolate forest:] & parke belonging to Mr. *Ghrame*, Master of the Buckhounds & Privy-purse to the King; where I went to visite his Lady & her sister, formerly both Mayds of Honor, & my deare friends: [9] the next day to *Windsor* about buisinesse with my L. Godolphin & L: Sunderland with whom I dind [(as also Lord Castle maine, late Ambassador to Rome)] & returned by *Cranburn* an house of my L. Godolphin, & thence again to Bagshot:

14 Went again to Cranburn, & dined there, return'd to Bagshot:

15 I went to visite my L. Clarendon &c at Swallowfild, where was my L: Cornbery just then arived from Denmark, whether he had accompanied the Prince of Denmark two months before & now came back: The miserable Tyrannie under which that nation lives, he related to us: the King keeping them under by an Army of above 40000 men all Germans, not daring to trust his owne subjects: notwithstanding which, that the *Danes* are exceedingly proude: The whole Country very poore & miserable: &c: here was my L: *Montrah* & Lady, after dinner I returned to Bagshot: 17th I went back to Wotton:

21 Mr. *Lucas* on: 11. Heb: 22: & so on 22 returned home to Says-Court, having ben 5 weekes absent, with my Bro: & friends, who entertained us very nobly: God be praised for his goodnesse, & this refreshment: after my many troubles, & let his mercy & providence ever preserve me.

27 I went to Lond, to resigne a Mortgage of 1000 pounds to my Lord Sunderland, being mony lent him in my name, but belonging to my Lord Godolphin, as part of his late Wifes (my ever dearest friend) portion: & now by his Lord-ships desire lent to the ⟨Exchequer⟩, in my name againe, the product both of this and 2000 pounds more, for the main-tenance of his sonn & heire Francis Godolphin &c: I returned this Evening:

Sept. 3 The Lo: Mayor &c sent me an Officer with a staff to be one of the Governors of St. Tho: Hospital:

4 Our Viccar proceeded on his former Text: The B: Comm: succeeded at which I participated:

Pomerid: The Curate ⟨on⟩ 1. *Cor:* 5. 7.

The *Turkes* beaten this summer by Emp: & Venetians exceedingly: persecution raging in France. Divers churches in France fired by lightning, Priests strucken, Consecrated hosts &c. burnt and destroyed, both at St. Malo, & *Paris* at the grand procession on *C. Christi* day.

13 I went to *Lambeth* & dined with my Lord Arch-bishop, after dinner I went into the Library which I found was exceed-ingly improved; there are also divers rare *Manuscripts* in a roome a part:

6 *Octob*: I was Godfather to sir Jo: Chartins sonn (the greate French Traveller), with the Earle of Bath, and the Countesse of Carlile: The Child was Christn'd in Greenewich Church with much solemnitie, and it was named *John*, which was also my L: of Bathes name &c: we all dined at sir Johns in the Queenes house, where was the Marquisse of Ruvignie, Young Lord Carteret, Sir Jo: Fenwick, & other persons of quality:

29 Was an Anabaptist very odd ignorant Mechanic, I thin⟨k⟩ a made Lord Mayor; The K: Q: Invited to feast at Guild-hall, together with *Dadi*, the *Popes Nuncio*—ô strange turne of affaires, That these who scandaliz'd the Church of England, as favourers of Popery (the Dissenters) should publiqly invite an Emissary from Rome, one who represented the very person of their Antichrist!

31 I was this day sixty-seaven yeares old: ô Lord, I beseech thee, teach me so to number my daies, that I may apply them to Wisedome, & prepare for my last day, & that of thy blessed Coming:

Nov: 5 Our Curate on 64 Psal 9 shewing the wonderfull deliverance that God gave his Church in this Nation from that most execrable designe: the History whereof he related at large; Inviting us to depend upon God, and celebrate this mercy &c.

30 Was our Annual feast of the R: Society: we continued my L: Carbery president another Yeare:

December 1 I went to visite severall of my friends, & returned home [2] The next day, leaving both my poore Wife & daughter very much Indisposed:

This season was Extraordinarily Wett & Tempestious.

10 I went to Lond to see my Wife who was Indisposed with a rhume, & staying some while to take the physitians Advice: My Son was now returned out of Devon Shire, where he had ben upon a Commission, from the Lords of the Tressury, about a Concealement of Land: I dined with the Secretary of the Admiralty [upon a petition for Mr. Fowler:] & returned home late:

20 I went with my Lord Chiefe-Justice Herbert, to see his house at Walton on the Thames: It is a barren place, he had built, to a very ordinary house a very handsome Library, designing more building to it, than the place deserves in my opinion: He desired my advice about the laying out of his Gardens &c: next day, we went to Waybridge, to see som pictures of the Dutchesse of Norfolcks, especialy the statue, or Christo in Gremio, said to be of M: Angelos; but, there are reasons to think it rather a copy, from some proportion in both the figures ill taken: I⟨t⟩ was now exposed to sale: I came to Lond: the thursday after, having be⟨en⟩ exceedingly well treated by my L. C. Justice: and so

1688. *Jan*: 1. Dr. Tenison at St. Martines; on: 1 Cor: 14. 40: The H: Sacrament followed, at which I communicated:

4 I having visited my Wife, (who had ben still Indispos'd) returned home:

12 I went to Lond. to visite my Wife still under her course of Physick, but (I tha⟨n⟩k God) growing better:

Mr. Slingsby, Master of the mint, being now under very deplorable circumstances, upon the Account of his Creditors, & especialy the King; I did my endeavor with the Lord⟨s⟩ of the Treasury, to be favorable to him:

My Lord Arran (eldest son to the Duke of Hamilton) being now married to my Lady Ann Spencer, eldest daughter of the Earle of Sunderland, Lord President of the Council: I & my family had most glorious favours, sent us: This wedding being celebrated with extraordinary splendor.

14 I went to salut & felicitate the new Lady Bride, & was most civily received by my Lord her husband, & the duke of Hamilton: which ceremony perform'd I returned home:

15 Was a solemn & particular office used at our, & all the Churche⟨s⟩ of London, & 10 miles about it, for thankgiving to God for her Majesties being with child:

The Afternoone being very tempestious, I went not to church:

22 I stayed at home all this weeke.

This Afternoone I went not to Church, being to finish a Religious Treatise I had undertaken.

I stirr'd not out this week.

29. Our *Lecturer* pre⟨a⟩ched on 5 Gal: 24: I went In the Afternoone to Greenewich to visite the Marquis de Ruvigny, where was publique prayers in the Chapell:

30: Being the Martyrdome day of K. Charles the First, our *Curate* made a florid Oration against the murder of that excellent Prince, with an Exhortation to Obedience: from the example of David 1. *Sam:* 24. 6.

I was not from home all this weeke:

Feb: 5 Our Lecturer proceeded on his ⟨former⟩ Text in Jobe: The holy Sacrament followed, I received: Pomerid: a stranger: on: 14. Joh: 6:

6: I went to Lond: about my *Quietus*.

12 Wednesday before My Daughter Evelyn, going in the Coach to visite in the Citty, a Jolt (the doore being not fast-shut) flung her quite out of the Coach upon her back, in such manner, as the hind-wheles passed over both her Thighes a little above the knees: Yet it pleased God, besides the bruse of the Wheele upon her flesh, she had no other harme: We let her blood, anointed, & made her keepe bed 2 days, after which ⟨s⟩he was able to walke & soone after perfectly well: Through God Almightys greate mercy to an Excellent Wife & a most dutifull & discreete daughter in Law:

17 After above 12 Weekes Indisposition, we now returned home much recovered:

I now receiv'd the sad tidings of my Niepce Montagues death, who died at Woodcot the 15th: There had ben unkindnesses & Injuries don our family by my Sister-in Law, her mother, which we did not deserve; & it did not thrive to the purposes of those who instigated her, to cause her da⟨u⟩ghter to cut-off an Intaile clandestinely: But Gods will be don, she has seene the ill effect of it, & so let it passe:

Mar. 15 I gave in my Account about the Sick & Wounded, in order to my quietus: & Visited some friends:

16 Dr. Jeane Divinity Profess: at Oxon: preached at W-hall on 3: *Mal:* 16. with an exhortation, to holy life & perseverance in our Religion, as the most pure, primitive & True, of all Professions of Christians under heaven.

I return'd home in the Afternoone:

18 The Lecturer on 17: Matt: 21: upon [which] he tooke occasion to Exhort, to a liberal & charitable Contribution to the reliefe of the French Protestants flying from the continual raging persecution at this time; for which there was a second Briefe, read in all the Churches:

21 I went to Lond: heard that excellent man Dr. Tenison at W:hall.

23 The Bish: of Oxford, Parker who so lately published, his extravagant Treatise about Transubstantiation & for abbrogating the Test & penal Laws, died: esteem'd a Violent, passionate haughty man, but being [yet] pressed to declare for the C. of Rome; he utterly refus'd it: A remarkable end:

The Fr: Tyrant, now finding he could make no proselytes amongst those Protestants of quality & others whom he had caused to be shut up in Dungeo⟨ns⟩ & confin'd to Nunneries & Monastries; gave them after so long Tryal a general releasement, & leave to go out of the Kingdom, but Utterly taking away their Estates, & their Children; so as greate numbers came daily into England & other places, where they were received & relieved with very Considerable Christian Charity: This providence and goodnesse of God to those who thus constantly held out; did so work upon those miserable poore soules, who to avoy'd the persecution, sign'd their renuntiation, & to save their Estates, went to Masse; That reflecting on what they had don, grew so afflicted in their Consciences, as not being longer able to support it; They Unanimously in infinite number thro all the french provinces; Acquaint the Magistrats & Lieutenants that being sorry for their Apostacy; They were resolved to returne to their old Religion, that they would go no more to Masse, but peace-ably assemble where they could, to beg pardon & worship God, but so without weapons, as not to give the least umbrage of Rebellion or sedition, imploring their pitty & commisseration: And accordingly meeting so from time to time, The Dragoon Missioners, popish Officers & Priests, fall upon them, murder & put to death who ever they could lay hold on, who without the least resistance embrace death, torture & hanging, with singing ⟨psalmes⟩ & praying for their persecutors to the last breath; yet still continuing the former Assembly of themselves in desert places, suffering with incredible Constancy, that through Gods mercy they might obtaine pardon for this Lapse: Such Examples of Christian behaviour has not been seene, since the primitive Persecution, by the Heathen: & doub⟨t⟩lesse God will do some signall worke in the end, if we can with patience & christian resolution hold out, & depend on his Providence:

28 I went to Lond: in the Evening, the next morning with Sir Charles Littleton to *Sheene* an house & estate given him by my Lord Brounchar, one who was ever noted for an hard, covetous, vicious man, had severall Bastards; but for his worldly Craft, & skill in gaming &c: few exceeding him: Coming to die, he bequeathed all his Land, House, furnitur &c intirely to Sir Charles, to whom he had no manner of Relation, but an antient friendship, contracted at the famous siege of Colchester 40 yeares before: It is a pretty place, fine gardens and well planted, & given to one worthy of them, Sir Charles being an honest Gent, & souldier; & brother to Sir Hen: Littleton of Worster shire, whose greate Estate he is to Inhe⟨r⟩ite, his Bro: being without Children: They are ⟨descendents⟩ of the greate Lawyer of that name & give same Armes & motto: He is married to one ⟨Mrs.⟩ Temple (formerly maide of Honor to the late Queene,) a beautifull Lady, & has many fine Children; so as none envy his good fortune.

After dinner (at his house) we went to see Sir William Tem-ples, neere to it: The most remarkeable thing, is his Orangerie & Gardens; where the wall Fruite-trees are most exquisitely nailed & applied, far better than in my life I had ever noted:

There are many good Pictures, especialy of V. dykes, in both these houses, & some few statues & small busts in the later:

From hence we went to *Kew*, to Visite Sir Hen: Capels, whose Orangerie & Myrtetum, are most beautifull, & perfectly well kept: He was contriving very high palisados of reedes, to shade his Oranges in during the Summer, & painting those reedes in oyle:

We return'd to Lond: in the Evening:

⟨30⟩ Dr. Megot, Deane of Winchester, preached at W:hall, on 10: Heb: 36:

Aprill 1 In the morning the first sermon was preach'd by Dr. Stillingfleete: Deane of St. Paules on 10: Luke 41. 42: The H. Communion follow'd, but was so interrupted, by the rude breaking in of multituds into the Chapell, zealous to heare the second sermon, to be preached by Dr. Ken: Bish: of Bathe & Wells; that the latter part of that holy Office could hardly be heard, or the Sacred Elements distributed, without greate trouble: The Princesse being come, The Bishop preached on 7: Mich: 8. 9. 10: Describing the Calamity of the Reformed Church of Judah, under the Babylonish persecution, for her sinns; & Gods certainely delivering her, upon her Repentance & patience, and therefore advising that her Enemy should not Insult over her calamity; for that though the Church should sit in the darke, & under all imaginable Circumstances of being deserted for her sinns; though the time should be long; she should certainely rise againe & be delivered, by him who would avenge her Enemys, as God did, upon the Edomites her apostate brother & neighbours, rejoicing in her Calamity, & the Babylonians designing her destruction: That yet by Gods providence from this Captive desolate state as Juda emerged; So should the now Reformed Church, where ever persecuted & Insulted over: & therefore exhorting to patience, & Reformation, and waiting on Gods Providence, for that Salvation should come, even out of the dust: Victory without [other] Weapons of his people [than prayer & ⟨reformation⟩]; That when they threw away their Swords, submitted to Tyrannous princes, God would take them up in his Churches defence, & revenge their wrongs: & therefore Exhorted all degrees of men, to a serious amendment of life; for the more speedy & Effectuall deliverance. This he preached with his accustom'd action, zeale & Energie, so as people flock'd from all quarters to heare him.

15 It was now a very dry, cold easterly windy, backward Spring:

The Turkish Empire in greate intestine Confusion: The French persecution still raging, multitud⟨e⟩s of Protestants & many very Considerable greate & noble persons flying hither, produced a second general Contribution: The papists, (by Gods providence) as yet making small progresse amongst us.

29 The weather was until now so cold & sharp, by an almost perpetual East wind, which had continued many moneths, that there was little appearance of any Spring; & yet the winter was very favourable as to frosts or Snow:

May 1: Met the foefees for the poore of Deptford:

2 To Lond: about my petition for allowances upon the Accompt of Commissioner for sick & wounded in the former war with Holland:

8: I returned home: His Majestie alarm'd by the greate Fleete of the Dut⟨c⟩h (whilst we had a very inconsiderable one & to our greate reproch) went down to chatham:

13 The Hollanders did now al'arme his Majestie with their fleete, so well prepar'd & out before we were in any readinesse, or had any considerable number to have encounter'd them had there ben occasion, to the greate reproch of the nation, whilst being in profound peace, there was a mighty Land Army, which there was no neede of, & no force by Sea, where onely was the apprehension; [at present, but was doub⟨t⟩lesse kept & increased in order to bring in & Countenance Popery, the K beginning to discover his intention by many Instances, perverted by the Jesuites against his first seeming resolution to alter nothing in the Church Established, so as it appeared that there can be no relyance ⟨o⟩n Popish promises.]

17 I went to Lond, to meete my Bro: G. Evelyn about our mutual concerne in the will of my Bro: Richard, by which, my Niepce Montague dying without issue, a considerable Estate ought to have returned to our Family, after the decease of her husband: but thro the fraude & unworthy dealing of her mother, (my sister in-Law), the intaile had ben cut off & a recovery pass'd & consequently the Estate given to her husband Montag⟨u⟩e, through the perswasion of my sister contrary to the intent of her husband my brother, & that to a son-in law who

had lived dissolutly & Scandalously with another woman, & his dishonesty made publiquely notorious: What should move my sister in Law, professing so greate love to the memory of her husband, to [cause my Niepce to] give away not onely this, but considerably more, to a son in law, who had no Issue, from all her husbands relations, was strangely spoken off, especialy to one who had so scandalously & so basely abused her da⟨u⟩ghter:

18 The King injoyning [the ministers] the Reading his declaration for giving liberty of Conscience (as it was styled) in all the Churches of England: This Evening six *Bishops*, *Bath* & Wells, *Peterborow*, *Ely*, *Chichester*, *St. Asaph*, & *Bristol*, (in the name of all the rest) came to his Majestie to petition him that he would not impose the reading of it to the severall Congregations under their diocesse: not that they were averse to the publishing of it, for want of due tendernes towards dissenters, in relation to whom they should be willing to come to such a temper, as should be thought fit, when that matter might come to be consider'd & settled in parliament & Convocation: But that the *declaration being founded upon such a dispencing power, as might at pleasure set aside all Lawes Ecclesiastical & Civil*, it appeared to them *Illegal*, as doing so to the parliaments in –61 & 72; & that it was a point of such Consequence, as they could not so far make themselves parties to it, as the Reading of it in the Church in the time of divine service amounted to.

The King was so far incensed at this Addresse, that he with threatning expressions commanded them to obey him in reading of it at their perils; & so dismis'd them:

20 I went to Church in White-hall Chapell, where after the morning lessons; The Declaration was read, by one of the *Coire* who used to reade the Chapters: Then followed the sermon, preached by Dr. *Scott* on 14 *John*: 17 making an eloquent [& pious] discourse upon the vicissitudes of worldly things. I heare it was also read in the Abby at Westminster; but almost universaly forborne throughout all London; the Consequences of which, a little time will shew:

I returned home in the Evening:

23 I went to Lond, 24 Ascension-day to Lond: the Scholemaster of St. Martines preached an excellent sermon: The holy Sacrament followed, of which I participated:

25 I visited Dr. Tenison, Secretary Pepys, of the Admiralty, Mr. Boile, Coll: Philips and severall of my Friends, all the discourse now being about the Bishops refusing to reade [the injunction for the abbrogation of] the Test &c: It seemes the Injunction came so crudely from the Secretarys office, that it was neither sealed nor sign'd in forme, nor had any Lawyer ben consulted; so as the Bishops who tooke all imaginable advice, put the Court to greate difficulties how to proceede against them: Greate were the Consults, and a Proclamation expected all this day; but no thing don: The action of the Bishop⟨s⟩ universaly applauded, & reconciling many adverse parties, Papists onely excepted, who were now exceedingly perplex'd, & violent courses every moment expected: Report was the Protestant Secular Lords & nobility would abett the Cleargy: God knows onely the event.

The Queene Dowager obstinately bent hitherto on her returne into Portugal, now on the suddaine, upon pretence of a greate debt owing her by his majesties, disabling, declares her resolution to stay:

Newes of the most prodigious Earthquake, that was almost ever heard of, subverting the Citty of *Lima* & Country in *Perù*, with the dreadfull Innundation following it:

27 Our *Curate* on 12 *Matt:* 36: my Wife being indispos'd we had prayers & sermon at home this afternoone: Came Sir J. Jardin to visite us:

June ⟨3⟩ Whitsonday, our *Viccar* on 4: *Eph:* 30: The holy Communion followed at which I participated: The Lord make me thankfull:

In the afternoone the Curate:

7 Dined at my house the Countesse of Sunderland, Bristol, Clancartie & severall other Ladys:

8 This day were the Arch-Bishop of Canterbery together with the Bishops of Ely, Chichester, St. Asaph, Bristol, Peterborow & Bath & Wells, sent from the Privy Council, Prisoners to the Tower, for refusing to give baile for their appearance (upon their not reading the Declaration for Liberty of Conscience) because in giving baile, they had prejudiced their Peerage: Wonderfull was the concerne of the people for them, infinite crowds of people on their knees, beging their blessing & praying for them as they passed out of the Barge; along the Tower wharfe &c:

10 A young Prince borne &c. [which will cost dispute.]

About two a clock, we heard the Toure Ordnance discharge, & the Bells ringing; for the Birth of a Prince of Wales; This was very surprizing, it being universaly given-out, that her Majestie did not looke til the next moneth:

13 I went to the Tower to see the Bishops now there in Prison, for not complying with his Majesties commands to Cause his declaration to be read in their Diocesse; where I visited the *A: Bish:* B: of Ely, Asaph, & Bath & Wells:

15 The Bish: came from the Tower to Westminster upon their *Habeas Corpus* & after divers houres dispute before the Judges, by their Counsel, upon security to appeare friday fortnight, were dismiss'd: Their Counsel alledged false Imprisonment & abatement of their Committment for want of some words: Denyed the paper given privately to the K. to be a seditious libel or that it was ever published: but all was over-ruled: W⟨r⟩ight, *Alibon,* Hollowell & Powell were the Judges: Finch, Sawyer, Pollixfen & Pemberton, their Counsel, who pleaded incomparably, [so as the Jury quitted them.] There was a lane of people from the Kings Bench to the water-side, upon their knees as the Bishops passed & repassed to beg their blessing: Bon fires made that night, & bells ringing, which was taken very ill at Court and an appearance of neere 60 Earles & Lords &c upon the bench in honor of the Bishops, & which did not a little comfort them; but indeede they were all along full of Courage & cherefull:

Note that they denyed to pay the Lieutennant of the Tower: (Hales who us'd them very surlily) any Fees, denying any to be due:

I Introduc'd Sir Jo: Hoskins Master of the Chancery to my Lord President, who received him being in bed: &c:

Supped at the E: of Clarendons, where I found the Bishops of St. Asaph, and Norwich &c:

17 Was the day of Thanksgiving in Lond: & 10 miles about, for the young Princes Birth, a forme of prayer made for the purpose by the B: of Rochester:

The night was solemniz'd with Bonfires & other Fire workes &c:

July 1 Dr. Tenison preach'd at St. Martines 10: Heb: 23. The holy Communion followed, which I received: The Lord blesse it to me:

2 I dind at my L. Godolphins where was the Duke of Grafton, L: Dover, &c:

3 I went with Dr. Godolphin [(& his bro: Sir William)] to St. Albans to see a library which he [would have] bought of the Widow of Dr. Cartwrite, late Arch-deacon of St. Albans, a very good collection of Books, especial Divinity: he was to give for them 300 pounds: so having seene the greate Church now newly repaired by a publique Contribution, we return'd that Evening:

12 I return'd home; The Camp now began at Hounslow, but the nation in high discontent:

The 2 Judges, who favour'd the Cause of the Bish: had their writ of Ease: greate wroth meditating against the Bish: Cleargy & Church:

Coll: *Titus*, Sir *H. Vane* (son of him who was executed for his Treason) & some others of the Presbyt: & Indep: party, Sworn of the Privy Council, hoping thereby to divert that party, from going-over to the Bishops & C: of England, which now they began to do: as foreseeing the designes of the papists to descend & take in their most hateful of heretiques (as they at other time believed them) to effect their owne ends, which was now evidently, the utter extirpation of the C. of Eng: first, & then the rest would inevitably follow:

14 Came to Visite me my Lord Chief-Justice Herbert.

16 Came to dine with us the Countesse of Sunderland, who staied 'til night:

17 I went to Lond: with my Wife &c: & This night were the fireworks plaied, which were prepar'd for the Queenes up-sitting: We stood at Mr. Pepys's Secretary of the Admiralty to greate advantage for the sight, & indeede they were very fine, & had cost some thousands of pounds about the pyramids & statues &c: but were spent too soone, for so long a preparation:

26 I went to Lambeth to visite the ArchBish: of Canterbery, I found him very cherefull: There was likewise at Dinner my Lord Clarendon & few others: I returned after evening prayers:

⟨29⟩ Preached, our Ministers Lond: Lecturer a very excellent sermon on 2 *Judges*, 1. 2. 3:

My Wife was ataqu'd with a suddaine fit of fainting, at dinner, but without any sensible convulsion; which yet to prevent, she was immediately let blood, & I blesse God soone restored:

Aug: 5 Our *Vicar* on 5 *Matt:* 8: The holy Communion follow'd of which I participated: The Curate on 9. Heb: 27:

10 To Lond. Din'd with Sir William Godolphin, return'd: [Dr. Tenison now told me there would suddainly be some greate thing discovered, which happened to be the P: of O: intended coming:]

14 I went to Lond: [15] the next day to *Althorp* in Northampton shire, it being 70 miles, which in 2 Coaches one [of 4 horses] that ⟨tooke⟩ me & my son up at white-hall & carried us to Dunstaple, where we arived & dined at noone, & another there of 6 horses, which carried us to Althorp 4 miles beyond N-hampton, by 7 a clocke that evening; both these Coaches laied for me alone, by that noble Countesse of Sunderland, who Invited me to her house at Althorp, where she entertaind me & my son with very extraordinary kindnesse, and convey'd us back againe to London in the very same noble manner, both going & coming, appointing a Dinner for us, at Dunstaple, which we found ready for us, as soone as we came to the Inn: I stayed with her Ladyship 'til the Thursday following.

18 Dr. Jessup the Minister of Althorp, who was my Lords Chaplaine, when Ambassador in France, preached on the shortest discourse I ever heard: but what was defective in the amplitude of his sermon, we found supplied in the largenesse, & convenience of the Parsonage house, which the Doctor (who had in spiritual advancements, at least 600 pounds per Annum) had new-built, fit for any person of quality to live in, with Gardens & all accommodations according.

20 My Lady carried us to my Lord of Northamptons Seate, a very strong large house built of stone, not altogether modern: they were now inlarging the Gardens, in which was nothing extraordinary but the Yron gate, opening into the Parke, which is indeede very good worke, wrought in flowers, painted with blew & gilded; & there is a very noble Walke of Elmes towards the front of the house by the Bowling Greene: I was not in any roomes of the house besides a lobby looking into the Garden, where my Lord, and his new Countesse (Sir St: Foxes daughter, whom I had known from a very Child) entertained the Countesse of Sunderland & her daughter the Countesse of Arran, (newly married to the son of the Duke of Hammilton) with so little good grace, & so dully, that our Visite was very short, & so we return'd to Althorp: which is 12 miles distant:

The Earle of Sunderlands House, or rather palace at Althorp, is a noble uniforme pile, in forme of an ⌗ built of brick & freestone, balustred, & a la moderne; The Hale is well, the Staircase incomparable, the roomes of State, Gallerys, Offices, & Furniture such as [may] become a greate Prince: It is situated in the midst of Gardens, exquisitely planted & kept, & all this in a parke wall'd with hewn stone; planted with rows & walkes of Trees; Canales & fish ponds, stored with Game: & what is above all this, Govern'd by a Lady, that without any shew of solicitude; keepes every thing in such admirable order both within & without, from the Garret, to the Cellar; That I do not believe there is any in all this nation or any other, exceeds her: all is in such exact order, without ostentation, but substantialy greate & noble; The meanest servant lodged so neate & cleanely, The Services at the several Tables, the good order & decenccy, in a word the intire Oeconomie perfectly becoming, a wise & noble person, & one whom for her distinguishing esteeme of me from a long & worthy friendship; I must ever honour & Celebrate: & wish, I do from my Soule; The Lord her Husband (whose parts & abilit(i)es are otherwise conspicuous) were as worthy of her, as by a fatal Apostacy, & Court ambition, he has made himselfe unworthy: This is what she deplores, & renders her as much affliction, as a Lady of a greate Soule & much prudence is capable of: The Countesse of Bristol her mother, a grave & honorable Lady has the comfort of seing her daughter & Grand-children under the same Oeconomie, especialy, Mr. Charles Spencer, a Youth of extraordinary hopes, very learned for his age & ingenious, & under a Governor of Extraordinary worth: Happy were it, could as much be said, ⟨of⟩ the Elder Bro: the Lord Spencer, who rambling about the world, dishonors both his name & family, adding sorrow to sorrow, to a Mother, who has taken all imaginable care of his Education: but vice more & more predominating, gives slender hopes of his reformation: He has another sister very Young, married to the Earle of Clancartie to a greate & fair Estate in Ireland, which [yet] gives no greate presage of worth; so universaly contaminated is the youth of this corrupt & abandoned age: But this is againe recompens'd by my *Lord Arran*, a sober & worthy Gent: & who has Espoused the Lady Ann Spencer, a young lady of admirable accomplishments & vertue:

23d I left this noble place, & Conversation on the 23d, passing through Northampton, which having lately ben burnt & reedified, is now become a Towne, that for the beauty of the buildings especialy the Church, & Towne-house, may compare with the neatest in Italy itselfe:

24 Hearing my poore wife, had ben ataqu'd with her late Indisposition I hasted home this morning, & God be pra(i)sed found her much amended.

Dr. Sprat: Bish of Rochester, writing a very honest & handsome letter to the Commissioners Ecclesiastical; excuses himselfe from sitting no longer among them, as by no meanes approving of their prosecution of the Cleargy who refus'd to reade his Majesties declaration for liberty of Conscience, in prejudice of the Church of England &c:

The French Arme & threaten the Election of the Elect: of Colin: The Dutch make extraordinary preparations both at sea & land, which (with the very small progresse popery makes amongst us) puts us to many difficulties:

The popish Irish Souldiers commit many murders & Insolences; The whole Nation dissaffected & in apprehensions: what the event will prove God onely knows:

After long trials of the Doctors, to bring up the little P: of Wales by hand (so-many of her Majesties Children having died Infants) not succeeding: A country Nurse (the wife of a Tile-maker) is taken to give it suck:

September 2 Our Viccar preached on his former Text: 5: *Matt:* 8: The holy Sacrament followed, at which I received, the L. Jesus make me thankfull:

THE REVOLUTION AND A NEW KING
AND QUEEN
(1688–1690)

18 I WENT to Lond: where I found the Court in the uttmost consternation upon report of the Pr: of Oranges landing, which put White-hall into so panic a feare, that I could hardly believe it possible to find such a change:

Writs issued now in order to the Parliament, & a declaration to back the good order of Elections, with greate professions of maintaining the Ch: of England: but without giving any sort of satisfaction to people, who now began to shew their high discontent at several things in the Government: how this will end, God onely can tell:

22 News of the French Investing Philipsburge: & of the Mar: Shombergs putting in 3000 men into Collin, upon the dispute of that Electors Interest against the Prince of Firstenberge: Appearances of wonderfull stirrs in this part of Europe, whilst the Emp: was successfull in Hungarie, having taken Belgrade: Earthquakes had now utterly demolished the antient *Smyrna*, & severall other places, both in Greece, Italy, & even the Spanish Indies, forerunners of greater Calamities: God Almight⟨y⟩ preserve his Church, & all who put themselves under the shadow of his Wings, 'til these things be over-past.

30 The *Court* &c in [so] extraordinary consternation upon assurance of the Pr: of Oranges intention of Landing, as the Writs which were sent forth to choose Parliament men, were recalled &c:

Octob: 6: I went to Lond: [7] The next day being Sonday Dr. Tenison viccar of St. Martins, preached on 2: *Tim:* 3. 16. shewing the Scripture to be our undoubted & onely Rule of Faith, & its perfection above all other Traditions & Writings, most excellently proved; after which the Communion was celebrated to neere 1000 devout people. This sermon chiefly occasioned by an impertinent Jesuite who in their Masse-house the Sunday before had disparaged the Scripture & railed at our Translation with extraordinary ignorance and impudence; which some present contradicting, they pulled him out of the Pulpit, & treated him very coursely, insomuch as it was like to create a very greate disturbance in the Citty:

Hourely dreate on expectation of the Pr: of Oranges Invasion still heightned to that degree, as his Majestie thought fit to recall the Writes of Summons of Parliament; to abbrogate the Commission for the dispencing power, [but retaining his owne right still to dispense with all Laws &] restore the ejected Fellows of Magdalen College Oxon: But in the meane time called over 5000 Irish, 4000 Scots; continue⟨s⟩ to remove protestants & put papists in to Portsmouth & other places of

Trust: & retaines the Jesuites about him, which gave no satisfaction to the nation, but increasing the universal discontent,
brought people to so desperate a passe as with uttmost expressions even passionately seeme to long for & desire the landing
of that Prince, whom they looked on as their deliverer from
popish Tyrannie, praying uncessantly for an Easterly Wind,
which was said to be the onely remora of his expedition, with a
numerous Army ready to make a descent; To such a strange
temper & unheard of in any former age, was this poore nation
reduc'd, & of which I was an Eye witnesse: The apprehension
was (& with reason) that his Majesties Forces, would neither at
land or sea oppose them with that viggour requisite to repell
Invaders:

The late Imprisoned Bishops, were now called to reconcile
matters, & the Jesuites hard at worke to foment confusions
amongst the Protestants, by their usual tricks &c: [Leter sent
the AB. of Cant informing from a good hand what was contriving by the Jesuits: &c]

9 I return'd the 9th—A paper of what the Bishops advised his
Majestie [was publish'd]

A [forme of] prayer, the Bishops were injoy⟨n⟩'d to prepare
[an office] against the feared Invasion.

A pardon published: Souldiers & Mariners daily pressed &c.

14 The Kings Birth-day, no Gunns from the Tower, as usualy:
The sunn Eclips'd at its rising: This day signal for the Victory of
William the Conqueror against Herold neere Battel in Sussex:
The wind (which had hitherto ben West) all this day East, won-
derfull expectation of the Dutch fleete.

Our *Viccar* proceeds ⟨on⟩ his former Text: a stranger in the
afternoone on 1. Cor: 15. ult: exhorting to an unmoveablenesse in
our Re⟨l⟩igion, these difficult times, &c:

Continual apprehensions of the Dutch Invasion, there were
pub: prayers ordered to be read in the Church [against it.]

27 I din'd with Sir W: Godolphin: [A Tumult in Lond on the
rabble demolishing a popish Chapell set up in the Citty.]

29 My Lady Sunderland acquainted me at large his
Majesties taking away the Seales from her husband, & of
her being with the Queene to interceede for him: It is conceiv'd he grew remisse of late in pursuing the Interest of the
Jesuitical Counsels, some reported one thing, some another;

but there was doubtlesse some seacret betraied, which time may discover:

There was a Council now cald, to which were summon'd the A:Bish of Cant. &⟨c⟩: Judges, Lord Major &c: Q: Dowager, all the Ladies & Lords, who were present at the Q: Consorts labour, upon oath to give testimonie of the Pr: of Wales's birth, which was recorded, both at the Council board, & at the Chancery a day or two after: This procedure was censur'd by some, as below his Majestie to condescend to, upon the talke of Idle people: Remarkable on this occasion, was the refusal of the A Bish: Marq: Halifax, Earles of Clarendon & Notinghams refusing to sit at the Council Table in their places, amongst Papists, & their bold telling his Majestie that what ever was don whilst such sate amongst them was unlawfull, & incurr'd præmunire: if at least, it be true, what I heard:

I din'd with my Lord Preston, now made Seccretary of state in place of the E. of Sunderland:

Visited Mr. Boile, where came in Duke Hamilton & E. of Burlington: The Duke told us many particulars of Mary Q: of Scots, and her amours with the Italian favorite &c:

30. I dined with the Secretary of the Admiralty, visited Dr. Tenison:

31. My Birthday, being the 68 yeare of my age: ô Blessed Lord, grant, that as I advance in yeare⟨s⟩, so I may improve in Grace: Be thou my protector this following yeare, & preserve me & mine from these dangers and greate confusions, which threaten a sad revolution to this sinfull Nation: Defend thy Church, our holy Religion, & just Lawes, disposing his Majestie to harken to sober & healing Counsels, that yet if it be thy blessed will we may still enjoy that happy Tranquility which hitherto thou hast continued to us. Amen: Amen:

I din'd at my sonns:

November 1. Dined with my L: Preston againe, with other company, at Sir St: Foxes:

Continual al'armes of the Pr: of Oranges landing, but no certainty: reports of his greate losses of horse in the storme; but without any assurance. A Man was taken with divers papers & printed Manifests, & carried to Newgate after examination at the Cabinet-Council: There was likewise a declaration of the States, for satisfaction of all publique Ministers in their

Dominions, the reason of their furnishing the Prince with their Vessels & Militia on this Expedition, which was delivered to all the Ambassadors & publique Ministers at the Hague except to the English & French:

There was in that of the Princes, an expression as if the Lords both Spiritual & Temporal &c had invited him over, with a deduction of the Causes of his enterprise: This made his Majestie Convene my L: of *Cant:* & the other Bishops now in Towne, to [give] them an account of what was in the *Manifesto*: & to enjoyne them to cleare themselves by ⟨some⟩ publique writing of this disloyal charge.

2 It was now certainly reported by some who saw the Pr: imbarke, and the fleete, That they sailed from Brill on Wednesday Morning, & that the Princesse of Orange was there, to take leave of her Husband, [3] & so I returned home.

4 Fresh reports of the Pr: being landed somewher about Portsmouth or Ile of Wight: wheras it was thought, it would have ben north ward: The Court in greate hurry—

5 Being the Anniversary of the powder plot, out *Viccar* preach'd on 76. Psal. 10. by divers Instances: shewing the disasters & punishments overtaking perfidious designes.

8 I went to Lond: heard the newes of the Prince of Oranges being landed at Tor-bay, with a fleete of neere 700 saile, so dreadfull a sight passing through the Channell with so favorable a Wind, as our Navy could by no meanes intercept or molest them: This put the King & Court into greate Consternation, now employed in forming an Army to incounter their farther progresse: for they were gotten already into Excester, & the season, & wayes very improper for his Majesties forces to march so greate a distance:

The A Bish of Cant, & some few of the other Bishops, & Lords in Lond. were sent for to White-hall, & required to set forth their abhorrency of this Invasion; They assured his Majestie they had never invited any of the Princes party or were in the least privy to this Invasion, & would be ready to shew all testimonies of their Loyalty &c: but as to a publique declaration, they being so few, desired that his majestie would call the rest of their brethren & peeres, that they might consult what was fit to do on this occasion, not thinking it convenient to publish any thing without them, & untill they had themselves seene the

Princes Manifest, in which it was pretended he was invited in by the Lords Sp: & temporal: This did not please his Majestie: So they departed: There came now out a Declaration, prohibiting all people to see or reade the Princes Manifest; in which was at large set-forth the cause of his Expedition, as there had ben on⟨c⟩e before one from the States: These are the beginnings of Sorrows, unlesse God in his Mercy prevent it, by some happy reconciliation of all dissentions amongst us, which nothing in likelihood can Effect but a free Parliament, but which we cannot hope to see, whilst there are any forces on either side: I pray God protect, & direct the King for the best, & truest Interest of his People: [I saw his Majestie touch for the Evil, Piters the Jesuit & F. Warner officiating in the Banqueting house]

I dined at Dr. Godolphins, with Mrs. Boscawen &c at her house warming in his prebends house near S. Paules: Lay at my sonns, & [9] returned home the next day.

11 My deare Wife fell very ill of the gravell &c in her kidnies this afternoone. God in mercy give her ease & comfort:

The Pr. of Orange increases every day in forces, several Lords go in to him; The King gos towards Salisbery with his Army; doubtfull of their standing by him, Lord Cornbery carrys some Regiments from him, marches to Honiton, the Princes head quarters; The Citty of Lond: in dissorder by the rabble &c who pull-downe the Nunery at St. Johns, newly bought by the Papists of my Lord Berkeley: The Queene [prepare⟨s⟩ to] ⟨go⟩ to Portsmouth for safty: to attend the issue of this commotion, which has a dreadfull aspect:

18 Our Viccar on his former Text, shewing the wonderfull deliverances of Gods church in its greatest necessities:

I went afternoone to Greenewich to visite the Marq: de Ruvigny, where a young man preached very excellently on 11. *Heb:* 6:

It was now very hard frost:

The King gos to Salisbery to rendevouze the Army, and returning back to Lond: Lord De la Mare appears for the Pr: in Cheshire: The nobility meete in Yorkshire: The ABish & some Bishops, & such peeres as were in Lond: addresse to his Majestie to call a Parliament: The King invites all forraine nations to come over: The French take all the Palatinat, & alarme the Germans more than ever:

29 I went to the R: Society, we adjourn'd Election of Præsident til 23. Aprill by reason of the publique commotions, yet
dined together as of custome on this day:

December 2 Dr. Tenison at St. Martins on: 36 Psal: 5. 6. 7:
I received the B: Sacrament.

Visited my L. Godolphin, then going with the Marquis of
Halifax, & E: of Notingham as Commissioner to the Prince
of Orange: He told me, they had little power: Plymoth declared
for the Prince & L: Bath: Yorke, Hull, Bristoll, all the eminent
nobility & persons of quality throut England declare for the
Protestant Rel⟨i⟩gion & Laws, & go to meete the Prince; who
every day sets forth new declarations &c: against the Papists:
The Greate favorits at Court, priest⟨s⟩ & Jesuites, flie or
abscond: Every thing (til now conceiled) flies abroad in publique
print, & is Cryed about the streetes: Expectations of the Pr:
coming to Oxon: Pr: of Wales & greate Treasure sent daily to
Portsmouth, Earle of Dover Governor: Addresse from the
Fleete not gratefull to his Majestie: The Popists in offices lay
down their Commissions & flie: Universal Consternation
amongst them: it lookes like a Revolution: Herbert, beates a
french fleete:

7 My son went towards Oxon: I returned home:

9 Our Lecturer on 122. Psal: 6: Pray for the peace of
Jerusalem: Lord Sunderland meditating flight, I writ to my
Lady, advised an Apologie:

13 I went to Lond: [The rabble people demolish all Papists
Chapells & severall popish Lords & Gent: house⟨s⟩, especialy
that of the Spanish Ambassador, which they pillaged & burnt
his Library &c:] 16 Dr. Tenison at St. Martins on: 8: Isay: 11:

I din'd at my L. Clarendons: The King flies to sea, [putts in at
Feversham for ballast is rudely detained by the people: comes
back to W⟨hite⟩hall.]

The Pr: of Orange now advanc'd to Windsor, is invited by the
King to St. James, the messenger sent was the E. of Feversham
the general of the forces: who going without Trumpet or passe-
port is detained prisoner by the Prince: The Prince accepts the
Invitation, but requires his Majestie to retire to some distant
place, that his owne Guards may be quartered about the palace
& Citty: This is taken heinously, so the King gos away privately
to Rochester: Is perswaded to come back: comes on the Sunday;

Goes to masse & dines in publique, a Jesuite says grace: [I was present] That night a Council, [17] his Majestie refuses to assent to all proposals; gos away againe to Rochester:

18 The Pr: comes to St. James, fills W-hall (the King taking barge to Gravesend at 12 a Clock) with Dut⟨c⟩h Guard: A Council of Peres meete about an Expedient to call a parliament: Adjourne to the House of Lords: The Chancelor, E. of Peterbor, & divers Priests & other taken: E: of Sunderland flies & divers others, Sir E: Hales, Walker & other taken & secured: All the world go to see the Prince at St. Jamess where is a greate Court, there I saw him & severall of my Acquaintance that come over with him: He is very stately, serious, & reserved: The Eng: souldiers &c. sent out of Towne to distant quarters: not well pleased: Divers reports & opinions, what all this will end in; Ambition & faction feared:

21 I visited L. Clarendon where was the Bishops of Ely & St. Asaph: we had much discourse of Afairs: I returned home:

24 The King passes into France, whither the queen & child wer gon a few days before.

26 The Peeres & such Commons as were members of the Parliament at Oxford, being the last of Charles the first: meeting, desire the Pr: of Orange to take on him the Government, & dispose of the publique Revenue 'til a Convention of Lords & Commons should meete in full body, appointed by his Circulary Letters to the Shires & Borrowghs 22. Jan:

I had now quartered upon me a Lieutenant Coll: & 8 horses:

30 Our Lecturer on 122. *Psal:* 6: Pomerid: a Stranger on 6. Eccles: This day Prayers for the Prince of Wales were first left off in our Church pew & pulpet.

Greate preparations of all the Princes of Europ, against the French &c: the Emp: making peace with the Turke:

168$\frac{8}{9}$; Jan: 1 Dined with me severall friends.

7 I returned home: on foote, it having ben a long frost & deepe snow, ⟨so⟩ as the Thames was almost quite frozen over.

15 I went to visite my Lord Archbish of Cant: where I found the Bishops of St. Asaph, Ely, Bath & Wells, Peterborow & Chichester; The Earle of Alesbery & Clarendon, Sir Geo: Makenzy Lord Advocate of Scotland, & then came in a Scotch Archbishop: &c. After prayers & dinner, were discoursed divers serious matters concerning the present state of the publique: &

sorry I was to find, there was as yet no accord in the judgements of those who both of the Lords & Commons were to convene: Some would have the princesse made Queene without any more dispute, others were for a Regency, There was a Torie part (as then called so) who were for ⟨inviting⟩ his Majestie againe upon Conditions, & there were Republicarians, who would make the Prince of Orange like a State-holder: The Romanists were also buisy among all these severall parties to bring them into Confusion; most for Ambition, or other Interest, few for Conscience and moderate resolutions: I found nothing of all this in this Assembly of Bishops, who were pleas'd to admitt me into their Discourses: They were all for a Regency, thereby to salve their Oathes, & so all publique matters to proceede in his Majesties name, thereby to facilitate the calling of a Parliament according to the Laws in being; this was the result of this meeting: My Lord of Cant: gave me greate thanks for the advertisement I sent his Grace in October, & assur'd me they tooke my counsel in that particular, & that it came very seasonable:

I found by the Lord Advocate of Scotland that the Bishops of Scotland, who were indeede very unworthy that Character & had don much mischiefe in that Church, were now coming about to the True Interest, more to save themselves in this conjuncture, which threatned the abolishing the whole Hierarchy in that Kingdome, than for Conscience: & therefore the Scotish Archbish: & Lord Advocate requested my L. of Cant: to use his best endeavors with the Prince, to maintaine the Church there in the same state as by Law at present settled: It now growing late, I after some private discourse, tooke my leave of his Grace, most of the Lords being gon: I beseech God of his infinite mercy to settle truth & peace amongst us againe:

It was now that the Triall of the Bishops was published in print:

23 I went to Lond, The greate Convention being assembled the day before, falling upon the greate Question about the Government, Resolved that K. *Jam:* 2d, having by the advise of Jesuites & other wicked persons, endeavored to subvert the Lawes of church & state, and Deserting the Kingdome [carrying away the Seales &c] without taking any care for the manegement of the Government, had by demise, abdicated himselfe, and wholy vacated his right: & They did therefore

desire the Lords Concurrence to their Vote, to place the Crowne upon the next heires: The Prince of Orange for his life, then to the Princesse his wife, & if she died without Issue to the Princesse of Denmark, & she failing to the heires of the Pr: Excluding for ever all possibility of admitting any Ro: Cath:

27 Dr. Tenison preached at St. Martines, on 6: *Gen:* 5: I din'd at the Admiralty, where was brought, a young Child not 12 yeares old, the sonn of one Dr. Clench, of the most prodigious maturity of memorie, & knowledge, for I cannot call it altogether memory, but [something more] extraordinary; Mr. Pepys & my selfe examining him not in any method, but [by] promiscuously questions, which required judgement & wonderfull discernement, to answere things so readily & pertinently: There was not any thing in Chronologie, Historie, Geographie, The several systemes of Astronomers, Courses of the starrs, Longitudes, Latitudes, doctrine of the Spheares, Sourses & courses of Rivers, Creekes, harbors, Eminent Citties, staples, boundaries & bearings of Countries, not onely in Europe but any other part of the Earth, which he did not readily resolve & demonstrate his knowledge of, readily drawing out, with his pen any thing that he would describe: He was able not onely to repeate the most famous things which are left us in any of the Greeke or Roman histories, Monarchie, Repub, Warrs, Colonies, Exploits by sea & land; but readily, besides all the Sacred stories of the Old & New Test: the succession of all the Monarches, Babylonish, Persian, Gr: Roman, with all the lower Emperors, Popes, Heresiarches, & Councils; What they were cald about, what they determined, [&] in the Controversie of Easter, The Tenets of the Gnostics, Sabellius, Arius, Nestorius; The difference twixt St. Cyprian & Stephen about rebaptization; The Schismes, we leaped from that to other things totaly different: To Olympic yeares, & Synchronismes; we asked him questions which could not be resolved without considerable meditation & judgement: nay, of some particulars of the Civil Lawes, of the Digest & Code: He gave a stupendous account of both Natural, & Moral Philosophie, & even in Metaphysics: Having thus exhausted our selves, rather than this wonderfull Child, or Angel rather, for he was as beautifull & lovely in Countenance, as in knowledge; we concluded, with asking him, if in all he had read, or heard of, he had ever met with any thing which was like, this Expedition of

the Pr: of Orange; with so small a force, to obtaine 3 greate ⟨Kingdoms⟩, without any Contest: He after a little thought, told us, that he knew of nothing did more resemble it, Than the coming of Constantin the Greate out of Brittane, thro: France & Italy, so tedious a March, to meete Maxentius, whom he over-threw at ponte Milvij, with very little conflict, & at the very gates of Rome, which he entered & was received with Triumph, & obtained the Empire, not of 3 Kingdomes onely, but of all the then known World: He was perfect in the Latine Authors, spake french naturaly, & gave us a description of France, Italy, Savoy, Spaine, Antient & modernly divided; as also of the antient Greece, S⟨c⟩ythia, & Northern Countries & Tracts, in a word, we left questioning farther with astonishment: This the child did without any set or formal repetition; as one who had learned things without booke, but, as if he minded other things going about the roome, & toying with a parat there, & as he was at dinner [(*tanquam aliud agens* as it were)] seeming to be full of play, of a lively & spiritfull temper, allways smiling, & exceed-ingly pleasant without the least levity, rudenesse or childish-nesse: His father assur'd us, he never imposed any thing to charge his memorie, by causing him to get things by heart, no, not the rules of Grammer; but his ⟨Tutor⟩ (who was a French-man) reading to him, in French first, & then in Latine: That he usualy plaied, amongst other boys 4 or 5 hours every day & that he was as earnest at play, as at his study: He was perfect in Arithmetic, & now newly entered into the Greek: In sum [(*Horesco referens*)] I had, read of divers, forward & præcoce, Youthes, & some I have known; but in my life, did never either heare or read of any like to this sweete Child, if it be lawfull to call him Child, who has more knowledge, than most men in the world: I counseled his father, not to set his heart too much upon this Jewell, *Immodicis brevis est ætas, et rara senectus*, as I my selfe learn'd by sad experience in my most deare child Richard many yeares since, who dying before he was six years old, was both in shape & Countenance, & pregnancy of learning, next to prodigie even in that tender-age, as I have given ample account in my præface to that Golden book of St. Chrysostome, which I published on that sad occasion &c:

28 The Votes of the House of Comm: being Carried up, by their chaire-man Mr. Hamden, to the Lords, [29] I got a

station by the Princes lodgings at the doore of the Lobby to the House, to heare much of the debate which held very long; The Lord Danby being in the chaire (for the Peres were resolved into a grand Committee of the whole house) after all had spoken, it comming to the question: It was carried out by 3 voices, again⟨s⟩t a *Regency*, which 51 of 54 were for, aledging the danger of dethroning   Kings, & scrupuling many passages & expressions of the Commons Votes; too long to set downe particularly, some were for sending to his Majestie with Conditions, others, that the K. could do no wrong, & that the mal-administration was chargeable on his Ministers. There were not above 8 or 9 Bish: & but two, against the Regency; The *Arch Bishop* was absent: & the Cleargie now began a new to change their note, both in pulpet & discourse, upon their old passive Obedience: so as people began to talke of the Bishops being cast out of the House: In short, things tended to dissatisfaction on both sides, add to this the morose temper of the Pr: of Orange, who shewed so little Countenance to the Noblemen & others, expecting a more gracious & cherefull reception, when they made their Court: The English Army likewise, not so in order, & firme to his Interest, nor so weaken'd, but that it might, give interruption: Ireland in a very ill posture, as well as Scotland; nothing yet towards any settlement: God of his infinite mercy, Compose these ⟨things⟩, that we may at lastt be a Nation & a church under some fixt and sober establishment:

30 Was the Anniversary of K: Ch: the Is Martyrdome; but in all the publique Offices & pulpet prayers, The Collects [& Litanys] for the King & Queene, were curtailed & mutilated: Dr. Sharp preached before the Common⟨s⟩; but was disliked & not so much as thanked for his sermon:

I went to St. Martin, where a stranger preached on *2: Apoc: 10* much against popery, with a touch at our Obligation of Loyalty to the King &c:

I came home afternoone, & at our church (the next ⟨day⟩ being appointed a Thanksgiving for deliverance by the P: of Orange, prayers purposly composed) our Lecturer, preached on 97: Psal: 1. a very honest Sermon, shewing our duty to God for the many signal deliverances of his Church, without entering into the politics.

Feb: ⟨3⟩ Our Lecturer on his former Text, shewing how all power flowes from God, & how absolutely necessary it is, that he should ⟨constitute⟩ his Vicegerents here, & how responsible they are that they governe justly; The fatal ends of those who have in all ages abused their power, & the hapinesse of religious Princes &c: The holy Communion follow'd, at which I received: Blessed be God.

6 The Kings Coronation day was ordred not to be observed, as hitherto it yearely had.

The Convention of L: & Comm: now declare the Pr: & princesse of Or: Q: & K of England, Fr: & Ireland (Scotland being an Independent Kingdome) The Pr & Princesse to enjoy it jointly during their lives, but the executive Authority to be vested in the Prince during life, though all proceedings to run in both names: & that it descend to the heires of both, & for want of such Issue to the Princesse Ann of Denmark, & in want of such to the heires of the body of the Pr: of Or: if he survive, & for defect, to devolve to the Parliament to choose as they think fit: These produc'd a Conference with the Lords, when also there was presented heads of such [new] laws as were to be enacted: & upon those Conditions they tis thought will be pro-claim'd: There was much contest about the Kings abdication, & whether he had vacated the Government: E. of Notingham & about 20 Lords & many Bishops, entred their protests &c, but the Concurrence was greater against them—The Princesse hourely Expected: Forces sending to Ireland, that K⟨ing⟩dome being in greate danger, by the E. of Tyrconnells Armie, & expec-tations from France: which K. is buisy to invade Flanders, & encounter the German Princes comming now to their Assis-tance: so as this is likely to be one of the most remarkable sum-mers for action, as has happed for many Ages:

21 At St. James's church preached Dr. Burnet, on 5. *Deut:* 29 relating to the obligation lying upon the nation, to walke worthy of Gods particular & signal deliverances of this Nation & Church:

22 I saw the new Queene & King, so proclaim'd, the very next day of her coming to White-hall, Wednesday 13. Feb. with won-derfull acclamation & general reception, Bonfires, bells, Gunns &c: It was believed that they both, especialy the Princesse, would have shewed some (seeming) reluctancy at least, of

assuming her Fathers Crowne & made some Apologie, testi-
fying her regret, that he should by his misgoverment necessitat
the Nation to so extraordinary a proceeding, which would have
shewed very handsomly to the world, (and according to
the Character give⟨n⟩ of her piety &c) & consonant to her husbands first Declaration, that there was no intention of Deposing
the King, but of Succoring the Nation; But, nothing of all this
appeared; she came into W-hall as to a Wedding, riant & jolly,
so as seeming to be quite Transported: rose early on the next
morning of her arival, and in her undresse (as reported) before
her women were up; went about from roome to roome, to see
the Convenience of White-hall: Lay in the same bed & appartment where the late Queene lay: & within a night or two, sate
downe to play at Basset, as the Q. her predecessor us'd to do:
smiled upon & talked to every body; so as no manner of change
seem'd in Court, since his Majesties last going away, save that
the infinite crowds of people thronged to see her, & that she
went to our prayers: This carriage was censured by many:
she seemes to be of a good nature, & that takes nothing to heart
whilst the Pr: her husband has a thoughtfull Countenance, is
wonderfull serious & silent, seemes to treate all persons alike
gravely: & to be very intent on affaires, both Holland, & Ireland
& France calling for his care: Divers Bishops, & Noble men
are not at all satisfied with this so suddain Assumption of the
Crown, without any previous, sending & offering some Conditions to the absent King: or, upon his not returning & assenting
to those Conditions within such a day: to have proclaim'd him
Regent &c. But the major part of both houses, prevailed to
make them King & Q: immediately, and a Crowne was tempting &c—This was opposed & spoke against with such vehe-
mency by my L. Clarendon (her owne Unkle) as putt him by all
preferments, which must doubtlesse, ⟨have⟩ been as greate, as
could have ben given him: My L: of Rochester his bro: overshot
himselfe by the same carriage & stiffnesse, which, their friends
thought, they might have well spared, when they saw how it was
like to be over-ruled, & that it had ben sufficient to have
declared their dissent with lesse passion, acquiescing in due-
time: The Æ of Cant, & some of the rest, upon scruple of
Conscience, & to salve the Oathes they had taken, entred their
protests, & hung off: Especially the Arch-Bishop, who had not

all this while so much as appeared out of Lambeth: all which incurred the wonder of many, who observed with what zeale they contributed to the Princes Expedition, & all this while also, rejecting any proposals of sending againe ⟨for⟩ the absented King: That they should now boggle & raise scrupuls, & such as created much division among people, greatly rejoicing the old Courtiers, & Papist⟨s⟩ especialy:

Another objection was the invalidity of what was don, by a Convention onely, & the as yet unabrogated Laws: which made them on the 22, make themselves a parliament, the new King passing the act with the Crowne on his head: This lawyers disputed; but necessity prevailed, the Government requiring a speedy settlement: And now innumerable were the Crowds who solicited for & expected Offices, most of the old ones turn'd out: Two or 3. White Staves were disposed of some days before, as L: Steward to the E. of Devonshire, Tress: of the Household to L: Newport, L. Cham: to the K, to my L: of Dorset &c: but there were yet none in offices of the Civil government, save: Pr: Seale to the Marq: of Halifax: A Council of 30 was chosen, L. Danby Presedent: but neither Chancellor, Tressurer, Judges &c not yet declared, A greate seale not yet finished: Thus far went things when I returned home (having visited divers of my old acquaintance &c) which was [23] on the Saturday:

Mar. 2 To Lond: 3d Dr. *Tenison* at St. Martins on: 16: Matt 26: The holy Communion follow'd, of which I participated.

8. Dr. Tillotson deane of Cant: an excellent discourse on 5. Matt: 44: exhorting to charity and forgivenesse of Enemies; I suppose purposly, The new Parliament now being furiously about Impeaching those who were obnoxious: & as their custome has ever ben going on violently, without reserve or moderation: whilst wise men were of opinion that the most notorious Offenders being named & excepted, an Act of Amnesty were more seasonable, to paciffie the minds of men, in so generall a discontent of the nation, especialy of those who did not expect to see the Government assum'd without any reguard to the absent King, or proving a spontaneous abdication, or that the Pr: of Wales was an Imposture, &c: 5 of the Bishops also still refusing to take the new Oath: In the interim to gratifie & sweeten the people, The Hearth Tax was remitted for ever: but what intended to supply it, besids present greate Taxes on land: is not

named: The King abroad furnished with mony & officers by the
French King going now for Ireland, Their wonderfull neglect of
more timely preventing that from hence, and disturbances in
Scotland, gives men apprehension of greate difficulties before
any settlement can be perfected here: [whilst] The Parliament
men dispose of the greate Offices amongst themselves: The Gr:
Seale, Treasury, Admiralty put into commission, of many unexperienc'd persons to gratifie the more: So as, by the present
prospect of things (unlesse God Almighty graciously interpose,
& give successe in Ireland, & settle Scotland) more Trouble
seemes to threaten this nation, than could be expected: In the
Interim, the New K. referrs all to the Parliament in the most
popular manner imaginable: but is very slow in providing
against all these menaces, besides finding difficulties in raising
men to send abroad, The former army (who had never don any
service hitherto, but received pay, and passed the summers in an
idle scene of a Camp at Hounslow) unwilling to engage, &
many of them dissaffected, & scarce to be trusted:

[28 I visited Mr. Boile where an Italian Traveller described
how farr he had ben in the desert of Africa and saw a Creature,
bodied like an ox, head like a pike fish, taile like a peacock:]

29 Good friday Morning at St. Martin, Dr. Tenison: on: 53.
Isah: ver: 3:

The Holy Sacrament follow'd at which I received:

I returned home after this: sermon:

The new King, much blamed for neglecting Ireland, now like
to be ruined by the L. Tyrconnel, & his popish party; too strong
for the Protestants; wonderfull uncertainty where King James
was, whether in France or Ireland: The Scotts seeme as yet to
favor King William, rejecting K James letter to them: yet declaring nothing positively: Souldiers in England, discontented: Parliament preparing the Coronation Oath: Presbyterians &
Dissenters displeased at the vote to preserve the protestant Religion as established by Law; without mentioning what they were
to have as to Indulgence: The Arch-Bishop of Cant, & the other
4: refusing to come to Parliament, it was deliberated whether
they should incurr premunire: but this was thought fit to be
let fall, & connived at, for feare of the people, to w⟨h⟩om
these prelates were very deare, for their opposing poper⟨y⟩:
Court Offices, distributed among the Parliament men: no

Considerable fleete as yet set forth: in summe: Things far from [the] settlement was expected by reason of the slothfull sickly temper of the new King: and unmindfullnesse of the Parliament, as to Ireland, which is like to prove a sad omission. The Confederats, beate the French out of the Palatinate, which they had most barbarously ruined:

31 Easter day: Our Viccar on 22 Matt: 29: The holy Communion follow'd, at which I received. The Curate on 1. Cor: 15. ver: 56. 57.

Aprill 7: Having taken cold after some preventing physick: I was not at Church this day, to my greate sorrow:

10 I went to Lond: was at the R. Society, where the very ingenious Mr. Waler brought in his Tables of knowing plants by a peculiar method: There was an extraordinary greate scorpion, sent the Society out of Africa, whose Eyes were in his back, like to spiders, but not so prominent:

11 I saw the procession both to, & from the Abby church of Westminster, with the greate feast in Westminster Hall &c: at the Coronation of the new K William & Q. Mary: That which was different from former Coronations, was, something altered in the Coronation Oath, concerning maintaining the Prot: Religion: &c: Dr. Burnet (now made L.B. of *Sarum*) preached on   with infinite applause: The parliament men had Scaffolds & places which tooke up one whole side of the Hall: & when the K & Q. had din'd. The Ceremonie of the Champion, & other services upon Tenures: The Parliament men were also feasted in the Exchequer Chamber: and had each of them a Medaile of Gold given them worth five & fourty shill: the K. & Q: effigies inclining one to another, on one side, the Reverse Jupiter throwing a bolt at Phaeton, the Word   which was but dull seing they might have had out of the poet something as apposite   The sculpture also very meane: Much of the splendor of the proceeding was abated, by the absence of divers who should have made it up: There being but as yet 5 Bish: 4. Judges, (no more at present, it seemes [as yet] sworn) & severall noblemen & greate Ladys wanting: But indeede the Feast was magnificent: The next day, went the H of Commons & kissed their new Majesties hands in the Banqueting house:

12 I went the next day afternoone [with the B: of St. Asaph] to visite my L. of Canterbery at Lambeth, who had excused himselfe

from officiating at the Coronation, (which the Bishop of Lond:
performed assisted by the A.B: of Yorke) we had much private &
free discourse with his Grace, concerning severall things, relating
to the Church, there being now a Bill of Comprehension to be
brought to the Commons from the Lords: I urg'd, that when they
went about to reforme some particulars in the Liturgie, Church
discipline, Canons &c: The Baptising in private Houses, without
necessity, might be reformd: as likewise the Burying dead bodies
so frequently in the Churches: The one proceeding meerely from
the pride of [the] Women, bringing that into Custome, which
was onely indulged in case of iminent danger: & out of necessity,
during the Rebellion and persecution of the Cleargy, in our late
Civil Warres &c: The other from the Avarice of the Minister, who
made in some opulent parishes, almost as much of permissions to
bury in the chancels & churches, as of their livings, and were paid
with considerable advantage & gifts, for baptising in Chambers:
To this the two Bishops, heartily assented: and promised their
indeavors to get it reformed: utterly disliking both practice⟨s⟩, as
novel, & undecent: We discoursed likewise concerning the greate
disturbance & prejudice it might cause should the new oath (now
upon the anvile) be imposed upon any, save such as were in [new]
office; without any retrospect to such as either had no office; or
had ben long in office, who likely had some scruples about taking a new othe, having already sworn fidelity to the Government,
as established by Law: and this we all knew to be the case of my L.
Arch Bishop & some other worthy persons, who were not so fully
satisfied with the Conventions abdicating the late K James, To
whom they had sworn alegiance &c: So I went back to Whit hall,
& thence home:

K. James now certainly in Ireland; with the Marshall
d'Aveaux, whom he made a Pr: Counselor, who immediatly
caused the King to remove the protestant Counselor⟨s⟩ (some
wheroff it seemes had continued to sit) telling him that his
Master the K of France would never assist him, if he did not
immediatly do it: by which tis apparent how this poore Prince is
menag'd by the French:

Scotland declare for K. William & Q: Mary, with the Reasons
of their laying K James aside [not as Abdicating but forfaiting his
right by maladministrat⟨ion⟩, the particulars mentioned] which
being published, I repeate not: proceeding with much more

caution & prudence than we did; who precipitated all things to the great reproch of the Nation, but all that was plainly menaged by some crafty, ill principled men: The new Pr: Council having a Republican Spirit, & manifestly undermining all future Succession of the Crown, and prosperity of the Church of England: which yet, I hope, they will not be able to accomplish so soone as they hope: though they get into all places of Trust and profit:

14: Our Viccar on 22. Matt: 29. 30:

The Curate in the Afternoone on 13. Romans 12: This was a more Seasonable Spring, than any we have had since the Restauration of K. Char. IId:

21 The Viccar proceeded on his former Text & sub: as also did the curate:

26 I heard the Lawyers plead before the Lords, the Writ of Error, in the Judgment of *Oates*, as to his charge of Perjurie, which they after debate referred to the Answer of Holloway &c: who were his Judges:

Then went with the B: of St. Asaph to Lambeth to visie the A Bishop: where they both entred into a discourse concerning the final destruction of Antichrist: both of them concluding, that the 3 Trumpet & Vial was now powering out; and my L. S. Asaph attributing the Killing of the two Witnesse⟨s⟩, to the utter destruction of the Cevenes Protestants, by the French & Duke of Savoy, & the other, the Waldenses & Pyrennean Christians (who by all appearances from good history had kept the Primitive faith from the very Apostles times till now): The doubt his Grace suggested, was whether it could be made ev⟨i⟩dent, that the present persecution had made so greate an havock of those faithfull people as of the other, & whether as yet, there were not some among them in being who met together: it being expedient from the Text: 11: Apoc: that they should be both slaine together: The⟨y⟩ both much approved of Mr. Meads way of Interpretation, and that he onely failed in resolving too hastily, upon the King of Swedens successes, (Gustavus Adolphus), in Germany: That It were good to employ some intelligent French Minister, to travell even as far as the Pyrennes, to understand the present state of the Churches there: It being a country, where no body almost traverses.

There now came certaine newes of K: James's being not onely landed in Ireland, but that by surprizing London Derry, he was become absolute Master of all that Kingdome: to the greate shame of our new King & Assembly at Westminster, who had ben so often solicited to provide against it, by timely succors, & which so easily they might have don: This is a terrible beginning of more troubles, especialy should an Armie come thence into Scotland; People being so generaly dissafected here & every where else; so as scarse would sea, or Landmen serve without compulsion:

A new Oath was now fabricating, for all the Cleargy to take, of obedience to the present Goverment, in abrogation of the former Oathes of Alegeance: which it is forseene, many Bishops, & others of the Cleargy will not take, the penalty being the losse of their dignit⟨i⟩e & spiritual preferment: so as this is thought to have ben ⟨driven⟩ on by the Presbyters & Comm: welth party, who were now in much credite with our new Governors: God in mercy, send us help, & direct the Counsel to his glory, & good of his Church:

May: 1 Being the Anniversary of the Feffees, for the poores Rents proceeding from the Charity of divers persons, our Viccar preached on: 11: Matt: 30: shewing the Ease of Christs Yoake: &c:

19 Matters publique went very ill in Ireland, Confusion & dissention amongst ourselves, stupidity, unconstancy, emulation, in the Governours, employing unskillfull men in greatest offices: No person of publique spirit, & ability appearing &c: threaten us with a very sad prospect what may be the conclusion: without Gods Infinite mercy: A fight by Admiral Herbert with the French, imprudently setting on them in a Creeke as they were landing men &c in Ireland: by which we came off with greate slaughter, & little honor: so strangely negligent, & remisse in preparing a timely & sufficient fleete. The S⟨c⟩ots Commissioners offer the Crowne &c to the new King, & Queene, upon Condition. [Act of Pole mony came forth sparing none:]

June 2: Our Viccar on 6: Heb: Last 3 verses: I received the holy Sacrament: Went in the afternoone to Greenewich to visite some French Gent: refugies:

Now came forth the Act of Indulgence for the disscenters, but not exempting them from paying dues to the Ch: of Eng: Cleargy, or serving in offices &c: according to law, with severall other Clauses:

A most splendid Ambassy from Holland to congratulate the Kings accession to the Crowne.

4. I went to Lond: [in my way Visited L: Arran, L. Peterboro, L: Preston in the Toure &c] the solemn Fast for Successe of the Fleete &c: was on [5] the next day carried on by the Bishop of Salisbury at Westminster Abby, before the Lords, and at St. Margarites before the Convention or Parliament by Dr. Tenison in the morning on   In which he did incomparably shew the sinn of selfe love, and how it was prejudicial to all brave and heroick actions &c:

7 I visited my L. A Bish: of Canterbery, to recommend Mr. Stringfellow to him, staied with him til about 7: a clock: he read to me, the Popes Excommunication of the French King &c:

8 I din'd with Mr. Pepys.

16 K: James's declaration was now dispersed, offring pardon to all if upon his landing or 20 days after, they should returne to their obedience:

Our Fleete, not yet at sea, & thro some prodigious sloth, & mens minding only their present Interest: The French riding master at Sea, taking many greate prises, to our wonderfull Reproch: No certaine newes from Ireland, various reports of Scotland, discontents at home: The K. of Denmark at last joyning with the Confederates: [& the two Northern Princes reconciled:]

The E. India Company like to be disolv'd by the Parliament for many arbitrarie actions:

Oates acquitted of perjurie to all honest mens admiration.

20 Dined with me the Countesses of Bristoll & Sunderland, Sir W: Godolphin, Dr. Tenison & Mrs. Penelope Godolphin: Brought newes of a plot discovered, upon which divers were sent to Tower & secured:

Twas now also reported that Col: Kirke had gotten into Lond: Derry with supplies: [but this proved false.]

23 An extraordinary Drowth, to the threatning of greate Wants, as to the fruits of the Earth:

⟨July⟩ 8 To Lond: [9] I sat for my Picture to Mr. *Kneller*, for Mr. Pepys late Secretary of the Admiralty, holding my *Sylva* in my right hand: It was upon his long and earnest request; & is plac'd in his Library: nor did Kneller ever paint better & more masterly work:

11 I dind at my L: Clarendons, it being his Ladys Weding day: when about 3 in the afternoone, so greate & unusual a storme of Thunder, raine and wind suddainly fell, as had not ben known in an age: many boates on the Thames were over wh⟨e⟩lmed, & such was the impetuosity of the wind, as carried up the waves in pillars & spouts, most dreadfull to behold, rooting up Trees, ruining some houses, & was indeede no other than an Hurocan:

The Co: of Sunderland told me, that it extended as far as *Althorp*, that very moment, which is about 70 miles from Lond: But I blesse Almighty God it did us no harme at Deptford, but at Greenewich it did much mischefe:

16 I went to Hampton Court, about buisinesse, the Council being there; A greate appartment, & spacious Garden with fountaines, was beginning in the Parke, at the head of the Canale: I return'd to Lond that evening:

19 I returned home: The Marishall de Scomberge, went now Generall towards Ireland, to the reliefe of Lond: Derry: Our Fleete lie before Brest: The Confederates, now passing the Rhyne, beseege Bonn, and Maence to obtaine a passage into France: A greate Victory gotten by the Muscovite, taking & burning *Procop*: A new Rebell against the Turks, unkle to Yegen Bassha threatens the destruction of that Tyrannie: All Europe in armes against France; & hardly in memory of an⟨y⟩ Historie, so universal a face of Warr: The Convention (or Parliament as some called it) sitting, exempt the Duke of Hanover from the Succession to the Crowne, which they seeme to confine to the present New King, his Wife, & Princesse Ann of Denmark, who is so monstroustly s⟨w⟩ollen, that its doubted, her being thought with child, may proove a Tympane onely: so as the [unhappy] family of Steuarts, seemes to be extinguishing: and then what government next, is likely to be set up, whether Regal & by Election, or otherwise, The Republicaries & Dissenters from the C. of England looking evidently that way: The Scots having now againe newly, voted downe Episcopacy there: Greate discontent still through the nation, at the slow proceedings of the King, & the incompetent Instruments

& Officers he advances to the greatest & most necessary charges:

24 I went to Lond; sate at Mr. Knellers for my picture, dined at Mr. Pepys', return'd that evening:

25 Came Mr. Knellar, with two other painters to visite me:

⟨August⟩ 2 I went to Lond, return'd that evening:

4 Mr. *Stringfellow* preached on: 16: *John* 13: The H: Communion followed, at which I participate⟨d⟩, *Deo laus & gloria*:

Marishal Schomberg went with forces to⟨w⟩ards Ireland, London Derry in exceeding want of reliefe:

6 I went to Lond: about buisnesse, returned the 8th: Lond: Derry relieved, Dundee slaine in Scotland.

11 Our Curate preached on 1. *Cor:* 3. 7, a very handsome discourse; The extreame heate of the Weather hindred me from Church in the Afternoone:

21: I went to Lond: to take leave of the Countesse of *Sunderland* going next day to Holland. I returned that Evening:

Octob: 6 Our Viccar on 22: Apoc. A visite kept me at home in the afternoone:

9 Came to visite us the [young] Marquis de Ru⟨v⟩ignie & one *Monsieur le Coque* a French Refugiè, who left greate Riches for his Religion, a very learned civill person: he married the sister of the Dutchesse de la Force &c.

31: My Birthday, being now 69 years old: Blessed Father who hast prolonged my years to this greate Age, & given me to see so greate & wonderfull Revolutions, preserved me amidst them, to this moment; accept I beseech thee the continuance of my Prayers & thankfull accknowledgements, and graunt to me the Grace to be working out my Salvation, & redeeme the Time, that thou mayst be glorified by me here, & my immortal Soule saved, when ever thou shall call for it, to perpetuate thy prayes to all eternity, in that heavenly Kingdome, where there is no more Changes, nor Vicissitudes, but rest & peace, & Joy & consummate felicity for ever: Grant this, ô heavenly Father, for the sake of the L. Jesus, thyne onely Sonn & our Saviour: Amen:

Nov 3 I received the H: Sacrament at St. Martines, Dr. Tenison preaching most excellently (as he allways dos) on: 3: *Luke* 5:

5 Bish: of St. Asaph Lord Almoner &c: preached before K. & Q: on 57: *Psal:* 7: the whole discourse being almost nothing save

an historical narrative of the C. of Englands several Deliverances, especialy that of this Anniversary, signalized, by that
of the P: of Oranges Birthday, & Marriage (which was on the
4th) & of his Landing at Tor-bay this day: which ended with a
splendid Ball, & other festival rejoicings:

In the Meane time, No, or not sufficient supplies, Ireland
gives greate apprehension of the successe of our Army there,
under the D: of Shomberg, K. James, being more powerfull in
Horse: & the Weather exceeding wet & stormy: [& we having
miserably lost all the past summer for want of prudent
menagement of affaires: The Convention vote a Tax of 2 Million &c:]

Card: Ottaboni (a Venetian) chosen Pope:

10 Our Viccar on his former Text: the Curate on 6: John: 37:
I received the B: Sacrament with my Wife at home, she as yet
not daring to adventure in the cold, which now (after a very wett
season) came on very severely:

17 The Assembly at Lond, now begin (too late) to consider
how miserably publique matters have ben maneiged; especialy as
to Ireland, the imbarging our Merchant ships now 15 moneths
for want of Convoys (which the Dutch afforded theirs with to
the immense prejudice of our Trade, & advantage of theirs)
besides the losse of so many of our best ships & other Vessells
both by accidents, & pirates:

A Convocation of the cleargy meete, about the Reforming of
our Liturgy, Canons &c: [obstructed by others of the Cleargy.]

27 I went to Lond [with my family] to Winter at Sohò in the
greate Square.

30 I went to the R: Society, where I was chosen one of the
Council, my Lord Penbrok president, we dined together:

December 1: Dr. Tenison preached at St. Martin on 1. Tim. 5.
21. against partiality and the factions now exceedingly disturbing
& threatning the publique: The H: Communion followed, at
which I was participal, praised be God.

I dind at Sir William Godolphins:

I spent most of this following weeke in receiving and returning Visites:

11 To Deptford to see my Grandson falln ill of a scarlet feaver
at the French Schoole at Greenewich, which, after blood letting
so abated that by Gods mercy I left him in an hopefull way.

1690. Jan: 5 Dr. Tenison at St. Martines on 2: Philip. 6. 7: against the Socinians: The holy Sacrament followed, at which I communicated:

Din'd with Sir W. Godolphin:

11 There was this night, so extraordinary a storme of win'd accompanied with snow & sharp weather, as had not ben known the like, in almost the memory of any man now living: greate was the harme it did in many places, blowing downe houses, Trees &c, killing divers people: it began about 2 in the morning and lasted til 5: being a kind of Hurecan, which Mariners observe, begin of late yeares to come northward, What mischiefe it has don at sea, where many of our Best ships are attending to convey the Q: of Sp⟨a⟩ine, together with a thousand merchants laden for several ports abroad, I almost tremble to think of:

This Winter has ben hithertoo, extremely wett, warme, & windy: Such as went before the death of the Usurper Cromwell, which was in a stormy day: The Death of the Queene of Bohemia, & what this portends, time will discover, God almighty avert the Judgements we deserve, if it be his blessed will:

24: The famous Infamous Tryal of my unworthy Nephew Montague at the Kings-bench, which indeede I heard with much regrett, that so vile and scandalous a Cause should have ben ⟨published⟩, the dammages being 6500 pounds: The immense wrong this proflygate wretch did my Niepce, drawing justly on him this disgrace: so vile a Cause had never ben brought to so publique an example:

⟨26⟩ A chaplain of the E. of Suffolke: on 2. Jam: 14: ⟨a⟩ more hopefull young preacher, for his matter, & manner of delivery I had seldom heard:

Extreame wet weather continues:

⟨30⟩ Anniversary K: Ch: Martyrdom: The Reader of St. Ann's: 3. Lament: 39: shewing for what sinns of this Nation, this Calamity fell upon it, & the way, by Confession & forsaking sinn, to obtaine pardon & prevent the like.

The Parliament, unexpectedly Prorogued til 2 April, to the discontent & surprizal of many members, who being exceeding averse from settling anything, proceeding with animosities, multiplying exceptions, against those whom they pronounc'd obnoxious, produc'd as universal a discontent, against K. William & themselves, as was before against K: James: The new King, also having with so much reproch lost now above a yeare, resolving an expedition into Ireland in person; Thought best to proroge this troublesome Session, now they had given him so much mony, & had no more use of them for the Present: it being also believed they should hardly meete againe, but in a new, & more authenticque Parliament:

About 150 of the Members, who were of the more royal part, meting at a Feast at the Apollo [Dunstan] Tavern: sent some of their company to the K. to assure him of their service; to whom he returned his Thanks, advising them to repaire to their several Countries & preserve the peace during his absence, & assuring them that he would be steady to his resolution of defending the Laws, and Religion established:

The great Lords, suspected to have counseled this Prorogation, universaly denying it; however it was believed, the chiefe Adviser was the Marquis of Carmardan &c—who now seemed to be most in favor:

Feb: 2: Dr. Tenison on 66 Psal: 12: The H: Sacrament follo⟨w⟩ed, at which I received.

The Parliament from a Prorogation, now Dissolved by Proclamation & another cald to meete on the 20th of March: This was a second surprize to the former members, & now the Court party, or as they call themselves, Ch: of England, are making their severall Interests in the Countries &c:

The Marques of Halifex lays down his office of L. Privy-Seale & pretends to retire:

WILLIAM III IN IRELAND – EVELYN
IS SEVENTY
(1690–1692)

16 THE DUTCHESSE of Monmoths Chaplain on *12: Heb:* 12 at St. Martins, an excellent discourse exhorting to Peace & Sanctitie, it being now at the time of very greate division & dissention in the nation: first amongst the Churchmen, among which the moderate & sober part, were for a speedy Reformation of divers

things, which were thought might be made in our Liturgie, for
the inviting of Dissenters: Others of the more stiff & ridigid
were for no Condescention at all, Bookes & pamphlets published every day pro & con: so as the Convocation Were for the
present forc'd to suspend any farther progresse; There was likewise a fierce & greate Canvasing about being elected in the new
Parliament to meete the next moneth.

The K: persists in his intentions to go in person for Ireland,
Whither the French are sending supplies to K: James, and wee
the Danish horse to Shomberge; The Confederates abroad
preparing also for the next Campagne, in which all Europe was
now engag'd, The *Emp:* having lost 4 Regiments, & flower of his
Armys, cut off by the Tartars; and much blamed for not accepting such advantagious Conditions as were offered him by the
Gr: Signor, from whom he had already recovered that goodly
K:dome of Hungrie, & gotten its Crowne settled on his son: so
as he might have ben in Condition to have diverted all his forces
on France, who had now an immense Army ready, & still threatning all the potentates of Christendome:

19 I dined with the Marqu(i)s of *Caermarthen* (late Lord
Danby) where was Lieutenant Gen: Duglas, a very considerable &
sober Commander, going for Ireland, & related to us the exceeding
neglect of the English Souldiers, perishing for want of Clothing &
necessarys this winter; & exceedingly magnifying their Courage &
bravery during all their hardships: There dined also my *Lord Lucas*
Lieutenant of The Towre, & The Bish: of St. Asaph &c:

The Privy Seale was now put againe into the hands of Commissioners, Mr. Cheny (who married my kindswoman,
Mrs. Pierpoint) Sir John Knatchbull, & Sir William Poultny:
I think I might have ben one of them, had I thought it seasonable, & would have ingaged my friends:

25 I went on foote to Kinsington, which K. Will: had bought
of my Lord of Notingham, & new altered, but it was yet a
patch'd building, yet with the Gardens a very sweete Villa, having to it the Parke, and the straite new way through the park:
I din'd with the *Bish:* of St. *Asaph*, Dr. Tenison & Stradling,
return'd that evening: News of some victory in Ireland.

Mar. 2 Dr. Tenison preached at St. Martins on 6. *Micha:* 8:
The holy Sacrament follow'd, of which I participated & was
wittnesse to my Lord Lumleys receiving &c:

Dined at Sir W: Godolphins, visited the Co: of Sunderland just now arrived from Holland.

7: I din'd with Mr. *Pepys*, late Secretary of the Admiralty, where was that excellent Shipwright, & sea-man (for so had he ben, as also Commissioner of the navy) Sir *Anthony Deane*, who amongst other discourses, & deploring the sad condition of our Navy, as now Govern'd by unexperienc'd men &c since this Revolution: Related to us, what exceeding advantage we of this ⟨nation⟩ had, by being the first who built Fregats: the first that was ever made, being that Vessel, which was afterward called the Constant Warwick; which Pet: of Chattham built for a tryal of making a Vessel that would saile swiftly, it was built with low Decks, the Gunns lying neere the water; & was so light & swift of sailing, that in a short time, he told us, she had ere the *Dut⟨c⟩h-War* was ended, taken as much mony from Privateers as would have laden her, & that more such being built, did in a year or two scoure our Channels, from being exceedingly infested by those of Dynkirk & others: And added that it were the best and onely infallible expedient, to be masters at sea, & able to destroy the greatest Navy of any enemy whatsoever, if instead of building huge greate ships, & 2d and 3d rates &c: they quite left off building them with such high decks, which he said was nothing but to gratifie Gentlemen Commanders who must have all their Effeminate accommodations, & for pomp, which would be the ruine of our Fleetes, if such persons were continued to command, they neither having Experience, nor [being] capable of learning, because they would not submitt to the fatigue & inconveniences, which bred seamen, could do, in those so otherwise usefull swift fregats: Which he made appeare, being to encounter the greatest ships, would be able to protect, set on, & bring off, those who should manege the Fireships, & that whatsoever [Prince] should first store himself with numbers of such (viz. Fireships) would thro the help and countenance of such Fregats, be certainly able to ruine, the greatest force, that, of never so vast ships, could be put to sea for fight, & that by reason of the dexterity of working those light & swift-sailing vessels, to guard the Fireships: & this he made so evident, that he concluded there would shortly be no other method of sea fight: & that our greate ships & Men of Warr, however stored with Gunns & men, must submit to whosoever should encounter them with far lesse number: He thereupon represented to us, the dreadfullnesse of these Fireships; & that he continualy observed in our last maritime warr with the Dut⟨c⟩h, that when ever an Enemys fireship, approch'd, the most valiant both of Commanders & common Sea-men & sailers, were in such feare and Consternation, that, though of all times, there was then most neede of the *Gunns,* boomes, & other Instruments, to keepe the misch⟨ie⟩f off; they grew pale & astonish'd, & as if possessed with a quite other meane soule, slung about, forsooke their gunns & worke, as in dispaire, everyone looking about, which way they might get out of their ship, though sure to be drown'd if they did so, or to be burnt to death if they staied: This he said was likly to prove hereafter the method of sea fights & that whatever King, got provision of this before his Neighbour potentats, must demonstrably destroy the other, & did therefore wish, it might not be the misfortune of England: especialy, if they continued to put the Gentlemen Commanders over experienced sea-men, upon accounte of their ignorance, effeminacy & Insolencie:

9 I din'd at the Bish: of S. *Asaphs,* (Almoner to the new Q:) where dined also the famous Lawyer Sir *Geo: Makenzie* (late Lord Advocate of Scotland) against whom, both the Bish: & myselfe had written & published books: both now most friendly reconciled: He discovered to us many particulars relating to Scotland, the present sad Condition of it, The inveterat hatred of the Presbyterians ther to the fam⟨i⟩ly of the Stewarts, the exceeding Tyrann⟨i⟩e of those Bigots, That they accknowledgd no superior over them on Earth, either in Civil or divine matters; That the people onely had the right of Government: in summ: Their implacable malice to the Episcopal order &C. of England &c: Upon which the Bishop, shewed us that the first Presbyters disenting from our discipline, were introduced by the Jesuite order, about the 20th yeare of Q: Elizabeth & that a famous Jesuite amongst them, faining himselfe a Protestant, was the first began to pray Extemporie, & brought in that which they since cald (& are still so fond of) praying by the Spirit: This *Jesuite* continued many years, befor he was discoverd, afterward died in Scotland, and is buried at   having yet on his Monument: *Rosa inter Spinas.*

11 I went againe to see Mr. Charletons Curiosities both of Art & nature; as also his full & rare collection of Medails: which taken alltogether in all kinds, is doubtlesse one of the most perfect assemblys of rarities that can be any where seene: I much admired the contorsions of the *Thea* roote, which was so perplext, large & intricate, (& with all hard as box) that it was wonderfull to consider:

30 This was the first time of my poore wifes going to church, after above a yeares Infirmity, for which God Almighty be praised:

Aprill 27 *Pomeridia* at White-hall, one of the chaplains: 3. Pro: 17:

The death of the duke of Loraine now happning put our new King here into great Melancholy, being so considerable a member of the Confederate Princes against France:

Discontents at the indiscreete government of affaires amongst us, and dissagreements among the Parliament men, had so intangld matters, that by a prodigal & carelesse menaging, the monys raised for the reduction of Ireland &c. things were here at such a stand, & the government so loose and neglected, (every body minding onely their own not the Publique), that we are like to fall into greate Confusion, Partys, Interests of private persons, animositie, & vice in aboundance:

May 4 Dr. Tenison at St. Martin on 1. James: 8. That all our threatning Calamitie proceeded from mens Vices, and they, for want of stable, Christian and Moral Principles, an universal atheistical, or sceptical, humor overspreading the nation: &c: The holy Communion follo⟨w⟩ed, at which I participated.

15 My Wife & family, who had ben all the past Winter in Lond: came home:

24 The Parliament adjourn'd, K. William preparing for Ireland. Citty Charter restored: Divers Excepted from Pardon: &c.

June 4: K: William set forth upon his Irish Expedition, leaving his Queene Regent during his absence &c:

10 I went to Lond: Mr. Pepys read to me his Remonstrance, shewed with what malice & ⟨injustice⟩ he was suspected, with Sir Ant: Deane, about the Timber of which the 30 ships were built by a late Act of Parliament: with the exceeding danger the present Fle⟨e⟩t would be shortly in by reason of the Ignorance & incompetency of those who now manag'd the

Admiralty & affaires of the Navy, of which he gave an accurate state, & shewed his greate abillitie: I retur⟨n⟩ed in the Evening:

15 [Trinity Sonday] Our Viccar on: 23 *Jer:* 10. Against Swearing: The Act of *Parliament* against Perjurie &c, having ben publiqly read before Sermon:

16 I went to Lond: Newes that K: William was safely landed in Ireland.

18 Fast day preached at St. Martin:

I went after all [publique] devotions were finish'd to visite the Bishop of St. Asaph (the Queens Almoner who was now entered upon the sole Regal Government during her husbands Absence) where⟨e⟩ was the Bishops of Lond. & Worcester & Deane of Paules Dr. Tenison &c: all of them not a little surpriz'd at what had happned in *Savoy*, among the *Voudois*, who being so neere their destruction & final extirpation by the French, as that they were generaly given up as to slaughter, & that every body expected to heare of their calamities & final destruction: It pleased God ⟨that⟩ the Duke of Savoy (hitherto joyning with the French in persecution of those poore Christians, & now pressed by the French to deliver ⟨Verrue⟩ & Turin as Cautionary to the French, upon their suspicion that he might at last come into the German Princes Confederacy) having seacretly concerted with the Confederats, & adjusted the Condition &c, not onely declared for the Confederats, but invited those poore Christians from their *dispersions* & *Latebræ* among the Mountains whither they had fled; but restor'd them to their Country, Dwellings, Exercise of the Religion, beged pardon for the ill usage they had received, & charging it upon the cruelty of the French, who forced him to it &c: These being the Remainder of those persecuted Christians, wh⟨om⟩ the Bishop had so long time, affirmed to be the 2 Wittnesses spoken of in the Revelation who should be Kild, & brought to life againe; It was looked on as an extraordinary thing, That this Prophetique Bish: should perswade two fugitive Ministers of the *Vodois* to returne to their Country, & furnish them with 20 pounds towards their Journey, at that very time, when it was believed nothing but universal destruction was to be expected, assuring them, & shewing them from the Text in the Apocalypse that their Country men should be returned safely to their Country, before they arived, let them make what hast they

could: This so hapning contrary to all expectation & appearance, did exceedingly credit the Bishops Confidence how that
prophesy of the Witnesses, should so come to passe, so just at
the time & very moneth of which he had spoken some yeares
before: I went afterwards with him to visite Mr. Boyle & Lady
Ranelagh his sister, to whom he explaind the necessity of its so
falling out by the Scriptures in a very wonderfull manner, which
he most skillfully & learnedly made out; with what events were
immediately to follow of the French Kings ruine, The Turkes,
& Calling of the Jewes to be neere at hand; but that the total
Kingdom of Antichrist, would yet not be utterly destroyed til
30 years, when Christ sho(u)ld begin the Milennium, not [as]
himselfe person(al)ly reigning in Earth Visibly; but that the
true Religion & universal peace, should obtaine thro all the
world: he shewed how Mr. Brightman, Mr. Meade, and other
Interpreters of their Events, failed, by mistaking & reckoning
the yeares as the Latines & others did, to consist of the present
Calculation & so many dayes to the yeare; wheras, the Apocalyps, reckons after the Persian account, as Daniel did whose
Visions St. John all along explains, as meaning onely the Christian Church: &c.

I return'd home this Evening.

24 Dined with & Visited me Mr. Pepys, Mr. Stuart & other
friends. Mr. P: sent the next day to the Gate-house, & severall
greate persons to the Towre, on suspicion of being affected to
K. James: amongst which was my Lord Earle of Clarendon,
unkle to the Queene.

[Mr. Pepys was the next morning imprisoned &c:]

July 6 I went to Lond: to heare Mr. Stringfellow preach at
St. James's Church as Dr. Tenison desired he would do, for trial,
whether his voice &c were fit for a Church he design'd him the
cure of upon my recommendation:

The whole Nation now exceedingly alarm'd by the French
fleete braving our Coast even to the very Thames mouth:
our Fleete commanded by debauched young men, & likewise
inferior in force, giving way to the Enemy, to our exceeding
reproch: God of his mercy defend this poore church & nation:
[Hollanders fleete beaten at sea:] K: William in Ireland taking a
passe, wounded in the shoulder with a Cannon bullet: greate
expectations from thence:

13 King William having vanquished K James in Ireland, there was much publique rejoicing: It seemes K. J: army would not stand, namely the Irish, but the English Irish & French made greate resistance: Shomberg was slaine, and Dr. Wa⟨l⟩ker, who so bravely defended L.derry: K.W: received a slight wound by the grazing of a cannon bullet on his shouldier, which yet he endured with very little interruption of his pursuit: Hamilton, who brake his word, about Tyrconells, was taken: K.J. is reported gon back to France: Droghedah & Dublin surrendered: and if K.W. be returning, one may say of him as of Cæsar, Veni, vidi, vici, for never was such a Kingdome won in so short an Expedition; But to alay much of this the French fleete having exceedingly beaten the Dutch fleete, & ours not daring to interpose, ride at present in our Chanell, threatning to Land, which causes an extraordinary alarme &c:

16 The publique fast: our Viccar preached on 18 Jer: 7. 8:

17 I went to London to visite some friends in the Toure, where asking for my Lord Clarendon (now with divers other Noble persons imprisoned upon suspicion of a plot) by mistake they directed me to the E. of Torrington who about 3 days before had ben sent for from the Fleete, was put into the Toure for his Cowardize and not fighting the French Fleete, which having beaten a Squadron of the Hollanders (whilst Torrington did nothing) did now ride masters at sea with that power as gave terror to the whole nation, in daily expectation of a descent, which God Almighty avert:

I returned in the Evening &c:

30 I went to Lond: Dined with Mr. Pepys now suffered to returne to his house in reguard of his Indisposition: I return'd home calling in at the R. Society, where Mr. Hook read a discourse of the cause of most hills & mountaines to be from subterranean eruptions &c:

Aug: 1 Came the Duke of Grafton to visite me, going now to his ship at the mouth of the River: [to transport him to Ireland where he was slaine.]

3 The Schole Master of Lewsham preached on 1 Joh: 2. 15: The holy Sacrament follow'd of which my Wife & I were participants, praised be God.

The French domineering still at sea, landed some souldiers at Tinmoth in Devon: & burned some poore houses:

10 Our Viccar on 3: *Amos*: 6:

The K: William having taken in Waterford, Duncannon & other places marches to Limrick, which Tyrconell seemes with 4000 french &c to hold out; &c. The French F⟨l⟩eete still hovering about the Western Coast, (we having 300 saile of rich Merchant Ships in the bay of Plimoth,) our Fleete begin to move towards them under 3 Admiralls in Commission: The Country in the West all on their Guard, A camp of about 4000 still on Blak-heath: The Germans and especialy that in Flanders very strong waiting to give battell to the French who are this yeare on the defence; The Duke of Savoy, waites joyning with some German troopes to block up Catenate the Fr: Gen: there:

[A very extraordinary fine season.]

12 So greate and long a storme of Thunder & lightning as had seldome ben seene in these countries.

13 I went to Lond: The season now much changed to wett & cold:

The French fleete returned to Brest & from our Coast, the Militia of the Trained Bands horse & foote which were up through out England now dismiss'd:

The French King having newes that King William was slaine, and his Army defeated in Ireland, causes such a Triumph at Paris & all over France, as was never heard of or almost read in any history, when in the midst of it, the unhappy K. James being vanquished, brought himselfe (by a speedy flight & escape) the sad tidings of his owne defeate, to the greate reproch of the French who made such unseasonable boasting:

15 I was desired to be one of the Baile of the Earle of Clarendon for his Lordships release out of the Tower, with divers other noblemen: [Bishop of St. Asaph expounds his Prophesys to me & Mr. Pepys &c:]

17 our Viccar proceeded on his former Text & subject:

Some greate designe in hand, by our preparation at Sea, now the Fr: fleete is gone home:

Limrick not yet reduc'd: Our Camp at Blakheath marching to Portsmouth.

That Sweete & hopefull youth Sir Charles Tuke, (after hopes of his recovery) dead of the wounds he receiv'd in the fight [of Boine], to the greate sorrow of all his friends, being

(I think) the last male of that noble family: to which my wife is related: A more virtuous young Gent: I never knew, he was learned for his age, having had the advantage of the choicest breading abroad, both as to Arts & Armes, had much Traveld; but was so unhappy to fall, in that unhappy side of an unfortunate King:

25 I went to Lond: about my Concerne with Sir C: Porter:

Limrick still holds out, we having received some losse [very] considerable by the negligence of Sir W: Poultnys son, who was to guard the Cannon: Galloway Entered by stratagem by the French who quitted Limric:

The weather very wett, & stormy, our Fleete at sea:

30 I came home: Our Merchant ships came safe from Plimouth:

31 Both Viccar & Curate proceeding on their former Texts.

No news from the Armys in Germany, but some uncertaine reports of Catinates having worsted the D. of Savoy: nothing yet from Ireland:

September 7 Our Viccar & Curate still on the same Text: The holy Sacrament followed of which I was partaker, the Lord make me thankfull:

Limrick proves yet a difficult piece; The unseasonable & most tempestuous season happning, the Naval expedition is hindred: No successe in Savoy, Catinates having (as reported) worsted the Duke, still in doubt:

14 Extremity of wet, cause the siege to be raised before Limrick: so as K.W. Returnes to England: re infectâ as to that plan: Lord Sydne⟨y⟩ &c left chiefe governors in that Kingdome as far as Conquered, which is neere three parts:

17 The publique fast, our Viccar preach'd on 13 Luke, 6 &c:

An extrordinary cold sharp Easte Wind, part of our fleete on some extraordinary designe.

21 The French Fleete againe on the Irish Coast: ours going to meete them:

Octo: 5 Corke surendred to K: Willia⟨m's⟩ forces upon discretion, the Duke of Grafton desperately wounded &c:

12 The Minister of Newington on 3: Phil: 10: both Morning & afternoon, very well:

The French Generall, with Tyrconell & their forces gon back to france, beaten out by K. William.

Corke Delivered: upon discretion; The Duke of Grafton mortaly wounded: [dies] Churchil: before Kingsale, [which he takes,] our Ships (most of them) come into Harbor: The Parliament siting & voting vast summs for the next yeares Warr: Tekelyes successe in Transylvania: The Swisse call a Dyet, press'd by the French: The Emperor Indiscreetely ingag'd by the Monks & Jesuites, to pursue the Warr against the Turks, neglected to make peace, whi(l)st France still gaines on & Indangers the Empire, & has Swallowed Savoy:

Very greate stormes of Wind:

The 8th of this moneth my Lord Spencer writ me word from Althorp out of N. hampton-shire that there happened an Earthquake the day before in the morning, which, tho short, sensibly shook the house: The like, & at the same very moment, (which was betweene 7 & 8 in the morning, viz, halfe an houre after 7:) the Gazette of this weeke aquainted us it so happned at Barnstable, Holy-head, & Dublin in Ireland: we were not at all sensible of it at Lond:

The Parliament voted the King 4 millions:

19 was held a day of Thanksgiving for the successe of K. Williams armes, & his owne escape in Ireland &c:

26 Our Viccar still on his former subject: 3. *Heb:* 12: The weather detain'd me at home in the afternoone:

KingSale at last surrendred; meane while K. James party burne all they have in their power of houses, & amongst them that stately palace of the Lord *Orories* which lately cost as reported 40000 pounds: By a disastrous accident a 3d rate ship (the Breda) firing blew up & destroied all the passengers in which wer 25 prisoner of War to set saile for England the very next day: Many excellent ships have we thus unfortunately lost this yeare beside aboundance taken by the Enemy:

The Turks retake Belgrade by storme putting all to the sword, & repassing the bridge at Esseck, with the successe of Tekely, threaten a reverse of their hitherto unprosperousnesse, & this, as too apparent by the tretchery of the Jesuites, who hindred the Emperor to make a most advantagious peace, by which France would have ben forc'd to abate of his so insolent progresse: poore Duke of Grafton, who came to take his leave of me, just as he imbarked for Ireland, is now dead of his wounds.

29 I came up to Lond: *Dover-streete* with part of my family, to Winter with my son:

31 My Birth-day, being now full 70 yeares of Age: Blessed be the Lord for the continuance of my health, & of all his mercies, hitherto hast thou brought me, To Thee alone be the accknowledgements from my Soule & all that is within me, which thou has⟨t⟩ preserved: Grant deare father the increase of thy Grace, with the yeares of my life, 'til in compassion thou bring me to the consummation of Glory in the life to come, Amen.

November 2 I received the B: Sacrament at St. Martines: Dr. Tenison preaching there on: 17: Pro: 27:

I dined with Sir William Godolphin: after prayers, visited Co: of Bristol:

3 Went to the Co: of Clancarty, to condole with her concerning her debauched & dissolut son, who had don so much mischef in Ireland, now taken & brought prisoner to the Toure:

23 Dr. Patrick B: of Chichester: on: 11. Isaiah: 9:

I din'd at Sir W: Godolphin:

Carried my Lord Godolphin (now resuming the Commission of the Treasury againe to all his friends wonder) Mr. Pepys Memoires:

December 1 R: Society St. Bartholomews day, I having been chosen President, by 21 Voices, with much difficulty, by all meanes [resolved] to avoyd it in this ill Conjuncture of publique affairs, with greate difficulty, devolved the Election on Sir Rob: Southwell, ⟨Secretary⟩ of State to the King William in Ireland:

The mild weather now growing to hard frost, greate apprehension of the French marching into Flanders: Matters universaly in great Confusion with us, nothing in any sort of apparent method for our preservation: The Lord Jesus avert our danger: Affairs in Savoy & among the Swisse Cantons, in very sad condition: Geneva in danger, The Kings Journey into Holland to meete the Confederats doubtfull &c:

28 Dr. Huff (president of Magd: in Oxon who was displac'd with several of the fellows, for not taking the oath: imposed by K James, now restor'd & made Bishop): at St. James church on 18 John 36: Afternoone at White hall Dr. Blagrave sub-Almoner on 10: *Mark*: 15:

Most of this moneth cold & frost: King preparing for his Journey into Holland hastens the parliament to dispatch all bills:

One Johnson a Knight executed at Tyburn for being Compl⟨i⟩ce with Campbel brother to the Lord Argile, for stealing away a young heiresse: &c:

31 I made up my Accompts for this yeare, paid wages &c: according to Costome—

1691

Jan. 4: Dr. Tenison at St. Martins on 3 Heb: 12: The H: Sacrament I received:

This weeke a plot discovered for a generall rising against the new Goverment, for which my Lord Clarendon, Lord Preston & others were sent to the Towre; I went to see my Lord Clar: the next day &c: The Bish: of Ely also searched for: Trial of Lord Preston (as no English Peer) hastened at the old Baily:

The Parliament adjourned, for the Kings Journy into Holland, but he is stayed by the exceding hard & now long frost.

18 My Lord Preston condemn'd about a designe to bring in K.Ja: by the French: Ashton executed: L: Clarendon in the Tower: Bishop of Ely, Mr. Graham &c: absconded &c:

King William gon into Holland.

Feb: 1 St. Martin: Dr. Tenison 1. Cor: 4: 20. Communion followed, I received:

Mar: 11 [Wednesday] At White-hall Dr. Wake 12 Rom: 18: I went to visite Lo: Clarendon, prisoner in the Tower, but was not suffered to come to him any neerer than the windowe &c:

13 Friday I went to visite Monsieur Justell, & the Library of St. James, in which this learned man had put the MSS: (which were in good number) into excellent order, which had laine many yeares neglected: Divers Medalls stolln & embeziled &c:

⟨19⟩ Thursday at St. James: ABishop of Tuam: Seeke the Lord whi⟨l⟩st he may be found.

Dined at Sir William Farmors who shewed me many good pictures, after dinner had a [french] servant that played rarely on the Lute: Sir William had now bought all the remaining statues collected with so much expense &c: by the famous Tho: Earle of Arundel E. Marshal &c: & sent them to his seate in Northampton shire:

25 My L. Sidny (pr: sec: of State) gave me a letter to my Lord Lucas Lieutenant of the Tower, to permitt me to visite my L. Clarendon, which this day I did, & dined with him, & afterwards made a step to my house at Deptford, where I staied til Aprill 4th:

⟨Aprill⟩ 10 Mons in *Hanalt* is delivered to the French, King William, not being prepared (though in person with an Army) to raise the siege, which greatly disappointed every body, in mighty expectation: But as the Spaniards had made no provision for the Army, & the Townesmen perswaded by the Priests, to deliver it, the Governor, fearing a mutiny & his Garison not ⟨able⟩ to suppresse it; The Towne was given up, before K: William, could be ready, though it had provision to have held out longer:

10 This night, a suddaine & terible Fire burnt downe all the buildings over the stone Gallery at W-hall, to the waterside, begining at the Appartments of the late Dut⟨c⟩hesse of Portsmouth (which had ben pulled down & rebuilt to please her [no lesse than] 3 times) & Consuming other Lodgings of such lewd Creatures, who debauched both K Char: 2d & others & were his destr⟨u⟩ction:

The King now returns out of Holland just at this Accident: Proclamation against Papists &c:

12 K: William now returned out of Holland:

16 I went to see Dr. Sloans Curiosities, being an universal Collection of the natural productions of Jamaica consisting of Plants, [fruits,] Corralls, Minerals, [stones,] Earth, shells, animals, Insects &c: collected by him with greate Judgement, several folios of Dried plants & one which had about 80: severall sorts of Fernes, & another of Grasses: &c: The Jamaica pepper in branch, leaves, flowers, fruits &c: [which] with his Journal, & other Philosophical & naturall discourses & observations is indeede very extraordinary and Copious, sufficient to furnish an excellent History of that Iland, to which I encouraged him, & exceedingly approved his Industry.

19 Dr. Young at W-hall 28: Job: 28.

The Arch-Bishop of Canterbury, Ely, Bath & Wells, Peterborow, Glocester & the rest who would not take the Oathes to K William now displac'd, & in their roomes Dr. Tillotson Deane of Paules made A.B of Cant: Patric removed from

Chichester to Ely, Comberland to Gloucester, ⟨Beveridge⟩, Comberland.

22 I went to visite my L. Clarendon & dined with him in the Tower:

24 I visited the C. & E. of Sunderland, now come to kisse the K. hand after his recesse in Holland: This is a Mysterie:

The K: is preparing to returne to the Confederat Army—

May ⟨3⟩ At St. Martins Dr. Tenison on 22: Luke: 19. Concerning the B: Sacrament: I Received:

[7 I visited the Earle of Clarindon prisoner in the Tower, kept there still about the late Plot, he told me he expected every day deliverance, and bespake me to stand with his Brother the E: of Rochester &c for security which I promised.]

King William gos now againe into Flanders.

7 I went to visite the A:B: of Cant: yet at Lambeth: I found him alone, & discoursing of the Times, especialy of the new Bishops design'd, he told me that by no Canon, or Law divine &c: they could justifie the removing the present Incumbents: That Dr. Beverwich, designed Bishop of Bath & Wells, came to aske his Advice, The AB: told him, That though he should give it, he believed he would not take it: The Doctor said he would: Why then says the AB: When they come to aske you, say *Nolo!* & say it from your heart: there's nothing Easier, than to resolve your selfe, what is to be don in the Case: The Doctor seem'd to Deliberate: what he will do, I know not; but Bishop Ken, who is to be put out, is exceedingly beloved of his D⟨i⟩ocesses: and if he (& the rest) should insist upon it, & plead their Interest as Freeholders, 'tis believed, there would be difficulty in their Case, & may indanger a Schisme & much disturbance: so as wise men thinke it had ben better to have let them alone, than to have proceeded with this rigour, to turne them out for refusing to sweare against their Conscience. I asked, at Parting, when his Grace removed, he sayd, that he had not yet received any summons: But I found the house altogether Disfurnished & his Bookes packing up:

10 At St. James, Dr. Tenison on: 15. Luke 13. [I stayed at the Communion.] In the Afternoone Mr. Wake on 4: Heb. 1.

Nothing yet don towards the delivery of my L. Clarendon, which he told me he thought would be within few days after I was to visite him: But I feare, since my L: Preston, 'tis said, has

Confess'd more, something may have ben added to his former Confessions, that may have retarded my L: Clarendons freedome &c:

12 I went to see the Hospital & Infirmarie for Emerited Souldiers lately built at Chelsey, which is indeede a very Magnificent, Compleat & excellent Foundation, the two Cutts from the Thames, Courts, and other accommodations wonderfull fine: The several wards for the souldiers, Infirmary for the sick, Dispensatory, Governors house & other officers, especialy the Refectory for 400 men, & Chapell; In the Refectory is a noble Picture of heroic argument in honor of Char: 2d painted by Virrio: also the Kings [James] Statue in Brasse, of the worke of Gibbons in the Court next the Cloister &c:

15 I returned with my family, home to my house in the Country, for the Summer:

⟨21⟩ Ascention Day I went to Lond, where at St. Martines, a young man preached on 1. Mat: 21: I received the holy Comunion:

This day died my Nephew John Evelyn of Wotton, onely son & heire of my Eldest Bro: Geo: who sent me word of it the next day: He had ben long, & so dangerously sick, a greate part of the Winter, that Physitians despaired of his Recovery; but on the suddaine he began so to mend, that though his limbs were weake, his Appetite, (before lost) Spirit, & cherefullnesse returned, so as he was thought past danger, & went not onely downe about the house, but tooke the aire abroad in the Coach, when unexpectedly, a Veine breaking carried him away, nothing being able to stop the flux, so greate was the sharpnesse of his blood, & weake the vessells, which inconveniences accompanied with a Palsy, was contracted by an habit of drinking much wine & strong waters to comply with other young intemperate men: He had else a very strong & robust body, and was a person of very good sense & parts: He died about 35 years of age, to the greate griefe of my Bro: & Joy (I believe) of his Wife, who never behaved herselfe so discreetely, as to give him any greate comfort, which made him at last, almost wish himselfe out of the World: He had had severall Children born, & lately a Son, a very pretty Child, & likely to live, but God was pleased to take them all to himselfe: So as now (there remaining onely Daughters, women grown, & of an Elder sons of my Bro:) according to the

Intailement; I became the next heire to my Bro: & our Paternal Estate, exceedingly far from my least expectation, or desert: The Lord God render me & mine worthy of this Providence, & that I may be a comfort to my Bro: whose prosperity I did ever wish & pray for:

June 1. I went, together with my son, & Bro: in Law Glanvil & his son, to Wotton, to solemnize the Funeral of my Nephew, which was performed the next day, very decently, & ordered by the Herauld, in the Afternoone, a very greate appearance of the Country being there: I being the chiefe Mourner, the Pal was held up, by Sir Fr: Vincent, Sir Rich: Onslow, Mr. Tho: Howard, son to Sir Robert, Auditer of the Exchequer & Cap: of the Kings Guard, Mr. Hyldiard, Mr. James; Mr. Herbert, Nephew to my L: Herbert of Cherbery & Co: German to my deceased Nephew: He was layed in the Vault at Wotton Church, in the bur⟨y⟩ing-place of that Family: an innumerable Concourse of Coaches & people accompan⟨y⟩ing the solemnity:

2 I stayed at Wotton with my Co: Geo: Evelyn of Nutfield & others of our relations, & returned to London the 3d, with promise of returning & staying longer with my Bro: to settle matters of concernement upon this change, so soone as I could finish some buisinesse, that would detaine me til after the ensuing Terme:

7: Dr. Tenison preached at St. Martins, on: 2: Ephes: 18. by many admirable Arguments, asserting the Divinity of the Holy-Ghost, against the Socinians, who now began exceedingly to broch their Heresy more than ever in England: The holy Sacrament followed, at which I received: it being Trinity Sonday: & first of the Moneth:

10 I went to visite my Lord Clarendon still prisoner in the Tower, though my L: Preston being pardoned, was now released: & so returned to my house at Deptford this Evening:

K. William raised the French siege before Liege: Our ⟨Navy⟩ set saile:

25 My wife & daughter, set out to the Bath &c:

July: 5 Our Viccar proceeded on the same Text: The Holy Comm: I received:

Afternoone the Curate of Wollwich on 2 Phil. 8. 9. 10 &c: The excessive heate & fullnesse inclined me to sleepe:

8 I went to Lond, to visite friends: 11. dined with Mr. Pepys where was Dr. Cumberland the new Bish: of Norwich, the other B: Dr. LLoyd, put out, for not acknowledging the Government; Comberland a very learned, excellent man:

Now also was possession given at Lambeth to Dr. Tillotson, by the Sherif, the Arch-Bishop Sancroft being gon, but leaving his Nephew to keepe possession, who refusing to do it upon the Queenes message, was dispossesed by the Sherif, & imprisoned: This stout demeanor of the few Bishops refusing to take the oaths to K: William &c: animated a greate party, to forsake the Churches, so as to threaten a Schisme: Though those who looked farther into the antient practise, found, that when (as formerly) there were Bishops displac'd, upon secular accounts, the people never refused to acc⟨k⟩nowledge the new Bishops, provided they were not heretics: The truth is, the whole Cleargy had till now stretched the duty of Passive Obedience, that their now proceedings against these Bishops, gave no little occasion of exceptions: But this not amounting to Heresy, there was a necessity of receiving the new Bishops, to prevent a failure of that Order in the Church:

Athlane taken in Ireland, & greate appearance of subduing that Kingdome this summer:

The D. of Savoy defends his Country with some better successe: whilst the French in Fland: avoyd K. Williams forces, who seekes to draw him to a Batell:

Greate speach of a suddaine peace twixt the Emp: & Turke: through the daily commotions at Constantinople:

No newes where either ours, or the French fleetes are, whilst our Merchants here are in extreame apprehension for their Smyrna Fleete, who being gon from Cales homeward, 'tis feared may hardly escape the French fleete.

The Government here, very loose & as it were on floates, the summ of all seeming to depend on the Issues of this summer:

I went to visite my L: Clarendon, in the Tower, whom I found gon into the Country [for aire], by the Queens permission, under the guard of his Warders:

15 The publique fast our Viccar on 21 Luke: 5. 6. 7:

My Wife & daughter went from my A Hungerford to the Bath on Saturday: where I blesse God she arived safe:

18. I went to Lond: in order to the hearing Mr. Stringfellow preach his first Sermon in the new erected Church of Trinity, to which I did recommend him to Dr. Tenison for the constant Preacher & Lecturer: This church being formerly built of Timber on Hounslow-heath by K. James for the Masse-Priests, being beged by Dr. Tenison Rector of St. Martines, was set up by that publique minded, charitable & pious Doctor neere my sons dwelling Dover-streete, chiefly at the Charge of the Doctor, who was pleased to receive Mr. Stringfellow to be the Minister for my sake, I knowing him to be both an excellent preacher, & a fit person: This Church, though erected in St. Martins (which is the Doctors Parish) he freely was not onely content, but was the sole industrious moover, that it might be made a separate Parish, in reguard, the building & inlargement of that quarter was so many & populous: Wherefore to countenance & introduce the new Minister, & take possession of a Gallery designed for my sonns family, I went to Lond:

19 The greate Victory of K: Williams Army in Ireland was now fresh & looked upon as decisive of that Warr, for the total reduction of that Iland: The Irish foote had 'tis sayd, much advantage by being intrenched, over numbered us in horse, but they forsaking the foote, a total route, greate slaughter, & losse of all the Canon & baggage followed: The French Gen: St. Ruth, (who had ben so cruel a slaughter man to the poore protestants in France,) slaine with divers of the best Commanders: nor was it cheape to us, neere 1000 kild, but of them 4 or 5000:

The Smyrna fleete arived safe in K.sale, very naro⟨w⟩ly escaping the French; & put to extraordinary suffering, by foule Weather carrying the⟨m⟩ far to the West: which yet was by Gods providence, the cause of their safty:

Greate rejoicing in Lond:

20 I returned to my house in Deptford:

Things prosper in Ireland: yet we lose Merchant ships by the Privateeres getting out of Dunkirk, notwithstanding our Men of War before it: greate apprehension of the Fleet laden with provision for the West Indies: our Merchants of Russias ships being taken:

24. Mr. Pepys dined with me:

26 Both our Viccar & Curate preached on their former Texts.

A most extraordinary hot season as I have knowne, yet refreshed with some Thunder showers:

Galloway rendred to the Kings forces.

28 I went to Wotton: upon my Bro: desire, to settle some concernes:

August 2: One Mr. Wye, Minister of Ware in Hartfordshire preached on: 1 John: 2: 17: No sermon in the Church the Afternoone: & the curacy ill served—

The hot season still continues:

16 So greate a Thunder & Lightning on thursday, & the like I had never heard ⟨or⟩ seene I ⟨think⟩ in my whole life; but the storme of wind & raine was not very violent; nor do I heare of any harme was don:

We lost our Barbados Fleete by the French:

Galloway taken, & Limrick besieging: K. William cannot tempt the French to a Battel: Our Fleete come In to lay up the greate ships, nothing don at sea, pretending that we cannot meete with the Frenche.

30 Mr. *Wye* at *Wotton* on 14. Apoc: 13:

In the afternoone onely prayers:

A greate Victory against the Turks & Limrick [still] besieging, nothing from the Confederats Army, or from the sea—

September 6 Mr. Morus at Wotton 1. *Joh:* 2. 15:

Greate storme at sea, & our losse of the Coronation & Harwich with above 600 men perishing:

Octob: 5: I returned to Deptford &c: [so soone as the paine of the gripes left me, which had come on me some day⟨s⟩ before:]

10 I went to Lond:

14 I returned home: *Limrick Surrendered*: A most pleasant Autumne:

Our Navy come-in without having performed any thing, yet greate losse of ships by negligence & unskilfull men governing both fleete & Navy: The Confederates did nothing this summer, prevented by the prudent Incampments of the French: so as this whole yeare lost both at Sea & Land: Excepting the taking of *Limrick*, which was the last & onely place in Ireland that hith⟨er⟩too held out: [but Conditions given very advantagious to the Enemy]

18 The Bish: of Rochester at Greenwich preached on 6 Luke 46: The Confirmation followed:

I din'd at my B: Glanvils: at Greenewich:

Afternoon the Curate preached on 1 Peter—12:—Drowsinesse surpriz'd me: & I sate inconveniently to heare:

The King now come back from Holland: The Parliament met: The D. of *Savoy* takes *Carmaliona* & besieges *Susa*: greate hopes of peace with the Turk:

25 Our Ambassador in Turky dead, a considerable losse of a prudent person, who had ben so usefull on this overture & hopes of a peace:

31 I was now 71 yeares old compleate: having passed this yeare by Gods infinit mercy in great health, & experience of his wonderfull providence, which I blesse God for, & by some more than ordinary solemn preparation for the Celebration of mercy & goodnesse to me, I received the H: Sacrament on

November 1 Our Viccar & Curate proceeding on their former Texts:

3 I came to Winter in Lond: with part of my Family from Deptford:

5 Mr. Stringfellow preached at Trinity Church on 2: Cor: 1. 10: This Festival was celebrated with Illuminations, that is, by setting up innumerable lights & candles in the windows towards the streete, in stead of Squibbs & Bonefires, much mischiefe having ben don by Squibbs: Illumination was the custome, long since in Italy, [& France:] & now introduced here:

The Parliament now sate:

7 I went to visite the Earle of Dover, who having it seems made his peace with the K. was come over: The Relation he gave of the strength of the Fr: King, & the difficulty of our forcing him to fight, or any way make Impression into France, was very wide from what we fancied:

8 A⟨n⟩ extraordinary dry & warme season, [without frost & like a new Spring:] such as had not ben know⟨n⟩ of many yeares.

Part of the Ks house at Kensingtowne burnt:

30 [St. Andrews day] We met at the R: Society, about Officers, continued Sir R: Southwell President, ⟨Chose⟩ the Council; &c: Dined together, &c:

A most unwonted warme & calme Winter:

The West India Fleete, so long lingering in Ireland, at last come safe home:

Decemb. 6: Mr. Stringfellow in the morning on his former Text:

In the Afternoone a stranger on 1. Cor: 15. 24:

Discourse of another plot, in which severall greate persons were named, but believed to be a foolish sham:

A proposal in the House of Comm: That whatever Officer in the whole nation received for sallary [above 500 pounds] or otherwise by virtue of his Office, he should contribute it wholy to the support of the War with France, & [this] upon their oathes:

Eight ships of the Barbados & Jamaica Fleete, taken by the French to an incredible losse, both of the ships, & greate rich lading &c:

[18 A very pretty Act or exercise of the Schoole boys where was my Grandson: Speeches & Orations, Verses in Gr: Lat: French: ending with a consort of voices of the boys, & then exercises in Mathematics]:

20 An exceeding dry & calme Winter no raine for many past moneths:

Afternoone the Bishop of Lincoln: on 3. Tit: 3:

After sermon I carried the Bish: home: [went] next morning to Depford, returned on Xmas Eve.

25 Christmas day was my daughter in Law brought well to bed of a Daughter, exactly at 12 at noone: Blessed be God.

28 Dined at Lambeth with the New AB: farr politer than the old man: the Effect of my Greenhouse Furnace, first set in practise by the AB: son in law &c.

30. Saw Mr. Charltons collection againe, the spider & bird, scorpion, other serpent &c:

31 Made up Accompts for the Yeare &c according to Costome:

1692

Jan: 1: N-yeres day, Dr. Birch at St. James's on 5: Gal: 6: The B: Sacrament follow'd at which I communicated.

This last week died that pious admirable Christian, excellent Philosopher, & my worthy Friend Mr. Boyle, a greate losse to the publique, & to all who knew that vertuous person: aged about 65:

6 At the Funeral of Mr. Boile, [at St. Martins] preached Dr. Burnet Bishop of Salisbery on 2: Eccles: 26: To a man that is good God giveth Knowledge & Wisedome & Joy: on which he made a Philosophical Discourse, Concerning the Acquisitions of

Mans knowledge, by the example of Salomon, who had made so many experiments of what this World, & the opportunities of his glorious Circumstances could attaine, and after all that there could be no Joy or true satisfaction in this knowledge, without its being applied to the Glory of God: Thence passed to Elogie due to Mr. Boyle, who made God & Religion the object and scope of all his excellent Tallents in the knowledge of Nature, who had arived to so high a degree in it, accompanied with such zeale and extraordinary piety, which he continualy shewed in the whole Course of his life: & particularly in his exemplary charity upon all occasions: That he gave 1000 pounds yearly to the distressed Refugies of France & Ireland, was at the Charge of Translating the Scripture into Irish, & Indian Tongues, & was now promoting a Turkish Translation, as he had formerly of Grotius de Veritate R.C. into Arabic, which he caused to be dispersed in those Eastern Countries; That he had setled a funds for Preachers who should preach expressly against Atheists, Libertins, Socinians ⟨&⟩ Jewes: besids given 8000 pounds now in his Will to Charitable uses, but that his private Charitys which no man knew of save himselfe were Extraordinary: He delated also of his greate learning in the Tongues, Heb: Greeke, his reading of the Fathers, & solid knowledge in Theologie, once deliberating about taking holy Orders, & that at a time when he might have made a greate figure in the Nation as to secular honor & Title, namely at the restauration of his Majestie Char: 2d: his feare of not being able to discharge so weighty a duty as the first made him decline the first, and his humility the other: He spake of his wonderfull comity and Civility to strangers, the greate Good he did by his experience in Medicine, & Chymistry, & to what noble ends he applied himselfe to that his darling studies, The works both pious & Usefull which he published, the exact life he led, & the happy End which he made: something was touched of his sister the Lady Ranelagh, who died but very few days before him: And truly all this was but his due, without any grain of flattery: It is certainly not onely England, but all the learned world suffred a publique losse in this greate & good man, & my particular worthy friend:

This Weeke was committed a most execrable Murder on Dr. Clench, by Villans, who under ⟨pretence⟩ of carrying him in a Coach to see a Patient strangled him in the Coach, & under pretence of sending the Coach-man a litle distance, left the poore man dead, & escaped themselves in the dusk of the Evening: This is that Doctor, father of that extraordinary learned Child, whom he brought me sometime to my house &c:

12 Was my Grandaughter Christned *Jane*, by Dr. Tenison Bishop of Lincolne, being the first Infant, that was ever Christened in Trinity Church: Godfather & Mothers, Mr. Pepys, Mrs. Steward, Mrs. Wiseman:

24 A frosty & very dry season still continued: Many persons die suddenly of Apoplexe, more than usualy in many years.

The Lord of Marboro, L: Gen: of K Williams Army in England, Gent of Bedchamber, &c. dismissed from all his Charges Military & other; & given to divers others: for his excessive taking bribes & Covetousnesse & Extortion upon all occasions from his inferior officers: Note this was the Lord who being intirely advanced by K James, the merit of his father being the prostitution of his Daughter (this Lords sister) to that King: Is now disgraced; & by none pittied, being also the first who betrayed & forsooke his Master K: James, who advanced him from the son of Sir Wi⟨nston⟩ Churchill, an officer of the Greene-Cloth.

29 Died my Sister Evelyn of Woodcot, who had made our family so unkind a returne of so neere Relation, by violating my Brothers Will, in causing her daughter my Niepce, to cut of an Intailement & give it to her husband Montague, a Vicious young man, who leaving no children, defrauded my Bro: George of Baynards an Estate worth neere 500 pounds per Ann: &c: I pray God forgive her:

30 The Bishop of Lincolne preached at Trinity-Church on being Anniversary of K. Charles the first: Text: 51 Psal: 14: shewing the heinousnesse of Bloudgil⟨t⟩inesse, & how (though the generation since that horrid Act, might think it signified nothing to them, as did the Pharises, who pretended they would not have don as their forefathers, in Killing the Prophets, whose sepulchers they built); yet they were liable to the gilt & punishment, & shewed the continuance of the same malice, in crucifying the Lord Jesus, & persecuting to death his Apostles: In like manner the wiccked murder commited this day, would & did still lie heavy on this Nation, for what their Fathers did, and was plainly seene by the confusions, plages, Fires and other Judgements & unsettlements both in church & state & the monstrous wicckednesse of mens lives in this nation ever since:

Feb: 7 An extraordinary Snow, in most parts now fell:

13 Being by the late Mr. Boile, made one of the Trustees for his Charitable Bequests, I went this morning to a Meeting of the Bishop of Lincolne, Sir Robert Ashwood,[1] & Serjeant Roderith; to settle that Clause in Mr. Boyles will, which he had left for Charitable Uses, & Especialy for the Appointing & Electing a Minister to preach one sermon the first Sonday every moneth ⟨except⟩ [the] 4 summer moneths, June, July, Aug: ⟨September⟩: expressly against Atheists, ⟨Deists⟩, Libertins, Jewes &c, without descending to any other Controversy whatever; for which is a fund left of 50 pounds per annum to be paid the Preacher quarterly & at the end of 3 years, to proceede to a new Election of some other able Divine, or to continue the same, according as we shold judge convenient; so we made choice of one Mr. Bently, a Chaplain to the Bishop of Worcester: Dr. Stillingfleete for our first preacher; & that the first sermon shold begin on the first Moneday of March, at St. Martins Church, Westminster, & the 2d ⟨on the first⟩ Monday of Aprill, at Bow-Church in the Citty & so *alternis vicibus*:

16 I sealed Articles with my Bro: Evelyn, by which he was to cut down 6500 pounds worth of Timber & no more; Also to leave standing the woods about the seate &c:

28 Mr. Stringfellow at Trinity church, on 7: Rom: 18:

The Lord Marborow (who so ungratefully left his old Master K James) for some misbehavior or words against the present King, discharged of all his greate places: & his Wife forbid to be in Court, & the Princesse of Denmarke, desired by the Queene to have her put from her service: The P: of D: refusing to do it, gos herselfe away from Court to Sion:

Divers new lords made, Sir H: Capel, Sir William Fermor &c: Change of Commissioners in the Treasury:

The Parliament adjourn'd: They are not well satisfied with affaires:

The buisinesse of the E. India: Comp: which they would have reformed, let fall:

The D: of Norfolck succeedes not in his endeavor to be devors'd: &c:

1 Evelyn's error for Sir Henry Ashurst.

WAR WITH FRANCE
(1692–1694)

Mar: 6 The King gos for Holland:

I had a sore fit of paine in my loynes, & feared gravell in my Kidneys.

20 My son was made one of the Commissioners of the Revenue & Tressury of Ireland, to which Imployment he had a mind, farr from my wishes, had it consisted with his Circumstances:

I went to visite the E. of Peterborow, who shewed me the picture of the Pr: of Wales, newly brought out of France, seeming in my opinion very much resembling the Q: his mother, & of a most vivacious Countenance:

Much discourse of an intended descent in France this Campagne:

Good friday, I receiv'd the holy Sacrament at St. Martines: in the Afternoone preached one Mr. Brampton on: 3. Gal: 13. a most pathetical & eloquent discourse: his action was very remarkable, & with Authority, such as I liked, but others not: his matter very good.

27 My Bro: sent me the Counterpart of the Articles about the Timber signed &c:

My son fell dangerously Ill of a Giddinesse & universal weakenesse, out of which it pleased God to recover him after 5 or 6 daies: blessed be his Mercy:

Aprill No Spring yet appearing.

The Queene Dowager went out of England towards Portugal, as pretended: against the advise of all her friends &c:

4 On: 17: Acts: 14: ad: 30th: So excellent a discourse, against the Epicurean Systeeme, as is not in few words to be recapitulated, shewing the extreame folly & weakenesse of those who question the existance of a Deity, or at least theire concerne for Mankind: He came to me to know whether I thought fit it should be published, or that there was any thing I desired should be altered therein: I tooke it for a Civilitye, & earnestly desired it might forthwith be printed, as one indeede of the most noble, learned, & Convincing discourses, that I had ever heard:

6 Being the day of publique Humiliation, Mr. *Stringfellow* preached at our church: on 17: Matt: 21.

17 K. James, sends a Letter written in his own hand, informing them of the Q: being ready to be brought abed, & therefore summons them to be at its birth by the middle of May, promising (as from the French King) they shall be permitted both to come & returne in safty: This Letter directed to severall of the Pr: Council, & one (tis sayd) to his daughter the regnant Queene:

20: Was at the R: Society, where was a discourse of the exceeding var⟨i⟩ation of the pole, within few years.

As much talk now & apprehension of the Invasion of the French upon our Coasts:

24 Greate talke of the French Invading; & of an universal rising: our Fleete begins to joyne with the Dutch, Souldiers march towards the Coasts &c:

⟨Unkindnesse ⟩ betweene the Q: & her sister: Very cold & unseasonable weather, scarse a leafe on the trees:

25 I went downe to my house to see my servant Jo: Strickland being taken sudainly sick: & returned the 27:

1. May: Our Minister Mr. Stringfellow preached on 1. *Tim:* 6. 6.

5 The Reports of an Invasion being now so hott, alarmed the Citty, Court & People exceedingly, nothing but securing & Imprisoning suspected persons; sending downe forces to the sea side, hastening out the Fleete, & an universal consternation what would be the event of all this expectation:

8: Continual discourse of the French Invasion, & no lesse of ours in France. The Eastern Winds, so constantly blowing, gave our Fleet time to unite, who were so tardy in preparation, that had not God thus wonderfully favored, they had in all probabillity ben upon us: Many daily secured, & proclamations out for more conspirator⟨s⟩, so called:

My Kindsman Sir Ed: Evelyn of long Ditton dyed suddenly, gave most of his Estate to daughters, from his brother, very unkindly:

22: Trinity Sonday, I heard a sermon at Greenewich of the Curate on: 1: Pet: 5: 7: Exhorting us to cast all our Care upon the Providence of God, doing our owne duty, illustrated by many Instances: & Indeede confirm'd by the Event which happened

this very weeke following: for within a day or two after (after all
our apprehensions of being invaded, & doubtfull of the event at
sea); it pleased Almighty God, to give us such a Victory at sea to
the utter ruine of the French Fleete, Admirall & all their best
men of Warr, Transport shipps &c: as perhaps never was greater
in this part of the World: I referr to the publique particulars:
The newes also of the Imperialists taking greate Waradine, [but
not certaine] & disturbances at Constantinople: The King being
yet with the Confederate Army in Flanders: The next expectation is what God will determine as to the Event of those forces
being on both ⟨sides⟩ so dreadfully greate &c:

My Servant falling into delirium, & past all hopes of recovery, did yet by the infinite mercy of God, come so to himselfe, as
to give us much comfort & so I Left him to the care of the
Physitian: returning to Lond 28:

29 I find that though this day, were set a part by a Law
expresse for the celebrating the memorable Birth, Returne &
Resta⟨u⟩ration of the Late King Char: 2d: There was no manner
of notice taken of it, or any part of the Office (annext to the
Comm prayer booke) made use of which I think was ill don:
In regard his Restauration not onely redeem'd us from Anarchy
& confusion but restored the Church of England as it were
miraculously:

There was a Thanksgiving read for the late Victory at
sea: &c:

June. Impatient expectation of hearing of the event of an
expected Battel at land for the raising the Seige of *Namur*, the
Armys on both sides being so very Greate K. Will: Eighty
foure tho⟨u⟩sand men, with 25000 horse: The French above
100000 &c:

5 At St. Martins Mr. *Linford* on: 12: *Rom:* 2:
The B: Comm: followed, of which I participated: Giving
Almighty God especial thanks for his gracious dealing with me
in the recovery of my Son, & Servants late dangerous sicknesse,
and for my Brothers kindnesse to me, in settling his Estate, &
making it irrevocable: for which I was much obliged to my Bro:
in Law Glanville:

9 I went to Windsor to carry my Grandson to Eaton Schoole,
where I met with My Lady Stonehouse & other of my daughter
in Laws relations, who came on purpose to see her before her

Journey into Ireland: We went to see the Castle, which we found furnish'd, & very neately kept as formerly, onely the Armes in the Gard Chambers & Keepe were removed & carried away:

The greate raines had so swelled the Rivers & Waters that K. Williams Army not being able to forrd over to ingage the French, the Towne of Namure was delivered, without almost any resistances, suppos'd to have ben bought, as usualy the Fr: King did all his Conquests: The Citadell yet holding out:

An exceeding greate storme of wind, ruined much fruit and tore the trees, stripping them of their leaves as it had ben winter in some places:

[16 My Bro: confirmed to me our paternal Estate without revocation &c.]

19 Proceeded on his former Text: [Holy Sacrament followed, which I received, the Lord be ever praysed] the season so wett that I did not go to Evening prayer.

An extraordinary wet season with Greate Floods:

The Castle of Namure yet holding out, but with little hope of reliefe, K. William not being able to come to a Battell:

[25 Came to visit me the Bishops of Lincoln & St. Asaph:]

26 The Castle of Namure taken by the French, to our greate dissappointment, the extraordinary raines hindring K. William & Confederats to passe the River & give battel to the Besiegers:

July: 3. Summer weather after extraordinary wett: nothing from sea or land.

25 We went to Mr. Hewers's to Clappham, who has a very excellent, usefull & Capacious House upon the Common: built by Sir *Den: Gauden*, & by him sold to Mr. *Ewers*, who got a very Considerable Estate in the Navy, in which, (from being Mr. Pepys's Cleark) he came to be one of the principal Officers, but was put out of all Employment upon the Revolution, as were all the best Officers, upon suspicion of being no friends to the change: & such put in their place, as were most shamefully Ignorant: & unfit: Mr. *Hewers* lives very handsomly and friendly to every body &c.

The deplorable Losse of many brave men upon an indiscreete endeavor of K. William to force the French Camp, &c:

Our Fleete was now sailing upon their long pretence of making a Des⟨c⟩ent in France:

31 The Fleet after having sail'd 100 leagues, the Admirals and Officers disagreeing, upon the time of yeare now so far spent, and the place where they were to land, returned back *re infecta*, to the greate dishonor of those who at the helme, concerted their matters so indiscreetely, or as others thought designingly:

This whole Summer was hitherto so exceedingly wet & rainy, as the like had not ben knowne since the yeare 1648, when Colchester was besieged; whilst in *Ireland* they had not knowne so greate a drowth:

⟨7 August⟩ I went to visite the *Bishop* of *Lincoln*, when amongst other things he told me that one Dr. Charlett, of University: Coll: in Oxon, was the person who wrot the Whole Duty of Man, that he read it to his pupils, & Communicated it to Dr. *Stern*: afterwards Arch Bishop of York; &c but would never suffer any of his pupils to have a copy of it:

Aug: 10: The publique Fast: at our Chapell preached a stranger on 13: Luke: 1. 2:

There came the sad newes of the Hurocan & Earthquake which has destroied almost the whole Iland & plantation of *Jamaica*, many Thousands perishing:

11 Went my Son, Wife & litle daughter, towards Ireland; there to reside one of the Commissioners of the Revenue: The Lord Jesus, accompany & blesse him, if it be his blessed will, & prosper him, & grant that I may yet see him in prosperity againe:

September 15 Happn'd an Earthquake, which though not so greate as to do any harme in England, was yet universal in all these parts of Europe; It shoke the House at Wotton, but was not perceived by any save a servant or two, who were making my bed, & another in a Garret, but I & the rest being at dinner below in the Parlor was not sensible of it. There had ben one in *Jamaica* this summer, which destroyed a world of people & almost ruin'd the whole Iland: God of his mercy, avert these Judgements, & make them to incite us to Repentance: This, of Jamaica, being prophanely & Ludicrously represented in a puppet play or some such lewd pass-time in the Faire at South-warke, caused the Queene to put-downe & abolish that idle & vicious mock-shew.

Octob: ⟨2⟩ This season was so exceedingly Cold by reason of a very long & tempestious North east Wind, as made this, usualy

⟨pleasant⟩ season, very uncomfortable: The D: of Savoy retires out of Dauphiny, burns Morbrun.

The K: daily looked for out of Flanders, the Campagne spent, and nothing advanced: Harbord dies at Belgrade, L. Paget sent Ambassador in his roome: No fruite at all kindly ripe this summer; blasted & unthriving:

23 The King now return'd out of Flanders:

A parliament in Ireland &c:

31 I had this day arived to my 72d yeare of Age, in health, though sometimes incomoded ⟨by⟩ pains in my kidneys, & difficulty of holding my water: I blesse the Almighty yet for these his infinite mercys ⟨in⟩ continuing my life thus long, unworthy of the least: beseching his divine Majestie to be with me through the Assistance of his Grace this following yeare, that I may worke ⟨out⟩ my Salvation and make my Calling & Election Sure: Amen: Amen:

November 1. At a meeting of the Feoffees for the poore, the Viccar on: 1 Tim: 6: 14:

6 There was a Vestry called, about repairing or new-building of the Church, which I thought unseasonable in reguard of the heavy Taxes, & other improper Circumstances, which I there declared, as also spake my opinion against the ill custome of burying in Churches &c:

10 The day of solemn Thanksgiving for our victory at sea against the French, safe returne of the King &c: one Mr. Thomas preached on 147: Psal: 11: 12:

This Afternoone went my Wife & part of my Family to our house in Dover streete to Winter in Lond.

20 A signal Robbery of the Tax mony brought out of the North Country towards Lond; set upon by severall desperat persons, who dismounted & stopt all Travellers on the Ro⟨a⟩de, & guarding them in a field, when the exploit was don, & The Treasure taken, killed all the Horses of those they had stay'd, to hinder the pursuit of them: 16 Horses they stabbed & then dismis'd those that they had dismounted &c: This done in Hartfordshire quære &c.

December 4: A chaplain of the L. Colraine, on 4: Eph: 36:

11 Mr. Stringfellow at our Church on 26: *Psal:* 6:

[14: We did, with much reluctancy gratifie Sir Jo: Rotheram, one of Mr. Boyls Trustees, admit the Bishop of Bath & Wells to be Lecturer for the next yeare, instead of Mr. Bently, who had so worthily acquitted himselfe ⟨we resolved⟩ to take him in againe the next yeare.]

30 Dined with me Mr. Pepys, Dr. Gale.

31 Made up Accompts for the Yeare according to Custome, Giving God thanks for his mercies hitherto:

1693⅔; Jan: 1: Mr. Stringfellow at our Church: 2. Luke: 21:

2 At St. Martins preached the Bishop of Bath & Welles Dr. Kidder [for Mr. Boyles Lecture] on 9. *John*: 29: Asserting the Doctrine of Christ, against the Jewes, with the usual Topics, but speaking nothing extraordinarily: This note I onely observed, that in comparing the Miracles of our B. Lord, & advancing them above those of Moses, both for numbers, greatenesse, & Effects, as being none for destruction, but for the good of Mankind, & the most charitable Instances: he observed, that the vaile of the Temple was not rent from the bottom to the Top, but from the Top to the bottome, to shew it was no effect of Wind, or Earthquake &c: but by an extraordinary designation &c:

The Court went now into Mourning for the ⟨E⟩lectresse of Bavaria: Furnes & Dixmude (lately taken & fortified) were surrendred to the French, without a blow struck, or rather deserted, before the French Army appeared, but whilst marching onely:

Contest in Parliament about a selfe denying Act, that no Parliament man should have any Office: It wanted onely two or 3 voices to have ben carried.

Duke of Norfolks Bill for the renewing his prosecution against his Dutchesse, for a divorce, thrown out: he having manedged it so very indiscreetely:

The quarell betweene Russell Admiral & L: Notingham, yet undertermined:

Feb: 4 After 5 days Trial, & extraordinary Contest, was the Lord Mohune acquitted by the Lords of the Murder of *Montford* the Player, notwithstanding that the Judges (from the pregnant witnesses of the fact) had declared him guilty: but whether in commiseration of his youth, being not 18 years old, though exceedingly dissolute, or upon what other reason (the King himselfe present, some part of the Trial, & satisfied they report, that he was culpable): 69 Lords acquitted him & onely 14: Condemn'd him.

Unheard of stories of the universal increase of Witches, men women Children devoting themselves to the Devil, in such numbers in New-England, That it threatened the subversion of the Government:

At the same time a Conspiracy among the Negros in the Barbados, to cut all the Throtes of their Masters, wonderfully detected by the over-hearing two of these slaves discourse of it to one another, & so preventing the execution:

5 Mr. Stringfellow on his former Text.

Afternoone Dr. Lancaster, on 32 Psal 7:

Hitherto an extraordinary mild Winter: France in the utmost Misery & poverty for want of Corne, & subsistance, whilst the ambitious King is intent to pursue his Conquests on the rest of his Neighbours both by sea & land:

Our Admiral Russell laid aside for not pursuing the advantage he had against the French the past summer: Three others chosen in his place:

[Dr. Burnets [B. of Salisbury] book burnt by the hangman for an expression of the Kings Title by Conquest, caused by a complaint of Jo: How a parliament member: little better than a mad man:]

19 [Proposals of a Marriage by Mr. Draper with my daughter Susanna, which I embraced:]

Hitherto an exceeding warme Winter such as had seldom ben known, & portending an unprosperous spring as to the fruits of the Earth, which in our Climate, require more Cold & Winterly weather:

The dreadfull & astonishing Earthquake swallowing up *Catanea* & other famous & antient Cities with above 100000 persons in S⟨i⟩cily on 11: January last, came now to ⟨be⟩ reported among us, which with what happened so lately in Jamaica in America & other parts: is to be greately deplored, & portentous of some extraordinary Revolutions, & terrorising ⟨Judgements⟩:

26 Mr. Stringfellow pursued his former subject.

I dined at my L: Sunderlands where I went to prayers, & so returned home: It being now an extraordinary deepe Snow, after almost no winter hithertoo: & a suddaine gentle Thaw:

The deplorable Earthquake hapning since that of *Sicily*, in Malta, neere as greate as the other:

Mar 12 Having ben much Indisposed the former weeke, I was not at Church til this day; for which God be praised: Mr. Stringfellow, proceeded on his former Text:

The Parliament Prorogu'd til May, without the Ks Assent to the Lords Advice or the Triennial Bill (though many other Acts pass'd, especialy for Money, even 4 s. in the pound &c very grievous) at which they rose not at all satisfied:

The K. resolves to go for Flanders in few days:

Direfull Effects of an Earthquake likewise in Malta:

30 I went to Deptford to take a little aire, & returned after one day: meeting the King by the way going with the Queene in Coach to Gravesend, & thence by Yacht pursuing his Journey to [31] Holland:

Aprill 25 Writing sealed for setling my Daughter⟨s⟩ Joyntur:

27 This day my Daughter Susanna was Married to William Draper Esquire, in the Chapell of Ely-house by my Lord Bishop of Lincoln [Dr. Tenison, since Arch Bishop of Cant:] I gave her in portion 4000 pounds: Her Joynture is 500 pounds a yeare: Which Marriage I pray Almighty God to give his Blessing to: She is a good Child, religious, [discreete,] Ingenious, & qualified with all the ornaments of her sex: especialy has a peculiar talent in Designe & Painting both in oyle & Miniature, & a genious extraordinary, for whatever hands can pretend to do with the Needle: Has the French Toung, has read most of the Greek & Roman Authors, Poets, using her talents with greate Modesty, Exquisitely shap'd, & of an agreable Countenance: This Character is due to her, though coming from her Father.

Much of this Weeke spent in Ceremonie, receiving Visites and Entertainments of Relations.

May Came to Visite my newly married daughter Divers Countesse⟨s⟩ & other Ladys of quality, & Gentlemen:

In which Ceremoni⟨o⟩us returnes a greate part of the week following was spent: Din'd with my L: Mulgrave where was L. Shomberg, Carbery, Maclesfield & divers other persons of quality.

11 My Daughter we accompanied to her Husbands house, where with many of his & our Relations we were magnificently treated & there we left her in an Appartment very richly addorned and furnish'd, & I hope in as happy a Condition as

could be wished: & with the greate satisfaction of all our friends for which God be praised:

14 Nothing yet of Acction from abroad: muttering of a designe of bringing out forces under colour of a descent: to be a standing Army for other purposes: Talke also of a declaration of the Fr: K: offering mighty advantages to the Confederats, exclusive to K. William &c & another of K. James's with an universal pardon, and referring the composing of all mistakes &c to a Parliament. These were yet but discourses, yet something is certainly under it:

25 Interrupted from the publique service of this day, (Ascention) I dined at my Lord ⟨Mulgraves⟩ &c.

Heidelberg taken by storme by the French &c: & burnt &c.

A Declaration or Manifesto from K. James, so writen as many thought to be very reasonable: & much more to the purpose than any of his former:

28 A stranger at St. James Chapell on ⟨2⟩: Cor: 7: 1.

Afternoone at St. James Church Dr. Hickman on 10: Acts 4:

Fine & seasonable weather made greate expectation of action both at Land & Sea.

Our Fleete very strong & now sailing to fight the French, which not being strong enough to encounter, tis believed they will avoyd us, & lie in weight for our Turkey Merchants, which would be to them a rich prize & to us an irr⟨e⟩parable losse, which might have ben prevented if leave had ben given for their sailing in feb:

The French in Flanders much superior to the Confederat forces; so as nothing but ruine threatens without Almightys wonderfull providence & mercy:

June 11 The same person & in the same place, & [on] same Text, directing how we should trie the Spirits, & those who pretend to extraordinary illuminations, Those false Prophets or Teachers gon out into the wor⟨l⟩d, & now more than ever, by which Atheisme, & at best Theisme, Sosinianisme, and other sects has overspread the nation:

I dined at Sir W: Godolphins, after Evening prayer visited the Dut⟨c⟩hesse of Grafton &c:

14 I returned with my Family to Deptford for the rest of the Summer.

21 I saw a greate Auction of Pictures exposed to be sold in the Banqueting house, White-Hall; they had ben my Lord Melfords, now Ambassador of K. James at Rome, & ingaged to his Creditors here: My Lord Mulgrave & Sir Ed Seymor came to my house & desired me to go along with them to the Sale: Divers more of the greate Lords &c were there who bought pictures, deare enough: There were some very excellent Paintings of V: Dikes, Rubens, Bassan; My L: Godolphin bought the boyes of Morella the Spaniard for 80 ginnies, deare enough: my Nephew Glanvill the old Earle of Arundels head of Rubens for 20 pounds. I(t) growing late I did not stay till all was sold but went immediately home to Deptford:

Extraordinary apprehension of our Turkey-Merchants fleetes falling a prey to the French in the Meditereane⟨an⟩, which if it should happen, it would be the most ruinous blow the Citty of London ever received of that Kind & influence the whole Kingdome: which God avert.

31 My Son in Law, his mother & my daughter, came now the first time to visite us at Says-Court:

July 17 I saw the Queenes rare Cabinets & China Collection, which was wonderfull rich & plentifull, but especialy a huge Cabinet, looking Glasse frame & stands all of Amber much of it white, with historical Basrelie⟨vos⟩ & statues with Medals carved in them, esteemed worth 4000 pounds, sent by the D. of Brandenburg, whose Country Prussia abounds with Amber, cast up by the sea &c: Divers other China, & Indian Cabinets, Schreens & Hangings: also her Library in which were many Bookes in English, French, Dutch, of all Sorts: also a Cuppord of Gold Plate, a Cabinet of silver Fillgrene which I think was our Q. Marys, & in my opinion with other Things, Cabinet pieces, should have ben generously sent her Majestie.

18 I din'd at my L Moulgraves, with E. of Devonshire; Mr. Hampden (a Scholar & fine Gent), Dr. Davenant, Sir H. Vane & others, & saw & indeede admired the *Venus* of Coreggio which my L. Mulgrave had newly bought of Mr. Daun for 250 pounds, one of the best paintings I ever saw: This day tooke leave of my son in law & daughter going their progresse amongst his friends into the Country for the rest of the summer.

19 The sad yet doubtfull newes of the taking of our Turkey Marchant⟨s⟩ & Convoy by the French neere Cape Vincent, which

if true as related, the greatest blow was ever given the Citty since the fire, & affecting the whole nation, & that by our wretched imprudence or tretchery: Also the losse of Huis, & ill successe in all our Concernes, forerunner of destruction for our folly & precipitous Change &c: God avert the deserved consequence:

Aug: 1 The long expected newes of the successe of a Battell, in Flander⟨s⟩ at Landun, gave us a sad account of our greate losse, who had much the better of the French from morning til 4 in the After noone, when fresh horse of the French turn'd the day, & got the feild, a most bloody fight, however the slaughter of the French much greater than ours: though they were double our number: viz: 80000 to 50000: The French lost aboundance of Officers, we but few: Count Solmes of our side Kild: Duke of Ormond much Wounded &c: on theirs, Duke of Berwick Taken & severall greate officers slaine: K William narrowly escaped, but doing the part of a greate Captain in the whole Conduct, but over powered by the Enemys horse, and as is sayd, by the cowardlinesse of Ginkle the Dutch Gen, who with severall Regiments did not come timely to the aide &c:

Our Fleete sailing towards Ushant, to waite the French; who had burnt & taken 60 of the Hollands Merchants & 2 men of War: Rooke our Admirall said to be come safe into Ireland, & the rest of our Merchant⟨s⟩ safe, put into Cales & other harbours: In summ we have thro negligence & want of honesty & Conduct, not at all prospered this summer in Flanders or at Sea: what will be don in Germany & Savoy we expect; The Turke makes no greate shew of doing much, through disturbance of the Asiatic forces: Denmarke marches to disturb his neighbours & is a pensioner of France:

Lord Capel Sir Cyril Wych & Mr. Duncomb, made Lord Justices in Ireland, my L: Sidney recald, & made Master of the Ordinance: &c:

5 Came to see me Mr. Justell, & the Earle of Castleton of Scotland & his son.

9 Fast day: our Viccar. 2. Sam: 24: 12. Shewing pride & sin the cause of all Calamity, punish'd both in Prince, & people: in all such exigences, nothing is to be don but to Repent, amend, bemone our sinns, & resigne our selves to Gods infinite Compassions: & Indeede so it was at this time that we had ben beaten with an extraordinary slaughter, Canon taken &c: Our

merchants ships burnt & ruined in the Mediterrane⟨an⟩, and every thing sadly declining; & all this for our late Injustice and disobedience, & the still reigning of sin among us:

Sept. 21 I went to Lond, to passe the deedes for the sale of that [part of] land in Deptford, sold to Mr. Vokey, & Mr. Tuffnel, to raise my daughter Drapers Portion, which was 4000 pounds: returned that Evening:

28 I went to Lond to finish the Conveyances & deeds of the sale of the land for my daughters portion & did receive 3000 pounds, which with 1000 before made up the summ of 4000: now paied to my Son Draper: & returned home this Saturday.

30 No newes of what was don in the Armies abroad, by reason of Contrary Winds &c:

Octob 1 Our Viccar proceeded on his former Text: the holy Communion followed, I received, The Lord, make me mindfull & Thankfull:

Seige of Charle-Roy.

31 An extraordinary & dangerous Indisposition, taken by a Cold, kept me within a full fortnight, so as I could not stir abroad without greate Danger; my Wife also surprized with her wonted winter Rheumatisme; but by Gods infinite Goodnesse both now much recovered; I am arived this day to the 73rd yeare of Age: The Lord Jesus make me thankfull for this & all his mercys, & so cause me to number the rest of my days, which by the Course of nature cannot be many, that I may apply them to that Wisdome which shall bring me to his Everlasting life in his heavenly kingdome: Amen.

A very wett: & uncomfortable season, & hitherto most unprosperous in all our publique Concernes: Charle-roy taken in Flanders: Roses in Catalognia; two battels lost in Savoy: & the siege of Pignoll there, and Belgrade in Hungary raised: Sad losse at sea by our Turky merchants: The King William Returned out of Holland yesterday; The Parliament sitting a day or two before, adjourned til tuesday next.

Nov: 5 The first Sonday of the moneth, & that I had ben at church since my late Indisposition: our Viccar on 2: Isa: 13: A discourse of the wonderfull preservations of his church in all Ages historicaly, the seacret yet sure workings of his providence to bring things about which he determines:

The holy Sacrament followed, at it I & my Wife received, the Lord make us mindfull & thankfull, restoring us both to health.

12 This weeke produced nothing observable: [save [L. Notingham laying down his being Secretary of State], the outing the Commissioners of the Admiralty, & restoring Mr. Russele to his Office againe.] The season continuing excedingly Wett, as had all this summer, if one might call it summer, in which there was no fruite, onely Corn very plentifull:

My Son Draper & Daughter, now with Child, came to see us; after their some moneths absence in Visiting their Relation in divers places of the Country &c and returned on Tuesday:

14 The Parliament examining the miscarriages of the Fleete the last summer:

In the Lottery set up after the Venetian manner by Mr. Neale, Sir R: Haddock, one of the Commissioners of the navy had the greatest Lot, 3000 pounds, my Coach-man 40 pounds, &c:

17 Cap: Youngs funerall I think the first who in the first warr of Cromwell against Spaine, tooke the Governor of Havana & other rich Prizes, & struck the first stroke against the Dut⟨c⟩h fleete in the first War with Holland in the time of the Rebellion &c, buried; a sober man & excellent sea man. Our Viccar preached the funeral sermon 7: *Micha* 9 shewing the duty of Patience & relyance on God for mercy, & submission to his Correction: The text chosen by the Cap: dying of the stone & greate age:

23 I went to Lond: to dispose of my sons house in Doverstreete: to Elect Mr. Bently [for the yeare to come, see next page*] Visited severall Friends:

26 St. James Chapel morning the Lecturer Dr. Hicks on: 7: Mich: 9:

Newes of Cap: Benbows exploit & seting fire on St. *Malows*, in manys opinion not well don, for the small damage we did them may infinitely indanger our Coasts, by their numerous Vessels   our Rivages lying so much more open to them, & many Gentlemens houses well furnish⟨ed⟩ &c within so few miles of the Coast: whereas all the French Townes & every small Dorp, is Walled, & so not obnoxious to sudden Incursions, I pray God we do not feele it reveng'd on us in the Summer:

30 R: Society St. Andrews Day, much againe Importuned to ⟨be⟩ Præsident, which as formerly I wholy refused; so as Sir Rob: Southwell was Continued for the following yeare: We all din'd at Pontacs, secundum Consuetudinem:

December 3 *I came to Lond to give my voice for Mr. *Bently* for proceeding on his former subject the following yeare; in Mr. Boyls Lecture in which he had ben interrupted by the importunity of Sir Jo: Rotheram, that the Bishop of Chichester might be chosen the yeare before: to the greate dissatisfaction of the Bishop of Lincolne & my selfe, & so we chose Mr. Bently againe for the yeare to come:

Parliament sitting, greate Complaint against the 3 Admirals for our ill successe the last summer:

2 million & halfe Voted for the sea service the next yeare: & what for the land forces & recruits, not yet determined:

Dutchesse of Graftons Appeale to the House of Lords for the protonotaries place, given the late Duke & to her son &c by K. Charles 2d: now challenged by the Lord C. Justice: The Judges severly Reprooved upon some thing they said.

Dr. Sancroft, the ejected A Bishop of Canterbury died:

10 The severe cold kept us within this Lords-day:

A very greate storme with Thunder & Lightning:

17 My Grandson came from *Eaton*, 12 years old, gotten into the 3d forme & a very pregnant hopefull fine Child, whom I pray God to blesse.

25 Christmas day our Viccar on 10 Matt. 2. ad 7: The holy Communion followed at which I & my wife Received:

My son Draper & daughter came & kept Xmas with us.

Making up Accompts according to Custome, & Giving A. God Thanks for his gracious preservation of me hithertoo:

169$\frac{3}{4}$. *Jan:* 1 Imploring the continuance of Gods Blessing & protection for the following yeare.

The Prince *Lewes* of *Baden* came to Lond, & was mightily feasted:

Danish Ships arested carrying Corne & Naval stores to France:

Talk of overtures of a generall Peace: Jubily Indicted:

A poore religious French Girle, much distorted in her feete & limbs of a long time, restored miraculously in a moment, as she was reading of that Chap   & saying that had she lived at that time she might have ben healed & did firmly believe God could yet do it if he pleased, see the Narrative Attested &c:

8 I went to London in order to Remove our Goods & furniture out of our House in Dover Streete in order to the letting of it:

11 Sup'd at Mr. Ed Sheldons where was Mr. Dryden the Poet, who now intending to Write no more Plays (intent upon the Translation of Virgil) read to us his Prologue & Epilogue to his last Valedictory Play, now shortly to be Acted:

21 Our Viccar on his former Text:

Lord: Maclesfild, Lord Warrington, & L: Westmorland all died within about one Weeke: Severall shot, hanged & made away with themselves:

The Prince of Baden exceedingly feasted:

30: Being the Anniversary of the Martyrdom of K. Charles I. a young man preached on 19 *Joh:* 15 Shewing in an excellent discourse, the Excellency of Kingly Government above all other, deriving it from Adam, The Patriarchs, God himselfe, That it was originaly in the Primogeniture, & so in a Manner continued in the Father over his children even thro the Ro: Emp: 'til *Justinian*: That Kings were allways so Sacred, even among the Heathen, as almost God in the Rites performed to many of them, *Cicero pro Deiotario* beginning his pleading with a wonder that a King should be brought as it were to the barr: This Reverence & submission to Kings he brought many suffrages for out of not onely the Pagans books & practise but out of divers of the Fathers of the Church under Heathen & Idolatrous Princes. Shewed the unnaturalnesse of subjects to destroy their owne King, especialy such a King as was this Martyr, & shewed how the Arguments brought by our Regicides to palliat their wicc⟨k⟩ed Action, were brought from Bellarmine &c & other Champions of the Papal Tyrannie: Ended with a Reflection on the sad Catastrophe of the Instruments of this Murder, the Confusions and Judgments since following, & the evils that yet threaten us without a serious Repentance for the time to Come; which I beseech God Grant us: Many passages in this Sermon, neerely touching the dethroning K. James, not easily to be answered.

The long frost now dissolved.

Feb: 11 Now ⟨w⟩as the greate Trial of Appeale of the Lord of Bath, & Montague before the Lords, for the Estate of the late Duke of Albemarle.

Mar: 22 Was Cristned my Nephew Glanvills daughter Eliz: borne in [Dover Streete] Trinity Parish neere St. James's.

Came the dismal newes of the disaster befalen our Turky merchants Fleete by Tempest, to the almost utter ruine of that Trade: The Convoy of 3 or 4 men of War, & divers Merchant ships with all thier Men & Lading perishing; so vast a losse as had hardly ever ben known; & worse than all that both our Warres & Conflicts with any Enemy had don us these hundred years:

Unreasonable Taxes & Impositions layed on us by the Parliament to maintaine an hithertoo successles Warr with France, maneged hitherto with so little discretion &c:

25 Dr. Goade, Minister of St. Martins, on 20. *Mat:* 9, against deferring Repentance til the deathbed, exceeding well pressed: This Doctor was likewise put in by the Queene upon the issue of her processe against the [B of] Lond.

28 I went to the Duke of Norfolck to desire him to make my Co: Evelyn of Nutfield one of the Dep: Lieutennants of Surrey, & intreate him to dismisse my old Bro, not now able by reason of age & Infirmity to serve: The Duke granted the one, but would not suffer my Brother to resigne his Commission; but keepe the honor of it during his life, though he could not act &c: professing very greate kindnesse to our Family &c.

Aprill 2 I returned home to my house:

Came about this time a Melancholy, Gent: very Learned & pious, to Visite me, & to desire my Acquaintance: his name was *Quin*: It seemes (as since the B: of Lincoln tells me) his Father cut his owne throate before the Altar in a church in Dublin:

12 Came the Countesse of Sunderland, Lady Sylvius, Mrs. Boscawen & Mrs. Den Godolphin to dine with us.

13 Came to see me Mr. Bently, Chaplain to the Bishop of Worcester, our Boylean Lecturer:

22 I return'd this Evening home, it being an extraordinary hot season.

Certaine report & undoubtedly confirmed of a firy exhalation rising out of the sea in Montgomery-shire, which spred it selfe a furlong broad & travelled many Miles in length; burning all Straw, hay, Thatch, grasse, but doing no harme to Trees, timber or any solid things: onely fires barnes & Thatched houses, leaving such a taint on the Grasse, as killed all the Cattell that eate of it: I my selfe saw the Attestations under the hands of the sufferers, This lasted many moneths:

The Berkley Castle sunk by the French, which comming from the E. Indies had ben worth 200000 pounds: The French also tooke our Castle of *Gambo* in Guiny; so as the Africa Actions fell to 30 pounds & the E. India to 80: so powerfull & vigilant & Industrious were the French, as with their Picaroons & men of War, ruined us in every place where we had any Trading, whilst neither English nor Dutch, with all their united forces, so far superior to them in number of ships, minded nothing, thro an accountable negligence:

Some Regiments of Highlande Dragoons, in their march thro England, men of huge stature & extremely well appointed, & disciplined: One of them being pursued by a Dutchman, whom it seemes he had reproch'd for cowardlinesse in our late fight when in church: The Highlander with his sword struck of his head with one blow, & cleft the scull of another Dutchman with him down to the chin:

A [very young] Gentleman named Wilson, the [younger] son of one that had not above 200 pounds per Annum: lived in the Garb & Equipage of the richest Noble man in the nation for House, Furniture, Coaches & 6 horses, & other saddle horses; Table & all things accordingly: Redeemed his Fathers Estate, gave portion to his sister; being challenged by one Laws a Scotsman, was now killed in Duel, not fairly, the quarell being because he tooke away his owne sister from lodging in a house, where this Laws had a Wench: which the Mistris of the lodging thinking a disparagement to her House, & loosing by it this Gentlewoman (namely Wilsons sister) who was a profitable Guest, Instigated the Scotchman to revenge it: Laws is taken & condemned for Murder: But the Mysterie is, how this so young gentleman, a sober young person, & very inoffensive, & of good fame, did so live in so extraordinary Equipage; it not being discovered by any possible industry, by any his most intimate Friends, no, tho' they had endeavoured to make him reveale it being in drink: But they could never find it out: It did not appeare he either was kept by Women or Play, or Coyning,

Padding; or that he had any dealing in Chymistry, but that he would sometimes say, that if he should live [to] never so greate an age, he had wherewith to maintain it in the same affluence. He was very young, Civil, well natured, of no greate force in Understanding, but very Indifferent parts: All which was subject of much discourse and admiration:

THE MOVE TO WOTTON – DEATH OF
MARY II – PEACE WITH FRANCE
(1694–1697)

24 TO LOND ABOUT settling some buisinesse in order to my going into Surrey. Calling at Gressham Coll: I went to visite Mr. Waller our Secretary, an extraordinary young Gent: & [of greate] accomplishments: skild in Mathematics, Anatomie, Musick, Painting both in Oyle and Miniature to a greate perfection, an excellent Botanist, Ingraves rarely in Brasse, writes in Latine, & is a poet, & with all this exceedingly modest: His house an Academy of it selfe: I carried him to see Brompton Parke, where he was in admiration at the store of rare plants & method he found in that noble nursery, & how well cultivated &c.

Greate Alterations among the Greate ones at Court, & among the Officers; new honors conferred; The Garter given the Earl of Shrewsbery, Secretary of State againe (upon the going out of L. of Notingham) the Duke Hamilton being dead at Edinburge:

The Parliament Prorogued til September.

A publique Bank of 140000 pounds set up by Act of Parliament among severall other Acts [& Lotteries] for mony to carry on the War:

The King went towards Flanders, but the Wind contrary returnes againe:

The whole moneth of ⟨April⟩, without a showre:

A greate Rising of People in Buckinghamshire, upon the declaration of a famous Preacher (& til now, reputed sober & religious man) that our Lord Christ appearing to him on the 16 of this moneth, told him he was now come downe, & would

appeare publicly at Pentecost & gather all the Saints Jew &
Gentile, & leade them to Jerusalem, & begin the *Millenium*,
& destroying & Judging the wiccked, deliver the government of
the world to them &c. This bringing greate multitude of people
to follow this Preacher, divers of the Zelous brought their
Goods, & considerable summs of mony, & began to live in imitation of the primitive Saints; minding no private concernes, but
were continualy dancing & singing Alalujas night & day; what
the end of it may be, I know not, if there be not timely care taken
to disperse them before they get to Lond: where there are such
multitudes of disscenters & sects, & a mobile so dangerous: &
so many discontents, so loose Government, in summ a whole
nation so unsettled & distracted: This brings to mind what
I lately happened to find in Alstedius, that the Thousand years
should indeede begin the very yeare 1694: It is in his Encyclope-
dia, my book printed neere 60 yeares since:

27 I dined with my son Draper, it being the wedding day of
my daughter.

May 4th. I went this day, with my Wife & 3 Servants from
Says-Court, & removing much furniture of all sorts, books, Pictures, Hangings, bedding &c: to furnish the Appartment my
Brother assign'd me; & now after more than 40 yeares, to spend
the rest of my dayes with him at Wotton, where I was borne;
leaving my House, & 3 servants at my house at Deptford (full
furnished) to my Son in Law Draper, to passe the summer in &
what longer time he thought good to make use of it: I Pray God
this solemn Remove may be to the Glory of his mercy, & the
good of my family:

20 The Wet hindred from going to Church, Prayers were here:

I by a slip downe some steps, brused my back; blessed be God
it was no worse:

27 Whitsonday Wotton Mr. Morus: 26 John: 14: The holy
Communion followed at which I received, the Lord make me
mindfull & thankfull:

There was no offering, & very few Communicants, of both
which I complained, & desired it might be reformed if possible;
The truth is, The present Incumbent, put in by my good natured
Brother, upon the importunity of Relations, was one who having
another fat living, tooke very little care of this parish, puting it
under an hireling tho' I believe a good man, but one altogether

without spirit or Vigour: The same did my Bro: to the next Parish in his Gift also, to a Relative of his Ladys, slothfull, & fitter to have ben any thing than a divine: The Lord pardon this fault & reforme it in his good time:

This weeke we had newes of my Lord Tiveots having Cut his owne Throat, through what discontent, not yet said: he had ben not many yeares past my Collegue in the Commission of the Privy-Seales, & old Acquaintance & one very sober & Religiously disposed: Lord what are [we] without thy continual Grace:

This very same Weeke we were also told that Coll: William Leg, bro: to the late Lord Dartmoth, made himselfe likewise away by the same desperate action: He indeede was a prophane wild Creature of whom I can say little good, ingaging me once at Hampton Court in a debauched Conversation: The Lord pardon:

My Lord Falkland (grandson to the learned Lord Falkland secretary of state to K: Charles 1: & slaine in his service:) died also now of the small pox: He was a pritty, briske understanding industrious young gent: had formerly ben faulty, now very much reclaimed: Had the fortune to marry a very greate fortune, besides fortunately intitled to a vast summ, being his share of the Spanish Wrack, taken up at the Expense of divers Adventurers: was now from a Scotch Vicount made an English Baron, designed Ambassador for Holland; had ben Treasurer of the Navy & advancing extreamly in the new Court: All this now gon in a moment, & I ⟨think⟩ the Title extinct in him, I know not whether the Estate devolves not to my Couse⟨n⟩ Carew &c: It was at my Lord Falklands, (whose Lady importuned us to let our daughter be with her some time) That that Deare Child tooke the same infection which kild her, some years before: The Lord be mercifull to us, & remove all his Judgements from us, restore health & peace & Trade:

June 3: Trinity Sonday Mr. *Edwards* Minister of Denton in Sussex, a Living in my Bro: Gift. The poore man suffered much by a fire, & was an object of Charity: he came to see his patron & preachèd on   perswading to the reading of the H: Scripture, by a description of all its Excellences & fullnesse beyond any other booke of the world:

10 Seasonable showers: Greate Expectations of Action from Fleete & Army:

⟨13⟩ June the publique Fast: Mr. *Wotton* (that extraordinary learned young man) preached incomparably on 4 Jonah: 9. 10: 11 verses:

After much Expectations & hopes of making a descent on Brest; we have ben fowly defeated to the losse of Col: Talmash one of the best Commanders, & some number of men: what event the Army in Flanders will be, is now our apprehensions, upon this so unprosperous a beginning the Campagne:

July 1 Mr. Duncomb, Minister of Albery, at Wotton on 1. *Joh:* 5. 4: A very religious & excellent discourse:

Very fine Haying weather, flying reports of a defeate given to the French by the Germans: which proved all false:

8 The first greate Banke for a fund of Mony, being now established by Acct of Parliament was now filled & compleated to the summ of 120000 pounds, & put under the government of the most able & wealthy Cittizens of Lond, by which all who adventured any summs had 4 per Centum, so long as it lay in the banke, & had power either to take it out againe at pleasure or Transferr it:

Never more glorious & steady Summer weather, Corne & all other fruits in extraordinary plenty generaly:

15 My Lord Berkley burnt Dieppe & Haverdegrace with the bombs in revenge of the defeate at Brest: This manner of destructive warring begun every where by the French, tho' it be exceeding ruinous, especialy falling on the poorer people, & is very barbarous, dos not seeme to tend to make any sooner end of the Warr but rather to exasperate, & incite to revenge:

Greate expectation of Action in Flanders, where the greate stresse of the quarrell lies: Admiral Russel gon with a greate fleete into the Mediterranean, to disturbe the seige of Barcelona &c:

Many Executed at London &c: for Clipping mony, which was now don to that intollerable degree, that there was hardly any mony stiring that was intrinsi⟨c⟩aly worth above halfe the value, to such a strange exorbitance things were arived, beyond that any age can shew example:

My son in law Draper came to visite us from Deptford &c:

August 4 I went to visite my Co: G: Evelyn of Nutfeild, where I found a Family of ten Children, five sonns, & as many

daughters: all of them beautifull Virgins, women growne &
extreamely well fashioned; all painted also in one piece very well
by Mr. Lutterell in Crayon upon Copper and seeming to be as
finely painted as the best Miniature: They are the Children of 2
most extraordinary beautifull Wives: The Boys were abroad at
Schoole: After dinner I returned againe, where I found my
poore Wife exceedingly afflicted with the stone, now of late
very much increasing her paine; from which I pray God to
deliver her.

5 Many persons seiz'd & secured about a plot:

12 No *Sermon* at the church this morning by the negligence of
the Parson:

Discourse of the French Landing in *Jamaica*; Parker escaped
out of the Toure, a greate summ to whomsoever shall apprehend him: many imprisoned, about a Plot: no Action of any
Armes: Unseasonable weather continues after a most promising
Harvest, & great plenty of all sorts of Fruite:

September 13 Hearing that my daughter Draper began to
Complaine & be uneasy of her greate belly, we went on the 13th
towards Deptford, hoping to get thither some competent time
before there would be neede of a Midwife: But were met upon
the way about Meecham, with the good newes of her being
delivered of a Boy the night before, about betweene 7 & 8 a
clocke: & so found her, after it seemes, a very sharp Conflict,
very well layd to all appearance, & so continuing without any
unusual Accident for 2 or 3 days; but after that seized with a
feavour, loosenesse, vapours & other evil symptoms which
increased upon her to that degree, that on [⟨21⟩] the friday
senight after, we had very little hopes of life: so as receiving the
B: Sacrament, we recomended her condition to Almighty God,
not expecting her to continue many hours after: But it pleased
God (of his infinite mercy) that escaping that night, Sir Tho
Melington & Dr. *Cade* (the physitians) gave us so⟨me⟩ hopes, &
so from thence day to day, her feavor, & fits abating, tho' very
slowly, exceeding thirst, & no sort of rest, put us into many
doubts what would be the issue of it: She is now God be praised
in some more ease, lesse thirsty, now & then sleepes; but still so
exceeding Weake & low in Spirits, as puts us in feare: God of his
infinite mercy restore her:

I never saw a finer or goodlier Child: The Baptisme is, against my will, deferr'd, expecting when Sir *T: Draper* (who is to be one of the Godfathers) can come downe, who it seemes is gon a journey, & returnes not til some days:

And this dangerous condition of my daughter hindering us from other duties; kept me from Church two Sondays: I was yet once [24] at London, but came backe againe the same evening.

Newes of the taking of *Huis* by storme:

Very fine & seasonable weather:

30: Dr. Holden at Deptford Church on: 8: *Rom.* 13: shewing what was meant by the flesh: Naturaly, the rational man as he is composed of flesh & blood: Thus the philosophers: But by *divines*, is understood all either disorderly or superfluous & sinfull gratifications of the senses, whereby the spiritual life is any way impeached: such as not onely all the more hainous sinns, but all sort of immoral Acctions whatsoever, all unnecessary pleasures, pomps, indulgences to ease, splendor, outward appearances, living without some calling or laudab⟨l⟩e Imployment for the benefit of the publique as well as ourselves, cares & solicitude for any thing, that may distract, desire of Riches, Honor, Reputation, yea even of learning for curiosity, or estemation of men; These & the like were all of them Carnal, whose end would be sorrow, & death eternal without Repentance, & Reformation, & therfore That a Christians Duty was to mortifie & withdraw his Affections from all such things, to strive to live [in] a modest course, to be content with humble & decent Circumstances, moderat & Indifferent for the things of this world; studious to do all the good he could, & so setting out the infinite pleasure & satisfaction of such a life beyond all the pleasures ⟨that⟩ this world could afford, in consideration of the tra⟨n⟩sitorinesse & uncertaintie of things; & the exceeding troubles which those who abound with them are obnoxious to: Instancing in that of a certaine Philosopher, recluse & studious person, who hapning to come to Rome, when a wondrous pompous Triumph was going thro the Citty, at which he was infinitly pleased & in admiration, of the happinesse of the Ceremonies, whilst it was mooving slowly thro the streetes; but at last it ended, & proved to be onely a short passage leaving nothing after it which lasted; the Consideration of which soone chang'd his thought of, the Happinesse & enjoyments of all he had seen & reckon'd upon; & went contentedly & choosingly back againe to his studious & innocent Recesse; where he enjoied so much tranquility: This was well applied: & brought to my thoughts, the many errors & follys of my past life, which I had seene, endeavored after, with no small Remorse; whoe had ben much hapier to have lived so: God Almighty of his Infinite Compassion, pardon all my Sinns, of this pride of life, & make me yet with all my power endeavor after this meeke, & humble state of life for the future if it be his heavenly will. Amen.

Oct: 2 My Daughter visibly mending of her hitherto dangerous Condition & giving us greate hopes of a perfect recovery, I went to Lond: about severall buisinesses:

5 I went to Paules to see the Choire now finished, as to the stone work & that part both without & within the scaffolds struck: some exceptions might yet perhaps be taken without ⟨as⟩ the placing Columns upon Pilasters, at the East Tribunal: As to the rest certainly a piece of Architecture without reproch: The pulling out of the Formes, like drawers from under the stalles, is very ingenious:

I went also to see the building begining neare St. Giles's where seaven streetes make a starr from a Doric Pillar plac'd in the middle of ⟨a⟩ Circular Area. Said to be built by Mr. Neale, Introducer of the late Lotteries in Imitation of those of Venice: now at this time set up here, for himselfe twise and now one of: 20000 for the state.

8 I Returned to Deptford finding my Daughter perfectly freed from her feavor:

11 This day Mr. Holden our Viccar Christned my Grandchild by the name of Thomas, being the Name of Sir Thomas Draper of Sunning Hill in Barkshire Unkle to my Son-in-Law, My selfe being the other Godfather: The Godmother the Lady Temple his Aunt: The Infant (much against my desire) being thus long from Baptis⟨m⟩e; by reason of Sir Thomass Indisposition which hindred him from comming abroad; & that my daughter had [not] ben recovered of her so late dangerous sicknesse:

November 22 Being to visite the B: of Lincoln newes came in of the death of the AB. of Canterbury, who few days before was struck with a paralytical palsey: [Died the same day & moneth that AB. Sancroft was put out, so tis said Lewes the XIII was borne the day & houre some yeares after Hen 4 was slaine.]

Having dispatched many Affaires in Lond, & Visited friends I returned to Deptford: the 23d.

23. An extraordinary sickly time especialy of the Small pox of which divers considerable persons died:

K. William had 2 fitts of an Ague:

The Gent in the North, imprisoned & tried for a Plot freed upon proofe of the perjury & vilany of the wittnesses.

Parliament Assembled: The State Lottery drawing, where one *Mr. Cock* a French Refugie, & a president in the parliament of Paris for the Reformed: drew a lot of 1000 pounds per ann:

24 I return'd to Deptford, & was so very ill of the cold I had taken that it turn'd to a Colick, so as I could not go the next Sonday to church, this indisposed me til 28.

29 Severall buisinesses carried me againe to Lond: I took leave of severall friends, [30] made the Bishop of Lincoln my Proxy to elect a fit person to succeede Mr. *Bentley* who now made the Kings Library-keeper at St. James, was laying downe Mr. Boyles Lecture: I spake then also to the Bishop, to assist the procuring an Acct of Parliament, to rectifie some things deficient in Mr. Boyles settlement of that particular:

I visited L: Marques of Normanby, & had much discourse concerning the King Chas 2d being poisoned: also concerning the *Quinquean* which the Physitians would not give the King, at a time when in a dangerous Ague it was the onely thing could ever cure him, out of envy, because it had ben brought into vogue by Mr. Tabore an Apothecary; Til Dr. Short (to whom the K. sent to have his opinion of it privately, he being reputed a papist, but was in troth a very honest good Christian): he sent him word, it was the onely thing could save his life, & then the King, injoyn'd his physitians to give it him, & was recovered: Being asked by this Lord why they would not prescribe it: Dr. Lower said, it would spoile their practise or some such expression: & at last confessed it was a Remedy fit onely for Kings:

Exception was taken that the late A.Bishop did not cause any of his Chaplins to use any Office for the sick during his sicknesse.

I went hence to the R: Society, where I was elected of the Council this yeare, much against my will, as likely to be absent most part of my time in Surry, whither I was going in a few days: I return'd to Deptford:

December 9 My Wife so dangerously ill of a defluction, that I was faine to returne the Coach which my Bro sent to carry us to Wotton:

I had newes that my deare & worthy Reverend ffriend Dr. Tenison Bishop of Lincoln, was now made Arch Bishop of Canterbery for which I thank God & rejoice, he being most worthy of it both for his Learning, Piety & Prudence: I told him the weeke before, that it would be so:

13 I went to Lond: to Congratulate the Bishop of Lincoln being now translated to Canterbery, who being my Proxie, gave my voice for the choise of Dr. Williams, to succeede Mr. Bently in Mr. Boyles Lecture:

15 I returned the Saturday: The small pox very mortal.

16 Our Viccar in the morning on 51 Psal: 18. it being a thanks-giving day for the preservation of King William & successe the past summer.

My wife amended blessed be God:

Exceeding sharp weather this week:

Mr. Wells Curate at Abinger had a letter from me to the A Bishop of Cant to procure him a living in Surrey neere Gildford, in place of one Mr. Gerey, who was unhappily killed, by reaching a Gun to his son in a Tree, watching to shoote some rabbets, the Cock being up as he delivered the but end of the piece to his son it went of & hitting the father in the forehead miserably slew him:

22 My son & daughter Draper went for Lond: to passe the rest of the winter there, having ben kindly with us till now, that my Wife recover'd from her late sicknesse & was able to leave her Chamber:

25 *Deptford* Our *Viccar* on 3. *Gen:* 2d. I received the holy Communion: God make me mindfull. Said the Queene ill of the small pox.

29 I went together with my Wife to Wotton, for the rest of the Winter; which with long frost & snow was I think the very

sharpest I ever past: The small pox increasing & exceedingl⟨y⟩ mortal: Queene Mary died theroff, full of Spotts: Died the 28: & I think was buried 2 or 3 days after: What this unexpected Accident may produce as to the present Government, many are the discourses, & a little time may shew: The K. seemed mightily afflicted, as indeede it behoved him:

30—the cold & frost so sharp as hindred us going to church.

31 Made up all my Accompts giving God thanks for his mercys hitherto.

169$\frac{4}{5}$ Jan: 1 Imploring the blessing of God for the yeare following.

8 I sent my Grandson John to Eaton, who had ben here at Wotton the Christmas:

13 So very fierce was the frost, as kept us still from church: The Thames frozen over; the Infection of the small pox &c: increased to 500 more this weeke than the former:

20 The frost & continual snows has now lasted neere 5 weekes, with that severity, as hindered me yet from going to our distant parish church to my no small sorrow: The small pox still raging: Greate expressions in most parts of England, & in Holland exceeding, for the death of the late Queene: The King & Princesse Ann (til now displeased with the Court, upon some suggestions, which made the two sisters strang to one another) now so fully reconciled, that she is invited to keepe her Court at White-hall (till now living privately at Berkely-house) & desired to take into her family divers servants of the Queene, to maintain which the King had assign'd her 5000 a quarter: Greate preparation in the meane time for a most magnificent funeral: All people in Mourning; Addresse⟨s⟩ of Condolence from all parts both at home, & from abroad:

Feb: 3 The weather & season had hitherto continued so very severe & the snow so deepe, & now so slabby, s⟨l⟩ippery & cold; as we could not be at church without danger: I do not know I have ben so many Sondays absent from it, above these 40 yeares, to my greate sorrow:

The Parliament are upon divers projects for mony, as chimny mony againe, mulcts of all Batchelors, Married men & children in order to a funds for a new lottery &c:

The long Frost intermitted but not quite gon:

10 This being the very first Sunday I had ben at church since I came into the Country, hindred by the severity of the weather &c: I now went to *Abenger*, where Mr. *Wotton* preached on: 6: Ephes: 13. In a very plaine & solid discourse:

17 Cald to Lond by Lord Godolphin one of the Lords of the Tress: offering me the Kings making me Treasurer of the Hospital designed to be for emerited sea-men &c: to be built at Greenewich, which I deliberated about &c.

20 Preached at St. James's Chap: coram Rege, the Bishop of Bangor, on All things work for the best to them who love God, applyed as most sermons now were, to the late death of the Queene, so universaly deplored:

21 I went to see the B: of Cant:

24 I saw the Q: lie in state at W.hall, all now in pompous mourning:

27 I dined with Sir Jo Jardine & a learned french divine of the Oratorians Converted &c: saw my pretty Godson:

Visited the Lord Marq: of Normanby &c who told me K. Char: had a designe to buy all Kings streete & build it nobly, it being the streete leading to Westminster: which the expense of the Q: funerall would have don; the pomp of which cost above 50000 pounds: very unseasonably & against her desire.

Mar: 5 Was the Queens funeral infinitely expensive, never so universal a Mourning, all the Parliament men had Cloaks given them: 400 poore women, all the streets hung, & the middle of the streets boarded & covered with black cloth: there was all the Nobility, Mayor & Aldermen, Judges, &c:

7 To the R: Society, where one lately come out of Poland among several curiosities presented an intire Plica Polonica or matted thick intangled matt of haire &c:

8 I tooke leave of my L. of Canterbery: & supped at the B: of Lichfild & Co: who related me the pious behaviour of the Queene in all her sicknesse which was admirable & the noble designe she had in hand, her expensive Charity, never enquiring of the opinion of the partys if objects of charity: that a Cabinet ⟨being⟩ opened some time after her decease, a paper was found wherein she had desired her body might not be opned or any expense on her funerall extraordinary when ever she should happen to dye; both which were not perform'd, finding this

paper too late after all was already prepared: Other excellent things under her owne hand to the very least of her debts, which were very small, & every thing in that exact method as seldom is found in any private persons: In summ such an admirable Creature (abating for her taking the Crown without a more due Apology) as dos if possible out do the Renowned Q: Eliz herselfe:

10 Dined at the Earle of Sunderland, with my Lord Spencer, newly married to the Lady Arbella daughter to the late Duke of Newcastle: my Lord shewed me his incomparable Library now againe improved by many books bought at the sale of Sir Charl Scarbrs, which was the very best collection especialy of Mathematical books that was I believe in all Europe: once designed for the Kings library of St. James but the Queene dying (who was the greate patronesse of that designe &c) it was let fall, and so miserably dissipated:

Now was pub: the new Edition of Cambdens Brit: with greate Additions, those to Surrey mine: so as I had one presented to me: Dr. Gale shewed me a MS. of some parts of the New Test. in vulg: Lect: that had belonged to a Monastery in the north of Scotland, which he esteemed to be above 800 yeares old: some considerable various readings observable as in 1. John: & Genealogies of St. Luke, left out &c: query more:

13 I went to see my house & family left at Deptford

24 *Easterday* Mr. *Duncomb*, parson of this Parish, which he hardly comes to above once a yeare, tho' but 7 or 8 miles off, preached at Wotton on 116 Psal. 11. 12. 13, in a florid discourse read out of his notes: The holy Sacrament followed, which he administered with very little reverence, leaving out many prayers & exhortations, nor was there any Oblations &c: This ought to be reformed; but my good Bro: did not well consider, when he gave away this Living and the next:

Very fine weather for the season: abating sharp Eastern winds.

The sermons now preached not onely in Lond, but almost thro the whole Nation, were upon the losse of the incomparable Queene, so universaly & worthily beloved & admired.

The latter part of this moneth sharp & severe cold, with much snow, & hard frost, no appearance of Spring:

Aprill 7 Abinger Mr. Wotton morning: 11. Isaih: 8. 9. 10:

Extreame Cold, no appearance of Spring: Lord Halifex died suddenly at Lond, the day his daughter was maried to E. of Notinghams son, at Burleigh, being upon the friday: Old Mr. Busby the s⟨c⟩hoolmaster at Westminster died:

12 I went to visie Mr. Wells, Curate of Abinger, a sweete natured well tempered man, & fellow of Kings Coll: in Cambridge, who died now of pleuresie, for which I am very sorry: [The Lord Marq *Halyfax* died at London, a very rich man, very witty in his younger days somewhat positive:]

14 The Wet weather stayed this family from Church:

Now after a most severe cold & snowy winter, without any [sufficient] shower for many mounthes; the wind continuing N. & East: & not a leafe appearing: The weather & wind now changing, some shower⟨s⟩ & remission of Cold:

Scio retaken by the Turks: Cassal besieged by the D: of Savoy:

21 The Spring now begins to appeare yet the trees hardly leav'd:

Sir T Cooke discovers what prodigious Bribes have ben given by some of the E. India Company [out] of the Stock, which makes an extraordinary Clamor.

An Act of Parliament to Tax all Batchelors, Widowers, Marriages, Burials &c: never so many Private Bill⟨s⟩ passed for unsettling Estates, shewing the wonderfull prodigality & decay of Families:

May: 5 I came to Deptford from Wotton: [9 went to Lond:] In order to the first meeting of the Commissioners for Erecting an Hospital for Sea-men at *Greenewich*: it was at the Gild-Hall; present L Archbishop of Cant: L: Keeper, L. Privy Seale, Lord Godolphin, Duke of Shrewsbery, Duke of Leedes, E. of Dorset, Monmouth: Comissioners of the Admiralty & Navy, Sir Rob: Clayton, Sir Chr Wren, & severall more: The Commission read by Mr. Lowndes Secretary to the Lords of the Tressury, Surveyor Gen:

13 The King went to Holland for this summers Action.

17 2d meeting of the Commissioners, & a Committe appointed to go to Greenwich to survey the place, I being one of them.

21 we went to survey Greenwich where we dined: Sir R. Clayton, Sir Chr. Wren, Mr. Travers the Kings Surveyor, Cap: Sanders, My selfe: dined there:

24 To Lond: where we made report of the state of Gr: House, & how the standing part might for 6000 pounds be made servicable at present & what Ground would be requisit for the whole designe:

My Lord *Keeper* ordered me to prepare a booke for Subscriptions, and a preamble to it. Went this Evening to Deptford:

29 I went to Lond: lay at Nephew Glanvils.

31 Met againe at G. Hall, Mr. Vanbrogh, was made Secretary to the Commissioners by my nomination of him to the Lords: which was all don that day: & he was ordred, to procure rolls of parchment for subscribers.

June 2 At St. *Margarets* the Bishop of St. Asaph 15 *Jo:* 26: I received the Holy Sac: in order to Capacitate me to be Tressurer of the Commission &c:

3 Next day—Westminster hall: Kings bench:

7 Commissioners Met at G.hall, scrupule & contest of L. Major, who would not meete as none of the Quorum; so as a new Commission was required: L: Keeper & the rest, thinking it yet too nice a punctillo:

I returned to Deptford this Evening:

9 Went afterwards to see Sir Jo: Mordens Charity or Hospital on Black-heath now building for the Reliefe of Merchands that have failed, a very worthy Charity & noble building:

14: Met at *Guild hall* but could do nothing for want of a ⟨*Quorum*⟩; Return'd.

July: 5 Guild hall an Accompt of Subscriptions amounting to about 7 or 8000 pounds.

6 I din'd at *Lambeth* making my first Visit to my L A Bishop, where was much company & greate cheere: After Prayers in the Evening, my Lord, made me stay, to shew me his house, furniture, & Garden, which was all very fine, & far beyond the usual *A Bishops*: not as affected by this A.B: but as being bought ready furnished of his predecessor: we discoursed of severall publique matters, particularly of the Princesse of Denmark, who made so little a figure & now after greate expectation, not with child &c: so I returned to Lond:

14 No sermon at church, but after Prayers the Names read of all the Parishioners in order to gathering the Tax of 4 shill &c for Marriage, burials, &c: a very imprudent & impertinent

dut⟨c⟩h Tax and especialy this reading the names, so most went out of all the Churches: Afternoone the Viccar preached on 24. Act: 16:

19: I dined at Sir *Purbeck Temples* [near Croyden]: his Lady Aunt to my Son in Law Draper, house excellently furnished &c: thence went with son & daughter to Wotton:

23 Dyed my Grandson & Godson Tho: Draper of a Convulsion fit at Nurse, just as they were about to have weaned it: A very hopefull, strong and lovely Child; to the very greate Griefe & affliction to us all, & especialy to my poore daughter, now big with another: The Lord pardon what ever in us might provoke him to deale thus severely & grant us his mercy in the preservation of my daughter with the fruite she now gos with: Amen:

28 Being rainy, we went not to church:

The seige of *Namur* has hitherto cost much blood: Cassale at last rendered on Conditions to be dismantled: An extraordinary Wet season.

Namur rendred, not yet the Castle:

Dixmude Betrayed & 3000 pris⟨o⟩ners—The Venetians had a greate Victory over the Turks:

Aug: 4 The Curate on 16 Luke last verse:

Cold unseasonable weather:

11 It was now so very cold, as that greater frosts were seldom seene somtimes in midst of winter, this succeeded much wet, & set harvest extremely backwards:

The wet last Sonday kept us from Church.

25 Mr. Offley at Abinger, on 26: *Matt:* 13. Concerning Mary Magdalens Anointing our B: Saviour: too much time spent in the Controversy whether it were the same Mary anointed him before &c without any neede of insisting on a nicity among the Country people here, the rest of his discourse but just tollerable: This was the first time I have heard him preach: He has this Living of my Bro: who too kindly bestowed both this & Wotton, to his Wifes Relations, without considering that two such good livings & so neere each other would ⟨have⟩ fitted one of the Learnedst & best preachers of England:

No newes but of the Castle of *Namure* still holding out, & of our Bombing of Calis: which is but a cruel & brutish way of making warr, tho' first begun by the Fr: King: The season very wett.

September

1 Namur Castle taken after one assault by Composition: The Fr. Army superior in number being in sight of: We & the Confederates losing many men, & commanders.

Greate stormes begin this moneth & unseasonable harvest:

7 My Wife went to Lond: to be at the Lying-in of my daughter:

10 Tuesday a quarter of an hour before 11, was my daughter Draper brought to bed of a daughter: for which God be praised:

15 My good & worthy friend Cap: Gifford, who that he might get some competency to live decently, adventured all he had in a Voyage of 2 years to the *E. Indies*, was with another greate ship, taken by some French Men-of-Warr, almost within sight of England, to the los(s)e of neere 700000 pounds: to my greate sorrow, & pity of his Wife: he being also a valiant & Industrious man: The losses of this sort to the Nation has ben immense; & all thro the negligence & little care of the Government, to secure the same neere our owne Coasts, of infinite more concernment to the publique than spending their time in bombing & ruining two or three paltry Towns, Calais, St. Malo &c in which so many poore Creatures are destroyed, without any benefit, or weakening our Enemys, who, tho' they began, ought not to have ben imitated by an hostility totally averse to humanity, & especialy to Christianity.

⟨22⟩ The Curate on 24 *Joss:* 23 being the Thanksgiving day appointed for the successe of the Kings & confederates against the French at Cassal & Namure:

29 Very cold weather: little Grandaughter Christned *Mary*: Godfather Mr. Roger Draper, my sister Draper (Niece Glan: standing for [her]): Sir Purbeque Temple unkle to my son Draper died sudenly: a greate funeral at *Adiscomb*, his lady being owne Aunt to my Son in Law, who hopes for a good fortune, there being no heire &c: I had most comfortable newes from my son of his perfect health in Ireland, for which I immediatly blessed God: & beseech him to confirme & improve it to the health of his soule:

There had ben a new meeting of the Commissioners about the Hosp: at Greenewich upon the new Commission, where my L. Major, Lord of Cant: Lord Keeper, &c appeared, but by reason of some Indisposition I could not be there:

I went to returne Mr. F⟨i⟩nches visit at Albury:

13 The King went a progresse into the North, to shew himselfe to the people &c against the calling the next Parliament, was every where complemented, but not so at Oxford as he expected, wherfore he hardly stayed an hour there, & having seene the Theatre, did not receive the Banquet prepared &c:

We now lost 3 most rich E. India Ships worth above 2 million.

I din'd with Dr. Gale at S. Paules S⟨c⟩hoole, who shewed me many incomparable passages out of some [antient] Platonists MSS. concerning the H. Trinity: which this greate & learned person would publish, with many other rare things, were he encouraged, and eased of the burden of Teaching.

19 Dind at Lambeth with L. ABishop: where was Dr Sherlock, Gale, Mr. Montague Chancellor of the Exchequer, Dr. Standing prebend of S. Paules, & the Deane of Granham &c. My wife return'd to Wotton.

20 The Parliament dissolved, another called:

25 The A Bishop & my selfe went alone to Hammersmith to visit & see Sir Sam: Moreland who was start-blind & could not see at all: a very Mortified sight & person: shewed us his Invention of Writing which was very ingenious, also his wooden Kalendar, which instructed him all by feeling, & other pretty & usefull Inventions of Mills, pumps &c. & the Pump he has erected that serves water to his Garden & to passengers, with an Inscription, & brings from a filthy part of the Thames, neere it, a most perfect & pure water: He had newly buried 200 pounds worth of Music books as he sayd 6. foote under ground, as being love songs & vanity, but playes himselfe on his Theorb, psalms & religious hymns. &c.

November 3. A stranger morning at St. Jamess Chappell on 7: Matt 13.

The B. Communion followed at which I received, after a most solemn preparation which I pray God I may remember.

The King in progresse as far as neere York: very mild weather the whole late moneth.

I dined at Sir W: Godolphins.

10 At White-Hall, morning, one Mr. Stanhop, Viccar of Lewisham on 13. Matt, the Parable of the Sower: This Mr. Stanhop, is certainly one of the most accomplish⟨ed⟩

preachers that in my life I ever heard, both for matter, eloquence, Action, Voice, Authority: & one of an excellent
Conversation: as I am told.

13 Famous & very chargeable Fireworkes (now the King
being returned from his progresse staying at Althorp 7 or 8 days,
at L. Sunderlands, & mightily entertained) were shewed befor
my L. Rumny, Master of the Ordinance, where the King stood,
viz. St. James's greate Square:

17 After sermon I spake to the AB. of Cant: to concerne
himse⟨l⟩fe for the restoring a roome belonging to St. Jame's
Library, where the books wante place.

20 At Gressam Colledge was brought the prospect of the
Ruines of Palmira, far exceeding any of the Roman extant,
the history will be in The Transactions:

21 I went to see Mr. Charletons Collection of Rarities:

23. I went to Lambeth, to continue Dr. Williams in the
Boylea⟨n⟩ Lecture the following year, being with the A Bishop
one of the Trustees &c. There dined with us the Bishops of
Lichfild, Lincoln, Norwich: Dr. Cowell the greate oriental
Traveler & divers others.

30 St. Andrews day we met & chose Mr. Montague Chancellor of the Exchequer, President, Sir R: Southwell having continued now 3 or 4 yeares.

Decemb: 1 St. James Chapell (before the King). Dr. Freeman:
on 4. John: The Time shall come when they shall worship the
Father in Spirit & Truth:

I dined at my Lord Sunderlands, now the greate favorite, &
underhand politician, but not adventuring on any Character, as
obnoxious to the people, for his having changed his Religion
twise &c:

Afternoone a Stranger on 1. Coloss: 6.

11 The Publique Fast for Successe next Campagne &c by the
Bishop of Lichfild & Coventry, on: 33. Deut: 26–27. That God
sometimes saves his people, deferring their ruine & Judgements:
This applyed by many Instances, & Judgments & Afflictions on
the Reformation, especialy in this Nation, which has so often
ben freed & saved from utter ruine: as first from the yoak &
bondage of Popery, Span: Invasion: –88: Gunpowder Treason,
Civil Warr, Plague, Fire, & lately againe from popish slavery –88
by the King present:

19. I went to see my House &c at Says-Court & return'd next day:

22 The Parliament wondrous Intent on ways to Reforme the Coine; setting out a Proclamation prohibiting the currency of half Crown &c which made much confusion among the people:

24. I Returned to Wotton, not without greate danger, loosing our way neere the precipice of Whitedowne, it being quite dark.

169$\frac{5}{6}$. *Jan:* 1. No Office at the parish church here; I implored the blessing of God to prosper me the now following year:

12 Greate confusion & distraction by reason of the clip'd mony & the difficulty found in reforming it. A clowdy season: Two suns seene:

19 The house of Comm: reject the Kings propose to give the revenue of the Principality of Wales to Banting[1] his favorite: mild uncertain weather.

26: A very wet season hindred our going to church:

Feb: 2: Greate Indisposition by paine in my kidnies, thro gravell &c: kept me from church this day also, but we had the Office by Mr. Wye &c:

This was an extraordinary wett season, tho temperate as to cold.

The Parliament intent on reforming the Coine, divers Wracks, at Sea.

The R: Sovraigne burnt at Chattham, that ship, which built 1637 was perhaps the original Cause of all the after trouble to this day:

An Earth quake in Dorset-shire by Portland, or rather a sinking of the ground suddenly for a large space, neere the quarries of stone, hindring the conveyance of that materi⟨a⟩ll for the finishing of St. Paules:

I was much afflicted with gravell:

9 Mr. Morus, on 6: *Luke* 46: *Socinianisme*, now wonderfully spreading in the Citty of Lond, & [their] books printed without any stop: &c:

23 They now began to Coine new Mony.

26 There was this weeke a Conspiracy of about 30 Knights, Gent, Captaines, many of them Irish & English Papists & non

1 Hans Willem Bentinck, earl of Portland.

Jurors or Jacobites (as calld) to murder K. William, upon the
first opportunity of his going either from Kensington, to hunting, or the Chappell, & upon a signal of fire to be given from
Dover C⟨l⟩iffe to Calis, an Invasion designed, where there were
in order to it, a very greate Army in readinesse, Men-of Warr &
transport ships innumerable to joyne with a general Insurrection
here, The Duke of Barwick being seacretly come to London to
head them, & K. James attending at Calis with the French
Army: but it being discovered by I think the Duke of   &
other of the Confederats, & by one of their owne party; & a
1000 pounds, to who soever could apprehend any of the 30
named: The whole designe was frustrated, most of the Ingaged
taken & secur'd: The Parliament, Citty & all the nation
congratulating the deliverance & Votings & Resolutions, that if
ever K. William should be Assassinated, it should be revenged
upon the Papists & Party throout the nation, an Act of Association drawing up to impower the Parliament to sit upon any such
Accident, til the Crowne should be dispos'd of according to the
late settlement at the Revolution; All Papists in the meane time
to be banished 10 miles from London; which put this nation
into an incredible disturbance & general Animosity against the
Fr: King, & K. James: The Militia of the Nation raised, several
Regiments sent for out of Flanders, & all things put into a posture to encounter a descent: which was so timed abroad, that,
whilst we were already much confused, & discontented upon the
greatnesse of the Taxes, and corruption of the mony &c, we had
likely to have had very few Men of Warr neere our Coasts; but
so it pleased God, the V Admiral Rooke wanting a Wind to pursue his Voyage to the Straites, That Squadron, with what other
forces at Portsmouth & other places, were still in the Channell,
& soone brought up to joyne with the rest of the Ships which
could be gotten together: so as there is hope this Plot may
be broken; It is certaine it had likely have ben very fatal to the
[danger of the] whole Nation, had it taken Effect; so as I looke
on it as a very greate deliverance & prevention by the Providence of God; for tho many did formerly pitty K. James's Condition, this designe of Assasination, & bringing over a French
Army, did much alienate many of his Friends, & was like to produce a more perfect establishment of K. William, it likewise so
much concerning the whole Confederacy: What it will yet end

in, God onely knows, may he of his Infinite mercy to this sinfull & miserably divided Church & nation, put an end to this bloody unchristian Warr, & restore peace & quietnesse:

Mar: 1 Mr. *Morus* pr: at Wotton on 16. Luke. 20. 21, very plainely & honestly:

The wind northerly & Easterly all this Weeke brought so many of our men of Warr together, & before the french Coast, that tho most of the French finding their designe detected & prevented, made a shift to get into Calais & Dunkirk roode, we wanting fireships & bombs, to encounter & disturbe them; but they were yet so ingag'd among the sands & flatts that tis said they cutt their Masts, & slung over their greate Gunns to lighten their Vessels: we are yet upon them, & what the Event will be must be expected: This deliverance is due onely to God: The French preparation was at once not onely to invade England, but Scotland & Ireland also; most seacretly & solemn⟨l⟩y Concerted, by all the French Commanders & politi-tians, that making the seate of the Warr here, the Confederats might at once be so distressed, as to submitt to his Arme⟨s⟩: but this God has in greate mercy prevented:

8 The greate Cold & other accidents keept us from going to the parish Church, this morning.

Divers of the Conspirators tried & condemn'd.

A greate Magazine of the French in Flanders burned:

15 *Vesuvius* breaking out, terrifies Naples:

Frost & Snow very cold ⟨season⟩.

Three of the unhappy wretches (whereoff one a Priest) executed this weeke for intending to assassinate the King; accknowledging their intention, but acquitting K. James, of instigating them to it in that manner, & dying very pene-tently: [Divers more in danger & some very Considerable persons:]

Greate frost & cold:

22 More of the Conspirators taken and condem'd: excessive cold weather, no leaves on the Trees:

29 Surpriz'd with a greate hoarsnesse & rheume hindr'd me from Church:

Aprill 6 I went to Lond about many Affairs, lay at my Son Drapers:

9 Visite Mr. Grahame in the fleete, imprisond on the Plot:

10 Now were the quarters of Sir W: Perkins & Mr. Friend, lately executed on the plot, set up with Perkins head on Temple barre, a dismal sight, which many pittied: I think there was never any such at Temple barre till now and one in K. Char: ⟨II⟩ Time, Sir Tho: Armestronge:

Still people secured on suspicion of the plot & more to be tried:

19 Greate offence taken at the 3. Ministers who absolved Sir W: Perkins & S. Friend at Tyburn; one of them (Snat) hapning to ⟨be⟩ a son of my old Schoolemaster: This produced much altercation on both sides, as to the canonicalnesse of the Action:

21 We had a meeting [at Gild-hall, L. Keeper & Mayor present &c:] of the Grand Committè about settling the draught of the Hospital for Sea-men &c:

23 I went to *Eaton*, din'd with Dr. Godolphin the Provost. The Scholemaster assured me that there had not ben in 20 yeares a more pregnant youth in that Place than my Grandson: I return'd that evening with Lady Jane Leueson & her daughter &c, who went to place Sir William Windham at that Schole:

I went to see the Kings house at Kensington with some Ladys: The House is very noble, tho not greate; the Gallerys furnished with all the best Pictures of all the Houses, of Titian, Raphel, Corregio, Holben, Julio Romano, Bassan, V: Dyke: Tintoret, & others, with a world of Porcelain; a pretty private Library; the Gardens about it very delicious:

26 At the Middle Temple in the morning preached Dr. Sharp on 3 Tit. 4. 5: 6: His prayer before sermon was one of the most excellently composed and comprehensive that I have heard:

[28 The stately Entry of the Venetian Ambassador: 50 footem⟨en⟩, many on horseback, 4 rich Coaches & infinite traine of Gallantry &c:]

More executions this weeke of the late Assassinates.

Oates dedicated a most villanous reviling booke against K. James, which he presumed to present K. William, who certainly could not but abhorr it, speaking so infamously & untruely of his late beloved Queenes owne father:

May: 2d. The King having nominated & left the same 7. Lords Justices to governe in his Absence this Campagne, went towards Flanders this morning.

I dined at Lambeth, being summon'd to meete with my Collegue Trustees, L: of Cant: Sir H. Ashurst, & Mr. Serjeant Rotheram, to consult about settling Mr. Boyles Lecture for a Perpetuity, which we concluded upon, by buying a Rent Charge of 50 pounds per Annum, with the stock in our hands &c:

4 Dr. Williams proceeded in the Boylean Lecture at St. Martins on 17. Act: 26: in a description of the whole Creation, & concluding with the wonderfull power, wisdom & providence of God, in bringing about the Redemption of Man kind by the seede of the Woman. See the printed discorse.

I went this afternoone to Deptford to take a little Country aire & see my little famely left there.

6 I went to Lambeth whither I had ben invited to meete at dinner the Co: of Sunderland & divers ladys, We din'd at the ArchBishops Wives Apartmen⟨t⟩ with his Grace & stayed late, yet I returned to Deptford that night.

13 I went to Lond: to Visie my Sonn, newly come out of Ireland, Indispos'd, with my Daughter his Wife &c: return'd next day:

17 Hindred for Church by the extreame wet weather:

22 Came up to Lond: summoned to meete the Lords &c at Guild-hal.

24 The French Fleete got out of the Mediterane⟨an⟩ to Brest, & out of Dunkirke where we had bin watching to prevent them, at an immense Charge.

Mony still continuing exceedingly scarse, so as none was either payed or received, but on Trust, the mint not supplying sufficient for common necessities:

An Association with an Oath required of all Lawyers & Officers, upon paine of Premunire, where men were obliged to renounce K. James as no rightfull King, & to revenge K. Williams death if happening by any Assa⟨ss⟩ination: This to be taken by all the Concerned by a day limited, so as the Courts of Chancery & K. Bench hardly heard any Cause all Easter Terme: so many crowding to take the Oath &c.

This was censur'd as a very intangling contrivance of the Parliament: In expectation that many in high office would lay downe, & others succeede:

Now were many Gent. discharged out of Prison, taken up on suspicion of the late Plot.

June 1. I went to Deptford to dispose of our Goods, being [in order to] lett it for 3 years to V. Admiral Benbow, with Conditions to keepe the Garden &c:

4: A Comitty meeting at W-hall, about the Hospital at Greenewich at Sir Chr: Wrenn, his Majesties Surveyor Gen: We made the first agreement with divers Workemen & for Materials, & gave the first Order for the proceding on the foundations, ordering payments to be Weekly to the Workmen & a general Accompt to be monethly:

I then received Orders from the Lords of the Tressury for the Kings 2000 pounds to be employed on that work:

11 Dined at my L: Pembroke L. Privy-Seale, a very worthy Gent: shewed me divers rare Pictures of very many of the old & best Masters, especially that of M: Angelo, a man gathering fruite to give a Woman, & a large booke of the best drawings of the old Masters:

Sir Jo: Fenwick one of the Conspiritors taken:

Greate Subscriptions in Scotland to their East India Company &c:

I let my House at Deptford to V: Admiral Benbow for 3 years &c.

The Spaniards receive an overthr⟨ow⟩ in Catalonia:

Want of current money to carry on not onely the smalest concernes, but for daily provisions in the Common Markets: Ginnys lowered to 22s: & greate summs daily transported into Holland, where it yeelds more, which with other Treasure sent thither to pay the Armies, nothing considerable coined of the new & now onely current stamp, breeding such a scarsity, that tumults are every day feared; no body either paying or receiving any mony; so Imprudent was the late Parliament, to damne the old (tho clip't & corrupted) 'til they had provided supplies. To this add the fraud of the Bankers & Goldsmiths who having gotten immense riches by extortion, keepe up their Treasure, in Expectation of a necessity of advancing its Value. *Duncumb* not long since, a meane Goldsmith, having made a purchase of neere 90000 pounds of the late D. of Buckinghams Estate, & reputed to have neere as much in Cash &c: Banks & Lotteries every day set up, besides Taxes intollerable, & what is worse & cause of all this, Want of Publique Spirite, in a Nation [daily] sinking under soe many Calamities.

18 The famous Tryal between my Lord of Bath & Lord Montague for an Estate of 11000 pounds a Yeare [left by the duke of Albemarle], wherein on several Trials had ben spent 20000 betweene the⟨m⟩; the E. of Bath was cast upon evident forgerie, to the greate dishonor of that family.

[20 I gave my Lord Cheny a Visite at Chelsey. I saw those ingenious Water works invented by Mr. Vinstanley wherein were some things very surprising & extraordinary.]

21 King of Poland died, a valiant prince that sav'd Vienna & indeede Europe from the Turk; but after that becoming a Pensioner of France, never did any brave thing after: to be sure the French will endeavour to advance some body of their Interest:

Greate offers of the Fr: King, to draw of the Duke of Savoy from the Confederats, & so likewise of the Emperor & K. of Spaine to keepe him steady:

25 A Triall at the Comm: Pleas betweene the Lady Purbec Temple & Mr. Temple [a Nephew of Sir Purbeck] concerning a Deede pretended to take place of several Wills; The Deede proved to be forged: The Cause went on my Ladys side: This [much] Concerning my Son in law Draper [appearing], I stayed almost all day in Court to heare the Cause: after which a greate supper was given to the Jury: being persons of the best Condition in Bucckinghamshire.

30 I went with a select committee of the Commissioners for the fabri⟨c⟩k of Greenewich Hospital, & with Sir Chr: Wren the Surveyor, where with him I laied the first stone of that intended foundation; precisely at 5 a clock in the Evening after we had dined together: Mr. Flamsted the Kings Astronomical Profes⟨s⟩or observing the punctual time by Instruments: Note that one of the workmen in helping to place the stone, being a Corner large stone, grating his fingers against the gravelly banke, some drops of blood fell upon it: We afterwards returned to Lond:

July 4. Note that my Lord Godolphin was the very first of the Subscriber⟨s⟩ who payed any mony towards this noble fabric:

The Weather began now to be very seasonable.

7 My Wife went back to Wotton:

I drank Epsom waters:

A northern wind altering the weat⟨h⟩er with a continual &
impetuous raine of 3 days & nights, it chang'd it into perfect
Winter.

Much discourse of a peace.

19 It now appeared that the Duke of Savoy had made a separate Peace with France, which caused a greate consternation
among the Confederates: much discoursing of some greate
Action in Flanders: Our Fleete had burnt & ruined many places
in the Ilands neere Rochell &c:

26 Mr. Benting came unexpectedly from the King, for supply
of mony to pay his Army, exceedingly disturbed us, so little
mony in the nation, that Exchequer Tallys (of which I had for
2000 pounds upon the best fonds in England the Post Office)
nobody would accept for 30 pounds per Cent advantage.

Aug: 2 At the mid: Temple an excellent sermon on 8: Rom: 9.
The H. Sacrament followed, the Lord make me thankfull:

In the Afternoone a stranger there on   How Christ
came not to bring peace but a sword in the Earth:

9 Lamenesse in one of my Legs, kept me from church this
morning: Afternoone at St. Clements, Mr. Adams: 8 Mark: 38:

I drank Epsom waters some days: nothing of publique this
weeke save the Bank lending the King 200000 pounds for the
Army in Flanders, that having don nothing against the Enemy,
had so exhausted the Treasure of the Nation that one could not
have borrowed mony under 14 or 15 per Cent on bills nor Exchequer Tallies ⟨on⟩ the best funds for 30 per Cent, so miserably had
we lost our best credit: Reasonable good harvest weather:

16 Severall Packetts failing from Flanders no tidings came
from abroad til late this weeke, without any thing of action from
the Armies, but that there was discourse of a peace; in the meane
time resolutions of the Confederats continuing the war in
⟨Piedmont⟩ uncertaine:

However 300000 pounds being carried over to our Armys,
made mony still more & more scarcy in England, so as one
could hardly borrow 100 pounds upon the publique security
under 13 or 14 per cent, nor on the Chequer for 30:

23 Uncertaine discourse of peace still; Clippers & abusers of
the publique Coine every day discovered, & all these disorders
evidently occasioned by the dishonesty of the Goldsmith &
Banker, &c:

29 I went to Lambeth, dined with the A Bishop: there had that morning ben a Court upon the Complaint against Dr. Watson the Bishop of Bristol suspended for Simonie; The AB: told me how unsatisfied he was with the Cannon Law, & how exceedingly unreasonable all their pleadings appeared to him: After dinner I mooved him for Dr. Bohune for a preferment promised me for him; & told him how much I had ben solicited to Bespeake his suffrage for the Deane of Carlisle, to succeede the Bishop of that Diocesse, now very old: As also concerning Okewood Chapell &c:

September. Very fine seasonable weather: & greate harvest after so cold & wet a summer, but greate scarcity in Scotland: The Queene of Spaine, reported to be irrecoverably sick & thought to be poyson'd: our parliament prorogu'd til October.

6. I went to Congratulate the Marriage of a Daughter of Mrs. Boscawen, to the son of Sir Phil: Meadows: she is niepce to my Lord Godolphin: They were Married at Lambeth 30 Aug: by the Arch-Bishop: a most vertuous discreete young Vergin & as hopefull a young Gentleman.

Certainty of the death of the Q: of Spaine & her child poison suspected: The French King in greate danger of dying also: much discourse still of peace: The Muscovites successe against the Tarter, taking Asseph: a tirrible battell twixt the Turke & Emperor, who tho' killing more, yet lost Heustler & Palfi, greate Generalls:

13 After confident discourses of the poysning the Q. of Spaine & cutting the Infant alive out of her belly when dead, & of the French Kings death, waigers layed of the truth, not one word was found true, so strangly was the nation given to lying:

After above 6 monethes being at Lond, about the Hospital at Greenwich, ⟨I⟩ return'd to Wotton, with my daughter Draper:

⟨20⟩ A Scotch-man preacher at Ockwood Chapell, preached this morning at Wotton on 16 *Matt* 24: In a long discourse, much action, vehement voice, much repetition in the Presbyterian way, yet the parson is Episcoparian, & the doctrine plaine & honest.

26 Came my Son-in Law Draper to Wootton. Princesse of Denmark ⟨m⟩iscarried of a son.

27 The next Lords day, the extreame wet season hindred us from going to parish-C⟨h⟩urch: This season so very wett, as

884 27 SEPTEMBER 1696–5 SEPTEMBER 1697

much hindred sowing Corne in many places &c: Which tho'
the⟨n⟩ in plenty with us, they in Scotland suffered greate Want:

Greate expectations of a general peace; the French in Savoy
beseige Valentia, greate contention in poland about Choosing a
King: The prince of Conty a Candidate: The battel twixt the
Chr: & Turke greate & to the losse on both sides: The weather
uncertaine:

Octob: 4. The Raine & ill weather hindred us againe from
the parish Church &c:

The King returned from Holland, nothing having ben don
by these greate Armies the whole Campagne:

The Duke of Savoy deserting the Confederates, upon proposal of a Mariage of his daughter to the Duke of Burgundy, &
insinuation of the French, now assists them in the Besieging
Valentia neer Milan:

November 8 The first frost now began very fiercely, but lasted
not: Reports of more plotts; & greate search for Jacobites as so
called:

15 So wonderfull & perpetual Rainy season without frost, but
exceeding greate storms wrecking many at sea, has not ben
knowne in any mans memory, so as hardly could they sow in
many places:

The famous Indian Pyrats executed:

29. The unseasonable weather againe hindred us from church
&c:

December. There hapning so swiftly an exceeding firce frost
after greate raines, & grew so very cold, that we had the office of
the day at home:

The French make greate preparations for some exploite,
reported to be for Ireland.

13. The continuance of [so] extreame a frost & snow as has
seldome been known, with my Indisposition, kept hitherto
longer from Church than I think I have ben above these 30 years:

31 Made up Accompts, with thanks to Almighty God for his
goodnesse & preservation the past yeare.

169$\frac{6}{7}$. *Jan:* 1 Beging Gods blessing the yeare entered into; we
had news of my daughter Draper being brought to bed safely of
a fine Boy, who was christened by my Bro: Evelyn by his name
George, whom God Almighty blesse & preserve.

17 The severe frost & weather not relenting, and freezing with snow, againe kept us from Church:

31 The weather continuing so exceeding fierce, so as since that tirrible winter 12 years since, the like had not ben known, much corne not coming up, much rotted by the extraordinary wett before the frost, and the ground so hard, as in many places now pl . . . threatning a Dirth: Mony yet so scarce &c: the Parliament are in greate distresse to furnish another Summers Campagne: besides people Mechanics begin to rise, as at the beginning of the greate Rebellion: peace much talked of, but nothing don; unheard of storms & losse at sea, Newfound Land surprized by the French: Confusion in Poland about a King; The K of Spaine not recovered: Conspirasies continualy against K William, for which this last week Sir J. *Fenwick*, was beheaded on Tower Hill: The Lord in mercy prevent further Calamities to this Church & nation.

Feb: 7 So severely greate has ben this still continuing frost, & snow, that divers sentinels doing their duty in the Armies & Townes kept by Garizons, that in Flanders many of them were frozen to death, within an houre or two before they were relieved tho so often: The Duke of Savoy now returning over the Mountain⟨s⟩, had many of his Guard & troops, Mules & Equipage lost in the Snow, the Duke himselfe hardly escaping:

Sir Jo: Fenwick, accused for having given consent or ben among some Conspirators, there being but one single Wittnesse, was yet Attainted. . . .[1]

⟨August 15?⟩ . . . The B: Communion followed of which I was participant with much Comfort: Blessed by God: Amen.

I dined with the Countesse of Sunderland & tooke leave of many friends: having now ben above 3 moneths in Towne.

17 I came to Wotton after above 3 moneths absence.

Sept: Very bright weather but with a sharp Eastern Wind: Uncertaine newes of the peace so neere Conclusion, the Fr: King, playing fast & loose, & manifestly deferring any positive resolution, I suppose in expectation of the successe of Poland & the returne of Pontis Exploit from Carth⟨a⟩gena:

5 Greate disturbances still in Poland about the Election; *Pointi* the french Admiral come with the booty from

1 One or more leaves are here missing from MS.

Carth⟨a⟩gena, dos not answer his losse of halfe his Men, &c: Ex⟨p⟩ectation still what the Treaty concerning Peace will end in:

9 My son, came in his melancholy Indisposition from Lond, hither, where his mother had ben to visie him:

12 We have had now the wellcome tidings of the Peace with France: with the Pr: of Conties Imbarkement for Poland, in hop of that Crown in competition with the Elector of Saxony, already Crow⟨n⟩'d which in probability will not be decided peaceably:

19 Greate preparation of Triumphal Arches &c to welcome the King coming out of flanders with the olive branch:

26 Certaine newes of the Emp: greate Victory over the Turkish Army in Hungary: 30000 slaine, the gr: Vissier killd, the Sultan fled, all his Tents, Artillery, & vast booty taken:

Octob: 3: It being a wet cold day, we went not to Church, officiating at home:

So greate were the stormes all this weeke, that there were nere 1000 poore men cast away going into the Texell, & many other disasters:

17 My Daughter Draper husband & family awakned in the night by the noise of fire, Escaped being all burnt in their bed, in the dead time of sleepe; by timely extinguishing it, in their owne chamber: for which God be ever praised:

31 Dr. Sherlock preached at the Temple. 3. *Gal:* 8. The Communion followed at which I received, it being my Birth-day, & 77th of my now old Age: for which blessed be the infinit mercy of God, whom I beseech to grant to me the year following & in greate Compassion to pitty & heale, & comfort my distressed miserable son, & sicke daughter, that we may yet live to magnify his goodnesse, to the salvation of our soules Amen.

Afternoone at the Savoy, a stranger on: 12. Heb. 14: Exhorting to peace & charity: The peace being now proclaymed; this was the subject of all the pulpits everywhere:

My intention was to have heard a recantation sermon of a considerable Abbot who came from France to professe the Reformed Religion: but the presse & multitude was so greate that I with many more, could not get into the French Church at the Savoy, & so I went to the Savoy parish-churche:

Greate preparations of fireworks & other pompes for the Kings returne: Contentions still in Poland twixt Conti, &

[D of] ⟨Saxony⟩: None got by this peace so much as Spaine who contributed least to it; the wonder is, why France who had such advantage should yeild to part with such Conquests, & having taken Barcellona which cost him so many brave men, & was so advantageous an acquist, besides successe in America; for that it was not want of men nor Mony appeared by those vast summes sent into Poland; & exceeding rich & chargeable expense for the Mariage of the D of Burgundy: But 'tis imputed to the decay of his owne health, his apprehension of the Dolphin, the importunitye of Mad: Maintenoon &c: In the mean time he keeps Strasburg which gives him entrance into Germany, when he pleases, secures the Swisse to him, having made such Conditions about Lorrain, ⟨as⟩ signify little when ever he think fit to breake: Nothing all this while don at all for the poore protestants or their interests, even in the palatinat it selfe, which shews, how little they were minded by us or any of the Confederats, since the D. of Sax, & others go over daily to the Papists, so as the peace is nothing that which it was hoped; The Queen of Eng: will have her Joynture, The K. her husband being dead by our Law: & this is all I can learne of this matter, at this Conjuncture.

November 5. A Bishop preached at W. Hall (present the AB. & B. of Lond, few other) on 33 Deut: 33. shewing by a parallel of deliverances of the Church of England, with that of the Israelites, the greate happinesse of this Church & people: He tooke occasion to discourse of the necessity of abso⟨l⟩ute Supremacy in every Government: ⟨as⟩ first In the Patriarchall state; every Patriarch having just vitæ & necis, absolutely over his own family: proved by Abr: intended Sacrifice of his own son, injoyning Circummcission &c not as Tyrants, but still under the precepts or Lawes delivered them from Noah & this the True Church kept to, til, after Jacob & Joseph's time; til their being made slaves in Egypt, which disturbed & disordered it; but then reverted naturaly to them again, & so continued, 'til God himselfe tooke it more immediately on him, & gave them other Laws, & other governance: The scope of his discourse was to shew, that every Governor or King has of right a Supremacy in his owne Dominion; & that the popes is an unjust & fraudulent & utterly illegal Supremacy, usurp'd, & has no right or title or just power to

impose on the Jurisdiction of other Bishops, & by his authority to bring in such strange Corruptions in the whole Church;
particularly instancing in divers of them, & predicting his
down fall, which God would one day bring about, & give his
Church a more generall delivery.

7 A prophesy in N damus raised wonderfull stirr & talke of
some Conspirasy upon the expected entry of the King; & a
report of the Duke of Barwicks with severall more being
seacretly come out of France to Lond, caused a proclamation for
the searching & seizing of them: 1000 pounds reward to any
should discover any of them. The Temple gates shutt & Inns of
Court searched, guards doubled &c:

14. The day being very wet keept me from going to church:
This evening the Towre guns &c fired & bells rung for news
of the Kings Landing.

16 Was the Kings Entry very pompous, but in nothing
approaching that at K. Cha: IId Restauration.

21 A notable pamphlet dispersed against a Standing Army, of
which there was a whisper as if it were intended to be proposed
to the approaching parliament [which produced many pamphlets Pro & Con:]

30. St. Andrews day at R. Society, many elected, we dined as
customarily together.

December 2 The Thanksgiving day for the peace, I went in
the morning to W. Hall, where was the K. & a very greate
Court: the Bishop of Salisbery preached, or rather made a florid
Panegyric on 2. Chro: 9. 7. 8: Shewing how neere ⟨to Solomon⟩
for successe & felicity this present K. was, & how God had
chosen him, & by many signal providences reserved him to
deliver this Church & nation, yea all Europ from the haughty &
insulting Enemy, Established us in this nation in our Religion &
propertys, & freed all our Neighbor nations from the ambition
of France, broken the power of Insulting foes, & don such
things by his Conduct & Courage that as the Q. of Sheba came
far to admire him, so a greate Prince (meaning the Zar of
Mus⟨c⟩ovy) came a farther, to see him who had don such wonders, concluded with that of the Text, that all this was that he
might do Justice & Judgement & govern his people righteously,
by encouraging the good, & rebuke the prophane & reform the
nation which now needed it, & for which God had preserved &

cald & set him up: This was the summ, but rather see the printed sermon:

The Evening concluded with fire-works & Illuminations, of [such] greate expence as would have erected ⟨a⟩ Triu⟨m⟩phal Arch of Marble & the fireworks in nothing answering expectation, but were the destruction of some spectators & of a person of quality a stranger:

SEVERE WINTERS – DEATH OF GEORGE EVELYN – EVELYN IS EIGHTY
(1697–1700)

3 DECEM: THE Parliament; when the K. made indeede an handsom speech; after he had given account of the peace, acquainted them with the deficiencys of the Revenue, & the necessity of maintaining a strong Navy at sea, & sufficient forces by Land, without mentioning a Standing Army, which was wisely done:

5. Was the first Sonday, St. Paules had had any service in ⟨it⟩, since it was Consumed at the Conflagration of the Citty; 1666: which I my selfe saw, & now ⟨w⟩as likewise my selfe there, the Quire being compleatly finished, & the Organ esteemed the best in Europe of I thin⟨k⟩ 40 stops; There were the Bishop of Lond, Lord Major & innumerable multitude, one Mr. Knight preaching (for Dr. Sherlock the Deane) on Epist Jude ver: 3. exhorting to Contend for the Faith once delivered, to the Church; most of which he applied against the Socinian doctrine now so rife: & this he did most excellently & to the satisfaction & Conviction I believe of all that heard him: The H. Sacrament followed, the B. of Lond. & Residentarys distributing the Elements: I was invited & dined with Dr. Godolphin, a Resider & Provost of Eaton.

In the afternoon preached Dr. Sherlock the deane, but the presse of people was so greate that I durst not venture, & so I heard a sermon on 17: Act: 31. at St. Martin Ludgate:

It was now most exceeding cold & frosty:

6 I went to Kensington, with the Sheriff, knights & chi⟨e⟩fe Gent of Surry to present their Addresse to the K, the D. of

Norfolk, promising to introduce it, but came so late that it was don before he came, This insignificant Ceremony, was brought in fashion in the Rebellious times, to accknowledge Cromwell & his son Richard, & so was practised in all the Kings reigns afterwards, in which people complemented the power with professions of loyalty, & standing by the(m) with their lives & fortunes what ever turne succeeded, but which they never meant to performe, but did the same to every one that got the power: I dined at Sir R. Onslows who treated almost all the Gentlemen of Surry; when we had halfe dined came in the D. of Norfolk to make his poore excuse: so I left them drinking healths.

19 The parliament vote the K. 700000 pounds for his life, for the Civil list:

December 23. I returned to Wotton, accompanied by Sir Cyr: Wych: where I found my son in the same sad Condition, & my Daughter in law dangerously ill of a flux. The Lord be gracious to both if it be his holy will in pitty & mercy.

25 Christmas day: Wotton, Mr. Morehouse, on 2. Heb: 16, an honest discourse shewing our infinite Obligation to our B. Saviour: I received the Holy Sacrament: The L. Jesus make me Thankfull.

26 Dr. Fullham (who lately married my Niepce) on: 29 Psal. last verse, a Thanksgiving Sermon upon the Peace, shewing with greate learning and eloquence that as piety & Religion is the meanes to procure peace, so to establish it.

31. Made up Accounts with thanks to A. God for his preservation of me the past yeare.

1697/8 New years day Beging Gods blessing for the Yeare entered into:

A greate Christmas kept at Wotton, open-house, much Company, my Son still melancholy, but by Gods mercy his wife recovering of her flux by drinking the Bath-Waters after all the Doctors could prescribe did not succeede.

I presented my Booke of Medals[1] &c to divers noblemen, before I suffered it to be exposed to sale.

Jan: 2 Excessive cold weather & piercing Winds:

---

1 *Numismata. A Discourse of Medals, Antient and Modern.*

White-hall utterly burnt to the ground, nothing but the walls & ruines left:

The Zar of Muscovy landed & came to Lond:

16 I made up all my private Accompts with J. Strickland:

17 Neither of these 2 Sondays could we go to the Church by reason of the Snow & extraordinary piercing weather: which lasted very severely

ffeb: 6. I missed being at Church by my owne fault having over tired my selfe the night before about dispatching letters, as also I was the Sonday next:

The Czar Emp: of *Moscovy*, having a mind to see the Building of Ships, hired my House at Says Court, & made it his Court & palace, lying & remaining in it, new furnish'd for him by the King:

Mar: 20 The Fr: Ambassador made a splendid Entry: The Czar gos to Portsmouth to se the representation of a sea fight. Duncomb quitted by the Lords, & sent to prison again by the Commons, having ben acquitted by the Lords but by one Voice:

I tooke some preventing Physic, but was much afflicted with palpitations of ♡.

Aprill 21 The Czar of Mosco⟨vy⟩ went from my house towards Russia, &c:

May 8 Extraordinary greate Snow, & frost, nipping & spoiling the Corne and other fruits universaly, & threatning famine, Corne at 9s. per bushell, & all thi⟨ng⟩s else extraordinary deare: The french K. preparing a greate Fleete, and army at Land, as is thought ready to invade Spaine & his dominion, expecting the death of that valetudinary King: Poland still in Confusion: The *Czar* landed in Holland:

My daugh⟨t⟩er Draper brought to bed of a fine Boy:

Continuance of extraordinary sharp weather.

19 Was my Grandson Draper Christen'd *William*; they would faine have had it Evelyn (making me Godfather as I was) but for some reasons I desired it might be William: Sir Jo: Conniers stood for me; The Godmother was one Mrs. Brent, a Relation of my Son in Laws, a very fine prudent Lady:

The Weather was so very Cold, wett & unseasonable as had not ben known by any almost alive, not onely in this nation but most part of Europe: all tree fruits ruined, & threatning the rest with famine.

22. It being very wett, I went not to our Church: this morning &c.

23 I came from Wotton to Lond: about suffering a Recovery, about a new, & unreasonable Settlement of the Estate in Surry, which I was advised not to do:

29 The Polish King & Cardinal Primate accorded: Earle of Bath lost his greate Cause which cost him 20000 pounds against my L. Mont: convicted of notorious forgery &c:—E. India-Comp: like to be broken & dissolved, to set up another who offered to subscribe two Millions, to the greate alarme of the other.

30 I dined at Mr. Pepyss, where I heard that rare Voice, Mr. *Pate*, who was lately come from *Italy*, reputed the most excellent singer, ever England had: he sang indeede many rare Italian Recitatives, &c: & severall compositions of the last Mr. Pursal, esteemed the best composer of any Englishman hitherto:

June 5 Dr. White late Bishop of Norwich ejected his Bishoprick for not complying with the Government, dying & buried in St. Greg: C-yard or Vault, at Paules, his Herse accompanyed with two other non jurar Bishops, Dr. Turner [Ely], & Lloyd:—with 40 other non jural Cleargy &c, would not stay the Office of the Burial, because, the Deane of Paules had appointed a Conformable Minister to reade the Office: at which all much wondered, there being nothing in the Burial Office, that mentions the present King:

9 I went to Deptford to view how miserably the Tzar of Moscovy had left my house after 3 moneths making it his Court, having gotten Sir Cr: Wren his Majesties Surveyor & Mr. London his Gardener to go down & make an estimat of the repairs, for which they allowed 150 pounds in their Report to the L: of the Treasury: Then I went to see the foundations of the Hall & Chapell, wharfe & other parts of the Greenwich Hospital: & so returned.

21 I went to see my L. of Canterbury at Lambeth who had ben indisposed.

Vote past for the New East India company, subscribing 2 millions, which was generaly looked upon as a greate hardship to the old & to the ruine of many Adventurers who had put their whole stock into ⟨the⟩ old Company.

July: 3. Minister of the Savoy Church on. 1. Thess: 5. 21 the H. Sacrament followed, I received.

6 The Parliament prorogued, on the 8 dissolved, & at the same moment a new one to sit in August following, a thing very rare:

8 I came to passe the rest of the summer ⟨at⟩ [my sonns house] in Berkly-streete, during my Brothers (or rather, my Neipces & Dr. Fullams) displeasure, because I could not assent to the alteration of a settlement of my Brothers gift freely to me: &c which I pray God to reconcile.

August 6. I din'd at Mr. Pepys, where was Cap: Dampier, who had ben a famous Buccaneere, brought hither the painted Prince Jolo, printed a Relation of his very strange adventures, which was very extraordinary, & his observations very profitable: Was now going abroad againe, by the Kings Incouragement, who furnished a ship of 290 Tunn: he seemed a [more] modest man, than one would imagine, by the relation of the Crue he had sorted with: He brought a map, of his observations of the Course of the winds in the South-Sea, & assured us that the Maps hithertoo extant, were all false as to the Pacifie-sea, which he makes on the S⟨o⟩uth of the line, that on the North, & running by the Coasts of *Perù*, being extremely tempestious:

21 I was now very much Indisposed, so as I was faine to keepe in, & tooke some Physick.

Nothing of Publique worth much notice, but that it was a very cold, wett, & winterlike season, little summer this quarter.

September 25 A report of many suddainly dying by being abroad some where in Barkshire in a stinking fogg:

Dr. Foy came to me to use my Interest with my L. Sunderland &c: with his Majestie for his being made Professor of Physick at Oxon: in the Kings Gift. I went also to my L. AB. of Cant: in his behalf:

November 5. I was hindred from church this Anniversary:

11 I visited Dr. Stillingfleete Bishop of Worcester.

Much snow falling winter comes fiercely on, so greate a frost seldom known to be in one night:

13 The snow & frost continue, I was at Gressh Colledge, where many Indian curiositys were presented, especialy the Chineze Barbers portable shop:

December The King now returned from Flanders, the Parliament began, 7 or 8 Candidats for to be the Speaker, Sir Tho. Littleton was chosen:

Very stormy weather.

7. Being one of the Council of the Society, I was named to be of the Comittè, to waite on our new President, my L. Chancellor, our Secretary Dr. Sloan, & Sir R. Southwell last ⟨Vice⟩ President, carrying our Book of Statutes; the officce of the President being read, his Lordship subscribed his name, & then tooke the Oathes according to our stat⟨ut⟩es as a Corporation, for the Improvement of Nat: Knowledge; Then his Lordship made a short Compliment, concerning the honour the Society had don him, & how ready he would be to promote us & so noble a designe, & come himselfe amongst us, as often as his attendance of the publique would permitt, & so we tooke our leave &c.

11 Of the many candidats for Speaker, it fell to Sir Tho: Littleton: The K of Spaine wonderfully recovered, & a Peace very likely to be concluded with the Turke:

25 Exceeding stormy, wett: Later end of the weeke freezin⟨g⟩, & on New Years day [a] very hard frost, but snow & raine afternoone, next day.

31 Accompts, with Thanks to Almighty God for his mercy to me: the past yeare.

1698/9 *Jan* 1 Beging the blessing of Almighty God, for his preservation of me the New Yeare.

The Parliament dismissed 3000 of the Kings standing Army, which should have ben 10000, Mr. Pelham, making a long speech against it, which was the more remarkable he being one of the Lords of the Treasury:

My Co: Perpoint died: She was Daughter to *Sir Jo. Evelyn* of Wil⟨t⟩shire, my Fathers Nephew, she was Widdow to William Perpoint, brother to the Marquess of Dorchester & mother to Evelyn Perpoint Earle of Kingston, a most excellent, & prudent Lady:

Unconstant Weather still continues:

15 The house of Comm: persist in refusing to consent that there should be above the number of 7000 to be a standing Army, & that no strangers be admitted of the number: which displeased the Court Party: our Country-man Sir R. Onslow

appeared against it also, which might reconcile him to the people who began to suspect him:

The Weather now sharp & seasonable: such prodigious stormes in Germany as the like had not ben know⟨n⟩, & did exceeding greate harme: The apprehension of an universal Famine thro Europe, puts France & other Countrys on making timely provisions: England as yet in tollerable plenty:

22 Sir R: Onslow & his sonn (a very hopefull Gent) came to Visite me:

30 Being the Fast on the Day of the Martyrdom of K. Charles: 1: preached a stranger on 9. Psal: 12. exaggerating the heynous sinn of murder, and especialy of that execrable one upon this day, & concluding with an Exhortation to repent & reforme, that the gilt of it may not yet live & continue on us or ours; & the judgements prevented which we of this land deserve &c:

Some Frost but exceeding Variable:

Feb 19 A most furious Wind, such as has seldom happened in many yeares, which did exceeding greate harme, to houses, ⟨&⟩ Trees, who with their falls killed severall people:

The Parliament having reduct the standing forces to 7000 onely, vote for the Navy 15000 pounds: Peace with the Turkes in Christendom, the French Kings pretences to a Treaty with Spaine for Succession to that Crowne, beginns to give jealosy of a new Warr:

The Ctzar of Moscovy, is building & preparing a Might⟨y⟩ Fleete in the Euxin.

Mar: 5 The old East India Company lost their buisinesse against the New Company by 10 Votes in Parliament: so many of their friends being absent by going to see a Tyger baited with dogs:

The persecuted Vodois banish⟨ed⟩ out of Savoy, received by the German Protestant princes: Magnificent entry of the Queene of the Romans at Vienna:

12 Mr. *Horneck* Son of late Minister of the Savoy, who was an Exile of Lituania (I think) preached an excellent sermon on 13. *Luke* 24:

24 Friday [To my exceeding griefe & affliction:] after a tedious [languishing] sicknesse contracted in Ireland, & increased here, died my onely remaining son John: ⟨who had⟩ now ben [6 years] one of the Kings Commissioners of the Revenue of that Kingdom, & performed his Employment both with

greate ability & reputation, aged 44 years & about 3 moneths: Leaving me one Grandson, now at Oxon, whom I beseech A. God to preserve, & be the remaining support of the Wotton family: Upon this Interruption I could not appeare at Church the following Sonday:

26 After an extraordinary storme came up the Thames a Whale which was 56. foote long: such, & a larger, & of the spout kind was kill'd there this moneth (that in June –58) this, 40 years after: See this Booke Anno ⟨1658⟩ June: 3. That yeare dyed Cromwell, as I think:

The most learned Dr. Stilling-fleete, Bishop of Worcester, died of the [Gout in the] Stomach, this Weeke: a Greate losse to the church;

[30 My deceased Son, was according to his desire Carried (being put into lead) into Surry, & layd amongst our Relations, in the Vault belonging to that family, accompanied by severall.]

Aprill: 5 A publique fast to Implore Gods mercy & deliverance of the poore persecuted Protestants of France, Cruely dispersed, put to death, sent to the Gallys, buried ignominiously & exposed, Their Children stolen from them & all they had: & to moove the Charity of the nation to relieve them: upon which I went to St. Jamess Chapell where Dr.—preached on 119 Psal: 53. Expressing the greate concern of *David* for feare of Gods judgements, upon consideration of the sinns of Israel in his Time; & exagerating the greate danger of both our owne nation & church for the prophanesse of the present Age, which may provoke God, to visite our Church & people with worse judgements, all sorts of wickednesse & prophanesse in life, & morals, Atheisme, Socinians, Schisme, Intemperance, Uncleanly, so abounding; that God having so signaly delivered us formerly, & of late from the Tyranny of Popery & Arbitrary government, & from a bloody War, be not provoked to bring all these & worse judgements upon us, except there be a thorow Reformation, which he earnestly pressed both small & greate to Endeavour: Shewing that when God is thereby Incensed even the most Righteous are many times, involved in the outward generall Calamity: Ending with an Exhortation to be liberall in our Contribution to our persecuted Breathren, for which this day was more especialy set apart.

Nothing of publique extraordinary.

9 The Duke of Devon: lost 1900 at an horse race at New merket &c:

The King preferring his young favorite D: of Albemarle to be first commander of his Guard: The Duke of Ormond layd down his Commission; this of the Dutch Dukes putting over his head, was exceedingly resented by every body.

16 In the morning Mr. Stringfellow on 6. Amos. 3. 4. 5. 6. This was to stir-up Charity, towards a Contribution for the Fr: Protestants, banished out of Savoy & Swisse.

Afternoone [at Whitehall] Dr: James: on: 34 Psal: 8: a very excellent sermon. This was at White-hall in the Banqueting-house now turned into a Chapell since the Palace was burnt:

I went afterwards to visite the Bishop of Lichfield, now named to be Bishop of Worcester, who entertained me with his old discourse concerning the Destruction of AntiChrist, inter-preting Daniel & the Revelation, with full Confidence of the Papacys fall, Frances Conversion, the final burning of Rome, which should certainly come to passe before the 36 years of the next Century, still persisting in his opinion, and as firmly believing it as an Article of Faith.

My Lord Spencer purchas'd an incomparable Library of   where-in among other rare Books, were severall, that were printed at the first Invention of that wonderfull Art, as particularly Tullys Offices: &c. There was a Homer & a Suidas in a very good greeke Character & good paper, almost as antient: This Gent, is a very fine Scholar, whom from a Child I have known: his Tutor was one *Florival* of Geneva:

My Grandson sent me a latin Epist⟨le⟩ from Oxon, giv-ing me account of the progresse of his studys there, & of his preparation for the receiving of the H. Eucharist, the first time, on Easter Sonday: I beseech God to blesse him, that he may proceede as he has hithertoo:

23 Rumor of the French equipping a greate Fleete & Army; which (as usualy) was spread, to get mony of the P: to raise more forces:

The Duke of Ormond disgusted by the putting the [now] favorite D. of A⟨l⟩bemarle, in his place of the Kings Guards; restored againe:

29 I went to Lambeth dined with the A:B. but my buisinesse was to get him to perswade the K: to purchase the late B: of

Worcesters Library, & build a place for his owne Library at
St. Jamess (which is too little &c) in the Parke:

[*May* 3 At a meeting of the R.S. I was nominated to be of the
Committè to waite on L. Chancellor to move the King to purchase the late B. of Worcesters Library.]

4 The Parliament was prorogued, the Kings speech not so
pleasing, seeming to intimate that they had not provided for the
necessitys of the nation, as to the publique arrears; & wishing
it may not appeare so by any inconvenience. The Court party
having very little influence this session: the forfeited Estates
in Ireland designed to be sold to discharge the publique debts,
but given to favorites, were by this session inquired into, &
some heats in the house of Peeres like to increase concerning
powers &c:

Rumour of the K: of Spains Indisposition againe &c:

8 Came my L. Privy-Seale to visite me, now made president
of the Council, some alterations made of Court Offices spoken
of. [L. Orford laid down his commission of Admiralty] The
Duke of Ormond restored to his Command.

All Lotterys 'til now cheating the people, to be no longer
permitted than to Christmas next, except that for the benefit
of Grinwich Hospital: Mr. Bridgeman, Chayre-man for the
Committe for carying on that Charitable Worke, died, a greate
losse to it: He was a Clerke of the Council, & a very industrious
usefull man:

I saw the Bishop of Norwich's [Dr. Moore] Library, one of
the best [& amplest] Collections of all sorts of good Bookes in
England, & he one of the most learned:

19 I went with the Commissioners to see how our fabrick at
Greenewich Hospital proceeded, & return'd that evening.

The weather extreamly hot & season dry:

28 Some sprinkling of Raine, but exceeding want of it: The
Parliament prorogued to 13 July:

The King went to Holland, having Constituted (as formerly)
9 persons to be Lords Justices & exercise the regal Government
in his absence: It was exceeding hot & dry weather &c:

June 4: Mr. ⟨Horneck⟩ at our Trinity Chapel, preached excellently on 2. Tim. 2: 19 (The Kings proclamation having ben read,
against blasphemy, & other Immoralitys): This young man was
the son of Dr. Honick, by nation about Poland or Lituania &c

& was long Minister of the Savoy, & Author of many pious Treatises:

Extraordinary drouth.

[June: 15:] After a long drowth we had a very refreshing Raine, but the day before it came, a dreadfull fire happened at Rotherith neere the Thames side, which besides divers ships that were burnt, destroyed & consum'd about 300 houses:

Now also died, the famous Dutchesse of Mazarine, in her time the richest Lady in Europ, Niepce to the greate Cardinal Mazarine, & married to the Richest subject in Europ, as is said: she was born at Rome, Educated in France, an extraordinary Beauty & Witt, but dissolute, & impatient of Matrimonial restraint, so as to be abandoned by her husband, came into England for shelter, liv'd on a pension given her here, & is reported to have hastned her death, by intemperan⟨t⟩ly drinking strong spirits &c: She has written her owne Story & Adventures & so has her other Extravagant sister, wife to the noble family *Colona*.

There died this weeke also *Conyers Seymor* son of Sir Ed: Seymor, kild in a Duel caused by a slight affront given him in St. Ja: Parke, by one that ⟨was⟩ envious at his Gallantry, for he was a new set-up vaine young fopp: who made a greate Eclat about the Town by his splendid Equipage, not setting any bounds to his pompous living; an Estate of 7000 pounds a yeare falling to him, not two years before, all which he left at about 2 or 23 years of age, to another Brother at Oxford: The general dissolution & Corruption & Atheisme of this period was now in as greate height in this nation among both sexes, as anywhere in Christendome.

19. Died suddenly my Co: Geo: Evelyn of Nutfield:

24 I went to Greenwich to see how the Hospital advanc't &c.

25 The heate has ben so extraordinary hot & dry now almost all this moneth as I remember not to have felt much greater in Italy &c: & this hapning after a winter, the wettest, tho not the coldest, that I ever remember since the siege of Colchester in the time of the Rebellion, almost 50 years since:

26. 28, after a yeares tedious altercations caused by one Dr. Fullham who had married a Grandaughter of my Bros, against the full Consent of her Relations, a Crafty & intriguing person, he so insinuated into my good Bro, after a few moneths, as to perswade my Bro: to require me, to cut off an Intaile of the

Estate he had given me, & that in Case, I should die without
Issue Male, it might fall to the Grandaughter, which by the reit-
erated settlements the law would not give him: My Bro: having
often professed, that he would have it descend to the name, &
I by no meanes willing it should be otherwise, & that the Patrimony of my Ancestors should be dissipated, sold or scattered,
among strangers, as it would soon have ben, & our name &
family extinguished, as it almost was, by Sir Jo: Evelyn of Godstone, Sir Jo: of Wilts, Sir Ed of Ditton, who leaving nothing to their name, 3 considerable Estates went away to the
female: My Bro: likewise, having amply provided portions to his
3 Grandaughters; & so many years persisting to have his Estate
Continue in the name: Was as I sayd, so wrought upon by
the Crafty Doctor as upon my refusal to alter the settlement, to
exhibit a Bill against me in Parliament now sitting, tho' I often
promised not to alter the settlement, but let it passe with the Con-
tingencys, offering in the meanetime, that provided the Mannor
of Wotton & Abinger might be reserved, to comply as to the
rest, that in Case I had no heir Male it should go to the Grand-
children: but when I found nothing would pacify the Doctor &
the rest, but the swallowing it all; I so answered my Bro: Bill,
shewing how absolutly it was conveyed to me; That the house of
Commons was so convinct of my Case, that they durst not proceede, I having so very greate an Interest among them in favour
of my right: So as hoping to fare better with the Lords, they
attempted all they could to gaine a party among them; but,
when they found I had not onely almost all the Bishops, & so
very many of the secular Lords, as were the most eminent speak-
ers, that they had no hope to prevaile there: My Bro: (who 'til
now they would not suffer, to accept of any Composition) did at
last, offer that if I would alowe him 6500 pounds, to inable him
to discharge [some of] his owne debts, & give legacys to his
Gr:-Children, he would make a new settlement, that should
more expressly Convey the whole Estate by an indefeasable
Inheritance, & being Tennant for life onely, oblige himself not
to make any farther wast of the woods & other spoile he had
begunn, & was in his power to do: To this, in reguard of his free
& original gift (tho most believed it had ben intended by my
Father but which my Bro: deneyed) & to quiet his Mind, &
indeede in Gratitude, I did consent to, The money to be payd by

1000 pounds a year for 7 years to begin after his decease: Now my good Bro: being sufficiently Convinct, & declaring that what he settled on me, was not onely absolutly in his power, to give his Estate as he pleased, and peremptorily affirming to the Doctor himselfe, that he would do it again if what he had settled was not sufficiently valid: Yet so dextrous was this Insinuating faire tongued & crafty man, assisted with the perpetual solicitation of the Women; that then they set on my Bro: with a Case of Conscience, & that tho' he had power to give the Estate as he had don, yet in Conscience he ought not to have don it: Upon this I sent my Case to the learned Bishop of Worcester Dr. Stillingflete, not more esteemed for his being an Excellent Lawyer, but a profound divine, who, as indeede did the A Bishop of Cant: Bishop of Ely, Chichester, Peterborough, Chester, Salisbery, Lichfield &c: who universaly affirm'd my Bro: was not obliged by Conscience to revoak what he had settled on me: And as to matter of Law, the other Lords, Dukes, Earles & Peers who were generaly for me, as were the Commons: I had so much the advantage, that, had I not ben tenderer of my Bro: reputation than some would have had me: I might have saved 6500 pounds: but I chose rather to incumber the Estate with it, than not to gratify my good Bro: notwithstanding the advantage I had, & least it should be said I was ungratefull; my designe & desire being nothing so much in all this Contest, but to preserve the patrimonial Estate to the famely: So as now, a settlement being made as strong as Law could do it, all was Reconciled: my Good Bro: having ben prevailed with, contrary to his own resolution, but suffers them to govern his as they pleased, & this in my absence, whilst I was cald to London about other affairs: to both our trouble & charge: The Writings were sealed 26. of June, & a Recovery suffered on 28:

After this finding my Occasions calling ⟨me⟩ so often to Lond: I tooke the remainder of the Time, my sonn, had in his lease of an house in Dover-streete, To which I now removed, finding my being at Wotton as yet Inconvenient: So as I resolved to continue at Lond: without removing my furniture at Wotton; having enough at Says Court, I furnished the house in Dover-street, & came to it on Saturday, July 1. from Berkley strete, where I had ben ever since I came from Wotton, in reguard of my unhapy Sons Indisposition: I pray God of his

infinit mercy, whose gracious providence has hitherto so wonderfully extricated me ⟨out⟩ of this, & other disturbances &
afflictions, to sanctifie it to me, and to blesse the remainder of
my life & now very old age with peace, & Charity, & assist me
with his Grace to the End:

2 [Died my Niepce Glanvill of the small pox, a pious, beautifull & excellent woman, she was daughter to my Co. Hales of
Kent, daughter of Sir J. Evelyn of Surry: she caught the infection of her owne Children whom she would needes attend in
that dissease:]

The Weather Continuing excessively hot:

6. At Doctors Commons tooke my Oath of Administration
of my Sonns Estate:

30 Greate Consultations abroad, how to secure the Princes of
Germany & other Dominions from France, in case of the Span-
ish Kings death, the French every day increasing his Army: The
Scots landed at *Darien* alarme the Spaniard, as dos the Ctzar
of Mosco the Turk: buisy about settling the Limits with the
Emp &c:

The Bishop of St. Davids depriv'd for Simony:

Aug: ⟨7?⟩ I went to Greenwich to refresh & take the aire for a
few days: & to see how our building went forward:

13 In the Afternoone, at Deptford, where they had built a
pretty decent new Church: The Curat preached on 5 Gal: 16:

I went to see the Blakesmith ⎱ profuse Gardens &c:
     Ankersmiths ⎰

Septr 1 My Daughter Draper was brought to bed of a Sonn,
and Christened on the 1 of September by the name of Richard,
his Godfather⟨s⟩ were Mr. Morley, Nephew to the late Bishop
of Winchester, & Mr. Sherwood, who maried a neere Relation
of my Sons in Law:

News of the Q. of Portugals death, caused by a feavor with
the boaring an hole in her Eare, for which according to the
method of that Country (not of Germany) they let her blood til
she breathed out her life:

The King of Spaine wonderfully & contrary to all hope
almost, recovering: Halfe the Citty of Mosco burnt, by the
throwing of Squibbs: K. William makes a general review of all
his Forces in the Netherlands: The old Duke of Tell gives him a
Visite in greate pomp:

2d: The Anniversary of London being burnt.

3—An Earthquake in Genoa & those parts: The K of Denmark dead:

9 I dined at Lambeth at the A. Bishop: where was the Bishop of Norwich a very learned man:

10 There was on Wednesday this weeke great expectations of the Effects of a very dismal Eclipse of the Sun, people expected by predictions of the Astrologer⟨s⟩ that it would be exceedingly darke: But tho' the morning were very Mirky, yet was the obscurity no other than on other clowdy days: But this I well remember, the whole Nation was affrited by Lilly the Almanack ⟨writer⟩, who foretold what a dreadfull Eclipse [that which was called Black monday] it would be, insomuch as divers persons were grievously in dread, & durst not peepe out of their house: Yet was that a very bright morning, & the darknesse much like this: It is now above 50 years since, it was indeede succeeded with many revolutions, cruell wars, twixt us & Holland, but this, was preceded by the Death of the K. of Denmark & Q. of Portugal: But thus superstitious people, not considering the natural Course of those Luminarys, looke on what ever haps of Extraordinary as their Effects, who ought to looke up to God the Author of Nature.

1 Octob: A strange Earthquake at New Batavia in the E. Indies, & the prodigious Effects of it, by a mountain breaking, burning, & raine & Inundation: & danger of that Citty &c:

4 Wednesday night departed this life my worthy & dear Bro: Geo: Evelyn at his house at Wotton in Surrey in the 83d yeare of his Age, & of such Infirmitys as are usualy incident to so greate an Age, but in perfect memory & understanding: A most worthy, Gentleman, Religious, Sober & Temperate, & of so hospitable a nature as no family in the whole County maintained that antient Custome of keeping (as it were) open house the whole yeare, did the like, or gave nobler & freer Entertainement to the whole County upon all occasions: so as his house was never free, there being sometime 20 persons more than his family, & some that stayed there all the summer to his no small expense, which created him the universal love of the Country: To this add, his being one of the Deputy Lieutenants of the County; and living to be the most antient Member of Parliament living: He was Born at Wotton, Went to Oxford, Trinity

Coll: from the Free Schole at Guilford, Thence to the Midle Temple, as gent: of the best quality did, tho' with no intention to study the Law as a Profession: He married the Daughter of *Colwall*, [of] a worthy & antient family in Leicester-⟨s⟩hire, by whome he had One son; she dying in 1643, left George her son an Infant, who being educated liberaly, after Traveling abroad, returning home, married one Mrs. Goare; by whom he had severall Children but left onely 3 daughters: He was a Young man of a good understanding, but over Indulging to his Ease & pleasure, grew so very Corpulent, contrary to the constitution of the rest of his fathers relations, that he died: after my Bro: his Father had married a most noble & honourable Lady, relict of Sir Jo Cotton, she being an Offley, a worthy & antient Staffordshire family by whom he had severall Children of both sexes: This lady dying left onely 2 daughters & a son: the younger daughter dyed, before Mariage: The other lived long [as] a Virgin, & was afterward married to Sir Cyrill Wych, a noble learned Gent: sonne to Sir   Wych: he had ben Ambassador at Constantinople: Sir Cyrill was afterwards Made one of the Lords Justices of Ireland: Before this Mariage her onely Bro: John Maried the daughter of Aresfeild of Sussex [of] an honorable family, whom he left a Widdow, without any Child living: He dying about Anno 1691 & his wife not many yeares after, without any heire: My Bro: resettled the whole Estate on me: His sister who maried S⟨ir⟩ C. Wych having had a portion of 6000 pounds to which what was added was worth above 300 pounds more: The 3 other Grandaughters, with what I added to theirs about 5000 pounds each: ⟨This⟩ my Bro: having seene performed, died this 5t of Octob: in a good old Age, & greate Reputation: & making his beloved Daughter my Lady Wych sole executrix (leaving me onely his Library & some Pictures of my Father, Mother &c:) She indeede buried him with extraordinary solemnity, rather as a Noble man, Than a privat Gent: There were I computed above 2000 people at the funerall, all the Gent of the County doing him the last honour: This performed [20th] I returned to Lond, where I came the day before, leaving my Concernes at Wotton, 'til my Lady should dispose of her selfe & family: & sending onely a servant thither to looke after my Concerns:

[31. I was this day 79 yeares old: Gods holy ⟨name⟩ be magnified, by the improvement of his grace & mercy & deliverances after the troubles of the yeare past.]

November ⟨4⟩ Great ceremony Balle & rejoicing it being the King⟨s⟩ birth day.

⟨5⟩ The day of the papists Conspiracy & Kings landing a stranger at our Chapell preached on   Psal: shewing by severall famous Instances, that the time of Gods deliverance of his Church is for the most part at the very article of its danger: That God had so universal a care of his people he instanced in that of 10: Daniel, where Michael withstood the Angel of Persia, & that his Church is under the protection of Gardian Angels, upon which he much inlarged, & so proceeded to the deliverance of the Day, namely the popish plot by powder, & the later designe to subject the nation to popery, & slavery, had not K. William prevented it most unexpectedly, as at the same moment: namely 5. November:

That it therefore behoved us to shew all thankfullnesse to God, by forsaking our sinns, & Charity to the poore, together with all other expressions of Gratitude &c.

Afternoone another: 3 Lament: 39.

There happned this Weeke so thick a Mist & fog; that people lost their way in the streetes, it being so exceedingly intense, as no light of Candle, Torches or Lanterns, yeilded any or very little direction: I was my selfe in it, and in extraordinary danger, robberys were committed betwene the very lights which were fixt between Lond: & K⟨e⟩nsington on both sides, and whilst Coaches & passengers were travelling: & what was strange, it beginning about 4 in the afternoone was quite gon by 8, without any wind to dissipate it. At the Thames they beate drumms, to direct the Watermen to make the shore, no lights being bright enough to penetrat the fogg:

The French persecution rages most inhumanely: My Lord President visited me.

24 The Parliament met & adjourned for a Weeke.

Horrible roberys, high-way men, & murders committed such as never was known in this Nation since Christian reformed: Atheism, Dissensions, prophanesse, [Blasphemy] among all sorts: portending some signal judgement, if not amended: upon

which a Society set on foote, who obliged themselves to endeavour the reforming of it, both in London & other places, which
began to punish offenders, & put the laws in more strict Execution: which God Almighty prosper.

Never was so gentle, Calme, dry, yet seasonable & temperate
weather thro all the seasons of the yeare, as this has ben:

December 3 The Pope sick, discourse of the K of Spaine
being relapsed: Greate Earthquake in Portugal: The Czar of
Moscovys warlike preparation. Weather so Calm, bright &
warm, as seldom so benigne in the midst of Aprill:

10: Mr. Stringfellow on his former Text:

Continuance of warm spring weather: The Parliament reverse
the prodigious donations of the Irish forfeitur, intended to be set
a part for dischargeing the vast national debt: And calling some
great persons in highest office in question for setting the greate
seale to an arch pyrates being pardon'd, & Comissioned to take &
bring other pyrats infesting Commerce, had turned pyrate again,
& brought prizes into the W: Indies, suspected to be conniued at,
upon ⟨shares⟩ of the prey: by which some greate men were
brought into suspicion: but the prevaling part in the house, called
Courtiers, out voted the Complaints, or Country part, as for
most part they do; not for being more in number, but more vigi-
lantly attending the house, thro neglect of their duty:

17 The Parliament adjourn some days, make a severe order for
the better attendance of the members: Discourse of K: James
indisposition at St. German. As mild weather still as in the
Spring:

$\frac{1699}{1700}$ Jan. 7: The Weather was at this time so mild as seldom
warmer in midst of Spring, such a season, I believ none alive had
know⟨n⟩ in these parts:

14: Dr. Lancaster imposing another Lecturer on our Chapell,
much against the inclination of those who frequented it; &, as
appears on some private grudge, dismisst, our excellent preacher
Mr. Stringfellow, who had ben put in & made the very first
preacher of that place, by the Bishop of Lincoln upon my recommendation, whilst the Bishop held the Vicarage of St. Martines, by a dispensation, which displeased the Bishop of
London: The person Dr. Lancaster put in, is one *Mr. Sandys*
who preached indifferently on: 1. Jo: 4. 11. Concerning brotherly
Charity:

The Scotch booke about *Darien*, burnt by the hang-man by Vote of Parliament: Very pleasant & absolute Spring weather. A Lady whose house was burnt in golden Square perishing in it: other houses burnt.

25 I went to Wotton, the first time, after my deare Brothers funerall, to settle my Interest & Concernes there, and furnish the house with necessarys, thro my Lady Wyche & Nephew [〈Glanvill〉] being Executors, having sold & disposed of what goods were left of my Brothers.

The season from hitherto being the most mild & gentle season that ever was (I think) known: now altering into sharp and hard frosts for some days:

28: Intermitting frosts & raine. The Parliament pursues the revocation of the Irish grants: Prohibits pintados, Musslin & other stuffs brought out of the E. Indies, as prejudicial to the Manufactures of England &c.

One Stephens preaching to the H. of Commons on K Charles I: Martyrdom 30 Jan: told them, that the observation of that day was never intended out of any detestation of his Murder, but to be a document to other Kings & Rulers, how they ought to behave themselves towards their Subjects, lest they came to the like End: This was so resented by the house, that whereas they used to desire these anniversary sermons to be printed, Stephen〈s〉 should not be thanked for his, ordering that none should for the future preach before them on solemn occasions, who was not either Deane, or Doctor of Divinity:

Feb: 4 The Parliament Incorporate the old E. India Company. Voted against the Scots invading or settling in [the] *Darien* as prejudicial to our trade with Spaine: Voted that the Exorbitant Numbers of Attourneys (now indeede swarming & evidently causing suits & disturbance, by eating out the Estate of people, provoking them to go to law &c) be lessened; Voted that it should not be in the power of *Popish* parents, to disinherit their Protestant Children:

Died the Duke of Beaufort, a person of greate honour, prudence & Estate:

March 3: I went to visite the Bishop of Worcester:

My Sonn in Law Draper, had left him now, by the death of his Aunt, my Lady Temple, in Land, Houses, plate & Jewells [Money] to the value of neere 20000 pounds.

6 I dined at the B: of Worcesters with the A Bishop of Cant, Earle of Clarendon & Countesse.

8: The season was now like to Aprill, for warmth, & mild-nesse, never the like observed in my remembrance.

The two young Northern Kings, lately comming to reign, & that during all these late disturbances in the rest of Europ, are now coming to a rupture; the Event of which may be very preju-dicial to all Europe:

13 [I] Was at the funerall of my *Lady Temple*, who was buried at Islington, brought from Adscomb neere Croydown: She left my son in Law Draper (her Nephew) the mansion house of Addscom, very nobly & compleatly furnished, with the Estate about it, which with the Jewells, money, plate &c, is computed to be worth neere 20000 pounds: She was a very prudent Lady: gave away many greate Legacys besids which 500 pounds to the poore of Islington, where her husband Sir P: Temple (both dying without Children) was buried.

Riga beseiged by the K. of Denmark, at diffrence with the K of Swede⟨n⟩, like to ingage the Northern Princes, who hitherto enjoyed greate quiet. Two young Monarchs emulating one another, & ambitious, strive to appeare who shall have the better, upon a small new ocasion: The weather now on the sud-den altered to hard frost & cold weather.

24 The Season was now so warme, gentle, & exceeding pleas-ant, as it could be expected in the most desierable Spring:

The nation being now grown to so unsufferable a passe, and height of Atheisme & profanesse: some Religious persons both in the Citty & Country, entred into a kind of fraternity to attempt a reformation, by a more than ordinary discountenanc-ing immorality & irreligion, upon all occasions; Into this Society entred divers persons of quality, & for that end, some Lectures, were set up, as in particular in the Citty of Lond: Bow-church or St. Paules, where preached the most Eminent of the Cleargy, after the reading of a declaration set forth by the King, to sup-presse this universal & growing wickednesse, which already began to take some effect, as to the Common Swearing & ⟨othes⟩ in the mouths of people of all ranks: & [25] this day preached Dr. Burnet Bishop of Salisbery, befor the Lord Mayor & a very greate Congregation: on 27: Pro: 5. & 6 verse, Open Rebuke is better than seacret love: applyed to the present designe of proceeding in their Indeavor of Reforming the publique dissolution.

27: The Duke of Norfolck divorc'd from his Wife by the Parliament: for Adultery with one Sir J. Germain a Dutch gamster of meane extraction, who had gotten much by Gaming (She was onely daughter to the Earle of Peterboro Mordaunt:) after long debates in Parliament, & undenyable proofe: The Duke having also leave to marry againe, by which (if he have Children) the Dukedome, will go from my late Lord Thomass Children, Papists indeede, but very hopefull & vertuous Gent: as was their father: The now Duke & Unkle, a dissolute protestant:

The Parliament did now nominate 14. Persons to go Commissioners into Ireland, in order to dispose of the Confiscated Estates in Ireland, towards payment of the Debts of this Nation contracted in the late Warr; [but] which the King had in greate measure given to some of his greate favorits of both sexes, Dutch & other of little merite, & very unseasonably ⟨as⟩ appeared: That this might be don, without suspition of Interest in the Parliament, but for the publique, It was determined that no Member of the House, should be of the Commission, & was therefore to be supplyed by severall Country Gent: & persons of quality, & reputed Integrity:

Aprill: 1. The Lecture instituted by Mr. Boyle, preached at St. Paules by Mr   on   very excellently, proving both by Scripture, prophane History, Reason, & whatever else can moraly be expected ⟨for⟩ the assertion of any Truth, That what is Writen, and delivered to us of our B: Savior, ⟨is⟩ of exceeding greater certainty & lesse liable to exceptions, than any Thing in other History whatsoever: These Sermons are all of them published:

The Lord Major, Sherifs, Aldermen &c went with a procession of the Children &c, brought-up in Christs Hospital: among which the 40 [Blew-Coate] Boys instructed in Mathematics & designed for the sea, with their mathematical Instruments in their hands, going to St. Brides according to custome:

3. I went, with Sir Chr: Wren, Surveyor of his Majesties Workes & Buildings, to Kensington, to present the King with the Model & several drafts ingraved, of the Hospital now erecting at Greenewich for Sea-Men, The A: Bish: of Cant:

introducing us; His Majestie receiving us with greate satisfaction, & incouraging the prosecution of the Work:

The Parliament drew now to a Conclusion of this Session.

10 The greate Contest betweene the Lords & Commons concerning the Lords power of amendments & rejection of certaine bills, tack't to the money bill, carried onely for the Commons for them against the Lords, was this days Event, which went so high, as every body almost believed would have either provoked the K to Adjourn, or dissolve them: But by Gods mercy and providence it is prevented: However this Tacking of Bills is a novell practise, suffered by Charles II. who being continualy in want of mony, let any thing passe rather than not have to feede his extravagant favorits &c:

Mr. Nagg our late lectur⟨er⟩ preached on 5: Hosea 15:

The greate contest betweene the Lords & Commons about passing the Bill for monys, to which they had tack't so many other considerable demands, (& which indeede was but a later practice caused by the continual want of mony to which Charles the 2d had brought himself by his profusion & favorits) was at last assented to, with greate difficulty, Voices being equal on both sides, & accidentaly carryed by one Voice; all the Bishops following the Court: going out save one: So as neere 60 Bills passt, to the greate triumph of the Commons, & Country part, but high regret of the Court, & those to whom the King had given large estates in Ireland, of lands, more necessary to discharge the prodigious arrears & debts of the publique, t⟨h⟩o it must be confessed, that this successe of theirs, must needes lessen the King, & the interest of the Court, which I foresee will be hard to recover; so apprehensive the Nation are of yeilding any advantage they have gotten, as being now the onely people in Europe who have preserved their libertys, & unwilling to come under a despotic power, as those in Fr: Denmark, Sweden & our neighbours grone under: And pity it is, that things should be brought to such extremitys; The government of this Nation being so equaly poised betweene King & Subject: But we are satisfied with nothing; & whilst there is no perfection on this side heaven, mi thinks both might be contented, without straining things too farr:

There passed among the rest a Law, that whatever Estate a Papist were intitled to, if he turn'd not protestant before 18 years of age, it should passe to his next protestant Heire: This indeede seemed an hard law; But not onely the barbarous usages of the French K: to his protestant subjects; but the indiscreete insolence of the popists here, going in triumphant & publique processions with their Bishops, with Banners & Trumpets, in divers places (as is said) in the Northern Countys, has brought it upon their party:

17 The rapine & miscarriages of those, who obtained vast gifts out of the forfaited Estates in Ireland, by the Kings bounty abus'd, & those persons of little; others of no merit, but rather of ill fame; was layd open & published by order of Parliament & Commissioners se⟨n⟩t over to inspect farther into this matter, it being to be applyed to discharge the debts of the nation, which was now mounted to a prodigious arrear:

The old E. India Company now confirm'd by Act of Parliament which before it wanting, Interlopers did greatly disturb it.

May: The Seale was taken from The L. Chancellor Summers, tho he had ben acquited by much majority of votes, for what was charged against him in the H. of Commons: This being in Terme time put some stop to affairs, the K. keeping the Seale, which many eminent lawyers refus'd to accept; considering the uncertainty of things in this fluctuating Conjuncture: It is certaine this Chancellor was a most excellent lawyer, a very learned ⟨man⟩ in all the polite literature, and an excellent Pen, & was Master of an handsome style of easy Conversation; but is said to make too much hast to be rich, as his predecessor & most in places, in this age did to a more prodigious excesse then was ever know⟨n⟩ in this nature. But the Commons had now, so mortified the Court party, and propriety & liberty so invaded in all the neighbour Kingdomes, that their jealosy made them cautious, & every day strengthen the Laws, which protected the people from Tyranny: besids the ⟨infinite⟩ Arrear, & Treasure which had brought the Nation into such debts, with other profusion, without any limitts &c:

There never had ben, in any mans memory, so glorious a Spring, such hope of aboundance of fruits of all kinds, & ⟨so⟩ propitious a yeare, & yet never a more profane, & atheistical age: most of the youth [& others] Atheist⟨s⟩, Theists, Arians, & Sectaries, which God of his mercy reforme:

10 The greate Tryal between Sir Walt: Clargis, & Mr. Sherwin, concerning the legitimacy of the late D: of Albemarle, on which depended an Estate of 1500 pounds a yeare: the Verdict was given for Sir Walter:

12 An Eastern-wind made it now very Cold: None would yet, accept of the Broad-seale.

19 Searjante Wright at last, accepted of the Great Seale of England.

24 I went from Dover Streete to Wotton for the rest of summer, whither I removed the rest of the goods from Says Court, to the House at Wotton.

June 2. Sweete seasonable ⟨weather⟩ & such a mixture of pleasant refreshings, as no man I think remembers so propitious a season, & likelinesse of a plentifull Harves⟨t⟩ both of Corn, & other fruits.

16 The Weather was now more like Aprill than summer: reports of the Cessation of Armes between the Northern Princes.

Mr. Creech fellow of All-Soules in Oxon: an Excellent Poet & Philosopher who published Lucretius with notes in Latine, & an English translation, with many other pieces, & ⟨seemed⟩ to be of a grave & sollid temper, was found hanged, none knowing upon what occasion or apparent discontent or Cause, his Circumstances being so very easy, for besides one of the best fello⟨w⟩ships in the University, he had a living, I am told worth 200 pounds per ann: This disaster much astonished me, who knew him, By this, we find, how greatly it concernes us to implore Gods Almighty Preventing, & Assistant Graces all the days of our life.

30 The King went into Holland: Never could be desir'd a more propitious season, aboundance of fruite of all sorts: Blessed be God:

July: ⟨7⟩: I was now visited with an attaque of a Feaver, accompanyed with the strangury, which detain'd me in bed & house neere a moneth & much weakned me; But it pleased God, as to mittigate & allay my feavor, so to abate of my other Infirmity also; for which forever be praise ascribed to him by me, & that thereby he has againe so gratiously advertiz'd me of my duty, to prepare for my latter end which now cannot be far off, at this greate Age of mine:

The death of the Duke of Gloucester, dying of the small-pox, is very astonishing, a hopefull child of 12 or 13 years old, & the onely Child of the Princesse *Ann* by the Prince of Den-marke, she having had & ben with child of many sonns & daughters, but commonly none living, & often misscarying: So as now there is none to succeede to this Crowne, according as lately settled by Parliament on the late Revolution, but ⟨on⟩ some Protestant Prince, the next I think being the Prince of Hanover,[1] Grandson, to the Q: of Bohemia, sister to K. Charles the first: otherwise, I think, descending (if the P: of Wales be utterly excluded) on the Dutchesse of Savoy, daugh-ter to the princes Henrietta, Sister to Charles the first: Wher the Crowne will now Settle, should the Princesse of Denmark breed no more to live, is matter of high speculation to the Politic:

My Son & daughter Draper came to Wotton to visite us: staying a fortnight with us.

Aug: 11. Was the first of my being in Condition to go to church, & give God thanks for my recovery: The Minister preached on 5 *Matt* 17:

The weather had for all this & last moneth, ben so seasonable & serene, as never in my memory was the like, God make us thankfull.

I had another attack of my Indisposition:

I consulted in order to the new making of my will, since I came to this Estate: My Gr-sonn came from Oxford for this Vaccation.

18 This being the first and onely yeare & time, I was obliged to turne [to] Husbandry, plowing & sowing, it pleased God ⟨t⟩o answer our hopes & labours by a most plentifull Harvest, which was brought home whilst the weather continued faire; for which God be blessed in the use of it: It turn'd to raine the next daye after: [My sonn ⟨and⟩ daughter⟨s⟩ 2d sonn, an Infant, ⟨died⟩, to our greate sorrow.]

25 The Minister preached on the same Chap: Ver: 30:

In the afternoone Explaination of that part of the Creede, which mentions the Resurrection:

1 George Louis, the future King George I.

September 1 The Marquis of Halifax, a very vertuous & hopefull ⟨young⟩ Noble man (& of which the Nation had very few) died now: much lamented.

September 13 A Considerable Estate in land, faire house, richly furnished, Plate, Mony &c being fallen to my Son in Law, Draper, at Adscome neere Croydon: I went with my Wife thither & stayed there til the 26, when I returned back to Wotton:

During the time of my being with my son & daughter: I went to see divers seats of the Gentry neere it, [16] as ⟨Marden⟩, a barren Warren, bought by Sir Ro: Clayton, who building there a pretty House, made such alteration by planting not onely with infinite store of the best fruit; but by so changing the natural situation of the hill, valleys & solitary mountains about it, that it represented rather some forrain Country, producing as it were spontaneously pines, fir, Cypresse, Yew, holly, Juniper intermingled with walks, mazes, precipices, & other so as one would easily fancy himself in some forrain Country, naturaly solitudinary, & exceedingly & pleasantly Exottique, the trees being come to their perfect growth & all preserved with uttmost Care, so as I, who had some years before seene it in its natural & baren condition was in admiration of it: The lande was purchased of Sir J. Evelyn of God-Stone, & by the Industry, & vast charge of this opulent Citizen, thus improved for pleasure & retirement: He & his Lady, entertained us with greate civility:

20: I went to see Bedington, the antient seate of the Carews formerly & in my remembrance, a noble old structure, capacious, & in forme of the buildings of the Age in Hen: 8. & Q. Eliz: ⟨time⟩ & proper for the old English hospitality, but now decaying with the house it selfe, heretofore adorned with ample Gardens, & the first Orange trees that ever were seene in England, planted in the open ground, & secured in Winter onely by a Tabernacle of boards, & stoves, removable in summer; thus standing 120 yeares large & goodly Trees & laden with fruite, but now in decay as well as the Grotts & other curiositys, Cabinets & fountaines in the house & abroade, thro the debauchery & negligence of the Heires, it being now fallen to a Child under age, & onely kept by a servant or two from utter delapidation. The Estate & Parke about it also in decay: the negligence of a few years, ruining the Elegances of many:

23: I went visite Mr. Pepys at Clapham, who has there a very noble, & wonderfully well furnished house, especialy with all the Indys & Chineze Curiositys, almost any where to be mett with, the Offices & Gardens exceedingly well accomodated ⟨for pleasure⟩ & retirement:

Octob: 13 The newes of the death of the Pope, who lived to this Jubily: more rumors of the K: of Spains death, & of the Ctzar of Moscovy coming to invade Sweden: The weather mild.

27 The King was now returned out of Holland: The Pope dead:

31 Being my Birth-day & now complete 80th yeare of my Age; I with my Soule render thanks to Almighty God, who of his infinit mercy, not onely brought me out of many troubles; but this yeare, restored me to health after a favourable surprize of an Ague & other infirmitys of so greate an Age, my sight, hearing, & other senses & facultys tollerable: To his praise, which, with the pardon of all my sinns past, I implore him to continue, & give me grace to acknowledge by my improvement of his goodnesse the insuing yeare, if it be his pleasure to protract my life, that I may be the better prepared for my last days, through the infinite merits of my B. Saviour, the Lord Jesus: Amen:

THE DEATHS OF JAMES II AND WILLIAM III
(1700–1702)

SEASONABLE, PEACEABLE & healthfull weather for the time of the yeare:

November 5 Came the newes of my deare Grandsons (the onely male of my family remaining) being fall'n ill of the Small-pox at Oxford, which after the dire effects it had, taking a way two of my Children (Women grown) exceedingly Afflicted me: But so it pleased my most mercyfull God, that, being let-blood, at his first complaint of uneasinesse; and the extraordinary Care of Dr. Mander, head of the Coll: & now Vice-chancelor, (who caused him to be brought out of his owne Chamber, & lodg'd in his owne Appartment, Bed & Bed-Chamber) with the advise of his Physitian, & care of his Tutor: That as they came out kindly, separatly, and but few: and no evil symtom accompanying: There was all faire hopes of his doing well, to our infinite Comfort, & refreshment; as ⟨appeared from⟩ the account, which was se⟨n⟩t us by letter every day since their appearance, by letters either from the V: Chan: himselfe, or his Tutor: for which Almighty-God be forever praised & depended on:

There was realy a Change of greate Officers at Court: my L. Godolphin returning to his former station of first Commissioner of the Treasury, and Sir Char: Hedges Secretary of State:

13 I came from Wotton with my family, to reside at Lond: This Winter:

The K of Spaine at last dead, bequeath'd [all] his Kingdoms and Territorys to the Duke of Anjou, grandchild of the French King, being about 17 years old: To the astonishment of all the world, till now amused, with a partition, to the Emp: Duke of Bavaria, & other expectant princes:

[Assurance of my Grandsons recovery: by a letter from himselfe:]

17 There was no other discourse at this time, amongst the Polit⟨it⟩ians & speculatists, save this great & stupendious Revolution of Spaine, given to the Fr: King⟨s⟩ Grandson by the will of that King: & it was looked on as a coup d'Adresse in the French, amusing our K. William and the rest, about a partition, without which the Spanish Counsels had never made this alteration; for they dreaded nothing so much as the dismembring of those Dominions, & this 'tis believed, induced them to make the King settle it by Will:

24 Our Min⟨i⟩ster preached on 2 Cor: 1: 10: shewing what Conscience was, & the sad estate of those who sin against Conscience, a tirrible discourse, which I besech God I may consider:

I was so Indisposed, when I came from Church, with an aguish distemper, as hinder⟨ed⟩ me from going in the afternoone:

⟨30⟩ St. Andrews-day we had a greate Assembly of the R. Society, where we continued my L. Summers (late L. High Chancellor) President:

December 1 The Court went now into deepe mourning for the K of Spaine & all the discourse was now, what must be the event of this wonderfull & surprising Revolution:

It began to freeze very sharply.

8 Greate alterations of Officers at Court & elsewhere: The L: C. Justice Treby died; who will succeede will soon be known. He was a learned man of that profession, of which we have now very few, never fewer: The Chancery requiring so little skill in deepe law-learning, so the practiser can Talke eloquently, & that Court so profitable, very few care to study the law to any purpose: In the Treasury my L. Godolphin resumes his place as first Lord Commissioner, & is made of the Cabinet Councell, my L. Marborow Master of the Ordinance in place of my L. Rumny, who is made Groom of the Stole: The Earle of Rochester gos L. Lieutennant to Ireland.

15 The Ctzar of Moscovy (who came with a greate Army to beseige Narva, & reduct that important place to greate straites) is defeated by the Swedes, the Seige raised, & a greate Batell fought, where in the losse on the Ctzars side were slayne 10000, The Artillery & Baggage Taken, The King in person, with a far unequal number, obtaining the Victory, to the joy of all those potentates, who dreaded the Ctzars having any thing to do in the Baltick, which was the aime of the barbarous Prince:

The New Spanish King writes to the French King in this style; to the most Christian King, my Brother & Grandfather:

Our Parliament dissolved, a new one is summoned for the 6t of Feb:

21 My Grandson came from Oxford to passe the Holydays here:

25 Mr. *Knag* [Christmas Day] preached at our Chapell on 1. John: 3. 8. The Communion followed, at which I was partaker: &c.

The season was very warme: The Parliament dissolved, another to be called & ⟨sit⟩ the 6 of Feb: & like to be greate Contests about Elections: The defeate of the *Czar* of Moscovy much greater than at first reported: The [new] Pope is Crowned. The French sends forces to secure Flanders, & especialy Milan, chalenged by the Emperor, as his feoffe, & fallen to him by the death of the K of Spaine without children, threatning to Invade

Italy: The Swisse & Venetian pressed by France to oppose his bringing any forces thro their Territorys are in greate per-plexit⟨y⟩ how to govern their Resolution: The French all this while pretending that he seeks onely to ballance Interests so as ⟨to⟩ Establish the Universal Peace, which no body believes. The Hollanders Augment their forces by sea & land & so doe the Portugals: in short, this Unexpected Revolution is likely to produce greate Changes.

1701. *Jan:* 3 [I finished the Sale of North Stoake in Sussex to Rob: Michel Esquire, appointed to be sold by my Brother for payment of portions to my Neepces & other incumbrances on the Estat]

There was extraordinary strivings among the Candidats at the Elections of Parliament men, in many Countys & Borows.

4 There fell so thick a Snow this night, as I have seldom known a greater in so short a time:

5: The Snow & exceeding sharp cold, hindred me from Church this Morning: In the Afternoone preached a young man on 2. *Titus* 14:

Extraordinary contention of Competitors at the Election for Parliament men, so as some had not don polling in a fortnight or 3 weekes:

The frost & Snow which so sudainly surpriz'd us, for a greater snow had scarse ben known to fall in one night: mealted away as sudainly by a gentle Thaw:

19 Very severe frost & such a Tempest, as threw downe divers chimnys, & did greate spoile at sea, blew downe above 20 ⟨Trees⟩ of mine at Wotton: &c:

Feb. 2 The minister of Wotton being sick the Curate of Abinger preached on 18 Ezek. 28.

Extraordinary hard & sharp cold, frost, & yet variable.

9 The Sermon was in the After-noone at Abinger on 1 Jacob: 27: I went to Visite Mr. Wy the Incumbent of Wotton, who was mortaly afflicted with a Cancer in his fauces, & not likely to recover:

10 I came back to Lond the 10th.

The Parliament met on the 6t: To whom the K. recommends their care about a Successor, the Pri: of Denmark not likely to have any child live: The shipping, & Harbours, The supply-ing the defects of the funds to pay of the greate debt of the

Nation, the burden of the poore Tax, the security of the Prot: Religion &c.

To which the⟨y⟩ returned Answer that they would besides all this endeavour the peace of Europ against all, its molesters &c:

But these Resolutions were so late & untimely, that the Fr: King, who had out witted all Europ by Contriving the K of Spaines will, that before they could do any thing Considerable by concerting matters of this exceeding greate Moment: with the Emperor, Hollanders & Northern princes, The French had seized on all Flanders, & the state of Millan, & pour'd into them greate Armies; so as the Dutch were forc't to owne the New King Philip: & all this may be imputed to our sole neglect of breaking-up the late Parliament, & not meeting of this til too late by a fatal stupidity: It was also Evident, that (for all the new lawes lately made, against Corruption in Elections) there was never know⟨n⟩ so much perjury, bribery & other enormous means used ⟨as⟩ in the Election of this Parliament, filled with young, debauched boys & worthlesse members: The old Speaker laid aside, & Mr. Harlow[1] (an able gent) Chosen: our County ⟨member⟩ Sir R. Onslow had a party for himsel⟨f⟩e: God Almight⟨y⟩ avert the sad fate which threatens all Christendom, especially the protestant part, thro this stupendous Revolution.

Parliament voting to stand by the King in maintaining his Leagues with other princes for the continuance of the peace of Europe:

The Hollanders recognize the new Sp: King:

27 By an Order of the house of Commons, I layed before the Speaker the State of the Accompt, what had ben received, & expended towards the building of the Marine Coll: at Greenwich of which I was Treasurer:

I had newes of the death of Mr. Wye, the Parson of Wotton, a very worthy, & good man, so the next presentation falling to me as Patron, I had some application to me very Early: But I had promised it, to Dr. Bohune, a learned person, & excellent preacher: He had ben my sones Tutor, and lived long in my family: To whom I now gave the presentation.

Mar. 18 I went to Greenewich, saw the progresse made of the new Hospital advancing: Thence to Says-Court, which I had now let

1 Robert Harley, created earl of Oxford 1711.

to the Lord Ca⟨r⟩naryon sonn to the Duke of Leedes, but the Lease was in the name of another:

The Parliament proceeding to purge corrupt members, and the French Kings preparation for war, exceedingly perplexing our Counsels & resolution: Cleare weather but with hard frost, & often haile & snow.

[28 I went to the funerall of my sister ⟨Draper⟩ who was buried at Edmonton in greate state & very . . . by my son & hers.]

Severall persons in greate places demited & left their Offices, both among the Lords Commissioners of the Treasury & chancery of the Exchequer, & others searched after by the H of Commons, absconded:

Dr. D'Avenant displeased the Cleargy (now met in Convocation) for a passage in his booke p: 40: I was very ill most part of the weeke.

The weather began to be more benigne after a long sharp season.

30 There was a fast Indicated for the 4 of Aprill: To beg of God his blessing & Assistance of our Governors & greate Councill of the Nation, for the preserving the publique Peace & Protestant Religion, both in this, & other Christian Nations.

There was a little Dutch Boy, of about 8 or 9 years old, who was by his parents carried about to shew, that had about the Circle or Iris of his Eyes, in one of them these letters *Deus meus*, & in that of his left Iris *Elohim* in the Hebrew Character: how this was impress'd, or don by artifice none could imagine, his parents affirming him to be so born, nor did it at all prejudice his sight, for flinging a small pin on the floore, he immediatly took it up, & seemed to be a lively playing boy: Everybody went to see this unusual phenomena: Physitians & philosophers with greate accuracy examining it, some affirmed it artificial, others tooke it for something almost supernaturall:

⟨April⟩ 4 A solemn fast Indicted for the whole Nation, to avert the consequences of the late Revolution: our Minister in the morning preached on 62 *Psal:* 8, Admonishing [to] a thoro Reformation of life, of faith & relyance on God, with recourse to his Mercy, & firme hope:

The continuance of this sharp & extraordinary dry and parching weather, affects us all generaly: The Duke of Norfolck died of an Apoplexy; & Mr. Tho: Howard of complicated disease, since his being cut of the stone, he was one of the Tellers of the Exchequer: The French every day gives more & more umbrage to the rest of Europe under pretence of his being guardian to the new K of Spaine his Grandson: preparations made with greate application every where to stemm this Inundation:

23d. I returned from Wotton by Greenwich, where my deare Wife being gon, thinking to have the benefit of the aire on the heath, for the recreation of her breath & lungs exceedingly still afflicted of the Cough, fell into a Feaver & Pleurisy, of which she was hardly relieved to my greate sorrow; but leaving her better the next day, businesse hastened me to Lond:

The House of Commons had Impeached 4 of the principal Officers of the Crowne, The Lord Summers, L. Halifax,[1] Lord Jersey, Lord Alford, unseasonably hindering other matters for the securing of the Nation & Government, in this unexpected & danger⟨ous⟩ Revolution.

25 I went to Greenwich, to cary Dr. Sloane to see my wife, & I stayed there 'til the 1 of May:

May 4 The Wind coming about more West & South, brought some small refreshment but not sufficient to the greate want of raine:

Some Kentish Gent: delivering a petition to the house of Comm: were sent to prison:

The Hollanders apprehending the French, now possessed of Flanders, desire 10000 Souldiers of the King, upon an Article of a former Treaty when they should at any time be attaqu'd by an Enemy.

11 It was now so greate a drouth, no raine considerable having fallen in some moneths, that a famine is feared, to all those other Judgements Impending on us, but which God avert:

My daughter Draper was delivered of a Daughter safely, for which God be praised; & my Wife gathering strength apace.

17 After an extraordinary drouth, God sent very plentifull showers, the wind coming West & South:

24 My Son-Drapers child Christened, & nam'd Susanna: My wife a Godmother came to Towne whence her hitherto sicknesse made her absent:

1 The former Charles Montagu, created Baron Halifax 1700.

June 1 Mr. Sands our Minister preached in the morning on 16: Mark: 16:

The Parliament were now intent upon the Tryal of my Lord Summers (late Chancelor), the Marquis of Halifax, [L. Alford] for counselling the K. in the buisinesse of the partition of the Spanish dominions & other misdemeanors; rather running into partys than much minding the danger of Europ by the preparation of the French: we had onely a good & chargeable fleete at sea, whilst the French neglected our preparation, whilst saving that Expense, he was wholy Intent on securing Millan, Flanders, & threatning Holland: The Emp. [forces] now also began to appeare on the confines of Italy: Venice, Portugal, The Pope, & divers other Princes & potentates, standing at Gaze irresolved what part ⟨to⟩ take, so over awed by the French: The Northern Kings of Poland, the Ctzar of Moscovy & Sweden actualy in Warr:

My Wife after a tedious sicknesse, much recovered I thanke God, came from Greenwich, where she had ben some time:

11 The parliament had now settled the Succession on the house of Hanover, of which there was an antient Lady of the Electoral palitine famely living, & the duke her son: with other usefull Accts that now passed: All the world being now big with expectation of action, the Emp: Army approaching Italy, & by this actualy gotten into it, against all mens expectation considering how the French had guarded the Avvenues: Nor were the Hollanders lesse industrious to keepe the French from Insulting on them, which the French every day threatened by the hostile preparations he made in Flanders: &c:

20 Most remarkable has this weeke ben, for the bold contest of the Commons, with the Lords upon the trials of the Impeached Lords: The Commons demanding a Conference for the trial of my L. Summers, which the Lords denyed; but proceeded on the trial of Summers [& acquitted him] without the Commons, who would not appeare because the Lords did it without the previous Conference of both houses which the Commons required: upon which they protested solemnly was contrary to the rules of Justice, & therefore null & voyd: & that it was an Invasion of the liberty of the Subject, & charging the ill Consequences that by this meanes delayed the supplys given by the Commons to protect the Nation from the power of

France: That Act not yet being past: How this will end God onely knows; but it was very unseasonable in this perilous Conjuncture: One ⟨thing⟩ is also observable, That all the Lords that were in greate Offices, entred their protests with the Commons:

Mr. Harcourt, who maneged this matter, & was one of the most powerfull & leading ⟨men⟩ of the Commons, dined with me the day after this contest:

The Emperors forces were gotten over the Mountaines, & into Italy against all the powers & obstacles of the French to stop them:

My Wife going into Surry, The Ax⟨l⟩etree of the Coach firing on Bansted downe, they endeavored to quench it, with the fat of the meate was caried with them and a bottle of sack, to refresh them on the way, no water neere them til they came to Letherhead.

22. Dr Lancaster preached both morning & after noone, upon 1. *Psal.* 1: I was so exceeding drowsy, that I could hardly lift my head up, in the afternoone, the weather & place being very hot:

The Parliament prorogu'd 'til *August*, & breaking up with much animosity betweene the 2 houses: The Lords, without granting a free Conference to the Commons, how the Trials of the Impeached Lords should be maneged, tryed & acquitted them, the Commons refusing to appeare, because the Lords began to try those Impeached peeres, against whom they had least to object, whilst the Commons (whose part it was so to do) insisted to have the L. Summers tried first: Who was most obnoxious: but the other being acquitted, & none appearing of the Commons, as so resolved: the Lord Summers was acquitted also: So as the King passing the mony bill, in a kind & wise speech, [thanking them for the supply & thanking them] recommending their care for the well governing of the nation during his absence, was now preparing for the Low-Countrys:

I went now to congratulate the arival of that worthy & Excellent person my L. Galloway who ⟨was⟩ newly come out of Ireland, where he behaved himselfe so honestly, & to the exceeding satisfaction of the people; was yet removed thence, for being a Frenchman; tho they had not a more worth⟨y⟩ valiant discre⟨e⟩t & trusty person in the 3 kingdoms on whom they could have relyed for his conduct & fitnesse, & one who had so deeply suffered, (as well as the Marquess his Father) by having their Estates confiscated & all they had, because Protestants: so this worthy Gent. design'd to go with his Majestie.—I also visit⟨ed⟩ the Co: of Sunderland, Earle of Kent, [Lord Kingston] E. of Pembroke now precedent of the Counsel, & one of the Lords Justices during the Kings Absence: the B. of Norwich [Sir R Onslow] and some other friends being myself preparing for the Country in few days:

It was now exceeding hot weather:

July   My Lord President, [Earle of Penbrok] Earle of Kent, Lord Cheny, did me the honor of Visits: I tooke leave of my Lord Godolphin one of the Lords Justices: & of my Lord Sommers newly acquitted of his Impeachment.

8 I went with my Family for the rest of the summer to Wotton, dined at my son Drapers at Adscomb.

I made a New Coach & Charriot this yeare:

19 A poore [old] Labourer falling off from the Hay Cart, not any considerable height, but pitching on his head, breaking his Collarbone, & doubtlesse disordering his braine, tho neither quite speechlesse, & let blood but without effect, died, to my exceeding sorrow & trouble, it being in my Haying:

Aug: Very fine summer weather after fine refreshing showers:

The Germans seeme yet to prosper in Italy, & the Sweed against the Poles & Moscovites: K. William is buisy in Holland to put those Countrys into a Condition of defence: [as] the French increase their forces in Flanders &c:

3 The weather changed (from heate not much lesse than in Italy or Spaine for some few days) to wett drip⟨p⟩ing & cold, with intermissions of faire: The Emperors forces penetrat so far into Italy, as after some advantageous encounters to Indanger the Milaneze thro the excellent Conduct of P: Eugenius: whilst also the K of Sweden carrys on his Victory against Poland & Russia, & is gotten Master of Mittau: K. William is still intent to fortify the Low Countrys most exposed to France which Ambassador is recald, as is ours also:

10 Our Doctor being gon to Salisbury to be Installed in the Prebend my Wife & I procured for him, Mr. Duncomb, the Minister of Albury supply⟨ed⟩ the Cure this afternoone with a very pious discourse of relyance on Gods deliverances:

Mr Finch, & Sir R. Onslow came to visite me at Wotton &c:

The weather very unconstant, & wett:

17 Very good harvest weather: & a hotter summer than has ben know⟨n⟩ in many yeares, some dayes little inferior in heate than in Spaine itselfe, but interrupted now & then with milder, agreable to this unconstant Climate: & at a certaine place in Lincolnshire a most dreadfull storme of haile, the stones so big as to kill aboundance of foales & spoile their Corne now ready to be reaped:

24 Dr. Bohun on 12: Rom: ult: which he preached on 27 July:

The Wether continued very seasonable: A pond of mine breaking I lost much fish: the progresse both of the Sweeds & Germans seeme considerably to prosper:

Sept. 7 The death of K. James hapning the 15 of this Moneth N. style after 2 or 3 days Indisposition, put an end to that unhapy Princes troubles, after a shorte & unprosperous Reigne, by his owne indiscreete attempting to bring in Popery, & make himselfe absolute, in imitation of the French, & impatience of the Jesuits & zeale of the Queene, to subduce the Kingdome & Religion to the Roman, which the nation would not indure: but thus was the Church of England againe preserved by Gods wonderfull providence:

There now died The Earle of Bath, after all his contest with the L. Montag⟨u⟩e, upon account of the Duke of Albemarles vast Estate pretended to by a Will, thought to be forged: This suit was worth the Lawyers (as is sayd) 10000 pounds: There died also this Earle of Baths Eldest son, the Lord Langsdowne, who shot himself dead, for what cause is not cleare, a very few days after his father: He was a most hopefull young man, & had so bravely behaved himself against the Turks at the seige of Vienna, that the Emp: made him a Count of the Empire: It was a [false] report that Sir Ed. Seymor [was also dead], a greate man, & long in the parliament, that had ben Speaker often, Tresurer of the Navy, & in many lucrative offices, of a haughty Spirit not thought at all sincere, but head of the party [at any time] prevailing in the Parliament:

14 our Doctor proceeded on his former Text:

The Prince of Wales was now proclaimed, K. of G.B. at Paris & so owned & visited by the F. King, Popes Nuntio & others:

[Upon which the English Ambassador was called home without taking leave or giving any notice to the French King:]

Nothing farther from abroad, but the Fr: Kings prohibiting our Ships to approch his ports, or bringing any merchandize into France, so as a Warr is in a maner begun: The Wind East & faire but very sharp.

29   Michaelmas day I kept Courts Leete & Barron
ad   every day this whole Weeke, in the Mannors & Lordships of *Milton*, *Westgate*, *Abinger*, *padington* & *padington penbrokis* &c.

Octob 4   on the last on Saturday at Wotton; being the first courts I kept since I came to this Estate in Surry: The Steward was Mr. Hervey, a Counsellor, Justice of Peace, & Member of Parliament & neighbour: I gave him 6 ginnys which was a ginny per diem, & Mr. Martin his Cleark 3. ginnys. I have employed him upon many other occasions:

6 It was very fine weather this weeke so sharp at the 2 first days, in which I tooke cold & was feavorishly disposed for a day or two, [12] which kept me from Church in the morning:

My Son in Law Draper with my daughter &c came to visie us:

The winter began very sharply sooner than usualy this moneth, with very bright & calme weather:

26 Oppressed with the Answer to many Letters, this afternoon, I was hindered from going to the publique Evening prayer:

There had ben very sharp winter frosts this Weeke, & some suddain raine at last:

30 We dined at my Co: *Husseys* with Sir R. Onslow & his family.

31 I was this day 81 years old Compleate in tollerable health considering my Great Age: *God* also delivered my Grandson sick at Oxford of the smalpox, for which and many other preservations, continuing my familys health, I rendred (as most bounden) my sincere Accknowledgements:

The weather grew suddainly Cold, hard frosts & snow.

November 2. The King returned from Holland: The frost relenting with seasonable weather: I planted the Elme walke in the back of the Meadow:

9 The parliament dissolved & to meete the 30 of next moneth, pretending that by the universal Addresse to the King, to revenge the Fr: Kings proclaiming this [supposed] P. of Wales &c: that they will give mighty assistance, as much ⟨as⟩ to say, what the present Parliament would not: which yet was held a very honest & good parliament, tho' requiring the tryal of divers Courtiers: But being thus dissolved, whether the next will be better much doubted, in the meane time, the favorit⟨s⟩ escape:

16 Sharp frost returned againe: Like to be much Competition amongst Candidats standing to be chosen members of the newly indicted ⟨parliament⟩ to begin [Jan: 30] my Interest much desired by severall Surry Gent:

28 I came with part of my family to Dover-Streete for the winter, leaving my Wife to come 3 or 4 days after:

30. Mr. Sands the Preacher at our Trinity Chapel, on 1 Mar: 3: The weather wett & mild:

A report of Lieges being given up to the french by the Elector.

December. very greate contention & competition about Elections, I gave my Vote & Interest to Sir R: Onslow, & Mr. Weston:

[The greate Lawyer Sir Barth. Shoor died almost suddenly much regretted.]

30 New Parliament met, chose Mr. Harlow speaker contrary to all Expectation, carying it from the Court-party against Sir T: Litleton.

31 Accompts lustration & thanks to Almighty God for his mercys this year:

$170\frac{1}{2}$ *Jan:* 4: A very rainy dark & uncomfortable weather:

The Lords 2d Addresse to the King, inciting never to desist from endeavouring to bring the F. King to relinquish all he has usurped & so fraudently gotten: by entering into the abused Alliances, with a vote of maintaining 80000 men for sea & land &c: The number of the Confederates being prodigiously greate: & Superior-to that of the Fr: by some hundred Thousands:

The K. of Sweden still so victorious, as threatening to besiege Warsow:

18 Unanimous votes & resolutions in both houses to assist the King joyning with the Confederats &c: Greate storms with lightning in many places which did greate mischief:

At our Chapel a stranger in the morning on 55 Isay: 5. 6: the holy Sacrament was Celebrated, & I communicated: The Lord graciously accept me:

Afternoone another Stranger on 3. *Lament*. 22: The weather was for the season exceeding warme, which made me drowsy: it having be⟨n⟩ a very moist & rany Winter hithertoo:

Continual wet & warme weather:

21 At the R: Society was read & approved the delineation [& description] of the Tables & Veines, by Mr. Cooper the Chirurgeon in order to their being Ingraven &c:

Feb: 8 The Surprize of Cremona, and accidental quitting of it againe, yet with such advantagious Circumstances & taking of Marishall Villroy, by Pr: Eugene: was the greate discourse of this weeke:

18 The season was wonderfully various, sunn, snow, haile, raine, wind in the same, day: and yet, generally hardly any sensible alteration of almost a constant warmth all the Winter hitherto:

The Germans still prosperous in Italy:

March ⟨8⟩ The King having had a fall from his horse as he was hunting, which broke his coller bone, & being himselfe much Indisposed before & Aguish, with his former long Cough & other weaknesse, put into a Feaver, died at Kensington this Sonday morning about 8 a clock, to the extraordinary disturbance of the whole Citty, & I feare, to the Interests of the whole nation, in this dangerous Conjuncture, without Gods Infinite mercy: Matters both abroad, & at home being in so loose a posture, & all Europe ready to breake out into the most dangerous Warr that it ever suffered, & this Nation especially being so unprovided of persons of the Experience, Conduct & Courage, just as we were concluding this Confederacy so long concerted with the Emp: & other Princes, to resist the deluge of the French: How this may concerne the measures hitherto taking: God onely knows: The Parliament sate all this day &, I think all last night, & Queene Ann Proclaym'ed at the usual places, & Ceremonys: These two days have ben warm & bright as Summer, all people else, especialy the Souldiers holding downe their heads: God has some greate thing to do, grant it may be to our good, & his Glory &c.

I carried to the Committe of the house of Comm: appointed to the Examination of the Accompt of what had ben received, & payed by me as Treasurer, for the Building of the new Hospital at Greenwich for Sea-men &c: which amounted to neere 100000 pounds:

11 There was orders published in print, after what manner the publique Mourning for the King was expected to be, as to the Clothes of persons of quality: In the meanetime, there seemed to be no sort of alteration, or Concerne in the people, upon the Kings death but all things pass't without any notice, as if he had still ben alive: Onely the Shopkeepers, who had provided store of Silke & other modish things, complained of the deadnesse of Trade they feared would insue: The Queene was proclaymed with the usual Ceremonies, the greate men, Lord Mayor & Aldermen &c: crouding to Kisse the Q: hands & felicitate her Accession to the Crown: The Wind not favoring, tho the weather like summer, no Intelligence from abroad.

22 Exceeding sharp weather: The Queene prescribed how all rankes should have their mourning clothes, for the death of the late King.

The states of Holland &c resolve to adhere to the late Kings confederation with the rest of the Imperial & German princes, in prosecution of their defence of the libertys of Europe against the French: E. of Malborow made Generalissimo & Knight of the Garte⟨r⟩: Ambassador Ext: to Holland: & they send Embassador hither to confirme the alliance &c.

ACCESSION OF ANNE – THE RENEWAL OF WAR – MARLBOROUGH'S VICTORIES – DEATH OF EVELYN
(1702–1706)

29 A NEW PROCLAMATION read in the churches against Immorality.

A proclamation concerning the Queens Coronation, to be on 23 of Aprill, to give notice to such as held Estates or offices for certaine Services then to be performed &c:

Aprill: 7 I dined with my L: Admiral Earle of Penbroke, gave him my Accompt of the Greenwich Hospital &c:

⟨9⟩ I being surprized with a Vertiginous Indisposition; I tooke a Vomite & afterward letting Blood, found much reliefe, thro Gods greate mercy:

It was a very rainy weeke, the wind altering to the S: W:

12 This morning, after a very tedious languishing, departed this life my Bro: in Law *Glanvill*, leaving a Son by my sister, & 2 Grand daughters: our Relation & friendship had ben long & greate, but much interupted by a displeasure he tooke both at me & my Wife, the Cause of which I could never learn or Imagin, unlesse my not concurring with him, as to his opinion of the Trinity: I hope yet he died in Charity & in a better persuasion: He was a man of Excellent parts. I pray God of his Infinite goodnesse pardon whatever pass'd between us during the late Settlement in Surry: *Et Requiescat in Pace:*

This night is buried the Body of the Late King William the IIId in Westminster Abbey.

This night died my B. in Law Glanvill after a tedious sicknesse: in the 84th yeare of his Age; & Willed his Body to be wrapt in Leade, and carried downe to Greenewich, where it was put on board in a yaght, and Buried in the Sea, between Dover & Calais about Godwin-Sands: which was don the Tuesday or Wednesday after, which made much discourse; he having no relation at all to the Sea. He was a Gent. of an Antient family in Devonshire, Married my Sister Jane, who left one Son: & by his prudent parcimony much improved his fortune: Was a greate friend where he tooke a fancy, & as greate an Enemy when he tooke displeasure: Subject to greate passions, positive: well spoken, of good natural parts; of a governing Spirit where he was intimate, Apt to take Exception, not easily reconciled, of greate Authority with my Bro: In person handsome, very Temperat: In his Judgement inclining to Socinianisme, upon which point we differing, he who till of late had much obliged me, on a suddaine withdrew his kindnesse to my greate prejudice. He died one of the   of the Alienation Office, & might have ben an extraordinary man, had he cultivated his parts:

Keyserwert beseiged by the Confederats begins the Warr abroad:

The exceeding sharp Eastern Wind made this Moneth hitherto very uncomfortable:

[21 I went to Greenewich to meete the Committe of Parliament, who were to make report of whatever the⟨y⟩ found the
state of the fabrique in: & which was advanced beyond their
Expectation]

23 Was Queene Ann Crowned with all possible magnificence
& Pomp, the AB of York preaching on   It was a bright
day, and every body much pleased & satisfied.

26 My Wife going to Wotton for a few days, to se what the
Workemen had don in repairing the house not yet finish'd: &
my steward came up with his Accompt I adjusted all the particulars, finding them very faire: & his Trust honestly
m⟨anaged⟩, amounting to 1900 pounds.

May not having the benefit of natural evacuation for severall days, I was very ill, & feavorish, but by Gods mercy
relieved, I began to be more at Ease, [3] so as I was able to go
to Church this After noone, when a young man preached on
12. Heb: 14.

The Report of the Comitty sent downe to Greenewich, to
Inspect how the Hospitall was advanc't & managed, together
with all the Accounts &c, was now delivered into the house of
Commons, to their greate Satisfaction:

My Lord Godolphin was made Lord High Treasurer of
England:

[6 I went to Congratulate him.]

31 This day was read a new prayer for a blessing of Successe to
our Armys, [War] being now proclaymed for the Assistance of
the Confederats against France & a solemn ⟨fast⟩ & Day of
humiliation indicted thro the whole Nation on the 10th of the
next month.

The Counter Scarp of Kyeserswert taken with the losse of
many Officers, the Earle of Huntington dangerously wounded:
Pr: Eugene in Italy in greate straits, overpowered by the numerous French, the Emperor failing to send supplys: The Swed⟨ish⟩
King takes Warsaw: Bergen Burnt in Norway, Upsall in
Sweden, the *Zars* of Moscovy Palace burnt, whether by accident
or Incendiarys not known.

June 10 We had severall most refreshing showers all this
Weeke: Little intelligence from abroad, by reason of Contrary
Winds: but by a sad & tragical accident & the Effect of
destr⟨action⟩, Mr. Fra: Godolphin, a Relation of my Lord
Treasurer, cut his own Throate, to the greate affliction of that

worthy family there being no known Cause of it, The Gent: being very rich; by an Estate left him of his bro [Ambassador] in Spaine: he was lately Governor of the Ilands of Silly: [Tis in the meane time sad to Consider how many of this Nation have murdered themselves of late year⟨s⟩ 15 or 16 in my remembrance.]

15 I dined at Lambeth at the Bishop of Cant: 17. I went to Clappham to visit Mr. Pepys &c.

19 Being elected a Member of the Society lately Incorporated for the Propagation of the Gospel in foreine parts, I subscribed 10 pounds per Annum towards the Carying it on: The A: Bishop of Cant: being absent, The L. Bishop of Lond. was [vice] President: when we agreed that every Missioner should besides the 20 pounds to set the person forth, should have out of the stock of the Corporation 50 pounds per Annum: til his Settlement there was worth 100 pounds per Annum: & [at] this meeting we sent a Young Divine to go to New Yorke.

15 I went to Lambeth & din'd with the Arch-Bishop, where were a greate many Divines amongst the rest the New-made Bishop of Carlisle Mr. N⟨i⟩cholson my worthy & learned Correspondent [here is a mistake of the days for I dined at Lambeth the 15th & at Mr Pepys the 18]

18 I went to Visite Mr. Pepys at Clapham.

27 I went to Wotton with my Family for the rest of the Summer, whether came my Son-in law Draper with his family to stay with us, his house at Adscome being New building, so as my family was now above 30.

July 5 The Doctor preached on 20 Acts: 21.

In the Afternoon Catechizing.

Uncertaine Weather, our Fleete was yet got thro the narrow: little newes from the Armys abroad, the K. of the Romans not yet got to the Army on the Rhyne, but the seige of Landau gos ⟨on⟩: Pr: Eugene is on the defensive in Italy, still endeavouring to blo⟨c⟩k up Mantua: The K. of Swed⟨en⟩ persists in Marching to Cracovia.

12 Our Doctor adds little to his former discourse of Faith, &c.

Very seasonable Hay-harvest Weather: Greate silence of newes from abroad, Our Fleete, forc't by Contrary winds to put in at Tor Bay, & in danger of loosing any opportunity of doing any Exploit on the Enemy, the yeare so far advanct:

19: The Weather excessively hot: & our Fleete at last gotten cleere of Silly:

26 Exceeding dry & hot weather. Parliament Members chosen in all Countys, most of Church of England principles: Divers of the peevish party, turn'd out of the Lieutenancy of the Citty:—In Surrey the Contest being greate for Knights of the Sheere, Tho Sir R. Onslow carried it for himselfe not without hazard, he could not hinder this ⟨an⟩tagonist Mr. Waysall from carying it against Mr. Weston:

Aug: 2. Our Doctor on 16 Luke ult:

In the Afternoon Catechism, he proceeded to assert the Divinity of Christ, against the late Arians, who being pinch'd by their praying to Christ, & yet deneying him God-head, & so Idolater, there is now a new sect of them, that totaly, leave off praying to him at all:

Some gentle showers, otherwise Temperate: *Landau* still beseiged, The K. of the Romans come to the Confederat Armys on the Rhyne: The pr: Eugene some losse, overpowered by the French: Our flete with a faire gale gotten past the Cape of Finister.

⟨9⟩ The Weather very wett & threatning the backward Harvest of Wheate: no tidings from our Fleete, & little very promising from other parts: Onely a very hopefull prospect of the future session of parliament, by more worthy Members carrying the Votes than in many Parliaments hitherto, which I pray God to prosper.

16 The Weather proving still faire & seasonable we have had an excellent Ha⟨r⟩vest, all mine brough⟨t⟩-in without any interruption, for which God be blessed, but especialy for the Victory ⟨of⟩ Pr: Eugenie of Savoy, over the French & Spanish in Italy, which is very considerable, the particular wheroff we shall have by the next: As also of the Successe of our Navy, & the Army of our Allys in Germany, &c of which there is greate probability of good successe:

23 Confirmation of Pr: Eugenes Victory killing above 7000 French & Span: lost 2000: uncertainty of the Fleete: Landaus seige gos on with successe:

Weather wonderfull Calm & seasonable.

30 The Queene gon to the Bath, was feasted at Oxford:

The weather began to chang into frequent & gentle seasonable Showers.

Prince Eugens Victory confirm'd: *Venlo* beseiged by the Confederates:

Our Queene gon to the Bath: [Landau taken by the Confederates.]

September 6. The weather very changable & towards the Equinoxus, very showery, & stormy: [Kaisarsworth surrendered to the Confederats.]

We had newes of our Fleetes sailing by Portugal, who supplyed them with what they pleased, & after landing neere Cales, tooke divers forts & harbours where were many Spanish & French ships: The Duke of Ormond publishing a Declaration of the Queenes sending him, to Vindicate & deliver the Spanish Monarchy from the insolent pretence of the French, & as Confederate with the rest of Europe, to assist the house of Austria & Emperor, as lawfull heirs: & not to usurp any thing, but to protect & receive, such loyal Spanyards as should declare for the Emp: & not upon any particular designes on their Country, but to free them from the French unjust usurpation: So as it is believed Our Fleete would be received at Cales &c:

My Gr:son returned from his Western Journey, in health, for which I thank Almighty God.

13 Our Doctor preached on 16 Luke ult; the very same he had preached not long before:—The Afternoon was so very Wett & stormy, that we did not go to Evening prayer at Church:

The Queene in her Journey to Bath, most magnificently entertained at Oxford, & all the Towns she went thro:

The Duke of Bavarias Surprizing of *Ulme* an Imperial Citty greatly exasperating the German Princes:

Weather uncertaine with raine & wind:

⟨20⟩ The Confederate forces march from *Venlo* which they tooke, to invest *Reurmonde*.

Aboundance of ships from the East Indies, & West, wher St. Christopher is taken &c, are come into the River, besides aboundance of Prizes, such as has not ben known in any Kings Reign since Q. Eliz: The Nation universaly pleased.

⟨27⟩ Being much indisposed, I did not go to church til the Afternoone:

Octob: Reurmond surrendered to the Confederats:

Doubtfull newes concerning taking of Cales: One Galion richly laden came into the Port of St. Luckar in Spaine: The Earle of Sunderland died:

4. Uncertaine Reports of some disadvantage hapning to our Expedition to Cales, & of the Plate flete being arived which we hope better of:

Prodigious Thunder Raine & lightning, hapning the beginning of this Weeke at London & the invirons, not reaching but very gently neere this place:

⟨11⟩ Nothing occurrs this Weeke but the taking of Liège by the Confederats: & the Queens return from Bath: &c.

18 Cleare weather & sharp frosts 'til the end of the weeke, Misty: no publique affairs but the meeting of the Parliament, & the Queens Speech; &c.

25 The Successe of our Armes with the Confederats, together with the newes of the Exploits of our Fleete in full recompence of our Miscarriage at Cales is so considerable, That I forbeare to describe it, till the particulars are published, which is hourely expected here in the Country, having at present sufficient assurance that it is true & greate, by the noise of the Tour Gunns, & other reports, for which God Almighty be praised:

The Parliament is met with wonderfull satisfaction & Kindnesse betweene it & the Royal Court at St. James:

My Lord Kent, a Relation to our Family is Dead, as also a sister of the E. of Kingston, wife to my L. Cheny:

31. Arived now to the 82d yeare of my Age, [Having read over all that past since this day twelve-month in these notes] with my Soule rendring my most solemne Thanks to the Lord, Humbly Imploring the pardon of my past life, sinns, & particularly of the Incursions, & frailtys &c not yet fully subdued; but that by the Assistance of his Grace I may yet be more than conqueror, making new Resolutions, & imploring that he will continue his blessed Assistance, & prepare me for my B: Saviours Comming, that I may obtaine a Comfortable Departure, after so long a terme as has ben hitherto indulged me: Finding by many Infirmitys this yeare (especialy nephritic pains) that I much decline: And yet of his infinite mercy retaining my Intellectuals, & senses in greate measure above most of my Greate Age: I have this yeare, much repaired the mansion house, & severall Tennants, payed some parte of my debts & Ingagements: My Wife

Children & Family in Health, for all which I most earnestly beseech Almighty God to accept of these my Accknowledgements, & that if it be his holy will to Continue me yet longer, that it may be to the praise of his infinite Grace, & Salvation of my Soule Amen:

November 1. There was now a full account of the particulars of the Successe of both our Land forces with the Confederates, our taking of so many fortifyed Townes & Territorys which the French had usurpt in Flanders & neerest parts of Germany, with the hapy escape of my L: Marborow our Generall, surprized by a party, as he was returning to Holland after this Winter Campagne: But of the Duke of Ormond (coming from Cales) taking sinking & destroying a greate part of the Spanish Plate-Fleete at Vigo, by a very bold & gallant attacking them in that Harbour to the number of 38 or 40 Ships, Gallions, Men of Warr & all their Equipage & of neer 1000 Cannon, plate & rich Lading &c, for which a day of publique Thanksgiving is appointed thro the whole nation: So as this summers Actions by these & the vast number of prizes (with little losse) & unwonted agreements of the Parliament, now met & sitting, such a concurence of Blessings & hope of Gods future favour, has not ben known in 100 yeares.

The forces also in Italy & on the Rhine prosperous beyond Expectation. Add to these the rich & numerous Returne of our Ships from the E. Indys & all other places.

8 There being so very slender a Congregation (not above 2 or 3) besides my Family the sermon prepared for the 5 of this moneth was put off to the Sonday: When the Doctor preached a very learned Sermon 1. Cor: 10: 7 concerning the Superstition of the Papists & the impossibility of our union with them, whilst they continued their Errors, shewing that they were the Schismatics: with an account of their bloody Conspiracys.

The weather now began to be Tempestuous.

The Duke of Ormonde now returned, with part of the ships & Galions, & every day more Coming home from the Action & successe at Vigo, & other prizes, greate Joy & satisfaction was over all the nation & publique Thanksgivings.

My kindsman Jo: Evelyn of Nutfeld a young & very hopefull young Gent: & member of parliament, having come to see me at

Wotton about 15 days past, died of the Small-pox at Lond: to my greate Sorrow, He left a Bro: a Commander in the Army in Flanders, who succeeds him in a faire Estate:

15 I was Christened this day of the moneth Anno 1620.

27 [By Gods goodnesse] After much wet, snow, cold & winterly weather, I had a faire journey from Woton with part of my family, my Wife & Grandson left there to come after:

There was greate rejoicing for the wonderfull prosperity of our forces by Sea and Land: Lord Marlborow return'd, Sir G: Rooke made a privy Counsellor, of all which the Bishop of Excester has handsomly mentioned in a very honest sermon preached at Paules, before the Queene & both houses; who were wonderfully Huzzas in their passage & most splendidly entertained in the Citty: & all this in so prosperous a Condition, that there has not ben so greate an Union in Parliament, Court, & people in memory of men of this nation, which God in mercy make us thankfull for & Continue—But to allay this in some sort, divers noble men & persons of quality, have ben sudenly taken away by Apoplexes, young, & old & of my Relations the Earle of Kent & two more of that family: also a grandson of the Earle of Rochester, The Earle of Derby: &c:

December. The Expectation now is what Effects we may find, as to the Treasure brought from Vigo, upon the breaking Bulke of the Spanish Gallion brought into the River, which being in ward & made up after an extraordinary manner in the holde was not begun to be opened till the 5t of this moneth, before 2 of the privy Council, 2 of the chiefe magistrats of the Citty, & Lord Treasurer: what therefore the List of the Summs is dos not yet appeare in publique:

The Weather is perfectly winterly, frost, snow, raine interchangeably:

13 I was so Indispos'd that I could not go to Church 'til the Afternoon when preached a stranger on ⟨xvii⟩ Act: 18.

There had ben high & reprochfull words betweene the Duke of Leedes & L. Halifax (Mountague) which product a Challenge of the Marquis of Carmarthen: but was speedily stopt by the peers:

Much Indisposition of health has detained me from going abroad 'til now: when on Christmas day, I went to our Chapell:

30 After: ⟨th⟩e excesse of honors conferred by the Queene on the E. of Marborow, to make him a knight of the Garter, & Duke for the successe of but one Campagne, ⟨that⟩ he should desire 5000 pounds a yeare out of the Post-office to be settled on him was by the parliament thought a bold & unadvised request, who had besides his owne considerable Estate, above 30000 pounds per Ann in places & Employments, with 50000 pounds at Interest: His Wife also (whose originall & his every body knew, & by what merit become such favorite, for his sister was a Miss to K. James the 2d when Duke of York, his Father but a cleark of the Green-Cloth, ingrossing all that stirred & was profitable at Court: But thus they married their daughter 1 to the Sonn of my L. Tress: Godolphin, another to the E. of Sunderland, 3. to the E. of Bridge-Water:) Thus suddainly rising was taken notice of & displeased those who had him til now in greate esteeme: He is indeed a very handsom proper well spoken, & affable person, & supplys his want of acquired knowledge by keeping good Company: In the meane time Ambition & love of riches has no End:

1703: Jan: 3 Having ben very much discomposed in my health, I was not able to go to our Chapell, till the 6t when the Lecturer on 2 Luke 11:

The Parliament was now upon Articles with the Dutch, that they should breake off all Commerce with France:

Newes of V: Ad: Benbos conflict with a squadron of the French in the West-Indies, in which he was wounded, yet did gallantly behave himselfe, & was sure of an extraordinary successe & prize, had not 4 of his Men of War, stood Spectators without comming to his assistance: for which 2 of their Commanders were tryed & executed by a Councell of Warr, a 3d condemned to perpetual Imprisonment, losse of pay & ⟨Incapacity⟩, the 4th died:

Sir R. Onslow & Mr. Oglethorp upon some words passing at a Comite, fought, Mr. Oglethorp was disarmed: he is the son of the late Sir Theophilus Oglethorp who has an Estate & seate about Godalming, a pretty young Gent: &c:

10: In the Morning I was Indisposed:

By reason of my greate paine in my Kidneys charged with gravell I could not stirr out:

The Parliament gave 100000 pounds per annum to Pr: George during his life: The Bill against occasional Conformity lost by one Vote:

Very warme, wett dull unconstant weather:

24 The weather strangly uncertaine:

The Parliament about the publique Accompts, now ready to rise: The French ⟨take⟩ one of our men of Warr transporting Recruits for Flanders: Corne & Provisions on the sudaine so cheape that farmers are unable to pay their rents: &c.

31 I was exceedingly drowsy, newly freed from my greate paine:

Feb [2 Mr. Adams preached his 2d Boylean lecture at Paules &c which I heard:]

I was some part of this Weeke very ill: [6] A grand Ball and much bravery, on the Queenes Birthday:

The Bishop of Lincolns wife, a melancholy woman flung her self out of a Window & died:

A famous Cause at the Kings bench twixt Mr. Fenwick & his Wife, which went for him, with a greate Estate:

10 Greate heates in the Parliament about Accompts, shewing that all the Taxes & Impositions appeared to have ben faithfully brought into the Chequer out of the Countys, & petitioning the Queene she would let them know what was become of them, & how there came to be a deficiency upon accurate Inspection:

Newes of the Confederate losses in Conflicts with the forces of Bavaria &c.

Very mild wet weather: I visited my L. of Cant, Bishop of Norwich, Worcester, & other persons of quality &c:

14 A Chaplain of my Lord Guilfords on 15 Luke 20 &c.

The severe frost broke: I sent store of Fruit Trees to Wotton:

The Lords & Commons differ concerning bringing persons in office to Accompt.

The K. of Portugal has received so greate returne of Treasure from Brazeele that we feare he will either stand newter or joyne in the Interest of France.

28 The duke of Marborow after all his prosperity riches & glory; lost his onely son, who died at Cambridge of the small pox, to the unexpressable sorrow of that family:

The Parliament now prorogued till: 23 Ap⟨ri⟩ll:

The weather raine, snow, haile, frost, cold . . . winds, so unseasonable a season as hardly here known:

Besides many greate Townes thrown-down in Italy by Earth-quake, At Rome not onely the remainder of the Amph⟨ithe⟩ater of Vespasian, but St. Peters church it selfe shaken, which made such a Consternation, that many forsook their houses & set up Tents in the fild &c.

A famous young woman, an Italian, was hired by our Com-medians to sing on the stage, during so many plays, for which they gave her 500 pounds: which part (which was her voice alone at the end of 3 Scenes) she performed with such modesty, & grace above all by her skill, as there was never any (of many Eunichs & others) did with their Voice, ever anything compar-able to her, she was to go hence to the Court of the K: of Prussia, & I believe carryed with her out of this vaine nation above 1000 pounds, every body coveting to heare her at their privat houses, especialy the noble men:

Upon the suddaine Calme, warme & delicate Weather:

The Earle of Marborow bur⟨y⟩ing his son in King's Coll: Chapell in Camb: where he died; tooke shiping a few days after for the Low Countrys to Command as generall:

March ⟨8th⟩ going out to Brompton parke to take the aire after my late Indisposition In walking in one of the Alleys, I hapned to stumble on a short stake left in the ground, which breaking my shin, kept me ⟨in⟩ greate paine, as yet it dos, remaining unhealed: & denying me to go to church this [14] being the 5t Sonday in Lent, to my grate sorrow: I beseech God to be mercifull to & heale me:

Many worthy persons came to visite me, Mr. Finch now new made Lord Gernsey:

Aprill: 11 I came downe out of my Confinement in my Bed & Chamber my leg being in a faire way of cure: It was still most gentle & seasonable weather: There was no Considerable news either from abroad [or at home.]

16 Came the Earle of Pembrock president of the Counsell to visite me.

⟨We⟩ had no good news from abroad or from the Confed-erats.

St. James Towne in Jamaica utterly burnt & destroyed by a casual fire.

May 2. In the morning I went to my L. Treasurers to recomend a Chaplaine &c. Thence to our Chapell where a young preacher [on 57 Isaiah 21] made a description of the unexpressible misery of persisting sinners, in their having no peace in this life, or that to come; both which he represented in that horror & Terror to come, with Exhortation to others, to avoide presumptuous sinns &c, to the Comfort of their lives & deaths & Eternal Blisse: ô that I had well considered this Text:

The past weeke was very Wett: newes of the Bavarians being hindred from Joyning the French, but the event of it doubtfull:

14 We came safe with our Family from Dover street to Wotton, ferying over by Lambeth, where I went to talke with my L. of Cant concerning suffrage for a Chaplaine of the Bishop of Norwich to be the next Lecturer for Mr. Boyles sermons.

I call'd in also at Clappham to visite Mr. Pepys now ⟨l⟩anguishing with small hope of recovery which much affected me.

16. The Usher of the free-Schole of Gilford preached an honest Instructive ⟨sermon⟩ Text 14 *John* 16. The H Communion followed at which most of my Family received: But thro divers Impertinences for the unpacking of our Goods, brought from Lond in the Wagon, I was not so prepared as I ought, which I pray God to pardon: The season was lovely, faire & temperat: But my self much Indisposed.

A greate part of this Weeke from hot, to cooler & showry weather.

26 This ⟨day⟩ dyed Mr. Sam: Pepys, a very worthy, Industrious & curious person, none in England exceeding him in the Knowledge of the Navy, in which he had passed thro all the most Considerable Offices, Clerk of the Acts, & Secretary to the Admiralty, all which he performed with greate Integrity: when K: James the 2d went out of England he layed down his Office, & would serve no more: But withdrawing himselfe from all publique Affairs, lived at Clapham with his partner (formerly his Cleark) Mr. Hewer, in a very noble House & sweete place, where he injoyed the fruit of his labours in g⟨r⟩eate prosperity, was universaly beloved, Hospitable, Generous, Learned in many things, skill'd in Musick, a very greate Cherisher of Learned men, of whom he had the Conversation. His Library & other Collections of Curiositys was one of the most Considerable;

The models of Ships especialy &c. Beside what he boldly published of an Account of the Navy, as he found & left it, He had
for divers years under his hand the History of the Navy, or,
Navalia (as he call'd it) but how far advancd & what will follow
of his, is left I suppose to his sisters son Mr. Jackson, a young
Gent: whom his Unkle had educated in all sorts of usefull learning, Travell abroad, returning with extraordinary Accomplishments, & worth to be his Heire: Mr: Pepys had ben for neere 40
years, so my particular Friend, that he now sent me Compleat
Mourning: desiring me to be one to hold up the Pall, at his magnificent Obsequies; but my present Indisposition, hindred me
from doing him this last Office:

The K. of Portugal has at last entred into the Confederacy
against France, Offensive & Defensive: The Weather was so
very Wett, as threatned greate losse to Farmers: &c:

26 Was kept a publique Fast. To implore Gods Mercy, & to
Assist the Confederate Armys, &c: A young person (designed
our Doctors Curate) preaching very well on

June The weather wet & cold, ill for Grasse & Haying: no
newes from abroade.

13 The raines have ben so greate, continual, & unseasonable,
as have hardly ben known in the memory of any alive; The
weather now neere Midsomer cold & so Wet, as threatens a
famine, after our murmuring at the Cheapnesse of Corne.
Change of weather about the Eclipse of the Moone, 18th of the
moneth:

July 11 I had this weeke a severe fit or two of a quartan Ague,
the 2d so sharp, as I was neere Expiring, but it ended in greate
sweats, & suddaine breaking-out of my face, with a sore Eye:
⟨But⟩ by Gods mercy, I was so well recovered, that a few days
after, I adventured to go [in Coach] as far as Adscome, 16 miles
from Wotton, to see my Son-in Laws new house, the Outsides
to the Covering being so excellent Brickwork, Based with Portland stone with the Pillasters, Windows & Contrivement
within, that I pronounce it, in all the points of good & solid
Architecture, to be one of the very best Gent: Houses in all
Surry, when finished, to which God give a Blessing: [17]
I returned that after noone to Wotton againe, with my Wife, &
Gr Children, though very weary.

18 My late severe Conflict, lasting me on Saturday the ⟨10th⟩ past, that I could not go to Church the next day: When the Doctor preached on 27 Pro. 23 Concerning the pride & Luxury of Apparell, which could be applyed to none save my Wife & Daughter, there being none in all the Parish else, but meane people, who [had no] more than sufficient to cloth them meanely enough &c upon which I told the Doctor that I conceived the sermon had ben more proper to St. James's or some other of the Theatrical Churches in Lond, where the Ladys & Women were so richly & wantonly dressed & full of Jewells: But this reproofe was taken so very ill of the Doctor, that falling into a very furious passion, he hardly spake to me of some days, but preach'd the very same Sermon this day: which was indeed very learned, & fit for a Gallant Congregation; but by no meanes with our poore Country people: Both my Wife & Children having no sort of habits ⟨but⟩ what was Universaly worne by the ordinary persons of their Condition; besides the sobriety & regularity of my owne domestick⟨s⟩: He now began to make a shuffling apology for his vehement discourse, that he meant it as one of the national sinns, ⟨we⟩ were to aske God pardon for & reforme, predicting great Judgements otherwise to succeede it: But all this while sayed not a Word of the pride of the Clergy, their long powdered Perruks, silke Casso⟨c⟩ks, Covetousnesse, suppression of those passions they themselves preach against: In the Afternoone he Catechized very well, concerning the duty of Parents &c:

The Season very warme & promising a plentyfull harvest:

Little newes of any Exploits of the Armys, the French in Flanders avoyding Engagements tho' provoked by the force of the Confederats.

25 There hapend the last weeke of this moneth so great & long continual Raine, as had not ben know⟨n⟩ of late years, & the last day of it & the Sunday following 1. Aug: Thunder lightning & raine, which hindered me from Morning Service &c at Church:

1 *Aug*. Nothing extraordinary this weeke, The wea⟨t⟩her pretty seasonable:

One of the younger Sonns of house of Hanover drowned:

10 I let out 4 ounces of Blood, which was perhaps too much at my greate Age, to try if it would help me, hithertoo

tormented with the Hæmerrhoids: it was very faulty blood, much serum, & I had that Evening no reliefe, but at night a kind of Aguish fit: The next day easier & on the next Sonday, I was able to go to Evening prayer: God be praised:

12 The new Commission for the proceeding in the R. Hospital at Greenwich was now sealed & open'd [at Windsor] at which was my Son Draper present, to whom I resign'd my office of Treasurer, During which from Anno 1696: was expended in Building &c: 89364: 14: 8:¼.

Sep: 5 The Doctor preached on 5 Job: 6.

The weather was very serene, sharp, & begining to freeze betime:

12 Nothing of Consequence at home this Weeke in Engl: The Weather from cold & sharp, turning to hot, storms, Thunder, lightning, yet seasonable enough:

From abroad the French taking B⟨r⟩izach: Commosions in Hungary & Turkey, but what most calamitous, the turning so many Thousands out of the principality ⟨of⟩ Orang, who lost their Estates, because of their Religion, & are received at Geneva, & the Swiss Cantons, though promised liberty to sell their Estates, by the Fr: King, whom they dare not Trust, after so unfaithfull a prince.

I was this week againe surprized with a 2d fit of most severe Ague, which so weakn'd me that I dared not stir-out to church: The Lord be gracious to me.

Octob. 3 It pleased God so far to restore me from my sharp Indisposition, after severall Weekes, that I could not go to Church: I went this Day to praise God for his mercy: The School-master of Gilford preached a very proper sermon on those Texts in 1 Corinth 11 Cap: 27. 28. 29.

The news from abroad was chiefly about the setting out of the K. of Spaine from Vienna to take shiping in Holland & transport him thither: The *Scevenies* grow exceedingly numerous: The Janizaries have deposed the Gr: Signor & set up his Bro: A greate Rising in Hung⟨a⟩ry: Gen: Stirumm has had the worst ⟨in⟩ a Conflict with the French, 1000 slaine, & Cannon & Bagage all taken: The Duke of Malbrough succeeds in his seiges: nothing looking toward peace twixt Sweden & Poland: The Scots discontented, which I pray God may be remedied, fomented doubtlesse by French Money, as are all the differences in Christendom.

24 The report of the breach of France & the D. of Savoy is confirmed, & of very greate Consequence: The Arch-Duke now as K of Spaine is just Imbarking for Portsmouth, w⟨h⟩ere a greate Convoy atends to cary him to Portugal:

31 The Scholemast⟨er⟩ of Gilford preached on 1. *Rom:* 20 against Atheisme, which wickednesse began to prevaile exceedingly in England &c.

This day being the Anniversary of my Birth, & 83 year of my Age, upon which examining what concerned me more particularly the past year, with the greate mercys of God preserving me & in some measure making my Infirmitys tollerable, I gave God most humble & hearty thanks, beseeching him to confirme to me the pardon of my sinns past, & to prepare me for a better life, by the vertue of his Grace & mercy for the sake of my B: Saviour:

The Weather was very mild & for most part serene:

November 7 Changeable Weather: [8] I had a sharp fit of an Ague againe this Evening, & tollerably at Ease otherways the rest of the Week, for which God be praised, preserving me from falling into the fire: The Parliament now met:

21 The wet & uncomfortable weather staying us from Church this Morning, our Doctor Officiated in my Family, at which were present above 20 Domesticks: upon: 1. Cor: 15-55. 56 On which he made an excellent discourse of the vanitys of this World, uncertaintys of life, & the unexpressible satisfaction & hapynesse of an holy life, & terrour of Judgement to the vicious & Impenitent, with pertinent Inferences, to prepare us for death & a future state: I gave him Thanks for his paines, and told him I tooke it kindly, as my Funerall Sermon:

26 The dismall Effects of the Hurecan & Tempest of Wind, raine & lightning thro all the nation, especial⟨y⟩ London, many houses demolished, many people killed: [27] & as to my owne losse, the subversion of Woods & Timber both left for Ornament, and Valuable materiall thro my whole Estate, & about my house, the Woods crowning the Garden Mount, & growing along the Park meadow; the damage to my owne dwelling, & Tennants farmes & Outhouses, is most Tragicall:

not to be paralleled with any thing hapning in our Age ⟨or⟩ in any history almost, I am not able to describe, but submitt to the Almight⟨y⟩ pleasure of God, with accknowledgement of his Justice for our National sinns, & my owne, who yet have not suffered as I deserved to: Every moment like Jobs Messengers, bring⟨s⟩ the sad Tidings of this universal Judgement: [See the History of this Storme.]

The Confederats forced to deliver that Important Town of Landaw, & losse ⟨of⟩ a Battell, by the too late Conjunction of the German forces meeting to have raised the Siege, as well as losses in Italy & other places, has given the French cause of Triumphe in shutting up this Campagnia, whilst the rest of the summer we had greater Advantage of him: The [new] K of Spaine, attempting to go on board the fleete designed for Portugal, was repelled to shore; since it had ben impossible to have sailed, We hourly dread to he⟨a⟩re what has happened at sea during this Tempest, & even in our very harbours.

The H of Commons balancing about their Votes concerning the Occasional Communicants:

28 The apprehension of catching cold that might stop the bleeding of my hæmeroids, til now exceedingly afflicting me, I was advise⟨d⟩ not to expose my selfe to the aire this Sunday being the first of Advent: But God I hope accepts of my Endeavour &c.

December 7 I remov'd with my family to Dover streete, saw the lamentable destruction of Houses & Trees thro all the Journey: & observed it had least injured those trees &c which grew in plaine exposed & perflatil grounds & places; but did most execution where it was pent in by the Villages & among the bottoms of hills:

I thank God I found all well at my house in Lond: But both house, Trees, Garden &c at Says-Court suffered very much:

News of sad losses of our Men of Warr by sea, & thousands of people &c: no newes yet from abroad.

12 The Scotts suspected of plotting, & Intelligence with France:

The Emperor in ill Condition not onely by the French taking Norimb⟨u⟩rg, but by the Rebellion in Hung⟨a⟩ry, where by his Oppressing the Protestants & Ragotski, they have become so strong & formidable, & take many strong Towns &c:

31 I made up my Accompts: payed wages, gave Rewards & Newyears-gift⟨s⟩ according to Custome &c.

We had newes of the K: of Spaine landing at Portsmouth & coming to Winsor.

170¾ Jan: 1 Rendring God prays for all his mercys & preservations of the yeare past, delivered & restor'd as I was, after many dangers, & Indispositions of Body: on the 2d being Sonday: Morning: Mr. Sandys on 2 *Ephes:* 10 [5 Ephes: 1. 2.]

The season was so very dark & Clowdy (as it had ben for many days) that the Doctor was f⟨a⟩ine to breake off his discourse abruptly, preaching out of his written notes: as they now generaly did all over England & not as formerly, (& [as] yet in all other Countrys) they preach'd Memoriter, which whether so well, I leave to others to Judge: Reading much hindring Action, which we in English pulpits are defective in: In the meane time written sermons being more studyed & methodical, have likewise greate advantages:

The Duke of Marlbery returned to Holland to concert matters with the States: The King of Spaine, landing at Portsmouth, came to Windsor where he was magnificently received by the Queen: & behav'd himself so nobly as every body was taken with his gracefull deportmen⟨t⟩, after 2 days (having presented the greate Ladys & others with very valuable Jewells) he went back to Portsmouth & immediately Imbark⟨ed⟩ for Spain with our Naval Guard.

16 My Lord Tressurer gave my Gr: Son, the office of Treasurer of the Revenue of the stampt parchment & paper: Sallary 300 pounds per annum.

[19 The publique fast, after the dreadfull storme, the Churches so crowded as few could get into them.]

The K. of Spaine driven back by contrary Winds to Portsmouth, & the weather stormy, disabled many of our Fleete:

31. This Fast (upon the day of the Martyrdom of K. Ch: 1.) was observed with more than usual sollemnity: Preached at our Chapell a Chaplaine of the L. Carmarthen on 1. Cor: 9: 27. Of the Ends & duty of fasting & humiliation, for the averting such Judgements & Calamitys as this days ⟨mark⟩ this Church & nation: in a very excellent discourse.

The K of Spaine still wind bound at Porchmouth.

Very warme weather:

Feb. 10 I went downe to see the lamentable destruction which the late dreadfull Tempest had made of my house & Gardens at S. Court & to take some order about the Repaires:

20 Nothing new from abroade, butt the states of Poland declaring the Thron vacant: A new funds which brings 120000 pounds into the Exchequer: See the Act.

29 Shrove Tuesday I new made my last Will & Testament with some alterations of the former:

Mar. The beginning of this moneth I was so Indisposed with Obstructions in my bowells, not having the benefit of Evacuation for severall days, that in my life I never suffered more torment, till after some Remedys it was removed & I restored againe for which God be Eternaly praised: So as after a Weeke I was alowed to take the aire:

The K. of Spaine was now certainly got to Lisbone, but his designed Queene the Princess of Brazeele, was dead of the smallpox:

12 A Chaplaine of the E. of Thannet preached on 1. Rom: 18: This was an afternoon sermon & the first I could go to, since my sicknesse:

[14 Came the L. AB of Canterbery to visite me]

Mild weather: The Parliament buisy in stating the pub. Accompt:

[15 I was at the R. Society Mr. Newton president]

19 A very wett unseasonable march, dissagreements among the Lords & Comm: about the Scotch Plotters⟨s⟩ Examinations, Lord of Nottingham complained of for some passage in a Gazett: Kracovia taken by the Sweeds.

26 Never greater expectation of news from Spaine, without any since the first arivall of the K. at Lisbon:

The season very wet but calm:

May 30th, I went from Dover-str: to Wotton for the rest of the Summer:

June 18 Dr. Bathurst Pres: of Trinity in Ox: (I think the oldest acquaintance now left me in all the wor⟨l⟩d), at 86 years age, both start blind, deafe, & memory lost, tho a person of admirable parts & learning no⟨w⟩ dying, was a serious alarm to me; God of his mercy grant that I may profit by it: He built a very handsom Chapell to that College & his owne Tomb. Gave a legacy of mony, & the 3d part of his library to Dr. Bohune, [his nephew] who now went hence to his funerall.

25 Nothing yet from the Army: & actions abroad, but general march to hinder the D. of Bavaria from farther progresse: The Polish, Sweeds & Hungarians still in hostillity:

⟨July⟩ 2. This week abounds with the news & assurance of the D of Marborow and Confederats signal Victory against the D of Bavaria &c: Lord *Godolphin* made a knight of the Garter:

23 The Confederat⟨s⟩ in Poland have chosen a new king: These are greate things.

Very seasonable Harvest Weather:

Aug: 6 All my Harvest brought in, & a sick-servant recovering: for which God be praised:

This weeke brought over hapy newes of the French & Bavarian Armys defeate by the Confederats, Especialy, by the vallour & Conduct of P: Eugene, & the Duke of Marborow, who vanquished, it, & tooke Marshall *Talard* their Generall prisoner: This was immediatly brought to the Queene, during the yet pursuite of the Enemys, written & sent by my *Co: Parcke* (an officer & Ayde de Camp) by the D: of Marlboro in such extreme hast, as he could not particularly describe the rest of the Circumstances & Event, which we hourely expect: But this has so exceedingly over Joyed us, that there is no thing but triumphs & demonstrations of Joy in the Citty & every where:

The weather a little variable, yet seasonable: God Almighty promote & improve this greate newes, to him be glory:

13 The Account of our Victory against the D: of *Bavaria* confirm'd but the particulars not yet come: The season excessive hot: The taking of *Gibraltar* ⟨*& Ce*⟩*uta* confirmed:

27 Still greater Confirmations of the Confederats Victory, the D. of Bavaria quite beaten out of his Country, who now sent their deputys to the Emp, to crave his protection & rescue their Country from utter Spoile: The D. of Marbrow marches over the Rhyne, Beseges Ulm & Landau: The Prisoners & spoile divided into 3 parts, to the Emp, English & Dutch: tis estimated the Fr: lost 40000 men kild & Taken, such a defeate as never was given in Europ these 1000 years:

The pope summons the Card primate of Poland to Rome, for crowning Vladislau their new King &c: this Victory breaks all the Fr: measures & designes, most providentialy for Europ:

Sept. 7. This day was celebrated the Thanksgiving for the late great Victory with the uttmost pomp & splendor by the Queene, Court, greate officers, Lord Major, Sheriffs, Companys &c the streets scaffolded from Temple-barr (where the L. M⟨a⟩yor presented her Majestie with the Sword, which she returned), every Company ranged under their Banners, & Citty Militia with out the rails, which were all hung with Cloth suitable to the Colour of the Banner, the L. Major, sherifs & Aldermen in their Scarlet roobs on their Caparisoned Horses: The knight Martiall & pensioners on horse, the Footguard: The Queene in a rich Coach with 8 Horse, none with her but the Dutchesse of Marl-brow, in a very plaine garment, The Q: full of Jewells, Musique & Trumpet⟨s⟩, at every Citty Company: The greate officers of the Crown & nobility & Bishops all in Coach of 6. Horses, besides innumerable Spectators in this order went to S. *Paules* where the Deane preached &c after which the Queene went back in the same order to St. James: The Citty & Companys, feasting all the Nobility & Bonfires and Illuminations at night: Note that there was Musick composed by the best Masters of that art, to accompany the Church musique & Anthems &c to all which (after a⟨n⟩ exceeding wet & stormy day) succeeded one of the most serene & Calmest bright-day⟨s⟩, as had ben all the yeare:

Our Curat also at Wotton, after the prayer (prescribt for the Occasion, exceedingly as to the psal⟨m⟩, lesson, & prayer) gave us an excellent Panegyrical & Eucharistical Sermon on   and this was solemnly observed all over England by publique Command: with Publique feasting &c:—I Invited severall of my Neighbours & Friends.

10 A sharp Conflict betweene Sir G: Rooke our Admirall in the Straits of Gibraltar with the French Fleete, which was beaten, but with a very greate losse of men on both sides, the particulars not as yet certaine: this was fought 16. Aug: No considerable news yet from Germany, the packet hindred by west winds:

17 Ulm taken, Landow besieged by the Confederats; A doubtfull fight in the Streites with the French fle⟨e⟩t, by Sir G Rooke, very many slaine on both sides; the K of Poland surprise⟨s⟩ ⟨Warsaw⟩:

Octob: 1 our Curate proceeded on the same Text: The holy Communion following, at which very few of the parish, so negligent people universaly are:

The weather exceedingly faire & seasonable, so as the yeare has ben wonderfully plentifull in all the fruits of the Earth, so as seldom a more propitious yeare has ben known, God make us thankfull.

The seige of *Landau* yet continuing, its redition is hourely expected: Sir G. Rooke & Mediteranean fleete come home safly: The losse on both sides very greate, but the Victory acknowledged on our side: The unhapy D. of Bavaria, retired to Flanders having lost his glorious Country:

22 The Queene [on one side] Lords & Comm: with extraordinary expressions of grace and kindnesse, congratulating their meeting, after the late Successes, & intimations of need of supplys to finish the humbling the French &c: & the Lords & Commons satisfaction of her government, & the like Congratulations of successe in Germany, gave hopes of a perfect and unanimous agrement of this Sessions just now begun:

31. Being my Birth-day, & 84th yeare of my life, After particular Reflection on my Concernes & passages of the yeare; I set some considerable time of this day a part, to recollect, & examine my State & Condition with giving God thanks, & acknowledging his infinite Mercys to me & mine, beging his blessing for the past, & imploring his protection &c for the yeare following:

November 5 our Curat preached on 107 Psal. 1. 2. Shewing the greate obligation we of this Church & Nation, have to blesse God for the deliverance of this Anniversary:

A Princes Dowager sister to the K: of Denmark, died, for which the Court ⟨went⟩ into mourning according to Custome:

13 My Wife went from Wotton to Lond, to be at the Labour of our Daughter Draper.

18: My Daughter brought to bed of a Girle.

19. Indisposed I went not to Church.

December 3. My little Grandaughter [at London] Christened *Evelyn* at the desire of the Father & mother: my Grandson being the Godfather:

6 I went from Wotton to Winter at *London* as formerly:

The Seige of Trarbach yet continuing: Uncertaine newes of the Seige of Gibraltar by the Spanyards:

9 my L. Clarendon presented me with the 3. Voll. of his Fathers History of the Rebellion: The D of Marbrough arived

in Eng: bringing the Count de Talard & many Prisoner⟨s⟩: Tra⟨r⟩bach surrendered, & the Houses of Parliament comple- ment him & his Victorys. [17] My Indisposition yet hindred me from going to church this day:

170$\frac{4}{5}$ Feb 9 I went to waite on my L. Tressurer where was the Victorious Duke of Marlborow, who came to me & tooke me by the hand with extraordinary familiarity & Civility, as for- merly he was used to doe without any alteration of his good nature. He had a most rich George in a Sardonix set with Dia- mond of an inestimable Value: for the rest very plaine: I had not seene him in 2 yeares & believed he had forgotten me:

21 Ash Wednesday

Such fine weather as ⟨has⟩ hardly ben known at this season without frost: Agues & Small pox much in every place; my poore Wife ill of a bastard pleurisy, from which I pray God to ffree her.

March. Nothing extraordinary from abroad: Temperat sea- son, yet many afflicted with Cold: my Wife delivered from a dangerous Pleurisy with losse of much blood:

11 Exceeding dry season: Greate losse by fire by the burn- ing of the out-houses and famous stable, at Burley full of rich goods & furnitur, of the E. of Notingham, by carelessnesse of a servant; as most of these accidents hapen by, & in a little before at Wilton my L. Pembrocks: The old Countesse of Northumberland dowager of Algernoon Piercy, Admirall of the Fleete to Chas: 1, dyed in the 83 year of her age, she was sister to the E. of Suffolke & left a greate Estate (her joyntur) to the D. of Sommerset: a most excellent religious Lady: No newes from abroad, save the holding out of Verru & Gibraltar:

The old Countesse of N-humberland died, a pious Lady, left much to the Duke of Somerset: & many young persons, Lords & others dyed sudenly of the S:pox: Sir Jo: Temple.

The Parliament prorogued, til may: nothing considerable from abroad, greate pressing for sea-men: [16] I waited on my L. Treasurer to whom was proposed my G-sons marriage with his Niepce, which he much approved of.

25 The Duke of Marlboro went to Holland, to Command in the ensuing Campan⟨ia⟩.

Apr. 4. The D. of Marborough landed in Holland:

9 I went [with my Gr: Son] for a few days to Wotton, returned the 14th, found my Wife had ben very ill in my absence of her old Cough: I myselfe much in paine by the Gravell,

22 Nothing of publique Importance, but the defeate of the French fleetes from relieving Gibraltar:

The Queene has ben magnificently treated at Cambridge, many Doctors & Graduats, & knights made: &c:

22 Nothing remarkable this Weeke; I after many moneth(s) indisposition, since I came to Towne: went to the meeting of the R. Society, where among other things there was a picture of one of the Electoral princes, Guards, a young fellow, who was 8 foote ½ in height, don by the person himselfe, in his livery-habite, with a huge broad-Sword by his side, studdied with gilt plate; sent to a Member of the Society out of Germany:—I also saw Sir Isaac Newtons (now made knight at the Queenes entertaining at Oxon) the burning Glasse which dos such wonders as that of the K. of France which cost so much, dos not come-neere, it penetrating Cast Iron of all Thicknesse, vitrifies Brick, mealts all sorts of mettals in a moment: That of the French kings, made I think at Lions, being all of one Piece of Mettal, & of a vast circumference, *this* made of 6 Concave Glasses not above a foote diameter: so plac'd about the middle Concave, that they prict their illuminated points all at once into the middle Concave focus where the rays meete & produce this Effect.

May. Very fine weather: The Baily of Westminster, hanged himselfe, he had an ill report, & indeede never was it known that so many made away with themselves as of these late yeares & age among us, among both men of quality & others:

13 The death of the Emperor, no mourning habits in our Court (as for all other Crown'd heads) because there was no notice taken in the Imperial Court, at the death of King William: The seige of Gibraltar raised:

18 I went to see Sir J. Jardine at Turnam Greene, the Gardens being very fine & exceedingly well planted with fruit: I went also to pay the Visit made me by the Earle of Chesterfeld:

3. *June* Trinity Sonday

I had this weeke a very greate & painefull fit of the stone which extreamly weakned me: The Lord in mercy looke on me & fortifie with patience.

4. I went to *Lambeth* & dined with the A. Bish where also dined the A:B of Dublin Dr. King, a Sharp ready man in politicks, as well as very Learned: Also the Earles of Sunderland, Manchester, Halifax, Chancellor of the Exchequer: with severall Divines &c; The Bishop of Rochester also: the Dinner was very splendid:

17 The season continued exceedingly dry & hot: I went to visite Dr. *Dikinson* the famous Chymist, where we had long Conversation about the Philosophers Elixir, which he believed attainable, & had seen projection himselfe, by one who went under the name of *Mundanus*, that sometime came among the Adepti &c: but was unknown as to his Country or aboade: of this the Doctor has written a Treatise in Latine full of very astonishing relations; he is a very learned person, formerly a fellow of Merton Coll in Oxon; where he practised Physick, but now altogether gave it over & lived retiredly, being very old & infirme, yet continued Chymistry &c:

I went to the R: Society, where were Tryals with Sir E Newtons Burning-glasse: which did strange things as to mealting whatever was held to it in a moment: one of the most difficult was common *Slate*, which lasted longer than Iron, Gold, brasse, Silver, flint, brick &c which it immediatly mealted, calcined & Vitrified: The Glasse was composed of 7 round burning glasses of about a foote diameter, so placed in a frame, as to cause all their Sun-beams to meete in one *focus* onely:

Excessive hot & ⟨dry⟩, & such a long time, as all the Country was burnt up:

Little don of military action abroad, thro' the tardinesse of the Germans, *Turin* in danger of a siege:

I went to Greenewich with my Wife, daughter, Gr Son, Mrs. Boscawen, & her daughter, then proposed as a Wife for him &c: To see the Hospital, which now began to take in wounded & emerited Sea-men, who were exceeding well provided for, the Buildings now going on very magnificent; dined at my servant, J. Strickland, & Returning visited Mr. Cresset my Tennant at Says Court: This by water:

24 ⟨So⟩me refreshing showrs, a greate fleete of Merchants from Lisbon came home, nothing else of ⟨m⟩oment:—I had a sore fall out of my bed accidentaly—without much harme God be praised.

July My L Treasurer made my Gr—son one of the Commissioners of the prizes, the sallary 500 pounds per Annum: Greate drowth—

6 I had a sore fit of the stone which much weakened me:

8 My Gr: son went this morning with Sir Sim: Harcourt the Solicitor Gen to Windsor to waite ⟨on⟩ my L. Treasurer, to whom I wrote to excuse my not being able to waite on him my selfe ⟨&c:⟩

There having for some time ben a proposal of Marying my Gr—Son to a daughter of Mrs. Bosca⟨wen⟩ Sister of my Lord Treasurer now far advanced:

A very signal Victory over the French in Flanders by the Duke of Marlborow, divers greate Officers Taken & Slaine, 1400 prisoners, 20 Cannons, & many standards taken &c:

The Hot & dry Weather very Excessive every thing burnt up:

14 I had this night a very severe fitt of [cold] Trembling, & heate after, with very greate pai⟨ne in my⟩ sides & backe & all over my Body, all symptoms of the stone: yet I crept to church wh⟨ere⟩ In the morning a stranger preached on 119 Psal: 115. & Dr. Lancaster in the Afternoone on the same Text: There was a Communion, at which I received ô Lord accept me:

I subscribed a contribution towards the Rebuilding of Oakewood Chapell in Su⟨rrey⟩ now after 200 years almost fallen downe:

22 ⟨The⟩ victory of the D. of Marborow over the D of Bavaria & French army in Flanders stil⟨l⟩ continues: We expect the further Event:

I was grievously afflicted with the stone all this Weeke: Little newes from abroad but the K. of Spaine in Portugal, going on board in our Fleete for the Mediterranean suppose⟨d⟩ an Expedition for Catalognia:

29 The Marriage Settlement of my Gr: son with a Daughter of Mrs. Boscawen; sister to my L. Treasurer, now finished, stays onely for the comming back of Sir Sym: Harcourt to examine the deeds & seale: he being yet in the Circuit:

31 I went with my Wife to Wotton:

Aug: 5. Dr. Bohun preached on 20 Acts: 21 Concerning the necessity of serious Repentance & danger of procrastination: upon which he Insisted every Sonday I was in the Country: where I stayed about severall necessary affaires 'til the 20; returning back by *Adscom*, & after dinner there returned to Lond: I now repaired another Mill, being with hewn stone (formerly of Timber as were all the rest) to my excessive Charge:

23 Mr. Solicitor being returned from the Judges Circuit: was finished my Gr:sons marriage settlement, & given to be Ingrossed, giving him my Intire Estate, reserving onely the possession of it during my life, and the absolute disposure of the personal Estate, to be disposed of by my Will: &c: The lease of the House, & intire furniture of my house at London I give absolutely to my deare Wife:

26 A stranger preached at our Chapell on 23 *Numb*. 10: How impossible it is to dye the death of the Righteous, without living the life of the Righteous, this he pressed so very seriously, & with that demonstration, & Advice, as extreamly affected me in particular, upon reflection of my greatest concerne as to my formerly spent life, & necessity of humiliation, & a thoro' resolution & endeavour to obtaine pardon of the past, & some earnests of Gods saving mercy, thro faith in my B: Saviour:

I was now very severely afflicted with the stone, & severall other Afflictions & Infirmitys of my greate Age:

Sept: 2. I was in excessive paine, no remedys working with me, by reason of a stopping in my Bowels, by being 6 days without Evacuation, in which Torment I continued two days, but was the next so relieved, that I was able to go take the aire, as far as Kensington, where I saw that House, [furniture] & the plantation about it, to my great admiration & Refreshment: It is a very noble Villa, the Gardens & Contrivances the worke of Mr. Wise, who was ther on purpose to receive me, & so returned I blesse God with much Ease & Refreshment &c:

September 6: Were Sealed the Writings &c. by which I settled my Estate on my Grandson, in order to his Marriage with Ann, Daughter to Mrs. Boscawen, sister to my L: Godolphin, L. High Treasurer of England:

9 This moneth has ben hithertoo exceeding dry, no Intelligence Certain from the Confederat army Abroad, but a report

of our Fleete landing at Barcelon: [The D: of Marlborow beseiging a small Towne.] & of a fight of P: Eugine in Savoy, the Event & Victory variously reported:

18 [Tuesday] my Gr: Son was Married by the Arch-Bishop of Cant: in Lambeth Chapell: to *Ann*, Daughter to Mrs. Boscawen, sister to the L. Godolphin, L. High Treasurer:—And, with aboundance of Relations on both sides, most magnificently Entertained with supper that night, by her Mother:

Most of the rest of this Weeke spent in receiving Visites of greate persons.

20 I went to visite my L. Treasurer:

21 I had 2 fitts of my Ague, in one night, which much weakened me:

26. We invited as many of the Re⟨l⟩ations of Mrs. Boscawen and of my L. Treasurer as were in Towne [&c.], to the number of 18 to Dinner, which was as greate as the solem⟨n⟩ity of Marriage of my Grandson &c required:

Octob: ⟨7⟩ The season now rainy & warme: Barcelona said to be taken, but the Prince of Hesse slayne, a greate losse:

11 I had a sore fit of the stone, which began like an Ague and much weakned me: The season very pleasant:

Mr. Cooper made L. Keeper, the seales taken from:
Cooper observing how uncertaine greate Officers are of continuing long in their places, would not accept of it, unlesse 2000 pounds a yeare were given them in pension, when ever he was put-out, in consideration of his losse of Practise: Though his predecessors how little while soever the⟨y⟩ had the Seale, got usualy 100000 pounds, & made them selves Barrons, which certainly must be by great Corruption; & those so frequent Changes an ill Symptom of the condition of the Government: Cooper an excellent Lawyer, but a vicious man:

A new Secretary of state: Lord Abington Lieutennant of the Tower displac'd & Lord Churchil Bro: to the Duke of Marlborow like to succeede: An indication of greate Unsteadynesse some where but thus the Crafty Whig-party (as called) began to change the face of the Court, in opposition to the *High Churchmen* which was another distinction of a party, from the Low church-men.

15 My Wife Gr:Son & his Wife went to Wotton, and returned on the 20th.

The weather began to be more rainy & cold after a glorious season.

21 The Parliament chose one Mr. Smith Speaker: There had never ben so greate an assembly of members on the first day of sitting: being [above] 450: The Votes both of . . . men as wel as ⟨the⟩ rest falling to those they called the Low-Church-men, contrary to all Expectation:

The taking of Barcelona confirmed:

27 I was very much indisposed, so as ⟨I⟩ could not go to Church next morning till the afternoone, when Dr. Lancaster preached on Jude 9:

[31. I am this day arived to the 85 yeare of Age, Lord teach me so to number the days to come that I may apply them to wisedom better than hitherto I have done, for J C sake.]

November A tennants house of mine was burnt down, but his Children left alone, & firing it, were saved:

Monsieur Rovignies ⟨arme⟩ in part shot off in the Warre against the S⟨p⟩aynard in Portugal: We had much losse by sea: Hard frost:

4 The Parliament now sitting, make extraordinary Complements to the Queene in answer to her Speech:

18: Nothing new, East-India fleete safely returned: I had a fit of the stone which for my sinns hindred me from going to Church & receive the B: Sacrament this morning:

The paine in my right kidny being very grate, I made bloody Waterr, & was much Indisposed:

Decemb 2 Nothing extraordinary save the Complyance of both hous⟨e⟩s of Parliament in most things proposed, which has not ben known in many yeares: They Granted the 25000 pounds towards the assistance of the K. of Spaine, now conqueror of Catalognia:

9. Extraordinary tempestious & rainy weather the weeke before.

An extraordinary wett-season & darke, severall Coaches & Travellers drowned, Great Innundations also in Italy &c: The small-pox tooke this Weeke away, Ed: Boscawen, a Brother of my Grandaughters, in the prime of his youth, just as an Estate fell-to him: To the greate griefe of his Disconsolate Mother & Family, there being onely his Elder Bro: remaining, a Gent of an Antient Family in Cornwall, & greate Estate: There also died the Lady Stonehouse, my Daughter in Laws, Mother, She died of a malignant feavor, at her son in Laws, Sir Simon Harcourt, Sollicitor Gen, ⟨so⟩ as all 3 familys were going into Mourning:

16 Being Advent Sonday: The B: of Salisbury preached in the morning & administered the Communion, Text: 6 Michaa: 8: with greate Earnestnesse & according to his manner much Action, did very well presse the dutys of the Text:

Afternoon Dr. Lancaster, on 7 Eccles: 29: I could ⟨hear⟩ little of this discourse, & was my selfe much Indisposed: yet went to Condole with Mrs. Boscawen:

[Some malicious Reflexions on my Lord Treasurer as if he had Corresponded with St. Germans in K. Williams Reigne &c. On⟨e⟩ Mr. Cæsar of the H of Commons was sent to the Tower:]

23 Nothing extraordinary from abroad, but great harme by stormes & Innundations, even at home: The Parliament settled the Succession in the protest⟨ant⟩ line: Remitted some prohibitions of bringing Commoditys out of Scotland:

1706. *Jan:* 1 Making up my Accompts for the past yeare, payed Wages, [Bills,] New years Gifts according to Custome, &c: Tho much Indisposed, & in so advanced an Age I went to our Chapell to give God publique Thanks: Beseeching Almighty God, to assist me with his Mercy & protection to me & my Family the Ensuing yeare, if he should yet Continue my Pilgrimage here, & bring me at last to a better life with him in his heavenly Kingdom.

Divers of our Friends & Relations dined with us this day.

6 Epiphany Exceedingly Indispos'd: I could not go to church, which I believe in very many yeares I have not omitted: And this whole Weeke, I had 3 fits of a shaking-fit, and feavor, with greate paines in the Kidneys, which much afflicted me:—Some Snow & sharp dayes:

13 I got to church in the Afternoone, but was exceeding drowsy: A Chap of the Bishop of Lond 2 Ephes: 17.

House of Comm, settling the Regency, in Case of the Q. death; & about ⟨admit⟩ting no officers Members in the future Elections.

I was much Indisposed most of this weeke:

20 A Lecturer in the morning on 7 Ecles: 14. The goodnesse of God, in giving us times to Consider of our ways & life in Affliction; the Infinite folly & madness to protract it, whilst

in health & prosperity, since Affliction one way or other will or may befalle us here.

The holy Sacrament followed, at which I received, The Lord make me mindfull.

Afternoone, another, on 11 Matt. 6: Christs being the Messias, doubted of by ⟨Johns⟩ disciples, & others, were sent to our B. Saviour to be convinced by his Miracles &c that he was the true Messias, which by reason of his meane appearance, they questioned: whilst ⟨John⟩ himselfe firmly belie⟨ved⟩ & affirmed, from the moment of the Voice & dove sent on him at his Bap⟨tism.⟩ The inference was, that [the] humility of our B. Lord, should teach us to Imitate ⟨his⟩ Grace in whomsoever, & not to be Scandalized or be offended upon such Circumstances in the faithfull: I was exceeding drowsy, which God in mercy pardon, for the rest better than before:

No Intelligence publique:

27 The Raine and a Thaw upon a deepe Snow, hindred me from going to Church.

My Infirmitys increasing, I was exceeding ill this whole weeke.

Feb. 3. A stranger at our Chapell on 19 Levit: 17, the necessity of warning a Brother or Christian, & method of Admonition, when we find any go astray or do amisse, with the Rules to be observed, according to the danger and natur of the fault &c.

Afternoon, a Scotchman, on   Let every one that names the L. Jesus depart from Evill, & increase in love of that profession.[1]

THE END

---

1 These are the last words of the Diary. Evelyn died at his house in Dover Street on 27 February and was buried at Wotton on 4 March. His epitaph follows on the next page.

Epitaph

Here lies the Body
of JOHN EVELYN Esq.
of this place second son
of RICHARD EVELYN Esq.
who having serv'd y^e Publick
in several employments, of which that
of Com'issioner of y^e Privy Seal in y^e
Reign of K. James y^e 2^d was most
Honourable: & perpetuated his fame
by far more lasting Monuments than
those of Stone, or Brass, his Learned
& usefull works fell asleep y^e 27th day
of February 170$\frac{5}{6}$ being y^e 86th Year
of his age in a full hope of a glorious
resurrection thro' faith in Jesus Christ.
Living in an age of extraordinary
events, & revolutions he learn't
(as himself asserted) this truth
which pursuant to his intention
is here declared
That all is vanity wch is not honest,
& that there's no solid Wisdom
but in real Piety.
Of five Sons, & three Daughters
borne to him from his most
vertuous, & excellent Wife
MARY sole daughter, & heiress
of Sr RICH^d BROWNE of Sayes
Court near Deptford in Kent
onely one daughter SUSANNA
married to WILL^m DRAPER
Esq. of Adscomb in this County
survived him, y^e two others
dying in y^e flower of their
age & all y^e Sons very young
except one nam'd JOHN, who
deceasd y^e 24th of March 169$\frac{8}{9}$
in y^e 45th year of his age,
leaving one son JOHN, & one
daughter ELIZABETH.

GLOSSARY

Albemarle, Duke of: *see* Monck, George.

Albemarle, Earl of: *see* Keppel, Arnold Joost van.

Aldobrandini, Hippolito (1536–1605): Italian Cardinal. Succeeded Innocent IX as Clement VIII in 1592.

Allix (Alex), Pierre (Peter) (1641–1717): Huguenot pastor and theologian who came to England with his family following the revocation of the Edict of Nantes and met with great encouragement. His eldest son, John Peter Allix, became a Doctor of Divinity, and was made Dean of Ely in 1730.

Anne, Queen (1665–1714): Reigned 1702–14. Last of the Stuart monarchs, daughter of the Catholic James II, but herself a Protestant, she succeeded her brother-in-law William III, presiding over the Act of Union with Scotland (1707). None of her five children born alive survived to adulthood.

Argyle, Marquis of: *see* Campbell, Archibald.

Arlington, Lord and Lady: *see* Bennet, Sir Henry.

Armorer, Sir Nicholas: Equerry to Charles II.

Arundel, Earl of: *see* Howard, Thomas.

Ashburnham, John (1603–71): Royalist. Groom of the Bedchamber to Charles I and Charles II. Described by Pepys as 'a pleasant man, and that hath seen much of the world, and more of the Court'. He was with Charles I during the rebellion, and represented Sussex in Parliament.

Ashley Cooper, Sir Anthony (1621–83): Statesman. He was one of the Cabal ministry who succeeded Clarendon to office in 1667, and was created Earl of Shaftesbury in 1672. He was Lord Chancellor 1672–3 but his animosity towards the Duke of York's Catholic marriage led to his dismissal. He thereafter joined the ranks of the Opposition as a champion of national liberties and of toleration for Dissenters, and is credited with founding the Whig party. He was the spokesman for the Exclusionists in the House of Lords, favouring the succession of the Protestant Duke of Monmouth, and in 1680 was sent to the Tower on a charge of treason. On release he fled to Holland, dying there two years later.

Aungier (Aunger), Gerald (d. 1655): Eldest son of Sir Francis Aungier. Created Master of the Rolls in 1609 and Baron Aungier in the Irish peerage in 1621.

Bargrave, Dr. John (1662–80): Dean of Canterbury and a great benefactor to the Cathedral Library there.

Barlow, Francis (d. 1702): English painter, known as 'the father of British sporting painting'.

Barlow, Lucy (1630?–58): Also known as Lucy Walter. Mistress of Charles II during his exile in Holland and France. She was the mother by him of James Scott, Duke of Monmouth, and a daughter, Mary.

Barrow, Isaac (1630–77): Master of Trinity College, Dublin.

Basire, Isaac (1607–76): Archdeacon of Northumberland and Prebendary of Durham. Chaplain in Ordinary to Charles II.

Bathurst, Dr Ralph (1620–1704): Friend of JE. MD 1654, FRS 1663. President of Trinity College, Oxford 1664–1705 (and Vice-Chancellor of the University 1673–6). Chaplain in Ordinary *c.* 1665– *c.* 1688; Dean of Wells 1670.

Beaufort, Duke of: *see* Somerset, Henry.

Benlowes (Benlous), Edward (1603?–76): English poet. Matriculated at St John's College, Cambridge, 1620. He was heir to a wealthy Catholic family though he converted to Protestantism in his later years.

Bennet, Sir Henry (c. 1620–85): Statesman. Fought with the Royalists and was wounded in the Civil War. Created Baron Arlington in 1665, 1st Earl of Arlington and a Knight of the Garter in 1672. Appointed Secretary of State in 1662, he was chiefly responsible for foreign policy. He opposed Clarendon, after whose fall in 1667 he became a member of the Cabal ministry. He scored a diplomatic coup in 1668 by engineering the Triple Alliance of England, Holland and Sweden, but two years later was also one of only two ministers (the other being Clifford) party to the Charles II's Secret Treaty of Dover (1670) with Louis XIV, which resulted in his impeachment in 1674. He was acquitted but resigned the secretaryship later that year in favour of his client, Sir Joseph Williamson. He was then appointed Lord Chamberlain (reappointed 1685) but never again enjoyed the same influence at court. He became a friend of JE. While he had Roman Catholic sympathies, he continued to practise the Protestant religion until his death-bed conversion. He married in 1665 Isabella (c. 1631–1718), daughter of Louis of Nassau, an illegitimate son of Maurice of Orange. Their daughter, Isabella (c. 1667–1723), became Countess of Arlington in her own right in 1685. Her first husband was the Duke of Grafton.

Berkeley, Lord John (1607–78): Royalist Commander in the Civil Wars. Created Baron Berkeley of Stratton in 1658. He was Lord-Lieutenant of Ireland in 1670, and Ambassador to France in 1674.

Blagge, Margaret: see Godolphin, Mrs. Margaret.

Blood (Bloud), Thomas (1618?–80): Irish adventurer and member of the Parliamentary army. He and three accomplices managed to steal the crown and orb from the Tower of London in 1671. All four were captured soon afterwards. To the astonishment of contemporaries, Charles II visited Blood in prison and later pardoned him.

Blount, Sir Henry (1602–82): Second son of Sir Thomas Pope Blount of Tittenhanger. He started in 1634 on a four-year tour of Turkey, Syria and Egypt and on his return published *A Voyage to the Levant*, which passed through many editions. He succeeded to the family estate in 1638 and was knighted the following year. He fought under the royal banner at Edgehill and afterwards changed sides and was employed by Cromwell as a commissioner for reforming the criminal code. On the return of Charles II he again switched sides.

Bobart, Jacob (1599–1680): Gardener and first Superintendant of the Oxford Physic Garden.

Bohemia, Elizabeth, Queen of (1596–1662): Sister of Charles I and widow of Frederick V, Elector Palatine (d. 1632). She was also known as the 'Winter Queen' of Bohemia (her husband was offered the crown by the Bohemian Protestants in 1619 but was defeated at the Battle of the White Mountain in 1620). Elizabeth lived in exile in Holland until the Restoration, when she came to England. Her 13 children included Carl Louis, restored as Elector Palatine in 1648, Princes Rupert and Maurice, who fought in the English Civil War, and Sophia, Electress of Hanover and mother of George I of England.

Bohun, Rev. Ralph (c. 1640–1716): Nephew of Ralph Bathurst. Fellow of New College Oxford, BCL 1665, DCL 1668. Tutor to

John Evelyn, jun., 1665–71, becoming a family friend. Rector of West Kingston, Wilts, 1674–1701. Presented to the rectory of Wotton by JE in 1701, when he also became Canon of Salisbury.

Borcht, Hendrik van der, the Elder (1583–1660): Flemish painter and etcher from Brussels who was in the service of the Earl of Arundel. He produced a portrait of JE.

Boyle, Elizabeth (d. 1673): Daughter of William Field, 1st Earl of Denbigh, she married Lewis, Viscount Boyle of Kinalmeaky, who fell at the Battle of Liscarrol in 1642. She was advanced to the peerage for life in 1660 as Countess of Guildford. She was for a time principal Lady of the Bedchamber to Henrietta Maria and became a Roman Catholic. For some time she had charge of Margaret Blagge.

Boyle, Robert (1627–91): English natural philosopher and chemist who made important contributions to experimental chemistry including the first quantitative measurements of gases and the formulation of Boyle's Law.

Boyle, Roger (1621–79): 1st Earl of Orrery. Irish statesman and dramatist.

Bradshaw, George: Rector of Ockham and JE's tutor at Oxford.

Bramhall, Dr. John (1593–1677): Anglican divine. Born in Yorkshire, he studied for the church, becoming chaplain to Archbishop Matthews, then Prebendary of York, and subsequently of Ripon. He went to Ireland on the invitation of Lord Wentworth, and was made Bishop of Derry. In 1641 his conduct laid him open to charges of high treason, and he quit the country till the return of Charles II, when he was created Archbishop of Armagh.

Brereton, William (1631–80): 3rd Lord Brereton, a founder member of the Royal Society.

Bristol, Earl and Countess of: see Digby, George, and Digby, Anne.

Brouncker, Sir William (1620?–84): 2nd Viscount Brouncker in the Irish peerage. Mathematician, music theorist and scientist. Nominated President of the Royal Society in its first charter (1662), serving until 1677. He was also Chancellor to Queen Catherine of Braganza, a Commissioner of the Admiralty, and Master of St Katherine's Hospital.

Brown, Francis (1610–82): 3rd Viscount Montagu, a zealous Royalist. He was married to Elizabeth (c. 1618–84), daughter of Henry Somerset, 1st Marquis of Worcester.

Browne, Sir Richard (1605–83): JE's father-in-law, married Elizabeth Prettyman (c. 1610–52), daughter of Sir John Prettyman of Dryfield, Glos. JE's wife, Mary Browne, was their only child. Sir Richard was Clerk of the Council 1641–72 and Resident at the French court for Charles I and Charles II, 1641–60. He provided in Paris a chapel for Anglican services, a home for Anglican divines and a cemetery for Protestants. He was created a baronet in 1649.

Browne, Sir Thomas (1605–82): Celebrated for his *Religio Medici*, published in 1642, a discussion of his attitude as a Christian and a doctor to God and the Church, faith and reason, the classical tradition, private friendship and national prejudice. Other important works include *Pseudodoxia Epidemica* (or *Vulgar Errors*) and *Hydriotaphia* (*Urn Burial*). After prolonged travel abroad he settled in Norwich to practise medicine in about 1637. He was knighted in 1671.

Bruce, Thomas (1600–63): 1st Earl of Elgin, in Scotland. Created Baron Bruce of Whorlton, Yorkshire, in the English peerage by Charles I in 1640.

Buckingham, Dukes of: *see* Villiers, George.

Butler, James (1610–88): 12th Earl, Marquis and 1st Duke of Ormond (1661), Anglo-Irish statesman, Royalist and soldier. The Marquis was a staunch friend of Strafford, even in his adversity, and an equally earnest partisan of the king, who bestowed upon him the Order of the Garter, and appointed him Lord-Deputy of Ireland, and Lord Steward of the Household. In the Civil Wars he exerted himself zealously in the royal cause till obliged to seek safety with his family in exile. He returned at the Restoration, and Charles II raised him to the English peerage by the titles of Baron Butler and Earl of Brecknock. He was Lord-Lieutenant of Ireland three times, but retired into private life on the accession of James II.

Butler, James (1665–1745): 2nd Duke of Ormond, son of Thomas Butler, Earl of Ossory. A supporter of the 1688 Revolution, he was a commander at the Battle of the Boyne and also fought under William III in the Netherlands. Co-operating with

Sir George Rooke's naval forces, he shared the honours of victory at Vigo Bay in 1702, where the Spanish treasure fleet was sunk.

Butler, Thomas (1634–80): Earl of Ossory. Irish nobleman, son of James Butler, 1st Duke of Ormond. Lieutenant-General of the army in Ireland (from 1665), he later joined the allied army in the Netherlands, winning great fame at the siege of Mons in 1678. He was also a naval commander who served with distinction in the Second and Third Dutch Wars. A man of letters as well as of action, he was an intimate friend of JE.

Caldwell, Mary: JE's sister-in-law, *see* Evelyn, Mrs. Mary.

Campbell, Archibald (1607–61): 8th Earl and 1st Marquis of Argyle. Scottish statesman, leader of the Covenanters and chief of the Campbell clan. He crowned Charles II King of Scots at Scone. He was beheaded in Edinburgh when Charles regained the throne of England.

Capel, Arthur (1632–83): 1st Earl of Essex and friend of JE. The son of a Royalist, the first Baron Capel, who had been executed in 1649, he was raised to the peerage after the Restoration. He married Lady Elizabeth Percy (1636–1718). He became a Privy Councillor in 1672 and was Lord Lieutenant of Ireland 1672–7 where his conscientious attempts to weed out corruption and patronage did not endear him to courtiers at home who were benefiting from it. He joined the Country party and on Danby's fall became a Commissioner of the Treasury but in 1680 resigned and allied himself with Shaftesbury and the Exclusionists. He took no part in the wilder schemes of the Whigs but was arrested as a result of the Rye Hill Plot and imprisoned in the Tower, where he committed suicide. He was succeeded by his 'hopeful son', Algernon (1670–1710). The daughter mentioned by JE in 1680 is Anne (c. 1675–1752), who married Charles Howard, 3rd Earl of Carlisle.

Carey, Elizabeth: *see* Mordaunt, Elizabeth, Viscountess Mordaunt.

Carey, Henry (c. 1580–1666): 4th Baron Hundson, created Viscount Rochford and Earl of Dover (1628). He had three daughters – Mary, who married Sir Thomas Wharton, Judith and Philadelphia.

Carlingford, Lord: *see* Taafe, Theobald.

Carnarvon, Earl of: *see* Dormer, Charles.

Carteret (Cartret), Sir George (*c.* 1610–80): Royalist, statesman and naval officer. Born on the island of Jersey, in the Channel Islands, he entered the navy at an early age and distinguished himself in the service, attracting the attention of the Duke of Buckingham. He was made Joint-Governor of Jersey and Comptroller of the Navy by Charles I. After the Restoration he was returned to Parliament for Portsmouth, and filled the offices of Vice-Chamberlain and Treasurer of the Navy.

Castlemaine, Lady: *see* Palmer, Barbara.

Catherine of Braganza (1638–1705): Queen consort of Charles II (married 1662) and daughter of John IV of Portugal. Catherine was immediately subjected to the humiliation of sharing Charles with his mistresses. Her Catholicism made her the subject of suspicion and she was in some danger during the Popish Plot, but always loyally protected by the king. The queen's inability to produce an heir gave rise to suggestions that Charles should divorce her and remarry, but he would never agree to this. Catherine remained in England after Charles's death until 1702 when she returned to Portugal, successfully acting as regent for her brother, Pedro II, in 1704.

Cave, Dr. William (1637–1713): Historian and chaplain to Charles II. He wrote a number of religious essays including some studies of primitive Christianity.

Cavendish, William (1617–84): 3rd Earl of Devonshire, also Knight of the Garter and Lord Steward of the Household. Married Elizabeth, *née* Cecil (1619–89), daughter of the Earl of Salisbury. Their son, also William Cavendish (1641–1707) was created 1st Duke of Devonshire in 1694.

Chardin, Sir John (1643–1713): French merchant and traveller who journeyed extensively in the East. His accounts of India and Persia were especially popular in his day. He spoke at the Royal Society, and was knighted by Charles II in 1681.

Charles I (1600–49): Son of James I, reigned 1625–49. Religious and constitutional crises dominated his reign. He ruled without Parliament (1629–40) but was obliged to recall Parliament to finance his war with Scotland. The ensuing dispute resulted in civil war in 1642. After the Royalist forces had been defeated, Charles was tried by special Parliamentary court and beheaded in 1649.

Charles II (1630–85): Succeeded his father in 1649. Proclaimed king in Scotland in 1651 but forced into exile after defeat by Cromwell at the battle of Worcester. Restored in 1660 after Cromwell's death and the collapse of his regime. He married the Portuguese princess Catherine of Braganza in 1662. Proved more adroit than his father in handling the religious and political strife of his reign, but it was exacerbated by his failure to produce a legitimate heir. Converted to Catholicism on his death-bed.

Charleton, Dr. Walter (1619–1707): Physican to Charles II during his exile. He returned with the king at the Restoration. He wrote on natural history, antiquities, theology, medicine and natural philosophy.

Chesterfield, Earl of: *see* Stanhope, Philip.

Chicheley (Chichley), Sir Thomas (1613–99): Master of the Ordinance (1670–4). Knighted in 1670.

Churchill, John (1650–1722): English statesman and general. The son of a country squire, he was page to the Duke of York (afterwards James II). In 1678 he married Sarah Jennings (1660–1744), maid of honour to Princess Anne, over whom she had great influence. He defeated the rebellion by the Duke of Monmouth in 1685 but then shifted his alliegance to William of Orange, who created him 1st Earl of Marlborough. He fell from grace when it became known that he was in secret correspondence with the deposed James II but was back in favour under Queen Anne. A brilliant soldier, he won many notable victories over the French during the War of the Spanish Succession, and in 1702 he was raised to a Duke and had Blenheim Palace built for him.

Clancarty, Countess of: *see* Fitzgerald, Elizabeth.

Clarendon, Countesses of: *see* Hyde, Flower; Hyde, Frances.

Clarendon, Earls of: *see* Hyde, Edward; Hyde, Henry.

Claude, John (d. 1687): Celebrated French Protestant minister, and a controversial writer. At the revocation of the Edict of Nantes he was ordered to quit France within 24 hours. He fled to England, where he died in 1687.

Clayton, Sir Robert (1629–1707): Merchant and politician. Married *c.* 1659 Martha Trott. Knighted 1671. Sheriff of London 1671–2. Lord Mayor 1679–80. He had a magnificent town house in Old Jewry: his family seat was at Marden in Surrey, purchased from JE's relations. Deprived of his aldermanship in 1683 as part of Charles II's drive to control municipal government. Whig in his sympathies, he supported the 1688 Revolution. Appointed a trustee for part of Buckingham's estate 1675; persuaded the king to found the Mathematics School (to teach navigation) at Christ's Hospital in 1673; Commissioner of Greenwich Hospital 1695.

Cleveland, Duchess of: *see* Palmer, Barbara.

Clifford, Sir Thomas (1630–73): Statesman. Became an MP in 1660, knighted in 1664. Appointed Comptroller of the Household and a Privy Councillor in 1666, and a Commissioner of the Treasury in 1667. He was a member of the Cabal ministry, though his appointment as Lord Treasurer in 1672 soured his relationship with his erstwhile patron, Lord Arlington. Created 1st Baron Clifford of Chudleigh in 1672. He was party to the Secret Treaty of Dover (1670), and in 1672 was the chief adviser on the Declaration of Indulgence, the Third Dutch War and the Stop of the Exchequer. A fellow Commissioner for the Sick and Wounded in 1664, he became a friend of JE. His interest in Catholicism, noted by JE, probably began in the 1660s. He felt unable to comply with the Test Act of 1673, resigned office and was received into the Roman Catholic Church.

Colbert, Charles, marquis de Croissy (Colbert de Croissy): French ambassador in England 1668–74. He was the brother of Jean Baptiste Colbert, the French statesman.

Collins, Captain John (1624–83): A contributor to the *Transactions* of the Royal Society, he wrote several mathematical works.

Compton, Dr. Henry (1632–1713): Anglican cleric. Abandoned a career in the army for the church and was ordained a priest in 1662. He became Bishop of London in 1675. A zealous Protestant, he was one of the seven bishops who presented grievances to James II. He was instrumental in bringing over William of Orange and placed the crown on his head at his coronation.

Condé (Condy), Louis II de Bourbon, Prince of (1621–86): French general. Played a prominent part in the war between France and Spain, defeating the Spaniards at Rocroi in 1643. At first took the side of the Court in the Fronde, but, considering himself ill-treated by Mazarin, led the Fronde of the Princes against him and later fought with the Spanish army against France. Restored to his rank in France after the Peace of the Pyrenees (1659), he led Louis XIV's armies against the Dutch, defeating the Prince of Orange (afterwards William III of England) in 1674.

Cooper, Samuel (1609–72): Fashionable miniaturist. He is well known for his characteristic painting of Cromwell.

Cooper, William: *see* Cowper.

Cottington, Francis, Baron Cottington (c. 1578–1652): Diplomat and statesman, created a baron in 1631. Spent much of his early career in Spain, where he became a secret Roman Catholic. Chancellor of the Exchequer 1629–42, Lord Treasurer 1643. In exile with the Royalists, he publicly embraced Catholicism and settled at Valladolid.

Cornbury, Lord and Lady: *see* Hyde, Henry, and Hyde, Flower.

Cotton, Mary, Lady Cotton (d. 1664): Born Offley, second wife of George Evelyn, JE's elder brother. Her mother's father was Lord Mayor of London in 1604–5; her sister was the wife of Sir Henry Herbert, Master of the Revels in the time of Charles I and Charles II; her brother also held office at court, and she herself was the widow of a Kentish knight, Sir John Cotton. She was the mother of John (1653–91) and Mary (1648–1723) Evelyn. Two other daughters – Jane and Elizabeth – died young, and several sons died as infants. She was godmother to JE's son George (1657–8).

Covel, Dr. John (1638–1722): Pastor and traveller whose journeys included extended trips to Greece and Italy. His diaries, drawings and maps are now in the British Museum. On his return he was made Chancellor of York, and later Master of Christ's College, Cambridge.

Coventry, Sir William (1628–86): Statesman. He was a member of the Privy Council of Charles II and was made a Knight of the Garter in 1665, and Commissioner of the Treasury in 1667. He was a principal instigator of the fall of Clarendon and was disappointed not to be appointed in his place. In 1669 he was sent to the Tower for challenging the Duke of Buckingham to a duel. He became prominent in the Country party, disapproving of Charles's pro-French policies and refusing further Court appointments. He remained moderate in his views and disapproved of the increasing violence of the Opposition. He retired from public life after the dissolution of the Cavalier Parliament in 1679.

Cowley, Abraham (1618–67): Poet and essayist. He began publishing poetry while still at school, and went on to study at Cambridge. During the Civil War he went with the queen to Paris, was sent on Royalist missions, and carried on her correspondence in cipher with the king. After the Restoration he retired to Chertsey. Principal works include *The Mistress* (1647), *Poems* (1656) and the political epic *The Civil War* (1679).

Cowper, William (c. 1665–1723): Lawyer and leading Whig politician, created a baron in 1706 and an earl in 1718. He was much involved in the negotiations for union between England and Scotland and was afterwards made the first Lord High Chancellor of Great Britain .

Craven (Cravons), William (1608–97): Eldest son of Sir William Craven, Lord Mayor of London. He distinguished himself during the Civil Wars and was created Viscount and Earl of Craven by Charles II in 1663.

Crewe, Sir Clipsby (Clepesby) (1599–1649): An MP twice in the 1620s. He was a friend of Herrick who addressed several poems to him.

Cromwell, Oliver (1599–1658): General and statesman. One of the principal commanders of the Parliamentary forces in the Civil War, and largely responsible for the trial and execution of Charles I in 1649, Cromwell became Lord Protector of the Commonwealth during the 1650s. He dissolved a number of Parliaments but refused Parliament's offer of the crown. His rule was notable for its Puritan reforms in the Church of England and for the establishment of the Commonwealth as a major Protestant power.

Cutler (Cuttler), Sir John (c. 1608–93): An eminent citizen of London, and member of the Grocers' Company. Besides being patron of the vicarage of Deptford he owned Upper Brockley Farm there. He was knighted in 1660.

Dampier, Captain William (1652–1715): Navigator and buccaneer whose works, including *Voyage Round the World* (1697), were widely read. He explored the coasts of Australia, New Britain and New Guinea between 1699 and 1701 for the British Admiralty.

Danby, Earl of: *see* Osborne, Sir Thomas.

Davenant (D'Avenant), Dr. Charles (1656–1714): Economist and politician, the eldest son of the poet Sir William Davenant. He was variously joint Inspector of Plays, Commissioner of Excise and Inspector-General of Exports and Imports. His chief work was the 5-volume *Essays on Trade*. The book referred to by JE (28 March 1701) was *Essays on the Balance of Power*.

De Vere, Aubrey (1626–1703): 20th Earl of Oxford. A Royalist and soldier, he was rewarded at the Restoration by a seat on the Privy Council and made a Knight of the Garter and Lord-Lieutentant of Essex.

Devonshire, Earl, Countess and Duke of: *see* Cavendish, William.

Dickinson, Dr. Edmund (1624–1707): Doctor, chemist and Fellow of Merton College. A talented alchemist, he conducted many experiments in a laboratory built for him by Charles II. He also acted as physician to the royal household of Charles II and James II.

Digby, Anne (d. 1697): Countess of Bristol and wife of the 2nd Earl (*see* below), whom she married in 1635. An Anglican, she was the daughter of Francis Russell, 4th Earl of Bedford, and mother of Lady Sunderland.

Digby, George (1612–77): 2nd Earl of Bristol. Suffered much for his Royalist loyalties, but was made a Knight of the Garter, and might have held important office, had he not, when abroad, become a Catholic.

Digby, Sir Kenelm (1603–65): Author, diplomat, naval commander (he defeated the French and Venetian fleets in 1628) and a founder member of the Royal Society. He discovered the necessity of oxygen to plant life; less scientifically, he believed that wounds could be cured by 'powder of sympathy'. In 1625 he secretly married the celebrated beauty Venetia Stanley.

Dives (Dyve), Sir Lewis (Lowes) (1599–1669): Royalist MP. Took part in the Civil War and was wounded at Worcester (1644). Made Sergeant-Major-General of Dorset in 1644, imprisoned in the Tower 1645–7, and afterwards served in Ireland, publishing an account of events there in 1650. He afterwards took refuge in France.

Dobson, William (1611–46): Portrait painter who succeeded Van Dyck in the employments he held under Charles I.

During the Civil War he was based in Oxford where he painted many of the leading Cavaliers. After the Royalist defeat he returned to London. He was later imprisoned for debt and died in poverty.

Dormer, Charles (1632–1709): 3rd Baron Dormer. He became 2nd Earl of Carnarvon in 1643 when his father was killed at Newbury, fighting for the king.

Dover, Earl of (d. 1668): see Carey, Henry; Jermyn, Henry (2).

Downing, Sir George (1624–84): Chaplain in Parliamentarian army 1646–9. Ambassador to the United Provinces 1657–65. Downing Street in London is named after him.

Doyley (D'oily), Sir William (c. 1614–77): MP for Norfolk 1654, 1659 and for Great Yarmouth 1660, 1661–77. Commissioner for Sick and Wounded (1664–7, 1672–4), and Agent for Tax Collectors (1664–7).

Draper, William (d. 1718): JE's son-in-law. His parents' names are unknown but he was a nephew of Sir Thomas Draper of Sunninghill; the family perhaps came from Islington. He was a member of various committees for Greenwich Hospital from 1696 onwards and was Treasurer, in succession to JE, from 1703 to 1715. He married JE's daughter Susanna in 1693.

Drebbell, Cornelius Van (1572–1634): Dutch scientist and inventor. Born in Alkmaar, Holland, he settled in London during the reign of Charles I. He is often credited with the invention of the submarine.

Ducy (Ducie), Sir William (c. 1615–79): Son of Sir Robert Ducy, wealthy Lord Mayor of London. Traveller and art-collector. He was made a Knight of the Bath in 1661 and created Viscount Downe in 1675. He bought Charlton House, not far from JE's Sayes Court, in 1658.

Duncombe, Sir Charles (1648–1711): A successful banker and goldsmith, he was charged with making false endorsements on Exchequer bills in 1698 and sent to the Tower. Though he confessed his guilt he was later released by the Lords. He became Lord Mayor in 1709.

Duport, Dr. James (1606–1679): Classical scholar. Son of the Master of Jesus' College, Cambridge, he was educated at Trinity College, Cambridge, and appointed Regius Professor of Greek there in 1632, though deprived of this post during the Protectorate. He was appointed chaplain to Charles II in 1660, when he was restored to his Greek

Professorship, created Doctor of Divinity, made Dean of Peterborough, and, in 1668, elected Master of Magdalen College.

Durell, Dr. John (1626–83): Dean of Windsor. Translated the Liturgy into French and Latin, and was the author *A Vindication of the Church of England Against Schismatics*.

Earle (Earles), Dr. John (1601–65): Scholar, author and cleric. Became tutor to Prince Charles in 1641 whom he afterwards served as chaplain during his exile in France. Returning to England at the Restoration, he was successively made Dean of Westminster, Clerk of the Closet, Bishop of Worcester (1662) and Bishop of Salisbury (1663). He was the author of *Microcosmographie* and of a Latin translation of the *Eikon Basilike*.

Ersfield: see Evelyn, Mrs. Catherine.

Essex, Earl of: see Capel, Arthur.

Evelyn, Anne (d. 1688): JE's niece, daughter of his younger brother Richard. She married William Montagu in 1670.

Evelyn, Anne, Lady Evelyn (1685–1752): Born Boscawen. Wife of JE's grandson Sir John Evelyn of Wotton, and niece of Sidney Godolphin.

Evelyn, Sir Edward, of Long Ditton (1626–92): JE's first cousin once removed. Sir Edward's grandfather, Thomas Evelyn of Long Ditton, was the eldest half-brother of JE's father, Richard Evelyn. Knighted 1676, created a baronet 1683. He had no male heirs and was succeeded by his daughters, Penelope, wife of Sir Joseph Alston, and Mary, wife of Sir William Glynn.

Evelyn, Mrs. Eleanor (1598–1635): Born Stansfield. JE's mother, wife of Richard Evelyn, sen. The couple had five children, all of whom survived to adulthood: Elizabeth (1614–34), Jane (1616–51), George (1617–99), JE (1620–1705) and Richard (1622–70).

Evelyn, Elizabeth (1614–34): JE's sister. First wife of Edward Darcy. Died shortly after giving birth to her first child, Elizabeth (1634–5).

Evelyn, Mrs. Elizabeth (c. 1628–92): Born Mynne. JE's sister-in-law, wife of his younger brother Richard, whom she married in 1648.

Evelyn, Elizabeth (1667–85): JE's daughter. Her married name is unknown.

Evelyn, Elizabeth (1684–1760): JE's grand-daughter, daughter of John Evelyn, jun.

Married Simon Harcourt, son of Viscount Harcourt, in 1709.

Evelyn, George, sen. (1526–1603): JE's grandfather, manufacturer of gunpowder and patriarch of the Evelyn family. His first wife was Rose Williams, and through their son Thomas Evelyn of Long Ditton (1551–1617) the Long Ditton and Huntercombe branches of the family were descended. Through their son John (1554–1627) the Wiltshire and Godstone branches were descended, and through their son Robert (b. c. 1556) the American branch was descended. His second wife was Joan Stint and the Wotton branch of the family descended from their son Richard (1590–1650), JE's father.

Evelyn, George: Traveller and architect. A first cousin of JE, his exact identification is uncertain. He is either George Evelyn, born 1593, son of JE's uncle Robert who emigrated to America, or George Evelyn of Huntercombe, Bucks (1593–1657), son of JE's uncle Thomas of Long Ditton.

Evelyn, George, of Wotton (1617–99): JE's elder brother. He was educated at the free school at Guildford and at Trinity College, Oxford. Inheriting the Wotton estate in 1640 he settled down to life as a local magnate. Married (1) Mary Caldwell, by whom he had one son, George (1644–76) and (2) Mary, Lady Cotton, whose surviving children were Mary (1648–1723) and John (1653–91). George became MP for Haslemere in 1661. He gravitated towards the Country party, and was later a Whig. He was returned as knight of the shire for Surrey in the short 'Exclusion' parliaments; in 1685 successful efforts were made by the Court party to prevent his re-election. He was returned for Surrey in the Convention parliament of 1689, but refused to stand again the following year in view of his age. He was noted for the old-fashioned hospitality which he maintained at Wotton.

Evelyn, George, of Huntercombe (1630–99): JE's first cousin once removed, grandson of his uncle Thomas Evelyn of Long Ditton. JE visited his house in July 1679.

Evelyn, George, of Nutfield (1641–99): JE's first cousin once removed, son of his first cousin Sir John of Godstone.

Evelyn, George, jun., of Wotton (1644–76): JE's nephew, son and heir of his elder brother George. He married Catherine Gore (b. c. 1648), a merchant's daughter. Three daughters survived to adulthood:

Catherine (b. 1671) who married George Fulham; Mary (b. 1673) and Elizabeth (1674–c. 95) who married Richard Dyott and left a daughter, Jane, who is mentioned in her great-grandfather's will in 1699.

Evelyn, George (1657–8): JE's fourth son.

Evelyn, George (b. and d. 1658): JE's nephew, son of Richard Evelyn.

Evelyn, Jane (1616–51): JE's sister, married William Glanville c. 1647. They had one son, also William (c. 1650–1718).

Evelyn, Jane (b. 1691): JE's granddaughter, daughter of his son John. She died in infancy.

Evelyn, John, of Kingston and Godstone (1554–1627): JE's uncle, manufacturer of gunpowder.

Evelyn, Sir John, of Godstone (1591–1664): JE's first cousin, son of the above, knighted 1641. MP for Bletchingly 1628, in the Long Parliament, and 1660. Married Thomasine Heynes. JE was friendly with him and he was godfather to his son John, b. 1655.

Evelyn, Sir John, of Godstone (1633–71): JE's first cousin once removed, son of the above. Created a baronet in 1660. He had no male heirs and left his Marden estate to his mistress, Mary Gittings.

Evelyn, Sir John, of West Dean and Everley (1601–85): Sometimes referred to as Sir John Evelyn of Wilts, he was JE's first cousin once removed, being the grandson of John Evelyn of Godstone, the diarist's uncle. He was knighted in 1623 and was MP for Ludgershall in the Short and Long Parliaments and for Stockbridge in 1660. A strong Parliamentarian, he was excluded from a pardon granted by Charles I to the inhabitants of Wiltshire (2 November 1642). He married Elizabeth, daughter of Robert Cockes of London in 1622 and was succeeded by his daughter Elizabeth Pierrepont (1639–99).

Evelyn, John Stansfield (1653–4): JE's second son.

Evelyn, John of Wotton (1653–91): JE's nephew, son of George Evelyn of Wotton. Married Katherine Eversfield in 1681. All their children died young.

Evelyn, John, jun. (1655–99): E's third son, and the only one to survive to adulthood. Married Martha Spencer in 1680. Two of their children survived infancy – John (1682–1763) and Elizabeth (1684–1760).

Evelyn, John of Nutfield (1677–1702): JE's first cousin twice removed, son of George

Evelyn of Nutfield. Became MP for Bletchingly in 1702.

Evelyn, Sir John (1682–1763): JE's grandson, son of John Evelyn, jun. He married Anne Boscawen, niece of Lord Godolphin, in 1705, and was made a baronet in 1713. He was succeeded by his eldest son, another John Evelyn, who became the second baronet.

Evelyn, Mrs. Katherine: Born Eversfield. Married JE's nephew John Evelyn of Wotton in 1681. She died before 1699.

Evelyn, Mrs. Martha (c. 1661–1726): Born Spencer. JE's daughter-in-law, wife of John Evelyn, jun. She was the daughter of Lady Stonhouse by her first husband, Richard Spencer.

Evelyn, Martha Maria (b. and d. 1683): JE's granddaughter, daughter of John and Martha Evelyn.

Evelyn, Mrs. Mary (d. 1644): JE's sister-in-law, born Caldwell, first wife of George Evelyn of Wotton, whom she married in 1640. She was the granddaughter of a gentleman owning an estate in the neighbouring parish of Albury. She left one child, George Evelyn, jun. (1644–76).

Evelyn, (Mrs.) Mary (d. 1664): Second wife of George Evelyn of Wotton: see Cotton, Mary, Lady Cotton.

Evelyn, Mrs. Mary (c. 1635–1709): JE's wife, daughter of Sir Richard Browne and Elizabeth Prettyman.

Evelyn, Mary (1648–1723): JE's niece. See Wyche, Mary, Lady Wyche.

Evelyn, Mary (1665–85): JE's daughter.

Evelyn, Richard, sen., (c.1589–1640): JE's father, married Eleanor Stansfield in 1614.

Evelyn, Richard, of Woodcote (1622–70): JE's younger brother, married Elizabeth Mynne in 1648. Only one daughter, Anne, survived to adulthood.

Evelyn, Richard (b. 1652): JE's nephew, son of George Evelyn. Presumably died before September 1656 when another Richard was baptised (who also died in infancy).

Evelyn, Richard (1652–8): JE's eldest son.

Richard (b. and d. 1664): JE's fifth son and second of the name.

Evelyn, Richard (b. 1664): JE's nephew, son of Richard Evelyn. He died in infancy.

Evelyn, Richard (1680–1): JE's grandson, son of John Evelyn, jun.

Evelyn, Stansfield (1655–6): JE's nephew, son of George Evelyn.

Evelyn, Susanna (1669–1754): JE's youngest daughter and only child to survive him.

She married William Draper in 1693. Two of their children survived to adulthood: William Draper (1698–1759) and Susanna (1701–72). At least four others died in infancy, including Thomas (1694–5).

Evelyn, Sir Thomas, of Long Ditton (1587–1659): JE's first cousin, eldest son of his uncle, Thomas Evelyn of Long Ditton.

Evelyn, Thomasine, Lady Evelyn (c. 1603–76): Born Heynes or Haines, wife of Sir John Evelyn of Godstone, JE's first cousin.

Fanshaw, Sir Richard (1608–66): Diplomat and man of letters. A staunch Royalist, he was ambassador to Portugal and subsequently to Spain after the Restoration.

Fell, Dr. John (1625–1686): Scholar, author and divine. Son of the Dean of Christchurch, Oxford, he began his studies at that college at the precocious age of 11. Later he was expelled for fighting for the king. After the Restoration he became Dean of Christchurch (1660–86), also serving as Vice-Chancellor of Oxford (in which capacity he received the gift of the Arundelian marbles on behalf of the University in 1667). He became Bishop of Oxford in 1676. Fell also contributed greatly to the development of the Oxford University Press, and was the subject of the well-known epigram beginning 'I do not love you, Dr. Fell'.

Ferrarius (Ferrari), Francisco Bernardino (1577–1669): Italian scholar who was selected by Frederick Borromeo, Archbishop of Milan, to travel and collect books and manuscripts for a library he was desirous of founding in that city. He collected a great number of works in all classes of literature, which with later editions, has since been known as the Ambrosian Library. He later became Prefect of the Ambrosian College.

Finch, Sir Heneage (1621–82): Lord Chancellor from 1675 to 1682. He was created Baron Finch of Daventry in 1674 and 1st Earl of Nottingham in 1681.

Finch, Sir John (1584–1660): Judge. He was Speaker of the House of Commons in 1627 and was made Attorney-General to the Queen (Henrietta Maria) in 1635. He was appointed Judge of the Common Pleas in 1636 and Lord Keeper of the Great Seal in 1637. In 1640 he was advanced to the peerage as Baron Finch of Fordwich.

Firmin, Thomas: Presumably Thomas Firmin (1632–97), the philanthropist. His interest in the relief of the fugitive Irish bishops and clergy led him to distribute the briefs for it.

Fitzgerald, Elizabeth (d. c. 1698): Countess of Clancarty, daughter of the Earl of Kildare. Her second husband, William Davis, was Chief Justice of the King's Bench of Ireland 1681–7. Her son, the 4th Earl of Clancarty, forfeited his vast estates for the services he had rendered James II.

Fitzroy, Henry (1663–90): Sailor and soldier. He was the second natural son of Charles II by the Duchess of Cleveland. He was created Earl of Euston in 1672, and Duke of Grafton in 1675. He commanded Royal troops in Somerset in the rebellion of Monmouth but later joined William of Orange. He died in battle at the storming of Cork while leading William's forces.

Flamstead, John (1646–1719): A distinguished astronomer who, in his day, rivalled Sir Isaac Newton in the comprehensiveness of his scientific knowledge. He was the first director of the Royal Greenwich Observatory, where he was charged by Charles II with the task of finding accurate measurements for longitude.

Fox, Sir Stephen (1627–1716): Statesman and financier, a friend of JE. He was made Paymaster of the Forces (1660–76) by Charles II and became a Commissioner of the Treasury in 1680, an office he filled for 23 years. He contributed £13,000 towards the founding of Chelsea Hospital. Unlike other statesmen of his day, he grew rich in the service of the nation without being suspected of corruption, and without forfeiting the esteem of his contemporaries.

Fulham, Dr. George (c. 1660–1702): Rector of Compton, Surrey 1685–1701, Prebendary of Winchester 1693, Archdeacon of Winchester 1700. Married Catherine Evelyn (1671–99), JE's great-niece, daughter of George Evelyn, jun.

Gale, Thomas (1636–1702): Greek Professor at Cambridge, Master of St. Paul's School, London, and subsequently Dean of York. He was the author of several scholastic works, and was counted among the most learned men of his time.

Gerard, Charles (1618–94): Royalist and soldier, created Baron Gerard of Brandon 1645 and Earl of Macclesfield 1679.

Gibbons (Gibson), Grinling (1648–1721): Celebrated wood carver and sculptor, who was discovered by JE and recommended by him to the king and to Sir Christopher Wren.

Gibbes (Gibbs), Dr. James Alban (1611–77): Physician and writer of Latin poetry. Born in Scotland, he was resident many years in Rome, where he died.

Glanville, Mrs. Frances (d. 1699): Daughter of Edward Hales and Elizabeth Evelyn (daughter of JE's cousin Sir John Evelyn of Godstone). She married JE's nephew William Glanville in 1691. The couple had at least two daughters, Elizabeth (b. 1694) and Frances (c. 1697–1719).

Glanville, William (c. 1618–1702): JE's brother-in-law. He married JE's sister Jane c. 1647. The couple had one son, also William.

Glanville, William (1650–1718): JE's nephew, son of the above. Became a barrister and an MP (1679, 1680). He married Frances Hales in 1691.

Godolphin, Francis (1678–1716): Only son of Sidney and Margaret Godolphin (see below). JE was appointed his trustee and also supervised his education. In 1698 he married Henrietta Churchill (1681–1733), eldest daughter of the Duke of Marlborough.

Godolphin, Mrs. Margaret (1652–78): Born Blagge. Orphan daughter of a Royalist colonel, maid of honour to the Duchess of York and later to the queen. Greatly loved by JE and frequently extolled by him as a model of piety and virtue in a depraved age. They made a compact of friendship in 1672. In 1675 she secretly married Sidney Godolphin, afterwards Lord Godolphin. She died in 1678 after the birth of her first child, Francis Godolphin, and her life was written by JE during the following decade. She is often represented by JE by two symbols: the pentacle and the sign for Libra.

Godolphin, Sidney (1645–1712): Statesman and friend of JE's. Created 1st Baron Godolphin in 1684, and 1st Earl of Godolphin in 1706. In 1679 he was appointed one of the Lords Commissioners of the Treasury under Charles II, rising to First Commissioner in 1684. On James II's accession he became Chamberlain to the Queen but returned to the Treasury two years later and continued in office under William III until 1696 and again in

1700–1702. Under Queen Anne he served as Lord Treasurer and chief minister for the Tories between 1702 and 1710.

Goring, Sir George (1585–1662): General. 1st Baron Goring 1628, created 1st Earl of Norwich 1644. He distinguished himself in the Civil Wars for his military services in the Royalist cause and later in the Netherlands as Lieutenant-General in the army of the king of Spain.

Grafton, Duke of: see Fitzroy, Henry.

Gramont (Grammont), Philebert, comte de (1621–1707): French courtier at the court of Louis XIV who was exiled after he tried to rival Louis in a love affair. He came to England where he became a prominent figure in the court of Charles II.

Grew, Dr. Nehemiah (1628–1711): English botanist and physician; one of the first to advocate the theory of different sexes in plants.

Guildford, Countess of: see Boyle, Elizabeth.

Gunning, Dr. Peter (1618–88): Born in Leyden, he came to England and was made Canon of Windsor by Charles II. He held the Mastership of St. John's College, Cambridge, and later the Bishopric of Ely. It was said of him by the king, 'He is a strange man for a divine; there is nothing he refuses to believe but the Bible'.

Gwyn, Nell (1650–87): Born Eleanor Gwyn, she was a popular comic actress and celebrated mistress of Charles II. She was originally an orange-seller in the theatre and made her debut at London's Theatre Royal in Dryden's *The Indian Emperor* in 1665. She became the mistress to the king in 1668 and bore him two sons. According to JE, the monarch's last words to his brother and successor James were 'that Nelly might not starve'.

Hale (Hales), Sir Matthew (1609–76): Judge. One of the Justices of the Bench in Cromwell's time, who distinguished himself through his impartiality and good judgement. After the Restoration he became Chief Baron of the Exchequer; then Chief Justice of the King's Bench. He was the author of numerous works including volumes on mathematics and philosophy.

Halifax: see Savile, Sir George.

Halley, Edmond (1656–1742): Astronomer, mathematician and Fellow of the Royal Society. Became Professor of Geometry at Oxford and was later appointed Astronomer Royal. Best known for recognizing that a bright comet (later named after him) had appeared several times, and for successsfully predicting its return.

Hampden, John (1653–96): Grandson of the opponent of ship money. Imprisoned in the Tower at the time of the Rye House Plot (1683) and fined. Condemned to death after the Monmouth Rebellion (1685) but pardoned the following year. He was also a scholar of repute.

Harley, Robert (1661–1724): Statesman. During William III's reign he acted with the Whigs, but under Queen Anne he became leader of the Tories and was Speaker of the House in three Parliaments. He was Secretary of State 1704–8, and appointed Lord High Treasurer in 1711 when he was also created Earl of Oxford and Mortimer. He later helped negotiate an end to the War of Spanish Succession. He was impeached upon the succession of the House of Hanover but acquitted.

Hartlib, Samuel (1600–62): Polish-born publisher, writer, and scholar who founded a school for the education of gentlemen's sons and published several works on agriculture. He arrived in England around 1630, and attained some celebrity in 1641 by the publication of a work describing various attempts to create a general union of Protestants of all denominations.

Hatton, Elizabeth, Baroness Hatton (d. 1672): Eldest daughter of Sir Charles Montagu of Boughton, and niece of Henry, Earl of Manchester. She married in 1630 Sir Christopher Hatton (1605–70), created a baron in 1643 for his services to the Royalist cause. He was appointed Governor of Guernsey after the Restoration.

Heinsius, Daniel (1580–1655): Dutch scholar and critic and Professor of History at Leyden, who edited numerous editions of the classics. In 1619, he was appointed Secretary to the States of Holland, at the Synod of Dort. The fame of his learning became so diffused that the Pope endeavoured to draw him to Rome.

Henrietta Anne (1644–70): Charles II's youngest and favourite sister, 'Minette'. She was raised as a Catholic at the French court and known as 'Madame' after her marriage in 1661 with Philippe, Duke of Orléans, brother of Louis XIV.

Henrietta Maria (1609–69): Daughter of Henri IV of France and Marie de Medici, queen consort of Charles I. Her Roman Catholicism heightened public concern about the religious sympathies of the court. From 1644 she lived mainly in France.

Henshaw, Thomas (1618–1700): Author and friend of JE. Trained as a lawyer but also served in the French army for some years. Gentleman of the Privy Council and French Under-Secretary to Charles II, James II and William III. An original Fellow of the Royal Society (1662). Envoy Extraordinary in Denmark 1671–4. His works include a translation of Samedo's *History of China* (1655) and an edition of Stephen Skinner's *Etymologicon Linguae Anglicanae* (1671).

Herbert, Arthur (1648–1716): Admiral and politician. Dismissed from office by James II, he actively supported the 1688 Revolution and was created Earl of Torrington in 1689. After retreating from the French fleet near Beachy Head in 1690, he was court-martialled and sent to the Tower. Though later acquitted, he was never again employed.

Hobbes, Thomas (1588–1679): Philosopher. In exile with the Royalists during the 1640s (he was sometime mathematical tutor to the Prince of Wales) he returned in 1651 and made his submission to Cromwell's government. His works include *De Corpore Politico* (1650), *Human Nature* (1650), *De Corpore* (1655) and *De Homine* (1658). The most famous of all, *Leviathan* (1651), a treatise of political philosophy, brought him into general disfavour with both Court and Church, but at the Restoration he was granted a pension by the king.

Hollar, Wenceslaus (1607–77): Sculptor and etcher, born in Prague, who came to England in the service of the Earl of Arundel in 1636. With the exception of an eight-year stay in Antwerp, he remained in England for the rest of his life.

Hooke, Robert (1635–1703): Physicist and architect. One of the leading scientists of 17th-century England, he was first Curator of Experiments at the Royal Society. As an architect, he designed the new Bethlehem Royal Hospital in Moorfields, which was compared by JE to the Tuileries in Paris.

Hooper, George (1640–1727): Dean of Canterbury, Bishop of St. Asaph, and later the Bishop of Bath and Wells.

Hopton, Sir Arthur (d. 1650): Uncle not, as stated by JE, brother to Sir Ralph, Lord Hopton, Royalist military hero.

Houblon (Houblons), Sir James (c. 1629–1700): Protestant refugee from Lille. One of the most eminent of the London merchants during the late 17th century and one of the first directors of the Bank of England (1694–1700).

Hough (Huff), Dr. John (1651–1743): President of Magdalen College, 1687. Bishop of Oxford (1690), Lichfield (1699) and Worcester (1717).

Howard, Elizabeth: Widow of William Howard, fourth son of the 1st Earl of Berkshire. Pepys describes her in 1669 as the Duke of York's housekeeper at the Treasurer's House in Deptford Dockyard. She and her two daughters, Dorothy Graham and Anne, Lady Sylvius, became friends of JE.

Howard, Henry (1628–84): Second son of Lord Mowbray and grandson of Thomas Howard, 2nd Earl of Arundel. Succeeded his elder brother as 6th Duke of Norfolk in 1677. JE often mentions this family. His son John spent much of his early boyhood with Howard's children, though fear of the earl's Catholicism eventually led Evelyn to withdraw him.

Howard, Henry (1655–1701): Son of the 6th Duke of Norfolk, inheriting the title in 1684 (previously styled Earl of Arundel). Brought up a Catholic, he conformed to the Church of England in 1678.

Howard, Henry Frederick (1608–52): Son of Lord Arundel. Irish Privy Councillor and Royalist soldier. In 1626 he married Elizabeth, eldest daughter of Esme Stuart, Earl of March, and afterwards Duke of Lennox. He was created 3rd Earl of Arundel in 1646 (styled Lord Mowbray 1640–46).

Howard, Philip Thomas (1629–94): Third son of Henry Frederick Howard, Baron Mowbray. Grand Almoner to Queen Catherine (1665), created a Cardinal in 1675.

Howard, Sir Robert (1626–1698): English dramatist, sixth son of Thomas Howard, 1st Earl of Berkshire. He held several important government posts under Charles II including Auditor of the Exchequer.

Howard, Thomas (1585–1646): 2nd Earl of Arundel and the first great English art collector and patron of arts. Part of his collection was eventually procured for the University of Oxford by JE.

Howard, Sir William (1614–80): A younger son of the above. Created Viscount

Stafford in 1640. In 1678 he was accused of complicity with the 'Popish Plot' and put on trial in Westminster Hall. He was found guilty by a majority of his peers and beheaded on Tower Hill in 1680.

Huygens, Christiaan (1629–95): Astronomer and scientist, inventor of the pendulum clock. His *Systema Saturnium* (1659) is an explanation of the rings of Saturn. He became a Fellow of the Royal Society in 1663.

Huygens, Constantine (1596–1687): Father of the above. A notable figure in the Dutch Renaissance, he was a poet and composer, and held the post of Secretary to the Princes of Orange (1625–50).

Hyde, Anne (1637–71): Daughter of the 1st Earl of Clarendon, Anne secretly married James, Duke of York, heir presumptive to the throne, in September 1660. Their two daughters both became queens of England – Mary II and Anne.

Hyde (Hide), Sir Edward (1609–74): Statesman and historian. Became adviser to Charles I and Charles II, sharing the latter's exile. He was Lord Chancellor after the Restoration until the unpopularity of the Court party and lack of success in the Second Dutch War led the king to force his resignation. He left the country to avoid impeachment by the Commons and died in exile. He wrote one of the earliest histories of the Civil Wars, *History of the Rebellion*, published posthumously (1702–4).

Hyde, Flower, Lady Clarendon (1641–1700): Born Backhouse. Twice widowed, she married Henry Hyde, then Lord Cornbury, in 1670 as his second wife.

Hyde, Frances, Lady Clarendon (1617–67): Second wife of Sir Edward Hyde, 1st Earl of Clarendon, whom she married in 1634.

Hyde, Lady Henrietta (Harriette) (*c*. 1645–87): Countess of Rochester. Daughter of Richard Boyle, Earl of Burlington; married, 1665, Clarendon's son, Laurence Hyde, created Earl of Rochester 1682.

Hyde, Henry (1638–1709): 2nd Earl of Clarendon, and eldest son of the 1st Earl. Styled Lord Cornbury 1661–74. Private secretary, then Lord Chamberlain (1665) and Treasurer (1670) to the queen. Keeper of Somerset House (1679). He was appointed Lord Privy Seal and Lord-Lieutenant of Ireland by James II but dismissed in 1687. Opposed Revolution settlement and was imprisoned in the Tower as a Jacobite (to

1690). He was elected a Fellow of the Royal Society in 1684.

Hyde, Laurence (1641–1711): Second son of the 1st Earl of Clarendon, created 1st Earl of Rochester (2nd creation) 1682. First Commissioner of the Treasury 1679–84, and one of Charles's chief ministers. Appointed Lord Treasurer by James II, 1685–7. Initially an opponent of the Revolution settlement, he emerged as leader of the Tories after 1688.

Hyde, Dr. Thomas (1638–1703): Orientalist and linguist. He was appointed Under-Keeper of the Bodleian Library in 1659 and, in 1665, Librarian-in-Chief. He also served as Prebend of Salisbury Cathedral and Canon of Christchurch, Oxford.

Hildyard (Hyldiard), Henry (1610–74): Compounded as a Royalist, 1646, an MP and Chamberlain of the Exchequer 1660–74. The Hildyards, also from Surrey, were family friends of JE. The eldest son, Henry (1636–1705) converted to Catholicism and went into exile after the Revolution, and Philip (d. 1693) was another Chamberlain of the Exchequer.

Ireton, Henry (1611–51): Parliamentarian general and regicide. Ireton married Cromwell's daughter Bridget, and acquired great influence in the Parliamentarian party. He took an active part in the Civil War from its outbreak, and in 1645 became Commissary General of Horse in the New Model Army. He went to Ireland as Cromwell's deputy in 1649 and died of fever during the siege of Limerick.

Innocentio decimo (Innocent X) (1574–1655): Also known as Giambattista Pamfili. Chosen as Pope in 1644.

James II (1633–1701); Second son of Charles I, reigned 1685–88. As Duke of York and heir presumptive to his brother, Charles II, James provoked a constitutional crisis when he converted to Catholicism. Attempts by Parliament to exclude him from the succession failed, but his religious policy resulted in the Revolution of 1688 and his deposition in favour of his eldest daughter Mary and her husband (also James's nephew), William of Orange, who were Protestants. James's move to win back his throne ended in failure at the battle of the Boyne in Ireland (1690) and he died in exile. By his first wife, Anne Hyde, James had two daughters, Mary and Anne, both of whom became queens of England: by his second wife, Mary of Modena, he had two children, the eldest of whom was James Edward, the 'Old Pretender' (1688–1766).

Jeffreys (Jeofries, etc.), Sir George (1648–89): The notorious 'Hanging Judge'. He embarked on a legal career in 1668 and by 1683 was Lord Justice of the King's Bench, having been knighted (1677) and created a baronet (1681) on the way. Currying royal favour, he readily subordinated impartiality to his political ambitions as in the trial of Algernon Sidney, who was convicted on the flimsiest of evidence of involvement in the Rye House Plot, and executed. James II created him first Baron Jeffreys, and Lord Chancellor, but his reputation as a judge became even more unsavoury after the 'Bloody Assizes', in which vengeance was wrought on followers of the Duke of Monmouth who had taken part in his rebellion. When James was deposed Jeffreys attempted to flee the country but was captured and died in the Tower of London.

Jermyn (German), Henry (1) (c. 1604–84): Courtier and favourite of Queen Henrietta Maria in whose household he began his career. He was MP for Bury St. Edmunds in the Long Parliament and an active and reckless Royalist. He was made 1st Baron Jermyn in 1643 and appointed Governor of Jersey in 1644. At the Restoration he was created 1st Earl of Albans. A strong supporter of Charles II's policy of friendship with France, he was Ambassador in Paris 1660–2 and returned there on missions in 1667 and 1669 in the lead-up to the Treaty of Dover. He was Lord Chamberlain 1671–4. In 1664 he obtained a grant of land in London near St. James's Palace, where Jermyn Street preserves the memory of his name.

Jermyn (Jarmine) Henry (2) (1636–1708): Nephew of the above. A Roman Catholic, he enjoyed a period of influence under James II, being appointed one of the Commissioners of the Treasury in 1687 and Governor of Portsmouth in 1688. He was created Baron Dover of Dover in 1685, and Earl of Dover in 1689 (Jacobite creation). He served under James in Ireland but appears to have surrendered to King William in 1690 and was subsequently pardoned. Dover Street in London is named after him.

Johnson, Rev. Samuel (1649–1703): Political divine, sometimes referred to as 'the Whig' to distinguish him from his great namesake. He was notorious for the rigour of his writings against the Court, especially for 'Julian the Apostate', directed at the Duke of York. For these he was fined and imprisoned, and degraded from the priesthood. He lived to see the Revolution, which placed William of Orange on the throne, whereupon he received a pension of £300 per annum.

Justell, Henry (1620–93): Born in France, he fled to England on the revocation of the Edict of Nantes, where he was appointed Keeper of the King's Library.

Joyliffe, George (1621–58): Anatomist and Fellow of the Royal College of Physicians. His discovery of the lymph ducts was published by Francis Glisson, 1654.

Ken, Dr. Thomas (1637–1711): Bishop of Bath and Wells (1684), hymn writer and chaplain to Charles II. Known for his benevolence, he was one of the seven bishops sent by James II to the Tower, yet he refused to acknowledge James's successor on the grounds that it would be a breach of his Consecration Oath, and was deprived in 1690.

Keppel, Arnold Joost van (1669–1718): Dutch supporter and companion of William III, Keppel was created Earl of Albemarle in 1695 and a Knight of the Garter in 1700. He returned to Holland after William's death and fought in the War of the Spanish Succession (1701–13).

Kercherus (Kircher, Kirker), Father Athanasius (1601–80): German Jesuit scholar. Renowned in his day as one of the world's greatest thinkers, he published many volumes on subjects as diverse as mathematics, Oriental studies, geology, medicine and hieroglyphics.

Kéroualle (Quirreval, etc.), Louise de, (1649–1734): Maid of Honour to the Duchess of Orléans, Charles II's sister.She came to England with instructions to entice Charles II into a union with Louis XIV. She became the king's mistress, was made Duchess of Portsmouth, and was his favourite till his death.

Keightley, Mrs. Rose (1596–1682/3): Daughter of JE's uncle Thomas Evelyn of Long Ditton, she was JE's first cousin and also his godmother. She married Thomas

Keightley, sen. in 1616. Two of their sons, Thomas (b. *c.* 1622) and William (b. *c.* 1621) converted to Catholicism.

Kneller, Sir Godfrey (1646–1723): German-born court painter to five monarchs of England (Charles II, James II, William III, Queen Anne, George I). He was knighted in 1692 by William III.

Kings of England: *see* Charles I, Charles II, James II, William III.

Lane, Jane (d. 1689): Sister of Colonel Lane, an officer in the army of Charles II. She assisted the king in effecting his escape after the battle of Worcester in 1651, when he travelled with her disguised as her servant, William Jackson. She subsequently became the wife of Clement Fisher, bart.

Laud (Lawd), William (1573–1645): Anglican cleric who became predominant in the Church of England on Charles I's accession in 1625, being made Bishop of London in 1628 and Archbishop of Canterbury in 1633. He supported the king in his struggle with the Commons and tried to enforce religious conformity. He interfered disastrously with the Scottish Church, was impeached by the Long Parliament, condemned, tried and executed. Laud gave some 1,300 manuscripts in 18 languages, and his collection of coins, to the Bodleian Library.

Lauderdale, Duke of: *see* Maitland, John.

Leech, Jane, Lady Leech (b. 1631): Born Jane Evelyn, daughter of Sir John Evelyn of Godstone, and JE's first cousin once removed. She married Sir William Leech of Squerryes in Westerham, Kent.

Leighton, Sir Elisha (Ellis) (d. 1685): An adventurer and dependant of Buckingham, he was Secretary to the Prize Office, and to the Duke of York. FRS 1663, expelled 1667.

L'Estrange, Sir Roger (1616–1704): Pamphleteer on the Royalist side before the Restoration and the Court side afterwards, he was one of the earliest of English journalists. He was a fierce and reckless advocate of High Church principles, and established a newspaper called the *Public Intelligencer*, which he afterwards changed to *London Gazette*, and ultimately to the *Observator*. He had the courage to oppose Oates when the Popish Plot was at its height. He was knighted by James II but after the 1688 Revolution was regarded by the Whigs as a grave threat to liberty

and was several times imprisoned. He supported himself by translations which include Aesop's *Fables* (1692).

Locke, John (1632–1704): Philosopher and political theorist, the founder of British Empiricism. His two most important works were published in 1690: *Two Treatises of Government* and *An Essay Concerning Human Understanding*. He was personal physician and adviser to the Earl of Shaftesbury and through him became involved in the politics of the period.

Louis XIV (1638–1715): King of France, reigned 1643–1715. His reign represented the high point of the Bourbon dynasty and of French power in Europe, during which French art and literature flourished. However, his almost constant wars of expansion united Europe against him and the Peace of Utrecht (1713–14) represented the ultimate failure of his attempts at European hegemony.

Lubicer: Thomas Baltzar (?1630–63), the violinist. He was from Lübeck, hence Evelyn's name for him.

Mackenzie (Mackenzy), Sir George (1636–1691): Scottish advocate who earned the nickname 'Bloody Mackenzie' for his heavy hand during the Scottish administration of Charles II.

Maitland, John (1616–82): 2nd Earl (1645) and 1st Duke (1672) of Lauderdale. Scottish statesman. Originally a subscriber to the Covenant he went over to Charles I during the Civil War, was later captured at the battle of Worcester (1651) and imprisoned until the Restoration. Charles II appointed him Secretary of State for Scotland. In 1667 he became a member of the Cabal ministry. He also sat on the Privy Council. His rule in Scotland was ruthless and unpopular, and his use of Highland troops to suppress the Covenanters in the southwest provoked an uprising in 1679. Despite attacks in Parliament, he kept his influence by intrigues until 1680, when his health broke.

Marlborough, Lord: *see* Churchill, John.

Mary II, Queen (1662–94): Daughter of James II, reigned 1689–94. On the insistence of Charles II, Mary and her sister Anne were brough up as Protestants in spite of their father's conversion to Catholicism, and she was invited to replace him on the throne after his deposition in 1688. This she did in conjunction with her husband, William of Orange (*see* William III). The couple had no children.

Mercator, Nicholas Kauffmann, known as Mercator (*c.* 1620–87): Mathematician and mechanician. Born in Holstein, he settled in England after the Restoration, where he was elected a Fellow of the Royal Society in 1661.

Merret, Christopher (1614–95): Celebrated physician and naturalist, Fellow of the Royal Society.

Middleton, John (*c.* 1608–74):
A Parliamentarian general in the Civil War, he subsequently fought for Charles II. He was created 1st Earl of Middleton in 1660 and was variously Commander-in-Chief of the Forces in Scotland, Governor of Edinburgh Castle and Commissioner of the Scottish Parliament until he clashed with the powerful Earl of Lauderdale and lost all his offices in 1663. He was Governor of Rochester 1663–7 and Lieutenant-General of the Kent Militia. In 1668 he was appointed Governor of Tangier.

Milton, Christopher (1615–93): Younger brother of the poet John Milton, he was made a judge in 1686, and later a Baron of the Exchequer.

Milton, John (1608–74): The poet. Until the publication of *Paradise Lost* in 1667, known principally as an author of subversive books and pamphlets on religion, rebellion, regicide and divorce. A propagandist for the cause of Parliament, he replied officially to *Eikon Basilike* (about the martyrdom of Charles I) with *Eikonoklastes* ('The Image Breaker') and to Salmasius's defence of Charles I with *Pro Populo Anglicano Defensio* (1651). At the Restoration he issued a last stand for Republicanism, *The Ready and Easy Way to Establish a Free Commonwealth*. He was fined and imprisoned but afterwards released.

Modena, Mary of (1658–1718): Daughter of Alfonso IV d'Este, Duke of Modena and the second wife of James, Duke of York, afterwards James II. Mary was a Catholic and by 1673, when they married, James had also converted to Catholicism. After the Revolution she spent the rest of her life in exile in France.

Monck (Monk), George (1608–70): General and admiral. He fought under Charles I in the Scottish war (1639), and under Cromwell during the Commonwealth, becoming Commander-in-Chief in Scotland in 1654. In 1659 he supported the recalled Rump Parliament when it came into conflict with the army leaders. In January 1660 his army marched to London and occupied the city. His intentions remained unclear until 1 May, when he recommended that Parliament should invite Charles II to return. When the restored king landed at Dover on 25 May, Monck was the first to greet him as he came ashore. Created Duke of Albemarle, he continued to command the army until his death, and as admiral of the fleet in 1666 he won a decisive victory over the Dutch.

Monconys, Balthasar de (1611–65): Frenchman, celebrated for his travels in the East, of which he published an account in three volumes.

Monmouth, Duke of: *see* Scott, James.

Montagu (Mountagu), Edward (1625–72): 1st Earl of Sandwich. Took part in the first Civil War on Parliament's side, though took no part in the second or in the trial and execution of the king. Held various offices under Cromwell, who was a personal friend, and, though he had no experience, was put in control of the fleet, presiding over the capture of the Spanish treasure fleet in 1657. He supported the Restoration and commanded the ship which brought Charles II to England. Established an English garrison in Tangiers, 1662. Took an active part in the Second Dutch War (victorious at Lowestoft, defeated at Bergen, 1665) but replaced by Albemarle as Commander-in-Chief. President of the Council for Foreign Plantations, 1671. Second-in-command of the fleet in the Third Dutch War, he was killed at the battle of Solebay.

Montagu, Viscount: *see* Brown, Francis.

Moore, Dr. John (d. 1714): Bishop of Norwich; afterwards Bishop of Ely. His collection of books was purchased by King George after his death for £6,000 and presented to the University of Cambridge.

Mordaunt, Elizabeth, Lady Peterborough (1603–71): Daughter of William Howard, Lord Howard of Effingham, and widow of the 1st Earl of Peterborough (d. 1643). She lived at Reigate Priory. She was the mother of Henry and John Mordaunt. JE was initimate with the family and took an active part in their business affairs.

Mordaunt, Elizabeth, Viscountess Mordaunt (d. 1679): Daughter of Thomas Carey

(1597–1634) and wife of John Mordaunt. JE had for some years been acquainted with her mother, who after Carey's death became Lady Herbert. Elizabeth became a close friend of JE and of Mrs. Godolphin. She left a collection of prayers, printed as her *Private Diarie* in 1856.

Mordaunt, Henry (1623–97): 2nd Earl of Peterborough, elder brother of JE's friend John Mordaunt. Privy Councillor 1683. He became a Catholic during the reign of James II and was imprisoned in the Tower for two years after the 1688 Revolution.

Mordaunt, John (1626–75): An ardent Royalist (for which he was put on trial and acquitted by just one vote during the Commonwealth), he campaigned for the return of Charles II, who in 1659 created him Baron Mordaunt of Reigate and Viscount Mordaunt of Avalon, and appointed him Constable of Windsor Castle. In 1656 he married Elizabeth Carey. Their eldest son Charles (1658–1735) succeeded to the earldom of Peterborough on the death of his uncle in 1697.

Morice, Sir William (1602–76): Secretary of State 1660–68.

Morison, Dr. Robert (1620–83): Scottish-born botanist and physician to Charles II. His skills as a botanist were so prized that he was appointed Regius Professor of Botany at Oxford.

Morley, Herbert (1616–67): Colonel. Educated at Lewes with JE. Became MP for Lewes in 1640. Fought on the Parliamentary side in the Civil War but would not act as one of the king's judges. Remained an MP for Sussex or Lewes throughout the Commonwealth period, also serving intermittently on the Council of State. As Lieutenant of the Tower of London he collected troops and opposed Lambert in 1659 but refused to negotiate for the king's return (in spite of JE's attempts to persuade him). With some help from JE he purchased a pardon in 1660.

Mowbray, Lord: *see* Howard, Henry Frederick.

Murray (Moray), Sir Robert (*c.* 1608–73): Scottish Royalist, statesman and scientist. Served in the French army, and joined the Scottish insurrection which ended in the defeat at Worcester (1651). He was knighted in 1643. In 1650 he was made Lord Justice Clerk and a Privy Councillor, appointments confirmed at the Restoration. According to the testimony of contemporaries he was universally esteemed and loved by men of all opinions. He was especially learned in geology, chemistry and natural history and was an original Fellow of the Royal Society, serving as President on several occasions between 1660 and 1662 when the office was elected monthly. Christiaan Huygens described him as the soul of the Society.

Nanteuil, Robert (1623–78): French draftsman, painter and printmaker who was the outstanding French portrait engraver of his age.

Needham, Dr. Jasper (1623–79): Personal physician to JE; performed an autopsy on his son Richard in 1658. JE also received advice from him when choosing books for his library.

Neve, La (1612?–78?): Artist better known as Cornelius De Neve.

Newton, Sir Adam (d. 1630): Tutor and secretary to Henry, Prince of Wales (d. 1612), eldest son of James I. Charlton House, which he built 1607–12, is still standing.

Newton, Sir Henry (1618–1701): Son of the above. The 3rd Baronet, a friend and neighbour of JE, he changed his surname to Puckering in 1654 and in 1656 went to live at Warwick Priory.

Newton, Sir Isaac (1642–1727): Mathematician and scientist. Attached to Trinity College, Cambridge from 1661 to 1696. Became Fellow of the Royal Society in 1672 and its President from 1703 until the end of his life. His great discoveries included the binomial theorem, differential calculus and the laws of gravitation which he applied to planetary and lunar motion in *Principia Mathematica* (1687). *Opticks* (1704) gave an account of his optical experiments and included the discovery that white light is made up of a mixture of colours. He sat in two Parliaments, was made Master of the Royal Mint in 1699, and knighted in 1705.

Nicholas, Sir John (*c.* 1623–1705): Eldest son of Sir Edward Nicholas (see below) and served as his secretary during the exile. KB 1661, MP from 1661 and one of the Clerks of the Council 1660–1705.

Nicholas, Sir Edward (1593–1669): Secretary of State ('Mr. Secretary') 1641–9 and 1654–62. Knighted 1641.

Northumberland, Earl of: *see* Percy, Algernon.

Norwich, Earl of: *see* Goring, Sir George.

Oates, Titus (1649–1705): Conspirator. Expelled from Merchant Taylors' School and twice sent down from Cambridge, Oates took holy orders and held several curacies and a naval chaplaincy from all of which he was dismissed. The same thing happened when he joined the Roman Catholic Church, at which point (1678) he concocted the story of the Popish Plot to murder the king and slaughter the Protestants. He perjured himself by making an affidavit before the magistrate Sir Edmund Berry Godfrey – whose murder in mysterious circumstances shortly afterwards proved very useful to him – and in spite of the inconsistencies of his evidence succeeded in creating a panic which led to the execution of many innocent Catholics, at the same time earning himself a pension of £600 and a suite in Whitehall. The Duke of York and the queen were both victims of his slanders. On the accession of the former in 1685 he was found guilty of perjury, flogged through the streets and imprisoned for life – only to be set free, with a pension, on the accession of William and Mary three years later.

Oldenburg, Henry (1615–77): A founder member of the Royal Society and its Secretary from 1663 until his death.

Ormond: *see* Butler.

Osborne, Sir Thomas (1631–1712): Statesman. Son of Sir Edward Osborne, Lieutenant-General of the Northern Forces. Commonly known by the title of Earl of Danby (1674) though he was subsequently made Marquis of Carmarthen (1689) and 1st Duke of Leeds (1694). Lord Treasurer and effectively chief minister from 1673, Danby was unpopular but an effective financial manager. His views on religion (strongly Anglican and anti-toleration) and foreign policy (anti-French) were in tune with the majority in the House, and he was never averse to offering bribes to encourage their support. His diplomatic triumph was the securing of a match between the Duke of York's daughter and heir, Mary, and the champion of Protestantism in Europe, William of Orange, but he could only pursue this public policy by acquiescence in the king's personal relations with Louis XIV and his acceptance of French money which bound him to support a policy the exact opposite of Danby's own. Impeachment threatened when the French king arranged for this complicity to be discovered to Parliament, and Danby was imprisoned in the Tower for five years. In 1688 he was one of the seven leaders who invited William III to England. A Tory, he was made Lord President of the Council, and after the retirement of his arch-enemy Halifax became the king's chief minister from 1690 to 1695, controlling Parliament by bribery as before. Unsuccessfully impeached for corruption in 1695, he began to lose influence and was compelled to resign from office in 1699. However, he continued to take an active part in politics until his death at the age of 80.

Ossory: *see* Butler.

Oughtred, Rev. William (1574–1660): Eminent mathematician and Anglican clergyman, credited as the inventor of the slide-rule (1622). His books include *An Easy Method of Geometrical Dialling* (1648) and *Trigonometry* (1657). In his *Clavis Mathematic* (1631) he introduced the signs × for multiplication and ∷ for proportion.

Owen, Sir John (1600–66): Welsh Royalist whose life had been forfeited for the part he took against Parliament, but was saved by the timely intervention of Colonel Hutchinson. The latter humanely spoke for him in the House, though Sir John was a perfect stranger to him; the colonel received scant gratitude for his pains.

Oxford, Earl of: *see* de Vere, Aubrey.

Packer, Philip (*c.* 1618–86): Barrister at the Middle Temple and an original Fellow of the Royal Society.

Palmer, Barbara (1640–1709). Born Barbara Villiers, and the cousin of the Duke of Buckingham, she married Roger Palmer in 1659 but became the mistress of Charles II the following year, and remained so throughout his reign, though principally during the 1660s. She was famously extravagant. She became Lady Castlemaine in 1661, her husband being granted the earldom, and Duchess of Cleveland in her own right in 1670. Of her six children, five were acknowledged by Charles, but she had other lovers, including the future Duke of Marlborough. She converted to Catholicism in 1673.

Papin, Denys (1647–*c.* 1712): French physician and mathematician who assisted Robert Boyle in his experiments and was afterwards Professor of Mathematics at Marburg.

Paston, Sir Robert (1631–83): Created Baron Paston and Viscount Yarmouth in 1673 and made Earl of Yarmouth in 1679. He was reputed a good scholar. He was the son of Sir William Paston (c. 1610–63), created a baronet in 1641.

Penn, Sir William (1621–70): Naval commander. He became Rear-Admiral in 1648 and distinguished himself in battle during the Second Dutch War (1665–7).

Penn, William (1644–1718): Son of the above. Quaker and founder of Pennsylvania, whom JE describes as having published 'a blasphemous book against the Deity of our blessed Lord', for which he was imprisoned in the Tower but released on his recantation (1669).

Pepys, Samuel (1633–1703): The diarist. Son of a London tailor, he entered the household of Sir Edward Montagu (afterwards Earl of Sandwich), a relation, and through his patronage followed a career in naval administration, ending as Secretary to the Admiralty. He also sat in Parliament 1673–9 and 1685–7. He was imprisoned in the Tower for complicity with the Popish plot 1679–80 but released and restored to office until displaced at the 1688 Revolution. His Diary (1660–69) was written in code and not deciphered until 1825.

Percy, Algernon (1602–68): 10th Earl of Northumberland, Charles I's Lord High Admiral (1637). A moderate Parliamentarian in the first Civil War, he opposed the king's trial and later supported the Restoration, becoming a Privy Councillor. His second wife, whom he married in 1642, was Elizabeth Howard (c. 1623–1705), daughter of the 2nd Earl of Suffolk. One of the first art collectors, Percy's Suffolk House gallery (later Northumberland House) was greatly admired by JE.

Peterborough: see Mordaunt.

Peters, Rev. Hugh (1598–1660): Independent divine. Minister in Salem, Massachusetts 1635–41. Back in England, threw himself into the civil conflict, his sermons winning recruits to the Parliamentarian army. Acted with the army in its dispute with Parliament. Accompanied Cromwell to Ireland in 1649. Made a chaplain to the Council of State in 1650 and during the Protectorate was a regular preacher at Whitehall. Executed in 1660 as an abettor of the execution of Charles I.

Petty, Sir William (1623–87): Inventor, physician, philosopher, author, political economist and entrepreneur, and one of the celebrities of the 17th century. Son of a Hampshire clothier, he attended grammar school but went to sea at 15, completing his education at Caen, in the Netherlands and in Paris, where he studied anatomy and medicine and practised as a physican. In 1647 he patented a copying-machine, which brought him to the intention of other scientists. He went on to hold a huge variety of posts including Professor of Anatomy at Oxford, Fellow of Brasenose, Professor of Music at Gresham College and Physician to the Army of Ireland. As Lord Deputy Commissioner in Ireland he executed for the Commonwealth the 'Down Survey' of forfeited lands, the first attempt on a large scale at carying out a survey scientifcally. He acquiesced in the Restoration, was knighted, and became an original member of the Royal Society. He was also appointed a Judge of the Admiralty in Ireland and a Commissioner of the Navy. Perhaps the most famous of his many books is his Treatise of Taxes and Contributions (1662) which considered the role of the state in the economy and touched on the labour theory of value. He married Elizabeth Fenton, widow of Sir Maurice Fenton, in 1667. Petty had twice refused a peerage, but Lady Petty was made Baroness Shelburne after his death.

Phillips, Edward (1630–96?): Author. Tutor to John Evelyn, jun. 1663–5. His mother was Milton's sister. Phillips gave JE some prominence in his edition of Baker's Chronicle (1665) and acknowledged him as a contributor to his dictionary, The New World of Words. He left JE's service for that of the Earl of Pembroke. In 1677 JE recommended him to Lord Arlington.

Pierce, Edward: Celebrated painter of landscape and architecture who worked under Van Dyck. He died a few years after the Restoration. His son, John, was also a painter.

Pierrepont, Mrs. Elizabeth (1639–99): Daughter of Sir John Evelyn of Wilts, married Robert Pierrepont. Their sons Robert, William and Evelyn Pierrepont became successively Earls of Kingston.

Pierrepont, Evelyn (c. 1655–1726): Son of the above. 5th Earl and (in 1715) 1st Duke of Kingston. Also created Marquis of Dorchester in 1706. A prominent figure in

982 GLOSSARY

fashionable society, he married Lady Mary
Fielding in 1687. One child of this marriage
was the celebrated Lady Mary Wortley
Montagu.

Plot, Robert (1640–96): Naturalist.
He acted as one of the Secretaries of the
Royal Society and was also the Royal
Historiographer and Keeper of the
Archives of the Heralds' College.

Porter, Endymion (1587–1649): Royalist, poet
and patron of the arts. Brought up in Spain,
he was involved in Buckingham's Spanish
diplomacy in the 1620s. He was Groom of
the Bedchamber to Charles I and one of
the agents employed by the king to build up
his great collection of pictures. An MP in
the Long Parliament, he was expelled in
1643 and went into exile, but compounded
with Parliament for a small fine in 1649.
He was painted by Van Dyck, and Jonson,
Herrick, D'Avenant and Dekker all
celebrated him in verse.

Portsmouth, Duchess of: see Kérouaille,
Louise de.

Poultney, Sir William (d. 1691): Distinguished
Parliamentarian, grandfather of 1st Earl of
Bath. He was a Commissioner of the Privy
Seal under William III.

Prideaux, Humphrey (1648–1724): Oriental
scholar and clergyman who took an active
role in the controversies of the day.
He became Dean of Norwich in 1702.

Pye, Sir Walter (1571–1635): Lawyer and
barrister of the Middle Temple. A favourite
of Buckingham, who obtained for him the
position of Attorney of the Court of Wards
and Liveries (1621). He was knighted in 1630.

Queens of England: see Henrietta Maria,
Catherine of Braganza, Mary of Modena,
Mary II, Anne.

Quirreval (Querouaille), Madame: see
Kérouaille, Louise de.

Ray, John (1628–1705): Celebrated naturalist
and author. He collected many thousands
of plants and animals, and laid the
foundations for botany as a serious science.
He was a contributor to the *Transactions*
of the Royal Society, having been elected
a Fellow in 1667.

Richardson, Sir Thomas: Judge. He was
made Lord Chief Justice of the Common
Pleas in 1626, and of the King's Bench in
1631.

Rochester, Earls of: see Hyde, Laurence;
Wilmot, John.

Rooke, Laurence (1623–62): Astronomy, and
subsequently Geometry Professor of
Gresham College.

Ross (Rosse), Rev. Alexander (1591–1654):
Scottish cleric and historian, master of a
free school in Southampton.

Rotiere, Philip: Engraver at the Royal Mint.
In 1667 he introduced the figure of
Britannica into the coinage, taking for his
model the king's favourite, Frances Stuart,
Duchess of Richmond.

Rupert, Prince (1619–82): Count Palatine
of the Rhine, third son of Elizabeth of
Bohemia (sister of Charles I) and
Frederick V, Elector Palatine. Fought as
a volunteer for the Prince of Orange in
the Thirty Years' War and came to England
in 1642 to fight for his uncle. He was a
distinguished if erratic cavalry leader and
general but when the tide began to turn
against him he was dismissed and spent
the 1650s on the Continent. After the
Restoration he served as a Privy Councillor
and as an admiral, seeing action in two
Dutch wars. He was First Lord of the
Admiralty 1673–9. He was an active
member of the Board of Trade and,
interested in promoting the development
of the colonies, was one of the chief
founders of the Hudson's Bay Company.
He was a keen scientist and inventor,
becoming a Fellow of the Royal Society in
1665, and also introduced mezzotints into
England.

Rustat, Toby (Tobias) (d. c. 1693): Attendant
of Charles II, both before and during his
reign, who carried messages between the
exiled Royals and the Royalists in hiding.
He was a great benefactor to Jesus College,
Cambridge, establishing a scholarship there
for the benefit of orphan sons of clergymen.

Ruvigny (Rouvigny, Rovigny, etc.), Henri de
Massue, 1st marquis de: French diplomat.
He was sent to the English court on a
number of special missions in the early
1660s, later becoming Envoy Extraordinary
(1667–8) and Ambassador (1674–6). He was
also Deputy-General of the Protestant
Churches of France from 1653. He and his
family fled from France after the revocation
of the Edict of Nantes (1685).

Ruvigny, Henri de Massue, 2nd marquis de
(1648–1720): Soldier and statesman. 1st Earl
of Galway, son of the above, raised to the
peerage by William III for his gallantry at
the battle of the Boyne, where his brother
also fought and was killed. Between 1697

and 1701 he was a Lord Justice and head of the administration in Ireland. He commanded afterwards both in Italy and Spain, where the fatal battle of Almanza put an end to his military glory.

St. Albans, Earl of: *see* Jermyn, Henry.

Sanderson, Sir William (1586–1676): Royalist and historian. He held the post of Gentleman of the Chamber to Charles II, and his wife that of 'mother of the maids'.

Sandwich, Earl of: *see* Montagu, Edward.

Saracins (or Sarazin), Jacques (1588–1660): Celebrated French sculptor. Founder (1648) and Rector (1654) of the Académie Royale, he was much employed by the royal family of France.

Savile (Savell), Sir George (1633–95): Statesman. Created Viscount Halifax 1668, Earl of Halifax 1679, Marquis 1682. He was active in passing through Parliament the Test Act of 1673; in 1680 he was instrumental in getting the Exclusion Bill rejected and in 1688 he took the popular side on the occasion of the trial of the bishops. On the accession of William III he was appointed Lord Privy Seal, exercising considerable influence. Halifax was consistent in his moderating principles, a fact not much appreciated at the time: he earned himself the disparaging title of 'Trimmer' which he defended in his *Character of a Trimmer* (pub. 1688).

Scarburgh, Sir Charles (1615–c. 1693): Physician. Deprived of his Fellowship at Caius College, Cambridge for Royalist sympathies, he practised medicine in London, becoming Lumleian Lecturer at the Royal College of Physicians in 1656. He was made one of the King's Physicians after the Restoration and received a knighthood.

Schott (Schotti), Casper (1608–66): German philosopher and mathematician. A favourite pupil of Father Kercherus, he taught in Rome and Palermo, and published several works in philosophy and natural history.

Scott, James (1649–85): Duke of Monmouth. Protestant pretender to the English throne. The eldest illegitimate son of Charles II (his mother was Lucy Barlow), he led a rebellion after the succession of the Catholic James II but was defeated in battle, captured, and beheaded.

Sedley (Sidly), Catherine (1657–1717): Mistress of James II c. 1677–1685/6, by whom she had a daughter, also Catherine. She was created

Countess of Dorchester in 1686. In 1696 she married Sir David Colyear, later Earl of Portmore, by whom she had two sons. Her father was the famous wit and dramatist Sir Charles Sedley.

Shaftesbury, Earl of : *see* Cooper, Sir Anthony Ashley.

Sidney (Sydney), Henry (1641–1704): Statesman. Son of Robert Sidney, 2nd Earl of Leicester, created Viscount Sydney of Sheppey 1689, Earl of Romney 1694. Played a prominent part in the 1688 Revolution and afterwards served as Secretary of State and Lord Lieutenant of Ireland, but his career faded under Queen Anne.

Simon, Dr. Patrick (1626–1707): Prebendary of Westminster, Dean of Peterborough and Bishop of Chichester. He was the author of several religious works in which he put himself forward as the champion of the Protestant party during the reign of James II.

Sirani, Elisabetta (Isabell) (1638–57): Daughter of Giovanni Andrea Sirani, a Bolognese artist. She was famous in her own right as a copyist of Guido, of whom her father was a pupil and imitator. Her sisters, Anna and Barbara, were also artists, but never reached the excellence of Elisabetta.

Slingsby, Henry (1621–90): Master of the Mint. He was active in the early days of the Royal Society, but expelled in 1675 for not paying his dues.

Snatt, Rev. Edward: JE's schoolmaster at Southover.

Somers (Summers), Sir John (1651–1716): Statesman and lawyer. He was Counsel for the seven bishops in June 1688 and one of the architects of the Revolution, presiding over the drafting of the Declaration of Rights. Made Solicitor-General and knighted 1689, Lord Keeper 1693; in 1695 with Montagu, Locke and Newton he planned the reform of the currency. As Baron Somers of Evesham he was appointed Lord High Chancellor of England in 1697. He possessed great influence, second only to that of Sunderland, with William III. In 1700 the unpopularity of William's standing army forced Somers to resign. He was impeached for his share in the secret partition treaties of 1698–9 but acquitted. On William's death he joined the Whig party, exercising considerable power until the fall of the junta in 1710.

Somerset, Henry (1629–99): 1st Duke of Beaufort (styled Lord Herbert 1629–67: 3rd Marquis of Worcester 1667, created Duke in 1682). He exerted himself against the Monmouth Rebellion in 1685 and in 1688 attempted to secure Bristol against the adherents of the Prince of Orange; upon whose elevation to the throne, the Duke, refusing to take the oaths, lived in retirement until his death.

Somerset, Lord John: Second son of Henry Somerset, 1st Marquis of Worcester, and nephew of Thomas Somerset (*see* below).

Somerset, Thomas (1579– *c.* 1650): Third son of Edward Somerset, 4th Earl of Worcester. He was created Viscount Somerset of Cashel in Ireland in 1626. His brother, Henry, the 5th Earl, was created Marquis of Worcester in 1642.

South, Dr. Robert (1634–1716): Prebendary of Westminster and Canon of Christchurch. One of the most eloquent preachers of the 17th century, he was celebrated for his wit in the pulpit.

Southampton, Earl of: *see* Wriothesley, Thomas.

Southwell, Sir Robert (1635–1702): Diplomat and government official. He was sent to Portugal in 1665 as Envoy Extraordinary, and in the same capacity to Brussels in 1671. He was subsequently Clerk of the Privy Council and was five times elected President of the Royal Society (1690–5).

Spanheim (Spanhemius), Ezekiel (1629–1710): Diplomat and author. Born in Geneva, he was sent by the Elector Palatine, Charles Louis, to whose son he had been tutor, to France as ambassador and from there to England, where he died.

Spencer, Robert (1640–1702): 2nd Earl of Sunderland, politician. Unprincipled even by the standards of the age, Sunderland served intermittently as a Secretary of State under Charles II and managed to retain power under James II in spite of having supported his exclusion from the throne. He later converted to Catholicism to please James (who none the less dismissed him), fled England after the 1688 Revolution but managed to negotiate his return both to the country and to royal favour, shedding his Catholicism on the way. As William's first political adviser, it was he who recommended that the king appoint his first Whig ministry in 1693. He was appointed Lord Chamberlain in 1697, but was driven out by public opinion.

Spencer, Anne (1646–1715): Countess of Sunderland, a friend of JE. Born Anne Digby, she was the daughter of the Earl of Bristol.

Sprat, Dr. Thomas (1635–1713): Dean of Westminster (1683–1713), Bishop of Rochester (1684). He was the biographer of Abraham Cowley and historian of the Royal Society.

Stansfield, John (d. 1627): JE's maternal grandfather.

Stanhope, Philip (1633–1713): 2nd Earl of Chesterfield, styled Lord Stanhope before 1656. In 1660 he married as his second wife Elizabeth Butler, Ossory's sister. He was Lord Chamberlain to the Queen 1662–5 and Chief Justice in Eyre of all the royal forests south of the Trent 1679–85.

Stapleton, Sir Robert (d. 1669): Member of a Yorkshire Catholic family, and Gentleman of the Bedchamber to Prince Charles (the future Charles II). He fought against the Parliamentarians at Edgehill and was afterwards knighted. He was a playwright, poet and translator, best known for his translations of Juvenal.

Strada, Famianus (1572–1649): Professor of Rhetoric in the Society of Jesus' College in Rome. Known to the English reader by his *Prolusions Academicæ*, in which he introduced clever imitations of the Latin poets.

Strafford, Earls of: *see* Wentworth, Sir Thomas; Wentworth, William.

Strickland, Sir Thomas (1621–94): Royalist and Roman Catholic. Made a Baronet by Charles I on the field at Edgehill, where he commanded a regiment of infantry. After the Restoration he was MP for Westmorland (expelled 1677), and Privy Purse to Charles II. He was subsequently one of James II's Privy Council, and followed him to France after the Revolution.

Sunderland, Lord and Lady: *see* Spencer, Robert, and Spencer, Anne.

Taafe, Theobald (d. 1677): Catholic Irish loyalist, son of 1st Viscount Taafe. Served the exiled Charles II and undertook a series of diplomatic missions after the Restoration. He was created Earl of Carlingford in 1662.

Talbot, Richard (*c.* 1630–91): Irish, Catholic Royalist soldier (also referred to by JE as 'Colonel Talbot') who entered the service of James, Duke of York, during his exile. He was arrested and exiled in 1678 for supposed complicity in the Popish Plot.

In 1685 James, now king, created him 1st
Earl of Tyrconnel, and 1st Duke in 1689.
He was sent to Ireland as commander-
in-chief of the army (independent of
Clarendon, the Lord Lieutenant), later,
displacing Clarendon, as Lord Deputy
(1687–88). Here he placed Catholics in
positions of control in the state and the
militia. His army joined the deposed
James II when he landed in Dublin in 1689.
After defeat at the battle of the Boyne in
1690 Tyrconnel went to France for aid,
returning to Ireland in 1691, where he died.

Taylor, Dr. Jeremy (1613–67): Divine, scholar
and writer. A protegé of Archbishop Laud,
he was several times imprisoned during the
Civil War and Commonwealth. He retired
to Carmarthenshire, writing his best-
known works there (*see* Chronology), but
also visited London where he held private
Anglican services at a time when they were
proscribed, and became JE's 'Ghostly
Father'. On the Restoration he was
appointed Bishop of Down and Connor.

Temple, Sir William (1628–99): Diplomat
and author. In 1668 became Ambassador to
The Hague, a post he held for much of the
next decade. He was largely responsible for
carrying through the Triple Alliance of
England, Holland and Sweden against
France (1668) and for arranging the
marriage of Princess Mary with William
of Orange in 1677. On return he twice
declined the office of Secretary of State,
and devoted himself to his writing (*see*
Chronology). Now famous as the recipient
of the published letters of Dorothy
Osborne, his wife.

Tenison, Dr. Thomas (1636–1715): Prelate.
Vicar of St. Martin in the Fields 1680,
where he endowed a free school and started
a library. Archdeacon of London 1689,
Bishop of Lincoln 1691, Archbishop of
Canterbury 1694. Strongly Whig and
Protestant in sympathy, he was high in the
favour of William III. His Latitudinarian
sympathies – he wished to win back
Nonconformists to the Anglican church by
making suitable concessions in rites and
ordinances – were shared by JE.

Thicknesse, James (c. 1620–1660s?):
University friend of JE. Son of Ralph
Thicknesse of Whitechapel. Matriculated
at Oxford in 1636, BA 1639, Fellow 1641,
MA 1642, expelled 1648 for the duration of
the Commonwealth, but restored in 1660.
JE mentions his unexpected death from an

ague in *De Vita Propria* without recording
the year.

Thynne (Thinn), Thomas (1648–82):
Courtier. He was the unfortunate victim of
a celebrated murder in Pall Mall, London,
in 1682. In 1681 he married Elizabeth, born
Percy, the young widow of Lord Ogle,
but the marriage was never consummated.
He had previously seduced, under promise
of marriage, a young lady who was said to
have been instrumental in his murder.
Hence the burlesque epitaph that did the
rounds at the time:

'Here lies Tom Thynne of Longleat Hall
Who never would have miscarried,
Had he married the woman he lay withal;
Or laid with the woman he married.'

Tonge (Tongue), Dr. Ezrereel (Israel)
(1621–80): Fellow of University College,
Oxford. A great opponent of the Roman
Catholics, he was Oates's accomplice in
'revealing' the Popish Plot. Among his
works were *The Jesuits Unmasked* (1678).

Torrington, Earl of: *see* Herbert, Arthur.

Tradescant, John the Younger (1608–62):
Traveller, horticulturalist, collector and
gardener, whose *Museum Tradescantianum*
(1656) was a catalogue to the museum in
south Lambeth founded by his father,
the elder John Tradescant (d. 1637?).
The museum contained a varied collection
of rarities which, after his death, was
bequeathed to Elias Ashmole and
subsequently formed the basis of the
Ashmolean Museum in Oxford.

Trenchard, Sir John (1640–94): Politician
and confidential friend of William III.
He was knighted by the king and made
Chief Justice of Chester. He was appointed
a Secretary of State in 1692.

Tuchet, Mervyn (1593–1631): 2nd Earl of
Castlehaven. He was convicted by a court
of 27 Lords, sitting in Westminster Hall,
for a number of sexual crimes and was
executed on Tower Hill in 1631.

Tuke, Sir Samuel (1610–73): JE's cousin and a
colonel in the army of Charles I. He was
also a playwright – his *Adventures of Five
Hours* was one of the most successful early
Restoration dramas.

Turner, Dr. Francis (1638–1700): Bishop of
Ely 1684 and one of the seven bishops sent
to the Tower for the petition to James II.

Turnor (Turner), Sir Edward (1617–70):
Speaker of the House of Commons 1661–71.
Subsequently Solicitor-General and Lord
Chief Baron of the Exchequer (1671–6).

Tyrconnel, Earl and Duke of: *see* Talbot, Richard.

Tyson, Dr. Edward (1649–1708): Physician and renowned anatomist. He was physican at the hospitals of Bethlehem and Bridewell and published numerous anatomical essays including the 'Anatomy of a Pigmy compared with a Monkey, an Ape, and a Man'.

Ussher, James (1581–1656): Irish prelate. Archbishop of Armagh, 1625. Went to England in 1640 and for eight years preached at Lincoln's Inn. Though consistent in his loyalty to the throne he was treated with favour by Cromwell. He was distinguished for his learning but also his charity and good temper. He was moderate in his views of church government and tried to find a way of embracing Puritans within the Anglican church. Of his numerous works the best known is *Annales Veteris et Novi Testamenti* (1650–54) which fixed the Creation precisely at 4004 BC.

Vanbrugh, William (*c.* 1657–1716): Secretary to the Commissioners for Greenwich Hospital 1695–1716; Deputy Comptroller, then Comptroller of the Household (1698–1716). A cousin of Sir John Vanbrugh, the playwright and architect.

Vanderborcht, Henry: *see* Borcht, Hendrik van der, the Elder.

Vane, Sir Henry (1613–62): Leading Parliamentarian and statesman of the Commonwealth, known as 'the younger' to distinguish him from his father, also Sir Henry Vane (1589–1654). He withdrew from government in 1653 following differences with Cromwell and in 1656 was imprisoned for his book *A Healing Question* which was critical of the Protectorate. (JE's 'foolish book': he mistakenly ascribes it to the older Vane). Vane was the author of a number of books on religious matters, and was in favour of complete liberty of conscience. Though a non-regicide, he was executed for treason after the Restoration, Charles II remarking that he was 'too dangerous a man to let live'.

Vesling, Johann (1598–1649): German Professor of Anatomy at the University of Padua. He had the care of the botanical garden there, and published a catalogue of its plants. Shortly afterwards, he travelled in Egypt, where he seems to have paid a good deal of attention to the artificial means of hatching poultry, then an Eygptian marvel.

Vic, Sir Henry de (d. 1672): English Resident at Brussels for Charles II. He was a Chancellor of the Order of the Garter, and was made Comptroller of the Household of the Duke of York in 1662.

Villiers, George (1592–1628): Court favourite of James I and Charles I. Created 1st Duke of Buckingham 1623; became one of the richest men in the country. He accompanied Charles, then Prince of Wales, to Spain in 1623 to promote his marriage with the Infanta: the mission failed. In 1627 his attempt to relieve Huguenots besieged at La Rochelle also ended in ignominious failure. Saved by the king fom impeachment by Parliament, he was assassinated a year later.

Villiers, George (1628–87): 2nd Duke of Buckingham. After his father's death, brought up with the children of Charles I. Fought with the Royalists in the Civil War. Married Mary Fairfax, daughter of the Parliamentarian General, Sir Thomas Fairfax, in 1657. In 1674 he killed the Earl of Shrewsbury in a duel over his wife the Countess who was Buckingham's mistress. One of the wildest *roués* of the Restoration court, he was also politically ambitious, and his exploits on several occasions ended with his being imprisoned in the Tower. He was partly responsible for the fall of Clarendon, was a member of the Cabal ministry which replaced him, and on its break-up in 1673 intrigued with the Whigs. He was the author of verses, satires, and the popular burlesque of Dryden's heroic dramas, *The Rehearsal*, and became a Fellow of the Royal Society.

Viner, Sir Robert (1631–88): A wealthy banker. As Lord Mayor, he entertained Charles II at the Guildhall. On his Majesty retiring, Sir Robert urged him to 'return and take t'other bottle'.

Wakeman, Sir George (*fl.* 1668–85): Doctor. A Royalist and a Roman Catholic who had been educated abroad, he was made a baronet in 1661 and appointed physician to Queen Catherine in 1670. He was accused by Titus Oates of planning to poison the king in 1678. Acquitted the following year, he went abroad but returned to London before 1685.

Waldegrave (Walgrave), Sir Henry (*c.* 1662–90): Married 1683 Henrietta

FitzJames, daughter of James II by Arabella Churchill. Created Baron Waldegrave in 1686. Comptroller of the King's Household 1687–8. Ambassador Extraordinary to France 1688. A Jacobite, he died in Paris.

Walker, Dr. George (1648–90): Irish clergyman, who distinguished himself as a soldier. After successfully defending Protestant Londonderry against the army of James II, he accompanied William III during his decisive campaign against his father-in-law. He was killed at the battle of the Boyne.

Walker, Obadiah (1616–99): Master of University College, Oxford.

Walker, Sir Edward (1612–77): Royalist. Celebrated for his knowledge of heraldry. He attended Charles II into exile, and was made first Clerk of the Privy Council after the Restoration, and subsequently Garter King-at-Arms.

Walker, Robert (1599–1658): Portrait painter chiefly patronized by Parliamentarians, among them Cromwell, Ireton and Fairfax.

Waller, Edmund (1606–87): Poet. An MP in the Long Parliament, he was imprisoned in the Tower 1643–4 for involvement in a Royalist plot, and afterwards banished. He returned to England in 1651. His *Poems* first appeared in 1645, *Divine Poems* in 1685.

Wallis, Dr. John (1616–1703): One of the earliest members of the Royal Society, to the *Transactions* of which he contributed many papers, and wrote several mathematical and theological works. He was Savilian Professor of Geometry at Oxford from 1649 to 1703. He was appointed chaplain to Charles II, and was often employed in deciphering intercepted correspondence, in which role he was considered remarkably adept.

Ward, Dr. Seth (1617–89): One of the founders of the Royal Society. He later became Bishop of Exeter and wrote numerous mathematical and astronomical works, as well as works opposing the philosopher Hobbes.

Warwick, Sir Philip (1609–83): Writer and politician. As an MP, he opposed Strafford's impeachment, and subsequently went to Oxford with the king, who employed him in 1646 as one of his commissioners to treat with Parliament. After the Restoration, he obtained the office of Secretary to the Lord Treasurer, which brought him into frequent

communication with JE. His *Memoirs of King Charles* contains a graphic account of Cromwell's first speech in the House of Commons.

Wentworth, Sir Thomas (1593–1641): Statesman and royal adviser. Created Baron Wentworth of Wentworth Woodhouse in 1628, Viscount Wentworth in 1628, and 1st Earl of Strafford in 1640. Viceroy of Ireland and Lord Deputy 1633–40, Lord Lieutenant 1641. He was impeached and executed for treason in 1641.

Wentworth, William (1626–95): 2nd Earl of Strafford, only son of Thomas Wentworth, 1st Earl of Strafford.

Wheeler, Sir Charles (*c.* 1619–83): Governor of the Leeward Islands 1671–2, recalled on account of incompetence the following year.

Whistler, Dr. Daniel (1619–84): Physician. Professor of Geometry at Gresham College, London, 1648. Fellow (1649) and later President (1683) of the Royal College of Physicians. His dissertation on rickets for the degree of MD in Leyden (1645) contains the earliest printed account of that disease. He was an original Fellow of the Royal Society.

Wilkins, Dr. John (1614–72): Scientist and theologian. Warden of Wadham College, Oxford 1648–59. In 1656 married Oliver Cromwell's sister, Robina, but switched allegiance following the Restoration. He was made Bishop of Chester in 1668. An original member of the Royal Society, he published a series of scientific and religious works including one on the practicality of journeying to the moon entitled *The Discovery of a New World.*

William III (1650–1702), reigned 1689–1702. The son of the Prince of Orange and Princess Mary, eldest daughter of Charles I, William became the champion of Protestantism in Europe and the principal challenger to the aspirations of Louis XIV. He was Stadtholder of the Netherlands from 1672, and married Mary, daughter of James II, in 1677. In 1688 he landed in England at the invitation of disaffected politicians, deposed James II, and, having accepted the Declaration of Rights, was crowned along with his wife the following year.

Williamson, Sir Joseph (1633–1701): Distinguished Parliamentarian and philanthropist, he was an original Fellow of the Royal Society and its President 1677–80.

Secretary of State 1674–8. He was the founder of a mathematical school at Rochester in Kent, in which David Garrick was one of the pupils placed under the first master.

Wilmot, Henry (1613–59): Only son of Charles, Viscount Wilmot of Athlone. He was made Baron Wilmot of Adderbury in 1643. He held a command in the King's Cavalry, in which he served with distinction at the battle of Roundway Down in 1643, and subsequently assisted Charles II to escape from the field of Worcester. He was created Earl of Rochester in 1652 in Paris.

Wilmot, John (1647–80): 2nd Earl of Rochester, son of the above. The poet and libertine.

Winstanley, Henry (1644–1703): Architect who built the first Eddystone Lighthouse, fourteen miles off the Plymouth coast, and perished in it when it was swept away by a great storm in 1703.

Worcester, Marquis of: see Somerset, Thomas.

Wotton, Rev. William (1666–1727): Scholar and friend of JE, best known for his *Reflections upon Ancient and Modern Learning* (1694).

Wriothesley, Thomas (1608–67): 4th Earl of Southampton, Lord Treasurer (1660–7) and one of Charles II's most loyal advisers. JE enjoyed much of his hospitality.

Wren, Sir Christopher (1632–1723): After an academic career as a scientist, Wren turned to architecture in the 1660s and was made Surveyor-General of the King's Works in 1669. His plans, like JE's, for the rebuilding of London after the Great Fire were not realized, but he did rebuild 52 London churches, including St. Paul's Cathedral. Greenwich Hospital, Greenwich Observatory and the partial rebuilding of Hampton Court are amongst his other works. He was a founder member and later President of the Royal Society.

Wright (Write), Michael (1617–94): Fashionable portrait painter of the day. A long account of him is given in Walpole's *Anecdotes of Painting*.

Wyche, Sir Cyril (c. 1632–1707): Barrister and MP, husband of Mary Evelyn, JE's niece. Born in Constantinople where his father, Sir Peter Wyche, was Ambassador. Served as Chief Secretary for Ireland 1676–82 and 1692–3. He was an original Fellow of the Royal Society. Mary Evelyn, whom he married in 1692, was his third wife.

Wyche, Mary, Lady Wyche (1648–1723): JE's niece, daughter of George Evelyn of Wotton, married Sir Cyril Wyche in 1692.

Yarborough (Yarbrow, Yearbrow), Henrietta Maria, Lady Yarborough: Eldest sister of Margaret Blagge, d. between 1709 and 1716. She married in 1664 Sir Thomas Yarborough (c. 1639–1716).

York, Duke of: see James II.

Zulecum (Zuylichem, etc): see Huygens.

INDEX

Note: Abbreviations used in the index are: Archb for Archbishop; Bp for Bishop; ChI and ChII for King Charles I and II of England; JII for King James II; JE for John Evelyn the diarist; RS for Royal Society; tr. for translation; WIII for King William III. Peers are listed under their titles; spelling is corrected to modern form. Extracts from the recension of the diary, *De Vita Propria*, are indicated by* following the page numbers.

JOSEPH CONRAD
Heart of Darkness
Lord Jim
Nostromo
The Secret Agent
Typhoon and Other Stories
Under Western Eyes
Victory

THOMAS CRANMER
The Book of Common Prayer
(UK only)

DANTE ALIGHIERI
The Divine Comedy

CHARLES DARWIN
The Origin of Species
The Voyage of the Beagle
(in 1 vol.)

DANIEL DEFOE
Moll Flanders
Robinson Crusoe

CHARLES DICKENS
Barnaby Rudge
Bleak House
David Copperfield
Dombey and Son
Great Expectations
Hard Times
Little Dorrit
Martin Chuzzlewit
The Mystery of Edwin Drood
Nicholas Nickleby
The Old Curiosity Shop
Oliver Twist
Our Mutual Friend
The Pickwick Papers
A Tale of Two Cities

DENIS DIDEROT
Memoirs of a Nun

JOHN DONNE
The Complete English Poems

FYODOR DOSTOEVSKY
The Adolescent
The Brothers Karamazov
Crime and Punishment
Demons
The Double and The Gambler
The Idiot
Notes from Underground

W. E. B. DU BOIS
The Souls of Black Folk
(US only)

GEORGE ELIOT
Adam Bede
Daniel Deronda
Middlemarch
The Mill on the Floss
Silas Marner

WILLIAM FAULKNER
The Sound and the Fury
(UK only)

HENRY FIELDING
Joseph Andrews and Shamela
(UK only)
Tom Jones

F. SCOTT FITZGERALD
The Great Gatsby
This Side of Paradise
(UK only)

PENELOPE FITZGERALD
The Bookshop
The Gate of Angels
The Blue Flower
(in 1 vol.)
Offshore
Human Voices
The Beginning of Spring
(in 1 vol.)

GUSTAVE FLAUBERT
Madame Bovary

FORD MADOX FORD
The Good Soldier
Parade's End

E. M. FORSTER
Howards End
A Passage to India

ELIZABETH GASKELL
Mary Barton

EDWARD GIBBON
The Decline and Fall of the
Roman Empire
Vols 1 to 3: The Western Empire
Vols 4 to 6: The Eastern Empire

J. W. VON GOETHE
Selected Works

NIKOLAI GOGOL
Dead Souls

IVAN GONCHAROV
Oblomov

GÜNTER GRASS
The Tin Drum

GRAHAM GREENE
Brighton Rock
The Human Factor

DASHIELL HAMMETT
The Maltese Falcon
The Thin Man
Red Harvest
(in 1 vol.)

THOMAS HARDY
Far From the Madding Crowd
Jude the Obscure
The Mayor of Casterbridge
The Return of the Native
Tess of the d'Urbervilles
The Woodlanders

JAROSLAV HAŠEK
The Good Soldier Švejk

NATHANIEL HAWTHORNE
The Scarlet Letter

JOSEPH HELLER
Catch-22

ERNEST HEMINGWAY
A Farewell to Arms
The Collected Stories
(UK only)

GEORGE HERBERT
The Complete English Works

HERODOTUS
The Histories

PATRICIA HIGHSMITH
The Talented Mr. Ripley
Ripley Under Ground
Ripley's Game
(in 1 vol.)

HINDU SCRIPTURES
(tr. R. C. Zaehner)

JAMES HOGG
Confessions of a Justified Sinner

HOMER
The Iliad
The Odyssey

VICTOR HUGO
Les Misérables

HENRY JAMES
The Awkward Age
The Bostonians
The Golden Bowl
The Portrait of a Lady
The Princess Casamassima
The Wings of the Dove
Collected Stories (2 vols)

SAMUEL JOHNSON
A Journey to the Western
Islands of Scotland

JAMES JOYCE
Dubliners
A Portrait of the Artist as
a Young Man
Ulysses

FRANZ KAFKA
Collected Stories
The Castle
The Trial

JOHN KEATS
The Poems

SØREN KIERKEGAARD
Fear and Trembling and
The Book on Adler

MAXINE HONG KINGSTON
The Woman Warrior and
China Men
(US only)

RUDYARD KIPLING
Collected Stories
Kim

THE KORAN
(tr. Marmaduke Pickthall)

CHODERLOS DE LACLOS
Les Liaisons dangereuses

GIUSEPPE TOMASI DI
LAMPEDUSA
The Leopard

WILLIAM LANGLAND
Piers Plowman
with (anon.) Sir Gawain and the
Green Knight, Pearl, Sir Orfeo
(UK only)

FRANÇOIS RABELAIS
Gargantua and Pantagruel

JOSEPH ROTH
The Radetzky March

JEAN-JACQUES
ROUSSEAU
Confessions
The Social Contract and
the Discourses

SALMAN RUSHDIE
Midnight's Children

JOHN RUSKIN
Praeterita and Dilecta

WALTER SCOTT
Rob Roy

WILLIAM SHAKESPEARE
Comedies Vols 1 and 2
Histories Vols 1 and 2
Romances
Sonnets and Narrative Poems
Tragedies Vols 1 and 2

MARY SHELLEY
Frankenstein

ADAM SMITH
The Wealth of Nations

ALEXANDER SOLZHENITSYN
One Day in the Life of
Ivan Denisovich

SOPHOCLES
The Theban Plays

MURIEL SPARK
The Prime of Miss Jean Brodie,
The Girls of Slender Means, The
Driver's Seat, The Only Problem
(1 vol.)

CHRISTINA STEAD
The Man Who Loved Children

JOHN STEINBECK
The Grapes of Wrath

STENDHAL
The Charterhouse of Parma
Scarlet and Black

LAURENCE STERNE
Tristram Shandy

ROBERT LOUIS STEVENSON
The Master of Ballantrae and
Weir of Hermiston
Dr Jekyll and Mr Hyde
and Other Stories

HARRIET BEECHER STOWE
Uncle Tom's Cabin

ITALO SVEVO
Zeno's Conscience

JONATHAN SWIFT
Gulliver's Travels

JUNICHIRŌ TANIZAKI
The Makioka Sisters

W. M. THACKERAY
Vanity Fair

HENRY DAVID THOREAU
Walden

ALEXIS DE TOCQUEVILLE
Democracy in America

LEO TOLSTOY
Collected Shorter Fiction (2 vols)
Anna Karenina
Childhood, Boyhood and Youth
The Cossacks
War and Peace

ANTHONY TROLLOPE
Barchester Towers
Can You Forgive Her?
Doctor Thorne
The Eustace Diamonds
Framley Parsonage
The Last Chronicle of Barset
Phineas Finn
The Small House at Allington
The Warden

IVAN TURGENEV
Fathers and Children
First Love and Other Stories
A Sportsman's Notebook

MARK TWAIN
Tom Sawyer
and Huckleberry Finn

JOHN UPDIKE
The Complete Henry Bech
(US only)
Rabbit Angstrom

This book is set in CASLON, designed and engraved by William
Caslon of WILLIAM CASLON & SON, Letter-Founders in
London, around 1740. In England at the beginning of
the eighteenth century, Dutch type was probably
more widely used than English. The rise
of William Caslon put a stop to the
importation of Dutch types
and so changed the his-
tory of English
typecutting.